myBusinessCourse

MW01492094

FREE WITH NEW COPIES OF THIS TEXTBOOK*

Scratch here for access code

YvJv4MVcfyuBFfgi

Scratch here for access code

Start using myBusinessCourse Today: www.mybusinesscourse.com

myBusinessCourse is a web-based learning and assessment program intended to complement your textbook and faculty instruction.

Student Benefits

- **eLectures**: These videos review the key concepts of each Learning Objective in each chapter.
- **Guided examples**: These videos provide step-by-step solutions for select problems in each chapter.
- **Auto-graded assignments**: Provide students with immediate feedback on select assignments. (**with Instructor-Led course ONLY**).
- **Quiz and Exam preparation**: myBusinessCourse provides students with additional practice and exam preparation materials to help students achieve better grades and content mastery.

You can access myBusinessCourse 24/7 from any web-enabled device, including iPads, smartphones, laptops, and tablets.

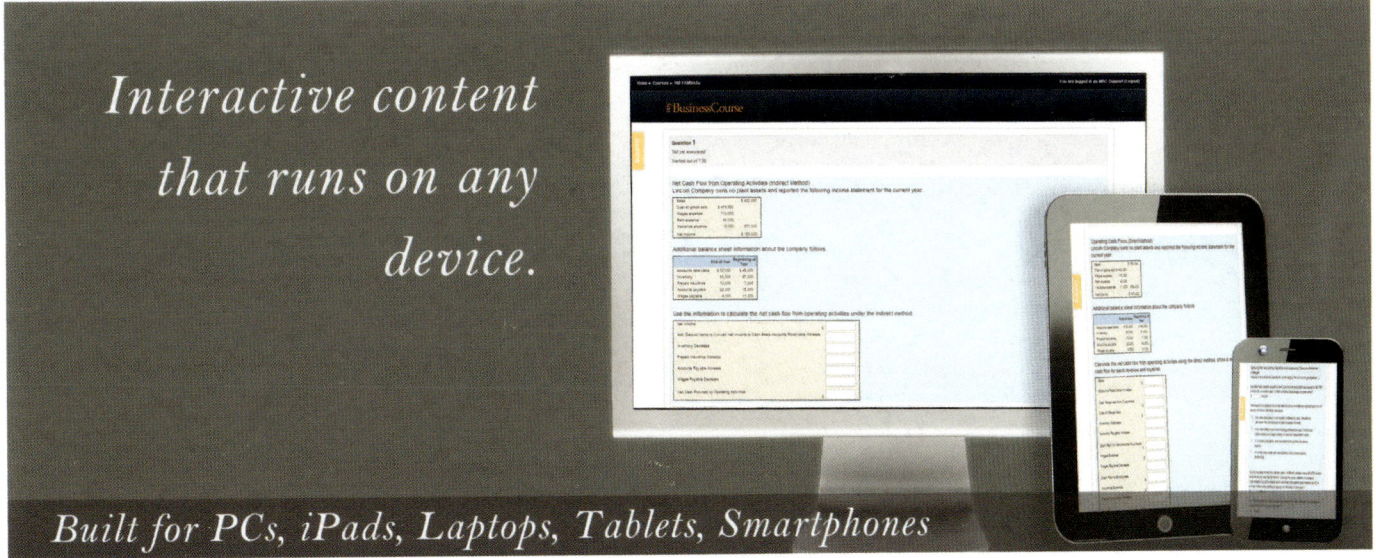

Interactive content that runs on any device.

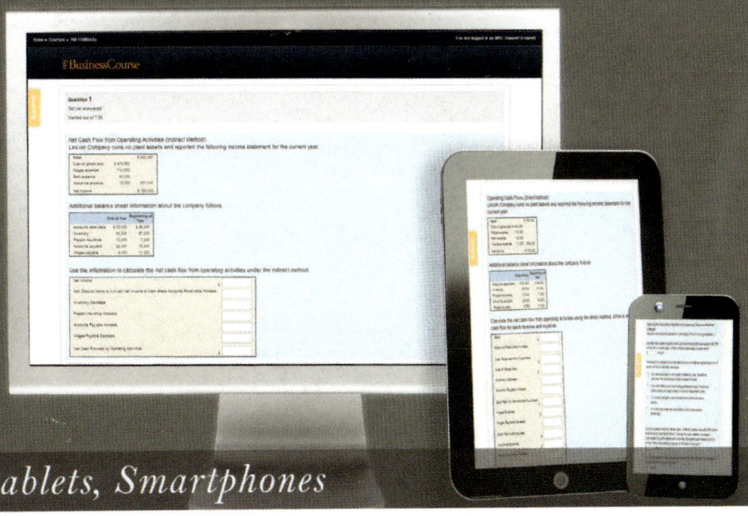

Built for PCs, iPads, Laptops, Tablets, Smartphones

***Each access code is good for one use only.** If the textbook is used for more than one course or term, students will have to purchase additional myBusinessCourse access codes. In addition, students who repeat a course for any reason will have to purchase a new access code. If you purchased a used book and the protective coating that covers the access code has been removed, your code may be invalid.

Access to myBusinessCourse is free ONLY with the purchase of a new textbook.

SEVENTH EDITION

Financial Accounting

MICHELLE L. HANLON
Massachusetts Institute of Technology

ROBERT P. MAGEE
Northwestern University

GLENN M. PFEIFFER
Chapman University

Cambridge
BUSINESS PUBLISHERS

To my husband, Chris, and to our children, Clark and Josie.

—MLH

To my wife, Peggy, and our family, Paul and Teisha, Michael and Heather, and grandchildren Sage, Caillean, Rhiannon, Corin, Connor, and Harri.

—RPM

To my wife, Kathie, and my daughter, Jaclyn.

—GMP

Photo credits:

Chapter 1: Shutterstock
Chapter 2: Shutterstock
Chapter 3: iStock
Chapter 4: Shutterstock
Chapter 5: Shutterstock
Chapter 6: Shutterstock
Chapter 7: Shutterstock
Chapter 8: iStock
Chapter 9: Shutterstock
Chapter 10: iStock
Chapter 11: Shutterstock
Chapter 12: Shutterstock

Cambridge Business Publishers

FINANCIAL ACCOUNTING, Seventh Edition, by Michelle L. Hanlon, Robert P. Magee, and Glenn M. Pfeiffer.

Student Edition ISBN: 978-1-61853-431-6

Bookstores & Faculty: To order this book, contact the company via email **customerservice@cambridgepub.com** or call 800-619-6473.

Students: To order this book, please visit the book's website and order directly online.

Printed in the United States.
10 9 8 7 6 5 4 3 2

About the Authors

The combined skills and expertise of Michelle Hanlon, Bob Magee, and Glenn Pfeiffer create the ideal team to author this exciting financial accounting textbook. Their combined experience in award-winning teaching, consulting, and research in the area of financial accounting and analysis provides a powerful foundation for this pioneering textbook.

Michelle L. Hanlon is the Howard W. Johnson Professor at the MIT Sloan School of Management. She earned her doctorate degree at the University of Washington. Prior to joining MIT, she was a faculty member at the University of Michigan. Professor Hanlon has taught undergraduates, MBA students, Executive MBA students, and Masters of Finance students. She has won many awards for her teaching and research, including the 2021 Outstanding Teacher Award, MIT Sloan School, 2020 Presidential Scholar, American Accounting Association, 2020 Distinguished Contribution to Accounting Literature Award, American Accounting Association, 2020 MIT Teaching with Digital Technology Award, and 2013 Jamieson Prize for Excellence in Teaching at MIT Sloan. Professor Hanlon's research focuses primarily on the intersection of financial accounting and taxation. She has published research studies in the *Journal of Accounting and Economics*, the *Journal of Accounting Research*, *The Accounting Review*, the *Review of Accounting Studies*, the *Journal of Finance*, the *Journal of Financial Economics*, the *Journal of Public Economics*, and others. She has won several awards for her research and has presented her work at numerous universities and conferences. Professor Hanlon has served on several editorial boards and currently serves as an editor at the *Journal of Accounting and Economics*. Professor Hanlon is a co-author on two other textbooks—*Intermediate Accounting* and *Taxes and Business Strategy*. She has testified in front of the U.S. Senate Committee on Finance and the U.S. House of Representatives Committee on Ways and Means about the interaction of financial accounting and tax policy and international tax policy. She served as a U.S. delegate to the American-Swiss Young Leaders Conference in 2010 and worked as an Academic Fellow at the U.S. House Ways and Means Committee in 2015.

Robert P. Magee is Keith I. DeLashmutt Professor Emeritus of Accounting Information and Management at the Kellogg School of Management at Northwestern University. He received his A.B., M.S. and Ph.D. from Cornell University. Prior to joining the Kellogg faculty in 1976, he was a faculty member at the University of Chicago's Graduate School of Business. For academic year 1980–81, he was a visiting faculty member at IMEDE (now IMD) in Lausanne, Switzerland.

Professor Magee's research focuses on the use of accounting information to facilitate decision-making and control within organizations. He has published articles in *The Accounting Review*, the *Journal of Accounting Research*, the *Journal of Accounting and Economics*, and a variety of other journals. He is the author of *Advanced Managerial Accounting* and co-author (with Thomas R. Dyckman and David H. Downes) of *Efficient Capital Markets and Accounting: A Critical Analysis*. The latter book received the Notable Contribution to the Accounting Literature Award from the AICPA in 1978. Professor Magee has served on the editorial boards of *The Accounting Review*, the *Journal of Accounting Research*, the *Journal of Accounting and Economics* and the *Journal of Accounting, Auditing and Finance*. From 1994–96, he served as Editor of *The Accounting Review*, the quarterly research journal of the American Accounting Association. He received the American Accounting Association's Outstanding Accounting Educator Award in 1999 and the Illinois CPA Society Outstanding Educator Award in 2000.

Professor Magee has taught financial accounting to MBA and Executive MBA students. He has received several teaching awards at the Kellogg School, including the Alumni Choice Outstanding Professor Award in 2003.

Glenn M. Pfeiffer is the Warren and Doris Uehlinger Professor of Business at the George L. Argyros School of Business and Economics and Provost Emeritus at Chapman University. He received his M.S. and Ph.D. from Cornell University after he earned a bachelors degree from Hope College. Prior to joining the faculty at the Argyros School, he held appointments at the University of Washington, Cornell University, the University of Chicago, the University of Arizona, and San Diego State University.

Professor Pfeiffer's research focuses on accounting and capital markets. He has investigated issues relating to lease accounting, LIFO inventory liquidation, earnings per share, management compensation, corporate reorganization, and technology investments. He has published articles in *The Accounting Review*, *Accounting Horizons*, the *Financial Analysts Journal*, the *International Journal of Accounting Information Systems*, the *Journal of High Technology Management Research*, *Economic Journal*, the *Journal of Accounting Education*, and several other academic journals. In addition, he has published numerous case studies in financial accounting and reporting.

Professor Pfeiffer teaches financial accounting and financial analysis to undergraduate, MBA, and Law students. He has also taught managerial accounting for MBAs. He has won several teaching awards at both the undergraduate and graduate levels.

Preface

Welcome to the seventh edition of *Financial Accounting* and, to adopters of the first six editions, thank you for the great success those editions have enjoyed. We wrote this book to equip students with the accounting techniques and insights necessary to succeed in today's business environment. It reflects our combined experience in teaching financial accounting to college students at all levels. For anyone who pursues a career in business, the ability to read, analyze, and interpret published financial reports is an essential skill. *Financial Accounting* is written for future business leaders who want to understand how financial statements are prepared and how the information in published financial reports is used by investors, creditors, financial analysts, and managers. Our goal is to provide the most engaging, relevant, and accessible textbook available.

TARGET AUDIENCE

Financial Accounting is intended for use in the first financial accounting course at either the undergraduate or graduate level; one that balances the preparation of financial statements with their analysis and interpretation. This book accommodates mini-courses lasting only a few days as well as extended courses lasting a full semester.

Financial Accounting is real-world oriented and focuses on the most salient aspects of accounting. It teaches students how to read, analyze, and interpret financial accounting data to make informed business decisions. To that end, it consistently incorporates **real company data**, both in the body of each chapter and throughout the assignment material.

REAL DATA INCORPORATED THROUGHOUT

Today's business students must be skilled in using real financial statements to make business decisions. We feel strongly that the more exposure students get to real financial statements, the more comfortable they become with the variety in financial statements that exists across companies and industries. Through their exposure to various financial statements, students will learn that, while financial statements do not all look the same, they can readily understand and interpret them to make business decisions. Because we update all of the examples throughout the chapters with the most recently available information, students will see the impact of recent events on financial statements, such as the impact of the COVID-19 pandemic. Furthermore, today's students must have the skills to go beyond basic financial statements to interpret and apply nonfinancial disclosures, such as note disclosures and supplementary reports. We expose students to the analysis and interpretation of real company data and nonfinancial disclosures through the use of focus companies in each chapter, the generous incorporation of note disclosures, financial analysis discussions in nearly every chapter, and an abundance of assignments that draw on real company data and disclosures.

Focus Companies for Each Chapter

Each chapter's content is explained through the accounting and reporting activities of real companies. Each chapter incorporates a "focus company" for special emphasis and demonstration. The enhanced instructional value of focus companies comes from the way they engage students in real analysis and interpretation. Focus companies were selected based on student appeal and the diversity of industries.

Chapter 1	Nike	**Chapter 7**	Home Depot
Chapter 2	Walgreens	**Chapter 8**	Procter & Gamble
Chapter 3	Walgreens	**Chapter 9**	Verizon
Chapter 4	CVS Health Corporation	**Chapter 10**	Deere & Co.
Chapter 5	PepsiCo	**Chapter 11**	Pfizer
Chapter 6	Microsoft Corporation	**Chapter 12**	Alphabet, Inc.

Road Maps

Each chapter opens with an Action Plan that identifies each learning objective for the chapter, the related page numbers, the reviews, and the assignments. This table allows students and faculty to quickly grasp the chapter contents and to efficiently navigate the desired topic.

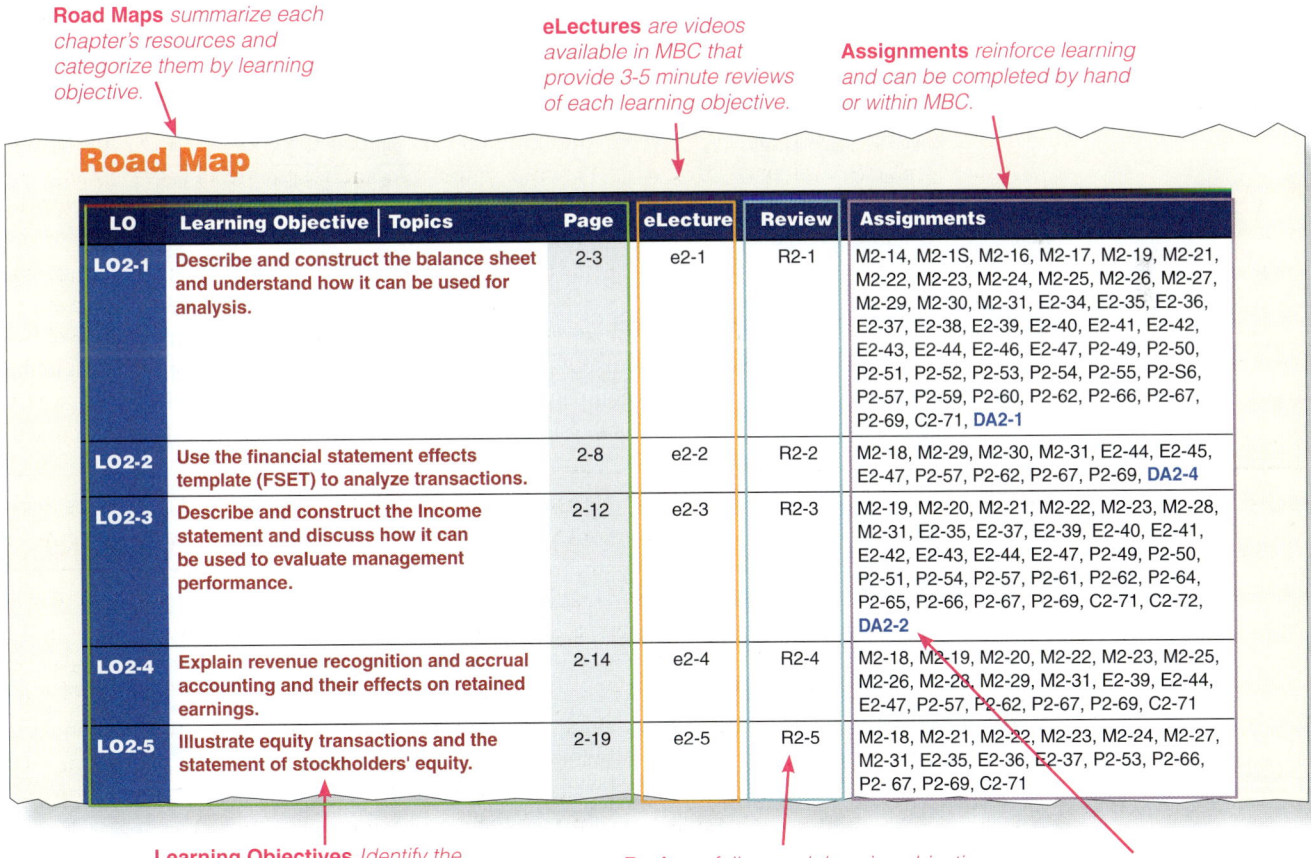

Road Maps *summarize each chapter's resources and categorize them by learning objective.*

eLectures *are videos available in MBC that provide 3-5 minute reviews of each learning objective.*

Assignments *reinforce learning and can be completed by hand or within MBC.*

Road Map

LO	Learning Objective | Topics	Page	eLecture	Review	Assignments
LO2-1	Describe and construct the balance sheet and understand how it can be used for analysis.	2-3	e2-1	R2-1	M2-14, M2-1S, M2-16, M2-17, M2-19, M2-21, M2-22, M2-23, M2-24, M2-25, M2-26, M2-27, M2-29, M2-30, M2-31, E2-34, E2-35, E2-36, E2-37, E2-38, E2-39, E2-40, E2-41, E2-42, E2-43, E2-44, E2-46, E2-47, P2-49, P2-50, P2-51, P2-52, P2-53, P2-54, P2-55, P2-S6, P2-57, P2-59, P2-60, P2-62, P2-66, P2-67, P2-69, C2-71, DA2-1
LO2-2	Use the financial statement effects template (FSET) to analyze transactions.	2-8	e2-2	R2-2	M2-18, M2-29, M2-30, M2-31, E2-44, E2-45, E2-47, P2-57, P2-62, P2-67, P2-69, DA2-4
LO2-3	Describe and construct the Income statement and discuss how it can be used to evaluate management performance.	2-12	e2-3	R2-3	M2-19, M2-20, M2-21, M2-22, M2-23, M2-28, M2-31, E2-35, E2-37, E2-39, E2-40, E2-41, E2-42, E2-43, E2-44, E2-47, P2-49, P2-50, P2-51, P2-54, P2-57, P2-61, P2-62, P2-64, P2-65, P2-66, P2-67, P2-69, C2-71, C2-72, DA2-2
LO2-4	Explain revenue recognition and accrual accounting and their effects on retained earnings.	2-14	e2-4	R2-4	M2-18, M2-19, M2-20, M2-22, M2-23, M2-25, M2-26, M2-28, M2-29, M2-31, E2-39, E2-44, E2-47, P2-57, P2-62, P2-67, P2-69, C2-71
LO2-5	Illustrate equity transactions and the statement of stockholders' equity.	2-19	e2-5	R2-5	M2-18, M2-21, M2-22, M2-23, M2-24, M2-27, M2-31, E2-35, E2-36, E2-37, P2-53, P2-66, P2- 67, P2-69, C2-71

Learning Objectives *Identify the key learning goals of the chapter.*

Reviews *follow each learning objective and require students to apply what they have just learned.* **Guided Example** *videos accompany the Reviews and demonstrate how to solve various types of problems. Reviews are also assignable in MBC.*

Data Analysis (DA) *exercises using Excel and Tableau are identified with blue font. Exercises are assignable in MBC.*

Note Disclosures and Management Disclosures

We incorporate note disclosure and other management disclosures, where appropriate, throughout the book. We explain the significance of the note disclosure and then demonstrate how to use the disclosed information to make managerial inferences and decisions. A representative sample follows.

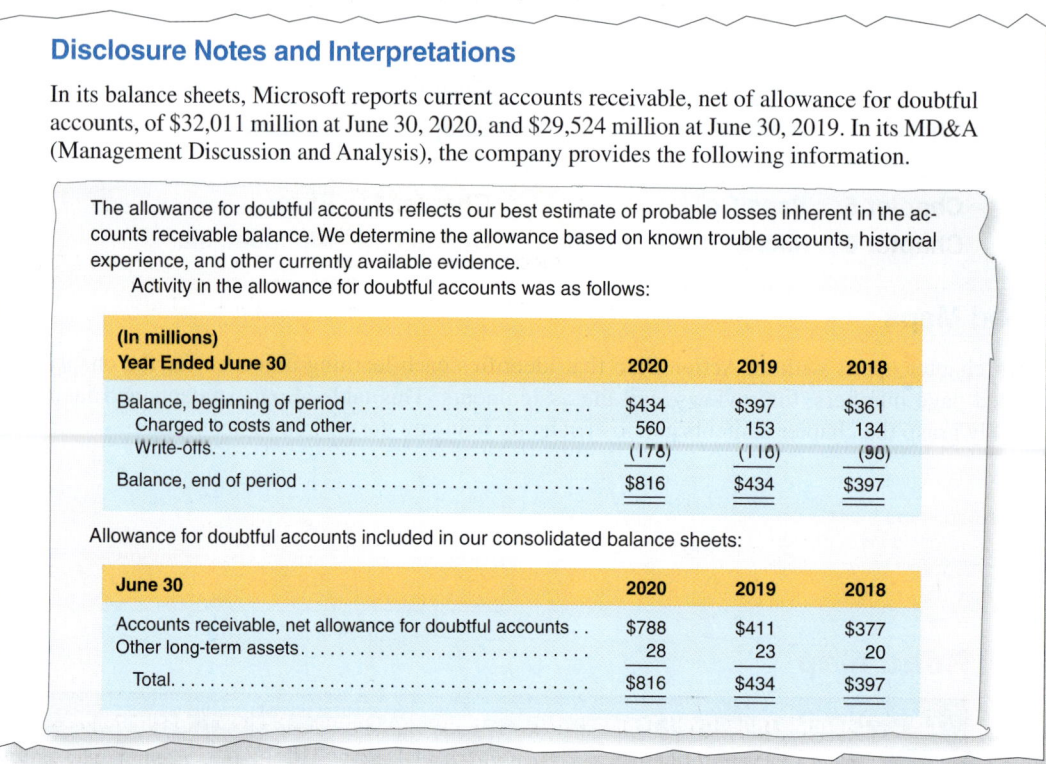

Disclosure Notes and Interpretations

In its balance sheets, Microsoft reports current accounts receivable, net of allowance for doubtful accounts, of $32,011 million at June 30, 2020, and $29,524 million at June 30, 2019. In its MD&A (Management Discussion and Analysis), the company provides the following information.

The allowance for doubtful accounts reflects our best estimate of probable losses inherent in the accounts receivable balance. We determine the allowance based on known trouble accounts, historical experience, and other currently available evidence.

Activity in the allowance for doubtful accounts was as follows:

(In millions) Year Ended June 30	2020	2019	2018
Balance, beginning of period	$434	$397	$361
Charged to costs and other	560	153	134
Write-offs	(178)	(116)	(98)
Balance, end of period	$816	$434	$397

Allowance for doubtful accounts included in our consolidated balance sheets:

June 30	2020	2019	2018
Accounts receivable, net allowance for doubtful accounts	$788	$411	$377
Other long-term assets	28	23	20
Total	$816	$434	$397

Financial Analysis Discussions

Each chapter includes a financial analysis discussion that introduces key ratios and applies them to the financial statements of the chapter's focus company. By weaving some analysis into each chapter, we try to instill in students a deeper appreciation for the significance of the accounting methods being discussed. One such analysis discussion follows.

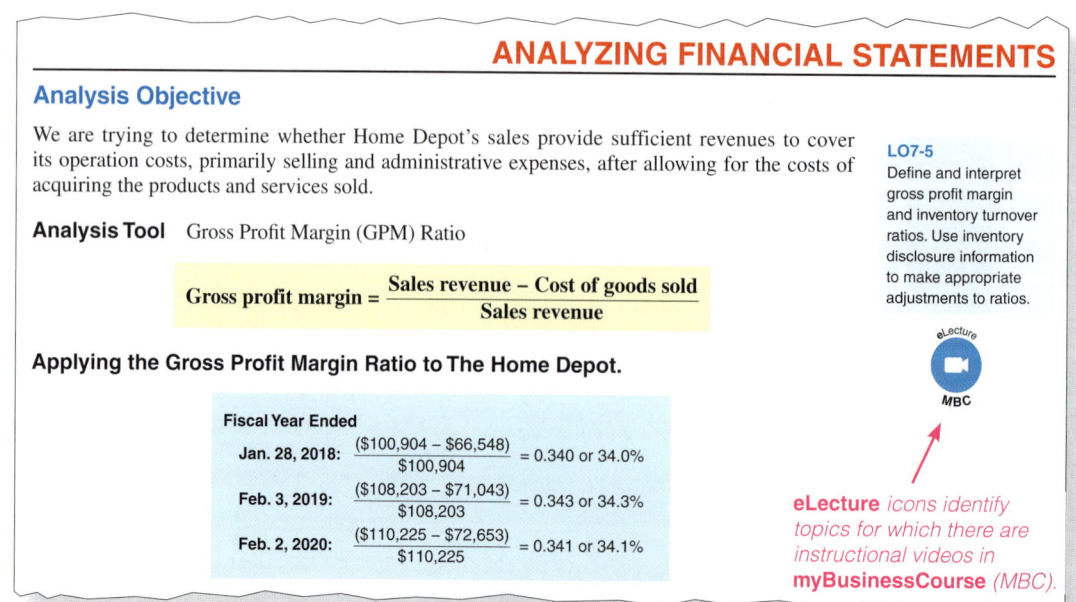

ANALYZING FINANCIAL STATEMENTS

Analysis Objective

We are trying to determine whether Home Depot's sales provide sufficient revenues to cover its operation costs, primarily selling and administrative expenses, after allowing for the costs of acquiring the products and services sold.

LO7-5 Define and interpret gross profit margin and inventory turnover ratios. Use inventory disclosure information to make appropriate adjustments to ratios.

eLecture MBC

Analysis Tool Gross Profit Margin (GPM) Ratio

$$\textbf{Gross profit margin} = \frac{\textbf{Sales revenue} - \textbf{Cost of goods sold}}{\textbf{Sales revenue}}$$

Applying the Gross Profit Margin Ratio to The Home Depot.

Fiscal Year Ended

Jan. 28, 2018: $\frac{(\$100{,}904 - \$66{,}548)}{\$100{,}904} = 0.340 \text{ or } 34.0\%$

Feb. 3, 2019: $\frac{(\$108{,}203 - \$71{,}043)}{\$108{,}203} = 0.343 \text{ or } 34.3\%$

Feb. 2, 2020: $\frac{(\$110{,}225 - \$72{,}653)}{\$110{,}225} = 0.341 \text{ or } 34.1\%$

***eLecture** icons identify topics for which there are instructional videos in **myBusinessCourse** (MBC).*

Assignments that Draw on Real Data

It is essential for students to be able to apply what they have learned to real financial statements. Therefore, we have included an abundance of assignments in each chapter that draw on recent, real data and disclosures. These assignments are readily identified by an icon in the margin that includes the company's ticker symbol and the exchange on which the company's stock trades. A representative example follows.

LO5-3 Homework MBC

Abbott Laboratories NYSE :: ABT
Bristol-Myers Squibb Company NYSE :: BMY
Johnson & Johnson NYSE :: JNJ
GlaxoSmithKline plc (ADR) NYSE :: GSK
Pfizer Inc. NYSE :: PFE
Moderna, Inc. NYSE :: MRNA

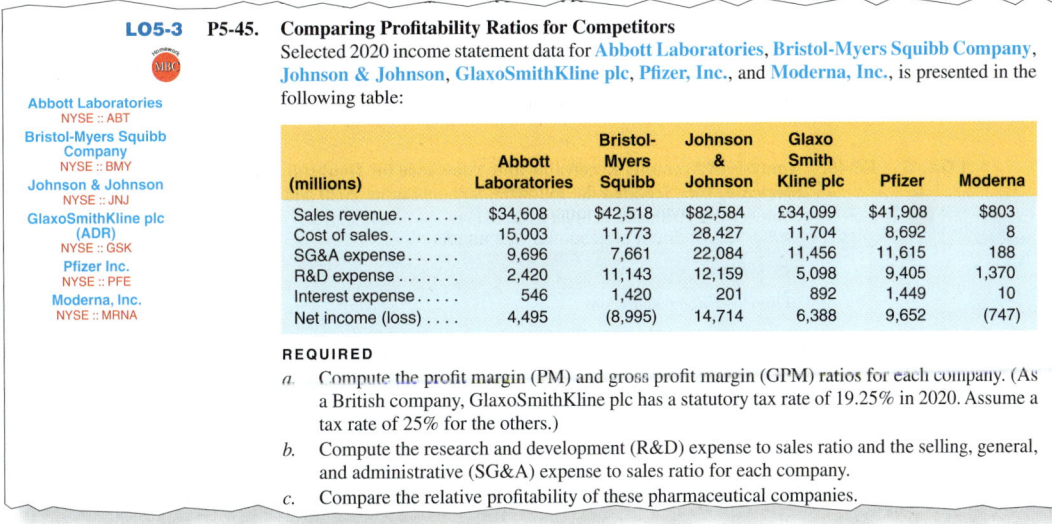

P5-45. Comparing Profitability Ratios for Competitors
Selected 2020 income statement data for Abbott Laboratories, Bristol-Myers Squibb Company, Johnson & Johnson, GlaxoSmithKline plc, Pfizer, Inc., and Moderna, Inc., is presented in the following table:

(millions)	Abbott Laboratories	Bristol-Myers Squibb	Johnson & Johnson	Glaxo Smith Kline plc	Pfizer	Moderna
Sales revenue.	$34,608	$42,518	$82,584	£34,099	$41,908	$803
Cost of sales.	15,003	11,773	28,427	11,704	8,692	8
SG&A expense.	9,696	7,661	22,084	11,456	11,615	188
R&D expense	2,420	11,143	12,159	5,098	9,405	1,370
Interest expense.	546	1,420	201	892	1,449	10
Net income (loss)	4,495	(8,995)	14,714	6,388	9,652	(747)

REQUIRED

a. Compute the profit margin (PM) and gross profit margin (GPM) ratios for each company. (As a British company, GlaxoSmithKline plc has a statutory tax rate of 19.25% in 2020. Assume a tax rate of 25% for the others.)

b. Compute the research and development (R&D) expense to sales ratio and the selling, general, and administrative (SG&A) expense to sales ratio for each company.

c. Compare the relative profitability of these pharmaceutical companies.

BALANCED APPROACH

As instructors of introductory financial accounting, we recognize that the first financial accounting course serves the general business students as well as potential accounting majors. *Financial Accounting* embraces this reality. This book **balances financial reporting, analysis, interpretation**, and **decision making** with the more standard aspects of accounting such as **journal entries**, **T-accounts**, and the **preparation of financial statements**.

3-Step Process: Analyze, Journalize, Post

One technique we use throughout the book to maintain a balanced approach is the incorporation of a 3-step process to analyze and record transactions. **Step 1** analyzes the impact of various transactions on the financial statements using the financial statement effects template (FSET). **Step 2** records the transaction using journal entries, and **Step 3** requires students to post the journal entries to T-accounts.

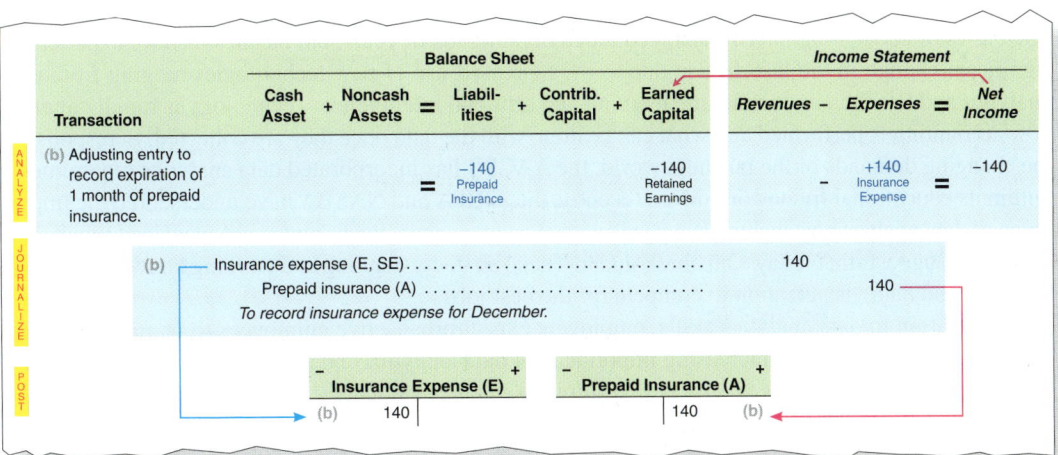

ANALYZE

	Balance Sheet									Income Statement				
Transaction	Cash Asset	+	Noncash Assets	=	Liabilities	+	Contrib. Capital	+	Earned Capital	*Revenues*	–	*Expenses*	=	*Net Income*
(b) Adjusting entry to record expiration of 1 month of prepaid insurance.				=	−140 Prepaid Insurance				−140 Retained Earnings		–	+140 Insurance Expense	=	−140

JOURNALIZE

		Dr.	Cr.
(b)	Insurance expense (E, SE).	140	
	Prepaid insurance (A)		140
	To record insurance expense for December.		

POST

– Insurance Expense (E) +	
(b) 140	

– Prepaid Insurance (A) +	
	140 (b)

The FSET captures each transaction's effects on the four financial statements: the balance sheet, income statement, statement of stockholders' equity, and statement of cash flows. For the balance sheet, we differentiate between cash and noncash assets to identify the cash effects of transactions. Likewise, equity is separated into the contributed and earned capital components (the latter includes retained earnings as its major element). Finally, income statement effects are separated into revenues, expenses, and net income (the updating of retained earnings is denoted with an arrow line running from net income to earned capital). The FSET provides a convenient means to represent financial accounting transactions and events in a simple, concise manner for assessing their effects on financial statements. To provide faculty flexibility to tailor instruction, all relevant end of chapter materials can be assigned using the journal entry approach or the FSET approach.

Assignments are organized to give instructors the flexibility to assign homework that emphasizes FSET and/or journal entries & T-accounts.

LO4, 5 Homework MBC

Steelcase, Inc.
NYSE :: SCS

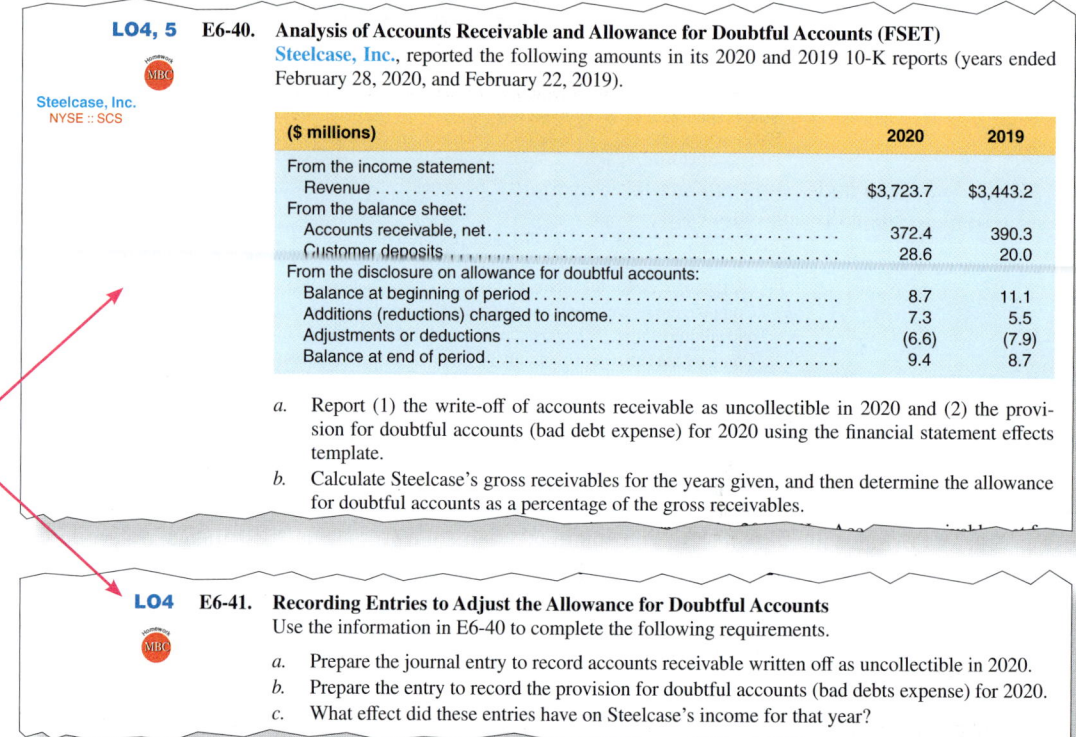

E6-40. Analysis of Accounts Receivable and Allowance for Doubtful Accounts (FSET)
Steelcase, Inc., reported the following amounts in its 2020 and 2019 10-K reports (years ended February 28, 2020, and February 22, 2019).

($ millions)	2020	2019
From the income statement:		
Revenue	$3,723.7	$3,443.2
From the balance sheet:		
Accounts receivable, net	372.4	390.3
Customer deposits	28.6	20.0
From the disclosure on allowance for doubtful accounts:		
Balance at beginning of period	8.7	11.1
Additions (reductions) charged to income	7.3	5.5
Adjustments or deductions	(6.6)	(7.9)
Balance at end of period	9.4	8.7

a. Report (1) the write-off of accounts receivable as uncollectible in 2020 and (2) the provision for doubtful accounts (bad debt expense) for 2020 using the financial statement effects template.

b. Calculate Steelcase's gross receivables for the years given, and then determine the allowance for doubtful accounts as a percentage of the gross receivables.

LO4 Homework MBC

E6-41. Recording Entries to Adjust the Allowance for Doubtful Accounts
Use the information in E6-40 to complete the following requirements.

a. Prepare the journal entry to record accounts receivable written off as uncollectible in 2020.
b. Prepare the entry to record the provision for doubtful accounts (bad debts expense) for 2020.
c. What effect did these entries have on Steelcase's income for that year?

DATA ANALYTICS & EXCEL SKILL DEVELOPMENT FOR CAREER READINESS

Data Analytics

The basics of accounting haven't changed much in hundreds of years, but businesses have experienced significant change in the last decade due to the increased use of new technologies ranging from data analytics and Blockchain to machine learning and artificial intelligence. Technology is rapidly altering how accounting is performed and what can be done with the data once they are collected. In response to the changing demands of the business world, the AACSB has incorporated data analytics requirements within its educational framework. More recently, the AICPA and NASBA have underscored the importance of data analytics by making it a significant element in the CPA Evolution Model Curriculum. The consensus suggests that today's business students need an understanding and working knowledge of data analytics and data visualization to compete for the best jobs.

In addition to data analytics skills, employers expect prospective employees to be proficient with Excel. In recognition of the increasing importance of data analytics and the need for Excel proficiency, the Seventh Edition includes several new features to enhance students' career readiness.

- In each chapter, we use data visualizations to depict financial information. It is important for students to become comfortable interpreting visual depictions of data.

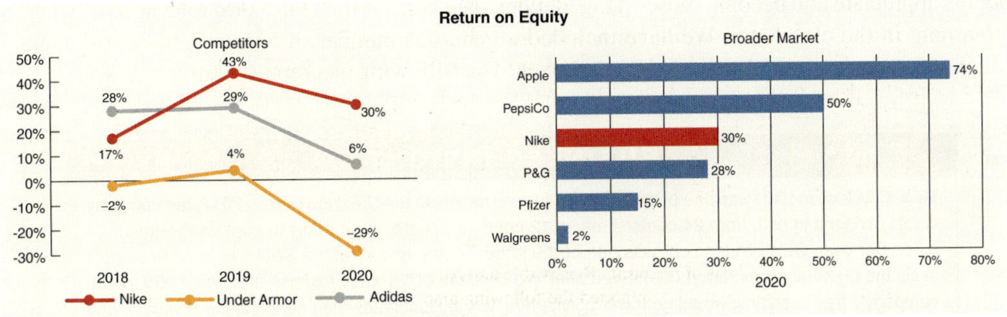

These companies do not have identical fiscal year-ends. For each fiscal year listed, balance sheets are dated from May 31 to December 31 of that year.

- Each chapter includes assignments that require students to use **Excel** and **Tableau** to hone data analysis and data visualization skills.

LO4-3 Data Analytics

DA4-1. Preparing and Interpreting Excel Visualizations Created from Income and Cash Flow Data
The Excel file associated with this exercise includes data extracted from Form 10-K reports for CVS Health Corporation (CVS) and Walgreens Boots Alliance (Walgreens Boots) for six years. In this exercise, we analyze changes to and the relations between net income and operating cash flows over a six-year period.

REQUIRED

1. Download Excel file DA4-1 found in myBusinessCourse.
2. Prepare a line chart for the six-year period for each company showing net income and operating cash flows. *Hint:* Highlight your data; click on Insert, Select line chart. There should be a separate line for net income and a separate line for operating cash flows. If necessary, edit the chart by opening the Chart Design tab and clicking Select Data. There should be two series.
3. Use the visualizations to answer the following questions.
   a. In what year(s) does net income exceed operating cash flows for CVS?
   b. In what year(s) do operating cash flows exceed net income for Walgreens Boots?
   c. Over the six-year period, which year showed the largest difference between net income and operating cash flows for CVS?

- **Appendix B** at the end of the book provides an overview of data analytics, data visualization, and best practices for the effective display of data.

DATA ANALYTICS

Data analytics can broadly be defined as the process of examining sets of data with the goal of discovering useful information from patterns found in the data. Increasingly, this process is aided by computers running programs ranging from basic spreadsheet software, such as Microsoft Excel and Google Sheets, to specialized software, such as Tableau or Power BI. This technology can reveal trends and insights that would otherwise be lost in the overwhelming amount of data.

LO1 Define Big Data and describe its four attributes.

eLecture MBC

Big Data

The concept of data analytics is intertwined with the concept of **big data**. Although no precise definition exists for big data, a commonly accepted definition is that big data is a collection of data that is both extremely large and also extremely complex, thus making its analysis beyond the scope of traditional tools. Important attributes of big data, commonly referred to as the four V's, are Volume, Variety, Velocity, and Veracity. **Volume** refers to the amount of data. According to IDC (a market intelligence company), there were 33 available zettabytes of data globally in 2018. IDC predicted

- MBC now contains a series of short videos that demonstrate the basic functions of Excel. These videos can be accessed within MBC as part of your MBC course.

INNOVATIVE PEDAGOGY

Business Insights

Students appreciate and become more engaged when they can see the real-world relevance of what they are learning in the classroom. We have included a generous number of current, real-world examples throughout each chapter in Business Insight boxes. The following is a representative example:

BUSINESS INSIGHT

General Electric (GE) was one of the biggest dividend payers in the U.S. However, in 2017, the company cut its dividend in half, from 24 cents/share to 12 cents per share, in an effort to save cash—about $4 billion per year. GE's dividend cut was one of the largest in the history of the S&P 500 and the biggest since the great recession era (2009). Even after this dividend cut, it was projected that about 85% of the company's free cash flow would go toward dividends, which illuminates the change in the company and its business over time. The stock price fell around 7% on the day the dividend cut was announced and almost 6% the next day (though other negative news was simultaneously announced, so not all of the price drop was likely due to the dividend news). In December of 2018, the company slashed the dividend further to only 1 cent per share.

Decision Making Orientation

One primary goal of a financial accounting course is to teach students the skills needed to apply their accounting knowledge to solving real business problems. With that goal in mind, **You Make the Call** boxes in each chapter encourage students to apply the material presented to solving actual business scenarios.

YOU MAKE THE CALL

You Are the Division Manager You are the division manager for a main operating division of your company. You are concerned that a declining PPE turnover is adversely affecting your division's profitability. What specific actions can you take to increase PPE turnover? [Answers on page 8-25]

Learning Objective Reviews

Financial accounting can be challenging—especially for students lacking business experience or previous exposure to business courses. To reinforce concepts presented in each chapter and to ensure student comprehension, we include a review problem at the conclusion of each learning objective. Answers to the review problems are included at the end of the chapter. Each review has a corresponding Guided Example video, available to students in myBusinessCourse (MBC), our online learning and homework system. In addition, each Review is assignable in MBC.

Review 6-4 LO6-4 **Estimating Uncollectible Accounts and Reporting Receivables**

GuidedExample MBC

Guided Example *icons denote the availability of a demonstration video in* **myBusinessCourse** *(MBC).*

At December 31, Engel Company had a balance of $770,000 in its Accounts Receivable account and an unused balance of $7,000 in its Allowance for Uncollectible Accounts. The company then analyzed and aged its accounts receivable as follows:

Current	$468,000
1–60 days past due	244,000
61–180 days past due	38,000
Over 180 days past due	20,000
Total accounts receivable	$770,000

In the past, the company experienced losses as follows: 1% of current balances, 5% of balances 1–60 days past due, 15% of balances 61–180 days past due, and 40% of balances over 180 days past due. The company bases its provision for credit losses on the aging analysis.

Required

a. What amount of uncollectible accounts (bad debts) expense will Engel report in its annual income statement?

b. Show how Accounts Receivable and the Allowance for Uncollectible Accounts appear in its December 31, balance sheet.

c. Assume that Engel's allowance for uncollectible accounts has maintained a historical average of 2% of gross accounts receivable. How do you interpret the level of the current allowance percentage?

Research Insights for Business Students

Academic research plays an important role in the way business is conducted, accounting is performed, and students are taught. It is important for students to recognize how modern research and modern business practice interact. Therefore, we periodically incorporate relevant research to help students understand the important relation between research and modern business.

RESEARCH INSIGHT

Accounting Conservatism and Cost of Debt Research indicates that companies applying more conservative accounting methods incur a lower cost of debt. Research also suggests that while accounting conservatism can lead to lower-quality accounting income (because such income does not fully reflect economic reality), creditors are more confident in the numbers and view them as more credible. Evidence also implies that companies can lower the required return demanded by creditors (the risk premium) by issuing high-quality financial reports that include enhanced note disclosures and detailed supplemental reports.

FLEXIBILITY FOR COURSES OF VARYING LENGTHS

Many instructors have approached us to ask about suggested chapter coverage based on courses of varying length. To that end, we provide the following table of possible course designs:

	15 Week Semester-Course	10 Week Quarter-Course	6 Week Mini-Course	1 Week Intensive-Course
Chapter 1	Week 1	Week 1	Week 1	Day 1
Chapter 2	Week 2 & 3	Week 2	Week 1 & 2	
Chapter 3	Week 3 & 4	Week 3 & 4	Week 2 & 3	Day 2
Chapter 4	Week 5 & 6	Week 4 & 5	Optional	Optional
Chapter 5	Week 6 & 7	Optional	Optional	Optional
Chapter 6	Week 7 & 8	Week 6	Week 3	Day 3
Chapter 7	Week 9	Week 7	Week 4	Day 4
Chapter 8	Week 10	Week 8	Week 5	
Chapter 9	Week 11 & 12	Week 9	Week 6	Day 5
Chapter 10	Week 12 & 13	Week 10	Week 6 (optional)	Skim
Chapter 11	Week 14	Optional	Optional	Optional
Chapter 12	Week 15	Optional	Optional	Optional

NEW IN THE 7TH EDITION

- We have expanded the coverage, resources, and assignments related to data analytics and Excel skill development in an effort to enhance career readiness.
- **Chapter Updates:** As appropriate, the text and assignments have been updated to reflect the latest FASB standards and other current information:
  - Chapter 4 incorporates restricted cash as part of total cash presented on the statement of cash flows.
  - Chapter 5 includes updated information on industry ratios that is referenced in real life examples not only in this chapter, but throughout the text.
  - Chapter 8 includes a discussion on digital assets with a supporting end of chapter assignment.

- Chapter 10 discusses the election in lease accounting to not separate lease and non-lease components.
- Chapter 11 reflects the new guidance on accounting for convertible instruments (including the impact on diluted EPS).
- Chapter 12 briefly discusses the recording of credit losses on available-for-sale debt securities and new guidance on the amortization of goodwill for private companies.
- Expanded the FSET presentation in Chapter 4 (transactions that impact the statement of cash flows) and in Chapter 10 (accounting for operating leases by the lessee).

- **Deere & Co.** replaced Delta Air Lines as the focus company of Chapter 10.
- In addition to the chapter-specific changes, there have been several changes that span the entire book. Some of these global changes include:
  - Added a Road Map to each chapter that summarizes the reviews and assignments for each learning objective in the chapter.
  - Added review problems to the end of each learning objective, replacing the mid-chapter and end of chapter reviews.
  - Expanded all end of chapter materials to allow for the assigning of either the journal entry approach or the FSET approach.
  - Updated numbers for examples, illustrations, and assignments that use real data
  - Updated note disclosures and other nonfinancial disclosures
  - Updated excerpts from the business and popular press
  - Nearly all of the assignments in each chapter have been revised with updated data or replaced with a new company focus.

TECHNOLOGY THAT IMPROVES LEARNING AND COMPLEMENTS FACULTY INSTRUCTION

95% of students who used MBC, responded that MBC helped them learn accounting.*

myBusinessCourse is an online learning and assessment program intended to complement your textbook and faculty instruction. Access to **myBusinessCourse** is FREE ONLY with the purchase of a new textbook, but access can be purchased separately.

MBC is ideal for faculty seeking opportunities to augment their course with an online component. MBC is also a turnkey solution for online courses. The following are some of the features of MBC.

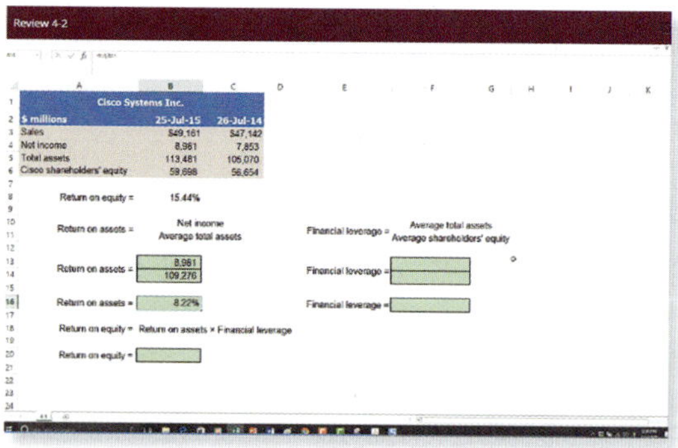

Increase Student Readiness

- **eLectures** cover each chapter's learning objectives and concepts. Consistent with the text and created by the authors, these videos are ideal for remediation and online instruction.
- **Guided Examples** are narrated video demonstrations created by the authors that show students how to solve select problems from the textbook.
- Immediate feedback with **auto-graded homework**.
- **Test Bank** questions that can be incorporated into your assignments.
- Instructor **gradebook** with immediate grade results.

86% of students said they would encourage their professor to continue using MBC in future terms.*

Make Instruction Needs-Based*

- Identify where your students are struggling and customize your instruction to address their needs.
- Gauge how your entire class or individual students are performing by viewing the easy-to-use gradebook.
- Ensure your students are getting the additional reinforcement and direction they need between class meetings.

* These statistics are based on the results of two surveys in which 2,330 students participated.

Provide Instruction and Practice 24/7

- Assign homework from your Cambridge Business Publishers' textbook and have MBC grade it for you automatically.
- With our Videos, your students can revisit accounting topics as often as they like or until they master the topic.
- Make homework due before class to ensure students enter your classroom prepared.
- For an additional fee, upgrade MBC to include the eBook and you have all the tools needed for an online course.

Integrate with LMS

myBusinessCourse integrates with many learning management systems, including **Canvas**, **Blackboard**, **Moodle**, **D2L**, **Schoology**, and **Sakai**. Your gradebooks sync automatically.

ADDITIONAL RESOURCES

Financial Accounting Bootcamp

This interactive tutorial is intended for use in programs that either require or would like to offer a tutorial that can be used as a refresher of topics introduced in the first financial accounting course. It is designed as an asynchronous, interactive, self-paced experience for students. Available Learning Modules (You Select) follow.

1. Introducing Financial Accounting (approximate completion time 2 hours)
2. Constructing Financial Statements (approximate completion time 4 hours)
3. Adjusting Entries and Completing the Accounting Cycle (approximate completion time 4 hours)
4. Reporting and Analyzing Cash Flows (approximate completion time 3.5 hours)
5. Analyzing and Interpreting Financial Statements (approximate completion time 3.5 hours)
6. Excel and Time-Value of Money Basics (approximate completion time 2 hours)

This is a separate, saleable item. Contact your sales representative to receive more information or email customerservice@cambridgepub.com.

Companion Casebook

Cases in Financial Reporting, 8th edition by Michael Drake (Brigham Young University), Ellen Engel (University of Illinois—Chicago), D. Eric Hirst (University of Texas—Austin), and Mary Lea McAnally (Texas A&M University). This book comprises 27 cases and is a perfect companion book for faculty interested in exposing students to a wide range of real financial statements. Each case deals with a specific financial accounting topic within the context of one (or more) company's financial statements. Each case contains financial statement information and a set of directed questions pertaining to one or two specific financial accounting issues. This is a separate, saleable casebook (ISBN 978-1-61853-122-3). Contact your sales representative to receive a desk copy or email customerservice@cambridgepub.com.

For Instructors

myBusinessCourse: An online learning and assessment program intended to complement your textbook and classroom instruction (see page xii for more details). Access to myBusinessCourse is FREE with the purchase of a new textbook and can also be purchased separately.

Solutions Manual: Created by the authors, the *Solutions Manual* contains complete solutions to all the assignment material in the text.

PowerPoint: The PowerPoint slides outline key elements of each chapter.

Test Bank: The Test Bank includes multiple-choice items, short essay questions, and problems.

Website: All instructor materials are accessible via the book's Website (password protected) along with other useful links and marketing information. www.cambridgepub.com

For Students

myBusinessCourse: An online learning and assessment program intended to complement your textbook and faculty instruction (see page xii for more details). This easy-to-use program grades assignments automatically and provides you with additional help when your instructor is not available. Access is free with new copies of this textbook (look for the page containing the access code towards the front of the book).

Student Solutions Manual: Created by the authors, the student Solutions Manual contains solutions to the even numbered assignments in the textbook. This is a **restricted** item that is only available to students after their instructor has authorized its purchase.

ACKNOWLEDGMENTS

This book has benefited greatly from the valuable feedback of focus group attendees, reviewers, students, and colleagues. We are extremely grateful to them for their help in making this project a success.

Ajay Adhikari
Hank Adler
Pervaiz Alam
Kris Allee
Bob Allen
Beverley Alleyne
Samuel Anderson
Dennis Applegate
Elizabeth Arnold
Lawrence Aronhime
Frances Ayres
Paul Bahnson
Jan Barton
Progyan Basu
Randy Beatty
James Benjamin
Anne Beyer
Robert Bowen
Kimberly Brickler-Ulrich
Rada Brooks
Helen Brubeck
Jacqueline Burke
Bruce Busta
Richard J. Campbell
Judson Caskey
Sumantra Chakravarty
Paul Chaney
Craig Chapman
Sean Chen
Hans Christensen
Paul Clikeman
Daniel Cohen
John Core
Erin Cornelsen
Steve Crawford
Somnath Das
Angela Davis
Mark Dawkins
David DeBoskey
Mark DeFond
Bruce Dehning
Bala G. Dharan
Timothy Dimond
Joe Dulin
Reed Easton
Ellen Engel
Bud Fennema
Tom Fields
Mark Finn
Linda Flaming
David Folsom
Elizabeth Foster
Micah Frankel
Henry Friedman
Christina Gehrke
George Geis
Elisabeth Gilgen
Jacqueline Gillette
Hubert Glover
Nancy Goble
Rajul Gokarn
Jeff Gramlich
Wayne Guay
Umit Gurun
Susan Hamlen
Rebecca Hann
Ling Harris
David Harvey
Rayford Harwell
Susan Hass
Joseph Hatch
Haihong He
Kenneth Henry
Eric Hirst
Jeffrey Hoopes
Robert Hoskin
Ying Huang
Marsha Huber
Glenn Huels
Richard E. Hurley
Robert L. Hurt
Marianne L. James
Ross Jennings
Jane Jollineau
Chris Jones
Januj Juneja
Jane Kennedy
Irene Kim
Jinhwan Kim
Michael Kimbrough
Ken Klein
Allison Koester
Kevin Koharki
Kalin Kolev
Gopal Krishnan
Yingxu Kuang
Susan Kulp
Benjamin Lansford
Stephanie Larocque
Cheol Lee
Zawadi Lemayian
Andrew Leone
Annette Leps
Alina Lerman
Xu Li
Thomas Lin
Brad Lindsey
Thomas J. Linsmeier
Jiangxia Liu
Frank Longo
Barbara Lougee
Luann Lynch
Jason MacGregor
Bill Magrogan
Lois Mahoney
Daphne Main
Cathy Margolin
Maureen Mascha
Dawn Matsumoto
Katie Maxwell
John McCauley
Bruce McClain
Harvey McCown
Katie McDermott
Marc McIntosh
Jeff McMillan
Greg Miller
Jeffrey Miller
Jeffrey Miller
Marilyn Misch
Stephen Moehrle
Matt Munson

Mark Myring
Sandeep Nabar
James Naughton
Karen Nelson
Christopher Noe
Walter O'Connor
Jose Oaks
Shailendra Pandit
Simon Pearlman
Marietta Peytcheva
Brandis Phillips
Kristen Portz
Richard Price
S.E.C. Purvis
Kathleen Rankin
Lynn Rees
Susan Riffe
Leslie Robinson
Paulette Rodriguez
Darren Roulstone
Debra Salbador
Anwar Y. Salimi
Haresh Sapra
Robert Scharlach
Steve Sefcik
Timothy Shields
Scott Showalter
Nemit Shroff
Andreas Simon
Robert Singer
Praveen Sinha
David Smith
Eric So
Kathleen Sobieralski
Robin Soffer
Gregory Sommers
Sri Sridharan
Vic Stanton
Jack Stecher
Doug Stevens
Tom Stober
Toby Stock
Phillip Stocken
William Stout
Rob Stussie
Shyam Sunder
Andrew Sutherland
Robert J. Swieringa
Thomas Tallerico
Mary Tarling
Robin Tarpley
Nicole Thibodeau
Patti Tilley
Rodrigo Verdi
Robert Walsh
Isabel Wang
Xue Wang
Rick Warne
Catherine Weber
Joe Weber
Lourdes White
Donna Whitten
Christopher Williams
Gayle Williams
Rahnl Wood
Jia Wu
Jason Xiao
Jennifer Yin
Teri Yohn
Rachel Yoon
Susan Young
Stephen Zeff
Yuping Zhao
Jian Zhou

The author team of this seventh edition of *Financial Accounting* would like to acknowledge the contributions of our colleague and friend, Tom Dyckman. Tom is well-known in the accounting academy for his scholarship, his teaching, his mentoring, and his service to the field. In addition, we know him as a generous collaborator from the first edition of *Financial Accounting* to the sixth. But with this seventh edition, he has chosen to pass the baton to us and enjoy a well-deserved retirement. We wish him and Ann many years in the warmer climes of Florida.

In addition, we are extremely grateful to George Werthman, Lorraine Gleeson, Jocelyn Mousel, Dana Zieman, Jill Sternard, Debbie McQuade, Terry McQuade, and the entire team at Cambridge Business Publishers for their encouragement, enthusiasm, and guidance.

Michelle Hanlon *Robert Magee* *Glenn Pfeiffer*

January 2022

Brief Contents

Contents

Chapter 1 Introducing Financial Accounting 1-1

Chapter 2 Constructing Financial Statements 2-1

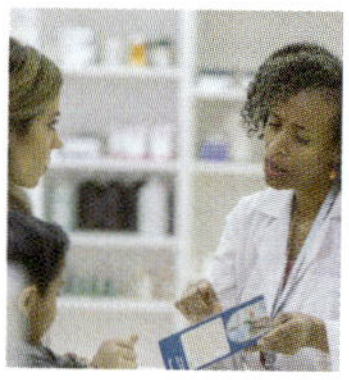

Chapter 3 Adjusting Accounts for Financial Statements **3-1**

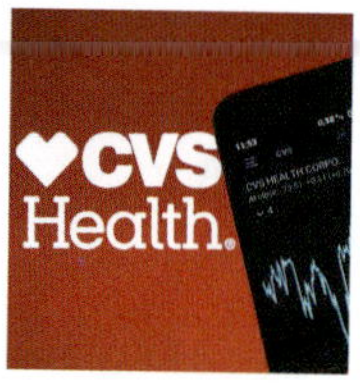

Chapter 4 Reporting and Analyzing Cash Flows **4-1**

Microsoft Azure

Doors
Automotive

Crest
DURACELL

verizon

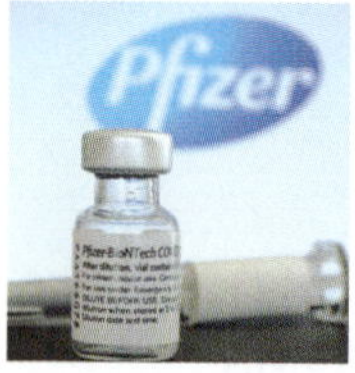

Chapter **11**
Reporting and Analyzing Stockholders' Equity **11-1**

Chapter **12**
Reporting and Analyzing Financial Investments **12-1**

Appendix A

Appendix B

Chapter 1

Introducing Financial Accounting

Learning Objectives identify the key learning goals of the chapter.

LEARNING OBJECTIVES

LO1-1 Identify the users of accounting information and discuss the costs and benefits of disclosure.

LO1-2 Describe a company's business activities and explain how these activities are represented by the accounting equation.

LO1-3 Identify the four key financial statements: balance sheet, income statement, statement of stockholders' equity, and statement of cash flows.

LO1-4 Describe how standardized accounting principles and a regulatory environment are important to financial statement integrity.

LO1-5 Compute two key ratios that are commonly used to assess profitability and risk—return on equity and the debt-to-equity ratio.

LO1-6 Appendix 1A: Explain the conceptual framework for financial reporting.

Road Maps summarize each chapter's resources and categorize them by learning objective.

Assignments reinforce learning and can be completed by hand or within MBC.

Road Map

LO	Learning Objective | Topics	Page	eLecture	Review	Assignments
LO1-1	Identify the users of accounting information and discuss the costs and benefits of disclosure.	1-3	e1-1	R1–1	M1-25, E1-28, E1-34, C1-49, C1-50, DA1-1
LO1-2	Describe a company's business activities and explain how these activities are represented by the accounting equation.	1-7	e1-2	R1–2	M1-19, M1-20, M1-21, E1-27, E1-29, E1-32, E1-33, P1-36, P1-37, P1-38, P1-43, C1-47
LO1-3	Identify the four key financial statements: balance sheet, income statement, statement of stockholders' equity, and statement of cash flows.	1-11	e1-3	R1–3	M1-22, M1-23, M1-24, E1-29, E1-30, E1-31, P1-37, P1-38, P1-39,P1-40, P1-41, P1-42, P1-43, P1-44, P1-45, C1-46, C1-47, C1-49
LO1-4	Describe how standardized accounting principles and a regulatory environment are important to financial statement integrity.	1-16	e1-4	R1–4	M1-26, E1-34, C1-50, DA1-3
LO1-5	Compute two key ratios that are commonly used to assess profitability and risk—return on equity and the debt-to-equity ratio.	1-21	e1-5	R1–5	E1-32, E1-33, P1-36, P1-43, P1-44, P1-45, C1-46, C1-47, C1-48, C1-49, DA1-2
LO1-6	Appendix 1A: Explain the conceptual framework for financial reporting.	1-25	e1-6	R1–6	E1-35

Learning Objectives identify the key learning goals of the chapter.

eLectures are videos available in MBC that provide 3-5 minute reviews of each learning objective.

Reviews follow each learning objective and require students to apply what they have just learned. Guided Example videos accompany the Reviews and demonstrate how to solve various types of problems. Reviews are also assignable in MBC.

Data Analysis (DA) exercises using Excel and Tableau are identified with blue font. Exercises are assignable in MBC.

A **Focus Company** *introduces each chapter and illustrates the relevance of accounting in everyday business.*

NIKE
www.Nike.com

Phil Knight majored in accounting and was a member of the track team at the University of Oregon. A few years after graduation, Knight teamed up with his former track coach, Bill Bowerman, to form a business called Blue Ribbon Sports to import, sell, and distribute running shoes from Japan. Blue Ribbon Sports, or BRS as it came to be known, was started on a shoestring—Knight and Bowerman each contributed $500 to start the business. A few years later, BRS introduced its own line of running shoes called Nike. It also unveiled a new logo, the now familiar Nike swoosh. Following the overwhelming success of the Nike shoe line, BRS officially changed its company name to Nike, Inc. Currently, the company is worth more than $120 billion. Knight is the former CEO and the Chairman, Emeritus of Nike, Inc.

Today, Nike, Inc. has sales in almost every country on the planet and, in the fiscal year ended May, 2021, Nike had total revenues of more than $37 billion and income of $2.5 billion. How does someone take a $1,000 investment and turn it into a company whose stock is worth more than $120 billion? Along the way, Nike management made countless decisions that ultimately led the company to where it is today. Each of these decisions involved identifying alternative courses of action and weighing their costs, benefits, and risks in light of the available information.

Accounting is the process of identifying, measuring, and communicating financial information to help people make economic decisions. People use accounting information to facilitate a wide variety of transactions, including assessing whether, and on what terms, they should invest in a firm, seek employment in a business, or continue purchasing its products. Accounting information is crucial to any successful business, and without it, most businesses would not even exist.

This book explains how to create and analyze financial statements, an important source of accounting information prepared by companies to communicate with a variety of users. We begin by introducing transactions between the firm and its investors, creditors, suppliers, employees, and customers. We continue by demonstrating how accounting principles are applied to these transactions to create the financial statements. Then we "invert" the process and learn how to analyze the firm's financial statements to assess the firm's underlying economic performance. Our philosophy is simple—we believe it is crucial to have a deep understanding of financial accounting to become critical readers and users of financial statements. Financial statements tell a story—a business story. Our goal is to understand that story and apply the knowledge gleaned from financial statements to make good business decisions.

Sources: Nike.com; Nike, Inc. 10-K Report for the year ended May 31, 2021; *Business Week* (October 2007, August 2009); *Portland Business Journal* (October 2007); *Fortune* (February 2012). For more on Phil Knight and Nike's history, see the book *Shoe Dog* (published by Scribner).

CHAPTER ORGANIZATION

***Chapter Organization** Charts visually depict the key topics and their sequence within the chapter.*

Introducing Financial Accounting

Demand for Accounting Information	Business Activities	Financial Statements	Financial Reporting Environment	Financial Statement Analysis
• Who Uses Financial Accounting Information? • Costs and Benefits of Disclosure	• Planning Activities • Investing Activities • Financing Activities • Operating Activities	• Balance Sheet • Income Statement • Statement of Stockholders' Equity • Statement of Cash Flows • Financial Statement Linkages	• Generally Accepted Accounting Principles • Regulation and Oversight • Role of the Auditor • A Global Perspective • Conceptual Framework (Appendix 1A)	• Profitability Analysis • Credit Risk Analysis

DEMAND FOR ACCOUNTING INFORMATION

LO1-1 Identify the users of accounting information and discuss the costs and benefits of disclosure.

eLecture MBC

***eLecture** icons identify topics for which there are instructional videos in **myBusinessCourse** (MBC). See the Preface for more information on MBC.*

Accounting can be defined as the process of recording, summarizing, and analyzing financial transactions. While accounting information attempts to satisfy the needs of a diverse set of users, the accounting information a company produces can be classified into two categories (see **Exhibit 1.1**):[1]

- **Financial accounting**—designed primarily for decision-makers outside of the company
- **Managerial accounting**—designed primarily for decision-makers within the company

EXHIBIT 1.1 Information Needs of Decision-makers Who Use Financial and Managerial Accounting

	Decision-Makers	Decisions	Information
Financial Accounting	• Investors and analysts • Creditors • Suppliers and customers	• Buy or sell stock? • Lend or not? • Purchase/sell goods or not?	• Sales and costs • Cash in and out • Assets and liabilities
Managerial Accounting	• Top management • Marketing teams • Production and operations	• Develop new strategy? • Launch a new product or not? • Manage operations	• Product sales and costs • Department performance reports • Budgets and quality reports

Financial accounting reports include information about company profitability and financial health. This information is useful to various economic actors who wish to engage in contracts with the firm, including investors, creditors, employees, customers, and governments. Managerial accounting information is not reported outside of the company because it includes proprietary information about the profitability of specific products, divisions, or customers. Company managers use managerial accounting reports to make decisions such as whether to drop or add products or divisions, or whether to continue serving different types of customers. This text focuses on understanding and analyzing financial accounting information.

[1] Businesses also have to compute a measure of income for income tax purposes in order to file tax returns in the jurisdictions that require them to file. This book is not about taxation, but we cover the accounting for income taxes in Chapter 10.

Who Uses Financial Accounting Information?

Demand for financial accounting information derives from numerous users including:

- Shareholders and potential shareholders
- Creditors and suppliers
- Managers and directors
- Financial analysts
- Other users

FYI features provide additional information that complements the text.

Shareholders and Potential Shareholders Corporations are the dominant form of business organization for large companies around the world, and corporate shareholders are one important group of decision-makers that have an interest in financial accounting information. A **corporation** is a form of business organization that is characterized by a large number of owners who are not involved in managing the day-to-day operations of the company.[2] A corporation exists as a legal entity that issues **shares of stock** to its owners in exchange for cash; therefore, the owners of a corporation are referred to as *shareholders* or **stockholders**.

FYI Shareholders of a corporation are its owners; although managers can own stock in the corporation, most shareholders are not managers.

CORPORATION

Because the shareholders are not involved in the day-to-day operations of the business, they rely on the information in financial statements to evaluate management performance and assess the company's financial condition.

In addition to corporations, sole proprietorships, partnerships, and limited liability companies are common forms of business ownership. A **sole proprietorship** has a single owner who typically manages the daily operations. Small family-run businesses, such as corner grocery stores, are commonly organized as sole proprietorships. A **partnership** has two or more owners who are also usually involved in managing the business. Many professionals, such as lawyers and CPAs, organize their businesses as partnerships. Many new businesses today start up as a limited liability company (LLC). An LLC allows for limited liability for the owners similar to a corporation, while allowing for more flexibility and other features that are similar to a partnership.

Most corporations begin as small, privately held businesses (sole proprietorships, partnerships, or an LLC). As their operations expand, however, they require additional capital to finance their growth. One of the principal advantages of a corporation over the other organizational forms of doing business is the ability to raise large amounts of cash by issuing (selling) stock. For example, as Nike grew from a small business with only two owners into a larger company, it raised the funds needed for expansion by selling shares of Nike stock to new shareholders. In the United States, large corporations can raise funds by issuing stock on organized exchanges, such as the **New York Stock Exchange (NYSE)** or **NASDAQ** (which is an acronym for the National Association of Securities Dealers Automated Quotations system). Corporations with stock that is traded on public exchanges are known as *publicly traded corporations* or simply *public corporations*. The raising of capital from a large group of outside shareholders leads to what is known as the separation of ownership and control. For example, as Nike sold more stock, the CEO (Knight) owned a smaller amount of the shares. In cases of such separation, which exists at most publicly traded firms, the information flow from the managers to the shareholders is very important.

Financial statements and the accompanying note disclosures provide information on the risk and return associated with owning shares of stock in the corporation, and they reveal how well management has performed. Financial statements also provide valuable insights into future performance by revealing management's plans for new products, new operating procedures, and new strategic directions for the company as well as for their implementation. Corporate management provides this information because the information reduces uncertainty about the company's future prospects which, in turn, increases the market price of its shares and helps the company raise the funds it needs to grow.

future performance

Creditors and Suppliers Few businesses rely solely on shareholders for the cash needed to operate the company. Instead, most companies borrow from banks or other lenders known as **creditors**. Creditors are interested in the potential borrower's ability to repay. They use financial

FYI Financial statements are typically required when a business requests a bank loan. (If the business is very small, then tax returns will often suffice).

[2] Most countries have business forms that are similar in structure to those of a U.S. corporation, though they are referred to by different names. For example, while firms that are incorporated in the United States have the extension "Inc." appended to their names, similar firms in the United Kingdom are referred to as a Public Limited Company, which has the extension "PLC."

Key Terms *are highlighted in bold, red font.*

accounting information to help determine loan terms, loan amounts, interest rates, and collateral. In addition, creditors' loans often include contractual requirements based on information found in the financial statements.

Suppliers use financial information to establish credit sales terms and to determine their long-term commitment to supply-chain relationships. Supplier companies often justify an expansion of *their* businesses based on the growth and financial health of their customers. Both creditors and suppliers rely on information in the financial statements to monitor and adjust their contracts and commitments with a company.

Managers and Directors Financial statements can be thought of as a financial report card for management. A well-managed company earns a good return for its shareholders, and this is reflected in the financial statements. In most companies, management is compensated, at least in part, based on the financial performance of the company. That is, managers often receive cash bonuses, shares of stock, or other *incentive compensation* that is linked directly to the information in the financial statements.

FYI The Sarbanes-Oxley Act requires issuers of securities to disclose whether they have a code of ethics for the senior officers.

Publicly traded corporations are required by law to have a **board of directors**. Directors are elected by the shareholders to represent shareholder interests and oversee management. The board hires executive management and regularly reviews company operations. Directors use financial accounting information to review the results of operations, evaluate future strategy, and assess management performance.

Both managers and directors use the published financial statements of *other companies* to perform comparative analyses and establish performance benchmarks. For example, managers in some companies are paid a bonus for financial performance that exceeds the industry average.

BUSINESS INSIGHT

Court cases involving corporations such as **Enron**, **Tyco**, and **WorldCom** (now **MCI**) have found executives, including several CEOs, guilty of issuing fraudulent financial statements. These executives have received substantial fines and, in some cases, long jail sentences. These trials have resulted in widespread loss of reputation and credibility among corporate boards.

Financial Analysts Many decision-makers lack the time, resources, or expertise to efficiently and effectively analyze financial statements. Instead, they rely on professional financial analysts, such as credit rating agencies like **Moody's** investment services, portfolio managers, and security analysts. Financial analysts play an important role in the dissemination of financial information and often specialize in specific industries. Their analysis helps to identify and assess risk, forecast performance, establish prices for new issues of stock, and make buy-or-sell recommendations to investors.

Other Users of Financial Accounting Information External decision-makers include many users of accounting information in addition to those listed above. For example, ***prospective employees*** often examine the financial statements of an employer to learn about the company before interviewing for or accepting a new job.

Labor unions examine financial statements in order to assess the financial health of firms prior to negotiating labor contracts on behalf of the firms' employees. ***Customers*** use accounting information to assess the ability of a company to deliver products or services and to assess the company's long-term reliability.

Government agencies rely on accounting information to develop and enforce regulations, including public protection, price setting, import-export, taxation, and various other policies.[3] Timely and reliable information is crucial to effective regulatory policy. Moreover, accounting information is often used to assess penalties for companies that violate regulations.

[3] A company's tax returns are distinctly different from its financial statements. Tax returns are prepared for tax authorities in order to comply with income tax rules. The financial statements are prepared to provide information to investors, creditors, and other decision-makers outside of the business.

Costs and Benefits of Disclosure

The act of providing financial information to external users is called **disclosure**. As with every decision, the benefits of disclosure must be weighed against the costs of providing the information.

One reason companies are motivated to disclose financial information to external decision-makers is that it often lowers financing and operating costs. For example, when a company applies for a loan, the bank uses the company's financial statements to help determine the appropriate interest rate. Without adequate financial disclosures in its financial statements, the bank is likely to demand a higher interest rate or perhaps not make the loan at all. Thus, in this setting, a benefit of financial disclosure is that it reduces the company's cost of borrowing.

While there are benefits from disclosing financial information, there are also costs. Besides the obvious cost of hiring accountants and preparing the financial statements, financial disclosures can also result in costs being imposed by competitors. It is common practice for managers to scrutinize the financial statements of competitors to learn about successful products, new strategies, innovative technologies, and changing market conditions. Thus, disclosing too much information can place a company at a competitive disadvantage. Disclosure can also raise investors' expectations about a company's future profitability. If those expectations are not met, they may bring litigation against the managers.

There are also political costs that are potentially associated with accounting disclosure. Highly visible companies, such as defense contractors and oil companies, are often the target of scrutiny by the public and by government officials. When these companies report unusually large accounting profits, they are often the target of additional regulation or increased taxes.

Stock market regulators impose disclosure standards for publicly traded corporations, but the nature and extent of the required disclosures vary substantially across countries. Further, because the requirements only set the minimum level of disclosure, the quantity and quality of information provided by firms will vary. This variation in disclosure ultimately reflects differences among companies in the benefits and costs of disclosing information to the public.

You Make The Call *requires you to assume various roles within a business and use your accounting knowledge to address an issue. Solutions are at the end of the chapter.*

YOU MAKE THE CALL

You are a Product Manager There is often friction between investors' needs for information and a company's desire to safeguard competitive advantages. Assume that you are the product manager for a key department at your company and you are asked for advice on the extent of information to disclose in the annual report on a potentially lucrative new product that your department has test marketed. What considerations affect the advice you provide and why? [Answer on page 1-29]

Review Problems *are self-study tools that require the application of accounting. To aid learning, solutions are provided at the end of the chapter.*

Identifying How Financial Statements Are Utilized by Different User Groups LO1-1 **Review 1-1**

For each accounting information user group (1 through 6), determine how it would utilize the financial statements of Macy's Inc., by selecting the relevant task from *a* to *f*.

Accounting Information User Group	Task Aided by Financial Statements
1. _e_ Shareholders	*a.* To assign a rating to Macy's debt, which indicates the chance of default.
2. _b_ Creditors	*b.* To determine whether to lend money to Macy's over a 10-year period.
3. _f_ Suppliers	*c.* To estimate your year-end bonus based on Macy's financial results.
4. _c_ Managers	*d.* To verify the amount of sales taxes due from Macy's Inc.
5. _a_ Financial analysts	*e.* To aid in the decision of whether to buy additional shares of Macy's stock.
6. _d_ Government agencies	*f.* As input in a decision to contractually sell a specified quantity of items at a set price to Macy's over the next two years.

GuidedExample MBC

Guided Example *icons denote the availability of a demonstration video in* **myBusinessCourse** *(MBC)—see the Preface for more on MBC.*

Solution on p. 1-39.

BUSINESS ACTIVITIES

LO1-2 Describe a company's business activities and explain how these activities are represented by the accounting equation.

eLecture MBC

Businesses produce accounting information to help develop strategies, attract financing, evaluate investment opportunities, manage operations, and measure performance. Before we can attempt to understand the information provided in financial statements, we must understand these business activities. That is, what does a business actually do? For example:

- Where does a company such as Nike find the resources to develop new products and open new retail stores?
- What new products should Nike bring to market?
- How much should Nike spend on product development? On advertising? On executive compensation?
- How does Nike's management determine if a product is a success?

Questions such as these define the activities of Nike and other companies.

Exhibit 1.2 illustrates the activities of a typical business. All businesses *plan* business activities, *finance* those activities, *invest* resources in those activities, and then engage in *operating* activities. Companies conduct all these activities while confronting a variety of *external forces,* including competition from other businesses, government regulation, economic conditions and market forces, and changing preferences of customers. The financial statements provide information that helps us understand and evaluate each of these activities.

EXHIBIT 1.2 Business Activities

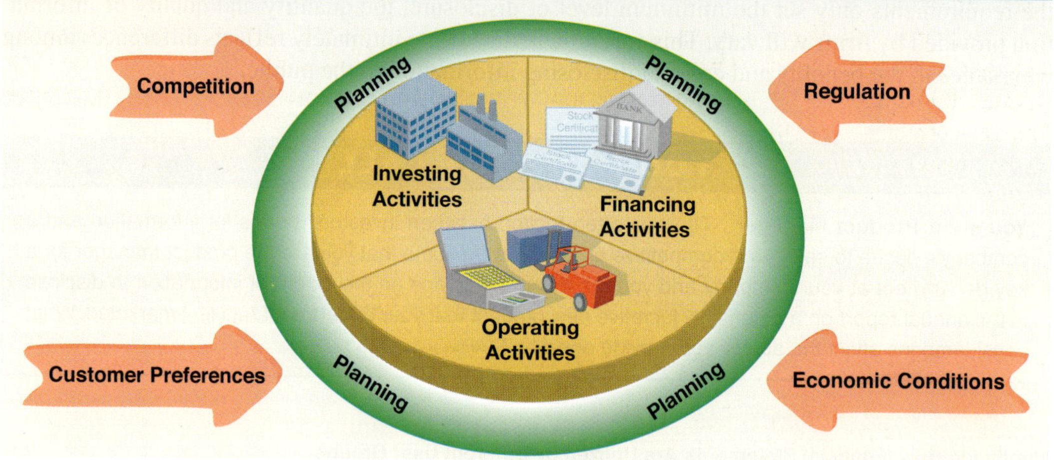

Planning Activities

A company's goals, and the strategies adopted to reach those goals, are the product of its **planning activities**. Nike, for example, states that its mission is "To bring inspiration and innovation to every athlete in the world," adding "If you have a body, you are an athlete." However, in its 2020 annual report to shareholders, for the year ended May 2020, Nike management suggests another goal that focuses on financial success and earning a return for the shareholders.

Excerpts *from recent financial statements are used to illustrate and reinforce concepts.*

> Our goal is to deliver value to our shareholders by building a profitable global portfolio of branded footwear, apparel, equipment, and accessories businesses. Our strategy is to achieve long-term revenue growth by creating innovative, "must have" products, building deep personal consumer connections with our brands, and delivering compelling consumer experiences through digital platforms and at retail.

As is the case with most businesses, Nike's primary goal is to create value for its owners, the shareholders. How the company plans to do so is the company's **strategy**.

A company's *strategic* (or *business*) *plan* describes how it plans to achieve its goals. The plan's success depends on an effective review of market conditions. Specifically, the company must assess both the demand for its products and services, and the supply of its inputs (both labor and capital). The plan must also include competitive analyses, opportunity assessments, and consideration of business threats. The strategic plan specifies both broad management designs that generate company value and tactics to achieve those designs.

Most information in a strategic plan is proprietary and guarded closely by management. However, outsiders can gain insight into planning activities through various channels, including newspapers, magazines, and company disclosures. Understanding a company's planning activities helps focus accounting analysis and place it in context.

Investing Activities

Assets

Investing activities consist of acquiring and disposing of the resources needed to produce and sell a company's products and services. These resources, called **assets**, provide future benefits to the company. Companies differ on the amount and mix of these resources. Some companies require buildings and equipment, while others have abandoned "bricks and mortar" to conduct business through the Internet.

Some assets that a company invests in are used quickly. For instance, a retail clothing store hopes to sell its spring and summer merchandise before purchasing more inventory for the fall and winter. Other assets are acquired for long-term use. Buildings are typically used for several decades. The relative proportion of short-term and long-term investments depends on the type of business and the strategic plan that the company adopts. For example, Nike has relatively few long-term assets because it outsources most of the production of its products to other companies.

The chart in **Exhibit 1.3** compares the relative proportion of short-term and long-term assets held by Nike and seven other companies, several of which are featured in later chapters. Nike has adopted a business model that requires very little investment in long-term resources. A majority of its investments are short-term assets. In contrast, **Verizon**, **PepsiCo**, and **Procter & Gamble** all rely heavily on long-term investments. These companies hold relatively small proportions of short-term assets. This mix of long-term and short-term assets is described in more detail in Chapter 2.

Real Companies *and* **Institutions** *are highlighted in bold, blue font.*

EXHIBIT 1.3 Relative Proportion of Short-Term and Long-Term Assets*

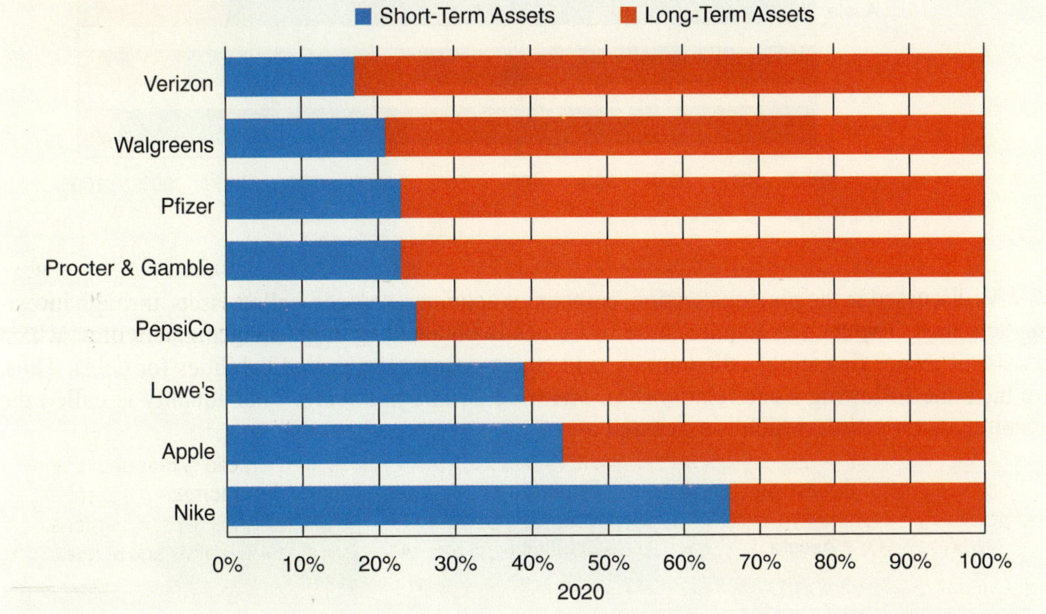

*These companies do not have identical fiscal year-ends. For each fiscal year listed (here and in the exhibits that follow), balance sheets are dated from January 31 to December 31 of that year. For example, Nike's fiscal year-end is May 31, 2020 while PepsiCo's fiscal year-end is December 26, 2020.

Financing Activities

Investments in resources require funding, and **financing activities** refer to the methods companies use to fund those investments. *Financial management* is the planning of resource needs, including the proper mix of financing sources.

Companies obtain financing from two sources: equity (owner) financing and creditor (nonowner) financing. *Equity financing* refers to the funds contributed to the company by its owners along with any income retained by the company. One form of equity financing is the cash raised from the sale (or issuance) of stock by a corporation. *Creditor* (or debt) *financing* is funds contributed by nonowners, which create *liabilities*. **Liabilities** are obligations the company must repay in the future. One example of a liability is a bank loan. We draw a distinction between equity and creditor financing for an important reason: creditor financing imposes a legal obligation to repay, usually with interest, and failure to repay amounts borrowed can result in adverse legal consequences such as bankruptcy. In contrast, equity financing does not impose an obligation for repayment.

Exhibit 1.4 compares the relative proportion of creditor and equity financing for Nike and other companies. PepsiCo uses liabilities to finance 85% of its resources. In contrast, **Walgreens Boots Alliance, Inc.** (Walgreens), relies more heavily on its equity financing, receiving 76% of its financing from creditors. **Pfizer** has the lowest proportion of creditor financing in this sample of companies, with just 59% of its assets financed by nonowners.

EXHIBIT 1.4 Relative Proportion of Credit and Equity Financing

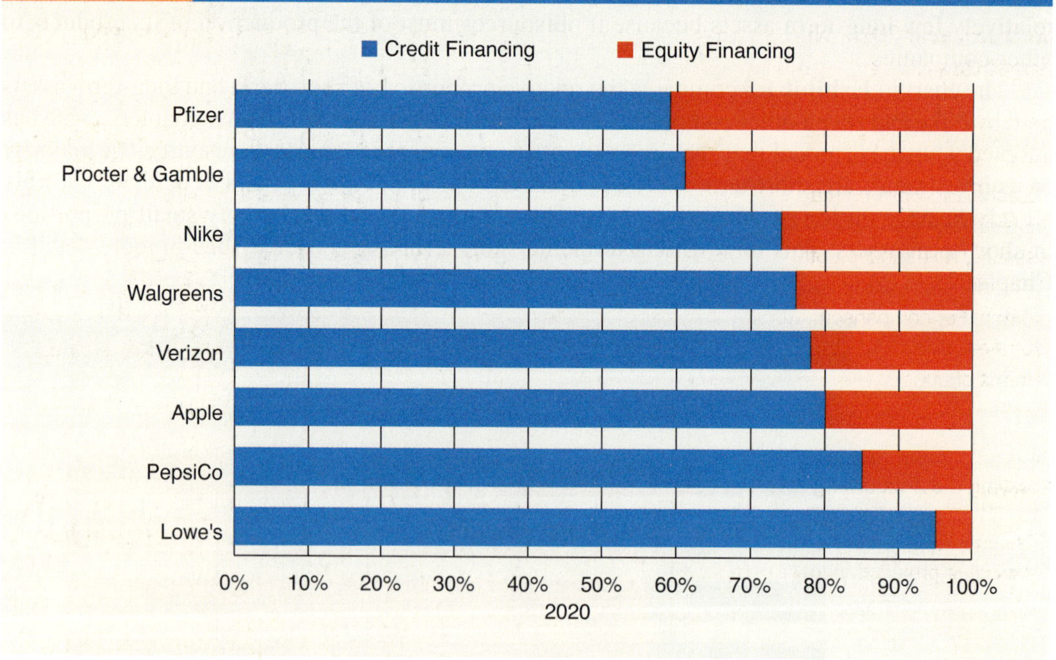

Infographics are used to convey difficult concepts and procedures.

As discussed in the previous section, companies acquire resources, called assets, through investing activities. The cash to acquire these resources is obtained through financing activities, which consist of owner financing, called equity, and creditor financing, called liabilities (or debt). Thus, we have the following basic relationship: *investing equals financing*. This equality is called the **accounting equation**, which is expressed as:

Investing	=	Financing	+	Owner Financing
Assets	=	**Liabilities**	+	**Equity**

At fiscal year-end 2020, the accounting equation for Nike was as follows ($ millions):

$$\$31,342 = \$23,287 + \$8,055$$

By definition, the accounting equation holds for all companies at all times. This relationship is a very powerful tool for analyzing and understanding companies, and we will use it often throughout the text.[4]

Operating Activities

Operating activities refer to the production, promotion, and selling of a company's products and services. These activities extend from a company's input markets, involving its suppliers, and to its output markets, involving its customers. Input markets generate *operating expenses* (or *costs*) such as inventory, salaries, materials, and logistics. Output markets generate *operating revenues* (or *sales*) from customers. Output markets also generate some operating expenses such as for marketing and distributing products and services to customers. When operating revenues exceed operating expenses, companies report *operating income*, also called *operating profit* or *operating earnings*. When operating expenses exceed operating revenues, companies report operating losses.

Revenue is the increase in equity resulting from the sale of goods and services to customers. The amount of revenue is determined *before* deducting expenses. An **expense** is the cost incurred to generate revenue, including the cost of the goods and services sold to customers as well as the cost of carrying out other business activities. **Income**, also called *net income*, equals revenues minus expenses and is the net increase in equity from the company's activities.

Income = **Revenues** − **Expenses**

For fiscal year 2020, Nike reported revenues of over $37 billion, yet its reported income was a fraction of that amount—just over $2.5 billion.

Business Insights *offer recent examples from the business news and popular press.*

BUSINESS INSIGHT

Each year, *Fortune* magazine ranks the 500 largest corporations in the United States based on total revenues. For 2021, which is based on fiscal 2020 financial results, Nike ranked 85th on the *Fortune 500* list with revenues of over $37 billion. The company also ranked 74th in profits, with net income of approximately $2.5 billion. For comparison, the largest corporation was **Walmart, Inc.**, with revenues of more than $559 billion and $13.5 billion in net income (ranking number 14 in terms of profit). (Source: http://fortune.com/fortune500/list)

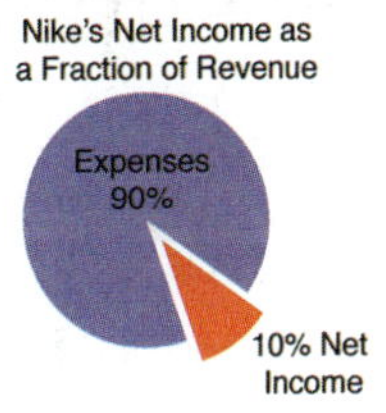

Applying the Accounting Equation and Computing Financing Proportions LO1-2 **Review 1-2**

Determine the missing amounts for each year below for Delta Air Lines, Inc., including the percentage of financing provided by owners and creditors.

($ millions)	Assets	Liabilities	Equity	% of Financing Provided by Owners	% of Financing Provided by Creditors
2019	?	$49,174	$15,358	?	?
2018	$60,266	?	$13,687	?	?
2017	$53,671	$41,141	?	?	?

GuidedExample MBC

Solution on p. 1-40.

[4] There are securities that do not neatly fit into either "debt" or "equity" classification, but rather have characteristics of both. These are known as debt-equity hybrid securities. Their existence does not alter the conceptual idea that assets are financed with debt and equity. A detailed discussion of these is beyond the scope of this textbook, but we describe these briefly in the chapters on debt and equity. For most ratio analyses in this introductory-level textbook, we include all these types of securities as either debt or equity for the sake of simplicity.

FINANCIAL STATEMENTS

LO1-3 Identify the four key financial statements: balance sheet, income statement, statement of stockholders' equity, and statement of cash flows.

eLecture MBC

Four financial statements are used to periodically report on a company's business activities. These statements are:

- **balance sheet**, which lists the company's investments and sources of financing using the accounting equation;
- **income statement**, which reports the results of operations;
- **statement of stockholders' equity**, which details changes in owner financing;
- **statement of cash flows**, which details the sources and uses of cash.

Exhibit 1.5 shows how these statements are linked across time. A balance sheet reports on a company's position at a point in time. The income statement, statement of stockholders' equity, and the statement of cash flows report on performance over a period of time. The three statements in the middle of **Exhibit 1.5** (period-of-time statements) link the balance sheet from the beginning of a period to the balance sheet at the end of a period. There is a fifth statement, a statement of comprehensive income, but it only comes into play for issues that arise in later chapters.

EXHIBIT 1.5 Financial Statement Links Across Time

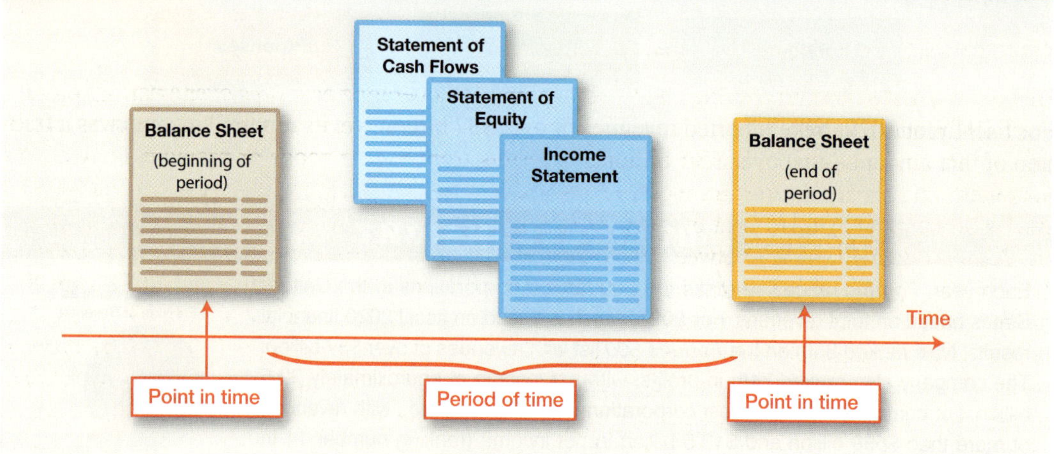

FYI The heading of each financial statement includes who, what, and when.

A one-year, or annual, reporting period is common, which is called the *accounting*, or *fiscal year*. Semiannual, quarterly, and monthly reporting periods are also common. *Calendar-year* companies have a reporting period that begins on January 1 and ends on December 31. Pfizer, Google, and Verizon are examples of calendar-year companies. Some companies choose a fiscal year ending on a date other than December 31. Seasonal businesses, such as retail stores, often choose a fiscal year that ends when sales and inventories are at their lowest level. For example, Home Depot, the retail home improvement store chain, ends its fiscal year on the Sunday closest to February 1, after the busy holiday season. Nike has a May 31 fiscal year. The heading of each statement identifies the (1) company name, (2) statement title, and (3) date or time period of the statement.

Balance Sheet

FYI The balance sheet is also known as the statement of financial position and the statement of financial condition.

A **balance sheet** reports a company's financial position at a point in time. It summarizes the result of the company's investing and financing activities by listing amounts for assets, liabilities, and equity. The balance sheet is based on the accounting equation, also called the *balance sheet equation*: Assets = Liabilities + Equity.

Nike's balance sheet for fiscal year 2020, which ended May 31, 2020, is reproduced in a reduced format in **Exhibit 1.6** and reports that assets are $31,342 million, liabilities are $23,287 million, and equity is $8,055 million, where owner financing is the sum of contributed capital of $8,302 million, retained earnings of $(191) million, a deficit, and other equity of $(56) million, a deficit. Thus, the balance sheet equation holds true for Nike's balance sheet: assets equal liabilities plus equity.

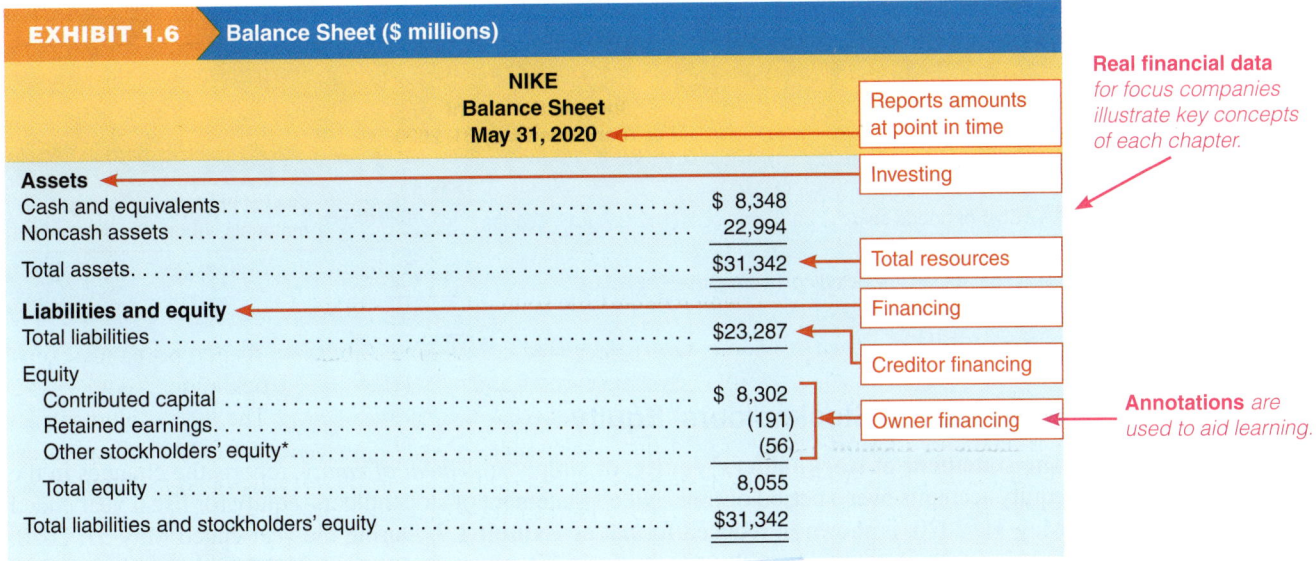

EXHIBIT 1.6 Balance Sheet ($ millions)

NIKE
Balance Sheet
May 31, 2020 ← Reports amounts at point in time

Assets ← Investing		
Cash and equivalents	$ 8,348	
Noncash assets	22,994	
Total assets	$31,342	← Total resources
Liabilities and equity ← Financing		
Total liabilities	$23,287	← Creditor financing
Equity		
Contributed capital	$ 8,302	← Owner financing
Retained earnings	(191)	
Other stockholders' equity*	(56)	
Total equity	8,055	
Total liabilities and stockholders' equity	$31,342	

* Other stockholders' equity includes accumulated other comprehensive income. Other components of stockholders' equity are discussed in Chapter 11.

Real financial data *for focus companies illustrate key concepts of each chapter.*

Annotations *are used to aid learning.*

Income Statement

The **income statement** reports the results of a company's operating activities over a period of time. It details amounts for revenues and expenses, and the difference between these two amounts is net income. Revenue is the increase in equity that results from selling goods or providing services to customers, and expense is the cost incurred to generate revenue. Net income is the increase in equity *after* subtracting expenses from revenues.

An important difference between the income statement and the balance sheet is that the balance sheet presents the company's position at a *point in time*, for instance December 31, 2020, while the income statement presents a summary of activity over a *period of time*, such as January 1, 2020, through December 31, 2020. Because of this difference, the balance sheet reflects the cumulative history of a company's activities. The amounts listed in the balance sheet carry over from the end of one fiscal year to the beginning of the next fiscal year, while the amounts listed in the income statement do not carry over from one year to the next.

Refer to Nike's income statement for the fiscal year ended May 31, 2020, shown in reduced format as **Exhibit 1.7**. It reports that revenues = $37,403 million, expenses = $34,864 million, and net income = $2,539 million. Thus, revenues minus expenses equals net income for Nike.

For manufacturing and merchandising companies, the **cost of goods sold** is an important expense that is typically disclosed separately in the income statement immediately following revenues. It is also common to report a subtotal for gross profit (also called gross margin), which is revenues less the cost of goods sold. The company's remaining expenses are then reported below gross profit. Nike's income statement is presented in this reduced format in **Exhibit 1.8**.

FYI The income statement is also known as a statement of income, statement of earnings, statement of operations, and statement of profit and loss.

FYI The term "gross" refers to an amount before subtractions, such as Gross Sales. An exception is made for the term Gross Profit (Gross Margin), defined as Sales less Cost of Goods Sold (Cost of Sales). When items are subtracted from a gross amount, the term "net" is generally used, as in the case of Net Sales (Gross Sales less returns and other items) or Net Income (Sales less all expenses).

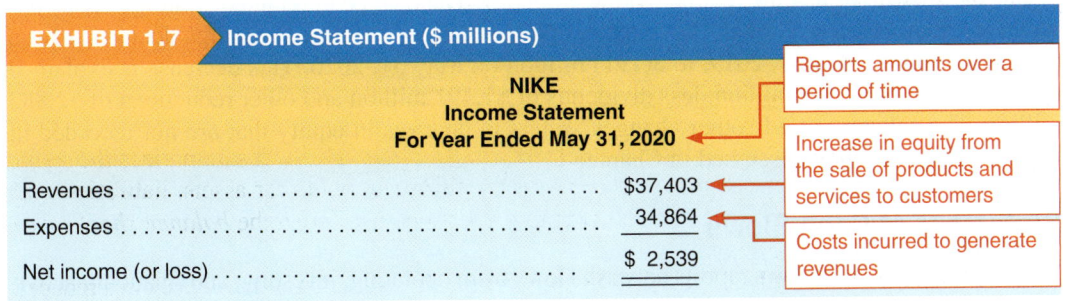

EXHIBIT 1.7 Income Statement ($ millions)

NIKE
Income Statement
For Year Ended May 31, 2020 ← Reports amounts over a period of time

Revenues	$37,403	← Increase in equity from the sale of products and services to customers
Expenses	34,864	← Costs incurred to generate revenues
Net income (or loss)	$ 2,539	

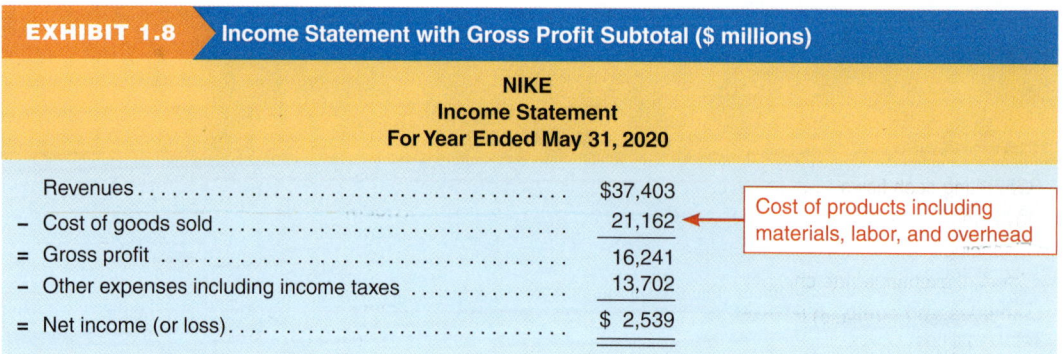

EXHIBIT 1.8 Income Statement with Gross Profit Subtotal ($ millions)

NIKE
Income Statement
For Year Ended May 31, 2020

	Revenues	$37,403
–	Cost of goods sold	21,162 ← Cost of products including materials, labor, and overhead
=	Gross profit	16,241
–	Other expenses including income taxes	13,702
=	Net income (or loss)	$ 2,539

Statement of Stockholders' Equity

The **statement of stockholders' equity**, or simply *statement of equity*, reports the changes in the equity accounts over a period of time. Nike's statement of stockholders' equity for fiscal year ended May 31, 2020, is shown in reduced format as **Exhibit 1.9**. During the year ended May 31, 2020, Nike's equity changed due to share issuance and income reinvestment. The exhibit details and classifies these changes into three categories:

- Contributed capital (includes common stock and additional paid-in capital)
- Retained earnings (includes cumulative net income or loss, and deducts dividends)
- Other stockholders' equity

EXHIBIT 1.9 Statement of Stockholders' Equity ($ millions)

NIKE
Statement of Stockholders' Equity
For Year Ended May 31, 2020 ← Reports amounts over a period of time

	Contributed Capital	Retained Earnings (Deficit)	Other Stockholders' Equity	Total Stockholders' Equity
Balance, May 31, 2019	**$7,166**	**$1,643**	**$ 231**	**$9,040** ← Beginning period amounts
Stock issuance	165	(9)		156
Net income		2,539		2,539 ← Change in balances over a period
Dividends		(1,491)		(1,491)
Other changes	971	(2,873)	(287)	(2,189)
Balance, May 31, 2020	**$8,302**	**$ (191)**	**$ (56)**	**$8,055** ← Ending period amounts

FYI Dividends are reported in the statement of equity, and not in the income statement.

Contributed capital represents the net amount received from issuing stock to shareholders (owners). **Retained earnings** (also called *earned capital*) represents the income the company has earned since its inception, minus the dividends it has paid out to shareholders. Thus, retained earnings equals the amount of income retained in the company. The change in retained earnings links consecutive balance sheets through the income statement. Nike's retained earnings decreased from $1,643 million on May 31, 2019, to $(191) million on May 31, 2020. This decrease is explained by net income of $2,539 million, less dividends of $1,491 million and other reductions of $2,882 million. The category titled "other changes" refers to changes in equity that are not recorded in income. This concept is discussed in Chapter 11.

Statement of Cash Flows

FYI Cash is critical to operations because it is necessary for purchasing resources and paying bills.

The **statement of cash flows** reports net cash flows from operating, investing, and financing activities over a period of time. Nike's statement of cash flows for fiscal year ended May 31, 2020, is shown in a reduced format in **Exhibit 1.10**. The statement reports that the cash balance increased by $3,882 million during the fiscal year. Operating activities provided $2,485 million (a cash inflow), investing activities used $1,028 million (a cash outflow), and financing activities provided $2,491 million (a cash inflow). These changes increased Nike's ending balance of cash to $8,348 million.

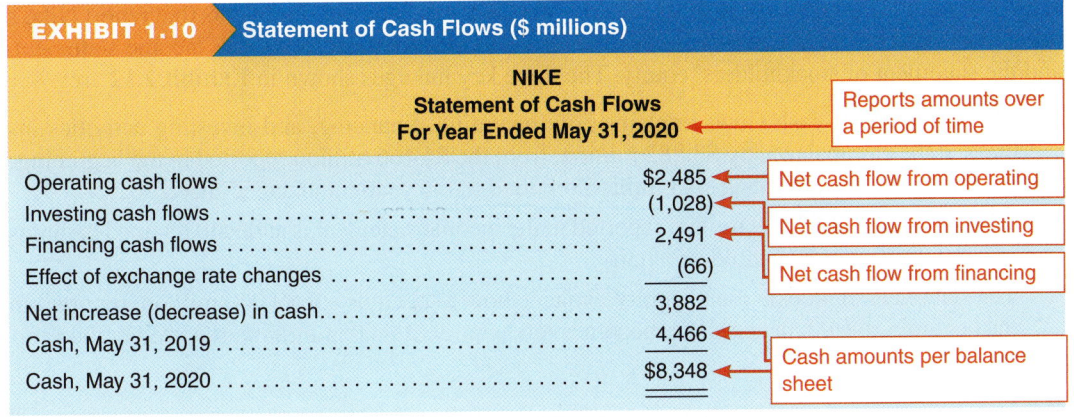

EXHIBIT 1.10 Statement of Cash Flows ($ millions)

NIKE
Statement of Cash Flows
For Year Ended May 31, 2020 ← Reports amounts over a period of time

Operating cash flows	$2,485	← Net cash flow from operating
Investing cash flows	(1,028)	← Net cash flow from investing
Financing cash flows	2,491	← Net cash flow from financing
Effect of exchange rate changes	(66)	
Net increase (decrease) in cash	3,882	
Cash, May 31, 2019	4,466	← Cash amounts per balance sheet
Cash, May 31, 2020	$8,348	← Cash amounts per balance sheet

FYI Common formatting for U.S. financial statements includes:
- Dollar sign next to first and last amount listed in a column
- Single underline before a subtraction or addition; double underline after a major total
- Assets listed in order of liquidity, which is nearness to cash
- Liabilities listed in order of due dates

Operating cash flow is the amount of cash generated from operating activities. This amount usually differs from net income due to differences between the time that revenues and expenses are recorded and the time that the related cash receipts and disbursements occur. For example, a company may report revenues for goods sold to customers this period, but not collect the payment until next period. Consistent with most companies, Nike's operating cash flows of $2,485 million do not equal its net income of $2,539 million. **Exhibit 1.11** compares net income and operating cash flows for Nike and several other companies. The exhibit shows that there is large variation across companies in the amount of net income and operating cash flows.

Both cash flow and net income are important for making business decisions. They each capture different aspects of firm performance and together help financial statement users better understand and assess a company's past, present, and future business activities.

EXHIBIT 1.11 Comparison of Net Income to Operating Cash Flows

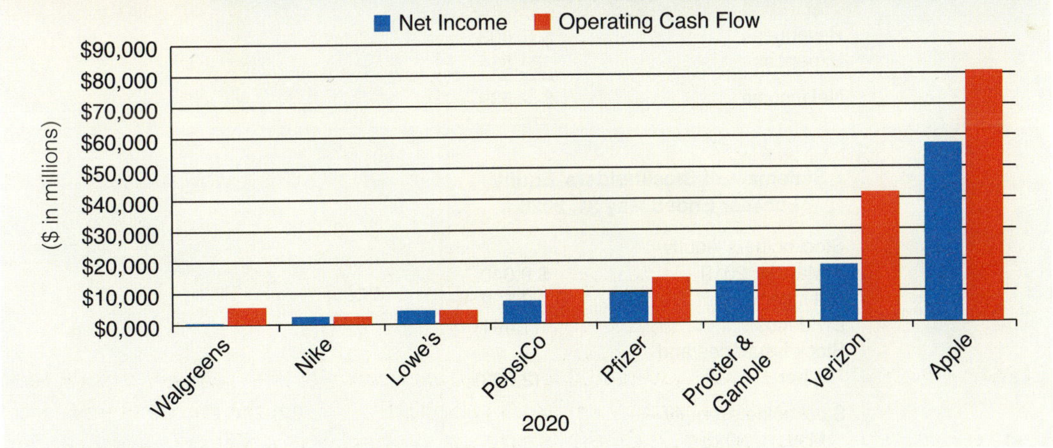

Financial Statement Linkages

A central feature of the accounting system is the linkage among the four primary statements, referred to as the *articulation* of the financial statements. Three of the key linkages are:

- The statement of cash flows links the beginning and ending cash in the balance sheet.
- The income statement links the beginning and ending retained earnings in the statement of stockholders' equity.
- The statement of stockholders' equity links the beginning and ending equity in the balance sheet.

Exhibit 1.12 demonstrates these links using Nike's financial statements from **Exhibits 1.6** through **1.10**. The left side of **Exhibit 1.12** presents Nike's beginning-year balance sheet for fiscal year 2020 (which is the same as the balance sheet for the end of fiscal year 2019), and the right side presents Nike's year-end balance sheet for fiscal year 2020. These balance sheets report Nike's investing and financing activities at the beginning and end of the fiscal year, two distinct points in time. The middle column of **Exhibit 1.12** presents the three financial statements that report Nike's fiscal year 2020 business activities over time: the statement of cash flows, the income statement, and the statement of stockholders' equity. The three key linkages shown in **Exhibit 1.12** are:

- The statement of cash flows explains how operating, financing, and investing activities increased the cash balance by $3,882 million, from the $4,466 million reported in the beginning-year balance sheet, to the $8,348 million reported in the year-end balance sheet.
- The net income of $2,539 million reported in the income statement is added to retained earnings in the statement of stockholders' equity.
- The statement of stockholders' equity explains how total equity of $9,040 million, reported in the beginning-year balance sheet, becomes total equity of $8,055 million, reported in the year-end balance sheet.

EXHIBIT 1.12 **Articulation of Nike Financial Statements ($ millions)**

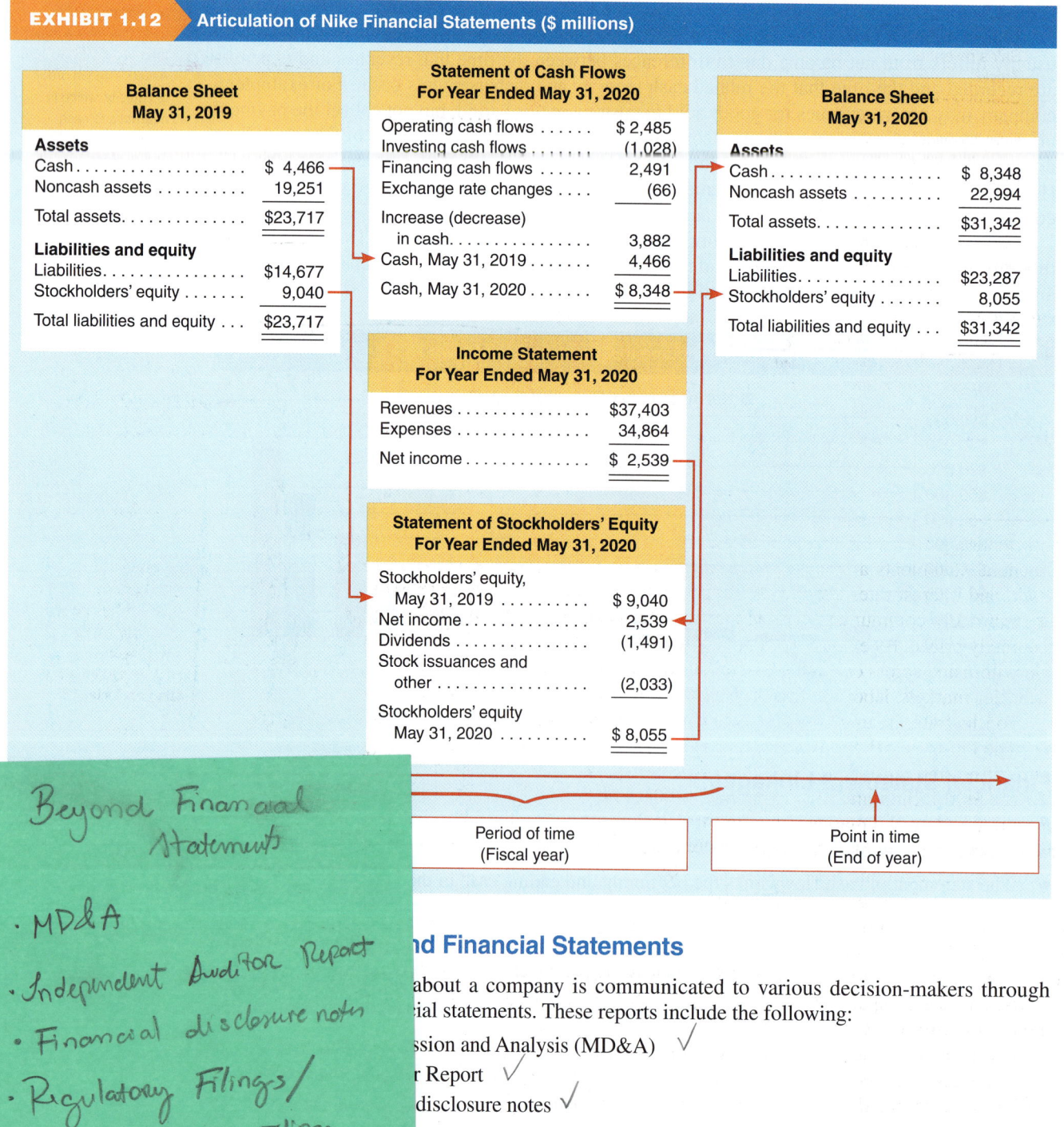

Balance Sheet
May 31, 2019

Assets	
Cash	$ 4,466
Noncash assets	19,251
Total assets	$23,717
Liabilities and equity	
Liabilities	$14,677
Stockholders' equity	9,040
Total liabilities and equity	$23,717

Statement of Cash Flows
For Year Ended May 31, 2020

Operating cash flows	$ 2,485
Investing cash flows	(1,028)
Financing cash flows	2,491
Exchange rate changes	(66)
Increase (decrease) in cash	3,882
Cash, May 31, 2019	4,466
Cash, May 31, 2020	$ 8,348

Income Statement
For Year Ended May 31, 2020

Revenues	$37,403
Expenses	34,864
Net income	$ 2,539

Statement of Stockholders' Equity
For Year Ended May 31, 2020

Stockholders' equity, May 31, 2019	$ 9,040
Net income	2,539
Dividends	(1,491)
Stock issuances and other	(2,033)
Stockholders' equity May 31, 2020	$ 8,055

Balance Sheet
May 31, 2020

Assets	
Cash	$ 8,348
Noncash assets	22,994
Total assets	$31,342
Liabilities and equity	
Liabilities	$23,287
Stockholders' equity	8,055
Total liabilities and equity	$31,342

Period of time
(Fiscal year)

Point in time
(End of year)

Beyond Financial Statements

· MD&A
· Independent Auditor Report
· Financial disclosure notes
· Regulatory Filings/ SEC Filings

nd Financial Statements

about a company is communicated to various decision-makers through ial statements. These reports include the following:

ssion and Analysis (MD&A) ✓
r Report ✓
disclosure notes ✓

- Regulatory filings, including proxy statements and other SEC filings

We describe and explain the usefulness of these additional information sources throughout the book.

Review Problems *are self-study tools that require the application of accounting. To aid learning, solutions are provided at the end of the chapter.*

Preparing Financial Statements

LO1-3 **Review 1-3**

Based in Germany, **Adidas** is one of **Nike**'s primary competitors. It markets athletic shoes and apparel under the Adidas and Reebok brands. It also sells Solomon ski equipment as well as TaylorMade golf equipment. Adidas's financial statements are reported in euros, the currency of the European Union. The statements are also prepared using International Financial Reporting Standards (IFRS). The following information is from the company's December 31, 2019, financial statements (€ millions):

GuidedExample MBC

Guided Example *icons denote the availability of a demonstration video in* **myBusinessCourse** *(MBC)—see the Preface for more on MBC.*

	2019
Cash and cash equivalents	€ 2,220
Cash flow from operations	2,819
Sales revenue	23,640
Stockholders' equity	7,058
Cost of goods sold	11,347
Cash flow used for financing	(2,273)
Total liabilities	13,622
Net other expenses	10,316
Noncash assets	18,460
Cash flow used for investing	(925)
Net income	1,977
Cash, beginning of year	2,629
Effect of exchange rates on cash	(30)

Required

a. Prepare Adidas's balance sheet at December 31, 2019, and its income statement and statement of cash flows for the fiscal year ended December 31, 2019.

b. Compare Adidas's revenue, net income, and cash flow from operations to that of Nike (as reported in this chapter). Assume an exchange rate of €1.00 = $1.12.

Solution on p. 1-40.

FINANCIAL REPORTING ENVIRONMENT

LO1-4 Describe how standardized accounting principles and a regulatory environment are important to financial statement integrity.

eLecture MBC

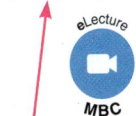

Learning Objectives *are repeated at the start of the section covering that topic.*

Information presented in financial statements is of critical importance to external decision-makers. Financial statements affect the prices paid for equity securities, such as a company's common stock, and interest rates attached to debt. To the extent that financial performance and condition are accurately communicated to business decision-makers, debt and equity securities are more accurately priced. By extension, financial reporting plays a crucial role in efficient resource allocation within and across economies. Accounting information contributes to the efficient operation of securities markets, labor markets, commodity markets, and other markets.

To illustrate, imagine the consequences of a breakdown in the integrity of financial reporting. The Enron scandal provides a case in point. At the beginning of 2001, **Enron** was one of the more, if not the most, innovative and respected companies in the United States. With revenues of over $100 billion and total company value of over $60 billion, it was the fifth largest U.S. corporation based on market value. In October 2001, the company released its third quarter earnings report to the public. Although operating earnings were higher than in previous years, the income statement contained a $1 billion "special charge." Financial analysts began investigating the cause of this charge and discovered that it was linked to related-party transactions and questionable accounting practices. Once it became clear to the capital markets that Enron had not faithfully and accurately reported its financial condition and performance, people became unwilling to purchase its securities. The value of its debt and equity securities dropped precipitously, and the company was unable to obtain the cash needed for operating activities. By the end of 2001, Enron was bankrupt!

Unfortunately, the demise of Enron didn't deter all cases of fraud. For example, **Luckin Coffee**, a China-based company whose shares had been trading on the Nasdaq, agreed to pay $180 million in penalties to the Securities and Exchange Commission (a federal commission described in the next section) in December 2020. The charges relate to a material overstatement of revenues and related expenses in order to falsely report a period of rapid growth. In another case, former executives of **FTE Networks** were charged with fraud by the Securities and Exchange Commission in July 2021. Among the charges were inflating revenue and keeping liabilities off of the balance sheet. These cases illustrate the importance of reliable financial reporting. Accountants recognize the importance of the information that they produce and, as a profession, they agree to follow a set of standards for the presentation of financial statements and the disclosure of related financial information. In the following paragraphs, we discuss these standards, or *principles*, as well as the institutional and regulatory environment in which accountants operate.

Generally Accepted Accounting Principles

Decision-makers who rely on audited financial statements expect that all companies follow similar procedures in preparing their statements. In response to these expectations, U.S. accountants have developed a set of standards and procedures called **generally accepted accounting principles (GAAP)**. GAAP is not a set of immutable laws. Instead, it is a set of standards and accepted practices, based on underlying principles, that are designed to guide the preparation of the financial statements. GAAP is subject to change as conditions warrant. As a result, specific rules are altered or new practices are formulated to fit changes in underlying economic circumstances or business transactions.

Some people mistakenly assume that financial accounting is an exact discipline—that is, companies select the proper standard to account for a transaction and then follow the rules. The reality is that GAAP allows companies considerable discretion in preparing financial statements. The choice of methods often yields financial statements that are markedly different from one company to another in terms of reported income, assets, liabilities, and equity amounts. In addition, financial statements depend on numerous estimates. Consequently, even though two companies may engage in the same transactions and choose the same accounting methods, their financial statements will differ because their managements have made different estimates about such things as the amount to be collected from customers who buy on credit, the length of time that buildings and equipment will be in use, and the future costs for product warranties.

Accounting standard setters walk a fine line regarding choice in accounting. On one hand, they are concerned that management discretion in preparing financial statements will lead to abuse by those seeking to influence the decisions of those who rely on the statements. On the other hand, they are concerned that companies are too diverse for a "one size fits all" financial accounting system. Ultimately, GAAP attempts to strike a balance by imposing constraints on the choice of accounting procedures, while allowing companies some flexibility within those constraints.

YOU MAKE THE CALL

You are a Financial Analyst Accountants, business leaders, and politicians have long debated the importance of considering the **economic consequences** of accounting standards (GAAP). Should accounting standards be designed to influence behavior and affect social or economic change considered by, say, a government body or other interested group? Alternatively, should such standards be designed simply to provide relevant and reliable information on which economic decisions can be made by others with a reasonable degree of confidence? What do you believe the objectives of financial reporting should be? [Answers on page 1-29.]

Regulation and Oversight

Following the U.S. stock market crash of 1929, the United States Congress passed the Securities Acts of 1933 and 1934. These acts were passed to require disclosure of financial and other information about securities being offered for public sale and to prohibit deceit, misrepresentations, and other fraud in the sale of securities. The 1934 Act created the **Securities and Exchange**

Commission (SEC) and gave it broad powers to regulate the issuance and trading of securities. The act also provided that companies with more than $10 million in assets and whose securities are held by more than 500 owners must file annual and other periodic reports, including a complete set of financial statements.

While the SEC has ultimate authority over financial reporting by companies in the United States, it has ceded the task of setting accounting standards to a professional body, the **American Institute of Certified Public Accountants (AICPA)**. Over the years, this process has resulted in three standard-setting organizations.

Currently, accounting standards are established by the **Financial Accounting Standards Board (FASB)**. The FASB is a seven-member board that has the primary responsibility for setting financial accounting standards in the United States. In 2009, the FASB codified the standards into the FASB Accounting Standards Codification. This is now the single source of authoritative, non-governmental U.S. GAAP.

BUSINESS INSIGHT

Accounting can be complicated—but rule-makers are trying to make it a little simpler.
The Financial Accounting Standards Board, which sets accounting rules for U.S. companies, launched the FASB Simplification Initiative in 2014. The objective of the initiative is to make financial reporting a little less complex and reduce costs for companies and their accountants, while maintaining or improving the quality of information reported.

The projects are relatively narrow, straightforward changes in accounting that clearly would help reduce complexity and that the board expects to be able to make relatively quickly, without the years of work that often accompany major revisions in accounting rules.

"Complexity in accounting can be costly to both investors and companies," FASB Chairman Russ Golden said. The simplification initiative, which FASB began in June 2014, "is focused on identifying areas that we can address quickly and effectively, without compromising the quality of information provided to investors."

Besides setting standards for financial accounting, the FASB has developed a framework to form the basis for future discussion of proposed standards and serve as a guide to accountants for reporting information that is not governed by specific standards. A summary of this *Conceptual Framework* is presented in Appendix 1A later in this chapter.

In the wake of the Enron, Tyco, AOL, Global Crossing, Halliburton, Xerox, Adelphia, Bristol-Myers Squibb, and WorldCom scandals, concerns over the quality of corporate financial reporting led Congress to pass the **Sarbanes-Oxley Act** in 2002. The goal of this act—sometimes referred to as SOX—was to increase the level of confidence that external users, particularly investors, have in the financial statements. To accomplish this objective, SOX imposed a number of requirements to strengthen audit committees and improve deficient **internal controls** by:

- increasing management's responsibility for accounting information,
- increasing the independence of the auditors,
- increasing the accountability of the board of directors,
- establishing adequate internal controls (policies and operating processes designed to prevent fraud and protect company resources).

SOX requires that the chief executive officer (CEO) and the chief financial officer (CFO) of a publicly traded corporation personally sign a statement attesting to the accuracy and completeness of financial statements. The prospect of severe penalties is designed to make these managers more vigilant in monitoring the financial accounting process. In addition, SOX established the **Public Company Accounting Oversight Board (PCAOB)** to approve auditing standards and monitor the quality of financial statements and audits.

The Sarbanes-Oxley Act is not without critics. One criticism is that the penalties imposed on management for misstatements or errors are too severe. Some argue that managers have become less forthcoming in their disclosures and more conservative in choosing accounting methods and making accrual estimates to avoid the possibility of heavy fines or criminal charges.

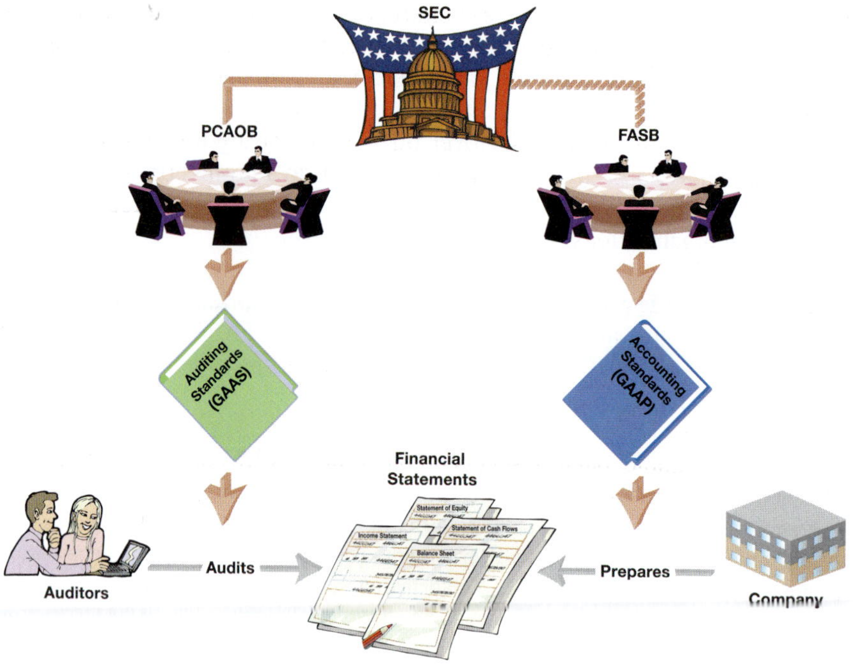

Role of the Auditor

What prevents a company from disclosing false or misleading information? For one thing, the financial statements are prepared by management, and management must take responsibility for what is disclosed. Management's reputation can be severely damaged by false disclosures when subsequent events unfold to refute the information. This situation can adversely affect the firm's ability to compete in capital, labor, and consumer markets. It can also lead to litigation and even criminal charges against management.

Even though management must personally attest to the accuracy and completeness of the financial statements, markets also demand assurances from independent parties. Therefore, the financial statements of publicly traded corporations must be **audited** by an *independent audit firm*. The auditors provide an opinion as to whether the statements *present fairly* and *in all material respects* a company's financial condition and the results of its operations.

The audit opinion is not a guarantee. Auditors only provide reasonable assurance that the financial statements are free of material misstatements. Even so, auditors provide a valuable service. Auditors effectively ensure that the information contained in the financial statements is reliable, thus increasing the confidence of outside decision-makers in the information they use to make investment, credit, and other decisions. Therefore, creditors and shareholders of privately held corporations often demand that the financial statements be audited as well.

Public corporations are required to establish audit committees whose purpose is not to audit but, rather, to appoint the audit firm and ensure that what is learned in the audit is disclosed to the firm's directors and shareholders.

YOU MAKE THE CALL

You are a Member of the Board of Directors Until recently accounting firms were permitted to earn money for consulting activities performed for clients they audited. Do you see any reason why this might not be an acceptable practice? Do you see any advantage to your firm from allowing such activity? [Answer on page 1-30.]

A Global Perspective

IFRS

Businesses increasingly operate in global markets. Consumers and businesses with access to the Internet can purchase products and services from anywhere in the world. Products produced in one country are often made with parts and materials imported from many different countries. Businesses outsource parts of operations to other countries to take advantage of better labor markets in those countries. Capital markets are global as well. Corporations whose securities trade on the New York Stock Exchange may also trade on exchanges in London, Toronto, Tokyo, or Hong Kong.

The globalization of capital markets, combined with the diversity of international accounting principles, led to an effort to increase comparability of financial information across countries. The **International Accounting Standards Board (IASB)** oversees the development of accounting standards outside the United States. Over 100 countries, including those in the European Union, require the use of **International Financial Reporting Standards (IFRS)** developed by the IASB.[5] The intention is to unify all public companies under one global set of reporting standards. The remaining major capital markets without an IFRS mandate are the U.S. (with no current plans to adopt), Japan (where voluntary adoption is permitted), and China (where standards are substantially converged and the country has plans to adopt).

Financial statements prepared under IFRS and U.S. GAAP are quite similar, yet important differences remain. For example, balance sheets prepared under IFRS often classify assets in reverse order of liquidity to those prepared under GAAP. Thus, intangible assets are listed first and cash last on the balance sheet. Both approaches require the same basic set of four financial statements, with explanatory disclosure notes. We shall examine some of the more important differences under a Global Perspective heading as they arise in future chapters. Websites maintained by the larger accounting firms as well as both the FASB and IASB provide considerable information.

Global Perspectives *examine issues related to similarities and differences in accounting practices of the U.S. and other countries.*

A GLOBAL PERSPECTIVE

Since 2007, the SEC allows foreign companies to report their financial results using international accounting standards rather than reconciling their financial statements to American rules. While this change made it easier for U.S. investors to purchase securities from around the world, a *New York Times* article referred to a "Tower of Babel in Accounting." The article raises concerns about the difficulty of comparing companies when their financial statements are based on diverse reporting standards. The situation is complicated by the fact that a number of developing countries have reserved the right to adopt exceptions to IFRS when deemed appropriate.

Identifying Roles in the Development and Regulation of Financial Reporting

LO1-4 **Review 1-4**

Guided Example MBC

Match each of the following terms with the most appropriate explanation of its relationship to financial reporting.

Terms: (a) Auditor, (b) FASB, (c) GAAP, (d) Internal controls, (e) Management, (f) PCAOB, (g) SEC

1. __c__ Set of authoritative standards and accepted practices that guide the preparation of financial statements in the U.S.
2. __g__ Organization that has the ultimate authority over financial reporting.
3. __b__ Currently codifies new accounting standards that guide financial reporting.
4. __f__ Approves auditing standards and monitors audits of public companies that are required to report annual results.
5. __e__ Takes responsibility for the accuracy and completeness of information disclosed in the financial statements.
6. __a__ Provides an opinion on the fair presentation of a company's financial reporting.
7. __d__ Helps ensure the accuracy of a company's financial reporting through a system of internal monitoring procedures and rules.

Solution on p. 1-40.

[5] Because it is international in its scope, the IASB has no legal authority to impose accounting standards on any country. Despite the push for comparability, not everyone is convinced that IFRS will improve the usefulness of accounting information. As one observer put it, "There is a real risk of a veneer of comparability that hides a lot of differences." A number of countries have reserved the right to adopt exceptions to IFRS when they deem them to be appropriate.

Each chapter includes a section on ***Analyzing Financial Statements*** *to emphasize the use of accounting information in making business decisions.*

ANALYZING FINANCIAL STATEMENTS

LO1-5
Compute two key ratios that are commonly used to assess profitability and risk—return on equity and the debt-to-equity ratio.

eLecture
MBC

The financial statements provide insights into the financial health and performance of a company. However, the accounting data presented in these statements are difficult to interpret in raw form. For example, knowing that Nike's net income was $2,539 million in the fiscal year ended May 2020 is, by itself, not very useful. Similarly, knowing the dollar amount of liabilities does not tell us whether or not Nike relies too heavily on creditor financing.

Financial analysts use a number of tools to help interpret the information found in the financial statements. They look at trends over time and compare one company to another. They calculate ratios using financial statement information to summarize the data in a form that is easier to interpret. Ratios also allow us to compare the performance and condition of different companies even if the companies being compared are dramatically different in size. Finally, ratios help analysts spot trends or changes in performance over time.

Throughout the book, we introduce ratios that are commonly used by financial analysts and other users who rely on the financial statements. Our goal is to develop an understanding of how to effectively use the information in the financial statements, as well as to demonstrate how these statements are prepared. In this chapter we introduce one important measure of **profitability** and one measure of financial **risk**.

Profitability Analysis

Profitability reveals whether or not a company is able to bring its product or service to the market in an efficient manner and whether the market values that product or service. Companies that are consistently unprofitable are unlikely to succeed in the long run.

A key profitability metric for stockholders and other decision-makers is company return on equity. This metric compares the level of net income with the amount of equity financing used to generate that income.

Analysis Objective

We are trying to determine Nike's ability to earn a return for its stockholders.

Analysis Tool Return on Equity

$$\textbf{Return on equity} = \frac{\textbf{Net income}}{\textbf{Average stockholders' equity*}}$$

*The average is computed by adding the beginning and ending balances of stockholders' equity and dividing by two.

Applying the Return on Equity Ratio to Nike

Fiscal Year Ended May 31:

2018: $\dfrac{\$1,933}{[(\$9,812 + \$12,407)/2]} = 0.174 \text{ or } 17.4\%$

2019: $\dfrac{\$4,029}{[(\$9,040 + \$9,812)/2]} = 0.427 \text{ or } 42.7\%$

2020: $\dfrac{\$2,539}{[(\$8,055 + \$9,040)/2]} = 0.297 \text{ or } 29.7\%$

Guidance Taken over time, ROE ratios that are over 10% and preferably increasing suggest the company is earning reasonable returns. For firms that are in more risky businesses, such as renewable power, even larger returns on equity would be appropriate, while firms in less risky endeavors, such as large food chains, would not be expected to generate as large returns.

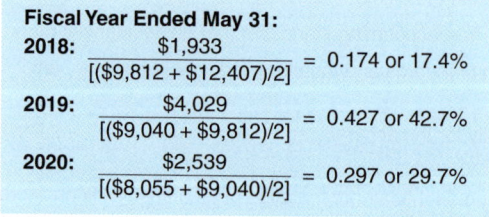

Nike in Context

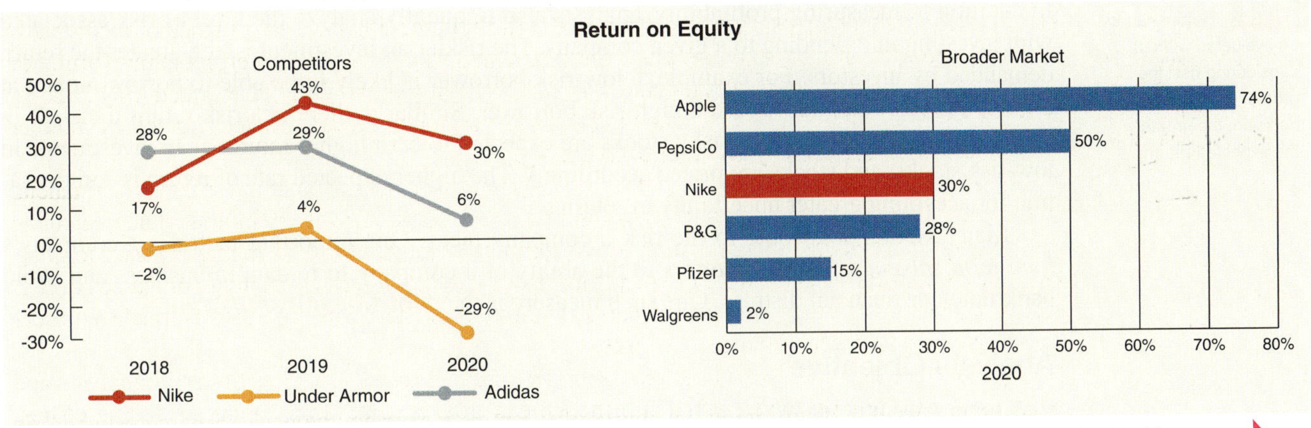

These companies do not have identical fiscal year-ends. For each fiscal year listed, balance sheets are dated from May 31 to December 31 of that year.

Data visualizations *are used throughout the text to convey financial information.*

Takeaways Over the time period covered by our calculations and by the chart, it is clear that Nike has done very well earning returns for its stockholders. Nike earned an ROE of over 42% for the year ended May 31, 2019 and almost 30% for the year ended May 31, 2020. These are exceptionally high ROE numbers and exceed the returns of its competitors, Adidas and Under Armor. Several new companies have entered the market, and Nike will need to continue developing new products to preserve its market leadership.

Other Considerations As with all ratios, care in their interpretation is essential. First, we need to be careful about comparing companies that operate in different product markets.

Second, regulation, such as applicable tax laws, can be different across countries and over time. In December of 2017 the U.S. enacted a new tax law known as the **Tax Cuts and Jobs Act (TCJA)**. (We discuss the TCJA in more detail in Chapter 10.) Many companies, including Nike, had to account for some of the provisions of the TCJA in the year that contained December 2017—for Nike this is the year that ended May 31, 2018. Nike's tax expense increased significantly, lowering net income. These one-time charges are part of the explanation of the lower ROE in 2018 computed above.[6]

Third, firms with different customer or supplier demographics can also produce different conclusions. Furthermore, different management policies toward assets and liabilities have their own unique effect on ratios across firms. For example, the conversion of inventories to sales can be subject to slowdowns that affect companies differently, within the same industry.

Fourth, these measures can be altered by management decisions designed solely for cosmetic effects such as improving current earnings or an important ratio. Thus, delaying inventory orders or filling sales orders early can lead to increasing net income and ROE in current periods to the detriment of future periods.

Finally, differences in the fiscal year-end of companies can influence a comparison of ROE ratios. If one company's fiscal year ends in May and another company's fiscal year ends in December, economic conditions may change between May and December, creating differences in ROE that are not due to differences in the operations of the two companies. For example, in 2020 the COVID-19 pandemic began to have an impact on businesses in March. The effect of the pandemic on a company's financial statements would depend on when the company's fiscal year ended. A company that had a fiscal year-end on June 30 might show a much different picture than a company with a December 31 fiscal year-end.

---

[6] The TCJA decreased the U.S. corporate statutory tax rate to 21% (from a graduated rate that topped out at 35%). However, the TCJA also required taxation of prior foreign earnings that many companies had not accrued U.S. tax on previously. This was the case for Nike, and it had to accrue a significant amount of U.S. tax (what Nike labels a transition tax in its report), leading to the higher tax expense for 2018. As a ballpark estimation, if we assume the same tax expense as in 2017 for Nike (and adjust earnings and equity accordingly), the ROE would have been 21.5% for 2018.

Credit Risk Analysis

FYI Return cannot be evaluated without considering risk; the greater the risk of any decision, the greater the expected return.

In addition to measuring profitability, analysts also frequently analyze the level of risk associated with investing in or lending to a given company. The riskier an investment is, the greater the return demanded by investors. For example, a low-risk borrower is likely to be able to borrow money at a lower interest rate than would a high-risk borrower. Similarly, there is a risk-return trade-off in equity returns. Investments in risky stocks are expected to earn higher returns than investments in low-risk stocks, and stocks are priced accordingly. The higher expected rate of return is compensation for accepting greater uncertainty in returns.

Many factors contribute to the risk a company faces. One important factor is a company's *long-term solvency*. **Solvency** refers to the ability of a company to remain in business and avoid bankruptcy or financial distress. One such measure is the **debt-to-equity (D/E) ratio**.

Analysis Objective

We are interested in determining the ability of a company to make the necessary interest and principal payments on its debt.

Analysis Tool Debt-to-Equity

$$\textbf{Debt-to-equity ratio} = \frac{\textbf{Total liabilities}}{\textbf{Total stockholders' equity}}$$

Applying the Debt-to-Equity Ratio to Nike

$$\textbf{May 31, 2018:}\ \frac{\$12{,}724}{\$9{,}812} = 1.30$$

$$\textbf{May 31, 2019:}\ \frac{\$14{,}677}{\$9{,}040} = 1.62$$

$$\textbf{May 31, 2020:}\ \frac{\$23{,}287}{\$8{,}055} = 2.89$$

Guidance Solvency is closely related to the extent a company relies on creditor financing. As the amount of creditor financing increases, the possibility of bankruptcy also increases. Short of bankruptcy, a company that has borrowed too much will occasionally find that the required interest payments are hurting the company's cash flow. The debt-to-equity ratio is an important measure used by analysts and others to assess a company's ability to make the necessary interest and principal payments on its debt.

Nike in Context

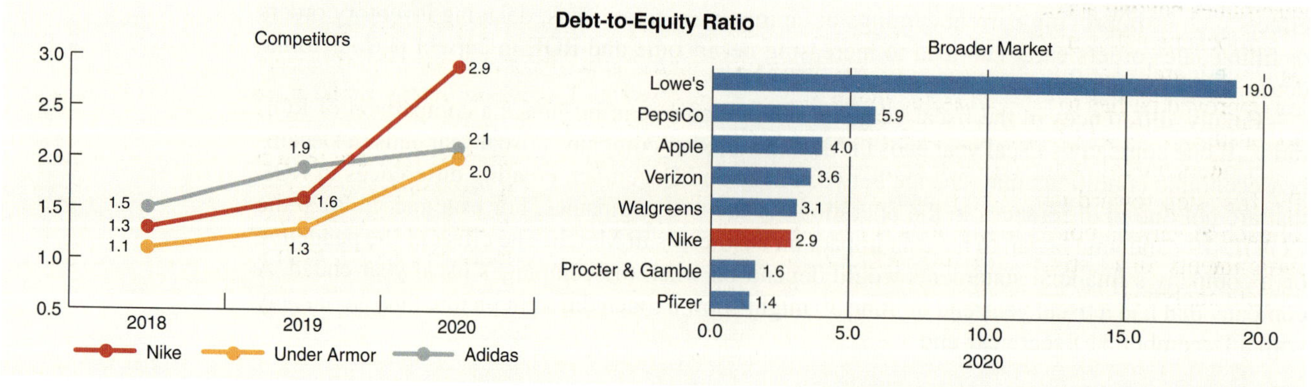

These companies do not have identical fiscal year-ends. For each fiscal year listed, balance sheets are dated from January 31 to December 31 of that year.

A debt-to equity ratio of one indicates that the company is using equal parts of debt and equity financing. Nike's debt-to-equity ratio has increased significantly since at least 2012, when it was 0.49.

The appropriate D/E ratio level depends on the nature of the business and will differ appreciably, as can be seen in the chart above. Typically, firms with large long-term commitments often reflected in fixed assets will find it appropriate to raise more capital through borrowing. The amount of debt relative to equity will also mirror the risk tolerance of the firm's management. If management believes it can earn a return above the debt interest cost, borrowing will increase the expected return to the owners.

Takeaways Nike's D/E ratio has increased over the three years presented. Nike's liabilities have been steadily increasing. Yet, stockholders' equity has not increased at the same pace. Indeed, by 2020, Nike has a significantly higher D/E ratio than its closest competitors. As we will discuss in Chapter 5, the ROE ratio discussed earlier and the D/E ratio are closely related. Nike's high ROE, relative to its competitors, can be explained in part by its higher D/E ratio. By relying more on debt financing, Nike is leveraging its profitability resulting in a higher ROE.

Other Considerations Comparisons with other companies in similar lines of business, such as Under Armour and Adidas, are always appropriate. New competitors, such as Quiksilver, could also prove insightful to examine in regard to strategic decisions. In Chapter 9, we will explore the accounting for liabilities in more depth. Balance sheets do not always recognize all obligations of a firm, and a careful reader will examine the disclosure notes to get a more complete picture of financial health in such comparisons. Nike might also consider increasing its debt level if profitable opportunities exist. The company has been, and remains, very successful, but new entrants are emerging indicating there is additional business to be had.

The chart shows that Nike has a similar and somewhat relatively lower D/E ratio when compared to the other companies we show. Procter & Gamble and Pfizer have lower D/Es, but Apple and PepsiCo have higher D/Es. Lowe's D/E is considerably higher than all other comparison companies.

There are other measures of profitability and risk that will be introduced in later chapters. Collectively, these ratios, when placed in the context of the company's business activities, help to provide a clear picture of the *drivers* of a company's financial performance and the factors affecting its financial condition. Understanding these performance drivers and their impact on the financial health of a company is key to effectively using the information presented in the financial statements.

Technology and Accounting

New technological innovations arise frequently, and they often increase the capabilities of businesses and make them more efficient. Recently, data analytics and blockchain technology have emerged as two prominent business-changing innovations. Many companies, including Amazon and Google, use data analysis throughout their organizations to make business decisions. **Data analytics** can broadly be defined as the process of examining large sets of data with the goal of discovering useful information from patterns found in the data. Business people employing data analytics can glean important insights from large data sets and identify opportunities for growth and operational efficiency. Data analysis has many applications, and you will encounter it in many disciplines beyond accounting.

Data Analytics

Blockchain was made famous as the underpinning technology used for digital currencies, such as Bitcoin and Ethereum. **Blockchain** is a distributed digital ledger that provides a secure means for approved parties to view recorded transactions. This technology has wide-ranging implications for business and is expected to greatly affect the way accountants perform audits.

Understanding what data analytics and blockchain technology are and how they are used is the first step toward developing marketable skills in each area, so we have included examples of each at various points in the book. Each chapter includes data analysis and data visualization assignments. In addition, **Appendix B** at the end of this book provides a more detailed discussion of data analytics.

ORGANIZATION OF THE BOOK

In the pages that follow Chapter 1, we will explore the financial accounting model and how it reflects an organization's activities and events. Chapters 2 and 3 are focused on building the balance sheet and the income statement from transactions and a set of required adjustments. This process requires a structure for "bookkeeping" and an understanding of the basic rules of the accounting language. When do we recognize revenue? When do we recognize an asset? We will look at these questions in a relatively simple setting.

In Chapter 4, we will construct the statement of cash flows. The balance sheet, income statement, and statement of cash flows are all built on the same underlying set of information, and they are each designed to give a different perspective on what's going on in the company. Chapter 5 shows how managers and investors organize financial information using ratios and how managers and investors use those ratios to compare companies and to make forecasts of the future.

While the first five chapters build the financial statement structure and its interpretation, the latter seven chapters are more topical. Accounting is not a cut-and-dried process, and financial reports can be affected by a variety of management decisions. So these seven chapters explore more sophisticated settings and analyses. We will find that financial reports rely on management estimates of future events and that sometimes management has the freedom to choose accounting methods that affect income and assets. And, when accounting practices don't allow reporting discretion, management's choice of transactions can make financial reports look more favorable.

Becoming an effective user of financial information requires an understanding of how the financial reports fit together and a willingness to explore the disclosure notes material to look for useful information. As we progress through *Financial Accounting* together, we will show you how to become a sophisticated reader of financial reports by looking at real companies and real financial statement information.

Review 1-5 LO1-5

Computing Return on Equity and Debt-to-Equity Ratios

GuidedExample MBC

Adidas, a major competitor of Nike, markets athletic shoes and apparel under the Adidas and Reebok brands. It also sells Solomon ski equipment and TaylorMade golf equipment. The following information is from Adidas's 2019 financial statements (Adidas's financial statements are reported in Euros, the currency of the European Union):

(millions)	Adidas
Net income (loss) (2019)	€ 1,977
Stockholders' equity (2019 year-end)	7,058
Stockholders' equity (2018 year-end)	6,364
Total liabilities (2019 year-end)	13,622

Required

a. Calculate the 2019 return on equity (ROE) ratio for Adidas.
b. Calculate the 2019 debt-to-equity ratio for Adidas.
c. Compare the profitability and risk of Adidas to that of Nike. Note: In your analysis, compare FY 2020 statements of Nike (12 months ended May 31, 2020) to 2019 statements of Adidas (12 months ended December 31, 2019).

Solution on p. 1-41.

APPENDIX 1A: Conceptual Framework for Financial Reporting

LO1-6 Explain the conceptual framework for financial reporting.

eLecture MBC

The Financial Accounting Standards Board (FASB) developed a conceptual framework for financial reporting which consists of a system of interrelated objectives that, if met, would help to identify desirable reporting standards. The FASB expects that the Board will most directly benefit from the conceptual framework by using the framework as a common foundation in the development of future standards. Both the IASB and the FASB issued new or amended conceptual frameworks in 2018. In addition, the FASB issued a new Chapter 8: *Notes to Financial Statements* (Statement of Financial Accounting Concepts No. 8). Chapter 8 is primarily about presentation and disclosure. FASB states that the intent is to aid the Board in identifying disclosures to be considered when setting disclosure requirements. The chapter is also intended to help the FASB improve its procedures and promote consistent decision making when determining disclosure requirements.

In this appendix, we focus on the objective for financial reporting as stated in the conceptual framework, as well as the characteristics of financial reporting that determine the degree of success in meeting that objective.

Objective of Financial Reporting

The objective of financial reporting is ***to provide information that is useful to present and potential equity investors, as well as lenders and other creditors, in making decisions about providing resources to the entity.*** The objective suggests that the information that is presented in financial statements is produced to 1) help the firm raise financing by providing information to equity investors and creditors about the financial health and performance of the firm, and 2) provide ongoing information to those deciding whether to buy, sell, or hold equity and debt securities (including whether to settle loans and other types of credit). Information that is intended for investors and creditors may also be useful to other users of the financial statements.

This objective may be met by providing information for the assessment of the amount, timing, and uncertainty of future (net) cash flows to the firm, which enables investors and creditors to assess the amount, timing, and uncertainty of the cash flows that they will receive. The objective of financial reporting is not to provide a value of a firm, but to provide information for users' own assessments of value.

Qualitative Characteristics of Useful Financial Information

The conceptual framework identifies ***relevance*** and ***faithful representation*** as two fundamental qualitative characteristics of financial information that are necessary to fulfill the objective described in the previous section. As the conceptual framework states, "Neither a faithful representation of an irrelevant phenomenon, nor an unfaithful representation of a relevant phenomenon, helps users make good decisions." In addition, the conceptual framework identifies several enhancing qualitative characteristics that affect the usefulness of relevant and faithfully represented information. These qualitative characteristics and their relationship to the basic objective are depicted in **Exhibit 1A.1** and discussed below.

EXHIBIT 1A.1 Conceptual Framework

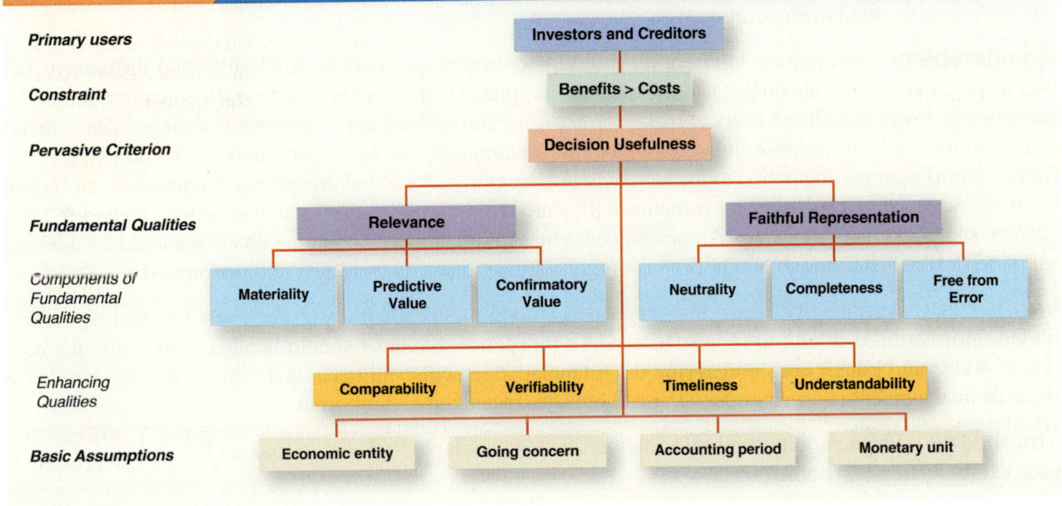

Relevance To be relevant, accounting information must have the ability to make a difference in a decision. Such information may be useful in making predictions about future performance of a company or in providing confirmatory feedback to evaluate past events.

MATERIALITY Materiality refers to whether a particular amount is large enough or important enough to affect the judgment of a reasonable decision-maker. In practice, materiality is typically judged by the relative size of an item (e.g., relative to total assets, sales revenues, or net income).

PREDICTIVE VALUE Financial information has predictive value if it can be used as an input in the decision processes employed by users to predict future outcomes. The information does not have to be a prediction or forecast itself, but if it can be used by others in making predictions, it has predictive value.

CONFIRMATORY VALUE Financial information has confirmatory value if it provides feedback about previous evaluations.

Faithful Representation In addition to being relevant, financial information must report the economic events that it purports to report. Financial reports describe where an organization is at a point in time and how it arrived at that location from a previous one. To a traveler, a map would provide a faithful representation if the traveler can use the map to discern his or her actual location.

Information is a perfectly faithful representation if it is ***complete***, ***neutral***, and ***free from error***. The objective stated in the conceptual framework does not expect to achieve such perfection, but the requirement of faithful representation for information provides a measuring stick for standard-setters when considering alternative reporting standards.

COMPLETENESS Financial information is complete if it enables the user to understand all the dimensions of an economic phenomenon. Achieving such completeness may require disclosure of additional numerical information (an asset's historical cost and its fair value) or descriptive information (ongoing litigation).

NEUTRALITY While lack of bias is desirable in any reporting system, the effects of financial reports on management and investors create significant incentives to report outcomes and to choose disclosures that portray the firm in a favorable light. In choosing accounting standards, standard-setters aspire to reduce the ability of organizations to bias financial reports and to give financial statement users the ability to identify those biases when they occur.

FREE FROM ERROR Free from error means there are no errors or omissions in the description of the phenomenon and that the process used to produce the reported information has been selected and applied with no errors in the process. A common misconception about accounting is that it consists solely of a historical record of a firm's economic activities. It is such a record, but it is also dependent on management's forecasts of the future. Financial reports are very dependent on forecasts of the future, and forecasts of the future are almost always wrong (though we hope not by much). In this context, "free from error" means that any estimates are described clearly as such, with an explanation of the estimating process.

Enhancing Qualitative Characteristics

For financial information that is relevant to investors and faithfully represents an economic phenomenon, the conceptual framework describes several additional qualitative characteristics that—when present—enhance the usefulness of that information.

Comparability Accounting information should enable users to identify similarities and differences between sets of economic phenomena. For instance, the financial statements of different companies should be presented in a way that allows users to make comparisons across companies concerning their activities, financial condition, and performance. In addition, the information supplied to decision-makers should exhibit conformity from one reporting period to the next with unchanging policies and procedures. Companies can choose to change accounting methods, and sometimes they are required to do so by standard-setters. However, such changes make it difficult to evaluate financial performance over time. Accounting changes should be rare and supported as the better means of reporting the organization's financial condition and performance.

Verifiability Verifiability means that consensus among independent observers could be reached that reported information is a faithful representation. An independent auditor should be able to examine the economic events and transactions underlying the financial statements and reach conclusions that are similar to those of management concerning how these events are measured and reported.

Timeliness Financial reporting information must be available to decision-makers before it loses its capacity to influence decisions.

Understandability Modern organizations engage in a wide variety of transactions, and this complexity can make it difficult for a general user of the financial statements to assess the amount, timing, and uncertainty of the organization's future cash flows. The conceptual framework endeavors to take into consideration the reporting requirements for "users who have a reasonable knowledge of business and economic activities and who review and analyze the information diligently."

The Cost Constraint

Financial reporting requirements impose costs on companies. There are the costs of gathering, processing, and verifying the information, as well as the costs of publicly disclosing information to competitors. These costs are ultimately borne by the companies' investors and should be justified by the benefits of the information produced.

Additional Underlying Basic Assumptions

While not a part of the conceptual framework, four assumptions underlie the preparation of financial statements. Knowing these assumptions is helpful in understanding how the statements are prepared and in interpreting the information reported therein. These assumptions include:

Separate Economic Entity For accounting purposes, the activities of a company are considered independent, distinct, and separate from the activities of its stockholders and from other companies.

Going Concern Companies are assumed to have continuity in that they can be expected to continue in operation over time. This assumption is essential for valuing assets (future benefits) and liabilities (future obligations).

Accounting Period While continuity is assumed, company operations must be reported periodically, normally each fiscal year. Interim reporting periods, such as quarterly or monthly reports, allow companies to supplement the annual financial statements with more timely information.

Monetary Unit The unit of measure is the monetary unit of the country in which the firm's accounting reports are issued. The dollar is the monetary unit in the United States.

YOU MAKE THE CALL

You are the Bank Loan Officer **Hertz**, the rental car firm, has a fleet of relatively new automobiles that it rents to customers for usually short periods. Suppose that Hertz applied to your bank for a loan and offered their fleet of cars as collateral. Would you, as the loan officer, be satisfied with the value shown on Hertz's balance sheet as a measure of the fleet's value? If not, what value would you prefer, and how might you estimate that value? [Answers on page 1-30.]

Identifying Conceptual Framework Topics

LO1-6 **Review 1-6**

GuidedExample MBC

The following topics 1 through 5 are discussed in the context of the FASB's conceptual framework.

1. Objective of financial reporting
2. Qualitative characteristics of useful financial information
3. Enhancing qualitative characteristics
4. Cost constraint
5. Accounting assumptions

Required

Listed below are subtopics of the above topics. Match the subtopics *a* through *j* with the topics 1 through 5.

a. ____	Completeness	*f.* ____	Materiality
b. ____	Cost effectiveness	*g.* ____	Predictive value
c. ____	Economic entity	*h.* ____	Provide information to investors and creditors
d. ____	Free from error	*i.* ____	Timeliness
e. ____	Going concern	*j.* ____	Verifiability

Solution on p. 1-41.

Summary *offers key bullet point takeaways for each Learning Objective.*

SUMMARY

Identify the users of accounting information, and discuss the costs and benefits of disclosure. (p. 1-3) **LO1-1**

- There are many diverse decision-makers who use financial information.
- The benefits of disclosure of credible financial information must exceed the costs of providing the information.

Describe a company's business activities, and explain how these activities are represented by the accounting equation. (p. 1-7) **LO1-2**

- To effectively manage a company or infer whether it is well managed, we must understand its activities as well as the competitive and regulatory environment in which it operates.
- All corporations *plan* business activities, *finance* and *invest* in them, and then engage in *operations.*
- Financing is obtained partly from stockholders and partly from creditors, including suppliers and lenders.
- Investing activities involve the acquisition and disposition of the company's productive resources called assets.
- Operating activities include the production of goods or services that create operating revenues (sales) and expenses (costs). Operating profit (income) arises when operating revenues exceed operating expenses.

Identify four key financial statements: balance sheet, income statement, statement of stockholders' equity, and statement of cash flows. (p. 1-11) **LO1-3**

- Four basic financial statements used to periodically report the company's progress are the balance sheet, the income statement, the statement of stockholders' equity, and the statement of cash flows. These statements articulate with one another.
- The balance sheet reports the company's financial position *at a point* in time. It lists the company's asset, liability, and equity items, and it typically aggregates similar items.

- The income statement reports the firm's operating activities to determine income earned, and thereby the firm's performance *over a period* of time.
- The stockholders' equity statement reports the changes in the key equity accounts *over a period* of time.
- The statement of cash flows reports the cash flows into and out of the firm from its operating, investing, and financing sources *over a period* of time.

LO1-4 **Describe how standardized accounting principles and a regulatory environment are important to financial statement integrity. (p. 1-16)**

- Generally Accepted Accounting Principles (GAAP) are established standards and accepted practices designed to guide the preparation of the financial statements.
- While the Securities and Exchange Commission (SEC) has ultimate authority over financial reporting by companies in the United States, it has ceded the task of setting accounting standards to the accounting profession.
- The Financial Accounting Standards Board (FASB) has the primary responsibility for setting financial accounting standards in the United States.
- The Sarbanes-Oxley Act established the Public Company Accounting Oversight Board (PCAOB) to approve auditing standards and monitor the quality of financial statements and audits.
- International Financial Reporting Standards (IFRS) are set by the International Accounting Standards Board (IASB).
- IFRS are an attempt to achieve a greater degree of commonality in financial reporting across different countries.

LO1-5 **Compute two key ratios that are commonly used to assess profitability and risk—return on equity and the debt-to-equity ratio. (p. 1-21)**

- **Return on equity (ROE)**—a measure of profitability that assesses the performance of the firm relative to the investment made by stockholders (equity financing)
- Return on equity (ROE) is an important profitability metric for stockholders.

$$\text{ROE} = \frac{\text{Net income}}{\text{Average stockholders' equity}}$$

- **Debt-to-equity ratio (D/E)**—a measure of long-term solvency that relates the amount of creditor financing to the amount of equity financing
- The debt-to-equity ratio is an important measure of long-term solvency, a determinant of overall company risk.

$$\text{D/E} = \frac{\text{Total liabilities}}{\text{Total stockholders' equity}}$$

LO1-6 **Appendix 1A: Explain the conceptual framework for financial reporting. (p. 1-25)**

- The conceptual framework includes, among other things, a statement of the *objectives* of financial reporting along with a discussion of the *qualitative characteristics* of accounting information that are important to users.

GUIDANCE ANSWERS . . . YOU MAKE THE CALL

You are a Product Manager There are at least two considerations that must be balanced—namely, the disclosure requirements and your company's need to protect its competitive advantages. You must comply with all minimum required disclosures. The extent to which you offer additional disclosures depends on the sensitivity of the information; that is, how beneficial it is to your existing and potential competitors. Another consideration is how the information disclosed will affect your existing and potential investors. Disclosures such as this can be beneficial in that they convey the positive investments that are available to your company. Still, there are many stakeholders influenced by your decision, and each must be given due consideration.

You are a Financial Analyst This question has received a lot of discussion from both sides under the title "Economic Consequences." On one side are those who maintain that accounting rules should not only reflect a rule's economic consequences but be designed to facilitate the attainment of a specific economic goal. One example is the case where the oil industry lobbied for an accounting rule that they and others believed would increase the incentive to explore and develop new oil deposits.

Those on the other side of the argument believe that accounting should try to provide data that is objective, reliable, and free from bias without considering the economic consequences of the decisions to be made. They believe that accounting rule makers have neither the insight nor the public mandate to attempt forecasts of the economic effects of financial reporting. Decisions that will affect the allocation of resources or that affect society's social structure should be made only by our elected representatives. While there are substantive points on both sides, we believe that it is the job of accounting rule makers to work toward the objective of financial reporting that reflects economic reality, subject to practical measurement limitations.

You are a Member of the Board of Directors In order to perform a thorough audit, a company's auditors must gain an intimate knowledge of its operations, its internal controls, and its accounting system. Because of this familiarity, the accounting firm is in a position to provide insights and recommendations that another consulting firm might not be able to provide. However, the independence of the auditor is critical to the credibility of the audit, and there is some concern that the desire to retain a profitable consulting engagement might lead the auditors to tailor their audit opinions to "satisfy the customer." Contrary to this concern, however, research finds that there is no evidence that auditors provide more optimistic audit reports for the companies they consult for. Rather, it appears that litigation and reputation concerns are reasonably effective in keeping auditors honest. Nevertheless, recent legislation in the United States now prohibits auditors from performing consulting services for their audit clients.

You are the Bank Loan Officer The value shown on Hertz's books will be the purchase price, though perhaps reduced for the time the fleet has been in use. However, the bank would want to know the current market value of the fleet, not its book value, and the bank would then adjust this market value. The current market value of a single car can be found in used-car market quotes. If the bank ultimately becomes the owner of the fleet, it will need to sell the cars, probably a few at a time through wholesalers. Therefore, the adjusted market value and the book value are likely to differ for several reasons, including:

1. Hertz would have been able to buy the fleet at a reduced value due to buying in large volume regularly (market value lower than used-car quotes).
2. Hertz is likely to have kept the cars in better condition than would the average buyer (market value higher than used-car quotes).
3. The bank would reduce the value by some percentage due to the costs associated with disposing of the fleet (including the wholesaler's discount) and the length of the bank loan (reduction to the value as otherwise determined).

KEY RATIOS

$$\text{Return on equity (ROE)} = \frac{\text{Net income}}{\text{Average stockholders' equity}} \qquad \text{Debt-to-equity (D/E)} = \frac{\text{Total liabilities}}{\text{Total stockholders' equity}}$$

Assignments with the MBC logo in the margin are available in myBusinessCourse. See the Preface of the book for details.

Multiple Choice *questions with answers are provided for each chapter.*

MULTIPLE CHOICE

1. Which of the following is a potential cost of the public disclosure of accounting information?
   a. Loss of competitive advantage caused by revealing information to competitors.
   b. Potential increased regulation and taxes due to reporting excessive profits in politically sensitive industries.
   c. Raising and then failing to meet the expectations of investors.
   d. All of the above are potential costs of disclosure.
2. Banks that lend money to corporations are considered
   a. creditors.
   b. stockholders.
   c. both *a* and *b* above.
   d. neither *a* nor *b* above.
3. Which of the following financial statements reports the financial condition of a company at a point in time?
   a. the balance sheet
   b. the income statement
   c. the statement of cash flows
   d. the statement of stockholders' equity
4. Which of the following is *not* one of the four basic financial reports?
   a. the balance sheet

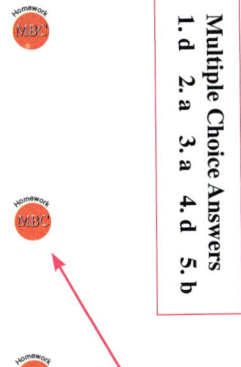

Multiple Choice Answers
1. d 2. a 3. a 4. d 5. b

Homework *icons indicate which assignments are available in* **myBusinessCourse** *(MBC). This feature is only available when the instructor incorporates MBC in the course.*

b. the income statement
c. the statement of stockholders' equity
d. the notes to the financial statements

Homework MBC

5. Which of the following expressions is a correct statement of the accounting equation?
a. Equity + Assets = Liability
b. Assets − (Liabilities + Equity) = 0
c. Liabilities − Equity = Assets
d. Liabilities + Assets = Equity

Superscript ^A denotes assignments based on Appendix 1A.

QUESTIONS

Q1-1. What are the three major business activities of a company that are motivated and shaped by planning activities? Explain each activity.

Q1-2. The accounting equation (Assets = Liabilities + Equity) is a fundamental business concept. Explain what this equation reveals about a company's sources and uses of funds and the claims on company resources.

Q1-3. Companies prepare four primary financial statements. What are those financial statements, and what information is typically conveyed in each?

Q1-4. Does a balance sheet report on a period of time or at a point in time? Also, explain the information conveyed in that report. Does an income statement report on a period of time or at a point in time? Also, explain the information conveyed in that report.

Q1-5. Warren Buffett, CEO of Berkshire Hathaway, and known as the "Sage of Omaha" for his investment success, has stated that his firm is not interested in investing in a company whose business model he does not understand through reading its financial statements. Would you agree? Name several information items (3 or 4) reported in financial statements that corporate finance officers would find particularly relevant in considering whether to invest in a firm.

Q1-6. Does a statement of cash flows report on a period of time or at a point in time? Also, explain the information and activities conveyed in that report.

Q1-7. Explain what is meant by the articulation of financial statements.

Q1-8. The trade-off between risk and return is a fundamental business concept. Briefly describe both risk and return and their trade-off. Provide some examples that demonstrate investments of varying risk and the approximate returns that you might expect to earn on those investments.

Q1-9. Why might a company voluntarily disclose more information than is required by GAAP?

Q1-10. Financial statements are used by several interested stakeholders. Develop a listing of three or more potential external users of financial statements and their applications.

Q1-11. What ethical issues might managers face in dealing with confidential information?

Q1-12. Return on equity (ROE) is an important summary measure of financial performance. How is it computed? Describe what this metric reveals about company performance.

Q1-13. Business decision-makers external to the company increasingly demand more financial information on business activities of companies. Discuss the reasons companies have traditionally opposed the efforts of regulatory agencies like the SEC to require more disclosure.

Q1-14. What are generally accepted accounting principles, and what organization presently establishes them?

Q1-15. What are International Financial Reporting Standards (IFRS)? Why are IFRS needed? What potential issues can you see with requiring all public companies to prepare financial statements using IFRS?

Q1-16. What is the primary function of the auditor? To what does the auditor attest in its opinion?

Q1-17.^A What are the objectives of financial accounting? Which of the financial statements satisfies each of these objectives?

Q1-18.^A What are the two fundamental qualitative characteristics and the six enhancing qualitative characteristics of accounting information? Explain how each characteristic improves the quality of accounting disclosures.

DATA ANALYTICS

DA1-1. Preparing Data Visualizations in Excel Using Doughnut Charts LO1-1

The Excel file associated with this exercise includes data obtained from the U.S. Bureau of Labor Statistics regarding the employers of (1) accountants and auditors and (2) financial analysts.[7] We will to create a data visualization for each employer group in Excel using a doughnut chart, a form of a pie chart.

REQUIRED

1. Download Excel file DA1-1 found in myBusinessCourse.
2. Create a new row in each dataset for "Other employers."
3. Add the applicable percentage to the new category, "Other employers." *Hint:* When creating a doughnut chart, we are showing proportions of a total. The total of the percentages for each dataset must add up to 100%.
4. Create a doughnut chart for each dataset. *Hint:* Highlight dataset, click on Insert, click on the Pie icon, click Doughnut. Do not include the dataset title when highlighting the dataset.
5. Update the features of your doughnut charts by either choosing one of the chart design templates or updating manually. *Hint:* You can add elements and change the chart style by using the Chart Layouts and Chart Styles tools on the Chart Design tab. The Chart Design tab appears when you click inside a chart.
6. Add percentages to each proportion of the doughnut charts. *Hint:* Right-click on your chart; click on Add data labels. Click on your chart labels to allow editing of color or font size.
7. Calculate the difference between the largest and smallest proportion in the doughnut chart for Dataset A.
8. Calculate the difference between the largest and smallest proportion in the doughnut chart for Dataset B.
9. List any employer categories that overlap between the two occupations.
10. List the formula type associated with the chart. *Hint:* Double-click on the doughnut chart in Dataset A, which will allow the formula to be visible in the formula bar.

DA1-2. Differentiating Between Different Types of Data Analytics LO1-5

For CPAs, we commonly consider four types of data analytics: descriptive analytics, diagnostic analytics, predictive analytics, and prescriptive analytics. To understand the differences between these four types, review Appendix B to this text and refer to *The Next Frontier in Data Analytics* by N. Tschakert, J. Kokina, S. Kozlowski, and M. Vasarhelyi in the *Journal of Accountancy* found at https://www.journalofaccountancy.com/issues/2016/aug/data-analytics-skills.html.

REQUIRED

For each of the following ten examples, indicate which type of data analytics best applies (descriptive, diagnostic, predictive, or prescriptive).

1. Analyzing the trends of collections over the past three years for a customer and using that information to estimate the customer's collection schedule over the upcoming year.
2. Preparing a horizontal analysis, showing changes in expenses over the prior year.
3. Analyzing a significant change in operating expenses over the prior year by drilling down to specific categories that were over budget, down to specific departments, down to specific time periods.
4. An analysis of inventory turns by product in conjunction with an analysis of web clicks for the related product resulted in a list of products to phase out over the next year.
5. Preparing a forecast of sales by major segment using a regression analysis.
6. The relation of a digital marketing campaign and resulting sales is used to budget sales in the following year given the plan for upcoming digital marketing campaigns.
7. An analysis of the relations between the costs of five recent digital marketing campaigns and resulting sales was used to recommend digital marking campaigns to pursue in the future.
8. Preparing monthly unaudited financial statements by department.
9. Examining trends in gross margin at a product level to understand the cause of a drop in overall gross margin.
10. Preparing a data visualization showing how many of the company's current customers are self-employed.

---

[7] Bureau of Labor Statistics, U.S. Department of Labor, Occupational Outlook Handbook, Accountants and Auditors, at https://www.bls.gov/ooh/business-and-financial/accountants-and-auditors.htm (visited August 18, 2021).

LO1-4 tableau Homework MBC Data Analytics

DA1-3. Preparing Executive Compensation Visualizations with Tableau: Part I, Part II, Part III
Refer to PB-17, PB-18, and PB-19 in Appendix B. This three-part problem uses Tableau to analyze compensation of chief executive officers and chief financial officers of S&P 500 companies.

DATA VISUALIZATION

Data Visualization

Data Visualization Activities are available in myBusinessCourse. These assignments use Tableau Dashboards to expose students to visual depictions of data and introduce students to data analytics through data visualizations. These exercises are easily assignable and auto graded by MBC.

MINI EXERCISES

LO1-2 Homework MBC — Macy's, Inc. NYSE :: M

M1-19. Financing and Investing Relations, and Financing Sources
Total assets of Macy's, Inc. equal $21,172 million, and its equity is $6,377 million. What is the amount of its liabilities? Does Macy's receive more financing from its owners or nonowners, and what percentage of financing is provided by its owners?

LO1-2 Homework MBC — Coca-Cola Company NYSE :: KO

M1-20. Financing and Investing Relations, and Financing Sources
Total assets of The Coca-Cola Company equal $86,381 million, and its liabilities equal $65,283 million. What is the amount of its equity? Does Coke receive more financing from its owners or nonowners, and what percentage of financing is provided by its owners?

LO1-2 Homework MBC — Hewlett-Packard NYSE :: HPE; General Mills NYSE :: GIS; Harley-Davidson NYSE :: HOG

M1-21. Applying the Accounting Equation and Computing Financing Proportions
Use the accounting equation to compute the missing financial amounts (a), (b), and (c). Which of these companies is more owner-financed? Which of these companies is more nonowner-financed?

($ millions)	Assets	=	Liabilities	+	Equity
Hewlett-Packard Enterprise Company . . .	$54,015.0		$37,919.0		$ (a)
General Mills	30,806.7		(b)		8,894.1
Harley-Davidson	(c)		8,724.2		1,804.0

LO1-3 Homework MBC — Apple Inc. NASDAQ :: AAPL

M1-22. Identifying Key Numbers from Financial Statements
Access the most recent 10-K for Apple Inc., at the SEC's EDGAR database for financial reports (www.sec.gov). What are Apple's dollar amounts for assets, liabilities, and equity at September 26, 2020? Confirm that the accounting equation holds in this case. What percent of Apple's assets is financed from creditor financing sources?

LO1-3 Homework MBC — Nike NYSE :: NKE

M1-23. Verifying Articulation of Financial Statements
Access the 10-K for Nike for the fiscal year ended May 31, 2019, at the SEC's EDGAR database of financial reports (www.sec.gov). Using its consolidated statement of stockholders' equity, prepare a table similar to **Exhibit 1.9** showing the articulation of its retained (reinvested) earnings for the year ended May 31, 2019. Was Nike more or less profitable in the fiscal year ended May 31, 2020, compared to the fiscal year ended May 31, 2019?

Ticker symbols are provided for companies so one can easily obtain additional information.

LO1-3 Homework MBC

M1-24. Identifying Financial Statement Line Items and Accounts
Several line items and account titles are listed below. For each, indicate in which of the following financial statement(s) you would likely find the item or account: income statement (IS), balance sheet (BS), statement of stockholders' equity (SE), or statement of cash flows (SCF).

a. Cash asset
b. Expenses
c. Noncash assets
d. Contributed capital
e. Cash outflow for land
f. Retained earnings
g. Cash inflow for stock issued
h. Cash outflow for dividends
i. Net income

LO1-1

M1-25. Ethical Issues and Accounting Choices
Assume that you are a technology services provider and you must decide whether to record revenue from the installation of computer software for one of your clients. Your contract calls for acceptance of the software by the client within six months of installation before payment is due. Although you have not yet received formal acceptance, you are confident that it is forthcoming. Failure to record these revenues will cause your company to miss Wall Street's earnings estimates. What stakeholders will be affected by your decision, and how might they be affected?

M1-26. Internal Controls and Their Importance
The Sarbanes-Oxley legislation requires companies to report on the effectiveness of their internal controls. What are internal controls and their purpose? Why do you think Congress felt it to be such an important area to monitor and report?

LO1-4

LOs link assignments to the Learning Objectives of each chapter.

EXERCISES

E1-27. Applying the Accounting Equation and Assessing Financing Contributions
Determine the missing amount from each of the separate situations (a), (b), and (c) below. Which of these companies is more owner-financed? Which of these companies is more creditor-financed?

LO1-2 · Homework MBC · Motorola Solutions NYSE :: MSI · Kraft Foods NASDAQ :: KHC · Merck & Co. NYSE :: MRK

($ millions)	Assets	=	Liabilities	+	Equity
a. Motorola Solutions, Inc.	$10,642		$?		$ (683)
b. The Kraft Heinz Company	?		49,701		51,749
c. Merck & Co., Inc.	84,397		58,396		?

E1-28. Financial Information Users and Uses
Financial statements have a wide audience of interested stakeholders. Identify two or more financial statement users that are external to the company. Specify two questions for each user identified that could be addressed or aided by use of financial statements.

LO1-1

E1-29. Applying the Accounting Equation and Financial Statement Articulation
Answer the following questions. (*Hint*: Apply the accounting equation.)

LO1-2, 3 · Homework MBC · Intel NASDAQ :: INTC · JetBlue Airways NASDAQ :: JBLU · Walt Disney Company NYSE :: DIS

a. Intel Corporation had assets equal to $153,091 million and liabilities equal to $72,053 million for a recent year-end. What was the total equity for Intel's business at year-end?

b. At the beginning of a recent year, JetBlue Airways Corporation's assets were $10,959 million, and its equity was $4,685 million. During the year, assets increased $959 million, and liabilities increased $845 million. What was its equity at the end of the year?

c. At the beginning of a recent year, The Walt Disney Company's liabilities equaled $91,132 million. During the year, assets increased by $7,565 million, and year-end assets equaled $201,549 million. Liabilities increased $12,905 million during the year. What were its beginning and ending amounts for equity?

E1-30. Financial Statement Relations to Compute Dividends
Colgate-Palmolive Company reports the following balances in its retained earnings.

LO1-3 · Homework MBC · Colgate-Palmolive NYSE :: CL

($ millions)	2019	2018
Retained earnings	$22,501	$21,615

During 2019, Colgate-Palmolive reported net income of $2,367 million.

a. Assume that the only changes affecting retained earnings were net income and dividends. What amount of dividends did Colgate-Palmolive pay to its shareholders in 2019?

b. This dividend amount constituted what percent of its net income?

E1-31. Calculating Gross Profit and Preparing an Income Statement
In 2019, Colgate-Palmolive Company reported sales revenue of $15,693 million and cost of goods sold of $6,368 million. Its net income was $2,527 million. Calculate gross profit and prepare an income statement using the format illustrated in **Exhibit 1.8**.

LO1-3 · Homework MBC · Colgate-Palmolive NYSE :: CL

E1-32. Applying the Accounting Equation and Calculating Return on Equity and Debt-to-Equity Ratio
At the end of 2019, Alphabet, Inc., reported stockholders' equity of $201,442 million and total assets of $275,909 million. Its balance in stockholders' equity at the end of 2018 was $177,628 million. Net income in 2019 was $34,343 million.

LO1-2, 5 · Homework MBC · Alphabet, Inc. NASDAQ :: GOOG

a. Calculate the return on equity ratio for Alphabet, Inc. for 2019.

b. Calculate its debt-to-equity ratio as of December 31, 2019. (*Hint:* Apply the accounting equation to determine total liabilities.)

E1-33. Applying the Accounting Equation and Computing Return on Equity and Debt-to-Equity Ratio
At the end of 2019, Daimler AG, reported stockholders' equity of €62,841 million and total assets of €302,438 million. Its stockholders' equity at the end of 2018 was €66,053 million. Net income in 2019 was €2,709 million.

LO1-2, 5 · Homework MBC · Daimler AG OTC :: DDAIF

a. Calculate Daimler's return on equity ratio for 2019.

b. Calculate Daimler's debt-to-equity ratio as of December 31, 2019.

LO1-1, 4 **E1-34. Accounting in Society**

Financial accounting plays an important role in modern society and business.

a. What role does financial accounting play in the allocation of society's financial resources?

b. What are three aspects of the accounting environment that can create ethical pressure on management?

LO1-6 **E1-35.[A] Basic Assumptions, Principles, and Terminology in the Conceptual Framework**

Match each item in the left column with the correct description in the right column.

____ 1. Relevance
____ 2. Verifiability
____ 3. Going concern
____ 4. Materiality
____ 5. Monetary unit
____ 6. Representational faithfulness
____ 7. Accounting period
____ 8. Comparability
____ 9. Timeliness
____10. Economic entity

a. Refers to whether or not a particular amount is large enough to affect a decision.

b. The activities of a business are considered to be independent and distinct from those of its owners or from other companies.

c. Accounting information should enable users to identify similarities and differences between sets of economic phenomena.

d. Financial reporting information must be available to decision-makers before it loses its capacity to influence decisions.

e. Information is useful if it has the ability to influence decisions.

f. Consensus among measures ensures that the information is free of error.

g. Accounting information should reflect the underlying economic events that it purports to measure.

h. The financial reports are presented in one consistent monetary unit, such as U.S. dollars.

i. A business is expected to have continuity in that it is expected to continue to operate indefinitely.

j. The life of a business can be divided into discrete accounting periods such as a year or quarter.

PROBLEMS

LO1-2, 5 **P1-36. Applying the Accounting Equation and Calculating Ratios**

Procter & Gamble
NYSE :: PG

The following table contains financial statement information for The Procter & Gamble Company ($ millions) for the fiscal years ended in June of each year:

Year	Assets	Liabilities	Equity	Net Income
2018	$118,310	$65,427	$?	$ 9,861
2019	?	67,516	47,579	3,966
2020	120,700	?	46,878	13,103

REQUIRED

a. Compute the missing amounts for assets, liabilities, and equity for each year.

b. Compute return on equity for 2019 and 2020. Let's assume that the median ROE for Fortune 500 companies is about 15%. How does P&G compare with this median?

c. Compute the debt-to-equity ratio for 2019 and 2020. Let's assume that the median debt-to-equity ratio for the Fortune 500 companies is 1.8. How does P&G compare to this median?

LO1-2, 3 **P1-37. Formulating Financial Statements from Raw Data**

General Mills
NYSE :: GIS

Following is selected financial information from General Mills, Inc., for its fiscal year ended May 31, 2020 ($ millions).

Cash and cash equivalents, end of year.	$ 1,677.8
Net cash from operations	3,676.2
Net sales.	17,626.6
Stockholders' equity, end of year	8,894.1
Cost of goods sold	11,496.7
Net cash from financing	(1,941.5)
Total liabilities, end of year	21,912.6
Other expenses, including income taxes	3,919.1
Noncash assets, end of year	29,128.9
Net cash from investing	(486.2)
Net income	2,210.8
Effect of exchange rate changes on cash.	(20.7)
Cash and cash equivalents, beginning of year.	450.0

REQUIRED

a. Prepare an income statement, balance sheet, and statement of cash flows for General Mills, Inc.

b. What portion of the financing is contributed by owners?

P1-38. Formulating Financial Statements from Raw Data

LO1-2, 3

Homework MBC

Abercrombie & Fitch
NYSE :: ANF

Following is selected financial information from Abercrombie & Fitch for its fiscal year ended February 1, 2020 ($ millions).

Cash asset, end of year	$ 692.2
Cash flows from operations	300.7
Net sales	3,623.1
Stockholders' equity, end of year	1,071.2
Cost of goods sold	1,472.2
Cash flows from financing	(147.9)
Total liabilities, end of year	2,478.5
Other expenses, including income taxes	2,105.9
Noncash assets, end of year	2,857.5
Cash flows from investing	(202.8)
Net income	45.0
Effect of exchange rate changes on cash	(3.6)
Cash asset, beginning of year	745.8

REQUIRED

a. Prepare an income statement, balance sheet, and statement of cash flows for Abercrombie & Fitch.

b. Determine the owner and creditor financing levels.

P1-39. Preparing Comparative Financial Statements from Raw Data

LO1-3

Homework MBC

Tilly's, Inc.
NYSE :: TLYS

Following is selected financial information for Tilly's, Inc.

($ thousands)	Feb. 1, 2020	Feb. 2, 2019
Cash and cash equivalents	$ 70,137	$ 68,160
Cash flow from operations	36,434	46,743
Cost of goods sold	432,592	417,582
Total liabilities	386,739	129,841
Total assets	546,640	293,168
Cash flow from financing	(27,948)	(25,526)
Sales revenue	619,300	598,478
Cash flow from investing	(6,509)	(6,259)
Other expenses, including income taxes	164,086	155,953

REQUIRED

Prepare balance sheets, income statements, and statements of cash flows for the years ended February 1, 2020 and February 2, 2019.

P1-40. Preparing Comparative Financial Statements from Raw Data

LO1-3

Homework MBC

Tesla, Inc.
NASDAQ :: TSLA

Following is selected financial information for Tesla, Inc.

($ millions)	Dec. 31, 2019	Dec. 31, 2018
Cash asset	$ 6,783	$ 4,277
Cash flow from operations	2,405	2,098
Cost of goods sold	20,509	17,419
Total liabilities	26,199	23,427
Total assets	34,309	29,740
Cash flow from financing	1,529	574
Sales revenue	24,578	21,461
Cash flow from investing	(1,436)	(2,337)
Other expenses, including income taxes	4,844	5,105
Effect of exchange rate changes on cash	8	(23)

REQUIRED

Prepare balance sheets, income statements, and statements of cash flows for the years ended December 31, 2019 and 2018.

P1-41. Formulating a Statement of Stockholders' Equity from Raw Data

LO1-3

Homework MBC

Crocker Corporation began calendar-year 2022 with stockholders' equity of $50,000, consisting of contributed capital of $35,000 and retained earnings of $15,000. During 2022, it issued additional stock for total cash proceeds of $15,000. It also reported $25,000 of net income, of which $12,500 was paid as a cash dividend to shareholders.

REQUIRED

Prepare the December 31, 2022, statement of stockholders' equity for Crocker Corporation.

LO1-3 Homework MBC

P1-42. Formulating a Statement of Stockholders' Equity from Raw Data

DP Systems, Inc., reports the following selected information at December 31, 2022 ($ millions):

Contributed capital, December 31, 2021 and 2022	$ 770
Retained earnings, December 31, 2021	3,412
Cash dividends, 2022	393
Net income, 2022	1,203

REQUIRED

Use this information to prepare its statement of stockholders' equity for 2022.

LO1-2, 3, 5 Homework MBC

Nokia
NYSE :: NOK

P1-43. Analyzing and Interpreting Return on Equity

Nokia Corp. manufactures, markets, and sells phones and other electronics. Stockholders' equity for Nokia was €15,401 million in 2019 and €15,371 million in 2018. In 2019, Nokia reported net income of €11 million on sales of €23,315 million.

REQUIRED

a. What was Nokia's return on equity for 2019?

b. Nokia's total assets were €39,128 million at the end of 2019. Compute its debt-to-equity ratio.

c. What were total expenses for Nokia in 2019?

LO1-3, 5 Homework MBC

Best Buy
NYSE :: BBY

P1-44. Presenting an Income Statement and Computing Key Ratios

Best Buy Co., Inc., reported the following amounts in its February 1, 2020, and February 2, 2019, financial statements.

($ millions)	2020	2019
Sales revenue	$43,638	$42,879
Cost of sales	33,590	32,918
Net income (loss)	1,541	1,464
Total assets	15,591	12,901
Stockholders' equity	3,479	3,306

REQUIRED

a. Prepare an income statement for Best Buy for the year ended February 1, 2020, using the format illustrated in **Exhibit 1.8**.

b. Calculate Best Buy's return on equity for the year ended February 1, 2020.

c. Compute Best Buy's debt-to-equity ratio as of February 1, 2020.

LO1-3, 5 Homework MBC

Facebook, Inc.
NASDAQ :: FB

P1-45. Preparing Income Statements and Computing Key Ratios

Facebook, Inc. reported the following amounts in its 2019 and 2018 financial statements.

($ millions)	Dec. 31, 2019	Dec. 31, 2018
Total assets	$133,376	$97,334
Total liabilities	32,322	13,207
Retained earnings	55,692	41,981
Revenue	70,697	55,838
Operating expenses	46,711	30,925
Other expenses, including income taxes	5,501	2,801

REQUIRED

a. Prepare income statements for Facebook for 2019 and 2018. Use the format illustrated in **Exhibit 1.8**.

b. Compute Facebook's return on equity ratio for 2019 and 2018. Facebook's stockholders' equity at the end of 2017 was $74,347 million.

c. Compute Facebook's debt-to-equity ratio for 2019 and 2018.

CASES AND PROJECTS

LO1-3, 5 Homework MBC

Starbucks Corporation
NASDAQ :: SBUX

C1-46. Preparing Comparative Income Statements and Computing Key Ratios

Starbucks Corporation reported the following data in its 2020 and 2019 10-K reports.

($ millions)	Sept. 27, 2020	Sept. 29, 2019
Total assets	$29,374.5	$19,219.6
Total liabilities	37,173.9	25,450.6
Sales revenue	23,518.0	26,508.6
Operating expenses	21,956.3	22,430.7
Other expenses, including income taxes	637.0	483.3

REQUIRED

a. Prepare income statements for Starbucks for the years ended September 27, 2020, and September 29, 2019. Use the format illustrated in **Exhibit 1.8**.

b. Compute Starbucks's return on equity ratio for 2020 and 2019. Starbucks stockholders' equity at September 30, 2018, was $1,175.8 million.

c. Compute Starbucks's debt-to-equity ratio for 2020 and 2019.

d. Assume that in 2019, Starbucks reported a lawsuit was in process where plaintiffs allege that Starbucks did not inform customers about the chemical acrylamide in their products (as required by California law). Starbucks did not record a liability (and expense), stating that the loss was possible but not probable. What would Starbucks's ROE have been if it had accrued a $2,000 million litigation liability (and expense)? What effect did this one-time charge have on the company's return on equity ratio? (*Hint:* Compute the ratio and include the litigation charge in other expenses, reduce stockholders' equity, and compare to the ratio computed in *b*.) Ignore tax effects.

e. Assume Starbucks disclosed information about the pending litigation in the disclosure notes to its 2018 financial statements (before the case was settled). Discuss the costs and benefits of disclosing this information in its 2018 annual report.

C1-47. Computing and Interpreting Key Ratios and Formulating an Income Statement

LO1-2, 3, 5

Homework MBC

The Gap NYSE :: GPS
Nordstrom NYSE :: JWN

Data from the financial statements of **The Gap, Inc.**, and **Nordstrom, Inc.**, are presented below.

($ millions)	The Gap	Nordstrom
Stockholders' equity, 2019	$ 3,316	$ 979
Stockholders' equity, 2018	3,553	873
Total assets, 2019	13,679	9,737
Total assets, 2018	8,049	7,886
Revenue, 2019	16,383	15,524
Cost of goods sold, 2019	10,250	9,932
Net income, 2019	351	496

REQUIRED

a. Compute the return on equity ratio for The Gap and Nordstrom for 2019. Which company earned the higher return for its shareholders?

b. Compute the debt-to-equity ratio for each company as of 2019. Which company relies more on creditor financing?

c. Prepare a 2019 income statement for each company using the format in **Exhibit 1.8**. For each firm, compute gross profit as a percentage of sales revenue.

d. Based on your answers to questions *a*, *b*, and *c*, compare these two retail companies. What might be the cause of any differences in the ratios that you computed?

C1-48. Computing and Interpreting Key Ratios

LO1-5

Homework MBC

JetBlue Airways NASDAQ :: JBLU
Southwest Airlines NYSE :: LUV

Data from the financial statements of **JetBlue Airways** and **Southwest Airlines** are presented below.

($ millions)	JetBlue Airways	Southwest Airlines
Total liabilities, 2019	$ 7,119	$16,063
Total liabilities, 2018	6,274	16,390
Total assets, 2019	11,918	25,895
Total assets, 2018	10,959	26,243
Revenue, 2019	8,094	22,428
Net income, 2019	569	2,300

REQUIRED

a. Compute the return on equity ratio for JetBlue and Southwest for 2019. Which company earned the higher return for its shareholders?

b. Compute the debt-to-equity ratio for each company as of December 31, 2019. Which company relies more on creditor financing?

c. For each firm, compute net income as a percentage of revenue in 2019.

d. Based on your answers to questions *a*, *b*, and *c*, compare these two competitors. What might be the cause of any differences in the ratios that you computed?

LO1-1, 3, 5 **C1-49. Interpreting Financial Statement Information**

Paula Seale is negotiating the purchase of an extermination firm called Total Pest Control. Seale has been employed by a national pest control service and knows the technical side of the business. However, she knows little about accounting data and financial statements. The sole owner of the firm, Meg Krey, has provided Seale with income statements for the past three years, which show an average net income of $86,400 per year. The latest balance sheet shows total assets of $342,000 and liabilities of $54,000. Seale brings the following matters to your attention and requests advice.

1. Krey is asking $360,000 for the firm. She has told Seale that because the firm has been earning 30% on its investment, the price should be higher than the net assets on the balance sheet. (Net assets equal total assets minus total liabilities.)
2. Seale has noticed no salary for Krey on the income statements, even though she worked half-time in the business. Krey explained that because she had other income, the firm only paid $21,600 in cash dividends to Krey (the sole shareholder). If she purchases the firm, Seale will hire a full-time manager for the firm at an annual salary of $43,200.
3. Krey's tax returns for the past three years report a lower net income for the firm than the amounts shown in the financial statements. Seale is skeptical about the accounting principles used in preparing the financial statements.

REQUIRED

a. How did Krey arrive at the 30% return figure in point 1? If Seale accepts Krey's average annual net income figure of $86,400, what would Seale's percentage return be, assuming that the net income remained at the same level and that the firm was purchased for $360,000?

b. Should the dividend to Krey affect the net income reported in the financial statements? What will Seale's percentage return be if she takes into consideration the $43,200 salary she plans to pay a full-time manager?

c. Could there be legitimate reasons for the difference between net income shown in the financial statements and net income reported on the tax returns, as mentioned in point 3? How might Seale obtain additional assurance about the propriety of the financial statements?

LO1-1, 4 **C1-50. Management, Auditing, and Ethical Behavior**

Jackie Hardy, CPA, has a brother, Ted, in the retail clothing business. Ted ran the business as its sole owner for 10 years. During this 10-year period, Jackie helped Ted with various accounting matters. For example, Jackie designed the accounting system for the company, prepared Ted's personal income tax returns (which included financial data about the clothing business), and recommended various cost control procedures. Ted paid Jackie for all these services. A year ago, Ted markedly expanded the business; Ted is president of the corporation and chairs the corporation's board of directors. The board of directors has overall responsibility for corporate affairs. When the corporation was formed, Ted asked Jackie to serve on its board of directors. Jackie accepted. In addition, Jackie now prepares the corporation's income tax returns and continues to advise her brother on accounting matters.

Recently, the corporation applied for a large bank loan. The bank wants audited financial statements for the corporation before it will decide on the loan request. Ted asked Jackie to perform the audit. Jackie replied that she cannot do the audit because the code of ethics for CPAs requires that she be independent when providing audit services.

REQUIRED

a. Why is it important that a CPA be independent when providing audit services?

b. Which of Jackie's activities or relationships impair her independence?

SOLUTIONS TO REVIEW PROBLEMS

Review 1-1

1. e 2. b 3. f 4. c 5. a 6. d

Review 1-2

($ millions)	Assets	Liabilities	Equity	% of Financing Provided by Owners	% of Financing Provided by Creditors
2019	$64,532	$49,174	$15,358	24%	76%
2018	$60,266	$46,579	$13,687	23%	77%
2017	$53,671	$41,141	$12,530	23%	77%

Review 1-3

ADIDAS
Balance Sheet (€ millions)
December 31, 2019

Cash and cash equivalents . . .	€ 2,220	Total liabilities	€13,622
Noncash assets	18,460	Stockholders' equity	7,058
Total assets.	€20,680	Total liabilities and stockholders' equity . . .	€20,680

ADIDAS
Income Statement (€ millions)
For Year Ended December 31, 2019

Sales revenue.	€23,640
Cost of goods sold	11,347
Gross profit.	12,293
Other expenses	10,316
Net income (loss)	€ 1,977

ADIDAS
Statement of Cash Flows (€ millions)
For Year Ended December 31, 2019

Cash flow from operations	€2,819
Cash flow from investing.	(925)
Cash flow from financing	(2,273)
Effect of exchange rates on cash	(30)
Net increase (decrease) in cash.	(409)
Cash, beginning of year	2,629
Cash, end of year	€2,220

b. Adidas reported revenues of €23,640 million (which is approximately equivalent to $26,477 million) compared to Nike's $37,403 million. Adidas reported net income of €1,977 million ($2,214 million) compared to Nike's $2,539 million. Adidas's operations produced cash flow of €2,819 million ($3,157 million), while Nike's cash flow from operations was $2,485 million. Hence, based on revenues, Nike is a larger company indicated by its substantially larger sales revenue. Its total assets of $31,342 million are also greater than Adidas' total assets of €20,680 million (or $23,162 million). Nike's operating cash flows and income are also larger than those of Adidas.

Review 1-4

1. GAAP 2. SEC 3. FASB 4. PCAOB 5. Management 6. Auditor 7. Internal controls

Review 1-5

a. $\text{ROE} = \dfrac{€1{,}977}{[(€6{,}364 + €7{,}058)/2]} = 0.295 \text{ or } 29.5\%$

b. $\text{Debt-to-equity} = \dfrac{€13{,}622}{€7{,}058} = 1.93$

c. One additional benefit to using ratios to analyze financial information is that ratios can be computed for amounts denominated in any currency. Thus, we can compare Adidas and Nike without translating euros into dollars. Adidas's ROE of 29.5% is almost identical to Nike's of 29.7%. This means that both companies earned a very similar return for their stockholders in 2019.

Adidas's debt-to-equity ratio is 1.93 compared to Nike's 2.89. This means that Nike relies more on debt financing, but again the companies are quite similar. A similar debt-to-equity ratio indicates a similar level of risk associated with an investment in either company.

Review 1-6

a. 2 *b.* 4 *c.* 5 *d.* 2 *e.* 5 *f.* 2 *g.* 2 *h.* 1 *i.* 3 *j.* 3

Chapter 2

Constructing Financial Statements

LEARNING OBJECTIVES

LO2-1 Describe and construct the balance sheet and understand how it can be used for analysis.

LO2-2 Use the financial statement effects template (FSET) to analyze transactions.

LO2-3 Describe and construct the income statement and discuss how it can be used to evaluate management performance.

LO2-4 Explain revenue recognition and accrual accounting and their effects on retained earnings.

LO2-5 Illustrate equity transactions and the statement of stockholders' equity.

LO2-6 Use journal entries and T-accounts to analyze and record transactions.

LO2-7 Compute net working capital, the current ratio, and the quick ratio, and explain how they reflect liquidity.

Road Map

LO	Learning Objective | Topics	Page	eLecture	Review	Assignments
LO2-1	Describe and construct the balance sheet and understand how it can be used for analysis.	2-3	e2-1	R2-1	M2-14, M2-1S, M2-16, M2-17, M2-19, M2-21, M2-22, M2-23, M2-24, M2-25, M2-26, M2-27, M2-29, M2-30, M2-31, E2-34, E2-35, E2-36, E2-37, E2-38, E2-39, E2-40, E2-41, E2-42, E2-43, E2-44, E2-46, E2-47, P2-49, P2-50, P2-51, P2-52, P2-53, P2-54, P2-55, P2-S6, P2-57, P2-59, P2-60, P2-62, P2-66, P2-67, P2-69, C2-71, DA2-1
LO2-2	Use the financial statement effects template (FSET) to analyze transactions.	2-8	e2-2	R2-2	M2-18, M2-29, M2-30, M2-31, E2-44, E2-45, E2-47, P2-57, P2-62, P2-67, P2-69, DA2-4
LO2-3	Describe and construct the Income statement and discuss how it can be used to evaluate management performance.	2-12	e2-3	R2-3	M2-19, M2-20, M2-21, M2-22, M2-23, M2-28, M2-31, E2-35, E2-37, E2-39, E2-40, E2-41, E2-42, E2-43, E2-44, E2-47, P2-49, P2-50, P2-51, P2-54, P2-57, P2-61, P2-62, P2-64, P2-65, P2-66, P2-67, P2-69, C2-71, C2-72, DA2-2
LO2-4	Explain revenue recognition and accrual accounting and their effects on retained earnings.	2-14	e2-4	R2-4	M2-18, M2-19, M2-20, M2-22, M2-23, M2-25, M2-26, M2-28, M2-29, M2-31, E2-39, E2-44, E2-47, P2-57, P2-62, P2-67, P2-69, C2-71
LO2-5	Illustrate equity transactions and the statement of stockholders' equity.	2-19	e2-5	R2-5	M2-18, M2-21, M2-22, M2-23, M2-24, M2-27, M2-31, E2-35, E2-36, E2-37, P2-53, P2-66, P2- 67, P2-69, C2-71
LO2-6	Use journal entries and T-accounts to analyze and record transactions.	2-21	e2-6	R2-6	M2-32, M2-33, E2-45, E2-48, P2-58, P2-63, P2-68, P2-70, DA2-3
LO2-7	Compute net working capital, the current ratio, and the quick ratio, and explain how they reflect liquidity.	2-30	e2-7	R2-7	E2-34, E2-36, E2-38, E2-41, E2-42, E2-46, P2-52, P2-55, P2-56, P2-59, P2-60

WALGREENS

www.walgreens.com

More than a hundred years have passed since Charles R. Walgreen, Sr. purchased his first pharmacy in 1901. In that time, the company that bears his name—created via a merger in 2014 of Walgreens and Alliance Boots GmbH—has grown remarkably. As of August 31, 2020, **Walgreens Boots Alliance, Inc.** (hereafter referred to as Walgreens) has a presence in all 50 states, and in more than 15 countries. The company employs roughly 331,000 people (450,000 people if equity method investees are included). The company has more than 13,000 retail locations and has one of the largest global pharmaceutical and wholesale distribution networks. The company continues to grow, adapt, and expand. In July 2020, the Company entered into an agreement with VillageMD to invest $1.0 billion. The Company and VillageMD plan to open 500 to 700 "Village Medical at Walgreens" physician-led primary care clinics in more than 30 U.S. markets.

Still, Walgreens faces a number of challenges. Pharmacy sales constitute a substantial portion of Walgreens' sales, and almost all of those are paid for by a third party. The success of that business depends significantly on factors like the growth of generic pharmaceuticals, legislative changes such as the Affordable Care Act, and the relationships with Pharmacy Benefit Managers. Furthermore, Walgreens faces competition from **CVS Health Corp.** and discount retailers like **Walmart Stores, Inc.**

Of course, the global Coronavirus pandemic presented unprecedented challenges, including store closures, then reduced hours and limited store capacity. Once the vaccines were developed and approved, Walgreens was crucial in the effort to administer the vaccine. The company operated with extended hours, launched mobile vaccine clinics, hosted vaccine clinics in medically underserved areas, and took other actions. As of the time of this writing, Walgreens has administered well over 5 million vaccine doses.

Walgreens has reported profits for many years, though 2020's profit was considerably lower (likely due to the pandemic). As we discovered in Chapter 1, companies like Walgreens prepare financial statements annually. These financial statements allow investors and creditors to assess the impact of changing economic conditions on the company's financial health and performance.

This chapter will introduce and explain financial statements using Walgreens as its prime example. The chapter also introduces some key accounting procedures such as transaction analysis, journal entries, and posting. The general ledger, key accounting assumptions, and basic accounting definitions are also introduced.

Sources: "In the beginning . . ." Walgreens history on the corporate website; Walgreens Boots Alliance, Inc., and Subsidiaries 2020 10-K annual report; Company press releases about vaccine access, *Fortune* magazine, *Wall Street Journal*, *Chicago Tribune*, *Bloomberg News* websites.

CHAPTER ORGANIZATION

Constructing Financial Statements

Reporting Financial Condition	Reporting Financial Performance	Reporting on Equity	Journalizing and Posting Transactions	Financial Statement Analysis
• Assets • Liabilities • Equity • Recording Balance Sheet Transactions • Financial Statement Effects Template	• Revenue Recognition • Accrual Accounting • Retained Earnings • Recording Income Statement Transactions	• Recording Equity Transactions • Statement of Stockholders' Equity	• T-Account • Debit and Credit System • Journal Entry • Analyze, Journalize, and Post	• Net Working Capital • Current Ratio • Quick Ratio

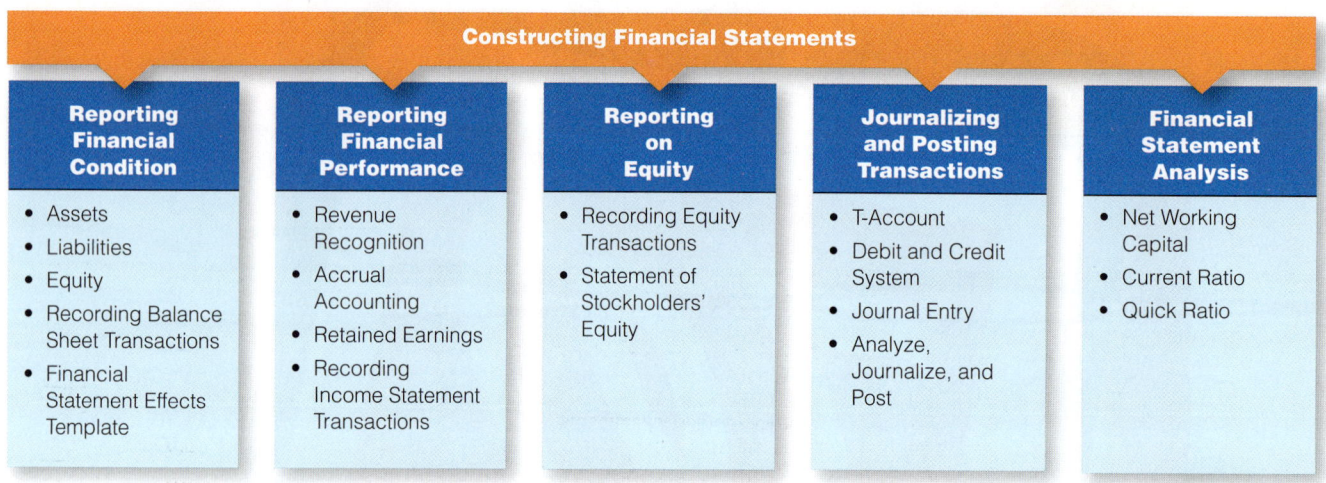

In Chapter 1, we introduced the four financial statements—the balance sheet, the income statement, the statement of cash flows, and the statement of stockholders' equity. In this chapter and in Chapter 3, we turn our attention to how the balance sheet and income statement are prepared. The statement of cash flows is discussed in detail in Chapter 4, and the statement of stockholders' equity is discussed in detail in Chapter 11.

REPORTING FINANCIAL CONDITION

LO2-1 Describe and construct the balance sheet and understand how it can be used for analysis.

eLecture

MBC

The balance sheet reports on a company's financial condition and is divided into three components: assets, liabilities, and stockholders' equity. It provides us with information about the resources available to management and the claims against those resources by creditors and shareholders. At the end of August 2020, Walgreens reports total assets of $87,174 million, total liabilities of $66,038 million, and equity of $21,136 million. Drawing on the **accounting equation**, Walgreens' balance sheet is summarized as follows ($ millions).

Assets	=	Liabilities	+	Equity
$87,174	=	$66,038	+	$21,136

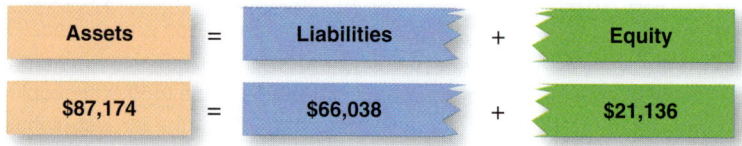

The balance sheet is prepared at a *point in time.* It is a snapshot of the financial condition of the company at that instant. For Walgreens, the above balance sheet amounts were reported at the close of business on August 31, 2020. Balance sheet accounts carry over from one period to the next; that is, the ending balance from one period becomes the beginning balance for the next period.

Walgreens' summarized 2020 and 2019 balance sheets are shown in **Exhibit 2.1**. These balance sheets report the assets and the liabilities and shareholders' equity amounts as of August 31, the company's fiscal year-end. Walgreens had $87,174 million in assets at the end of August 31, 2020, with the same amount reported in liabilities and shareholders' equity. Companies report their audited financial results on a yearly basis.[1] Many companies use the calendar year as their fiscal year. Other companies prefer to prepare their yearly report at a time when business activity is at a low level. Walgreens is an example of the latter reporting choice.

Assets

An **asset** is a resource owned or controlled by a company and expected to provide the company with future economic benefits. When a company incurs a cost to acquire future benefits, we say that cost is capitalized and an asset is recorded. An asset must possess two characteristics to be reported on the balance sheet:

[1] Companies also report quarterly financial statements, and these are reviewed by the independent accountant, but not audited.

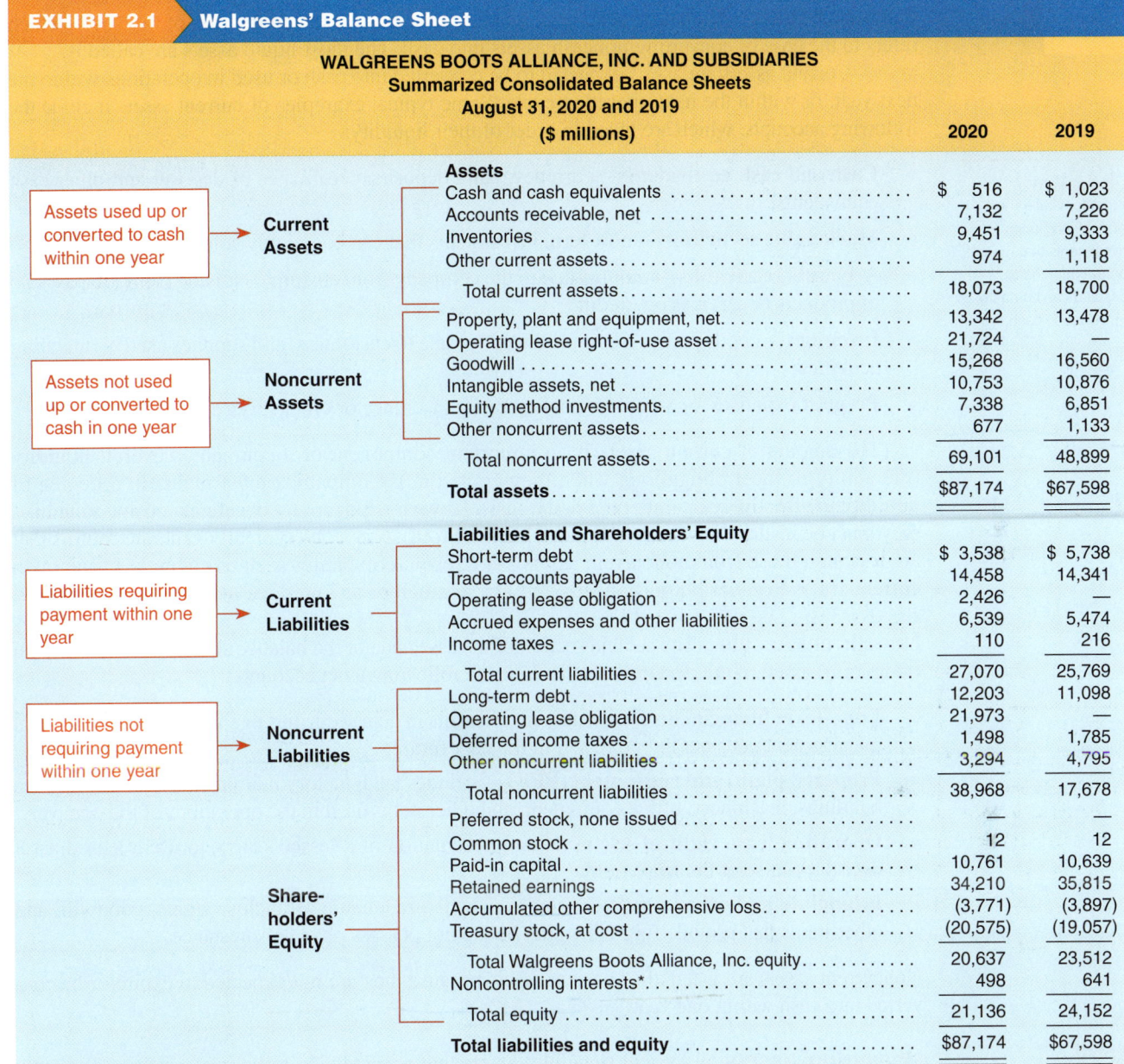

EXHIBIT 2.1 Walgreens' Balance Sheet

WALGREENS BOOTS ALLIANCE, INC. AND SUBSIDIARIES
Summarized Consolidated Balance Sheets
August 31, 2020 and 2019
($ millions)

Classification	Line item	2020	2019
	Assets		
Assets used up or converted to cash within one year → **Current Assets**	Cash and cash equivalents	$ 516	$ 1,023
	Accounts receivable, net	7,132	7,226
	Inventories	9,451	9,333
	Other current assets	974	1,118
	Total current assets	18,073	18,700
Assets not used up or converted to cash in one year → **Noncurrent Assets**	Property, plant and equipment, net	13,342	13,478
	Operating lease right-of-use asset	21,724	—
	Goodwill	15,268	16,560
	Intangible assets, net	10,753	10,876
	Equity method investments	7,338	6,851
	Other noncurrent assets	677	1,133
	Total noncurrent assets	69,101	48,899
	Total assets	$87,174	$67,598
	Liabilities and Shareholders' Equity		
Liabilities requiring payment within one year → **Current Liabilities**	Short-term debt	$ 3,538	$ 5,738
	Trade accounts payable	14,458	14,341
	Operating lease obligation	2,426	—
	Accrued expenses and other liabilities	6,539	5,474
	Income taxes	110	216
	Total current liabilities	27,070	25,769
Liabilities not requiring payment within one year → **Noncurrent Liabilities**	Long-term debt	12,203	11,098
	Operating lease obligation	21,973	—
	Deferred income taxes	1,498	1,785
	Other noncurrent liabilities	3,294	4,795
	Total noncurrent liabilities	38,968	17,678
Shareholders' Equity	Preferred stock, none issued	—	—
	Common stock	12	12
	Paid-in capital	10,761	10,639
	Retained earnings	34,210	35,815
	Accumulated other comprehensive loss	(3,771)	(3,897)
	Treasury stock, at cost	(20,575)	(19,057)
	Total Walgreens Boots Alliance, Inc. equity	20,637	23,512
	Noncontrolling interests*	498	641
	Total equity	21,136	24,152
	Total liabilities and equity	$87,174	$67,598

*** Noncontrolling interests arise from the practice of consolidating subsidiaries that are controlled, but not wholly owned. Chapters 11 and 12 provide a brief introduction to this topic.**

1. It must be owned or controlled by the company.
2. It must possess probable future benefits that can be measured in monetary units.

The first requirement, that the asset must be owned or controlled by the company, implies that the company has legal title to the asset or has the unrestricted right to use the asset. This requirement presumes that the cost to acquire the asset has been incurred, by paying cash, by trading other assets, or by assuming an obligation to make future payments.

The second requirement indicates that the company expects to receive some future benefit from ownership of the asset. Benefits can be the expected cash receipts from selling the asset or from selling products or services produced by the asset. Benefits can also refer to the receipt of other noncash assets, such as accounts receivable or the reduction of a liability (e.g., when assets are given up to settle debts). It also requires that a monetary value can be assigned to the asset.

Companies acquire assets to yield a return for their shareholders. Assets are expected to produce revenues, either directly (e.g., inventory that is sold) or indirectly (e.g., a manufacturing plant that produces inventories for sale). To create shareholder value, assets must yield resources that are in excess of the cost of the funds utilized to acquire the assets.

Current Assets The assets section of a balance sheet is presented in order of **liquidity**, which refers to the ease of converting noncash assets into cash. The most liquid assets are called **current assets**. Current assets are assets expected to be converted into cash or used in operations within the next year, or within the next operating cycle. Some typical examples of current assets include the following accounts, which are listed in order of their liquidity:

FYI Cash equivalents are short-term, highly liquid investments that mature in three months or less and can be easily converted to cash.

- **Cash** and **cash equivalents**—currency, bank deposits, certificates of deposit, and other cash equivalents;
- **Marketable securities**—short-term investments that can be quickly sold to raise cash;
- **Accounts receivable**—amounts due to the company from customers arising from the past sale of products or services on credit;
- **Inventory**—goods purchased or produced for sale to customers, and supplies used in operating activities;
- **Prepaid expenses**—costs paid in advance for insurance or other services.

The amount of current assets is an important component of a company's overall liquidity (the ability to meet obligations when they come due). Companies must maintain a degree of liquidity to effectively operate on a daily basis. However, current assets are expensive to hold—they must be insured, monitored, financed, and so forth—and they typically generate returns that are less than those from noncurrent assets. As a result, companies seek to maintain just enough current assets to cover liquidity needs, but not so much so as to reduce income unnecessarily.

Noncurrent Assets The second section of the asset side of the balance sheet reports noncurrent (long-term) assets. **Noncurrent assets** include the following asset accounts:

- **Long-term financial investments**—investments in debt securities or shares of other firms that management does not intend to sell in the near future;
- **Property, plant, and equipment (PPE)**—includes land, factory buildings, warehouses, office buildings, machinery, office equipment, and other items used in the operations of the company;
- **Operating lease right-of-use asset**—representation of a lessee's right to use a leased asset over the course of the lease term.
- **Intangible and other assets**—includes patents, trademarks, franchise rights, goodwill, and other items that provide future benefits but do not possess physical substance.

Noncurrent assets are listed after current assets because they are not expected to expire or be converted into cash within one year.

FYI Excluded assets often relate to self-developed, knowledge-based assets, like organizational effectiveness and technology. This is one reason that knowledge-based industries are so difficult to analyze. Yet, excluded assets are presumably reflected in company market values. This fact can explain why the firm's market capitalization (its share price multiplied by the number of shares) is often greater than the book value shown on the balance sheet.

Measuring Assets Physical (tangible) assets that are intended to be used, such as inventory and property, plant, and equipment, are reported on the balance sheet at their **historical cost** (with adjustments for depreciation in some cases). Historical cost refers to the original acquisition cost. The use of historical cost to report asset values rather than market, or fair, value in these cases is because fair value is not often **verifiable**. The historical cost is more verifiable and considered more **representationally faithful** because the acquisition cost (the amount of cash paid to purchase the asset) can be objectively determined and accurately measured. The disadvantage of historical costs is that some assets can be significantly undervalued on the balance sheet. For example, the land in Anaheim, California, on which Disneyland was built more than 65 years ago, was purchased for a mere fraction of its current fair value.

Some assets, such as marketable securities, are reported at current value or **fair value**. The current value of these assets can be easily obtained from online price quotes or from reliable sources such as **The Wall Street Journal**. Reporting certain assets at fair value increases the **relevance** of the information presented in the balance sheet. Relevance refers to how useful the information is to those who use the financial statements for decision-making. For example, marketable securities are intended to be sold for cash when cash is needed by the company to pay its obligations. Therefore, the most relevant value for marketable securities is the amount of cash that the company would receive if the securities were sold.

Only those asset values that have probable future benefits are recorded on the balance sheet. For this reason, some of a company's most important assets are often not reflected among the reported assets of the company. For example, the well-recognized Walgreens logo does not appear as an asset on the company's balance sheet. The image of Mickey Mouse and that of the Aflac Duck are also absent from **The Walt Disney Company**'s and **Aflac Incorporated**'s balance sheets. Each of these items is referred to as an unrecognized intangible asset. These intangible assets and others, such as the Coke bottle silhouette, the Kleenex name, or a well-designed supply chain, are measured and reported on the balance sheet only when they are purchased from a third party (usually in a merger). As a result, *internally created* intangible assets, such as the Mickey Mouse image, are not reported on a balance sheet, even though many of these internally created intangible assets are of enormous value.

Liabilities and Equity

Liabilities and equity represent the sources of capital to the company that are used to finance the acquisition of assets. **Liabilities** represent the firm's obligations for borrowed funds from lenders or bond investors, as well as obligations to pay suppliers, employees, tax authorities, and other parties. These obligations can be interest-bearing or non-interest-bearing. **Equity** represents capital that has been invested by the shareholders, either directly via the purchase of stock (when issued by the company), or indirectly in the form of earnings that are reinvested in the business and not paid out as dividends (retained earnings). We discuss liabilities and equity in this section.

The liabilities and equity sections of Walgreens' balance sheets for 2020 and 2019 are reproduced in the lower section of **Exhibit 2.1**. Walgreens reports $66,038 million of total liabilities and $21,136 million of equity as of its 2020 fiscal year-end. The total of liabilities and equity equals $87,174—the same as the total assets—because the shareholders have the residual claim on the company.

A liability is a probable future economic sacrifice resulting from a current or past event. The economic sacrifice can be a future cash payment to a creditor, or it can be an obligation to deliver goods or services to a customer at a future date. A liability must be reported in the balance sheet when each of the following three conditions is met:

1. The future sacrifice is probable.
2. The amount of the obligation is known or can be reasonably estimated.
3. The transaction or event that caused the obligation has occurred.

When conditions 1 and 2 are satisfied, but the transaction that caused the obligation has not occurred, the obligation is called an **executory contract** and no liability is reported. An example of such an obligation is a purchase order. When a company signs an agreement to purchase materials from a supplier, it commits to making a future cash payment of a known amount. However, the obligation to pay for the materials is not considered a liability until the materials are delivered. Therefore, even though the company is contractually obligated to make the cash payment to the supplier, a liability is not recorded on the balance sheet. However, information about purchase commitments and other executory contracts is useful to investors and creditors, and the obligations, if material, should be disclosed in the notes to the financial statements. In its annual report, Walgreens reports open inventory purchase orders of $2,227 million at the end of fiscal year 2020.

Current Liabilities Liabilities on the balance sheet are listed according to maturity. Obligations that are due within one year or within one operating cycle are called **current liabilities**. Some examples of common current liabilities include:

- **Accounts payable**—amounts owed to suppliers for goods and services purchased on credit. Walgreens uses another common name for this account—trade accounts payable.
- **Accrued liabilities**—obligations for expenses that have been recorded but not yet paid. Examples include accrued compensation payable (wages earned by employees but not yet paid), accrued interest payable (interest on debt that has not been paid), and accrued taxes (taxes due).
- **Short-term borrowings**—short-term debt payable to banks or other creditors.
- **Operating lease obligation**—an obligation to make payments arising from a lease, measured on a discounted basis. Includes amount scheduled to be repaid within one year.

- **Deferred (unearned) revenues**—an obligation created when the company accepts payment in advance for goods or services it will deliver in the future. The preferred terms for this are contract liability or performance obligation; these are sometimes also called advances from customers or customer deposits.
- **Current maturities of long-term debt**—the current portion of long-term debt that is due to be paid within one year.

Noncurrent Liabilities **Noncurrent liabilities** (also noncurrent liabilities) are obligations to be paid after one year. Examples of noncurrent liabilities include:

FYI Borrowings are often titled **Notes Payable**. When a company borrows money, it normally signs a promissory note agreeing to pay the money back (including interest)—hence, the title notes payable.

- **Long-term debt**—amounts borrowed from creditors that are scheduled to be repaid more than one year in the future. Any portion of long-term debt that is due within one year is reclassified as a current liability called *current maturities of long-term debt.*
- **Operating lease obligation**—an obligation to make payments arising from a lease, measured on a discounted basis. Includes amounts scheduled to be repaid more than one year in the future.
- **Other long-term liabilities**—various obligations, such as warranty and deferred compensation liabilities and long-term tax liabilities, that will be satisfied at least a year in the future. These items are discussed in later chapters.

Detailed information about a company's noncurrent liabilities, such as payment schedules, interest rates, and restrictive covenants, are provided in the notes to the financial statements.

BUSINESS INSIGHT

How Much Debt Is Reasonable? On August 31, 2020, Walgreens reports total assets of $87,174 million, liabilities of $66,038 ($27,070 current + $38,968 noncurrent) million, and equity of $21,136 million. This means that Walgreens finances 76% of its assets with borrowed funds and 24% with shareholder investment. Liabilities represent claims for fixed amounts, while shareholders' equity represents a flexible claim (because shareholders have a residual claim). Companies must monitor their financing sources and amounts because borrowing too much increases risk, and investors must recognize that companies may have substantial obligations (like Walgreens' inventory purchase commitment) that do not appear on the balance sheet.

Stockholders' Equity Equity reflects capital provided by the shareholders of the company. It is often referred to as a *residual interest.* That is, stockholders have a claim on any assets that are not needed to meet the company's obligations to creditors. The following are examples of items that are typically included in stockholders' equity:

Contributed Capital

- **Common stock**—the capital received from the primary owners of the company. Total common stock is divided into shares. One share of common stock represents the smallest fractional unit of ownership of a company.[2]
- **Additional paid-in capital**—amounts received from the common shareholders in addition to the par value or stated value of the common stock.
- **Treasury stock**—the amount paid for its own common stock that the company has reacquired, which reduces contributed capital.

Earned Capital

- **Retained earnings**—the accumulated earnings that have not been distributed to stockholders as dividends.
- **Accumulated other comprehensive income or loss**—accumulated changes in equity that are not reported in the income statement; discussed in Chapters 11 and 12.

The equity section of a balance sheet consists of two basic components: contributed capital and earned capital. **Contributed capital** is the net funding that a company has received from issuing

[2] Many companies' common shares have a par value, but that value has little economic significance. For instance, Walgreens' shares have a par value of $0.01 per share, while the market price of the stock is about $51 at the time of this writing. In most cases, the sum of common stock (at par) and additional paid-in capital represents the value of stockholders' contributions to the business in exchange for shares.

and reacquiring its equity shares. That is, the funds received from issuing shares less any funds paid to repurchase such shares. In 2020, Walgreens' equity section reports $21,136 million in equity. Its contributed capital is a deficit balance of $9,802 million ($12 million in common stock plus $10,761 million in [additional] paid-in capital minus $20,575 million in treasury stock). Note that for Walgreens, their contributed capital is negative because they have repurchased so many shares. This situation is not uncommon.

Earned capital is the cumulative net income (and losses) retained by the company (not paid out to shareholders as dividends). Earned capital typically includes retained earnings and accumulated other comprehensive income or loss. Walgreens' earned capital is $30,439 million ($34,210 million in retained earnings minus $3,771 million in accumulated other comprehensive loss). Other comprehensive income is discussed in Chapters 11 and 12.

RETAINED EARNINGS There is an important relation for retained earnings that reconciles its beginning and ending balances as follows:

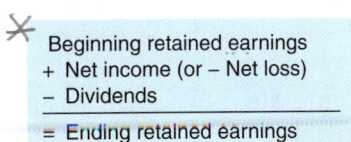

Beginning retained earnings
+ Net income (or – Net loss)
– Dividends
= Ending retained earnings

This relation is useful to remember, even though there are other items that sometimes affect retained earnings. We revisit this relation after our discussion of the income statement and show how it links the balance sheet and income statement.

FYI **Equity** is a term used to describe owners' claims on the company. For corporations, the terms **shareholders' equity** and **stockholders' equity** are also used to describe owners' claims. We use all three terms interchangeably.

Classifying Balance Sheet Accounts

LO2-1 **Review 2-1**

Guided Example MBC

Assume Schaefer's Pharmacy, Inc., has the following detailed accounts as part of its accounting system. Enter the letter of the balance sheet category A through E in the space next to the balance sheet items numbered 1 through 20. Enter an **X** in the space if the item is not reported on the balance sheet.

A. Current assets	C. Current liabilities	E. Equity
B. Noncurrent assets	D. Noncurrent liabilities	X. Item not reported on balance sheet

____ 1. Accounts receivable
____ 2. Short-term notes payable
____ 3. Land
____ 4. Retained earnings
____ 5. Intangible assets
____ 6. Common stock
____ 7. Repairs expense
____ 8. Equipment
____ 9. Treasury stock
____ 10. Investments (noncurrent)
____ 11. Operating lease right-of-use asset
____ 12. Cash
____ 13. Buildings
____ 14. Accounts payable
____ 15. Prepaid insurance
____ 16. Borrowings (due in 25 years)
____ 17. Marketable securities (current)
____ 18. Inventories
____ 19. Additional paid-in capital
____ 20. Unearned revenue

Solution on p. 2-53.

Analyzing and Recording Transactions for the Balance Sheet

LO2-2 Use the financial statement effects template (FSET) to analyze transactions.

eLecture MBC

The balance sheet is the foundation of the accounting system. Every event, or transaction, that is recorded in the accounting system must be recorded so that the following accounting equation is maintained:

Assets = Liabilities + Equity

We use this fundamental relation throughout the book to help us assess the financial impact of transactions. This is our "step 1" when we encounter a transaction. Our "steps 2 and 3" are to journalize those financial impacts and then post them to individual accounts to emphasize the linkage from entries to accounts. (Steps 2 and 3 are explained later in this chapter.)

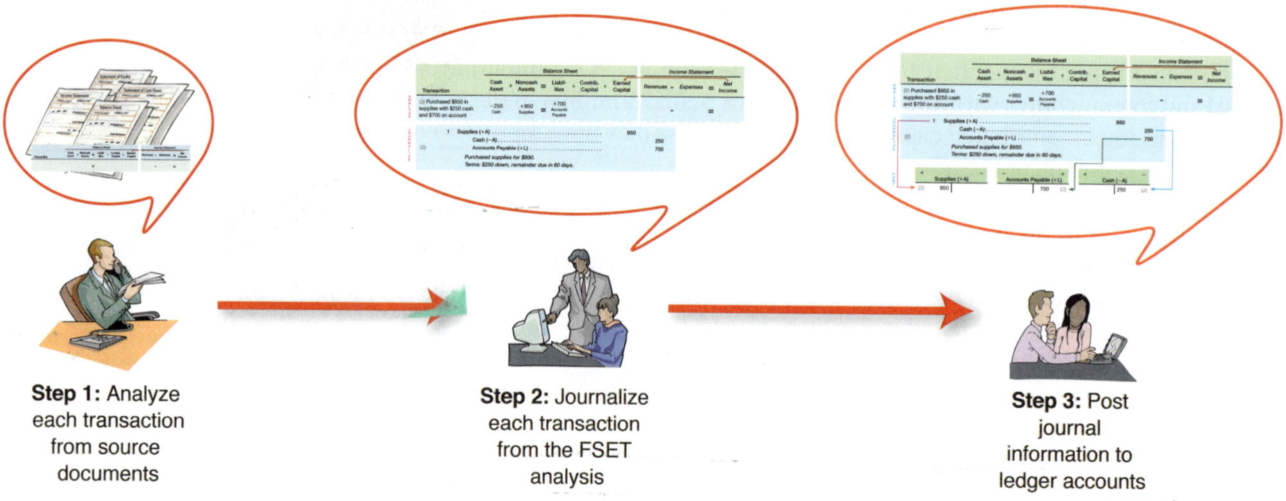
Step 1: Analyze each transaction from source documents
Step 2: Journalize each transaction from the FSET analysis
Step 3: Post journal information to ledger accounts

Financial Statement Effects Template To analyze the financial impacts of transactions, we employ the following **financial statement effects template (FSET)**.

	Balance Sheet									Income Statement				
Transaction	Cash Asset	+	Noncash Assets	=	Liabil-ities	+	Contrib. Capital	+	Earned Capital	*Revenues*	−	*Expenses*	=	*Net Income*
				=							−		=	

The template accomplishes several things. First and foremost, it captures the transaction that must be recorded in the accounting system. That "recording" function is our focus for the next several pages. But accounting is not just recording financial data; it is also the reporting of information that is useful to financial statement readers. So, the template also depicts the effects of the transaction on the four financial statements: balance sheet, income statement, statement of stockholders' equity, and statement of cash flows. For the balance sheet, we differentiate between cash and noncash assets to identify the cash effects of transactions. Likewise, equity is separated into the contributed and earned capital components. (The latter includes retained earnings as its major element.) Likewise, income statement effects are separated into revenues, expenses, and net income. (The updating of retained earnings is denoted with an arrow line running from net income to earned capital.) Finally, the template proves the accounting equation; transactions must be recorded in a manner such that assets less liabilities equals shareholders' equity. This template provides a convenient means to demonstrate the relationships among the four financial statements and of representing financial accounting transactions and events in a simple, concise manner for analyzing, journalizing, and posting.

The Account An **account** is a mechanism for accumulating the effects of an organization's transactions and events. For instance, an account labeled "Merchandise Inventory" allows a retailer's accounting system to accumulate information about the receipts of inventory from suppliers and the delivery of inventory to customers.

Before a transaction is recorded, we first analyze the effect of the transaction on the accounting equation by asking the following questions:

- What accounts are affected by the transaction?
- What is the direction and magnitude of each effect?

To maintain the equality of the accounting equation, each transaction must affect (at least) two accounts. For example, a transaction might increase assets and increase equity by equal amounts. Another transaction might increase one asset and decrease another asset, while yet another might decrease an asset and decrease a liability. These *dual effects* are what constitute the **double-entry accounting system**.

The account is a record of increases and decreases for each important asset, liability, equity, revenue, or expense item. The **chart of accounts** is a listing of the titles (and identification codes) of all accounts for a company.[3] Account titles are commonly grouped into five categories: assets, liabilities, equity, revenues, and expenses. The accounts for Natural Beauty Supply, Inc. (introduced below), follow:

Assets	Equity
110 Cash	310 Common Stock
120 Accounts Receivable	320 Retained Earnings
130 Other Receivables	**Revenues and Income**
140 Inventory	410 Sales Revenue
150 Prepaid Insurance	420 Interest Income
160 Security Deposit	**Expenses**
170 Fixtures and Equipment	510 Cost of Goods Sold
175 Accumulated Depreciation—Fixtures and Equipment	520 Wages Expense
Liabilities	530 Rent Expense
210 Accounts Payable	540 Advertising Expense
220 Interest Payable	550 Depreciation Expense—Fixtures and Equipment
230 Wages Payable	560 Insurance Expense
240 Taxes Payable	570 Interest Expense
250 Gift Card Liability	580 Tax Expense
260 Notes Payable	

Each transaction entered in the template must maintain the equality of the accounting equation, and the accounts cited must correspond to those in its chart of accounts.

Transaction Analysis Using FSET To illustrate the effect of transactions on the accounting equation and, correspondingly, the financial statements, we consider the business activities of Natural Beauty Supply, Inc. Natural Beauty Supply was established to operate as a retailer of organic beauty and health care products, though the owners hoped that they also would become a wholesale provider of such products to local salons. The company began business on November 1, 2021. The following transactions occurred on the first day of business:

(1) Nov. 1 Investors contributed $20,000 cash to launch Natural Beauty Supply, Inc. (NBS), in exchange for 10,000 shares of NBS stock.

(2) Nov. 1 NBS borrowed $5,000 cash from a family member of the company's founders by signing a note. The $5,000 must be paid back on November 30, 2021, with interest of $50.

(3) Nov. 1 NBS arranged to rent a storefront location for six months and began to use the property. The landlord requires payment of $1,500 at the end of each month. NBS paid a $2,000 security deposit that will be returned at the end of the lease.[4]

(4) Nov. 1 NBS purchased, on account (i.e., to be paid later), and received $17,000 of inventory consisting of natural soaps and beauty products.

Let's begin by analyzing the financial statement effects of the first transaction. At the beginning of its life, Natural Beauty Supply has accounts that show no balances, so the financial statements would be filled with zeroes. In the company's very first transaction, shareholders invested $20,000 cash in Natural Beauty Supply, and the company issued 10,000 shares of common stock, which increased equity (contributed capital). This transaction is reflected in the following financial statements effects template.

---

[3] Accounting systems at large organizations have much more detail in their account structures than we use here. The account structure's detail allows management to accumulate information by responsibility center or by product line or by customer.

[4] This lease is for less than one year, so the lease itself will not be accounted for on the balance sheet. Leases are covered more fully in Chapter 10.

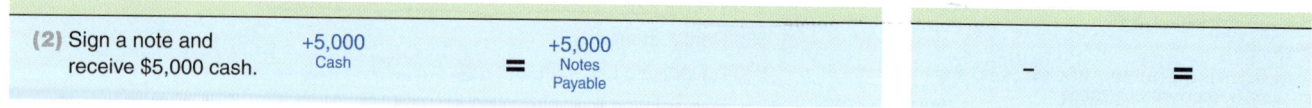

	Balance Sheet									Income Statement				
Transaction	**Cash Asset**	+	**Noncash Assets**	=	**Liabil-ities**	+	**Contrib. Capital**	+	**Earned Capital**	***Revenues***	−	***Expenses***	=	***Net Income***
(1) Issue stock for $20,000 cash.	+20,000 Cash			=			+20,000 Common Stock				−		=	

Assets (cash) and equity (common stock) increased by the same amount, and the accounting equation remains in balance (as it always must).

In the second transaction, Natural Beauty Supply borrowed cash by signing a note (loan agreement) with a family member. This transaction increased cash (an asset) and increased notes payable (a liability) by the same amount. The notes payable liability recognizes the obligation to repay the family member.

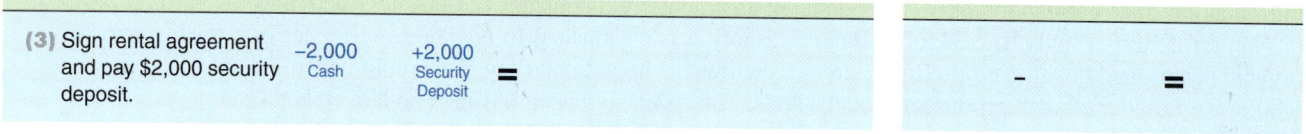

(2) Sign a note and receive $5,000 cash.	+5,000 Cash			=	+5,000 Notes Payable						−		=	

At this point, Natural Beauty Supply would not record anything for the interest that will eventually be paid. Interest expense occurs with the passage of time, and at the moment of borrowing on November 1, there is no interest obligation to be recognized.

Also on November 1, 2021, Natural Beauty Supply arranged for rental of a location and paid a security deposit that it expects to be returned at a future date. This transaction decreased cash (an asset) and increased security deposits (another asset). We'll assume that Natural Beauty Supply hopes to move to a more upscale location within a year, so the security deposit is considered a current asset.

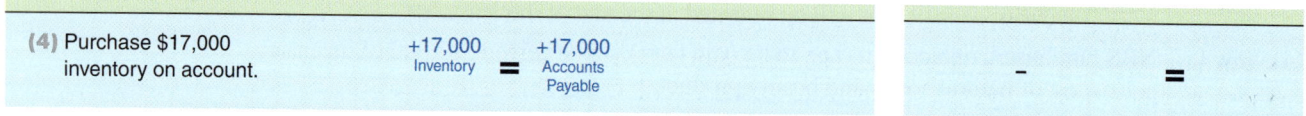

(3) Sign rental agreement and pay $2,000 security deposit.	−2,000 Cash		+2,000 Security Deposit	=							−		=	

Like the case of interest expense, Natural Beauty Supply would make no entry for rent expense on November 1 because the obligation to pay for the use of the location occurs with the passage of time.

Finally, Natural Beauty Supply purchased and received $17,000 of inventory on credit. This transaction increased inventory (an asset) by $17,000 and increased accounts payable (a liability) by $17,000, recognizing the obligation to the supplier. This transaction is recorded as follows:

(4) Purchase $17,000 inventory on account.			+17,000 Inventory	=	+17,000 Accounts Payable						−		=	

To summarize, the description of each transaction appears in the first column of the template. Then the financial statement effects of that transaction are recorded with a + or a – in the appropriate columns of the template. Under each number, the account title within that column of the balance sheet or income statement is entered. So far, Natural Beauty Supply's activities have not affected the revenue or expense accounts of the income statement.

After each transaction, the equality of the accounting equation is maintained. If we so choose, we can prepare a balance sheet at any time, reflecting the transactions up to that point in time. At the end of the day on November 1, 2021, Natural Beauty Supply's balance sheet appears as follows:

NATURAL BEAUTY SUPPLY, INC.
Balance Sheet
November 1, 2021

Assets		**Liabilities and Equity**	
Cash	$23,000	Notes payable	$ 5,000
Inventory	17,000	Accounts payable	17,000
Security deposit	2,000	Total current liabilities	22,000
Total current assets	42,000	**Equity**	
		Common stock	20,000
Total assets	$42,000	Total liabilities and equity	$42,000

Using the Financial Statement Effects Template to Analyze Transactions LO2-2 **Review 2-2**

Assume that Schaefer's Pharmacy, Inc., enters into the following transactions. Report each of the following transactions in the financial statement effects template.

a. Issued common stock for $20,000 cash.
b. Purchased inventory costing $8,000 on credit.
c. Purchased equipment costing $10,000 for cash.
d. Paid suppliers $3,000 cash for part of the inventory purchased in *b*.

GuidedExample MBC

Solution on p. 2-53.

REPORTING FINANCIAL PERFORMANCE

LO2-3 Describe and construct the income statement and discuss how it can be used to evaluate management performance.

eLecture MBC

While balance sheets provide useful information about the structure of a company's resources and the claims on those resources at a point in time, they provide little sense of recent movement or trajectory. The retained earnings balance represents the amount earned (but not paid out in dividends) over the entire life of the company. Looking at the difference between points in time doesn't provide a complete picture about what happened between those points in time. For that perspective, we need the income statement to see whether our business activities generated more resources than they used. For instance, Walgreens' retained earnings decreased by $1,605 million over fiscal year 2020, but that amount does not convey the volume or types of activities that resulted in this decrease.

Walgreens' fiscal year summarized 2020 Statement of Earnings is shown in **Exhibit 2.2**. Walgreens reported net earnings of $424 million on revenues of $139,537 million, or about $0.003 of each revenue dollar ($424 million/$139,537 million). The remaining $0.997 of that revenue dollar relates to costs incurred to generate the revenues, such as the costs of products sold and equipment used, wages, advertising and promotion, interest, and taxes. Interpretation of this $0.003 amount requires further analysis, as shown in Chapter 5, but we can compare it to previous amounts of $0.029 in fiscal year 2019, and $0.038 in fiscal year 2018.

FYI The income statement is also called the statement of earnings or the statement of operations or the profit and loss statement. Walgreens uses all three terms (profit, income, and earnings) in **Exhibit 2.2**.

To analyze an income statement, we need to understand some terminology. **Revenues** result in increases in **net assets** (assets minus liabilities) that are caused by the company's transferring goods or services to customers. **Expenses** result from decreases in net assets (assets minus liabilities) that are caused by the company's revenue-generating activities, including costs of products and services sold, operating costs like depreciation, wages and advertising, nonoperating costs like interest on debt and, finally, taxes on income. The difference between revenues and expenses is **net income** when revenues exceed expenses, or **net loss** when expenses exceed revenues. The connection to the balance sheet can be seen in that reporting net income means that revenues exceeded expenses, which in turn means that the company's business activities increased its net assets.

P/L statement

Operating expenses are the usual and customary costs that a company incurs to support its main business activities. These include cost of goods sold expense, selling expenses, depreciation expense, amortization expense, and research and development expense. Not all of these expenses are recognized in the period in which cash is disbursed. For example, depreciation expense is recognized in the time period during which the asset is used, not in the period when it was first acquired in exchange for cash. In contrast, other expenses, such as compensation expense, are

FYI The terms "revenues" and "sales" are often used interchangeably.

EXHIBIT 2.2 Walgreens' Income Statement

WALGREENS BOOTS ALLIANCE, INC. AND SUBSIDIARIES
Summarized Consolidated Statement of Earnings
Year ended August 31, 2020
($ millions)

Net sales	$139,537
Cost of sales	111,520
Gross profit	28,017
Selling, general and administrative expenses	27,045
Equity earnings in AmerisourceBergen	341
Operating income	1,312
Interest expense, net	639
Other income	70
Earnings before income tax provision	743
Income tax provision	360
Post tax earnings from other equity method investments	41
Net earnings	424
Net loss attributable to noncontrolling interests*	(32)
Net earnings attributable to Walgreens Boots Alliance, Inc.	$ 456

Per the Walgreens 10-K, certain amounts in the Consolidated Condensed Financial Statements may not add due to rounding.
*Noncontrolling interests arise from the practice of consolidating subsidiaries that are controlled, but not wholly owned. Chapters 11 and 12 provide a brief introduction to this topic.

recognized in the period when the services are performed, which is often before cash is actually paid to employees. Walgreens' operating expenses in 2020 were $138,565 million ($111,520 million + $27,045 million).[5]

Nonoperating revenues and expenses relate to the company's financing and investing activities and include interest revenue and interest expense. Business decision-makers and analysts usually segregate operating and nonoperating activities as they offer different insights into company performance and condition. Walgreens' income statement reports net nonoperating expenses in 2020 of $569 million ($639 million – $70 million), followed by tax expenses of $360 million.

It is helpful to separately identify 1) income from continuing operations and 2) income from nonrecurring items. Many readers of financial statements are interested in forecasting future company performance and focus their analysis on sources of operating income that are expected to *persist* into the future. Nonrecurring revenues and expenses are unlikely to arise in the future and are largely irrelevant to predictions of future performance. Consequently, many decision-makers identify transactions and events that are unlikely to recur and separate them from operating income in the income statement. These nonrecurring items are described in greater detail in Chapter 6.

Review 2-3 LO2-3

Preparing an Income Statement

GuidedExample MBC

Assume that Schaefer's Pharmacy, Inc.'s records show the following amounts at December 31. Use this information, as necessary, to prepare its annual income statement. (Ignore income taxes.)

Cash	$ 3,000	Cash dividends	$ 1,000
Accounts receivable	12,000	Revenues	45,000
Office equipment	32,250	Cost of goods sold	20,000
Inventory	26,000	Insurance expense	5,000
Land	10,000	Wages expense	8,000
Accounts payable	7,500	Utilities expense	2,000
Common stock	45,750	Other expenses	4,000

Solution on p. 2-53.

[5] Walgreens also reports $341 million in equity earnings in AmerisourceBergen, a company in which Walgreens invested. The operations of AmerisourceBergen are similar enough to Walgreens' operations that they include this as a component of operating income.

Accrual Accounting for Revenues and Expenses

LO2-4
Explain revenue recognition, accrual accounting, and their effects on retained earnings.

eLecture
MBC

The income statement's ability to measure a company's periodic performance depends on the proper timing of revenues and expenses. Revenue should be recorded when the company has transferred goods or services to customers, in an amount that reflects how much the company expects to be entitled from the transfer—even if there is not an immediate increase in cash. This is called **revenue recognition**, a topic that receives more detailed attention in Chapter 6. Expenses are recognized when assets are diminished (or liabilities increased) as a result of earning revenue or supporting operations, even if there is no immediate decrease in cash. This is called **expense recognition**. **Accrual accounting** refers to this practice of recognizing revenues as goods and services are transferred to customers through the company's operations and recognizing expenses as the assets used and obligations incurred in carrying out those operations.

An important consequence of accrual accounting for revenues and expenses is that the balance sheet depicts the resources of the company (in addition to cash) and the obligations that the company must fulfill in the future. Accrual accounting is required under U.S. GAAP (and the International Financial Reporting Standards, IFRS) because it is considered to provide the most useful information for making business decisions and evaluating business performance. (That is not to say that information on cash flows is not important—but it is conveyed by the statement of cash flows discussed in Chapter 4.)

Walgreens' net sales in 2020 were $139,537 million. **Cost of goods sold** (cost of sales) is an expense item in the income statements of manufacturing and merchandising companies. It represents the cost of products that are delivered to customers during the period. The difference between revenues (at selling prices) and cost of goods sold (at purchase price or manufacturing cost) is called **gross profit**. Gross profit for merchandisers and manufacturers is an important number because it represents the remaining income available to cover all of the company's overhead and other expenses (selling, general and administrative expenses, research and development, interest, and so on). Walgreens' gross profit in 2020 is calculated as total net revenues less cost of sales, which equals $28,017 million ($139,537 million − $111,520 million).

The principles of revenue and expense recognition are crucial to income statement reporting. To illustrate, assume a company purchases inventories for $100,000 cash, which it sells later in that same period for $150,000 cash. The company would record $150,000 in revenue when the inventory is delivered to the customer, because at that point, the company has fulfilled its responsibilities in the exchange with the customer. Also assume that the company pays $20,000 cash for sales employee wages during the period. The income statement is designed to tell how effective the company was at generating more resources than it used, and it would appear as follows (ignoring income taxes for the moment):

Revenues	$150,000
Cost of goods sold	100,000
Gross profit	50,000
Wages expense	20,000
Net income (earnings)	$ 30,000

In this illustration, there is a correspondence between each of the revenues/expenses and a cash inflow/outflow within the accounting period. Net income was $30,000, and the increase in cash was $30,000.

However, that need not be the case under accrual accounting. Suppose that the company sells its product on **credit** (also referred to as *on account*) rather than for cash. Does the seller still report sales revenue? The answer is yes. Under GAAP, revenues are reported when a company has transferred goods or services to its customers. This means that the company has satisfied its agreed upon performance obligations—no material contingencies remain. The seller reports an accounts receivable asset on its balance sheet, and revenue can be recognized before cash collection.

FYI Purchase of inventories on credit or on account means that the buyer does not pay the seller at the time of purchase. The buyer reports a liability (accounts payable) on its balance sheet that is later removed when payment is made. The seller reports an asset (accounts receivable) on its balance sheet until it is removed when the buyer pays.

Credit sales mean that companies can report substantial sales revenue and assets without receiving cash. When such receivables are ultimately collected, no further revenue is recorded because it was recorded earlier when the revenue recognition criteria were met. The collection

FYI Sales on credit will not always be collected. The potential for uncollectable accounts introduces additional risk to the firm.

FYI **Cash accounting** recognizes revenues only when received in cash and expenses only when paid in cash. This approach is not acceptable under GAAP.

of a receivable merely involves the decrease of one asset (accounts receivable) and the increase of another asset (cash), with no resulting increase in net assets.

Next, consider a different situation. Assume that the company sells gift cards to customers for $9,500. Should the $9,500 received in cash be recognized as revenue? No. Even though the gift cards were sold and cash was collected, there has been no transfer of goods or services to the customer. The revenue from gift cards is recognized when the product or service is provided. For example, revenue can be recognized when a customer purchases an item of merchandise using the gift card for payment. Hence, the $9,500 is then recorded as an increase in cash and an increase in *gift card liabilities*, a liability, with no resulting increase in net assets.

The proper timing of revenue recognition suggests that the expenses incurred in generating that revenue be recognized in the same fiscal period. Thus, if merchandise inventory is purchased in one period and sold in another, the cost of the merchandise should be retained as an asset until the items are sold. It would not be proper to recognize expense when the inventory was purchased or the cash was paid. Accurate income determination requires the proper timing of revenue and expense recognition, and the exchange of cash is *not* the essential ingredient.

We have already seen that when a company incurs a cost to acquire a resource that produces benefits in the future (for example, merchandise inventory for future sale), it recognizes an asset. That asset represents costs that are waiting to be recognized as expenses in the future, when these assets are used to produce revenue or to support operations. When inventory is delivered to a customer, we recognize that the asset no longer belongs to the selling company. The inventory asset is decreased, and cost of goods sold is recognized as an expense.

The same principle applies when employees earn wages for work in one period, but are paid in the next period. Wages expense must be recognized when the liability (obligation) is *incurred*, regardless of when they are paid. If the company in the illustration doesn't pay its employees until the following reporting period, it recognizes a wages payable liability of $20,000 and, because this decreases net assets, it would recognize a wage expense of the same amount.

When wages are paid in the next reporting period, both cash and the wages payable liability are decreased. No expense is reported when the wages are paid because the expense is recognized when the employees worked to generate sales in the prior period.

Accrual accounting principles are crucial for reporting the income statement revenues and expenses in the proper period, and these revenues and expenses provide a more complete view of the inflows and outflows of resources (including cash) for the firm. Was an outflow of cash supposed to produce benefits in the current period or in a future period? Was an inflow of cash the result of past operations or current operations? The accrual accounting model uses the balance sheet and income statement to answer such questions and to enable users of financial statements to make more timely assessments of the firm's economic performance.

However, accrual accounting's timeliness requires management to estimate future events in determining the amount of expenses incurred and revenue earned. The precise amount of cash to be received or disbursed may not be known until a later date. In the case of wages, the amount of the accrual is known with certainty. In other cases (e.g., incentive bonuses), it may not and thus require an estimate.

Retained Earnings

Net income for the period is added to the company's retained earnings, which, in turn, is part of stockholders' equity. The linkage between the income statement and the beginning- and end-of-period balance sheets, which we called articulation in Chapter 1, is achieved by tying net income to retained earnings because net income is, by definition, the *change* in retained earnings resulting from business activities during an accounting period. This link is highlighted by the red arrow at the top of the financial statement effects template (FSET).[6] There are typically other adjustments to

[6] In the FSET, we show that each transaction that affects the income statement also affects retained earnings. This approach is useful for *analyzing* the effect of the transaction on both the income statement and the balance sheet. However, the impact of net income on retained earnings is *recorded* only once each accounting period, after all of the revenues and expenses have been recorded. This recording procedure is explained later in this chapter and in Chapter 3.

retained earnings. The most common adjustment is for dividend payments to stockholders. **Exhibit 2.3** provides the annual adjustments to retained earnings for Walgreens.

EXHIBIT 2.3 Walgreens' Retained Earnings Reconciliation

WALGREENS BOOTS ALLIANCE, INC. AND SUBSIDIARIES
Year Ended August 31, 2020
($ millions)

Retained earnings, August 31, 2019	$35,815
Add: Net earnings attributable to Walgreens Boots Alliance, Inc.	456
	36,271
Less: Cash dividends declared	1,618
Less: Adoption of new accounting standard	442
Retained earnings, August 31, 2020	$34,210

Per the Walgreens 10-K, certain amounts in the Consolidated Condensed Financial Statements may not add due to rounding.

Analyzing and Recording Transactions for the Income Statement

Earlier, we introduced the financial statement effects template as a tool to illustrate the effects of transactions on the balance sheet. In this section, we show how this template is used to analyze transactions that may affect the current period's income statement. To do so, we extend our illustration of Natural Beauty Supply (NBS) to reflect the following events in 2021:

(5) Nov. 2 NBS paid $670 to advertise in the local newspaper for November.

(6) Nov. 18 NBS paid $13,300 cash to its suppliers in partial payment for the earlier delivery of inventory.

(7) Nov. — During the month of November, NBS sold and delivered products to retail customers. The customers paid $7,000 cash for products that had cost NBS $4,000.

(8) Nov. — During the month of November, sales and deliveries to wholesale customers totaled $2,400 for merchandise that had cost $1,700. Instead of paying cash, wholesale customers are required to pay for the merchandise within ten working days.

(9) Nov. — NBS employed a salesperson who earned $1,400 for the month of November and was paid that amount in cash.

(10) Nov. 24 NBS received an order from a wholesale customer to deliver products in December. The agreed price of the products to be delivered is $700, and the cost is $450.

(11) Nov. 25 NBS introduced holiday gift certificates, which entitle the recipient to a one-hour consultation on the use of NBS's products. $300 of gift certificates were sold for cash, but none were redeemed before the end of November.

(12) Nov. 30 NBS received $1,450 in partial payment from customers billed in (8).

(13) Nov. 30 NBS repaid the loan and interest in (2).

(14) Nov. 30 NBS paid $1,680 for a twelve-month fire insurance policy. Coverage begins on December 1.

(15) Nov. 30 NBS paid $1,500 to the landlord for November rent.

In the fifth transaction, Natural Beauty Supply gave cash in return for advertising for the month of November. This payment does not create a benefit for future periods, so it does not create an asset. Nor does the payment discharge an existing obligation. Therefore, it decreases NBS's net assets (assets minus liabilities). The purpose of this decrease in net assets is to generate revenues for the company, so it is reported as an expense in the income statement.

We begin by entering the decrease in cash and an increase in expenses. (The minus sign in front of expenses ensures that the accounting equation still holds.) Recording the expense allows the income statement to keep track of the flows of assets and liabilities that result from the company's operations.

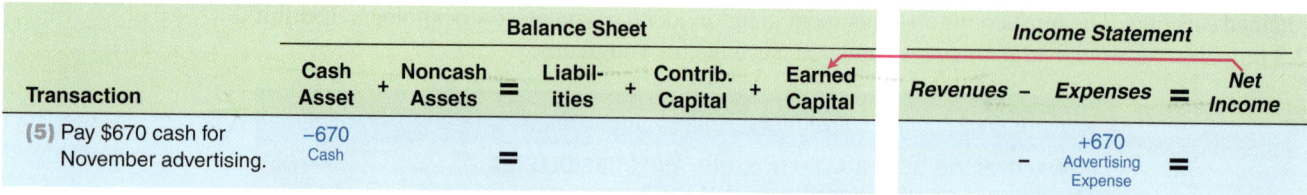

	Balance Sheet						Income Statement				
Transaction	**Cash Asset** +	**Noncash Assets**	=	**Liabil-ities** +	**Contrib. Capital** +	**Earned Capital**	***Revenues***	−	***Expenses***	=	***Net Income***
(5) Pay $670 cash for November advertising.	−670 Cash		=					−	+670 Advertising Expense	=	

However, the FSET goes further than recording the accounting entry. It also depicts the effects of the expense on net income and of net income on retained earnings. So, the complete FSET description of transaction (5) is as follows. The FSET uses color to differentiate between the accounting entry (in blue) and the resulting effect on net income and retained earnings (in black).

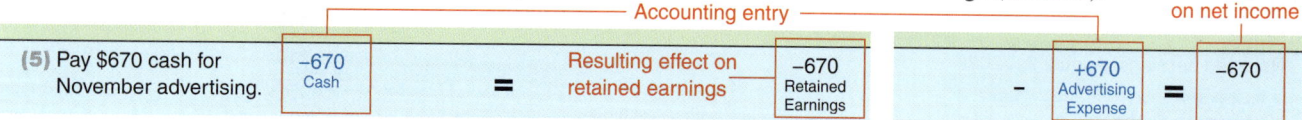

Accounting entry — Resulting effect on retained earnings — Resulting effect on net income

Transaction	Cash Asset	Noncash Assets	=	Liabilities	Contrib. Capital	Earned Capital	Revenues	−	Expenses	=	Net Income
(5) Pay $670 cash for November advertising.	−670 Cash		=			−670 Retained Earnings		−	+670 Advertising Expense	=	−670

In the sixth transaction, Natural Beauty Supply made a partial payment of $13,300 in cash to the suppliers who delivered inventory on November 1. This transaction decreases cash by $13,300 and decreases the accounts payable liability by $13,300. The income statement is not affected by this payment. The cost of merchandise is reflected in the income statement when the merchandise is sold, not when it is paid for (as we will see shortly).

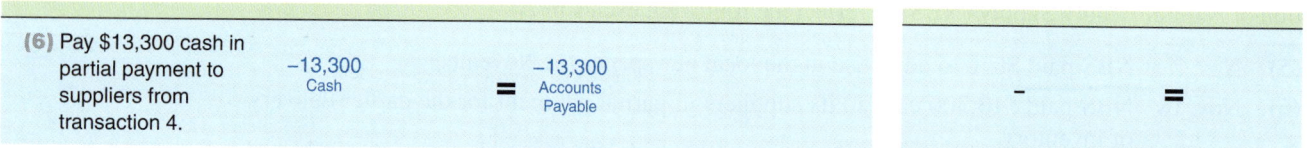

Transaction	Cash Asset	Noncash Assets	=	Liabilities	Contrib. Capital	Earned Capital	Revenues	−	Expenses	=	Net Income
(6) Pay $13,300 cash in partial payment to suppliers from transaction 4.	−13,300 Cash		=	−13,300 Accounts Payable				−		=	

In transaction seven, Natural Beauty Supply sold and delivered products to customers who paid $7,000 in cash. NBS's transfer of products to customers results in the recognition of revenue in the income statement and an increase in net assets (cash) on the balance sheet. As in transaction 5, the FSET also depicts the impact of these sales on net income and on the retained earnings balance.

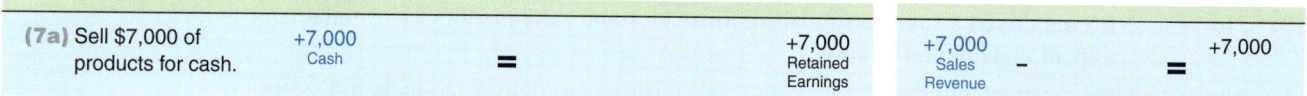

Transaction	Cash Asset	Noncash Assets	=	Liabilities	Contrib. Capital	Earned Capital	Revenues	−	Expenses	=	Net Income
(7a) Sell $7,000 of products for cash.	+7,000 Cash		=			+7,000 Retained Earnings	+7,000 Sales Revenue	−		=	+7,000

At the same time, NBS must recognize that these sales transactions involved an exchange, and cash was received while inventory costing $4,000 was delivered. Transaction (7b) recognizes that NBS no longer has this inventory and that this decrease in net assets produces an expense called cost of goods sold. In this way, the income statement portrays the increases in net assets (revenues) and the decreases in net assets (expenses like cost of goods sold and advertising) from the company's operating activities. (Again, the minus sign in front of all expenses ensures that the accounting equation remains balanced.)

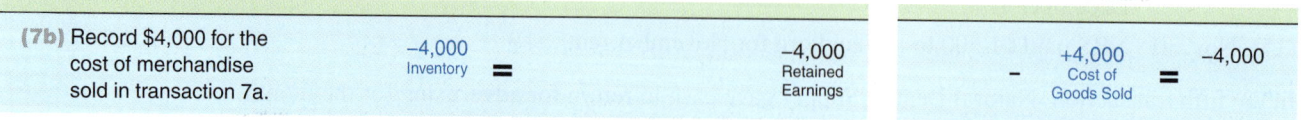

Transaction	Cash Asset	Noncash Assets	=	Liabilities	Contrib. Capital	Earned Capital	Revenues	−	Expenses	=	Net Income
(7b) Record $4,000 for the cost of merchandise sold in transaction 7a.		−4,000 Inventory	=			−4,000 Retained Earnings		−	+4,000 Cost of Goods Sold	=	−4,000

The eighth transaction is similar to the previous one, except that Natural Beauty Supply's customers will pay for the products ten days after they were delivered. Should NBS recognize revenue on these sales? The products have been delivered, so the revenue has been earned.[7] Therefore, NBS should recognize that it has a new asset—accounts receivable—equal to $2,400, and that it has earned revenue in the same amount. As above, NBS would also record cost of goods sold to recognize the cost of inventory delivered to the customers.

[7] In Chapter 6, we consider the possibility that a customer might not pay the receivable. For the time being, we assume that the receivables' collectability is assured.

Transaction	Cash Asset	+	Noncash Assets	=	Liabilities	+	Contrib. Capital	+	Earned Capital	Revenues	−	Expenses	=	Net Income
(8a) Sell $2,400 of products on account.			+2,400 Accounts Receivable	=					+2,400 Retained Earnings	+2,400 Sales Revenue	−		=	+2,400
(8b) Record $1,700 for the cost of merchandise sold in transaction 8a.			−1,700 Inventory	=					−1,700 Retained Earnings		−	+1,700 Cost of Goods Sold	=	−1,700

The ninth entry records wage expense. In this case, wages were paid in cash. Cash is decreased by $1,400, and this decrease in net assets results in a recognition of wages expense in the income statement (with resulting decreases in net income and retained earnings).

Transaction	Cash Asset	+	Noncash Assets	=	Liabilities	+	Contrib. Capital	+	Earned Capital	Revenues	−	Expenses	=	Net Income
(9) Record $1,400 in wages to employees.	−1,400 Cash			=					−1,400 Retained Earnings		−	+1,400 Wages Expense	=	−1,400

Transaction ten involves a customer order for products to be delivered in December. This transaction is an example of an *executory contract*, which does not require a journal entry (just like Walgreens' open purchase orders for inventory described earlier). NBS does not record revenue because it has not yet delivered the products.

Transaction	
(10) Receive customer order.	Memorandum entry for customer order

In transaction eleven, Natural Beauty Supply sold gift certificates for $300 cash, but none were redeemed. In this case, NBS has received cash, but revenue cannot be recognized because no goods or services have been transferred to the customers. Rather, NBS has accepted an obligation to provide services in the future when the gift certificates are redeemed. This obligation is recognized as a liability titled Gift Card Liability.

Transaction	Cash Asset	+	Noncash Assets	=	Liabilities	+	Contrib. Capital	+	Earned Capital	Revenues	−	Expenses	=	Net Income
(11) Sell gift certificates for $300 cash.	+300 Cash			=	+300 Gift Card Liability						−		=	

In transaction twelve, NBS received $1,450 cash as partial payment from customers billed in transaction eight. Cash increases by $1,450 and accounts receivable decreases by $1,450. Recall that revenues are recorded when goods or services are transferred to customers (transaction 8), not when cash is received.

Transaction	Cash Asset	+	Noncash Assets	=	Liabilities	+	Contrib. Capital	+	Earned Capital	Revenues	−	Expenses	=	Net Income
(12) Receive $1,450 cash as partial payment from customers billed in transaction 8.	+1,450 Cash		−1,450 Accounts Receivable	=							−		=	

In transaction thirteen on November 30, Natural Beauty Supply paid back the family member who had loaned money to the business. The cash payment was the agreed-upon $5,050 ($5,000 principal and $50 interest). The repayment of the principal does not change the net assets of NBS; cash goes down by $5,000, and the note payable liability goes down an equal amount. However, the payment of $50 interest does cause the net assets to decrease, and this net asset decrease creates an interest expense in the income statement.

Transaction	Cash Asset	+	Noncash Assets	=	Liabilities	+	Contrib. Capital	+	Earned Capital	Revenues	−	Expenses	=	Net Income
(13) Pay interest of $50 and repay principal of $5,000.	−5,050 Cash			=	−5,000 Notes Payable				−50 Retained Earnings		−	+50 Interest Expense	=	−50

In the fourteenth transaction, NBS paid an annual insurance premium of $1,680 for coverage beginning December 1. NBS will receive the benefits of the insurance coverage in the future, so insurance expense will be recognized in those future periods. At this time, a noncash asset titled prepaid insurance is increased by $1,680, and cash is decreased by the same amount.

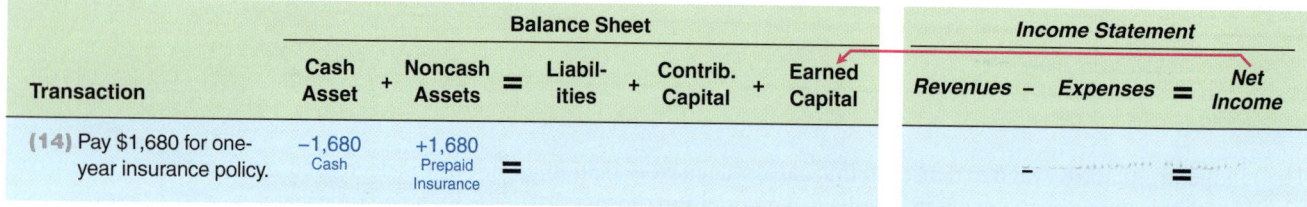

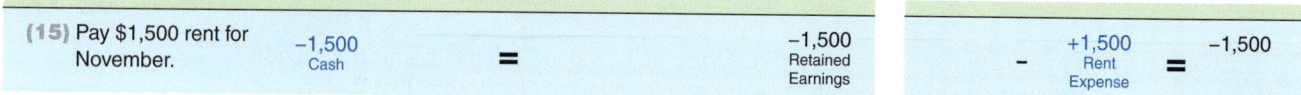

	Balance Sheet										Income Statement				
Transaction	Cash Asset	+	Noncash Assets	=	Liabil-ities	+	Contrib. Capital	+	Earned Capital		Revenues	–	Expenses	=	Net Income
(14) Pay $1,680 for one-year insurance policy.	−1,680 Cash		+1,680 Prepaid Insurance	=								–		=	
(15) Pay $1,500 rent for November.	−1,500 Cash			=					−1,500 Retained Earnings			–	+1,500 Rent Expense	=	−1,500

In the last transaction of the month of November, Natural Beauty Supply paid $1,500 cash to the landlord for November's rent. This $1,500 reduction of net assets is balanced by rent expense in the income statement.

We can summarize the revenue and expense entries of these transactions to prepare an income statement for Natural Beauty Supply for the month ended November 30, 2021.

NATURAL BEAUTY SUPPLY, INC.
Income Statement
For Month Ended November 30, 2021

Sales revenue	$9,400
Cost of goods sold	5,700
Gross profit	3,700
Wages expense	1,400
Rent expense	1,500
Advertising expense	670
Operating income	130
Interest expense	50
Net income	$ 80

Review 2-4 LO2-4

Preparing a Retained Earnings Statement

GuidedExample MBC

Use the information from Review 2-3 to complete the following requirements. Assume that Schaefer's Pharmacy, Inc., reports the following selected financial information for the year ended December 31.

Retained earnings, Dec. 31	$30,000	Dividends	$ 1,000
Net income	$ 6,000	Retained earnings, Jan. 1	$25,000

a. Prepare the current year retained earnings reconciliation for this company.

b. Suppose that you discover that the company had not recorded digital marketing expense of $750 that had been incurred but was not due to be paid until next year. What impact would this information have on your answer to part *a* (if any)?

Solution on p. 2-54.

REPORTING ON EQUITY

eLecture MBC

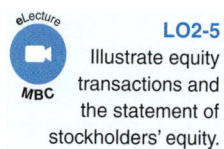

LO2-5 Illustrate equity transactions and the statement of stockholders' equity.

Analyzing and Recording Equity Transactions

Earlier we recorded the effect of issuing common stock on the balance sheet of Natural Beauty Supply. To complete our illustration, we record one final equity transaction: a dividend payment.

(16) Nov. 30 Natural Beauty Supply paid a $50 cash dividend to its shareholders.

To record the dividend payment, we decrease cash and decrease retained earnings.

Transaction	Cash Asset	+	Noncash Assets	=	Liabil-ities	+	Contrib. Capital	+	Earned Capital	Revenues	−	Expenses	=	Net Income
(16) Pay $50 cash dividend to shareholders.	−50 Cash			=					−50 Retained Earnings		−		=	

No revenue or income is recorded from a stock issuance. Similarly, no expense is recorded from a dividend. This is always the case. Companies cannot report revenues and expenses from capital transactions (transactions with stockholders relating to their investment in the company).

The FSET entries can be accumulated by account to determine the ending balances for assets, liabilities and equity. Natural Beauty Supply's balance sheet for November 30, 2021, appears in **Exhibit 2.4**. The balance in retained earnings is $30 (net income of $80 less the cash dividend of $50).

EXHIBIT 2.4 Natural Beauty Supply's Balance Sheet

NATURAL BEAUTY SUPPLY, INC.
Balance Sheet
November 30, 2021

Assets		Liabilities	
Cash	$ 8,100	Accounts payable	$ 3,700
Accounts receivable	950	Gift card liability	300
Inventory	11,300	Total current liabilities	4,000
Prepaid insurance	1,680	Equity	
Security deposit	2,000	Common stock	20,000
Total current assets	24,030	Retained earnings	30
		Total equity	20,030
Total assets	$24,030	Total liabilities and equity	$24,030

Statement of Stockholders' Equity

The statement of stockholders' equity is a reconciliation of the beginning and ending balances of selected stockholders' equity accounts. The statement of stockholders' equity for Natural Beauty Supply for the month of November is in **Exhibit 2.5**.

EXHIBIT 2.5 Natural Beauty Supply's Statement of Stockholders' Equity

NATURAL BEAUTY SUPPLY, INC.
Statement of Stockholders' Equity
For Month Ended November 30, 2021

	Contributed Capital	Earned Capital	Total Equity
Balance, November 1, 2021	$ 0	$ 0	$ 0
Common stock issued	20,000	—	20,000
Net income	—	80	80
Cash dividends	—	(50)	(50)
Balance, November 30, 2021	**$20,000**	**$30**	**$20,030**

This statement highlights three main changes to Natural Beauty Supply's equity during November.

1. Natural Beauty raised $20,000 in equity capital during the month.
2. Natural Beauty Supply earned net income of $80. That is, its business activities increased the company's net assets by $80 during the month.
3. Natural Beauty Supply declared a $50 cash dividend.

At this point, we can make the important observation that the various financial statements are not the result of independent processes. That is, the process of constructing the income statement is closely tied to the process of constructing the balance sheet. When we think about the fact that revenues reflect how much the company expects to receive from its delivery of goods to customers, and expenses measure the outflow of assets and increases in liabilities resulting from generating revenues and supporting operations, it should be apparent that an error on the income statement will, in all likelihood, lead to an error in the balance sheet. Understanding the connections among the various statements is a key step in becoming an effective reader of financial information.

YOU MAKE THE CALL

You are an Analyst Colgate-Palmolive Company reported a balance in retained earnings of $22,501 million on December 31, 2019. This amount compares to $21,615 million one year earlier at the end of 2018. In 2019, Colgate-Palmolive Company reported net income of $2,367 million. Why did the company's retained earnings go up by less than reported net income? [Answer on page 2-33.]

Review 2-5 LO2-5 **Preparing a Balance Sheet and a Statement of Stockholders' Equity**

GuidedExample MBC

a. Use the listing of accounts and figures reported in Review 2-3 along with the ending retained earnings from Review 2-4, part *a* to prepare the December 31 balance sheet for Schaefer's Pharmacy, Inc.

b. Assuming that no new shares of common stock were issued during the year, prepare the company's statement of stockholders' equity for the year.

Solution on p. 2-54.

JOURNALIZING AND POSTING TRANSACTIONS

LO2-6 Use journal entries and T-accounts to analyze and record transactions.

eLecture MBC

The financial statement effects template is a useful tool for illustrating the effects of a transaction on the balance sheet, income statement, statement of stockholders' equity, and statement of cash flows. However, when representing individual transactions or analyzing individual accounts, the accounting system records information in journal entries (step 2) that are collected in individual accounts. This section introduces the basics of that system. It also introduces the T-account as a useful tool for learning debits and credits and for representing accounts in the ledger (step 3).

T-Account

Accountants commonly use a graphic representation of an account called a **T-account**, so named because it looks like a large T. The typical form of a T-account is:

Account Title	
Debits	Credits
(Dr.)	(Cr.)
Always the left side	Always the right side

FYI Recall that an account is a record of increases and decreases in asset, liability, equity, revenue, or expense items.

One side of the T-account is used to record increases to the account, and the other side is used to record decreases.

Accountants record individual transactions using the journal entry. A **journal entry** is an accounting entry in the financial records (journals) of a company. The journal entry is the *bookkeeping* aspect of accounting. Even if you never make a journal entry for a company, you will interact with accounting and finance professionals who do and who will use this language. Further, journal entries and T-accounts can help in reconstructing transactions and interpreting their financial effects.

Debit and Credit System

Accountants describe increases and decreases in accounts using the terms **debit** and **credit**. The left side of each account is the debit side (abbreviated Dr.), and the right side of each account is the credit side (abbreviated Cr.). In some accounts, increases are recorded on the debit (left) side of the account, and decreases are recorded on the credit (right) side of the account. In other accounts, just the opposite is true—increases are credits and decreases are debits. An easy way to remember what the words "debit" and "credit" reflect is to visualize a balance sheet in "T" account form with assets on the left and liabilities and equity on the right as follows:

FYI "Debit" and "credit" are accounting terms meaning left and right, respectively.

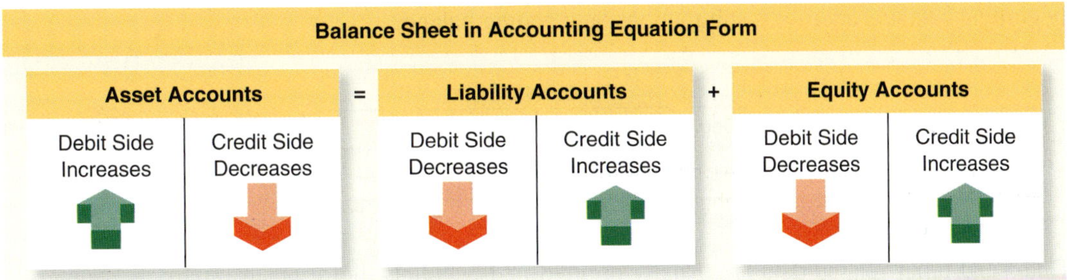

FYI In our everyday speech, the words "debit" and "credit" are often imbued with value connotations. For example, "To her credit, she took responsibility for the incident." But there are no value connotations within the accounting system. Every good event is recorded with both a debit and a credit, and the same is true for every bad event.

Thus, assets are assigned a *normal debit balance* because they are on the left side. Liabilities and equity are assigned a *normal credit balance* because they are on the right side. So, to reflect an increase in an asset, we debit the asset account. To reflect an increase in a liability or equity account, we credit the account. Conversely, to reflect a decrease in an asset account, we credit it. To reflect a decrease in a liability or equity account, we debit it. (There are exceptions to these normal balances; one case is accumulated depreciation, which is explained in Chapter 3.)

The balance sheet must always balance (assets = liabilities + equity). So too must total debits equal total credits in each journal entry. There can, however, be more than one debit and one credit in an entry. These so-called **compound entries** still adhere to the rule: *total debits equal total credits for each entry.* This important relation is extended below to show the *expanded accounting equation* in T-account form with the inclusion of debit (Dr.) and credit (Cr.) rules. Equity is expanded to reflect increases from stock issuances and revenues and to reflect decreases from dividends and expenses.

FYI The rule that total debits equal total credits for each entry is known as double-entry accounting, or the duality of accounting.

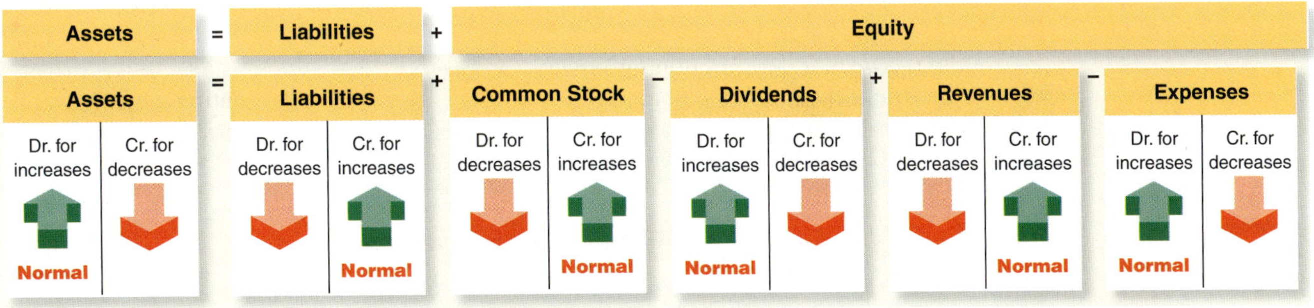

Income (revenues less expenses) feeds directly into retained earnings. Also, anything that increases equity is a credit and anything that decreases equity is a debit. So, to reflect an increase in revenues (which increases retained earnings and, therefore, equity), we credit the revenue account, and to reflect an increase in an expense account (which reduces retained earnings and, therefore, equity), we debit it.

To summarize, the following table reflects the use of the terms "debit" and "credit" to reflect increases and decreases to the usual balance sheet and the income statement relations.

FYI The **normal balance** of any account is on the side on which increases are recorded.

Accounting Relation		Debit	Credit
Balance sheet	Assets (A)	Increase	Decrease
	Liabilities (L)	Decrease	Increase
	Equity (SE)	Decrease	Increase
Income statement	Revenue (R)	Decrease	Increase
	Expense (E)	Increase	Decrease

T-Account with Debits and Credits

To illustrate use of debits and credits with a T-account, we use the Cash T-account for NBS transactions 1, 2, 3, and 4 (see page 2-10 for the transactions). There is a beginning balance of $0 on the left side (which is also the ending balance of the previous period). Increases in cash have been placed on the left side of the Cash T-account, and decreases have been placed on the right side. Transactions (1) and (2) increased the cash balance, while transaction (3) decreased it. Transaction (4) does not involve cash.

The ending balance of cash is $23,000. An account balance is determined by totaling the left side and the right side columns and entering the difference on the side with the larger total. The T-account is an extremely simple record that can be summarized in terms of four elements: beginning balance, additions, subtractions, and ending balance.

+	Cash (A)		−
Beg. bal.	0		
(1)	20,000	2,000	(3)
(2)	5,000		
End. bal.	23,000		

Dates and other related data are usually omitted in T-accounts, but it is customary to *key* entries with a number or a letter to identify the similarly coded transaction. The number or letter is keyed to the journal entry (discussed next) that identifies the transaction involved. The type and number of accounts used by a business depend on the complexity of its operations and the degree of detail demanded by managers.

The Journal Entry

FYI We denote the transaction's effect on assets, liabilities, equity, revenues, and expenses in parentheses for each journal entry.

The journal entry records each transaction (step 2) by summarizing the debits and credits. To illustrate the use of journal entries and T-accounts (step 3), assume that Walgreens: (1) Paid employees $1,200 cash wages, recognizing that amount as an expense, and (2) Paid $9,500 cash to acquire equipment. The journal entries and T-accounts reflecting these two transactions follow. The T-accounts can be viewed as an abbreviated representation of the company *ledger,* which is a listing of all accounts and their dollar balances.

Journal Entries

(1)	Wages expense (+E, −SE)	1,200	
	Cash (−A)		1,200
(2)	Equipment (+A)	9,500	
	Cash (−A)		9,500

General Ledger Effects in T-Account Form

+	Cash (A)		−
	1,200		(1)
	9,500		(2)

+	Equipment (A)		−
(2)	9,500		

+	Wages Expense (E)		−
(1)	1,200		

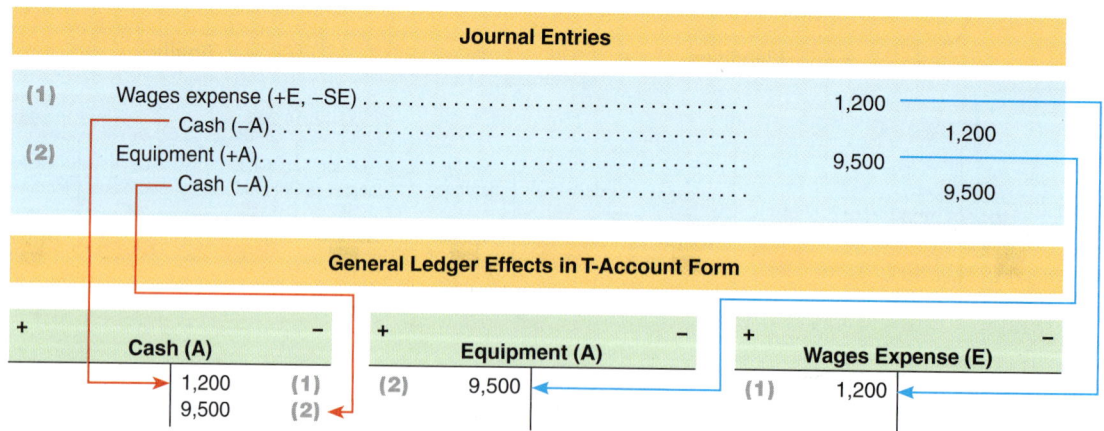

For journal entries, debits are recorded first followed by credits. Credits are commonly indented. The dollar amounts are entered in both the debit (left) column and the credit (right) column. In practice, recordkeepers also enter the date. An alternative presentation is to utilize the abbreviation *Dr* to denote debits and *Cr* to denote credits that precede the account title. We use the first approach in this book.

Analyze, Journalize, and Post

To illustrate the use of journal entries and T-accounts to record transactions, we return to Natural Beauty Supply and reexamine the same transactions recorded earlier in the financial statement effects template. The following layout illustrates our three-step accounting process of analyzing, journalizing, and posting. The FSET is followed by the journal entry. A debit in the journal entry is posted to the debit side of the relevant T-Account, shown with a blue arrow. A credit in the journal entry is posted to the credit side of the relevant T-Account, shown with a red arrow.

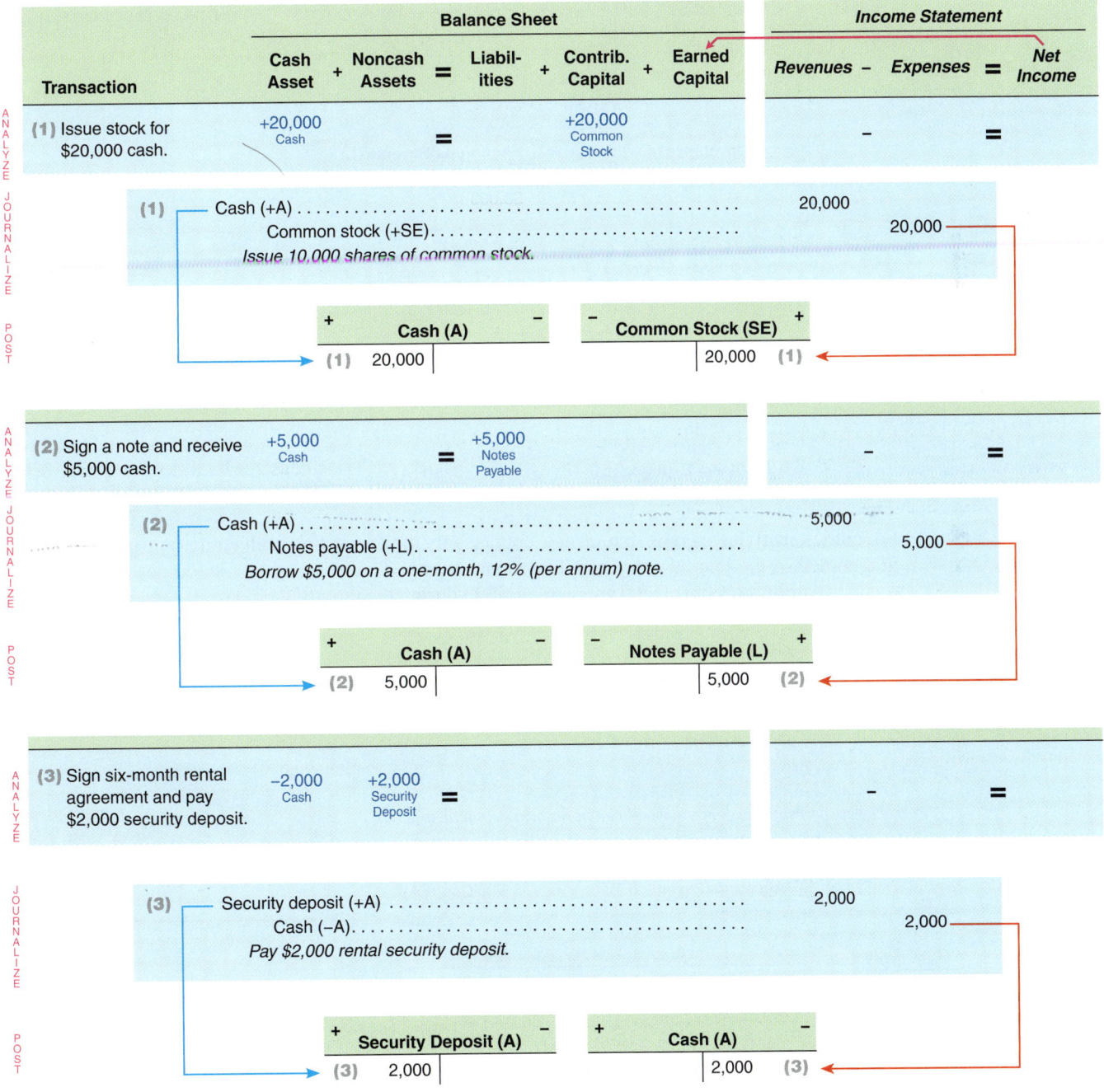

	Balance Sheet									*Income Statement*				
Transaction	**Cash Asset**	+	**Noncash Assets**	=	**Liabil-ities**	+	**Contrib. Capital**	+	**Earned Capital**	***Revenues***	−	***Expenses***	=	***Net Income***
ANALYZE **(1)** Issue stock for $20,000 cash.	+20,000 Cash			=			+20,000 Common Stock				−		=	

JOURNALIZE

		Debit	Credit
(1)	Cash (+A)	20,000	
	Common stock (+SE).		20,000
	Issue 10,000 shares of common stock.		

POST

+	Cash (A)	−
(1)	20,000	

−	Common Stock (SE)	+
	20,000	**(1)**

Transaction	Cash Asset	+	Noncash Assets	=	Liabilities	+	Contrib. Capital	+	Earned Capital	Revenues	−	Expenses	=	Net Income
ANALYZE **(2)** Sign a note and receive $5,000 cash.	+5,000 Cash			=	+5,000 Notes Payable						−		=	

JOURNALIZE

		Debit	Credit
(2)	Cash (+A)	5,000	
	Notes payable (+L).		5,000
	Borrow $5,000 on a one-month, 12% (per annum) note.		

POST

+	Cash (A)	−
(2)	5,000	

−	Notes Payable (L)	+
	5,000	**(2)**

Transaction	Cash Asset	+	Noncash Assets	=	Liabilities	+	Contrib. Capital	+	Earned Capital	Revenues	−	Expenses	=	Net Income
ANALYZE **(3)** Sign six-month rental agreement and pay $2,000 security deposit.	−2,000 Cash		+2,000 Security Deposit	=							−		=	

JOURNALIZE

		Debit	Credit
(3)	Security deposit (+A)	2,000	
	Cash (−A).		2,000
	Pay $2,000 rental security deposit.		

POST

+	Security Deposit (A)	−
(3)	2,000	

+	Cash (A)	−
	2,000	**(3)**

continued

continued from previous page

ANALYZE

Transaction	Cash Asset	+	Noncash Assets	=	Liabilities	+	Contrib. Capital	+	Earned Capital	Revenues	−	Expenses	=	Net Income
(4) Purchase $17,000 inventory on account.			+17,000 Inventory	=	+17,000 Accounts Payable						−		=	

JOURNALIZE

		Debit	Credit
(4)	Inventory (+A)	17,000	
	Accounts payable (+L)		17,000
	Purchase inventory on account.		

POST

+ Inventory (A) −	
(4) 17,000	

− Accounts Payable (L) +	
	17,000 (4)

ANALYZE

Transaction	Cash Asset	+	Noncash Assets	=	Liabilities	+	Contrib. Capital	+	Earned Capital	Revenues	−	Expenses	=	Net Income
(5) Pay $670 cash for November advertising.	−670 Cash			=					−670 Retained Earnings		−	+670 Advertising Expense	=	−670

JOURNALIZE

		Debit	Credit
(5)	Advertising expense (+E, −SE)	670	
	Cash (−A)		670
	Record advertising expense.		

POST

+ Advertising Expense (E) −	
(5) 670	

+ Cash (A) −	
	670 (5)

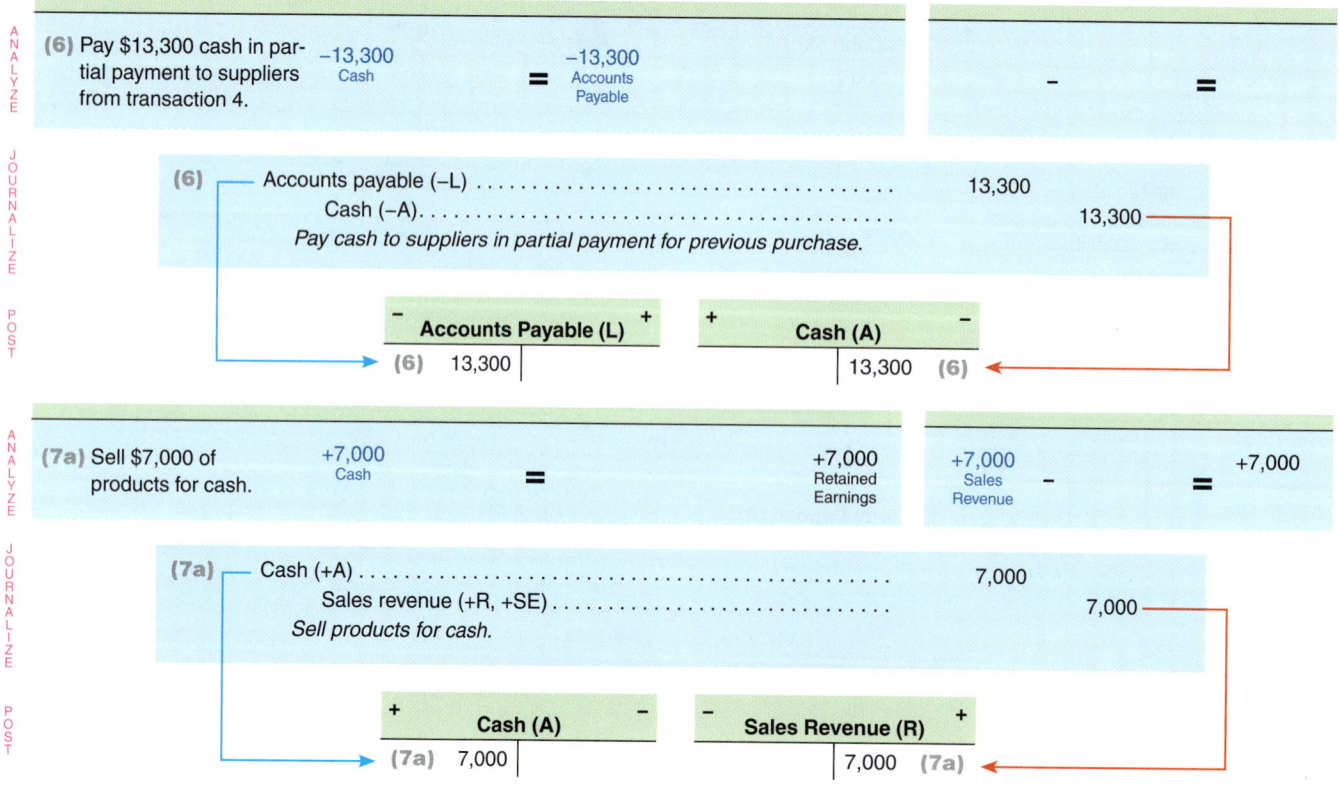

For entries involving income statement accounts, only the transaction itself (**blue type** in the FSET) is recorded in the journal entry and T-account posting. The resulting effects on net income and retained earnings occur (**black type** in the FSET) during the reporting process.

ANALYZE

Transaction	Cash Asset	+	Noncash Assets	=	Liabilities	+	Contrib. Capital	+	Earned Capital	Revenues	−	Expenses	=	Net Income
(6) Pay $13,300 cash in partial payment to suppliers from transaction 4.	−13,300 Cash			=	−13,300 Accounts Payable						−		=	

JOURNALIZE

		Debit	Credit
(6)	Accounts payable (−L)	13,300	
	Cash (−A)		13,300
	Pay cash to suppliers in partial payment for previous purchase.		

POST

− Accounts Payable (L) +	
(6) 13,300	

+ Cash (A) −	
	13,300 (6)

ANALYZE

Transaction	Cash Asset	+	Noncash Assets	=	Liabilities	+	Contrib. Capital	+	Earned Capital	Revenues	−	Expenses	=	Net Income
(7a) Sell $7,000 of products for cash.	+7,000 Cash			=					+7,000 Retained Earnings	+7,000 Sales Revenue	−		=	+7,000

JOURNALIZE

		Debit	Credit
(7a)	Cash (+A)	7,000	
	Sales revenue (+R, +SE)		7,000
	Sell products for cash.		

POST

+ Cash (A) −	
(7a) 7,000	

− Sales Revenue (R) +	
	7,000 (7a)

continued

continued from previous page

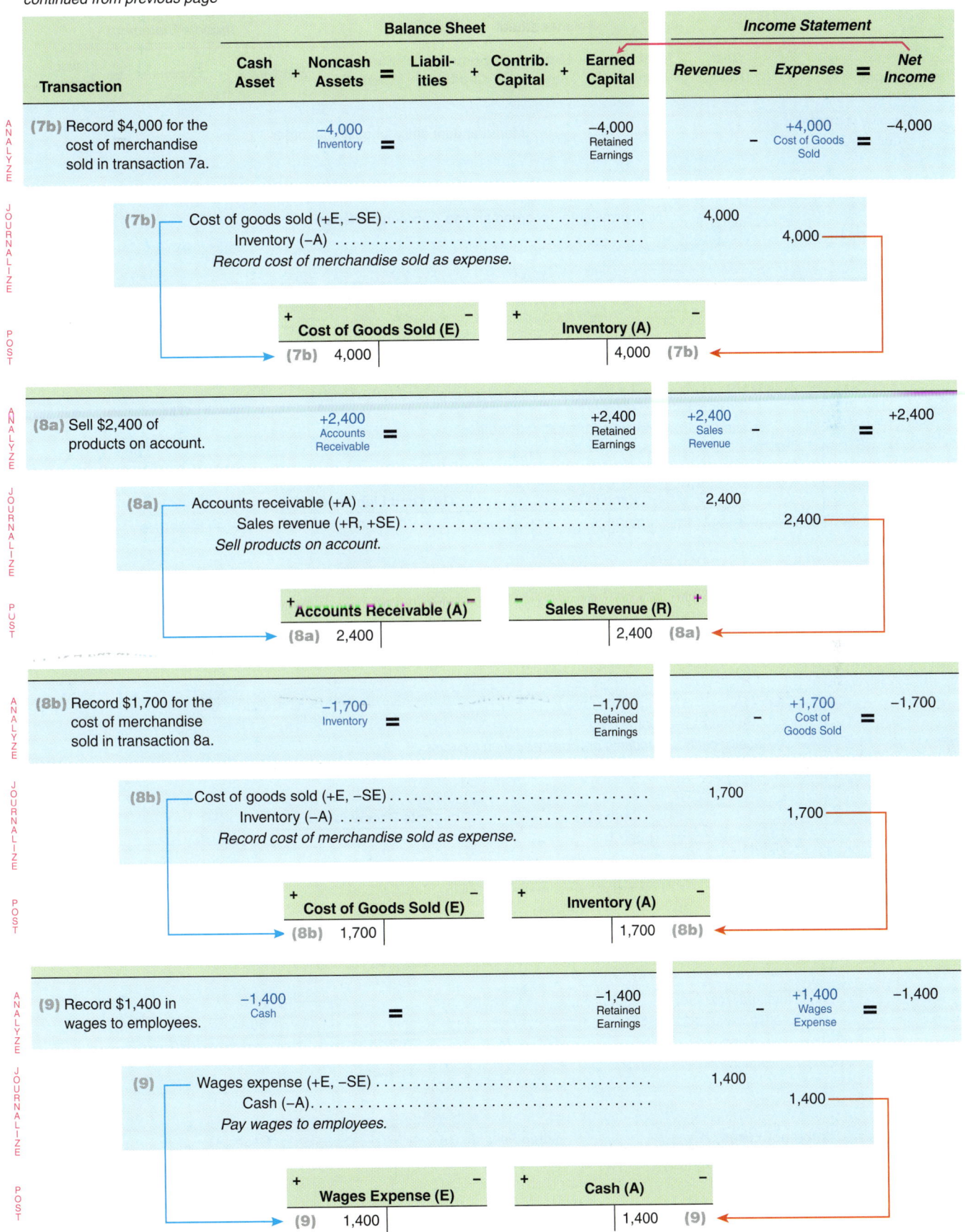

ANALYZE

Transaction	Cash Asset	+ Noncash Assets	=	Liabil-ities	+ Contrib. Capital	+ Earned Capital	*Revenues*	−	*Expenses*	=	*Net Income*
(7b) Record $4,000 for the cost of merchandise sold in transaction 7a.		−4,000 Inventory	=			−4,000 Retained Earnings		−	+4,000 Cost of Goods Sold	=	−4,000

JOURNALIZE

(7b) Cost of goods sold (+E, −SE)	4,000	
Inventory (−A)		4,000
Record cost of merchandise sold as expense.		

POST

+ Cost of Goods Sold (E) −	
(7b) 4,000	

+ Inventory (A) −	
	4,000 (7b)

ANALYZE

Transaction	Cash Asset	+ Noncash Assets	=	Liabil-ities	+ Contrib. Capital	+ Earned Capital	*Revenues*	−	*Expenses*	=	*Net Income*
(8a) Sell $2,400 of products on account.		+2,400 Accounts Receivable	=			+2,400 Retained Earnings	+2,400 Sales Revenue	−		=	+2,400

JOURNALIZE

(8a) Accounts receivable (+A)	2,400	
Sales revenue (+R, +SE)		2,400
Sell products on account.		

POST

+ Accounts Receivable (A) −	
(8a) 2,400	

− Sales Revenue (R) +	
	2,400 (8a)

ANALYZE

Transaction	Cash Asset	+ Noncash Assets	=	Liabil-ities	+ Contrib. Capital	+ Earned Capital	*Revenues*	−	*Expenses*	=	*Net Income*
(8b) Record $1,700 for the cost of merchandise sold in transaction 8a.		−1,700 Inventory	=			−1,700 Retained Earnings		−	+1,700 Cost of Goods Sold	=	−1,700

JOURNALIZE

(8b) Cost of goods sold (+E, −SE)	1,700	
Inventory (−A)		1,700
Record cost of merchandise sold as expense.		

POST

+ Cost of Goods Sold (E) −	
(8b) 1,700	

+ Inventory (A) −	
	1,700 (8b)

ANALYZE

Transaction	Cash Asset	+ Noncash Assets	=	Liabil-ities	+ Contrib. Capital	+ Earned Capital	*Revenues*	−	*Expenses*	=	*Net Income*
(9) Record $1,400 in wages to employees.	−1,400 Cash		=			−1,400 Retained Earnings		−	+1,400 Wages Expense	=	−1,400

JOURNALIZE

(9) Wages expense (+E, −SE)	1,400	
Cash (−A)		1,400
Pay wages to employees.		

POST

+ Wages Expense (E) −	
(9) 1,400	

+ Cash (A) −	
	1,400 (9)

continued

continued from previous page

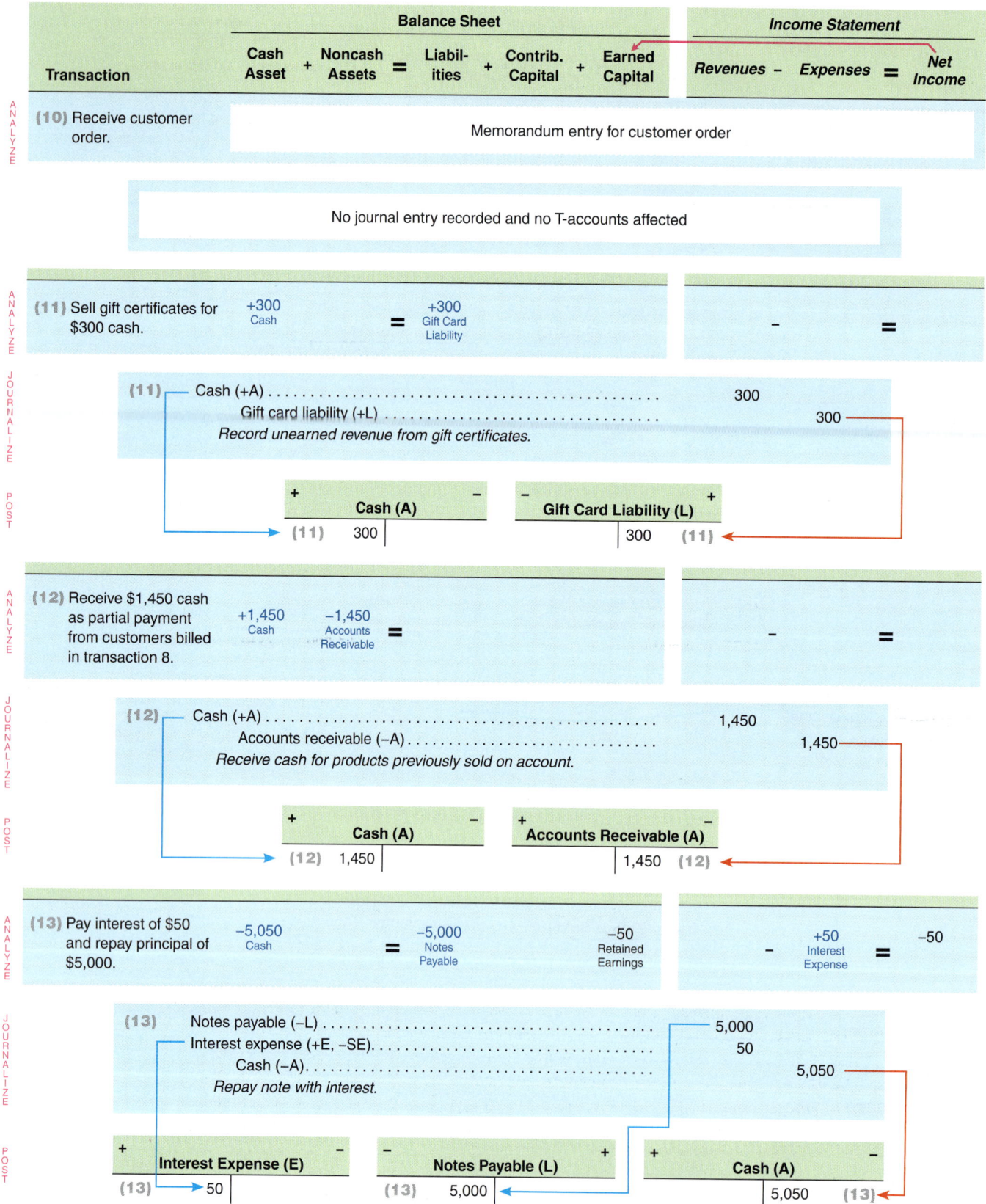

Transaction	Cash Asset	+	Noncash Assets	=	Liabil-ities	+	Contrib. Capital	+	Earned Capital	Revenues	–	Expenses	=	Net Income
(10) Receive customer order.	Memorandum entry for customer order													
(11) Sell gift certificates for $300 cash.	+300 Cash			=	+300 Gift Card Liability						–		=	
(12) Receive $1,450 cash as partial payment from customers billed in transaction 8.	+1,450 Cash		–1,450 Accounts Receivable	=							–		=	
(13) Pay interest of $50 and repay principal of $5,000.	–5,050 Cash			=	–5,000 Notes Payable				–50 Retained Earnings		–	+50 Interest Expense	=	–50

(10) No journal entry recorded and no T-accounts affected

(11) Journalize

		Debit	Credit
(11)	Cash (+A)	300	
	Gift card liability (+L)		300
	Record unearned revenue from gift certificates.		

Post

+ Cash (A) –	
(11) 300	

– Gift Card Liability (L) +	
	300 (11)

(12) Journalize

		Debit	Credit
(12)	Cash (+A)	1,450	
	Accounts receivable (–A)		1,450
	Receive cash for products previously sold on account.		

Post

+ Cash (A) –	
(12) 1,450	

+ Accounts Receivable (A) –	
	1,450 (12)

(13) Journalize

		Debit	Credit
(13)	Notes payable (–L)	5,000	
	Interest expense (+E, –SE)	50	
	Cash (–A)		5,050
	Repay note with interest.		

Post

+ Interest Expense (E) –	
(13) 50	

– Notes Payable (L) +	
(13) 5,000	

+ Cash (A) –	
	5,050 (13)

continued

continued from previous page

ANALYZE

Transaction	Cash Asset	+	Noncash Assets	=	Liabil-ities	+	Contrib. Capital	+	Earned Capital	*Revenues*	–	*Expenses*	=	*Net Income*
	Balance Sheet									***Income Statement***				
(14) Pay $1,680 for one-year insurance policy.	–1,680 Cash		+1,680 Prepaid Insurance	=							–		=	

JOURNALIZE

(14) Prepaid insurance (+A).	1,680	
Cash (–A).		1,680
Pay insurance premium.		

POST

+ Prepaid Insurance (A) –	
(14) 1,680	

+ Cash (A) –	
	1,680 (14)

ANALYZE

Transaction	Cash Asset	+	Noncash Assets	=	Liabil-ities	+	Contrib. Capital	+	Earned Capital	*Revenues*	–	*Expenses*	=	*Net Income*
(15) Pay $1,500 rent for November.	–1,500 Cash			=					–1,500 Retained Earnings		–	+1,500 Rent Expense	=	–1,500

JOURNALIZE

(15) Rent expense (+E, –SE).	1,500	
Cash (–A).		1,500
Record payment of November rent.		

POST

+ Rent Expense (E) –	
(15) 1,500	

+ Cash (A) –	
	1,500 (15)

ANALYZE

Transaction	Cash Asset	+	Noncash Assets	=	Liabil-ities	+	Contrib. Capital	+	Earned Capital	*Revenues*	–	*Expenses*	=	*Net Income*
(16) Pay $50 cash dividend to shareholders.	–50 Cash			=					–50 Retained Earnings		–		=	

JOURNALIZE

(16) Retained earnings (–SE)	50	
Cash (–A).		50
Pay a cash dividend.		

POST

– Retained Earnings (SE) +	
(16) 50	

+ Cash (A) –	
	50 (16)

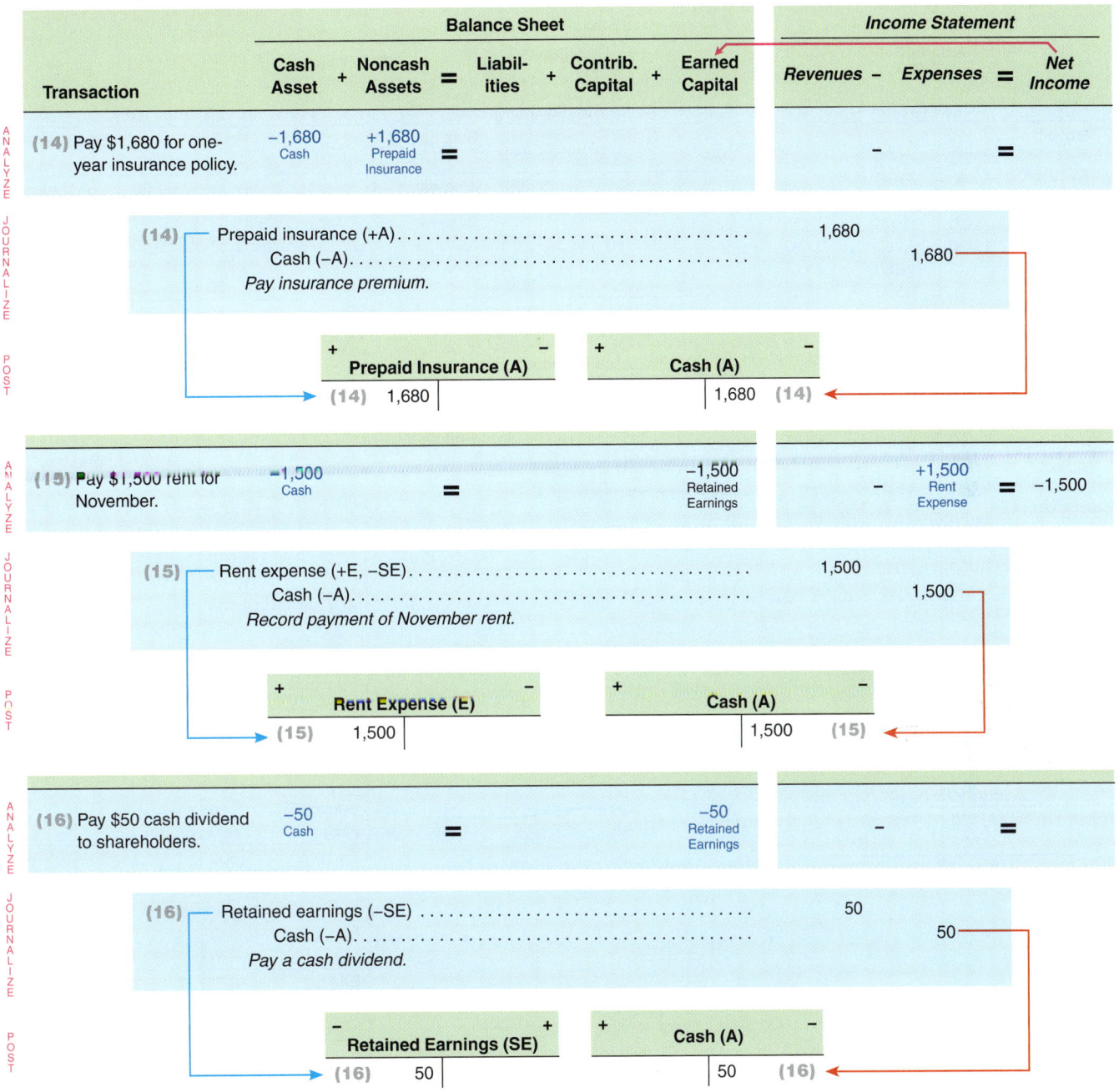

As shown each of the journal entries is posted to the appropriate T-accounts, which represent the general ledger. The complete general ledger reflecting each of these sixteen transactions follows, reflecting how the balance sheet and income statement are produced by the same underlying process. **The dashed line around the six equity accounts indicates those that are reported in the income statement before becoming part of retained earnings.** Each balance sheet T-account starts with an opening balance on November 1 (zero in this case), and the ending balances are the starting balances for December. Income statement T-accounts do not have an opening balance, for reasons we explore in Chapter 3.

As always, we see that: Assets = Liabilities + Equity. Specifically, $24,030 assets ($8,100 + $950 + $11,300 + $1,680 + $2,000) = $4,000 liabilities ($3,700 + $300) + $20,030 equity ($20,000 – $50 + $9,400 – $5,700 – $1,400 – $1,500 – $670 – $50).

General Ledger

Assets = Liabilities + Equity

Assets

Cash (A) (+ / −)

	+	−	
Beg. bal.	0		
(1)	20,000	2,000	(3)
(2)	5,000	670	(5)
(7a)	7,000	13,300	(6)
(11)	300	1,400	(9)
(12)	1,450	5,050	(13)
		1,680	(14)
		1,500	(15)
		50	(16)
End bal.	8,100		

Accounts Receivable (A) (+ / −)

	+	−	
Beg. bal.	0		
(8a)	2,400	1,450	(12)
End bal.	950		

Inventory (A) (+ / −)

	+	−	
Beg. bal.	0		
(4)	17,000	4,000	(7b)
		1,700	(8b)
End bal.	11,300		

Prepaid Insurance (A) (+ / −)

	+	−	
Beg. bal.	0		
(14)	1,680		
End bal.	1,680		

Security Deposit (A) (+ / −)

	+	−	
Beg. bal.	0		
(3)	2,000		
End bal.	2,000		

Liabilities

Accounts Payable (L) (− / +)

	−	+	
		0	Beg. bal.
(6)	13,300	17,000	(4)
		3,700	End bal.

Gift Card Liability (L) (− / +)

	−	+	
		0	Beg. bal.
		300	(11)
		300	End bal.

Notes Payable (L) (− / +)

	−	+	
		0	Beg. bal.
(13)	5,000	5,000	(2)
		0	End bal.

Equity

Common Stock (SE) (− / +)

	−	+	
		0	Beg. bal.
		20,000	(1)
		20,000	End bal.

Retained Earnings (SE) (− / +)

	−	+	
		0	Beg. bal.
(16)	50		
End bal.	50		

Sales Revenue (R) (− / +)

	−	+	
		0	Beg. bal.
		7,000	(7a)
		2,400	(8a)
		9,400	End bal.

Cost of Goods Sold (E) (+ / −)

	+	−	
Beg. bal.	0		
(7b)	4,000		
(8b)	1,700		
End bal.	5,700		

Wages Expense (E) (+ / −)

	+	−	
Beg. bal.	0		
(9)	1,400		
End bal.	1,400		

Rent Expense (E) (+ / −)

	+	−	
Beg. bal.	0		
(15)	1,500		
End bal.	1,500		

Advertising Expense (E) (+ / −)

	+	−	
Beg. bal.	0		
(5)	670		
End bal.	670		

Interest Expense (E) (+ / −)

	+	−	
Beg. bal.	0		
(13)	50		
End bal.	50		

Assets = $24,030 = **Liabilities = $4,000** + **Equity = $20,030**

Review 2-6 LO2-6

Reporting Using the FSET and Preparing Journal Entries and the General Ledger

Assume that the following accounts appear in the ledger of M.E. Carter, a financial consultant to companies in the retail sector. Cash; Accounts Receivable; Office Equipment; Prepaid Subscriptions; Accounts Payable; Note Payable; Common Stock; Retained Earnings; Fees Earned; Salaries Expense; Rent Expense; Interest Expense; and Utilities Expense. For each of the following 11 transactions:

continued

continued from previous page

a. Analyze and enter each into the financial statement effects template.
b. Prepare journal entries for each of the transactions, set up T-accounts for each of the ledger accounts, and post the journal entries to those T-accounts—key all entries with the number identifying the transaction.
c. Prepare the general ledger in T-account form, enter the financial effects of all transactions, and determine the ending balance for each account.

(1) M.E. Carter started the firm by contributing $15,500 cash to the business in exchange for common stock.
(2) The firm purchased $10,400 in office equipment, issuing a long-term note payable for $4,400 with the remainder on account.
(3) Paid $700 cash for this period's office rent (on a short-term lease).
(4) Paid $9,600 cash for subscriptions to online financial databases covering the next three periods.
(5) Billed clients $11,300 for services rendered.
(6) Made $1,000 cash payment on account for the equipment purchased in transaction 2.
(7) Paid $2,800 cash for assistant's salary for this period.
(8) Collected $9,400 cash from clients previously billed in transaction 5.
(9) Received $180 invoice for this period's utilities; it is paid early in the next period.
(10) Paid $1,500 cash for dividends to shareholders.
(11) Paid $225 cash for interest on the note payable for the period.

Solution on p. 2-55.

ANALYZING FINANCIAL STATEMENTS

Analysis Objective

We are trying to determine if Walgreens has sufficient funds to pay its short-term debts as they come due. To accomplish this task, we employ several measures of liquidity. We introduce three such measures below to assess liquidity.

LO2-7 Compute net working capital, the current ratio, and the quick ratio, and explain how they reflect liquidity.

eLecture MBC

Analysis Tool Net Working Capital

Net working capital = Current assets − Current liabilities

Applying Net Working Capital to Walgreens

2018: $17,846 − $21,667 = $(3,821)
2019: $18,700 − $25,769 = $(7,069)
2020: $18,073 − $27,070 = $(8,997)

Guidance A company's net working capital is determined primarily by the time between paying for goods and employee services and the receipt of cash from sales for cash or on credit. This cycle is referred to as the firm's **cash operating cycle** (see **Exhibit 2.6**). The cash operating cycle can provide additional resources through trade credit financing. For example, inventory is typically bought on credit with terms that allow payment to be deferred for 30 to 90 days without penalty. The delay in payment allows the cash to be invested, thereby increasing the cash to be used in the following operating cycle. Of course, the reluctant supplier of the credit strives to reduce this payment delay, for example, through discounts for early payment.

A company's net working capital is a broad measure including all current assets even though some of them—inventories for one—require time to turn them into cash. Later in the book, we will discover that the accounting for some components of working capital, like inventory, needs to be adjusted with information found in the disclosure notes.

EXHIBIT 2.6 Operating Cycle

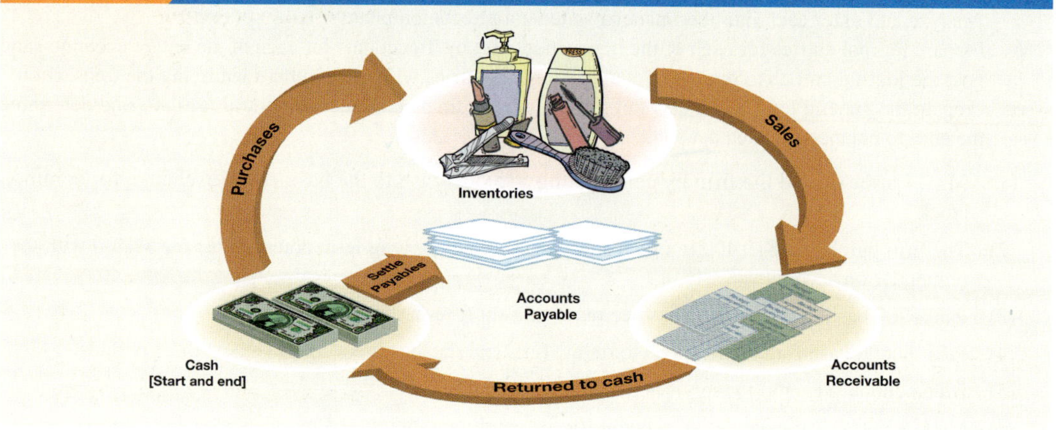

Analysis Tool Current Ratio

$$\text{Current ratio} = \frac{\text{Current asset}}{\text{Current liabilities}}$$

Applying the Current Ratio to Walgreens

$$\textbf{2018: } \frac{\$17,846}{\$21,667} = 0.82$$

$$\textbf{2019: } \frac{\$18,700}{\$25,769} = 0.73$$

$$\textbf{2020: } \frac{\$18,073}{\$27,070} = 0.67$$

Guidance The current ratio is just a different form of net working capital and as such simply provides a different viewpoint. Current ratios exceeding one indicate a positive net working capital. However, for firms that find difficulty in predicting sales and collections, a higher current ratio is desirable, as discussed in Chapter 5. Companies generally prefer a current ratio greater than one but less than two. The ratio allows us to discern whether the company is likely to have difficulty meeting its short-term obligations. The current ratio has additional value as a ratio because net working capital depends on the size of the company. This is useful when comparing companies as below.

Walgreens in Context

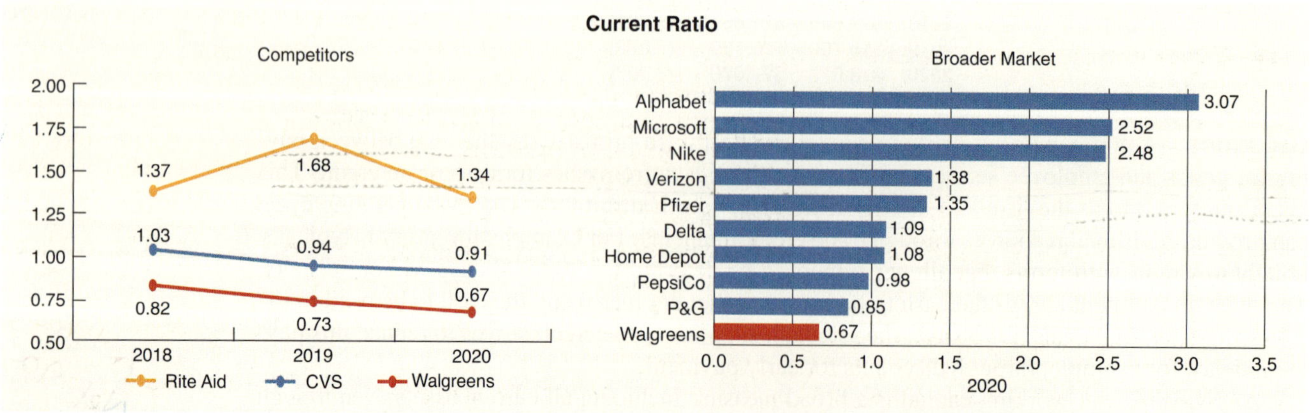

These companies do not have identical fiscal year-ends. For each fiscal year listed, balance sheets are dated from February 2 to December 31 of that year.

Analysis Tool Quick Ratio

$$\text{Quick ratio} = \frac{\text{Cash} + \text{Short-term securities} + \text{Accounts receivable}}{\text{Current liabilities}}$$

Applying the Quick Ratio to Walgreens

$$\textbf{2018:}\quad \frac{(\$785 + \$0 + \$6{,}573)}{\$21{,}667} = 0.34$$

$$\textbf{2019:}\quad \frac{(\$1{,}023 + \$0 + \$7{,}226)}{\$25{,}769} = 0.32$$

$$\textbf{2020:}\quad \frac{(\$516 + \$0 + \$7{,}132)}{\$27{,}070} = 0.28$$

Guidance The quick ratio is a more restrictive form of the current ratio in that it excludes inventories. Only those assets that are cash, or near cash, are considered in this liquidity measure, making it a more stringent test of liquidity.

Walgreens in Context

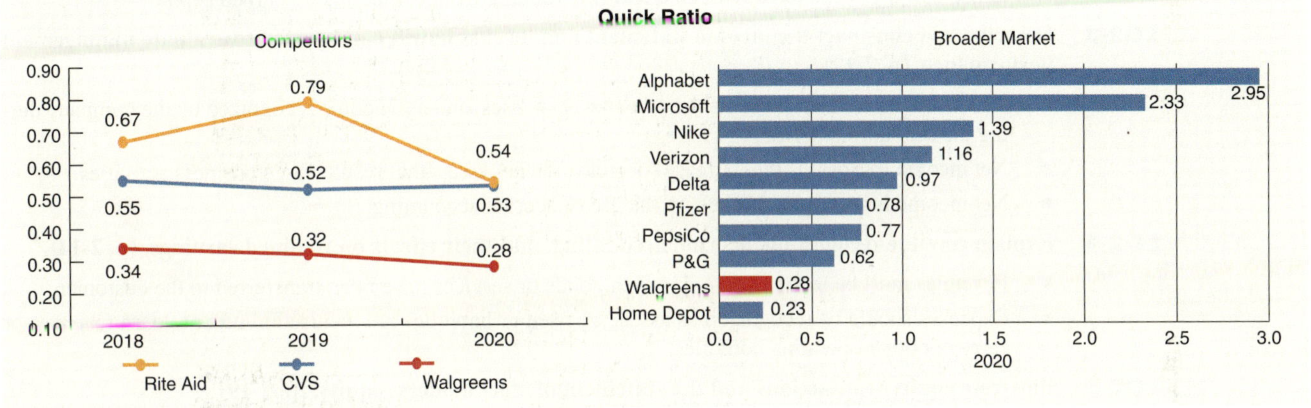

These companies do not have identical fiscal year-ends. For each fiscal year listed, balance sheets are dated from February 2 to December 31 of that year.

Takeaways Over the three-year period covered by our calculations, we can see that Walgreens is in a relatively weaker position with respect to liquidity compared to its competitors and the broader market. Its net working capital is negative in each of the three years, and has become more negative over this time period. The current and quick ratios have declined over the three years as well. So there may be some cause for concern for Walgreens in terms of liquidity, but this is offset by Walgreens's strong, positive operating cash flow, which will help them meet liquidity needs going forward.

Other Considerations The ratios above tell us about retail pharmacy chains and some other companies in other industries. It is important to note that companies with different operating cycles are likely to exhibit different values at optimal levels of activity. For example, grocery stores will have few current assets but consistent, large operating cash inflows that ensure sufficient liquidity despite current ratios less than one. Additionally, companies that efficiently manage inventories, receivables, and payables can also operate with current ratios less than one. Walmart Inc., for instance, uses its strong market power to extract extended credit terms from suppliers while simultaneously enforcing short payment periods on customers.

Computing Working Capital, Current Ratio, and Quick Ratio LO2-7 **Review 2-7**

Using the information from Review 2-6, compute the following ratios on end-of-year balances for M.E. Carter.

a. Working capital
b. Current ratio
c. Quick ratio

GuidedExample MBC

Solution on p. 2-58.

SUMMARY

LO2-1 **Describe and construct the balance sheet and understand how it can be used for analysis. (p. 2-3)**

- Assets, which reflect investment activities, are reported (in order of their liquidity) as current assets (expected to be used typically within a year) and noncurrent assets.
- Assets are reported at their historical cost and not at market values (with a few exceptions) and are restricted to those that can be reliably measured.
- Not all assets are reported on the balance sheet; a company's self-developed intellectual capital, often one of its more valuable assets, is one example.
- For an asset to be recorded, it must be owned or controlled by the company and carry future economic benefits.
- Liabilities and equity are the sources of company financing; they are ordered by maturity dates.

LO2-2 **Use the financial statement effects template (FSET) to analyze transactions. (p. 2-8)**

- The FSET captures the effects of transactions on the balance sheet, income statement, statement of stockholders' equity, and statement of cash flows.
- Income statement effects are separated into revenues, expenses, and net income. The updating of retained earnings is denoted with an arrow line running from net income to earned capital.

LO2-3 **Describe and construct the income statement and discuss how it can be used to evaluate management performance. (p. 2-12)**

- The income statement presents the revenues, expenses, and net income recognized by the company during the accounting period.
- Net income (or loss) is the increase (decrease) in net assets that results from business activities.
- Net income is determined based on the use of accrual accounting.

LO2-4 **Explain revenue recognition, accrual accounting, and their effects on retained earnings. (p. 2-14)**

- Revenues must be recognized only when goods or services have been transferred to the customer.
- Expenses should be recognized as assets are used or liabilities are incurred in order to earn revenues or carry out other operating activities.

LO2-5 **Illustrate equity transactions and the statement of stockholders' equity. (p. 2-19)**

- The statement of stockholders' equity reports transactions resulting in changes in equity accounts during the accounting period.
- Transactions between the company and its owners, such as dividend payments, are not reported in the income statement.

LO2-6 **Use journal entries and T-accounts to analyze and record transactions. (p. 2-21)**

- Transactions are recorded in the accounting system using journal entries.
- Journal entries are posted to a general ledger, represented by "T-accounts."
- Accountants use "debits" and "credits" to record transactions in the accounts.

LO2-7 **Compute net working capital, the current ratio, and the quick ratio, and explain how they reflect liquidity. (p. 2-30)**

- Net working capital: an indicator of a firm's ability to pay its short-term debts computed as the difference between current assets and current liabilities.
- Current ratio (CR): A measure of liquidity indicating the degree of coverage of current liabilities by current assets.
- Quick ratio (QR): A measure of the ability to cover current liabilities using only cash and cash equivalents (such as money market accounts), short-term securities, and accounts receivable.

GUIDANCE ANSWERS . . . YOU MAKE THE CALL

You are an Analyst Often, the answer in such a case is dividends. Indeed, in 2019, Colgate-Palmolive Company paid cash dividends of $1,472 million. The net income and dividend payments and, in Colgate-Palmolive's case a $9 million amount classified as "other," account for the change in retained earnings ($22,501 million – $21,615 million = $2,367 million – $1,472 million – $9 million). On occasion, companies pay dividends in excess of their earnings (or pay dividends even when earning losses), resulting in a decrease in retained earnings over the period.

KEY RATIOS

Net working capital = Current assets − Current liabilities

$$\text{Current ratio} = \frac{\text{Current assets}}{\text{Current liabilities}} \qquad \text{Quick ratio} = \frac{\text{Cash + Short-term securities + Accounts receivable}}{\text{Current liabilities}}$$

Assignments with the MBC logo in the margin are available in myBusinessCourse. See the Preface of the book for details.

MULTIPLE CHOICE

1. Which of the following conditions must exist for an item to be recorded as an asset?
   a. Item is not owned or controlled by the company.
   b. Future benefits from the item cannot be reliably measured.
   c. Item must be a tangible asset.
   d. Item must be expected to yield future benefits.

2. Company assets that are excluded from the company financial statements
   a. are presumably reflected in the company's stock price.
   b. include all of the company's intangible assets.
   c. are known as intangible assets.
   d. include investments in other companies.

3. If an asset declines in value, which of the following must be true?
   a. A liability also declines.
   b. Equity also declines.
   c. Either a liability or equity also declines or another asset increases in value.
   d. Neither *a* nor *b* can occur.

4. Which of the following is true about accrual accounting?
   a. Accrual accounting requires that expenses always be recognized when cash is paid out.
   b. Accrual accounting is required under GAAP.
   c. Accrual accounting recognizes revenue only when cash is received.
   d. Recognition of a prepaid asset is not an example of accrual accounting.

5. Which of the following options accurately identifies the effects a cash sale of an iPhone has on Apple's accounts?
   a. Accounts receivable increases, sales revenue increases, cost of goods sold increases, and inventory decreases.
   b. Cash increases, sales revenue increases, cost of goods sold decreases, and inventory decreases.
   c. Accounts receivable increases, sales revenue increases, cost of goods sold decreases, and inventory decreases.
   d. Cash increases, sales revenue increases, cost of goods sold increases, and inventory decreases.

Multiple Choice Answers
1. d 2. a 3. c 4. b 5. d

QUESTIONS

Q2-1. The balance sheet consists of assets, liabilities, and equity. Define each category and provide two examples of accounts reported within each category.

Q2-2. Two important concepts that guide income statement reporting are the revenue recognition principle and the expense recognition principle. Define and explain each of these two guiding principles.

Q2-3. GAAP is based on the concept of accrual accounting. Define and describe accrual accounting.

Q2-4. What is the statement of stockholders' equity? What information is conveyed in that statement?

Q2-5. What are the two essential characteristics of an asset?

Q2-6. What does the concept of liquidity refer to? Explain.

Q2-7. What does the term "current" denote when referring to assets?

Q2-8. Assets are often recorded at historical costs even though current market values might, arguably, be more relevant to financial statement readers. Describe the reasoning behind historical cost usage.

Q2-9. Identify three intangible assets that are likely to be excluded from the balance sheet because they cannot be reliably measured.

Q2-10. How does the quick ratio differ from the current ratio?

Q2-11. What three conditions must be satisfied to require reporting of a liability on the balance sheet?

Q2-12. Define net working capital. Explain how increasing the amount of trade credit can reduce the net working capital for a company.

Q2-13. On December 31, Miller Company had $525,000 in total assets and owed $165,000 to creditors. If this corporation's common stock totaled $225,000, what amount of retained earnings is reported on its December 31 balance sheet?

DATA ANALYTICS

LO2-1

Data Analytics

DA2-1. Preparing Basic Data Visualization in Excel of the Balance Sheet
The Excel file associated with this exercise includes total liabilities, common stock, and retained earnings balances as of December 31 for Monona Inc. We will prepare data visualizations focusing on how these amounts relate to each other and how the relations are expressed through proportions.

REQUIRED

1. Download Excel file DA2-1 found in myBusinessCourse.
2. Prepare a doughnut chart showing total liabilities, total common stock, and total retained earnings as components of total liabilities plus stockholders' equity. *Hint:* Highlight the dataset and open the Insert tab. Click on the Pie icon in the Charts group and click on Doughnut.
3. Display a percentage label in each section of your chart. *Hint:* Right-click inside the doughnut, select Format data labels, select Percentage. Deselect Value if necessary.
4. List the formula for the chart data range. *Hint:* Click inside the chart. Open the Chart Design tab and click Select Data. The formula is in the Chart data range field.
5. List the percentage amount (or combination of percentage amounts) on the doughnut chart that reflect the stockholders' equity proportion.
6. List the larger percentage: either the total liabilities proportion or the total equity proportion of the pie chart.
7. List the percentage amount (or combination of percentage amounts) on the doughnut chart that reflect the total assets proportion.
8. List the dollar amount of total assets.

LO2-3

Data Analytics

DA2-2. Preparing a Basic Data Visualization in Excel to Highlight Changes in Expenses Over Time
The Excel file associated with this exercise includes three years of operating expenses of Starbucks Corporation reported in recent reports on Form 10-K. We will use data visualizations to analyze the trends of expenses over this three-year period.

REQUIRED

1. Download Excel file DA2-2 found in myBusinessCourse.
2. Create a data visualization within the worksheet in Excel, through the Sparkline feature: Line option. *Hint:* Highlight the cells with numeric data and click on Insert, click on Sparklines, click on Line. Next, select where to place Sparklines by highlighting the empty cells in the column to the right of your last column of data.
3. Format the Sparklines by adding color markers to the high and low points of your chart and adding thickness to the chart lines. *Hint:* Highlight your Sparkline and under the Sparkline tab, click on High Point and Low Point and choose your desired color scheme from the options listed in the Style Group. To add thickness, click on Sparkline Color and Weight to make an adjustment.
4. Determine which Sparkline (and, thus, pattern of activity) is most similar to the Sparkline for Product and distribution.
5. Determine which Sparkline is most similar to the Sparkline for Store operating expenses.

LO2-6

Data Analytics

DA2-3. Explaining the Role of Artificial Intelligence in Accounting
Artificial intelligence (AI) is the simulation of human intelligence through the use of machines. Machines are programmed to sense, recognize speech, problem solve, learn, act, or react. In a post by Nigel Duffy and Karsten Fuser called "Six Ways the CFO Can Use Artificial Intelligence Today" (found at https://www.ey.com/en_us/ai/six-ways-the-cfo-can-use-artificial-intelligence-today), the authors outline several uses of AI. Match a specific example that applies to each of the six uses of AI summarized by the authors.

CATEGORY OF AI USAGE

1. Customer data and predictive behavior
2. Beyond the book value
3. Management of bad debt
4. Fraud
5. Money laundering
6. Taking drudgery out of finance

SPECIFIC EXAMPLE OF AI USAGE

a. ___ Using natural language processing software to review thousands of pages of contracts to identify possible lease agreements.

b. ___ Applying minute-by-minute pricing based upon correlations between customer demographics, type of product, and payment method with the goal of maximizing revenues.

c. ___ Using AI to predict which customers will pay and when they will pay, analyzing data such as the company's credit rating, industry type, purchase history, and contact transactions.

d. ___ A lender assesses the fair value of collateral by assessing thousands of variables including market data and data specific to the collateral.

e. ___ Using AI to analyze trends in all recorded expenses, detecting patterns by certain employees.

f. ___ Classification of suspicious transactions according to the risk that they resulted in illegally obtained money.

DA2-4. Preparing Tableau Visualizations of Basic Financial Information LO2-2

Refer to PB-20 in Appendix B. This problem requires the creation of Tableau visualizations of financial information of S&P 500 companies from balance sheet, income statement and statement of cash flows data.

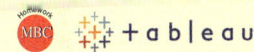

Homework MBC

Data Analytics

DATA VISUALIZATION

Data Visualization Activities are available in myBusinessCourse. These assignments use Tableau Dashboards to expose students to visual depictions of data and introduce students to data analytics through data visualizations. These exercises are easily assignable and auto graded by MBC.

Data Visualization

MINI EXERCISES

M2-14. Determining Retained Earnings and Net Income Using the Balance Sheet LO2-1

The following information is reported for Kinney Corporation at the end of the year.

Homework MBC

Accounts receivable	$ 46,000	Retained earnings	$?
Accounts payable	22,000	Supplies inventory	18,000
Cash	16,000	Equipment	276,000
Common stock	220,000		

a. Compute the amount of retained earnings reported at the end of the year.

b. If the amount of retained earnings at the beginning of the year was $60,000, and $24,000 in cash dividends were declared and paid during the year, what was the company's net income for the year?

M2-15. Applying the Accounting Equation to the Balance Sheet LO2-1

Determine the missing amount in each of the following separate company cases.

Homework MBC

	Assets	Liabilities	Equity
a.	$280,000	$119,000	$?
b.	?	44,800	39,200
c.	130,200	?	72,800

M2-16. Applying the Accounting Equation to the Balance Sheet LO2-1

Determine the missing amount in each of the following separate company cases.

Homework MBC

	Assets	Liabilities	Equity
a.	$300,000	$84,000	$?
b.	?	34,400	8,800
c.	702,400	?	337,600

LO2-1 Homework MBC

M2-17. Applying the Accounting Equation to Determine Unknown Values

Determine the following for each separate company case:

a. The stockholders' equity of Jensen Corporation, which has assets of $360,000 and liabilities of $260,800.

b. The liabilities of Sloan & Dechow, Inc., which has assets of $494,400 and stockholders' equity of $132,000.

c. The assets of Clem Corporation, which has liabilities of $320,000, common stock of $160,000, and retained earnings of $148,000.

LO2-2, 4, 5 Homework MBC

M2-18. Analyzing Transaction Effects on Equity

Would each of the following transactions increase, decrease, or have no effect on equity?

a. Paid cash to acquire supplies.

b. Paid cash for dividends to shareholders.

c. Paid cash for salaries.

d. Purchased equipment for cash.

e. Shareholders invested cash in business in exchange for common stock.

f. Rendered service to customers on account.

g. Rendered service to customers for cash.

LO2-1, 3, 4 Homework MBC

M2-19. Identifying and Classifying Financial Statement Items

For each of the following items, identify whether they would most likely be reported in the balance sheet (B) or income statement (I).

a.	Machinery	_____	*e.*	Common stock	_____	*i.*	Taxes expense	_____
b.	Supplies expense	_____	*f.*	Factory buildings	_____	*j.*	Cost of goods sold	_____
c.	Prepaid advertising	_____	*g.*	Receivables	_____	*k.*	Long-term debt	_____
d.	Advertising expense	_____	*h.*	Taxes payable	_____	*l.*	Treasury stock	_____

LO2-3, 4 Homework MBC

M2-20. Computing Net Income

Healy Corporation recorded service revenues of $200,000 during the year, of which $140,000 were for credit and $60,000 were for cash. Moreover, of the $140,000 credit sales, it collected $40,000 cash on those receivables before year-end. The company also paid $120,000 cash for current year's wages.

a. Compute the company's net income for the year.

b. Suppose you discover that employees had earned an additional $20,000 in wages during the year, but this amount had not been paid. Would annual net income change? If so, by how much?

LO2-1, 3, 5 Homework MBC

M2-21. Classifying Items in Financial Statements

Next to each item, indicate whether it would most likely be reported on the balance sheet (B), the income statement (I), or the statement of stockholders' equity (SE).

a.	Liabilities	_____	*d.*	Revenues	_____	*g.*	Assets	_____
b.	Net income	_____	*e.*	Stock issuance	_____	*h.*	Expenses	_____
c.	Cash	_____	*f.*	Dividends	_____	*i.*	Equity	_____

LO2-1, 3, 4, 5 Homework MBC

M2-22. Classifying Items in Financial Statements

For each of the following items, indicate whether it is most likely reported on the balance sheet (B), the income statement (I), or the statement of stockholders' equity (SE).

a.	Accounts receivable	_____	*e.*	Notes payable	_____
b.	Prepaid insurance	_____	*f.*	Supplies expense	_____
c.	Net income	_____	*g.*	Land	_____
d.	Stockholders' equity	_____	*h.*	Supplies	_____

LO2-1, 3, 4, 5 Homework MBC

M2-23. Classifying Items in Financial Statements

For each of the following items, indicate whether it is most likely reported on the balance sheet (B), the income statement (I), or the statement of stockholders' equity (SE).

a.	Cash (year-end balance)	_____	*e.*	Dividends	_____
b.	Advertising expense	_____	*f.*	Accounts payable	_____
c.	Common stock	_____	*g.*	Inventory	_____
d.	Printing fee revenue	_____	*h.*	Equipment	_____

LO2-1, 5 Homework MBC

L Brands, Inc.
NYSE :: LB

M2-24. Determining Company Performance and Retained Earnings Using the Accounting Equation

Use your knowledge of accounting relations to complete the following table for L Brands, Inc. (All amounts are in $ millions.)

Fiscal Year Ending	February 2, 2019	February 1, 2020
Beginning retained earnings (deficit)	$(1,460)	$(1,482)
Net income (loss)	?	(366)
Dividends paid	(666)	?
Other net changes in retained earnings	0	(2)
Ending retained earnings (deficit)	$(1,482)	$(2,182)

M2-25. Analyzing the Effect of Transactions on the Balance Sheet LO2-1, 4 Homework MBC

Following the example in *a* below, indicate the effects of transactions *b* through *i* on assets, liabilities, and equity, including identifying the individual accounts affected.

a. Rendered legal services to clients for cash
ANSWER: Increase assets (Cash)
Increase equity (Service Revenues)

b. Purchased office supplies on account

c. Issued additional common stock in exchange for cash

d. Paid amount due on account for office supplies purchased in *b*

e. Borrowed cash (and signed a six-month note) from bank

f. Rendered legal services and billed clients

g. Paid cash to acquire a desk lamp for the office

h. Paid cash to cover interest on note payable to bank

i. Received invoice for this period's utilities

M2-26. Analyzing the Effect of Transactions on the Balance Sheet LO2-1, 4 Homework MBC

Following the example in *a* below, indicate the effects of transactions *b* through *i* on assets, liabilities, and equity, including identifying the individual accounts affected.

a. Paid cash to acquire a computer for use in office
ANSWER: Increase assets (Office Equipment)
Decrease assets (Cash)

b. Rendered services and billed client

c. Paid cash to cover rent for this period

d. Rendered services to client for cash

e. Received amount due from client in *b*

f. Purchased an office desk on account

g. Paid cash to cover this period's employee salaries

h. Paid cash to cover desk purchased in *f*

i. Declared and paid a cash dividend

M2-27. Constructing a Retained Earnings Reconciliation from Financial Data LO2-1, 5 Homework MBC

Johnson & Johnson
NYSE :: JNJ

Following is financial information from Johnson & Johnson for the year ended December 29, 2019. Prepare the 2019 fiscal-year retained earnings reconciliation for Johnson & Johnson ($ millions).

Retained earnings, Dec. 30, 2018	$106,216	Dividends	$9,917
Net earnings	15,119	Retained earnings, Dec. 29, 2019	?
Other retained earnings changes	(759)		

M2-28. Analyzing Transactions to Compute Net Income LO2-3, 4 Homework MBC

Guay Corp., a start-up company, provided services that were acceptable to its customers and billed those customers for $175,000 in 2021. However, Guay collected only $140,000 cash in 2021, and the remaining $35,000 of 2021 revenues were collected in 2022. Guay employees earned $100,000 in 2021 wages that were not paid until the first week of 2022. How much net income does Guay report for 2021? For 2022 (assuming no new transactions)?

M2-29. Analyzing Transactions Using the Financial Statement Effects Template (FSET) LO2-1, 2, 4 Homework MBC

Report the effects for each of the following independent transactions using the financial statement effects template. If no entry should be made, answer "No entry."

Transaction	Cash Asset	+	Noncash Assets	=	Liabil-ities	+	Contrib. Capital	+	Earned Capital	Revenues	–	Expenses	=	Net Income
a. Issue common stock for $30,000 cash.				=							–		=	
b. Pay $3,000 insurance in advance.				=							–		=	
c. Purchase computer equipment for $10,500 cash.				=							–		=	
d. Purchase and receive $19,500 of inventory on account (i.e., pay supplier later)				=							–		=	
e. Pay supplier of inventory in part (d)				=							–		=	

LO2-1, 2 **M2-30. Analyzing Transactions Using the Financial Statement Effects Template (FSET)** Report the effects for each of the following independent transactions using the financial statement effects template. If no entry should be made, answer "No entry."

Transaction	Cash Asset	+	Noncash Assets	=	Liabil-ities	+	Contrib. Capital	+	Earned Capital	Revenues	–	Expenses	=	Net Income
a. Borrow €28,500 from local bank.				=							–		=	
b. Pay €4,500 insurance premium for coverage for following year.				=							–		=	
c. Purchase vehicle for €48,000 cash.				=							–		=	
d. Purchase and receive €3,750 of office supplies on account (i.e., pay supplier later).				=							–		=	
e. Place order for €1,500 of additional supplies to be delivered next month.				=							–		=	

LO2-1, 2, 3, 4, 5 **M2-31. Analyzing Transactions Using the Financial Statement Effects Template (FSET)** Report the effects for each of the following independent transactions using the financial statement effects template. If no entry should be made, answer "No entry."

Transaction	Cash Asset	+	Noncash Assets	=	Liabil-ities	+	Contrib. Capital	+	Earned Capital	Revenues	–	Expenses	=	Net Income
a. Receive merchandise inventory costing $18,000, purchased with cash.				=							–		=	
b. Sell half of inventory in (a) for $15,000 on credit.				=							–		=	
c. Place order for $10,000 of additional merchandise inventory to be delivered next month.				=							–		=	

continued

continued from previous page

Transaction	Balance Sheet: Cash Asset	+	Noncash Assets	=	Liabilities	+	Contrib. Capital	+	Earned Capital	Income Statement: *Revenues*	–	*Expenses*	=	*Net Income*
d. Pay employee $8,000 for compensation earned during the month.				=							–		=	
e. Pay $14,000 rent for use of premises during the month (lease term < 12 months).				=							–		=	
f. Receive full payment from customer in part (b).				=							–		=	

M2-32. Journalizing Business Transactions LO2-6

Refer to the transactions in M2-31. Prepare journal entries for each of the transactions (*a*) through (*f*).

M2-33. Posting to T-Accounts LO2-6

Refer to the transactions in M2-31. Set up T-accounts for each of the accounts referenced by the transactions and post the amounts for each transaction to those T-accounts. (The T-accounts will not have opening balances.)

EXERCISES

E2-34. Constructing Balance Sheets and Computing Working Capital LO2-1, 7

The following balance sheet data are reported for Beaver, Inc., on May 31.

Accounts receivable	$27,450	Accounts payable	$ 7,800
Notes payable	30,000	Cash	18,300
Equipment	82,500	Common stock	63,750
Supplies	24,600	Retained earnings	?

Assume that on June 1, only the following two transactions occurred.

June 1 Purchased additional equipment costing $22,500, giving $3,000 cash and a $19,500 note payable.
Declared and paid a $10,500 cash dividend.

a. Prepare its balance sheet on May 31.
b. Prepare its balance sheet on June 1.
c. Calculate its net working capital on June 1. (Assume that Notes Payable are noncurrent.)

E2-35. Applying the Accounting Equation to Determine Missing Data LO2-1, 3, 5

For each of the four separate situations 1 through 4 that follow, compute the unknown amounts referenced by the letters *a* through *d* shown.

	1	2	3	4
Beginning				
Assets	$50,400	$21,600	$50,400	$ (d)
Liabilities	33,480	9,000	34,200	16,200
Ending				
Assets	54,000	46,800	61,200	72,000
Liabilities	31,140	(b)	27,000	34,200
During Year				
Common Stock Issued	3,600	8,100	(c)	6,300
Revenues	(a)	50,400	32,400	43,200
Expenses	15,300	37,800	19,800	30,600
Cash Dividends Paid	9,000	2,700	1,800	11,700

LO2-1, 5, 7 Homework MBC

E2-36. Preparing Balance Sheets, Computing Income, and Applying the Current and Quick Ratios
Balance sheet information for Lang Services at the end of Year 2 (the most recent year) and Year 1 is:

	December 31, Year 2	December 31, Year 1
Accounts receivable	$68,400	$52,500
Notes payable	5,400	4,800
Cash	30,000	24,000
Equipment	96,000	81,000
Supplies	14,100	12,600
Accounts payable	75,000	75,000
Stockholders' equity	?	?

a. Prepare Lang Services' balance sheet for December 31 of each year.

b. Lang Services raised $15,000 cash through issuing additional common stock early in Year 2, and it declared and paid a $51,000 cash dividend in December Year 2. Compute its net income or loss for Year 2.

c. Calculate the current ratio and quick ratio for Year 2.

d. Assume the industry average is 1.5 for the current ratio and 1.0 for the quick ratio. Comment on Lang's current and quick ratios relative to the industry.

LO2-1, 3, 5 Homework MBC

E2-37. Constructing Balance Sheets and Determining Income
Following is balance sheet information for Lynch Services at the end of Year 2 (the most recent year) and Year 1.

	December 31, Year 2	December 31, Year 1
Accounts payable	$ 9,000	$ 13,500
Cash	34,500	30,000
Accounts receivable	63,000	49,500
Land	60,000	60,000
Building	375,000	390,000
Equipment	64,500	67,500
Mortgage payable	135,000	150,000
Supplies	30,000	27,000
Common stock	330,000	330,000
Retained earnings	?	?

a. Prepare balance sheets on December 31 of each year.

b. The firm declared and paid a cash dividend of $15,000 in December Year 2. Compute its net income for Year 2.

LO2-1, 7 Homework MBC

E2-38. Constructing Balance Sheets and Applying the Current and Quick Ratios
The following balance sheet data are reported for Brownlee Catering on September 30.

Accounts receivable	$ 68,000	Accounts payable	$ 96,000
Notes payable	48,000	Cash	40,000
Equipment	136,000	Common stock	110,000
Supplies inventory	36,000	Retained earnings	?

Assume that on October 1, only the following two transactions occurred:

October 1 Purchased additional equipment costing $44,000, giving $12,000 cash and signing a $32,000 note payable.
Declared and paid a cash dividend of $12,000.

REQUIRED

a. Prepare Brownlee Catering's balance sheet at September 30.

b. Prepare the company's balance sheet at the close of business on October 1.

c. Calculate Brownlee's current and quick ratios on September 30 and October 1. (Assume that Notes Payable are noncurrent.)

d. The October 1 transactions have decreased Brownlee's current and quick ratios, reflecting a decline in liquidity. Identify two transactions that would increase the company's liquidity.

LO2-1, 3, 4 Homework MBC

E2-39. Constructing Financial Statements from Transaction Data
Yost Corporation commences operations at the beginning of January. It provides its services on credit and bills its customers $45,000 for January sales to be collected in February. Its employees

also earn January wages of $18,000 that are not paid until the first of February. Complete the following statements for the month-end of January.

Income Statement		Balance Sheet	
Sales	$	Cash	$ 12,000
Wages expense		Accounts receivable	
Net income (loss)	$	Total assets	$
		Wages payable	$
		Common stock	12,000
		Retained earnings	
		Total liabilities and equity	$

E2-40. Classifying Balance Sheet and Income Statement Accounts

LO2-1, 3

Homework MBC

Procter & Gamble NYSE :: PG

Following are selected accounts for The Procter & Gamble Company for June 30, 2020.

($ millions)	Amount	Classification
Net sales	$ 70,950	
Income tax expense	2,731	
Retained earnings	100,239	
Net earnings	13,103	
Property, plant and equipment (net)	20,692	
Selling, general and administrative expense	19,994	
Accounts receivable	4,178	
Total liabilities	73,822	
Stockholders' equity	46,878	
Cost of products sold	35,250	

a. Indicate the appropriate classification of each account as appearing in either its balance sheet (B) or its income statement (I).

b. Using the data, compute the amount that Procter & Gamble reported for total assets.

E2-41. Classifying Balance Sheet and Income Statement Accounts and Computing Current Ratio

LO2-1, 3, 7

Homework MBC

Shoprite Holdings Ltd JSE :: SHP

Shoprite Holdings Ltd is an African food retailer listed on the Johannesburg Stock Exchange. The following accounts are selected from its annual report for the fiscal year ended June 28, 2020. The amounts are in millions of South African rand.

(rand millions)	Amount	Classification
Sales of merchandise	R 156,855	
Depreciation and amortization	5,031	
Reserves (Retained earnings)	13,141	
Property, plant and equipment	18,265	
Cost of goods and services	119,323	
Trade and other payables	20,157	
Total assets	82,726	
Total equity	19,994	
Employee benefits expense	12,585	
Total noncurrent assets	42,789	
Total noncurrent liabilities	30,159	

a. Indicate the appropriate classification of each account as appearing in either its balance sheet (B) or its income statement (I).

b. Using the data, compute Shoprite's total liabilities on June 28, 2020.

c. Calculate Shoprite's current ratio as of June 28, 2020.

E2-42. Classifying Balance Sheet and Income Statement Accounts and Computing Quick Ratio

LO2-1, 3, 7

Homework MBC

El Puerto de Liverpool OTCMKTS :: ELPQF

El Puerto de Liverpool (Liverpool) is a large retailer in Mexico. The following accounts are selected from its annual report for the fiscal year ended December 31, 2019. The amounts are in thousands of Mexican pesos.

(pesos thousands)	Amount	Classification
Total revenue	$126,244,910	
Retained earnings	97,320,175	
Inventory	23,340,421	
Administration expenses	34,317,814	
Total assets	200,561,869	
Long-term debt	31,707,410	
Financing costs	6,512,917	
Total current assets	77,082,460	
Total stockholders' equity	109,074,538	
Prepaid expenses	1,804,877	
Total noncurrent liabilities	48,983,414	

a. Indicate the appropriate classification of each account as appearing in either its balance sheet (B) or its income statement (I).

b. Determine Liverpool's total liabilities and current liabilities as of December 31, 2019.

c. Calculate Liverpool's quick ratio as of December 31, 2019. (Assume that Liverpool only has five types of current assets—cash, marketable securities, accounts receivable, inventory, and prepaid expenses.)

LO2-1, 3 Homework MBC

Kimberly-Clark
NYSE :: KMB

E2-43. Classifying Balance Sheet and Income Statement Accounts and Computing Debt-to-Equity
Following are selected accounts for Kimberly-Clark Corporation for 2020.

($ millions)	Amount	Classification
Net sales	$19,140	
Cost of goods sold	12,318	
Retained earnings	7,567	
Net income	2,352	
Property, plant and equipment, net	8,042	
Marketing research and general expenses	3,632	
Accounts receivable, net	2,235	
Total liabilities	16,626	
Total stockholders' equity	897	

a. Indicate the appropriate classification of each account as appearing in either its balance sheet (B) or its income statement (I).

b. Using the data, compute its amounts for total assets and for total expenses.

c. Compute Kimberly-Clark's debt-to-equity ratio. (Debt-to-equity was defined in Chapter 1.)

LO2-1, 2, 3, 4 Homework MBC

E2-44. Analyzing Transactions Using the Financial Statement Effects Template (FSET)
Record the effect of each of the following independent transactions using the financial statements effects template provided. Confirm that Assets = Liabilities + Equity for each transaction.

	Balance Sheet									Income Statement				
Transaction	Cash Asset	+	Noncash Assets	=	Liabil-ities	+	Contrib. Capital	+	Earned Capital	*Revenues*	–	*Expenses*	=	*Net Income*
(1) Receive €75,000 in exchange for common stock.				=							–		=	
(2) Borrow €15,000 from bank.				=							–		=	
(3) Purchase €3,000 of supplies inventory on credit.				=							–		=	
(4) Receive €22,500 cash from customers for services provided.				=							–		=	

continued

continued from previous page

Transaction	Cash Asset	+	Noncash Assets	=	Liabil-ities	+	Contrib. Capital	+	Earned Capital	Revenues	−	Expenses	=	Net Income
(5) Pay €3,000 cash to supplier in transaction 3.				=							−		=	
(6) Receive order for future services with €5,250 advance payment.				=							−		=	
(7) Pay €7,500 cash dividend to shareholders.				=							−		=	
(8) Pay employees €9,000 cash for compensation earned.				=							−		=	
(9) Pay €750 cash for interest on loan in transaction 2.				=							−		=	
Totals				=							−		=	

E2-45. Recording Transactions Using Journal Entries and T-Accounts LO2-2, 6

Use the information in Exercise 2-44 to complete the following.

a. Prepare journal entries for each of the transactions (1) through (9).

b. Set up T-accounts for each of the accounts used in part *a* and post the journal entries to those T-accounts. (The T-accounts will not have opening balances.)

E2-46. Constructing Balance Sheets and Interpreting Liquidity Measures LO2-1, 7

The following balance sheet data are reported for Bettis Contractors on June 30.

Accounts payable	$ 7,120	Common stock	$80,000
Cash	11,760	Retained earnings	?
Supplies	24,400	Notes payable	24,000
Equipment	78,400	Accounts receivable	7,360
Land	20,000		

Assume that during the next two days only the following three transactions occurred:

July 1 Paid $4,000 cash toward the notes payable owed.
2 Purchased equipment for $8,000, paying $1,600 cash and a $6,400 note payable for the remaining balance.
2 Declared and paid a $4,400 cash dividend.

a. Prepare a balance sheet on June 30.

b. Prepare a balance sheet on July 2.

c. Calculate its current and quick ratios on June 30. (Notes payable is a noncurrent liability.)

d. Assume the industry average is 3.0 for the current ratio and 2.0 for the quick ratio. Comment on Bettis' current and quick ratios relative to the industry.

E2-47. Analyzing Transactions Using the Financial Statement Effects Template (FSET) LO2-1, 2, 3, 4

Record the effect of each of the following independent transactions using the financial statement effects template provided. Confirm that Assets = Liabilities + Equity.

	Balance Sheet									Income Statement				
Transaction	**Cash Asset**	+	**Noncash Assets**	=	**Liabilities**	+	**Contrib. Capital**	+	**Earned Capital**	***Revenues***	−	***Expenses***	=	***Net Income***
(1) Receive $80,000 cash in exchange for common stock.				=							−		=	
(2) Purchase $8,000 of inventory on credit.				=							−		=	
(3) Sell inventory for $12,000 on credit.				=							−		=	
(4) Record $8,000 for cost of inventory sold in 3.				=							−		=	
(5) Collect $12,000 cash from transaction 3.				=							−		=	
(6) Acquire $20,000 of equipment by signing a note.				=							−		=	
(7) Pay wages of $4,000 in cash.				=							−		=	
(8) Pay $20,000 on a note payable that came due.				=							−		=	
(9) Pay $8,000 cash dividend.				=							−		=	
Totals				=							−		=	

LO2-6 Homework MBC

E2-48. Recording Transactions Using Journal Entries and T-Accounts
Use the information in Exercise 2-47 to complete the following.

a. Prepare journal entries for each of the transactions 1 through 9.

b. Set up T-accounts for each of the accounts used in part *a* and post the journal entries to those T-accounts. (The T-accounts will not have opening balances.)

PROBLEMS

LO2-1, 3 Homework MBC

Comcast Corporation
NASDAQ :: CMCSA
Apple Inc.
NASDAQ :: AAPL
Nike, Inc.
NYSE :: NKE
Target Corporation
NYSE :: TGT
Harley-Davidson, Inc.
NYSE :: HOG

P2-49. Comparing Operating Characteristics Across Industries
Review the following selected income statement and balance sheet data for fiscal years ending in 2019.

($ millions)	Sales	Cost of Sales	Gross Profit	Net Income	Assets	Liabilities	Equity
Comcast Corporation....	$108,942	$ 34,400	$74,542	$13,323	$263,414	$178,168	$85,246
Apple Inc.	260,174	161,782	98,392	55,256	338,516	248,028	90,488
Nike Inc...............	39,117	21,643	17,474	4,029	23,717	14,677	9,040
Target Corporation......	78,112	54,864	23,248	3,281	42,779	30,946	11,833
Harley-Davidson Inc.	4,573	3,230	1,343	424	10,528	8,724	1,804

REQUIRED

a. Compare and discuss how these companies finance their operations.

b. Which companies report the highest ratio of income to assets (net income/total assets)? Suggest a reason for this result.

c. Which companies have the highest estimated ROE? Is this result a surprise? Explain.

LO2-1, 3 Homework MBC

HP Inc.
NYSE :: HPQ

P2-50. Comparing Operating Characteristics Within an Industry
Selected data from HP Inc. on October 31, 2020, follow.

($ millions)	Sales	Cost of Sales	Gross Profit	Net Income	Assets	Liabilities	Equity
HP Inc.	$56,639	$46,202	$10,437	$2,844	$34,681	$36,909	$(2,228)

REQUIRED

a. Using the data for **Apple Inc.** in P2-49, compare and discuss the two companies on the basis of how they finance their operations.

b. Which company reports the higher ratio of income to assets (net income/total assets)? Suggest a reason for this result.

c. Which firm has the higher gross margin (gross profit as a percentage of sales)? What factors might account for the difference?

Apple inc.
NASDAQ :: AAPL

P2-51. Comparing Operating Characteristics Within an Industry

LO2-1, 3

Homework MBC

Review the following selected income statement and balance sheet data for **Verizon Communications Inc.** as of December 31, 2019.

Verizon Communications Inc.
NYSE :: VZ

($ millions)	Sales	Cost of Sales	Gross Profit	Net Income	Assets	Liabilities	Equity
Verizon Communications Inc. . . .	$131,868	$54,726	$77,142	$19,788	$291,727	$228,892	$62,835

REQUIRED

a. Using the data for **Comcast Corporation** in P2-49, compare and discuss how Verizon and Comcast finance their operations.

b. Which company reports the higher ratio of income to assets (net income/total assets)? Suggest a reason for this result.

Comcast Corporation
NASDAQ :: CMCSA

P2-52. Comparing Operating Structure Across Industries

LO2-1, 7

Homework MBC

Review the following selected income statement and balance sheet data from the fiscal years ending in 2020.

($ millions)	Current Assets	Non-current Assets	Total Assets	Current Liab.	Non-current Liab.	Total Liab.	Equity
3M*	$ 14,982	$ 32,362	$ 47,344	$ 7,948	$ 26,465	$ 34,413	$12,931
Abercrombie & Fitch**	1,265	2,284	3,549	815	1,663	2,478	1,071
Apple†	143,713	180,175	323,888	105,392	153,157	258,549	65,339

* Manufacturer of consumer and business products
** Retailer of name-brand apparel at premium prices
† Computer company

3M Company
NYSE :: MMM
Abercrombie & Fitch Co.
NYSE :: ANF
Apple Inc.
NYSE :: AAPL

REQUIRED

a. Compare and discuss how these companies finance their operations.

b. Which company has the greatest net working capital? Which company has the highest current ratio? Do you have concerns about any firm's net working capital position? Explain.

P2-53. Preparing a Balance Sheet, Computing Net Income, and Understanding Equity Transactions

LO2-1, 5

Homework MBC

At the beginning of the year, Barth Company reported the following balance sheet.

Assets		Liabilities and Equity	
Cash	$ 7,200	Accounts payable	$18,000
Accounts receivable	22,050	Equity	
Equipment	15,000	Common stock	71,250
Land	75,000	Retained earnings	30,000
Total assets	$119,250	Total liabilities and equity	$119,250

REQUIRED

a. At the end of the year, Barth Company reported the following assets and liabilities: Cash, $13,200; Accounts Receivable, $27,600; Equipment, $13,500; Land, $75,000; and Accounts Payable, $11,250. Prepare a year-end balance sheet for Barth. (*Hint:* Report equi*Hint:*ty as a single total.)

b. Assuming that Barth did not issue any common stock during the year but paid $18,000 cash in dividends, what was its net income or net loss for the year?

c. Assuming that Barth issued an additional $20,250 common stock early in the year but paid $31,500 cash in dividends before the end of the year, what was its net income or net loss for the year?

LO2-1, 3 Homework MBC

Abercrombie & Fitch Co. NYSE :: ANF
Nordstrom, Inc. NYSE :: JWN

P2-54. Analyzing and Interpreting the Financial Performance of Competitors

Abercrombie & Fitch Co. and Nordstrom, Inc., are major retailers that concentrate in the higher-end clothing lines. Following are selected data from their 2019 fiscal-year ended February 1, 2020, financial statements:

($ millions)	ANF	JWN
Total liabilities and equity	$3,549	$ 9,737
Net income	45	496
Net sales	3,623	15,132
Total liabilities	2,478	8,758

REQUIRED

a. What is the total amount of assets at (1) ANF and (2) JWN? What are the total expenses for each company (1) in dollars and (2) as a percentage of sales?

b. What is the return on equity (ROE) for (1) ANF and (2) JWN? ANF's total equity at the beginning of 2019 is $1,219 million and JWN's beginning 2019 equity is $873 million. (ROE was defined in Chapter 1.)

LO2-1, 7 Homework MBC

Kimberly-Clark Corp NYSE :: KMB

P2-55. Analyzing Balance Sheet Numbers from Incomplete Data and Interpreting Liquidity Measures

Selected balance sheet amounts for Kimberly-Clark Corp, a consumer products company, for four recent years follow:

($ millions)	Current Assets	Noncurrent Assets	Total Assets	Current Liabilities	Noncurrent Liabilities	Total Liabilities	Equity
2017	$?	$ 9,940	$15,151	$5,858	$8,350	$14,208	$?
2018	5,041	?	14,518	6,536	?	?	18
2019	5,057	10,226	?	?	8,141	?	223
2020	?	12,349	17,523	6,443	?	16,626	?

REQUIRED

a. Compute the missing balance sheet amounts for each of the four years shown.

b. What types of accounts would you expect to be included in current assets? In noncurrent assets?

c. Calculate Kimberly-Clark's working capital and current ratio for 2019 and 2020.

d. Assume that the industry average is 2.0 for the current ratio. Comment on Kimberly-Clark's liquidity measures relative to the industry.

LO2-1, 7 Homework MBC

Macy's, Inc. NASDAQ:: M

P2-56. Analyzing and Interpreting Balance Sheet Data and Interpreting Liquidity Measures

Selected balance sheet amounts for Macy's, Inc., a retail company, for four recent fiscal years ending in the following calendar years:

($ millions)	Current Assets	Noncurrent Assets	Total Assets	Current Liabilities	Noncurrent Liabilities	Total Liabilities	Equity
2017	$7,626	$12,225	$?	$5,647	$9,882	$15,529	$?
2018	?	11,937	19,381	?	8,645	13,720	?
2019	7,445	?	19,194	5,232	?	12,758	6,436
2020	6,810	14,362	?	5,750	?	14,795	?

REQUIRED

a. Compute the missing balance sheet amounts for each of the four years shown.

b. What asset category do you expect to constitute the majority of the company's current assets?

c. Calculate Macy's current ratio for fiscal years 2017 and 2020.

d. If the industry average debt-to-asset ratio is 0.4 and the industry average current ratio for 2020 is 1.8, how would you characterize Macy's financial condition?

P2-57. Analyzing Transactions Using the Financial Statement Effects Template and Preparing an Income Statement (FSET)

LO2-1, 2, 3, 4

Homework MBC

On December 1, R. Lambert formed Lambert Services, which provides career and vocational counseling services to graduating college students. The following transactions took place during December, and company accounts include the following: Cash, Accounts Receivable, Land, Accounts Payable, Notes Payable, Common Stock, Retained Earnings, Counseling Services Revenue, Supplies Expense, Advertising Expense, Interest Expense, Salary Expense, and Utilities Expense.

1. Raised $21,000 cash through common stock issuance.
2. Paid $2,250 cash for supplies and training materials.
3. Received $1,500 invoice for December advertising expenses.
4. Borrowed $45,000 cash from bank and signed note payable for that amount.
5. Received $3,600 cash for counseling services rendered.
6. Billed clients $20,400 for counseling services rendered.
7. Paid $6,600 cash for secretary salary.
8. Paid $1,110 cash for December utilities.
9. Declared and paid a $2,700 cash dividend.
10. Purchased land for $39,000 cash to use for its own facilities.
11. Paid $300 cash to bank as December interest expense on note payable.

REQUIRED

a. Report the effects for each of the separate transactions 1 through 11 using the financial statement effects template. Total all columns and prove that (1) assets equal liabilities plus equity on December 31, and (2) revenues less expenses equal net income for December.

b. Prepare an income statement for the month of December.

P2-58. Recording Transactions in Journal Entries and T-Accounts

LO2-6

Homework MBC

Use the information in Problem 2-57 to complete the following requirements.

REQUIRED

a. Prepare journal entries for each of the transactions 1 through 11.

b. Set up T-accounts for each of the accounts used in part *a* and post the journal entries to those T-accounts.

P2-59. Analyzing and Interpreting Balance Sheet Data and Interpreting Liquidity Measures

LO2-1, 7

Homework MBC

Apple Inc.
NYSE :: AAPL

Selected balance sheet amounts for Apple Inc., a retail company, for four recent fiscal years follow:

($ millions)	Current Assets	Non-current Assets	Total Assets	Current Liabilities	Non-current Liabilities	Total Liabilities	Stockholders' Equity
2017	$128,645	$?	$375,319	$?	$140,458	$241,272	$134,047
2018	131,339	234,386	?	116,866	?	258,578	107,147
2019	162,819	175,697	?	?	142,310	248,028	?
2020	?	180,175	323,888	105,392	?	258,549	65,339

REQUIRED

a. Compute the missing balance sheet amounts for each of the four years shown.

b. What asset category would you expect to constitute the majority of Apple's current assets? Of its long-term assets?

c. Is the company conservatively financed; that is, is it financed by a greater proportion of equity than of debt?

d. Calculate the current ratio for 2017 and 2020.

e. Assume the industry average is 1.0 for the current ratio. Comment on Apple's current ratio relative to the industry.

P2-60. Analyzing Balance Sheet Numbers from Incomplete Data and Interpreting Liquidity Measures

LO2-1, 7

Homework MBC

Alibaba Group Holding Ltd
NYSE :: BABA

Selected balance sheet amounts for Alibaba Group Holding Ltd, a China-based online and mobile commerce company, for three recent fiscal years ending March 31 follow:

(millions of US $)	Current Assets	Non-current Assets	Total Assets	Current Liabilities	Non-current Liabilities	Total Liabilities	Equity
2018	$40,949	$?	$?	$21,651	$?	$44,270	$70,056
2019	?	103,529	143,801	?	22,176	53,120	90,681
2020	?	120,052	185,429	34,159	28,325	?	?

REQUIRED

a. Compute the missing balance sheet amounts for each of the three years shown.

b. What asset category do you expect to constitute the majority of the company's current assets?

c. Calculate Alibaba's current ratio for fiscal years 2018 and 2020.

d. Calculate net working capital for 2018 and 2020.

LO2-3 Homework MBC

P2-61. Analyzing and Interpreting Income Statement Data

Nike, Inc.
NYSE :: NKE

Selected income statement information for Nike, Inc., a manufacturer of athletic footwear, for four recent fiscal years ending May 31 follows.

($ millions)	Revenues	Cost of Goods Sold	Gross Profit	Operating Expenses	Operating Income	Other Expenses	Net Income
2017	$34,350	$19,038	$?	$10,563	$4,749	$509	$?
2018	36,397	?	15,956	11,511	4,445	?	1,933
2019	?	21,643	17,474	12,702	4,772	743	?
2020	37,403	21,162	16,241	?	3,115	?	2,539

REQUIRED

a. Compute the missing amounts for each of the four years shown.

b. Compute the gross profit margin (gross profit/sales) for each of the four years and comment on its level and any trends that are evident.

c. What would you expect to be the major cost categories constituting its operating expenses?

LO2-1, 2, 3, 4 Homework MBC

P2-62. Analyzing Transactions Using the Financial Statement Effects Template and Preparing an Income Statement (FSET)

On June 1, a group of pilots in Melbourne, Australia, formed Outback Flights by issuing common stock for $25,000 cash. The group then leased several amphibious aircraft and docking facilities, equipping them to transport campers and hunters to outpost camps owned by various resorts in remote parts of Australia. The following transactions occurred during June, and company accounts include the following: Cash, Accounts Receivable, Prepaid Insurance, Accounts Payable, Common Stock, Retained Earnings, Flight Services Revenue, Rent Expense, Entertainment Expense, Advertising Expense, Insurance Expense, Wages Expense, and Fuel Expense.

1. Issued common stock for $25,000 cash.
2. Paid $2,400 cash for June rent of aircraft, dockage, and dockside office. The leases are all for less than 12 months—the company is evaluating the business model before they purchase.
3. Received $800 invoice for the cost of a reception to entertain resort owners in June.
4. Paid $450 cash for June advertising in various sport magazines.
5. Paid $900 cash for insurance premium for July.
6. Rendered flight services for various groups for $11,350 cash.
7. Billed client $1,450 for transporting personnel, and billed various firms for $6,500 in flight services.
8. Paid $750 cash to cover accounts payable.
9. Received $6,600 on account from clients in transaction 7.
10. Paid $8,000 cash to cover June wages.
11. Received $1,750 invoice for the cost of fuel used during June.
12. Declared and paid a $1,500 cash dividend.

REQUIRED

a. Report the effects for each of the separate transactions 1 through 12 using the financial statement effects template. Total all columns and prove that (1) assets equal liabilities plus equity on June 30 and (2) revenues less expenses equal net income for June.

b. Prepare an income statement for the month of June.

P2-63. Recording Transactions in Journal Entries and T-Accounts
LO2-6
Homework MBC

Use the information in Problem 2-62 to complete the following requirements.

REQUIRED

a. Prepare journal entries for each of the transactions 1 through 12.

b. Set up T-accounts for each of the accounts used in part *a* and post the journal entries to those T-accounts.

P2-64. Analyzing and Interpreting Income Statement Numbers from Incomplete Data
LO2-3
Homework MBC
Starbucks Corporation
NASDAQ :: SBUX

Selected income statement information for **Starbucks Corporation**, a coffee-related restaurant chain, for four recent fiscal years follows.

($ millions)	Revenues	Cost of Sales	Gross Profit	Operating Expenses	Operating Income	Other Expenses	Net Income
2017	$?	$7,065.8	$15,321.0	$?	$4,134.7	$1,249.8	$?
2018	24,719.5	?	16,788.8	?	?	(634.7)	4,518.0
2019	26,508.6	8,526.9	?	13,903.8	4,077.9	?	3,594.6
2020	?	7,694.9	15,823.1	14,261.4	1,561.7	637.0	?

REQUIRED

a. Compute the missing amounts for each of the four years shown.

b. Compute the gross profit margin (gross profit/sales) for each of the four years and comment on its level and any trends that are evident.

c. What would you expect to be the major cost categories constituting its operating expenses?

P2-65. Analyzing, Reconstructing, and Interpreting Income Statement Data
LO2-3
Homework MBC
Siemens AG
OTCMKTS :: SIEGY

Selected income statement information for **Siemens AG**, a global technology company, for four fiscal years follows:

(€ millions)	Revenues	Cost of Goods Sold	Gross Profit	Operating Expenses	Operating Income	Other Expense	Net Income
2017	82,863	57,820	25,043	?	7,571	?	6,094
2018	83,044	?	24,863	18,677	?	?	6,120
2019	?	36,848	21,635	15,343	6,292	644	?
2020	57,139	36,953	?	15,147	?	839	4,200

REQUIRED

a. Compute the missing amounts for each of the four years shown.

b. Per the annual report, the company engaged in a restructuring effort effective in 2019 (including changes in reportable segments). Assuming all else constant, what were the effects of the restructuring on the firm's gross profit margin (gross profit/sales)?

c. What would we expect to be the major cost categories constituting Siemens' operating expenses?

P2-66. Preparing the Income Statement, Statement of Stockholders' Equity, and Balance Sheet
LO2-1, 3, 5
Homework MBC

The records of Geyer, Inc., show the following information after all transactions are recorded for the year.

Notes payable	$ 8,000	Supplies	$12,200
Service fees earned	135,200	Cash	29,600
Supplies expense	19,400	Advertising expense	3,400
Insurance expense	3,000	Salaries expense	60,000
Miscellaneous expense	400	Rent expense (short-term lease)	15,000
Common stock (beg. year)	8,000	Retained earnings (beg. year)	12,400
Accounts payable	3,600		

In addition, Geyer, Inc., raised $2,800 cash through the issuance of additional common stock during this year, and it declared and paid a $27,000 cash dividend near year-end.

REQUIRED

a. Prepare its income statement for the year.

b. Prepare its statement of stockholders' equity for the year.

c. Prepare its balance sheet at December 31.

LO2-1, 2, 3, 4, 5 **P2-67. Analyzing Transactions Using the Financial Statement Effects Template and Preparing Financial Statements (FSET)**

Homework MBC

Schrand Aerobics, Inc., specializes in offering aerobics classes. On January 1, its beginning account balances are as follows: Cash, $10,000; Accounts Receivable, $10,400; Equipment, $0; Notes Payable, $5,000; Accounts Payable, $2,000; Common Stock, $11,000; Retained Earnings, $2,400; Services Revenue, $0; Insurance Expense, $0; Advertising Expense, $0; Wages Expense, $0; Utilities Expense, $0; Interest Expense, $0. The following transactions occurred during January.

1. Paid $1,200 cash toward accounts payable.
2. Paid $7,200 cash for insurance.
3. Billed clients $23,000 for January classes.
4. Received $1,000 invoice from supplier for T-shirts given to January class members as an advertising promotion.
5. Collected $20,000 cash from clients previously billed for services rendered.
6. Paid $4,800 cash for employee wages.
7. Received $1,360 invoice for January utilities expense.
8. Paid $40 cash to bank as January interest on notes payable.
9. Declared and paid $1,800 cash dividend to stockholders.
10. Paid $8,000 cash on January 31 to purchase sound equipment.

REQUIRED

a. Using the financial statement effects template, enter January 1 beginning amounts in the appropriate columns of the first row. (*Hint:* Beginning balances for columns can include amounts from more than one account.)

b. Report the effects for each of the separate transactions 1 through 10 in the financial statement effects template set up in part *a*. Total all columns and prove that (1) assets equal liabilities plus equity at January 31, and (2) revenues less expenses equal net income for January.

c. Prepare its income statement for January.

d. Prepare its statement of stockholders' equity for January.

e. Prepare its balance sheet at January 31.

LO2-6 **P2-68. Recording Transactions in Journal Entries and T-Accounts**

Homework MBC

Use the information in Problem 2-67 to complete the following requirements.

REQUIRED

a. Prepare journal entries for each of the transactions 1 through 10.

b. Set up T-accounts, including beginning balances, for each of the accounts used in part *a*. Post the journal entries to those T-accounts.

LO2-1, 2, 3, 4, 5 **P2-69. Analyzing Transactions Using the Financial Statement Effects Template and Preparing Financial Statements (FSET)**

Homework MBC

Kross, Inc., provides appraisals and feasibility studies. On January 1, its beginning account balances are as follows: Cash, $12,100; Accounts Receivable, $26,700; Notes Payable, $4,500; Accounts Payable, $1,100; Retained Earnings, $22,400; and Common Stock, $10,800. The following transactions occurred during January, and company accounts include the following: Cash, Accounts Receivable, Vehicles, Accounts Payable, Notes Payable, Services Revenue, Rent Expense, Interest Expense, Salary Expense, Utilities Expense, Common Stock, and Retained Earnings.

1. Paid $1,800 cash for January rent (short-term lease < 12 months).
2. Received $15,900 cash on customers' accounts.
3. Paid $900 cash toward accounts payable.
4. Received $2,900 cash for services performed for customers.
5. Borrowed $9,000 cash from bank and signed note payable for that amount.
6. Billed the city $11,200 for services performed, and billed other credit customers for $3,500 in services.
7. Paid $7,200 cash for salary of assistant.
8. Received $800 invoice for January utilities expense.
9. Declared and paid a $10,800 cash dividend.
10. Paid $17,700 cash to acquire a vehicle (on January 31) for business use.
11. Paid $100 cash to bank for January interest on notes payable.

REQUIRED

a. Using the financial statement effects template, enter January 1 beginning amounts in the appropriate columns of the first row. (*Hint:* Beginning balances for columns can include amounts from more than one account.)

b. Report the effects for each of the separate transactions 1 through 11 in the financial statement effects template set up in part *a*. Total all columns and prove that (1) assets equal liabilities plus equity on January 31, and (2) revenues less expenses equal net income for January.

c. Prepare its income statement for January.

d. Prepare its statement of stockholders' equity for January.

e. Prepare its balance sheet at January 31.

P2-70. Recording Transactions in Journal Entries and T-Accounts

LO2-6

Homework MBC

Use the information in Problem 2-69 to complete the following requirements.

REQUIRED

a. Prepare journal entries for each of the transactions 1 through 11.

b. Set up T-accounts, including beginning balances, for each of the accounts used in part *a*. Post the journal entries to those T-accounts.

CASES AND PROJECTS

C2-71. Constructing Financial Statements from Cash Data

LO2-1, 3, 4, 5

Homework MBC

Sarah Penney operates the Wildlife Picture Gallery, selling original art and signed prints received on consignment (rather than purchased) from recognized wildlife artists throughout the country. The firm receives a 30% commission on all art sold and remits 70% of the sales price to the artists. All art is sold on a strictly cash basis.

Sarah began the business on March 1. The business received a $15,000 loan from a relative of Sarah to help her get started; it took on a note payable agreeing to pay the loan back in one year. No interest is being charged on the loan, but the relative does want to receive a set of financial statements each month. On April 1, Sarah asks for your help in preparing the statements for the first month.

Sarah has carefully kept the firm's checking account up to date and provides you with the following complete listing of the cash receipts and cash disbursements for March.

Cash Receipts	
Original investment by Sarah Penney	$ 9,750
Loan from relative	15,000
Sales of art	142,500
Total cash receipts	167,250
Cash Disbursements	
Payments to artists for sales made	81,000
Payment of March rent for gallery space	1,350
Payment of March wages to staff	7,350
Payment of airfare for personal vacation of Sarah (vacation will be in April)	750
Total cash disbursements	90,450
Cash balance, March 31	$ 76,800

Sarah also gives you the following documents she has received:

1. A $525 invoice for March utilities; payment is due by April 15.
2. A $2,550 invoice from Careful Express for the shipping of artwork sold in March; payment is due by April 10.
3. Sarah signed a short-term lease for the gallery space; as an incentive to sign the lease, the landlord reduced the first month's rent by 25%; the monthly rent starting in April is $1,800.

In your discussions with Sarah, she tells you that she has been so busy that she is behind in sending artists their share of the sales proceeds. She plans to catch up within the next week.

REQUIRED

From the above information, prepare the following financial statements for Wildlife Picture Gallery: (*a*) income statement for the month of March; (*b*) statement of stockholders' equity for the month of March; and (*c*) balance sheet as of March 31.

LO2-3 **C2-72. Financial Records and Ethical Behavior**

Andrea Frame and her supervisor are sent on an out-of-town assignment by their employer. At the supervisor's suggestion, they stay at the Spartan Inn (across the street from the Luxury Inn). After three days of work, they settle their lodging bills and leave. On the return trip, the supervisor gives Andrea what appears to be a copy of a receipt from the Luxury Inn for three nights of lodging. Actually, the supervisor indicates that he prepared the Luxury Inn receipt on his office computer and plans to complete his expense reimbursement request using the higher lodging costs from the Luxury Inn.

REQUIRED

What are the ethical considerations that Andrea faces when she prepares her expense reimbursement request?

SOLUTIONS TO REVIEW PROBLEMS

Review 2-1

1. A	2. C	3. B	4. E	5. B	6. E	7. X	8. B	9. E	10. B
11. B	12. A	13. B	14. C	15. A	16. D	17. A	18. A	19. E	20. C

Review 2-2

	Balance Sheet									Income Statement				
Transaction	Cash Asset	+	Noncash Assets	=	Liabil-ities	+	Contrib. Capital	+	Earned Capital	*Revenues*	–	*Expenses*	=	*Net Income*
(a) Issue common stock for $20,000.	+20,000 Cash			=			+20,000 Common Stock				–		=	
(b) Purchase $8,000 of inventory on credit.			+8,000 Inventory	=	+8,000 Accounts Payable						–		=	
(c) Purchase equipment for $10,000 cash.	–10,000 Cash		+10,000 Equipment	=							–		=	
(d) Pay suppliers $3,000 cash.	–3,000 Cash			=	–3,000 Accounts Payable						–		=	
Totals	+7,000		+18,000	=	+5,000		+20,000							
	Assets			=	Liabilities	+	Equity							

Review 2-3

SCHAEFER'S PHARMACY, INC.
Income Statement
For Year Ended December 31

Revenues		$45,000
Expenses		
Cost of goods sold	$20,000	
Wages expense	8,000	
Insurance expense	5,000	
Utilities expense	2,000	
Other expenses	4,000	
Total expenses		39,000
Net income		$ 6,000

Review 2-4

a.

SCHAEFER'S PHARMACY, INC.
Retained Earnings Reconciliation
For Year Ended December 31

Retained earnings, Jan. 1	$25,000
Add: Net income	6,000
Less: Dividends	(1,000)
Retained earnings, Dec. 31	$30,000

b.

SCHAEFER'S PHARMACY, INC.
Retained Earnings Reconciliation
For Year Ended December 31

Retained earnings, Jan. 1	$25,000
Add: Net income	5,250
Less: Dividends	(1,000)
Retained earnings, Dec. 31	$29,250

Review 2-5

a.

SCHAEFER'S PHARMACY, INC.
Balance Sheet
December 31

Cash	$ 3,000	Accounts payable	$ 7,500
Accounts receivable	12,000		
Inventory	26,000		
Office equipment	32,250	Common stock	45,750
Land	10,000	Retained earnings	30,000
Total assets	$83,250	Total liabilities and equity	$83,250

b.

SCHAEFER'S PHARMACY, INC.
Statement of Stockholders' Equity
For Year Ended December 31

	Contributed Capital	Earned Capital	Total Equity
Balance, January 1	$45,750	$25,000	$70,750
Common stock issued	—	—	0
Net income	—	6,000	6,000
Cash dividends	—	(1,000)	(1,000)
Balance, December 31	$45,750	$30,000	$75,750

Review 2-6

a.

Transaction	Balance Sheet: Cash Asset	+ Noncash Assets	= Liabilities	+ Contrib. Capital	+ Earned Capital	Income Statement: Revenues	− Expenses	= Net Income
(1) Issue common stock for cash.	+15,500 Cash			+15,500 Common Stock				
(2) Purchase office equipment on account.		+10,400 Office Equipment	+6,000 Accounts Payable +4,400 Note Payable					
(3) Pay rent expense.	−700 Cash				−700 Retained Earnings		+700 Rent Expense	−700
(4) Pay for subscriptions in advance.	−9,600 Cash	+9,600 Prepaid Subscriptions						
(5) Bill clients for services rendered.		+11,300 Accounts Receivable			+11,300 Retained Earnings	+11,300 Fees Earned		+11,300
(6) Pay toward accounts payable.	−1,000 Cash		−1,000 Accounts Payable					
(7) Pay salary for assistant.	−2,800 Cash				−2,800 Retained Earnings		+2,800 Salaries Expense	−2,800
(8) Collect cash from clients billed earlier.	+9,400 Cash	−9,400 Accounts Receivable						
(9) Recognize utility expense.			+180 Accounts Payable		−180 Retained Earnings		+180 Utilities Expense	−180
(10) Pay cash dividends.	−1,500 Cash				−1,500 Retained Earnings			
(11) Pay cash for interest.	−225 Cash				−225 Retained Earnings		+225 Interest Expense	−225
Totals	9,075	+ 21,900	= 9,580	+ 15,500	+ 5,895	11,300	− 3,905	= 7,395
	Assets		= Liabilities	+ Equity				

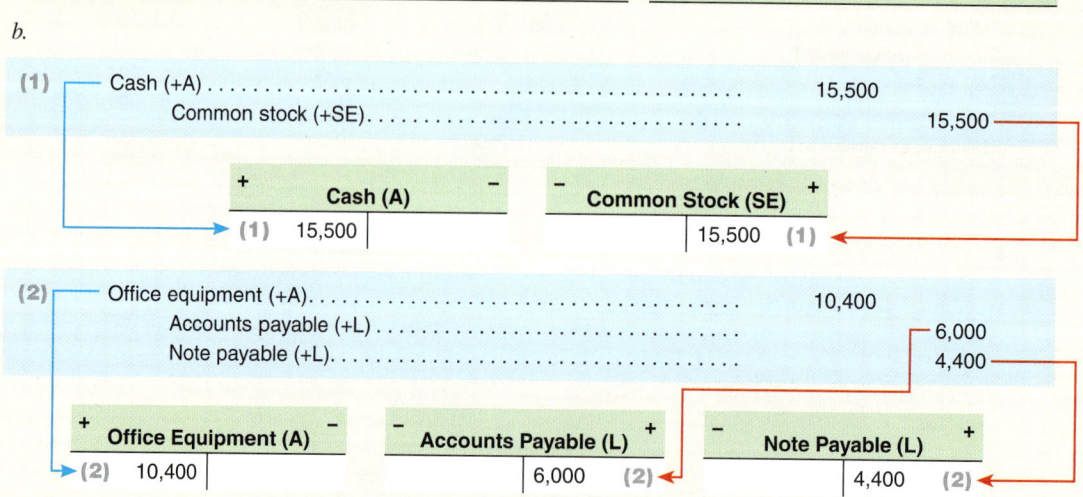

b.

(1)

	Debit	Credit
Cash (+A)	15,500	
Common stock (+SE)		15,500

+ Cash (A) −		− Common Stock (SE) +	
(1) 15,500			15,500 (1)

(2)

	Debit	Credit
Office equipment (+A)	10,400	
Accounts payable (+L)		6,000
Note payable (+L)		4,400

+ Office Equipment (A) −		− Accounts Payable (L) +		− Note Payable (L) +	
(2) 10,400			6,000 (2)		4,400 (2)

continued

continued from previous page

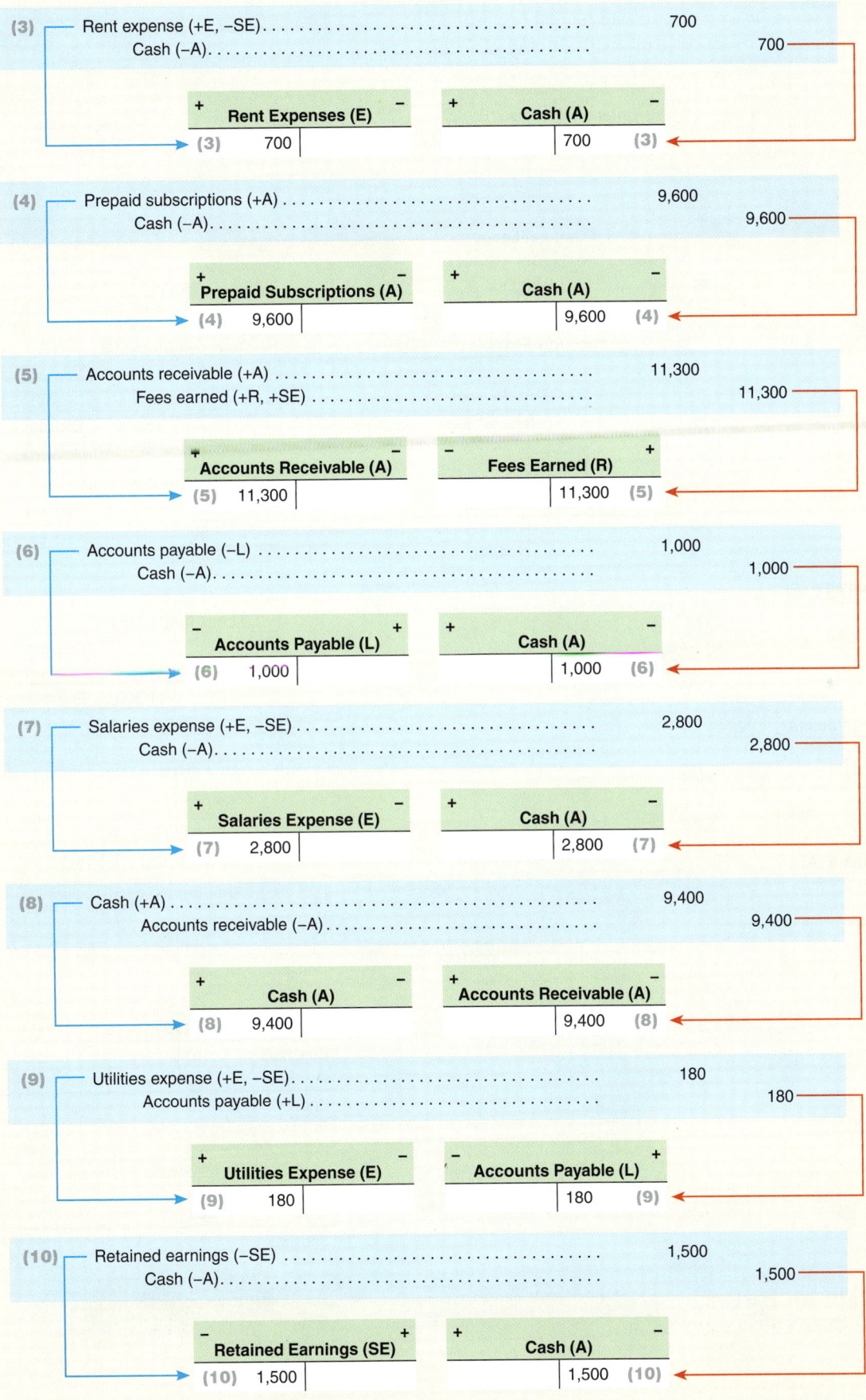

(3)	Rent expense (+E, −SE)	700	
	Cash (−A)		700

+ Rent Expenses (E) −		+ Cash (A) −	
(3) 700			700 (3)

(4)	Prepaid subscriptions (+A)	9,600	
	Cash (−A)		9,600

+ Prepaid Subscriptions (A) −		+ Cash (A) −	
(4) 9,600			9,600 (4)

(5)	Accounts receivable (+A)	11,300	
	Fees earned (+R, +SE)		11,300

+ Accounts Receivable (A) −		− Fees Earned (R) +	
(5) 11,300			11,300 (5)

(6)	Accounts payable (−L)	1,000	
	Cash (−A)		1,000

− Accounts Payable (L) +		+ Cash (A) −	
(6) 1,000			1,000 (6)

(7)	Salaries expense (+E, −SE)	2,800	
	Cash (−A)		2,800

+ Salaries Expense (E) −		+ Cash (A) −	
(7) 2,800			2,800 (7)

(8)	Cash (+A)	9,400	
	Accounts receivable (−A)		9,400

+ Cash (A) −		+ Accounts Receivable (A) −	
(8) 9,400			9,400 (8)

(9)	Utilities expense (+E, −SE)	180	
	Accounts payable (+L)		180

+ Utilities Expense (E) −		− Accounts Payable (L) +	
(9) 180			180 (9)

(10)	Retained earnings (−SE)	1,500	
	Cash (−A)		1,500

− Retained Earnings (SE) +		+ Cash (A) −	
(10) 1,500			1,500 (10)

continued

continued from previous page

		Debit	Credit
(11)	Interest Expense (+E, −SE)	225	
	Cash (−A).		255

+ Interest Expense (E) −

(11)	225		

+ Cash (A) −

		225	(11)

c.

General Ledger

Assets = Liabilities + Equity

Assets

+ Cash (A) −

Beg. bal.	0		
(1)	15,500	700	(3)
(8)	9,400	9,600	(4)
		1,000	(6)
		2,800	(7)
		1,500	(10)
		225	(11)
End. bal.	9,075		

+ Accounts Receivable (A) −

Beg. bal.	0		
(5)	11,300	9,400	(8)
End. bal.	1,900		

+ Prepaid Subscriptions (A) −

Beg. bal.	0		
(4)	9,600		
End. bal.	9,600		

+ Office Equipment (A) −

Beg. bal.	0		
(2)	10,400		
End. bal.	10,400		

Liabilities

− Accounts Payable (L) +

		0	Beg. bal.
(6)	1,000	6,000	(2)
		180	(9)
		5,180	End. bal.

− Note Payable (L) +

		0	Beg. bal.
		4,400	(2)
		4,400	End. bal.

Equity

− Common Stock (SE) +

		0	Beg. bal.
		15,500	(1)
		15,500	End. bal.

− Retained Earnings (SE) +

		0	Beg. bal.
(10)	1,500		
End. bal.	1,500		

− Fees Earned (R) +

		0	Beg. bal.
		11,300	(5)
		11,300	End. bal.

+ Salaries Expense (E) −

Beg. bal.	0		
(7)	2,800		
End. bal.	2,800		

+ Rent Expense (E) −

Beg. bal.	0		
(3)	700		
End. bal.	700		

+ Utilities Expense (E) −

Beg. bal.	0		
(9)	180		
End. bal.	180		

+ Interest Expense (E) −

Beg. bal.	0		
(11)	225		
End. bal.	225		

Assets = $30,975 = **Liabilities = $9,580** + **Equity = $21,395**

Review 2-7

a. Working capital: Current assets ($9,075 + $1,900 + $9,600) – Current liabilities ($5,180) = $15,395

b. Current ratio: $20,575/$5,180 = 4.0

c. Quick ratio: ($9,075 + $1,900)/$5,180 = 2.1

Chapter 3

Adjusting Accounts for Financial Statements

LEARNING OBJECTIVES

LO3-1 Analyze transactions and review the process of journalizing and posting transactions.

LO3-2 Describe the adjusting process and illustrate adjusting entries.

LO3-3 Prepare financial statements from adjusted accounts.

LO3-4 Describe the process of closing temporary accounts.

LO3-5 Analyze changes in balance sheet accounts.

Road Map

LO	Learning Objective | Topics	Page	eLecture	Review	Assignments
LO3-1	Analyze transactions and review the process of journalizing and posting transactions.	3-3	e3-1	R3–1	M3-21, M3-22, M3-23, M3-24, M3-25, M3-26, M3-29, M3-30, M3-34, M3-35, M3-36, M3-37, E3-41, E3-42, E3-45, E3-48, E3-49, P3-51, P3-52, P3-54, P3-56, P3-61, P3-62, P3-63, P3-64, P3-71, P3-74, P3-75, P3-76, C3-78, C3-79, C3-80, C3-81, C3-82, DA3-1
LO3-2	Describe the adjusting process and illustrate adjusting entries.	3-11	e3-2	R3–2	M3-25, M3-26, M3-27, M3-28, M3-29, M3-30, M3-34, M3-35, M3-36, M3-37, E3-39, E3-40, E3-41, E3-42, E3-43, E3-44, E3-45, E3-48, E3-49, P3-51, P3-52, P3-53, P3-54, P3-55, P3-56, P3-57, P3-58, P3-61, P3-62, P3-63, P3-64, P3-65, P3-66, P3-67, P3-68, P3-71, P3-72, P3-73, P3-74, P3-75, P3-76, C3-77, C3-78, C3-79, C3-80, C3-81, C3-82
LO3-3	Prepare financial statements from adjusted accounts.	3-19	e3-3	R3–3	M3-31, E3-50, P3-56, P3-59, P3-68, P3-69, P3-74, P3-76, C3-78, DA3-2, DA3-3
LO3-4	Describe the process of closing temporary accounts.	3-24	e3-4	R3–4	M3-32, M3-33, M3-36, E3-38, E3-41, E3-47, E3-50, P3-56, P3-59, P3-60, P3-68, P3-69, P3-70, P3-74, P3-76, C3-78
LO3-5	Analyze changes in balance sheet accounts.	3-27	e3-5	R3–5	M3-27, M3-28, M3-29, M3-34, E3-43, E3-44, E3-45, E3-46, E3-48, E3-49, P3-51, P3-52, P3-56, P3-67, P3-68, P3-71, P3-72, P3-73, P3-74, P3-75, P3-76, C3-77, C3-78, C3-79, C3-81, C3-82

WALGREENS
www.walgreens.com

Walgreens Boots Alliance, Inc., is anchored by iconic brands, Walgreens in the United States and Boots in the United Kingdom. The company strives to meet customer needs through many retail locations and digital platforms. The company also works to shape the future of healthcare by bringing more innovative healthcare offerings to customers and patients and by working on government and employer efforts to control healthcare costs.

Walgreen's U.S. retail segment operates 9,021 (as of August 2020) drugstores in 50 states, the District of Columbia, Puerto Rico, and the U.S. Virgin Islands. About 78 percent of the U.S. population lives within five miles of a Walgreens or Duane Reade pharmacy. They sell prescription and non-prescription drugs, as well as a wide assortment of retail products, including health and wellness, beauty, personal care, consumables and general merchandise. Walgreens filled approximately 818 million prescriptions in fiscal 2020, including immunizations.

Because the financial statements should reflect the firm's underlying economic reality, Walgreens' management will need to "adjust" or "update" its financial statements to reflect the changes in its strategy and performance. Accounting adjustments are a key part of creating the financial statements, and they are central to the difference between accrual and cash accounting. While cash accounting only records transactions that involve cash receipts and disbursements, accrual accounting records revenues when they are earned (even if cash has not yet been received) and expenses as they are incurred (regardless of when the cash disbursement associated with that expense is made). The quality, or lack thereof, of the financial statements often hinges on the quality of those adjustments. Thus, understanding how and why accounting adjustments occur is fundamentally important to those who wish to analyze and interpret the financial statements.

This chapter describes the need for adjustments, how they are prepared, their financial statement effect, and the need for ethics and oversight in this process. We illustrate how financial statements are prepared from those adjusted accounts. Then, we end the chapter with the closing process for the financial statements. Such "closing of the books" enables firms to report their performance for the year and then "open the books" anew for the next period.

Sources: United States Segment | Walgreens Boots Alliance About Us | Company & Corporate Info | Walgreens Boots Alliance

CHAPTER ORGANIZATION

Adjusting Accounts for Financial Statements

Analyzing and Recording Transactions	Adjusting the Accounts	Constructing Financial Statements	Closing Temporary Accounts	Financial Statement Analysis
• Accounting Cycle • Review of Analyzing and Journalizing Transactions	• Preparing an Unadjusted Trial Balance • Identifying and Recording Adjustments	• Preparing an Adjusted Trial Balance • Preparing Financial Statements	• Performing the Closing Process • Preparing a Post-Closing Trial Balance	• Analyzing Changes in Balance Sheet Accounts

The double-entry accounting system introduced in Chapter 2 provides us with a framework for the analysis of business activities, and we use that framework to record transactions and create financial reports. This chapter describes more fully the procedures companies use to account for the operations of a business during a specific time period. All companies, regardless of size or complexity, perform accounting steps, known as the *accounting cycle*, to accumulate and report their financial information. An important step in the accounting cycle is the *adjusting* process that occurs at the end of every reporting period. This chapter focuses on the accounting cycle with emphasis on the adjusting process.

ACCOUNTING CYCLE

LO3-1 Analyze transactions and review the process of journalizing and posting transactions.

eLecture MBC

Companies engage in business activities. These activities are analyzed for their financial impact, and the results from that analysis are entered into the accounting information system. When management and others want to know where the company stands financially and what its recent performance tells about future prospects, the financial data often require adjustment prior to financial statements being prepared. At the end of this adjustment process, the company *closes the books.* This closing process prepares accounts for the next accounting period.

The process described constitutes the major steps in the **accounting cycle**—a sequence of activities to accumulate and report financial statements. The steps are: analyze, record, adjust, report, and close. **Exhibit 3.1** shows the sequence of major steps in the accounting cycle.

EXHIBIT 3.1 Accounting Cycle—Abbreviated

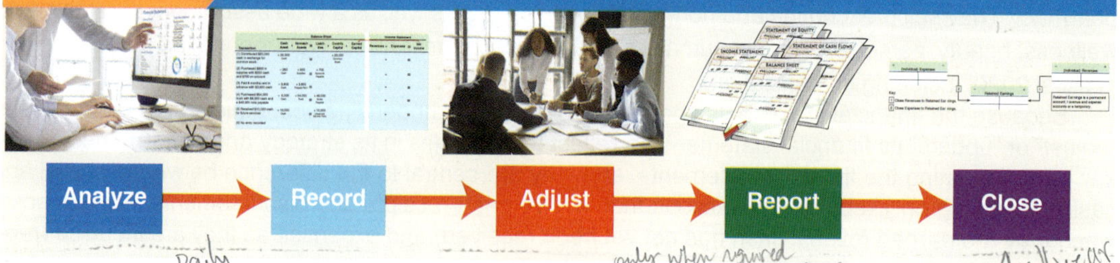

The steps in the accounting cycle do not occur with equal frequency. That is, companies analyze and record daily transactions throughout the accounting period, but they adjust and report only when management requires financial statements, often monthly or quarterly, but at least annually. Closing occurs once during the accounting cycle, at the period-end.

The annual (one-year) accounting period adopted by a company is known as its **fiscal year**. Companies with fiscal year-ends on December 31 are said to be on a **calendar year**. About 60% of U.S. companies are on a calendar-year basis. Many companies prefer to have their accounting year coincide with their "natural" year; that is, the fiscal year ends when business is slow. For example,

L Brands, Inc., a specialty retailer, ends its fiscal year on the Saturday nearest January 31. Starbucks Corporation ends its fiscal year on the Sunday nearest to September 30. The Manchester United Ltd., a professional soccer team, ends its fiscal year on June 30, during its off-season.

ANALYZING, RECORDING, AND POSTING

The purpose of this section is to (1) review the analysis and recording of transactions as described in Chapter 2, and (2) to extend the Natural Beauty Supply example to illustrate the process of adjusting and closing accounts in the following sections. Natural Beauty Supply's fiscal year-end is December 31.

Review of Accounting Procedures

The **chart of accounts** for Natural Beauty Supply is in **Exhibit 3.2**, and lists the titles and numbers of all accounts found in its general ledger. The account titles are grouped into the five major sections of the general ledger (assets, liabilities, equity, revenues, and expenses). We saw in Chapter 2 that the recording process involves analyzing, journalizing, and posting. The **general journal**, or *book of original entry*, is a tabular record where business activities are captured in debits and credits and recorded in chronological order before they are posted to the general ledger. The word *journalize* means to record a transaction in a **journal**. Each transaction entered in the journal must be stated in terms of equal dollar amounts of debits and credits—the double-entry system at work. The account titles cited must correspond to those in the general ledger (per the chart of accounts).

EXHIBIT 3.2 Chart of Accounts for Natural Beauty Supply

Assets	**Equity**
110 Cash	310 Common Stock
120 Accounts Receivable	320 Retained Earnings
130 Other Receivables	
140 Inventory	**Revenues and Income**
150 Prepaid Insurance	410 Sales Revenue
160 Security Deposit	420 Interest Income
170 Fixtures and Equipment	
175 Accumulated Depreciation—Fixtures and Equipment	**Expenses**
	510 Cost of Goods Sold
	520 Wages Expense
Liabilities	530 Rent Expense
210 Accounts Payable	540 Advertising Expense
220 Interest Payable	550 Depreciation Expense—Fixtures and Equipment
230 Wages Payable	
240 Taxes Payable	560 Insurance Expense
250 Gift Card Liability	570 Interest Expense
260 Notes Payable	580 Tax Expense

After transactions are journalized, the debits and credits in each journal entry are transferred to their related general ledger accounts. This transcribing process is called posting to the general ledger, or simply **posting**. Journalizing and posting occur simultaneously when recordkeeping is automated.

Review of Recording Transactions

In Chapter 2, we recorded the November activities of Natural Beauty Supply (NBS) and created the end-of-November financial statements. As NBS continues its activities into the next month, the end-of-November balance sheet provides the starting point for December. **Exhibit 3.3** provides a summary of Natural Beauty Supply's December 2021 transactions.

EXHIBIT 3.3 Transactions for Natural Beauty Supply for December 2021

Event	Date	Description
(17)	Dec. 1	NBS signed a three-year note to borrow $11,000 cash from a financial institution. NBS will pay interest on the first business day of every month (starting in January) at the rate of 12% per year or 1% per month. The $11,000 principal is due at the end of three years.
(18)	Dec. 1	NBS purchased and installed improved fixtures and equipment for $18,000 cash.
(19)	Dec. 10	NBS paid $700 to advertise in the local newspaper for December.
(20)	Dec. 20	NBS paid $3,300 cash to its suppliers in partial payment for the delivery of inventory in November.
(21)	Dec. —	During the month of December, NBS sold products costing $5,000 to retail customers for $8,500 cash.
(22)	Dec. —	During the month of December, sales to wholesale customers totaled $4,500 for merchandise that had cost $3,000. Instead of paying cash, wholesale customers are required to pay for the merchandise within ten business days.
(23)	Dec. —	$1,200 of gift cards were sold during the month of December. Each gift card entitles the recipient to a one-hour consultation on the use of NBS' products.
(24)	Dec.	NBS employed salespersons who were paid $1,625 in cash in December.
(25)	Dec. —	During the month of December, NBS received $3,200 in cash from wholesale customers for products that had been delivered earlier.
(26)	Dec. 28	NBS purchased and received $4,000 of inventory on account.
(27)	Dec. 31	NBS paid $1,500 to the landlord for December rent related to the short-term lease NBS entered into in November.
(28)	Dec. 31	NBS paid $50 cash dividend to its shareholders.

Most of these transactions are similar to those that we analyzed in Chapter 2. Each of the transactions involves an exchange of some kind. Suppliers provide inventory and employees provide labor services in exchange for cash or the promise of future cash payments. Customers receive products in exchange for cash or a promise to pay cash in the future. For each of these items, we analyze, journalize, and post as shown in Chapter 2.

NBS has the opportunity to secure long-term financing from a financial institution and signs a note that must be paid back at the end of three years. Cash increases, and a noncurrent liability increases. Interest payments are made at the start of every month, beginning on January 2, 2022, but no entry is made for interest until time passes and an interest obligation is created.

ANALYZE

	Balance Sheet									Income Statement				
Transaction	Cash Asset	+	Noncash Assets	=	Liabil-ities	+	Contrib. Capital	+	Earned Capital	Revenues	−	Expenses	=	Net Income
(17) Sign note and receive $11,000 cash.	+11,000 Cash			=	+11,000 Notes Payable						−		=	

JOURNALIZE

		Debit	Credit
(17)	Cash (+A)	11,000	
	Notes payable (+L)		11,000
	Borrow $11,000 on a three-year note.		

POST

+ Cash (A) −	
(17) 11,000	

− Notes Payable (L) +	
	11,000 (17)

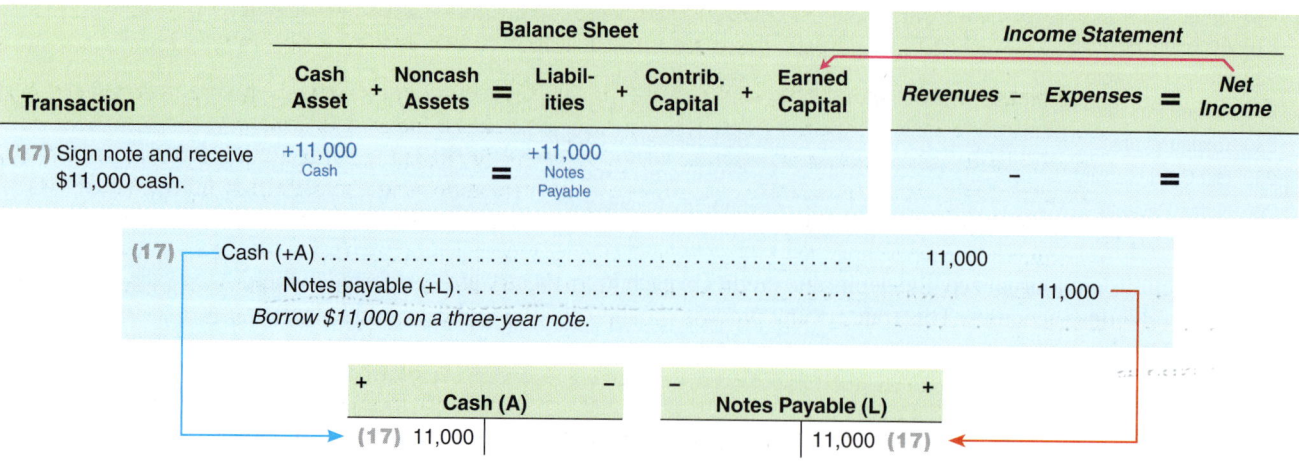

NBS pays $18,000 cash to purchase improved fixtures and equipment for its store location. One asset (cash) decreases, while a noncurrent asset (fixtures and equipment) is increased.

ANALYZE

Transaction	Balance Sheet: Cash Asset	+ Noncash Assets	= Liabilities	+ Contrib. Capital	+ Earned Capital	Income Statement: Revenues	− Expenses	= Net Income
(18) Pay $18,000 cash for fixtures and equipment.	−18,000 Cash	+18,000 Fixtures and Equipment						

JOURNALIZE

		Debit	Credit
(18)	Fixtures & equipment (+A)	18,000	
	Cash (−A)		18,000
	Purchase fixtures and equipment for cash.		

POST

+ Fixtures & Equipment (A)	−
(18) 18,000	

+ Cash (A)	−
	18,000 (18)

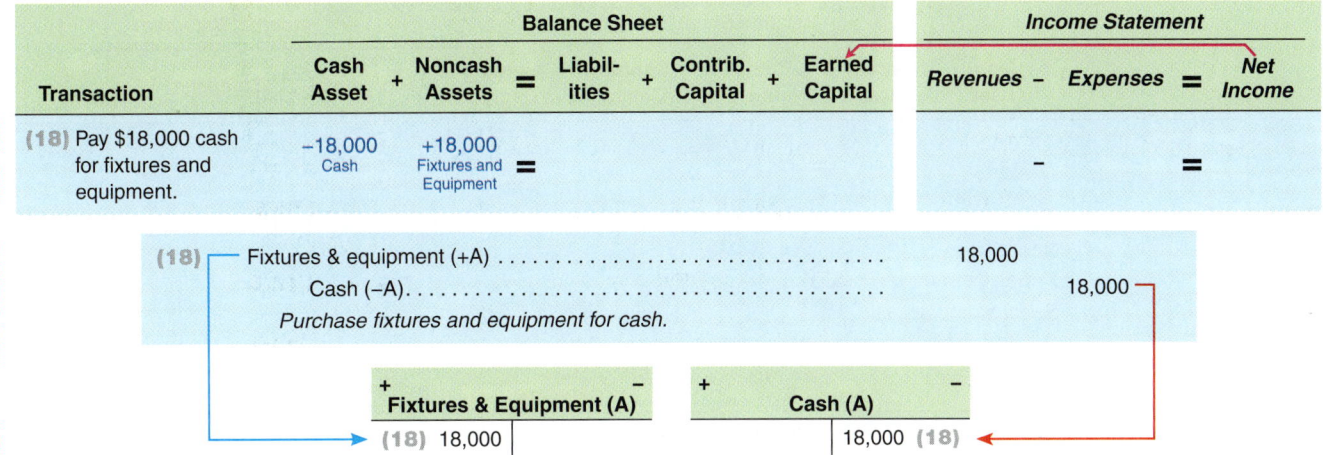

Transactions (19) and (20) are similar to ones that we saw in Chapter 2. The expenditure for advertising results in an expense that decreases net income and ultimately, retained earnings. The payment to suppliers fulfills (in part) an obligation that appeared in the November 30 balance sheet.

ANALYZE

Transaction	Cash Asset	+ Noncash Assets	= Liabilities	+ Contrib. Capital	+ Earned Capital	Revenues	− Expenses	= Net Income
(19) Pay $700 cash for December advertising.	−700 Cash				−700 Retained Earnings		+700 Advertising Expense	−700

JOURNALIZE

		Debit	Credit
(19)	Advertising expense (+E,−SE)	700	
	Cash (−A)		700
	Record advertising expense.		

POST

+ Advertising Expense (E)	−
(19) 700	

+ Cash (A)	−
	700 (19)

ANALYZE

Transaction	Cash Asset	+ Noncash Assets	= Liabilities	+ Contrib. Capital	+ Earned Capital	Revenues	− Expenses	= Net Income
(20) Pay $3,300 cash to suppliers.	−3,300 Cash		−3,300 Accounts Payable					

JOURNALIZE

		Debit	Credit
(20)	Accounts payable (−L)	3,300	
	Cash (−A)		3,300
	Pay cash to suppliers for previous purchases.		

POST

− Accounts Payable (L)	+
(20) 3,300	

+ Cash (A)	−
	3,300 (20)

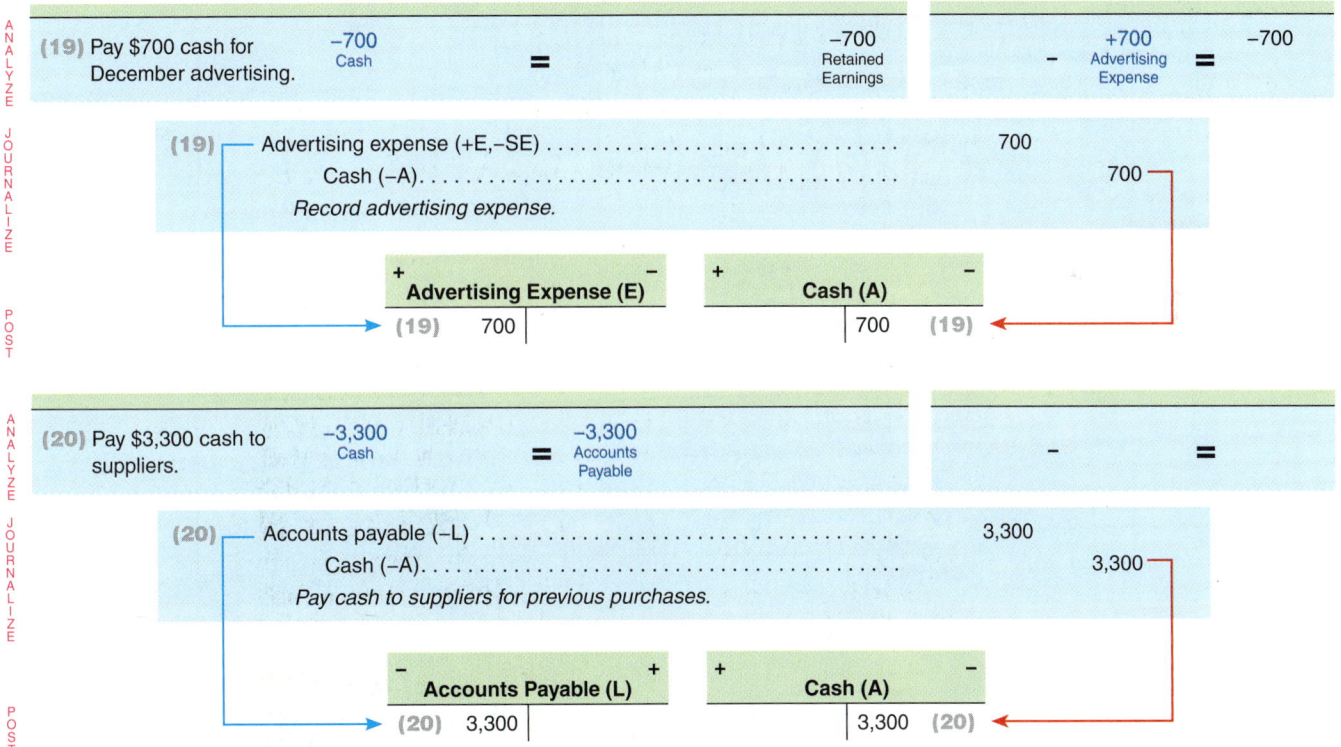

Sales to customers in (21), (22), and (23) are also similar to transactions in Chapter 2, and they are accounted for in similar fashion. Revenue is recognized when products are delivered to customers, rather than when cash is received. When cash is received after delivery, an accounts receivable asset is recorded; when cash is received before delivery, a performance obligation liability is recorded. In this case, NBS uses the account title "Gift Card Liability."[1] Cost of goods sold expense is recognized when the associated revenue is recognized.

[1] The Gift Card Liability represents NBS' obligation to deliver services to customers when the gift cards are redeemed. Companies sometimes use the terms "deferred revenue" or "unearned revenue" to refer to these liabilities. We use the preferred terms "performance obligation," "contract liability," or a more descriptive account title such as "Gift Card Liability" wherever possible.

Transaction	Cash Asset	+	Noncash Assets	=	Liabil-ities	+	Contrib. Capital	+	Earned Capital	Revenues	−	Expenses	=	Net Income
ANALYZE **(21a)** Sell $8,500 of products for cash.	+8,500 Cash			=					+8,500 Retained Earnings	+8,500 Sales Revenue	−		=	+8,500

JOURNALIZE

(21a) Cash (+A)	8,500	
Sales revenue (+R,+SE)		8,500
Sell products for cash.		

POST

+ Cash (A) −	
(21a) 8,500	

− Sales Revenue (R) +	
	8,500 **(21a)**

Transaction	Cash Asset	+	Noncash Assets	=	Liabil-ities	+	Contrib. Capital	+	Earned Capital	Revenues	−	Expenses	=	Net Income
ANALYZE **(21b)** Record $5,000 for the cost of merchandise sold in transaction 21a.			−5,000 Inventory	=					−5,000 Retained Earnings		−	+5,000 Cost of Goods Sold	=	−5,000

JOURNALIZE

(21b) Cost of goods sold (+E,−SE)	5,000	
Inventory (−A)		5,000
Record cost of merchandise sold as expense.		

POST

+ Cost of Goods Sold (E) −	
(21b) 5,000	

+ Inventory (A) −	
	5,000 **(21b)**

Transaction	Cash Asset	+	Noncash Assets	=	Liabil-ities	+	Contrib. Capital	+	Earned Capital	Revenues	−	Expenses	=	Net Income
ANALYZE **(22a)** Sell $4,500 of products on account.			+4,500 Accounts Receivable	=					+4,500 Retained Earnings	+4,500 Sales Revenue	−		=	+4,500

JOURNALIZE

(22a) Accounts receivable (+A)	4,500	
Sales revenue (+R,+SE)		4,500
Sell products on account.		

POST

+ Accounts Receivable (A) −	
(22a) 4,500	

− Sales Revenue (R) +	
	4,500 **(22a)**

Transaction	Cash Asset	+	Noncash Assets	=	Liabil-ities	+	Contrib. Capital	+	Earned Capital	Revenues	−	Expenses	=	Net Income
ANALYZE **(22b)** Record $3,000 for the cost of merchandise sold in transaction 22a.			−3,000 Inventory	=					−3,000 Retained Earnings		−	+3,000 Cost of Goods Sold	=	−3,000

JOURNALIZE

(22b) Cost of goods sold (+E,−SE)	3,000	
Inventory (−A)		3,000
Record cost of merchandise sold as expense.		

POST

+ Cost of Goods Sold (E) −	
(22b) 3,000	

+ Inventory (A) −	
	3,000 **(22b)**

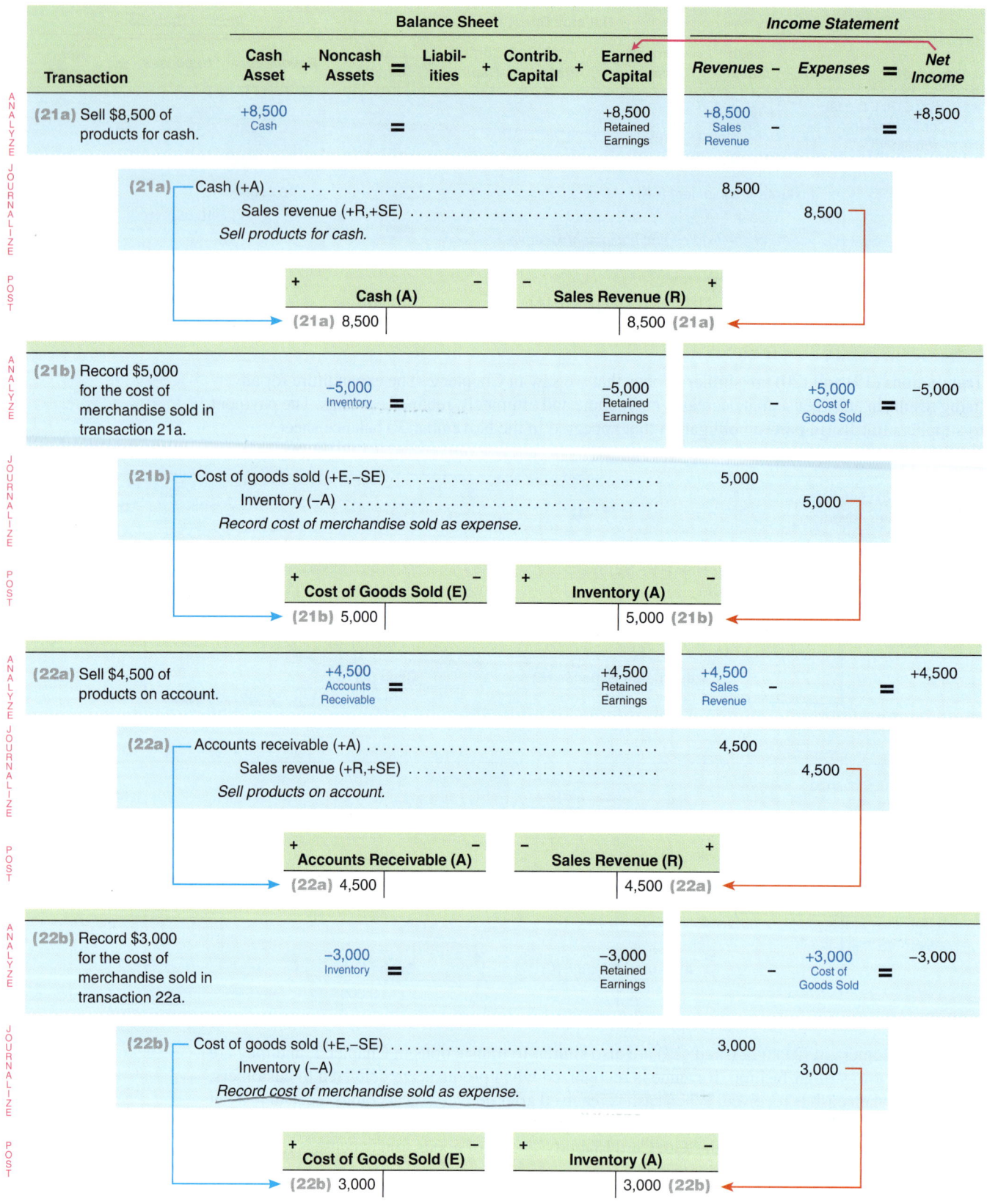

continued

ANALYZE

Transaction	Cash Asset	+	Noncash Assets	=	Liabilities	+	Contrib. Capital	+	Earned Capital	Revenues	–	Expenses	=	Net Income
(23) Sell gift cards for $1,200 cash.	+1,200 Cash			=	+1,200 Gift Card Liability						–		=	

JOURNALIZE

		Debit	Credit
(23)	Cash (+A)	1,200	
	Gift Card Liability (+L)		1,200
	Record unearned revenue from gift cards.		

POST

+ Cash (A) –		– Gift Card Liability (L) +	
(23) 1,200			1,200 (23)

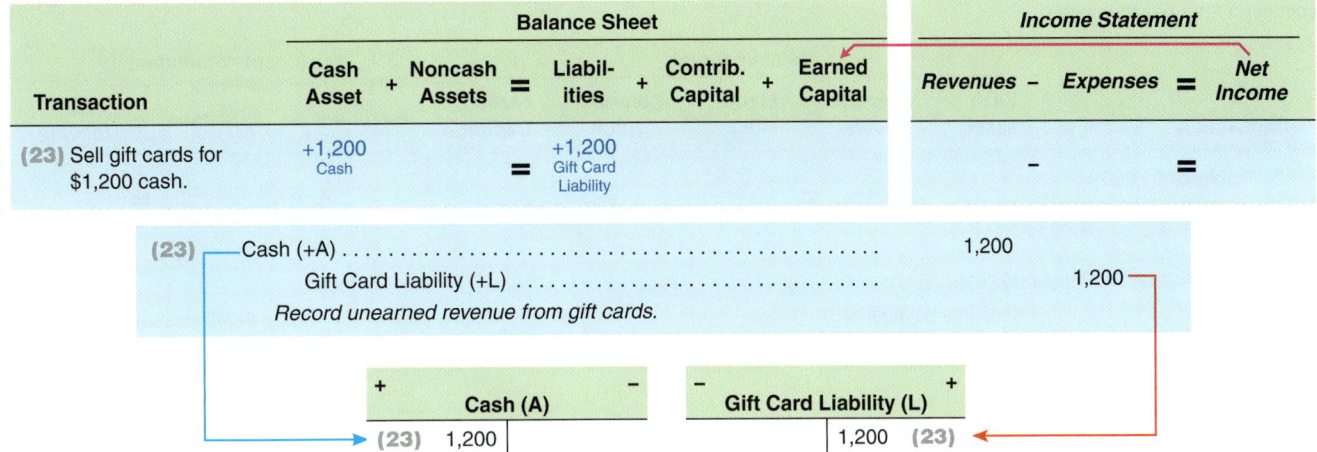

The final five transactions in December also are similar to transactions that NBS had in November. Payment of wages to the employee is reflected in a wage expense. Cash received from wholesale (credit) customers does not cause revenue; rather, the increase in cash is balanced by a decrease in accounts receivable. Purchase of inventory on account does not create an expense—the cost of the inventory is held in the inventory asset account until it is purchased by a customer. Payments to the landlord are balanced by a rent expense in the income statement. The cash dividend to shareholders decreases an asset (cash) and shareholders' equity (retained earnings) but does not affect the income statement.

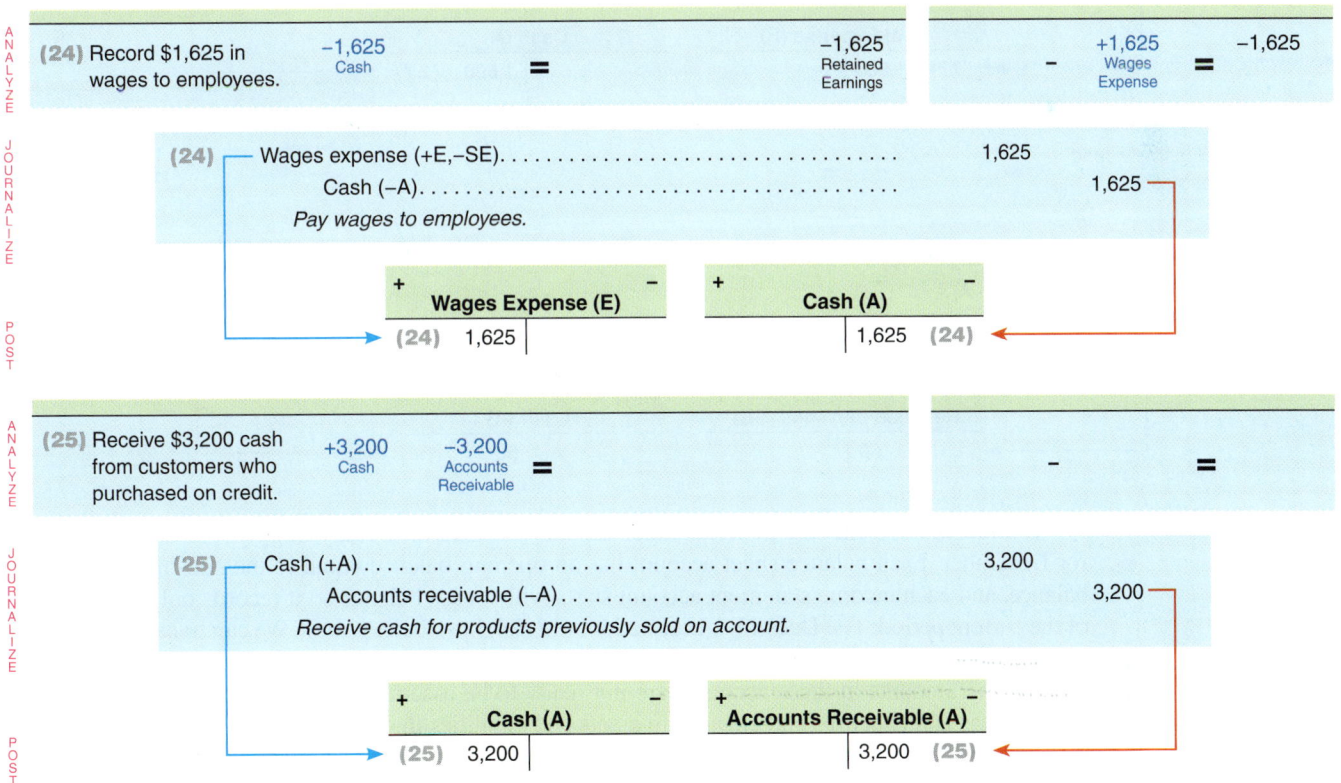

ANALYZE

Transaction	Cash Asset	+	Noncash Assets	=	Liabilities	+	Contrib. Capital	+	Earned Capital	Revenues	–	Expenses	=	Net Income
(24) Record $1,625 in wages to employees.	–1,625 Cash			=					–1,625 Retained Earnings		–	+1,625 Wages Expense	=	–1,625

JOURNALIZE

		Debit	Credit
(24)	Wages expense (+E,–SE)	1,625	
	Cash (–A)		1,625
	Pay wages to employees.		

POST

+ Wages Expense (E) –		+ Cash (A) –	
(24) 1,625			1,625 (24)

ANALYZE

Transaction	Cash Asset	+	Noncash Assets	=	Liabilities	+	Contrib. Capital	+	Earned Capital	Revenues	–	Expenses	=	Net Income
(25) Receive $3,200 cash from customers who purchased on credit.	+3,200 Cash		–3,200 Accounts Receivable	=							–		=	

JOURNALIZE

		Debit	Credit
(25)	Cash (+A)	3,200	
	Accounts receivable (–A)		3,200
	Receive cash for products previously sold on account.		

POST

+ Cash (A) –		+ Accounts Receivable (A) –	
(25) 3,200			3,200 (25)

continued

continued from previous page

ANALYZE

Transaction	Cash Asset	+	Noncash Assets	=	Liabilities	+	Contrib. Capital	+	Earned Capital	*Revenues*	−	*Expenses*	=	*Net Income*
(26) Purchase $4,000 inventory on account.			+4,000 Inventory	=	+4,000 Accounts Payable						−		=	

JOURNALIZE

		Debit	Credit
(26)	Inventory (+A)	4,000	
	Accounts payable (+L)		4,000
	Purchase inventory on account.		

POST

+ Inventory (A) −	
(26) 4,000	

− Accounts Payable (L) +	
	4,000 (26)

ANALYZE

Transaction	Cash Asset	+	Noncash Assets	=	Liabilities	+	Contrib. Capital	+	Earned Capital	*Revenues*	−	*Expenses*	=	*Net Income*
(27) Pay $1,500 rent for December.	−1,500 Cash			=					−1,500 Retained Earnings		−	+1,500 Rent Expense	=	−1,500

JOURNALIZE

		Debit	Credit
(27)	Rent expense (+E,−SE)	1,500	
	Cash (−A)		1,500
	Record payment of December rent.		

POST

+ Rent Expense (E) −	
(27) 1,500	

+ Cash (A) −	
	1,500 (27)

ANALYZE

Transaction	Cash Asset	+	Noncash Assets	=	Liabilities	+	Contrib. Capital	+	Earned Capital	*Revenues*	−	*Expenses*	=	*Net Income*
(28) Pay $50 cash dividend to shareholders.	−50 Cash			=					−50 Retained Earnings		−		=	

JOURNALIZE

		Debit	Credit
(28)	Retained earnings (−SE)	50	
	Cash (−A)		50
	Pay a cash dividend.		

POST

− Retained Earnings (SE) +	
(28) 50	

+ Cash (A) −	
	50 (28)

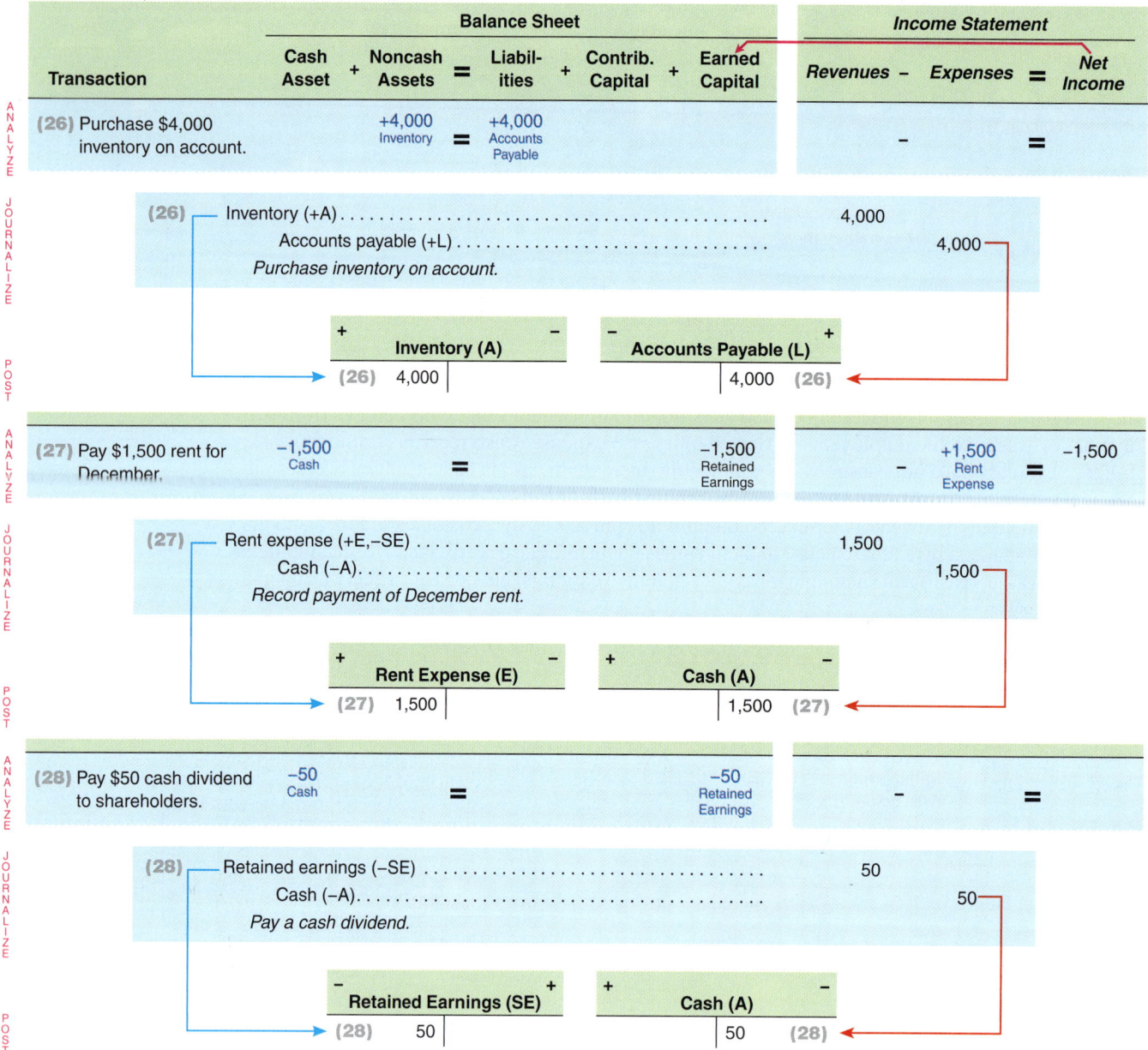

Exhibit 3.4 presents the general ledger accounts of Natural Beauty Supply in T-account form for December. Each balance sheet account has an opening balance equal to the end-of-November balance, and each income statement account starts with a zero balance so it records only the events of the current period. The December transactions (17–28) have been posted. We can trace each of the postings from the transactions above to these ledger accounts.

But the amounts in these accounts are not ready to be assembled into financial reports. There are revenues and expenses and changes in assets and liabilities that occur with the passage of time.[2] Accounting for these items is essential for us to determine how well a company has performed in an accounting period and to assess its financial standing.

[2] Natural Beauty Supply's November activities in Chapter 2 were carefully chosen so we could produce financial statements without adjusting entries. But, as **Exhibit 3.1** depicts, the adjusting process is an essential part of the accounting cycle.

EXHIBIT 3.4 General Ledger for Natural Beauty Supply before Adjustments

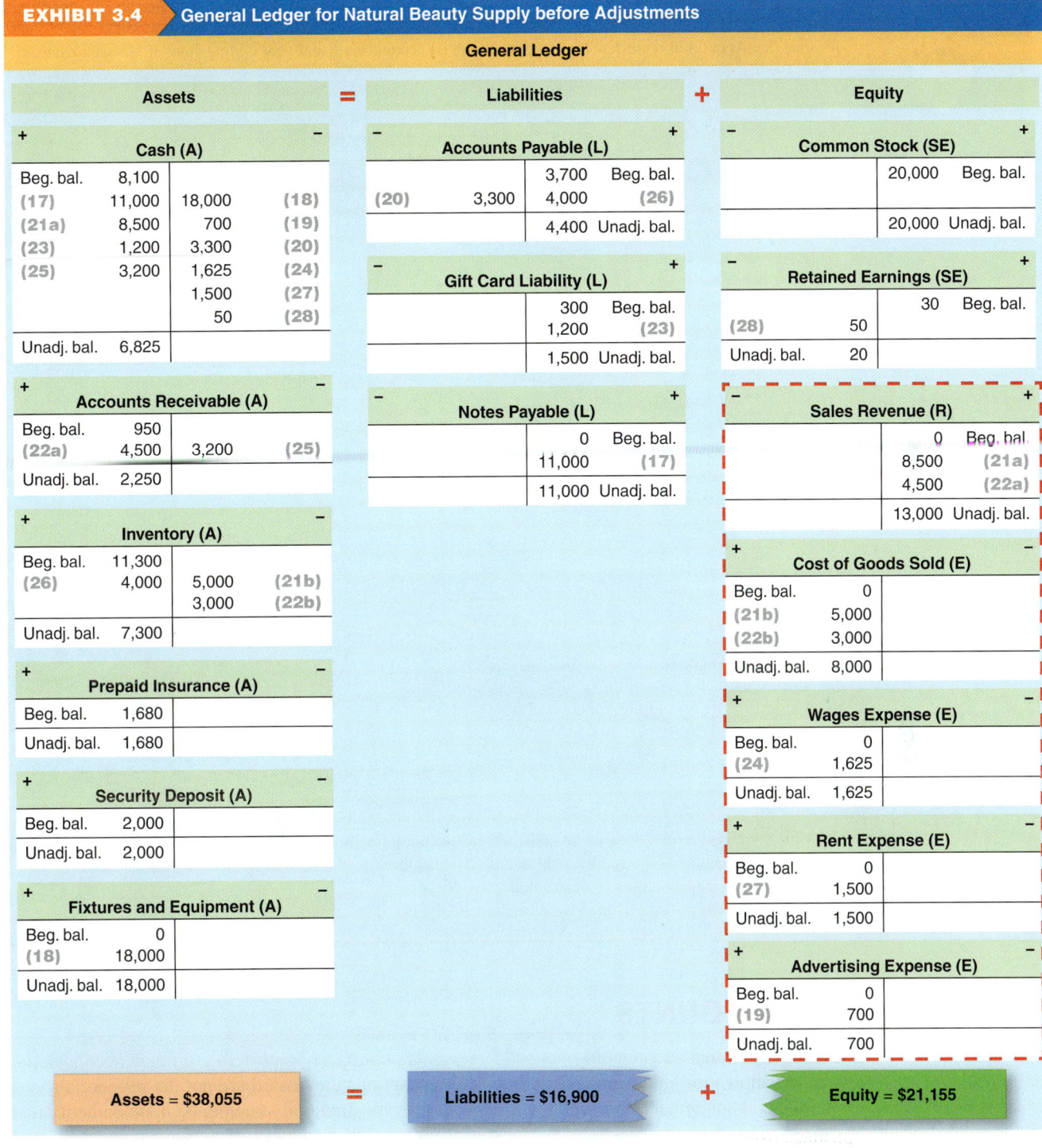

General Ledger

Assets = Liabilities + Equity

Assets

Cash (A)

+			−
Beg. bal.	8,100		
(17)	11,000	18,000	(18)
(21a)	8,500	700	(19)
(23)	1,200	3,300	(20)
(25)	3,200	1,625	(24)
		1,500	(27)
		50	(28)
Unadj. bal.	6,825		

Accounts Receivable (A)

+			−
Beg. bal.	950		
(22a)	4,500	3,200	(25)
Unadj. bal.	2,250		

Inventory (A)

+			−
Beg. bal.	11,300		
(26)	4,000	5,000	(21b)
		3,000	(22b)
Unadj. bal.	7,300		

Prepaid Insurance (A)

+			−
Beg. bal.	1,680		
Unadj. bal.	1,680		

Security Deposit (A)

+			−
Beg. bal.	2,000		
Unadj. bal.	2,000		

Fixtures and Equipment (A)

+			−
Beg. bal.	0		
(18)	18,000		
Unadj. bal.	18,000		

Liabilities

Accounts Payable (L)

−			+
		3,700	Beg. bal.
(20)	3,300	4,000	(26)
		4,400	Unadj. bal.

Gift Card Liability (L)

−			+
		300	Beg. bal.
		1,200	(23)
		1,500	Unadj. bal.

Notes Payable (L)

−			+
		0	Beg. bal.
		11,000	(17)
		11,000	Unadj. bal.

Equity

Common Stock (SE)

−			+
		20,000	Beg. bal.
		20,000	Unadj. bal.

Retained Earnings (SE)

−			+
		30	Beg. bal.
(28)	50		
Unadj. bal.	20		

Sales Revenue (R)

−			+
		0	Beg. bal.
		8,500	(21a)
		4,500	(22a)
		13,000	Unadj. bal.

Cost of Goods Sold (E)

+			−
Beg. bal.	0		
(21b)	5,000		
(22b)	3,000		
Unadj. bal.	8,000		

Wages Expense (E)

+			−
Beg. bal.	0		
(24)	1,625		
Unadj. bal.	1,625		

Rent Expense (E)

+			−
Beg. bal.	0		
(27)	1,500		
Unadj. bal.	1,500		

Advertising Expense (E)

+			−
Beg. bal.	0		
(19)	700		
Unadj. bal.	700		

Assets = \$38,055 = **Liabilities = \$16,900** + **Equity = \$21,155**

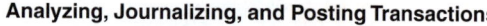

Review 3-1 LO3-1

Analyzing, Journalizing, and Posting Transactions

GuidedExample MBC

Assume that Atwell Laboratories, Inc., operates with an accounting fiscal year ending June 30. Its trial balance as of May 31 is as follows.

ATWELL LABORATORIES, INC.
Trial Balance
May 31

	Debit	Credit
Cash	$ 500	
Accounts receivable	8,000	
Prepaid insurance	6,000	
Supplies	30,200	
Equipment	270,000	
Accumulated depreciation—equipment*		$ 60,000
Accounts payable		4,000
Contract liability		4,000
Fees revenue		142,300
Wages expense	54,000	
Rent expense	22,000	
Common stock		120,400
Retained earnings		60,000
Totals	$390,700	$390,700

*Accumulated depreciation, a contra asset account, will be discussed in the next section.

The following five transactions took place in June by the company.

1. Paid $4,000 in cash for wages for June.
2. Received $6,500 in cash for services provided in June.
3. Purchased $1,100 supplies on account.
4. Performed $1,200 of services on account in June.
5. Paid suppliers $2,000 on account.

Required

a. Show the impact of the transactions listed above using the FSET.
b. Show the impact of the transactions listed above using journal entries.
c. Prepare T-accounts with the May 31 balances as beginning balances, enter the transactions from part b, and determine the unadjusted ending balances.
d. Prepare Atwell's June 30 unadjusted trial balance.

Solution on p. 3-50.

ADJUSTING THE ACCOUNTS

LO3-2 Describe the adjusting process and illustrate adjusting entries.

eLecture MBC

It is important that accounts in financial statements be properly reported. For many accounts, the balances shown in the general ledger after all transactions are posted are not the proper balances for financial statements. So, when it is time to prepare financial statements, management must review account balances and make proper adjustments to these balances. The adjustments required are based on accrual accounting and generally accepted accounting principles. This section focuses on this adjustment process.

Preparing an Unadjusted Trial Balance

The T-accounts in **Exhibit 3.4** show balances for each account after recording all transactions. This set of balances is called an **unadjusted trial balance** because it shows account balances before any adjustments are made. The purpose of an unadjusted trial balance is to be sure the general ledger is in balance before management adjusts the accounts. Showing all general ledger account balances in one place also makes it easier to review accounts and determine which account balances require adjusting. Natural Beauty Supply's unadjusted trial balance at December 31 is shown in **Exhibit 3.5**.

EXHIBIT 3.5 Unadjusted Trial Balance

NATURAL BEAUTY SUPPLY
Unadjusted Trial Balance
December 31, 2021

	Debit	Credit
Cash	$ 6,825	
Accounts receivable	2,250	
Inventory	7,300	
Prepaid insurance	1,680	
Security deposit	2,000	
Fixtures & equipment	18,000	
Accounts payable		$ 4,400
Gift card liability		1,500
Notes payable		11,000
Common stock		20,000
Retained earnings	20	
Sales revenue		13,000
Cost of goods sold	8,000	
Wages expense	1,625	
Rent expense	1,500	
Advertising expense	700	
Totals	$49,900	$49,900

FYI Even if the unadjusted trial balance shows an equal amount of debits and credits, this does not mean that the general ledger is correct. Journal entries could have been omitted or falsified, or the accounts used or the amounts involved may have been wrong. Thus, the equality of debits and credits is a necessary, but not a sufficient, condition for the financial statements to be correct.

Types of Adjustments

Accrual adjustments are caused by a variety of accounting practices. There are some revenues and expenses that arise with the passage of time, rather than in a transaction. There are asset and liability values that change over time or that require estimation based on recent events. All of these require adjustments before proper financial statements can be produced.

Adjusting entries have two common characteristics. First, they occur at the end of a reporting period, just before the construction of financial statements. Second, they (almost) never involve cash. Changes in cash require a transaction, and adjusting entries do not involve the recording of transactions.

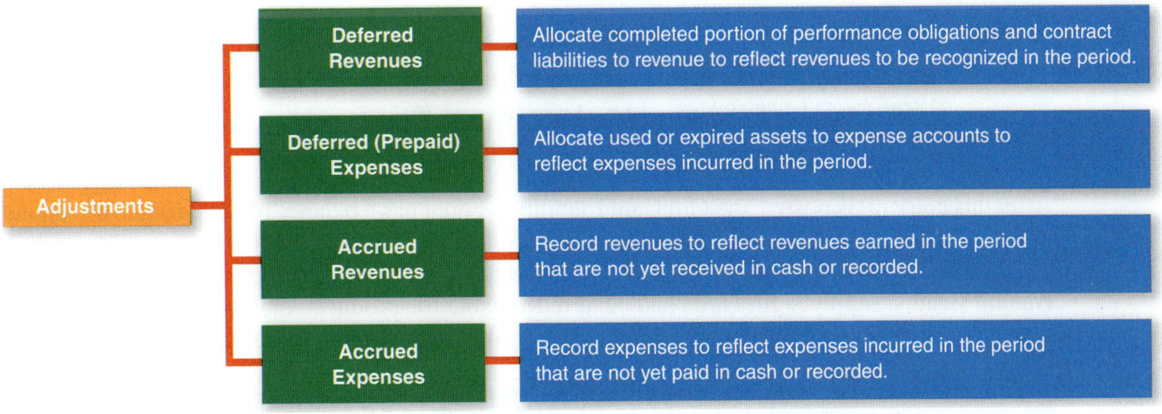

Through the course of this book, we will encounter quite a few required adjusting entries, but we will start with four general types of adjustments made at the end of an accounting period.

Journal entries made to reflect these adjustments are known as **adjusting entries**. Each adjusting entry usually affects a balance sheet account (an asset or liability account) and an income statement account (an expense or revenue account). The first two types of adjustments—allocating assets to expense and allocating unearned revenues to revenue—are often referred to as **deferrals**. The distinguishing characteristic of a deferral is that the adjustment deals with an amount previously recorded in a balance sheet account; the adjusting entry decreases the balance sheet account and increases an income statement account. The last two types of adjustments—accruing expenses and accruing revenues—are often referred to as **accruals**. The unique characteristic of an accrual is that the adjustment deals with an amount not previously recorded in any account; this type of adjusting entry increases both a balance sheet account and an income statement account. Both accruals and deferrals allow revenue to be recognized when it is earned and the expenses of the period to reflect asset decreases and liability increases from generating revenues or supporting that period's operations. Let's consider each of these adjustments in more detail.

FYI Chapter 2 explained that revenue recognition is key to determining net income under accrual accounting, which recognizes revenues when services are performed or when goods are sold and recognizes expenses in the period that they help to generate the recorded revenues.

Type 1: Deferred Revenue—Allocating Performance Obligation Liabilities to Revenue Companies often receive fees for products or services before those products or services are rendered. Such transactions are recorded by debiting Cash and crediting a performance obligation liability account for the **deferred revenue** (the account could have other names such as unearned revenue or contract liability). This account reflects the obligation for performing future services or delivering a product in the future. As services are performed or products are delivered, revenue should be recognized. At period-end, an adjusting entry is used to record the revenue in the current accounting period and reduce the liability account that was previously recorded.[3]

DEFERRED REVENUE During November and December, Natural Beauty Supply sold gift cards that entitled the recipient to a one-hour consultation with a salesperson on the use of natural and organic health and beauty products. When the gift cards were purchased, NBS recognized a gift card liability that reflected the obligation to provide these services. During the month of December, gift cards totaling $900 were redeemed. On December 31, Natural Beauty Supply made the adjustment (a) in the following template, journal entry, and T-accounts to recognize the (partial) fulfillment of the obligation and to recognize the $900 of revenue to which it is now entitled. The $900 increase in sales revenue is reflected in net income and carried over to retained earnings.

ANALYZE

	Balance Sheet									*Income Statement*				
Transaction	Cash Asset	+	Noncash Assets	=	Liabil-ities	+	Contrib. Capital	+	Earned Capital	*Revenues*	–	*Expenses*	=	*Net Income*
(a) Adjusting entry for gift certificates redeemed in December.				=	−900 Gift Card Liability				+900 Retained Earnings	+900 Sales Revenue	–		=	+900

JOURNALIZE

		Debit	Credit
(a)	Gift card liability (−L)	900	
	Sales revenue (+R,+SE)		900
	To record redemption of gift cards.		

POST

− Gift Card Liability (L) +	
(a) 900	

− Sales Revenue (R) +	
	900 (a)

After this entry (a) is posted, the Gift Card Liability account has a balance of $600 for the remaining gift certificates outstanding, and the Sales Revenue account reflects the $900 earned in December.

In this case, the cost of the salesperson's time has already been recognized as an expense. If Natural Beauty Supply's gift cards had been redeemable for products, then we would have recognized a Cost of Goods Sold expense for the items purchased with the redeemed certificates.

YOU MAKE THE CALL

You are the Chief Accountant REI requires customers of its travel-vacation business to make an initial deposit equal to $400 when the trip is reserved and to make full payment two months before departure. REI's refunding policy is to return the entire deposit if the customer informs REI of the trip's cancellation three or more months in advance of the trip. REI will refund all but the $400 deposit if the customer cancels between 60 and 90 days prior to the trip or if the customer cancels between 30 and 60 days prior to the trip, REI will retain 50% of the total amount paid. There is no refund if notification occurs within 30 days of the trip. REI's cancellation rate is very low. How should you account for deposits, and when should revenue be recorded? [Answers on page 3-29]

[3] Note that there are some conditions under which a contract liability would be recorded even before cash is received from the customer. For example, if the contract is not cancelable and the due date for payment has passed. This is beyond the scope of this book and not common.

Other examples of revenues received in advance include rental payments received in advance by real estate management companies, insurance premiums received in advance by insurance companies, subscription revenues received in advance by magazine and newspaper publishers, and membership fees received in advance by health clubs. In each case, a performance obligation liability account is set up when the advance payment is received. Later, an adjusting entry is made to reflect the revenues earned from the services provided or products delivered during the period.

Type 2: Deferred (Prepaid) Expenses—Allocating Assets to Expenses Many cash outlays benefit several accounting periods. Examples are purchases of buildings, equipment, and supplies; prepayments of advertising; and payments of insurance premiums covering several periods. These outlays are added to (debited to) an asset account when the expenditure occurs. Then at the end of each accounting period, the estimated portion of the outlay that has expired in that period or has benefited that period is transferred to an expense account.

We can usually see when adjustments of this type are needed by inspecting the unadjusted trial balance for costs that benefit several periods. Looking at the December 31 trial balance of Natural Beauty Supply (**Exhibit 3.5**), for example, adjustments are required to record the costs of prepaid insurance and the fixtures and equipment for the month of December.

FYI Many transactions reflected in ledger accounts affect net income of more than one period. Likewise, other events that are not yet recorded in accounts affect the current period's income. The adjusting process identifies these situations to record the proper revenues and expenses in the current period.

PREPAID INSURANCE On November 30, Natural Beauty Supply paid one year's insurance premium in advance and debited the $1,680 payment to Prepaid Insurance, an asset account. As each day passes and the insurance coverage is being used, insurance expense is being incurred, and the Prepaid Insurance asset is decreasing. It is not necessary to record insurance expense on a daily basis because financial statements are not prepared daily. At the end of an accounting period, however, an adjustment must be made to recognize the proper amount of Insurance Expense for the period and to decrease Prepaid Insurance by that amount. On December 31, one month's insurance coverage has been used up, so Natural Beauty Supply transfers $140 ($1,680/12 months) from Prepaid Insurance to Insurance Expense. This entry is identified as adjustment (b) in the template, journal entry, and T-accounts.

ANALYZE

	Balance Sheet									Income Statement				
Transaction	Cash Asset	+	Noncash Assets	=	Liabil-ities	+	Contrib. Capital	+	Earned Capital	Revenues	−	Expenses	=	Net Income
(b) Adjusting entry to record expiration of 1 month of prepaid insurance.			−140 Prepaid Insurance	=					−140 Retained Earnings		−	+140 Insurance Expense	=	−140

JOURNALIZE

		Debit	Credit
(b)	Insurance expense (+E, −SE)	140	
	Prepaid insurance (−A)		140
	To record insurance expense for December.		

POST

+ Insurance Expense (E) −	
(b) 140	

+ Prepaid Insurance (A) −	
	140 (b)

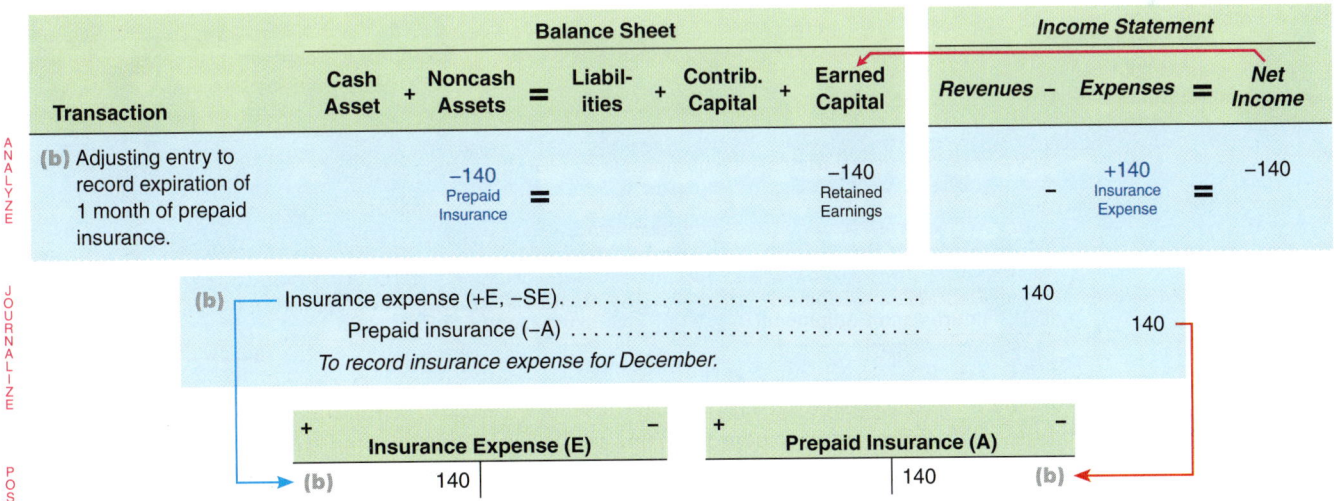

The posting of this adjusting entry creates the proper Insurance Expense of $140 for December in the Insurance Expense ledger account and reduces the Prepaid Insurance balance to the (eleven-month) amount that is prepaid as of December 31, which is $1,540.

Examples of other prepaid expenses for which similar adjustments are made include prepaid advertising. When advertising services are purchased in advance, the payment is debited to Prepaid Advertising. At the end of an accounting period, an adjustment is needed to recognize the cost of any of the prepaid advertising used during the period. The adjusting entry debits (increases) Advertising Expense and credits (decreases) Prepaid Advertising.

a accounts are used to provide more information to users of financial statements. For example, Accumulated Depreciation is a contra asset reported in the balance sheet that enables users to estimate asset age. For Natural Beauty Supply, the December 31 balance sheet reveals that its Fixtures and Equipment is nearly new as its accumulated depreciation is only $375, which is 1/48 of the $18,000 original cost.

DEPRECIATION The process of allocating the costs of equipment, vehicles, and buildings to the periods benefiting from their use is called **depreciation**. Each accounting period in which such assets are used must reflect a portion of their cost as expense because these assets helped generate revenue or support operations for those periods. This periodic expense is known as *depreciation expense*. Periodic depreciation expense is an estimate. The procedure we use here estimates the annual amount of depreciation expense by dividing the asset cost by its estimated useful life. (We assume that the entire asset cost is depreciated—so-called zero salvage value; later in the book we consider salvage values other than zero.) This method is called **straight-line depreciation** and is used by the great majority of companies in their financial reports.

Expenses are recorded when business activities reduce net assets. But when we record depreciation expense, the asset amount is not reduced directly. Instead, the reduction is recorded in a **contra asset** account (labeled XA in the journal entries and T-accounts) called *Accumulated Depreciation*. **Contra accounts** are so named because they are used to record reductions in or offsets against a related account. The Accumulated Depreciation account normally has a credit balance and appears in the balance sheet as an offset against (or reduction in) the related asset amount. Use of the *contra asset* Accumulated Depreciation allows the original cost of the asset to be reported in the balance sheet, followed (and reduced) by the accumulated depreciation. Let's consider an example.

The fixtures and equipment purchased by Natural Beauty Supply for $18,000 are expected to last for four years. Straight line depreciation recorded on the equipment is $4,500 per year ($18,000/4 years), or $375 per month ($18,000/48 months). At December 31, Natural Beauty Supply makes adjustment (c), as shown in the following template, journal entry, and T-accounts.

The introduction of contra assets requires a new column in the FSET for these accounts.[4] Increases in a contra asset decrease the net balance of the company's long-term assets. The new column is preceded by a minus sign to indicate that increases in contra assets create a decrease in the asset side of the accounting equation.

ANALYZE

	Balance Sheet													Income Statement				
Transaction	Cash Asset	+	Noncash Assets	−	Contra Assets	=	Liabil-ities	+	Contrib. Capital	+	Earned Capital		Revenues	−	Expenses	=	Net Income
(c) Adjusting entry for depreciation on fixtures and equipment for December.				−	+375 Accumulated Depreciation	=					−375 Retained Earnings			−	+375 Depreciation Expense	=	−375

JOURNALIZE

		Dr.	Cr.
(c)	Depreciation expense—Fixtures and equipment (+E, −SE)	375	
	Accumulated depreciation—Fixtures and equipment (+XA, −A)		375
	To record depreciation on fixtures and equipment.		

POST

+ Depreciation Expense—Fixtures and Equipment (E) −	
(c) 375	

− Accumulated Depreciation—Fixtures and Equipment (XA) +	
	375 (c)

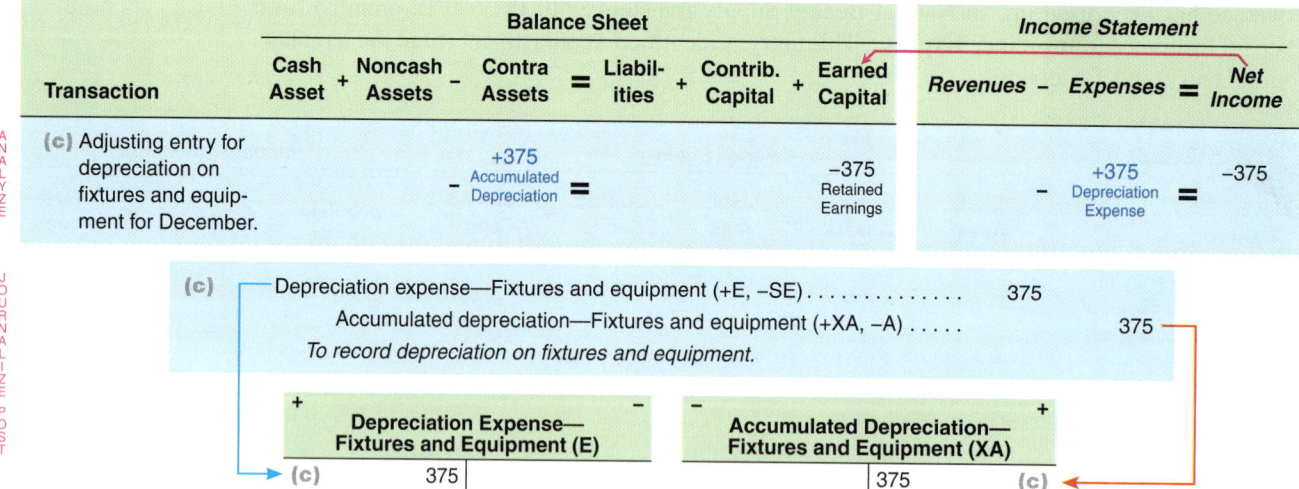

When this entry is posted, it properly reflects the cost of using this asset during December, and the $375 depreciation expense appears in the December income statement. On the balance sheet, the accumulated depreciation is an offset to the asset amount. The resulting balance (cost less accumulated depreciation), which is the asset's **book value**, represents the unexpired asset cost to be allocated as an expense in future periods. For example, the December 31, 2021, balance sheet reports the equipment with a book value of $17,625, as follows.

Fixtures and equipment	$18,000	
Less: Accumulated depreciation.	375	
Fixtures and equipment, net.	$17,625	(book value)

[4] Our practice is to include a separate FSET column where contra assets are required, but not to do so all the time. As we progress through the topics in this text, we will also see examples of contra liability accounts and contra equity accounts.

In each subsequent month, $375 is recognized as depreciation expense, and the Accumulated Depreciation contra asset is increased by the same amount (from $375 to $750 to $1,125 and so on). As a result, the book value of the fixtures and equipment is decreased by $375 each month. In Chapter 8, we will see the same principles applied to certain intangible assets.

FYI An increase in the contra asset account Accumulated Depreciation reduces the book value of the asset.

Type 3: Accrued Revenues Revenue should be recognized when the company has transferred goods or services to customers, and in an amount that reflects the amount to which the company expects to be entitled from the transfer. Yet, a company often provides services during a period that are neither paid for by customers nor billed before the end of the period. Such values should be included in the firm's current period income statement, reflecting the company's fulfillment of its agreement with the customer. To properly account for such situations, end-of-period adjusting entries are made to reflect any revenues or income earned, but not yet billed or received. Such accumulated revenue is often called **accrued revenue** or **accrued income**.

ACCRUED SALES REVENUE/INCOME At the end of December, Natural Beauty Supply learns that its bank has decided to provide interest on checking accounts for small businesses like NBS. Each month, NBS earns interest income based on the average balance in its checking account. The interest is paid into NBS' checking account on the fifth business day of the following month. Based on its average daily balance, NBS earned $30 in interest during December.

In this instance, Natural Beauty Supply does not receive the interest payment until January. Nevertheless, the company earned interest during the month of December. Therefore, it should recognize an interest receivable (or "other receivables") asset and interest income in the income statement. (We could also call this interest revenue, but the term "interest income" is more commonly used for nonfinancial companies.) The entry in the FSET, the journal entry, and the T-account posting is:

ANALYZE

	Balance Sheet									*Income Statement*				
Transaction	Cash Asset	+	Noncash Assets	=	Liabil-ities	+	Contrib. Capital	+	Earned Capital	*Revenues*	–	*Expenses*	=	*Net Income*
(d) Adjusting entry for interest income.			+30 Other Receivables	=					+30 Retained Earnings	+30 Interest Income	–		=	+30

JOURNALIZE

(d)	Other receivables (+A)	30	
	Interest income (+R,+SE)		30
	To record interest income.		

POST

+ Other Receivables (A) –	
(d) 30	

– Interest Income (R) +	
	30 (d)

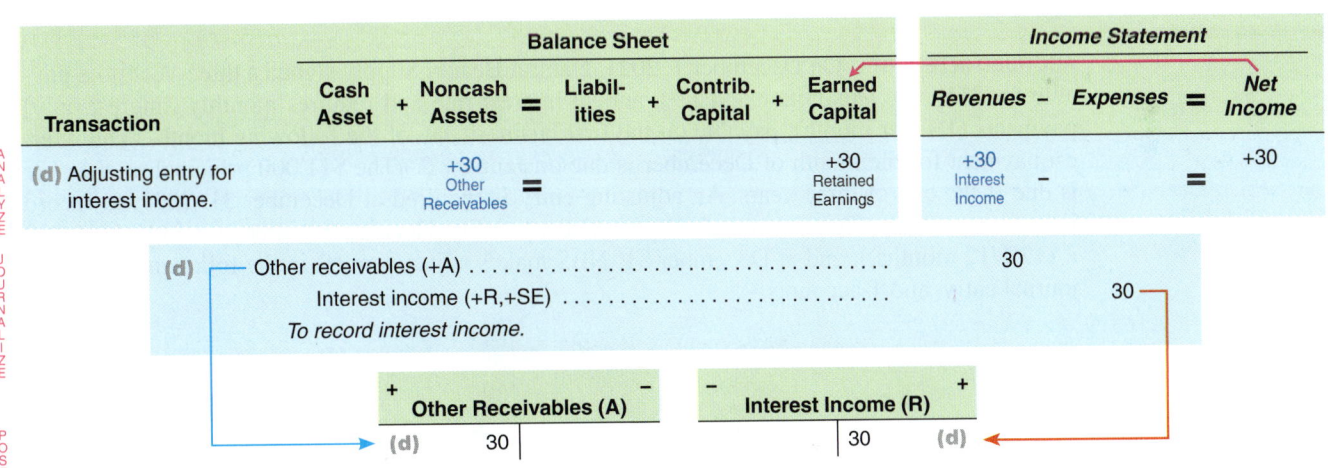

Type 4: Accrued Expenses Companies often incur expenses before paying for them. Wages, interest, utilities, and taxes are examples of expenses that are incurred before cash payment is made. Usually the payments are made at regular intervals of time, such as weekly, monthly, quarterly, or annually. If the accounting period ends on a date that does not coincide with a scheduled cash payment date, an adjusting entry is required to reflect the expense incurred since the last cash payment. Such an expense is referred to as an **accrued expense**. Natural Beauty Supply has three such required adjustments for December 31: one for wages, one for interest, and one for income tax.

ACCRUED WAGES Natural Beauty Supply employees are paid on a weekly basis. Recall that wages of $1,625 were paid during December in transaction 24. However, as of December 31, the company's employees have earned wages of $480 that will be paid in January. Wages expense of $480 must be recorded in the income statement for December because there is now an obligation to compensate employees, who helped generate revenues for December.

ANALYZE

Transaction	Cash Asset	+	Noncash Assets	=	Liabilities	+	Contrib. Capital	+	Earned Capital	Revenues	−	Expenses	=	Net Income
(e) Adjusting entry to record wages earned but not yet paid.				=	+480 Wages Payable				−480 Retained Earnings		−	+480 Wages Expense	=	−480

JOURNALIZE

(e)	Wages expense (+E, −SE)	480	
	Wages payable (+L)		480
	To record accrued wages earned for December.		

POST

+ Wages Expense (E) −	
(e) 480	

− Wages Payable (L) +	
	480 (e)

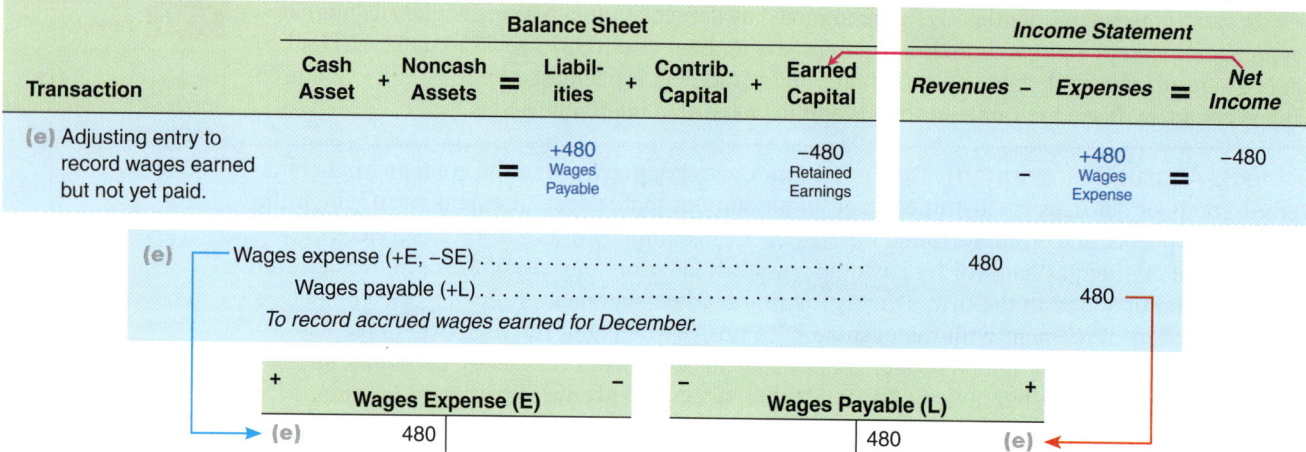

This adjustment enables the firm to reflect as December expense the cost of all wages *incurred* during the month rather than just the wages *paid*. In addition, the balance sheet shows the liability for unpaid wages at the end of the period.

When the employees are paid in January, the following entry is made.

Jan.	Wages payable (−L)	480	
	Cash (−A)		480

This entry eliminates the liability recorded in Wages Payable at the end of December and reduces Cash for the wages paid.

ACCRUED INTEREST On December 1, 2021, Natural Beauty Supply signed a three-year note payable for $11,000. This note has a 12% annual interest rate and requires monthly (interest-only) payments (1% per month), payable on the first business day of the following month. (The interest payment for the month of December is due on January 2.) The $11,000 principal on the note is due at the end of three years. An adjusting entry is required at December 31, 2021, to record interest expense for December and to recognize a liability. December's interest is $110 [$11,000 × (12%/12 months)], and at December 31, NBS makes adjustment (f) in the following template, journal entry, and T-accounts.

ANALYZE

Transaction	Cash Asset	+	Noncash Assets	=	Liabilities	+	Contrib. Capital	+	Earned Capital	Revenues	−	Expenses	=	Net Income
(f) Adjusting entry to record interest owed but not yet paid.				=	+110 Interest Payable				−110 Retained Earnings		−	+110 Interest Expense	=	−110

JOURNALIZE

(f)	Interest expense (+E, −SE)	110	
	Interest payable (+L)		110
	To record December interest on note payable.		

POST

+ Interest Expense (E) −	
(f) 110	

− Interest Payable (L) +	
	110 (f)

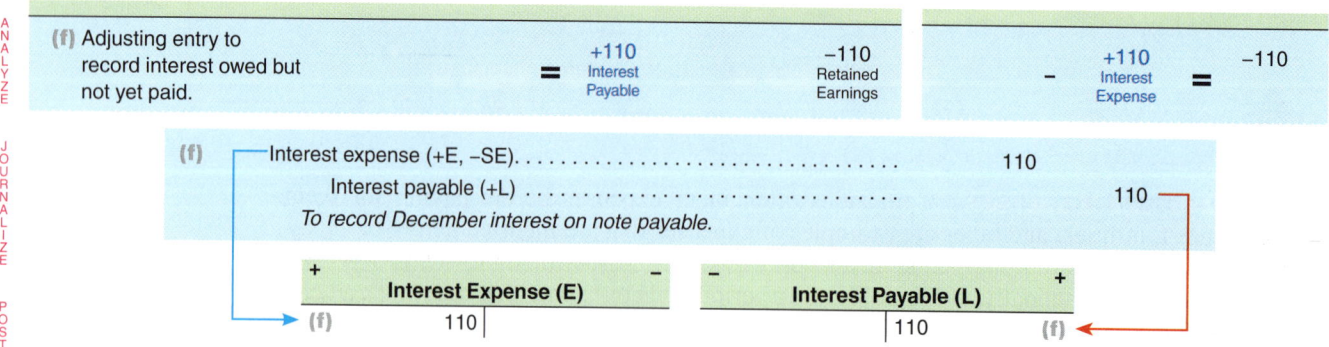

When these entries are posted to the general ledger, the accounts show the correct interest expense for December and the interest liability for one month's interest on the note that has accrued by December 31.

ACCRUED INCOME TAX Describing this at a high level for now (Chapter 10 will cover the topic in more detail), Natural Beauty Supply is required to pay income taxes based on how much it earns. Using an estimated 25% tax rate, income tax expense for December 2021 is $250, computed as ($13,900 sales revenue + $30 interest income − $8,000 cost of goods sold − $1,500 rent expense − $2,105 wages expense − $700 advertising expense − $375 depreciation expense − $140 insurance expense − $110 interest expense) × 25%. Even if the tax payments are not actually made until 2022 (for example, when the company files their tax return), there is an obligation created as a result of the operations in December 2021. Natural Beauty Supply makes adjustment (g) for taxes in the following template, journal entry, and T-accounts.

ANALYZE

	Balance Sheet									Income Statement				
Transaction	**Cash Asset**	+	**Noncash Assets**	=	**Liabilities**	+	**Contrib. Capital**	+	**Earned Capital**	***Revenues***	−	***Expenses***	=	***Net Income***
(g) Adjusting entry for estimated income tax.				=	+250 Tax Payable				−250 Retained Earnings		−	+250 Tax Expense	=	−250

JOURNALIZE

		Dr.	Cr.
(g)	Tax expense (+E, −SE)	250	
	Taxes payable (+L)		250
	To record estimated income tax for December 2021.		

POST

+ Tax Expense (E) −		− Taxes Payable (L) +	
(g) 250			250 (g)

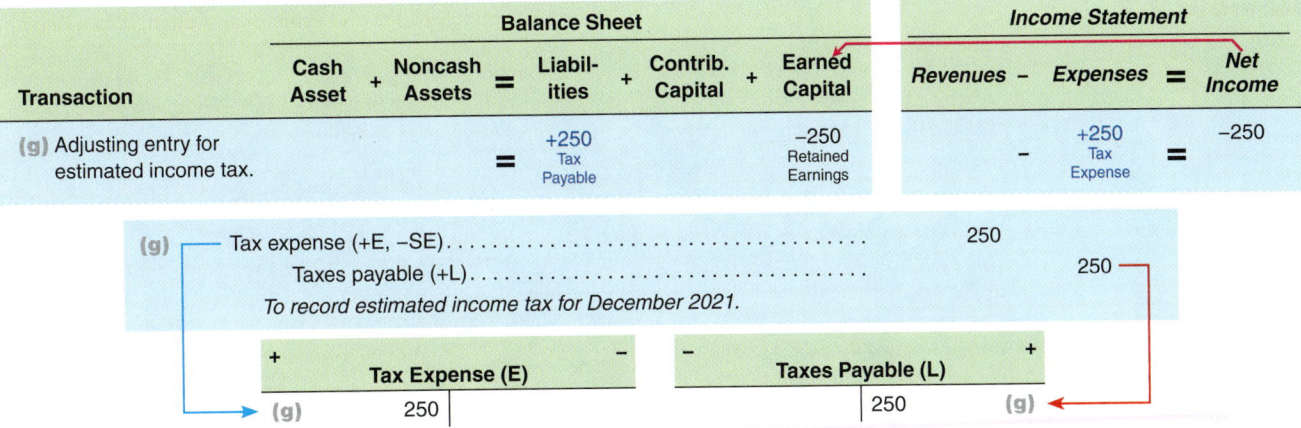

Exhibit 3.6 summarizes the four types of accounting adjustments, the usual journal entries required for each, and their financial impacts on the balance sheet and income statements.

EXHIBIT 3.6 Summary of Accounting Adjustments

Accounting Adjustment	Examples	Adjusting Entry	Financial Effects if *Not* Adjusted: Balance Sheet	Financial Effects if *Not* Adjusted: Income Statement
Deferrals: Deferred revenues	Delivery on advances from clients, gift cards, and subscribers	Dr. Liability Cr. Revenue	Liability overstated Equity understated	Revenue understated
Deferred (Prepaid) Expenses	Expiration of prepaid rent for short-term leases, insurance, and advertising; depreciation of buildings and equipment	Dr. Expense Cr. Asset (or Contra asset)	Asset overstated Equity overstated	Expense understated
Accruals: Accrued revenues	Earned but not received service, sales, and interest revenues	Dr. Asset Cr. Revenue	Asset understated Equity understated	Revenue understated
Accrued expenses	Incurred but unpaid wages, interest, and tax expenses	Dr. Expense Cr. Liability	Liability understated Equity overstated	Expense understated

Ethics and Adjusting Entries

When companies engage in transactions, there is some evidence of the exchange. Cash increases or decreases; asset and liability levels change. Adjusting entries are much more dependent on estimation processes. What was the value of service provided to customers? What obligations have arisen in the past period without a transaction? What is their value? What is the expected useful life of our depreciable assets?

The usefulness of financial performance measures such as net income depends on these questions being answered to the best of management's ability. However, there often are pressures not to provide the most accurate information. For instance, an estimate might convey information about management's strategy that could be used by competitors. Or, the financial community may have set expectations for performance that management cannot meet by executing its current business plan. In these circumstances, managers are sometimes pressured to use the discretion inherent in the reporting process to meet analysts' expectations or to disguise a planned course of action.

The financial reporting environment described in Chapter 1 imposes significant controls on financial reporting because that reporting process is important to thc health of the economy.

Managers who do not report accurately and completely are potentially subject to severe penalties. Moreover, adjusting entry estimates have a "self-correcting" character. Underestimating expenses today means greater expenses tomorrow; overestimating revenues today means lower revenues tomorrow.

Review 3-2 LO3-2

Record Adjusting Entries and Prepare an Adjusted Trial Balance

GuidedExample MBC

Use the unadjusted June 30 trial balance for Atwell Laboratories, Inc., completed in Review 3-1 as the starting point for this review. Assume that the company's accounts are adjusted and closed at the company's fiscal year end of June 30. The company summarized the following additional information.

1. Atwell acquired a two-year insurance policy on January 1. The policy covers fire and casualty; Atwell had no coverage prior to January 1.
2. An inventory of supplies was taken on June 30, and the amount available was $6,300.
3. All equipment was purchased on July 1, three years earlier, for $270,000. The equipment's life is estimated at 9 years. Assume the entire asset cost is depreciated over its useful life.
4. Atwell received a $4,000 cash payment on April 1 from Beave Clinic for diagnostic work to be provided uniformly over the next 4 months, beginning April 1. The amount was credited to Contract Liability. The service was provided per the agreement.
5. Unpaid and unrecorded wages at June 30 were $600.
6. Atwell has a short-term rental for $2,000 per month. Atwell has not yet made or recorded the payment for June.

In addition to the unadjusted accounts listed above, Atwell's ledger includes the following accounts, all with zero balances: Insurance Expense; Depreciation Expense; Supplies Expense; Wages Payable; and Rent Payable.

Required

a. Show the impact of the necessary adjusting entries using the FSET.
b. Show the impact of the necessary adjusting entries using journal entries.
c. Prepare T-accounts with the June 30 unadjusted balances as beginning balances and enter the adjusting entries from part *b*.
d. Prepare Atwell's June 30 adjusted trial balance by entering the adjusting journal entries into the T-accounts.

Solution on p. 3-52.

CONSTRUCTING FINANCIAL STATEMENTS FROM ADJUSTED ACCOUNTS

LO3-3 Prepare financial statements from adjusted accounts

This section explains the preparation of financial statements from the adjusted financial accounts.

Preparing an Adjusted Trial Balance

eLecture MBC

After adjustments are recorded and posted, the company prepares an adjusted trial balance. The **adjusted trial balance** lists all the general ledger account balances after adjustments. Much of the content for company financial statements is taken from an adjusted trial balance. **Exhibit 3.7** shows the general ledger accounts for Natural Beauty Supply after adjustments, in T-account form.

The adjusted trial balance at December 31 for Natural Beauty Supply is prepared from its general ledger accounts and is in the right-hand two columns of **Exhibit 3.8**. We show the unadjusted balances along with the adjustments to highlight the adjustment process.

EXHIBIT 3.7 General Ledger for Natural Beauty Supply after Adjustments

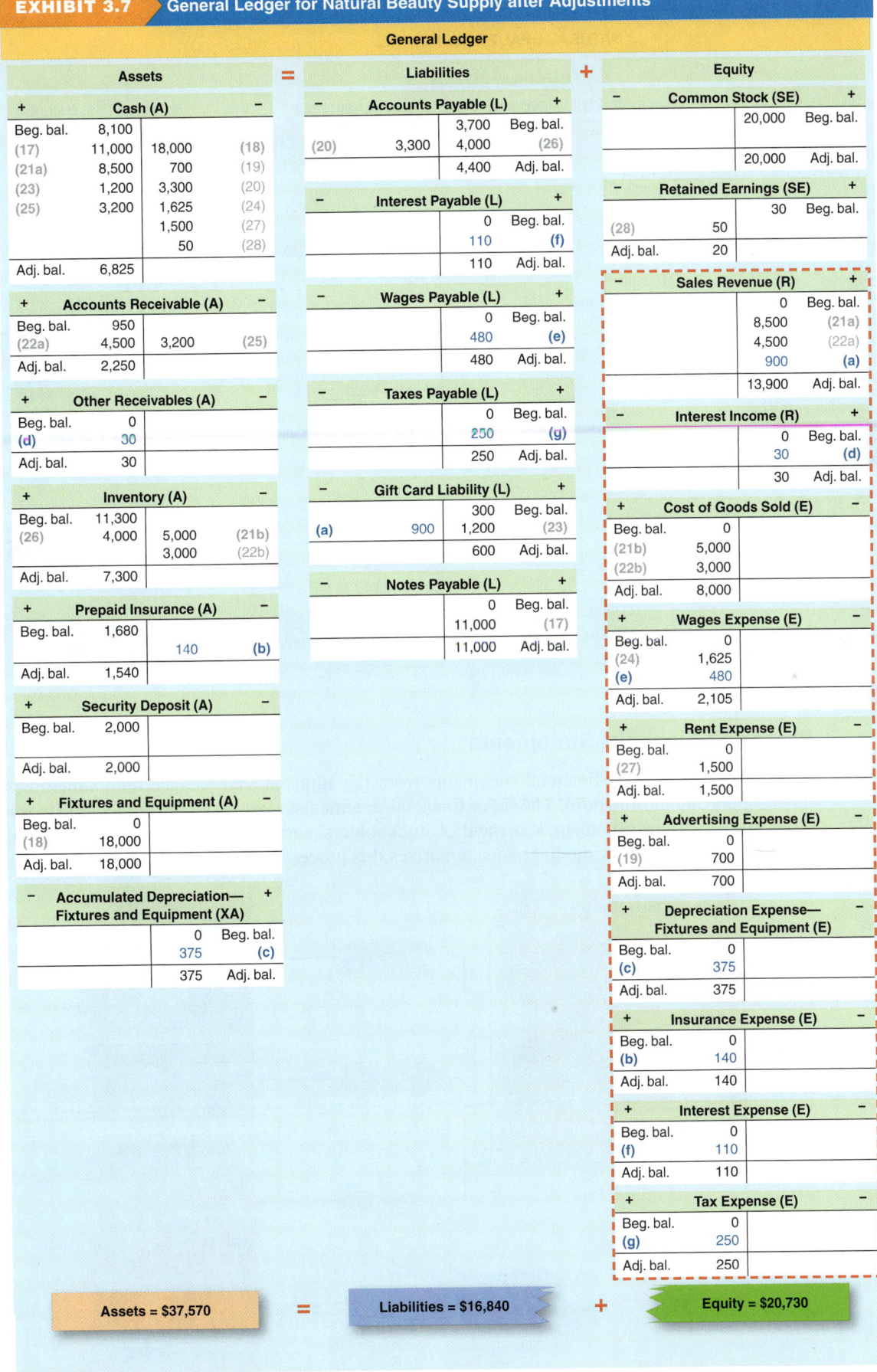

General Ledger

Assets =

+ Cash (A) −

Beg. bal.	8,100		
(17)	11,000	18,000	(18)
(21a)	8,500	700	(19)
(23)	1,200	3,300	(20)
(25)	3,200	1,625	(24)
		1,500	(27)
		50	(28)
Adj. bal.	6,825		

+ Accounts Receivable (A) −

Beg. bal.	950		
(22a)	4,500	3,200	(25)
Adj. bal.	2,250		

+ Other Receivables (A) −

Beg. bal.	0		
(d)	30		
Adj. bal.	30		

+ Inventory (A) −

Beg. bal.	11,300		
(26)	4,000	5,000	(21b)
		3,000	(22b)
Adj. bal.	7,300		

+ Prepaid Insurance (A) −

Beg. bal.	1,680		
		140	(b)
Adj. bal.	1,540		

+ Security Deposit (A) −

Beg. bal.	2,000		
Adj. bal.	2,000		

+ Fixtures and Equipment (A) −

Beg. bal.	0		
(18)	18,000		
Adj. bal.	18,000		

− Accumulated Depreciation—Fixtures and Equipment (XA) +

		0	Beg. bal.
		375	(c)
		375	Adj. bal.

Liabilities +

− Accounts Payable (L) +

		3,700	Beg. bal.
(20)	3,300	4,000	(26)
		4,400	Adj. bal.

− Interest Payable (L) +

		0	Beg. bal.
		110	(f)
		110	Adj. bal.

− Wages Payable (L) +

		0	Beg. bal.
		480	(e)
		480	Adj. bal.

− Taxes Payable (L) +

		0	Beg. bal.
		250	(g)
		250	Adj. bal.

− Gift Card Liability (L) +

		300	Beg. bal.
(a)	900	1,200	(23)
		600	Adj. bal.

− Notes Payable (L) +

		0	Beg. bal.
		11,000	(17)
		11,000	Adj. bal.

Equity

− Common Stock (SE) +

		20,000	Beg. bal.
		20,000	Adj. bal.

− Retained Earnings (SE) +

		30	Beg. bal.
(28)	50		
Adj. bal.	20		

− Sales Revenue (R) +

		0	Beg. bal.
		8,500	(21a)
		4,500	(22a)
		900	(a)
		13,900	Adj. bal.

− Interest Income (R) +

		0	Beg. bal.
		30	(d)
		30	Adj. bal.

+ Cost of Goods Sold (E) −

Beg. bal.	0		
(21b)	5,000		
(22b)	3,000		
Adj. bal.	8,000		

+ Wages Expense (E) −

Beg. bal.	0		
(24)	1,625		
(e)	480		
Adj. bal.	2,105		

+ Rent Expense (E) −

Beg. bal.	0		
(27)	1,500		
Adj. bal.	1,500		

+ Advertising Expense (E) −

Beg. bal.	0		
(19)	700		
Adj. bal.	700		

+ Depreciation Expense—Fixtures and Equipment (E) −

Beg. bal.	0		
(c)	375		
Adj. bal.	375		

+ Insurance Expense (E) −

Beg. bal.	0		
(b)	140		
Adj. bal.	140		

+ Interest Expense (E) −

Beg. bal.	0		
(f)	110		
Adj. bal.	110		

+ Tax Expense (E) −

Beg. bal.	0		
(g)	250		
Adj. bal.	250		

Assets = $37,570 = **Liabilities = $16,840** + **Equity = $20,730**

EXHIBIT 3.8 Unadjusted and Adjusted Trial Balances

NATURAL BEAUTY SUPPLY, INC.
Trial Balance
December 31, 2021

	Unadjusted Trial Balance		Adjustments		Adjusted Trial Balance	
	Debit	Credit	Debit	Credit	Debit	Credit
Cash	$ 6,825				$ 6,825	
Accounts receivable	2,250				2,250	
Other receivables			(d) $ 30		30	
Inventory	7,300				7,300	
Prepaid insurance	1,680			(b) $ 140	1,540	
Security deposit	2,000				2,000	
Fixtures and equipment	18,000				18,000	
Accumulated depreciation				(c) 375		$ 375
Accounts payable		$ 4,400				4,400
Interest payable				(f) 110		110
Wages payable				(e) 480		480
Taxes payable				(g) 250		250
Gift card liability		1,500	(a) 900			600
Notes payable		11,000				11,000
Common stock		20,000				20,000
Retained earnings	20				20	
Sales revenue		13,000		(a) 900		13,900
Interest income				(d) 30		30
Cost of goods sold	8,000				8,000	
Wages expense	1,625		(e) 480		2,105	
Rent expense	1,500				1,500	
Advertising expense	700				700	
Depreciation expense			(c) 375		375	
Insurance expense			(b) 140		140	
Interest expense			(f) 110		110	
Tax expense			(g) 250		250	
Totals	$49,900	$49,900	$2,285	$2,285	$51,145	$51,145

Preparing Financial Statements

A company prepares its financial statements from the adjusted trial balance (and sometimes other supporting information). The set of financial statements consists of (and is prepared in the order of) the income statement, statement of stockholders' equity, balance sheet, and statement of cash flows. The following diagram summarizes this process.

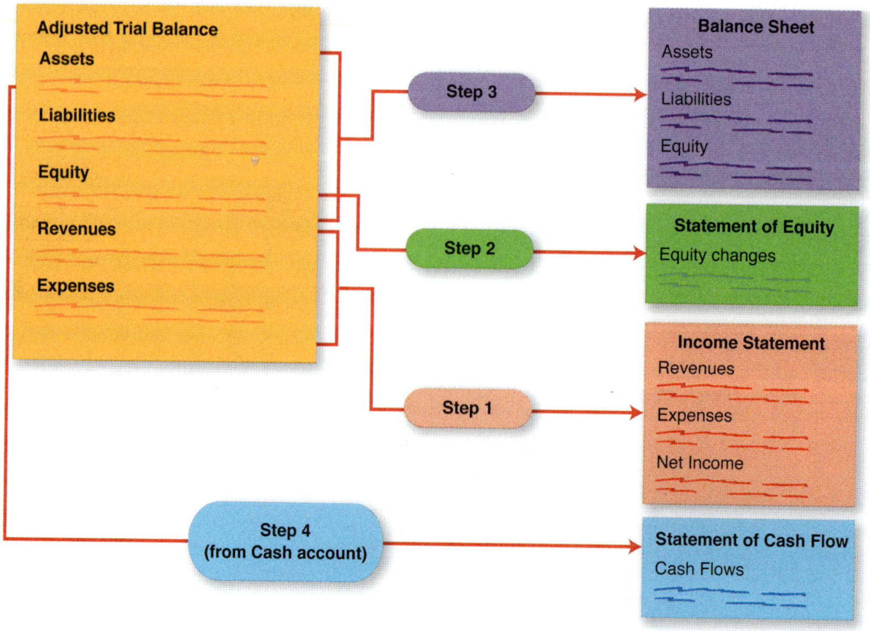

Income Statement The income statement reports a company's revenues and expenses. Natural Beauty Supply's adjusted trial balance contains two revenue/income accounts and eight expense accounts. The revenues and expenses are reported in Natural Beauty Supply's income statement for December, as shown in **Exhibit 3.9**. Its net income for December is $750.

EXHIBIT 3.9 Income Statement

NATURAL BEAUTY SUPPLY, INC.
Income Statement
For Month Ended December 31, 2021

Sales revenue	$13,900
Cost of goods sold	8,000
Gross profit	5,900
Wages expense	2,105
Rent expense	1,500
Advertising expense	700
Depreciation expense	375
Insurance expense	140
Operating income	1,080
Interest income	00
Interest expense	(110)
Income before tax expense	1,000
Tax expense	250
Net income	$ 750

Statement of Stockholders' Equity The statement of stockholders' equity reports the events causing the major equity components to change during the accounting period. **Exhibit 3.10** shows Natural Beauty Supply's statement of stockholders' equity for December. A review of its common stock account in the general ledger provides some of the information for this statement—namely, its balance at the beginning of the period and stock issuances during the period. The net income (or net loss) amount comes from the income statement. Dividends during the period are reflected in the retained earnings balance from the adjusted trial balance.

EXHIBIT 3.10 Statement of Stockholders' Equity

NATURAL BEAUTY SUPPLY, INC.
Statement of Stockholders' Equity
For Month Ended December 31, 2021

	Contributed Capital	Earned Capital	Total Equity
Balance, November 30, 2021	$20,000	$ 30	$20,030
Net income	—	750	750
Common stock issued	—	—	—
Cash dividends	—	(50)	(50)
Balances, December 31, 2021	$20,000	$730	$20,730

FYI Financial statements are most commonly prepared for annual and quarterly accounting periods. A request for a bank loan is an example of a situation that can lead to financial statement preparation for a non-accounting period.

Balance Sheet The balance sheet reports a company's assets, liabilities, and equity. The assets and liabilities for Natural Beauty Supply's balance sheet at December 31, 2021, shown in **Exhibit 3.11**, come from the adjusted trial balance in **Exhibit 3.8**. The amounts reported for Common Stock and Retained Earnings in the balance sheet are taken from the statement of stockholders' equity for December (**Exhibit 3.10**).

EXHIBIT 3.11 Balance Sheet

NATURAL BEAUTY SUPPLY, INC.
Balance Sheet
December 31, 2021

Assets			**Liabilities**	
Cash		$ 6,825	Accounts payable	$ 4,400
Accounts receivable		2,250	Interest payable	110
Other receivables		30	Wages payable	480
Inventory		7,300	Taxes payable	250
Prepaid insurance		1,540	Gift card liability	600
Security deposit		2,000	Current liabilities	5,840
Current assets		19,945	Notes payable	11,000
Fixtures and equipment	$18,000		Total liabilities	16,840
Less: Accumulated depreciation	375		**Equity**	
Fixtures and equipment, net		17,625	Common stock	20,000
			Retained earnings	730
Total assets		$37,570	Total liabilities and equity	$37,570

Review 3-3 LO3-3

Preparing Financial Statements

GuidedExample
MBC

Use the adjusted June 30 trial balance for Atwell Laboratories, Inc., completed in Review 3-2 as the starting point for this review.

Required

Prepare the company's June 30 balance sheet and its income statement and statement of stockholders' equity for the year ended June 30.

Solution on p. 3-54.

FYI The income statement, statement of stockholders' equity, and statement of cash flows report on periods of time. These statements illustrate the accounting period concept—the concept that useful statements can be prepared for arbitrary time periods within a company's life span. The purpose of adjusting entries is to obtain useful statements for specific time periods.

Statement of Cash Flows The statement of cash flows is formatted to report cash inflows and outflows by the three primary business activities:

- *Cash flows from operating activities* Cash flows from the company's transactions and events that relate to its primary operations.
- *Cash flows from investing activities* Cash flows from acquisitions and divestitures of investments and long-term assets.
- *Cash flows from financing activities* Cash flows from issuances of and payments toward equity, borrowings, and long-term liabilities.

The net cash flows from these three sections yield the change in cash for the period.

In analyzing the statement of cash flows, we should not necessarily conclude that the company is better off if cash increases and worse off if cash decreases. It is not the cash change that is most important, but the reasons for the change. For example, what are the sources of the cash inflows? Are these sources mainly from operating activities? To what uses have cash inflows been put? Such questions (and their answers) are key to properly using the statement of cash flows. In Chapter 4, we examine the statement of cash flows more closely and answer these questions. The procedures for preparing a statement of cash flows are discussed in the next chapter. For completeness, we present Natural Beauty Supply's statement of cash flows for December in **Exhibit 3.12**.

EXHIBIT 3.12 Statement of Cash Flows

NATURAL BEAUTY SUPPLY, INC. Statement of Cash Flows For Month Ended December 31, 2021	
Cash Flows from Operating Activities	
Cash received from customers	$12,900
Cash paid for inventory	(3,300)
Cash paid for wages	(1,625)
Cash paid for rent	(1,500)
Cash paid for advertising	(700)
Net cash provided by operating activities	5,775
Cash Flows from Investing Activities	
Cash paid for fixtures and equipment	(18,000)
Net cash used for investing activities	(18,000)
Cash Flows from Financing Activities	
Cash received from loans	11,000
Cash paid for dividends	(50)
Net cash provided by financing activities	10,950
Net change in cash	(1,275)
Cash balance, November 30, 2021	8,100
Cash balance, December 31, 2021	$ 6,825

CLOSING TEMPORARY ACCOUNTS

LO3-4 Describe the process of closing temporary accounts.

eLecture MBC

The chart of accounts contains two different types of accounts. Income statement accounts (revenues, expenses, etc.) are used to measure the net assets generated and used in a specific accounting period. As such, their end-of-period balances are reported in the income statement for that period. We use those balances to construct the statements of stockholders' equity and cash flows. But then these account balances have served their purpose, and we must get them ready to do the same thing for the following accounting period. Specifically, we must set their balances to zero so they can accumulate the revenues and expenses for that following period. For this reason, income statement accounts are called **temporary accounts**. Their end-of-period values do not carry over to the next reporting period.

In contrast, balance sheet account balances do carry over to the next reporting period. For example, the end-of-period balance in accounts receivable is the beginning-of-period balance for the next period. Therefore, balance sheet accounts are referred to as **permanent accounts**.

Permanent Accounts			Temporary Accounts	
Assets	Liabilities	Equity Contributed capital Retained earnings	Revenues	Expenses

The **closing process** takes the end-of-period balances in the temporary accounts and moves them to a permanent account—the Retained Earnings account. A temporary account is *closed* when an entry is made that changes its balance to zero. The entry is equal in amount to the account's balance but is opposite to the balance as a debit or credit. An account that is closed is said to be closed *to* the account that receives the offsetting debit or credit. Thus, a closing entry simply transfers the balance of one account to another account. When closing entries bring temporary account balances to zero, the temporary accounts are then ready to accumulate data for the next accounting period.

Closing Process

The Retained Earnings account can be used to close the temporary revenue and expense accounts.[5] The entries to close temporary accounts are:

[5] *All* revenue and expense accounts are temporary accounts, so they are closed to retained earnings at the end of the reporting period. In addition, companies often use a temporary account entitled Dividends Declared to record the amount of shareholder dividends declared during a reporting period. This account would accumulate a debit balance (because it reduces equity) and is closed to retained earnings at the end of the reporting period.

1. **Close revenue accounts.** Debit each revenue account for an amount equal to its balance, and credit Retained Earnings for the total of revenues.
2. **Close expense accounts.** Credit each expense account for an amount equal to its balance, and debit Retained Earnings for the total of expenses.

After these temporary accounts are closed, the difference equals the period's net income (if revenues exceed expenses) or net loss (if expenses exceed revenues), and that difference is now included in Retained Earnings. The closing process is graphically portrayed as follows.

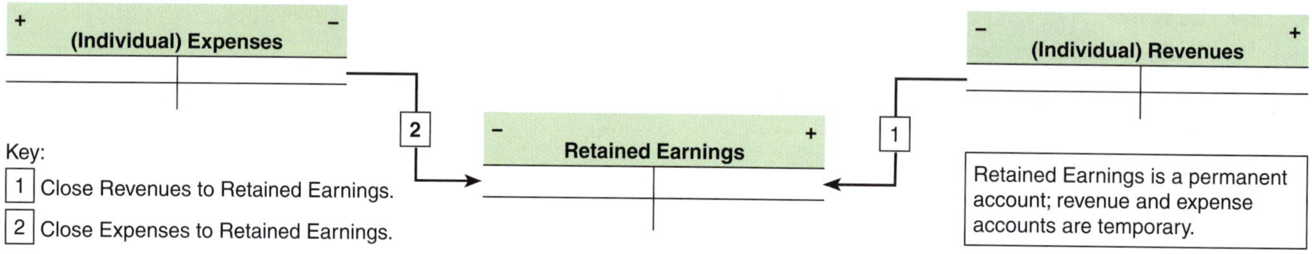

Closing Steps Illustrated

Exhibit 3.13 illustrates the entries for closing revenues and expenses for Natural Beauty Supply. The effects of these entries in T-accounts are shown after the journal entries. (We do not show the financial statement effects template for closing entries because the template automatically closes revenues and expenses to the Retained Earnings account as they occur—see earlier transactions for examples.)

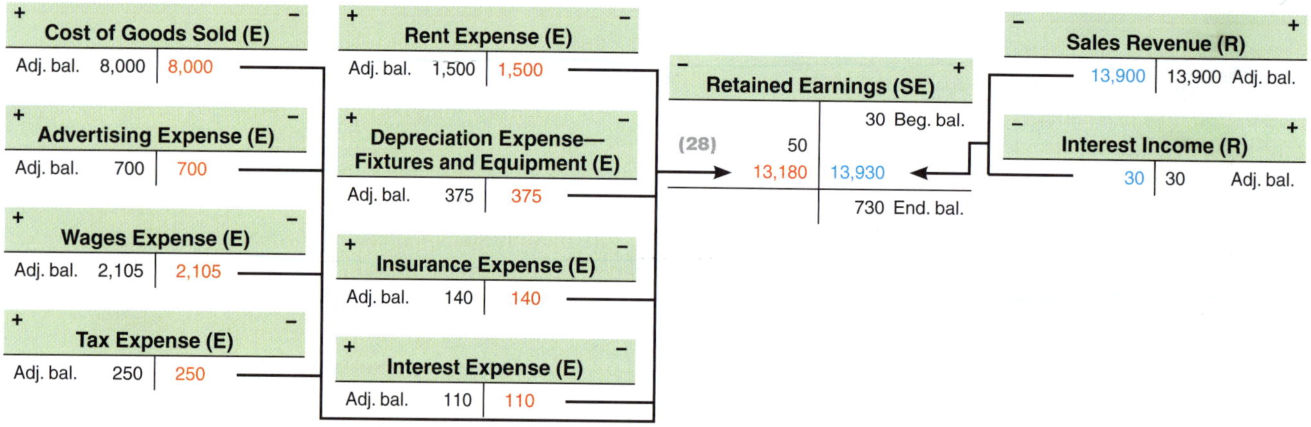

EXHIBIT 3.13 Closing Revenues and Expenses*

1	Dec. 31	Sales revenue (−R)	13,900	
		Interest income (−R)	30	
		Retained earnings (+SE)		13,930
2	Dec. 31	Retained earnings (−SE)	13,180	
		Cost of goods sold (−E)		8,000
		Wages expense (−E)		2,105
		Rent expense (−E)		1,500
		Advertising expense (−E)		700
		Depreciation expense (−E)		375
		Insurance expense (−E)		140
		Interest expense (−E)		110
		Tax expense (−E)		250

* The two entries in this exhibit can be combined into a single entry where the credit (debit) to retained earnings would be net income (loss).

After these two steps, the net adjustment to the Retained Earnings account is a credit equal to the company's net income of $750, computed as $13,930 less $13,180. The Retained Earnings account in this case is increased by $750. We also recall that Natural Beauty Supply paid a cash dividend of $50 (transaction 28), which reduces retained earnings and results in the ending balance of $730.

Preparing a Post-Closing Trial Balance

After closing entries are recorded and posted to the general ledger, all temporary accounts have zero balances. At this point, a **post-closing trial balance** is prepared. A balancing of this trial balance is evidence that an equality of debits and credits has been maintained in the general ledger throughout the adjusting and closing process and that the general ledger is in balance to start the next accounting period. Only balance sheet accounts appear in a post-closing trial balance because all income statement accounts have balances of zero. The post-closing trial balance for Natural Beauty Supply is shown in **Exhibit 3.14**.

EXHIBIT 3.14 Post-Closing Trial Balance

NATURAL BEAUTY SUPPLY, INC.
Post-Closing Trial Balance
December 31, 2021

	Debit	Credit
Cash	$ 6,825	
Accounts receivable	2,250	
Other receivables	30	
Inventory	7,300	
Prepaid insurance	1,540	
Security deposit	2,000	
Fixtures and equipment	18,000	
Accumulated depreciation		$ 375
Accounts payable		4,400
Interest payable		110
Wages payable		480
Taxes payable		250
Gift card liability		600
Notes payable		11,000
Common stock		20,000
Retained earnings		730
Totals	$37,945	$37,945

Subsequent Events

There is usually a few weeks' delay between the end of the fiscal reporting period and the issuing of the financial reports for that period. What happens if a significant event occurs (e.g., a fire at a production facility, an acquisition, etc.) during that interim? Should the previous period's financial statements be changed to reflect the event?

If the event doesn't provide information about the company's condition on the balance sheet date, then the answer is no. So, neither the fire nor the acquisition would be reported in the previous period's financial statements. Such events should be disclosed in a note, if they are material.

SUMMARIZING THE ACCOUNTING CYCLE

The sequence of accounting procedures known as the accounting cycle occurs each fiscal year (period) and represents a systematic process for accumulating and reporting financial data of a company. **Exhibit 3.15** expands on **Exhibit 3.1** to include descriptions of the five major steps in the accounting cycle.

EXHIBIT 3.15 Accounting Cycle

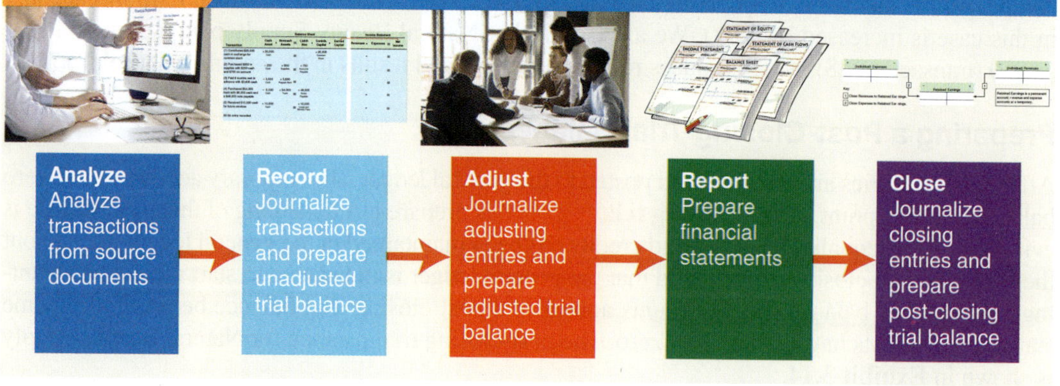
Analyze
Analyze transactions from source documents
Record
Journalize transactions and prepare unadjusted trial balance
Adjust
Journalize adjusting entries and prepare adjusted trial balance
Report
Prepare financial statements
Close
Journalize closing entries and prepare post-closing trial balance

Review 3-4 LO3-4

Preparing Closing Entries

GuidedExample MBC

Use the adjusted June 30 trial balance for Atwell Laboratories, Inc., completed in Review 3-2 as the starting point for this review.

Required

a. Prepare Atwell's closing journal entries.

b. Post entries from part *a* to T-accounts (key the entries).

Solution on p. 3-55.

FINANCIAL STATEMENT ANALYSIS

Using Information on Levels and Flows

LO3-5 Analyze changes in balance sheet accounts.

eLecture MBC

A careful reader of financial statements must differentiate between those things that depict *levels* and those that depict *flows* or *changes*. The balance sheet portrays levels of resources and claims on those resources at a point in time, and the income statement portrays changes in those levels over a period of time. Knowing how the levels and flows relate to each other can be a very useful tool for analysis.

For instance, suppose that a service business has an inventory of office supplies. On July 1, an inventory count determined that the business has $2,400 of supplies inventory on hand. During the third calendar quarter, there were deliveries of office supplies with a cost of $5,700. And, at the end of the third quarter—on September 30—an inventory count finds $1,900 of supplies on hand. What amount of supplies expense should be recognized for the quarter?

Finding the answer to this question is easier if we recall the transactions that can affect the supplies inventory account, and that these transactions (changes) must lead from the beginning inventory level to the ending inventory level. At present, we know of two such transactions: the purchase of supplies inventory and the usage of supplies inventory.

(a)	Supplies inventory (+A).	5,700	
	Cash (−A) or Accounts payable (+L)		5,700
	Purchase supplies inventory.		
(b)	Supplies expense (+E, −SE).	?	
	Supplies inventory (−A)		?
	Record expense for supplies used.		

The supplies inventory T-account must look like the following:

+	Supplies Inventory (A)		−
Beg. bal.	2,400		
(a)	5,700	?	(b)
End. bal.	1,900		

An FSET version of this analysis would look like the following, with the only noncash account being supplies inventory, and assuming that the supplies inventory purchase was made with cash.

Transaction	Balance Sheet: Cash Asset	+ Supplies Inventory	= Liabilities	+ Contrib. Capital	+ Earned Capital	Income Statement: Revenues	− Expenses	= Net Income
Beg. bal.		2,400 Supplies Inv						
(a) Purchase office supplies	−5,700 Cash	+5,700 Supplies Inv =				−		=
(b) Office supplies taken for use in client service activities		−? Supplies Inv =			−? Retained Earnings	−	+? Supplies Expense	= −?
End. bal.		1,900 Supplies Inv						

Balancing the account requires that $2,400 + $5,700 − ? = $1,900, and the value that satisfies this condition is $6,200. That amount would be recorded as supplies expense for the quarter.

This application of the account structure is a simple one. But, suppose that a separate source of information (e.g., scanner data) told us that $5,900 in supplies had been taken from inventory for client service activities. When put into the FSET/T-account analysis above, this new fact would imply an additional $300 in supplies had been removed for reasons such as breakage, obsolescence, or pilferage.

As we progress through the topics in future chapters, we will find that accounting reports do not always provide the information that is most useful for assessment of a company's current performance or standing. In those cases, we can often use the more detailed T-accounts and journal entries or the FSET to analyze levels and changes and to develop the numbers that do a better job of answering important questions.

Analyzing Changes in Balance Sheet Accounts LO3-5 **Review 3-5**

GuidedExample MBC

The following excerpts were obtained from the trial balance of Lazer Inc.

	Beg. Bal.	End. Bal.
Accounts receivable	$ 45,000	$ 63,000
Supplies inventory	13,000	12,300
Accounts payable	55,000	65,000
Retained earnings	180,000	187,000

Required

a. If sales on account were $200,000, what were cash collections for the period?
b. If $18,200 of supplies inventory was used during the period, what was the total of supplies inventory purchases for the period?
c. If $160,000 was paid on account for the period, what were the new charges on account this period?
d. If net income for the period was $10,000, what were dividends paid during the period?

Solution on p. 3-56.

SUMMARY

LO3-1 Analyze transactions and review the process of journalizing and posting transactions. (p. 3-3)

- The major steps in the accounting cycle are
  a. Analyze *b.* Record *c.* Adjust *d.* Report *e.* Close
- Transactions are initially recorded in a journal; the entries are in chronological order, and the journal shows the total effect of each transaction or adjustment.
- Posting is the transfer of information from a journal to the general ledger accounts.

LO3-2 Describe the adjusting process and illustrate adjusting entries. (p. 3-11)

- Adjusting entries achieve the proper recognition of revenues and the proper matching of expenses with those revenues; adjustments are summarized as follows.

Adjustment	Adjusting Entry
Adjusting prepaid (deferred) expenses	Increase expense Decrease asset
Adjusting unearned (deferred) revenues	Decrease liability Increase revenue
Accruing expenses	Increase expense Increase liability
Accruing revenues	Increase asset Increase revenue

LO3-3 Prepare financial statements from adjusted accounts. (p. 3-19)

- An income statement, statement of stockholders' equity, balance sheet, and statement of cash flows are prepared from an adjusted trial balance and other information.

LO3-4 Describe the process of closing temporary accounts. (p. 3-24)

- *Closing the books* means closing (yielding zero balances) revenues and expenses—that is, all temporary accounts. Revenue and expense account balances are transferred (closed) to the Retained Earnings account.

LO3-5 Analyze changes in balance sheet accounts. (p. 3-27)

- The combination of balance sheet levels and income statement flows allows a financial statement reader to infer the effects of transactions and adjustments that are not disclosed directly.

GUIDANCE ANSWERS . . . YOU MAKE THE CALL

You are the Chief Accountant Deposits represent a liability and should be included in REI's current liabilities at the time the cash or check is received. The account that would be used may have several names, including advances, trip deposits, contract liabilities, or performance obligations. Revenue should not be recognized until goods are transferred or services are provided to the customer. In this instance, REI should not recognize revenues until the trip has been completed. It is not unusual for events to occur that result in a refund of some portion or even all of the traveler's total payment. In the present case involving a low cancellation rate, waiting until the trip is over is not only conservative reporting, but is likely more efficient bookkeeping as well.

Assignments with the MBC logo in the margin are available in myBusinessCourse. See the Preface of the book for details.

MULTIPLE CHOICE

1. An end-of-period journal entry made to reflect accrual accounting is called
   a. a posted journal entry.
   b. an adjusting journal entry.
   c. an erroneous journal entry.
   d. a compound journal entry.

2. Posting refers to the process whereby journal entry information is transferred from
   a. journal to general ledger accounts.
   b. general ledger accounts to a journal.
   c. source documents to a journal.
   d. a journal to source documents.

3. Which of the following is an example of an adjusting entry?
a. Recording the purchase of supplies on account
b. Recording depreciation expense on a truck
c. Recording cash received from customers for services rendered
d. Recording the cash payment of wages to employees

4. A piece of equipment was placed in service on January 1, 2020. The cost of the equipment was $30,000, and it is expected to have no value at the end of its eight-year life. Using straight-line depreciation, what amounts will be seen for depreciation expense and accumulated depreciation for fiscal (and calendar) year 2022?

	Fiscal Year 2022 Depreciation Expense	Fiscal Year-End 2022 Accumulated Depreciation
a.	$ 3,750	$ 3,000
b.	–0–	30,000
c.	3,750	11,250
d.	11,250	11,250

5. When a customer places an order, Custom Cakes requires a deposit equal to the full purchase price. However, Custom Cakes does not recognize revenue until the completed cake is delivered. During the month of November, Custom Cakes received $48,000 in customer deposits. The balance in its customer deposits liability was $8,000 at the beginning of November and $12,000 at the end of November. How much revenue did Custom Cakes recognize during the month of November?
a. $52,000
b. $48,000
c. $44,000
d. $8,000

Multiple Choice Answers
1. b 2. a 3. b 4. c 5. c

QUESTIONS

Q3-1. What are the five major steps in the accounting cycle? List them in their proper order.

Q3-2. What does the term "fiscal year" mean?

Q3-3. What are three examples of source documents that underlie business transactions?

Q3-4. What is the nature and purpose of a general journal?

Q3-5. Explain the process of posting.

Q3-6. What is an adjusting journal entry?

Q3-7. What is a chart of accounts? Give an example of a coding system for identifying different types of accounts.

Q3-8. Why is the adjusting step of the accounting cycle necessary?

Q3-9. What four different types of adjustments are frequently necessary at the close of an accounting period? Give examples of each type.

Q3-10. On January 1, Prepaid Insurance was debited with the cost of a two-year premium, $2,448. What adjusting entry should be made on January 31 before financial statements are prepared for the month?

Q3-11. What is a contra account? What contra account is used in reporting the book value of a depreciable asset?

Q3-12. A building was acquired on January 1, 2014, at a cost of $3,200,000, and its depreciation is calculated using the straight-line method. At the end of 2018, the accumulated depreciation contra asset for the building is $640,000. What will be the balance in the building's accumulated depreciation contra asset at the end of 2025? What is the building's book value at that date?

Q3-13. The publisher of *International View*, a monthly magazine, received two-year digital subscriptions totaling $12,600 on January 1. (a) What entry should be made to record the receipt of the $12,600? (b) What entry should be made at the end of January before financial statements are prepared for the month?

Q3-14. Globe Travel Agency pays an employee $525 in wages each Friday for the five-day workweek ending on that day. The last Friday of January falls on January 27. What adjusting entry should be made on January 31, the fiscal year-end?

Q3-15. The Bayou Company earns interest amounting to $400 per month on its investments. The company receives the interest every six months, on December 31 and June 30. Monthly financial statements are prepared. What adjusting entry should be made on January 31?

Q3-16. Which groups of accounts are closed at the end of the accounting year?

Q3-17. What are the two major steps in the closing process?

Q3-18. What is the purpose of a post-closing trial balance? Which of the following accounts should *not* appear in the post-closing trial balance: Cash; Unearned Revenue; Prepaid Rent; Depreciation Expense; Utilities Payable; Supplies Expense; and Retained Earnings?

Q3-19. Dehning Corporation is an international manufacturer of films and industrial identification products. Included among its prepaid expenses is an account titled Prepaid Catalog Costs; in recent years, this account's size has ranged between \$2,500,000 and \$4,000,000. The company states that catalog costs are initially capitalized and then written off over the estimated useful lives of the publications (generally eight months). Discuss the Dehning Corporation's handling of its catalog costs.

Q3-20. At the beginning of January, the first month of the accounting year, the supplies account had a debit balance of \$990. During January, purchases of \$310 worth of supplies were debited to the account. Although only \$750 of supplies were still available at the end of January, the necessary adjusting entry was omitted. How will the omission affect (a) the income statement for January, and (b) the balance sheet prepared at January 31?

DATA ANALYTICS

LO3-1 **DA3-1. Matching Chart Types and Aims to Data Measures**

In the process of preparing a data visualization, determine which chart would be best suited for each data measure and determine what is the aim of that particular chart. Refer to Appendix B for a description of each chart type.

Data Measure	Chart Type	Aim of Chart
a. Relation of daily clicks on digital ads with daily online sales	__ Bar chart	__ Compare different categories
b. Sales by major city for a company's best-selling product	__ Pie chart	__ Analyze changes over time
c. Level of eight types of digital marketing expenses for the year	__ Line chart	__ Show parts that make up a whole
d. Common stock and retained earnings portions of total equity	__ Scatter plot	__ Show correlation between two variables
e. Ten-year trend in digital marketing expense	__ Map chart	__ Show differences across geographic locations

LO3-3 **DA3-2. Preparing Basic Visualization in Excel of Changes in Sales Data Over Time**

The Excel file associated with this exercise includes daily sales for the month of December for Strickland Inc. In this exercise, we determine which sales amounts appear to be outliers which means that they differ significantly from the other daily sales amounts.

REQUIRED

1. Download Excel file DA3-2 found in myBusinessCourse.
2. Prepare a line chart for the month of December. *Hint:* Highlight the data and open the Insert tab. Click the Line chart in the Charts group and select one of the 2-D lines. Do not include the column titles or the total row when highlighting the data.
3. Add a trendline to the chart. *Hint:* Right-click on the line in your chart to view the option to add a linear trendline.
4. Describe the position of the trendline on the chart on December 18.
5. List the point(s) (if any) on the chart that are positioned over +/–\$1,200 beyond the trendline. *Hint:* Use the gridlines on the chart to help you visually detect outliers.

LO3 **DA3-3. Displaying Key Performance Indicators in Excel**

A key performance indicator (KPI) is a quantifiable measure used to track a company's overall performance. Managers can create a KPI dashboard, which is a data visualization that displays all indicators in one central location. This allows a manager to conveniently track and monitor key operational data. Information in KPI dashboards may even be updated in real time. For this exercise, we use the data included in the Excel file associated with this exercise for Wakeboards Inc. to create a data visualization (dashboard). Wakeboards Inc. manufactures and sells three types of wakeboards to 50 customers located primarily in oceanside cities in the U.S.

REQUIRED

1. Download Excel file DA3-3 found in myBusinessCourse.
2. Create the following six PivotCharts arranged as one KPI dashboard using the data included in file DA3-3.
   a. Top five customers for Model 1 in a bar chart. *Hint:* Click anywhere inside the data table and open the Insert tab. Click PivotTable in the Tables group. Add the PivotTable to a new worksheet. Drag Customer Name to Rows; Model 1 Sales Units to Values. In the PivotTable,

open the dropdown menu next to RowLabels and select Top 10 in the Values Filter menu. Change to Top 5. Click anywhere inside the PivotTable and open the PivotTable Analyze tab. Click PivotChart in the Tools group. Select Bar. Click inside the bars and click Format Data Labels.

b. Top five customers for Model 2 in a bar chart. *Hint:* Highlight all cells in the PivotTable created in part *a*. Right-click and select Copy. Move to another location on the same worksheet. Right-click and select Paste. Make the appropriate changes to the second PivotTable.

c. Top five customers for Model 3 in a bar chart.

d. Sales in units by model by month in a line chart. *Hint:* Months in Rows; Model 1, 2, and 3 Sales Units fields to Values.

e. Most recent monthly sales (December) in a pie chart showing the proportion by Model number. *Hint:* Months in Columns; Model 1, 2, and 3 Sales Units fields to Values.

f. Sales in units by customer by month with a slicer for Customer name and Months. *Hint:* Customer Name and Months fields to Rows; Model 1, 2, and 3 Sales Units fields to Values. Click inside the chart and open the PivotTable Analyze tab. Click Insert Slicer and select Customer Name and Months. Slicers are used to filter the data included in PivotTables.

3. Use the visualizations to answer the following questions.

a. List the third largest customer for Model 1.

b. List the first largest customer for Model 2.

c. List the fifth largest customer for Model 3.

d. List the peak month for sales of Model 1.

e. List the quantity of sales in December for Model 2.

f. List the quantity of sales of Model 1, Model 2, and Model 3 for Marina Inc. in June.

DATA VISUALIZATION

Data Visualization Activities are available in myBusinessCourse. These assignments use Tableau Dashboards to expose students to visual depictions of data and introduce students to data analytics through data visualizations. These exercises are easily assignable and auto graded by MBC.

Data Visualization

MINI EXERCISES

M3-21. Recording Transactions in the Financial Statement Effects Template (FSET) LO3-2

Homework MBC

Creative Designs, a firm providing art services for advertisers, began business on June 1. The following transactions occurred during the month of June.

June 1 Anne Clem invested $30,000 cash to begin the business in exchange for common stock.
2 Paid $2,500 cash for June rent (short-term lease).
3 Purchased $16,000 of office equipment on account.
6 Purchased $9,500 of art materials and other supplies; paid $4,500 cash with the remainder due within 30 days.
11 Billed clients $11,750 for services rendered.
17 Collected $8,100 cash from clients on their accounts.
19 Paid $7,500 cash toward the account for office equipment suppliers (see June 3).
25 Paid $2,200 cash for dividends.
30 Paid $900 cash for June utilities.
30 Paid $5,800 cash for June salaries.

REQUIRED

Record the above transactions for June using the financial statement effects template.

M3-22. Journalizing Transactions and Posting to T-Accounts LO3-1

Homework MBC

Use the information from M3-21 to complete the following requirements.

a. The following accounts in its general ledger are needed to record the transactions for June: Cash; Accounts Receivable; Supplies; Office Equipment; Accounts Payable; Common Stock; Retained Earnings; Service Fee Revenue; Rent Expense; Utilities Expense; and Salaries Expense. Record the above transactions for June in journal entry form.

b. Set up T-accounts for each of the ledger accounts and post the entries to them (key the numbers in T-accounts by date).

LO3-1 Homework MBC

M3-23. Recording Transactions in the Financial Statement Effects Template (FSET)
Minute Maid, a firm providing housecleaning services, began business on April 1. The following transactions occurred during the month of April.

April 1 A. Falcon invested $13,500 cash to begin the business in exchange for common stock.
2 Paid $4,200 cash for six months' lease on van for the business.
3 Borrowed $15,000 cash from bank and signed note payable agreeing to repay it in 1 year plus 10% interest.
3 Purchased $8,200 of cleaning equipment; paid $3,800 cash with the remainder due within 30 days.
4 Paid $6,400 cash for cleaning supplies.
7 Paid $500 cash for advertisements to run in newspaper during April.
21 Billed customers $5,500 for services performed.
23 Paid $4,400 cash on account to cleaning equipment suppliers (see April 3).
28 Collected $4,000 cash from customers on their accounts.
29 Paid $1,500 cash for dividends.
30 Paid $2,600 cash for April wages.
30 Paid $1,480 cash to service station for gasoline used during April.

REQUIRED
Record the above transactions for April using the financial statement effects template.

LO3-1 Homework MBC

M3-24. Journalizing Transactions and Posting to T-Accounts
Use the information from M3-23 to complete the following requirements.

a. The following accounts in its general ledger are needed to record the transactions for April: Cash; Accounts Receivable; Supplies; Prepaid Van Lease; Equipment; Accounts Payable; Notes Payable; Common Stock; Retained Earnings; Cleaning Fees Earned; Van Fuel Expense; Advertising Expense; and Wages Expense. Record the above transactions for April in journal entry form.

b. Set up T-accounts for each of the ledger accounts and post the entries to them (key the numbers in T-accounts by date).

LO3-1, 2 Homework MBC

M3-25. Recording Transactions and Adjustments in the Financial Statement Effects Template (FSET)
Deluxe Building Services offers custodial services on both a contract basis and an hourly basis. On January 1, Deluxe collected $50,250 in advance on a six-month contract for work to be performed evenly during the next six months. Assume that Deluxe closes its books and issues financial reports on a monthly basis.

a. Prepare the entry on January 1 to record the receipt of $50,250 cash for contract work using the financial statements effect template.

b. Prepare the adjusting entry to be made on January 31 for the contract work done during January using the financial statements effect template.

c. At January 31, a total of 45 hours of hourly rate custodial work was unbilled. The billing rate is $19 per hour. Prepare the adjusting entry needed on January 31 using the financial statements effect template. (The firm uses the account Fees Receivable to reflect amounts due but not yet billed.)

LO3-1, 2 Homework MBC

M3-26. Journalizing Transactions and Adjusting Accounts
Using the information from M3-25, prepare entries for parts *a*, *b*, and *c* in journal entry form.

LO3-2, 5 Homework MBC

M3-27. Adjusting Accounts Using the Financial Statement Effects Template (FSET)
Selected accounts of Ideal Properties, a real estate management firm, are shown below as of January 31 before any adjusting entries have been made.

Unadjusted Account Balances	Debits	Credits
Prepaid insurance	$10,800	
Supplies inventory	2,895	
Office equipment	8,928	
Unearned rent liability		$ 7,875
Salaries expense	4,650	
Rent revenue		22,500

Monthly financial statements are prepared. Using the following information, report the adjusting entries necessary on January 31 using the financial statements effect template.

1. Prepaid Insurance represents a three-year premium paid on January 1.
2. Supplies of $1,275 were still available on January 31.
3. Office equipment—purchased on January 1—is expected to last eight years.
4. On January 1, Ideal Properties collected six months' rent in advance from a tenant renting space for $1,310 per month.
5. Accrued employee salaries of $735 have not been recorded as of January 31.

M3-28. Journalizing Transactions and Adjusting Accounts
Using the information from M3-27, prepare entries for parts 1–5 in journal entry form.

LO3-2, 5
Homework MBC

M3-29. Inferring Transactions from Financial Statements (FSET)
El Puerto de Liverpool (Liverpool) is a large retailer in Mexico. The following accounts are selected from its annual report for the fiscal year ended December 31, 2019. For the fiscal year ended December 31, 2019, Liverpool purchased merchandise inventory costing 89,500,425 thousand Mexican pesos. Assume that all purchases were made on account. The following T-accounts reflect information contained in the company's 2019 and 2018 balance sheets in thousands of Mexican pesos.

LO3-1, 2, 5
Homework MBC
El Puerto de Liverpool
OTCMKTS :: ELPQF

+ Inventories (A)	–
12/31/2018 Bal. 20,673,219	
12/31/2019 Bal. 23,340,421	

– Suppliers (Accounts Payable)	+
	23,694,308 12/31/2018 Bal.
	22,070,209 12/31/2019 Bal.

a. Prepare the entry using the financial statement effects template to record Liverpool's purchases for the 2019 fiscal year.

b. What amount did Liverpool pay in cash to its suppliers for the fiscal year ended December 31, 2019? Explain. Assume that Suppliers (Accounts payable) is affected only by transactions related to inventory.

c. Prepare the entry using the financial statement effects template to record cost of goods sold for the year ended December 31, 2019.

M3-30. Inferring Transactions from Financial Statements
Using the information from M3-29, prepare entries for parts *a* and *c* in journal entry form.

LO3-1, 2
Homework MBC

M3-31. Preparing a Statement of Stockholders' Equity
On December 31, Year 1, the credit balances of the Common Stock and Retained Earnings accounts were $36,000 and $21,600, respectively, for Architect Services Company. Its stock issuances for Year 2 totaled $7,200, and it paid $11,640 cash toward dividends in Year 2. For the year ended December 31, Year 2, the company had net income of $35,880. Prepare a Year 2 statement of stockholders' equity for Architect Services.

LO3-3
Homework MBC

M3-32. Applying Closing Procedures
Assume you are in the process of closing procedures for Echo Corporation. You have already closed all revenue and expense accounts to the Retained Earnings account. The total debits to Retained Earnings equal $247,400 and total credits to Retained Earnings equal $277,900. The Retained Earnings account had a credit balance of $79,200 at the start of this current year. What is the post-closing ending balance of Retained Earnings at the end of this current year?

LO3-4
Homework MBC

M3-33. Preparing Closing Entries Using Journal Entries and T-Accounts
The adjusted trial balance at December 31 for Smith Company includes the following selected accounts.

LO3-4
Homework MBC

Adjusted Account Balances	Debit	Credit
Commissions revenue		$127,350
Wages expense	$54,000	
Insurance expense	2,850	
Utilities expense	12,300	
Depreciation expense	14,700	
Retained earnings		108,150

a. Prepare entries to close these accounts in journal entry form.

b. Set up T-accounts for each of these ledger accounts, enter the balances above, and post the closing entries to them. After these entries are posted, what is the post-closing balance of the Retained Earnings account?

LO3-1, 2, 5 **M3-34. Inferring Transactions from Financial Statements (FSET)**

Homework MBC

Amazon.com Inc.
NASDAQ :: AMZN

Amazon.com Inc. is one of the world's leading e-commerce companies, with over $386 billion in revenues for the fiscal year ended December 31, 2020. For the year ended December 31, 2020, Amazon's cost of goods sold was $233,307 million. Assume that all purchases were made on account. The following T-accounts reflect information contained in the company's 2020 and 2019 balance sheets (in millions).

+ Inventories		−
12/31/2019 Bal.	20,497	
12/31/2020 Bal.	23,795	

− Accounts Payable	+	
	47,183	12/31/2019 Bal.
	72,539	12/31/2020 Bal.

a. Prepare the entry using the financial statement effects template to record cost of goods sold for the year ended December 31, 2020.

b. Prepare the entry using the financial statement effects template to record Amazon's inventory purchases for the year ended December 31, 2020. (Assume all purchases are made on account.)

c. What amount did Amazon pay in cash to its suppliers for the year ended December 31, 2020?

LO3-1, 2 **M3-35. Inferring Transactions from Financial Statements**

Homework MBC

Using the information from M3-34, prepare entries for parts *a* and *b* in journal entry form.

LO3-1, 2, 4 **M3-36. Preparing Entries Across Two Periods**

Homework MBC

Hatcher Company closes its accounts on December 31 each year. On December 31, 2021, Hatcher accrued $1,200 of interest income that was earned on an investment but not yet received or recorded. (The investment will pay interest of $1,800 cash on January 31, 2022.) On January 31, 2022, the company received the $1,800 cash as interest on the investment. Prepare journal entries to:

a. Accrue the interest earned on December 31, 2021;

b. Close the Interest Income account on December 31, 2021 (the account has a year-end balance of $4,800 after adjustments); and

c. Record the cash receipt of interest on January 31, 2022.

LO3-1, 2 **M3-37. Inferring Transactions from Financial Statements (FSET)**

Homework MBC

Using the information from M3-36, prepare entries for parts *a* and *c* using the financial statement effects template.

EXERCISES

LO3-4 **E3-38. Journalizing and Posting Closing Entries**

Homework MBC

The adjusted trial balance as of December 31 for Brooks Consulting Company contains the following selected accounts.

Adjusted Account Balances	Debit	Credit
Service fees		€60,500
Rent expense	€15,600	
Salaries expense	34,200	
Supplies expense	4,200	
Depreciation expense	7,700	
Retained earnings		50,250

a. Prepare entries to close these accounts in journal entry form.

b. Set up T-accounts for each of the ledger accounts, enter the balances above, and post the closing entries to them. After these entries are posted, what is the post-closing balance of the Retained Earnings account?

LO3-2 **E3-39. Preparing Adjusting Entries (FSET)**

Homework MBC

For each of the following separate situations, prepare the necessary adjustments using the financial statement effects template.

1. Unrecorded depreciation on equipment is $915.
2. On the date for preparing financial statements, an estimated utilities expense of $585 has been incurred, but no utility bill has yet been received or paid.

Hartford Financial Services Group
NYSE :: HIG

3. On the first day of the current period, fees for professional journal subscriptions for four periods were paid and recorded as a $4,200 debit to Prepaid subscriptions and a $4,200 credit to Cash.
4. Nine months ago, the **Hartford Financial Services Group** sold a one-year policy to a customer and recorded the receipt of the premium by debiting Cash for $936 and crediting Contract Liabilities for $936. No adjusting entries have been prepared during the nine-month period. Hartford's annual financial statements are now being prepared.
5. At the end of the period, employee wages of $1,448 have been incurred but not yet paid or recorded.
6. At the end of the period, $450 of interest income has been earned but not yet received or recorded.

E3-40. Preparing and Journalizing Adjusting Entries LO3-2

Homework MBC

Using the information from E3-39, prepare necessary adjustments in journal entry form.

E3-41. Preparing Adjusting and Closing Entries Across Two Periods LO3-1, 2, 4

Homework MBC

Norton Company closes its accounts on December 31 each year. The company works a five-day work week and pays its employees every two weeks. On December 31, Norton accrued $6,200 of salaries payable. On January 7 of the following year, the company paid salaries of $15,000 cash to employees. Prepare journal entries to:

a. Accrue the salaries payable on December 31;

b. Close the Salaries Expense account on December 31 (the account has a year-end balance of $275,000 after adjustments); and

c. Record the salary payment on January 7.

E3-42. Preparing Adjusting Entries (FSET) LO3-1, 2

Homework MBC

Using the information from E3-41, prepare entries for parts *a* and *c* using the financial statement effects template.

E3-43. Analyzing Accounts Using Adjusted Data LO3-2, 5

Homework MBC

Selected T-account balances for Fields Company are shown below as of January 31; adjusting entries have already been posted. The firm uses a calendar-year accounting period but prepares *monthly* adjustments.

+ Supplies (A) −	
Jan. 31 Bal. 1,600	

+ Supplies Expense (E) −	
Jan. 31 Bal. 1,920	

+ Prepaid Insurance (A) −	
Jan. 31 Bal. 1,148	

+ Insurance Expense (E) −	
Jan. 31 Bal. 164	

− Wages Payable (L) +	
	1,000 Jan. 31 Bal.

+ Wages Expense (E) −	
Jan. 31 Bal. 6,400	

+ Truck (A) −	
Jan. 31 Bal. 17,400	

− Accumulated Depreciation—Truck (XA) +	
	5,220 Jan. 31 Bal.

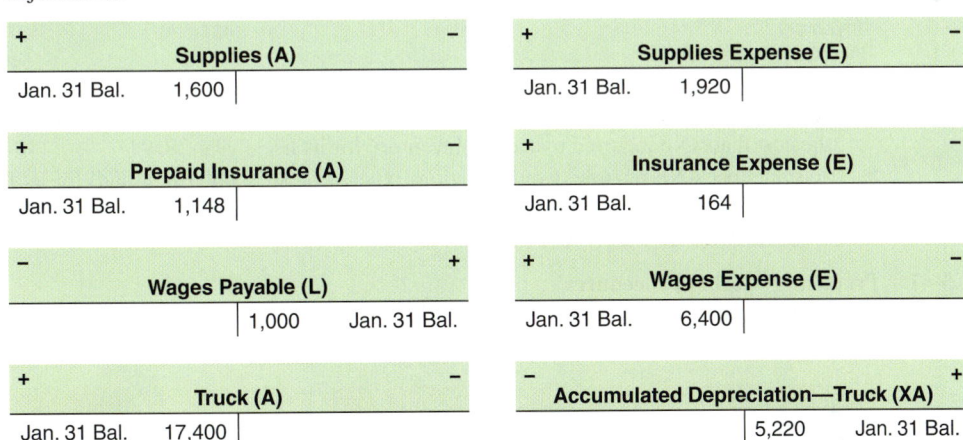

a. If the amount in Supplies Expense represents the January 31 adjustment for the supplies used in January, and $1,240 worth of supplies were purchased during January, what was the January 1 beginning balance of Supplies?

b. The amount in the Insurance Expense account represents the adjustment made at January 31 for January insurance expense. If the original insurance premium was for one year, what was the amount of the premium, and on what date did the insurance policy start?

c. If we assume that no beginning balance existed in wages payable or wages expense on January 1, how much cash was paid as wages during January?

d. If the truck has a useful life of five years, what is the monthly amount of depreciation expense, and how many months has Fields owned the truck?

E3-44. Preparing Adjusting Entries (FSET) LO3-2, 5

Homework MBC

Jake Thomas began Thomas Refinishing Service on July 1. Selected accounts are shown below as of July 31, before any adjusting entries have been made.

Unadjusted Account Balances	Debit	Credit
Prepaid rent	$8,520	
Prepaid advertising	945	
Supplies inventory	4,500	
Performance obligation liability		$ 900
Refinishing fees revenue		3,750

Using the following information, prepare the adjusting entries necessary on July 31 using the financial statement effects template.

1. On July 1, the firm paid one year's advance rent of $8,520 in cash (assume lease qualifies as short-term).
2. On July 1, $945 cash was paid to the local newspaper for an advertisement to run daily for the months of July, August, and September.
3. Supplies still available at July 31 total $1,650.
4. At July 31, refinishing services of $1,200 have been performed but not yet recorded or billed to customers. The firm uses the account Fees Receivable to reflect amounts due but not yet billed.
5. A customer paid $900 in advance for a refinishing project. At July 31, the project is one-half complete.

LO3-1, 2, 5 Homework MBC

E3-45. Preparing Adjusting Entries

Use the information from E3-44 to answer the following requirements.

a. Prepare necessary adjustments on July 31 in journal entry form.

b. Set up T-accounts for each of the ledger accounts, enter the balances above, and post the adjusting entries to them.

LO3-5 Homework MBC

Abercrombie & Fitch Co.
NYSE :: ANF

E3-46. Inferring Transactions from Financial Statements

Abercrombie & Fitch Co. (ANF) is a specialty retailer of casual apparel. The following information is taken from ANF's fiscal 10-K report for the fiscal year 2019, which ended February 3, 2020. (All amounts in $ thousands.)

Selected Balance Sheet Data	February 1, 2020	February 2, 2019
Inventory	$434,326	$437,879
Accrued compensation	58,588	65,156

a. ANF reported Cost of Goods Sold of $1,472,155 (thousand) for its fiscal year 2019. What was the cost that ANF incurred to acquire inventory for its fiscal year 2019?

b. Assume that ANF reported Compensation Expense of $650,000 (thousand) for its fiscal year 2019. What amount of compensation was paid to its employees for fiscal year 2019?

c. Where would you expect ANF to report its balance of Accrued Compensation?

LO3-4 Homework MBC

E3-47. Preparing Closing Procedures

The adjusted trial balance of Parker Corporation, prepared December 31, contains the following selected accounts.

Adjusted Account Balances	Debit	Credit
Service fees revenue		$74,000
Interest income		1,760
Salaries expense	$33,440	
Advertising expense	3,440	
Depreciation expense	6,960	
Income tax expense	7,920	
Retained earnings		34,160

a. Prepare entries to close these accounts in journal entry form.

b. Set up T-accounts for each of the ledger accounts, enter the balances above, and post the closing entries to them. After these entries are posted, what is the post-closing balance of the Retained Earnings account?

LO3-1, 2, 5 Homework MBC

Ethan Allen Interiors Inc.
NYSE :: ETH

E3-48. Inferring Transactions from Financial Statements (FSET)

Ethan Allen Interiors Inc., a leading manufacturer and retailer of home furnishings and accessories, sells products through an exclusive network of approximately 300 design centers. All of Ethan Allen's products are sold by special order. Customers generally place a deposit equal to 25%

to 50% of the purchase price when ordering. Orders take 4 to 12 weeks to be delivered. Selected fiscal-year information from the company's balance sheets is as follows ($ thousands):

Selected Balance Sheet Data	2020	2019
Inventories	$126,101	$162,389
Customer deposits and deferred revenues	64,031	56,714

a. In fiscal 2020, Ethan Allen reported total sales revenue of $589,837 (thousand). Assume that the company collected customer deposits equal to $175,000 (thousand) over the year. Prepare entries using the financial statement effects template to record customer deposits and its sales revenue for fiscal year 2020.

b. Ethan Allen's cost of goods sold for 2020 was $266,705 (thousand). Prepare the adjusting entry using the financial statement effects template that it made to record inventory acquisitions.

c. Where would you expect Ethan Allen to report its Customer Deposits?

E3-49. Inferring Transactions from Financial Statements LO3-1, 2, 5 Homework MBC

Use the information from E3-48 to record necessary adjustments in journal entry form for parts *a* and *b*.

E3-50. Preparing Financial Statements and Closing Procedures LO3-3, 4 Homework MBC

Solomon Corporation's adjusted trial balance for the year ending December 31 is:

SOLOMON CORPORATION Adjusted Trial Balance December 31	Debit	Credit
Cash	$ 6,000	
Accounts receivable	9,750	
Equipment	117,000	
Accumulated depreciation		$ 21,000
Notes payable		15,000
Common stock		64,500
Retained earnings		18,900
Service fees revenue		106,500
Rent expense	27,000	
Salaries expense	55,650	
Depreciation expense	10,500	
Totals	$225,900	$225,900

a. Prepare its income statement and statement of stockholders' equity for the current year, and its balance sheet for the current year-end. Cash dividends were $12,000, and there were no stock issuances or repurchases.

b. Prepare entries to close its temporary accounts in journal entry form.

c. Set up T-accounts for each of the ledger accounts, enter the balances above, and post the closing entries to them. After these entries are posted, what is the post-closing balance of the Retained Earnings account?

PROBLEMS

P3-51. Recording Transactions and Adjusting Entries Using the Financial Statement Effects Template (FSET) LO3-1, 2, 5 Homework MBC

B. Lougee opened Lougee Roofing Service on April 1. Transactions for April are as follows:

Apr. 1 Lougee contributed $13,800 cash to the business in exchange for common stock.
1 Paid $3,360 cash for two-year premium toward liability insurance effective immediately.
2 Paid $7,500 cash for the purchase of a used truck.
2 Purchased $3,600 of ladders and other equipment; paid $1,200 cash, with the balance due in 30 days.
5 Purchased $1,400 of supplies on account.
5 Received an advance of $2,100 cash from a customer for roof repairs to be done during April and May.

Apr. 12 Billed customers $6,600 for roofing services performed.
18 Collected $5,800 cash from customers on their accounts.
29 Paid $810 cash for truck fuel used in April.
30 Paid $120 cash for April digital marketing ads.
30 Paid $3,000 cash for assistants' wages.
30 Billed customers $4,800 for roofing services performed.

REQUIRED

a. Record these transactions for April using the financial statement effects template.

b. Supplies still available on April 30 amount to $480; and depreciation for April was $125 on the truck and $75 on equipment; and roofing services were completed by April 30 representing one-fourth of the roofing fees received in advance. Prepare entries to adjust the books for Insurance Expense, Supplies Expense, Depreciation Expense—Trucks, Depreciation Expense—Equipment, and Roofing Fees Revenue using the financial statement effects template.

LO3-1, 2, 5 **P3-52. Journalizing and Posting Transactions, and Preparing a Trial Balance and Adjustments**

Homework MBC

REQUIRED

Use the information from P3-51 to complete the following.

a. Set up a general ledger in T-account form for the following accounts: Cash; Accounts Receivable; Supplies; Prepaid Insurance; Trucks; Accumulated Depreciation—Trucks; Equipment; Accumulated Depreciation—Equipment; Accounts Payable; Contract Liability; Common Stock; Roofing Fees Revenue; Fuel Expense; Advertising Expense; Wages Expense; Insurance Expense; Supplies Expense; Depreciation Expense—Trucks; and Depreciation Expense—Equipment.

b. Record these transactions for April in journal entry form.

c. Post these entries to their T-accounts (key numbers in T-accounts by date).

d. Prepare an unadjusted trial balance as of April 30.

e. Prepare the adjusting entries and post the adjusting entries to their T-accounts.

LO3-2 **P3-53. Recording Adjusting Entries Using the Financial Statement Effects Template (FSET)**

Homework MBC

SnapShot Company, a commercial photography studio, has just completed its first full year of operations on December 31. General ledger account balances *before* year-end adjustments follow; no adjusting entries have been made to the accounts at any time during the year. Assume that all balances are normal.

Cash	$ 6,450
Accounts receivable	11,400
Prepaid software subscription contract	37,800
Prepaid insurance	8,910
Supplies	12,750
Equipment	68,400
Accounts payable	5,730
Performance obligations	7,800
Common stock	72,000
Photography fee revenue	103,440
Wages expense	33,000
Utilities expense	10,260

An analysis of the firm's records discloses the following.

1. Photography services of $2,775 have been rendered, but customers have not yet paid or been billed. The firm uses the account Fees Receivable to reflect amounts due but not yet billed.
2. Equipment, purchased January 1, has an estimated life of 10 years.
3. Utilities expense for December is estimated to be $1,200, but the bill will not arrive or be paid until January of next year.
4. The balance in Prepaid Software Subscription Contract represents the amount paid on January 1 for a 2-year contract for high-functioning photo editing software and its updates.
5. In November, customers paid $7,800 cash in advance for photos to be taken for the holiday season. When received, these fees were credited to Performance Obligations. By December 31, all of the services related to these fees had been performed.
6. A 3-year insurance premium paid on January 1 was debited to Prepaid Insurance.
7. Supplies available at December 31 are $4,560.
8. At December 31, wages expense of $1,125 has been incurred but not paid or recorded.

REQUIRED
Prepare the company's adjusting entries using the financial statement effects template.

P3-54. Preparing an Unadjusted Trial Balance and Adjustments LO3-1, 2

Homework MBC

REQUIRED
Use the information from P3-53 to complete the following.

a. Prove that debits equal credits for SnapShot's unadjusted account balances by preparing its unadjusted trial balance at December 31.

b. Prepare its adjusting entries in journal entry form.

c. Set up T-accounts, enter the balances above, and post the adjusting entries to them.

P3-55. Recording Adjusting Entries Using the Financial Statement Effects Template (FSET) LO3-2

Homework MBC

Murdock Carpet Cleaners ended its first month of operations on June 30. Monthly financial statements will be prepared. The unadjusted account balances are as follows.

MURDOCK CARPET CLEANERS
Unadjusted Trial Balance
June 30

	Debit	Credit
Cash	$ 2,950	
Accounts receivable	1,130	
Prepaid insurance	7,740	
Supplies	6,300	
Equipment	11,100	
Accounts payable		$ 1,900
Common stock		5,000
Retained earnings		13,240
Service fees revenue		11,630
Wages expense	2,550	
	$31,770	$31,770

The following information is available.

1. The balance in Prepaid insurance was the amount paid on June 1 for the first four months' insurance.
2. Supplies available at June 30 were $2,050.
3. Equipment, purchased June 1, has an estimated life of five years.
4. Unpaid and unrecorded employee wages at June 30 were $525.
5. Utility services used during June were estimated at $750. A bill is expected early in July.
6. Fees earned for services performed but not yet billed on June 30 were $950. The company uses the account Accounts Receivable to reflect amounts due but not yet billed.

REQUIRED
Prepare its adjusting entries at June 30 using the financial statement effects template.

P3-56. Preparing Adjusting Entries, Financial Statements, and Closing Entries LO3-1, 2, 3, 4, 5

Homework MBC

REQUIRED
Use the information from P3-55 to complete the following.

a. Prepare the company's adjusting entries at June 30 in journal entry form.

b. Set up T-accounts, enter the balances above, and post the adjusting entries to them.

c. Prepare its income statement for June and its balance sheet at June 30.

d. Prepare entries to close its temporary accounts in journal entry form.

e. Post the closing entries to the T-accounts.

P3-57. Preparing Adjusting Entries Using the Financial Statement Effects Template (FSET) LO3-2

Homework MBC

The following information relates to the December 31 adjustments for Kwik Print Company. The firm's fiscal year ends on December 31.

1. Weekly employee salaries for a five-day week total $3,600, payable on Fridays. December 31 of the current year is a Tuesday.
2. Kwik Print has $40,000 of notes payable outstanding at December 31. Interest of $380 has accrued on these notes by December 31 but will not be paid until the notes mature next year.
3. During December, Kwik Print provided $1,800 of printing services to clients who will be billed on January 2. The firm uses the account Fees Receivable to reflect amounts due but not yet billed.

4. Starting December 1, all maintenance work on Kwik Print's equipment is handled by Richardson Repair Company under an agreement whereby Kwik Print pays a fixed monthly charge of $500. Kwik Print paid six months' service charge in advance on December 1, debiting Prepaid Maintenance for $3,000.
5. The firm paid $1,800 cash on December 15 for a series of radio commercials to run during December and January. One-third of the commercials have aired by December 31. The $1,800 payment was debited to Prepaid Advertising.
6. Starting December 16, Kwik Print rented 400 square feet of storage space from a neighboring business using a short-term lease. The monthly rent of $1.00 per square foot is due in advance on the first of each month. Nothing was paid in December, however, because the neighbor agreed to add the rent for the one-half of December to the January 1 payment.
7. Kwik Print invested $7,500 cash in securities on December 1 and earned interest of $35 on these securities by December 31. No interest payment will be received until January, and the end-of-December market value of the securities remains at $7,500.
8. Annual depreciation on the firm's equipment is $4,350. No depreciation has been recorded during the year.

REQUIRED

Prepare its adjusting entries required at December 31 using the financial statement effects template.

LO3-2 Homework MBC **P3-58. Preparing Adjusting Entries**

REQUIRED

Use the information from P3-57 to prepare adjusting entries in journal entry form.

LO3-3, 4 Homework MBC **P3-59. Preparing Financial Statements and Closing Entries**

The following adjusted trial balance is for Trueman Consulting Inc. at December 31. The company had no stock issuances or repurchases during the year.

	Debit	Credit
Cash	$ 1,350	
Accounts receivable	1,635	
Supplies	1,530	
Prepaid insurance	750	
Equipment	3,200	
Accumulated depreciation—equipment		$ 540
Accounts payable		430
Long-term notes payable		3,500
Common stock		500
Retained earnings		1,645
Service fees revenue		29,200
Rent expense	6,000	
Salaries expense	16,700	
Supplies expense	2,350	
Insurance expense	1,625	
Depreciation expense—equipment	360	
Interest expense	315	
	$35,815	$35,815

REQUIRED

a. Prepare its income statement and statement of stockholders' equity for the year and its balance sheet at December 31.

b. Prepare entries to close its accounts in journal entry form.

LO3-4 Homework MBC **P3-60. Preparing Closing Entries**

The following adjusted trial balance is for Wilson Company at December 31.

	Debit	Credit
Cash	$ 10,200	
Accounts receivable	9,600	
Prepaid insurance	4,320	
Equipment	86,400	
Accumulated depreciation		$ 14,400
Accounts payable		720
Common stock		30,000
Retained earnings		22,920
Service fees revenue		116,640
Miscellaneous income		5,040
Salaries expense	51,360	
Rent expense	16,080	
Insurance expense	2,160	
Depreciation expense	9,600	
Income tax expense	10,560	
Income tax payable		10,560
	$200,280	$200,280

REQUIRED

a. Prepare closing entries in journal entry form.

b. After the firm's closing entries are posted, what is the post-closing balance for the Retained Earnings account?

c. Prepare its post-closing trial balance.

P3-61. Preparing Entries Across Two Periods Using the Financial Statement Effects Template (FSET) LO3-1, 2

Homework MBC

The following selected accounts appear in Shaw Company's unadjusted trial balance at December 31, the end of its fiscal year. (All accounts have normal balances.)

Prepaid advertising	$ 1,700	Performance obligations	$ 7,600
Wages expense	61,300	Service fees revenue	121,800
Prepaid insurance	4,800	Rental income	6,900

REQUIRED

a. Prepare its adjusting entries at December 31 using the financial statement effects template and the following additional information.

1. Prepaid advertising at December 31 is $1,100.
2. Unpaid and unrecorded wages earned by employees in December are $1,800.
3. Prepaid insurance at December 31 is $3,200.
4. Performance obligations represent service fees collected in advance of when the services are provided to customers. Performance obligations at December 31 are $4,200.
5. Rent revenue of $1,400 owed by a tenant is not recorded at December 31.

b. Prepare entries on January 4 of the following year using the financial statement effects template to record (1) payment of $3,400 cash in wages, which includes the $1,800 accrued at December 31 and (2) cash receipt of the $1,400 rent revenue owed from the tenant.

P3-62. Preparing Entries Across Two Periods LO3-1, 2

Homework MBC

REQUIRED

Use the information from P3-61 to prepare journal entries in journal entry form for parts *a* and *b*.

P3-63. Recording Transactions and Adjustments Using the Financial Statement Effects Template (FSET) LO3-1, 2

Homework MBC

Market-Probe, a market research firm, had the following transactions in June, its first month of operations.

June 1 B. May invested $33,000 cash in the firm in exchange for common stock.

1 The firm purchased the following: office equipment, $15,360; office supplies, $4,000. Terms are $6,200 cash with the remainder due in 60 days. (Make a compound entry requiring two credits.)

2 Paid $1,400 cash for June rent owed to the landlord on a short-term lease.

2 Contracted for three months' advertising in a local newspaper at $400 per month and paid for the advertising in advance.

2 Signed a six-month contract with a customer to provide research consulting services at a rate of $4,500 per month. Received two months' fees in advance. Work on the contract started immediately.

June 10 Billed various customers $8,100 for services rendered.
12 Paid $5,000 cash for two weeks' salaries (5-day week) to employees.
15 Paid $1,700 cash to employee for travel expenses to conference.
18 Paid $700 cash to post office for bulk mailing of research questionnaire (postage expense).
26 Paid $5,000 cash for two weeks' salaries to employees.
28 Billed various customers $7,300 for services rendered.
30 Collected $10,900 cash from customers on their accounts.
30 Paid $2,100 cash for dividends.

REQUIRED

a. Record these transactions using the financial statement effects template.

b. Prepare adjusting entries using the financial statement effects template that reflect the following information at June 30:
- Office supplies available, $2,100
- Accrued employee salaries, $1,100
- Estimated life of office equipment is 8 years

Adjusting entries must also be prepared for advertising and service fees per information in the June transactions.

LO3-1, 2 **P3-64. Journalizing and Posting Transactions, and Preparing a Trial Balance and Adjustments**

Homework MBC

REQUIRED

Use the information from P3-63 to complete the following.

a. Set up a general ledger in T-account form for the following accounts: Cash; Accounts Receivable; Office Supplies; Prepaid Advertising; Office Equipment; Accumulated Depreciation—Office Equipment; Accounts Payable; Salaries Payable; Contract Liabilities; Common Stock; Retained Earnings; Service Fees Revenue; Salaries Expense; Advertising Expense; Supplies Expense; Rent Expense; Travel Expense; Depreciation Expense—Office Equipment; and Postage Expense.

b. Record these transactions in journal entry form.

c. Post these entries to their T-accounts (key numbers in T-accounts by date).

d. Prepare an unadjusted trial balance at June 30.

e. Prepare adjusting entries in journal entry form that reflect the following information at June 30:
- Office supplies available, $2,100
- Accrued employee salaries, $1,100
- Estimated life of office equipment is 8 years

Adjusting entries must also be prepared for advertising and service fees per information in the June transactions.

f. Post all adjusting entries to their T-accounts.

LO3-2 **P3-65. Preparing Adjusting Entries Using the Financial Statement Effects Template (FSET)**

Homework MBC

DeliverAll, a mailing service, has just completed its first full year of operations on December 31. Its general ledger account balances *before* year-end adjustments follow; no adjusting entries have been made to the accounts at any time during the year. Assume that all balances are normal.

Cash	$ 1,900	Accounts payable	$ 4,180
Accounts receivable	4,100	Common stock	7,700
Prepaid advertising	1,380	Mailing fees earned	68,000
Supplies	5,100	Wages expense	31,100
Equipment	33,800	Other compensation expense expense	6,000
Notes payable	6,000	Utilities expense	2,500

An analysis of the firm's records reveals the following.

1. The balance in Prepaid Advertising represents the amount paid for newspaper advertising for one year. The agreement, which calls for the same amount of space and cost each month, covers the period from February 1 of this year to January 31 of the following year. DeliverAll did not advertise during its first month of operations.
2. Equipment, purchased January 1, has an estimated life of eight years.
3. Utilities expense does not include expense for December, estimated at $400. The bill will not arrive until January of the following year.
4. At year-end, employees have earned an additional $1,100 in wages that will not be paid or recorded until January.

5. Supplies available at year-end amount to $1,300.
6. At year-end, unpaid interest of $360 has accrued on the notes payable.
7. The company offers no retirement plan but as part of the compensation contract, the company pays other compensation of $500 per month payable on the first of each month, plus an amount equal to 1/2% of annual mailing fees earned. This is payable within 15 days after the end of the year.

REQUIRED

Prepare adjusting entries using the financial statement effects template.

P3-66. Preparing an Unadjusted Trial Balance and Adjusting Entries **LO3-2**

Homework MBC

REQUIRED

Use the information from P3-65 to answer the following.

a. Prove that debits equal credits for its unadjusted account balances by preparing its unadjusted trial balance at December 31.

b. Prepare its adjusting entries in journal entry form.

c. Set up T-accounts, enter the balances above, and post the adjusting entries to them.

P3-67. Preparing Adjusting Entries Using the Financial Statement Effects Template (FSET) **LO3-2, 5**

Homework MBC

Wheel Place Company began operations on March 1 to provide automotive wheel alignment and balancing services. On March 31 the unadjusted balances of the firm's accounts are as follows.

WHEEL PLACE COMPANY
Unadjusted Trial Balance
March 31

	Debit	Credit
Cash	$ 2,280	
Accounts receivable	4,500	
Prepaid insurance	5,700	
Supplies	4,440	
Equipment	43,740	
Accounts payable		$ 3,050
Service contract liability		1,200
Common stock		46,100
Service revenue		14,990
Wages expense	4,680	
Totals	$65,340	$65,340

The following information is available.

1. The balance in Prepaid insurance was the amount paid on March 1 to cover the first 6 months' insurance.
2. Supplies available on March 31 amount to $2,060.
3. Equipment has an estimated life of nine years and a zero salvage value.
4. Unpaid and unrecorded wages at March 31 were $670.
5. Utility services used during March were estimated at $470; a bill is expected early in April.
6. The balance in Service Contract Liability was the amount received on March 1 from a car dealer to cover alignment and balancing services on cars sold by the dealer in March and April. Wheel Place agreed to provide the services at a fixed fee of $600 each month.

REQUIRED

Prepare adjusting entries using the financial statement effects template.

P3-68. Preparing and Posting Adjusting Entries, Preparing Financial Statements, Preparing Closing Entries **LO3-2, 3, 4, 5**

Homework MBC

REQUIRED

Use the information from P3-67 to answer the following.

a. Prepare its adjusting entries at March 31 in journal entry form.

b. Set up T-accounts, enter the balances above, and post the adjusting entries to them.

c. Prepare its income statement for March and its balance sheet at March 31.

d. Prepare entries to close its temporary accounts in journal entry form and post the closing entries to the T-accounts.

LO3-3, 4 Homework MBC

P3-69. Preparing Financial Statements and Closing Entries

Trails, Inc., publishes magazines for skiers and hikers. The company's adjusted trial balance for the year ending December 31 is:

TRAILS, INC.
Adjusted Trial Balance
December 31

	Debit	Credit
Cash	$ 5,100	
Accounts receivable	12,900	
Supplies	6,300	
Prepaid insurance	1,395	
Office equipment	99,000	
Accumulated depreciation		$ 16,500
Accounts payable		3,150
Subscription liabilities		15,000
Salaries payable		5,250
Common stock		37,500
Retained earnings		34,830
Subscription revenue		252,450
Advertising revenue		74,550
Salaries expense	150,345	
Printing and mailing expense	128,400	
Rent expense (for a short-term lease)	13,200	
Supplies expense	0,150	
Insurance expense	2,790	
Depreciation expense	8,250	
Income tax expense	2,400	
Totals	$439,230	$493,230

REQUIRED

a. Prepare its income statement and statement of stockholders' equity for the year and its balance sheet at December 31. There were no cash dividends and no stock issuances or repurchases during the year.

b. Prepare entries to close its accounts in journal entry form.

LO3-4 Homework MBC

P3-70. Preparing Closing Entries

The following adjusted trial balance is for Mayflower Moving Service at December 31.

MAYFLOWER MOVING SERVICE
Adjusted Trial Balance
December 31

	Debit	Credit
Cash	$ 7,600	
Accounts receivable	10,500	
Supplies	4,600	
Prepaid advertising	6,000	
Trucks	56,600	
Accumulated depreciation—trucks		$ 20,000
Equipment	15,200	
Accumulated depreciation—equipment		4,200
Accounts payable		2,400
Service contract liabilities		5,400
Common stock		10,000
Retained earnings		31,100
Service fees revenue		145,000
Wages expense	59,600	
Rent expense	20,400	
Insurance expense	5,800	
Supplies expense	10,200	
Advertising expense	12,000	
Depreciation expense—trucks	8,000	
Depreciation expense—equipment	1,600	
Totals	$218,100	$218,100

REQUIRED

a. Prepare closing entries in journal entry form.

b. After its closing entries are posted, what is the post-closing balance for the Retained Earnings account?

c. Prepare Mayflower's post-closing trial balance.

P3-71. Preparing Entries Across Two Periods Using the Financial Statement Effects Template (FSET) LO3-1, 2, 5 Homework MBC

The following selected accounts appear in Zimmerman Company's unadjusted trial balance at December 31, the end of its fiscal year. (All accounts have normal balances.)

Prepaid maintenance	$ 6,750	Commission revenue	$210,000
Supplies	21,000	Wage expense	27,000
Performance obligations	21,250		

Additional information is as follows.

1. On September 1, the company entered into a prepaid equipment maintenance contract. Zimmerman Company paid $6,750 to cover maintenance service for 6 months, beginning September 1. The $6,750 payment was debited to Prepaid Maintenance.
2. Supplies available on December 31 are $8,000.
3. Performance obligations at December 31 are $10,000.
4. Commission revenue where services have been performed but the amounts for which have not yet been billed at December 31 are $7,000. (*Hint:* Debit Commissions Receivable.)
5. Zimmerman Company's compensation plan calls for salary of $2,250 per month payable on the first of each month, plus an annual amount equal to 1% of annual commission revenue. This additional compensation is payable on January 10 of the following year. (*Hint:* Use the adjusted amount of commission revenue in computing the additional compensation.)

REQUIRED

a. Prepare Zimmerman Company's adjusting entries at December 31 using the financial statement effects template.

b. Prepare entries on January 10 of the following year using the financial statement effects template to record (1) the billing of $11,500 in commissions (which includes the $7,000 of commissions not billed at December 31) and (2) the cash payment of the additional compensation owed for the current year. (*Hint for part (1)*: Zimmerman Company has two receivable accounts—Commissions Receivable is used for services performed, but not yet billed, and Accounts Receivable for amounts that are related to services performed and billed to the customer.)

P3-72. Preparing Entries Across Two Periods LO3-2, 5 Homework MBC

Use the information from P3-71 to answer the following. Prepare the adjusting entries from part *a* and the transactions in part *b* in journal entry form.

P3-73. Preparing Adjusting Entries (FSET) LO3-2, 5 Homework MBC

Fischer Card Shop is a small retail shop. Fischer's balance sheet at year-end 2021 is as follows.

FISCHER CARD SHOP
Balance Sheet
December 31, 2021

Cash		$12,750	Accounts payable	$ 7,800
Inventories		18,000	Wages payable	150
Prepaid insurance		5,700	Total current liabilities	7,950
Total current assets		36,450	Total equity (includes retained earnings)	35,250
Equipment	$11,250		Total liabilities and equity	$43,200
Less accumulated depreciation	4,500			
Equipment, net		6,750		
Total assets		$43,200		

The following information details transactions and adjustments that occurred during 2022.

1. Sales total $218,775 in 2022; all sales were cash sales.
2. Inventory purchases total $114,300 in 2022; at December 31, 2022, inventory totals $21,750. Assume all purchases were made on account.
3. Accounts payable totals $6,150 at December 31, 2022.
4. Annual insurance premiums of $36,000 was paid on March 1, 2022, covering the next 12 months. The balance in prepaid insurance at December 31, 2021, was the balance remaining from the advance premium payment in 2021.

5. Wages are paid every other week on Friday; during 2022, Fischer paid $18,750 cash for wages. At December 31, 2022, Fischer owed employees unpaid and unrecorded wages of $525.
6. Depreciation on equipment totals $2,550 in 2022.

REQUIRED

Prepare any necessary transaction entries for 2022 and adjusting entries at December 31, 2022, using the financial statement effects template.

LO3-1, 2, 3, 4, 5 **P3-74. Preparing Adjusting Entries, Financial Statements, and Closing Entries**

Homework MBC

REQUIRED

Use the information from P3-73 to answer the following.

a. Prepare any necessary transaction entries for 2022 and adjusting entries at December 31, 2022, in journal entry form.
b. Set up T-accounts, enter the balances above, and post the transactions and adjusting entries to them.
c. Prepare its income statement for 2022 and its balance sheet at December 31, 2022.
d. Prepare entries to close its temporary accounts in journal entry form and post the closing entries to the T-accounts.

LO3-1, 2, 5 **P3-75. Recording Entries and Adjusting Entries (FSET)**

Homework MBC

Rhoades Tax Services began business on December 1. Its December transactions are as follows.

Dec.	1	Rhoades invested $50,000 in the business in exchange for common stock
	2	Paid $3,000 cash for December rent to Bomba Realty (short-term lease).
	2	Purchased $2,700 of supplies on account.
	3	Purchased $23,750 of office equipment, paying $11,750 cash with the balance due in 30 days.
	8	Paid $2,700 cash on account for supplies purchased December 2.
	14	Paid $2,250 cash for assistant's wages for 2 weeks' work.
	20	Performed consulting services for $7,500 cash.
	28	Paid $2,250 cash for assistant's wages for 2 weeks' work.
	30	Billed clients $18,000 for December consulting services.
	31	Paid $4,500 cash for dividends.

Additional information:

1. Supplies available at December 31 are $1,775.
2. Accrued wages payable at December 31 are $675.
3. Depreciation for December is $300.
4. Rhoades has spent 45 hours on an involved tax fraud case in December. When completed in January, his work will be billed at $125 per hour. (The account Fees Receivable is used to reflect amounts earned but not yet billed.)

REQUIRED

Record (a) these transactions and (b) any necessary adjusting entries using the financial statement effects template.

LO3-1, 2, 3, 4, 5 **P3-76. Applying the Entire Accounting Cycle**

Homework MBC

REQUIRED

Use the information from P3-75 to answer the following.

a. Set up a general ledger in T-account form for the following accounts: Cash; Fees Receivable; Supplies; Office Equipment; Accumulated Depreciation—Office Equipment; Accounts Payable; Wages Payable; Common Stock; Retained Earnings; Consulting Revenue; Supplies Expense; Wages Expense; Rent Expense; and Depreciation Expense.
b. Record the above transactions in journal entry form.
c. Post these entries to their T-accounts (key numbers in T-accounts by date).
d. Prepare an unadjusted trial balance at December 31.
e. Journalize the adjusting entries at December 31 in journal entry form, drawing on the information above. Then post adjusting entries to their T-accounts and prepare an adjusted trial balance at December 31.
f. Prepare a December income statement and statement of stockholders' equity and a December 31 balance sheet.
g. Record its closing entries in journal entry form. Post these entries to their T-accounts.
h. Prepare a post-closing trial balance at December 31.

CASES AND PROJECTS

C3-77. Preparing Adjusting Entries (FSET) LO3-2, 5

Seaside Surf Shop began operations on July 1 with an initial investment of $40,000. During the initial 3 months of operations, the following cash transactions were recorded in the firm's checking account.

Cash receipts		Cash payments	
Initial investment by owner	$ 40,000	Rent	$ 19,200
Collected from customers	64,800	Fixtures and equipment	20,000
Borrowed from bank 7/1	8,000	Merchandise inventory	49,600
Total cash receipts	$112,800	Salaries	4,800
		Other expenses	10,400
		Total cash payments	$104,000

Additional information

1. Most sales were for cash; however, the store accepted a limited amount of credit sales; at September 30, customers owed the store $7,200.
2. Rent was paid on July 1 for six months (short-term lease).
3. Salaries of $2,400 per month are paid on the 1st of each month for salaries earned in the month prior.
4. Inventories are purchased for cash; at September 30, inventory worth $16,800 was available.
5. Fixtures and equipment were expected to last five years with zero salvage value.
6. The bank charges 12% annual interest (1% per month) on its bank loan.

REQUIRED

Prepare any necessary adjusting entries at September 30 using the financial statement effects template.

C3-78. Preparing Adjusting Entries, Financial Statements, and Closing Entries LO3-1, 2, 3, 4, 5

REQUIRED

Use the information from C3-77 to answer the following.

a. Prepare any necessary adjusting entries at September 30 in journal entry form.

b. Set up T-accounts and post the adjusting entries to them.

c. Prepare its initial three-month income statement and its balance sheet at September 30. (Ignore taxes.)

d. Analyze the statements from part *c* and assess the company's performance over its initial three months.

C3-79. Analyzing Transactions, Impacts on Financial Ratios, and Loan Covenants LO3-1, 2, 5

Wyland Consulting, a firm started three years ago by Reyna Wyland, offers consulting services for material handling and plant layout. Its balance sheet at the close of the year is as follows.

WYLAND CONSULTING
Balance Sheet
December 31

Assets			Liabilities	
Cash		$ 5,100	Notes payable	$ 45,000
Accounts receivable		34,315	Accounts payable	6,300
Supplies		19,800	Contract liabilities	16,950
Prepaid insurance		6,750	Wages payable	600
Equipment	$102,750		Total liabilities	68,850
Less: accumulated depreciation	35,960	66,790	**Equity**	
			Common stock	12,000
			Retained earnings	51,905
Total assets		$132,755	Total liabilities and equity	$132,755

Earlier in the year Wyland obtained a bank loan of $45,000 cash for the firm. One of the provisions of the loan is that the year-end debt-to-equity ratio (ratio of total liabilities to total equity) cannot exceed 1.0. Based on the above balance sheet, the ratio at the end of the year is 1.08. Wyland is concerned about being in violation of the loan agreement and requests assistance in reviewing the situation. Wyland believes that she might have overlooked some items at year-end. Discussions with Wyland reveal the following.

1. On January 1 the firm paid a $6,750 insurance premium for 2 years of coverage; the amount in Prepaid Insurance has not yet been adjusted.
2. Depreciation on the equipment should be 10% of cost per year; the company inadvertently recorded 15% for the year.
3. Interest on the bank loan has been paid through the end of the year.
4. The firm concluded a major consulting engagement in December, doing a plant layout analysis for a new factory. The $9,000 fee has not been billed or recorded in the accounts.
5. On December 1, the firm received a $16,950 advance payment from Croy Corporation for consulting services to be rendered over a 2-month period. This payment was credited to the Contract Liabilities account. One-half of this fee was earned by December 31.
6. Supplies costing $7,200 were available on December 31; the company has made no entry in the accounts.

REQUIRED

a. What portion of the company is financed by debt versus equity (called the debt-to-equity ratio and defined in Chapter 1) at December 31?

b. Is the firm in violation of its loan agreement? Prepare computations to support the correct total liabilities and total equity figures at December 31.

LO3-1, 2 **C3-80. Ethics, Accounting Adjustments, and Auditors**

It is the end of the accounting year for Juliet Javetz, controller of a medium-sized, publicly held corporation specializing in toxic waste cleanup. Within the corporation, only Javetz and the president know that the firm has been negotiating for several months to land a large contract for waste cleanup in Western Europe. The president has hired another firm with excellent contacts in Western Europe to help with negotiations. The outside firm will charge an hourly fee plus expenses but has agreed not to submit a bill until the negotiations are in their final stages (expected to occur in another 3 to 4 months). Even if the contract falls through, the outside firm is entitled to receive payment for its services. Based upon her discussion with a member of the outside firm, Javetz knows that its charge for services provided to date will be $150,000. This is a material amount for the company.

Javetz knows that the president wants negotiations to remain as secret as possible so that competitors will not learn of the contract the company is pursuing in Europe. In fact, the president recently stated to her, "Now is not the time to reveal our actions in Western Europe to other staff members, our auditors, or the readers of our financial statements; securing this contract is crucial to our future growth." No entry has been made in the accounting records for the cost of contract negotiations. Javetz now faces an uncomfortable situation. The company's outside auditor has just asked her if she knows of any year-end adjustments that have not yet been recorded.

REQUIRED

a. What are the ethical considerations that Javetz faces in answering the auditor's question?

b. How should Javetz respond to the auditor's question?

LO3-1, 2, 5 **C3-81. Inferring Adjusting Entries from Financial Statements (FSET)**

Homework MBC

Lady G's Fashions, a specialty retailer of women's apparel, markets its products through retail stores and catalogs. Selected information from its Year 1 and Year 2 balance sheets is as follows.

Selected Balance Sheet Data ($ thousands)	Year 1	Year 2
Prepaid catalog expenses (asset)	$ 7,788	$ 8,612
Advertising credits receivable	42	1,068
Gift certificate liability	12,216	14,106

The following excerpts are from Lady G's Fashions accompanying note disclosures:

- Catalog costs in the direct segment are considered direct response advertising and as such are capitalized as incurred and amortized over the expected sales life of each catalog, which is generally a period not exceeding six months.
- The Company periodically enters into arrangements with certain national magazine publishers, whereby the Company includes magazine subscription cards in its catalog mailings in exchange for advertising credits or discounts on advertising.

REQUIRED

a. Assume that Lady G's Fashions spent $125,100 to design, print, and mail catalogs in Year 2. Also assume that it received advertising credits of $1,698. Prepare the entry using the financial statement effects template that Lady G's Fashions would have recorded when these costs were incurred.

b. Prepare the adjusting entry using the financial statement effects template that would be necessary to record its amortization of prepaid catalog costs.

c. How do advertising credits expire? Prepare the adjusting entry using both the financial statement effects template that Lady G's Fashions would record to reflect the change in advertising credits.

d. Assume that Lady G's Fashions sold gift certificates valued at $38,350 in Year 2. Prepare the entry using the financial statement effects template that Lady G's Fashions would make to record these sales. Next, prepare the entry using the financial statement effects template that it makes to record merchandise sales to customers who pay with gift certificates.

C3-82. Inferring Adjusting Entries from Financial Statements **LO3-1, 2, 5**

Homework MBC

REQUIRED

Using the information from C3-81, prepare entries in journal entry form for parts *a* through *d*.

SOLUTIONS TO REVIEW PROBLEMS

Review 3-1

a.

	Balance Sheet									Income Statement				
Transaction	Cash Asset	+	Noncash Assets	=	Liabil-ities	+	Contrib. Capital	+	Earned Capital	Revenues	−	Expenses	=	Net Income
(1) Paid $4,000 for wages	−4,000 Cash			=					−4,000 Retained Earnings		−	+4,000 Wages Expense	=	−4,000
(2) Receipt of $6,500 for services provided.	+6,500 Cash			=					+6,500 Retained Earnings	+6,500 Fees Revenue	−		=	+6,500
(3) Purchase of $1,100 in supplies on account.			+1,100 Supplies	=	+1,100 Accounts Payable						−		=	
(4) Performed $1,200 of services on account.			+1,200 Accounts Receivable	=					+1,200 Retained Earnings	+1,200 Fees Revenue	−		=	+1,200
(5) Paid suppliers $2,000 on account.	−2,000 Cash			=	−2,000 Accounts Payable						−		=	

b.

		Debit	Credit
(1)	Wages expense (+E, −SE)	4,000	
	Cash (−A)		4,000
(2)	Cash (+A)	6,500	
	Fees revenue (+R, +SE)		6,500
(3)	Supplies (+A)	1,100	
	Accounts payable (+L)		1,100
(4)	Accounts receivable (+A)	1,200	
	Fees revenue (+R, +SE)		1,200
(5)	Accounts payable (−L)	2,000	
	Cash (−A)		2,000

c.

General Ledger

Assets = Liabilities + Equity

Assets

Cash (A) (+ / −)

Beg. bal.	500	4,000	(1)
(2)	**6,500**	**2,000**	(5)
End. bal.	1,000		

Accounts Receivable (A) (+ / −)

Beg. bal.	8,000	
(4)	**1,200**	
End. bal.	9,200	

Prepaid Insurance (A) (+ / −)

Beg. bal.	6,000	
End. bal.	6,000	

Supplies (A) (+ / −)

Beg. bal.	30,200	
(3)	**1,100**	
End. bal.	31,300	

Equipment (A) (+ / −)

Beg. bal.	270,000	
End. bal.	270,000	

Accumulated Depreciation—Equipment (XA) (− / +)

	60,000	Beg. bal.
	60,000	End. bal.

Liabilities

Accounts Payable (L) (− / +)

(5)	2,000	4,000	Beg. bal.
		1,100	(3)
		3,100	End. bal.

Contract Liability (L) (− / +)

	4,000	Beg. bal.
	4,000	End. bal.

Equity

Common Stock (SE) (− / +)

	120,400	Beg. bal.
	120,400	End. bal.

Retained Earnings (SE) (− / +)

	60,000	Beg. bal.
	60,000	End. bal.

Fees Revenue (R) (− / +)

	142,300	Beg. bal.
	6,500	(2)
	1,200	(4)
	150,000	End. bal.

Rent Expense (E) (+ / −)

Beg. bal.	22,000	
End. bal.	22,000	

Wages Expense (E) (+ / −)

Beg. bal.	54,000	
(1)	**4,000**	
End. bal.	58,000	

Assets = $257,500 = **Liabilities = $7,100** + **Equity = $250,400**

d.

ATWELL LABORATORIES, INC.
Unadjusted Trial Balance
June 30

	Debit	Credit
Cash	$ 1,000	
Accounts receivable	9,200	
Prepaid insurance	6,000	
Supplies	31,300	
Equipment	270,000	
Accumulated depreciation—equipment		$ 60,000
Accounts payable		3,100
Contract liability		4,000
Fees revenue		150,000
Wages expense	58,000	
Rent expense	22,000	
Common stock		120,400
Retained earnings		60,000
Totals	$397,500	$397,500

Review 3-2

a.

	Balance Sheet											Income Statement				
Transaction	Cash Asset	+	Noncash Assets	−	Contra Assets	=	Liabil-ities	+	Contrib. Capital	+	Earned Capital	Revenues	−	Expenses	=	Net Income
(1) Adjustment to record insurance expense.			−1,500 Prepaid Insurance	−		=					−1,500 Retained Earnings		−	+1,500 Insurance Expense	=	−1,500
(2) Adjustment to record supplies expense.			−25,000 Supplies	−		=					−25,000 Retained Earnings		−	+25,000 Supplies Expense	=	−25,000
(3) Adjustment to record depreciation expense.				−	+30,000 Accumulated Depreciation —Equipment	=					−30,000 Retained Earnings		−	+30,000 Depreciation Expense	=	−30,000
(4) Adjustment to record fees revenue.				−		=	−3,000 Contract Liability				+3,000 Retained Earnings	+3,000 Fees Revenue	−		=	+3,000
(5) Adjustment to record wages expense.				−		=	+600 Wages Payable				−600 Retained Earnings		−	+600 Wages Expense	=	−600
(6) Adjustment to record rent expense.				−		=	+2,000 Rent Payable				−2,000 Retained Earnings		−	+2,000 Rent Expense	=	−2,000

b.

		Debit	Credit
(1)	Insurance expense (+E, −SE)	1,500	
	Prepaid insurance (−A)		1,500
	Record insurance expired $6,000 × (6 months/24 months).		
(2)	Supplies expense (+E, −SE)	25,000	
	Supplies (−A)		25,000
	Record supplies used ($31,300 − $6,300).		
(3)	Depreciation expense (+E, −SE)	30,000	
	Accumulated depreciation—Equipment (+XA, −A)		30,000
	Record depreciation [($270,000 − $0) ÷ 9 years].		
(4)	Contract liability (−L)	3,000	
	Fees revenue (+R, +SE)		3,000
	Record fees earned.		
(5)	Wages expense (+E, −SE)	600	
	Wages payable (+L)		600
	Record employee wages incurred.		
(6)	Rent expense (+E, −SE)	2,000	
	Rent payable (+L)		2,000
	Record rent owed.		

c.

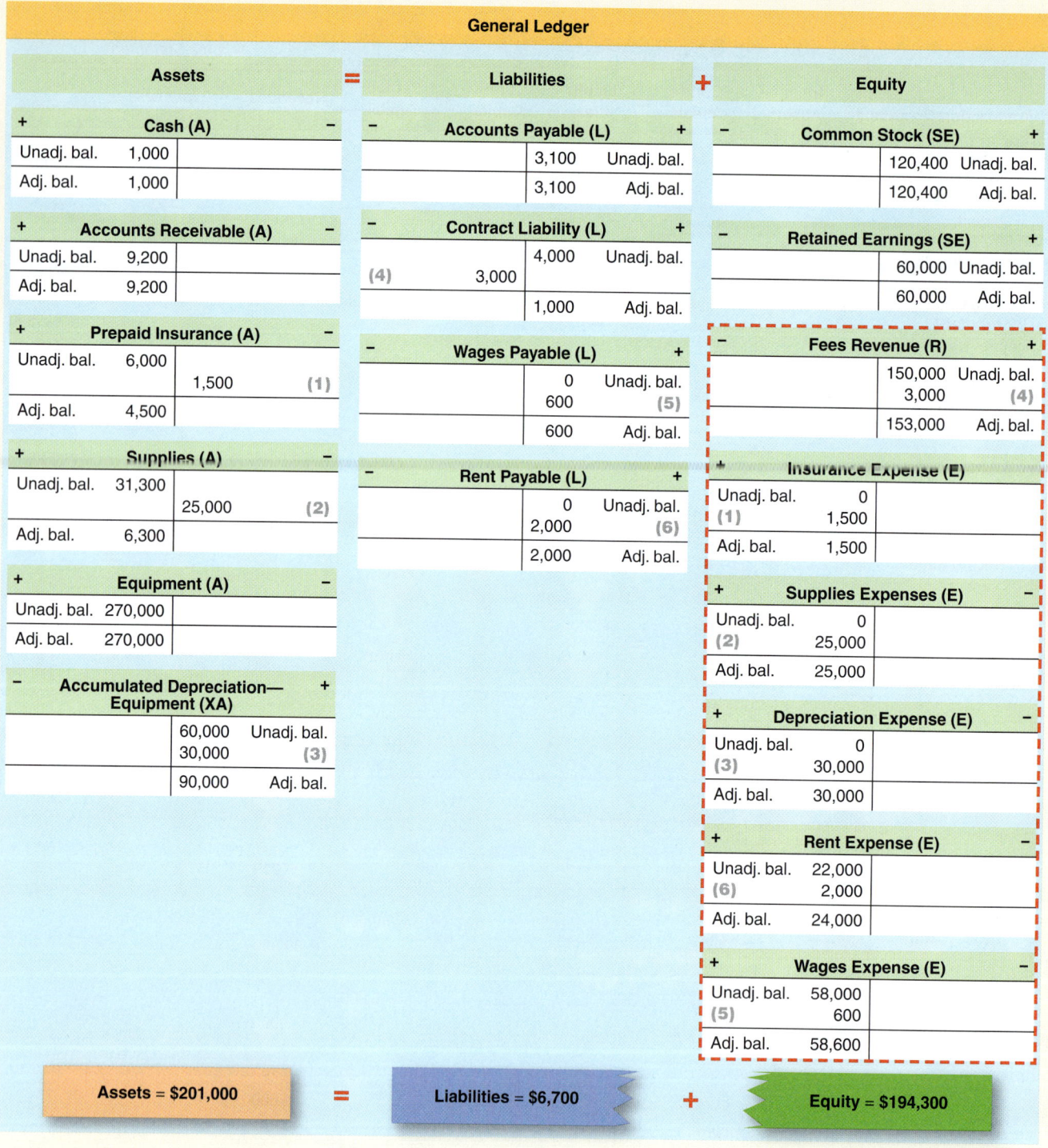

General Ledger

Assets = Liabilities + Equity

Assets

Cash (A) (+ / −)

Unadj. bal.	1,000		
Adj. bal.	1,000		

Accounts Receivable (A) (+ / −)

Unadj. bal.	9,200		
Adj. bal.	9,200		

Prepaid Insurance (A) (+ / −)

Unadj. bal.	6,000		
		1,500	(1)
Adj. bal.	4,500		

Supplies (A) (+ / −)

Unadj. bal.	31,300		
		25,000	(2)
Adj. bal.	6,300		

Equipment (A) (+ / −)

Unadj. bal.	270,000		
Adj. bal.	270,000		

Accumulated Depreciation—Equipment (XA) (− / +)

		60,000	Unadj. bal.
		30,000	(3)
		90,000	Adj. bal.

Liabilities

Accounts Payable (L) (− / +)

		3,100	Unadj. bal.
		3,100	Adj. bal.

Contract Liability (L) (− / +)

		4,000	Unadj. bal.
(4)	3,000		
		1,000	Adj. bal.

Wages Payable (L) (− / +)

		0	Unadj. bal.
		600	(5)
		600	Adj. bal.

Rent Payable (L) (− / +)

		0	Unadj. bal.
		2,000	(6)
		2,000	Adj. bal.

Equity

Common Stock (SE) (− / +)

		120,400	Unadj. bal.
		120,400	Adj. bal.

Retained Earnings (SE) (− / +)

		60,000	Unadj. bal.
		60,000	Adj. bal.

Fees Revenue (R) (− / +)

		150,000	Unadj. bal.
		3,000	(4)
		153,000	Adj. bal.

Insurance Expense (E) (+ / −)

Unadj. bal.	0		
(1)	1,500		
Adj. bal.	1,500		

Supplies Expenses (E) (+ / −)

Unadj. bal.	0		
(2)	25,000		
Adj. bal.	25,000		

Depreciation Expense (E) (+ / −)

Unadj. bal.	0		
(3)	30,000		
Adj. bal.	30,000		

Rent Expense (E) (+ / −)

Unadj. bal.	22,000		
(6)	2,000		
Adj. bal.	24,000		

Wages Expense (E) (+ / −)

Unadj. bal.	58,000		
(5)	600		
Adj. bal.	58,600		

Assets = $201,000 = **Liabilities = $6,700** + **Equity = $194,300**

d.

ATWELL LABORATORIES, INC.
Adjusted Trial Balance
June 30

	Debits	Credits
Cash	$ 1,000	
Accounts receivable	9,200	
Prepaid insurance	4,500	
Supplies	6,300	
Equipment	270,000	
Accumulated depreciation—equipment		$ 90,000
Accounts payable		3,100
Rent payable		2,000
Wages payable		600
Contract liability		1,000
Fees revenue		153,000
Wages expense	58,600	
Rent expense	24,000	
Insurance expense	1,500	
Supplies expense	25,000	
Depreciation expense	30,000	
Common stock		120,400
Retained earnings		60,000
Totals	$430,100	$430,100

Review 3-3

ATWELL LABORATORIES, INC.
Balance Sheet
June 30

Assets			**Liabilities**	
Cash		$ 1,000	Accounts payable	$ 3,100
Accounts receivable		9,200	Contract liability	1,000
Prepaid insurance		4,500	Wages payable	600
Supplies		6,300	Rent payable	2,000
Total current assets		21,000	Total current liabilities	6,700
Equipment, original cost	$270,000		**Equity**	
Less accumulated depreciation	90,000	180,000	Common stock	120,400
			Retained earnings	73,900
Total assets		$201,000	Totals liabilities and equity	$201,000

ATWELL LABORATORIES, INC.
Income Statement
For Year Ended June 30

Fees revenue		$153,000
Expenses		
Insurance expense	$ 1,500	
Supplies expense	25,000	
Depreciation expense	30,000	
Rent expense	24,000	
Wages expense	58,600	
Total expense		139,100
Net income		$ 13,900

ATWELL LABORATORIES, INC.
Statement of Stockholders' Equity
For Year Ended June 30

	Common Stock	Retained Earnings	Total
Balance at June 30, prior year	$120,400	$60,000	$180,400
Net Income	—	13,900	13,900
Balance at June 30, current year	$120,400	$73,900	$194,300

Atwell's statement of stockholders' equity is much simpler than the usual statement because we have focused on the adjustment and closing process. In doing so, we did not consider additional activities in which corporations commonly engage, such as paying dividends, issuing stock, and repurchasing stock. (Requirements did not ask for a statement of cash flows. The next chapter is devoted to the statement of cash flows.)

Review 3-4

a.

Retained earnings (−SE)	139,100	
Insurance expense (−E)		1,500
Supplies expense (−E)		25,000
Depreciation expense (−E)		30,000
Rent expense (−E)		24,000
Wages expense (−E)		58,600

Fees revenue (−R)	153,000	
Retained earnings (+SE)		153,000

b.

General Ledger

Assets = Liabilities + Equity

Assets

Cash (A) (+ / −)

Unadj. bal.	1,000		
Adj. bal.	1,000		

Accounts Receivable (A) (+ / −)

Unadj. bal.	9,200		
Adj. bal.	9,200		

Prepaid Insurance (A) (+ / −)

Unadj. bal.	6,000		
		1,500	(1)
Adj. bal.	4,500		

Supplies (A) (+ / −)

Unadj. bal.	31,300		
		25,000	(2)
Adj. bal.	6,300		

Equipment (A) (+ / −)

Unadj. bal.	270,000		
Adj. bal.	270,000		

Accumulated Depreciation—Equipment (XA) (− / +)

		60,000	Unadj. bal.
		30,000	(3)
		90,000	Adj. bal.

Liabilities

Accounts Payable (L) (− / +)

		3,100	Unadj. bal.
		3,100	Adj. bal.

Contract Liability (L) (− / +)

		4,000	Unadj. bal.
(4)	3,000		
		1,000	Adj. bal.

Wages Payable (L) (− / +)

		0	Unadj. bal.
		600	(5)
		600	Adj. bal.

Rent Payable (L) (− / +)

		0	Unadj. bal.
		2,000	(6)
		2,000	Adj. bal.

Equity

Common Stock (SE) (− / +)

		120,400	Unadj. bal.
		120,400	Adj. bal.

Retained Earnings (SE) (− / +)

		60,000	Unadj. bal.
(a)	139,100	153,000	(b)
		73,900	Adj. bal.

Fees Revenue (R) (− / +)

		150,000	Unadj. bal.
(b)	153,000	3,000	(4)
		0	Adj. bal.

Insurance Expense (E) (+ / −)

Unadj. bal.	0		
(1)	1,500	1,500	(a)
Adj. bal.	0		

Supplies Expense (E) (+ / −)

Unadj. bal.	0		
(2)	25,000	25,000	(a)
Adj. bal.	0		

Depreciation Expense (E) (+ / −)

Unadj. bal.	0		
(3)	30,000	30,000	(a)
Adj. bal.	0		

Rent Expense (E) (+ / −)

Unadj. bal.	22,000		
(6)	2,000	24,000	(a)
Adj. bal.	0		

Wages Expense (E) (+ / −)

Unadj. bal.	58,000		
(5)	600	58,600	(a)
Adj. bal.	0		

Assets = $201,000 = **Liabilities = $6,700** + **Equity = $194,300**

Review 3-5

a. $182,000 *b.* $17,500 *c.* $170,000 *d.* $3,000

Chapter 4 Reporting and Analyzing Cash Flows

LEARNING OBJECTIVES

LO4-1 Explain the purpose of the statement of cash flows and classify cash transactions by type of business activity: operating, investing, or financing.

LO4-2 Construct the operating activities section of the statement of cash flows using the direct method.

LO4-3 Reconcile cash flows from operations to net income and use the indirect method to compute operating cash flows.

LO4-4 Construct the investing and financing activities sections of the statement of cash flows.

LO4-5 Examine the sale of investing assets and the disclosure of noncash activities.

LO4-6 Compute and interpret ratios that reflect a company's liquidity and solvency using information reported in the statement of cash flows.

LO4-7 Appendix 4A: Use a spreadsheet to construct the statement of cash flows.

Road Map

LO	Learning Objective | Topics	Page	eLecture	Review	Assignments
LO4-1	Explain the purpose of the statement of cash flows and classify cash transactions by type of business activity: operating, investing, or financing.	4-3	e4-1	R4–1	M4-21, M4-22, M4-23, M4-24, M4-29, C4-58, C4-59
LO4-2	Construct the operating activities section of the statement of cash flows using the direct method.	4-7	e4-2	R4–2	M4-25, M4-27, M4-30, M4-31, E4-34, E4-38, E4-41, E4-43, E4-44, P4-47, P4-49, P4-51, P4-53, C4-59
LO4-3	Reconcile cash flows from operations to net income and use the indirect method to compute operating cash flows.	4-17	e4-3	R4–3	M4-21, M4-23, M4-25, M4-26, M4-27, M4-28, M4-29, E4-35, E4-42, E4-44, P4-45, P4-46, P4-48, P4-50, P4-51, P4-52, P4-53, P4-54, P4-55, P4-56, C4-57, C4-58, C4-59, DA4-1
LO4-4	Construct the investing and financing activities sections of the statement of cash flows.	4-19	e4-4	R4–4	M4-21, E4-39, P4-46, P4-48, P4-50, P4-51, P4-52, P4-53, P4-54, P4-55, P4-56, C4-57, C4-58, C4-59
LO4-5	Examine the sale of investing assets and the disclosure of noncash activities.	4-23	e4-5	R4–5	M4-24, E4-36, E4-37, E4-38, E4-39, P4-48, P4-50, P4-52, P4-53, P4-54, P4-55, C4-57, C4-58, C4-59
LO4-6	Compute and interpret ratios that reflect a company's liquidity and solvency using information reported in the statement of cash flows.	4-29	e4-6	R4–6	E4-32, E4-33, E4-35, E4-43, P4-46, P4-48, P4-50, P4-52, P4-55, P4-56, C4-59, DA4-2
LO4-7	Appendix 4A: Use a spreadsheet to construct the statement of cash flows.	4-33	e4-7	R4–7	E4-42, P4-55

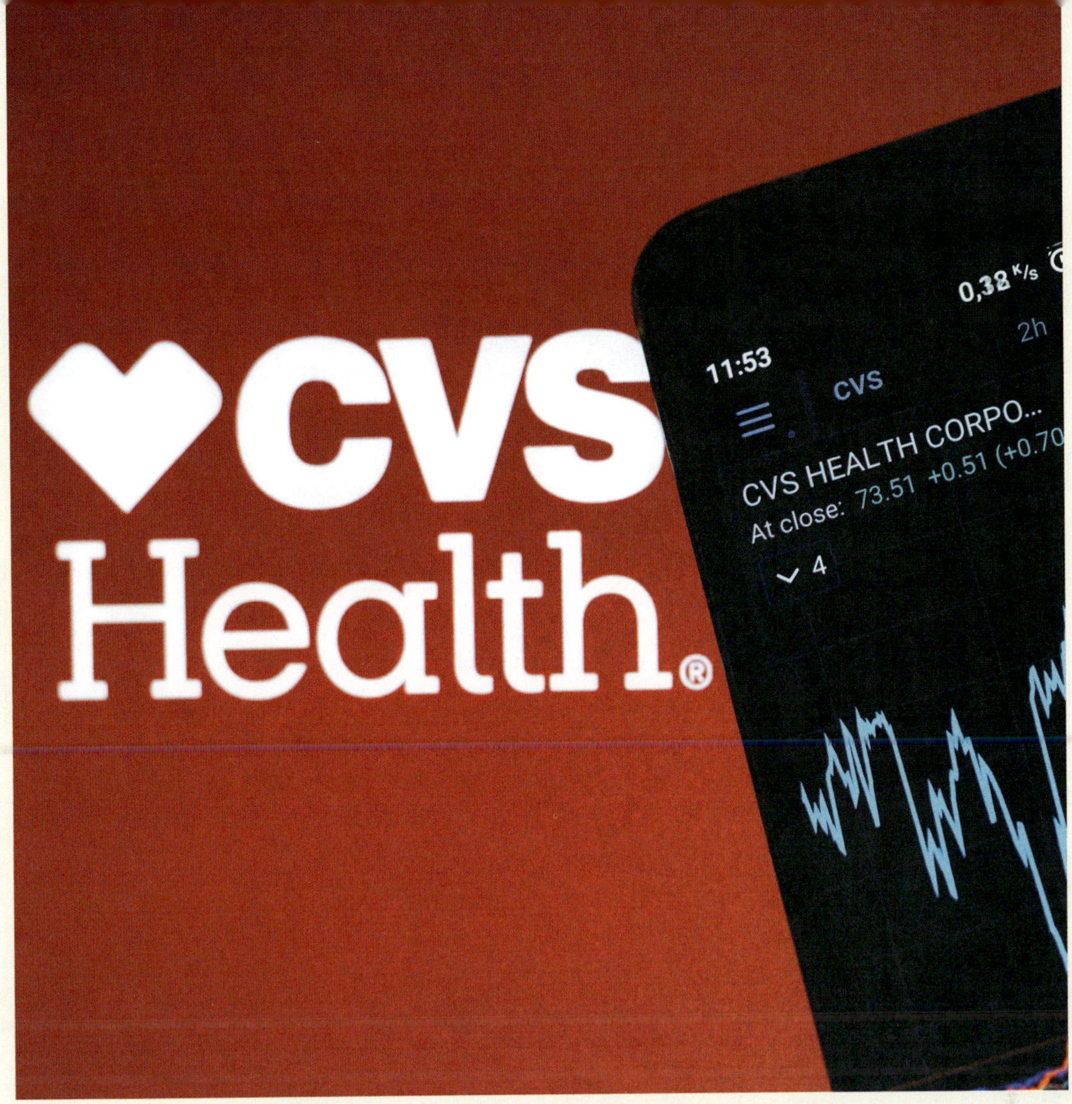

CVS HEALTH CORPORATION
www.cvshealth.com

Like **Walgreens Boots Alliance** (Walgreens), **CVS Health** started small, with a single store in Lowell, Massachusetts, in 1963, where CVS stood for Consumer Value Stores. The company soon grew in number of stores and expanded beyond health and beauty products to include pharmaceuticals. CVS made frequent use of acquisitions to increase the number of stores and the geographic reach of the company. In its 2020 annual report, CVS Health reports that it had more than 9,900 retail locations and almost 300,000 colleagues working at the company.

CVS Health operates at the intersection of two industries—retail and healthcare. In retail, almost all companies are affected by the rapid growth of online retailers and the decline in "bricks and mortar" businesses. And, the political pressure on healthcare costs affects an assortment of parties besides the ultimate consumer—pharmacies, insurance companies, pharmacy benefit managers, and pharmaceutical companies. Over time, CVS Health has expanded beyond its pharmacies into pharmacy benefit management to streamline costs, to provide better service to customers, and to maintain market competitiveness. In November 2018, CVS Health expanded its scope further by acquiring an insurance company, **Aetna, Inc.** The Aetna acquisition further expanded CVS Health's role in the pharmacy market, giving it an opportunity to improve operations and customer service. In addition, analysts suggest the merger provides some protection against online retail companies who might enter the pharmacy market.

However, that acquisition came at a cost, in the form of increased debt service costs and dividends to an increased number of outstanding shareholders. Where do we look to find out how successful CVS Health has been in meeting the challenges of these cost increases in the pandemic environment? For CVS Health, the 2020 statement of cash flows discloses that the company's increased cash inflows enabled it to maintain its dividend and reduce its outstanding debt by a substantial amount.

As we will discover in this chapter, a business must make sure that its cash inflows are adequate to fund new investments, meet obligations to creditors as they come due, and pay dividends to shareholders, in addition to meeting the challenges posed by unforeseen events like the COVID-19 pandemic. Even a profitable company can fail if it does not have a healthy cash flow. We will also discover why it is important to look at the statement of cash flows along with the income statement and balance sheet when trying to assess the financial health of a company.

Sources: CVS Health Corporation, Form 10-K 2020; www.cvshealth.com/about/company-history; "Leveraging cash flow's effect on valuation," *CFO Dive, cfodive.com* May 3, 2021.

CHAPTER ORGANIZATION

Reporting and Analyzing Cash Flows

Purpose of the Statement of Cash Flows	Framework for the Statement of Cash Flows	Preparing the Statement of Cash Flows	Analysis of Cash Flows
• What Do We Mean by Cash? • What Does a Statement of Cash Flows Look Like?	• Operating Activities • Investing Activities • Financing Activities • Usefulness of Classifications	• Cash Flows from Operating Activities • Cash Flows from Investing and Financing Activities • Additional Detail in the Statement of Cash Flows • Preparing the Statement of Cash Flows Using a Spreadsheet (Appendix 4A)	• Operating Cash Flow to Current Liabilities • Operating Cash Flow to Capital Expenditures • Free Cash Flow

PURPOSE OF THE STATEMENT OF CASH FLOWS

LO4-1 Explain the purpose of the statement of cash flows and classify cash transactions by type of business activity: operating, investing, or financing.

eLecture MBC

In addition to the balance sheet and the income statement, corporations are required to report a statement of cash flows. The **statement of cash flows** tells us how a company generated cash (cash inflows) and how it used cash (cash outflows). The statement of cash flows complements the income statement and the balance sheet by providing information that neither the income statement nor the balance sheet can provide. For instance, slower collection of receivables doesn't affect income, but it does reduce the amount of cash coming into the company.

Understanding the statement of cash flows helps us understand trends in a firm's **liquidity** (ability to pay near-term liabilities and take advantage of investment opportunities), and it helps us assess a firm's **solvency** (ability to pay long-term liabilities). With information about how cash was generated or used, creditors and investors are better able to assess a firm's ability to settle its liabilities and pay dividends to shareholders. A firm's need for outside financing is also better evaluated when using cash flow data. Over time, the statement of cash flows permits users to observe and assess management's investing and financing policies. For example, a business that is not generating enough cash flow internally, i.e., from operations, must get cash from borrowing, issuing shares, or selling off its assets.

The statement of cash flows also provides information about a firm's ability to generate sufficient amounts of cash to respond to unanticipated needs and opportunities. Information about past cash flows, particularly cash flows from operations, helps in assessing a company's financial flexibility. An evaluation of a firm's ability to survive an unexpected drop in demand, for example, should include a review of its past cash flows from operations. The larger these cash flows, the greater is the firm's ability to withstand adverse changes in economic conditions.

So, whether we are a potential investor, loan officer, future employee, supplier, or customer, we greatly benefit from an understanding of the cash inflows and outflows of a company.

What Do We Mean by "CASH"?

FYI A cash equivalent is a short-term, highly liquid investment that is easily converted to cash and is close enough to maturity that its market value is not sensitive to interest rate changes.

The statement of cash flows explains the change in a firm's cash *and* cash equivalents. **Cash equivalents** are short-term, highly liquid investments that are (1) easily convertible into a known cash amount and (2) close enough to maturity that their market value is not sensitive to interest rate changes (generally, investments with remaining maturities of three months or less). Treasury bills, commercial paper (short-term notes issued by corporations), and money market funds are typical examples of cash equivalents.

In some situations, a portion of a company's cash balances may not be immediately available for use. For instance, a lender might require a borrowing company to keep a minimum balance of cash. Such restricted cash is not included in cash and cash equivalents on the balance sheet, but rather in a separate asset account called **restricted cash**, with a note describing the restrictions. For instance, CVS Health reports a balance of cash and cash equivalents of $7,854 million in its balance sheet, plus another $276 million in restricted cash that is included in "other assets."

However, the statement of cash flows describes the total flows of cash, including unrestricted cash and cash equivalents plus restricted cash and cash equivalents, as can be seen at the bottom of **Exhibit 4.1**. The addition of cash equivalents is done because the purchase and sale of investments in cash equivalents are considered to be part of a firm's overall management of cash rather than a source or use of cash. As statement users evaluate and project cash flows, for example, it should not matter whether the cash is readily available in a cash register or safe, deposited in a bank account, or invested in cash equivalents. Consequently, transfers back and forth between a firm's cash on hand, its bank accounts, and its investments in cash equivalents are not treated as cash inflows and cash outflows in its statement of cash flows. When discussing the statement of cash flows, managers generally use the word *cash* rather than the phrases cash, cash equivalents, and restricted cash. We will follow the same practice.

What Does a Statement of Cash Flows Look Like?

Exhibit 4.1 reproduces CVS Health Corporation's statement of cash flows for the fiscal year ended on December 31, 2020. During this fiscal year, CVS Health generated $15,865 million in cash from its operations.

Investing activities used $5,534 million in cash, and financing activities used another $8,155 million of cash. Over the entire year, the company's cash balance increased by $2,176 million and ended the year at $8,130 million on December 31, 2020.

EXHIBIT 4.1 CVS Health Corporation Statement of Cash Flows

CVS HEALTH CORPORATION
Consolidated Statement of Cash Flows
For the Fiscal Year Ended December 31, 2020

In millions	
Cash flows from operating activities	
Cash receipts from customers	$264,327
Cash paid for inventory and prescriptions dispensed by retail network pharmacies	(158,636)
Insurance benefits paid	(55,124)
Cash paid to other suppliers and employees	(29,763)
Interest and investment income received	894
Interest paid	(2,904)
Income taxes paid	(2,929)
Net cash provided by operating activities	15,865
Cash flows from investing activities	
Proceeds from sales and maturities of investments	6,467
Purchases of investments	(9,639)
Purchases of property and equipment	(2,437)
Proceeds from sale-leaseback transactions	101
Acquisitions (net of cash acquired)	(866)
Proceeds from sale of subsidiaries and other assets	840
Net cash used in investing activities	(5,534)
Cash flows from financing activities	
Proceeds from issuance of long-term debt	9,958
Repayments of long-term debt	(15,631)
Derivative settlements	(7)
Dividends paid	(2,624)
Proceeds from exercise of stock options	264
Payments for taxes related to net share settlement of equity awards	(88)
Other	(27)
Net cash used in financing activities	(8,155)
Net increase in cash, cash equivalents, and restricted cash	2,176
Cash, cash equivalents, and restricted cash at the beginning of the period	5,954
Cash, cash equivalents, and restricted cash at the end of the period	**$ 8,130**

FRAMEWORK FOR THE STATEMENT OF CASH FLOWS

The statement of cash flows classifies cash receipts and payments into one of three categories: operating activities, investing activities, or financing activities. Classifying cash flows into these categories identifies the effects on cash of each of the major activities of a firm. The combined effects on cash of all three categories explain the net change in cash for the period. The period's net change in cash is then reconciled with the beginning and ending amounts of cash.

Operating Activities

FYI Cash flows from operating activities (cash flows from operations) refer to cash inflows and outflows directly related to the firm's primary day-to-day business activities.

A company's income statement mainly reflects the transactions and events that constitute its operating activities. The cash effects of these operating transactions and events determine the net cash flow from operating activities. The usual focus of a firm's **operating activities** is on selling goods or rendering services, but the activities are defined broadly enough to include any cash receipts or payments that are not classified as investing or financing activities. For example, CVS Health Corporation reports cash received from customers and for interest. The company paid cash to suppliers (of pharmaceuticals and other items) and employees and tax authorities and to lenders for interest. The following are examples of cash inflows and outflows relating to operating activities.

Cash Inflows

1. Cash receipts from customers for sales made or services rendered (or in anticipation of future deliveries of goods or services).
2. Cash receipts of interest and dividends.[1]
3. Other cash receipts that are not related to investing or financing activities, such as rentals, lawsuit settlements, and refunds received from suppliers.

Cash Outflows

1. Cash payments to employees or suppliers.
2. Cash payments to purchase inventories.
3. Cash payments of interest to creditors.[1]
4. Cash payments of taxes to government.
5. Other cash payments that are not related to investing or financing activities, such as contributions to charity and lawsuit settlements.

Investing Activities

FYI Cash flows from investing activities are cash inflows and outflows related to acquiring or selling productive assets and the investments in securities of other entities.

A firm's transactions involving (1) the acquisition and disposal of property, plant, and equipment (PPE) assets and intangible assets, (2) the purchase and sale of government securities and securities of other companies, including stocks, bonds, and other securities that are not classified as cash equivalents, and (3) the lending and subsequent collection of money constitute the basic components of its **investing activities**. The related cash receipts and payments appear in the investing activities section of the statement of cash flows and, if material in amount, inflows and outflows should be reported separately (not as a net amount). Examples of these cash flows follow:

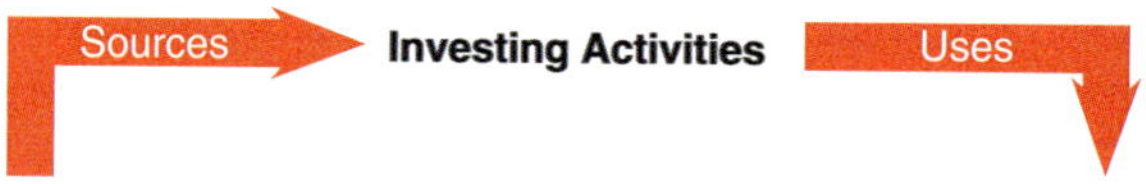

Cash Inflows

1. Cash receipts from sales of property, plant, and equipment (PPE) assets and intangible assets.
2. Cash receipts from sales of investments in government securities and securities of other companies (including divestitures).
3. Cash receipts from repayments of loans by borrowers.

Cash Outflows

1. Cash payments to purchase property, plant, and equipment (PPE) assets and intangible assets.
2. Cash payments to purchase government securities and securities of other companies (including acquisitions).
3. Cash payments made to lend money to borrowers.

Financing Activities

FYI Cash flows from financing activities are cash inflows and outflows related to external sources of financing (owners and nonowners).

A firm engages in **financing activities** when it receives cash from shareholders, returns cash to shareholders, borrows from creditors, and repays amounts borrowed. Cash flows related to these

[1] Many financial statement readers believe that interest and dividends received should be considered cash inflows from investing activities and that interest payments should be considered cash outflows from financing activities. In fact, when the reporting standard was passed by the Financial Accounting Standards Board, three of the seven members dissented from the standard for this reason (among others). The majority based their decision on "the view that, in general, cash flows from operating activities should reflect the cash effects of transactions and other events that enter into the determination of net income." (Statement of Financial Accounting Standards No. 95, paragraph 88.)

transactions are reported in the financing activities section of the statement of cash flows and again, inflows and outflows should be reported separately (not as a net amount) if material. Examples of these cash flows follow:

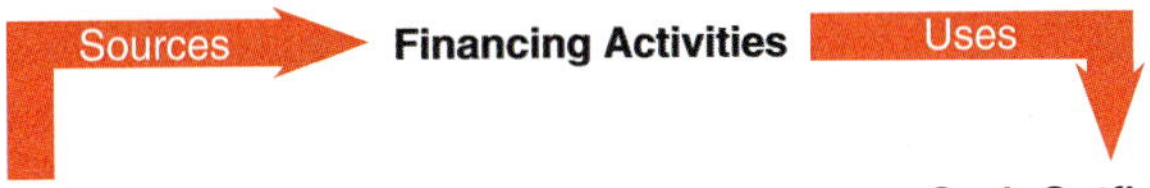

Cash Inflows

1. Cash receipts from issuances of common stock and preferred stock and from sales of treasury stock.
2. Cash receipts from issuances of bonds payable, mortgage notes payable, and other notes payable.

Cash Outflows

1. Cash payments to acquire treasury stock.
2. Cash payments of dividends.
3. Cash payments to settle outstanding bonds payable, mortgage notes payable, and other notes payable.

Paying cash to settle such obligations as accounts payable, trade notes payable, wages payable, interest payable, and income tax payable are operating activities, not financing activities, because they are related to the daily operations of the company such as buying and selling inventory. Also, cash received as interest and dividends and cash paid as interest (not dividends) are classified as cash flows from operating activities. However, cash paid to shareholders as dividends is classified as cash flows from financing activities.

FYI **Treasury stock** refers to the amount paid by a company to purchase its own common stock.

A GLOBAL PERSPECTIVE

Under U.S. accounting principles, payments for interest expense and receipts for interest and dividend income are considered part of cash from operations. International Financial Reporting Standards allow companies to report interest payments as part of either operating activities or financing activities and to report interest and dividend receipts as part of either operating activities or investing activities.

IFRS

Usefulness of Classifications

The classification of cash flows into three categories of activities helps financial statement users interpret cash flow data. To illustrate, assume that Faultless, Inc., Peerless Co., and Dauntless Ltd. each reports a $100,000 cash increase during the current year. Information from their current-year statements of cash flows is summarized in **Exhibit 4.2**.

EXHIBIT 4.2 Summary Information for Three Competitors

	Faultless	Peerless	Dauntless
Net cash provided by operating activities	$100,000	$ 0	$ 0
Cash flows from investing activities			
Sale of property, plant, and equipment	0	100,000	0
Cash flows from financing activities			
Issuance of notes payable	0	0	100,000
Net increase in cash.	$100,000	$100,000	$100,000

One of the keys to evaluating a company's worth is estimating its future cash inflows based on the information available. Companies that can generate a stream of future cash inflows are worth more than those with a single cash inflow. In **Exhibit 4.2**, each company's net cash increase was the same, but the source of the increase varied by company. This variation affects the analysis of the cash flow data, particularly for potential creditors who must evaluate the likelihood of obtaining repayment in the future for any funds loaned to the company. Based only on these cash flow data, a potential creditor would feel more comfortable lending money to Faultless than to either Peerless or Dauntless. This choice is because Faultless' cash increase came from its operating activities, and operations tend to be continuing. Both Peerless and Dauntless could only break even on their cash flows from operations. Also, Peerless' cash increase came from the sale of property, plant, and equipment (PPE) assets—a source of cash that is not likely to recur regularly. Dauntless' cash increase came entirely from borrowed funds. This means Dauntless faces additional cash burdens in the future when the interest and principal payments on the note payable become due.

BUSINESS INSIGHT

Objectivity of Cash Usefulness of financial statements is enhanced when the underlying data are objective and verifiable. Measuring cash and the changes in cash are among the most objective measurements that accountants make. Thus, the statement of cash flows is arguably the most objective financial statement. This characteristic of the statement of cash flows is welcomed by those investors and creditors interested in evaluating the quality of a firm's income.

Review 4-1 LO4-1

Classifying Cash Flows

GuidedExample MBC

Assume CVS Health Corporation executed the following transactions during the year. Indicate whether the transaction creates a cash inflow (In) or outflow (Out). Next, determine how each item should be classified in the statement of cash flows: an operating activity (O), an investing activity (I), or a financing activity (F). For example: $50,000 cash received for the sale of snack foods. Answer: In/O

1. ____ $250,000 cash paid to purchase a warehouse
2. ____ $120,000 cash paid for interest on a loan
3. ____ $850,000 cash paid to employees as wages
4. ____ $20,000,000 cash raised through the issuance of stock
5. ____ $450,000 cash paid to the government for taxes
6. ____ $350,000 cash received as part of a settlement of a legal case
7. ____ $630,000 cash received from the sale of long-term securities
8. ____ $75,000 cash received from the sale of used office equipment
9. ____ $500,000 cash dividend paid to shareholders
10. ____ $90,000 cash received as interest earned on a government bond

Solution on p. 4-60.

PREPARING THE STATEMENT OF CASH FLOWS—OPERATING ACTIVITIES

LO4-2 Construct the operating activities section of the statement of cash flows using the direct method.

eLecture MBC

In Chapter 3's **Exhibit 3.12**, we presented a statement of cash flows for Natural Beauty Supply (hereafter, NBS) for the month of December 2021. This statement is reproduced in **Exhibit 4.3**. The statement details how NBS' cash balance decreases by $1,275 in December, from $8,100 to $6,825. The statement was prepared by examining all of the cash transactions that occurred during the month and then grouping them according to the type of activity each represents—operating, investing, or financing—as illustrated in the cash T-account below. Transaction (17) was the loan, so that goes in the financing activity section; transaction (18) was the purchase of fixtures and equipment and belongs in the investing activity section; and so on.

		+ Cash (A)	–	
	Beg. bal.	8,100		
Operating activities	(21)	8,500	700	(19)
	(23)	1,200	3,300	(20)
	(25)	3,200	1,625	(24)
			1,500	(27)
Investing activities			18,000	(18)
Financing activities	(17)	11,000	50	(28)
	End. bal.	6,825		

An alternative presentation of the transactions affecting cash can be organized by activity using the Financial Statement Effects Template (FSET). Those items involving cash are gathered inside the red box and then categorized according to the type of activity—operating, investing, or financing—that generated them.

	Balance Sheet									Income Statement				
Transaction	Cash asset	+	Noncash asset	=	Liabil-ities	+	Contrib. Capital	+	Earned Capital	Revenue	–	Expense	=	Net income
Beg. Bal.	8,100 Cash													
Operating activities														
(19)	−700 Cash			=					−700 Retained Earnings		–	+700 Advertising Expense	=	−700
(20)	−3,300 Cash			=	−3,300 Accts Payable						–		=	
(21)	+8,500 Cash			=					+8,500 Retained earnings	+8,500 Sales Revenue	–		=	+8,500
(23)	+1,200 Cash			=	+1,200 Gift Card Liability						–		=	
(24)	−1,625 Cash			=					−1,625 Retained Earnings		–	+1,625 Wage Expense	=	−1,625
(25)	+3,200 Cash		−3,200 Accts Receivable	=							–		=	
(27)	−1,500 Cash			=					−1,500 Retained Earnings		–	+1,500 Rent Expense	=	−1,500
Investing activities														
(18)	−18,000 Cash		+18,000 Fixtures and Equipment	=							–		=	
Financing activities														
(17)	+11,000 Cash			=	+11,000 Notes Payable						–		=	
(28)	−50 Cash			=					−50 Retained Earnings		–		=	
End. Bal.	6,825 Cash													

Whether one uses T-accounts or the FSET, the approach to preparing the statement of cash flows is straightforward and doesn't require any additional bookkeeping steps, other than those introduced in Chapters 2 and 3.

However, for many companies, the number and variety of cash transactions that occur each period are so large that such an approach is often impractical. A company with revenues and assets and liabilities in the billions of dollars, like CVS Health, for example, has thousands of cash transactions each day. It has accounts with several different banks in numerous locations and regularly transfers cash from one account to another or back and forth between cash accounts and cash equivalents, as needed. For such a company, simply listing the cash transactions is not practical.

An alternative to this approach of compiling a list of cash flows is to reconcile the information in the income statement and balance sheet to prepare the statement of cash flows. The statement of cash flows complements the balance sheet and the income statement. The balance sheet details the financial position of the company at a given point in time. Comparing two balance sheets prepared at the beginning and at the end of a period reveals changes that transpired during the accounting period. These changes are explained by the income statement and the statement of cash flows. Both the income statement and the statement of cash flows summarize the events and transactions of the business during the accounting period, and as such, provide complementary descriptions of a company's activities. While the statement of cash flows provides information that is not explicitly found in either of the other two statements, it must articulate with the balance sheet and income statement to present a complete picture of company activities.

EXHIBIT 4.3 NBS Statement of Cash Flows (Direct Method)

NATURAL BEAUTY SUPPLY, INC.
Statement of Cash Flows
For the Month Ended December 31, 2021

Cash Flows from Operating Activities		
Cash received from customers (entries 21, 23, 25)	$12,900	
Cash paid for inventory (entry 20)	(3,300)	
Cash paid for wages (entry 24)	(1,625)	
Cash paid for rent (entry 27)	(1,500)	
Cash paid for advertising (entry 19)	(700)	
Net cash provided by operating activities		$ 5,775
Cash Flows from Investing Activities		
Cash paid for fixtures and equipment (entry 18)	(18,000)	
Net cash used for investing activities		(18,000)
Cash Flows from Financing Activities		
Cash received from loans (entry 17)	11,000	
Cash paid for dividends (entry 28)	(50)	
Net cash provided by financing activities		10,950
Net change in cash		(1,275)
Cash balance, November 30, 2021		8,100
Cash balance, December 31, 2021		$ 6,825

One of the characteristics of the accounting system is that when an entry changes Net Income without a change in Cash, then it must change another account on the balance sheet. And, when an operating cash flow occurs without a change in Net Income, then there must be a change in some other balance sheet account. Therefore, we can start with information from the income statement and then use the balance sheet (and some additional information) to prepare the statement of cash flows. **Exhibit 4.4** presents the income statement and comparative balance sheets for NBS. We will use the data from these financial statements to prepare NBS' reconciliation of Net Income to Cash from Operating Activities.

EXHIBIT 4.4 NBS Income Statement and Comparative Balance Sheet

NATURAL BEAUTY SUPPLY
Income Statement
For the Month Ended December 31, 2021

Sales revenue		$13,900
Cost of goods sold		8,000
Gross profit		5,900
Operating expenses:		
Rent	$1,500	
Wages	2,105	
Advertising	700	
Depreciation	375	
Insurance	140	
Total operating expenses		4,820
Operating income		1,080
Interest income		30
Interest expense		(110)
Income before taxes		1,000
Income tax expense		350
Net income		$ 650

NATURAL BEAUTY SUPPLY
Comparative Balance Sheets

	12/31/21	**11/30/21**
Assets:		
Cash	$ 6,825	$ 8,100
Other receivables	30	
Accounts receivable	2,250	950
Inventory	7,300	11,300
Prepaid insurance	1,540	1,680
Security deposit	2,000	2,000
Fixtures and equipment	18,000	
Accumulated depreciation	(375)	
Total assets	$37,570	$24,030
Liabilities:		
Accounts payable	$ 4,400	$ 3,700
Gift card liability	600	300
Wages payable	480	
Interest payable	110	
Taxes payable	350	
Notes payable	11,000	
Stockholders' equity:		
Common stock	20,000	20,000
Retained earnings	630	30
Total liabilities and equity	$37,570	$24,030

Converting Revenues and Expenses to Cash Flows from Operating Activities

We know from Chapter 3 that net income consists of revenues and expenses. We also know that these are often not cash transactions. For example, sales on account will be considered revenue but are not cash inflows until collected. Depreciation is an expense but is not a current-period cash outflow. (The cash outflow presumably occurred when the underlying asset was acquired in a past investing transaction.) We can compute cash flow from operating activities by making adjustments to the revenues and expenses presented in the income statement. The adjustment amounts represent differences between revenues, expenses, gains, and losses recorded under accrual accounting and the related operating cash inflows and outflows. The adjustments are added to or subtracted from net income, depending on whether the related cash flow is more or less than the accrual amount.

Convert Sales Revenues to Cash Received from Customers To illustrate this adjustment procedure for revenues and cash receipts from customers, consider the Chapter 3 transactions and adjusting entry that occurred for NBS in December 2021:

(21) Dec. 20 During the month of December, NBS sold products costing $5,000 to retail customers for $8,500 cash.
(22) Dec. — During the month of December, sales to wholesale customers totaled $4,500 for merchandise that had cost $3,000. Instead of paying cash, wholesale customers are required to pay for the merchandise within ten working days.
(23) Dec. — $1,200 of gift certificates were sold during the month of December. Each gift certificate entitles the recipient to a one-hour consultation on the use of NBS' products.
(25) Dec. — During the month of December, NBS received $3,200 in cash from wholesale customers for products that had been delivered earlier.
(a) Dec. 31 Gift certificates worth $900 were redeemed during the month.

We enter the revenue and cash receipts implications of each of these into the Financial Statement Effects Template (FSET) on the following page. Whenever there is a difference between the revenue recognized and the cash received, that difference affects an operating asset (accounts receivable) or an operating liability (gift card liability). For instance, in transaction (22a), NBS recognizes credit sales revenue. That is, revenue increases, but cash does not, and the accounting equation is kept by increasing accounts receivable, an operating asset. When NBS received cash in advance of revenue recognition, as in transaction (23), the balancing entry is in gift card liability, an operating liability. We will find that when an operating transaction affects cash or income—but not both—the operating assets and operating liabilities serve as a temporary buffer between the two.

The total of each of these columns is given in the last row, and because each individual entry is balanced, the totals are balanced.

	Balance Sheet									Income Statement				
Transaction	Cash Asset	+	Noncash Assets	=	Liabil-ities	+	Contrib. Capital	+	Earned Capital	Revenues	–	Expenses	=	Net Income
(21a) Sell $8,500 of products for cash.	+8,500 Cash			=					+8,500 Retained Earnings	+8,500 Sales Revenue	–		=	+8,500
(22a) Sell $4,500 of products on account.			+4,500 Accounts Receivable	=					+4,500 Retained Earnings	+4,500 Sales Revenue	–		=	+4,500
(23) Sell gift certificates for $1,200 cash.	+1,200 Cash			=	+1,200 Gift Card Liability						–		=	
(25) Receive $3,200 cash from customers who purchased on credit.	+3,200 Cash		−3,200 Accounts Receivable	=							–		=	
(a) Adjusting entry for gift certificates redeemed in December.				=	−900 Gift Card Liability				+900 Retained Earnings	+900 Sales Revenue	–		=	+900
Total changes	+12,900 Cash	+	+1,300 Accounts Receivable	=	+300 Gift Card Liability	+	0	+	+13,900 Retained Earnings	+13,900 Sales Revenue	–	0	=	+13,900

We can see that December's revenue was $13,900, and NBS collected $12,900 from customers during the month. Accounts receivable increased by $1,300 over the month, and gift card liability increased by $300. The FSET maintains the accounting equation at every entry, so we know that the equality will hold for the totals in the last row.

Cash flow (receipts)	+	Change in accounts receivable	=	Change in gift card liability	+	Net income (Sales revenue)
$12,900	+	**$1,300**	=	**$300**	+	**$13,900**

And this relationship can be rewritten as the following:

Cash flow	=	Net income	−	Change in accounts receivable	+	Change in gift card liability
$12,900	=	**$13,900**	−	**$1,300**	+	**$300**

So, when we start with net income and then subtract the change in accounts receivable and add the change in gift card liability, we convert the revenues in net income into the cash receipts from customers needed for cash from operations.

Convert Cost of Goods Sold to Cash Paid for Merchandise Purchased As a second illustration, let's examine the December 2021 transactions involving NBS' inventory and its suppliers (**Exhibit 3.3** in Chapter 3).

(20) Dec. 20 NBS paid $3,300 cash to its suppliers in partial payment for the delivery of inventory in November.

(21) Dec. — During the month of December, NBS sold products costing $5,000 to retail customers for $8,500 cash.

(22) Dec. — During the month of December, sales to wholesale customers totaled $4,500 for merchandise that had cost $3,000. Instead of paying cash, wholesale customers are required to pay for the merchandise within ten working days.

(26) Dec. 28 NBS purchased and received $4,000 of inventory on account.

When a company like NBS purchases inventory for future sale, we know that the purchase will be followed by two events in the normal course of business. One event is that NBS will have to pay the supplier in cash according to the terms of the purchase, resulting in a cash outflow. The other event is the sale of that inventory to a customer of NBS, resulting in a cost of goods sold expense on the income statement. But these two events do not necessarily occur at the same point in time. As we enter these events into the FSET, we see that the differences between cash payments for inventory and cost of goods sold expense are buffered by inventory, an operating asset, and accounts payable, an operating liability.

	Balance Sheet									Income Statement				
Transaction	Cash Asset	+	Noncash Assets	=	Liabil-ities	+	Contrib. Capital	+	Earned Capital	Revenues	−	Expenses	=	Net Income
(20) Pay $3,300 cash to suppliers.	−3,300 Cash			=	−3,300 Accounts Payable						−		=	
(21b) Record $5,000 for the cost of merchandise sold in transaction 21a.			−5,000 Inventory	=					−5,000 Retained Earnings		−	+5,000 Cost of Goods Sold	=	−5,000
(22b) Record $3,000 for the cost of merchandise sold in transaction 22a.			−3,000 Inventory	=					−3,000 Retained Earnings		−	+3,000 Cost of Goods Sold	=	−3,000
(26) Purchase $4,000 inventory on account.			+4,000 Inventory	=	+4,000 Accounts Payable						−		=	
Total changes	−3,300 Cash	+	−4,000 Inventory	=	+700 Accounts Payable	+	0	+	−8,000 Retained Earnings	0	−	+8,000 Cost of Goods Sold	=	−8,000

Again, the FSET keeps the accounting equation with every entry, so we know that the total changes in the last row must also conform to the accounting equation.

Cash flow (payments)	+	Change in inventory	=	Change in accounts payable	+	Net income (COGS expense)
–$3,300	+	**–$4,000**	=	**$700**	+	**–$8,000**

And this relationship can be written as the following:

Cash flow	=	Net income	–	Change in inventory	+	Change in accounts payable
–$3,300	=	**–$8,000**	–	**(–$4,000)**	+	**$700**

The change in inventory is negative for NBS during December 2021, so when we subtract the change in inventory above, we must subtract a negative number, making a positive adjustment. (That is, –(–$4,000) = +$4,000.) And, when we subtract the change in inventory from net income and add the change in accounts payable to net income, we convert the (minus) cost of goods sold expense to the (minus) payments to suppliers we need for the cash from operations.

Stepping back to look at the big picture, we begin to see a pattern. The cash flow effect of an item is equal to its income statement effect, minus the change in any associated operating asset(s) plus the change in any associated operating liability(ies). That pattern can be confirmed as we look at the remaining necessary adjustments.

Convert Wages Expense to Cash Paid to Employees To determine the adjustment needed for transactions involving employees, we look at the two entries from Chapter 3 related to the wages earned and paid during the month of December 2021.

	Balance Sheet									Income Statement				
Transaction	Cash Asset	+	Noncash Assets	=	Liabil-ities	+	Contrib. Capital	+	Earned Capital	Revenues	–	Expenses	=	Net Income
(24) Record $1,625 in wages to employees.	–1,625 Cash			=					–1,625 Retained Earnings		–	+1,625 Wages Expense	=	–1,625
(e) Adjusting entry to record wages earned but not yet paid.				=	+480 Wages Payable				–480 Retained Earnings		–	+480 Wages Expense	=	–480
Total changes	–1,625 Cash	+	0	=	+480 Wages Payable	+	0	+	–2,105 Retained Earnings	0	–	+2,105 Wages Expense	=	–2,105

Using the same approach as above, the FSET tells us the following about the totals:

Cash flow (payments)	=	Change in wages payable	+	Net income (wage expense),

which can be rewritten as

Cash flow	=	Net income	+	Change in wages payable
–$1,625	=	**–$2,105**	+	**$480**

NBS recorded more wage expense than it paid to its employees, and that additional expense goes into an operating liability, wages payable. If wages payable had decreased over the period, it would imply that NBS had paid more to its employees than they had earned during the period (perhaps because they were owed compensation from a prior period).

Convert Rent Expense to Cash Paid for Rent and Advertising Expense to Cash Paid for Advertising The December 2021 entries for rent and advertising are presented in the FSET below.

Transaction	Cash Asset	+ Noncash Assets	= Liabilities	+ Contrib. Capital	+ Earned Capital	*Revenues*	− *Expenses*	= *Net Income*
	Balance Sheet					***Income Statement***		
(19) Pay $700 cash for December advertising.	−700 Cash		=		−700 Retained Earnings		− +700 Advertising Expense	= −700
(27) Pay $1,500 rent for December.	−1,500 Cash		=		−1,500 Retained Earnings		− +1,500 Rent Expense	= −1,500
Total changes	−2,200 Cash	+ 0	= 0	+ 0	+ −2,200 Retained Earnings	0	− +2,200 Advertising and Rent Expense	= −2,200

For these items, the amount paid is exactly equal to the amount recorded as expense, so no adjustment is necessary. The amounts included for advertising and rent in the determination of net income are exactly what we want in the cash from operations. If NBS had paid rent in advance or promised to pay later for its advertising, then operating assets and/or liabilities would have been created, and an adjustment would have been necessary (as we see in the case immediately following).

Other Adjustments There are five more items in NBS' income statement that require adjustment to arrive at the amount of cash from operations for the month of December. Four of these items are insurance expense, interest income, interest expense, and income tax expense. These items involved only adjusting entries during the month of December, so there were no cash flows involved, and we present the adjustments in an abbreviated fashion below.

(b) Adjusting entry to record expiration of 1 month of prepaid insurance.		−140 Prepaid insurance	=		−140 Retained Earnings		− +140 Insurance Expense	= −140
Total changes	0 Cash	+ −140 Prepaid Insurance	= 0	+ 0	+ −140 Retained Earnings	0	− +140 Insurance Expense	= −140

Cash flow + Change in prepaid insurance = Net income, or

Cash flow = Net income − Change in prepaid insurance, or
$0 (zero) = −$140 − (−$140)

(d) Adjusting entry for interest income earned.		+30 Other Receivables	=		+30 Retained Earnings	+30 Interest Income	−	= +30
Total changes	0 Cash	+ +30 Other Receivables	= 0	+ 0	+ +30 Retained Earnings	+30 Interest Income	− 0	= +30

Cash flow + Change in other receivables = Net income, or

Cash flow = Net income − Change in other receivables, or
$0 (zero) = $30 − $30

(f) Adjusting entry to record interest owed but not yet paid.			= +110 Interest Payable		−110 Retained Earnings		− +110 Interest Expense	= −110
Total changes	0 Cash	+ 0	= +110 Interest Payable	+ 0	+ −110 Retained Earnings	0	− +110 Interest Expense	= −110

Cash flow = Change in interest payable + Net income, or

Cash flow = Net income + Change in interest payable, or
$0 (zero) = −$110 + $110

	Balance Sheet										Income Statement				
Transaction	Cash Asset	+	Noncash Assets	−	Contra Assets	=	Liabil-ities	+	Contrib. Capital	+	Earned Capital	Revenues	−	Expenses	=	Net Income
(g) Adjusting entry for estimated income tax.				−		=	+350 Taxes Payable				−350 Retained Earnings		−	+350 Tax Expense	=	−350
Total changes	0 Cash	+	0	−		=	+350 Taxes Payable	+	0	+	−350 Retained Earnings	0	−	+350 Tax Expense	=	−350

Cash flow = Change in taxes payable + Net income, or

Cash flow = Net income + Change in taxes payable, or
$0 (zero) = −$350 + $350

Each of the above four items involved only an adjusting entry (i.e., an entry at the end of the fiscal period). Adjusting entries rarely involve cash, so the adjustment simply cancels out the item in the income statement. We will see more examples in later chapters (e.g., write-downs of physical or intangible assets, restructuring charges, etc.).

Eliminate Depreciation Expense and Other Noncash Operating Expenses
NBS recorded an adjusting entry for depreciation at the end of December 2021 for $375. That entry into the FSET was the following.

Transaction	Cash Asset	+	Noncash Assets	−	Contra Assets	=	Liabil-ities	+	Contrib. Capital	+	Earned Capital	Revenues	−	Expenses	=	Net Income
(c) Adjusting entry for depreciation on fixtures and equipment for December.				−	+375 Accumulated Depreciation	=					−375 Retained Earnings		−	+375 Depreciation Expense	=	−375
Total changes	0 Cash	+	0	−	+375 Accumulated Depreciation	=	0	+	0	+	−375 Retained Earnings	0	−	+375 Depreciation Expense	=	−375

We can see that this entry reduced net income by $375, but it had no effect on cash. When we look at the total impact of this entry on the FSET (in the last row), its effect can be written in the following way.

Cash flow − Change in accumulated depreciation (for depreciation expense) = Net income,

or

Cash flow = Net income + Depreciation expense
$0 (zero) = −$375 + $375

So, NBS' net income of $650 for December includes a depreciation expense of $375 that did not involve any cash outflow. When we add back depreciation expense (and similar items like amortization expense), we move the net income number one step closer to cash from operations.

Would increasing depreciation expense increase the cash flows from operations? That question is more complex than it initially appears. In Chapter 8, we will find that companies use different depreciation methods for tax reporting and financial reporting, and in Chapter 10 we will see how differences between tax and financial reporting are reconciled. Increasing the tax depreciation expense reduces taxable income and the amount of tax that has to be paid. Increasing depreciation expense in financial reports to shareholders has no effect on the amount of taxes paid and, therefore, no effect on the amount of cash generated.

A General Rule . . . with a Note of Caution The relationships illustrated in the above examples suggest a general rule that we can use to prepare the statement of cash flows:

> The difference between a revenue or an expense reported in the income statement and a related cash receipt or expenditure reported in the statement of cash flows will be reflected in the balance sheet as a change in one or more balance sheet accounts.

More specifically, all the above reconciliation adjustments for NBS can be summarized in a pattern:

Net income + Adjustments = Cash from operations

Or, more particularly

Net income + Depreciation expense − Change in operating assets + Change in operating liabilities = Cash from operations

By "operating assets," we mean receivables, inventories, prepaid expenses, and similar assets. "Operating liabilities" refers to accounts and wages payable, accrued expenses, unearned revenues, taxes payable, interest payable, and similar items. Investing assets (like investment securities and property, plant, and equipment) and financing liabilities (like notes payable and long-term debt) would not be included in these adjustments.

Exhibit 4.5 summarizes the basic adjustments needed to convert the revenues, expenses, gains, and losses presented in the income statement to cash receipts and payments presented in the statement of cash flows from operating activities. (The adjustments for nonoperating gains and losses will be discussed shortly.)

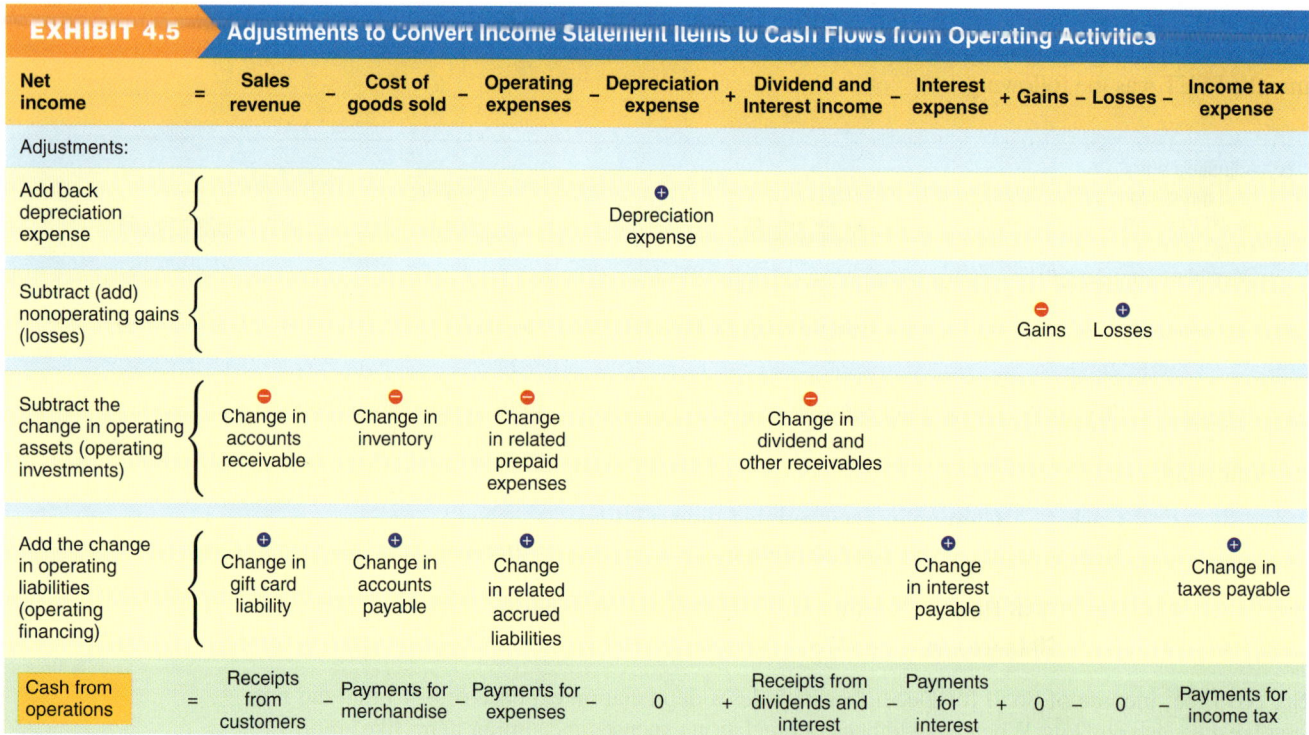

EXHIBIT 4.5 Adjustments to Convert Income Statement Items to Cash Flows from Operating Activities

Net income	= Sales revenue	− Cost of goods sold	− Operating expenses	− Depreciation expense	+ Dividend and Interest income	− Interest expense	+ Gains	− Losses	− Income tax expense
Adjustments:									
Add back depreciation expense				(+) Depreciation expense					
Subtract (add) nonoperating gains (losses)							(−) Gains	(+) Losses	
Subtract the change in operating assets (operating investments)	(−) Change in accounts receivable	(−) Change in inventory	(−) Change in related prepaid expenses		(−) Change in dividend and other receivables				
Add the change in operating liabilities (operating financing)	(+) Change in gift card liability	(+) Change in accounts payable	(+) Change in related accrued liabilities			(+) Change in interest payable			(+) Change in taxes payable
Cash from operations	= Receipts from customers	− Payments for merchandise	− Payments for expenses	− 0	+ Receipts from dividends and interest	− Payments for interest	+ 0	− 0	− Payments for income tax

We have now applied the adjustments to convert each accrual revenue and expense to the corresponding operating cash flow. We use these individual cash inflows and outflows to prepare the operating activities section of the statement of cash flows. The adjustments to convert revenues and expenses to operating cash flows are summarized in **Exhibit 4.6**, and this information can be used to produce NBS' cash from operating activities by using the information in the income statement and balance sheet.

Like all general rules, this one provides useful insights, but it also has limitations. As we learn more and more about business activities and the accounting for them, we find the need for refinements of this general rule. For instance, in Chapter 12, we will see that operating assets and liabilities can increase from acquisitions (an investing activity) as well as from operations. But for the time being, the general rule is a useful way to approach the calculation and interpretation of operating cash flow.

EXHIBIT 4.6 **Converting Revenues and Expenses to Cash Inflows and Outflows from Operating Activity (Natural Beauty Supply)**

	Net income	= Sales revenue	+ Interest income	− Cost of goods sold	− Wages expense	− Rent expense	− Advertising expense	− Insurance expense	− Interest expense	− Depreciation expense	− Income tax expense
	$ 650	= $13,900	+ 30	− 8,000	− 2,105	− 1,500	− 700	− 140	− 110	− 375	− 350
Adjustments:											
Add back depreciation expense										⊕ 375 Depreciation expense	
Subtract the change in operating assets (operating investments)		⊖ 1,300 Change in accounts receivable	⊖ 30 Change in other receivables	⊖ (−4,000)* Change in inventory				⊖ (−140)* Change in prepaid insurance			
Add the change in operating liabilities (operating financing)		⊕ 300 Change in gift card liability		⊕ 700 Change in accounts payable	⊕ 480 Change in wages payable				⊕ 110 Change in interest payable		⊕ 350 Change in taxes payable
	$5,775	= $12,900	+ 0	− 3,300	− 1,625	− 1,500	− 700	− 0	− 0	− 0	− 0
	Cash from operations	= Receipts from customers	+ Receipts for interest	− Payments for merchandise	− Payments to employees	− Payments for rent	− Payments for advertising	− Payments for insurance	− Payments for interest	− 0	− Payments for income tax

* When the change in an operating asset is negative, subtracting that negative amount results in a positive adjustment.

Preparing Operating Activities Section of the Statement of Cash Flows—Direct Method LO4-2 **Review 4-2**

The income statement and comparative balance sheets for Mug Shots, Inc., (a photography studio) are presented below. Use the information in these financial statements and the frameworks in **Exhibits 4.5** and **4.6** to compute Mug Shots' cash flow from operating activities using the direct method.

GuidedExample MBC

MUG SHOTS, INC.
Income Statement
For Month Ended December 31

Revenue		
Sales revenue		$31,000
Expenses		
Cost of goods sold	$16,700	
Wages expense	4,700	
Interest expense	300	
Advertising expense	1,800	
Rent expense	1,500	
Depreciation expense	700	
Total expenses		25,700
Income before taxes		5,300
Income tax expense		1,855
Net income		$ 3,445

MUG SHOTS, INC.
Comparative Balance Sheets

	Dec. 31	Nov. 30
Assets		
Cash	$10,700	$ 5,000
Accounts receivable	2,500	
Inventory	32,300	24,000
Prepaid rent	7,500	9,000
Equipment	30,000	18,000
Accumulated depreciation	(700)	
Total assets	$82,300	$56,000
Liabilities		
Accounts payable	$25,000	$24,000
Interest payable	300	
Wages payable	2,200	
Income tax payable	1,855	
Unearned revenue	500	
Notes payable	30,000	12,000
Equity		
Common stock	20,000	20,000
Retained earnings	2,445	
Total liabilities and equity	$82,300	$56,000

Solution on p. 4-60.

Reconciling Net Income and Cash Flow from Operating Activities

LO4-3
Reconcile cash flows from operations to net income and use the indirect method to compute operating cash flows.

eLecture MBC

We now have two metrics to consider when examining the operations of a company over a period of time—net income and cash from operations. For December 2021, NBS reported net income of $650 and cash from operations of $5,775. For its fiscal year ended December 31, 2020, CVS Health Corporation reported net income of $7,192 million and cash from operations of $15,865 million. While both net income and cash from operations measure aspects of operations over the same time period, they can sometimes be very far apart, as seen in the following table.

	2020 ($ millions; US$ unless otherwise noted)	
	Net Income	**Cash from Operations**
Delta Air Lines, Inc.	$(12,385)	$ (3,793)
Southwest Airlines Co.	(3,074)	(1,127)
American Airlines Group, Inc.	(8,885)	(6,543)
Target Corporation	3,281	7,117
Walmart, Inc.	15,201	25,255
Amazon.com, Inc.	21,331	66,064
Alphabet Inc.	40,269	65,124
Facebook, Inc.	29,146	38,747
Tesla, Inc.	862	5,943
BMW Group	€3,857	€13,251
Ford Motor Company	(1,276)	24,269
Toyota Motor Corporation	913	5,764
Carmax, Inc.	888	(237)
AutoNation, Inc.	382	1,208

It would be natural for a financial statement reader to want to understand the source(s) of the differences between net income and cash from operations. So, companies that present their statement of cash flows like CVS Health Corporation must also present a reconciliation of net income to cash from operations. The reconciliation for CVS Health's fiscal year ending December 31, 2020, is in **Exhibit 4.7**.

EXHIBIT 4.7 CVS Health Corporation Income to Operating Cash Flows Reconciliation

CVS HEALTH CORPORATION
CONSOLIDATED STATEMENT OF CASH FLOWS
For the Fiscal Year Ended December 31, 2020
RECONCILIATION OF NET INCOME TO NET CASH PROVIDED BY OPERATING ACTIVITIES

In millions	
Net income	**$ 7,192**
Adjustments required to reconcile net income to net cash provided by operating activities	
Depreciation and amortization	4,441
Stock-based compensation	400
(Gain) loss on sale of subsidiaries	(269)
Loss on early extinguishment of debt	1,440
Deferred income taxes	(570)
Other noncash items	72
Change in operating assets and liabilities, net of effects from acquisitions:	
Accounts receivable, net	(1,510)
Inventories	(973)
Other assets	364
Accounts payable and pharmacy claims and discounts payable	2,769
Health care costs payable and other insurance liabilities	(231)
Other liabilities	2,740
Net cash provided by operating activities	**$15,865**

This reconciliation leads to the same number that was presented in the operating section of **Exhibit 4.1**, but in a very different format. How is it produced? It is constructed using the same adjustment process depicted in **Exhibits 4.5** and **4.6**.

CVS Health's reconciliation contains a couple of entries that we did not see for Natural Beauty Supply. A company's income statement may contain gains and losses related to nonoperating activities. Examples include gains and losses from the sale of subsidiaries and the loss on the early extinguishment of debt. Because these gains and losses are included in income but are not related to operating activities, **Exhibit 4.5** shows that we omit them as we convert income statement items to various cash flows from operating activities. The cash flows relating to these gains and losses are reported in the investing activities or financing activities sections of the statement of cash flows. NBS had no nonoperating gains or losses in December, but CVS Health made an adjustment to remove a $269 million gain on the sale of subsidiaries (an investing activity) and a $1,440 million loss on the early extinguishment of debt (a financing activity).

Another adjustment involves stock-based compensation. Corporations often use their common stock to reward employees and to provide incentives for future performance. The value of such grants must be recognized in income as an expense, but it is an expense that does not involve cash. Therefore, the amount expensed—$400 million for CVS Health in 2020—is added back in reconciling net income to cash flow from operations.

CVS Health also makes a negative $570 million adjustment for deferred income taxes. Deferred income taxes occur when companies use different accounting methods for tax and financial reporting and are beyond our scope for the moment. It will be covered later in Chapter 10.

Cash Flow from Operating Activities Using the Indirect Method

Two alternative formats may be used to report the net cash flow from operating activities: the direct method and the indirect method. *Both methods report the same amount of net cash flow from operating activities.* Net cash flows from investing and financing activities are prepared in the same manner under both the indirect and the direct methods; only the format for cash flows from operating activities differs.

For Natural Beauty Supply, we computed cash flow from operating activities using the direct method. The **direct method** presents the components of cash flow from operating activities as a list of gross cash receipts and gross cash payments. This format is illustrated in **Exhibit 4.3** and by CVS Health Corporation's statement in **Exhibit 4.1**.

The direct method is logical and relatively easy to follow. In practice, however, nearly all operating activities sections in the statements of cash flows are presented using what is called the **indirect method**. Under this method, the reconciliation of net income to operating cash flow (e.g., **Exhibit 4.7**) is used for the presentation of cash flow from operations. The cash flow from operations section begins with net income and applies a series of adjustments to net income to convert it to net cash flow from operating activities. However, the adjustments to net income are not cash flows themselves, so the indirect method does not report any detail concerning individual operating cash inflows and outflows. In fact, there are no cash flows in the indirect method operating section of the statement of cash flows, except the subtotal—cash flow from operations. The **Apple Inc.** statement of cash flows on page 4-53 is an example.

While accounting standard-setters prefer the direct method presentation, it is not very popular with reporting companies. In the U.S., surveys have found that fewer than 5% of companies use the direct method presentation. The indirect method is popular because (1) it is easier and less expensive to prepare than the direct method and (2) companies that use the direct method are required to present a supplemental disclosure showing the reconciliation of net income to cash from operations (thus, essentially requiring the company to report both methods for cash from operations). International standard-setters also have stated a preference for the direct method, and its use is more frequent than in the U.S. But the indirect method of presenting cash flow from operations is used by a significant majority of companies.

FYI Managers can boost declining sales by lengthening credit periods or by lowering credit standards. The resulting increase in accounts receivable can cause net income to outpace operating cash flow. Consequently, many view a large receivables increase as a warning sign.

The procedure for presenting indirect method cash flows from operations uses the same approach that we applied above to convert income statement items to operating cash flows. In fact, the indirect method can be viewed as a "short-cut" calculation of the process shown in **Exhibit 4.5**. That is:

Net income ± Adjustments = Cash flow from operating activities

In **Exhibit 4.5**, revenue and expense components of the income statement are presented in the orange row that totals to net income. The yellow rows list the adjustments, and cash receipts and payments are listed in the green row at the bottom. The total of the green row is cash flow from operating activities. The indirect method skips the listing of individual revenues and expenses and starts with net income. After adjustments, we have total cash flow from operating activities, but not individual receipts and payments.

Cash flow from December's operating activities for NBS is presented using the indirect method in **Exhibit 4.8**. The calculation begins with the December net income of $650 and ends with cash flow from operating activities, $5,775. The total cash flow from operating activities is the same amount as was computed in **Exhibit 4.6** using the direct method. If we compare **Exhibit 4.6** and **Exhibit 4.8**, we see that the two exhibits are very similar. The only difference is that all of the revenues and expenses are listed in the orange row at the top of **Exhibit 4.6**, while **Exhibit 4.8** lists only the total—net income. Similarly, the green row at the bottom of **Exhibit 4.6** lists all of the cash inflows and outflows, while the bottom line of **Exhibit 4.8** lists only the net cash flow from operating activities. In both exhibits, the center rows list the adjustments.

EXHIBIT 4.8 NBS Cash Flow from Operating Activities—Indirect Method

Net income	$ 650	
Adjustments:		
Add back depreciation expense	375	
Subtract:		
Change in accounts receivable	1,300	
Change in other receivables	30	
Change in inventory	(4,000)*	
Change in prepaid insurance	(140)*	
Add:		
Change in gift card liability	300	
Change in accounts payable	700	
Change in wages payable	480	
Change in interest payable	110	
Change in taxes payable	350	
Total adjustments	5,125	
Cash flow from operating activities		$5,775

* When the change in an operating asset is negative, subtracting that negative amount results in a positive adjustment.

Review 4-3 LO4-3 Reconciling Cash Flows from Operations to Net Income

GuidedExample MBC

Refer to the financial statements for Mug Shots, Inc., presented in Review 4-2. Compute cash flows from operating activities for Mug Shots, Inc., using the indirect method.

Solution on p. 4-60.

PREPARING THE STATEMENT OF CASH FLOWS—INVESTING AND FINANCING ACTIVITIES

LO4-4 Construct the investing and financing activities sections of the statement of cash flows.

eLecture MBC

The remaining sections of the statement of cash flows focus on investing and financing activities. Investing activities are concerned with transactions affecting noncurrent (and some current) noncash assets. Financing activities are concerned with raising capital from owners and creditors. The presentation of the cash effects of investing and financing transactions is not affected by the method of presentation (direct or indirect) of cash flows from operating activities.

Accounting standard-setters (both in the United States and International) require that financing and investing items be presented in the statement of cash flows using gross amounts instead of net amounts. In **Exhibit 4.1**, CVS Health reports that it spent $9,639 million in cash to purchase investments in 2020, and it received $6,467 million in cash from the sale and maturities of investments. It would not be acceptable to show the net amount—an outflow of $3,172 million—as a single item unless one of the components is consistently immaterial.

Cash Flows from Investing Activities

Investing activities cause changes in noncash asset accounts. Usually the accounts affected (other than cash) are noncurrent operating asset accounts such as property, plant, and equipment assets and investing assets like marketable securities and long-term financial investments. Cash paid for acquisitions of other companies would be included as well. To determine the cash flows from investing activities, we analyze changes in all noncash asset accounts not used in computing net cash flow from operating activities. Our objective is to identify any investing cash flows related to these changes.

Purchases of noncash assets cause cash outflow. Conversely, a sale of a noncash asset results in cash inflow. This relationship is highlighted in the following decision guide:

Cash flows increase due to:	Cash flows decrease due to:
Sales of assets	Purchases of assets

NBS had only one investing transaction during December—the purchase of fixtures and equipment for $18,000. Any change in the Fixtures and Equipment account in the balance sheet is usually the result of one or both of the following transactions: (1) buying assets, or (2) selling assets.[2] Buying and selling nonoperating assets are classified as investing transactions. NBS' entry to record the purchase of fixtures and equipment for cash is as follows:

	Balance Sheet									Income Statement				
Transaction	Cash Asset	+	Noncash Assets	=	Liabil-ities	+	Contrib. Capital	+	Earned Capital	*Revenues*	−	*Expenses*	=	*Net Income*
(18) Pay $18,000 cash for fixtures and equipment.	−18,000 Cash		+18,000 Fixtures and Equipment	=							−		=	

ANALYZE

(18) Fixtures & equipment (+A)	18,000	
Cash (−A)		18,000
Purchase fixtures and equipment for cash.		

JOURNALIZE

+ Fixtures & Equipment (A) −	
(18) 18,000	

+ Cash (A) −	
	18,000 (18)

POST

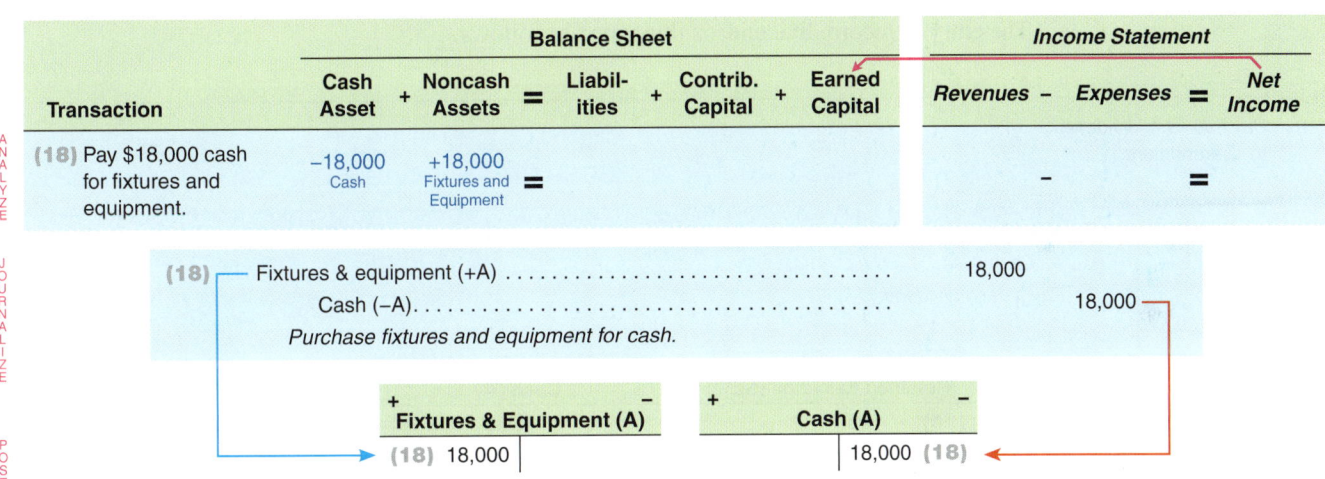

The resulting $18,000 cash outflow is listed in the statement of cash flows under cash flow used for investing activities.

Cash Flows from Financing Activities

Financing activities cause changes in financial liabilities and stockholders' equity accounts. Financial liabilities include current liability items like seasonal bank borrowing and the current portion of long-term debt due within the next year, plus noncurrent items like long-term debt issues and longer term borrowing from financial institutions. Cash receipts from the issuance of these liabilities and cash payments to settle outstanding principal balances are considered cash flows from financing activities. Stockholders' equity accounts include contributed capital (common stock, additional paid-in-capital, and treasury stock) and retained earnings. Transactions with shareholders are always considered part of a company's financing activities. This relationship is highlighted in the following decision guide:

Cash flows increase due to:	Cash flows decrease due to:
Taking on a financial liability or issuing shares	Repaying principal on a financial liability or paying dividends to shareholders or making share repurchases

[2] The Accumulated Depreciation—Fixtures and Equipment contra-asset account is affected by depreciation expense and selling assets.

NBS had two financing transactions during December. It borrowed $11,000 on a three-year note, resulting in an increase in cash, and it paid $50 in cash dividends to shareholders. The entry to record the $11,000 note is illustrated as:

ANALYZE

	Balance Sheet									Income Statement				
Transaction	Cash Asset	+	Noncash Assets	=	Liabil-ities	+	Contrib. Capital	+	Earned Capital	Revenues	−	Expenses	=	Net Income
(17) Sign note and receive $11,000 cash.	+11,000 Cash			=	+11,000 Notes Payable						−		=	

JOURNALIZE

(17)	Cash (+A)	11,000	
	Notes payable (+L)		11,000
	Borrow $11,000 on a three-year note.		

POST

+ Cash (A) −		− Notes Payable (L) +	
(17) 11,000			11,000 (17)

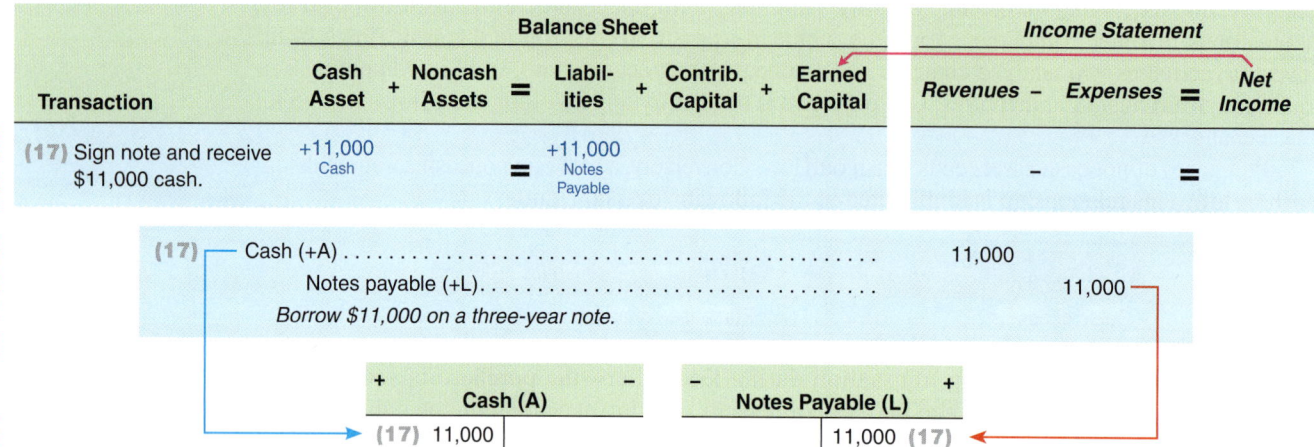

The resulting $11,000 cash inflow is listed in the statement of cash flows under cash flow from financing activities.

The entry to record dividends is illustrated as follows:

ANALYZE

Transaction	Cash Asset	+	Noncash Assets	=	Liabil-ities	+	Contrib. Capital	+	Earned Capital	Revenues	−	Expenses	=	Net Income
(28) Pay $50 cash dividend to shareholders.	−50 Cash			=					−50 Retained Earnings		−		=	

JOURNALIZE

(28)	Retained earnings (−SE)	50	
	Cash (−A)		50
	Pay a cash dividend.		

POST

− Retained Earnings (SE) +		+ Cash (A) −	
(28) 50			50 (28)

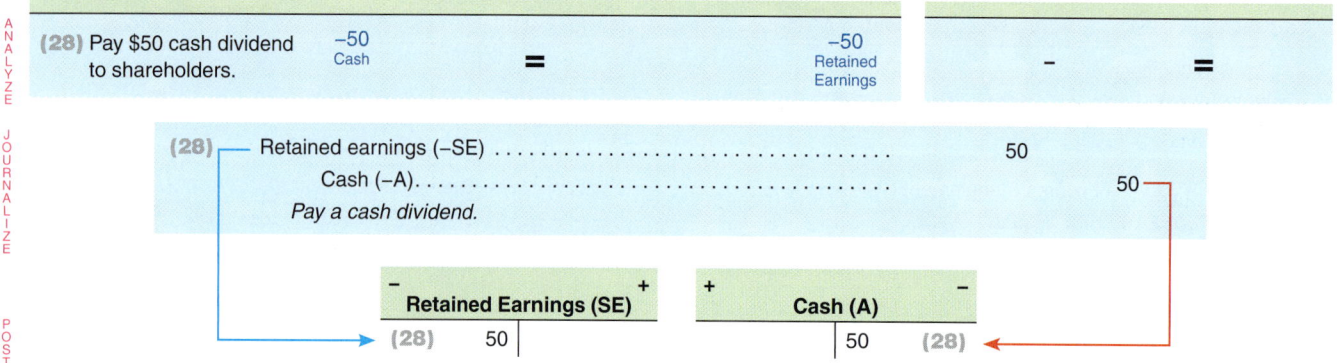

This dividend payment is a financing cash outflow and would be deducted from cash flow from financing activities.

When using the indirect method for the cash flow from operating activities, we should remember that there are some balance sheet accounts that will be affected by more than one type of activity. For instance, the balance in retained earnings will be affected by net income (which is going to appear in the operations section) and shareholder dividends (which will appear in the financing section).

The statement of cash flows lists cash flows from operating activities first (using either the direct or the indirect method), followed by cash flows from investing activities, then cash flows from financing activities. Once all three categories of cash flows have been listed, we total the three amounts to arrive at net cash flow for the period. The final step is to reconcile the cash balance from the beginning of the period to the ending balance. The completed statement of cash flows for NBS using the indirect method for operating cash flows is presented in **Exhibit 4.9**. We see from this statement that operating activities produced a cash inflow of $5,775, while investing activities resulted in a cash outflow of $18,000, and financing activities resulted in a cash inflow of $10,950. The sum of these three amounts ($5,775 − $18,000 + $10,950) equals the change in cash for December of −$1,275 ($6,825 − $8,100).

YOU MAKE THE CALL

You are the Chief Accountant. In its annual report for fiscal year 2020 (ending January 30, 2021), **Kohl's Corporation** reported that its cash used in investing activities decreased by almost 85% from the previous year, in part due to the "sale of real estate." Proceeds for the sale of real estate produced cash inflows of $197 million and gains on sale of $127 million. How would these amounts be reflected in the company's statement of cash flows? [Answer on page 4-36.]

EXHIBIT 4.9 NBS Statement of Cash Flows—Indirect Method

NATURAL BEAUTY SUPPLY
Statement of Cash Flows
For the Month Ended December 31, 2021

Operating activities:		
Net income	$ 650	
Adjustments:		
Add back Depreciation expense	375	
Subtract:		
Change in accounts receivable	1,300	
Change in other receivables	30	
Change in inventory	(4,000)*	
Change in prepaid insurance	(140)*	
Add:		
Change in gift card liability	300	
Change in accounts payable	700	
Change in wages payable	480	
Change in interest payable	110	
Change in taxes payable	350	
Total adjustments	5,125	
Cash flow from operating activities		$5,775
Investing activities:		
Purchase of fixtures and equipment	(18,000)	
Cash flow used for investing activities		(18,000)
Financing activities:		
Bank note	11,000	
Dividends paid	(50)	
Cash flow from financing activities		10,950
Net decrease in cash		(1,275)
Cash, November 30, 2021		8,100
Cash, December 31, 2021		$ 6,825

* When the change in an operating asset is negative, subtracting that negative amount results in a positive adjustment.

FYI The net cash inflow or outflow for the period is the same amount as the increase or decrease in cash and cash equivalents for the period from the balance sheet.

Preparing a Complete Statement of Cash Flows

LO4-4 **Review 4-4**

Refer to the financial statements for Mug Shots, Inc., in Review 4-2. Prepare a complete statement of cash flows for December using the indirect method for cash flows from operating activities. Follow the format used in **Exhibit 4.9**.

GuidedExample MBC

Solution on p. 4-61.

ADDITIONAL DETAIL IN THE STATEMENT OF CASH FLOWS

LO4-5
Examine the sale of investing assets and the disclosure of noncash activities

eLecture

MBC

There are two additional types of transactions that we must explore to understand the statement of cash flows. The first of these is the sale of investing assets like equipment or an investment security. The transaction itself isn't very complicated, but the use of the indirect method for operating cash flows makes it seem so. And, companies often engage in investing and financing activities that do not involve cash (e.g., acquiring another company through an exchange of stock). This section explores the accounting for these two types of transactions and their effect on the statement of cash flows.

Case Illustration Natural Beauty Supply did not have any disposals of assets or repayments of debt in December 2021, so there is no adjustment to make in this case. However, let's consider the financial statements of One World Café, a coffee shop that is located next door to NBS. The income statement and comparative balance sheet for One World Café are presented in **Exhibit 4.10**. The statement of cash flows is presented in **Exhibit 4.11**.

EXHIBIT 4.10 One World Café Income Statement and Comparative Balance Sheets

ONE WORLD CAFÉ, INC.
Income Statement
For Year Ended December 31, 2021

Revenue		
Sales revenue		$390,000
Expenses		
Cost of goods sold	$227,000	
Wages expense	82,000	
Advertising expense	9,800	
Depreciation expense	17,000	
Interest expense	200	
Loss on sale of plant assets	2,000	
Total expenses		338,000
Income before taxes		52,000
Income tax expense		17,000
Net income		$ 35,000

ONE WORLD CAFÉ, INC.
Comparative Balance Sheets
At December 31

	2021	2020
Assets		
Cash	$ 8,000	$ 12,000
Accounts receivable	22,000	28,000
Inventory	94,000	66,000
Prepaid advertising	12,000	9,000
Plant assets, at cost	208,000	170,000
Less accumulated depreciation	(72,000)	(61,000)
Total assets	$272,000	$224,000
Liabilities		
Accounts payable	$ 27,000	$ 14,000
Wages payable	6,000	2,500
Income tax payable	3,000	4,500
Notes payable	5,000	—
Equity		
Common stock	134,000	125,000
Retained earnings	97,000	78,000
Total liabilities and equity	$272,000	$224,000

For One World Café, creation of the statement of cash flows requires information that cannot be discerned from the income statement and balance sheet. (After all, the statement of cash flows is *supposed* to provide additional information!) In particular, the following events occurred during the year.

- Plant assets were purchased for cash.
- Obsolete plant assets, with original cost of $12,000 and accumulated depreciation of $6,000, were sold for $4,000 cash, resulting in a $2,000 loss.
- Additional common stock was issued for cash.
- Cash dividends of $16,000 were declared and paid during the year.
- One World Café acquired $5,000 of plant assets by issuing notes payable.

Reviewing One World Café's comparative balance sheet, we see that plant assets at cost increased from $170,000 to $208,000, an increase of $38,000. In addition, the accumulated depreciation contra-asset increased by $11,000 from $61,000 to $72,000. However, these are *net* increases, and we need information on the individual components of the increases. Consequently, we need to determine the gross amounts to ensure the statement of cash flows we create properly presents the gross amounts in the investing activities section.

EXHIBIT 4.11 Statement of Cash Flows for One World Café

ONE WORLD CAFÉ, INC.
Statement of Cash Flows
For Year Ended December 31, 2021

Cash flows from operating activities		
Net income	$35,000	
Add (deduct) items to convert net income to cash basis		
Add back depreciation	17,000	
Add back loss on sale of plant assets	2,000	
Subtract change in:		
Accounts receivable	(6,000)*	
Inventory	28,000	
Prepaid advertising	3,000	
Add change in:		
Accounts payable	13,000	
Wages payable	3,500	
Income tax payable	(1,500)	
Net cash provided by operating activities		$44,000
Cash flows from investing activities		
Purchase of plant assets	(45,000)	
Proceeds from sale of plant assets	4,000	
Net cash used for investing activities		(41,000)
Cash flows from financing activities		
Issuance of common stock	9,000	
Payment of dividends	(16,000)	
Net cash flows used for financing activities		(7,000)
Net cash decrease		(4,000)
Cash at beginning of year		12,000
Cash at end of year		$ 8,000

* When the change in an operating asset is negative, subtracting that negative amount results in a positive adjustment.

In addition to the changes in plant assets and accumulated depreciation, notes payable increased by $5,000 in 2021. The best way to fully understand what happened to cause the changes in balance sheet accounts during the year, and the impact of these changes on cash flows, is to "work backward" to reconstruct the investing and financing transactions using journal entries and T-accounts, especially the plant assets and accumulated depreciation accounts.

Gains and Losses on Investing and Financing Activities

The focus of the income statement is on the revenues and expenses that are generated by a company's transactions with customers, suppliers, employees, and other operating activities. But the income statement also contains gains and losses that result from investing or financing transactions. Gains and losses from the sale of investments, property, plant, and equipment, or intangible assets result from investing activities, not operating activities. A gain or loss from the retirement of bonds payable is an example of a financing gain or loss. When these transactions occur, the income statement does not show a revenue and an expense, but rather shows only the net amount as a gain or loss.

The full cash flow effect from these types of events is reported in the investing or financing sections of the statement of cash flows. To illustrate, we record the sale of Old World Café's obsolete plant assets at a loss with the following FSET entry:

	Balance Sheet											Income Statement				
Transaction	Cash Asset	+	Noncash Assets	−	Contra Asset	=	Liabilities	+	Contrib. Capital	+	Earned Capital	*Revenues*	−	*Expenses*	=	*Net Income*
(1)	+4,000 Cash		−12,000 Plant Assets		−6,000 Accumt Dep'n	=					−2,000 Retained Earnings		−	+2,000 Loss on Sale of Plant Assets	=	−2,000

Or, using the journal entry and T-accounts shown below.

(1)	Cash (+A)	4,000	
	Accumulated depreciation (−XA, +A)	6,000	
	Loss on sale of plant assets (+E, −SE)	2,000	
	Plant assets (−A)		12,000

Cash (A)

+		−
(1)	4,000	

Plant Assets (A)

+			−
Beg. bal.	170,000		
		12,000	(1)

Accumulated Depreciation (XA)

−			+
		61,000	Beg. bal.
(1)	6,000	17,000	Depreciation
		72,000	End. bal.

Loss (E)

+		−
(1)	2,000	

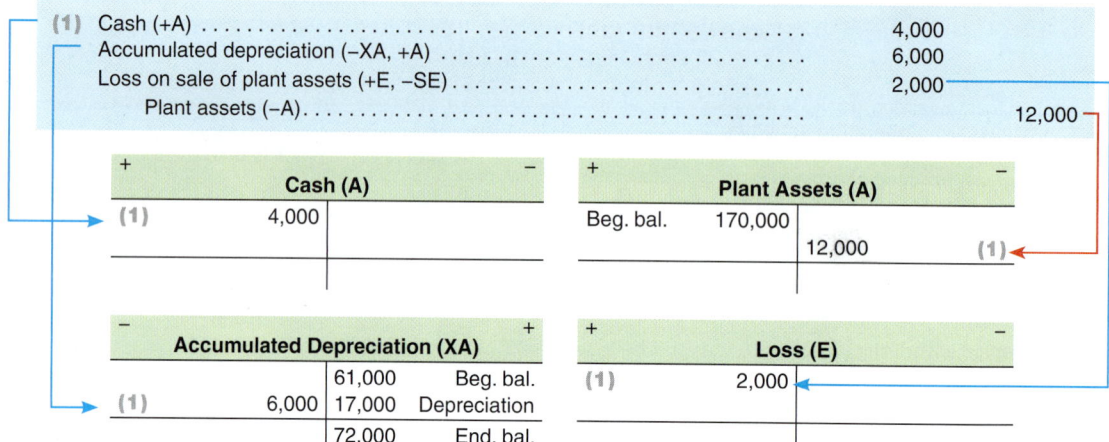

The $4,000 of cash received from this sale should be listed as a cash inflow under cash flows from investing activities, and it can be seen in **Exhibit 4.11**. The $4,000 cash flow is equal to the $6,000 net book value of the plant assets that were sold ($12,000 − $6,000) less the $2,000 loss on the sale.

If we were using the direct method to report the cash flows from operating activities, we wouldn't need to take any additional steps. But an indirect method operating cash flows starts with net income, and Old World Café's net income includes a $2,000 loss from this investing transaction (**Exhibit 4.10**). So, when we add back the investing loss to net income (or subtract an investing gain), we remove the effect of this investing transaction from the determination of cash flows from operating activities. It's one more step in the adjustments that are needed to reconcile net income to the cash flows from operating activities.

In Chapter 9, we will find that companies can experience financing gains (losses) from the early retirement of their debt. These gains and losses appear in the income statement, but they result from financing activities. In an indirect method statement of cash flows, the financing gains (losses) must be subtracted from (added to) net income to determine cash flows from operating activities.

We also see that the accumulated depreciation account started with a credit balance of $61,000, and the obsolete asset sale reduced this by $6,000 to $55,000. But the balance sheet in **Exhibit 4.10** tells us that the ending (credit) balance is $72,000. The difference is due to $17,000 depreciation expense for the year.

YOU MAKE THE CALL

You are the Securities Analyst You are analyzing a company's statement of cash flows. The company extends credit to customers that purchase its products. You see that the company has sold some of its accounts receivable to another company, receiving cash in return. As a result, the sale of receivables is reported as an asset sale, which reduces receivables and yields a gain or loss on sale. This action increases the company's operating cash flows. How should you interpret these items in the statement of cash flows? [Answer on p. 4-37.]

Noncash Investing and Financing Activities

In addition to reporting how cash changed from one balance sheet to the next, cash flow reporting is intended to present summary information about a firm's investing and financing activities. Many of these activities affect cash and are therefore already included in the investing and financing sections of the statement of cash flows. Some significant investing and financing events, however, do not affect current cash flows. Examples of **noncash investing and financing activities** are the issuance of stocks, bonds, or leases in exchange for property, plant, and equipment (PPE) assets or intangible assets; the exchange of long-term assets for other long-term assets; and the conversion of long-term debt into common stock.

To illustrate the effect of noncash transactions on the preparation of the statement of cash flows, consider One World Café's purchase of $5,000 of plant assets that was financed with notes payable. The FSET entry to record the purchase is as follows:

	Balance Sheet											Income Statement			
Transaction	Cash Asset	+	Noncash Assets	−	Contra Asset	=	Liabil-ities	+	Contrib. Capital	+	Earned Capital	Revenues	− Expenses	=	Net Income
(2)			+5,000 Plant Assets	−		=	+5,000 Notes Payable						−	=	

Or, using the journal entry and T-accounts shown below.

		Debit	Credit
(2)	Plant assets (+A)	5,000	
	Notes payable (+L)		5,000

Plant Assets (A) (+ / −)

	Debit (+)	Credit (−)	
Beg. bal.	170,000		
		12,000	(1)
(2)	5,000		

Notes Payable (L) (− / +)

	Debit (−)	Credit (+)	
		0	Beg. bal.
		5,000	(2)
		5,000	End. bal.

Because this purchase did not use any cash, it is not presented in the statement of cash flows. Only those capital expenditures that use cash are listed as cash flows from investing activities. That is, cash flows from investing activities should reflect the actual amount of cash spent to purchase plant assets or investment assets.

Noncash investing and financing transactions generally do affect *future* cash flows. Issuing notes payable to acquire equipment, for example, requires future cash payments for interest and principal on the notes and should produce future operating cash flows from the equipment. Alternatively, converting bonds payable into common stock eliminates future cash payments related to the bonds but may carry the expectation of future cash dividends. Knowledge of these types of events, therefore, is helpful to users of cash flow data who wish to assess a firm's future cash flows.

Information on noncash investing and financing transactions is disclosed in a schedule that is separate from the statement of cash flows. The separate schedule is reported either immediately below the statement of cash flows or among the notes to the financial statements.

Solving for Purchases of Plant Assets The remaining entry affecting plant assets is the purchase of plant assets for cash. The amount of plant assets purchased can be determined by solving for the missing amount in the Plant Assets T-account:

Plant Assets (A) (+ / −)

	Debit (+)	Credit (−)	
Beg. bal.	170,000		
		12,000	(1)
(2)	5,000		
(3)	X		
End. bal.	208,000		

Balancing the account requires that we solve for the unknown amount:

$$\$170{,}000 + \$5{,}000 + X - \$12{,}000 = \$208{,}000$$
$$X = \$45{,}000$$

Thus, plant assets costing $45,000 were purchased for cash. This amount is listed as a cash outflow under cash flows for investing activities.

The same analysis can be portrayed using the FSET. The column for Plant assets yields the same $45,000 answer for cash purchases of plant assets.

Transaction	Cash Assets	+	Noncash Assets	−	Contra Assets	=	Liabilities	+	Contrib. Capital	+	Earned Capital	Revenues	−	Expenses	=	Net Income
Beg. Bal.			170,000 Plant Assets													
(1)	+4,000 Cash		−12,000 Plant Assets	−	−6,000 Accum Dep'n	=					−2,000 Retained Earnings		−	+2,000 Loss on Sale of Plant Assets	=	−2,000
(2)			+5,000 Plant Assets	−		=	+5,000 Notes Payable						−		=	
(3)	−X Cash		+X Plant Assets	−		=							−		=	
End. Bal.			208,000 Plant Assets													

Examining the statement of cash flows for One World Café in **Exhibit 4.11**, we see that two cash flows are listed under investing activities: (1) a $45,000 cash outflow for the purchase of plant assets, and (2) a $4,000 cash inflow from the sale of plant assets. The purchase of plant assets costing $5,000 by issuing notes payable is not listed; nor is the increase in notes payable listed under financing activities.

Appendix 4A at the end of this chapter introduces a spreadsheet approach that can be used to prepare the statement of cash flows. The appendix uses the One World Café financial statements as the illustration.

The Effects of Foreign Currencies on the Statement of Cash Flows

Multinational companies often engage in transactions that involve currencies other than U.S. dollars and may hold assets that were acquired with foreign currencies or liabilities that must be repaid in foreign currencies. Also, part of a company's cash balance may be held in a currency other than dollars. If the company prepares its financial statements in U.S. dollars, these foreign currency amounts must be converted, or *translated*, into dollars before preparing the financial statements. The process of translating transactions based in many currencies into one common currency for financial statement presentation is beyond the scope of an introductory text. However, foreign exchange rates fluctuate, and these fluctuations can have an effect on the statement of cash flows.

The statement of cash flows explains the change in the cash balance during the fiscal year, but part of this change may be due to changes in the dollar value of foreign currencies. This amount is typically small and it is not a cash flow, but it is included in the statement of cash flows so that we can accurately reconcile the beginning balance in cash to the ending balance. The statement of cash flows for Nike, Inc., was summarized in Chapter 1 in **Exhibit 1.10** and is repeated here for illustration. In contrast, CVS Health reported that "the effects of foreign currency remeasurements were not material" for fiscal year 2020.

NIKE
Statement of Cash Flows
For the Year Ended May 31, 2020
($ millions)

Operating cash flows	$2,485
Investing cash flows	(1,028)
Financing cash flows	2,491
Effect of exchange rate changes	(66)
Net increase in cash and cash equivalents	3,882
Cash and equivalents, beginning of year	4,466
Cash and equivalents, end of year	$8,348

Supplemental Disclosures

If the direct method is used in the statement of cash flows, a reconciliation of net income to cash flows from operating activities is also required. If the indirect method is used, two separate supplemental disclosures are required—cash paid for interest and cash paid for income taxes. All companies must disclose the amount and nature of all noncash investing and financing transactions, in addition to the firm's policy for determining which highly liquid, short-term investments are treated as cash equivalents.

One World Café Case Illustration One World Café incurred $200 of interest expense, which was paid in cash. It also reported income tax expense of $17,000 and reported a decrease in income taxes payable of $1,500 ($4,500 – $3,000). Thus, One World Café paid $18,500 ($17,000 + $1,500) in income taxes during 2021. It also had the noncash investment in plant assets costing $5,000, which was financed with notes payable. One World Café would provide the following disclosure:

Supplemental cash flow information	
Cash payments for interest	$ 200
Cash payments for income taxes	18,500
Noncash transaction—investment in plant assets financed with notes payable	5,000

When some portion of a firm's cash and cash equivalent assets is held for a specific purpose and not available for immediate use (i.e., restricted cash), it is reported separately from the balance sheets' cash and cash equivalent amounts. The amount of restricted cash and the nature of the restrictions must be disclosed. However, the beginning and ending cash balances in the statement of cash flows include both unrestricted and restricted cash.

For instance, suppose that Old World Café's new borrowing carried with it a requirement that it keep a minimum cash balance of $500 with the lender. On the balance sheet, the company's ending cash balance would have been $7,500, rather than $8,000, and a $500 asset would appear labeled restricted cash. But for the statement of cash flows, the closing balance would be *Cash and restricted cash* equal to $8,000, and information on the nature of the restrictions should be disclosed in the notes to the financial statements.

Reconstructing Investing Cash Flows LO4-5 **Review 4-5**

GuidedExample MBC

The balance sheet of Jack's Snacks, Inc., reports the following amounts:

	End-of-Year	Beginning-of-Year
Property, plant, and equipment at cost	$670,000	$600,000
Accumulated depreciation	(150,000)	(140,000)
Property, plant, and equipment, net	$520,000	$460,000

Additional information

During the year, Jack's Snacks disposed of a used piece of equipment. The original cost of the equipment was $80,000 and, at the time of disposal, the accumulated depreciation on the equipment was $60,000. The purchaser of the used piece of equipment paid in cash, and Jack's Snacks reported a gain of $35,000 on the disposal.

All acquisitions of new property, plant, and equipment were paid for in cash.

Required

a. How much cash did Jack's Snacks receive from the used equipment disposal? How would this amount be reported on the statement of cash flows?

b. How much cash did Jack's Snacks spend to acquire new property, plant, and equipment during the year? How would this amount be reported on the statement of cash flows?

c. How much depreciation expense did Jack's Snacks record during the year?

d. Now assume that Jack's Snacks issued common stock (instead of using cash) to acquire the new property, plant, and equipment. How would this transaction be reported on the statement of cash flows?

Solution on p. 4-61.

ANALYZING FINANCIAL STATEMENTS

LO4-6 Compute and interpret ratios that reflect a company's liquidity and solvency using information reported in the statement of cash flows.

eLecture MBC

Cash is a special resource for companies because of its flexibility. At short notice, it can be used to fulfill obligations and to take advantage of investment opportunities. When companies run short of cash, their suppliers may be reluctant to deliver and lenders may be able to take over control of decision making. In Chapter 2, we introduced the current ratio, which compares the level of current assets to the level of current liabilities at a point in time. But the statement of cash flows gives us the opportunity to compare a company's ongoing cash generating activities to its obligations and to its investment opportunities.

Interpreting Indirect Method Cash from Operations

We want to interpret the cash flows from operations presented using the indirect method.

When companies use the indirect method to present their cash flows from operating activities, it is difficult to interpret the numbers presented to adjust net income to cash from operating activities. For instance, in **Exhibit 4.11**, One World Café reports $6,000 for the change in accounts receivable. Does that mean that the company received cash payments of $6,000 from its customers? It does not! Every item in the reconciliation has to be interpreted relative to the net income at the top. Net income includes revenue of $390,000, and the adjustment addition of $6,000 means that One World Café received payments of $390,000 + $6,000 = $396,000 from its customers.

The $3,500 adjustment for wages payable does not mean that One World Café received payments of $3,500 from its employees. Rather, the company paid its employees $3,500 less than it recognized as wage expense in determining net income. The adjustment for income tax payable was $(1,500), but that doesn't mean that One World Café's tax payments totaled $1,500 for the year. Rather, the $35,000 net income already reflects a charge for tax expense of $17,000, so the adjustment means that One World's payments for income tax totaled $17,000 + $1,500 = $18,500. Depreciation expense is added back not because it increases cash, but because it is an expense that doesn't require a cash outflow.

How should we interpret the changes in operating assets and liabilities? These assets and liabilities are a function of both the scale of the business and the practices of the business. If we're selling to 10% more customers this year, then we would expect an increase in receivables of about 10% over the previous year. If the increase is substantially more than that amount, then there must have been some other change as well. Perhaps increasing sales required that we give more favorable payment terms and customers are taking longer to pay. Such a development could cause an investor to question the "quality" of the company's earnings. If sales are constant and accounts payable are increasing, that may imply that the company is taking longer to pay its suppliers. That change would appear as a positive adjustment in the indirect method cash from operations, but it may indicate an unfavorable development for the company.

The indirect method may also alert us to gains and losses from nonoperating transactions. These gains and losses are often in "other income" in the income statement, and therefore it's easy for a financial statement reader to miss them. The fact that gains must be subtracted and losses must be added back in the indirect cash from operations gives them a prominence that they don't have in the income statement.

Analysis Objective

We are trying to gauge CVS Health Corporations' generation of cash from its operating activities relative to its average short-term obligations found in the balance sheet.

Analysis Tool Operating Cash Flow to Current Liabilities (OCFCL)

$$\textbf{Operating cash flow to current liabilities} = \frac{\textbf{Operating cash flow}}{\textbf{Average current liabilities*}}$$

*The average is computed by adding the beginning and ending balances of current liabilities and dividing by two.

Applying the Operating Cash Flow to Current Liabilities Ratio to CVS Health Corporation

$$\textbf{2018: } \frac{\$8,865}{\$37,329} = 0.24 \text{ or } 24\%$$

$$\textbf{2019: } \frac{\$12,848}{\$48,656} = 0.26 \text{ or } 26\%$$

$$\textbf{2020: } \frac{\$15,865}{\$57,660} = 0.28 \text{ or } 28\%$$

Guidance CVS Health Corporation's OCFCL is lower than the retail industry average. CVS Health's business is relatively low-margin, which means that it requires a large flow of resources to generate profits and cash from operations, and that large volume of activity results in high levels of current liabilities relative to the cash generated. The OCFCL ratio complements the current ratio and quick ratio introduced in Chapter 2. CVS Health's current ratio is 0.91, also lower than average for the retail industry, and its quick ratio of 0.53 is slightly higher than the industry average.

CVS Health Corporation in Context

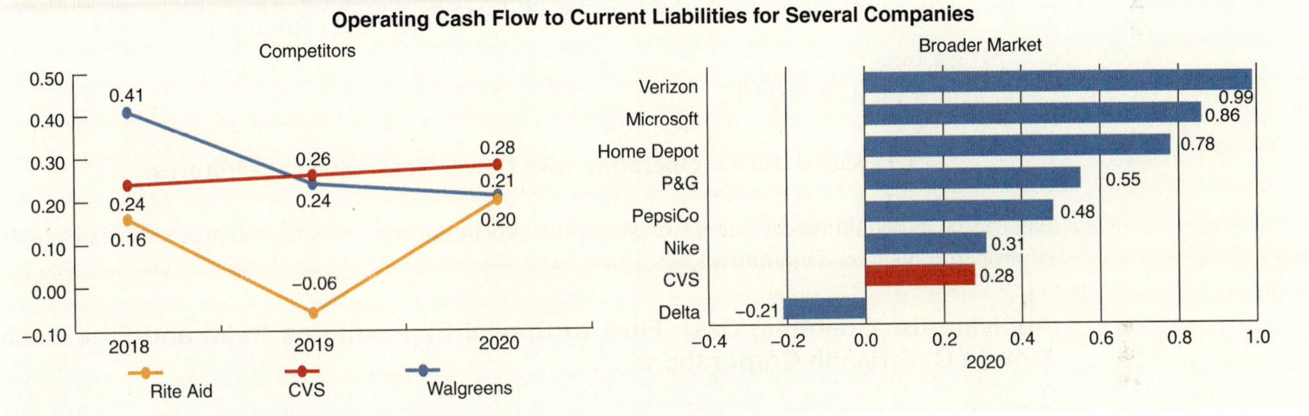

These companies do not have identical fiscal year-ends. For each fiscal year listed, balance sheets are dated from February 2 to December 31 of that year.

Takeaways Over the past three years, CVS Health's OCFCL ratio has risen steadily and now compares favorably to the two competitors that are included in the chart on the left. Both Walgreen's and Rite Aid's ratios are below the industry average, with Walgreens showing a more stable ratio. Rite Aid is consistently below these other companies. The 2020 increase in CVS Health's OCFCL ratio is largely due to a 23% increase in cash from operations. The comparison of focus companies' OCFCLs in the right-hand chart shows a range from −0.21 for Delta Air Lines to a high of almost one for Verizon. Delta Air Lines was affected significantly by the COVID-19 pandemic, which resulted in an unusual negative value for cash flows from operation. Other than Delta, CVS Health is lower than any of these companies.

Other Considerations There are some transactions that change both the numerator and the denominator, like using cash to pay current operating liabilities. Such a transaction would decrease both the numerator and the denominator, and these changes have an indeterminate effect on the ratio. Paying \$100 to a creditor decreases operating cash flow and ending current liabilities by \$100, with the average current liabilities decreasing by \$50. If the OCFCL is below 2.0 prior to the transaction, it will be even lower after the transaction. If the OCFCL is greater than 2.0 prior to the transaction, it will be even higher after the transaction. Delaying a payment to the creditor would have the opposite effect.

It is also important to take a look at the components of current liabilities. Sometimes there is a large portion of long-term debt that comes due and increases current liabilities for one year. Or, in the case of Delta Air Lines, about 25% of their current liabilities represent unearned revenue from customers who have purchased tickets in advance of travel (like the gift certificates at NBS). For this liability, Delta doesn't have to pay someone; they just need to keep flying.

Analysis Objective

We wish to determine CVS Health's ability to fund the capital expenditures needed to maintain and grow its operations and to make acquisitions.

Does CVS Health generate enough cash from its operations to make its capital investments? If it does not, then the company will have to finance those investments by selling other investments, by borrowing (resulting in future interest costs), by getting cash from shareholders, or by reducing cash balances. If it generates more cash than needed for capital expenditures, then the additional cash can be used to grow the business (e.g., by acquisition) or to distribute cash to investors. Two measures may be used in making this assessment. The first of these measures, operating cash flow to capital expenditures, is a ratio that facilitates comparisons with other companies. The second, free cash flow,[3] is a monetary amount that reflects the funds available for investing in new ventures, buying back stock, paying down debt, or returning funds to stockholders in the form of dividends. The concept is also used in mergers and acquisitions to indicate cash that would be available to the acquirer for investment.

Analysis Tools Operating Cash Flow to Capital Expenditures (OCFCX)

$$\textbf{Operating cash flow to capital expenditures} = \frac{\textbf{Operating cash flow}}{\textbf{Annual capital expenditures}}$$

Free Cash Flow (FCF)

$$\textbf{Free cash flow} = \textbf{Operating cash flow} - \textbf{Net capital expenditures}$$

Net capital expenditures are equal to cash capital expenditures minus the cash proceeds of disposals of property, plant, and equipment.

Applying the Operating Cash Flow to Capital Expenditures Ratio and Free Cash Flow to CVS Health Corporation

	OCFCX	FCF*
2018:	$\frac{\$8,865}{\$2,037}$ = 4.35 or 435%	\$ 8,865 − \$2,037 = \$ 6,828
2019:	$\frac{\$12,848}{\$2,457}$ = 5.23 or 523%	\$12,848 − \$2,457 = \$10,391
2020:	$\frac{\$15,865}{\$2,437}$ = 6.51 or 651%	\$15,865 − \$2,437 = \$13,428

*CVS Health did not report proceeds from the sale of property and equipment.

Guidance Operating cash flows to capital expenditures ratios that exceed 1.0 (or free cash flows that are positive) mean that the company can make its capital investments without obtaining additional financing or reducing its cash balances. The excess cash could be used to reduce borrowing, make acquisitions, or it could be returned to shareholders. CVS Health's merger with Aetna in 2018 required more than $40 billion in cash, and CVS Health increased its debt to a level exceeding its long-term target. The company's OCFCX and FCF values have increased significantly across these years, and the company has used this growth in cash flow to repay significant amounts of debt while maintaining dividend payments to shareholders.

[3] Free cash flow can be defined in several ways, but it always includes a measure of the cash resources generated by the company's current operations minus a measure of the cash required to sustain those operations. One of the simpler, more common definitions is presented here.

CVS Health Corporation in Context

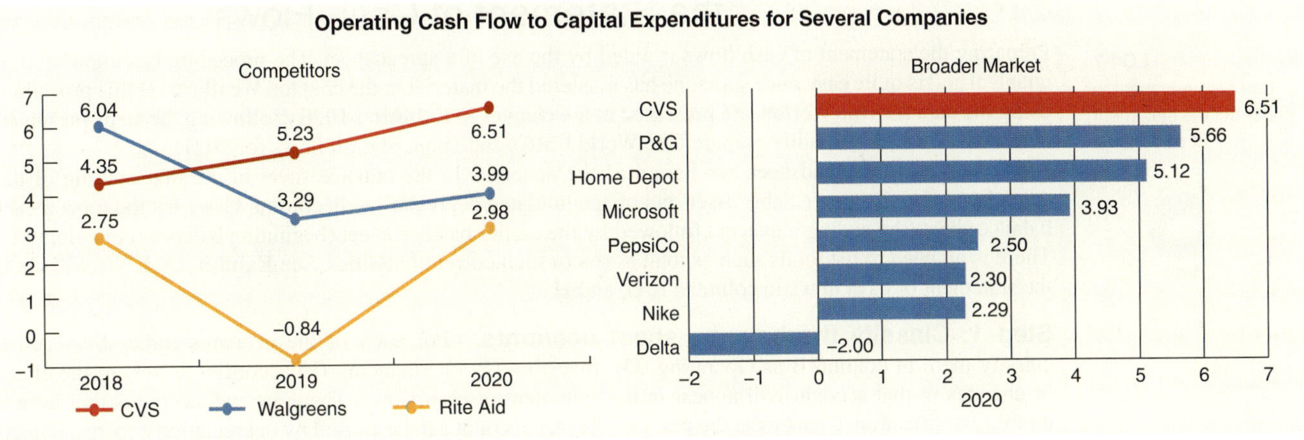

Takeaways OCFCX increased steadily over the last three years for CVS Health, and its OCFCX is higher than Walgreens and Rite Aid. Like CVS Health, Walgreens and Rite Aid have used the additional cash flow to acquire other businesses and repay long-term debt. But CVS Health's merger with Aetna has resulted in an increase in cash flow from operations that is greater than the increase in capital expenditures. CVS Health has used that growth to repay debt that was used to purchase Aetna, to make new investments, and to maintain dividends to shareholders. The OCFCX values for the focus companies show that many of them—with the exception of Delta—were able to weather the pandemic with cash flows adequate to conduct operations.

Other Considerations Measurement of cash flows is regarded as more objective than measures of income and less dependent on management judgments and estimates. But it may be subject to "lumpy" behavior from management's decisions, particularly for smaller companies. Capital expenditures may differ significantly from year to year if management takes on large, but infrequent, projects. A series of high values of OCFCX followed by a low value might mean deterioration in cash generating performance, but it might also mean that management has been accumulating cash in anticipation of a major project.

RESEARCH INSIGHT

Is the Statement of Cash Flows Useful? Some analysts rely on cash flow forecasts to value common stock. Research shows that both net income and operating cash flows are correlated with stock prices, but that stock prices are more highly correlated with net income than with cash flows. So, do we need both statements? Evidence suggests that by using *both* net income and cash flow information, we can improve our forecasts of *future* cash flows. Also, net income and cash flow together are more highly correlated with stock prices than either net income or cash flow alone. This result suggests that, for purposes of stock valuation, information from the statement of cash flows complements information from the income statement.

Calculating Ratios to Assess Liquidity and Solvency LO4-6 **Review 4-6**

Refer to One World Café's statement of cash flows and comparative balance sheets from **Exhibits 4.10** and **4.11** to complete the following.

GuidedExample MBC

Required

1. Calculate the operating cash flow to current liabilities (OCFCL) ratio for One World Café and interpret your findings. Assume that the notes payable are due within the year and are a current liability.
2. Calculate One World Café's operating cash flow to capital expenditures (OCFCX) ratio. What observations can you make about your findings?
3. Calculate the free cash flow (FCF) for One World Café.

Solution on p. 4-63.

APPENDIX 4A: A Spreadsheet Approach to Preparing the Statement of Cash Flows

LO4-7
Use a spreadsheet to construct the statement of cash flows.

eLecture MBC

Preparing the statement of cash flows is aided by the use of a spreadsheet. The procedure is somewhat mechanical and is quite easy once someone has mastered the material in the chapter. We illustrate this procedure using the data for One World Café presented in the chapter in **Exhibit 4.10**. By following the steps presented below, we are able to readily prepare One World Café's statement of cash flows for 2021.

To set up the spreadsheet, we list all of the accounts in the balance sheet in the first column of the spreadsheet. We list depreciable assets net of accumulated depreciation. In column C, we list the most recent balance sheet (the ending balances) followed by the earlier balance sheet (beginning balances) in column D. There is no need to list totals such as total assets or total current liabilities. See **Exhibit 4A.1**. We will build the statement of cash flows in columns F, G, and H.

Step 1: Classify the balance sheet accounts. For each of the accounts (other than cash), classify them in column B as Operating (O), Investing (I), or Financing (F) according to where the effect of changes in that account will appear in the statement of cash flows. There are two accounts that have a double classification. Changes in the plant assets, net account can be caused by depreciation expense (which will appear in the indirect method cash from operations) and by investing activities, so we label it as (O, I). Changes in the retained earnings account are caused by net income (which appears in the indirect method cash from operations) and dividends, so we label it as (O, F).

For those rows labeled I or F, insert two rows below: one for increases in the account and one for decreases in the account because we must report increases and decreases separately. For plant assets, net, insert three rows below: one for depreciation expense, one for plant asset acquisitions, and one for plant asset sales. For retained earnings, insert two rows below: one for net income and one for dividends.

EXHIBIT 4A.1 Cash Flow Spreadsheet for One World Café

	A	B	C	D	E	F	G	H	I	J
1						Effect of Change on Cash Flow				
2		O, I or F?	2021	2020	Change	Operating	Investing	Financing	No Effect on Cash	Total F, G, H, I
3	**Assets**									
4	Cash		8,000	12,000	(4,000)					
5										
6	Accounts receivable	O	22,000	28,000	(6,000)	6,000				6,000
7	Inventory	O	94,000	66,000	28,000	(28,000)				(28,000)
8	Prepaid advertising	O	12,000	9,000	3,000	(3,000)				(3,000)
9	Plant assets, net	O,I	136,000	109,000	27,000					
10	Depreciation expense					17,000				
11	Plant assets purchased						(45,000)		(5,000)	(27,000)
12	Plant assets sold					2,000	4,000			
13										
14	**Liabilities**									
15	Accounts payable	O	27,000	14,000	13,000	13,000				13,000
16	Wages payable	O	6,000	2,500	3,500	3,500				3,500
17	Income tax payable	O	3,000	4,500	(1,500)	(1,500)				(1,500)
18	Notes payable	F	5,000	—	5,000					
19	New borrowing								5,000	5,000
20	Borrowing repayments									
21										
22	**Shareholders' Equity**									
23	Common stock	F	134,000	125,000	9,000					
24	New issue of common stock							9,000		9,000
25	Repurchase of common stock									
26	Retained earnings	O,F	97,000	78,000	19,000					
27	Net income					35,000				19,000
28	Dividends							(16,000)		
29										
30	**Totals**					44,000	(41,000)	(7,000)	—	(4,000)

Step 2: Compute the changes in the balance sheet accounts. Subtract the beginning balances in each account from the ending balances and record these in column E. We highlight the change in the cash balance because this is the amount that we are trying to explain. At this point it is useful to verify that the change in cash is equal to the changes in liabilities plus the changes in stockholders' equity minus the changes in noncash assets:

Δ Cash = Δ Liabilities + Δ Stockholders' Equity – Δ Noncash Assets

In effect, we're going to use changes on the right-hand side of this equation to explain the changes in cash on the left-hand side.

Step 3: Handle the accounts that have single classifications. For those accounts that are operating-only assets (accounts receivable, inventory, prepaid expenses, etc.), we enter in column F the *negative* of the value in column E. The $28,000 increase in inventories in column E results in $(28,000) for the operating cash flows in column F. Changes in assets have the opposite effect on cash. Increases in assets have a negative effect on cash, while decreases in assets lead to positive adjustments to cash.

For those accounts that are operating only liabilities (accounts payable, wages payable, taxes payable, etc.), we enter in column F the value in column E. The $13,000 increase in accounts payable produces a $13,000 entry in column F.

For those accounts that are financing only (notes payable, common stock), we enter in column H the cash effect(s) of the change in column E. For example, we must be aware that the common stock account could have changed due to both issuing stock for cash and repurchasing stock for cash. For One World Café, there was only a $9,000 inflow due to a new stock issue in column H. (We will deal with the notes payable changes in the next step.)

One World Café has no assets that are investing only, but for such accounts (marketable securities, investments, etc.), we would again make entries for increases and decreases separately. And, because these are assets, the change in the balance sheet has the opposite sign of the entry in the cash flow columns. For instance, if One World Café had invested $10,000 in a financial security, its investments asset would increase, and we would put an entry of $(10,000) in column G.

Step 4: Enter the effect of investing/financing transactions that do not involve cash. We know from the information provided about One World Café that it arranged the purchase of $5,000 of plant assets by signing a note payable for the same amount. This transaction affected an investing asset and a financing liability at the same time, and we put the effects into column I. $5,000 is put in the new borrowing row (19), and $(5,000) is put in the plant assets purchased row (11). This transaction will not appear in the statement of cash flows in columns F, G, and H, but it does explain some of the changes in the company's assets and liabilities.

Step 5: Analyze the change in retained earnings. Some accounts require special attention because the change in the account balance involves two types of cash flow effects. For example, the change in retained earnings is actually two changes—net income, which is related to operations, and dividends, which is a financing cash outflow.

One World Café's retained earnings increased by $19,000. It reported net income of $35,000, which is listed as an operating item (because we're using the indirect method), and paid dividends of $16,000, a cash outflow listed under financing activities. For clarity, it is helpful to list each of these changes on a separate line. Thus, we have inserted two lines into the spreadsheet immediately below retained earnings—the first for net income and the second for dividends. The $35,000 inflow and the $16,000 outflow net to $19,000.

Step 6: Analyze the change in plant assets. A change in depreciable assets is actually the result of both operating and investing items. The change in plant assets can be explained by looking at the individual transactions that caused the change. As was the case with retained earnings, it is helpful to list each of these transactions in a separate row in the spreadsheet. Thus, we have inserted three rows into the spreadsheet immediately below the change in plant assets. First, we recall that One World Café reported depreciation expense of $17,000, which reduced its plant assets, net. This is listed in the first row under plant assets as a positive adjustment to cash flow from operations because cash flow effects on the asset side have the opposite sign.

In the next row, we list purchases of plant assets. One World Café purchased plant assets for $45,000 in cash, which is listed under investing as a cash outflow in column F. There was also the $5,000 purchase of plant assets that was financed with notes payable. This transaction did not affect cash, so it's in column I.

In the third row below plant assets, we list the sale of plant assets. One World Café sold plant assets for $4,000 cash, recognizing a loss of $2,000. The loss is listed in the operations column (as a positive adjustment to operating cash flow), and the proceeds from the sale are listed under investing as a cash inflow in column F.

When all of the balance sheet changes have been analyzed, the change for each account should add up to the sum of the effect on operating, investing, and financing cash flows, plus the amount in the "no effect" column. That is, for each change listed in the spreadsheet in column E, we can add columns F, G, H, and I to get the change in the balance sheet account in column J. For retained earnings: $35,000 – $16,000 = $19,000. For assets, the total will be the *negative* of the change. Adding up entries for plant assets: $17,000 – $45,000 – $5,000 + $2,000 + $4,000 = –$27,000, which is minus the amount in column E, row 9.

Step 7: Total the columns. We add up the effects listed in columns F, G, H, and I to get the cash flow subtotals. One World Café had cash flow from operations of $44,000, investing cash flows of –$41,000, and financing cash flows of –$7,000. The total for the "no effect" column (column I) should be $0 because the entries in this column had no effect on cash flow. Finally, we add up these totals to make sure that the cash flow effects equal the change in cash: $44,000 – $41,000 – $7,000 – $0 = –$4,000. If the totals do not add up to the change in cash, then there must be an error in analyzing one or more of the balance sheet changes. For example, if we had forgotten to subtract dividends, then the cash flow effects in columns F, G, and H would not add up to the change in retained earnings listed in column E. Likewise, if we had mistakenly omitted the sale of plant assets, then the change in plant assets would not add up correctly. Totaling the columns and rows is a check to verify that our analysis is complete and correct.

Step 8: Prepare the statement of cash flows. Starting with operating cash flows (column F), we list each of the items in the statement of cash flows. We start with net income and then add depreciation and the loss on the sale of plant assets. Then we list the remaining adjustments, starting with the change in accounts receivable and working down the column. Next, we do the same for the items listed in the investing (column G) and financing (column H) sections of the statement of cash flows. The resulting statement is identical to the statement presented in **Exhibit 4.11**.

Review 4-7 LO4-7

Using a Spreadsheet to Create a Statement of Cash Flows

The comparative balance sheets and income statement information for Rocky Road Bicycles, Inc., are as follows.

ROCKY ROAD BICYCLES, INC.
Comparative Balance Sheets

At December 31	2021	2020
Assets		
Cash	$ 106,000	$ 96,000
Accounts receivable	156,000	224,000
Inventory	752,000	528,000
Prepaid rent	68,000	72,000
Plant assets	1,692,000	1,360,000
Less accumulated depreciation	(562,000)	(488,000)
Total assets	$2,212,000	$1,792,000
Liabilities		
Accounts payable	$ 216,000	$ 112,000
Wages payable	18,000	20,000
Income tax payable	44,000	36,000
Equity		
Common stock	1,142,000	1,000,000
Retained earnings	792,000	624,000
Total liabilities and equity	$2,212,000	$1,792,000

Additional Information

- Rocky Road reported net income of $326,000 in 2021.
- Depreciation expense was $122,000 in 2021.
- Rocky Road sold plant assets during 2021. The plant assets originally cost $88,000, with accumulated depreciation of $48,000, and were sold for a gain of $16,000.
- Rocky Road declared and paid a $158,000 cash dividend in 2021.

Required

Use a spreadsheet to create a statement of cash flows for Rocky Road Bicycles, Inc.

Solution on p. 4-64.

SUMMARY

LO4-1 Explain the purpose of the statement of cash flows and classify cash transactions by type of business activity: operating, investing, or financing. (p. 4-3)

- The statement of cash flows summarizes information about the flow of cash into and out of the business.
- Operating cash flow includes any cash transactions related to selling goods or rendering services, as well as interest payments and receipts, tax payments, and any transaction not specifically classified as investing or financing.

- Investing cash flow includes acquiring and disposing of plant assets, buying and selling securities, including securities of other companies, and lending and subsequently collecting funds from a borrower.
- Financing cash flow includes all cash received or paid to shareholders, including stock issued or repurchased and dividends paid. In addition, it includes amounts borrowed and repaid to creditors.

Construct the operating activities section of the statement of cash flows using the direct method. (p. 4-7) LO4-2

- The direct method presents net cash flow from operating activities by showing the major categories of operating cash receipts and payments.
- The operating cash receipts and payments are usually determined by converting the accrual revenues and expenses to corresponding cash amounts.

Reconcile cash flows from operations to net income and use the indirect method to compute operating cash flows. (p. 4-17) LO4-3

- Because operating cash flow differs from net income, a reconciliation of these two amounts helps financial statement users understand the sources of this difference.
- The indirect method reconciles net income and operating cash flows by making adjustments for noncash revenues and expenses and changes in balance sheet accounts related to operations.

Construct the investing and financing activities sections of the statement of cash flows. (p. 4-19) LO4-4

- Investing activities capture cash flows from the purchase and disposal of long-term assets such as property, plant, and equipment as well as from the purchase (disposal) of other companies (subsidiaries). Cash flows related to the purchase and disposal of investing assets such as marketable securities and long-term financial investment would be included as well.
- Cash obtained from the issuance of securities or borrowings, and any repayments of debt, are disclosed in the financing section. Cash dividends are also included in this section. Interest payments are included in the operating section of the statement.

Examine the sale of investing assets and the disclosure of noncash activities. (p. 4-23) LO4-5

- Cash receipts from asset disposals are included in the investing section. Because cash receipts include any gain on sale (or reflect any loss), the gain (loss) must be subtracted from (added to) net income in the operating section to avoid double-counting.
- Some events, for example assets donated to the firm, provide resources to the business that are important but which do not involve cash outlays. These events are disclosed separately, along with the statement of cash flows, as supplementary disclosures or in the notes.

Compute and interpret ratios that reflect a company's liquidity and solvency using information reported in the statement of cash flows. (p. 4-29) LO4-6

- Interpreting indirect method cash from operations requires reference to those items that comprise net income. Each adjustment is intended to modify an income statement item to bring it to cash from operations.
- Two ratios of importance that are based on cash flows include:
  - Operating cash flow to current liabilities—a measure of the adequacy of current operations to cover current liability payments.
  - Operating cash flow to capital expenditures—a reflection of a company's ability to replace or expand its activities based on the level of current operations.
- Free cash flow is defined as: Cash flow from operations − Net capital expenditures.
- Free cash flow is a measure of a company's ability to apply its resources to new endeavors.

Appendix 4A: Use a spreadsheet to construct the statement of cash flows. (p. 4-33) LO4-7

- A spreadsheet helps to prepare the statement of cash flows by classifying the effect of each change in the balance sheet as operating, investing, financing, or not affecting cash.
- The spreadsheet approach relies on the key relationship:

Cash = Liabilities + Stockholders' equity − Noncash assets

GUIDANCE ANSWERS . . . YOU MAKE THE CALL

You are the Chief Accountant In its annual report for fiscal year 2020, Kohl's Corporation would report an increase of $197 million as "proceeds from sale of real estate" in the investing section of its statement of cash flows. The indirect method cash flow from operations of that statement would show an adjustment of a negative $127 million for "Gain on sale of real estate."

You are the Securities Analyst A company's operating activities are the "engine" that produces the cash flows that allow the investment necessary for growth and the funds that may be returned to the sources of capital. Accounting standards say that cash flows from operating activities include cash receipts from sales of goods or services, *including receipts from collection or sale of accounts*. So, receipts from the sale of accounts receivable should be included in cash from operations, along with ordinary cash receipts from customers. However, an analyst should consider the circumstances of the sale of receivables. Is such a sale part of the company's regular practices, enabling it to cut its borrowing or increase its growth? Or, if the sale is a new transaction, does it indicate that the company is having difficulty collecting from its customers or experiencing unusual expenditures or financing problems? Companies will almost always sell receivables at a discount—how much is it giving up to have access to the cash today? Many analysts argue that operating cash flows do not increase as a result of such transactions and that analysts should adjust the statement of cash flows to classify the sale of receivables as a financing activity.

KEY RATIOS

$$\text{Operating cash flow to current liabilities} = \frac{\text{Operating cash flow}}{\text{Average current liabilities}}$$

$$\text{Operating cash flow to capital expenditures} = \frac{\text{Operating cash flow}}{\text{Annual capital expenditures}}$$

$$\text{Free cash flow} = \text{Operating cash flow} - \text{Net capital expenditures}$$

Assignments with the MBC logo in the margin are available in myBusinessCourse. See the Preface of the book for details.

MULTIPLE CHOICE

Multiple Choice Answers
1. a 2. c 3. d 4. c 5. c

1. Which of the following is not disclosed in a statement of cash flows?
a. A transfer of cash to a cash equivalent investment
b. The amount of cash at year-end
c. Cash outflows from investing activities during the period
d. Cash inflows from financing activities during the period

2. Which of the following events appears in the cash flows from investing activities section of the statement of cash flows?
a. Cash received from customers
b. Cash received from issuance of common stock
c. Cash purchase of equipment
d. Cash payment of dividends

3. Which of the following events appears in the cash flows from financing activities section of the statement of cash flows?
a. Cash purchase of equipment
b. Cash purchase of bonds issued by another company
c. Cash received as repayment for funds loaned
d. Cash purchase of treasury stock

4. Tyler Company has a net income of $73,500 and the following related items:

Depreciation expense	$ 7,500
Accounts receivable increase	3,000
Inventory decrease	15,000
Accounts payable decrease	6,000

Using the indirect method, what is Tyler's net cash flow from operations?
a. $63,000
b. $69,000
c. $87,000
d. $57,000

5. Refer to information in Review 4-2. Assume that notes payable are not due within the coming year and are classified as a noncurrent liability. The operating cash flow to current liabilities ratio for Mug Shots, Inc., in December is
   a. 6.4%.
   b. 2.9%.
   c. 2.6%.
   d. impossible to determine from the data provided.

Homework MBC

Superscript A denotes assignments based on Appendix 4A.

QUESTIONS

Q4-1. What is the definition of *cash equivalents*? Give three examples of cash equivalents.

Q4-2. Why are cash equivalents included with cash in a statement of cash flows?

Q4-3. What are the three major types of activities classified on a statement of cash flows? Give an example of a cash inflow and a cash outflow in each classification.

Q4-4. In which of the three activity categories of a statement of cash flows would each of the following items appear? Indicate for each item whether it represents a cash inflow or a cash outflow:
   a. Cash purchase of equipment.
   b. Cash collection on loans.
   c. Cash dividends paid.
   d. Cash dividends received.
   e. Cash proceeds from issuing stock.
   f. Cash receipts from customers.
   g. Cash interest paid.
   h. Cash interest received.

Q4-5. Traverse Company acquired a $5,000,000 building by issuing $5,000,000 worth of bonds payable. In terms of cash flow reporting, what type of transaction is this? What special disclosure requirements apply to a transaction of this type?

Q4-6. Why are noncash investing and financing transactions disclosed as supplemental information to a statement of cash flows?

Q4-7. Companies are sometimes required to maintain minimum balances of cash for contractual reasons, making the cash unavailable for general business purposes. How does such an arrangement affect the financial statements of the reporting company?

Q4-8. What is the difference between the direct method and the indirect method of presenting net cash flow from operating activities?

Q4-9. In determining net cash flow from operating activities using the indirect method, why must we add depreciation back to net income? Give an example of another item that is added back to net income under the indirect method.

Q4-10. Vista Company sold for $49,000 cash land originally costing $35,000. The company recorded a gain on the sale of $14,000. How is this event reported in a statement of cash flows using the indirect method?

Q4-11. A firm uses the indirect method. Using the following information, what is its net cash flow from operating activities?

Homework MBC

Net income	$132,000
Accounts receivable decrease	19,500
Inventory increase	13,500
Accounts payable decrease	5,250
Income tax payable increase	2,250
Depreciation expense	9,000

Q4-12. What separate disclosures are required for a company that reports a statement of cash flows using the indirect method to report cash flows from operating activities?

Q4-13. If a business had a net loss for the year, under what circumstances would the statement of cash flows show a positive net cash flow from operating activities?

Q4-14. A firm is converting its accrual revenues to corresponding cash amounts using the direct method. Sales on the income statement are $740,000. Beginning and ending accounts receivable on the balance sheet are $46,400 and $35,200, respectively. What is the amount of cash received from customers?

Homework MBC

Homework MBC **Q4-15.** A firm reports $129,000 wages expense in its income statement. If beginning and ending wages payable are $5,850 and $4,200, respectively, what is the amount of cash paid to employees?

Homework MBC **Q4-16.** A firm reports $51,600 advertising expense in its income statement. If beginning and ending prepaid advertising are $7,200 and $9,120, respectively, what is the amount of cash paid for advertising?

Homework MBC **Q4-17.** Rusk Company sold equipment for $10,200 cash that had cost $70,000 and had $58,000 of accumulated depreciation. How is this event reported in a statement of cash flows using the direct method to report the operating activities section?

Q4-18. What separate disclosures are required for a company that reports the operating activities section of a statement of cash flows using the direct method?

Q4-19. How is the operating cash flow to current liabilities ratio calculated? Explain its use.

Q4-20. How is the operating cash flow to capital expenditures ratio calculated? Explain its use.

DATA ANALYTICS

LO4-3 Data Analytics Homework MBC

DA4-1. Preparing and Interpreting Excel Visualizations Created from Income and Cash Flow Data
The Excel file associated with this exercise includes data extracted from Form 10-K reports for CVS Health Corporation (CVS) and Walgreens Boots Alliance (Walgreens Boots) for six years. In this exercise, we analyze changes to and the relations between net income and operating cash flows over a six-year period.

REQUIRED

1. Download Excel file DA4-1 found in myBusinessCourse.
2. Prepare a line chart for the six-year period for each company showing net income and operating cash flows. *Hint:* Highlight your data; click on Insert, Select line chart. There should be a separate line for net income and a separate line for operating cash flows. If necessary, edit the chart by opening the Chart Design tab and clicking Select Data. There should be two series.
3. Use the visualizations to answer the following questions.
   a. In what year(s) does net income exceed operating cash flows for CVS?
   b. In what year(s) do operating cash flows exceed net income for Walgreens Boots?
   c. Over the six-year period, which year showed the largest difference between net income and operating cash flows for CVS?
   d. What is a likely cause of the difference shown between net income and operating cash flows for the year identified in part *c*?
   e. For Walgreens Boots, in what year were net income and operating cash flows most similar?
   f. For CVS, in what year were net income and operating cash flows most similar?
   g. How would you compare the trend of operating cash flows for CVS vs. Walgreens Boots?

LO4-6 Data Analytics Homework MBC

DA4-2. Analyzing Cash Flow Ratio Trends by Industry Segment
The Excel file associated with this exercise includes Compustat data for S&P 500 companies for Year 1 through Year 5. For this exercise, we analyze trends in cash flow ratios by industry segment. The current cash debt coverage ratio is a liquidity ratio that measures whether a company can pay its *current* debts with cash provided from operating activities. The cash debt coverage ratio is a solvency ratio that measures a company's ability to pay *all* debts with cash provided from operating activities. In both cases, an increase in the ratio is generally viewed as favorable because it indicates that the company has a stronger ability to pay off obligations.

PART 1 PREPARING THE DATA

1. Download Excel file DA4-2 found in myBusinessCourse.
2. Format the worksheet as a table. *Hint:* Highlight data in worksheet by clicking on keys Alt and A simultaneously. Select Insert, Table.
3. Sort data in table by Segment and delete all rows in the Financials and Real Estate Segments. Companies in these industries rarely report current assets or liabilities. *Hint:* Because this worksheet is formatted as a table, you can sort by any row using the dropdown at the column head.
4. Add a column to calculate average current liabilities for Years 2 through 5. *Hint:* Use the IF function to calculate the amount (the average current liabilities for that year). If the company name agrees to the company name in the previous cell (Company Name column), then calculate the average; otherwise, put "n/a" in the cell. Year 1 will always be n/a.

5. Copy and Paste Special—Values back into the same cells. This will allow you to sort by other columns in the table without causing a recalculation error. *Hint:* To quickly highlight a long column, double-click on the bottom right corner of the first cell in the column.
6. Add a column to calculate average liabilities for Years 2 through 5. *Hint:* Use similar steps as in part 4.
7. Create a ratio column to calculate the current cash debt coverage ratio and a ratio column to calculate the cash debt coverage ratio. Sort your worksheet in ascending order by each ratio column and eliminate any rows with errors due to incomplete information (such as a Year 1 calculation) or where the answer is zero and it indicates an error or missing information.
8. Eliminate extreme outliers by deleting any company's information where it shows a ratio over +/–60. Be sure to eliminate all years of data of any company considered an outlier.
9. Check your output by answering the following questions:
   a. What is the Current cash debt coverage ratio for XRX for Year 3?
   b. What is the Cash debt coverage ratio for GD for Year 2?
   c. What is Cash flow from operations for HD for Year 5?
   d. How many rows are included for the Materials segment? *Hint:* Sort your worksheet by segment and then by the Materials column and view the "Count" at the bottom right of your screen.

Current Cash Debt Coverage

$$\frac{\text{Cash provided by operating activities}}{\text{Average current liabilities}}$$

Cash Debt Coverage

$$\frac{\text{Cash provided by operating activities}}{\text{Average total liabilities}}$$

PART 2 CREATING A PIVOTTABLE

1. Create a PivotTable showing the average current cash debt coverage ratio and cash debt coverage ratio by segment by year. *Hint:* Drag Year then Segment to Rows and Current cash debt coverage and Cash debt coverage to Values. *Hint:* Right-click on a numeric field, select Value Field Settings, and change to Average.
2. Format your table to show two decimal places. *Hint:* Right-click on any item in the column to format and click on Number Format to update.
3. Eliminate totals from your chart. *Hint:* Click on the Design tab (it will be highlighted when you click anywhere in your PivotTable), Grand totals, Off for rows & columns.
4. Answer the following questions:
   a. Which industry segment has the highest average current cash debt coverage ratio in Year 2?
   b. Which industry segment has the lowest average current cash debt coverage ratio in Year 3?
   c. Which industry segment has the highest average cash debt coverage ratio in Year 5?
   d. Which industry segment has the lowest average cash debt coverage ratio in Year 5?
   e. What company had the largest current cash debt coverage ratio listed in the Telecommunications segment in Year 5? *Hint:* Double-click on the ratio amount in the PivotTable for Telecommunications, Year 5 to open up a new sheet with the supporting detail.

PART 3 PREPARING AND ANALYZING A PIVOTCHART

1. Create a PivotChart of the Cash Debt Coverage Ratio using a line chart.
2. Add a Slicer for Segment. *Hint:* Click inside the chart, click PivotChart Analyze, and click Add Slicer.
3. Describe the trend in each segment from Year 2 through Year 5.

DATA VISUALIZATION

Data Visualization Activities are available in myBusinessCourse. These assignments use Tableau Dashboards to expose students to visual depictions of data and introduce students to data analytics through data visualizations. These exercises are easily assignable and auto graded by MBC.

Data Visualization

MINI EXERCISES

M4-21. Identifying the Impact of Account Changes on Cash Flow from Operating Activities (Indirect Method)

LO4-1, 3, 4

Homework MBC

Target
NYSE :: TGT

The following account information was presented as adjustments to net income in the 2019 fiscal year statement of cash flows for **Target Corporation**. Determine whether each item would be a positive adjustment or a negative adjustment to net income in determining cash from operations. ($ millions).

a. Operating activities increased accounts payable by $140.
b. Operating activities decreased inventories by $505.
c. Early extinguishment of debt resulted in a loss of $10.
d. Depreciation and amortization expense was $2,604.
e. Operating activities decreased other assets by $18.

LO4-1 Homework MBC

M4-22. Classifying Cash Flows

For each of the items below, indicate whether the cash flow relates to an operating activity, an investing activity, or a financing activity.

a. Cash receipts from customers for services rendered.
b. Sale of long-term investments for cash.
c. Acquisition of plant assets for cash.
d. Payment of income taxes.
e. Bonds payable issued for cash.
f. Payment of cash dividends declared in previous year.
g. Purchase of short-term investments (not cash equivalents) for cash.

LO4-1, 3 Homework MBC

General Mills, Inc.
NYSE :: GIS

M4-23. Classifying Components of the Statement of Cash Flows

The following table presents selected items from a recent statement of cash flows of **General Mills, Inc.** For each item, determine whether the amount would be disclosed in the statement of cash flows under operating activities, investing activities, or financing activities. (General Mills uses the indirect method of reporting cash flows from operating activities.)

GENERAL MILLS, INC. Selected Items from Its Statement of Cash Flows	
1.	Payment of long-term debt
2.	Change in receivables
3.	Depreciation and amortization
4.	Change in prepaid expenses
5.	Dividends paid
6.	Stock-based compensation
7.	Cash received from sales of assets and businesses
8.	Net earnings
9.	Change in accounts payable
10.	Proceeds from common stock issued
11.	Purchases of land, buildings, and equipment

LO4-1, 5 Homework MBC

M4-24. Classifying Cash Flows

For each of the items below, indicate whether it is (1) a cash flow from an operating activity, (2) a cash flow from an investing activity, (3) a cash flow from a financing activity, (4) a noncash investing and financing activity, or (5) none of the above.

a. Paid cash to retire bonds payable at a loss.
b. Received cash as settlement of a lawsuit.
c. Acquired a patent in exchange for common stock.
d. Received advance payments from customers on orders for custom-made goods.
e. Gave large cash contribution to local university.
f. Invested cash in 60-day commercial paper (a cash equivalent).

LO4-2, 3 Homework MBC

M4-25. Reconciling Net Income and Cash Flow from Operations Using FSET

For the year, Beyer GmbH had the following summary information available concerning its operating activities. The company had no investing or financing activities this year.

1.	Sales of merchandise to customers on credit	€253,700
2.	Sales of merchandise to customers for cash	45,750
3.	Cost of merchandise sold on credit	160,050
4.	Cost of merchandise sold for cash	31,700
5.	Purchases of merchandise from suppliers on credit	175,800
6.	Purchases of merchandise from suppliers for cash	23,850
7.	Collections from customers on accounts receivable	241,700
8.	Cash payments to suppliers on accounts payable	170,100
9.	Operating expenses (all paid in cash)	86,150

REQUIRED

a. Enter the items above into the Financial Statement Effects Template. Under noncash assets, use two separate columns for accounts receivable and inventories. Calculate the totals for each column.

b. What was the company's net income for the year? What was the cash flow from operating activities? (Use the direct method.)

c. Indicate the direction and amounts by which each of the following accounts changed during the year.
1. Accounts receivable
2. Merchandise inventory
3. Accounts payable

d. Using your results above, prepare the operating activities section of the statement of cash flows using the indirect format.

M4-26. Calculating Net Cash Flow from Operating Activities (Indirect Method) LO4-3 Homework MBC

The following information was obtained from Galena Company's comparative balance sheets. Assume that Galena Company's annual income statement showed depreciation expense of $12,000, a gain on sale of investments of $13,500, and net income of $67,500. Calculate the net cash flow from operating activities using the indirect method.

	Ending	Beginning
Cash	$ 28,500	$ 13,500
Accounts receivable	66,000	52,500
Inventory	82,500	73,500
Prepaid rent	9,000	12,000
Long-term investments	31,500	51,000
Plant assets	225,000	159,000
Accumulated depreciation	60,000	48,000
Accounts payable	36,000	30,000
Income tax payable	6,000	9,000
Common stock	181,500	138,000
Retained earnings	159,000	136,500

M4-27. Reconciling Net Income and Cash Flow from Operations Using FSET LO4-2, 3 Homework MBC

For the year, Riffe Enterprises had the following summary information available concerning its operating activities. The company had no investing or financing activities this year.

1.	Sales of services to customers on credit	$384,600
2.	Sales of services to customers for cash	23,100
3.	Employee compensation earned	263,350
4.	Cash payment in advance to landlord for offices	74,550
5.	Cash paid to employees for compensation	260,800
6.	Rental expense for offices used over the year	58,950
7.	Collections from customers on accounts receivable	362,050
8.	Operating expenses (all paid in cash)	61,400
9.	Depreciation expense	11,500

REQUIRED

a. Enter the items above into the Financial Statement Effects Template. Under noncash assets, use three separate columns for accounts receivable and prepaid rent and the accumulated depreciation contra-asset. Calculate the totals for each column.

b. What was the company's net income for the year? What was the cash flow from operating activities? (Use the direct method.)

c. Indicate the direction and amounts by which each of the following accounts changed during the year.
1. Accounts receivable
2. Prepaid rent
3. Accumulated depreciation
4. Wages payable

d. Using your results above, prepare the operating activities section of the statement of cash flows using the indirect format.

LO4-3 Homework MBC

M4-28. Calculating Net Cash Flow from Operating Activities (Indirect Method)
Weber Company had a $16,800 net loss from operations for the year. Depreciation expense for the year was $6,880, and a cash dividend of $4,800 was declared and paid. Balances of the current asset and current liability accounts at the beginning and end of the year follow. Did Weber Company's operating activities for the year provide or use cash? Use the indirect method to determine your answer.

	Ending	Beginning
Cash	$ 2,800	$ 5,600
Accounts receivable	12,800	20,000
Inventory	40,000	42,400
Prepaid expenses	4,800	7,200
Accounts payable	9,600	6,400
Accrued liabilities	4,000	6,080

LO4-1, 3 Homework MBC

Nordstrom, Inc.
NYSE :: JWN

M4-29. Classifying Statement of Cash Flows Components and Determining Their Effects
The following table presents selected items from a recent statement of cash flows of Nordstrom, Inc.

a. For each item, determine whether the amount would be disclosed in the statement of cash flows under operating activities, investing activities, or financing activities. (Nordstrom uses the indirect method of reporting.)

b. For each item, determine whether it will appear as a positive or negative in determining the net increase in cash and cash equivalents.

NORDSTROM, INC.
Consolidated Statement of Cash Flows—Selected Items

1. Decrease in accounts receivable
2. Capital expenditures
3. Proceeds from long-term borrowings
4. Increase in deferred income tax net liability
5. Principal payments on long-term borrowings
6. Increase in merchandise inventories
7. Increase in prepaid expenses and other assets
8. Proceeds from issuances under stock compensation plans
9. Increase in accounts payable
10. Net earnings
11. Payments for repurchase of common stock
12. Increase in accrued salaries, wages, and related benefits
13. Cash dividends paid
14. Depreciation and amortization expenses

LO4-2 Homework MBC

M4-30. Calculating Operating Cash Flows (Direct Method)
Calculate the cash flow for each of the following cases.

a. Cash paid for rent:

Rent expense	$90,000
Prepaid rent, beginning of year	15,000
Prepaid rent, end of year	12,000

b. Cash received as interest:

Interest income	$24,000
Interest receivable, beginning of year	4,500
Interest receivable, end of year	5,550

c. Cash paid for merchandise purchased:

Cost of goods sold	$147,000
Inventory, beginning of year	28,500
Inventory, end of year	33,000
Accounts payable, beginning of year	16,500
Accounts payable, end of year	10,500

M4-31. Calculating Operating Cash Flows (Direct Method)

LO4-2

Homework MBC

Chakravarthy Company's current year income statement reports the following:

Sales	$412,500
Cost of goods sold	275,000
Gross profit	$137,500

Chakravarthy's comparative balance sheets show the following (accounts payable relate to merchandise purchases):

	End of Year	Beginning of Year
Accounts receivable	$35,500	$30,000
Inventory	54,500	48,000
Accounts payable	15,500	18,500

Compute Chakravarthy's current-year cash received from customers and cash paid for merchandise purchased.

EXERCISES

E4-32. Comparing Firms Using Ratio Analysis

LO4-6

Homework MBC

Consider the following 2020 data for several pharmaceutical firms ($ millions). (None of the firms reported the proceeds from disposals of property, plant, and equipment.)

	Average Current Liabilities	Cash from Operations	Expenditures on PPE
Merck & Co., Inc.	$24,774	$10,253	$4,684
Pfizer Inc.	31,612	14,403	2,252
Abbott Laboratories	11,385	7,901	2,177
Johnson & Johnson	39,229	23,536	3,347

Merck & Co.
NYSE :: MRK
Pfizer Inc.
NYSE :: PFE
Abbott Laboratories
NYSE :: ABT
Johnson & Johnson
NYSE :: JNJ

a. Compute the operating cash flow to current liabilities (OCFCL) ratio for each firm.
b. Compute the free cash flow for each firm.
c. Comment on the results of your computations.

E4-33. Comparing Firms Using Ratio Analysis

LO4-6

Homework MBC

Consider the following data for several firms from 2020 ($ millions):

	Average Current Liabilities	Cash from Operations	Expenditures on PPE	Proceeds from the Sale of PPE
Walmart, Inc.	$77,634	$25,255	$10,705	$321
The Coca-Cola Company	20,787	9,844	1,177	189
Target Corporation	14,751	7,117	3,027	63

Walmart Inc.
NYSE :: WMT
The Coca-Cola Company
NYSE :: KO
Target Corporation
NYSE :: TGT

a. Compute the operating cash flow to current liabilities (OCFCL) ratio for each firm.
b. Compute the free cash flow for each firm.
c. Comment on the results of your computations.

E4-34. Preparing a Statement of Cash Flows (Direct Method)

LO4-2

Homework MBC

Use the following information about the annual cash flows of Mason Corporation to prepare a statement of cash flows under the direct method. Refer to **Exhibit 4.3** for the appropriate format.

Cash balance, end of year	$ 9,000
Cash paid to employees and suppliers	111,000
Cash received from sale of land	30,000
Cash paid to acquire treasury stock	7,500
Cash balance, beginning of year	12,000
Cash received as interest	4,500
Cash paid as income taxes	8,250
Cash paid to purchase equipment	66,750
Cash received from customers	145,500
Cash received from issuing bonds payable	22,500
Cash paid as dividends	12,000

LO4-3, 6 Homework MBC

E4-35. Calculating Net Cash Flow from Operating Activities (Indirect Method)
Lincoln Company owns no plant assets and reported the following income statement for the current year:

Sales		$562,500
Cost of goods sold	$352,500	
Wages expense	82,500	
Rent expense	31,500	
Insurance expense	11,250	477,750
Net income		$ 84,750

Additional balance sheet information about the company follows:

	End of Year	Beginning of Year
Accounts receivable	$40,500	$36,750
Inventory	45,000	49,500
Prepaid insurance	6,000	5,250
Accounts payable	16,500	13,500
Wages payable	6,750	8,250

Use the information to

a. Calculate the net cash flow from operating activities under the indirect method.

b. Compute its operating cash flow to current liabilities (OCFCL) ratio. (Assume current liabilities consist of accounts payable and wages payable.)

LO4-5 Homework MBC

E4-36. Accounting Sleuth: Reconstructing Entries
Meubles Fischer SA had the following balances for its property, plant, and equipment accounts (in thousands of euros):

	Sept. 30 Year 3	Sept. 30 Year 4
Property, plant, and equipment at cost	€2,000	€2,400
Accumulated depreciation	(700)	(780)
Property, plant, and equipment, net	€1,300	€1,620

During fiscal Year 4, Meubles Fischer acquired €200 thousand in property by signing a mortgage, plus another €600 thousand in equipment for cash. The company also received €200 thousand in cash from the sale of used equipment, and its income statement reveals a €40 thousand gain from this transaction.

a. What was the original cost of the used equipment that Meubles Fischer SA sold during fiscal Year 4?

b. How much depreciation had been accumulated on the used equipment at the time it was sold?

c. How much depreciation expense did Meubles Fischer SA recognize in its fiscal Year 4 income statement?

E4-37. Accounting Sleuth: Reconstructing Entries

LO4-5

Homework MBC

Kasznik Ltd. had the following balances for its property, plant, and equipment accounts (in millions of pounds):

	Dec. 31 Year 7	Dec. 31 Year 8
Property, plant, and equipment at cost	£525	£549
Accumulated depreciation	(234)	(249)
Property, plant, and equipment, net	£291	£300

During Year 8, Kasznik Ltd. paid £84 million in cash to acquire property and equipment, and this amount represents all the acquisitions of property, plant, and equipment for the period. The company's income statement reveals depreciation expense of £51 million and a £15 million loss from the disposal of used equipment.

a. What was the original cost of the used equipment that Kasznik Ltd. sold during Year 8?

b. How much depreciation had been accumulated on the used equipment at the time it was sold?

c. How much cash did Kasznik Ltd. receive from its disposal of used equipment?

E4-38. Reconciling Changes in Balance Sheet Accounts

LO4-2, 5

Homework MBC

Walgreens Boots Alliance, Inc.
NYSE :: WBA

The following table presents selected items from the 2020 and 2019 balance sheets and 2020 income statement of Walgreens Boots Alliance, Inc.

WALGREENS BOOTS ALLIANCE, INC. ($ millions)

Selected Balance Sheet Data	2020	2019	Selected Income Statement Data	2020
Inventories	$ 9,451	$ 9,333	Cost of merchandise sold	$111,520
Property and equipment, less accumulated depreciation	13,342	13,478	Depreciation expense*	1,500
Trade accounts payable	14,458	14,341	Net earnings	424
Retained earnings	34,210	35,815		

*Includes amortization on capitalized system development costs and software included in property, plant, and equipment.

a. Compute the cash paid for merchandise inventories in 2020. Assume that trade accounts payable is only for merchandise purchases.

b. Compute the net cost of property acquired in 2020.

c. Compute the cash dividends paid in 2020.

E4-39. Analyzing Investing and Financing Cash Flows

LO4-4, 5

Homework MBC

During the year, Paxon Corporation's long-term investments account (at cost) increased $30,000, which was the net result of purchasing stocks costing $160,000 and selling stocks costing $130,000 at a $12,000 loss. Also, its bonds payable account decreased $20,000, the net result of issuing $260,000 of bonds and retiring bonds with a book value of $280,000 at an $18,000 gain. What items and amounts appear in the (a) cash flows from investing activities and (b) cash flows from financing activities sections of its annual statement of cash flows?

E4-40. Reconciling Changes in Balance Sheet Accounts

LO4-4, 5

Homework MBC

The following table presents selected items from the Year 6 (the more recent year) and Year 5 balance sheets and Year 6 income statement of Andrews, Inc.

ANDREWS, INC.

Selected Balance Sheet Data	Year 6	Year 5	Selected Income Statement Data	Year 6
Property and equipment, cost	$1,050,000	$1,041,000	Depreciation expense	$41,600
Accumulated depreciation	815,000	780,000	Gain on sale of property and equipment	600
Retained earnings	215,000	195,000	Net income	34,050

Andrews, Inc., reported expenditures for property and equipment of $12,600 in Year 6. In addition, the company acquired property and equipment valued at $3,000 in a noncash transaction in Year 6.

a. What was the original cost of the property and equipment that Andrews, Inc., sold during Year 6? What was the accumulated depreciation on that property and equipment at the time of sale?

b. Compute the cash proceeds from the sale of property and equipment in Year 6.

c. Prepare the journal entry to describe the sale of property and equipment.

d. Determine the cash dividends paid in Year 6.

LO4-2 **E4-41. Calculating Operating Cash Flows (Direct Method)**

Homework MBC

Calculate the cash flow for each of the following cases.

a. Cash paid for advertising:

Advertising expense	$74,400
Prepaid advertising, beginning of year	13,200
Prepaid advertising, end of year	18,000

b. Cash paid for income taxes:

Income tax expense	$35,000
Income tax payable, beginning of year	8,500
Income tax payable, end of year	5,800

c. Cash paid for merchandise purchased:

Cost of goods sold	$215,000
Inventory, beginning of year	36,000
Inventory, end of year	30,000
Accounts payable, beginning of year	12,000
Accounts payable, end of year	14,500

LO4-3, 4, 7 **E4-42.^A Preparing a Statement of Cash Flows (Indirect Method)**

Homework MBC

The following financial statements were issued by Hoskins Corporation for the fiscal year ended December 31, Year 8. All amounts are in millions of U.S. dollars.

Balance Sheets		Dec. 31 Year 7		Dec. 31 Year 8
Assets				
Cash		$ 900		$ 1,650
Accounts receivable		1,800		4,500
Inventory		1,200		1,500
Prepaid expenses		1,200		450
Current assets		5,100		8,100
Property, plant, and equipment at cost	$18,600		$18,300	
Less accumulated depreciation	(6,300)		(5,250)	
Property, plant, and equipment, net		12,300		13,050
Total assets		$17,400		$21,150
Liabilities and Shareholders' Equity				
Accounts payable		$ 1,200		$ 2,400
Income tax payable		600		300
Short-term debt		3,600		8,100
Current liabilities		5,400		10,800
Long-term debt		3,000		0
Total liabilities		8,400		10,800
Contributed capital		2,400		2,400
Retained earnings		6,600		7,950
Total shareholders' equity		9,000		10,350
Total liabilities and shareholders' equity		$17,400		$21,150

Income Statement	Year 8
Sales revenues	$19,500
Cost of goods sold	10,200
Gross profit	9,300
Selling, general, and administrative expenses	4,350
Depreciation expense	1,050
Operating income	3,900
Interest expense	1,050
Income before income tax expense	2,850
Income tax expense	750
Net income	$2,100

Additional information:

1. During fiscal Year 8, Hoskins Corporation acquired new equipment for $3,600 in cash. In addition, the company disposed of used equipment that had original cost of $3,900 and accumulated depreciation of $2,100, receiving $1,800 in cash from the buyer.
2. During fiscal Year 8, Hoskins Corporation arranged short-term bank financing and borrowed $4,500, using a portion of the cash to repay all of its outstanding long-term debt.
3. During fiscal Year 8, Hoskins Corporation engaged in no transactions involving its common stock, although it did declare and pay in cash a common stock dividend of $750.

REQUIRED

Using the spreadsheet approach from the chapter appendix, prepare a statement of cash flows (all three sections) for Hoskins Corporation's fiscal Year 8, using the indirect method for the cash from operations section.

E4-43. Analyzing Operating Cash Flows (Direct Method) LO4-2, 6 Homework MBC

Refer to the information in Exercise 4-35. Calculate the net cash flow from operating activities using the direct method. Show a related cash flow for each revenue and expense. Also, compute its operating cash flow to current liabilities (OCFCL) ratio. (Assume current liabilities consist of accounts payable and wages payable.)

E4-44. Interpreting Cash Flow from Operating Activities LO4-2, 3 Homework MBC

Carter Company's income statement and cash flow from operating activities (indirect method) are provided as follows ($ thousands):

Income Statement	
Revenue	$800
Cost of goods sold	430
Gross profit	370
Operating expenses	220
Operating income	150
Interest expense	50
Income before taxes	100
Income tax expense	30
Net income	$ 70

Cash Flow from Operating Activities	
Net income	$ 70
Plus depreciation expense	140
Operating asset adjustments	
Less increase in accounts receivable	(50)
Less increase in inventories	(100)
Less increase in prepaid rent	(10)
Plus increase in accounts payable	130
Plus increase in income tax payable	10
Cash flow from operating activities	$190

a. For each of the four statements below, determine whether the statement is true or false.

b. If the statement is false, provide the (underlined) dollar amount that would make it true.

1. Carter collected $750 from customers in the current period.
2. Carter paid $0 interest in the current period.
3. Carter paid $40 in income taxes in the current period.
4. If Carter increased the depreciation expense (for financial reporting to shareholders) by $100, it would increase its cash from operations by $100.

PROBLEMS

LO4-3 **P4-45. Reconciling and Computing Operating Cash Flows from Net Income**

Homework MBC

Petroni Company reports the following selected results for its calendar year.

Net income	$202,500
Depreciation expense	37,500
Gain on sale of assets	7,500
Accounts receivable increase	15,000
Accounts payable increase	9,000
Prepaid expenses decrease	4,500
Wages payable decrease	6,000

REQUIRED

Prepare the operating section only of Petroni Company's statement of cash flows for the year under the indirect method of reporting.

LO4-3, 4, 6 **P4-46. Preparing a Statement of Cash Flows (Indirect Method)**

Homework MBC

Wolff Company's income statement and comparative balance sheets follow.

WOLFF COMPANY
Income Statement
For Year Ended December 31, Year 5

Sales		$762,000
Cost of goods sold	$516,000	
Wages expense	103,200	
Insurance expense	9,600	
Depreciation expense	20,400	
Interest expense	10,800	
Income tax expense	34,800	694,800
Net income		$ 67,200

WOLFF COMPANY
Balance Sheets

	Dec. 31 Year 5	Dec. 31 Year 4
Assets		
Cash	$ 13,200	$ 6,000
Accounts receivable	49,200	38,400
Inventory	108,000	72,000
Prepaid insurance	6,000	8,400
Plant assets	300,000	234,000
Accumulated depreciation	(81,600)	(61,200)
Total assets	$394,800	$297,600
Liabilities and Stockholders' Equity		
Accounts payable	$ 8,400	$ 12,000
Wages payable	10,800	7,200
Income tax payable	8,400	9,600
Bonds payable	156,000	90,000
Common stock	108,000	108,000
Retained earnings	103,200	70,800
Total liabilities and equity	$394,800	$297,600

Cash dividends of $34,800 were declared and paid during Year 5. Also in Year 5, plant assets were purchased for cash, and bonds payable were issued for cash. Bond interest is paid semiannually on June 30 and December 31. Accounts payable relate to merchandise purchases.

REQUIRED

a. Compute the change in cash that occurred during Year 5.

b. Prepare a Year 5 statement of cash flows using the indirect method.

c. Compute and interpret Wolff's
(1) operating cash flow to current liabilities ratio, and
(2) operating cash flow to capital expenditures ratio.

P4-47. Computing Cash Flow from Operating Activities (Direct Method) LO4-2

Refer to the income statement and comparative balance sheets for Wolff Company presented in P4-46.

Homework MBC

REQUIRED

a. Compute Wolff Company's cash flow from operating activities using the direct method. Use the format illustrated in **Exhibit 4.5** in the chapter.

b. What can we learn from the direct method that may not be readily apparent when reviewing a statement of cash flows prepared using the indirect method?

P4-48. Preparing a Statement of Cash Flows (Indirect Method) LO4-3, 4, 5, 6

Arctic Company's income statement and comparative balance sheets follow.

Homework MBC

ARCTIC COMPANY
Income Statement
For Year Ended December 31, Year 8

Sales		$582,400
Cost of goods sold	$427,200	
Wages expense	152,000	
Advertising expense	24,800	
Depreciation expense	17,600	
Interest expense	14,400	
Gain on sale of land	(20,000)	616,000
Net loss		$ (33,600)

ARCTIC COMPANY
Balance Sheets

	Dec. 31, Year 8	Dec. 31, Year 7
Assets		
Cash	$ 39,200	$ 22,400
Accounts receivable	33,600	40,000
Inventory	85,600	90,400
Prepaid advertising	8,000	10,400
Plant assets	288,000	177,600
Accumulated depreciation	(62,400)	(44,800)
Total assets	$392,000	$296,000
Liabilities and Stockholders' Equity		
Accounts payable	$ 13,600	$ 24,800
Interest payable	4,800	—
Bonds payable	160,000	—
Common stock	196,000	196,000
Retained earnings	41,600	75,200
Treasury stock	(24,000)	—
Total liabilities and stockholders' equity	$392,000	$296,000

During Year 8, Arctic sold land for $56,000 cash that had originally cost $36,000. Arctic also purchased equipment for cash, acquired treasury stock for cash, and issued bonds payable for cash in Year 8. Accounts payable relate to merchandise purchases.

REQUIRED

a. Compute the change in cash that occurred during Year 8.

b. Prepare a Year 8 statement of cash flows using the indirect method.

c. Compute and interpret Arctic's
(1) operating cash flow to current liabilities ratio, and
(2) operating cash flow to capital expenditures ratio.

LO4-2 **P4-49. Computing Cash Flow from Operating Activities (Direct Method)**

Homework MBC

Refer to the income statement and comparative balance sheets for Arctic Company presented in P4-48.

REQUIRED

a. Compute Arctic Company's cash flow from operating activities using the direct method. Use the format illustrated in **Exhibit 4.5** in the chapter.

b. What can we learn from the direct method that may not be readily apparent when reviewing a statement of cash flows prepared using the indirect method?

LO4-3, 4, 5, 6 **P4-50. Preparing a Statement of Cash Flows (Indirect Method)**

Homework MBC

Dair Company's income statement and comparative balance sheets follow.

DAIR COMPANY
Income Statement
For Year Ended December 31, Year 8

Sales		$525,000
Cost of goods sold	$330,000	
Wages and other operating expenses	71,250	
Depreciation expense	16,500	
Amortization expense	5,250	
Interest expense	7,500	
Income tax expense	27,000	
Loss on bond retirement	3,750	461,250
Net income		$ 63,750

DAIR COMPANY
Balance Sheets

	Dec. 31, Year 8	Dec. 31, Year 7
Assets		
Cash	$ 20,250	$ 13,500
Accounts receivable	39,750	36,000
Inventory	77,250	81,750
Prepaid expenses	9,000	7,500
Plant assets	270,000	252,000
Accumulated depreciation	(65,250)	(63,000)
Intangible assets	32,250	37,500
Total assets	$383,250	$365,250
Liabilities and Shareholders' Equity		
Accounts payable	$ 24,000	$ 19,500
Interest payable	3,000	5,250
Income tax payable	4,500	6,000
Bonds payable	45,000	90,000
Common stock	189,000	171,000
Retained earnings	117,750	73,500
Total liabilities and equity	$383,250	$365,250

During Year 8, the company sold for $12,750 cash old equipment that had cost $27,000 and had $14,250 accumulated depreciation. Also in Year 8, new equipment worth $45,000 was acquired in exchange for $45,000 of bonds payable, and bonds payable of $90,000 were retired for cash at a loss. A $19,500 cash dividend was declared and paid in Year 8. Any stock issuances were for cash.

REQUIRED

a. Compute the change in cash that occurred in Year 8.

b. Prepare a Year 8 statement of cash flows using the indirect method.

c. Prepare separate schedules showing
(1) cash paid for interest and for income taxes and
(2) noncash investing and financing transactions.

d. Compute its
(1) operating cash flow to current liabilities ratio,
(2) operating cash flow to capital expenditures ratio, and
(3) free cash flow.

P4-51. Interpreting the Statement of Cash Flows

LO4-2, 3, 4

CVS Health Corp.
NYSE :: CVS

Homework MBC

For this question, refer to the information in **Exhibits 4.1** and **4.7**.

a. Based on the information presented in its statement of cash flows, what amount of revenues should CVS Health report in its 2020 income statement?

b. Why is "stock-based compensation" listed under "Adjustments necessary to reconcile net income to net cash provided by operating activities"?

c. Why does CVS Health not list the effect of exchange rate changes on cash and cash equivalents in its statement of cash flows?

d. Using three bullet points, explain what CVS Health did with the nearly $16 billion in cash that was provided by operating activities is 2020.

P4-52. Preparing a Statement of Cash Flows (Indirect Method)

LO4-3, 4, 5, 6

Homework MBC

Rainbow Company's income statement and comparative balance sheets follow.

RAINBOW COMPANY
Income Statement
For Year Ended December 31, Year 8

Sales		$375,000
Dividend income		7,500
Total revenue		382,500
Cost of goods sold	$220,000	
Wages and other operating expenses	65,000	
Depreciation expense	19,500	
Patent amortization expense	3,500	
Interest expense	6,500	
Income tax expense	22,000	
Loss on sale of equipment	2,500	
Gain on sale of investments	(1,500)	337,500
Net income		$ 45,000

RAINBOW COMPANY
Balance Sheets

	Dec. 31, Year 8	Dec. 31, Year 7
Assets		
Cash and cash equivalents	$ 9,500	$ 12,500
Accounts receivable	20,000	15,000
Inventory	51,500	38,500
Prepaid expenses	5,000	3,000
Long-term investments	—	28,500
Land	95,000	50,000
Buildings	222,500	175,000
Accumulated depreciation—buildings	(45,500)	(37,500)
Equipment	89,500	112,500
Accumulated depreciation—equipment	(21,000)	(23,000)
Patents	25,000	16,000
Total assets	$451,500	$390,500
Liabilities and Stockholders' Equity		
Accounts payable	$ 10,000	$ 8,000
Interest payable	3,000	2,500
Income tax payable	4,000	5,000
Bonds payable	77,500	62,500
Preferred stock ($100 par value)	50,000	37,500
Common stock ($5 par value)	189,500	182,000
Paid-in capital in excess of par value—common	66,500	62,000
Retained earnings	51,000	31,000
Total liabilities and equity	$451,500	$390,500

During Year 8, the following transactions and events occurred:

1. Sold long-term investments costing $28,500 for $30,000 cash.
2. Purchased land for cash.
3. Capitalized an expenditure made to improve the building.
4. Sold equipment for $7,000 cash that originally cost $23,000 and had $13,500 accumulated depreciation.

5. Issued bonds payable at face value for cash.
6. Acquired a patent with a fair value of $12,500 by issuing 125 shares of preferred stock at par value.
7. Declared and paid a $25,000 cash dividend.
8. Issued 1,500 shares of common stock for cash at $8 per share.
9. Recorded depreciation of $8,000 on buildings and $11,500 on equipment.

REQUIRED

a. Compute the change in cash and cash equivalents that occurred during Year 8.
b. Prepare a Year 8 statement of cash flows using the indirect method.
c. Prepare separate schedules showing (1) cash paid for interest and for income taxes and (2) noncash investing and financing transactions.
d. Compute its (1) operating cash flow to current liabilities ratio, (2) operating cash flow to capital expenditures ratio, and (3) free cash flow.

LO4-2, 3, 4, 5 Homework MBC

P4-53. Preparing a Statement of Cash Flows (Direct Method)
Refer to the data for Rainbow Company in Problem 4-52.

REQUIRED

a. Compute the change in cash that occurred in Year 8.
b. Prepare a Year 8 statement of cash flows using the direct method. Use one cash outflow for "cash paid for wages and other operating expenses." Accounts payable relate to inventory purchases only.
c. Prepare separate schedules showing (1) a reconciliation of net income to net cash flow from operating activities and (2) noncash investing and financing transactions.

LO4-3, 4, 5 Apple Inc. NASDAQ :: AAPL Homework MBC

P4-54. Interpreting Cash Flow Information
The 2020 statement of cash flows for **Apple Inc.** is presented below (all $ amounts in millions):

APPLE INC. Consolidated Statement of Cash Flows Year Ended September 30, 2020	
Cash and cash equivalents, beginning of the year	$ 50,224
Operating activities	
Net income	57,411
Adjustments to reconcile net income to cash generated by operating activities:	
Depreciation, and amortization	11,056
Share-based compensation expense	6,829
Deferred income tax expense	(215)
Other	(97)
Changes in operating assets and liabilities:	
Accounts receivable, net	6,917
Inventories	(127)
Vendor nontrade receivables	1,553
Other current and noncurrent assets	(9,588)
Accounts payable	(4,062)
Deferred revenue	2,081
Other current and noncurrent liabilities	8,916
Cash generated by operating activities	80,674
Investing activities	
Purchases of marketable securities	(114,938)
Proceeds from maturities of marketable securities	69,918
Proceeds from sales of marketable securities	50,473
Payments for acquisition of property, plant, and equipment	(7,309)
Payments made in connection with business acquisitions, net	(1,524)
Purchases of nonmarketable securities	(210)
Proceeds from nonmarketable securities	92
Other	(791)
Cash used in investing activities	(4,289)

continued

continued from previous page

Financing activities	
Proceeds from issuance of common stock	880
Payments for taxes related to net share settlement of equity awards	(3,634)
Payments for dividends and dividend equivalents	(14,081)
Repurchases of common stock	(72,358)
Proceeds from issuance of term debt, net	16,091
Repayments of term debt	(12,629)
Repayments of commercial paper, net	(963)
Other	(126)
Cash used in financing activities	(86,820)
Increase (decrease) in cash and cash equivalents	(10,435)
Cash and cash equivalents, end of the year	$ 39,789
Supplemental cash flow disclosure:	
Cash paid for income taxes, net	$ 9,501
Cash paid for interest	$ 3,002

REQUIRED

a. Did Apple's accounts receivable go up or down in 2020? Apple reported net sales of $274,515 in its fiscal 2020 income statement. What amount of cash did Apple collect from customers during the year? (Ignore the Vendor nontrade receivables account, which relates to Apple's suppliers.)

b. Apple's cost of goods sold was $169,559 million in 2020. Assuming that accounts payable applies only to the purchase of inventory, what amount did Apple pay to purchase inventory in 2020?

c. At September 30, 2020, Apple reported a balance of $36.8 billion in property, plant, and equipment, net of accumulated depreciation, and its disclosure notes revealed that depreciation expense on property, plant, and equipment was $9.7 billion for fiscal 2020. What was the balance in property, plant, and equipment, net of accumulated depreciation at the end of fiscal 2019?

d. Apple lists stock-based compensation as a positive amount—$11,056 million—under cash flow from operating activities. Why is this amount listed here? Explain how this amount increases cash flow from operating activities.

P4-55.[A] Preparing the Statement of Cash Flows Using a Spreadsheet

LO4-3, 4, 5, 6, 7
Snack Food Inc.

The table below provides the balance sheets for Snack Food Inc. for the fiscal years ended December 31, Year 6 and Year 5.

	Year Ended	
Consolidated Balance Sheets ($ thousands)	**Year 6**	**Year 5**
Assets		
Cash	$ 1,610	$ 940
Accounts receivable, net	8,540	8,870
Inventories	4,590	4,200
Prepaid expenses	1,030	1,090
Income tax receivable	20	390
Total current assets	15,790	15,490
Property, plant, and equipment at cost	78,560	77,900
Accumulated depreciation	60,930	58,310
Property, plant, and equipment, net	17,630	19,590
Cash surrender value of life insurance	360	510
Other	740	780
Total assets	$34,520	$36,370

continued

continued from previous page

Liabilities & stockholders' equity		
Liabilities		
Checks outstanding in excess of bank balances	$ —	$ 860
Accounts payable	3,390	3,240
Salaries payable	100	90
Current portion of long-term debt	670	640
Line of credit outstanding	—	2,260
Other accrued expenses	4,130	4,020
Total current liabilities	8,290	11,110
Note payable to bank, noncurrent	4,290	4,980
Capital lease obligation	170	—
Bonds payable	740	740
Deferred income taxes, net	2,110	2,180
Total liabilities	15,600	19,010
Stockholders' equity		
Common stock at par	7,380	7,380
Additional paid-in capital	5,450	5,250
Retained earnings	16,600	15,240
Treasury shares, at cost	(10,510)	(10,510)
Total stockholders' equity	18,920	17,360
Total liabilities and stockholders' equity	$34,520	$36,370

Additional information (in $ thousands):

1. Net income for Year 6 was $2,550.
2. Depreciation expense for Year 6 was $3,110.
3. Accounts for other assets and for the life insurance asset should be classified as operating.
4. Checks outstanding in excess of bank balances should be treated as an operating liability.
5. During Year 6, Snack Food Inc. sold used property, plant, and equipment, receiving $50 in cash and recognizing a gain of $50.
6. For Year 6, debt proceeds (encompassing the liabilities for current portion of long-term debt, line of credit outstanding, and note payable to bank, noncurrent) were zero and debt repayments were $2,920.
7. During Year 6, Snack Food Inc. acquired a long-term asset in a noncash transaction. At the time of the transaction, the asset and the liability were both valued at $200. The asset is included under property, plant, and equipment in the balance sheet, and it is being depreciated. The associated financial liability is included on the balance sheet under the "capital lease obligation" liability. During Year 6, Snack Food Inc. repaid $30 of principal on this obligation.
8. During Year 6, Snack Food Inc. recognized an expense of $200 for stock-based compensation. The expense increased additional paid-in capital by the same amount.

REQUIRED

a. Set up a spreadsheet to analyze the changes in Snack Food's comparative balance sheets. Use the format illustrated in **Exhibit 4A.1**.

b. Prepare a statement of cash flows (including operations, investing and financing) for Snack Food Inc. for Year 6 using the indirect method for the operating section.

c. Using information in the statement of cash flows prepared in part *b*, compute (1) the operating cash flow to current liabilities ratio and (2) the operating cash flow to capital expenditures ratio.

LO4-3, 4, 6 **P4-56. Managing Cash Flows**

Homework MBC

Amazin, Inc., is a specialty online wholesaler that has just completed initial financing and acquired the physical facilities to support its operations. The management team is optimistic about the company's growth opportunities as they begin operations, but they also recognize that there are significant risks for any young company's survival. The current financial condition is shown in the following balance sheet.

Balance Sheet (in $ thousands)	
Assets	
Cash	$ 800
Accounts receivable	—
Property, plant, and equipment at cost	1,200
Total assets	$2,000
Liabilities and shareholders' equity	
Accounts payable	—
Contributed capital	2,000
Retained earnings	—
Total liabilities and shareholders' equity	$2,000

Amazin's management team has "benchmark" financial projections for the first quarter of operation. Revenue is forecasted to be $2,000 thousand in Q1. Cost of goods sold will be 40% of revenue, depreciation will be $150 thousand for the quarter, and selling, general, and administrative expenses (SG&A) will be 30% of revenue. This benchmark case is based on the assumption that customers will pay for purchases in the subsequent quarter, and Amazin, Inc., will be able to delay the payments to suppliers for the same length of time.

Amazin's growth plans will require capital expenditures of $300 thousand in Q1 and subsequent quarters. The dynamic nature of the company's operations means that these physical assets have a useful life of only eight quarters. The family and friends who funded the start-up are expecting dividends equal to 20% of profits. (Taxes may be ignored.)

REQUIRED

a. Produce projected income statement, statement of cash flows, and ending balance sheet for Q1.

b. One team member suggests a more aggressive approach to growth. By increasing SG&A from 30% of revenue to 33%, revenue would increase from $2,000 thousand to $2,400 thousand. What would be the effect of such a change on Amazin's income statement? On its cash flows and financial position?

c. One team member notes that suppliers are not going to be pleased to wait a quarter to be paid. Relative to the benchmark plan, he forecasts that cost of goods sold expense would be lower by 10% if suppliers were paid promptly. What would be the effect of such a change on Amazin's income statement? On its cash flows and financial position?

CASES AND PROJECTS

C4-57. Analyzing a Projected Statement of Cash Flows and Loan Covenants LO4-3, 4, 5

Homework MBC

The president and CFO of Lambert Co. will be meeting with their bankers next week to discuss the short-term financing needs of the company for the next six months. Lambert's controller has provided a projected income statement for the next six-month period, and a current balance sheet along with a projected balance sheet for the end of that six-month period. These statements and additional information are presented below ($ millions).

LAMBERT CO. Projected Six-Month Income Statement	
Revenues	$1,200
Cost of goods sold	600
Gross profit	600
Selling and administrative expense	150
Depreciation expense	360
Income before income taxes	90
Income taxes	36
Net income	$ 54

LAMBERT CO. Current and Projected Six-Month Balance Sheets	Current	6-Month Projected
Cash	$ 150	$???
Accounts receivable	540	660
Inventory	600	540
Total current assets	1,290	???
Property, plant, and equipment, cost	1,200	1,500
Less accumulated depreciation	(450)	(660)
Property, plant, and equipment, net	750	840
Total assets	$2,040	$???
Accounts payable	$ 450	$ 540
Income taxes payable	60	30
Short-term borrowing	150	???
Long-term debt	600	540
Total liabilities	1,260	???
Common stock at par	300	375
Retained earnings	480	444
Total liabilities and shareholders' equity	$2,040	$???

Additional Information (already reflected in the projected income statement and balance sheet):

- Lambert's current long-term debt includes $300 that is due within the next six months. During the next six months, the company plans to take advantage of lower interest rates by issuing new long-term debt that will provide $240 in cash proceeds.
- During the next six months, the company plans to dispose of equipment with an original cost of $375 and accumulated depreciation of $150. An appraisal by an equipment broker indicates that Lambert should be able to get $225 in cash for the equipment. In addition, Lambert plans to acquire new equipment at a cost of $675.
- A small issue of common stock for cash ($75) and a cash dividend to shareholders ($90) are planned in the next six months.
- Lambert's outstanding long-term debt imposes a restrictive loan covenant on the company that requires Lambert to maintain a debt-to-equity ratio below 1.75.

REQUIRED

The CFO says, "I would like a clear estimate of the amount of short-term borrowing that we will need six months from now. I want you to prepare a forecasted statement of cash flows that we can take to the meeting next week."

Prepare the required statement of cash flows, using the indirect method to compute cash flow from operating activities. The forecasted statement should include the needed amount of short-term borrowing and should be consistent with the projected balance sheet and income statement, as well as the loan covenant restriction.

LO4-1, 3, 4, 5 Homework MBC

C4-58. Reconstructing Journal Entries and T-Accounts from Completed Financial Statements
Lundholm Company's comparative balance sheets, income statement, and statement of cash flows for July are presented below:

LUNDHOLM COMPANY Comparative Balance Sheets	July 1	July 31
Cash	$ 900	$ 1,776
Accounts receivable	9,750	10,200
Inventory	3,600	2,700
Prepaid rent	—	600
Current assets	14,250	15,276
Fixtures and equipment at cost	2,850	3,930
Accumulated depreciation	(1,200)	(1,320)
Plant and equipment, net	1,650	2,610
Total assets	$15,900	$17,886

continued

continued from previous page

Accounts payable	$ 4,500	$ 4,650
Salaries and wages payable	150	105
Taxes payable	—	561
Bank loan payable	2,400	—
Current liabilities	7,050	5,316
Long-term loan	—	3,000
Common stock	6,900	6,900
Retained earnings	1,950	2,670
Total liabilities and shareholders' equity	$15,900	$17,886

LUNDHOLM COMPANY
Income Statement
Month Ended July 31

Revenue		$5,700
Operating expenses:		
Cost of goods sold	$2,700	
Salaries and wages	1,050	
Rent	300	
Depreciation	225	
Total operating expenses		4,275
Operating income		1,425
Interest expense		24
Income before taxes		1,401
Income taxes		561
Net income		$ 840

LUNDHOLM COMPANY
Statement of Cash Flows
Month Ended July 31

Operating activities:	
Net income	$ 840
Adjustments:	
Depreciation	225
Increase in accounts receivable	(450)
Decrease in inventory	900
Increase in prepaid rent	(600)
Increase in accounts payable	150
Decrease in salaries and wages payable	(45)
Increase in taxes payable	561
Total adjustments	741
Cash flow from operating activities	1,581
Investing activities:	
Proceeds from disposal of fixtures and equipment	15
Purchases of fixtures and equipment	(1,200)
Cash flow used for investing activities	(1,185)
Financing activities:	
Loan repayment	(2,400)
Proceeds from new loan	3,000
Dividends paid to shareholders	(120)
Cash flow from financing activities	480
Net increase in cash	876
Cash balance, July 1	900
Cash balance, July 31	$1,776

REQUIRED

a. Set up T-accounts and enter beginning and ending balances for each account in Lundholm Company's balance sheet.

b. Provide a set of *summary journal entries* for July that would produce the financial statements presented above. For simplicity, you may assume that all of Lundholm Company's sales are made on account and that all of its purchases are made on account. One such entry is provided as an example.

(1)	Accounts receivable (+A)	5,700	
	Sales revenue (+R, +SE)		5,700

c. Post the journal entries from part *b* to T-accounts and verify ending balances.

LO4-1, 2, 3, 4, 5, 6
Daimler AG
ETR :: DAI

C4-59. Interpreting the Statement of Cash Flows

The statement of cash flows for Daimler AG follows:

DAIMLER AG
Consolidated Statement of Cash Flows
Year Ended December 31, 2020 (€ millions)

Profit before income taxes	€ 6,339
Depreciation and amortization/impairments	8,957
Other noncash expense and income	(836)
Gains (−)/losses (+) on disposals of assets	131
Change in operating assets and liabilities	
Inventories	2,039
Trade receivables	1,339
Trade payables	(299)
Receivables from financial services	2,397
Vehicles on operating leases	1,822
Other operating assets and liabilities	653
Dividends received from equity-method investments	1,783
Income taxes paid	(1,993)
Cash provided by operating activities	22,332
Additions to property, plant, and equipment	(5,741)
Additions to intangible assets	(2,819)
Proceeds from disposals of property, plant, and equipment and intangible assets	365
Investments in shareholdings	(661)
Proceeds from disposals of shareholdings	259
Acquisition of marketable debt securities and similar investments	(3,792)
Proceeds from sales of marketable debt securities and similar investments	5,941
Other	27
Cash used for investing activities	(6,421)
Change in short-term financing liabilities	(3,263)
Additions to long-term financing liabilities	53,713
Repayment of long-term financing liabilities	(59,953)
Dividend paid to shareholders of Daimler AG	(963)
Dividends paid to noncontrolling interests	(282)
Proceeds from issuance of share capital	31
Acquisition of treasury shares	(30)
Cash used for financing activities	(10,747)
Effect of foreign exchange rate changes on cash and cash equivalents	(999)
Net increase in cash and cash equivalents	4,165
Cash and cash equivalents at the beginning of the period	18,883
Cash and cash equivalents at the end of the period	€23,048

REQUIRED

a. Daimler begins its statement of cash flows with before-tax income of €6,339 million, then adds €8,957 million for depreciation and amortization. Why is Daimler adding depreciation and amortization to net income in this computation?

b. Why does Daimler add €131 million of losses on disposals of assets in its indirect method cash flows from operating activities? If these losses are all created by disposals of property, plant, and equipment and intangible assets, what was the book value of the assets Daimler disposed of during fiscal year 2020?

c. Daimler shows a positive €2,039 million for inventories in the statement of cash flows. Does this mean that Daimler paid €2,039 million for inventories in 2020? Explain.

d. Compute Daimler's free cash flow for 2020. How did the company finance its investing activities?

e. Daimler reports a net cash inflow from operating activities of €22,332 million, despite reporting pre-tax income of €6,339 million. What principal activities account for this difference? Does this raise concerns about the health of Daimler AG?

f. Why does Daimler list the "effect of foreign exchange rate changes on cash and cash equivalents" in its statement of cash flows? What does this amount represent?

SOLUTIONS TO REVIEW PROBLEMS

Review 4-1

1. Out/I 2. Out/O 3. Out/O 4. In/F 5. Out/O 6. In/O 7. In/I 8. In/I 9. Out/F 10. In/O

Review 4-2

MUG SHOTS, INC.
Computation of Cash Flow from Operating Activities
For Month Ended December 31

	Net income $3,445	= Sales revenue $31,000	– Cost of goods sold 16,700	– Wage expenses 4,700	– Interest expense 300	– Advertising expense 1,800	– Rent expense 1,500	– Depreciation expense 700	– Income tax expense 1,855
Adjustments: Add depreciation expense								+ 700 Depreciation expense	
Subtract (add) non-operating gains (losses)									
Subtract the change in operating assets (operating investments)		− 2,500 Change in accounts receivable	− 8,300 Change in inventory				− (−1,500) Change in prepaid rent		
Add the change in operating liabilities (operating financing)		+ 500 Change in unearned revenue	+ 1,000 Change in accounts payable	+ 2,200 Change in wages payable	+ 300 Change in interest payable				+ 1,855 Change in income tax payable
	$700 Cash from operations	= $29,000 Receipts from customers	– 24,000 Payments for merchandise	– 2,500 Payments for wages	– 0 Payments for interest	– 1,800 Payments for advertising	– 0 Payments for rent	– 0	– 0 Payments for income tax

Review 4-3

MUG SHOTS, INC.
Cash Flow from Operating Activities—Indirect Method

Net income		$3,445
Adjustments:		
Add back depreciation expense	$ 700	
Subtract changes in:		
Accounts receivable	(2,500)	
Inventory	(8,300)	
Prepaid rent..	1,500	
Add changes in:		
Unearned revenue....................................	500	
Accounts payable	1,000	
Wages payable	2,200	
Interest payable....................................	300	
Income tax payable	1,855	
Total adjustments		(2,745)
Cash flow from operating activities		$ 700

Review 4-4

MUG SHOTS, INC. Statement of Cash Flows For Month Ended December 31		
Cash flow from operating activities		
Net income	$ 3,445	
Add back depreciation	700	
Subtract changes in:		
Accounts receivable	(2,500)	
Inventory	(8,300)	
Prepaid rent	1,500	
Add changes in:		
Accounts payable	1,000	
Unearned revenue	500	
Income tax payable	1,855	
Wages payable	2,200	
Interest payable	300	
Net cash provided by operating activities		$700
Cash flow from investing activities		
Purchase of equipment	(12,000)	
Net cash used for investing activities		(12,000)
Cash flow from financing activities		
Bank loan	18,000	
Payment of dividend	(1,000)	
Net cash provided by financing activities		17,000
Net cash increase		5,700
Cash, beginning of period		5,000
Cash, end of period		$10,700

Review 4-5

There are three entries that affected the balance sheet accounts of Property, Plant, and Equipment at cost and Accumulated Depreciation. We know some of the amounts involved, but not all. Let P be the proceeds on the sale of used equipment, let A be the cash spent to acquire new property, plant, and equipment, and let D be the year's depreciation expense. Here are the entries:

a. Disposal—use T-account or FSET

DR Cash (+A)	P	
DR Accumulated depreciation (−XA, +A)	60,000	
CR Property, plant, and equipment at cost (−A)		80,000
CR Gain on equipment disposal (+R, +SE)		35,000

Or

Transaction	Cash Assets	+	Noncash Assets	−	Contra Assets	=	Liabil-ities	+	Contrib. Capital	+	Earned Capital	Revenues	−	Expenses	=	Net Income
	P Cash		−80,000 PPE at Cost	−	−60,000 Accum Dep'n	=					+35,000 Retained Earnings	+35,000 Gain on Equipment Disposal	−		=	+35,000

(Balance Sheet: Cash Assets through Earned Capital; Income Statement: Revenues through Net Income)

The value of P must be $55,000 because Jack's Snacks reported a gain of $35,000 on selling an asset with book value of $20,000 (= $80,000 − $60,000). The company would report an inflow of cash of $55,000 in the investing section of the statement of cash flows.

b. Acquisition—use T-account or FSET

DR Property, plant, and equipment at cost (+A)	A	
CR Cash (−A)		A

Or

Transaction	Cash Assets	+	Noncash Assets	−	Contra Assets	=	Liabil-ities	+	Contrib. Capital	+	Earned Capital	Revenues	−	Expenses	=	Net Income
	−A Cash		+A PPE at Cost	−		=							−		=	

We can determine the cost of acquired assets by looking at the account for Property, Plant, and Equipment at Cost.

+ Property, Plant, and Equipment at Cost (A)			−
Beg. bal.	600,000		
Purchases	A	80,000	Disposal
End. bal.	670,000		

Or

Transaction	Cash Assets	+	Noncash Assets	−	Contra Assets	=	Liabil-ities	+	Contrib. Capital	+	Earned Capital	Revenues	−	Expenses	=	Net Income
Beg. Bal.			600,000 PPE, at cost													
Disposal	+55,000 Cash		−80,000 PPE, at Cost	−	−60,000 Accum Dep'n	=					+35,000 Retained Earnings	+35,000 Gain on Equipment Disposal	−		=	+35,000
Purchase	−A Cash		+A PPE, at Cost	−		=							−		=	
End. Bal.			670,000 PPE, at Cost													

The value of A, i.e., the amount spent on acquiring PPE, must have been $150,000. The company would report an outflow of cash of $150,000 in the investing section of the statement of cash flows.

c. Depreciation expense—use T-account or FSET

DR Depreciation expense (+E, −SE)	D	
CR Accumulated depreciation (+XA, −A)		D

Or

Transaction	Cash Assets	+	Noncash Assets	−	Contra Assets	=	Liabil-ities	+	Contrib. Capital	+	Earned Capital	Revenues	−	Expenses	=	Net Income
				−	+D Accum Dep'n	=					−D Retained Earnings		−	+D Dep'n Expense	=	−D

We can determine the depreciation expense by looking at the T-account or FSET column for the Accumulated Depreciation contra-asset.

− Accumulated Depreciation (XA)			+
		140,000	Beg. bal.
Disposal	60,000	D	Deprec. Exp.
		150,000	End. bal.

Or

	Balance Sheet							Income Statement				
Transaction	Cash Assets +	Noncash Assets −	Contra Assets	=	Liabilities +	Contrib. Capital +	Earned Capital	Revenues −	Expenses	=	Net Income
Beg. Bal.			140,000 Accum Dep'n								
Disposal	+55,000 Cash	−80,000 PPE, at Cost	− −60,000 Accum Dep'n	=			+35,000 Retained Earnings	+35,000 Gain on Equipment Disposal	−	=	+35,000
Dep'n expense			− +D Accum Dep'n	=			−D Retained Earnings		− +D Dep'n Expense	=	−D
End. Bal.			150,000 Accum Dep'n								

The depreciation expense for the year, D, must have been $70,000 because the contra-asset increased by $10,000 even though the disposal decreased it by $60,000.

d. The acquisition of property, plant, and equipment through the issuance of stock would be included in the disclosure notes of the company as a noncash transaction. Neither the investing nor financing sections of the statement of cash flows would be affected by the transaction.

Review 4-6

1. We assume that One World Café's notes payable are classified as current liabilities. If so, current liabilities are $41,000 ($27,000 + $6,000 + $3,000 + $5,000) in 2021 and $21,000 ($14,000 + $2,500 + $4,500) in 2020.
   $44,000 / [($41,000 + $21,000)/2] = 1.42
   One World Café is generating cash flows from operations in excess of its current liabilities. Assuming that this continues, it should have no difficulty meeting its obligations.
2. $44,000 / $45,000 = 0.98
   One World Café spent a little more on plant capacity than it generated through operations. However, for a small business, capital expenditures are often irregular. Thus, this ratio is not alarmingly low.
3. $44,000 – ($45,000 – $4,000) = $3,000.

Review 4-7

Cash Flow Spreadsheet for Rocky Road Bicycles, Inc.

	A	B	C	D	E	F	G	H	I	J
1		O, I,				Effect of Change on Cash Flow			No Effect	Total
2		or F?	2021	2020	Change	Operating	Investing	Financing	on Cash	F, G, H, I
3	Assets									
4	Cash		106,000	96,000	10,000					
5										
6	Accounts receivable	O	156,000	224,000	(68,000)	68,000				68,000
7	Inventory	O	752,000	528,000	224,000	(224,000)				(224,000)
8	Prepaid rent	O	68,000	72,000	(4,000)	4,000				4,000
9	Plant assets, net	O, I	1,130,000	872,000	258,000					
10	Depreciation expense					122,000				
10	Plant assets purchased						(420,000)			(258,000)
12	Plant assets sold					(16,000)	56,000			
13										
14	Liabilities									
15	Accounts payable	O	216,000	112,000	104,000	104,000				104,000
16	Wages payable	O	18,000	20,000	(2,000)	(2,000)				(2,000)
17	Income tax payable	O	44,000	36,000	8,000	8,000				8,000
18	Notes payable	F								
19	New borrowing									—
20	Borrowing repayments									
21										
22	Shareholders' Equity									
23	Common stock	F	1,142,000	1,000,000	142,000					
24	New issue of common stock							142,000		142,000
25	Repurchase of common stock									
26	Retained earnings	O, F	792,000	624,000	168,000					
27	Net income					326,000				168,000
28	Dividends							(158,000)		
29										
30	Totals					390,000	(364,000)	(16,000)	—	10,000

$390,000 – $364,000 – $16,000 = $10,000.

ROCKY ROAD BICYCLES, INC.
Statement of Cash Flows
For Year Ended December 31, 2021

Cash flows from operating activities		
Net income	$326,000	
Add (deduct) items to convert net income to cash basis		
Depreciation	122,000	
Gain on sale of plant assets	(16,000)	
Accounts receivable	68,000	
Inventory	(224,000)	
Prepaid rent	4,000	
Accounts payable	104,000	
Wages payable	(2,000)	
Income tax payable	8,000	
Net cash provided by operating activities		$390,000
Cash flows from investing activities		
Purchase of plant assets	(420,000)	
Proceeds from sale of plant assets	56,000	
Net cash used for investing activities		(364,000)
Cash flows from financing activities		
Issuance of common stock	142,000	
Payment of dividends	(158,000)	
Net cash used for financing activities		(16,000)
Net cash increase		10,000
Cash at beginning of year		96,000
Cash at end of year		$106,000

Chapter

5 Analyzing and Interpreting Financial Statements

LEARNING OBJECTIVES

LO5-1 Prepare and analyze common-size financial statements.

LO5-2 Compute and interpret measures of return on investment, including return on equity (ROE), return on assets (ROA), and return on financial leverage (ROFL).

LO5-3 Disaggregate ROA into profitability (profit margin) and efficiency (asset turnover) components.

LO5-4 Compute and interpret measures of liquidity and solvency.

LO5-5 Appendix 5A: Measure and analyze the effect of operating activities on ROE.

LO5-6 Appendix 5B: Prepare financial statement forecasts.

Road Map

LO	Learning Objective | Topics	Page	eLecture	Review	Assignments
LO5-1	Prepare and analyze common-size financial statements.	5-4	e5-1	R5-1	M5-15, M5-16, M5-19, M5-20, E5-35
LO5-2	Compute and interpret measures of return on investment, including return on equity (ROE), return on assets (ROA), and return on financial leverage (ROFL).	5-8	e5-2	R5-2	M5-14, M5-17, M5-21, M5-22, E5-25, E5-26, E5-27, E5-28, E29, E5-30, E5-31, E5-34, P5-36, P5-38, P5-41, C5-49, DA5-1, DA5-5
LO5-3	Disaggregate ROA into profitability (profit margin) and efficiency (asset turnover) components.	5-11	e5-3	R5-3	M5-14, M5-17, M5-21, M5-22, M5-24, E5-25, E5-27, E5-28, 29, E5-30, E5-31, E5-34, P5-36, P5-38, P5-41, P5-45, P5-46, C5-47, C5-48, C5-49, DA5-4
LO5-4	Compute and interpret measures of liquidity and solvency.	5-15	e5-4	R5-4	M5-18, M5-23, E5-32, E5-33, P5-37, P5-39, P5-42, C5-49, DA5-2, DA5-6
LO5-5	Appendix 5A: Measure and analyze the effect of operating activities on ROE.	5-23	e5-5	R5-5	P5-40, P5-43
LO5-6	Appendix 5B: Prepare financial statement forecasts.	5-25	e5-6	R5-6	E5-35, P5-44, DA5-3

PEPSICO
www.pepsico.com

PepsiCo Chief Executive Officer and Chairman of the Board, Ramon Laguarta, has faced a variety of challenges since he became CEO in 2018. The company operates in very competitive markets for beverages (**The Coca-Cola Company**) and for snack foods (**Kellogg Company**, **Nestlé S. A.**, **Snyder's-Lance, Inc.**). Consumer tastes change constantly, and so a company like PepsiCo must adjust to consumer trends with products that meet changing consumer demands. On August 3, 2021, PepsiCo announced the sale of Tropicana, Naked, and other select juice brands to PAI Partners (a private equity firm), resulting in pre-tax cash proceeds of approximately $3.3 billion. Ramon Laguarta stated that this divestiture will "free us to concentrate on our current portfolio of diverse offerings, including growing our portfolio of healthier snacks, zero-calorie beverages, and products like SodaStream, which are focused on being better for people and the planet."

As is the case in most companies, PepsiCo's management employs a number of financial measures to assess the performance and financial condition of its operating units. These measures include ratios related to profitability and asset utilization as well as return on investment. An analysis of these measures affects significant decisions such as the sale of PepsiCo's juice brands. PepsiCo reported that although its juice businesses delivered approximately $3 billion in net revenue in 2020, its operating profit margins for juice businesses were below PepsiCo's overall operating margin in 2020. Now with a significant cash infusion from the sale, PepsiCo is able to invest in other product offerings that have the potential to be more profitable, while meeting customer demands.

This chapter focuses on the analysis of information reported in the financial statements. We discuss a variety of measures that provide insights into a company's performance to answer questions such as: Is it managed efficiently and profitably? Does it use assets efficiently? Is the performance achieved with an optimal amount of debt? We pay especially close attention to measures of return. In Chapter 1, we introduced one such return metric—namely, return on equity (ROE). In this chapter, we review ROE and add another return metric—return on assets (ROA).

ROE and ROA differ by the use of debt financing, or financial leverage. Companies can increase ROE by borrowing money and using these funds to finance investment in operating assets. However, debt financing can increase company risk and, if not used judiciously, can have a detrimental effect on ROE and even lead to financial distress. In the latter part of this chapter, we examine metrics that measure liquidity and solvency that allow us to assess that risk.

In its shift to healthier snacks, PepsiCo formed a joint venture with **Beyond Meat Inc.**, in 2021 in order to develop and produce snack and beverage products made from plant-based proteins. PepsiCo indicated that the joint venture will allow them the ability to create and scale new snack options. These efforts are being made to meet consumer demands for more nutritious product offerings while PepsiCo scales back from more high-sugar product offerings such as juice drinks.

Sources: PepsiCo annual report 2020; PepsiCo press releases, January 2021, August 2021; *reuters.com*, August 2021

CHAPTER ORGANIZATION

Analyzing and Interpreting Financial Statements

Common-Size Statements	Return on Investment	Liquidity and Solvency	Appendices
• Vertical Analysis • Horizontal Analysis	• Return on Equity • Return on Assets • Return on Financial Leverage • Disaggregating ROA into Profit Margin and Asset Turnover	• Short-Term Liquidity: Current Ratio and Quick Ratio • Long-Term Solvency: Debt-to-Equity and Times Interest Earned • Limitations of Ratio Analysis	• Analyzing Core Operating Activities • Preparing Financial Statement Forecasts

INTRODUCTION

Companies prepare financial statements to be used. These statements are used by investors who rely on financial statement information to assess investment risk, forecast income and dividends, and estimate value. They are used by creditors to assess credit risk and monitor outstanding loans for compliance with debt covenants. And, as the PepsiCo example illustrates, they are used by management to evaluate the performance of operating units. **Financial statement analysis** identifies relationships between numbers within the financial statements and trends in these relationships from one period to the next. The goal is to help users such as investors, creditors, and managers interpret the information presented in the financial statements.

Financial statement analysis is all about making comparisons. Accounting information is difficult to interpret when the numbers are viewed in isolation. For example, a company that reports net income of $7 million may have had a good year or a bad year. However, if we know that total sales were $100 million, assets total $90 million, and the previous year's net income was $6 million, we have a better idea about how well the company performed. If we go a step further and compare these numbers to those of a competing company or to an industry average, we begin to make an assessment about the relative quality of management, the prospects for future growth, overall company risk, and the potential to earn sustainable returns.

Assessing the Business Environment

Financial statement analysis cannot be undertaken in a vacuum. A meaningful interpretation of financial information requires an understanding of the business, its operations, and the environment in which it operates. That is, before we begin crunching the numbers, we must consider the broader business context in which the company operates. This approach requires starting with the Management's Discussion and Analysis section of the financial reports and asking questions about the company and its business environment, including:

- *Life cycle*—At what stage in its life is this company? Is it a start-up, experiencing the growing pains that often result from rapid growth? Is it a mature company, reaping the benefits of its competitive advantages? Is it in decline?
- *Outputs*—What products does it sell? Are its products new, established, or dated? Do its products have substitutes? Are its products protected by patents? How complicated are its products to produce?
- *Customers*—Who are its customers? How often do customers purchase the company's products? What demographic trends are likely to have an effect on future sales?
- *Competition*—Who are the company's competitors? How is it positioned in the market relative to its competition? Is it easy for new competitors to enter the market for its products? Are its products differentiated from competitors' products? Does it have any cost advantages over its competitors?

- *Inputs*—Who are the company's suppliers? Are there multiple supply sources? Does the company depend on one (or a few) key supply source creating the potential for high input costs?
- *Labor*—Who are the company's managers? How effective are they? Is the company unionized? Does it depend on a skilled or educated workforce?
- *Technology*—What technology does the company employ to produce its products? Does the company outsource production? What transport systems does the company rely on to deliver its products?
- *Capital*—To what extent does the company rely on public markets to raise needed capital? Has it recently gone public? Does it have expansion plans that require large sums of cash to carry out? Is it planning to acquire another company? Is it in danger of defaulting on its debt?
- *Political*—How does the company interact with the communities, states, and countries in which it operates? What government regulations affect the company's operations? Are any proposed regulations likely to have a significant impact on the company?

These are just a few of the questions that we should ask before we begin analyzing a company's financial statements. Ultimately, the answers will help us place our numerical analysis in the proper context so that we can effectively interpret the accounting numbers.

In this chapter, we introduce the tools that are used to analyze and interpret financial statements. These tools include common-size financial statements that are used in vertical and horizontal analysis and ratios that measure return on investment and help to assess liquidity and solvency.

VERTICAL AND HORIZONTAL ANALYSIS

LO5-1
Prepare and analyze common-size financial statements.

eLecture MBC

Companies come in all sizes, a fact that presents difficulties when making comparisons between firms and over time. **Vertical analysis** is a method that attempts to overcome this obstacle by restating financial statement information in ratio (or percentage) form. Specifically, it is common to express components of the income statement as a percent of net sales, and balance sheet items as a percent of total assets. This restatement is often referred to as **common-size financial statements**, and it facilitates comparisons across companies of different sizes as well as comparisons of accounts within a set of financial statements.

Exhibit 5.1 presents PepsiCo's summarized comparative balance sheets for 2020 and 2019. Next to the comparative balance sheets are common-size balance sheets for the same two years. Vertical analysis helps us interpret the composition of the balance sheet. For example, as of the end of 2020, 24.7% of PepsiCo's assets were current assets and 23.0% were property, plant, and equipment. Intangible assets made up a greater share of the company's total assets. In addition, 85.4% of PepsiCo's total assets were financed with liabilities—up from 81.1% in 2019. Long-term debt obligations were 43.4% of total assets in 2020, but as recently as 2014, long-term liabilities were 33.8% of total assets. This significant change in liabilities can be attributed, in part, to the historically low interest rates of the recent past. Financial statement analysts should be aware of changes that produce significant changes in financial statement relationships. It is not uncommon for companies to use lower-cost debt financing to finance expansion, especially if low stock prices discourage management from issuing common stock. However, increasing debt levels are a concern if profits and cash flows are not growing fast enough to cover the rising interest and principal payments.

In **Exhibit 5.2**, we present PepsiCo's summarized comparative income statements for 2020 and 2019, along with common-size income statements for the same years. Vertical analysis reveals that cost of sales is 45.2% of net revenue, up from 44.9% in 2019. Selling, general, and administrative expenses increased as a percentage of revenue compared to the year before—40.5% versus 39.8%. An increase in selling, general, and administrative expenses could be due to higher marketing and advertising costs, supply chain or distribution improvements, or increased management costs. We also need to recognize the potential higher operating costs that may have been caused by the COVID-19 pandemic in 2020.

EXHIBIT 5.1 PepsiCo Comparative Balance Sheets

PEPSICO, INC.
Balance Sheets and Common-Size Balance Sheets
December 30, 2020 and December 31, 2019

	As Reported ($ millions)		As a Percentage of Total Assets	
	2020	**2019**	**2020**	**2019**
Assets				
Current assets				
Cash and cash equivalents	$ 8,185	$ 5,509	8.8%	7.0%
Short-term investments	1,366	229	1.5%	0.3%
Accounts and notes receivable, net	8,404	7,822	9.0%	10.0%
Inventories	4,172	3,338	4.5%	4.2%
Prepaid expenses and other current assets	874	747	0.9%	1.0%
Total current assets	23,001	17,645	24.7%	22.5%
Property, plant, and equipment, net	21,369	19,305	23.0%	24.6%
Amortizable intangible assets, net	1,703	1,433	1.8%	1.8%
Goodwill	18,757	15,501	20.2%	19 .7%
Other indefinite-lived intangible assets	17,612	14,610	19.0%	18.6%
Investments in noncontrolled affiliates	2,792	2,683	3.0%	3.4%
Deferred income taxes	4,372	4,359	4.7%	5.5%
Other assets	3,312	3,011	3.6%	3.8%
Total assets	$92,918	$78,547	100.0%	100.0%
Liabilities and equity				
Current liabilities				
Short-term debt obligations	$ 3,780	$ 2,920	4.1%	3.7%
Accounts payable and other current liabilities	19,592	17,541	21.1%	22.3%
Total current liabilities	23,372	20,461	25.2%	26.0%
Long-term debt obligations	40,370	29,148	43.4%	37.1%
Deferred income taxes	4,284	4,091	4.6%	5.2%
Other liabilities	11,340	9,979	12.2%	12.7%
Total liabilities	79,366	63,679	85.4%	81.1%
Total equity	13,552	14,868	14.6%	18.9%
Total liabilities and equity	$92,918	$78,547	100.0%	100.0%

Note: Percentages are rounded amounts, and thus, they may not exactly sum to totals and subtotals.

EXHIBIT 5.2 PepsiCo Comparative Income Statements

PEPSICO, INC.
Income Statements and Common-Size Income Statements
Fiscal Years Ended December 30, 2020 and December 31, 2019

	As Reported ($ millions)		As a Percentage of Net Revenue	
	2020	**2019**	**2020**	**2019**
Net revenue	$70,372	$67,161	100.0%	100.0%
Cost of sales	31,797	30,132	45.2%	44.9%
Gross profit	38,575	37,029	54.8%	55.1%
Selling, general, and administrative expenses	28,495	26,738	40.5%	39.8%
Operating profit	10,080	10,291	14.3%	15.3%
Other pension and retiree medical benefits expense	117	(44)	0.2%	(0.1)%
Net interest expense and other	(1,128)	(935)	(1.6)%	(1.4)%
Income before income taxes	9,069	9,312	12.9%	13.8%
Provision for taxes	1,894	1,959	2.7%	2.9%
Net income	$ 7,175	$ 7,353	10.2%	10.9%

Horizontal analysis examines changes in financial data across time. Comparing data across two or more consecutive periods is helpful in analyzing company performance and in predicting future performance. **Exhibit 5.3** presents a horizontal analysis of a few selected items from PepsiCo's income statement—revenue, operating income, and net income. The dollar amounts reported in each year from 2016 through 2020 are shown for each item along with a percentage change for each item. The amount of the change for a given year is computed by subtracting the amount for the prior year from the amount for the current year. The change is then divided by the reported amount for the prior year to get the percentage change. For example, PepsiCo's percentage change in net revenue was +4.8% in 2020, computed as follows:

$$+4.8\% = \frac{\$70{,}372 \text{ million} - \$67{,}161 \text{ million}}{\$67{,}161 \text{ million}}$$

Exhibit 5.3 highlights some important information in PepsiCo's income statement. The table shows that revenue per year has been increasing for the last four years. Most recently, revenue increased in 2020 by nearly 5% over 2019 reflecting factors like the increase in snack food sales. Operating profit (operating income) has fluctuated over recent years. Part of the decrease in 2020 the company has attributed to the effects of the COVID-19 pandemic for charges such as projections of customer defaults and incremental frontline incentive pay. Interpreting these numbers requires looking into factors that affect the company but are beyond its control, e.g., fluctuations in raw material prices, international currencies, and the pandemic.

EXHIBIT 5.3 Horizontal Analysis of Selected Income Statement Items

PEPSICO, INC.
Revenue, Operating Profit, and Net Income
($ millions and percent changes)

	2020	2019	2018	2017	2016[1]
Revenue	$70,372	$67,161	$64,661	$63,525	$62,799
	4.8%	3.9%	1.8%	1.2%	
Operating profit	$10,080	$10,291	$10,110	$10,276	$ 9,804
	−2.1%	1.8%	−1.6%	4.8%	
Net income	$ 7,175	$ 7,353	$12,559	$ 4,908	$ 6,379
	−2.4%	−41.5%	155.9%	−23.1%	

Horizontal analysis is useful in identifying unusual changes that might not be obvious when looking at the reported numbers alone. At the same time, it is important to look at both the percentage change and the reported dollar amount. If a reported amount is close to $0 in one year, the percentage change will likely be very large the following year, even if the amount reported in that year is small. Similarly, if reported earnings is negative one year and positive the next, the percentage change will be negative even though the earnings increased. Horizontal analysis that is based on a denominator that is negative or zero is not meaningful.

Preparing Common-Size Income Statements and Balance Sheets LO5-1 **Review 5-1**

Following are summarized 2020 and 2019 income statements and balance sheets for The Coca-Cola Company.

GuidedExample MBC

Required

Prepare common-size income statements and balance sheets for Coca-Cola. Comment on any noteworthy relationships that you observe.

continued

[1] One feature of PepsiCo's annual reporting practices is that its fiscal year is 52 weeks long in most years, but every five or six years, it is 53 weeks long. 2016 was a 53-week year, so the percentage increase in 2017's revenues is really a little better than +1.2%.

continued from previous page

THE COCA-COLA COMPANY AND SUBSIDIARIES
Consolidated Statements of Income
($ millions)

Year Ended December 31	2020	2019
Net operating revenues	$33,014	$37,266
Cost of goods sold	13,433	14,619
Gross profit	19,581	22,647
Selling, general, and administrative expenses	9,731	12,103
Other operating charges	853	458
Operating income	8,997	10,086
Interest income	370	563
Interest expense	1,437	946
Equity income (loss)—net	978	1,049
Other income (loss)—net	841	34
Income before taxes	9,749	10,786
Income taxes	1,981	1,801
Consolidated net income	$ 7,768	$ 8,985

THE COCA-COLA COMPANY AND SUBSIDIARIES
Consolidated Balance Sheets
($ millions)

December 31	2020	2019
Assets		
Current assets		
Cash and cash equivalents	$ 6,795	$ 6,480
Short-term investments	1,771	1,467
Marketable securities	2,348	3,228
Trade accounts receivable, net	3,144	3,971
Inventories	3,266	3,379
Prepaid expenses and other assets	1,916	1,886
Total current assets	19,240	20,411
Equity method investments	19,273	19,025
Other investments	812	854
Other assets	6,184	6,075
Deferred income tax assets	2,460	2,412
Property, plant, and equipment, net	10,777	10,838
Trademarks with indefinite lives	10,395	9,266
Goodwill	17,506	16,764
Other intangible assets	649	736
Total assets	$87,296	$86,381
Liabilities and equity		
Current liabilities		
Accounts payable and accrued expenses	$11,145	$11,312
Loans and notes payable	2,183	10,994
Current maturities of long-term debt	485	4,253
Accrued income taxes	788	414
Total current liabilities	14,601	26,973
Long-term debt	40,125	27,516
Other liabilities	9,453	8,510
Deferred income tax liabilities	1,833	2,284
Total liabilities	66,012	65,283
Total equity	21,284	21,098
Total liabilities and equity	$87,296	$86,381

Solution on p. 5-49.

RETURN ON INVESTMENT

Common-size financial statements and percentage changes are useful, but there is a limit to what we can learn from this type of analysis. While vertical and horizontal analysis focuses on relationships within a particular financial statement—either the income statement or the balance sheet—many of the questions that we might ask about a company can be answered only by comparing amounts between statements. For example, return on investment measures are ratios that divide some measure of performance—typically reported in the income statement—by the average amount of investment as reported in the balance sheet.

LO5-2
Compute and interpret measures of return on investment, including return on equity (ROE), return on assets (ROA), and return on financial leverage (ROFL).

eLecture
MBC

In this section, we discuss three important return metrics—return on equity (ROE), return on assets (ROA), and return on financial leverage (ROFL). We also examine return on investment in detail by disaggregating ROA into performance drivers that capture profitability and efficiency.

Return on Equity (ROE)

Return on equity (ROE) is the primary summary measure of company performance and is defined as:

$$\text{ROE} = \frac{\text{Net income}}{\text{Average stockholders' equity}}$$

ROE relates net income to the average investment by shareholders as measured by total stockholders' equity from the balance sheet. The net income number in the numerator measures the performance of the firm for a specific period (typically a fiscal year). Therefore, in order to accurately capture the return for that period, we use the average level of stockholders' equity for the same period as the denominator. The average is computed by adding the beginning and ending stockholders' equity balances and then dividing by two.

FYI Whenever we compare an income statement amount with a balance sheet amount, the balance sheet amount should be the *average* balance for the period (beginning balance plus ending balance divided by 2) rather than the year-end balance.

ROE	2020	2019	2018	2017	2016
PepsiCo	50.5%	49.9%	98.2%	44.3%	54.9%

PepsiCo's ROE was 50.5% in 2020. This return is computed as $7,175 million/[($13,552 million + $14,868 million)/2]. PepsiCo's ROE has been consistently high over the past 5 years, ranging from a low of 44.3% in 2017 to a high of 98.2% in 2018. The 98.2% return in 2018 is something of an anomaly due to the effects of the Tax Cuts and Jobs Act of 2017 (examined in Chapter 10).

ROE is widely used by analysts, investors, and managers as a key overall measure of company performance. Billionaire investor Warren Buffett highlights ROE as part of his acquisition criteria: "businesses earning good returns on equity while employing little or no debt." Companies can use debt to increase their return on equity, but too much debt increases risk because the failure to make required debt payments is likely to yield many legal consequences, including bankruptcy. This is one reason why many analysts focus on returns generated by assets used in operations, rather than on returns produced by increasing the amount of debt financing. Next, we discuss each of these sources of return in more detail.

Return on Assets (ROA)

ROE measures the return on the investment made by the firm's stockholders. In contrast, **return on assets (ROA)** measures the return earned on each dollar that the firm invests in assets. By focusing on the asset side of the balance sheet, ROA captures the returns generated by the firm's operating and investing activities, without regard for how those activities are financed. ROA is defined as:

$$\text{Return on assets (ROA)} = \frac{\text{Earnings without interest expense (EWI)}}{\text{Average total assets}}$$

Average total assets is computed in much the same way that we calculated average stockholders' equity for ROE. We add the beginning and ending balances in total assets and then divide by two. The numerator in this ratio, **earnings without interest expense (EWI)**, is defined to be:

Earnings without interest expense (EWI) =

Net income + [Interest expense × (1 – Statutory tax rate)]

EWI measures the income generated by the firm before taking into account any of its financing costs. Interest costs should be excluded from the ROA calculation so that return is measured without the effect of debt financing. Because interest expense is subtracted when net income is calculated, it must be added back to net income when we compute EWI. However, interest expense is tax deductible and, as such, it reduces the firm's tax obligation. That is, interest expense produces a tax *savings* for the firm. This tax savings is equal to the interest expense times the statutory tax rate. In order to eliminate the full effect of interest cost on EWI, we must add back the interest expense *net* of the resulting tax savings. To accomplish this, we multiply the interest expense by (1 – the statutory tax rate). This amount is then added to net income to get EWI. Thus, we can compute ROA as follows:

$$\textbf{Return on assets (ROA)} = \frac{\textbf{Net income + [Interest expense} \times \textbf{(1 – Statutory tax rate)]}}{\textbf{(Beginning total assets + Ending total assets)/2}}$$

ROA is an important measure of how well a company's management has utilized assets to earn a profit. If ROA is high, the firm can pay its interest costs to creditors and still have sufficient resources left over to distribute to stockholders as a dividend or to reinvest in the firm.

PepsiCo's ROA was 9.5% in 2020. PepsiCo's return is computed as follows:[2]

$$\text{ROA} = \frac{\$7{,}175 \text{ million} + [\$1{,}252 \text{ million} \times (1 - 0.25)]}{(\$92{,}918 \text{ million} + \$78{,}547 \text{ million})/2} = 9.5\%$$

While PepsiCo reports "Net interest expense and other" on its consolidated statement of income of $1,128 million, the company reports interest expense for 2020 of $1,252 million (a component of this $1,128 million amount) in its 10-K. PepsiCo's return on assets fluctuated from a high of 17.4% in 2018 to a low of 7.4% in 2017, although the 2017 and 2018 figures are affected by the one-time effects of the Tax Cuts and Jobs Act (TCJA) in late 2017.

Return on Financial Leverage (ROFL)

The principal difference between ROE and ROA is the effect that liabilities (including debt financing) have on the return measure. ROA is calculated so that it is independent of financing costs, whereas ROE is computed net of the cost of debt financing. **Financial leverage** refers to the effect that liabilities (including debt financing) have on ROE. A firm's management can increase the return to shareholders (ROE) by effectively using financial leverage. On the other hand, too much financial leverage can be risky. To help gauge the effect that financial leverage has on a firm, the **return on financial leverage (ROFL)** is defined as:

ROFL = ROE – ROA

This return metric captures the amount of ROE that can be attributed to financial leverage. In the case of PepsiCo, the 2020 ROFL is 41.0% (50.5% – 9.5%). Over the past 5 years, financial leverage has had a significant impact on PepsiCo's ROE performance, as illustrated in **Exhibit 5.4**. The height of each bar in the chart reflects PepsiCo's ROE for that year. Each bar is split into two components—ROA for the same year (the lower portion of each bar) and ROFL (the upper portion of each bar).

[2] The statutory federal tax rate for corporations has been 35% (per U.S. tax code) since the early 1990s. Beginning in 2018, the federal income tax rate for corporations was reduced to 21%, with the transition producing many one-time tax expense effects as described above for PepsiCo. To make the mental math simpler, we will use income tax rate approximations of 35% in years prior to 2018 and 25% for years 2018 and thereafter. Most companies provide components of income tax expense as percentages in the income tax note disclosure that may be used for more detailed analysis.

EXHIBIT 5.4 Contribution of Financial Leverage to PepsiCo's ROE

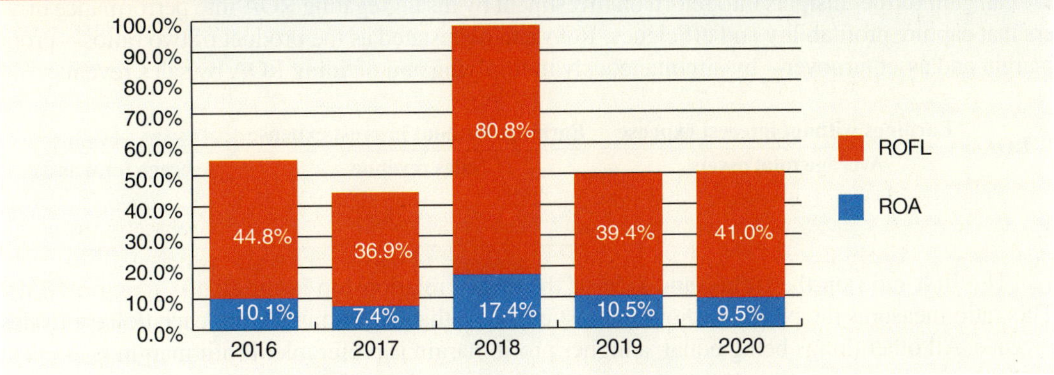

In **Exhibit 5.5**, we compare the ROE, ROA, and ROFL of PepsiCo to that of several other companies featured in this text. As in **Exhibit 5.4**, the height of each bar represents the company's ROE for 2020. The lower portion of each bar is the company's ROA, and the upper portion reflects the contribution of financial leverage (ROFL). The chart suggests that PepsiCo's ROE is influenced to a greater extent by financial leverage than the other companies.

EXHIBIT 5.5 ROE, ROA, and ROFL for PepsiCo and Comparison Companies*

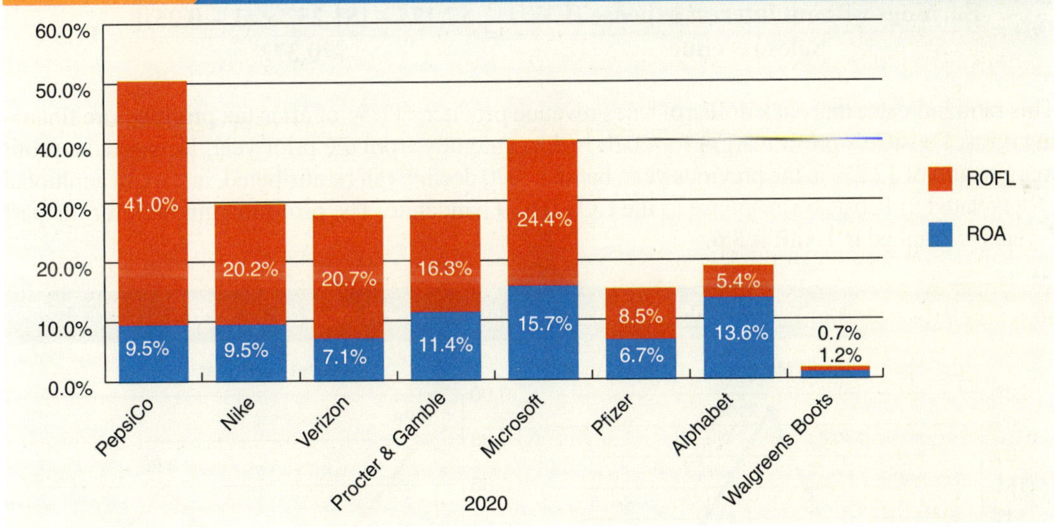

*These companies do not have identical fiscal year-ends; 2020 balance sheets are dated from May 31 to December 31 of 2020.

Later in this chapter, we examine the effects of financial leverage more closely and discuss several ratios that measure liquidity and solvency. These ratios help us to evaluate the risk associated with using financial leverage.

Calculating ROE, ROA, and ROFL LO5-2 **Review 5-2**

Required

Refer to the financial statements for the Coca-Cola Company presented in Review 5-1. Calculate Coca-Cola's ROE, ROA, and ROFL for 2020. Assume a 25% statutory tax rate for this year.

GuidedExample MBC

Solution on p. 5-50.

Disaggregating ROA

LO5-3 Disaggregate ROA into profitability (profit margin) and efficiency (asset turnover) components.

eLecture MBC

We can gain further insights into return on investment by disaggregating ROA into performance drivers that capture profitability and efficiency. ROA can be restated as the product of two ratios—profit margin and asset turnover—by simultaneously multiplying and dividing ROA by sales revenue:

$$\text{ROA} = \frac{\textbf{Earnings without interest expense}}{\textbf{Average total assets}} = \underbrace{\frac{\textbf{Earnings without interest expense}}{\textbf{Sales revenue}}}_{\text{Profit Margin}} \times \underbrace{\frac{\textbf{Sales revenue}}{\textbf{Average total assets}}}_{\text{Asset Turnover}}$$

The first ratio on the right-hand side of the above relationship is the **profit margin (PM)**. This ratio measures the profit, without interest expense, that is generated from each dollar of sales revenue. All other things being equal, a higher profit margin is preferable. Profit margin is affected by the level of gross profit that the company earns on its sales (sales revenue minus cost of goods sold), which depends on product prices and the cost of manufacturing or purchasing its product. It is also affected by operating expenses that are required to support sales of products or services. These include wages and salaries, marketing, research and development, as well as depreciation and other **capacity costs**. Finally, profit margin is affected by the level of competition, which affects product pricing, and by the company's operating strategy, which affects operating costs, especially discretionary costs such as advertising and research and development.

PepsiCo's profit margin ratio was 11.5% in 2020, computed as follows ($ millions):

$$\textbf{Profit margin (PM)} = \frac{\textbf{Earnings without interest expense (EWI)}}{\textbf{Sales revenue}} = \frac{\$7{,}175 + [\$1{,}252 \times (1 - 0.25)]}{\$70{,}372} = 11.5\%$$

This ratio indicates that each dollar of sales revenue produces 11.5¢ of after-tax profit before financing costs. PepsiCo's profit margin for 2020 is down slightly from the prior year. It reported a profit margin ratio of 12.2% in the previous year, but the 2020 decline can be attributed, in part, to additional costs related to PepsiCo's response to the COVID-19 pandemic. The profit margin ratio for the past 5 years is graphed in **Exhibit 5.6**.

EXHIBIT 5.6 PepsiCo's Profit Margin and Asset Turnover Ratios, 2016–2020

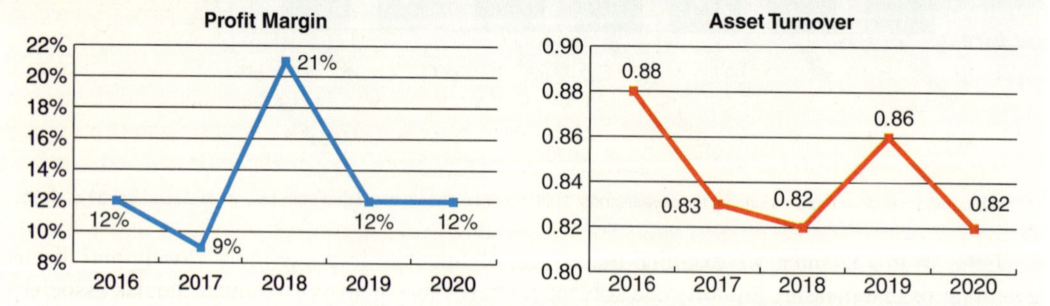

The **asset turnover (AT)** ratio reveals insights into a company's productivity and efficiency. This metric measures the level of sales generated by each dollar that a company invests in assets. A high asset turnover ratio suggests that assets are being used efficiently so, all other things being equal, a high asset turnover ratio is preferable. The ratio is affected by inventory management practices, credit policies, and most of all, the technology employed to produce a company's products or deliver its services.

The asset turnover ratio can be improved by increasing the level of sales for a given level of assets or by efficiently managing assets. For many companies, efficiently managing working capital—primarily inventories and receivables—is the easiest way to limit investment in assets and increase turnover. On the other hand, it is usually more difficult to increase asset turnover by managing investment in long-term assets. Capital intensive companies, such as those in the telecommunications or energy production industries, tend to have lower asset turnover ratios (often less than 1.0) because the production technology employed by these firms requires a large investment in property, plant, and equipment. Retail companies, on the other hand, tend to have a relatively small investment in plant assets. As a result, they tend to have higher asset turnover ratios (sometimes over 3.0).[3]

PepsiCo's asset turnover ratio in 2020 is computed as follows ($ millions):

$$\textbf{Asset turnover (AT)} = \frac{\textbf{Sales revenue}}{\textbf{Average total assets}} = \frac{\$70{,}372}{(\$92{,}918 + \$78{,}547)/2} = 0.821$$

The ratio indicates that each dollar of assets generates 82.1¢ in sales revenue each year. Over the past five years, PepsiCo's asset turnover has ranged from 0.821, both in 2020 and 2017, to 0.877 in 2016, as illustrated by the graphic in **Exhibit 5.6**. The 2020 decline in AT results from the larger increase in assets over the prior year relative to the increase in sales revenue over the prior year.

YOU MAKE THE CALL

You are the Entrepreneur You are analyzing the performance of your start-up company. Your analysis of ROA reveals the following (industry benchmarks in parentheses): ROA is 16% (10%), PM is 18% (17%), and AT is 0.89 (0.59). What interpretations do you draw that are useful for managing your company? [Answer, page 5-32.]

Trade-Off Between Profit Margin and Asset Turnover ROA is the product of profit margin and asset turnover. By decomposing ROA in this way, we can identify the source of PepsiCo's decline in ROA between 2019 and 2020:

	ROA	=	Profit Margin	×	Asset Turnover
2019:	10.5%	=	12.22%	×	0.860
2020:	9.5%	=	11.53%	×	0.821

Between 2019 and 2020, PepsiCo's profit margin declined from 12.22% to 11.53% while, at the same time, asset turnover declined from 0.860 to 0.821. Both ROA and AT decreased in 2020 relative to 2019. These changes are most likely due to the impact of the pandemic. It will be interesting to watch how PepsiCo responds in 2021 and beyond.

Basic economics tells us that any successful business must earn an acceptable return on investment if it wants to attract capital from investors and survive. Yet, there are an infinite number of combinations of asset turnover and profit margin that will yield a given ROA. The trade-off between profit margin and asset turnover is heavily influenced by a company's business model. A company can attempt to increase its ROA by targeting higher profit margins or by increasing its asset turnover. To an extent, this trade-off is the result of strategic decisions made by management. However, to a greater extent, the relative mix of margin and turnover is dictated by the industry in which the company operates. As mentioned earlier, one determinant of a company's profit margin is its competitive environment, while asset turnover is heavily influenced by the production technology employed. For this reason, companies in the same industry tend to exhibit similar combinations of margin and turnover while comparisons between industries can exhibit much greater variation. That is, within a given industry, differences in the mix of profit margin and asset turnover often reflect the specific strategy employed by each individual firm, while variations between industries are caused by differences in the competitive environment and production technology of each industry.

This trade-off is illustrated in **Exhibit 5.7**. The solid curved line represents the median ROA for all companies over the period from 2018–2020. Each point along that curve represents a combination of asset turnover and profit margin that yields the average ROA. Industries that are plotted near the upper-left side of the chart are those that achieve their ROA targets by maintaining a high asset turnover. These industries are often characterized by intense competition and low profit margins. On the other hand, industries in the lower right-hand portion of the chart have lower asset turnover ratios because they typically employ capital-intensive production technologies. At the same time, the competitive environment within these industries allows companies to achieve higher profit margins to offset the lower turnover ratios.

[3] Historically, these ratios have also been affected by leasing, the use of contract manufacturers, and other methods of using assets that do not appear on the balance sheet. The new accounting procedures for leasing are discussed in Chapter 10. As of 2019, leasing is no longer a method for off-balance-sheet financing of assets.

EXHIBIT 5.7 Profit Margin and Turnover Across Industries (2018–2020)

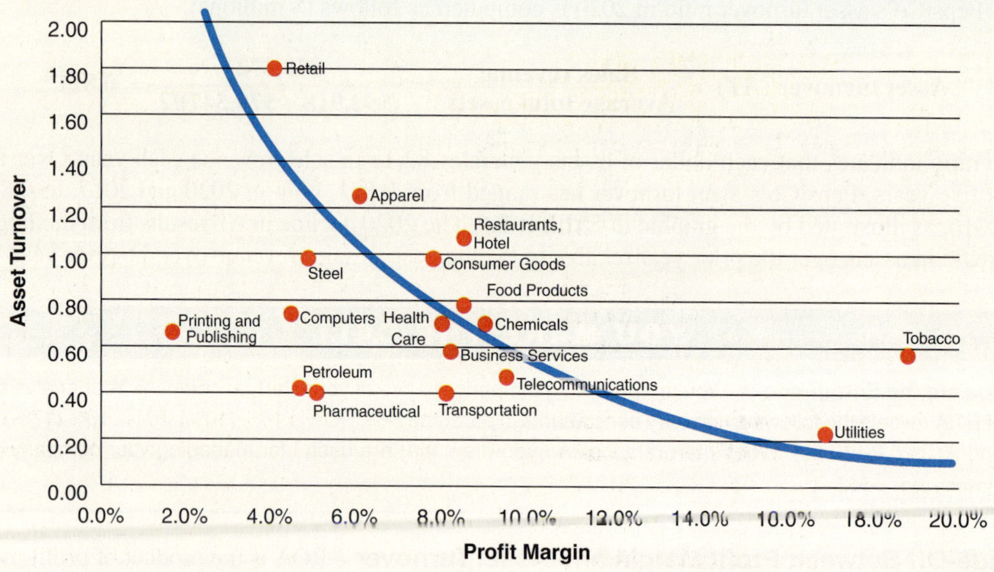

BUSINESS INSIGHT

The DuPont Model Disaggregation of return on equity (ROE) into three components—profitability, turnover, and financial leverage—was initially introduced by the **E.I. DuPont de Nemours and Company** to aid its managers in performance evaluation. DuPont realized that management's focus on profit alone was insufficient because profit can be increased simply by adding investments in low-yielding, but safe, assets. Further, DuPont wanted managers to think like investors and to manage their portfolio of activities using investment principles that allocate scarce investment capital to competing projects based on a goal of maximizing return on investment.

The basic DuPont model disaggregates ROE as the product of three ratios as follows:

$$\text{ROE} = \underbrace{\frac{\text{Net income}}{\text{Sales}}}_{\text{Net Profit Margin}} \times \underbrace{\frac{\text{Sales}}{\text{Average total assets}}}_{\text{Asset Turnover}} \times \underbrace{\frac{\text{Average total assets}}{\text{Average stockholders' equity}}}_{\text{Financial Leverage}}$$

An important limitation of the DuPont model is that net profit margin is measured using net income in the numerator rather than earnings without interest expense (EWI). This means that this measure of profitability is affected by financial leverage—as financial leverage increases, interest expense increases and the net profit margin decreases. As a consequence, the model fails to adequately separate the effects of operating profitability on ROE from the effects of financial leverage. Despite this limitation, the DuPont model is widely used as a simple, straightforward way to disaggregate ROE.

Further Disaggregation of Profit Margin and Asset Turnover While disaggregation of ROA into profit margin and asset turnover yields useful insights into the factors driving company performance, analysts, investors, creditors, and managers often disaggregate these measures even further. The purpose of this analysis is to be more precise about the specific determinants of profitability and efficiency.

To disaggregate profit margin (PM), we examine gross profit on products sold and individual expense accounts that contribute to the total cost of operations. The key ratios include the gross profit margin and expense-to-sales ratios. **Gross profit margin (GPM)** is defined as:

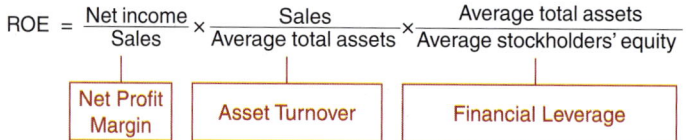

$$\textbf{Gross profit margin (GPM)} = \frac{\textbf{Sales revenue} - \textbf{Cost of goods sold}}{\textbf{Sales revenue}}$$

PepsiCo's GPM is 54.8% ([$70,372 million – $31,797 million]/$70,372 million). That is, just over half (54.8¢) of every sales dollar is gross profit, while slightly less than half (45.2¢) goes to cover the cost of products sold.

Gross profit margin measures the percentage of each sales dollar that is left over after product costs are subtracted. It is easily determined by looking at the common-size income statement. This ratio is discussed in more detail in Chapter 7.

An **expense-to-sales (ETS)** ratio measures the percentage of each sales dollar that goes to cover a specific expense item and is computed by dividing the expense by sales revenue. Expense items that might be examined with ETS ratios include selling, general, and administrative (SG&A) expenses, advertising expense, or research and development (R&D) expense, among others. Which specific ETS ratio is appropriate depends on the company being analyzed. For instance, advertising expense is an important expense item for a consumer products company, such as PepsiCo, while R&D expense is important for an R&D intensive pharmaceutical company, such as **Pfizer**. Analysts study trends in ETS ratios over time in an effort to uncover clues that might explain changes in profit margin and make predictions about future profitability.

PepsiCo's SG&A ETS ratio is computed by dividing selling, general, and administrative expenses by net revenue. The resulting ETS ratio is 40.5% ($28,495 million/$70,372 million). This ratio indicates that 40.5¢ of every sales dollar goes to pay marketing and administrative costs. This ETS ratio is relatively high because this expense item includes PepsiCo's advertising expenditures. Further analysis of SG&A expenses as described in the notes might look for trends in advertising expenses over time or PepsiCo's expenses relative to competitors.

To disaggregate asset turnover (AT), we examine individual asset accounts and compare them to sales or cost of goods sold. We focus on three specific turnover ratios—accounts receivable turnover (ART), inventory turnover (INVT), and property, plant, and equipment turnover (PPET).

Accounts receivable turnover (ART) is defined as follows:

$$\textbf{Accounts receivable turnover (ART)} = \frac{\textbf{Sales revenue}}{\textbf{Average accounts receivable}}$$

ART measures how many times receivables have been turned (collected) during the period. More turns indicate that accounts receivable are being collected more quickly, while low turnover often indicates difficulty with a company's credit policies. PepsiCo's ART is 8.7 times ($70,372 million/[{$8,404 million + $7,822 million}/2]).

A variation on this measure is days-sales-outstanding = 365/ART = 42.0 for PepsiCo. It implies that—on average—PepsiCo waits 42 days to be paid by its customers. ART is discussed in Chapter 6.

Inventory turnover (INVT) is defined as:

$$\textbf{Inventory turnover (INVT)} = \frac{\textbf{Cost of goods sold}}{\textbf{Average inventory}}$$

INVT measures the number of times during a period that total inventory is turned (sold). A high INVT indicates that inventory is managed efficiently. Retail companies, such as **Walmart** and **Home Depot**, focus a great deal of management attention on maintaining a high INVT ratio. PepsiCo's INVT is 8.5 times ($31,797 million/[{$4,172 million + $3,338 million}/2]). A variation on this measure is days-inventory = 365/INVT = 42.9 for PepsiCo. It implies that—on average—PepsiCo's inventory stays in the company for almost 43 days before it's delivered to a customer and becomes cost of goods sold expense. This ratio is discussed further in Chapter 7.

Property, plant, and equipment turnover (PPET) measures the sales revenue produced for each dollar of investment in PP&E. It is computed as the ratio of sales to average PP&E assets:

$$\textbf{Property, plant, and equipment turnover (PPET)} = \frac{\textbf{Sales revenue}}{\textbf{Average PP\&E}}$$

PPET provides insights into asset utilization and how efficiently a company operates given its production technology. PepsiCo's PPET is 3.5 times ($70,372 million/[{$21,369 million + $19,305 million}/2]). This ratio is revisited in Chapter 8.

In the next section, we examine ratios that focus on liquidity and solvency. These ratios help us evaluate the risk associated with debt financing and weigh the costs and benefits of financial leverage. **Exhibit 5.8** presents a schematic summary of the disaggregation of ROE. It identifies the two primary components of ROE—ROA and ROFL—and highlights the disaggregation of ROA into profit margin and asset turnover, along with the drivers of these ratios. In addition, the link between ROFL and liquidity and solvency analysis is highlighted.

EXHIBIT 5.8 ROE Disaggregation

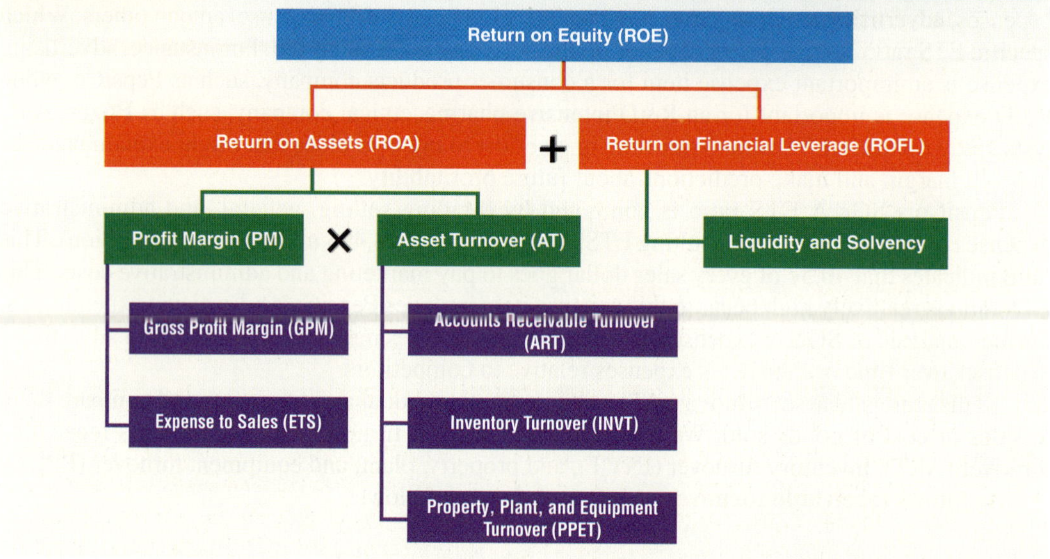

Review 5-3 LO5-3

Disaggregating the Return on Equity Ratio into its Components

GuidedExample MBC

Required

Refer to the financial statements for the Coca-Cola Company presented in Review 5-1.

1. Calculate Coca-Cola's profit margin (PM) and asset turnover (AT) ratios for 2020.
2. Show that ROA = PM × AT using Coca-Cola's financial data.
3. Calculate Coca-Cola's gross profit margin (GPM), accounts receivable turnover (ART), inventory turnover (INVT), and property, plant, and equipment turnover (PPET) ratios for 2020.
4. Evaluate Coca-Cola's ratios in comparison to those of PepsiCo.

Solution on p. 5-50.

LIQUIDITY AND SOLVENCY

LO5-4 Compute and interpret measures of liquidity and solvency.

eLecture MBC

Companies can use debt to increase financial leverage and boost ROE. The increase in ROE due to the use of debt is called *return on financial leverage (ROFL)*. The primary advantage of debt financing is that it is typically less costly than equity financing for two reasons. For the borrower, interest payments to lenders are tax-deductible, so paying $1 in interest reduces pre-tax income by $1 and reduces tax payments by *t*, the statutory tax rate. If the tax rate were 25%, the effective cost of $1 in interest to $(1 – 0.25) = $0.75. In addition, lenders require a lower rate of return than shareholders because they are subject to less risk than shareholders. Interest payments have priority over share dividends. And, in the event a firm fails, creditors collect their investment first, while shareholders receive any residual.

Exhibit 5.9 illustrates a comparison between two companies—one (Company A) is financed with 100% equity and the other (Company B) is financed with 50% debt and 50% equity. Both companies have $1,000 in (average) assets and EWI of $100, producing an ROA of 10% ($100/$1,000). Because Company A does not use liability financing, average equity equals average total assets. Also, it reports no interest expense in its income statement, so net income equals EWI. Therefore, for Company A, ROE = ROA, and its ROFL = 0%.

EXHIBIT 5.9 The Effect of Debt Financing on ROE (ROA > interest rate)

	Company A	Company B
Assets (average)	$1,000	$1,000
EWI	100	100
ROA (EWI/Assets)	10%	10%
Equity (average)	$1,000	$ 500
Debt	0	500
Interest expense (4% of debt)	0	20
Net income (EWI – interest)	100	80
ROE (Net income/equity)	10%	16%
ROFL (ROE – ROA)	0%	6%

In contrast, Company B has $500 of equity financing and $500 of debt financing. It reports interest expense of $20 ($500 × 4%), leaving net income of $80 ($100 – $20). Company B's ROE is 16% ($80/$500), which means that its ROFL is 6% (16% – 10%). Company B has made effective use of debt financing to increase its ROE. As long as a company's ROA is greater than its cost of debt, its ROFL will be positive.[4]

We might further ask: If a higher ROE is desirable, why don't companies use as much debt financing as possible? The answer is that there are risks associated with debt financing. As the amount of debt in a company's balance sheet increases, so does the burden of interest costs on income and debt payments on cash flows. In the best of times, financial leverage increases returns to stockholders (ROE). In contrast, when earnings are depressed, financial leverage has the effect of making a bad year even worse. In the worst case, too much debt can lead to financial distress and even bankruptcy.

To illustrate how debt financing can reduce shareholder returns, **Exhibit 5.10** compares Company A and Company B in a year when reported profits are lower than in the previous example. Both companies have $1,000 in (average) assets, and both report EWI of $30, producing an ROA of 3% ($30/$1,000). Company A does not use liability financing, so its ROE = 3%, and its ROFL = 0%. Because Company B has $500 of equity and $500 of debt, it reports interest expense of $20 ($500 × 4%), leaving net income of $10 ($30 – $20). Company B's ROE is 2% ($10/$500), which means that its ROFL is –1% (2% – 3%). That is, for Company B, the use of financial leverage has a negative effect on ROE. As this example illustrates, whenever ROA is less than the interest rate on the debt, debt financing reduces the return to shareholders.

EXHIBIT 5.10 The Effect of Debt Financing on ROE (ROA < interest rate)

	Company A	Company B
Assets (average)	$1,000	$1,000
EWI	30	30
ROA (EWI/Assets)	3%	3%
Equity (average)	$1,000	$ 500
Debt	0	500
Interest expense (4% of debt)	0	20
Net income (EWI – interest)	30	10
ROE (Net income/equity)	3%	2%
ROFL (ROE – ROA)	0%	–1%

As a general rule, shareholders benefit from increased use of debt financing provided that the assets financed with the debt earn a return that exceeds the cost of the debt. However, increasing levels of debt result in successively higher interest rates charged by creditors. At some point, the cost of debt exceeds the return on assets that a company can expect from the debt financing. Thereafter, further debt financing does not make economic sense. The market, in essence, places a limit on the amount that a company can borrow.

In addition, creditors usually require a company to execute a loan agreement that places various restrictions on its operating activities. These restrictions, called **covenants**, help safeguard debtholders in the face of increased risk. This occurs because debtholders do not have a voice on the board of directors

[4] The interest cost on debt is tax deductible. Therefore, the relevant cost of debt to use to compare to ROA is the after-tax interest rate.

like stockholders do. These debt covenants impose a "cost" on the company beyond that of the interest rate, and these covenants are more stringent as a company increases its reliance on debt financing.

The median ratio of total liabilities to stockholders' equity, which measures the relative use of debt versus equity in a company's capital structure, is approximately 1.5 for large, publicly traded companies. This means that the typical company relies more on debt financing than on equity. However, the relative use of debt varies considerably across industries as illustrated in **Exhibit 5.11**.

EXHIBIT 5.11 Median Ratio of Liabilities to Equity for Selected Industries (2018–2020)

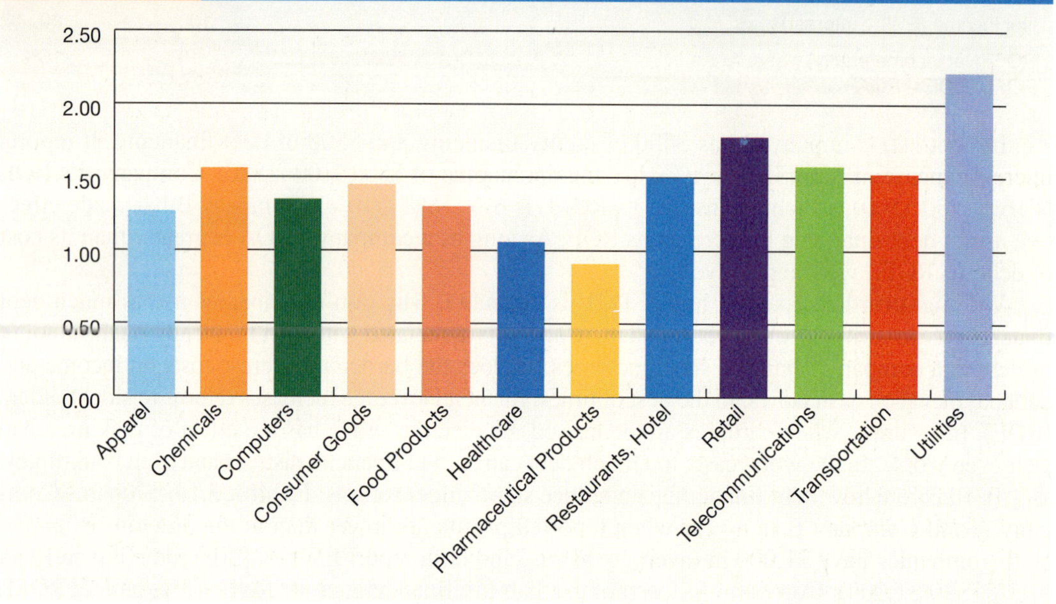

Companies in the utilities industry have relatively high proportions of debt. Because the utilities industry is regulated, profits and cash flows are relatively certain and stable and, as a result, utility companies can support a higher debt level. The chemicals and telecommunications industries also utilize a relatively high proportion of debt. These industries are not regulated, but their heavy investments in property, plant, and equipment require significant long-term debt. At the lower end of debt financing are pharmaceuticals and apparel companies. Historically, these industries have been characterized by relatively uncertain profits and cash flows. In addition, success in these industries depends heavily on intellectual property and human resources devoted to research and product development. These "assets" do not appear on the balance sheet and cannot be used as collateral when borrowing funds. Consequently, they use less debt in their capital structures.

To summarize, companies can effectively use debt to increase ROE. Although it reduces financing costs, debt increases **default risk**: the risk that the company will be unable to repay debt when it comes due. Because of this risk, analysts carefully examine a company's financial statements to determine if it is using debt financing effectively and judiciously.

The core of our analysis relating to debt is the examination of a company's ability to generate cash to *service* its debt (that is, to make required debt payments of both interest and principal). Analysts, investors, and creditors are primarily concerned about whether the company has sufficient cash available or, alternatively, whether it is able to generate the required cash in the future to cover its debt obligations. The analysis of available cash is called **liquidity analysis**. The analysis of the company's ability to generate sufficient cash in the future is called **solvency analysis** (so named because a bankrupt company is said to be "insolvent").

Liquidity Analysis

Liquidity refers to cash availability: how much cash a company has, and how much it can raise on short notice. The most common ratios used to assess the degree of liquidity are the current ratio and the quick ratio, which were first introduced in Chapter 2, as well as the operating cash flow to current liabilities ratio, which was introduced in Chapter 4. Each of these ratios links required near-term payments to cash available in the near term.

Current Ratio *Current assets* are those assets that a company expects to convert into cash within the next operating cycle, which is typically a year. *Current liabilities* are those liabilities that come due within the next year. An excess of current assets over current liabilities (Current assets – Current liabilities) is known as *net working capital* or simply **working capital**. Positive working capital implies more expected cash inflows than cash outflows in the short run. The **current ratio** expresses working capital as a ratio and is computed as follows:

$$\text{Current ratio (CR)} = \frac{\text{Current assets}}{\text{Current liabilities}}$$

A current ratio greater than 1.0 implies positive working capital. Both working capital and the current ratio consider existing balance sheet data only and ignore cash inflows from future sales or other sources. The current ratio is more commonly used than working capital because ratios allow comparisons across companies of different sizes. Generally, companies prefer a higher current ratio; however, an excessively high current ratio indicates inefficient asset use. Furthermore, a current ratio less than 1.0 is not always problematic for at least two reasons:

1. A cash-and-carry company (like a grocery store) can have little or no receivables (and a low current ratio), but consistently large operating cash inflows ensure the company will be sufficiently liquid. A company can efficiently manage its working capital by minimizing receivables and inventories and maximizing payables. **The Kroger Company** and **Walmart**, for example, use their buying power to exact extended credit terms from suppliers. Consequently, because both companies are essentially cash-and-carry companies, their current ratios are less than 1.0 and both are sufficiently liquid.
2. A service company will typically report little or no inventories among its current assets. In addition, some service companies do not report significant accounts receivable. If short-term borrowings and accrued expenses exceed cash and temporary investments, a current ratio of less than 1.0 would result. **United Airlines Holdings, Inc.**, is an example of such a firm.

The aim of current-ratio analysis is to discern if a company is having, or is likely to have, difficulty meeting its short-term obligations. If a company cannot cover its short-term debts with cash provided by operations, it may need to liquidate current assets to meet its obligations. **PepsiCo**'s current ratio was 0.98 ($23,001 million/$23,372 million) at December 26, 2020. At the end of fiscal year 2019, its current ratio was 0.86 ($17,645 million/$20,461 million).

Quick Ratio The **quick ratio** is a variant of the current ratio. It focuses on quick assets, which are those assets likely to be converted to cash within a relatively short period of time, usually less than 90 days. Specifically, quick assets include cash, short-term securities, and accounts receivable; they exclude inventories and prepaid assets. The quick ratio is defined as follows:

$$\text{Quick ratio (QR)} = \frac{\text{Cash + Short-term securities + Accounts receivable}}{\text{Current liabilities}}$$

The quick ratio reflects on a company's ability to meet its current liabilities without liquidating inventories that could require markdowns. It is a more stringent test of liquidity than the current ratio and may provide more insight into company liquidity in some cases.

At the end of 2020, PepsiCo's quick ratio was 0.77 ([$8,185 million + $1,366 million + $8,404 million]/$23,372 million), which was up from 0.66 in 2019 ([$5,509 million + $229 million + $7,822 million]/$20,461 million). **Exhibit 5.13** shows that the median food products company has a quick ratio well below 1.0, and slightly below PepsiCo's value.

Operating Cash Flow to Current Liabilities The **operating cash flow to current liabilities (OCFCL)** ratio was introduced in Chapter 4 and is defined as follows:

$$\text{Operating cash flow to current liabilities (OCFCL)} = \frac{\text{Cash flow from operations}}{\text{Average current liabilities}}$$

Cash flow from operations is taken directly from the statement of cash flows. It represents the net amount of cash derived from operating activities during the year. Ultimately, the ability of a company to pay its debts is determined by whether its operations can generate enough cash to cover debt payments. Thus, a higher OCFCL ratio is generally preferred by analysts.

PepsiCo reported an OCFCL ratio of 0.48 in 2020 ($10,613 million/[($23,372 million + $20,461 million)/2]). Its 2019 OCFCL ratio was 0.45 ($9,649 million/[($20,461 million + $22,138 million)/2]). PepsiCo's OCFCL ratio has decreased slightly since 2016, though it increased a bit in 2020. The slight increase in 2020 is consistent with increases in the CR and QR. In Chapter 4 we saw that reductions in inventory and receivables increased operating cash flows. As a consequence, the improvement may not be sustainable, and continued improvement is certainly limited. **Exhibit 5.12** provides a plot of all three liquidity ratios over the past 5 years.

EXHIBIT 5.12 **PepsiCo's Liquidity Ratios, 2016–2020**

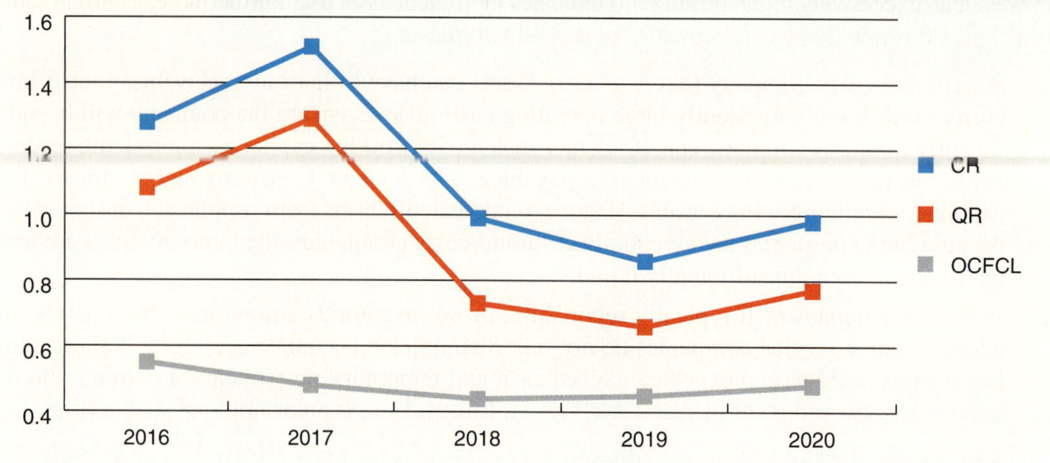

Cash Burn Rate The **cash burn rate (CBR)** is used when a company's free cash flow (cash from operations minus net investments in property, plant, and equipment) is negative. Free cash flow can be negative in a variety of circumstances—for young companies working to become established (e.g., **Tesla**) or for established companies that have run into financial distress (e.g., **Sears**). For 2020, **Blue Apron Holdings, Inc.**, reported that its cash flows used in operations were $5.4 million, and its net investments in property and equipment were $6.0 million, making free cash flow a negative $11.4 million. Blue Apron's cash burn rate would be the following:

Cash burn rate = Free cash flow in the period ÷ number of days in the period
= –$11.4 million ÷ 365 days = –$31 thousand/day

In its efforts to attract and retain subscribers, Blue Apron is using cash at the rate of $31 thousand per day. This represents a significant improvement over the prior years, when the cash burn rate was $59 thousand per day in 2019 and $252 thousand per day in 2018.

Naturally, the interpretation of the cash burn rate depends on the depth of the company's pockets. In its June 30, 2020, balance sheet, Blue Apron reports cash and cash equivalents of $44.1 million, so it would appear that the company can, if necessary, continue on its present course for quite a while. As expected, this cash balance is down from the December 31, 2018, balance of $95.6 million. (We don't calculate PepsiCo's cash burn rate because its free cash flow is positive.)

Solvency Analysis

Solvency refers to a company's ability to meet its debt obligations, including both periodic interest payments and the repayment of the principal amount borrowed. Solvency is crucial because an insolvent company is a failed company. There are two general approaches to measuring solvency. The first approach uses balance sheet data and assesses the proportion of capital raised from creditors. The second approach uses income statement data and assesses the profit generated relative to debt payment obligations. We discuss each approach in turn.

Debt-to-Equity The **debt-to-equity ratio (D/E)**, which was introduced in Chapter 1, is a useful tool for the first type of solvency analysis. It is defined as follows:

$$\text{Debt-to-equity ratio} = \frac{\text{Total liabilities}}{\text{Total stockholders' equity}}$$

This ratio conveys how reliant a company is on creditor financing (which are fixed claims) compared with equity financing (which are flexible or residual claims). A higher ratio indicates less solvency and more risk. PepsiCo's debt-to-equity ratio is 5.9 for 2020 ($79,366 million/$13,552 million). In 2019, its ratio was 4.3 ($63,679 million/$14,868 million). As seen in the chart below, the debt-to-equity ratio declined in 2018, remained steady in 2019, but increased in 2020. Like many large companies, PepsiCo has returned cash to shareholders in the form of dividends and share buybacks and increased debt to take advantage of unusually low interest rates. At some point, the increase in the debt-to-equity ratio may have an impact on PepsiCo's ability to borrow at favorable interest rates. PepsiCo's debt-to-equity ratio is well above the average of approximately 1.31 for other companies in the food industry.

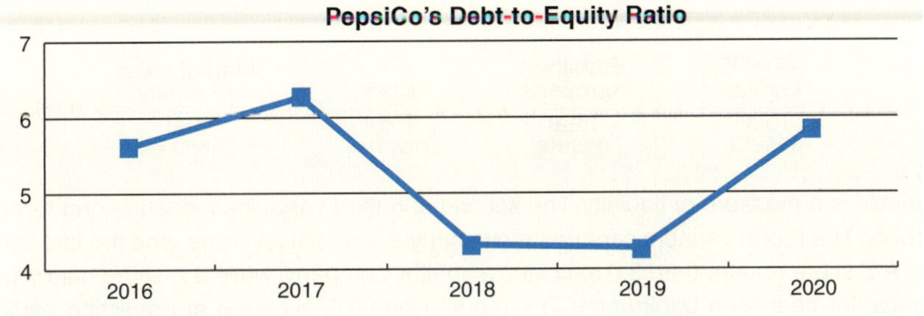

In practice, analysts use a variety of solvency measures that are similar to the debt-to-equity ratio. One variant of this ratio considers a company's *long-term* debt divided by equity. This approach assumes that current liabilities are repaid from current assets (so-called self-liquidating). Thus, it assumes that creditors and stockholders need only focus on the relative proportion of long-term capital.

Times Interest Earned The second type of solvency analysis compares profits to liabilities. This approach assesses how much operating profit is available to cover debt obligations. A common measure for this type of solvency analysis is the **times interest earned (TIE)** ratio (see Chapter 9) defined as follows:

$$\text{Times interest earned} = \frac{\text{Earnings before interest expense and taxes}}{\text{Interest expense}}$$

The times interest earned ratio reflects the operating income available to pay interest expense. The underlying assumption is that only interest needs to be paid because the principal will be refinanced. This ratio is sometimes abbreviated as EBIT/I. The numerator is similar to earnings without interest (EWI), but it is *pretax* instead of after tax.

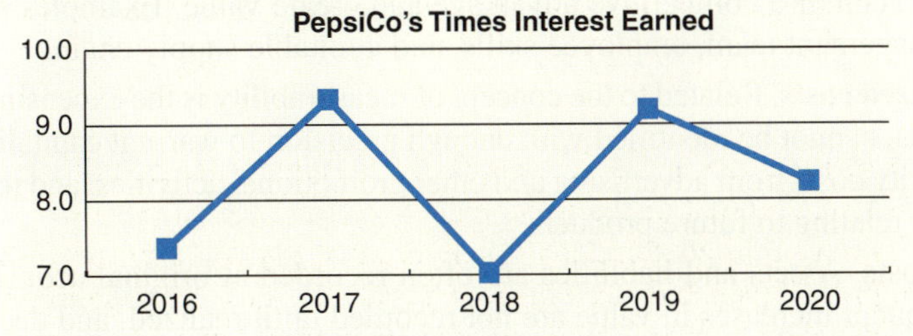

Management wants this ratio to be sufficiently high so that there is little risk of default. PepsiCo's TIE ratio was 8.24 times in 2020 ([$9,069 million + $1,252 million]/$1,252 million), which is down significantly from 9.20 times in 2019 ([$9,312 million + $1,135 million]/$1,135 million). Over the 5-year period between 2016 and 2020, PepsiCo's TIE ratio has ranged from a low of 7.03 in 2018 to a high of 9.34 in 2017. The current level of this ratio suggests that PepsiCo is more than capable of earning income that is sufficient to cover its financing costs.

There are many variations of solvency and liquidity analysis and the ratios used. The basic idea is to construct measures that reflect a company's credit risk exposure. There is not one "best" financial leverage ratio. Instead, as financial statement users, we want to use measures that capture the risk we are most concerned with. It is also important to compute the ratios ourselves to ensure we know what is included and excluded from each ratio.

RESEARCH INSIGHT

Using Ratios to Predict Bankruptcy Several research studies have examined the use of various financial ratios, such as those discussed in this chapter, to predict financial distress of large companies. In a pioneering study, Professor Edward Altman used discriminant analysis to develop a method for scoring a company's credit risk and using that score to predict bankruptcy. Altman's model produced a **Z-score** as follows:

$$\text{Z-score} = 1.2 \times \frac{\text{Working capital}}{\text{Total assets}} + 1.4 \times \frac{\text{Retained earnings}}{\text{Total assets}} + 3.3 \times \frac{\text{EBIT}}{\text{Total assets}} + 0.6 \times \frac{\text{Market value of equity}}{\text{Total liabilities}} + 0.99 \times \frac{\text{Sales}}{\text{Total assets}}$$

The first variable is a measure of liquidity. The second and third variables measure long-term and short-term profitability. The fourth variable captures a company's financial leverage, and the last variable is asset turnover. A Z-score greater than 3.0 indicates a healthy company, while a Z-score below 1.8 suggests a high potential for near-term bankruptcy. The model was 95% accurate at predicting bankruptcy one year in advance and 72% accurate two years in advance. Today, credit scoring models similar to Altman's Z-score are used by nearly all financial institutions and many other businesses to evaluate credit risk. (Altman, E., "Financial Ratios, Discriminant Analysis and the Prediction of Corporate Bankruptcy," *Journal of Finance*, September, 1968.)

Limitations of Ratio Analysis

The quality of financial statement analysis depends on the quality of financial information. We ought not blindly analyze numbers; doing so can lead to faulty conclusions and suboptimal decisions. Instead, we need to acknowledge that current accounting rules (GAAP) have limitations and be fully aware of the company's environment, its competitive pressures, and any structural and strategic changes. **Exhibit 5.13** shows how ratios can differ significantly across industries, so comparisons to companies with similar customers, technologies, and competitive pressures will be most meaningful. Even within industries, there may be differences in strategy that create big differences in ratio values. There can be other factors that limit the usefulness of financial accounting information for ratio analysis.

GAAP Limitations Several limitations in GAAP can distort financial ratios. Limitations include:

1. **Measurability**. Financial statements reflect what can be reliably measured. This results in nonrecognition of certain assets, often internally developed assets, the very assets that are most likely to confer a competitive advantage and create value. Examples are brand name, a superior management team, employee skills, and a reliable supply chain.
2. **Non-capitalized costs**. Related to the concept of measurability is the expensing of costs relating to "assets" that cannot be identified with enough precision to warrant capitalization. Examples are brand equity costs from advertising and other promotional activities, and research and development costs relating to future products.
3. **Historical costs**. Assets and liabilities are often recorded at original acquisition or issuance costs. Subsequent increases in value are not recorded until realized, and declines in value are recognized only if deemed permanent.

Thus, GAAP balance sheets omit important and valuable assets. Our analysis of ROE, including that of liquidity and solvency, must consider that assets can be underreported and that ratios can be distorted. We discuss many of these limitations in more detail in later chapters.

EXHIBIT 5.13 Industry Ratios: Medians of Companies with Market Capitalization > $500 Million (2018–2020)

	ROE	ROA	ROFL	PM	GPM	AT	ART	INVT	PPET	DE	TIE	CR	QR	OCFCL
Apparel	13.1%	7.4%	6.0%	6.2%	50.9%	1.23	9.90	2.84	6.38	1.27	11.02	2.08	0.99	0.47
Business Services	10.7%	4.1%	4.1%	8.3%	53.3%	0.59	5.59	34.60	8.16	1.30	4.08	1.37	1.19	0.35
Chemicals	13.0%	6.2%	6.0%	9.1%	35.0%	0.70	5.91	4.46	2.48	1.58	5.67	1.93	1.12	0.55
Computers	5.7%	3.6%	2.1%	4.6%	42.5%	0.74	4.83	7.47	8.63	1.36	5.80	1.53	1.33	0.34
Consumer Goods	15.1%	7.3%	7.7%	7.8%	47.4%	0.98	8.06	5.09	5.65	1.45	13.07	1.57	0.94	0.48
Food Products	12.1%	6.1%	4.9%	8.6%	34.5%	0.79	12.44	5.73	3.70	1.31	5.90	1.61	0.73	0.59
Healthcare	8.8%	5.8%	2.5%	8.0%	33.0%	0.70	6.38	30.39	4.49	1.07	3.73	1.51	1.19	0.69
Petroleum	4.3%	2.9%	0.8%	4.8%	32.8%	0.43	5.81	11.30	0.82	1.09	3.48	1.35	0.96	0.85
Pharmaceutical	2.8%	2.1%	0.1%	5.2%	70.2%	0.41	5.39	2.34	4.36	0.92	3.04	2.96	2.33	0.38
Printing & Publishing	1.5%	1.3%	0.2%	1.7%	54.1%	0.67	6.08	12.96	6.25	2.15	6.51	1.29	0.84	0.33
Restaurants, Hotel	6.1%	6.6%	2.9%	8.5%	22.1%	1.07	21.71	62.47	2.35	1.51	4.01	0.97	0.78	0.70
Retail	14.2%	6.8%	7.2%	4.1%	31.7%	1.80	41.60	5.60	5.38	1.79	6.66	1.29	0.42	0.46
Steel	8.2%	5.5%	2.2%	5.0%	18.0%	0.98	7.96	5.46	2.42	1.16	5.24	2.12	1.11	0.37
Telecommunications	9.0%	4.1%	3.3%	9.5%	49.9%	0.47	5.27	22.61	1.43	1.60	3.77	1.02	0.78	0.58
Tobacco	15.4%	11.5%	10.0%	18.8%	64.4%	0.57	25.61	2.32	9.07	3.15	8.93	0.99	0.50	0.55
Transportation	11.2%	5.2%	4.0%	8.2%	31.3%	0.41	11.08	30.89	0.57	1.54	3.38	0.96	0.81	0.59
Utilities	9.8%	4.2%	5.6%	16.8%	33.9%	0.24	7.01	13.96	0.34	2.22	2.80	0.69	0.43	0.58
Overall	9.8%	5.1%	3.9%	7.1%	36.9%	0.68	6.90	6.21	3.63	1.33	4.82	1.63	1.05	0.51

Company Changes Many companies regularly undertake mergers, acquire new companies, and divest subsidiaries. Such major operational changes can impair the comparability of company ratios across time. Companies also change strategies, such as product pricing, R&D, and financing. We must understand the effects of such changes on ratios and exercise caution when we compare ratios from one period to the next. Companies also behave differently at different points in their life cycles. For instance, growth companies possess a different profile than do mature companies. Seasonal effects also markedly impact analysis of financial statements at different times of the year. Thus, we must consider life cycle and cyclicality when we compare ratios across companies and over time.

Conglomerate Effects Few companies are pure-play; instead, most companies operate in several businesses or industries. Most publicly traded companies consist of a parent company and multiple subsidiaries, often pursuing different lines of business. PepsiCo reports financial information for six separate business segments. Most heavy equipment manufacturers, for example, have finance subsidiaries, (**Ford Motor Credit Company** and **Caterpillar Financial Services Corporation** are subsidiaries of **Ford** and **Caterpillar**, respectively.) Financial statements of such conglomerates are consolidated and include the financial statements of the parent and its subsidiaries. Consequently, such consolidated statements are challenging to analyze. Typically, analysts break the financials apart into their component businesses and separately analyze each component. Fortunately, companies must report financial information (albeit limited) for major business segments in their 10-Ks.

Means to an End Ratios reduce, to a single number, the myriad complexities of a company's operations. No one number can accurately capture the qualitative aspect of a company. Ratios cannot hope to capture the innumerable transactions and events that occur each day between a company and various parties. Ratios cannot meaningfully convey a company's marketing and management philosophies, its human resource activities, its financing activities, its strategic initiatives, and its product management. In our analysis we must learn to look through the numbers and ratios to better understand the operational factors that drive financial results. Successful analysis seeks to gain insight into what a company is really about and what the future portends. Our overriding purpose in analysis is to understand the past and present to better predict the future. Computing and examining ratios is just one step in that process.

Review 5-4 LO5-4

Computing and Interpreting Liquidity and Solvency Ratios

GuidedExample MBC

Refer to the income statements and balance sheets for the Coca-Cola Company presented in Review 5-1 earlier in this chapter.

Required

Compute the following liquidity and solvency ratios for Coca-Cola and interpret your results in comparison to those of PepsiCo.

1. Current ratio
2. Quick ratio
3. Debt-to-equity ratio
4. Times interest earned

Solution on p. 5-50.

APPENDIX 5A: Analyzing and Interpreting Core Operating Activities

LO5-5 Measure and analyze the effect of operating activities on ROE.

eLecture MBC

In Chapter 4, we analyzed cash flows by grouping them into three categories—operating, investing, and financing. Similarly, the income statement and balance sheet can be formatted to distinguish between operating and nonoperating (investing and financing) activities. In this appendix, we consider the effect of operating activities on the return on investment. The distinction between returns earned from operating activities and those generated by nonoperating activities is important. Operations provide the primary value drivers for stockholders. It is for this reason that many analysts argue that operating activities must be executed successfully if a company expects to remain profitable in the long run.

Operating activities refer to the core transactions and events of a company. They consist of those activities required to deliver a company's products and services to its customers. A company is engaged in operating activities when it conducts research and development, establishes supply chains, assembles administrative support, produces and markets its products, and follows up with after-sale customer service. Although nonoperating activities, namely investing and financing activities, are important and must be managed well, they are not the primary value drivers for investors and creditors.

Operating returns are measured by the **return on net operating assets (RNOA)**. This return metric is defined as follows:

$$\text{RNOA} = \frac{\textbf{Net operating profit after taxes (NOPAT)}}{\textbf{Average net operating assets (NOA)}}$$

In order to calculate this ratio, we must first classify the income statement and balance sheet accounts into operating and nonoperating components so that we can assess each separately. First, we will consider operating components of the income statement and the calculation of NOPAT. Then, we consider operating and nonoperating components of the balance sheet and the calculation of NOA.

Reporting Operating Activities in the Income Statement The income statement reports operating activities through accounts such as sales revenue, cost of goods sold, selling, general, and administrative (SG&A) expenses, depreciation, rent, insurance, wages, advertising, and R&D expenses. These activities create the most long-lasting effects on profitability and cash flows. Nonoperating items in the income statement include interest expense on borrowed funds and interest and dividend income on investments as well as gains and losses on those investments.

A commonly used measure of operating income is **net operating profit after taxes (NOPAT)**. NOPAT is calculated as:

$$\textbf{NOPAT} = \textbf{Net income} - [(\textbf{Nonoperating revenues} - \textbf{Nonoperating expenses}) \times (1 - \textbf{Statutory tax rate})]$$

NOPAT is an important measure of profitability. It is similar to net income except that NOPAT focuses exclusively on after-tax *operating* performance.

Computation of NOPAT requires that we separate nonoperating revenues and expenses from operating sources of income. Companies often report income from operations as a subtotal (before income taxes) within the income statement. These numbers should be interpreted with caution. Currently, there are no requirements within GAAP that specify which revenue and expense items should be included in operating income. As a consequence, some nonoperating items may be included (as part of SG&A expense, for example). PepsiCo has investments in affiliated companies that distribute its snack foods in certain parts of the world. PepsiCo's income from these investments is included in its SG&A expense in the income statement, but the amount is not disclosed. While this income might appear to be nonoperating, most analysts would argue that this amount should be included in the calculation of NOPAT for PepsiCo because these distribution operations are part of the core operating activities of the business.

The tax rate used to compute NOPAT above is the corporate statutory tax rate. As we have done throughout the book, we use the federal statutory tax rate of 35% for 2017 and earlier and 25% for 2018 and later.[5] PepsiCo's 2020 NOPAT can be computed using this tax rate:

$$\textbf{NOPAT} = \$7{,}175 \text{ million} - [(\$117 \text{ million} - \$1{,}128 \text{ million}) \times (1 - 0.25)] = \$7{,}933.3 \text{ million}$$

PepsiCo's NOPAT is greater than its net income of $7,175 million in 2020. The difference between net income and NOPAT is the interest expense on its debt, interest income on its investments, as well as other pension and retiree medical benefits income.

Reporting Operating Activities in the Balance Sheet The balance sheet also reflects both operating and nonoperating activities. The asset side of the balance sheet reports resources devoted to operating activities in accounts such as cash, receivables, inventories, property, plant, and equipment, and intangible assets. Among liabilities, accounts payable, accrued expenses, and some long-term liabilities such as deferred compensation and pension benefits arise out of operating activities. In addition, accrued and deferred income taxes are generally considered operating liabilities.

Investments in securities of other companies are usually considered nonoperating. The exception is that some equity-type investments are related to operations. PepsiCo's investment in its snack foods distributors is an example of this type of investment. Equity investments are discussed further in Chapter 12. Among a company's liabilities, short-term and long-term debt accounts are classified as nonoperating. These include accounts such as notes payable, interest payable, current maturities of long-term debt, lease liabilities, and long-term debt.

PepsiCo reported short-term investments of $1,366 million in 2020 ($229 million in 2019), which were nonoperating. It also reported long-term investments in non-controlled affiliates of $2,792 million in 2020 ($2,683 million in 2019). These long-term investments are the aforementioned equity investments in companies distributing PepsiCo's snack foods, and most analysts would consider them to be part of operations. PepsiCo's note disclosures show that its noncurrent Other assets account included nonoperating assets of $493 million in 2020 ($385 million in 2019). Its nonoperating liabilities included short-term debt obligations of $3,780 million in 2020 ($2,920 million in 2019) and long-term debt obligations of $40,370 million in 2020 ($29,148 million in 2019).

By subtracting total operating liabilities from total operating assets, we get **net operating assets (NOA)**.[6] PepsiCo's NOA for 2020 and 2019 is calculated as follows ($ millions):

	2020	2019
Operating assets	$92,918 – $1,366 – $493 = $91,059	$78,547 – $229 – $385 = $77,933
Operating liabilities	$79,366 – $3,780 – $40,370 = $35,216	$63,679 – $2,920 – $29,148 = $31,611
NOA	$55,843	$46,322

Given NOPAT and NOA, we can compute PepsiCo's RNOA as follows:

$$\textbf{RNOA} = \frac{\textbf{NOPAT}}{\textbf{Average NOA}} = \frac{\$7{,}933.3 \text{ million}}{(\$55{,}843 \text{ million} + \$46{,}322 \text{ million})/2} = 15.5\%$$

PepsiCo's ROE was 50.5% in 2020. Its RNOA was 15.5%, which represents 31% of the total return earned by stockholders.

Disaggregating RNOA

We gain further insights into operating returns by disaggregating RNOA into operating profit margin and asset turnover. RNOA can be presented as the product of net operating profit margin (NOPM) and net operating asset turnover (NOAT). We define **net operating profit margin (NOPM)** as the amount of operating profit produced as a percentage of each sales dollar. NOPM is similar to the profit margin (PM) ratio defined in the

[5] In the calculation of NOPAT, we want the tax rate used to compute financial accounting income. For total net income, this would be the GAAP effective tax rate (described in Chapter 10). Using the federal statutory tax rate is reasonable when there are no 'permanent differences' (discussed in Chapter 10). However, permanent differences do exist in some cases, and when they do, some nonoperating sources of revenue and expense are not taxed at the statutory rate. For example a significant part of dividend income received from investments of stock of other corporations is excluded from taxable income. A detailed review of the company's tax note is required to attempt to work out whether an effective rate on nonoperating income would be appropriate. We use the statutory rate for simplicity in this introductory book.

[6] Total operating assets can be computed by subtracting nonoperating assets from total assets. Similarly, we can determine operating liabilities either by adding up the operating items or by subtracting the nonoperating items from total liabilities.

chapter, except that it excludes all nonoperating revenues and expenses from the calculation. PepsiCo's NOPM was 11.3% in 2020, computed as:

$$\text{NOPM} = \frac{\text{NOPAT}}{\text{Sales revenue}} = \frac{\$7{,}933.3 \text{ million}}{\$70{,}372 \text{ million}} = 11.3\%$$

The ratio indicates that each dollar of sales revenue generated 11.3¢ of after-tax operating profit. PepsiCo's NOPAT is very close to PepsiCo's EWI because the primary nonoperating item in the company's income statement is interest expense. Thus, its NOPM is almost identical to its profit margin of 11.5%.

Net operating asset turnover (NOAT) is defined as the ratio of sales revenue to average net operating assets (NOA). NOAT captures the amount of sales revenue generated by each dollar of net investment in operating assets. PepsiCo's NOAT is 1.38 times, computed as:

$$\text{NOAT} = \frac{\text{Sales revenue}}{\text{Average NOA}} = \frac{\$70{,}372 \text{ million}}{(\$55{,}843 \text{ million} + \$46{,}322 \text{ million})/2} = 1.38$$

This ratio suggests that each dollar of investment in net operating assets generates $1.38 of sales revenue. This ratio is considerably higher than PepsiCo's asset turnover (AT) ratio of 0.821. This difference is caused by the difference between net operating assets (NOA) and total assets. NOAT is computed using average NOA in the denominator rather than average total assets. Thus, nonoperating assets are excluded, and operating assets are presented net of operating liabilities. The resulting denominator is, therefore, considerably smaller.

PepsiCo's RNOA is 15.5%. This return can be disaggregated into the product of NOPM and NOAT as follows:

$$\text{RNOA} = \text{NOPM} \times \text{NOAT}$$
$$15.5\% = 11.27\% \times 1.378$$

Review 5-5 LO5-5 Measuring the Effects of Operating Activities on ROE

Refer to the financial statements of the Coca-Cola Company presented in Review 5-1. For 2020, calculate Coca-Cola's return on net operating assets (RNOA) and then disaggregate RNOA into net operating profit margin (NOPM) and net operating asset turnover (NOAT). Assume a statutory tax rate of 25% and that equity method investments, other assets, and other liabilities are operating items.

Solution on p. 5-51.

APPENDIX 5B: Financial Statement Forecasts

LO5-6 Prepare financial statement forecasts.

The ability to forecast future financial activities is an important aspect of many business decisions. We might, for example, wish to estimate the value of a company's common stock before purchasing its shares. Or, we might want to evaluate the creditworthiness of a prospective borrower. We might also be interested in comparing the financial impact of alternative business strategies or tactics. For each of these decision contexts, a forecast of future earnings and cash flows would be relevant to such an evaluation.

Financial statement forecasts are hypothetical statements prepared to reflect specific assumptions about the company and its transactions. These forecasts are prepared for future periods based on assumptions about the future activities of a business. By varying the assumptions, forecasts of statements allow us to ask "what if" questions about the future activities of the company, the answers to which provide the necessary inputs underlying most business decisions.

In this appendix, we present a common, yet simple method for preparing financial statement forecasts. This method proceeds in seven steps:

1. Forecast sales revenue.
2. Forecast operating expenses, such as cost of goods sold and SG&A expenses.
3. Forecast operating assets and liabilities, including accounts receivable, inventory, property, plant, and equipment, accounts payable, and prepaid and accrued expenses.
4. Forecast nonoperating assets, liabilities, contributed capital, revenues, and expenses.
5. Forecast net income, dividends, and retained earnings.
6. Forecast the amount of cash required to balance the balance sheet.
7. Prepare a statement of cash flows based on the forecasted income statement and balance sheet.

Step 1. Forecast Sales Revenue

The sales forecast is the crucial first step in the preparation of financial statement forecasts because many of the accounts in the income statement and balance sheet depend on their relation to the sales forecast.

The general method for forecasting sales is to assume a revenue growth rate and apply that rate to the current sales revenue amount:

Forecasted revenues = Current revenues × (1 + Revenue growth rate)

A good starting point for estimating the revenue growth rate is the historical rate of sales growth. This is obtained by using data from the horizontal analysis discussed earlier in the chapter. For example, over the past four years, PepsiCo has experienced an average sales growth of 2.9% per year. Once we have this historical rate as a starting point, we can then adjust the growth rate up or down based on other relevant information. For example, we might attempt to answer the following questions:

- How will future sales be affected by economic conditions? What will happen in the economy in the coming year? Do we expect economic growth or a recession? How will economic growth vary in various markets, such as the United States, Europe, Asia, and Latin America? How will foreign currency exchange rates come into play?
- What changes are expected from the company? Are there any new strategic initiatives planned? Is the company planning to open new stores or launch new products, new advertising campaigns, or new pricing tactics? Do we expect any acquisitions of other businesses?
- What changes in the competitive environment do we expect? Are new competitors entering the market? How will existing competitors respond to changes in the company's strategy? How will substitute products affect sales?

To answer each of the above questions, we rely on a variety of information sources, not the least of which is the management's discussion and analysis (MD&A) section of the company's 10-K report. We can also use publicly available information from competitors, suppliers, customers, industry organizations, and government agencies to provide some insight into trends that can have an effect on future revenues. Our objective is to be able to adjust the historical growth rate up or down to reflect the insights we gain from reviewing this additional information. Revenue for 2020 increased by about 4.8% over 2019. Therefore, we forecast the 2021 revenue to be $73,891 million ($70,372 million × 1.05).

Step 2. Forecast Operating Expenses

Given our forecast of sales revenue, we then turn to forecasting operating expenses. We rely on the common-size income statement as a starting point to identify the relationship between operating expense items and sales revenue. That is, we use the expense-to-sales (ETS) ratio for each operating expense item to compute the forecasted expense:

Forecasted operating expense = Forecasted revenues × ETS ratio

While historical ETS ratios provide a good place to start, we may want to adjust these ratios up or down based on observed trends or any additional information that we might have. For example, when we examined PepsiCo's common-size income statements, we learned that cost of goods sold increased to 45.2% of sales in 2020, up from 44.9% in 2019. Will this trend continue into 2021? What are the effects of developments in the sugar market or from tariffs on imported aluminum? What about PepsiCo's cost-cutting efforts over recent years? Or, do we anticipate that this expense item will revert to historical levels in relation to sales? Will the ETS ratios post-pandemic be similar to pre-pandemic levels? As was the case with the sales forecast, there are numerous sources of information that are potentially useful for making adjustments to the historical relationships.

For the purpose of illustration, we assume that 2021 Cost of sales will increase to 45.5% of revenues ($33,990 million) and that Selling, general, and administrative expenses will drop slightly to 40% of revenues in 2021 ($29,556 million).

Step 3. Forecast Operating Assets and Liabilities

The sales forecast can also be used to forecast operating assets and liabilities. The relationship between operating assets and revenues is based on asset turnover analysis. For example, when we compute accounts receivable turnover (ART), sales revenue is divided by average accounts receivable. When forecasting accounts receivable, we assume a relationship between sales revenue and year-end accounts receivable:

$$\textbf{Forecasted accounts receivable} = \frac{\textbf{Forecasted sales revenue} \times \textbf{Reported accounts receivable}}{\textbf{Reported sales revenue}}$$

PepsiCo reports accounts and notes receivable of $8,404 million in 2020, which is 11.94% of the reported sales revenue of $70,372 million. The forecasted accounts receivable for 2021 is, therefore, $8,823 million ($73,891 million × 11.94%).

The same procedure can be used to forecast other operating assets, such as inventories, prepaid expenses and property, plant, and equipment, as well as operating liabilities such as accounts payable and accrued expenses. Intangible assets, including Goodwill, arise when one company acquires another. Goodwill and some intangibles are not amortized after purchase (more in Chapter 12), but some do get amortized. Forecasting these values requires forecasts of PepsiCo's acquisitions in 2021. For this illustration, we assume no acquisitions in 2021, no impairments of nonamortizable intangibles, and the amortization of intangible assets in 2021 is $90 million, the same as in 2020.

Step 4. Forecast Nonoperating Assets, Liabilities, Revenues, and Expenses

While operating expenses, assets, and liabilities tend to be related to sales revenue, this is typically not the case for nonoperating items. Instead, nonoperating revenues, such as interest and dividend income, tend to be related to investments, while nonoperating expense, namely interest expense, is related to debt financing. As a starting point, we forecast each of these items by assuming no change from the current amounts. For example, PepsiCo reported long-term debt of $40,370 million in 2020 along with short-term obligations of $3,780 million. We forecast the same level of debt financing in 2021. Likewise, net interest expense and other should remain the same at $1,128 million.

There may be information in the notes or in the MD&A section of the 10-K report to suggest other assumptions. For example, the notes typically reveal the amount of long-term debt that will come due in each of the next five years. This information can be used to adjust the balance in short-term obligations because current maturities of long-term debt would be included under this item. Nevertheless, an assumption of no change is a good place to start.

Step 5. Forecast Net Income, Dividends, and Retained Earnings

Once we have forecasts of sales revenue (from step 1), operating expenses (step 2), and nonoperating revenues and expenses (step 4), we can calculate pretax earnings, income tax expense, and net income. Income tax expense is forecasted by multiplying pretax income by the effective tax rate:

Forecasted income tax expense = Forecasted pretax income × Effective tax rate

The **effective tax rate** is the average tax rate applied to pretax earnings and is computed by dividing reported income tax expense by reported pretax earnings. PepsiCo's effective tax rate was 20.9% in 2020 ($1,894 million/$9,069 million). Although this rate can be adjusted up or down based on additional information, we apply a 25% effective tax rate to compute 2021 forecasted income taxes. This assumption results in forecasted income taxes of $2,426 million ($9,704 million × 25%) and forecasted net income of $7,278 million ($9,704 million – $2,426 million). PepsiCo's forecasted 2021 income statement is presented in **Exhibit 5B.1** alongside its 2020 reported income statement.

EXHIBIT 5B.1 PepsiCo Income Statement Forecast

PEPSICO, INC.
2020 Income Statement and 2021 Income Statement Forecast

($ millions)	Forecast 2021	As Reported 2020
Net revenue ($70,372 × 1.05)	$73,891	$70,372
Cost of sales ($73,891 × 0.455)	33,620	31,797
Selling, general, and administrative expenses ($73,891 × 0.40)	29,556	28,495
Operating profit	10,715	10,080
Other pension and retiree medical benefits income/(expense) (no change)	117	117
Net interest expense and other (no change)	(1,128)	(1,128)
Income before income taxes	9,704	9,069
Provision for income taxes ($9,704 × 0.25)	2,426	1,894
Net income	$ 7,278	$ 7,175

Our forecast of dividends relies on the **dividend payout ratio**, defined as dividend payments divided by net income.

Forecasted dividends = Forecasted net income × Dividend payout ratio

PepsiCo paid cash dividends of $5,509 million in 2020, which is 76.8% of its net income of $7,175 million. In 2019, PepsiCo had a dividend payout ratio of 72.1%. Using a dividend payout ratio of 75%, we forecast 2021 dividends to be $5,459 million ($7,278 million × 75%).

Next, we can forecast retained earnings using the forecasts of net income and dividends:

Forecasted retained earnings = Beginning retained earnings + Forecasted net income − Forecasted dividends

Throughout this chapter, we have presented PepsiCo's stockholders' equity as a single amount, without separating retained earnings from contributed capital. Contributed capital increases when common stock is issued, and it decreases when common stock is repurchased. PepsiCo has repurchased shares every year for the past eleven years but indicated that it does not expect to repurchase any additional shares in 2021. Thus, total forecasted stockholders' equity in 2021 will equal $15,371, computed as follows:

Forecasted stockholders' equity	=	Beginning stockholders' equity	+	Forecasted net income	−	Forecasted dividends
$15,371 million	=	**$13,552 million**	+	**$7,278 million**	−	**$5,459 million**

Step 6. Forecast Cash

If the forecasts of all other components of the balance sheet are in place, we can then forecast the cash balance. This forecast is simply a "plug" amount that makes the balance sheet balance:

Forecasted cash = Forecasted liabilities + Forecasted stockholders' equity − Forecasted noncash assets

It is possible that the resulting forecast of cash will be negative or unreasonably small or large. If this occurs, we then revisit steps 4 and 5. If the cash forecast is negative or too low, we adjust our forecast of short-term debt and interest expense to reflect increased borrowing to cover cash needs. If the cash forecast is too large, we can assume that excess cash is invested in marketable securities and increase the amount of interest income. In either case, we then modify our forecast of income taxes, net income, dividends, and retained earnings before recalculating the cash forecast.

PepsiCo's 2021 balance sheet forecast is presented in **Exhibit 5B.2**, alongside the company's 2020 actual balance sheet. The cash balance is forecasted to increase, from $8,185 million in 2020 to $9,725 million in 2021.

EXHIBIT 5B.2 PepsiCo Balance Sheet Forecast

PEPSICO, INC.
2020 Balance Sheet and 2021 Balance Sheet Forecast

($ millions)	Forecast 2021	As Reported 2020
Assets		
Cash and cash equivalents (plug to balance)	$ 9,725	$ 8,185
Short-term investments (no change)	1,366	1,366
Accounts and notes receivable, net ($73,891 × 11.94%)	8,823	8,404
Inventories ($73,891 × 5.93%)	4,382	4,172
Prepaid expenses and other current assets ($73,891 × 1.24%)	916	874
Total current assets	25,212	23,001
Property, plant, and equipment, net ($73,891 × 30.37%)	22,441	21,369
Amortizable intangible assets, net ($1,703 − $90)	1,613	1,703
Goodwill (no change)	18,757	18,757
Other indefinite-lived intangible assets (no change)	17,612	17,612
Investments in noncontrolled affiliates (no change)	2,792	2,792
Deferred income taxes ($73,891 × 6.21%)	4,589	4,372
Other assets ($73,891 × 4.71%)	3,480	3,312
Total assets	$96,496	$92,918
Liabilities and equity		
Short-term obligations (no change)	$ 3,780	$ 3,780
Accounts payable and other current liabilities ($73,891 × 27.84%)	20,571	19,592
Total current liabilities	24,351	23,372
Long-term debt obligations (no change)	40,370	40,370
Deferred income taxes ($73,891 × 6.09%)	4,500	4,284
Other liabilities ($73,891 × 16.11%)	11,904	11,340
Total liabilities	81,125	79,366
Total equity ($13,552 + $7,278 − $5,459)	15,371	13,552
Total liabilities and equity	$96,496	$92,918

Step 7. Prepare the Statement of Cash Flows Forecast

Once we have a forecast of the income statement and balance sheet, we can prepare a forecast of the statement of cash flows using the methods illustrated in Chapter 4. To do so, we need a forecast of depreciation expense (if that item is not explicitly listed as an operating expense in the income statement). The procedure for forecasting depreciation expense is the same as was used for other operating expenses—we simply use the depreciation ETS ratio.

PepsiCo reported depreciation and amortization expense of $2,548 million in 2020, which was 3.62% of sales revenue. Using this ETS ratio, we can forecast depreciation expense of $2,675 million in 2021 ($73,891 million × 3.62%). Using this forecast, along with other items forecasted earlier, we can prepare the statement of cash flows, which is presented in **Exhibit 5B.3**.

Additional Considerations

Forecasts of financial statements are based on a set of assumptions about the future. Any decisions that are based on such statements are only as good as the quality of these assumptions. Therefore, it is important that we appreciate the effect that each assumption has on the forecasted amounts. To this end, it is often helpful to use **sensitivity analysis** to examine the effect of alternative assumptions on the forecasted statements. For example, we might prepare three different forecasted income statements—one using our "most-likely" assumption for the sales forecast, and one each for the "best-case" and "worst-case" scenarios. In some situations, a change in the sales forecast can have a dramatic effect on net income and cash flows, particularly in the presence of large fixed costs. Sensitivity analysis helps to identify these effects before a decision is made so that costly mistakes can be avoided.

It is also important to remember that these statements are predictions about the future and, as such, are bound to be wrong. That is, we expect that there will be **forecast errors**—differences between the forecasted and the actual amounts. The goal of a good forecast is accuracy, which means that we want the forecast errors to be as small as possible. Generating forecasted statements using a computer is relatively easy, and the efficiency and precision of spreadsheet software can provide a false sense of confidence in the numbers. Spreadsheets routinely calculate forecasted amounts to the "nth" decimal place whether or not such precision is justified. However, an amount forecasted to the nearest penny may not be useful if the forecast is off by millions of dollars. It is better to be imprecisely accurate than to be precisely inaccurate.

EXHIBIT 5B.3 PepsiCo Statement of Cash Flow Forecast

PEPSICO, INC.
2021 Statement of Cash Flows Forecast

($ millions)	2021 Forecast
Operating activities:	
Net income	$ 7,278
Adjustments:	
Depreciation and amortization ($73,891 × 3.62%)	2,548
Minus change in accounts and notes receivable	(419)
Minus change in inventories	(210)
Minus change in prepaid expenses and other current assets	(42)
Minus change in deferred income taxes	(217)
Minus change in other assets	(168)
Plus change in accounts payable and other current liabilities	979
Plus change in deferred income taxes	216
Plus change in other liabilities	564
Cash flow from operations	10,529
Investing activities:	
Investment in property, plant, and equipment [$2,548 + ($22,441 – $21,369) + ($1,613 – $1,703)]	(3,530)
Cash used for investing activities	(3,530)
Financing activities:	
Dividends paid	(5,459)
Cash used for financing activities	(5,459)
Net decrease in cash ($10,529 – $3,530 – $5,459)	1,540
Cash and cash equivalents, 2020	8,185
Cash and cash equivalents, 2021	$ 9,725

Preparing a Forecast Income Statement and Balance Sheet

LO5-6 **Review 5-6**

GuidedExample MBC

Refer to the income statements and balance sheets of the Coca-Cola Company presented in Review 5-1.

Required

Make the following assumptions:

- 2021 sales revenue increases 5% from 2020 to $34,665 million.
- Operating expenses increase in 2021 in proportion to sales revenue.
- Operating assets and liabilities increase based on their 2020 relation to sales revenue. Classify "deferred and accrued taxes," "Other assets," and "Other liabilities" as operating.
- Nonoperating revenues, expenses, assets (including investments and intangible assets), and liabilities do not change from 2020 to 2021. Assume no change for equity income or equity method investments.
- Dividend payout is 60% of net income.
- Income tax rate is 25%.

Prepare a forecast income statement and balance sheet for 2021.

Solution on p. 5-51.

SUMMARY

Prepare and analyze common-size financial statements. (p. 5-4) LO5-1

- Vertical analysis restates items in the income statement as a percentage of sales revenue and items in the balance sheet as a percentage of total assets.
- Horizontal analysis examines the percentage change from one year to the next for specific items in the income statement and balance sheet.

Compute and interpret measures of return on investment, including return on equity (ROE), return on assets (ROA), and return on financial leverage (ROFL). (p. 5-8) LO5-2

- ROE is the primary measure of company performance. It captures the return earned by shareholder investment in the firm.
- ROA measures the return earned on the firm's investment in assets. It is not affected by the way those assets are financed.
- ROFL is the difference between ROE and ROA and measures the effect that financial leverage has on ROE.

Disaggregate ROA into profitability (profit margin) and efficiency (asset turnover) components. (p. 5-11) LO5-3

- ROA can be disaggregated as the product of profit margin (PM) and asset turnover (AT).
- PM can be analyzed further by examining the gross profit margin and expense-to-sales ratios.
- AT can be analyzed further by examining accounts receivable turnover (ART), inventory turnover (INVT), and property, plant, and equipment turnover (PPET).
- The trade-off between PM and AT is determined by the company's strategy and its competitive environment.

Compute and interpret measures of liquidity and solvency. (p. 5-15) LO5-4

- The current ratio (CR) and quick ratio (QR) measure short-term liquidity by comparing liquid assets to short-term obligations. The operating cash flow to current assets ratio (OCFCL) and the cash burn rate (CBR) relate a company's cash flows to its existing obligations and liquid resources.
- The debt-to-equity ratio (D/E) and times interest earned ratio (TIE) measure long-term solvency by comparing sources of financing and the level of earnings to the cost of debt (interest).

Appendix 5A: Measure and analyze the effect of operating activities on ROE. (p. 5-23) LO5-5

- Net operating profit after taxes (NOPAT) measures the portion of income that results from a business' core operating activities.
- Return on net operating assets (RNOA), defined as NOPAT/average net operating assets, measures the return on a company's net investment in operating assets.

Appendix 5B: Prepare financial statement forecasts. (p. 5-25) LO5-6

- Financial statement forecasts are prepared for future periods based on assumptions about the future activities of the business.
- Financial statement forecasts can be used to evaluate the effects of alternative actions or assumptions on the financial statements.

KEY RATIOS

RETURN MEASURES

$$\text{Return on equity (ROE)} = \frac{\text{Net income}}{\text{Average stockholders' equity}}$$

$$\text{Earnings without interest expense (EWI)} = \text{Net income} + [\text{Interest expense} \times (1 - \text{Statutory tax rate})]$$

$$\text{Return on assets (ROA)} = \frac{\text{Earnings without interest expense (EWI)}}{\text{Average total assets}}$$

$$\text{Return on financial leverage (ROFL)} = \text{ROE} - \text{ROA}$$

PROFITABILITY RATIOS

$$\text{Profit margin (PM)} = \frac{\text{Earnings without interest expense (EWI)}}{\text{Sales revenue}}$$

$$\text{Gross profit margin (GPM)} = \frac{\text{Sales revenue} - \text{Cost of goods sold}}{\text{Sales revenue}}$$

$$\text{Expense-to-sales (ETS)} = \frac{\text{Individual expense items}}{\text{Sales revenue}}$$

TURNOVER RATIOS

$$\text{Asset turnover (AT)} = \frac{\text{Sales revenue}}{\text{Average total assets}}$$

$$\text{Accounts receivable turnover (ART)} = \frac{\text{Sales revenue}}{\text{Average accounts receivable}}$$

$$\text{Inventory turnover (INVT)} = \frac{\text{Cost of goods sold}}{\text{Average inventory}}$$

$$\text{Property, plant, and equipment turnover (PPET)} = \frac{\text{Sales revenue}}{\text{Average PP\&E}}$$

LIQUIDITY RATIOS

$$\text{Current ratio (CR)} = \frac{\text{Current assets}}{\text{Current liabilities}}$$

$$\text{Quick ratio (QR)} = \frac{\text{Cash} + \text{Short-term securities} + \text{Accounts receivable}}{\text{Current liabilities}}$$

$$\text{Operating cash flow to current liabilities (OCFCL)} = \frac{\text{Operating cash flow}}{\text{Average current liabilities}}$$

$$\text{Cash burn rate} = \frac{\text{Free cash flow in the period}}{\text{Number of days in the period}}$$

SOLVENCY RATIOS

$$\text{Times interest earned (TIE)} = \frac{\text{Earnings before interest expense and taxes (EBIT)}}{\text{Interest expense}}$$

$$\text{Debt-to-equity (D/E)} = \frac{\text{Total liabilities}}{\text{Total stockholders' equity}}$$

Assignments with the MBC logo in the margin are available in myBusinessCourse.
See the Preface of the book for details.

MULTIPLE CHOICE

1. Which of the following ratios would not be affected by an increase in cost of goods sold?
   a. ROA
   b. INVT
   c. QR
   d. PM

2. A company has the following values: PM = 0.07; EWI = \$3,770; Average total assets = \$74,800. AT equals
   a. 0.05
   b. 0.72
   c. 0.36
   d. AT is not determinable because its sales are not reported.

3. A company's current ratio is 2 and its quick ratio is 1. What can be said about the sum of the company's cash + short-term securities + accounts receivable?
   a. The sum exceeds the current liabilities.
   b. The sum is equal to the sum of the current liabilities.
   c. The sum is equal to 1/2 of the total current liabilities.
   d. None of the above is correct.

4. A company's interest expense is $250,000 and its net income is $7 million. If the company's effective tax rate is 30%, what is the company's times interest earned (TIE) ratio?
   a. 90
   b. 41
   c. 32
   d. 16

5. If a company's ROFL is negative, which of the following is *not* true?
   a. ROA > ROE
   b. The D/E ratio is negative.
   c. ROA < net interest rate
   d. The company likely has a low TIE ratio.

Multiple Choice Answers
1. c 2. b 3. b 4. b 5. b

GUIDANCE ANSWERS . . . YOU MAKE THE CALL

You are the Entrepreneur Your company is performing substantially better than its competitors. Namely, your ROA of 16% is markedly superior to competitors' ROA of 10%. However, ROA disaggregation shows that this is mainly attributed to your AT of 0.89 versus competitors' AT of 0.59. Your PM of 18% is essentially identical to competitors' PM of 17%. Accordingly, you will want to maintain your AT because further improvements are probably difficult to achieve. Importantly, you are likely to achieve the greatest benefit with efforts at improving your PM of 18%, which is only marginally better than the industry norm of 17%.

Superscript A(B) denotes assignments based on Appendix 5A (5B).

QUESTIONS

Q5-1. Explain in general terms the concept of return on investment. Why is this concept important in the analysis of financial performance?

Q5-2. (a) Explain how an increase in financial leverage can increase a company's ROE. (b) Given the potentially positive relation between financial leverage and ROE, why don't we see companies with 100% financial leverage (entirely nonowner financed)?

Q5-3. Gross profit margin [(Sales revenue − Cost of goods sold)/Sales revenue] is an important determinant of profit margin. Identify two factors that can cause gross profit margin to decline. Is a reduction in the gross profit margin always bad news? Explain.

Q5-4. Explain how a reduction in operating expenses as a percentage of sales can produce a short-term gain at the cost of long-term performance.

Q5-5. Describe the concept of asset turnover. What does the concept mean, and why is it so important to understanding and interpreting financial performance?

Q5-6. Explain what it means when a company's ROE exceeds its ROA.

Q5-7. What are common-size financial statements? What role do they play in financial statement analysis?

Q5-8. How does a firm go about increasing its AT ratio? What strategies are likely to be most effective?

Q5-9.[A] What is meant by the term "net" in net operating assets (NOA)?

Q5-10. Why is it important to disaggregate ROA into profit margin (PM) and asset turnover (AT)?

Q5-11. What insights do we gain from the graphical relation between profit margin and asset turnover?

Q5-12. Explain the concept of liquidity and why it is crucial to company survival.

Q5-13. Identify at least two factors that limit the usefulness of ratio analysis.

DATA ANALYTICS

LO5-2

Data Analytics

MBC

DA5-1. Critically Analyzing a Visualization in Excel

The financial information in the Excel file associated with this exercise was obtained from 10-K reports for **Costco Wholesale Corporation**. In this exercise, we examine how changing the starting point (baseline) of the y-axis from 0.0 impacts the chart that is created. The chart that is created for Costco examines return on equity over a five-year period. The return on equity ratio measures the return of the stockholders' investment in the company. An increase in the ratio generally means that the company is more efficiently using its equity to generate profits.

REQUIRED

1. Download Excel file DA5-1 found in myBusinessCourse.
2. Calculate the return on equity for Costco for Year 2 through Year 6 in Excel. Carry your answers to three decimal places.
3. Create a line chart showing the return on equity for Year 2 through Year 6. Note that when you use the default setting, the y-axis starts at point 0.0. *Hint:* Highlight data; click Insert, Line. You may need to edit the data selections. Right-click inside the chart, Select Data. The Series (y-axis) should be the ROE; the Category (x-axis) should be Years 2–6.
4. Create a second line chart showing the return on equity for Year 2 through Year 6. For this second chart, change the scale of the y-axis to start at 0.17 and to end at 0.27. *Hint:* Right-click inside the y-axis scale and select Format Axis. Set Minimum bound as 0.17 and Maximum bound as 0.27 on the column chart icon tab.
5. Indicate which of the following descriptions best depicts the trends in Chart 1 and the description that best depicts the trends in Chart 2:
   a. Return on equity increased sharply from Year 2 to Year 4, stabilized for a year and dropped more rapidly in Year 5.
   b. Return on equity gradually increased from Year 2 to Year 4, and remained fairly stable through Year 6.
6. Compute the percentage change in ROE from Year 2 to Year 3, Year 3 to Year 4, Year 4 to Year 5, and Year 5 to Year 6 in Excel.
7. Compare Chart 1 to Chart 2.

Return on equity

$$\frac{\text{Net income}}{\text{Average stockholders' equity}}$$

LO5-4

Data Analytics

MBC

DA5-2. Analyzing the Liquidity of Companies by Industry Segments in Excel

The Excel file associated with this exercise includes Compustat data for S&P 500 companies for five years. In this exercise, we will prepare the data in the Excel file and convert the information in the data file to a PivotTable. Lastly, we will prepare a PivotChart to discern data trends in liquidity by industry segment, measured through the current ratio.

REQUIRED

PART 1 PREPARING DATA; CREATING A PIVOTTABLE; MINING DATA

1. Download Excel file DA5-2 found in myBusinessCourse.
2. Add a column to the worksheet in the Excel file that computes the current ratio per each row of data.
3. Sort data in the current ratio column in ascending order to group together rows where errors appear. *Hint:* Use the filter button in the column heading field to sort the data.
4. Identify the industry that had the most instances in which current assets and current liabilities were not provided which resulted in errors in the current ratio column. *Hint:* Use the filter button in the current ratio column heading field and select only those rows with errors (#DIV/0 rows). Then use the filter button in the column heading of the Segment field to sort the column in alphabetical order.
5. Delete all rows in the worksheet where errors appeared in the current ratio calculated cell. *Hint:* Start by clearing the filter in the Current Ratio column. If necessary, re-sort Current Ratio column in ascending order.
6. Create a PivotTable displaying the average current ratio for years 1 through 5 by industry segment. *Hint:* To create a PivotTable, click anywhere inside the table. Open Insert tab and select PivotTable in the Tables group. Add the PivotTable to a new worksheet. Drag Segment to Columns, drag Year to Rows, and drag Current ratio to Values. Select Value Field Settings in the dropdown menu next to Current Ratio in the Values box. Select Average in the Summarize Value Field box.
7. List for each year the industry that has the highest and lowest current ratio.

Current Ratio

$$\frac{\text{Current assets}}{\text{Current liabilities}}$$

8. List the company with the highest and lowest current ratio for the Health Care segment in Year 4. *Hint:* Double-click on the average current ratio for Health Care in Year 4 to automatically open up a new sheet that holds the supporting details.

PART 2 CREATING A PIVOTCHART AND ANALYZING TRENDS

1. Create a visualization through a PivotChart in the form of a line chart of the current ratio by industry segment over the five-year period. *Hint:* Click anywhere inside the PivotTable created in Part 1. Open the PivotTable Analyze tab and click PivotChart in the Tools group. Click Line.
2. Based only on the visualization, answer the following questions.
   a. What two industries appear to have had the least fluctuation from year to year?
   b. What three industries appear to have had the most fluctuation from year to year?
3. Describe the trend in liquidity from Year 1 to Year 5 for the Consumer Staples segment.

DA5-3. Forecasting Sales Using Excel

LO5-6 Homework MBC Data Analytics

The Excel file associated with this exercise includes weekly data for Clack Inc. including cash sales, number of ad impressions, and number of ad clicks. Ad impressions are the number of times that a digital advertisement is displayed on a person's screen. Ad clicks are the number of times that a user clicks on a digital advertisement. In this exercise, we examine the relation between the number of ad impressions and cash sales and the relation between the number of ad clicks and cash sales. Understanding the relations of ad impressions and ad clicks to cash sales can help us determine if future cash sales can be predicted given future estimates of ad impressions or ad clicks.

REQUIRED

1. Download Excel file DA5-3 found in myBusinessCourse.
2. Create a scatter chart in Excel using the 106 weeks of actual data to determine whether there is a relation between the number of ad impressions and cash sales. *Hint:* Highlight the data to be included in the chart. Use Ctrl to select data in non-contiguous cells. Open the Insert tab and click the Scatter chart in the Charts group.
3. List the category of the x-value and the category of the y-value.
4. Add a trendline to the chart and display the regression equation and R-squared value. *Hint:* Right-click inside the data points on your chart, select Add trendline, check the Display equation on chart, check Display R-squared value on chart.
5. List the R-squared and the equation. *Hint:* The R-squared (a number from 0 to 1) reveals how close the estimated values that make up the trendline correspond to the actual data (portrayed in the scatter plot). The closer the R-squared is to 1, the better the fit of the actual data to the trendline.
6. Create a second scatter chart in Excel using the 106 weeks of actual data to determine whether there is a relation between the number of ad clicks and cash sales.
7. List the category of the x-value and the category of the y-value.
8. Add a trendline to the chart and display the regression equation and R-squared value.
9. List the R-squared and the equation.
10. Determine whether ad impressions or ad clicks are a better indicator of cash sales.
11. Determine the average click-through rate, rounded to four decimal places. *Hint:* The average click-through rate is the ratio of ad clicks to impressions determined from the 106 weeks of actual data provided
12. Estimate ad clicks for Weeks 3 through 14 of Year 3. *Hint:* Use the average click-through rate to estimate ad clicks for the estimated periods.
13. Use the equation with the best fit to the trendline to estimate cash sales for Weeks 3 through 14 of Year 3. List the estimated sales amounts. *Hint:* Estimated cash sales = $x multiplied by predictor (either ad impressions or ad clicks) + fixed cost.

DA5-4. Preparing Tableau Visualizations to Analyze the Use of Assets Through Asset Turnover

LO5-3 Homework MBC tableau Data Analytics

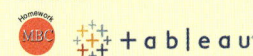

Refer to PB-26 in Appendix B. This problem uses Tableau to analyze asset utilization of S&P 500 companies in certain segments through the asset turnover ratio.

DA5-5. Preparing Tableau Visualizations to Decompose Return on Equity Using the Dupont Method: Part 1, Part II, Part III

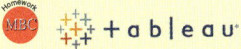

LO5-2 Homework MBC tableau Data Analytics

Refer to PB-29, PB-30, and PB-31 in Appendix B. This three-part problem uses Tableau to decompose the return on equity ratio of S&P 500 companies using the DuPont method. The final part of the problem includes the creation of an interactive dashboard.

LO5-4 tableau Homework MBC Data Analytics

DA5-6. Preparing Tableau Visualizations to Analyze Liquidity Through the Current Ratio
Refer to PB-27 in Appendix B. This problem uses Tableau to analyze liquidity of S&P 500 companies through the current ratio. The visualization is exported to PowerPoint for communication purposes.

DATA VISUALIZATION

Data Visualization

Data Visualization Activities are available in myBusinessCourse. These assignments use Tableau Dashboards to expose students to visual depictions of data and introduce students to data analytics through data visualizations. These exercises are easily assignable and auto graded by MBC.

MINI EXERCISES

LO5-2, 3 Homework MBC

M5-14. Return on Investment, DuPont Analysis, and Financial Leverage
The following table presents selected annual financial information for Sunder Company.

SUNDER COMPANY Selected Annual Financial Data	
Balance Sheet:	
Average total assets	$1,500,000
Average total liabilities	750,000
Average stockholders' equity	750,000
Income statement:	
Sales revenue	$1,500,000
Earnings before interest (net of tax)	30,000
Interest expense (net of tax)	22,500
Net income	7,500

a. Compute Sunder's ROE, ROA, and ROFL for the year.
b. Use the DuPont analysis described in the Business Insight on page 5-13 to disaggregate ROE.
c. How did the use of financial leverage affect Sunder's ROE during the year? Explain.

LO5-1 Homework MBC Target Corporation NYSE :: TGT

M5-15. Common-Size Balance Sheets
Following is the balance sheet for Target Corporation. Prepare Target's common-size balance sheets as of February 1, 2020, and February 2, 2019.

($ millions)	February 1, 2020	February 2, 2019
Assets		
Cash and cash equivalents	$ 2,577	$ 1,556
Inventory	8,992	9,497
Other current assets	1,333	1,466
Total current assets	12,902	12,519
Property and equipment, net	26,283	25,533
Operating lease assets	2,236	1,965
Other noncurrent assets	1,358	1,273
Total assets	$42,779	$41,290
Liabilities and shareholders' investment		
Accounts payable	$ 9,920	$ 9,761
Accrued and other current liabilities	4,406	4,201
Current portion of long-term debt and other borrowings	161	1,052
Total current liabilities	14,487	15,014
Long-term debt and other borrowings	11,338	10,223
Noncurrent operating lease liabilities	2,275	2,004
Deferred income taxes	1,122	972
Other noncurrent liabilities	1,724	1,780
Total noncurrent liabilities	16,459	14,979
Total shareholders' investment	11,833	11,297
Total liabilities and shareholders' investment	$42,779	$41,290

M5-16. Common-Size Income Statements

LO5-1 Homework MBC — Target Corporation NYSE :: TGT

Following is the income statement for Target Corporation. Prepare Target's common-size income statement for the fiscal year ended February 1, 2020.

($ millions)	Fiscal Year Ended February 1, 2020
Sales	$78,112
Cost of sales	54,864
Selling, general, and administrative expenses	16,233
Depreciation and amortization (exclusive of depreciation included in cost of sales)	2,357
Operating income	4,658
Net interest expense	477
Net other (income)/expense	(9)
Earnings from continuing operations before income taxes	4,190
Provision for income taxes	921
Net earnings from continuing operations	3,269
Discontinued operations, net of tax	12
Net earnings	$ 3,281

M5-17. Compute ROA, Profit Margin, and Asset Turnover

LO5-2, 3 Homework MBC — Target Corporation NYSE :: TGT

Refer to the financial information for Target Corporation, presented in M5-15 and M5-16.

a. Compute its return on assets (ROA) for the fiscal year ending February 1, 2020. Compute two ROA measures: one using net earnings from continuing operations and one using net earnings. Assume a statutory tax rate of 25%.

b. Disaggregate ROA into profit margin (PM) and asset turnover (AT). Confirm that ROA = PM × AT.

M5-18. Analysis and Interpretation of Liquidity and Solvency

LO5-4 Homework MBC — Target Corporation NYSE :: TGT

Refer to the financial information of Target Corporation in M5-15 and M5-16 to answer the following.

a. Compute Target's current ratio and quick ratio on February 1, 2020, and February 2, 2019. Comment on any observed trends.

b. Compute Target's times interest earned for the year ended February 1, 2020, and its debt-to-equity ratios on February 1, 2020, and February 2, 2019. Comment on any trends observed.

c. Summarize your findings in a conclusion about the company's liquidity and solvency. Do you have any concerns about Target's ability to meet its debt obligations?

M5-19. Common-Size Balance Sheets

LO5-1 Homework MBC — 3M Company NYSE :: MMM

Following is the balance sheet for 3M Company. Prepare common-size balance sheets for 2020 and 2019.

3M COMPANY AND SUBSIDIARIES December 31 ($ millions)	2020	2019
Assets		
Current assets		
Cash and cash equivalents	$ 4,634	$ 2,353
Marketable securities—current	404	98
Accounts receivable—net of allowances of $233 and $161	4,705	4,791
Total inventories	4,239	4,134
Prepaids	675	704
Other current assets	325	891
Total current assets	14,982	12,971
Property, plant, and equipment—net	9,421	9,333
Operating lease right of use assets	864	858
Goodwill	13,802	13,444
Intangible assets—net	5,835	6,379
Other assets	2,440	1,674
Total assets	$47,344	$44,659

continued

continued from previous page

3M COMPANY AND SUBSIDIARIES December 31 ($ millions)	2020	2019
Liabilities and shareholders' equity		
Current liabilities		
Short-term borrowings and current portion of long-term debt	$ 806	$ 2,795
Accounts payable	2,561	2,228
Accrued payroll	747	702
Accrued income taxes	300	194
Operating lease liabilities—current	256	247
Other current liabilities	3,278	3,056
Total current liabilities	7,948	9,222
Long-term debt	17,989	17,518
Pension and postretirement benefits	4,405	3,911
Operating lease liabilities	609	607
Other liabilities	3,462	3,275
Total liabilities	$34,413	$34,533
Total equity	12,931	10,126
Total liabilities and equity	$47,344	$44,659

LO5-1 **M5-20. Common-Size Income Statements**

3M Company
NYSE :: MMM

Following is the income statement for 3M Company. Prepare common-size income statements for 2020 and 2019.

3M COMPANY AND SUBSIDIARIES Year Ended December 31 ($ millions)	2020	2019
Net sales	$32,184	$32,136
Operating expenses		
Cost of sales	16,605	17,136
Selling, general, and administrative expenses	6,929	7,029
Research, development, and related expenses	1,878	1,911
Gain on sale of businesses	(389)	(114)
Total operating expenses	25,023	25,962
Operating income	7,161	6,174
Other expense (income), net	450	462
Income before income taxes	6,711	5,712
Provision for income taxes	1,318	1,130
Income of consolidated group	5,393	4,582
Income (loss) from unconsolidated subsidiaries, net of taxes	(5)	—
Net income including noncontrolling interest	$ 5,388	$ 4,582

LO5-2, 3 **M5-21. Compute ROA, Profit Margin, and Asset Turnover**

3M Company
NYSE :: MMM

Refer to the balance sheet and income statement information for 3M Company, presented in M5-19 and M5-20.

a. Compute 3M's 2020 return on assets (ROA). Interest expense for 2020 (included in "Other expense (income), net") is reported as $529 million. Use 25% as the statutory tax rate.

b. Disaggregate ROA into profit margin (PM) and asset turnover (AT). Confirm that ROA = PM × AT.

LO5-2, 3 **M5-22. Compute ROA, Profit Margin, and Asset Turnover for Competitors**

Urban Outfitters, Inc.
NASDAQ :: URBN
TJX Companies
NYSE :: TJX

Selected balance sheet and income statement information from Urban Outfitters, Inc., and TJX Companies, clothing retailers in the high-end and value-priced segments, respectively, follows.

Company ($ millions)	2019 Sales	2019 Earnings Without Interest Expense (EWI)	2019 Total Assets	2018 Total Assets
Urban Outfitters	$ 3,984	$ 169	$ 3,316	$ 2,161
TJX Companies	41,717	3,280	24,145	14,326

a. Compute the 2019 return on assets (ROA) for both companies.

b. Disaggregate ROA into profit margin (PM) and asset turnover (AT) for each company. Confirm that ROA = PM × AT.

c. Discuss differences observed with respect to PM and AT, and interpret these differences in light of each company's business model.

M5-23. Compute and Interpret Liquidity and Solvency Ratios
Selected balance sheet and income statement information from Verizon Communications, Inc., follows.

LO5-4
Homework MBC
Verizon Communications, Inc.
NYSE :: VZ

($ millions)	2020	2019
Current assets	$ 54,594	$ 37,473
Current liabilities	39,660	44,868
Total liabilities	247,209	228,892
Equity	69,272	62,835
Earnings before interest and taxes	28,214	27,463
Interest expense	4,247	4,730
Net cash flow from operating activities	41,768	35,746

a. Compute the current ratio for each year and discuss any change in liquidity. How does Verizon's current ratio compare to the median for the telecommunications industry in **Exhibit 5.13**? What additional information about the numbers used to calculate this ratio might be useful in helping us assess liquidity? Explain.

b. Compute times interest earned, the debt-to-equity, and the operating cash flow to current liabilities ratios for each year and discuss any trends for each. (In 2018, current liabilities totaled $37,930 million.) Compare Verizon's ratios to those that are typical for its industry (refer to **Exhibit 5.13**). Do you have any concerns about the extent of Verizon's financial leverage and the company's ability to meet interest obligations? Explain.

c. Verizon's capital expenditures are expected to remain high as it seeks to respond to competitive pressures to upgrade the quality of its communication infrastructure. Assess Verizon's liquidity and solvency in light of this strategic direction.

M5-24. Computing Turnover Ratios for Companies in Different Industries
Selected data from 2020 financial statements of The Procter & Gamble Company, CVS Health Corporation, and Valero Energy Corporation are presented below.

LO5-3
Homework MBC
The Procter & Gamble Company
NYSE :: PG
CVS Health Corporation
NYSE :: CVS
Valero Energy Corporation
NYSE :: VLO

($ millions)	Procter & Gamble	CVS Health	Valero Energy
Sales	$70,950	$268,706	$64,912
Cost of sales	35,250	163,981	65,652
Average receivables	4,565	20,680	7,549
Average inventories	5,258	18,006	6,526
Average PP&E	20,982	12,325	29,827
Average total assets	117,898	226,582	52,819

a. Compute the asset turnover (AT) ratio for each company.

b. Compute the accounts receivable turnover (ART), inventory turnover (INVT), and PP&E turnover (PPET) for each company.

c. Discuss any differences across these three companies in the turnover ratios computed in *a* and *b*.

EXERCISES

E5-25. Compute and Interpret ROA, Profit Margin, and Asset Turnover of Competitors
Selected 2020 balance sheet and income statement information for McDonald's Corporation and Yum! Brands, Inc., follows.

LO5-2, 3
Homework MBC
McDonald's Corporation
NYSE :: MCD
Yum! Brands, Inc.
NYSE :: YUM

($ millions)	Sales Revenue	Interest Expense	Net Income	Average Total Assets
McDonald's	$19,208	$1,218	$4,731	$50,069
Yum! Brands	5,652	543	904	5,542

a. Compute the return on assets (ROA) for each company. Use the 25% statutory tax rate.

b. Disaggregate ROA into profit margin (PM) and asset turnover (AT) for each company.

c. Discuss any differences in these ratios for each company. Your interpretation should reflect the distinct business strategies of each company.

LO5-2 Homework MBC

E5-26. Compute ROA, ROE, and ROFL and Interpret the Effects of Leverage
Basic income statement and balance sheet information is given below for six different cases. For each case, the assets are financed with a mix of non-interest-bearing liabilities, 10% interest-bearing liability, and stockholders' equity. In all cases, assume the statutory tax rate is 40%.

Case	A	B	C	D	E	F
Average assets	$1,500	$1,500	$1,500	$1,500	$1,500	$1,500
Non-interest-bearing liabilities	0	0	0	0	300	300
Interest-bearing liabilities	0	375	750	750	0	450
Average shareholders' equity	1,500	1,125	750	750	1,200	750
Earnings before interest and taxes (EBIT)	180	180	180	120	150	120

a. For each case, calculate the return on equity (ROE), return on assets (ROA), and return on financial leverage (ROFL).

b. Consider cases A, B, and C. How does increasing leverage affect the three ratios? Why does the ROE grow from case A to case C?

c. Consider cases C and D. When does leverage work in favor of shareholders? Does that hold for case E?

d. Case F has two types of liabilities. How does ROA compare to the rate on interest-bearing liabilities? Does leverage work in favor of the shareholders? Why?

LO5-2, 3 Homework MBC

CVS Health Corporation
NYSE :: CVS

Walgreens Boots Alliance, Inc.
NASDAQ :: WBA

E5-27. Compute, Disaggregate, and Interpret Competitors' Rates of Return
Selected balance sheet and income statement information for the drug retailers **CVS Health Corporation** and **Walgreens Boots Alliance** follows. Assume a statutory tax rate of 25%.

($ millions)	CVS Health	Walgreens Boots
Sales revenue—2020	$268,706	$139,537
Interest expense—2020	2,907	639
Net income—2020	7,192	424
Total assets—2020	230,715	87,174
Total assets—2019	222,449	67,598
Stockholders' equity—2020	69,701	21,136
Stockholders' equity—2019	64,170	24,152

a. Compute the 2020 return on assets (ROA) for each company.

b. Disaggregate ROA into profit margin (PM) and asset turnover (AT) for each company.

c. Compute the 2020 return on equity (ROE) and return on financial leverage (ROFL) for each company.

d. Discuss any differences in these ratios for each company. Identify the factor(s) that drives the differences in ROA observed from your analyses in parts *a* through *c*.

LO5-2, 3 Homework MBC

Intel Corporation
NASDAQ :: INTC

E5-28. Compute, Disaggregate, and Interpret ROE
Selected fiscal year balance sheet and income statement information for the computer chip maker, **Intel Corporation**, follows ($ millions).

Balance Sheet Information ($ millions)	2020	2019	2018
Total assets	$153,091	$136,524	$127,963
Total shareholders' equity	81,038	77,659	74,982
Income Statement Information ($ millions)	**2020**	**2019**	**2018**
Sales revenue	$ 77,867	$ 71,965	$ 70,848
Interest expense	629	489	468
Net income	20,899	21,048	21,053

a. Calculate Intel's return on equity (ROE) for fiscal years 2020 and 2019.

b. Calculate Intel's return on assets (ROA) and return on financial leverage (ROFL) for each year. Is financial leverage working to the advantage of Intel's shareholders? Use a statutory tax rate of 25%.

c. Use the DuPont formulation in the Business Insight on page 5-13 to analyze the variations in Intel's ROE over this period. How does this analysis differ from your answers to *a* and *b* above?

LO5-2, 3 Homework MBC

E5-29. Return on Investment, Financial Leverage, and DuPont Analysis
The following tables provide information from the recent annual reports of HD Rinker, AG.

Balance Sheets (€ millions)	2022	2021	2020	2019
Total assets	€4,886	€5,161	€5,738	€5,578
Total liabilities	4,776	3,979	3,991	4,078
Total shareholders' equity	110	1,182	1,747	1,500

Income Statements (€ millions) 52 Weeks Ended	2022	2021	2020
Sales revenue	€8,291	€7,690	€6,906
Earnings before interest and income taxes	1,178	1,167	710
Interest expense	197	166	190
Earnings before income taxes	981	1,001	520
Income tax expense	302	357	162
Net earnings	€ 679	€ 644	€ 358

a. Calculate HD Rinker's return on equity (ROE) for fiscal years 2022, 2021, and 2020.

b. Calculate HD Rinker's return on assets (ROA) and return on financial leverage (ROFL) for each year. Is financial leverage working to the advantage of HD Rinker's shareholders? Use a statutory tax rate of 25%.

c. Use the DuPont formulation in the Business Insight on page 5-13 to analyze the variations in HD Rinker's ROE over this period. How does this analysis differ from your answers to *a* and *b* above?

E5-30. Compute, Disaggregate, and Interpret ROE and ROA

LO5-2, 3 Homework MBC

ODP Corp. NASDAQ :: ODP

Selected balance sheet and income statement information from The ODP Corporation follows ($ millions).

Sales	Interest Expense	Net Loss	Total Assets		Stockholders' Equity	
2020	2020	2020	2020	2019	2020	2019
$9,710	$42	$(319)	$5,558	$7,311	$1,880	$2,173

a. Compute the 2020 return on equity (ROE), return on assets (ROA), and return on financial leverage (ROFL). Use 25% as the statutory tax rate.

b. Disaggregate ROA into profit margin (PM) and asset turnover (AT).

c. What inferences do we draw from PM compared to AT? How do these ratios compare to industry medians?

E5-31. Compute, Disaggregate, and Interpret ROE and ROA

LO5-2, 3 Homework MBC

Intuit Inc. NASDAQ :: INTU

Selected balance sheet and income statement information from the software company, Intuit Inc., follows ($ millions).

Sales	Interest Expense	Net Income	Total Assets		Stockholders' Equity	
2020	2020	2020	2020	2019	2020	2019
$7,679	$14	$1,826	$10,931	$6,283	$5,106	$3,749

a. Compute the 2020 return on equity (ROE), return on assets (ROA), and return on financial leverage (ROFL). Use 25% as the statutory tax rate.

b. Disaggregate the ROA from part *a* into profit margin (PM) and asset turnover (AT).

c. What can we learn by comparing PM to AT? What explanation can we offer for the relation between ROE and ROA observed and for Intuit's use of financial leverage?

E5-32. Compute and Interpret Liquidity and Solvency Ratios

LO5-4 Homework MBC

Tesla, Inc. NASDAQ :: TSLA

Selected balance sheet, income statement, and the statement of cash flows information from Tesla, Inc., for 2020 and 2019 follows ($ millions).

December 31	2020	2019
Cash and cash equivalents	$19,384	$ 6,268
Net receivables	1,886	1,324
Inventory	4,101	3,552
Other current assets	1,346	959
Current assets	26,717	12,103
Current liabilities	14,248	10,667
Total liabilities	28,418	26,199
Stockholders' equity	23,730	8,110

continued

continued from previous page

Year Ended December 31	2020
Income before income taxes	$1,154
Interest expense	748
Cash flows from operating activities	5,943
Capital expenditures	3,157

a. Compute the current ratio and quick ratio for each year and discuss any trend in liquidity. Do you believe the company is sufficiently liquid? How should the balance in restricted cash affect your analysis?

b. Compute the debt-to-equity ratio for 2020 and 2019 and the times-interest-earned ratio for 2020. Discuss the trend in the debt-to-equity ratio.

c. In 2018, Tesla had a cash burn rate of approximately $8,000 per day. Compute the cash burn rate for 2020. Analyze your results.

LO5-4 **E5-33. Compute and Interpret Liquidity and Solvency Ratios**

Homework MBC

Siemens AG
OTCMKTS :: SIEGY

Selected balance sheet and income statement information from **Siemens, AG**, for 2018 through 2020 follows (€ millions).

	Total Current Assets	Total Current Liabilities	Cash Flow from Operations	Pretax Income	Interest Expense	Total Liabilities	Stockholders' Equity
2018	€64,570	€47,874	€8,425	€8,050	€1,089	€90,869	€48,046
2019	70,370	50,723	8,456	6,933	965	99,265	50,984
2020	52,968	34,117	8,862	5,672	815	84,074	39,823

a. Compute the current ratio for each year and discuss any trend in liquidity. Also compute the operating cash flow to current liabilities (OCFCL) ratio for each year. (In 2017, current liabilities totaled €46,077 million.) Do you believe the company is sufficiently liquid? Explain. What additional information about the accounting numbers comprising this ratio might be useful in helping you assess liquidity? Explain.

b. Compute times interest earned and the debt-to-equity ratio for each year and discuss any trends for each.

c. What is your overall assessment of the company's liquidity and solvency from the analyses in *a* and *b*? Explain.

LO5-2, 3 **E5-34. Compute, Disaggregate, and Interpret ROE and ROA**

Homework MBC

The Gap, Inc.
NYSE :: GPS

Income statements for **The Gap, Inc.**, follow, along with selected balance sheet information ($ millions).

THE GAP, INC.
Consolidated Statement of Earnings

Fiscal Year Ended	Feb. 1, 2020	Feb. 2, 2019
Net sales	$16,383	$16,580
Cost of goods sold and occupancy expenses	10,250	10,258
Gross profit	6,133	6,322
Operating expenses	5,559	4,960
Operating income	574	1,362
Interest expense	76	73
Interest income	(30)	(33)
Income before income taxes	528	1,322
Income taxes	177	319
Net income	$ 351	$ 1,003

THE GAP, INC.
Selected Balance Sheet Data

	Feb. 1, 2020	Feb. 2, 2019
Merchandise inventories	$ 2,156	$2,131
Total assets	13,679	8,049
Total stockholders' equity	3,316	3,553

a. Compute the return on equity (ROE), return on assets (ROA), and return on financial leverage (ROFL) for the fiscal year ended February 1, 2020. Assume a statutory tax rate of 25%.

b. Disaggregate ROA into profit margin (PM) and asset turnover (AT).

c. Compute the gross profit margin (GPM) and inventory turnover (INVT) ratios for the fiscal year ended February 1, 2020.

d. Assess the Gap's performance. What are the most important drivers of the Gap's success?

E5-35.[B] Common-Size and Forecast Income Statements

LO5-1, 6

Homework MBC

The Gap, Inc.
NYSE :: GPS

Refer to the income statements for The Gap, Inc., presented in E5-34.

a. Prepare common-size income statements for fiscal years 2019 (ending February 1, 2020) and 2018 (ending February 2, 2019).

b. Prepare an income statement forecast for the fiscal year 2020 (ending January 30, 2021), based on the following assumptions:

- Net sales total $14,000 million.
- Cost of goods sold and occupancy expenses are 62% of sales.
- Operating expenses total 35% of sales.
- Interest income and interest expense are unchanged from the 2019 amounts.
- The Gap's effective tax rate on income before taxes is 25% in 2020.

c. Given the Gap's business strategy, what are the factors that ultimately determine the accuracy of the income statement forecast prepared in *b*?

PROBLEMS

P5-36. Analysis and Interpretation of Return on Investment for Competitors

LO5-2, 3

Homework MBC

Nike, Inc.
NYSE :: NKE

Adidas Group, AG
OTCMKTS :: ADDYY

Balance sheets and income statements for Nike, Inc., and Adidas Group follow. Refer to these financial statements to answer the requirements.

	NIKE, INC. Balance Sheets ($ millions) May 31		ADIDAS GROUP, AG Balance Sheets (€ millions) December 31	
	2020	2019	2019	2018
Assets				
Current assets:				
Cash and cash equivalents	$ 8,348	$ 4,466	€ 2,220	€ 2,629
Short-term investments	439	197	836	548
Accounts receivable, net	2,749	4,272	2,625	2,418
Inventories	7,367	5,622	4,085	3,445
Prepaid expenses and other current assets	1,653	1,968	1,170	773
Total current assets	20,556	16,525	10,934	9,813
Property, plant, and equipment, net	4,866	4,744	2,380	2,237
Operating lease right-of-use assets, net	3,097	—	2,931	—
Goodwill and identifiable intangible assets, net	497	437	2,421	2,285
Deferred income taxes and other assets	2,326	2,011	2,013	1,277
Total assets	$31,342	$23,717	€20,680	€15,612
Liabilities and shareholders' equity				
Current liabilities:				
Short-term debt	$ 251	$ 15	€ 43	€ 66
Accounts payable	2,248	2,612	2,703	2,300
Current portion of operating lease liabilities	445	—	733	—
Accrued liabilities	5,184	5,010	2,437	2,305
Income taxes payable	156	229	618	268
Other current liabilities	—	—	2,219	1,895
Total current liabilities	8,284	7,866	8,754	6,834
Long-term debt	9,406	3,464	1,595	1,609
Operating lease liabilities	2,913	—	2,399	—
Other noncurrent liabilities	2,684	3,347	874	805
Total shareholders' equity	8,055	9,040	7,058	6,364
Total liabilities and shareholders' equity	$31,342	$23,717	€20,680	€15,612

Note: Amounts in the Adidas reports are rounded amounts, and thus, they may not exactly sum to totals and subtotals.

	NIKE, INC. Income Sheets ($ millions) Year Ended May 31		ADIDAS GROUP, AG Income Sheets (€ millions) Year Ended Dec. 31	
	2020	2019	2019	2018
Revenues	$37,403	$39,117	€23,640	€21,915
Cost of sales	21,162	21,643	11,347	10,552
Gross profit	16,241	17,474	12,293	11,363
Total selling and administrative expense	13,126	12,702	9,633	8,995
Operating profit	3,115	4,772	2,660	2,368
Interest expense (income), net	89	49	166	47
Other expense (income), net	139	(78)	(64)	(57)
Income before income taxes	2,887	4,801	2,558	2,378
Income tax expense	348	772	640	669
Net income from continuing operations	2,539	4,029	1,918	1,709
Gain (loss) from discontinued operations, net of tax	—	—	59	(5)
Net income	$ 2,539	$ 4,029	€ 1,977	€ 1,704

REQUIRED

a. Compute return on equity (ROE), return on assets (ROA), and return on financial leverage (ROFL) for Nike and Adidas in the most recent year. The corporate tax rate in Germany, where Adidas is headquartered, is about 30%. Assume a statutory tax rate of 25% for Nike.

b. Disaggregate the ROA's computed into profit margin (PM) and asset turnover (AT) components. Which of these factors drives ROA for each company?

c. Compute the gross profit margin (GPM) and operating expense-to-sales ratios for each company. How do these companies' profitability measures compare?

d. Compute the accounts receivable turnover (ART), inventory turnover (INVT), and property, plant, and equipment turnover (PPET) for each company. How do these companies' turnover measures compare?

e. Nike's fiscal year ends on May 31, 2020, while Adidas' fiscal year ends on December 31, 2019 (a difference of five months). How does this difference affect your analysis of ROE and ROA for these two companies?

f. Nike's financial statements are prepared in accordance with U.S. GAAP, while Adidas, a German company, follows IFRS rules. How does this difference in financial reporting standards affect your comparison of these companies' financial statements?

LO5-4 Homework MBC

Nike, Inc.
NYSE :: NKE
Adidas Group, AG
OTCMKTS :: ADDYY

P5-37. Analysis and Interpretation of Liquidity and Solvency for Competitors
Refer to the financial statements of Nike and Adidas presented in P5-36.

REQUIRED

a. Compute each company's current ratio and quick ratio for each year. Comment on any changes that you observe.

b. Compute each company's times interest earned ratio and debt-to-equity ratio for each year. Comment on any observed changes.

c. Compare these two companies on the basis of liquidity and solvency. Do you have any concerns about either company's ability to meet its debt obligations?

LO5-2, 3 Homework MBC

The Home Depot, Inc.
NYSE :: HD
Lowe's Companies, Inc.
NYSE :: LOW

P5-38. Analysis and Interpretation of Return on Investment for Competitors
Balance sheets and income statements for The Home Depot, Inc., and Lowe's Companies, Inc., follow. Refer to these financial statements to answer the requirements.

($ millions)	HOME DEPOT, INC. Balance Sheets		LOWE'S COMPANIES Balance Sheets	
	2/2/20	2/3/19	1/31/20	2/1/19
Assets				
Current assets:				
Cash and cash equivalents	$ 2,133	$ 1,778	$ 716	$ 511
Short-term investments	—	—	160	218
Receivables, net	2,106	1,936	—	—
Merchandise inventories	14,531	13,925	13,179	12,561
Other current assets	1,040	890	1,263	938
Total current assets	19,810	18,529	15,318	14,228
Net property and equipment	22,770	22,375	18,669	18,432
Operating lease right-of-use assets	5,595	—	3,891	—
Goodwill	2,254	2,252	303	303
Long-term investments	—	—	372	256
Other assets	807	847	918	1,289
Total assets	$51,236	$44,003	$39,471	$34,508
Liabilities and shareholders' equity				
Current liabilities:				
Short-term debt and current maturities of long-term debt	$ 2,813	$ 1,339	$ 2,538	$ 1,832
Accounts payable	7,787	8,811	7,659	8,279
Accrued salaries and related expenses	1,494	1,506	684	662
Deferred revenue	2,116	1,782	1,219	1,299
Income taxes payable	55	11	—	—
Current operating lease liabilities	828	—	501	—
Other current liabilities	3,282	3,267	2,581	2,425
Total current liabilities	18,375	16,716	15,182	14,497
Long-term debt, excluding current maturities	28,670	26,807	16,768	14,391
Long-term operating lease liabilities	5,066	—	3,943	—
Deferred income taxes	706	491	—	—
Other long-term liabilities	1,535	1,867	1,606	1,976
Total liabilities	54,352	45,881	37,499	30,864
Total shareholders' equity	(3,116)	(1,878)	1,972	3,644
Total liabilities and shareholders' equity	$51,236	$44,003	$39,471	$34,508

($ millions)	HOME DEPOT, INC. Income Statements		LOWE'S COMPANIES Income Statements	
	FY 2019	FY 2018	FY 2019	FY 2018
Net sales	$110,225	$108,203	$72,148	$71,308
Cost of sales	72,653	71,043	49,205	48,401
Gross profit	37,572	37,160	22,943	22,908
Operating expenses:				
Selling, general, and administrative	19,740	19,513	15,367	17,413
Depreciation and amortization	1,989	1,870	1,262	1,477
Impairment loss	—	247	—	—
Operating income	15,843	15,530	6,314	4,018
Interest and other (income) expense:				
Interest and investment income	(73)	(77)	—	—
Interest expense	1,201	1,051	691	624
Earnings before provision for income taxes	14,715	14,556	5,623	3,394
Provision for income taxes	3,473	3,435	1,342	1,080
Net earnings	$ 11,242	$ 11,121	$ 4,281	$ 2,314

REQUIRED

a. Compute return on equity (ROE), return on assets (ROA), and return on financial leverage (ROFL) for each company in fiscal year 2019. Assume a statutory tax rate of 25% for these years.

b. Disaggregate the ROA's computed into profit margin (PM) and asset turnover (AT) components. Which of these factors drives ROA for each company?

c. Compute the gross profit margin (GPM) and operating expense-to-sales ratios for each company. How do these companies' profitability measures compare?

d. Compute the accounts receivable turnover (ART), inventory turnover (INVT), and property, plant, and equipment turnover (PPET) for each company. How do these companies' turnover measures compare?

e. Compare and evaluate these competitors' performance in 2019.

LO5-4 Homework MBC

Home Depot, Inc.
NYSE :: HD
Lowe's Companies, Inc.
NYSE :: LOW

P5-39. Analysis and Interpretation of Liquidity and Solvency for Competitors

Refer to the financial statements of Home Depot and Lowe's presented in P5-38.

REQUIRED

a. Compute each company's current ratio and quick ratio for each year. Comment on any changes that you observe.

b. Compute each company's times interest earned ratio and debt-to-equity ratio for each year. Comment on any observed changes.

c. Compare these two companies on the basis of liquidity and solvency. Do you have any concerns about either company's ability to meet its debt obligations?

LO5-5 Homework MBC

Home Depot, Inc.
NYSE :: HD
Lowe's Companies, Inc.
NYSE :: LOW

P5-40.[A] Analysis of the Effect of Operations on ROE

Refer to the financial statements of Home Depot and Lowe's presented in P5-38.

REQUIRED

a. Compute each company's net operating profit after taxes (NOPAT) for fiscal year 2019 and net operating assets (NOA) for fiscal year 2019 and 2018. Classify other assets and other liabilities (both current and noncurrent) as operating assets and liabilities in the balance sheet. Assume a 25% tax rate. *Hint:* The impairment loss is part of operations.

b. Compute each company's return on net operating assets (RNOA) for fiscal year 2019.

c. Compute the fiscal year 2019 net operating profit margin (NOPM) and net operating asset turnover (NOAT) for each company.

d. Compare operating returns for these two companies. How does RNOA compare to ROA? What insights are gained by focusing on operating returns?

LO5-2, 3 Homework MBC

United Parcel Service, Inc.
NYSE :: UPS

P5-41. Analysis and Interpretation of Profitability

Balance sheets and income statements for United Parcel Service, Inc., (UPS) follow. Refer to these financial statements to answer the following requirements.

UNITED PARCEL SERVICE, INC.
Income Statement

Years Ended December 31 ($ millions)	2020	2019	2018
Revenue	$84,628	$74,094	$71,861
Operating expenses:			
Compensation and benefits	44,529	38,908	37,235
Repairs and maintenance	2,365	1,838	1,732
Depreciation and amortization	2,698	2,360	2,207
Purchased transportation	15,631	12,590	13,409
Fuel	2,582	3,289	3,427
Other occupancy	1,539	1,392	1,362
Other expenses	7,600	5,919	5,465
Total operating expenses	76,944	66,296	64,837
Operating profit	7,684	7,798	7,024
Other income and (expense):			
Investment income (expense) and other	(5,139)	(1,493)	(400)
Interest expense	(701)	(653)	(605)
Total other income and (expense)	(5,840)	(2,146)	(1,005)
Income before income taxes	1,844	5,652	6,019
Income tax expense	501	1,212	1,228
Net income	$ 1,343	$ 4,440	$ 4,791

UNITED PARCEL SERVICE, INC.
Balance Sheet

December 31 ($ millions)	2020	2019	2018
Assets			
Current assets:			
Cash and cash equivalents	$ 5,910	$ 5,238	$ 4,225
Marketable securities	406	503	810
Accounts receivable, net	10,750	9,552	8,958
Assets held for sale	1,197	—	—
Other current assets	1,953	1,810	2,217
Total current assets	20,216	17,103	16,210
Property, plant, and equipment, net	32,254	30,482	26,576
Operating lease right-of-use assets	3,073	2,856	—
Goodwill	3,367	3,813	3,811
Intangible assets, net	2,274	2,167	2,075
Investments and restricted cash	25	24	170
Deferred income tax assets	527	330	141
Other noncurrent assets	672	1,082	1,033
Total assets	$62,408	$57,857	$50,016
Liabilities and shareholders' equity			
Current liabilities:			
Current maturities of long-term debt, commercial paper, and finance leases	$ 2,623	$ 3,420	$ 2,805
Current maturities of operating leases	560	538	—
Accounts payable	6,455	5,555	5,188
Accrued wages and withholdings	3,569	2,552	3,047
Self-insurance reserves	1,085	914	810
Accrued group welfare and retirement plan contributions	927	793	715
Other current liabilities	1,797	1,641	1,522
Total current liabilities	17,016	15,413	14,087
Long-term debt and finance leases	22,031	21,818	19,931
Noncurrent operating leases	2,540	2,391	—
Pension and postretirement benefit obligations	15,817	10,601	8,347
Deferred income tax liabilities	488	1,632	1,619
Other noncurrent liabilities	3,847	2,719	2,995
Total liabilities	61,739	54,574	46,979
Total shareowners' equity	669	3,283	3,037
Total liabilities and shareowners' equity	$62,408	$57,857	$50,016

REQUIRED

a. Compute ROA and disaggregate it into profit margin (PM) and asset turnover (AT) for 2020 and 2019. Comment on the drivers of the ROA. Assume a 25% tax rate for this period.

b. Compute any expense to sales (ETS) ratios that you think might help explain UPS' profitability.

c. Compute return on equity (ROE) for 2020 and 2019.

d. Comment on the difference between ROE and ROA. What does this relation suggest about UPS' use of debt?

P5-42. Analysis and Interpretation of Liquidity and Solvency

LO5-4
Homework MBC
United Parcel Service
NYSE :: UPS

Refer to the financial information of United Parcel Service in P5-41 to answer the following requirements.

REQUIRED

a. Compute its current ratio and quick ratio for 2020 and 2019. Comment on any observed trends.

b. Compute its times interest earned and its debt-to-equity ratios for 2020 and 2019. Comment on any trends observed.

c. Summarize your findings in a conclusion about the company's liquidity and solvency. Do you have any concerns about its ability to meet its debt obligations?

P5-43.[A] Computing and Analyzing Operating Returns

LO5-5
Homework MBC
United Parcel Service
NYSE :: UPS

Refer to the financial statements of United Parcel Service in P5-41 to answer the following requirements.

REQUIRED

a. Compute net operating profit after taxes (NOPAT) for 2020 and net operating assets (NOA) for 2020 and 2019. Assume a tax rate of 25%.

b. Compute the return on net operating assets (RNOA) for 2020. What percentage of UPS' ROE is generated by operations?

c. Decompose RNOA by computing net operating profit margin (NOPM) and net operating asset turnover (NOAT) for 2020.

d. What can be inferred about UPS from these ratios?

LO5-6 Homework MBC

United Parcel Service
NYSE :: UPS

P5-44.[B] Preparing Financial Statement Forecasts

Refer to the financial statements of United Parcel Service in P5-41 to answer the following requirements. The following assumptions should be useful:

- UPS' sales forecast for 2021 is $90,000 million.
- Operating expenses and operating profits increase in proportion to sales.
- Interest expense is unchanged in 2021, and Investment (income) expense is forecasted to be ($1,500).
- Income taxes are 25% of pretax earnings.
- Marketable securities and Investments and restricted cash are unchanged in 2021, and there are no assets held for sale in 2021; all other assets (except cash) increase in proportion to sales.
- Long-term debt and finance leases, non-current operating leases, current maturities of long-term debt and of operating leases are unchanged in 2021; all other liabilities increase in proportion to sales.
- Dividends are 50% of net income. Income and dividends are the only changes to stockholders' equity in 2021.

REQUIRED

a. Prepare an income statement forecast for 2021.

b. Prepare a balance sheet forecast for 2021.

LO5-3 Homework MBC

Abbott Laboratories
NYSE :: ABT
Bristol-Myers Squibb Company
NYSE :: BMY
Johnson & Johnson
NYSE :: JNJ
GlaxoSmithKline plc (ADR)
NYSE :: GSK
Pfizer Inc.
NYSE :: PFE
Moderna, Inc.
NYSE :: MRNA

P5-45. Comparing Profitability Ratios for Competitors

Selected 2020 income statement data for Abbott Laboratories, Bristol-Myers Squibb Company, Johnson & Johnson, GlaxoSmithKline plc, Pfizer, Inc., and Moderna, Inc., is presented in the following table:

(millions)	Abbott Laboratories	Bristol-Myers Squibb	Johnson & Johnson	Glaxo Smith Kline plc	Pfizer	Moderna
Sales revenue	$34,608	$42,518	$82,584	£34,099	$41,908	$803
Cost of sales	15,003	11,773	28,427	11,704	8,692	8
SG&A expense	9,696	7,661	22,084	11,456	11,615	188
R&D expense	2,420	11,143	12,159	5,098	9,405	1,370
Interest expense	546	1,420	201	892	1,449	10
Net income (loss)	4,495	(8,995)	14,714	6,388	9,652	(747)

REQUIRED

a. Compute the profit margin (PM) and gross profit margin (GPM) ratios for each company. (As a British company, GlaxoSmithKline plc has a statutory tax rate of 19.25% in 2020. Assume a tax rate of 25% for the others.)

b. Compute the research and development (R&D) expense to sales ratio and the selling, general, and administrative (SG&A) expense to sales ratio for each company.

c. Compare the relative profitability of these pharmaceutical companies.

LO5-3 Homework MBC

Best Buy Co., Inc.
NYSE :: BBY
The Kroger Co.
NYSE :: KR
Nordstrom, Inc.
NYSE :: JWN
ODP Corp.
NASDAQ :: ODP
Walgreens Boots Alliance, Inc.
NASDAQ :: WBA

P5-46. Comparing Profitability and Turnover Ratios for Retail Companies

Selected financial statement data for Best Buy Co., Inc., The Kroger Co., Nordstrom, Inc., ODP Corp., and Walgreens Boots Alliance, Inc., is presented in the following table:

($ millions)	Best Buy	Kroger	Nordstrom	ODP Corp.	Walgreens Boots
Sales revenue	$43,638.0	$122,286.0	$15,524.0	$9,710.0	$139,537.0
Cost of sales	33,590.0	95,294.0	9,932.0	7,578.0	111,520.0
Interest expense	64.0	603.0	151.0	42.0	639.0
Net income	1,541.0	1,512.0	496.0	(319.0)	424.0
Average receivables	1,082.0	1,647.5	163.5	727.0	7,179.0
Average inventories	5,291.5	8,293.5	1,949.0	981.0	9,392.0
Average PP&E	2,419.0	21,753.0	4,050.0	627.5	13,410.0
Average total assets	14,246.0	41,687.0	8,811.5	6,434.5	77,386.0

REQUIRED

a. Compute return on assets (ROA), profit margin (PM), and asset turnover (AT) for each company. Assume a statutory tax rate of 25%. Discuss the relative importance of PM and AT for each company.

b. Compute accounts receivable turnover (ART), inventory turnover (INVT), and property, plant, and equipment turnover (PPET) for each company. Discuss any difference that you observe.

c. Compute the gross profit margin (GPM) for each company. How does the GPM differ across companies? Does this difference seem to correlate with differences in ART or INVT? Explain.

CASES AND PROJECTS

C5-47. Management Application: Gross Profit and Strategic Management LO5-3

One way to increase overall profitability is to increase gross profit. This can be accomplished by raising prices and/or by reducing manufacturing costs.

REQUIRED

a. Will raising prices and/or reducing manufacturing costs unambiguously increase gross profit? Explain.

b. What strategy might you develop as a manager to (i) yield a price increase for your product or (ii) reduce product manufacturing cost?

C5-48. Management Application: Asset Turnover and Strategic Management LO5-3

Increasing net operating asset turnover requires some combination of increasing sales and/or decreasing net operating assets. For the latter, many companies consider ways to reduce their investment in working capital (current assets less current liabilities). This can be accomplished by reducing the level of accounts receivable and inventories or by increasing the level of accounts payable.

REQUIRED

a. Develop a list of suggested actions to achieve all three of these objectives as manager.

b. Examine the implications of each. That is, describe the marketing implications of reducing receivables and inventories and the supplier implications of delaying payment. How can a company achieve working capital reduction without negatively impacting its performance?

C5-49. Ethics and Governance: Earnings Management LO5-2, 3, 4

Companies are aware that analysts focus on profitability in evaluating financial performance. Managers have historically utilized a number of methods to improve reported profitability that are cosmetic in nature and do not affect "real" operating performance. These are typically subsumed under the general heading of "earnings management." Justification for such actions typically includes the following arguments:

- Increasing stock price by managing earnings benefits shareholders; thus, no one is hurt by these actions.
- Earnings management is a temporary fix; such actions will be curtailed once "real" profitability improves, as managers expect.

REQUIRED

a. Identify the affected parties in any scheme to manage profits to prop up stock price.

b. Do the ends (of earnings management) justify the means? Explain.

c. To what extent are the objectives of managers different from those of shareholders?

d. What governance structure can you envision that might prohibit earnings management?

SOLUTIONS TO REVIEW PROBLEMS

Review 5-1

THE COCA-COLA COMPANY AND SUBSIDIARIES
Consolidated Statements of Income
($ millions)

Year Ended December 31	2020	2019
Net operating revenues	100.0%	100.0%
Cost of goods sold	40.7%	39.2%
Gross profit	59.3%	60.8%
Selling, general, and administrative expenses	29.5%	32.5%
Other operating charges	2.6%	1.2%
Operating income	27.2%	27.1%
Interest income	1.1%	1.5%
Interest expense	4.4%	2.5%
Equity income (loss)—net	3.0%	2.8%
Other income (loss)—net	2.5%	0.1%
Income before taxes	29.4%	29.0%
Income taxes	6.0%	4.8%
Consolidated net income	23.4%	24.2%

THE COCA-COLA COMPANY AND SUBSIDIARIES
Common Size Balance Sheets

December 31	2020	2019
Assets		
Current assets		
Cash and cash equivalents	7.8%	7.5%
Short-term investments	2.0%	1.7%
Marketable securities	2.7%	3.7%
Trade accounts receivable, net	3.6%	4.6%
Inventories	3.7%	3.9%
Prepaid expenses and other current assets	2.2%	2.2%
Total current assets	22.0%	23.6%
Equity method investments	22.1%	22.0%
Other investments	0.9%	1.0%
Other assets	7.1%	7.0%
Deferred income tax assets	2.8%	2.8%
Property, plant, and equipment, net	12.3%	12.5%
Trademarks with indefinite lives	11.9%	10.7%
Goodwill	20.1%	19.4%
Other intangible assets	0.8%	1.0%
Total assets	100.0%	100.0%
Liabilities and equity		
Current liabilities		
Accounts payable and accrued expenses	12.8%	13.1%
Loans and notes payable	2.5%	12.7%
Current maturities of long-term debt	0.6%	4.9%
Accrued income taxes	0.9%	0.5%
Total current liabilities	16.8%	31.2%
Long-term debt	46.0%	31.9%
Other liabilities	10.8%	9.9%
Deferred income taxes	2.1%	2.6%
Total liabilities	75.7%	75.6%
Total equity	24.3%	24.4%
Total liabilities and equity	100.0%	100.0%

Note: Percentages are rounded amounts, and thus, they may not exactly sum to totals and subtotals.

Operating income, income before taxes, and consolidated income as a percentage of sales remained relatively flat from 2019 to 2020. Also, the mix between debt and equity financing changed very little between years (liabilities are approximately 76% of total assets for each year). Current assets as a percentage of total assets dropped slightly from 23.6% in 2019 to 22.0% in 2019 due to a drop in short-term investments and trade accounts receivable as a percentage of total assets in 2020 compared to 2019. The most significant change over the prior year was the increase in long-term debt as a percentage of total assets over the prior year (46% in 2020 vs. 32% in 2019). This caused a drop in current liabilities as a percentage of total assets in 2020 compared to 2019.

Review 5-2

($ MILLIONS)

$$\text{ROE} = \frac{\$7{,}768}{(\$21{,}284 + \$21{,}098)/2} = 0.3666 \text{ or } 36.66\%$$

$$\text{ROA} = \frac{\$7{,}768 + [\$1{,}437 \times (1 - 0.25)]}{(\$87{,}296 + \$86{,}381)/2} = 0.1019 \text{ or } 10.19\%$$

$$\text{ROFL} = 0.3666 - 0.1019 = 0.2647 \text{ or } 26.47\%$$

Review 5-3

($ MILLIONS)

$$\text{PM} = \frac{\$7{,}768 + [\$1{,}437 \times (1 - 0.25)]}{\$33{,}014} = 0.2679 \text{ or } 26.79\%$$

$$\text{AT} = \frac{\$33{,}014}{(\$87{,}296 + \$86{,}381)/2} = 0.3802 \text{ times}$$

$$26.79\% \times 0.3802 = 10.19\%$$

$$\text{GPM} = \frac{\$33{,}014 - 13{,}433}{\$33{,}014} = 0.5931 \text{ or } 59.31\%$$

$$\text{ART} = \frac{\$33{,}014}{(\$3{,}144 + \$3{,}971)/2} = 9.2801 \text{ times}$$

$$\text{INVT} = \frac{\$13{,}433}{(\$3{,}266 + \$3{,}379)/2} = 4.0430 \text{ times}$$

$$\text{PPET} = \frac{\$33{,}014}{(\$10{,}777 + \$10{,}838)/2} = 3.0547 \text{ times}$$

PepsiCo and Coca-Cola have similar business models, and both companies achieve high returns on the capital invested by their shareholders. PepsiCo has a much higher ROE (51% vs. 37% for Coca-Cola), and Coca-Cola has a slightly higher ROA (10.2% vs. 9.5% for PepsiCo). Most of the cause of the difference in ROE is due to the fact that PepsiCo has a much higher ROFL (41.0% vs. 26.5% for Coca-Cola), caused by its higher use of liabilities as a source of financing. Coca-Cola has a higher GPM and PM, while PepsiCo achieves a higher turnover of total assets. Closer analysis of turnover ratios reveals that ART is similar, implying that they employ similar credit policies. PepsiCo's inventory turns over significantly more quickly than Coca-Cola's inventory, perhaps reflecting differences in their product mix (e.g., PepsiCo's snack foods). This difference plays a significant role in PepsiCo's superior asset turnover. The two companies' PPET ratios are essentially identical, so utilization of fixed assets is not a factor in PepsiCo's higher total asset turnover.

Review 5-4

($ MILLIONS)

$$\text{Current ratio} = \frac{\$19{,}240}{\$14{,}601} = 1.318$$

$$\text{Quick ratio} = \frac{\$6{,}795 + \$4{,}119 + \$3{,}144}{\$14{,}601} = 0.963$$

$$\text{Debt-to-equity ratio} = \frac{\$66{,}012}{\$21{,}284} = 3.101$$

$$\text{Times interest earned} = \frac{\$9{,}749 + \$1{,}437}{\$1{,}437} = 7.784$$

Coca-Cola is more liquid than PepsiCo, as indicated by a higher current ratio (1.32 vs. 0.98) and a higher quick ratio (0.96 vs. 0.77). In addition, PepsiCo has a much higher debt-to-equity ratio than Coca-Cola (5.9 vs. 3.1), suggesting that PepsiCo is relying more on debt financing. This is consistent with the higher ROFL ratio computed in Review 5-2. Nevertheless, neither company has significant issues related to solvency. Both report reasonably high times-interest-earned ratios (8.24 for PepsiCo and 7.78 for Coca-Cola).

Review 5-5

($ MILLIONS)

Operating assets:
2020: $87,296 – $4,119 – $812 = $82,365
2019: $86,381 – $4,695 – $854 = $80,832

Operating liabilities:
2020: $66,012 – $2,183 – $485 – $40,125 = $23,219
2019: $65,283 – $10,994 – $4,253 – $27,516 = $22,520

Net operating assets (NOA):
2020: $82,365 – $23,219 = $59,146
2019: $80,832 – $22,520 = $58,312
NOPAT = $7,768 – [($370 – $1,437 + $841) × (1 – 0.25)] = $7,937.5

$$\text{RNOA} = \frac{\$7,937.5}{(\$59,146 + \$58,312)/2} = 13.5\%$$

$$\text{NOPM} = \frac{\$7,937.5}{\$33,014} = 24.04\%$$

$$\text{NOAT} = \frac{\$33,014}{(\$59,146 + \$58,312)/2} = 0.562$$

Review 5-6

THE COCA-COLA COMPANY AND SUBSIDIARIES
Forecasted Statements of Income
($ millions)

Year Ended December 31	2021
Net operating revenues	$34,665 (5% growth)
Cost of goods sold ($34,665 × 40.7%)	14,109
Gross profit	20,556
Selling, general, and administrative expenses ($34,665 × 29.5%)	10,226
Other operating charges ($34,665 × 2.6%)	901
Operating income	9,429
Interest income (unchanged)	370
Interest expense (unchanged)	1,437
Equity income (loss)—net (unchanged)	978
Other income (loss)—net (unchanged)	841
Income from continuing operations before income taxes	10,181
Income taxes from continuing operations ($10,181 × 25%)	2,545
Consolidated net income	$ 7,636

THE COCA-COLA COMPANY AND SUBSIDIARIES
Forecasted Balance Sheet
($ millions)

December 31	2021
Assets	
Current assets	
Cash and cash equivalents	$ 9,662
Short-term investments (unchanged)	1,771
Marketable securities (unchanged)	2,348
Trade accounts receivable, net ($34,665 × 9.5%)	3,293
Inventories ($34,665 × 9.9%)	3,432
Prepaid expenses and other assets ($34,665 × 5.8%)	2,011
Total current assets	22,517
Equity method investments (unchanged)	19,273
Other investments (unchanged)	812
Other assets ($34,665 × 18.7%)	6,482
Deferred income tax assets ($34,665 × 7.5%)	2,600
Property, plant, and equipment, net ($34,665 × 32.6%)	11,301
Trademarks with indefinite lives (unchanged)	10,395
Goodwill (unchanged)	17,506
Other intangible assets (unchanged)	649
Total assets	$91,535
Liabilities and shareholders' equity	
Current liabilities	
Accounts payable and accrued expenses ($34,665 × 33.8%)	$11,717
Loans and notes payable (unchanged)	2,183
Current maturities of long-term debt (unchanged)	485
Accrued income taxes ($34,665 × 2.4%)	832
Total current liabilities	15,217
Long-term debt (unchanged)	40,125
Other liabilities ($34,665 × 28.6%)	9,914
Deferred income taxes ($34,665 × 5.6%)	1,941
Total liabilities	67,197
Total equity [$21,284 + 7,636 – (0.60 × 7,636)]	24,338
Total liabilities and equity	$91,535

Chapter 6

Reporting and Analyzing Revenues, Receivables, and Operating Income

LEARNING OBJECTIVES

LO6-1 Describe and apply the criteria for determining when revenue is recognized.

LO6-2 Illustrate revenue and expense recognition when the transaction involves future deliverables and/or multiple elements.

LO6-3 Illustrate revenue and expense recognition for long-term projects.

LO6-4 Estimate and account for uncollectible accounts receivable.

LO6-5 Calculate return on net operating assets, net operating profit after taxes, return on net operating assets, net operating profit margin, accounts receivable turnover, and average collection period.

LO6-6 Discuss earnings management and explain how it affects analysis and interpretation of financial statements.

LO6-7 Appendix 6A: Describe and illustrate the reporting for nonrecurring items.

Road Map

LO	Learning Objective | Topics	Page	eLecture	Review	Assignments
LO6-1	Describe and apply the criteria for determining when revenue is recognized.	6-5	e6-1	R6-1	M6-14, M6-15, M6-17, E6-28, E6-29, E6-30, E6-31, E6-37, E6-47, E6-48, C6-50, C6-59, C6-61, DA6-1, DA6-2
LO6-2	Illustrate revenue and expense recognition when the transaction involves future deliverables and/or multiple elements.	6-8	e6-2	R6-2	M6-17, M6-26, M6-27, E6-29, E6-30, E6-31, E6-34, E6-35, E6-47, E6-48, E6-49, E6-50, P6-58, C6-59, C6-60, C6-61, C6-62, C6-63
LO6-3	Illustrate revenue and expense recognition for long-term projects.	6-11	e6-3	R6-3	M6-13, M6-16, E6-29, E6-30, E6-31, E6-32, E6-33, P6-52
LO6-4	Estimate and account for uncollectible accounts receivable.	6-14	e6-4	R6-4	M6-18, M6-19, M6-20, M6-21, M6-22, M6-24, M6-25, E6-38, E6-39, E6-40, E6-41, E6-42, E6-43, E6-44, E6-45, P6-54, P6-55, P6-56, P6-57, C6-52, C6-53, DA6-3, DA6-4, DA6-5
LO6-5	Calculate return on net operating assets, net operating profit after taxes, return on net operating assets, net operating profit margin, accounts receivable turnover, and average collection period.	6-22	e6-5	R6-5	M6-21, M6-23, E6-36, E6-40, E6-46, P6-51, P6-54, P6-55, C6-62
LO6-6	Discuss earnings management and explain how it affects analysis and interpretation of financial statements.	6-27	e6-6	R6-6	M6-28, E6-37, P6-53, C6-59, C6-60, C6-61
LO6-7	Appendix 6A: Describe and illustrate the reporting for nonrecurring items.	6-29	e6-7	R6-7	E6-46, P6-51, C6-64

MICROSOFT CORPORATION

www.microsoft.com

Microsoft Corporation has adopted a broad mission—to provide technology that will "empower every person and every organization on the planet to achieve more." To accomplish that objective, the company provides a wide range of software, services, devices, and solutions.

In its early years, Microsoft concentrated on software products—operating systems and productivity tools. Microsoft's current products include operating systems, productivity applications, server and business solution applications, tools to manage servers and to develop software, and video games. The company's products also include personal computers, tablets, and gaming equipment.

The technology industry is notable for quick, substantial changes, with formidable competition. Microsoft has expanded its offerings in cloud computing services that include software, platforms, content, and consulting. The company is one of the world's two largest providers of cloud computing. This service area is where Microsoft is experiencing significant growth. From 2018 to 2020, revenue from products increased by 5%, while revenue from services increased by 63%. But the coronavirus pandemic that appeared in the latter part of the company's 2020 fiscal year has affected some lines of business favorably (e.g., Personal Computing), while others were not (e.g., LinkedIn).

Profitability is the primary measure by which financial statement users gauge a company's success in efficiently offering products and services that receive a favorable response from customers. In this chapter, we focus on how companies report operating income. Operating income is determined by decisions about how and when to recognize revenues and expenses. In addition, the income statement also includes nonrecurring (or transitory) items, such as restructuring charges. Transitory items are often important events reflecting very large dollar amounts and are distinguished by the fact that they are unlikely to recur in subsequent years. Understanding how such nonrecurring items are reported is crucial to interpreting a company's profitability.

Microsoft's performance cannot be measured by profits alone. To control costs and improve operating profits, Microsoft must effectively manage operating assets. For example, accounts receivable is an important operating asset at Microsoft—accounting for almost 20% of its operating assets. By extending credit to customers on favorable credit terms, Microsoft stimulates sales. However, extending credit exposes the company to collectibility risk—the risk that some customers will not pay the amounts owed. In addition, accounts receivable do not earn interest and involve administrative costs associated with billing and collection. Hence, management of receivables is critical to financial success. This chapter describes the reporting of receivables. The reporting of other operating assets is covered in subsequent chapters.

Sources: Microsoft Corporation Annual Report 10-K 2020.

CHAPTER ORGANIZATION

Reporting and Analyzing Revenues, Receivables, and Operating Income

Reporting Operating Income
- Revenue Recognition
- Accounting for Transactions with Future Deliverables
- Accounting for Long-Term Projects

Reporting Receivables
- Allowance for Uncollectible Accounts
- Disclosures and Interpretations

Analyzing Financial Statements
- Net Operating Profit After Taxes
- Return on Net Operating Assets
- Net Operating Profit Margin
- Accounts Receivable Turnover
- Average Collection Period

Further Considerations
- Earnings Management
- Reporting Nonrecurring Items (Appendix A)

REPORTING OPERATING INCOME

The income statement is the primary source of information about recent company performance. This information is used to predict future performance for investment purposes and to assess the creditworthiness of a company. The income statement is also used to evaluate the quality of management.

This section describes the information reported in the income statement and its analysis implications. The central questions that the income statement attempts to answer are:

- How profitable has the company been recently?
- How did it achieve that profitability?
- Will the current profitability level persist?

To answer these three profitability questions, it is not enough to focus on a company's net income. Rather, we must use the various classifications within the income statement to see how profits were achieved and what the future prospects look like. **Exhibit 6.1** provides a schematic of the primary income statement classifications.

EXHIBIT 6.1 Income Statement Classifications

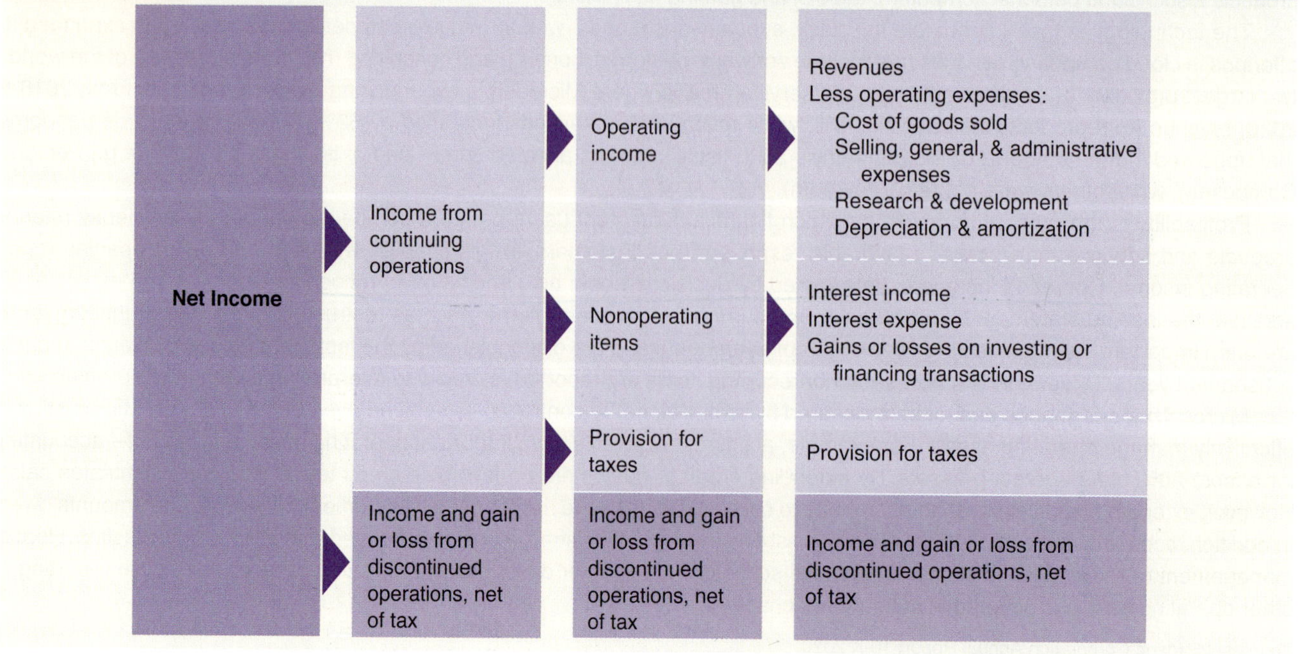

Operating activities refer to the primary transactions and events of a company. These include the purchase of goods from suppliers, the employment of personnel, the conversion of materials into finished products, the promotion and distribution of goods, the sale of goods and services to customers, and post-sale customer support. Operating activities are reported in the income statement under items such as sales, cost of goods sold, and selling, general, and administrative expenses (including research and development). They represent a company's primary activities, which must be executed successfully for a company to remain consistently profitable.

Nonoperating activities relate to the financial (borrowing) and securities investment activities of a company. These activities are typically reported in the income statement under items such as interest income and expenses, dividend revenues, and gains and losses on sales of securities. Distinguishing income components by operating versus nonoperating is an important part of effective financial statement analysis because operating activities drive company performance. It is of interest, for example, to know whether company profitability results from operating activities or whether poorly performing operating activities are being masked by income from nonoperating activities.

FYI When analyzing a company's income statement, it is important to distinguish operating activities from nonoperating activities and recurring activities from nonrecurring activities.

All the line items in income from continuing operations are presented before taxes, with the final line item being provision for income taxes, or tax expense. Microsoft's 2018 provision for income taxes includes the one-time effect of the Tax Cuts and Jobs Act that was enacted at the end of calendar year 2017. The accounting for income taxes is discussed more fully in Chapter 10.

If the company has income or gain/loss items that qualify as discontinued operations, these will be presented after income from continuing operations for the current year and for other income statements presented. Discontinued operations are reported net of income tax expense or benefit. The appendix at the end of this chapter provides a more detailed description of nonrecurring items. Finally, many large corporations report something called **net income attributable to noncontrolling interests**. Such an amount arises when a company consolidates a subsidiary that it controls, but for which it holds less than 100% ownership. This topic is covered in later chapters.

Exhibit 6.2 presents the 2020, 2019, and 2018 income statements (sometimes called statements of operations) for Microsoft Corporation. Microsoft has no discontinued operations during this time period, so income from continuing operations is the same as net income. Like many companies, Microsoft presents operating income as a subtotal in its income statement. Microsoft's operating income is computed by subtracting its total operating expenses (including cost of revenue, research and development, sales and marketing, and general and administrative) from total sales revenues. Nonoperating income and expenses, such as interest income and expense, and other income and expense are added to or deducted from the subtotal for operating income.

EXHIBIT 6.2 Distinguishing Operating and Nonoperating Sources of Income

MICROSOFT CORPORATION
Income Statements

(In millions, except per share amounts)	2020	2019	2018
Revenue:			
Product	**$68,041**	$ 66,069	$ 64,497
Service and other	**74,974**	59,774	45,863
Total revenue	**143,015**	125,843	110,360
Cost of revenue:			
Product	**16,017**	16,273	15,420
Service and other	**30,061**	26,637	22,933
Total cost of revenue	**46,078**	42,910	38,353
Gross margin	**96,937**	82,933	72,007
Research and development	**19,269**	16,876	14,726
Sales and marketing	**19,598**	18,213	17,469
General and administrative	**5,111**	4,885	4,754
Operating income	**52,959**	42,959	35,058
Other income, net	**77**	729	1,416
Income before income taxes	**53,036**	43,688	36,474
Provision for income taxes	**8,755**	4,448	19,903
Net income	**$44,281**	$ 39,240	$ 16,571

At this time, GAAP does not have specific rules for classifying revenue and expense items as either operating or nonoperating, so management must use judgment in reporting, and financial statement users must be careful to examine each revenue and expense item to determine if it is appropriately listed as part of operating income. Specifically, sales, cost of goods sold, and most selling, general, and administrative expenses are categorized as operating activities. Alternatively, investment-related income from dividends and interest is nonoperating, as is interest expense. Gains and losses on debt retirements and sales of investments are also nonoperating.[1]

While we think of Microsoft as a provider of software, hardware, and services, it had approximately $123 billion (41% of its total assets) invested in financial instruments (mostly government and government-backed securities) at 2020 fiscal year-end. And these assets provided close to $2.7 billion in interest and dividend income for 2020. So, making predictions about Microsoft's profitability for 2021 would be improved by separating the results of its product and service operations from those of its investing activities. In addition, operating income is the normal focus of business unit managers in a company—financing activities and investments in financial instruments and tax administration are usually determined at the central corporate level.

Revenue Recognition

LO6-1 Describe and apply the criteria for determining when revenue is recognized.

eLecture MBC

Revenue is one of the most important metrics of a company's operating success. The objective of almost all operating activities is to obtain a favorable response from customers, and revenue is a primary indicator of how customers view the company's product and service offerings. Companies can improve profits by reducing costs, but the effects of those improvements are limited unless revenues are increasing. Accordingly, growth in revenue is carefully monitored by management and by investors, as exemplified by the attention given to "same-store sales growth" in the retail industry.[2]

Revenue recognition refers to the timing and amount of revenue reported by the company. The decision of when to recognize revenue depends on certain criteria. Determining whether the criteria for revenue recognition are met is often subjective and requires judgment. Therefore, financial statement readers should pay careful attention to companies' revenue recognition, particularly when companies face market pressures to meet income targets. Indeed, many SEC enforcement actions against companies for inaccurate and sometimes fraudulent financial reporting are for improper (usually premature) revenue recognition.

Sales transactions between companies and their customers generally consist of an exchange in which the company provides a product or a service and, in return, receives a payment (usually, but not necessarily, a payment in cash). For many companies, this is a simple process—the customer walks into the convenience store, selects a soft drink, pays the store clerk for the soft drink, and then consumes the soft drink on the way home. The convenience store's revenue is the amount paid by the customer for the soft drink as the customer walks out with it (minus any sales taxes collected on behalf of government entities).

But other company/customer arrangements can be quite complicated, with delivery of the product and/or service occurring over time and with payments not coinciding with delivery. Revenue is such a vital component of companies' financial results, accounting standard setters formulated a broad principle and a process that is applied to almost all situations. The core principle is the following.

> An entity should recognize revenue to depict the transfer of goods or services to customers in an amount that reflects the consideration to which the entity expects to be entitled in exchange for those goods and services.

---

[1] To further complicate matters, the classification of some items in the income statement as nonoperating is not consistent with their classification in the cash flow statement. Specifically, interest and dividend income and interest expense are classified as operating in the cash flow statement and nonoperating in most income statements. Of course, the distinction between operating and nonoperating items depends on the company's business. For Microsoft, interest income and expense would be classified as nonoperating, but for a financial institution (e.g., a bank), those same items would be considered part of their operations. Purchases and sales of production equipment would be considered nonoperating for Microsoft, but operating for a company in the business of buying and selling used equipment.

[2] For a retail company, sales growth can come from increased sales at existing locations or from sales at recently opened locations—the former coming from customers' increased liking for the company's offerings and the latter coming from increased availability (which costs more to achieve). Quarterly same store sales growth uses only those locations that have been open for the current quarter and the quarter one year prior.

To accomplish this principle, companies follow a five-step process.

Step 1: Identify the contract with a customer.
Step 2: Identify the performance obligations in the contract.
Step 3: Determine the transaction price.
Step 4: Allocate the transaction price (if necessary).
Step 5: Recognize revenue when or as the entity satisfies a performance obligation.

The first step is to determine whether the transaction has commercial substance, that is it changes the future cash flows of the entity.[3] The word "contract" is used here in a general sense—it may refer to a legal document, but it can also reflect an oral agreement or be implied by the entity's (i.e., the seller's) customary business practices. The agreement must create enforceable rights and obligations for the parties.

The second step breaks the contract down into distinct "**performance obligations**" that the entity agrees to perform. Essentially, the entity must determine how many distinct goods and services it has agreed to provide to the customer. These are the "deliverables" for the entity, and the accounting standards require the performance obligations to be distinct from each other. That is, the customer can benefit from each performance obligation on its own or together with readily accessible resources. For instance, if the entity regularly sells the good or service separately, then it can be distinct. For instance, a manufacturer's product warranty is *not* a separate performance obligation if the warranty terms are set to assure the customer that the product will perform as promised. Ford Motor Company's base warranty comes with every vehicle and is not considered a separate performance obligation. On the other hand, a customer may purchase a ticket for travel on an airline, and that purchase would be comprised of transportation services on the scheduled flight *and* frequent flyer miles that can be used for travel in the future. Are the frequent flyer miles a separate performance obligation? The answer is yes, because airlines sell frequent flyer miles separately from travel services.[4] On the other hand, if there are multiple goods and/or services, but they require significant integration or coordination, then there is only one deliverable.

For the third step, the transaction price is the amount of consideration to which the entity expects to be entitled in exchange for transferring promised goods or services.[5] The accounting standard allows for "**variable consideration**," which may include (but is not limited to) price concessions, volume discounts, rebates, refunds, credits, incentives, performance bonuses, and royalties. Determining variable consideration can require significant estimation by the entity's management, and the standard has features that are intended to control undue optimism on the part of management. Consider the following from United Technologies Corporation's 10-K regarding revenue recognition.

> We consider the contractual consideration payable by the customer and assess variable consideration that may affect the total transaction price, including contractual discounts, contract incentive payments, estimates of award fees, unfunded contract value under U.S. Government contracts, and other sources of variable consideration, when determining the transaction price of each contract.
>
> We include variable consideration in the estimated transaction price when there is a basis to reasonably estimate the amount. These estimates are based on historical experience, anticipated performance, and our best judgment at the time.

If there are multiple performance obligations, then Step 4 requires that the transaction price from Step 3 be allocated to these individual performance obligations based on their stand-alone selling prices. This process is simple if stand-alone selling prices are readily available. But if such

[3] Suppose Companies A and B each have an inventory of 10,000 units of the same item, with unit costs of $100. They each arrange to sell the inventory to the other for $3 million. Could they each recognize $3 million in revenue and $1 million in cost of goods sold? No, because the transactions leave their future cash flows unaffected, i.e., lacking commercial substance.

[4] If the contract involves providing a series of distinct goods or services that are substantially the same, then the series is treated as a single performance obligation that is satisfied over time. For example, a company might agree to provide nightly cleaning services for an office. While one could treat each day's cleaning as a separate performance obligation, it was deemed easier to view the cleaning contract as a single performance obligation that is fulfilled over time.

[5] Amounts collected for third parties (e.g., sales taxes) are not included in the entity's revenue.

prices do not exist, then the company must estimate the stand-alone selling prices. For example, if the stand-alone selling prices of performance obligations A and B are $150 and $350 respectively, and the entity agrees to deliver them to the customer for a combined price of $400, then it should recognize $120 (= $400 × (150/(150 + 350))) when A is delivered and $280 = $400 × [350/(150 + 350)] when B is delivered.

Finally, Step 5 requires that the entity recognize revenue as it satisfies a performance obligation. A performance obligation is considered to be satisfied when the customer obtains control, i.e., when the customer obtains the ability to direct the use of and obtain substantially all of the remaining benefits of the asset/service that constitutes the performance obligation. In some cases, the customer obtains control over time, but if control does not transfer over time, then it is presumed to transfer at a point in time.

In many instances, the sole performance obligation is to deliver a product or service to the customer. Delivery doesn't refer only to transportation to the customer's location, but rather the transfer of title and the risks and rewards of ownership to the customer. Revenue recognition complications arise if there is uncertainty about collectability or when the sale is contingent on product performance, product approval, or similar contingencies. In some industries, it is standard practice to allow customers to return the product within a specified period of time. When these uncertainties are substantial, companies may have to reconsider the first step in the revenue recognition process. That is, does the delivery have commercial substance?

But for many companies, returns and uncollectible accounts are either immaterial in amount or relatively easy to predict based on history of a large number of similar transactions. The expected returns are estimated and reduce the reported revenue from the sale.

As noted earlier, revenue is a key performance indicator for almost every company, and there exists a wide variety of practices used in formulating a sales contract between a company and its customers. Given that diversity, the process to determine when to recognize revenue and how much revenue to recognize requires substantial judgment on the part of management. Therefore, it's important for the financial statement reader to check the disclosure notes describing a company's practices.

BUSINESS INSIGHT

Performance Obligations and Product Returns at The Gap, Inc. Following is an excerpt from The Gap, Inc.'s accounting policies as reported in its annual financial statements:

> For online sales and catalog sales the Company has elected to treat shipping and handling as fulfillment activities, and not a separate performance obligation. Accordingly, we recognize revenue for our single performance obligation related to online sales and catalog sales at the time control of the merchandise passes to the customer, which is generally at the time of shipment. We also record an allowance for estimated returns based on our historical return patterns and various other assumptions that management believes to be reasonable . . .

The Gap's policy regarding product returns is consistent with GAAP in that expected returns are estimated and deducted from sales at the time that the sale is recorded. This represents the amount to which the company "expects to be entitled" when it makes the sale. If returns cannot be estimated at that point in time, then GAAP would assess that there was not a contract with the customer, and no revenue would be recognized at that point.

The term "delivery" does not refer solely to transportation to the customer's location, but also the transfer of title and of the control of the item's benefits. In a **consignment** sale, a *consignor* delivers product to a *consignee* but retains ownership until the consignee sells the product to the ultimate customer. As long as ownership remains with the consignor, a sale has not taken place. Only when the consignee sells the product should the consignor record the sale revenue. Also at that point, the consignee, who has been acting as an agent for the consignor, will recognize the commission earned (not the full purchase price paid by the ultimate customer).

Identifying the Steps in the Revenue Recognition Process

LO6-1 Review 6-1

GuidedExample MBC

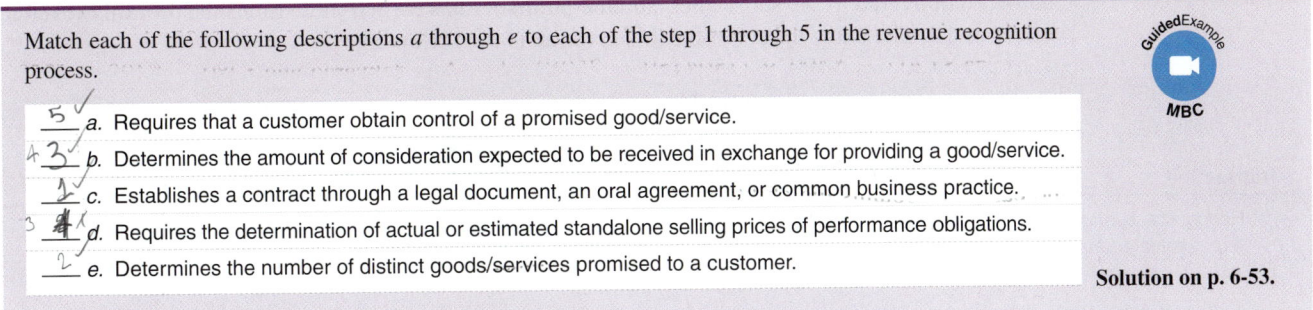

Match each of the following descriptions *a* through *e* to each of the step 1 through 5 in the revenue recognition process.

____ *a.* Requires that a customer obtain control of a promised good/service.

____ *b.* Determines the amount of consideration expected to be received in exchange for providing a good/service.

____ *c.* Establishes a contract through a legal document, an oral agreement, or common business practice.

____ *d.* Requires the determination of actual or estimated standalone selling prices of performance obligations.

____ *e.* Determines the number of distinct goods/services promised to a customer.

Solution on p. 6-53.

Revenue Recognition Subsequent to Customer Purchase

LO6-2 Illustrate revenue and expense recognition when the transaction involves future deliverables and/or multiple elements.

eLecture MBC

There are many businesses in which customers purchase a product or a service prior to its delivery. For instance, a customer may pay for a year's subscription to a periodical. The publisher receives the cash at the start of the subscription, but it recognizes revenue as it fulfills its performance obligation to deliver the periodical to the subscriber. Or, a homeowner may pay for the upcoming year's casualty insurance, but the insurance company can only recognize revenue as it fulfills its performance obligation to provide insurance coverage over that year.

In settings where a company's customers pay for the product or service prior to its delivery, the company must recognize a **contract liability**. The term "contract liability" refers to an entity's obligation to transfer goods or services to a customer for which the entity has received consideration (or the amount is due) from the customer. Such contract liabilities are frequently labeled as **unearned revenue** or **deferred revenue**[6] or some other descriptive term. Then this liability is reduced, and revenue recognized, as the performance obligation is fulfilled.

Suppose that on January 1, a subscriber pays $36 for an annual subscription to a monthly magazine. At the time of payment, the publisher would make the following entry:

ANALYZE

Transaction	Balance Sheet: Cash Asset	+	Noncash Assets	=	Liabil-ities	+	Contrib. Capital	+	Earned Capital	Income Statement: Revenues	−	Expenses	=	Net Income
(1) Receive $36 payment for one-year subscription.	+36 Cash			=	+36 Unearned Revenue						−		=	

JOURNALIZE

Cash (+A)	36	
Unearned revenue (+L)		36

POST

+ Cash (A) −	
(1) 36	

− Unearned Revenue (L) +	
	36 (1)

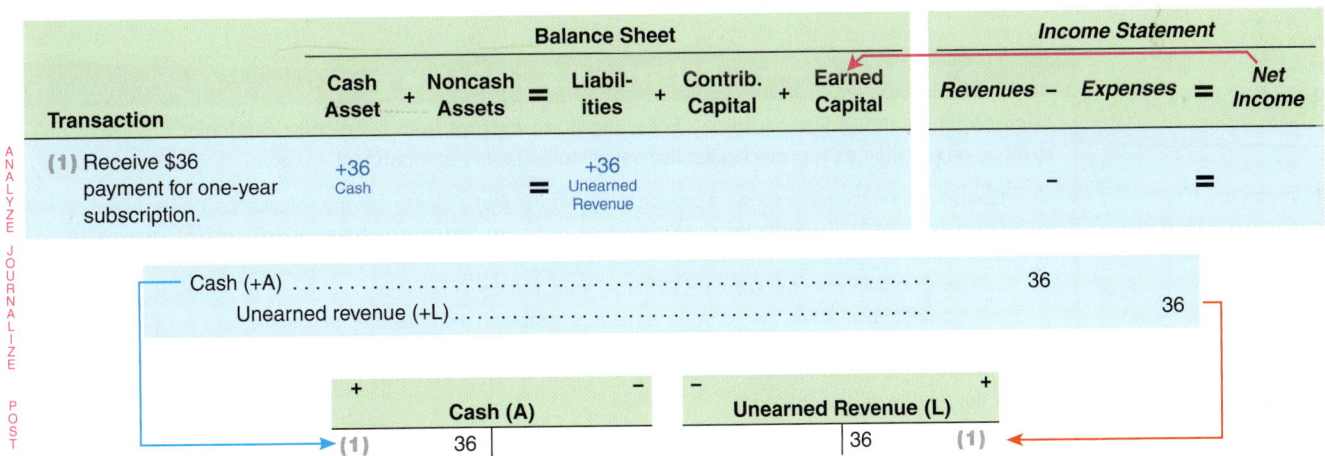

The unearned revenue liability represents the publisher's obligation—not to make a payment, but to provide the promised publication. Most liabilities reflect obligations to make a future payment, but unearned revenue is one of a handful of *contract liabilities* that represent an obligation for future performance.

---

[6] The term used for a contract liability may be particular to the company's business. For instance, **Delta Air Lines** shows an Air Traffic Liability of $4,044 million in its December 31, 2020, annual report, which represents customers' purchases of tickets in advance of their flights. **The Allstate Corporation** uses the term *Unearned Premiums*.

On March 31, at the end of its first quarter, the publisher would recognize that three magazines had been delivered to the subscriber, and the publisher has earned three times the monthly revenue of $3, or $9. The entry to recognize this revenue is the following.

ANALYZE

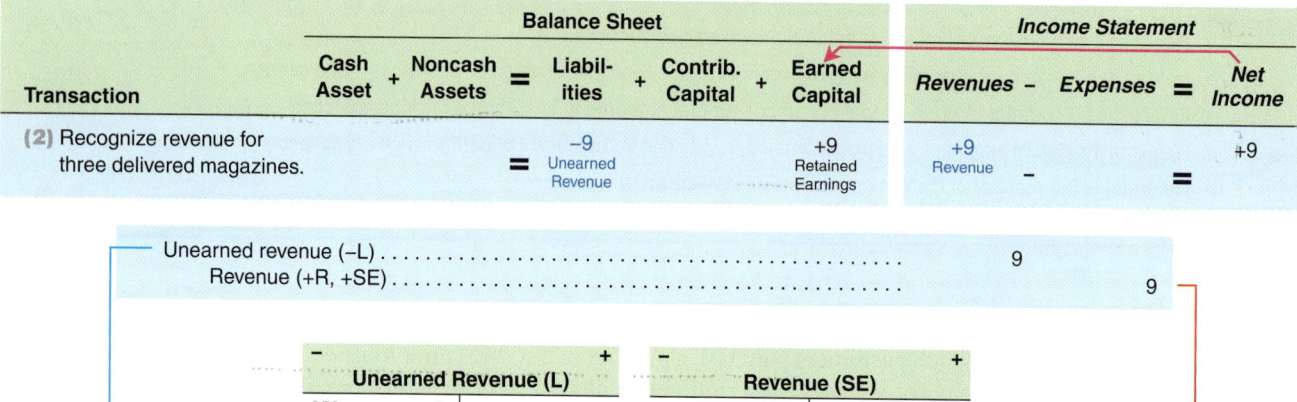

	Balance Sheet									Income Statement				
Transaction	**Cash Asset**	+	**Noncash Assets**	=	**Liabilities**	+	**Contrib. Capital**	+	**Earned Capital**	***Revenues***	–	***Expenses***	=	***Net Income***
(2) Recognize revenue for three delivered magazines.				=	−9 Unearned Revenue				+9 Retained Earnings	+9 Revenue	–		=	+9

JOURNALIZE

Unearned revenue (−L)	9	
Revenue (+R, +SE)		9

POST

− Unearned Revenue (L) +	
(2) 9	

− Revenue (SE) +	
	9 (2)

The same entries would be made until the subscription expired. In the March 31 balance sheet, the publisher would have an unearned revenue liability of $27, reflecting the remaining obligation for nine months of subscription delivery. And, the quarter's indirect method operating cash flows would include $9 in revenue (in net income) and the $27 increase in unearned revenue liability which, in total, reflect the $36 received from the customer.

Unearned revenue is seen in a growing number of financial statements as companies increase the use of gift cards as well as their promises of future deliveries of products and service due to the changing nature of products and services in the economy and in an effort to build a continuing relationship with their customers. From the point of view of a financial analyst, one implication of revenue deferral is that the change in revenue from one period to the next is not equal to the change in customer purchases over the same period. In the case of our publisher with one-year subscriptions, quarterly revenue is actually a composite of subscriber purchases over the current

BUSINESS INSIGHT

Microsoft's Revenue Recognition Following is an excerpt from Microsoft Corporation's policies on revenue recognition as reported in its disclosure notes to its recent annual report.

> Licenses for on-premises software provide the customer with a right to use the software as it exists when made available to the customer. Customers may purchase perpetual licenses or subscribe to licenses, which provide customers with the same functionality and differ mainly in the duration over which the customer benefits from the software. Revenue from distinct on-premises licenses is recognized upfront at the point in time when the software is made available to the customer. In cases where we allocate revenue to software updates, primarily because the updates are provided at no additional charge, revenue is recognized as the updates are provided, which is generally ratably over the estimated life of the related device or license . . . .
>
> Judgment is required to determine the SSP [Stand-alone Selling Price] for each distinct performance obligation. We use a single amount to estimate SSP for items that are not sold separately, including on-premises licenses sold with SA [Software Assurance] or software updates provided at no additional charge. We use a range of amounts to estimate SSP when we sell each of the products and services separately and need to determine whether there is a discount to be allocated based on the relative SSP of the various products and services.
>
> In instances where SSP is not directly observable, such as when we do not sell the product or service separately, we determine the SSP using information that may include market conditions and other observable inputs. We typically have more than one SSP for individual products and services due to the stratification of those products and services by customers and circumstances. In these instances, we may use information such as the size of the customer and geographic region in determining the SSP.

Microsoft emphasizes that judgment is required at many points in the revenue recognition process, from estimating the total selling price, to identifying distinct performance obligations, to allocating the total price to the performance obligations, and finally recognizing when the performance obligations are fulfilled.

quarter plus the last three quarters and, therefore, not an ideal indicator of how current customers are responding to the publisher's offerings. Both the revenue and unearned revenue accounts need to be analyzed to obtain a complete picture.

A revenue recognition complication arises when an agreement with a customer requires that two or more products or services (i.e., performance obligations) are sold under the same agreement for one lump-sum price. These bundled sales are commonplace in the software industry, where developers sell software, training, maintenance, and customer support in one transaction. In this case, the company must allocate the total consideration to the separate performance obligations based on their stand-alone selling price (estimated, if necessary). Revenue allocated to the performance obligations that have not yet been fulfilled (such as maintenance and customer support) must be deferred, with revenue recognized as those performance obligations are fulfilled in future periods.

To illustrate revenue recognition for a multiple performance obligation arrangement (or bundled sale), assume that Software Innovations, Inc., develops marketing software designed to track customer questions and comments on the Internet and through social media. The software license sells for $125,000 and includes user training for up to 12 individuals and customer support for three years. Software Innovations estimates that the software, if licensed without training or customer support, would sell for $120,000. In addition, it estimates that the value of the user training services, if sold separately, would be $18,000 and the customer support would sell for $12,000. Software Innovations would allocate the $125,000 sales price as illustrated in **Exhibit 6.3**.

EXHIBIT 6.3 Allocation of the Sales Price in a Multiple Performance Obligation Arrangement

Performance Obligation	Estimated Value	Percent of Total Value		Bundle Sales Price		Sales Price Allocated to Each Performance Obligation
Software license	$120,000	80%	×	$125,000	=	$100,000
Training	18,000	12	×	125,000	=	15,000
Customer support	12,000	8	×	125,000	=	10,000
Total	$150,000	100%				$125,000

The sale would be recorded as revenue for the portion that was allocated to software and as deferred (or unearned) revenue for that portion that was allocated to training and customer support:

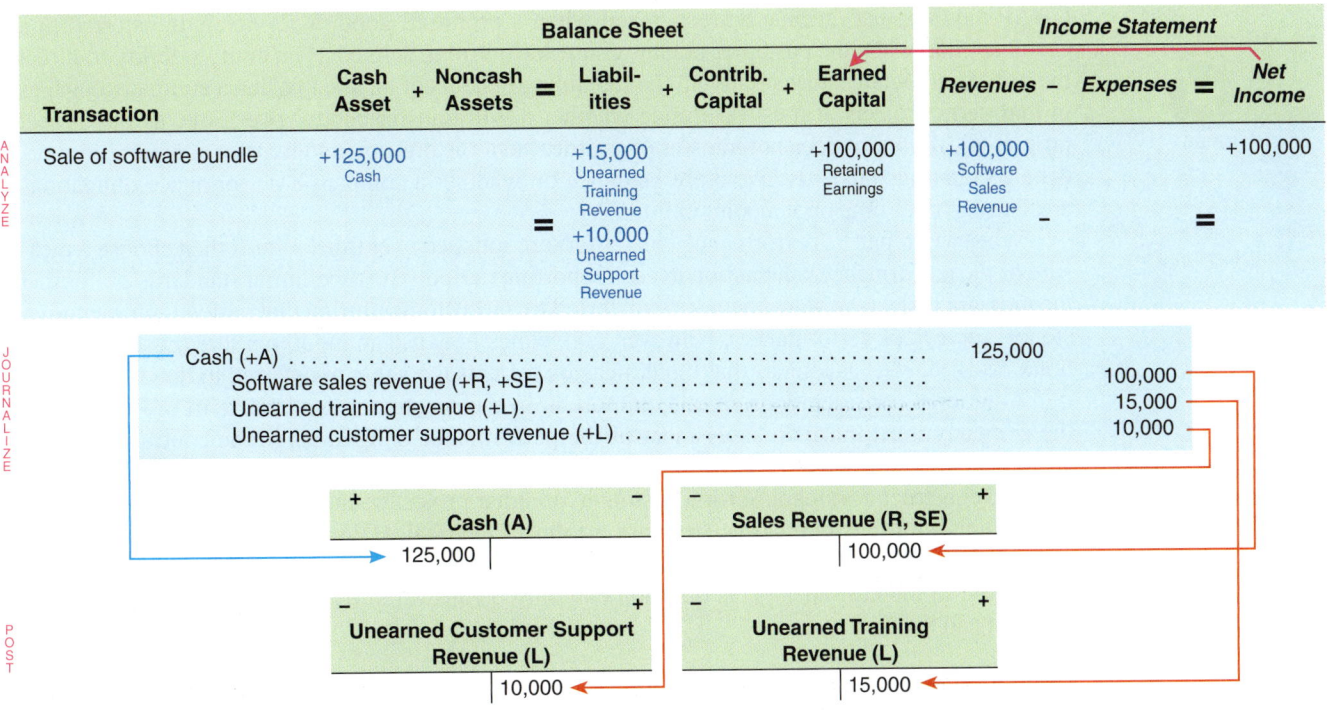

ANALYZE

	Balance Sheet									Income Statement				
Transaction	Cash Asset	+	Noncash Assets	=	Liabilities	+	Contrib. Capital	+	Earned Capital	Revenues	−	Expenses	=	Net Income
Sale of software bundle	+125,000 Cash			=	+15,000 Unearned Training Revenue +10,000 Unearned Support Revenue				+100,000 Retained Earnings	+100,000 Software Sales Revenue	−		=	+100,000

JOURNALIZE

Cash (+A)	125,000	
Software sales revenue (+R, +SE)		100,000
Unearned training revenue (+L)		15,000
Unearned customer support revenue (+L)		10,000

POST

+ Cash (A) −	
125,000	

− Sales Revenue (R, SE) +	
	100,000

− Unearned Customer Support Revenue (L) +	
	10,000

− Unearned Training Revenue (L) +	
	15,000

The unearned training revenue would be recognized as training services are provided. Software Innovations might recognize 1/12 of the $15,000, or $1,250 for each individual trained. The unearned customer support revenue would be recognized over time ($10,000/3 = $3,333 each year).

Review 6-2 LO6-2

Analyzing Deferred Revenue Charges

GuidedExample

MBC

In its annual report for fiscal year 2020, Electronic Arts, Inc., included the following disclosure in the notes accompanying the financial statements.

> Games with Services. Our sales of Games with Services are evaluated to determine whether the software license, future update rights, and the online hosting are distinct and separable. Sales of Games with Services are generally determined to have three distinct performance obligations: software license, future update rights, and the online hosting.
>
> Since we do not sell the performance obligations on a stand-alone basis, we consider market conditions and other observable inputs to estimate the stand-alone selling price for each performance obligation. For Games with Services, generally 75 percent of the sales price is allocated to the software license performance obligation and recognized at a point in time when control of the license has been transferred to the customer (which is usually at or near the same time as the booking of the transaction). The remaining 25 percent is allocated to the future update rights and the online hosting performance obligations and recognized ratably as the service is provided (over the Estimated Offering Period).

In its income statement for the fiscal year ended March 31, 2020, Electronic Arts reported *Total net revenue* of $5,537 million. At the beginning of that fiscal year, the company had a liability for *Deferred net revenue (online-enabled games)* of $1,100 million. At the end of the fiscal year, that liability was $945 million, a decrease of $155 million.

Required

a. What would cause the *Deferred net revenue (online-enabled gaming)* liability to go down over the fiscal year?

b. What was the amount of online-enabled games purchased by Electronic Arts' customers in the fiscal year ended March 31, 2020? How might that information be useful for a financial statement reader?

Solution on p. 6-53.

LO6-3 Illustrate revenue and expense recognition for long-term projects.

eLecture

MBC

Revenue Recognition for Long-Term Projects Challenges can arise in determining revenue recognition for companies with long-term production/service processes (spanning more than one reporting period), such as consulting firms, construction companies, and defense contractors. GAAP requires that revenue be recognized when a promised good or service is transferred to a customer, i.e., when the customer obtains control. Control is defined as an entity's ability to direct the use of and obtain substantially all the remaining benefits of an asset. When a company engages in long-term projects, it must determine whether it will transfer control over time, as the project progresses. If control does not transfer over time, then it is presumed to transfer at a point in time. (The accounting standards give more guidance on whether a company's performance obligations are satisfied over time or at a point in time.)

When a company's performance obligations are satisfied over time, it must then choose a measure of the performance satisfaction in each reporting period. The accounting standards prefer that the measure reflect the value that was transferred to the customer during that period (contract milestones, surveys of performance). However, companies may use an input measure (costs incurred, hours worked, etc.) as long as that input measure reflects the value transferred to the customer.

Additional considerations are also important in the accounting for long-term projects. First, the company must make an assessment of the performance obligations in the contract with the customer. Are there separate performance obligations, or only one? A construction company may agree to construct a warehouse for a customer, and that project could include several facets—site preparation, utilities, foundation, structure, roofing, electrical, HVAC, and so on. Does the company have separate performance obligations for each of these, or just one—to deliver a functioning warehouse to the customer? This question can only be answered by careful consideration of the contract and the circumstances.

PERFORMANCE OBLIGATION SATISFIED OVER TIME To illustrate the revenue recognition when the performance obligation is satisfied over time, assume that Built-Rite Construction signs a $10 million contract to construct a building for a customer. Built-Rite estimates $7.5 million in construction costs, yielding an expected gross profit of $2.5 million. Based on its review of the contract, Built-Rite determines that the building construction is a single performance obligation satisfied over time. In addition, the construction costs incurred reflect the amount of value transferred to the customer during a reporting period, so Built-Rite can use the "cost-to-cost"[7] measure of performance.

In the first year of construction, Built-Rite incurs $4.5 million in construction costs. The remaining $3.0 million are incurred during the second year. The amount of revenue and gross profit that Built-Rite would report each year (in millions) is illustrated in **Exhibit 6.4**.

EXHIBIT 6.4 Performance Obligation Satisfied over Time Based on Cost-to-Cost

Year	Measure of Value Transferred	Revenue Recognized	Expense Recognized	Gross Profit
1	$4.5/$7.5 = 60%	$10.0 × 60% = $ 6.0	$4.5	$1.5
2	$3.0/$7.5 = 40%	$10.0 × 40% = 4.0	3.0	1.0
Total	100%	$10.0	$7.5	$2.5

Using this method, Built-Rite would report $1.5 million in gross profit in the first year and $1.0 million in the second year. The timing of revenue and gross profit coincides with the transfer of value to the customer.

When a company's performance obligation is satisfied over time and cost is used to assess performance, it requires an estimate of the total cost to completion. This estimate is initially made at the start of the contract, usually used to bid the contract. However, estimates are inherently prone to error. If total completion costs are underestimated, the percentage of completion is overestimated (the denominator is too small), and too much revenue and gross profit are recognized in the early years of the project. Therefore, the reliability of the reported performance depends on the quality of judgments made by the company's management.

PERFORMANCE OBLIGATION SATISFIED AT A POINT IN TIME In some circumstances, the company will determine that its performance obligation is not satisfied over time, but rather at a point in time. If Built-Rite Construction had determined that its performance obligation to construct the customer's building was not satisfied until delivery of the completed building to the customer, the revenue and gross profit would be reported as in **Exhibit 6.5**.

EXHIBIT 6.5 Performance Obligation Satisfied over Time versus at a Point in Time

Performance Obligation Satisfied over Time			Performance Obligation Satisfied at a Point in Time		
	Year 1	Year 2		Year 1	Year 2
Revenues	$6.0	$4.0	Revenues	$0.0	$10.0
Expenses	4.5	3.0	Expenses	0.0	7.5
Gross profit.	$1.5	$1.0	Gross profit.	$0.0	$ 2.5

The total revenue and gross profit are the same under either method. The only difference is in the timing of the income statement reporting. Revenue and gross profit will show more variability when the performance obligation is satisfied at the end of the process.

TIMING DIFFERENCES BETWEEN REVENUES AND CASH RECEIPTS It is very likely that Built-Rite would have received some cash payments from the customer during the construction period, perhaps as advances or based on milestones in the construction process. However, the recognition of revenue is tied to the completion of performance obligations, which may differ from the measures used to determine progress payments. If a company receives payment prior to completion of the performance obligation, then it should recognize a **contract liability**, like deferred revenue or unearned revenue. If the project progress entitles the company to payment, it would also recognize an account receivable.

[7] That is, the cost incurred compared to the estimated total cost. This approach is often referred to as "percentage-of-completion."

In addition, the company should recognize revenue in the amount to which it expects to be entitled for completing the performance obligation. So, if a contract includes an incentive payment for timely completion of the project, the company should recognize its estimate of the amount of incentive that it expects to receive, prior to the actual receipt of that payment at the end of the contract. This contract arrangement can result in the company recognizing revenue when it cannot yet send an invoice to the customer. That is, the company is not yet entitled to an unconditional right to future payment. When such revenue is credited, the account debited is referred to as a **contract asset** (sometimes referred to as unbilled receivables). A contract asset represents an amount that the company expects to receive from the customer for performance to date, but for which it is not yet entitled to payment.

As an example, suppose Built-Rite's contract with the customer allows it to bill the customer for half the project once 60% of the work is complete at the end of year 1. The entry made to reflect revenue recognized for year 1 would be the following (all amounts in $ millions):

	Balance Sheet									Income Statement				
Transaction	**Cash Asset**	+	**Noncash Assets**	=	**Liabil-ities**	+	**Contrib Capital**	+	**Earned Capital**	**Revenues**	−	**Expenses**	=	**Net Income**
ANALYZE: Recognize year 1 revenue			+5 Accounts Receivable +1 Contract Assets	=					+6 Retained Earnings	+6 Construction Revenue	−		=	+6

JOURNALIZE

Accounts receivable (+A). 5
Contract assets (+A) 1
  Construction revenue (+R, +SE). 6
Recognize year 1 revenue on construction

POST

+ Accounts receivable (A) −	
5	

− Construction revenue (R, SE) +	
	6

+ Contract assets (A) −	
1	

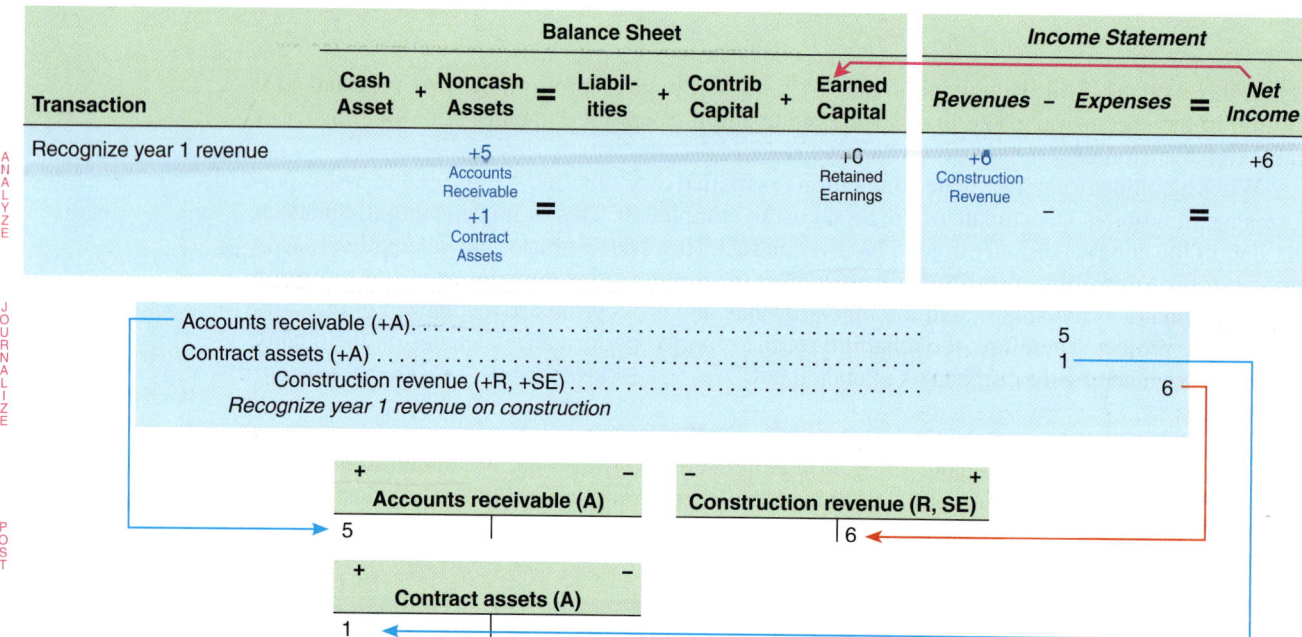

On completion of the project at the end of year 2, Built-Rite would recognize as revenue the 40% of the project completed. It would bill the customer for this amount *plus* the amount of revenue previously held as contract assets.

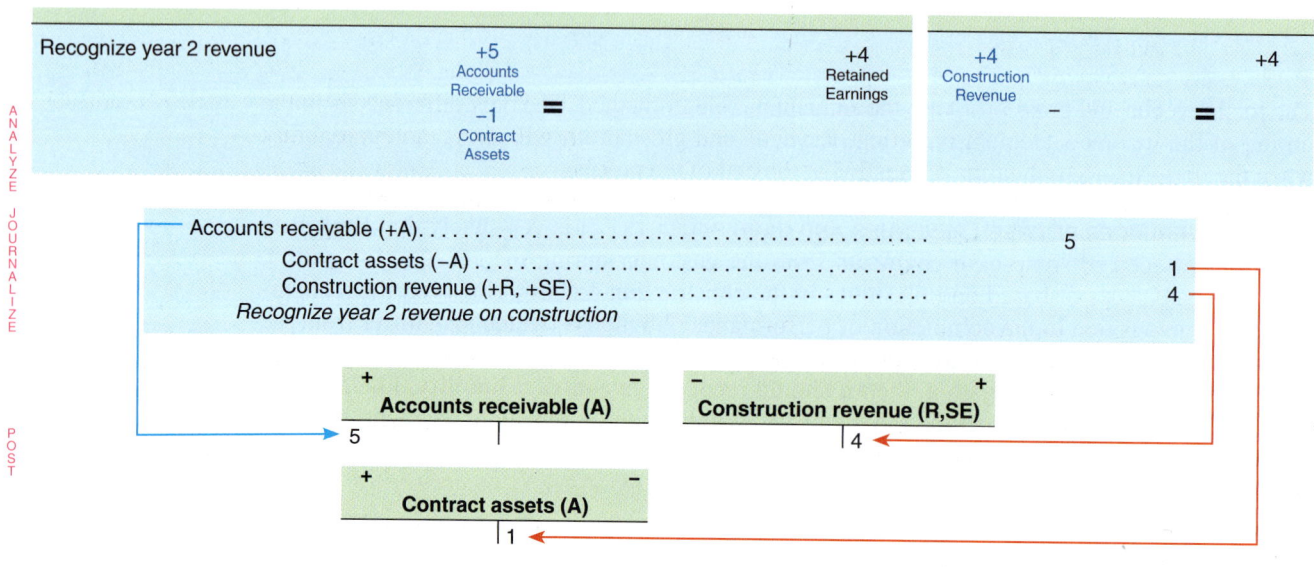

Transaction	Cash Asset	+	Noncash Assets	=	Liabil-ities	+	Contrib Capital	+	Earned Capital	Revenues	−	Expenses	=	Net Income
ANALYZE: Recognize year 2 revenue			+5 Accounts Receivable −1 Contract Assets	=					+4 Retained Earnings	+4 Construction Revenue	−		=	+4

JOURNALIZE

Accounts receivable (+A). 5
  Contract assets (−A) 1
  Construction revenue (+R, +SE). 4
Recognize year 2 revenue on construction

POST

+ Accounts receivable (A) −	
5	

− Construction revenue (R,SE) +	
	4

+ Contract assets (A) −	
	1

BUSINESS INSIGHT

Fluor Corporation engages in engineering and construction activities for its customers. The following excerpts from its 2019 10-K are taken from its disclosure note on revenue recognition.

> "We recognize engineering and construction contract revenue over time as we provide services to satisfy our performance obligations. We generally use the cost-to-cost percentage-of-completion measure of progress as it best depicts how control transfers to our clients. The cost-to-cost approach measures progress towards completion based on the ratio of contract cost incurred to date compared to total estimated contract cost. Engineering and construction contracts are generally accounted for as a single unit of account (a single performance obligation) and are not segmented between types of services on a single project . . ."
>
> "The nature of our contracts gives rise to several types of variable consideration, including claims, unpriced change orders, award and incentive fees, liquidated damages, and penalties. We consider variable consideration in the development of our project forecasts so that our forecasted revenue reflects the amount of consideration we expect to be probable of recovering without a significant reversal . . ."

In its December, 31, 2019, balance sheet, Fluor Corporation reports *Contract assets* of $882 million (11.1% of total assets) and *Contract liabilities* of $1,120 million (17.6% of total liabilities). The contract assets represent revenue that has been recognized but not yet billed to the customer. When Fluor bills a customer for an amount that exceeds the recognized revenue, the excess is reported as a contract liability.

Recording Revenue Transactions

LO6-3 **Review 6-3**

GuidedExample MBC

Haskins, Inc., has reached an agreement with a customer, Skaife Corporation, to deliver 200 units of a customized product. The standard billing price per unit is $1,000, and there are no discounts. At the time of the agreement on April 6, Skaife Corporation provides a $40,000 cash deposit to Haskins, Inc. Haskins agrees to deliver 120 units to Skaife Corporation on May 31 and, at that time, Haskins can send an invoice for $50,000 to be paid by Skaife Corporation on June 15. The remaining 80 units are to be delivered on July 15, accompanied by an invoice for the remaining amount of the total $200,000 purchase price to be paid on July 31.

Required

Assume that Haskins, Inc., has no uncertainties about its own ability to meet the terms of the contract or about Skaife Corporation's ability and willingness to pay.

a. Report the effects of the above events on Haskins' revenues using the financial statement effects template (leaving out the accounting for Haskins' costs).

b. Prepare journal entries to record the events identified in part a and post to T-accounts.

Solution on p. 6-53.

REPORTING ACCOUNTS RECEIVABLE

LO6-4 Estimate and account for uncollectible accounts receivable.

eLecture MBC

Receivables are usually a major part of operating working capital. They must be carefully managed because they represent a substantial asset for most companies. GAAP requires companies to report revenues in the amount to which they expect to be entitled and receivables in the amount to which they have an unconditional right to payment. But the balance sheet value of receivables should be the amount they expect to collect, necessitating an estimation of uncollectible accounts. These estimates determine the amount of receivables reported on the balance sheet as well as revenues and expenses reported on the income statement. Accordingly, it is important that companies accurately assess uncollectible accounts and report them. It is also necessary that readers of financial reports understand management's accounting choices and the effects of those choices on reported balance sheets and income statements.

FYI The phrase "trade receivables" refers to accounts receivable from customers.

When companies sell to other companies, they usually do not expect cash upon delivery as is common with retail customers. Instead, they offer credit terms, and the resulting sales are called **credit sales** or *sales on account.*

FYI Receivables are claims held against customers and others for money, goods, or services.

Companies establish credit policies (to determine which customers receive credit) by weighing the expected losses from uncollectible accounts against the expected profits generated by offering credit. Sellers know that some buyers will be unable to pay their accounts when they become due. Buyers, for example, can suffer business downturns that are beyond their control and which limit their cash available to meet liabilities. They must, then, make choices concerning which of their liabilities to pay. Liabilities to the IRS, to banks, and to bondholders are usually paid because those creditors have enforcement powers and can quickly seize assets and disrupt operations, leading to bankruptcy and eventual liquidation. Buyers also try to cover their payroll because they cannot exist without employees. Then, if there is cash remaining, these customers will pay suppliers to ensure a continued flow of goods.

When a customer faces financial difficulties, suppliers are often the last creditors to receive payment and are often not paid in full. Consequently, there is risk in the collectibility of accounts receivable. This *collectibility risk* is crucial to analysis of accounts receivable.

Accounts receivable are reported on the balance sheet of the seller at **net realizable value**, which is the net amount that the seller expects to collect. Microsoft reports $32,011 million of accounts receivable in the current asset section of its 2020 balance sheet. Its receivables are reported net of allowances for doubtful accounts of $788 million. This means that the total amount owed to Microsoft by customers is $32,799 million ($32,011 million + $788 million), but the company *estimates* that $788 million of these receivables will be uncollectible. Thus, only the net amount that Microsoft expects to collect is reported on the balance sheet.

FYI Receivables are classified into three types: (1) current or noncurrent, (2) trade or nontrade, (3) accounts receivable or notes receivable. **Notes receivable** and **notes payable** are discussed in Chapter 9.

We might ask why the management of Microsoft would sell to companies from whom they do not expect to collect the amounts owed.[8] The answer is they would not *if* they knew beforehand who those companies were. That is, Microsoft probably cannot identify those companies that constitute the $788 million in uncollectible accounts as of its statement date. Yet, Microsoft knows from past experience that a certain portion of its receivables will prove uncollectible. GAAP requires a company to estimate the dollar amount of uncollectible accounts each time it issues its financial statements (even if it cannot identify specific accounts that are uncollectible) and to report its accounts receivable at the resulting *net realizable value* (total receivables less an **allowance for doubtful (uncollectible) accounts**).

Determining the Allowance for Uncollectible Accounts

The amount of expected uncollectible accounts is usually estimated based on an **aging analysis**. When aging the accounts, an analysis of receivables is performed as of the balance sheet date. Specifically, each customer's account balance is categorized by the number of days or months that the related invoices are outstanding. Based on prior experience, assessment of current economic conditions, or other available statistics, uncollectible (bad debt) percentages are applied to each of these categorized amounts, with larger percentages applied to older accounts. The result of this analysis is a dollar amount for the allowance for uncollectible accounts (also called allowance for doubtful accounts) at the balance sheet date.

To illustrate, **Exhibit 6.6** shows an aging analysis for a seller that began operations this year and is owed $100,000 of accounts receivable at year-end. Those accounts listed as current consist of those outstanding that are still within their original credit period. Accounts listed as 1–60 days past due are those 1 to 60 days past their due date. This classification would include an account that is 45 days outstanding for a net 30-day invoice. This same logic applies to all aged categories.

EXHIBIT 6.6 Aging of Accounts Receivable

Age of Accounts Receivable	Receivable Balance	Estimated Percent Uncollectible	Accounts Estimated Uncollectible
Current	$ 50,000	2%	$1,000
1–60 days past due	30,000	3	900
61–90 days past due	15,000	4	600
Over 90 days past due	5,000	8	400
Total	$100,000		$2,900

[8] GAAP requires that companies distinguish between amounts that they expected to receive that turned out to be uncollectible and amounts that represent an "implied price concession." For example, suppose a healthcare provider treats an uninsured patient, and the list price of the services is $10,000. But it is common for the healthcare company to accept, say, $1,500 from uninsured patients receiving such services. Should the healthcare company report revenue of $10,000 and $8,500 of bad debt expense? GAAP says that if there is an expectation that the healthcare company will accept the lower amount, then it should recognize $1,500 in revenue, not $10,000.

The calculation illustrated in **Exhibit 6.6** also reflects the seller's experience with uncollectible accounts, which manifests itself in the uncollectible percentages for each aged category. For example, on average, 3% of buyers' accounts that are 1–60 days past due prove uncollectible for this seller. Hence, it estimates a potential loss of $900 for those $30,000 in receivables for that aged category.

One possible means of estimating uncollectible accounts is to use a percentage of sales as an estimate of bad debt expense. That approach might satisfy as an estimate for the forecasting of future period financial statements, but it ignores the actual payments made by customers, making it less accurate and not acceptable under U.S. GAAP.

In the past, investments in many financial instruments were valued at their acquisition cost until there was some evidence that a loss had occurred. Financial standard setters require that companies use a current expected credit loss model (CECL). CECL requires that companies use their historical loss rate, adjusted for current conditions, to value such investments, even at the point of initial investment. The aging-of-accounts described above is one such approach for the valuation of trade receivables and similar instruments.

Reporting the Allowance for Uncollectible Accounts

How does the accounting system record this estimate? The amount that appears in the balance sheet as accounts receivable represents a collection of individual accounts—one or more receivables for each customer. Because we need to keep track of exactly how much each customer owes us, we cannot simply subtract estimated uncollectibles from individual accounts receivable.

In Chapter 3, we introduced contra-asset accounts to record accumulated depreciation. A contra-asset account is directly associated with an asset account but serves to offset the balance of the asset account. To record the estimated uncollectible accounts without disturbing the balance in accounts receivable, we use another contra-asset—the allowance for uncollectible accounts.

To illustrate, we use the data from **Exhibit 6.6**. The summary journal entry to reflect credit sales follows.

ANALYZE

Transaction	Cash Asset	+	Noncash Assets	=	Liabil-ities	+	Contrib. Capital	+	Earned Capital	Revenues	−	Expenses	=	Net Income
					Balance Sheet					**Income Statement**				
(1) Sell $100,000 of products on account.			+100,000 Accounts Receivable	=					+100,000 Retained Earnings	+100,000 Sales Revenue	−		=	+100,000

JOURNALIZE

(1) Accounts receivable (+A)	100,000	
Sales revenue (+R, +SE)		100,000

POST

+ Accounts Receivable (A) −	
(1) 100,000	

− Sales Revenue +	
	100,000 (1)

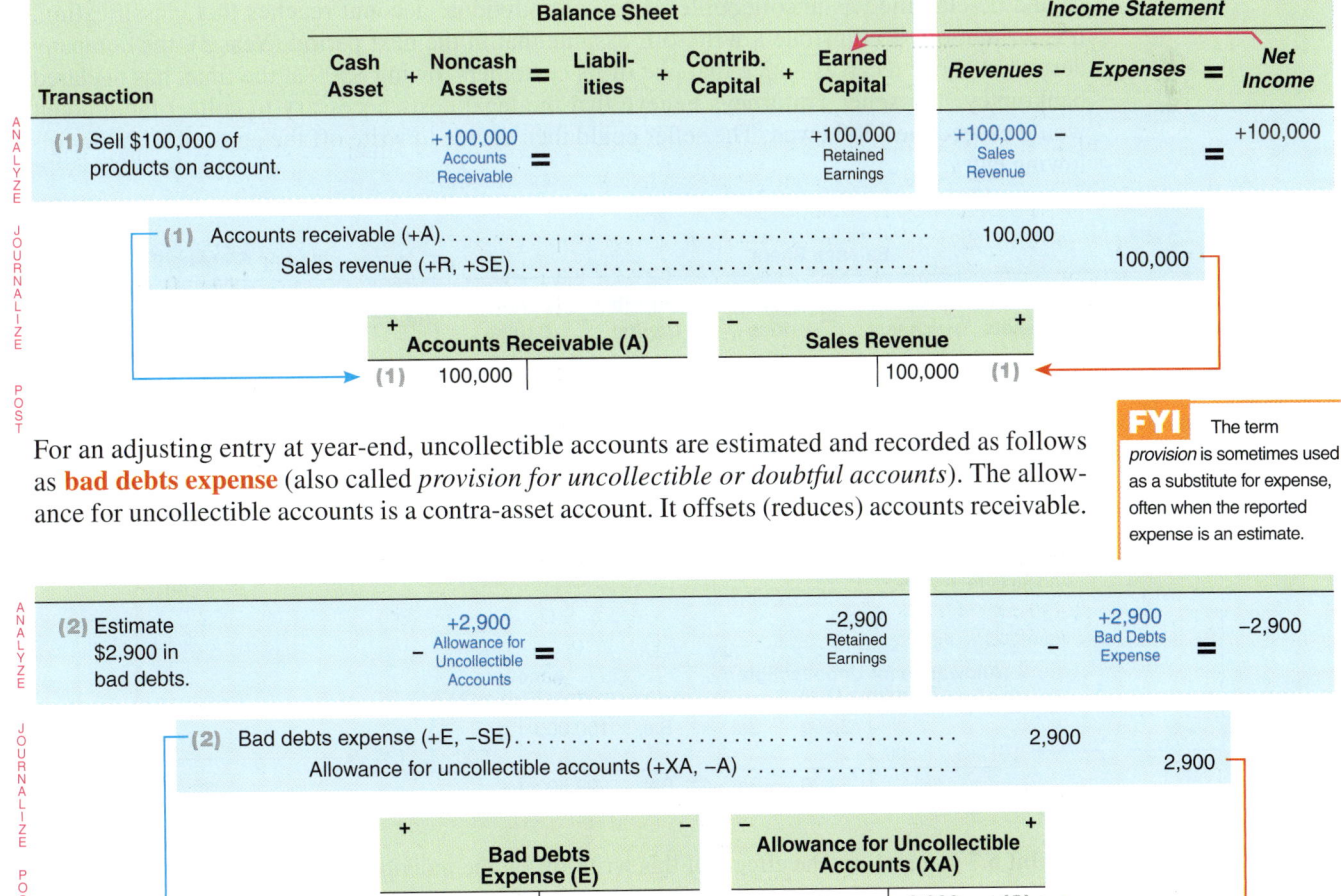

For an adjusting entry at year-end, uncollectible accounts are estimated and recorded as follows as **bad debts expense** (also called *provision for uncollectible or doubtful accounts*). The allowance for uncollectible accounts is a contra-asset account. It offsets (reduces) accounts receivable.

FYI The term *provision* is sometimes used as a substitute for expense, often when the reported expense is an estimate.

ANALYZE

Transaction	Cash Asset	+	Noncash Assets	=	Liabilities	+	Contrib. Capital	+	Earned Capital	Revenues	−	Expenses	=	Net Income
(2) Estimate $2,900 in bad debts.		−	+2,900 Allowance for Uncollectible Accounts	=					−2,900 Retained Earnings		−	+2,900 Bad Debts Expense	=	−2,900

JOURNALIZE

(2) Bad debts expense (+E, −SE)	2,900	
Allowance for uncollectible accounts (+XA, −A)		2,900

POST

+ Bad Debts Expense (E) −	
(2) 2,900	

− Allowance for Uncollectible Accounts (XA) +	
	2,900 (2)

This accounting treatment serves three purposes. First, the balance in accounts receivable is reported in the balance sheet net of estimated uncollectible accounts as follows:

Accounts receivable, net of $2,900 in allowances	$97,100

The $97,100 is the estimated net realizable value of the accounts receivable. Second, the original value of accounts receivable is preserved. The individual accounts that add up to the $100,000 in accounts receivable have not been altered. Third, bad debts expense of $2,900, which is part of the cost of offering credit to customers, is recognized against the $100,000 sales generated on credit and reported in the income statement. Bad debts expense is usually included in SG&A expenses.

The allowance for uncollectible accounts is increased by bad debts expense (estimated provision for uncollectibles) and decreased when an account is written off. Because the allowance for uncollectible accounts is a contra-asset account, credit entries increase its balance. The greater the balance in the contra-asset account, the more the corresponding asset account is offset.

BUSINESS INSIGHT

Expense or reduction in revenue? Technically speaking, bad debts expense is not really an expense. It is, instead, a reduction of revenue. Although it is correct under current GAAP to record this item as a subtraction from sales revenue, companies commonly record bad debts expense as part of selling expenses to emphasize that this amount is a cost of offering credit to customers.

Recording Write-Offs of Uncollectible Accounts

Companies have collection processes and policies to determine when an overdue receivable should be classified as uncollectible. When an individual account reaches that classification, it is written off. To illustrate a write-off, assume that in the next period (Year 2), the company described above receives notice that one of its customers, owing $500 at the time, has declared bankruptcy. The seller's attorneys believe that the legal costs necessary to collect the amount would exceed the $500 owed. The seller could then decide to write off the account with the following entry.

ANALYZE

Transaction	Cash Asset	+	Noncash Assets	−	Contra Asset	=	Liabilities	+	Contrib. Capital	+	Earned Capital	Revenues	−	Expenses	=	Net Income
	Balance Sheet											***Income Statement***				
(3) Write off $500 in accounts receivable.*			−500 Accounts Receivable	−	−500 Allowance for Uncollectible Accounts	=							−		=	

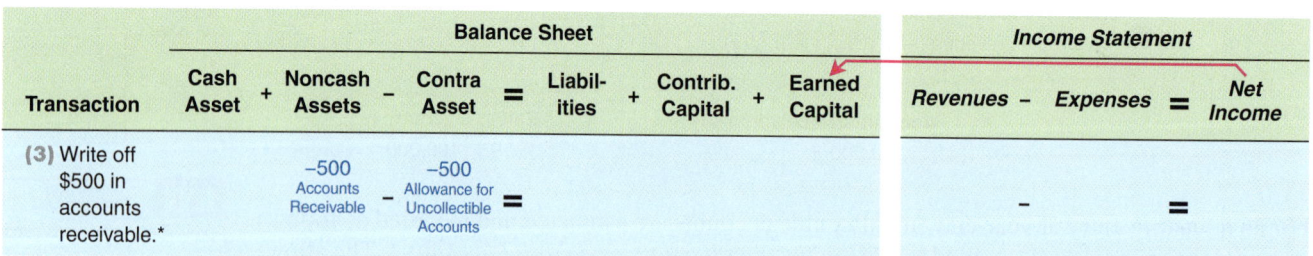

*There is no effect on accounts receivable, net of the allowance for uncollectible accounts. Consequently, there is no *net* effect on the balance sheet.

JOURNALIZE

	Debit	Credit
(3) Allowance for uncollectible accounts (−XA, +A)	500	
Accounts receivable (−A)		500

POST

− Allowance for Uncollectible Accounts (XA) +			
		2,900	Bal.
(3)	500		
		2,400	Bal.

+ Accounts Receivable (A) −			
Bal.	100,000		
		500	(3)
Bal.	99,500		

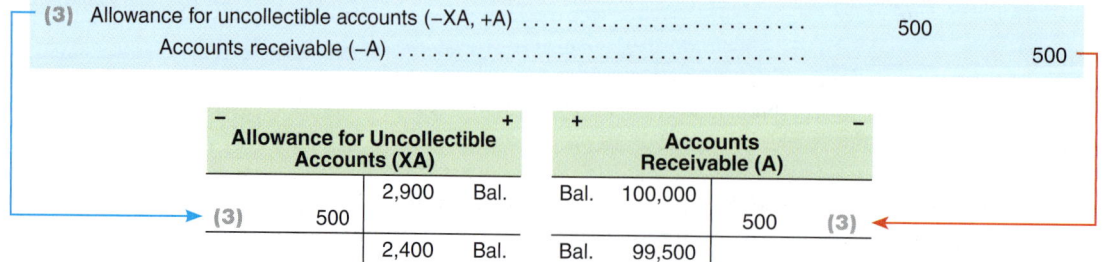

Exhibit 6.7 summarizes the effects of this write-off on the individual accounts.

EXHIBIT 6.7 Effects of an Accounts Receivable Write-Off

	Before Write-Off	Effects of Write-Off	After Write-Off
Accounts receivable	$100,000	$ (500)	$99,500
Less: Allowance for uncollectible accounts.	2,900	500	2,400
Accounts receivable, net of allowance	$ 97,100		$97,100

The net amount of accounts receivable that is reported in the balance sheet after the write-off is the same amount that was reported before the write-off. This is always the case. The individual account receivable was reduced and the contra-asset was reduced by the same amount. Also, no entry was made to the income statement. The expense was estimated and recorded in the period when the credit sales were recorded.[9]

To complete the illustration, assume that management's aging of accounts at the end of Year 2 shows that the ending balance in the allowance account should be $3,000, so another $600 should be added to the allowance account at the end of Year 2. This $600 amount would reflect sales made in Year 2, as well as the seller's experience with collections during Year 2. The entry to record the Year 2 provision follows.

ANALYZE

Transaction	Cash Asset	+ Noncash Assets	− Contra Asset	= Liabil-ities	+ Contrib. Capital	+ Earned Capital	Revenues	− Expenses	= Net Income
(4) Estimate $600 in bad debts.			+600 Allowance for Uncollectible Accounts			−600 Retained Earnings		+600 Bad Debts Expense	−600

(Balance Sheet: Cash Asset through Earned Capital; Income Statement: Revenues through Net Income)

JOURNALIZE

(4) Bad debts expense (+E, −SE).	600	
Allowance for uncollectible accounts (+XA, −A)		600

POST

+ Bad Debts Expense (E) −			
(4)	600		

− Allowance for Uncollectible Accounts (XA) +			
		2,900	Bal.
(3)	500	600	(4)
		3,000	Bal.

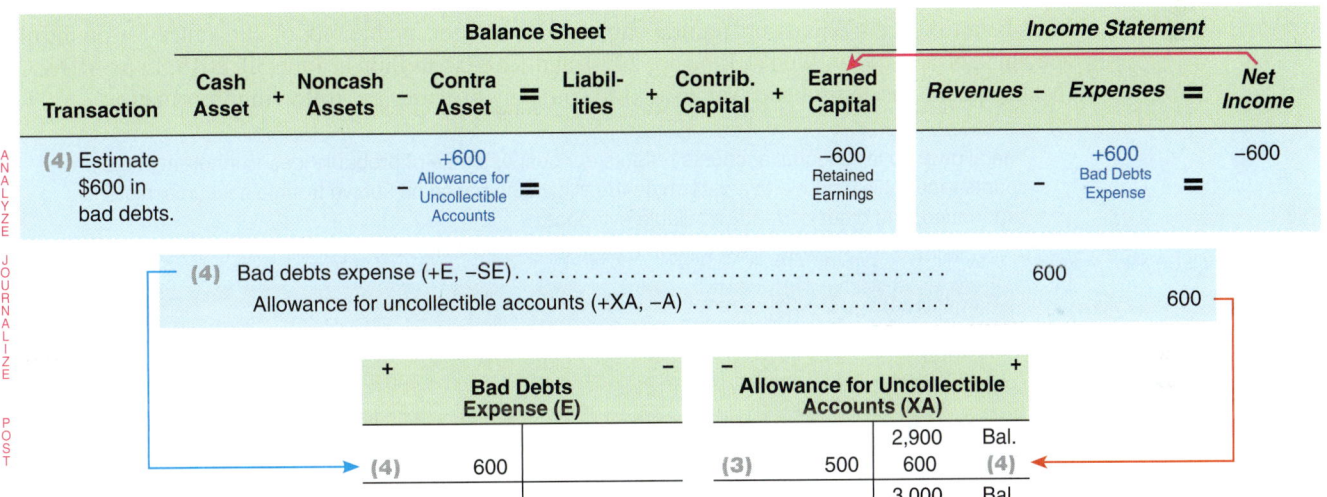

This entry is the same (albeit with a different dollar amount) as the entry made to record the estimate in Year 1. A reconciliation of allowance for uncollectible accounts for the two years follows.

	Year 1	Year 2
Allowance for uncollectible accounts, beginning balance.	$ 0	$2,900
Add: provision for uncollectible accounts (bad debts expense estimate)	2,900	600
Subtract: write-offs of uncollectible accounts receivable	0	(500)
Allowance for uncollectible accounts, ending balance	$2,900	$3,000

To summarize, the *main balance sheet and income statement effects occur when the provision is made to the allowance for uncollectible accounts.* Accounts receivable (net) is reduced, and that reduction is reflected in the income statement as bad debts expense (usually part of selling, general, and administrative expenses). The net income reduction yields a corresponding equity reduction (via reduced retained earnings). Importantly, the main financial statement effects are at the point of *estimation*, not upon the event of *write-off.* In this way, the net accounts receivable reflects the most up-to-date judgments about future customer payments, and bad debts expense is recognized

[9] Suppose a previously written off account is unexpectedly paid, often referred to as a *recovery*. If that occurs, the write-off entry (3) is reversed (reinstating the receivable and increasing the allowance), and the payment of this reinstated receivable is accounted for in the usual fashion.

as a cost of achieving the current period's sales and incorporates any changes in management's assessment of the likelihood that customers will pay.

ANALYSIS INSIGHT

In Chapter 4, we looked at the relationship between revenues and cash collected from customers. If a company offers credit to its customer (and receives no payments in advance of sales), then cash collected from customers equals revenue minus the change in accounts receivable. *But* which accounts receivable—gross or net? And what do we do with bad debts and/or write-offs?

The interesting thing about these questions is that there isn't one answer, but two!

Cash received from customers = Revenue – Bad debt expense – Change in Accounts receivable, net,

Or

Cash received from customers = Revenue – Write-offs – Change in Accounts receivable, gross.

Both formulas give the same answer.

Disclosure Notes and Interpretations

In its balance sheets, Microsoft reports current accounts receivable, net of allowance for doubtful accounts, of $32,011 million at June 30, 2020, and $29,524 million at June 30, 2019. In its MD&A (Management Discussion and Analysis), the company provides the following information.

The allowance for doubtful accounts reflects our best estimate of probable losses inherent in the accounts receivable balance. We determine the allowance based on known trouble accounts, historical experience, and other currently available evidence.

Activity in the allowance for doubtful accounts was as follows:

(In millions) **Year Ended June 30**	**2020**	**2019**	**2018**
Balance, beginning of period	$434	$397	$361
Charged to costs and other	560	153	134
Write-offs	(178)	(116)	(98)
Balance, end of period	$816	$434	$397

Allowance for doubtful accounts included in our consolidated balance sheets:

June 30	**2020**	**2019**	**2018**
Accounts receivable, net allowance for doubtful accounts	$788	$411	$377
Other long-term assets	28	23	20
Total	$816	$434	$397

In Microsoft's 10-K report filed with the Securities and Exchange Commission, it discloses that its provision for doubtful accounts (bad debts expense) was $560 million, $153 million, and $134 million in fiscal years 2020, 2019, and 2018, respectively. Based on this information, we could construct a reconciliation of Microsoft's allowance for doubtful accounts (for both current and long-term receivables) as presented in **Exhibit 6.8**.

EXHIBIT 6.8 Reconciliation of Microsoft's Allowance for Doubtful Accounts

Allowance for Doubtful Accounts ($ millions)	
Balance at June 30, 2019	$434
Provision for doubtful accounts	560
Write-offs	(178)
Balance at June 30, 2020	$816

The disclosure notes may also disclose whether or not a company has *pledged* its accounts receivable as collateral for a short-term loan. If this is the case, a short-term loan is presented in the liabilities section of the balance sheet, and a disclosure note explains the arrangement. As an alternative to borrowing, a company may *factor* (or sell) its accounts receivable to a bank or other financial institution. If the receivables have been factored, the bank or other financial institution accepts all responsibility for collection. Consequently, the receivables do not appear on the balance sheet of the selling company because they have been sold.

The reconciliation of Microsoft's allowance account provides insight into the level of its annual provision (bad debts expense) relative to its write-offs. In 2020, Microsoft wrote off $178 million in uncollectible accounts while recording a provision for doubtful accounts (bad debts expense) of $560 million. Because the provision exceeded the write-offs, the total allowance increased from $434 million in 2019 to $816 million in 2020.

Microsoft's bad debts expense (or provision) more than tripled in 2020, though the magnitude is small relative to the size of their sales revenue. The company reported allowance for doubtful accounts of $788 million in 2020 and $411 million in 2019, an increase from 1.4% of accounts receivable to 2.4%. The changes in bad debts expense, both in absolute amount and as a percentage of sales revenue, could be caused by several factors. For example, the creditworthiness of Microsoft's customers may have changed due to the coronavirus pandemic. These changes can be caused by changing economic conditions or changes in Microsoft's credit policies (including collection efforts). Of course, it also could mean that Microsoft expects these changes to occur in the coming months.

The magnitude of Microsoft's uncollectible accounts relative to the company's overall size and profitability makes it an unlikely place for earnings management. But companies in other industries (banking, publishing, retail) often have receivables that require substantial adjustments for expected returns or uncollectible accounts. For instance, the publisher **John Wiley & Sons, Inc.**, reports accounts receivable of $309.4 million in its April 30, 2020, balance sheet, but this amount is net of an allowance for doubtful accounts of $18.3 million. In addition, the company has recognized a print book sales return reserve net liability balance of $19.6 million. So, Wiley only expects to collect about 88% of the amounts it has billed customers. For such companies, modest changes in expectations of returns or collections can have a material effect on reported income. Wiley reports that a 1% change in the estimated return rate would decrease net income by $1.3 million.

Experience tells us that many companies have used the allowance for uncollectible accounts to shift income from one period into another. For instance, a company may overestimate its allowance in some years. Such an overestimation may have been unintentional, or it may have been an intentional attempt to manage earnings by building up a reserve (during good years) that can be drawn down in subsequent periods in order to increase reported income. Such a reserve is sometimes called a **cookie jar reserve**. Alternatively, a company may underestimate its provision in some years. This underestimation may be unintentional, or it may be an attempt to boost earnings to achieve some desired target. Looking at the patterns in the reconciliation of the allowance for uncollectible accounts may provide some indicators of this behavior.[10]

The MD&A section of a company's 10-K report often provides insights into changes in company policies, customers, or economic conditions to help explain changes in the allowance account. Further, the amount and timing of the uncollectible provision is largely controlled by management. Although external auditors assess the reasonableness of the allowance for uncollectible accounts, auditors do not possess the inside knowledge of management and are, therefore, at an information disadvantage, particularly if a dispute arises.

Some insight can be gained by comparing Microsoft's allowance to those of its competitors. **Exhibit 6.9** illustrates that Microsoft's allowance as a percentage of total receivables is at the lower end of other technology companies, **IBM**, **Intuit Inc.**, and **Alphabet Inc.** These percentages increased for all of these companies, probably reflecting the economic upheavals of the coronavirus pandemic.

---

[10] See McNichols, Maureen and G. Peter Wilson, "Evidence of Earnings Management from the Provision for Bad Debts," *Journal of Accounting Research*, Supplement 1988.

EXHIBIT 6.9 Allowance for Doubtful Accounts as a Percentage of Gross Receivables

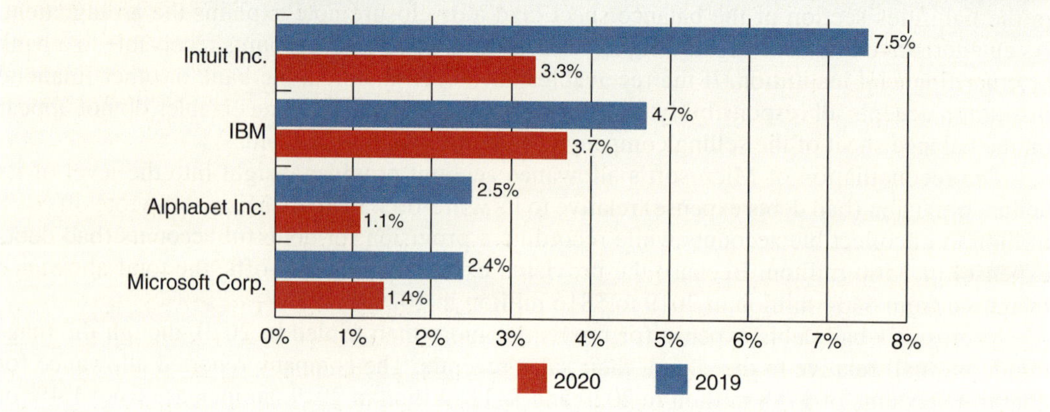

These companies do not have identical fiscal year-ends. For each fiscal year listed above, balance sheets are dated from June 30 to December 31 of that year.

Ultimately, a company makes two representations when reporting accounts receivable (net) in the current asset section of its balance sheet:

1. It expects to collect the asset amount reported on the balance sheet (remember, accounts receivable are reported net of allowance for uncollectible accounts).
2. It expects to collect the asset amount within the next year (implied from its classification as a current asset).

From an analysis viewpoint, we scrutinize the adequacy of a company's provision for its uncollectible accounts. If the provision is inadequate, the cash ultimately collected will be less than what the company is reporting as net receivables.

The financial statement effects of uncollectible accounts are at the point of estimation, not at the time of a write-off. Nevertheless, it is important to remember that management sets the size of the allowance, albeit with auditor assurances.

Review 6-4 LO6-4

Estimating Uncollectible Accounts and Reporting Receivables

GuidedExample MBC

At December 31, Engel Company had a balance of $770,000 in its Accounts Receivable account and an unused balance of $7,000 in its Allowance for Uncollectible Accounts. The company then analyzed and aged its accounts receivable as follows:

Current	$468,000
1–60 days past due	244,000
61–180 days past due	38,000
Over 180 days past due	20,000
Total accounts receivable	$770,000

In the past, the company experienced losses as follows: 1% of current balances, 5% of balances 1–60 days past due, 15% of balances 61–180 days past due, and 40% of balances over 180 days past due. The company bases its provision for credit losses on the aging analysis.

Required

a. What amount of uncollectible accounts (bad debts) expense will Engel report in its annual income statement?

b. Show how Accounts Receivable and the Allowance for Uncollectible Accounts appear in its December 31, balance sheet.

c. Assume that Engel's allowance for uncollectible accounts has maintained a historical average of 2% of gross accounts receivable. How do you interpret the level of the current allowance percentage?

continued

continued from previous page

d. Report the effects for each of the following summary transactions in the financial statement effects template.
1. Bad debts expense estimated at the amount determined in part *a*.
2. Write off $5,000 in customer accounts.

e. Prepare journal entries for each transaction in part *d*, and then post the amounts to the appropriate T-accounts. **Solution on p. 6-54.**

ANALYZING FINANCIAL STATEMENTS

LO6-5
Calculate return on net operating assets, net operating profit after taxes, return on net operating assets, net operating profit margin, accounts receivable turnover, and average collection period.

We began this chapter with a discussion of operating income and revenues and proceeded to examine receivables. We now introduce ratios that will aid in our analysis of income, revenue, and receivables. The first ratio is a measure of performance that relates the firm's operating achievements to the resources available. The next ratio, net operating profit margin, relates operating profit to sales. The last two ratios, accounts receivable turnover ratio and the average collection period, aid in the analysis of receivables. Before we discuss these ratios, we examine a commonly used measure of operating profit first introduced in Chapter 5: net operating profit after taxes (NOPAT).

Net Operating Profit After Taxes (NOPAT)

eLecture MBC

Net operating profit after taxes (NOPAT) is a widely used measure of operating profitability. NOPAT is calculated as follows:

NOPAT = Net income − [(Nonoperating revenues − Nonoperating expenses) × (1 − Statutory tax rate)]

As described in Appendix A of Chapter 5, we assume that the applicable statutory tax rate on nonoperating revenues and expenses is equal to 25%. To illustrate the calculation of NOPAT, refer to Microsoft's income statement presented in **Exhibit 6.2**. Microsoft reported net income of $44,281 million in 2020. It also reported Other income, net of $77 million. Therefore, Microsoft's NOPAT for 2020 is $44,223 million {$44,281 million − [$77 million × (1 − 0.25)]}. In 2019, Microsoft's NOPAT was $38,693 million {$39,240 million − [$729 million × (1 − 0.25)]}, with the 14% increase in 2020 largely explained by increased demand in Microsoft's products and service (reflected by a 14% increase in sales revenue).

NOPAT is an important measure of profitability. It is similar to net income except that NOPAT focuses exclusively on after-tax operating performance, while net income measures the overall performance of the company and includes both operating and nonoperating components. NOPAT is used as a performance measure by management and analysts alike, and it is also used in a number of ratios, such as the net operating profit margin.

Next, we examine two ratios that allow us to compare operating profitability across firms.

Analysis Objective

We want to gauge the profitability of a company's operations.

Analysis Tool Return on net operating assets (RNOA).

$$\textbf{Return on net operating assets (RNOA)} = \frac{\textbf{NOPAT}}{\textbf{Average net operating assets}}$$

Applying the Ratio to Microsoft

$$\textbf{2018:}\ \text{RNOA} = \frac{\$15{,}509}{\$43{,}796} = 0.354 \text{ or } 35.4\%$$

$$\textbf{2019:}\ \text{RNOA} = \frac{\$38{,}693}{\$50{,}469} = 0.767 \text{ or } 76.7\%$$

$$\textbf{2020:}\ \text{RNOA} = \frac{\$44{,}223}{\$62{,}292} = 0.710 \text{ or } 71.0\%$$

Microsoft's average total assets for fiscal 2020 total $293,934 ([$301,311 million + $286,556 million]/2), but $122,707 of this amount represents average investments in marketable securities. So, average operating assets are $171,227 million. Microsoft also reports average operating liabilities of $108,935 million. Subtracting this amount from average operating assets gives average net operating assets of $62,292 million.

BUSINESS INSIGHT

What constitutes "cash," and when is cash operating and when is it nonoperating? To compute RNOA in this book, we make a simplifying assumption and consider marketable securities and other investments as nonoperating assets, but we consider cash to be an operating asset. This is a matter of judgment for the financial statement user when doing financial statement analysis. The categorization of investment securities as cash or as investments varies across firms. At the end of fiscal 2020, Microsoft had balances of cash and cash equivalents of $13.6 billion and short-term investments of $123.0 billion. But they also disclosed that these amounts—plus cash flow from operations—are expected to be "sufficient to fund our operating activities" and "cash commitments for investing and financing activities," making it difficult to draw a clear distinction between operating and non-operating investments. Other companies include investments in a separate line item on the balance sheet (either in current, long-term assets, or some in each).

Guidance **Return on net operating assets (RNOA)** is conceptually similar to return on assets (ROA) except that it excludes all nonoperating components of income and investment from the calculation. The resulting ratio is a measure of how well the company is performing relative to its core objective. A company can use investments in securities and financial leverage to report a satisfactory level of profit and return overall, even when its primary operating activities are not performing well. RNOA can reveal weaknesses in a company's operating strategy that are not readily apparent from overall measures such as return on equity and return on assets. Microsoft has a very healthy RNOA, though we know that the denominator does not provide an asset value for the company's self-developed intellectual assets. NOPAT grew in 2020, but average net operating assets grew faster, in significant part due to an increase in property and equipment.

Microsoft in Context

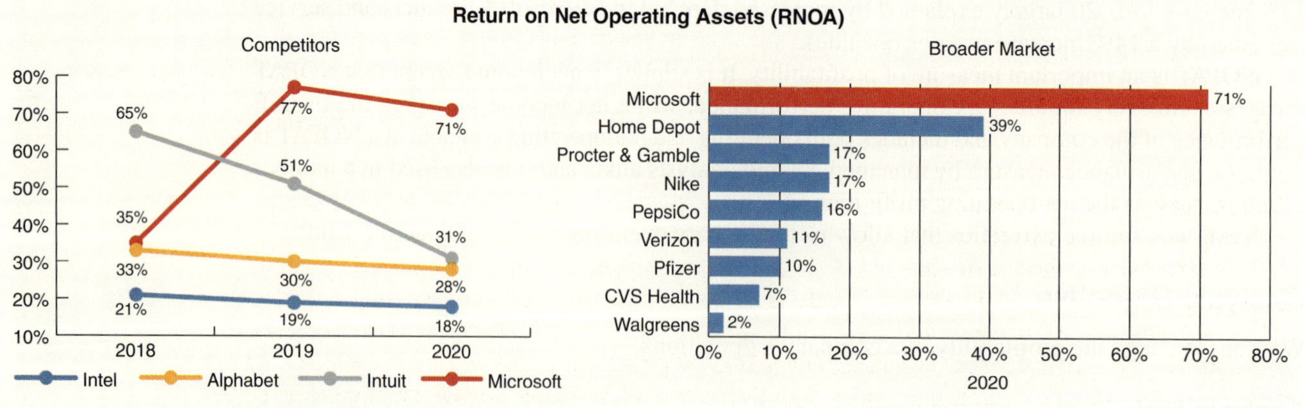

For each fiscal year listed above and in later charts, balance sheets are dated from February 2 to December 31 of that year.

A variation on RNOA is the **return on capital employed**. This ratio examines the return on net operating assets *before* income taxes and is often used to measure performance of business units and division managers within a large organization. Operating managers generally do not have responsibility for income taxes or financing activities. (These functions are typically the responsibility of central management.) Consequently, return on capital employed excludes income taxes and focuses exclusively on the resources made available to the unit manager.

Microsoft does not provide enough information to calculate return on capital employed for individual business units, but we can do so for the company as a whole. From **Exhibit 6.2**, we see that 2020 pretax operating income is $52,959 million. Average net operating assets for 2020, adjusted for income tax assets and liabilities, total $95,930.0 million.[11] Thus, Microsoft's return on capital employed is 55.2% ($52,959 million/$95,930.0 million) for 2020.

Analysis Tool Net operating profit margin (NOPM)

$$\textbf{Net operating profit margin (NOPM)} = \frac{\textbf{NOPAT}}{\textbf{Sales revenue}}$$

Applying the Ratio to Microsoft

$$\textbf{2018:}\ \text{NOPM} = \frac{\$15{,}509}{\$110{,}360} = 0.141 \text{ or } 14.1\%$$

$$\textbf{2019:}\ \text{NOPM} = \frac{\$38{,}693}{\$125{,}843} = 0.307 \text{ or } 30.7\%$$

$$\textbf{2020:}\ \text{NOPM} = \frac{\$44{,}223}{\$143{,}015} = 0.309 \text{ or } 30.9\%$$

Guidance Profit margins are commonly used to compare a company to its competitors and to evaluate the performance of business segments. **Net operating profit margin (NOPM)** is a useful summary measure that focuses on the overall operating profitability of the company relative to its sales revenue.

Microsoft in Context

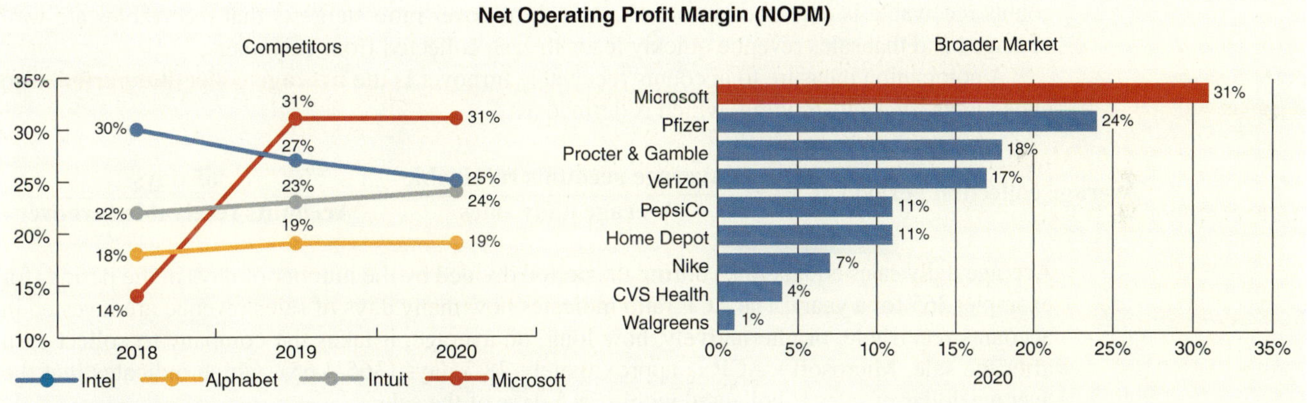

Takeaways Both of Microsoft's return metrics are at the high end of these comparison groups, reflecting returns to its intellectual assets. Retail businesses, such as **Walgreens Boots** and **CVS Health**, tend to have lower operating profit margins than companies in other industries. Retail companies rely more heavily on turnover of operating assets to produce returns, relative to other industries, to achieve a higher value of RNOA. As noted in the introduction, Microsoft's product revenue is not growing, while its service revenue has increased by two-thirds in the past two years. But the margin on its services is significantly lower than the margin on products, so maintaining the same levels of NOPM in the future will be a challenge.

As emphasized in Chapter 5, the calculation of ratios is never the end of the analysis, but rather the beginning. So, the patterns that we see in these ratios should be examined further. For instance, the US Congress enacted a tax reduction at the end of 2017 that had a significant, one-time effect on many companies' tax expense—a topic that we will explore in Chapter 10. Another issue for companies like Microsoft is the recognition of intellectual property assets. In earlier chapters, we explored the differing accounting rules for asset purchases and R&D activities. The former are

[11] Because we use operating profit before taxes, accrued income taxes payable, long-term income taxes and deferred income taxes (assets and liabilities) should be excluded when computing net operating assets for this ratio. Microsoft reported average long-term income taxes of $29,522.0 million, average deferred tax liabilities of $218.5 million, and average income taxes payable of $3,897.5 million. Thus, the average net operating assets used to calculate return on capital employed equals $62,292.0 million + ($29,522.0 million + $218.5 million + $3,897.5 million) = $95,930.0 million.

recognized as assets on the balance sheet, while the latter are not—a factor that could influence the denominator in RNOA calculations.

Analysis Objective

We want to evaluate a company's management of its receivables.

Analysis Tool Accounts receivable turnover (ART) and average collection period (ACP)

$$\textbf{Accounts receivable turnover (ART)} = \frac{\textbf{Sales revenue}}{\textbf{Average accounts receivable}}$$

Applying the Accounts Receivable Turnover Ratio to Microsoft

$$\textbf{2018:}\ \text{ART} = \frac{\$110{,}360}{(\$22{,}431 + \$26{,}481)/2} = 4.51 \text{ times}$$

$$\textbf{2019:}\ \text{ART} = \frac{\$125{,}843}{(\$26{,}481 + \$29{,}524)/2} = 4.49 \text{ times}$$

$$\textbf{2020:}\ \text{ART} = \frac{\$143{,}015}{(\$29{,}524 + \$32{,}011)/2} = 4.65 \text{ times}$$

Guidance **Accounts receivable turnover** measures the number of times each year that accounts receivable is converted into cash. A high turnover ratio suggests that receivables are well managed and that sales revenue quickly leads to cash collected from customers.

A companion measure to accounts receivable turnover is the **average collection period**, also called *days sales outstanding*, which is defined as:

$$\textbf{Average collection period (ACP)} = \frac{\textbf{Average accounts receivable}}{\textbf{Average daily sales}} = \frac{\textbf{365 days}}{\textbf{Accounts receivable turnover}}$$

Average daily sales equals sales during the period divided by the number of days in the period (for example, 365 for a year). The ACP ratio indicates how many days of sales revenue are invested in accounts receivable, or alternatively, how long, on average, it takes the company to collect cash after the sale. Microsoft's ACP is approximately 78.5 days (365/4.65), which indicates that the average dollar of sales is collected within 78.5 days of the sale.

Microsoft in Context

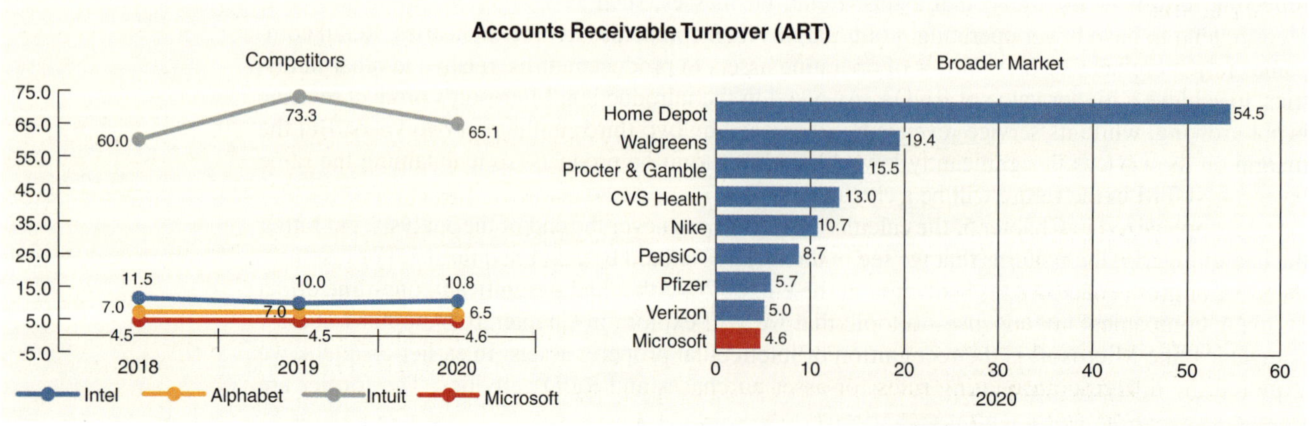

Takeaways The accounts receivable turnover and the average collection period yield valuable insights on at least two dimensions:

1. *Receivables quality.* A change in receivables turnover (and collection period) provides insight into accounts receivable quality. If turnover slows (collection period lengthens), the reason could be deterioration in collectibility of receivables. However, before reaching this conclusion, consider at least three alternative explanations:
   a. A seller can extend its credit terms. If the seller is attempting to enter new markets or take market share from competitors, it may extend credit terms to attract buyers.
   b. A seller can take on longer-paying customers. For example, facing increased competition, many computer and automobile companies began leasing their products, thus reducing the cash outlay for customers and stimulating sales. The change in mix away from cash sales and toward leasing had the effect of reducing receivables turnover and increasing the collection period.
   c. The seller can increase the allowance provision. Receivables turnover is often computed using net receivables (after the allowance for uncollectible accounts). Overestimating the provision reduces net receivables and increases turnover.
2. *Asset utilization.* Asset turnover is an important measure of financial performance, both by managers for internal performance goals, as well as by the market in evaluating companies. High-performing companies must be both efficient (controlling margins and operating expenses) and productive (getting the most out of their asset base). An increase in receivables ties up cash because the receivables must be financed, and slower-turning receivables carry increased risk of loss. One of the first "low-hanging fruits" that companies pursue in efforts to improve asset utilization is efficiency in receivables collection.

Other Considerations Accounts receivable are sometimes used by companies to obtain financing. This is done in one of two ways: (1) the company can use accounts receivable as collateral for a short-term loan in a transaction called *securitization*, or (2) the company can sell its receivables, which is referred to as *factoring*. A thorough discussion of these transactions is beyond the scope of this text. Nonetheless, if a firm uses securitization or factoring of receivables to obtain short-term financing, the amount of accounts receivable listed on the balance sheet is altered which, in turn, affects the ART ratio.

YOU MAKE THE CALL

You are the Receivables Manager You are analyzing your receivables turnover report for the period, and you are concerned that the average collection period is lengthening, causing a drop in cash flow from operations. What specific actions can you take to reduce the average collection period? [Answers on page 6-32]

Computing NOPAT, RNOA, NOPM, ART, and ACP LO6-5 **Review 6-5**

GuidedExample MBC

The following data were taken from the 2019 10-K reports of Comcast Corporation and Charter Communications:

($ millions)	Comcast Corp	Charter Communications
Sales revenue	$108,942	$ 45,764
Net income	13,323	1,992
Nonoperating revenues	438	0
Nonoperating expenses	4,567	4,080
Accounts receivable, net (end-of-year)	11,292	2,227
Accounts receivable, net (beginning-of-year)	11,104	1,733
Operating assets (end-of-year)	261,165	148,188
Operating assets (beginning-of-year)	249,538	146,130
Operating liabilities (end-of-year)	70,785	30,299
Operating liabilities (beginning-of-year)	66,123	29,031

continued

continued from previous page

Required

a. Compute the following for each company:
1. Net operating profit after taxes (NOPAT). Assume a 25% statutory tax rate.
2. Return on net operating assets (RNOA).
3. Net operating profit margin (NOPM).
4. Accounts receivable turnover (ART).
5. Average collection period (ACP).

b. Compare these two companies based on the ratios computed in (*a*). What inferences can you make about these competitors?

Solution on p. 6-56.

EARNINGS MANAGEMENT

LO6-6 Discuss earnings management and explain how it affects analysis and interpretation of financial statements.

eLecture MBC

FYI Earnings management involves earnings quality and management ethics. For the latter, management must consider both legal and personal ethical standards of conduct.

Management choices about transactions, accounting principles, estimates, disclosure, and presentation of income components are an inevitable part of financial reporting. Earnings management occurs when management uses this discretion to mask the underlying economic performance of a company.

There are many motives for earnings management, but these motives generally fall into one of two categories:

1. A desire to mislead some financial statement users about the financial performance of the company to gain economic advantage, or
2. A desire to influence legal contracts that use reported accounting numbers to specify contractual obligations and outcomes.[12]

Most earnings management practices relate to aggressive revenue or expense recognition practices. However, financial statement presentation can also be a concern. Below, we identify several examples of potentially misleading reporting.

- *Overly optimistic (or overly pessimistic) estimates.* The use of estimates in accrual accounting is extensive. For instance, revenue recognition requires estimates of things like future discounts and performance awards and the stand-alone value of individual performance obligations. Depreciation expense depends on estimates of useful life, and bad debts expense depends on estimates of future customer payments. Although changes in estimates may be warranted by changes in business conditions, they can have a significant effect on reported net income and, thereby, may provide opportunities for managers to report income that is better (or worse) than it should be.
- *Channel stuffing.* **Channel stuffing** arises when a company uses its market power over customers or distributors to induce them to purchase more goods than necessary to meet their normal needs. Or, the seller may offer significant price reductions to encourage buyers to stock up on its products. Channel stuffing usually occurs immediately before the end of an accounting period and boosts the seller's revenue for that period (while increasing the buyer's inventory). The practice is not illegal, and revenue may be recorded, as long as the transactions meet the necessary criteria for revenue recognition.
- *Strategic timing and disclosure of transactions and nonrecurring gains and losses.* Management has some discretion over the timing of transactions that can affect financial statements. If management has an asset (e.g., a tract of land) with book value less than market value, it can choose when to sell the asset to recognize a gain and maintain steady improvements in net income. This practice is known as **income smoothing**. In some cases, these smoothing effects are reported in combination with other items, making it more difficult to separate recurring amounts from nonrecurring amounts. Or, a company could take a **big bath** by recording a nonrecurring loss in a period of already depressed income. Concentrating bad news in a single period reduces the amount of bad news recognized in other periods. Given adequate disclosure, the astute reader

[12] See Healy, Paul M., and James M. Wahlen, "A Review of Earnings Management Literature and Its Implications for Standard Setting," *Accounting Horizons*, December 1999, and Graham, John R., Campbell R. Harvey, and Shiva Rajgopal, "The Economic Implications of Corporate Financial Reporting," *Journal of Accounting & Economics,* December 2005.

of the financial statements will separate nonrecurring income items from persistent operating income, making these income management tactics transparent.

- *Mischaracterizing transactions as arm's-length.* Transfers of inventories or other assets to related entities typically are not recorded until later **arm's-length** sales occur. Sometimes sales are disguised as being sold to unrelated entities to inflate income when (1) the buyer is a related party to the seller, or (2) financing is provided or guaranteed by the seller, or (3) the buyer is a special-purpose entity that fails to meet independence requirements. This financial reporting practice is not consistent with GAAP and may be fraudulent.

FYI An arm's-length transaction is any transaction between two unrelated parties.

The consequence of earnings management is that the usefulness of the information presented in the income statement is compromised. **Quality of earnings** is a term that analysts often use to describe the extent to which reported income reflects the underlying economic performance of a company. Financial statement users must be careful to examine the quality of a company's earnings before using that information to evaluate performance or value its securities.[13]

YOU MAKE THE CALL

You are the Controller While evaluating the performance of your sales staff, you notice that one of the salespeople consistently meets his quarterly sales quotas but never surpasses his goals by very much. You also discover that his customers often return an unusually large amount of product at the beginning of each quarter. What might be happening here? How would you investigate for potential abuse? [Answer on page 6-32]

RESEARCH INSIGHT

Non-GAAP Income Nonrecurring items in income, such as discontinued operations and restructuring charges, make it difficult for investors to determine what portion of income is sustainable into the future. In its 2020 10-K annual report, Microsoft Corporation provided non-GAAP income numbers for 2019 and 2018 (none for 2020). Microsoft's 2019 GAAP numbers included a $2.6 billion tax gain from a one-time transfer of intangible properties for 2019, and the non-GAAP adjustments removed this amount, making non-GAAP net income $2.6 billion lower than GAAP net income. The 2018 adjustment was more substantial. The 2017 Tax Cuts and Jobs Act produced one-time accounting effects for companies like Microsoft. The one-time increase in tax expense was $13.7 billion for Microsoft, resulting in a decrease in net income of 35% from 2017 to 2018. But that $13.7 billion is added to GAAP net income to create a non-GAAP net income that omits this transitory item.

Microsoft has used its non-GAAP adjustments to let financial statement readers see the one-time items affecting its current financial results, but that should not be present in future results. This disclosure should improve forecasts of results for future years. But there may be a temptation for a company to be more strategic in reporting non-GAAP results. Research, however, provides no evidence that more exclusions via non-GAAP income lead to more predictable future cash flows. More important, investors appear to be misled by the exclusions at the time of the non-GAAP income release. The Securities and Exchange Commission has issued Regulation G for non-GAAP disclosures by public companies. Among other requirements, it states that non-GAAP reports be reconciled to the most directly comparable GAAP measure.

Identifying the Financial Statement Effect of Managing Earnings — LO6-6 Review 6-6

Determine the financial statement impact (overstatement, understatement, or no impact) of each of the following adjustments made by management with the intent to manage earnings. Consider each item separately, and consider the effect only in the period of the adjustment.

GuidedExample MBC

continued

[13] See Dechow, Patricia, Weili Ge, and Catherine Schrand, "Understanding Earnings Quality: A Review of the Proxies, Their Determinants, and Their Consequences," *Journal of Accounting and Economics*, December, 2010.

continued from previous page

			Impact on	
	($ millions)	**Revenues**	**Expenses**	**Net Income**
a.	Increasing the estimate of the useful life of equipment.			
b.	Offering deep discounts in products at year-end, which encourages customers to stock up on product.*			
c.	Expensing in the current year (a pandemic period) amounts prepaid pertaining to maintenance work for the upcoming year.			
d.	Underestimating the expected collectibility of overdue accounts receivable amounts.			
e.	Recognizing sales on products held at a third-party's warehouse, awaiting shipment to customers.*			

Solution on p. 6-56.

*Assume selling price exceeds costs.

APPENDIX 6A: Reporting Nonrecurring Items

LO6-7 Describe and illustrate the reporting for nonrecurring items.

eLecture MBC

In addition to categorizing income statement elements as either operating or nonoperating, it is useful to separate **recurring** components of income from those sources that are **nonrecurring**. Isolating nonrecurring earnings components is useful for two reasons. First, to evaluate company performance or management quality, it is helpful to make comparisons of current performance with prior years and with other companies facing similar economic circumstances. It is easier to make these comparisons if we focus on recurring income components. Nonrecurring income components are likely to be specific to one company and one accounting period, making them irrelevant for comparative purposes. Second, estimation of company value involves forecasts of income and cash flows. Such forecasts are better when we can identify any nonrecurring effects in income and cash flows and then eliminate them from projections. Recurring earnings and cash flows are more **persistent** and, therefore, more useful in estimating company value.

Accounting standards attempt to distinguish some nonrecurring income components. Two of the most common nonrecurring items are:

- **Discontinued operations**—income related to business units that the company has discontinued and sold or plans to sell.
- **Restructuring charges**—expenses and losses related to significant reorganization of a company's operations.

Discontinued Operations

Discontinued operations refer to separately identifiable components of the company that management sells or intends to sell. Recent guidance for discontinued operations (ASU 2014-08) provides that only disposals representing a strategic shift in operations should be reported as discontinued operations. Examples include a disposal of a major geographical segment, a major line of business, or a major equity investment. The new guidance was issued because of concerns that too many disposals of small asset groups were being classified as discontinued operations.

The income or loss of the discontinued operations (net of tax), and the after-tax gain or loss on sale of the unit, are reported in the income statement below income from continuing operations. The segregation of discontinued operations means that its revenues and expenses are *not* reported with revenues and expenses from continuing operations.

To illustrate, assume that Chapman Company's income statement results were the following.

	Continuing Operations	Discontinued Operations	Total
Revenues	$10,000	$3,000	$13,000
Expenses	7,000	2,000	9,000
Pretax income	3,000	1,000	4,000
Tax expense (40%)	1,200	400	1,600
Net income	$ 1,800	$ 600	$ 2,400

The reported income statement would then appear with the separate disclosure for discontinued operations (shown in bold, separately net of any related taxes) as follows.

Revenues	$10,000
Expenses	7,000
Pretax income	3,000
Tax expense (40%)	1,200
Income from continuing operations	1,800
Income from discontinued operations, net of income taxes	**600**
Net income	$ 2,400

Revenues and expenses reflect the continuing operations only, and the (persistent) income from continuing operations is reported after deducting the related tax expense. Results from the (transitory) discontinued operations are collapsed into one line item and reported separately net of any related taxes. The same is true for any gain or loss from sale of the discontinued operation's net assets. The net income figure is unchanged by this presentation, but our ability to evaluate and interpret income information is greatly improved.

FYI Income, gains, and losses from discontinued operations are reported separately from other items to alert readers to their transitory nature.

Exit or Disposal Costs

Exit or disposal costs include but are not limited to **restructuring costs**. Exit and disposal costs typically include activities such as consolidating production facilities, reorganizing sales operations, outsourcing product lines, or discontinuing product lines within a business unit or that do not represent a strategic shift in operations. These costs should be separately disclosed if material, but if not material are not required to be shown as a separate line item on the income statement. Often these costs, such as restructuring costs, are material in nature and are shown as a separate line item or are detailed in the notes to the financial statements. These costs are considered transitory because many companies do not engage in restructuring activities every year. As such, these costs should be classified to a transitory category for analysis purposes even though the costs are included in income from continuing operations. Restructuring costs include, but are not limited to, the following types of costs:

FYI Management's ability to reduce income using restructuring charges and later reverse some of that charge (creating subsequent period income) reduces earnings quality. U.S. GAAP requires disclosures that enable a financial statement reader to track the restructuring activities and to identify any reversals that occur.

1. Employee severance costs
2. Costs to consolidate and close facilities, including asset write-downs

The first of these, **employee severance costs**, represent accrued (estimated) costs for termination of employees as part of a restructuring program. The second part of restructuring costs consists of **asset write-downs**, also called *write-offs* or *charge-offs*. Restructuring activities usually involve closure or relocation of manufacturing or administrative facilities. This process can require the write-down of long-term assets (such as plant assets) and the write-down of inventories that are no longer salable at current carrying costs.

Information summarized from the 2020 10-K financial reports of GANNETT CO., INC.:

Over the past several years, in furtherance of the Company's cost-reduction and cash-preservation plans, the Company has engaged in a series of individual restructuring programs designed primarily to right-size the Company's employee base, consolidate facilities, and improve operations, including those of recently acquired entities. . .

Severance and consolidation costs can be summarized as follows for fiscal year 2020 (in $ thousands):

Restructuring charges	Severance and related costs	Facility consolidation and other restructuring-related expenses
Publishing	$55,655	$ 5,197
Digital Marketing Solutions	6,320	343
Corporate and other	24,322	53,894
Total	$86,297	$59,434

The liability for severance and related costs at the end of 2020 is reported as follows (in $ thousands):

Balance at December 31,2019	$ 30,785
Restructuring provision included in Integration and reorganization costs	86,297
Cash payments	(86,139)
Balance at December 31, 2020	$ 30,943

The restructuring reserve balance is expected to be paid out over the next twelve months.

At the end of fiscal year 2020, GANNETT CO., had an outstanding liability for restructuring costs of $30,943 thousand. That balance represents the costs charged to income prior to December 31, 2020 (but not yet paid) and consists of employee severance and "related" obligations.

RESEARCH INSIGHT

Restructuring Costs and Managerial Incentives Research has investigated the circumstances and effects of restructuring costs. Some research finds that stock prices increase upon announcement of a restructuring as if the market appreciates the company's candor. Research also finds that many companies that reduce income through restructuring costs later reverse those costs, resulting in a substantial income boost for the period of reversal. These reversals often occur when their absence would have yielded an earnings decline. Whether or not the market responds favorably to trimming the fat or simply disregards such transitory items as uninformative, managers have incentives to exclude such income-decreasing items from operating income. These incentives are contractually based, extending from debt covenants and restrictions to managerial bonuses.

YOU MAKE THE CALL

You are the Financial Analyst You are analyzing the financial statements of a company that has reported a large restructuring cost, involving both employee severance and asset write-downs, in its income statement. How do you interpret and treat this cost in your analysis of its current and future period profitability? [Answer on page 6-32]

Review 6-7 LO6-7

Reporting Nonrecurring Items

GuidedExample MBC

On April 30 of the current year, Singh Corporation decided to close its operations in Fiji. During the first four months of the year (January through April) these operations had reported a loss of $120,000. Singh paid its employees $12,000 in severance pay. The assets of this operation were sold at a loss of $18,000. The tax rate in Fiji is 30%.

Required

a. If this closure is recorded as discontinued operations, how should it be presented in Singh's income statement?

b. If this closure is classified as a restructuring charge, how would it be presented in Singh's income statement?

c. What would determine whether this event should be reported as discontinued operations or a restructuring charge?

Solution on p. 6-56.

SUMMARY

LO1 **Describe and apply the criteria for determining when revenue is recognized. (p. 6-5)**

- Revenue is recognized as a company fulfills the performance obligations in its contract with a customer.

LO2 **Illustrate revenue and expense recognition when the transaction involves future deliverables and/or multiple elements. (p. 6-8)**

- When customers pay prior to the delivery of all elements of the product (or service) package, a contract liability must be recognized.
- When a company recognizes a contract liability, its reported revenue for a period does not coincide with the purchases made by customers in that period.

LO3 **Illustrate revenue and expense recognition for long-term projects. (p. 6-11)**

- When a company engages in long-term projects, it must determine whether it will transfer control over time, as the project progresses. If it does, then its performance obligation on the contract is fulfilled over time.
- When a company engages in long-term projects, it must determine whether it transfers control over time, as the project progresses. If it does not, then its performance obligation on the contract is fulfilled at a point in time.

- If the long-term project's performance obligations are satisfied over time, the revenue recognition should reflect the value transferred to the customer during the period.

Estimate and account for uncollectible accounts receivable. (p. 6-14) **LO4**

- Uncollectible accounts are usually estimated by aging the accounts receivable.
- Estimated uncollectible accounts are recorded as a contra-asset called allowance for uncollectible accounts.
- Write-offs of uncollectible accounts are deducted from accounts receivable and from the allowance account.

Calculate return on net operating assets, net operating profit after taxes, return on net operating assets, net operating profit margin, accounts receivable turnover, and average collection period. (p. 6-22) **LO5**

- Net operating profit after taxes (NOPAT) and the net operating profit margin (NOPM) are measures of the profitability of operating activities.
- Return on net operating assets (RNOA) measures after-tax operating performance relative to available net operating assets; similarly, return on capital employed is a pretax measure that is used to evaluate business unit performance.
- Accounts receivable turnover (ART) and average collection period (ACP) measure the ability of the company to convert receivables into cash through collection.

Discuss earnings management and explain how it affects analysis and interpretation of financial statements. (p. 6-27) **LO6**

- Earnings management occurs when management uses its discretion to mask the underlying economic performance of a company.
- The consequence of earnings management is that the usefulness of the information presented in the income statement is compromised.

Appendix 6A: Describe and illustrate the reporting for nonrecurring items. (p. 6-29) **LO7**

- Income or loss from discontinued operations is a transitory (nonrecurring) item that is reported net of income taxes after earnings from continuing operations.
- Restructuring charges include asset write-downs and employee severance costs. Even though these charges are typically reported among earnings from continuing operations, they are classified as transitory for analysis purposes.

GUIDANCE ANSWERS . . . YOU MAKE THE CALL

You are the Receivables Manager First, you must realize that the extension of credit is an important tool in the marketing of your products, often as important as advertising and promotion. Given that receivables are necessary, there are some methods we can use to speed their collection. (1) We can better screen the customers to whom we extend credit. (2) We can negotiate advance or progress payments from customers. (3) We can use bank letters of credit or other automatic drafting procedures so that billings need not be sent. (4) We can make sure products are sent as ordered to reduce disputes. (5) We can improve administration of past due accounts to provide for more timely notices of delinquencies and better collection procedures.

You are the Controller The salesperson may be channel stuffing or recording sales without a confirmed sales order. The unusual amount of returns suggests that sales revenues are most likely being recognized prematurely. To investigate, you could examine specific sales orders from customers who returned goods early in the following quarter or contact customers directly. Most companies delay bonuses until after an appropriate return period expires and only credit the sales staff with net sales.

You are the Financial Analyst There are two usual components to a restructuring charge: asset write-downs (such as inventories, property, plant, and goodwill) and severance costs. Write-downs occur when the cash flow generating ability of an asset declines, thus reducing its current market value below its book value reported on the balance sheet. Arguably, this decline in cash flow generating ability did not occur solely in the current year and, most likely, has developed over several periods. Delays in loss recognition, such as write-downs of assets, are not uncommon. Thus, prior period income is arguably not as high as reported, and the current period loss is not as great as is reported. Turning to severance costs, their recognition can be viewed as an investment decision by the company that is expected to increase future cash flows (through decreased wages). If this cost accrual is capitalized on the balance sheet, current period income is increased and future period income would bear the amortization of this "asset" to match against future cash flow benefits from severance. This implies that current period income is not as low as reported; however, this adjustment is not GAAP because such severance costs cannot be capitalized. Yet, we can make such an adjustment in our analysis.

KEY RATIOS

Net operating profit after taxes (NOPAT)

NOPAT = Net income − [(Nonoperating revenues − Nonoperating expenses) × (1 − Statutory tax rate)]

Return on net operating assets (RNOA)

$$\text{RNOA} = \frac{\text{NOPAT}}{\text{Average net operating assets}}$$

Accounts receivable turnover (ART)

$$\text{ART} = \frac{\text{Sales revenue}}{\text{Average accounts receivable}}$$

Net operating profit margin (NOPM)

$$\text{NOPM} = \frac{\text{Net operating profit after taxes (NOPAT)}}{\text{Sales revenue}}$$

Average collection period (ACP)

$$\text{ACP} = \frac{\text{Average accounts receivable}}{\text{Average daily sales}} = \frac{365}{\text{Accounts receivable turnover (ART)}}$$

$$\text{Return on capital employed} = \frac{\text{Income from operations before taxes}}{\text{Average net operating assets}}$$

Assignments with the MBC logo in the margin are available in myBusinessCourse. See the Preface of the book for details.

MULTIPLE CHOICE

Multiple Choice Answers
1.c 2.b 3.d 4.d 5.a 6.d

1. Which of the following best describes the condition(s) that must be present for the recognition of revenue from a contract with a customer?
- *a.* Cash payment must have been received from the customer.
- *b.* All of the performance obligations must be fulfilled.
- *c.* One of the contract's performance obligations must be fulfilled.
- *d.* There must be no uncertainty about the amount to be received from the customer.

2. When multiple products or services are bundled and sold for one price, the revenue should be
- *a.* recognized when the bundle of products or services is sold.
- *b.* allocated among the distinct performance obligations and recognized as each of these is fulfilled.
- *c.* deferred until all elements of the bundle are delivered to the customer.
- *d.* recognized when the customer pays cash for the bundle of products or services.

3. A construction company engages in a contract to build a production facility for a customer. The construction company should recognize revenue as the construction progresses only:
- *a.* if it receives advance cash payments from the customer.
- *b.* if it retains title to the project until completion.
- *c.* if there are no contingent payments (e.g., bonuses, penalties) in the contract with the customer.
- *d.* if title to the project transfers to the customer as the project progresses.

4. When management selectively excludes some revenues, expenses, gains, and losses from earnings calculated using generally accepted accounting principles, it is an example of
- *a.* income smoothing.
- *b.* big bath accounting.
- *c.* cookie jar accounting.
- *d.* non-GAAP reporting.

5. If bad debts expense is determined by estimating uncollectible accounts receivable, the entry to record the write-off of a specific uncollectible account would decrease
- *a.* allowance for uncollectible accounts.
- *b.* net income.
- *c.* net book value of accounts receivable.
- *d.* bad debts expense.

6. If management intentionally underestimates bad debts expense, then net income is
- *a.* overstated and assets are understated.
- *b.* understated and assets are overstated.
- *c.* understated and assets are understated.
- *d.* overstated and assets are overstated.

Superscript A denotes assignments based on Appendix 6A.

QUESTIONS

Abercrombie & Fitch
NYSE :: ANF

Q6-1. What is the process that guides firms in the recognition of revenue? What does each of the steps mean? How does this process work for a company like **Abercrombie & Fitch Co.**, a clothing retailer? How would it work for a construction company that builds offices under long-term contracts with developers?

Q6-2. Why are discontinued operations reported separately from continuing operations in the income statement?

Q6-3. Identify the two typical categories of restructuring costs and their effects on the balance sheet and the income statement.

Q6-4. Explain the concept of a *big bath* and why restructuring costs are often identified with this event.

Q6-5. Why might companies want to manage earnings? Describe some of the tactics that some companies use to manage earnings.

Q6-6. What is the concept of *non-GAAP income* or *pro forma income,* and why has this income measure been criticized?

Q6-7. Why does GAAP allow management to make estimates of amounts that are included in financial statements? Does this improve the usefulness of financial statements? Explain.

Q6-8. How might earnings forecasts that are published by financial analysts encourage companies to manage earnings?

Q6-9. Explain how management can shift income from one period into another by its estimation of uncollectible accounts.

Q6-10. During an examination of Wallace Company's financial statements, you notice that the allowance for uncollectible accounts has decreased as a percentage of accounts receivable. What are the possible explanations for this change?

Q6-11. Under what circumstances would it be correct to say that a company would be better off with more uncollectible accounts?

Q6-12. The FASB allows the aging-of-accounts to report bad debt expense and estimated uncollectibles, but not the percentage-of-sales method. Why?

DATA ANALYTICS

LO1

Data Analytics

DA6-1. Preparing and Interpreting Sales Data in Excel
Wakeboards Inc. manufactures and sells three types of wakeboards to 50 customers located primarily in oceanside cities in the U.S. The Excel file associated with this exercise contains daily sales data for its three different models over the past year. Using this file, we will drill down to and rank sales by model number, by customer name, by time period.

PART 1 CREATING PIVOTTABLE ONE

1. Download Excel file DA6-1 found in myBusinessCourse.
2. Prepare a PivotTable showing sales by customer by month. *Hint:* With your cursor on a cell in the worksheet, click on Insert, PivotChart. Drag month into Columns and Customer name into Rows, and desired Model (such as Model 1) into Values.
3. Answer the following questions based upon data in your PivotTable.
   a. How many units of Model 1 did Villager Store purchase for the year?
   b. How many units of Model 1 did Carmel Sports purchase in April?
   c. How many units of Model 2 did West Loop Inc. purchase during the year?
   d. How many units of Model 2 did Marina Inc. purchase in July?
   e. How many units of Model 3 did East Beach purchase in May? What dates were the purchases? *Hint:* Double-click on the total purchases by the customer in May and a worksheet will automatically open with the date details.
4. Apply conditional formatting to the PivotTable, highlighting all monthly orders > 50 units of Model 1. *Hint:* Highlight cells in the month column of the table; then under the Home tab, click on Conditional formatting in the Styles group. Click Highlight cell rules, Greater than and specify your rule.
5. List the companies with four or more orders that are greater than 50 units of Model 1.

PART 2 CREATING PIVOTTABLE TWO

1. Prepare a second PivotTable showing the total sales of Model 1 by month. *Hint:* Drag Months to Columns and Model 1 Sales Units to Values.
2. List the amount of the highest monthly sales and the month in which it occurs.
3. Calculate the number of months where unit sales fall below 500 units.

LO2 **DA6-2. Preparing Excel Visualizations to Analyze Industry Trends Over Time**

Data Analytics

The file associated with this exercise includes data extracted from the Estimates of Monthly Retail and Food Services Sales by Kind of Business obtained at the United States Census Bureau at https://www.census.gov/retail/index.html. In this exercise, we will analyze the trends in sales of *automobile and other motor vehicles* over a five-year period.

REQUIRED

1. Download Excel file DA6-2 found in myBusinessCourse.
2. Transpose the data so that it is shown in a column instead of a long row. *Hint:* Copy, Paste Special, Transpose.
3. Prepare a line chart showing trends in the sales of automobile and other motor vehicle dealers from 2017 to 2021. *Hint:* Highlight data and open Insert tab. Click Line graph in Charts group and select one of the 2-D graphs.
4. Answer the following questions using the visualization for reference.
   a. What was the lowest month of sales during the period of January 2017 to June of 2021?
   b. What was the peak month of sales during the period of January 2017 to June of 2021?
   c. How would you describe the trends in 2020 through the first half of 2021?
   d. What is a likely cause of the low point described in part *a*?

LO4 **DA6-3. Preparing Accounts Receivable Aging Using Excel**

Data Analytics

A review of open invoices of Sketchers Inc. results in a schedule shown in the Excel file associated with this exercise. For this exercise, we convert the list of open invoices into an accounts receivable aging schedule.

PART 1 CLEANING THE DATA

1. Download Excel file DA6-3 found in myBusinessCourse.
2. Separate the items listed in one column in the worksheet into three columns using Text to Columns feature under the Data tab.
3. Determine which method to use to divide the data into columns, delimited or fixed width.
4. List the invoice that required a manual adjustment after applying the Text to columns feature.
5. Create a new column in your worksheet that calculates the number of days the invoices are outstanding. *Hint:* Enter: Dec 31 (the date of reference) in a new cell; next, in a new column, for each invoice, subtract the cell holding each invoice date from the cell holding Dec 31 (using an absolute reference). Add $ before the column and row cell reference in a formula to make it absolute. Absolute references don't change when formulas are copied. Change the format in your new column to Number, if necessary. Add headings to your columns.
6. Determine how many days invoice #204 is outstanding based upon data included in your worksheet.

PART 2 CREATING A PIVOTTABLE

1. Create a PivotTable which results in an aging schedule that lists invoices in categories of (1) less than 30 days due, (2) 31–60 days due, (3) 60–90 days due, and (4) greater than 90 days due. *Hint:* After selecting your data and creating a PivotTable, drag Days outstanding to Rows, and drag Amount to Values. PivotTables are created by highlighting the data, including column titles, and clicking PivotTable on the Insert tab. To group your PivotTable into 30-day increments, right-click on the first column, select Group, and enter 1 for "starting," enter 90 for "ending," and enter 30 for "by." Lastly, drag Invoice to Rows to show invoices within each aging category.
2. Determine the total amount in each category, 1–30, 31–60, 61–90, and >91 based on data in the PivotTable.
3. Determine how many invoices are in the 61–90 day category based on data in the PivotTable. *Hint:* Copy the PivotTable from 1. Remove Invoice number from Rows. Open the dropdown menu next to Sum of Amount in the Values box and select Value Field Settings. Select Count in the Summarize value field by box.
4. Create a new PivotTable, updating the aging categories to show aging categories by 30 days through 180 days past due.

5. Determine the total amount in each category, 1–30, 31–60, 61–90, 91–120, 121–150, 151–180 and >181.
6. Determine how many invoices are in the 151–180 category.

DA6-4. Preparing Tableau Visualizations of Accounting Receivable Aging LO4
Refer to PB-23 in Appendix B. This problem uses Tableau to create accounts receivable aging visualizations based on invoice data provided for Hugo Enterprises.

Homework MBC +tableau Data Analytics

DA6-5. Preparing Tableau Visualizations of Accounting Receivable Aging LO4
Refer to PB-24 in Appendix B. This problem uses Tableau to create accounts receivable aging visualizations based on invoice data provided for Javier Enterprises.

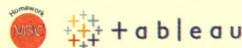

Homework MBC +tableau Data Analytics

DATA VISUALIZATION

Data Visualization Activities are available in myBusinessCourse. These assignments use Tableau Dashboards to expose students to visual depictions of data and introduce students to data analytics through data visualizations. These exercises are easily assignable and auto graded by MBC.

Data Visualization

MINI EXERCISES

M6-13. Computing Revenues on Long-Term Projects LO3
In 2021, Bartov Corporation agreed to build a warehouse for $1,900,000. Expected costs for the warehouse follow: 2022, $300,000; 2023, $750,000; and 2024, $375,000. Assume that Bartov completed the warehouse on time and on budget, that Bartov's performance obligation for the warehouse is fulfilled over time and that the costs incurred provide a close approximation of the value conveyed to the customer. Compute revenues, expenses, and income for each year 2022 through 2024.

Homework MBC

M6-14. Assessing Revenue Recognition of Companies LO1
Identify and explain when each of the following companies should recognize revenue.

a. **The GAP Inc.**: The GAP is a retailer of clothing items for all ages.
b. **Merck & Company Inc.**: Merck engages in the development, manufacturing, and marketing of pharmaceutical products. It sells its drugs to retailers like **CVS Health Corporation** and **Walgreens Boots Alliance, Inc.**
c. **Deere & Company**: Deere manufactures heavy equipment. It sells equipment to a network of independent distributors, who in turn sell the equipment to customers. Deere provides financing and insurance services both to distributors and to customers.
d. **Bank of America Corporation**: Bank of America is a banking institution. It lends money to individuals and corporations and invests excess funds in marketable securities.
e. **Johnson Controls Inc.**: Johnson Controls manufactures products for the U.S. government under long-term contracts.

The GAP Inc. NYSE :: GPS
Merck & Company Inc. NYSE :: MRK
CVS Health Corporation NYSE :: CVS
Walgreens Boots Alliance, Inc. NYSE :: WBA
Deere & Company NYSE :: DE
Bank of America Corporation NYSE :: BAC
Johnson Controls, INC. NYSE :: JCI

M6-15. Estimating Revenue Recognition with Right of Return LO1
The Unlimited Company offers an unconditional return policy for its retail clothing business. It normally expects 2% of sales at retail selling prices to be returned at some point prior to the expiration of the return period, and returned items cannot be resold. Assuming that it records total sales of $10 million for the current period, how much net revenue would it report for this period?

Homework MBC

M6-16. Accounting for Long-Term Contracts LO3
Halsey Building Company signed a contract to build an office building for $20,000,000. The scheduled construction costs follow.

Homework MBC

Year	Cost
Year 1	$ 4,500,000
Year 2	7,500,000
Year 3	3,000,000
Total	$15,000,000

The building should be completed in Year 3.

For each year, compute the revenue, expense, and gross profit reported for this construction project under each of the following assumptions:

a. Halsey's performance obligation to build the office building is fulfilled as construction proceeds, and the cost incurred is an accurate reflection of the value transferred to the customer.

b. Halsey's contract does not transfer ownership rights to the customer until the building is completed.

LO1, 2 Homework MBC

M6-17. Explaining Revenue Recognition and Bundled Sales

A.J. Smith Electronics is a retail consumer electronics company that also sells extended warranty contracts for many of the products that it carries. The extended warranty provides coverage for three years beyond expiration of the manufacturer's warranty. In 2022, A.J. Smith sold extended warranties amounting to $2,040,000. The warranty coverage for all of these begins in 2023 and runs through 2025. The total expected cost of providing warranty services on these contracts is $600,000 and is expected to be incurred evenly over the three-year warranty period.

a. How should A.J. Smith recognize revenue on the extended warranty contracts? Assume that providing the warranty coverage is considered a single performance obligation that is fulfilled over time.

b. Estimate the revenue, expense, and gross profit reported from these contracts in the year(s) that the revenue is recognized.

c. Also in 2022, as a special promotion, A.J. Smith sold a digital camera (retail price $300), a digital photograph printer (retail price $125), and an extended warranty contract for each (total retail price $75) as a package for a special price of $399. The extended warranty covers the period from 2023 through 2025. The company sold 240 of these camera–printer packages. Compute the revenue that A.J. Smith should recognize in each year from 2022 through 2025.

LO4 Homework MBC

M6-18. Reporting Uncollectible Accounts and Accounts Receivables (FSET)

Mohan Company estimates its uncollectible accounts by aging its accounts receivable and applying percentages to various aged categories of accounts. Mohan computes a total of $4,200 in estimated losses as of December 31. Its Accounts Receivable has a balance of $196,000, and its allowance for Uncollectible Accounts has an unused balance of $1,000 before adjustment at December 31.

a. What is the amount of bad debts expense that Mohan will report during the year?

b. Show the effect of the adjustment to the allowance for Uncollectible Accounts in the financial statement effects template.

c. Determine the net amount of accounts receivable reported in current assets at December 31.

LO4 Homework MBC

M6-19. Analyzing the Allowance for Uncollectible Accounts Using T-Accounts

Using the information in M6-18, set up T-accounts for both Bad Debt Expense and Allowance for Uncollectible Accounts. Enter any beginning balances and effects from the information provided (including your results from parts *a* and *b*). Explain the numbers for each of your T-accounts.

LO4

M6-20. Explaining the Allowance Method for Accounts Receivable

At a recent board of directors meeting of Ascot, Inc., one of the directors expressed concern over the allowance for uncollectible accounts appearing in the company's balance sheet. "I don't understand this account," he said. "Why don't we just show accounts receivable at the amount owed to us and get rid of that allowance?" Respond to that director's question. Include in your response (a) an explanation of why the company has an allowance account, (b) what the balance sheet presentation of accounts receivable is intended to show, and (c) how the concept of expense recognition relates to the analysis and presentation of accounts receivable.

LO4, 5 Homework MBC

M6-21. Analyzing the Allowance for Uncollectible Accounts

Following is the current asset section from the Ralph Lauren Corporation balance sheet:

Ralph Lauren Corporation
NYSE :: RL

($ millions)	March 28, 2020	March 30, 2019
ASSETS		
Current assets:		
Cash and cash equivalents	$1,620.4	$ 584.1
Short-term investments	495.9	1,403.4
Accounts receivable, net of allowances of $276.2 million and $192.2 million	277.1	398.1
Inventories	736.2	817.8
Income tax receivable	84.8	32.1
Prepaid expenses and other current assets	160.8	359.3
Total current assets	$3,375.2	$3,594.8

The 2020 allowance consists of $204.7 for returns and $71.5 for uncollectible accounts. The amounts for 2019 were $176.5 and $15.7.

a. Compute the gross amount of accounts receivable for both 2020 and 2019. Compute the percentage of the allowance for uncollectible accounts relative to the gross amount of accounts receivable for each of these years.

b. How do you interpret the change in the percentage of the allowance for uncollectible accounts relative to total accounts receivable computed in part *a*?

c. Ralph Lauren reported net sales of $6,159.8 million in 2020. Compute its accounts receivable turnover and average collection period.

M6-22. Analyzing Accounts Receivable Changes LO4 Homework MBC

The comparative balance sheets of Sloan Company reveal that accounts receivable (before deducting allowances) increased by $21,000 during the year. During the same time period, the allowance for uncollectible accounts increased by $2,940. If sales revenue was $168,000 during the year and bad debts expense was 2% of sales, how much cash was collected from customers during the year?

M6-23. Evaluating Accounts Receivable Turnover for Competitors LO5 Homework MBC

The Procter & Gamble Company NYSE :: PG
Colgate-Palmolive Company NYSE :: CL

The Procter & Gamble Company and Colgate-Palmolive Company report the following sales and accounts receivable balances ($ millions):

	Procter & Gamble			Colgate-Palmolive	
Fiscal Year	Net Sales	Accounts Receivable	Fiscal Year	Sales	Accounts Receivable
June 30, 2020. . . .	$70,950	$4,178	December 31, 2019	$15,693	$1,440
June 30, 2019. . . .	67,684	4,951	December 31, 2018	15,544	1,400

a. Compute accounts receivable turnover and average collection period for both companies.

b. Identify and discuss a potential explanation for the difference between these competitors' accounts receivable turnover.

M6-24. Analyzing Accounts Receivable Changes (FSET) LO4 Homework MBC

During the year, Grant Corporation recorded credit sales of $2,560,000 and bad debts expense of $33,600. Write-offs of uncollectible accounts totaled $31,200, and one account, worth $9,600 that had been written off in an earlier year, was collected during the year.

a. Report each of the above transactions in the financial statement effects template to show the effect of these entries on the balance sheet and income statement.

b. If net accounts receivable increased by $220,000, how much cash was collected from credit customers during the year? Report the transaction in the financial statement effects template.

M6-25. Recording Accounts Receivable Changes LO4 Homework MBC

Using the information from M6-24:

a. Prepare journal entries to record each of these transactions.

b. If net accounts receivable increased by $176,000, how much cash was collected from credit customers during the year? Prepare a journal entry to record cash collections.

c. Set up T-accounts and post each of the transactions in parts *a* and *b* to them.

M6-26. Analyzing Unearned Revenue Changes LO2 Homework MBC

Finn Publishing Corp. produces a monthly publication aimed at competitive swimmers, with articles profiling current stars of the sport, advice from coaches, and advertising by swimwear companies, training organizations, and others. The magazine is distributed through newsstands and bookstores, and by mail to subscribers. The most common subscription is for twelve months. When Finn Publishing receives payment of an annual subscription, it records an Unearned Revenue liability that is reduced by 1/12th each month as publications are provided.

The table below provides four years of revenues from the income statement and unearned revenue from the balance sheet. (All amounts in $ thousands.)

Fiscal Year	Revenue	Unearned Revenue Liability (End of Year)
Year 1	$72,000	$30,000
Year 2	82,500	36,000
Year 3	93,000	39,000
Year 4	93,000	37,000

a. Calculate the growth in revenue from Year 1 to Year 2, Year 2 to Year 3, and Year 3 to Year 4.

b. Calculate the amount of customer purchases in Year 2, Year 3, and Year 4. Customer purchases are defined as sales made at newsstands and bookstores, plus the amount paid for new or renewal subscriptions. Again, calculate the growth rates from Year 2 to Year 3 and from Year 3 to Year 4.

c. Explain the differences in growth rates between parts *a* and *b* above.

LO2 M6-27. Applying Revenue Recognition Criteria

Commtech, Inc., designs and sells cellular phones. The company creates the technical specifications and the software for its products, though it outsources the production of the phones to an overseas contract manufacturer. Commtech has arrangements to sell its phones to the major wireless communications companies who, in turn, sell the phones to end customers packaged with calling plans.

The product life cycle for a phone model is about six months, and Commtech recognizes revenue at the time of delivery to the wireless communications company. The product team for the CD924 model has met to consider a possible modification to the phone. The software team has developed an improved global positioning application for a new phone model, and this application works in the CD924. It could be uploaded to existing phones through the wireless networks.

Marketing's analysis of focus groups and customer feedback is that further sales of the CD924 would be enhanced significantly if the new application were made available. The software engineers have demonstrated that the new GPS application can be successfully sent wirelessly to the CD924.

However, the finance manager points out that Commtech's financial statements have been based on the assumption that the company's phones do not involve multiple performance obligations, like upgrades. All revenue is recognized at the point of sale to the wireless communications companies. Like many communications hardware companies, Commtech has been under pressure to demonstrate its financial performance. Offering an upgrade to the CD924's navigation capabilities would probably be viewed as a significant deliverable in terms of customer value, and the finance manager says that "the accounting won't let us do it."

How should the product team proceed?

LO6 M6-28. Earnings Management and the Allowance for Doubtful Accounts

Verdi Co. builds and sells PC computers to customers. The company sells most of its products for immediate payment but also extends credit to some customers. The industry is competitive, and in the most recent year many competitors showed declines in revenue. However, Verdi Co. showed stable revenues. It is later revealed that Verdi Co. made sales and extended credit to customers previously deemed to have credit scores too low for the company to extend credit. The company did not disclose this practice in its financial statements or elsewhere.

a. Explain how this practice would have enabled Verdi Co. to show stable sales.

b. How should Verdi Co. have accounted for these additional sales and related receivables in its financial statements?

c. How would the actions by Verdi Co. in the current period affect financial statements in future periods if the customers cannot pay for the computers they purchased on credit?

EXERCISES

LO1, 2, 3 E6-29. Assessing Revenue Recognition Timing

L Brands, Inc. NYSE :: LB
Boeing Company NYSE :: BA
United Natural Foods, Inc. NYSE :: UNFI
Wells Fargo & Company NYSE :: WFC
Harley-Davidson, Inc. NYSE :: HOG
Gannett Co., Inc. NYSE::GCI

Discuss and justify when each of the following businesses should recognize revenues:

a. A clothing retailer like **L Brands, Inc.**

b. A contractor like **The Boeing Company** that performs work under long-term government contracts.

c. An operator of grocery stores like **United Natural Foods, Inc.**

d. A residential real estate developer who constructs only speculative houses and later sells these houses to buyers.

e. A banking institution like **Wells Fargo & Company** that lends money for home mortgages.

f. A manufacturer like **Harley-Davidson, Inc.**

g. A publisher of newspapers like **Gannett Co., Inc.**

LO1, 2, 3 E6-30. Contract Assets and Liabilities (FSET)

Homework MBC

Haskins, Inc., has reached an agreement with a customer, Skaife Corporation, to deliver 300 units of a customized product. The standard billing price per unit is $1,000, and there are no discounts, so Skaife Corporation will pay $300,000 in total. At the time of the agreement on April 6, Skaife Corporation provides a $60,000 cash deposit to Haskins, Inc. Haskins agrees to deliver 180 units to Skaife Corporation on May 31 and at that time, Haskins can send an invoice for $75,000 to be paid by Skaife Corporation on June 15. The remaining 120 units are to be delivered on July 15, accompanied by an invoice for the remaining amount of the total $300,000 purchase price to be paid on July 31.

REQUIRED

Assume that Haskins, Inc., has no uncertainties about its own ability to meet the terms of the contract or about Skaife Corporation's ability and willingness to pay. Report the events described above in the financial statement effects template (leaving out the accounting for Haskins, Inc.'s costs).

E6-31. Recording Contract Assets and Liabilities

LO1, 2, 3 — Homework MBC

Using the information from E6-30, provide the journal entries to record the events (leaving out the accounting for Haskin, Inc.'s costs).

E6-32. Constructing and Assessing Income Statements for Long-Term Project

LO3 — Homework MBC

General Electric Company NYSE :: GE
Eversource Energy NYSE :: ES

Assume that General Electric Company agreed in February 2022 to construct an electricity generating facility for Eversource Energy, a utility serving the Boston area. The contract price of $600 million is to be paid as follows: $240 million at the time of signing; $120 million on December 31, 2022; and $240 million at completion in May 2023. General Electric incurred the following costs in constructing the power plant: $120 million in 2022, and $360 million in 2023. The construction of the power generating facility is considered to be a single performance obligation.

a. Compute the amount of General Electric's revenue, expense, and income for both 2022 and 2023 assuming that its performance obligation is fulfilled over time and that the costs it incurs are reflective of the value conveyed to Eversource.

b. Compute the amount of GE's revenue, expense, and income for both 2022 and 2023 assuming that its performance obligation to construct the facility is fulfilled at a point in time (at the completion of construction).

c. What performance ratios would be affected by the different contract terms in parts (a) and (b)?

E6-33. Distinct Performance Obligations

LO3 — Homework MBC

Floyd Corporation is a large engineering and construction company that designs and builds office buildings, apartment buildings, distribution warehouses, and other structures for its customers. Projects usually begin with a design and engineering phase, followed by construction of the customer's facility. The design/engineering and construction activities take place in separate divisions of Floyd Corporation, and these two divisions bill separately for their work.

A typical three-year project might have the following pattern of work and billing (in $ millions).

	Design/Engineering		Construction		Total	
Year	Cost Incurred	Billings to Customer	Cost Incurred	Billings to Customer	Cost Incurred	Billings to Customer
1	$14	$20	$ 0	$ 0	$14	$20
2	4	6	30	24	34	30
3	2	4	20	36	22	40
Total	$20	$30	$50	$60	$70	$90

REQUIRED

a. Assume that Floyd Corporation determines that the work of the design/engineering division and the construction division are separate performance obligations, that these performance obligations are satisfied over time, and that cost incurred is reflective of the value transferred to the customer. For years 1, 2, and 3, determine the amount that Floyd Corporation will recognize in revenue and expense. What is the margin percentage reported in each year?

b. Assume that Floyd Corporation determines that the work of the design/engineering division and the construction division requires too much coordination to be considered separate performance obligations. The combined performance obligation is satisfied over time, and cost incurred is reflective of the value transferred to the customer. For years 1, 2, and 3, determine the amount that Floyd Corporation will recognize in revenue and expense. What is the margin percentage reported in each year?

c. If this is a typical project, how does the performance obligation assessment affect the company's financial statements? For example, how is the debt-to-equity ratio (total liabilities ÷ total shareholders' equity) affected?

LO2 **E6-34. Accounting for Contracts with Multiple Performance Obligations (FSET)**

Homework MBC

Amazon.com
NASDAQ :: AMZN

Amazon.com, Inc., provides the following description of its revenue recognition policies in its second quarter of 2020 10-K report.

> ***Revenue***
> Revenue is measured based on the amount of consideration that we expect to receive, reduced by estimates for return allowances, promotional discounts, and rebates. Revenue also excludes any amounts collected on behalf of third parties, including sales and indirect taxes. In arrangements where we have multiple performance obligations, the transaction price is allocated to each performance obligation using the relative stand-alone selling price. We generally determine stand-alone selling prices based on the prices charged to customers or using expected cost plus a margin.
> A description of our principal revenue generating activities is as follows:
>
> *Retail sales*—We offer consumer products through our online and physical stores. Revenue is recognized when control of the goods is transferred to the customer, which generally occurs upon our delivery to a third-party carrier or, in the case of an Amazon delivery, to the customer.
>
> *Third-party seller services*—We offer programs that enable sellers to sell their products in our stores and fulfill orders through us. We are not the seller of record in these transactions. The commissions and any related fulfillment and shipping fees we earn from these arrangements are recognized when the services are rendered, which generally occurs upon delivery of the related products to a third-party carrier or, in the case of an Amazon delivery, to the customer.
>
> *Subscription services*—Our subscription sales include fees associated with Amazon Prime memberships and access to content including digital video, audiobooks, digital music, ebooks, and other non-AWS subscription services. Prime memberships provide our customers with access to an evolving suite of benefits that represent a single stand-ready obligation. Subscriptions are paid for at the time of or in advance of delivering the services. Revenue from such arrangements is recognized over the subscription period.
>
> *AWS*—Our AWS sales arrangements include global sales of compute, storage, database, and other services. Revenue is allocated to services using stand-alone selling prices and is primarily recognized when the customer uses these services, based on the quantity of services rendered, such as compute or storage capacity delivered on-demand. Certain services, including compute and database, are also offered as a fixed quantity over a specified term, for which revenue is recognized ratably. Sales commissions we pay in connection with contracts that exceed one year are capitalized and amortized over the contract term.
>
> *Other*—Other revenue primarily includes sales of advertising services, which are recognized as ads are delivered based on the number of clicks or impressions.

a. What is an "arrangement with multiple performance obligations? How are revenues recognized in such arrangements?

b. Suppose that Amazon.com sells a Fire Tablet with a one-year membership in Amazon Prime. Assume that the device has a stand-alone selling price of $165, and a one-year Prime membership costs $180. Suppose the price charged for the combination is $300, and a customer buys the combination on July 1. What amount of revenue would Amazon recognize in the third calendar quarter (July through September)? How would the remaining revenues be recognized?

c. Report the July 1 transaction described in part b using the financial statement effects template.

LO2 **E6-35. Recording Entries for Contracts with Multiple Performance Obligations**

Homework MBC

Referring to the information in E6-34, record the July 1 transaction described in part *b* in journal entry form.

LO5 **E6-36. Computing NOPAT, NOPM, and RNOA**

Homework MBC

LVMH
OTCMKTS::LVMUY

LVMH Moët Hennessy Louis Vuitton SE (LVMH) is a French multinational luxury goods conglomerate headquartered in Paris. The following information is selected from their 2020 annual report.

(€ millions)	2020	2019
Revenue	44,651	53,670
Operating income	7,972	11,273
Net financial income/(expense)	(608)	(559)
Net income	4,702	7,171
Operating assets	107,932	95,592
Operating liabilities	45,139	45,431

LVMH has an income tax rate of approximately 30%.

a. Compute LVMH's net operating profit after taxes (NOPAT) for 2020 and 2019.

b. Compute LVMH's net operating profit margin (NOPM) for each year.

c. Compute LVMH's return on net operating assets (RNOA) for 2020.

E6-37. Applying Revenue Recognition Criteria LO1, 6

Simpyl Technologies, Inc., manufactures electronic equipment used to facilitate control of production processes and tracking of assets using RFID and other technologies. Since its initial public offering in 1996, the company has shown consistent growth in revenue and earnings, and the stock price has reflected that impressive performance.

Operating in a very competitive environment, Simpyl Technologies provides significant bonus incentives to its sales representatives. These representatives sell the company's products directly to end customers, to value-added resellers, and to distributers.

Consider the four situations below. In each case, determine whether Simpyl Technologies can recognize revenue at this time. Describe the reasons for your judgment.

a. When selling directly to the end customer, Simpyl Technologies requires a sales contract with authorized signatures from the customer company. At the end of Simpyl's fiscal year, sales representative A asks to book revenue from a customer. The customer's purchasing manager has confirmed the intention to complete the purchase, but the contract has only one of the two required signatures. The second person is traveling and will return to the office in a few days (but after the end of Simpyl's fiscal year). The inventory to fulfill the order is sitting in Simpyl's warehouse. Can Simpyl recognize revenue at this time?

b. Sales representative B has an approved contract to deliver units that must be customized to meet the customer's specifications. Just prior to the end of the fiscal year, the uncustomized units are shipped to an intermediate staging area where they will be reconfigured to meet the customer's requirements. Can Simpyl recognize revenue on the basic, uncustomized units at this time?

c. Sales representative C has finalized an order from a value-added reseller who regularly purchases significant volumes of Simpyl's products. The products have been delivered to the customer at the beginning of the fiscal year, and Simpyl Technologies has no further responsibilities for the items. However, the sales representative (with the regional sales manager) is still conducting negotiations with the value-added reseller as to the volume discounts that will be offered for the current year. Can Simpyl recognize revenue on the items delivered to the customer?

d. Sales representative D has finalized an order from a distributor, and the items have been delivered. However, an examination of the distributor's financial condition shows that it does not have the resources to pay Simpyl for the items it has purchased. It needs to sell those items, so the resulting proceeds can be used to pay Simpyl. Can Simpyl recognize revenue on the items delivered to the distributor?

E6-38. Reporting Uncollectible Accounts and Accounts Receivable (FSET) LO4 Homework MBC

LaFond Company analyzes its accounts receivable at December 31 and arrives at the aged categories below along with the percentages that are estimated as uncollectible.

Age Group	Accounts Receivable	Estimated Loss %
Current (not past due)	$375,000	0.5%
1–30 days past due	135,000	1.0
31–60 days past due	30,000	2.0
61–120 days past due	16,500	5.0
121–180 days past due	9,000	10.0
Over 180 days past due	6,000	25.0
Total accounts receivable	$571,500	

At the beginning of the fourth quarter, there was a credit balance of $6,525 in the Allowance for Uncollectible Accounts. During the fourth quarter, LaFond Company wrote off $5,745 in receivables as uncollectible.

a. What amount of bad debts expense will LaFond report for the year?

b. What is the balance of accounts receivable that it reports on its December 31 balance sheet?

c. Report (1) the write-off of accounts receivable as uncollectible and (2) bad debt expense calculated in part a using the financial statement effects template.

d. Suppose LaFond wrote off $1,500 more in receivables in the quarter. Or, $1,500 less. How would that affect the bad debt expense for the fourth quarter? How does the aging of accounts deal with the inevitable differences between estimated cash collections and actual cash collections?

LO4 Homework MBC

E6-39. Analyzing T-Accounts in Accounting for Uncollectible Accounts
Referring to the information in E6-38, set up T-accounts for both Bad Debts Expense and the Allowance for Uncollectible Accounts. Enter any unadjusted balances along with the dollar effects of the information described (including your results from parts *a* and *b*). Explain the numbers in each of the T-accounts.

LO4, 5 Homework MBC

Steelcase, Inc.
NYSE :: SCS

E6-40. Analysis of Accounts Receivable and Allowance for Doubtful Accounts (FSET)
Steelcase, Inc., reported the following amounts in its 2020 and 2019 10-K reports (years ended February 28, 2020, and February 22, 2019).

($ millions)	2020	2019
From the income statement:		
Revenue	$3,723.7	$3,443.2
From the balance sheet:		
Accounts receivable, net	372.4	390.3
Customer deposits	28.6	20.0
From the disclosure on allowance for doubtful accounts:		
Balance at beginning of period	8.7	11.1
Additions (reductions) charged to income	7.3	5.5
Adjustments or deductions	(6.6)	(7.9)
Balance at end of period	9.4	8.7

a. Report (1) the write-off of accounts receivable as uncollectible in 2020 and (2) the provision for doubtful accounts (bad debt expense) for 2020 using the financial statement effects template.

b. Calculate Steelcase's gross receivables for the years given, and then determine the allowance for doubtful accounts as a percentage of the gross receivables.

c. Calculate Steelcase's accounts receivable turnover for 2020. (Use Accounts receivable, net for the calculation.)

d. How much cash did Steelcase receive from customers in 2020?

LO4 Homework MBC

E6-41. Recording Entries to Adjust the Allowance for Doubtful Accounts
Use the information in E6-40 to complete the following requirements.

a. Prepare the journal entry to record accounts receivable written off as uncollectible in 2020.

b. Prepare the entry to record the provision for doubtful accounts (bad debts expense) for 2020.

c. What effect did these entries have on Steelcase's income for that year?

LO4 Homework MBC

E6-42. Analyzing and Reporting Receivable Transactions and Uncollectible Accounts (Using Percentage-of-Sales Method)
At the beginning of the year, Penman Company had the following (normal) account balances in its financial records:

Accounts receivable	$61,000
Allowance for uncollectible accounts	3,950

During the year, its credit sales were $586,500, and collections on credit sales were $575,000. The following additional transactions occurred during the year:

Feb. 17	Wrote off Nissim's account, $1,800.
May 28	Wrote off White's account, $1,200.
Dec. 15	Wrote off Ohlson's account, $450.
Dec. 31	Recorded the provision for uncollectible accounts at 0.8% of credit sales for the year. (*Hint*: The allowance account is increased by 0.8% of credit sales regardless of any prior write-offs.)

Compute and show how accounts receivable and the allowance for uncollectible accounts are reported in its December 31 balance sheet.

LO4 Homework MBC

E6-43. Estimating Bad Debts Expense and Reporting of Receivables (FSET)
At December 31, Sunil Company had a balance of $562,500 in its accounts receivable and an unused balance of $6,300 in its allowance for uncollectible accounts. The company then aged its accounts as follows:

Current	$456,000
0–60 days past due	66,000
61–180 days past due	27,000
Over 180 days past due	13,500
Total accounts receivable	$562,500

The company has experienced losses as follows: 1% of current balances, 5% of balances 0–60 days past due, 15% of balances 61–180 days past due, and 40% of balances over 180 days past due. The company continues to base its provision for credit losses on this aging analysis and percentages.

a. What amount of bad debts expense does Sunil report on its annual income statement?

b. Show how accounts receivable and the allowance for uncollectible accounts are reported in its December 31 balance sheet.

c. Report the increase in bad debt expense calculated in part a using the financial statement effects template.

E6-44. Analyzing T-Accounts in Accounting for Uncollectible Accounts LO4 Homework MBC

Using the information from E6-43, set up T-accounts for both Bad Debts Expense and the Allowance for Uncollectible Accounts. Enter any unadjusted balances along with the dollar effects of the information described (including your results from parts *a* and *b* in E6-43). Explain the numbers in each of the T-accounts.

E6-45. Estimating Uncollectible Accounts and Reporting Receivables over Multiple Periods LO4 Homework MBC

Barth Company, which has been in business for three years, makes all of its sales on credit and does not offer cash discounts. Its credit sales, customer collections, and write-offs of uncollectible accounts for its first three years follow:

Year	Sales	Collections	Accounts Written Off
Year 1	$600,800	$586,400	$4,240
Year 2	700,800	691,200	4,640
Year 3	777,600	750,400	5,200

a. Barth uses the allowance method of recognizing credit losses that provides for such losses at the rate of 1% of sales. (This means the allowance account is increased by 1% of credit sales regardless of any write-offs and unused balances.) What amounts for accounts receivable and the allowance for uncollectible accounts are reported on its balance sheet at the end of Year 3? What total amount of bad debts expense appears on its income statement for each of the three years?

b. Comment on the appropriateness of the 1% rate used to provide for bad debts based on your results in part *a*. (*Hint*: T-accounts can help with this analysis.)

E6-46.[A] Evaluating Business Segment Information LO5, 7 Homework MBC

Hewlett-Packard
NYSE :: HPQ

Hewlett-Packard Company reports that its "operations are organized into three segments for financial reporting purposes: Personal Systems, Printing and Corporate Investments" with the last segment encompassing HP Labs and incubation projects. The company provides the following information about these business segments:

($ millions)	2020	2019
Total net revenues		
Personal systems	$38,997	$38,694
Printing	17,641	20,066
Corporate investments	2	2
Earnings (loss) from continuing operations		
Personal systems	2,312	1,898
Printing	2,495	3,202
Corporate investments	(69)	(96)
Total assets		
Personal systems	14,697	14,092
Printing	14,170	14,309
Corporate investments	3	4

a. Calculate the 2020 return on capital employed for each segment. (Base the calculation on total assets instead of net operating assets in the denominator. HP does not disclose operating assets and liabilities by segment.)

b. Which segment is more profitable? Which is growing more quickly?

c. The Corporate Investments segment is dwarfed by the other two reporting segments. Why would HP's management want to keep Corporate Investments separate rather than combining it with one of the others?

LO1, 2 Homework MBC

E6-47. Analyzing Unearned Revenue Liabilities (FSET)

The Metropolitan Opera Association, Inc., was founded in 1883 and is widely regarded as one of the world's greatest opera companies. The Metropolitan's performances run from September to May, and the season may consist of more than two dozen different operas. Many of the opera's loyal subscribers purchase tickets for the upcoming season prior to the end of the opera's fiscal year-end at July 31. In its annual report, the Metropolitan recognizes a Deferred Revenue liability that is defined in their disclosure notes as follows: "Advance ticket sales, representing the receipt of payments for ticket sales for the next opera season, are reported as deferred revenue in the consolidated balance sheets." Ticket sales are recognized as box office revenue "on a specific performance basis."

Fiscal Year Ended July 31	Revenues (Box Office and Tours)	Deferred Revenue
2019	$85,054	$42,108
2018	86,688	49,615
2017	88,514	42,649
2016	87,582	46,609

a. What revenue recognition principle(s) drive The Metropolitan Opera's deferral of advance ticket purchases?

b. Report (1) ticket sales revenue (box office and tours) for the fiscal year 2019 and (2) advance sales for the fiscal year 2020 season using the financial statement effects template. (Assume that advance ticket sales extend no further than the next year's opera season.)

c. The Metropolitan Opera's season changes every year. At the end of each fiscal year, management of the opera can observe the revenue generated by the season just concluded and its subscribers' enthusiasm for the upcoming season. How might that information be used in managing the organization?

LO1, 2 Homework MBC

E6-48. Analyzing Unearned Revenue Liabilities

Using the information from E6-47, re-create the summary journal entries to recognize ticket sales revenue (box office and tours) for The Metropolitan Opera's fiscal year 2019 and advance sales for the fiscal year 2020 season. (Assume that advance ticket sales extend no further than the next year's opera season.)

LO2 Homework MBC

E6-49. Accounting for Membership Fees and Rewards Program (FSET)

BJ's Wholesale Club Holdings, Inc. NYSE::BJ

BJ's Wholesale Club Holdings, Inc., provides the following description of its revenue recognition policies for membership fees and its reward program.

Performance Obligations

The Company identifies each distinct performance obligation to transfer goods (or bundle of goods) or services. The Company recognizes revenue as it satisfies a performance obligation by transferring control of the goods or services to the customer . . .

Merchandise sales—The Company recognizes sale of merchandise at clubs and gas stations when the customer takes possession of the goods and tenders payment . . .

BJ's Perks Rewards and My BJ's Perks programs—The Company's BJ's Perks® Rewards membership program allows participating members to earn 2% cash back, up to a maximum of $500 per year, on qualified purchases made at BJ's. The Company also offers a co-branded credit card program, the My BJ's Perks® program, which allows My BJ's Perks® Mastercard credit card holders to earn up to 5% cash back on eligible purchases made at BJ's up to 2% cash back on purchases made with the card outside of BJ's. Cash back is in the form of electronic awards issued in $20 increments that may be used online or in-club at the register and expire six months from the date issued.

Earned rewards may be redeemed on future purchases made at the Company. The Company recognizes revenue for earned rewards when customers redeem such rewards as part of a purchase at one of the Company's clubs or the Company's website. The Company accounts for these transactions as multiple element arrangements and allocates the transaction price to separate performance obligations using their relative fair values. The Company includes the fair value of award dollars earned in deferred revenue at the time the award dollars are earned . . .

continued

continued from previous page

> *Membership*—The Company charges a membership fee to its customers. That fee allows customers to shop in the Company's clubs, shop on the Company's website, and purchase gasoline at the Company's gas stations for the duration of the membership, which is generally 12 months. Because the Company has the obligation to provide access to its clubs, website, and gas stations for the duration of the membership term, the Company recognizes membership fees on a straight-line basis over the life of the membership . . .

The following data were extracted from income statement, balance sheet, and disclosure notes of BJ's 10-K annual report for 2020:

($ millions)	Fiscal Year Ended February 1, 2020	
Net sales	$12,889	
Membership fee income	302	
Total revenues	$13,191	
	February 1, 2020	**February 2, 2019**
Deferred revenue—membership fees	$ 144.0	$134.4

a. Explain BJ's accounting for membership fees.

b. Report (1) membership fees collected in cash in the first half of fiscal year 2020 and (2) membership fee revenue recognized over that period using the financial statement effects template.

E6-50. Accounting for Membership Fees and Rewards Program LO2

Homework MBC

Using the information from E6-49:

a. Prepare journal entries to record (1) membership fees collected in cash in the first half of fiscal year 2020 and (2) membership fee revenue recognized over that period.

b. Explain BJ's accounting for its BJ's Perks Rewards program that provides 2% cash back, up to a maximum of $500 per year on qualified purchases made at BJ's.

PROBLEMS

P6-51.[A] Identifying Operating and Nonrecurring Income Components LO5, 7

Homework MBC

DowDuPont Inc.
BYSE :: DWDP

The following information comes from recent **DowDuPont, Inc.**, income statements.

(In millions, except per share amounts) For the Years Ended December 31	2019	2018
Net sales	$42,951	$49,604
Cost of sales	36,657	41,074
Research and development expenses	765	800
Selling, general, and administrative expenses	1,590	1,782
Amortization of intangibles	419	469
Restructuring, goodwill impairment, and asset-related charges—net	3,219	221
Integration and separation costs	1,063	1,179
Equity in earnings (losses) of nonconsolidated affiliates	(94)	555
Sundry income (expense)—net	461	96
Interest income	81	82
Interest expense and amortization of debt discount	933	1,063
Income (loss) from continuing operations before income taxes	(1,247)	3,749
Provision for income taxes on continuing operations	470	809
Income (loss) from continuing operations, net of tax	(1,717)	2,940
Loss from discontinued operations, net of tax	445	1,835
Net income (loss)	$ (1,272)	$ 4,775

REQUIRED

a. Identify the components in its statement that you would consider operating.

b. Identify those components that you would consider nonrecurring.

c. Compute net operating profit after taxes (NOPAT) and net operating profit margin (NOPM) for each year. Use an income tax rate of 25%.

LO3 **P6-52. Performance Obligation Fulfilled Over Time**

Homework MBC

Philbrick Company signed a three-year contract to develop custom sales training materials and provide training to the employees of Elliot Company. The contract price is $1,500 per employee, and the number of employees to be trained is 400. Philbrick can send a bill to Elliot at the end of every training session. Once developed, the custom training materials will belong to Elliot Company, but Philbrick does not consider them to be a separate performance obligation.

The expected number to be trained in each year and the expected development and training costs follow.

	Number of Employees	Development and Training Costs Incurred
Year 1	125	$ 91,000
Year 2	200	112,000
Year 3	75	42,000
Total	400	$245,000

REQUIRED

a. For each year, compute the revenue, expense, and gross profit reported assuming revenue is recognized over time using . . .

1. the number of employees trained as a measure of the value provided to the customer.
2. the cost incurred as a measure of the value provided to the customer.

b. Assume that Philbrick's costs are $18,750 to develop the custom training materials at the beginning of the contract and then $500 for each employee trained. Which method do you believe is more appropriate in this situation? Explain.

LO6 **P6-53. Incentives for Earnings Management**

Harris Corporation pays senior management an annual bonus from a bonus pool. The size of the bonus pool is determined as follows.

Reported Net Income	Bonus Pool
Less than or equal to $12 million	$0
Greater than $12 million, but less than or equal to $24 million	10% of income in excess of $12 million
Greater than $24 million	$1 million

REQUIRED

a. Assume that senior management expects current earnings to be $25 million and next year's earnings to be $22 million. What incentive does management of Harris Corporation have for managing earnings?

b. Assume that senior management expects current earnings to be $20 million and next year's earnings to be $29 million. What incentive does management of Harris Corporation have for managing earnings?

c. Assume that senior management expects current earnings to be $11 million and next year's earnings to be $14 million. What incentive does management of Harris Corporation have for managing earnings?

d. How might the bonus plan be structured to minimize the incentives for earnings management?

LO4, 5 **P6-54. Interpreting Accounts Receivable and Uncollectible Accounts (FSET)**

Mattel, Inc.
NASDAQ::MAT
Homework MBC

Mattel, Inc., designs, manufactures, and markets a broad variety of toy products worldwide that are sold to its customers and directly to consumers. The company's brands include American Girl, Fisher-Price, Hot Wheels, and Barbie. The following information is taken from the company's 10-K annual report for its fiscal year ending December 31, 2019.

($ millions)	2019	2018	2017
Accounts receivable	$954.9	$992.1	$1,150.1
Allowance for doubtful accounts	18.5	22.0	25.4
Accounts receivable, net	936.4	970.1	1,124.7

Activity in the allowance for doubtful accounts for the past three fiscal years is as follows:

($ millions)	2019	2018	2017
Balance at beginning of year	$22.0	$25.4	$21.4
Charged to income	1.0	40.9	17.6
Deductions[a]	4.5	44.3	13.6
Allowance at end of year	18.5	22.0	25.4

[a] Includes write-offs, recoveries of previous write-offs, and currency translation adjustments.

Mattel's revenues were $4,504.6 million and $4,514.8 million for fiscal years 2019 and 2018, respectively.

REQUIRED

a. What amount did Mattel report as accounts receivable, net in its December 31, 2019, balance sheet?

b. Report (1) bad debts expense and (2) write-offs of uncollectible accounts in fiscal 2019 using the financial statement effects template. (Assume that Deductions did not include recoveries or foreign currency adjustments.)

c. Assume that Mattel experienced a $0.5 million recovery of a previously written-off receivable. Report the transaction using the financial statement effects template.

d. Compute the ratio of allowance for doubtful accounts to gross accounts receivable for fiscal 2018 and 2019.

e. Compute Mattel's accounts receivable turnover and average collection period for 2018 and 2019. (Use Accounts receivable, net for the calculation.)

f. What might be the cause of the changes that you observe in parts *d* and *e*?

P6-55. Accounting for Receivables and Uncollectible Accounts LO4

Homework MBC

Use the information from P6-54 to complete the following requirements.

a. Prepare journal entries to record bad debts expense and write-offs of uncollectible accounts in fiscal 2019. (Assume that Deductions did not include recoveries or foreign currency adjustments.)

b. Post the entries in part a to T-accounts.

c. Now suppose Mattel experienced a $0.5 million recovery of a previously written-off receivable. How should the company record this recovery?

P6-56. Accounting for Product Returns (FSET) LO4

Homework MBC

The GAP, Inc.
NYSE :: GPS

In its income statement for fiscal year 2019, **The Gap, Inc.**, reported net sales of $16,383 million and cost of goods sold and occupancy expenses of $10,250 million, resulting in a gross profit of $6,133 million. In its disclosure notes, The Gap reports that "We also record an allowance for estimated merchandise returns based on our historical return patterns and various other assumptions that management believes to be reasonable, which is presented on a gross basis on our Consolidated Balance Sheet."

When The Gap accounts for estimated sales returns, it makes two entries. First, it reduces sales revenue by the returns' expected sales price and recognizes a sales return allowance as a liability for the same amount. Then, The Gap reduces cost of goods sold by the returns' expected cost and recognizes a right of return merchandise asset for that same amount.

At the end of fiscal year 2019, The Gap reported a sales return allowance liability of $74 million and a right of return merchandise asset of $36 million.

REQUIRED

a. What was the estimated gross profit margin on the items The Gap expected to be returned following fiscal year 2019? How does that compare with the gross profit margin reported in the income statement for the first quarter of fiscal year 2019? What might account for the difference?

b. Suppose The Gap sells 150 units of an item for $50 each, and its gross profit on each unit is $20. Further, suppose The Gap expects that 15 of the units will be returned. Using the financial statement effects template, report (1) the sale of 150 units (for cash) along with the expected returns, and (2) the subsequent return of items by 15 customers who receive a cash refund. Assume that the units are undamaged and can be sold to other customers.

P6-57. Accounting for Product Returns LO4

Homework MBC

Use the information from P6-56 part *b* to complete the following requirements.

a. What entries will be made to record the sale of 150 units (for cash) and the expected returns?

b. What entry is made when 15 customers subsequently return the items and receive a cash refund? Assume that the units are undamaged and can be sold to other customers.

LO2 **P6-58. Analyzing Unearned Revenue Changes**

Homework MBC

Take-Two Interactive Software, Inc.
NASDAQ :: TTWO

Take-Two Interactive Software, Inc. (TTWO) is a developer, marketer, publisher, and distributor of video game software and content to be played on a variety of platforms. There is an increasing demand for the ability to play these games in an online environment, and TTWO has developed this capability in many of its products. In addition, TTWO maintains servers (or arranges for servers) for the online activities of its customers.

TTWO considers that its products have multiple performance obligations. The first performance obligation is to provide software to the customer that enables the customer to play the game offline or online. That performance obligation is fulfilled at the point at which the software is provided to the customer. In addition, TTWO's customers benefit from "online functionality that is dependent on our online support services and/or additional free content updates." This second performance obligation is fulfilled over time, and the estimated time period for which an average user plays the software product is judged to be a faithful depiction of the fulfillment of this performance obligation.

At the beginning of fiscal year 2020, TTWO had a deferred net revenue liability of $843,302 thousand. When that fiscal year ended on March 31, 2020, the deferred net revenue liability was $777,784 thousand. Revenue for the fiscal year was $3,088,970 thousand.

REQUIRED

a. What would cause the *deferred net revenue* liability to go down over the quarter?

b. What was the amount of online-enabled games purchased by TTWO's customers in the 2020 fiscal year? Were the purchases greater or less than the revenue recognized in the income statement? How might that information be useful for a financial statement reader?

CASES AND PROJECTS

LO1, 2, 6 **C6-59. Revenue Recognition and Refunds (FSET)**

Groupon, Inc.
NASDAQ :: GRPN
Homework MBC

From the annual 2019 10-K of **Groupon, Inc.**:

REVENUE RECOGNITION

Service revenue

Service revenue primarily represents the net commissions earned from selling goods or services on behalf of third-party merchants. Those transactions generally involve a customer's purchase of a voucher through one of our online marketplaces that can be redeemed by the customer with a third-party merchant for goods or services (or for discounts on goods or services). Service revenue from those transactions is reported on a net basis as the purchase price collected from the customer less the portion of the purchase price that is payable to the third-party merchant. We recognize revenue from those transactions when our commission has been earned, which occurs when a sale through one of our online marketplaces is completed and the related voucher has been made available to the customer. . . .

Product revenue

We generate product revenue from direct sales of merchandise inventory to customers through our Goods category. For product revenue transactions, we are the primary party responsible for providing the good to the customer, we have inventory risk and we have discretion in establishing prices. As such, product revenue is reported on a gross basis as the purchase price received from the customer. Product revenue, including associated shipping revenue, is recognized when title passes to the customer upon delivery of the product.

Variable Consideration for Unredeemed Vouchers

For merchant agreements with redemption payment terms, the merchant is not paid its share of the sale price for a voucher sold through one of our online marketplaces until the customer redeems the related voucher. If the customer does not redeem a voucher with such merchant payment terms, we retain all of the gross billings for that voucher, rather than retaining only our net commission. We estimate the variable consideration from vouchers that will not ultimately be redeemed using our historical voucher redemption experience and recognize that amount as revenue at the time of sale. We only recognize amounts in variable consideration when we believe it is probable that a significant reversal of revenue will not occur in future periods, which requires us to make significant estimates of future redemptions. . . .

REQUIRED

a. Assume that Groupon sells an Invicta Chronograph watch in its Product marketplace. The price of the watch is $120, and the watch cost Groupon $60. Using the financial statement effects template, illustrate how Groupon would record the sale of the watch.

b. Assume that Groupon sells a restaurant voucher in its Local marketplace. The consumer pays $120, and Groupon will pay the restaurant $60 after the consumer has redeemed the voucher at the restaurant. The consumer has 60 days to redeem the voucher. Using the financial statement effects template, illustrate how Groupon would record the sale of the voucher. Assume that the consumer will redeem the voucher with certainty.

c. Refer to the facts presented in part *b* above. Assume that Groupon estimates that 10% of the Groupon customers will not redeem the voucher within the 60-day period. How does this change the entry in part *b*?

C6-60. Revenue Recognition and Refunds LO1, 2, 6 MBC

Use the information from C6-59, record journal entries to illustrate the transactions in parts *a*, *b*, and *c*.

C6-61. Interpreting Revenue Recognition Policies and Earnings Management LO1, 2, 6 Under Armour, Inc. NYSE::UAA

On May 3, 2021, the Securities and Exchange Commission filed an Accounting and Auditing Enforcement Release (AAER) concerning the sports apparel company, Under Armour, Inc. The document contained the following information.

> This matter concerns Under Armour's failure to disclose material information about its revenue management practices that rendered statements it made misleading . . . Under Armour has emphasized its consistent revenue growth . . . For 26 consecutive quarters, beginning in the second quarter of 2010, Under Armour's reported year-over-year revenue growth exceeded 20%, and Under Armour repeatedly highlighted this growth streak in earnings calls and earnings releases.

But starting with the third quarter of 2015, Under Armour's internal revenue forecasts indicated that it would not exceed the growth targets, and the company began a practice of "pull forward," i.e., accelerating the fulfillment of customer orders that were scheduled for a future quarter to allow revenue to be recognized in the current quarter. Sometimes customers were offered price discounts or favorable credit terms. This practice of pulling forward is not in itself illegal, but failure to disclose the practice made the financial statements misleading.

Year	Quarter	Revenue "pulled forward" from succeeding quarter ($ millions)
2015	3rd	$ 45.0
2015	4th	99.0
2016	1st	17.5
2016	2nd	10.0
2016	3rd	65.0
2016	4th	172.0

The table shows the amount of pull forward that was required to meet growth targets, and the practice had grown to the point that the $172 million for the fourth quarter of 2016 represented 13% of its quarterly revenue. Under Armour offered and sold company stock during this period.

Under Armour agreed to a "cease and desist" order from the SEC and a $9 million civil penalty. Shareholder lawsuits are pending at the time of this writing.

REQUIRED

1. Why do companies feel it is so important to meet analyst growth forecasts?
2. If you were an analyst covering Under Armour, how would knowledge of the "pull forward" have affected your assessment of the company?
3. Is a practice of "pull forward" to meet growth forecasts a sustainable one? How can companies like Under Armour prevent earnings management in circumstances such as this?

LO2, 4, 5

Homework MBC

John Wiley and Sons, Inc.
NYSE :: JW

C6-62. Accounting for Doubtful Accounts and Returns (FSET)

John Wiley and Sons, Inc., publishes books, periodicals, software, and other digital content. Its April 30, 2020, balance sheet reported the following amounts for accounts receivable ($ thousands):

April 30	2020	2019
Accounts receivable, net	$309,384	$306,631

Wiley's income statement provided the following detail of operating income ($ thousands):

Year Ended April 30	2020	2019
Revenue	$1,831,483	$1,800,069
Costs and Expenses		
Cost of sales	591,024	554,722
Operating and administrative expenses	997,355	963,582
Impairment of goodwill and intangible assets	202,348	0
Restructuring and related charges	32,607	3,118
Amortization of intangibles	62,436	54,658
Operating expenses	$1,885,770	$1,576,080

Wiley normally charges operating and administrative expenses for estimated doubtful accounts. The company provided the following supplemental information concerning doubtful accounts and returns in its disclosure notes ($ thousands):

	Balance at Beginning of Period	Charged to Expenses and Other	Deductions from Reserves	Balance at End of Period
Year ended April 30, 2020				
Allowance for sales returns	$18,542	$48,829	$47,729	$19,642
Allowance for doubtful accounts	14,307	5,470	1,442	18,335
Year ended April 30, 2019				
Allowance for sales returns	$18,628	$37,483	$37,569	$18,542
Allowance for doubtful accounts	10,107	5,279	1,079	14,307

Net sales return reserves are reflected in the following accounts of the Consolidated Statements of Financial Position—increase (decrease):

April 30	2020	2019
Increase in inventories, net	$ 8,686	$ 3,739
Decrease in accrued royalties	(4,441)	(3,653)
Increase in contract liabilities	32,769	25,934
Print book sales return reserve net liability balance	$(19,642)	$(18,542)

REQUIRED

a. Using the financial statement effects template, report bad debts expense and accounts receivable write-offs for 2019 and 2020.

b. Compute the allowance for doubtful accounts as a percentage of accounts receivable. What might account for the change from 2019 and 2020?

c. Wiley has also established an allowance for returns. How do returns differ from doubtful accounts? Under what circumstances might this difference affect the accounting for returns?

d. Calculate the accounts receivable turnover ratio and average collection period for 2020 using net accounts receivable.

LO2, 4

Homework MBC

C6-63. Accounting for Doubtful Accounts and Returns

Use the information from C6-62 to complete the following requirements.

a. Prepare journal entries to record bad debts expense and accounts receivable write-offs for 2019 and 2020.

b. Post the entries from part a to the Allowance for doubtful accounts T-account.

LO7

3M Company
NYSE: MMM

C6-64.[A] Interpreting Restructuring Charges

The following is from the most recent 10-K report of 3M Company for the year ended December 31, 2020.

3M COMPANY AND SUBSIDIARIES
Consolidated Statement of Income

(Millions, except per share amounts)	2020
Net sales	$32,184
Operating expenses	
Costs of sales	16,605
Selling, general, and administrative expenses	6,929
Research, development, and related expenses	1,878
Gain on sale of businesses	(389)
Total operating expenses	25,023
Operating income	7,161
Other expense (income), net	450
Income before income taxes	6,711
Provision for income taxes	1,318
Net income including noncontrolling interest	$ 5,393

In its disclosure notes, 3M provided the following information about the gain on sale of businesses in the income statement.

> ***Gain on Sale of Businesses:***
> During the first quarter of 2020, the Company recorded a pre-tax gain of $2 million ($1 million loss after tax) related to the sale of its advanced ballistic-protection business and recognition of certain contingent consideration. During the second quarter of 2020, the Company recorded a pretax gain of $387 million ($304 after tax) related to the sale of substantially all of its drug delivery business.

In addition, 3M provided information about restructuring charges for fiscal year 2020:

> ***Operational/Marketing Capability Restructuring***
> In late 2020, 3M announced it would undertake certain actions to further enhance its operations and marketing capabilities to take advantage of certain global market trends while de-prioritizing investments in slower-growth end markets. During the fourth quarter of 2020, management approved and committed to undertake associated restructuring actions impacting approximately 2,100 positions resulting in a pre-tax charge of $137 million. 3M is planning further actions under this initiative primarily in the second half of 2021. This aggregate initiative, spanning 2020 and 2021, is expected to impact approximately 2,900 positions worldwide with an expected pre-tax charge of $250 to $300 million. . . .
>
> ***Divestiture-Related Restructuring***
> During the second quarter of 2020, following the divestiture of substantially all of the drug delivery business (see Note 3), management approved and committed to undertake certain restructuring actions addressing corporate functional costs and manufacturing footprint across 3M in relation to the magnitude of amounts previously allocated/burdened to the divested business. These actions affected approximately 1,300 positions worldwide and resulted in a second quarter 2020 pre-tax charge of $55 million, within Corporate and Unallocated. . . .
>
> ***Other Restructuring***
> Additionally, in the second quarter of 2020, management approved and committed to undertake certain restructuring actions addressing structural enterprise costs and operations in certain end markets as a result of the COVID-19 pandemic and related economic impacts. These actions affected approximately 400 positions worldwide and resulted in a second quarter 2020 pre-tax charge of $58 million. . . .

REQUIRED

a. Describe where on the income statement the above described restructuring charges and gain on sale of businesses are included.

b. Describe how an analyst of the company should treat these items when making financial statement projections.

c. What incentives might management have to either overstate or understate the above described restructuring charges? Describe how future financial statements would be affected if the costs were overstated or understated when these charges were recorded in 2020.

SOLUTIONS TO REVIEW PROBLEMS

Review 6-1

a. Step 5 *b.* Step 3 *c.* Step 1 *d.* Step 4 *e.* Step 2

Review 6-2

(All dollar amounts are in millions.)

a. The *Deferred net revenue* liability increases when Electronic Arts sells a game, and it decreases when the company recognizes revenue from providing post-sale services to customers. So a decrease means that the amount sold was less than the amount recognized.

b. Electronic Arts' sales to customers equals its *Total net revenue* plus the change in the *Deferred net revenue* liability, or $5,537 + (–$155) = $5,382. A financial statement reader should recognize that the reported revenues are a weighted average of customer purchases made in the current period and in prior periods. Changes in the deferred revenue liability can be a useful indicator of the revenue in future income statements.

Review 6-3

a.

		Balance Sheet					Income Statement		
	Transaction	Cash Asset +	Noncash Assets =	Liabilities +	Contrib. Capital +	Earned Capital	Revenues –	Expenses =	Net Income
ANALYZE	April 6	+40,000 Cash		+40,000 Contract Liability					
ANALYZE	May 31		+50,000 Accounts Receivable +30,000 Contract Assets	–40,000 Contract Liability		+120,000 Retained Earnings	+120,000 Revenue		+120,000
ANALYZE	June 15	+50,000 Cash	–50,000 Accounts Receivable						
ANALYZE	July 15		+110,000 Accounts Receivable –30,000 Contract Assets			+80,000 Retained Earnings	+80,000 Revenue		+80,000
ANALYZE	July 31	+110,000 Cash	–110,000 Accounts Receivable						

b.

April 6 JOURNALIZE

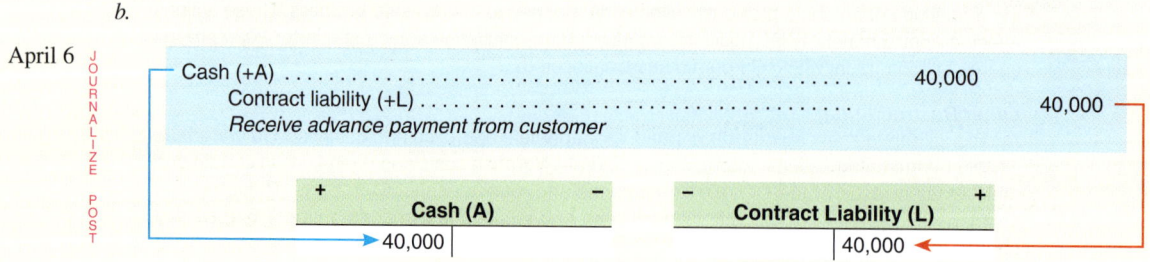

Cash (+A)	40,000	
Contract liability (+L)		40,000
Receive advance payment from customer		

POST

+ Cash (A) –		– Contract Liability (L) +	
40,000			40,000

JOURNALIZE

May 31		Dr.	Cr.
	Accounts receivable (+A)	50,000	
	Contract assets (+A)	30,000	
	Contract liability (-L)	40,000	
	Revenue (+R, +SE)		120,000
	Recognize year 1 revenue on contract		

POST

+ Accounts Receivable (A) −	
50,000	

− Revenue (R,SE) +	
	120,000

+ Contract Assets (A) −	
30,000	

− Contract Liability (L) +	
40,000	

JOURNALIZE

June 15		Dr.	Cr.
	Cash (+A)	50,000	
	Accounts receivable (−A)		50,000
	Receive payment from customer		

POST

+ Cash (A) −	
50,000	

+ Accounts Receivable (A) −	
	50,000

JOURNALIZE

July 15		Dr.	Cr.
	Accounts receivable (+A)	110,000	
	Revenue (+R, +SE)		80,000
	Contract asset (−A)		30,000
	Recognize year 2 revenue on contract		

POST

+ Accounts Receivable (A) −	
110,000	

− Revenue (R,SE) +	
	80,000

+ Contract Assets (A) −	
	30,000

JOURNALIZE

July 31		Dr.	Cr.
	Cash (+A)	110,000	
	Accounts receivable (−A)		110,000
	Receive payment from customer		

POST

+ Cash (A) −	
110,000	

+ Accounts Receivable (A) −	
	110,000

Review 6-4

a. As of December 31

Current	$468,000	×	1%	=	$ 4,680	
1–60 days past due	244,000	×	5%	=	12,200	
61–180 days past due	38,000	×	15%	=	5,700	
Over 180 days past due	20,000	×	40%	=	8,000	
Amount required					$30,580	
Unused allowance balance					7,000	
Provision					$23,580	Annual bad debts expense

b. Current assets section of balance sheet.

Accounts receivable, net of $30,580 in allowances	$739,420

c. Engel Company has markedly increased the percentage of the allowance for uncollectible accounts to gross accounts receivable—from the historical 2% to the current 4% ($30,580/$770,000). There are at least two possible interpretations:

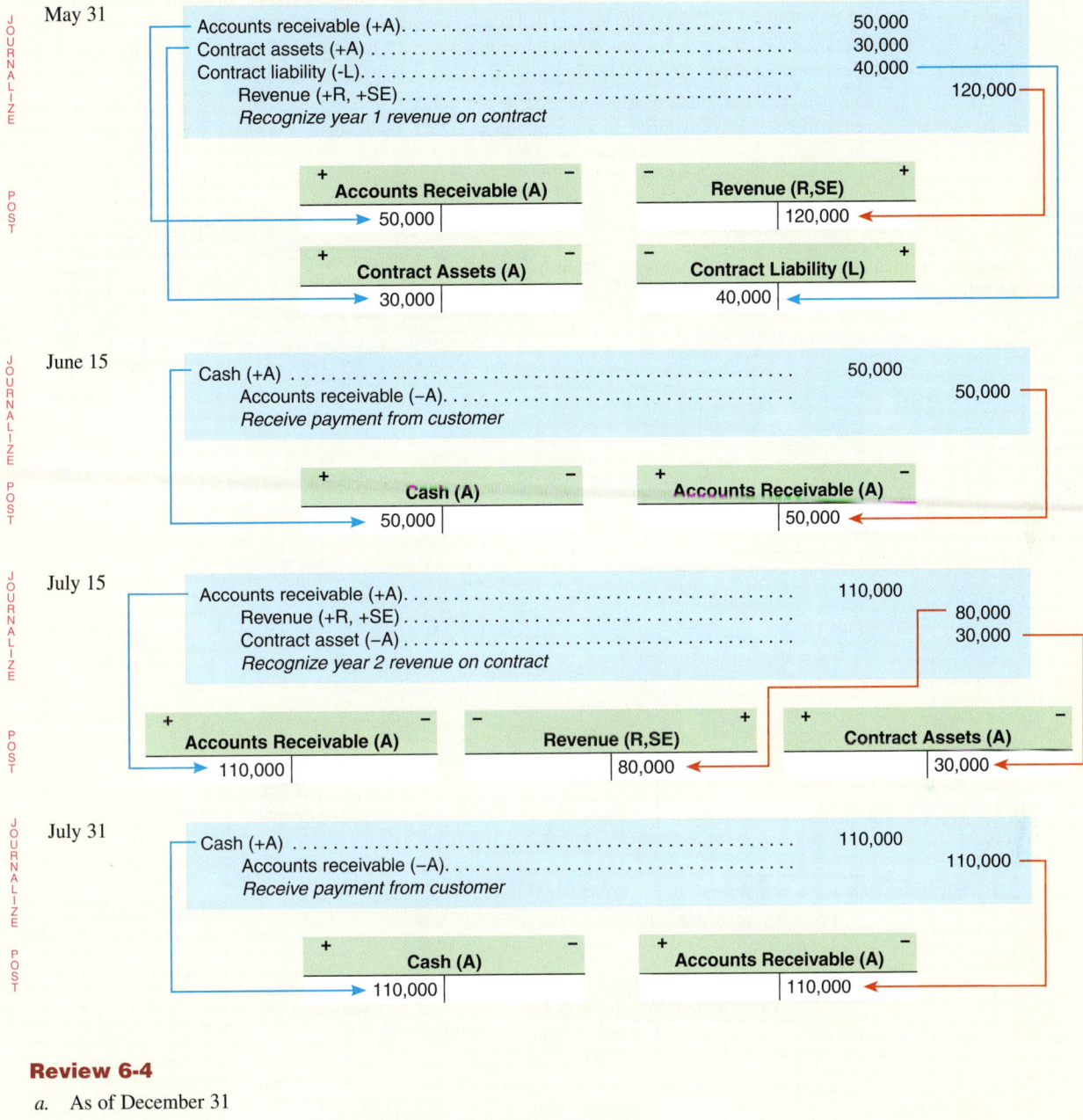

1. The quality of Engel Company's receivables has declined. Possible causes include the following: (1) sales can stagnate and the company can feel compelled to sell to lower-quality accounts to maintain sales volume; (2) it may have introduced new products for which average credit losses are higher; and (3) its administration of accounts receivable can become lax.
2. The company has intentionally increased its allowance account above the level needed for expected future losses so as to reduce current period income and "bank" that income for future periods (income shifting).

d.

	Balance Sheet						Income Statement		
Transaction	**Cash Asset**	**+ Noncash Assets**	**− Contra Asset**	**= Liabilities**	**+ Contrib. Capital**	**+ Earned Capital**	***Revenues***	***− Expenses***	***= Net Income***
ANALYZE **(a)** Estimate $23,580 in bad debts.			+23,580 Allowance for Uncollectible Accounts			−23,580 Retained Earnings		+23,580 Bad Debts Expense	−23,580
ANALYZE **(b)** Write off $5,000 in accounts receivable.*		−5,000 Accounts Receivable	−5,000 Allowance for Uncollectible Accounts						

* There is no effect on net accounts receivable.

e.

JOURNALIZE

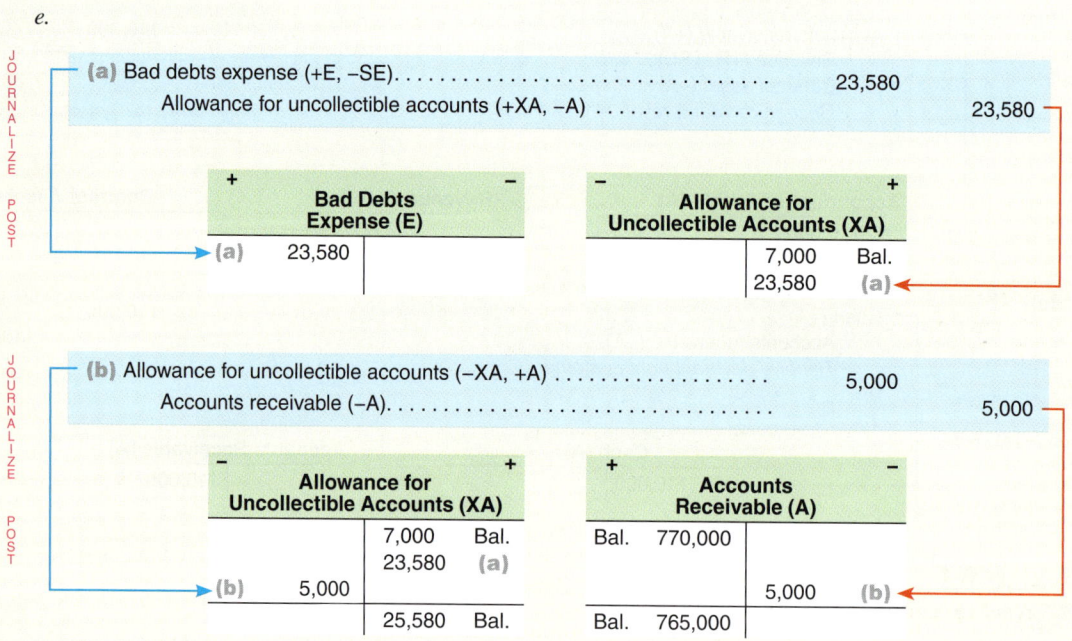

(a) Bad debts expense (+E, −SE)	23,580	
Allowance for uncollectible accounts (+XA, −A)		23,580

POST

+ Bad Debts Expense (E) −

(a) 23,580	

− Allowance for Uncollectible Accounts (XA) +

	7,000 Bal.
	23,580 (a)

JOURNALIZE

(b) Allowance for uncollectible accounts (−XA, +A)	5,000	
Accounts receivable (−A)		5,000

POST

− Allowance for Uncollectible Accounts (XA) +

	7,000 Bal.
	23,580 (a)
(b) 5,000	
	25,580 Bal.

+ Accounts Receivable (A) −

Bal. 770,000	
	5,000 (b)
Bal. 765,000	

Review 6-5

a.

($ millions)	Comcast (Xfinity)	Charter Communications
NOPAT	\$13,323 – [(\$438 – \$4,567) × (1 – 0.25)] = \$16,419.75	\$1,992 – [(\$0 – \$4,080) × (1 – 0.25)] = \$5,052.00
Average net operating assets	[(\$261,165 – \$70,785) + (\$249,538 – \$66,123)]/2 = \$186,897.5	[(\$148,188 – \$30,299) + (\$146,130 – \$29,031)]/2 = \$117,494.00
Return on net operating assets	\$16,419.75/\$186,897.5 = 0.088	\$5,052.00/\$117,494 = 0.043
Net operating profit margin	\$16,419.75/\$108,942.00 = 0.151	\$5,052.00/\$45,764 = 0.110
Accounts receivable turnover	\$108,942/[(\$11,292 + \$11,104)/2] = 9.73	\$45,764/[(\$2,227 + \$1,733)/2] = 23.11
Average collection period	365/9.73 = 37.5 days	365/23.11 = 15.8 days

b. Comcast is considerably bigger, with revenues almost two-and-a-half times of Charter and NOPAT roughly three times bigger. But average operating assets was only about 60% higher. So, it appears that Comcast is able to leverage its size to produce greater returns, in relation to both its operating assets and its revenues. The difference might be ascribed to competitive environment or management capabilities.

There is a significant difference in the companies' handling of receivables, with Charter waiting about 15.8 days to collect, while Comcast is more than twice as long (37.5 days). Both companies collect more quickly than the industry median ART of 5.27 (69.3 days) from Exhibit 5.13.

Review 6-6

	Revenues	Impact on Expenses	Net Income
a.	No impact	Understatement	Overstatement
b.	Overstatement	Overstatement	Overstatement
c.	No impact	Overstatement	Understatement
d.	No impact	Overstatement	Understatement
e.	Overstatement	Overstatement	Overstatement

Review 6-7

a. A loss from discontinued operations of \$105,000 would be reported below income from continuing operations. The loss is net of tax and is calculated as follows:
\$105,000 = (\$120,000 + \$12,000 + \$18,000) × (1 – 30%).

b. A restructuring charge of \$30,000 (\$12,000 + \$18,000) would be reported as part of operating income. The loss is before taxes. The tax effect of the restructuring charge would be included in the provision for income taxes (income tax expense).

c. Singh could report this loss as discontinued operations only if the closure represented a separate business unit within the company and the closure represents a strategic shift in operations. Otherwise, it must be reported as a restructuring charge.

Chapter 7 Reporting and Analyzing Inventory

LEARNING OBJECTIVES

LO7-1 Interpret disclosures of information concerning operating expenses, including manufacturing and retail inventory costs.

LO7-2 Account for inventory and cost of goods sold using different costing methods.

LO7-3 Apply the lower of cost or net realizable value rule to value inventory.

LO7-4 Evaluate how inventory costing affects management decisions and outsiders' interpretations of financial statements.

LO7-5 Define and interpret gross profit margin and inventory turnover ratios. Use inventory disclosure information to make appropriate adjustments to ratios.

LO7-6 Appendix 7A: Analyze LIFO liquidations and the impact they have on the financial statements.

Road Map

LO	Learning Objective | Topics	Page	eLecture	Review	Assignments
LO7-1	Interpret disclosures of information concerning operating expenses, including manufacturing and retail inventory costs.	7-3	e7-1	R7-1	M7-13, M7-14, M7-I5, M7-16, M7-18
LO7-2	Account for inventory and cost of goods sold using different costing methods.	7-7	e7-2	R7-2	M7-19, M7-20, M7-21, M7-22, M7-23, M7-25, M 7-26, E7-29, E7-30, E7-32, E7-33, E7-34, P7-36, P7-37, P7-39, C7-40, C7-41
LO7-3	Apply the lower of cost or net realizable value rule to value inventory.	7-13	e7-3	R7-3	M7-27, E7-31, DA7-1
LO7-4	Evaluate how inventory costing affects management decisions and outsiders' interpretations of financial statements.	7-14	e7-4	R7-4	M7-19, E7-29, E7-32, E7-33, E7-34, P7-36, P7-37, P7-39, C7-40, C7-41
LO7-5	Define and interpret gross profit margin and inventory turnover ratios. Use inventory disclosure information to make appropriate adjustments to ratios.	7-20	e7-5	R7-5	M7-17, M7-24, E7-28, E7-34, E7-35, P7-36, P7-37, P7-38, C7-40, DA7-2, DA7-3, DA7-4
LO7-6	Appendix 7A: Analyze LIFO liquidations and the impact they have on the financial statements.	7-25	e7-6	R7-6	E7-29, E7-32, E7-33, P7-39, C7-40

HOME DEPOT
www.HomeDepot.com

The Home Depot, Inc., is the world's largest home improvement retailer. At February 2, 2020, the company operated 2,291 retail stores worldwide and reported sales of just over $110 billion. This performance represents the tenth year of increasing revenues.

The One Home Depot strategy focuses on using the digital experience to leverage the capabilities of its more than 400,000 associates and the scale of the company. "Connect stores to online, and online to stores." This approach requires digital tools for associates and customers to connect with products in the stores, as well as improvements in the online customer experience.

A key element of Home Depot's operating strategy is inventory management. Inventory represents one of the largest assets on Home Depot's balance sheet. A typical Home Depot store carries 30,000 to 40,000 products during the year, ranging from garden supplies to hardware and lumber to household appliances. These stores are stocked through a sophisticated logistics program designed to ensure product availability for customers and low supply chain costs. The fiscal 2019 annual report states that the company "continued to focus on optimizing our supply chain network and improving our inventory, transportation and distribution productivity." As of February 2, 2020, the company operated a network of 200 distribution centers and 150 fulfillment centers to facilitate delivery speed. The company also utilizes its retail stores as a network of locations for customers who shop online. Online sales have grown approximately $1 billion in each of the last six years, and more than 50 percent of the time, online customers choose to pick up their order in the company's stores.

In this chapter, we examine the reporting of inventory and cost of goods sold. For most retail and manufacturing businesses, cost of goods sold and the related inventory management costs represent the largest source of expenses in the income statement. Carrying large stocks of inventory is costly for any business. The more that a business can minimize the resources tied up in merchandise or materials, while still meeting customer demand, the more profitable it will be. Moreover, excessive inventory balances can indicate poor inventory management, obsolete products, and weakening sales. We explore accounting methods designed to measure inventory costs and determine cost of goods sold. We also look at measures that help us assess the effectiveness of inventory management practices for companies such as The Home Depot.

Sources: The Home Depot, Inc. 2019–2020 10-K reports; The Home Depot does not end its fiscal year on December 31, but rather on the Sunday closest to January 31. So, "Fiscal Year 2019" actually ended on February 2, 2020. One interesting aspect of this practice is that most of The Home Depot's fiscal years have 52 weeks, but periodically a fiscal year will have 53 weeks. (Fiscal Year 2018 was the most recent year of this event.)

CHAPTER ORGANIZATION

Reporting and Analyzing Inventory			
Reporting Operating Expenses	**Inventory Costing Methods**	**Financial Statement Effects and Disclosure**	**Analyzing Financial Statements**
• Expense Recognition • Recording and Reporting Inventory Costs • Manufacturing Inventory	• FIFO • LIFO • Average Cost • Lower of Cost or NRV	• Disclosure Notes • Income Statement Effects • Balance Sheet Effects • Cash Flow Effects	• Gross Profit Analysis • Inventory Turnover • LIFO Liquidation (Appendix 7A)

REPORTING OPERATING EXPENSES

LO7-1 Interpret disclosures of information concerning operating expenses, including manufacturing and retail inventory costs.

eLecture MBC

In Chapter 6, we introduced the concept of operating income and discussed issues surrounding revenue recognition and how best to measure and report a company's performance. But the amount of revenue from customers must be interpreted relative to the resources that were required to achieve it. Operating expenses include the costs of acquiring the products (and services) that customers purchase, plus the costs of selling efforts, administrative functions, and any other activities that support the operations of the company. Careful examination of these costs allows financial statement users to judge management's performance, to identify emerging problems, and to make predictions of future performance. For instance, we may address the following questions.

- Are the company's costs of providing products and services increasing or decreasing?
- Is the company able to maintain its margins in the face of changes in costs or competition?
- Does management's ability to judge customer tastes and preferences allow it to avoid overstocks of unpopular inventory and the resulting price discounts that reduce margins?

In this chapter, we begin our examination of operating expenses by studying inventory and cost of goods sold. The reporting of inventory and cost of goods sold is important for three reasons. First, cost of goods sold is often the largest single expense in a company's income statement, and inventory may be one of the largest assets in the balance sheet. Consequently, information about inventory and cost of goods sold is critical for interpreting the financial statements. Second, in order to effectively manage operations and resources, management needs accurate and timely information about inventory quantities and costs. Finally, alternative methods of accounting for inventory and cost of goods sold can distort interpretations of margins and turnovers unless the information in the financial statement disclosure notes is used.

Expense Recognition Principles

In addition to determining when to recognize revenues to properly measure and report a company's performance, we must also determine when to recognize expenses. In general, expenses are recognized when assets are diminished (or liabilities increased) as a result of earning revenue or supporting operations, even if there is no immediate decrease in cash. Expense recognition can be generally divided into the following three approaches.

- **Direct association.** Any cost that can be *directly* associated with a specific source of revenue should be recognized as an expense at the same time that the related revenue is recognized. For a merchandising company (a retailer or a wholesaler), an example of direct association is recognizing cost of goods sold and sales revenue when the product is delivered to the customer. The cost of acquiring the inventory is recorded in the inventory asset account where it remains until the item is sold. At that point, the inventory cost is removed from the inventory asset and transferred to expenses. The future costs of any obligations arising from current revenues should also be estimated and recognized as liabilities and matched as expenses against those revenues. An example of such an expense is expected warranty costs, a topic covered in Chapter 9.

  For a manufacturing company, the accounting system distinguishes between *product costs* and *period costs*. Product costs are incurred to benefit the company's manufacturing activities and include raw materials, production workers and supervisors, depreciation on equipment and facilities, utilities, and so on. Even though some of these costs cannot be directly associated with a unit of production, the accounting system accumulates product costs and assigns them to inventory assets until the unit is sold. All costs not classified as product costs are considered period costs.

- **Immediate recognition**. Many period costs are necessary for generating revenues and income but cannot be directly associated with specific revenues. Some costs can be associated with all of the revenues of an accounting period, but not with any specific sales transaction that occurred during that period. Examples include most administrative and marketing costs. These costs are recognized as expenses in the period when the costs are incurred. Other expense items, such as research and development (R&D) expense, are recognized immediately because of U.S. GAAP requirements.
- **Systematic allocation**. Costs that benefit more than one accounting period and cannot be associated with specific revenues or assigned to a specific period must be allocated across all of the periods benefited. The most common example is depreciation expense. When an asset is purchased, it is capitalized (recorded in an asset account). The asset cost is then converted into an expense over the duration of its useful life according to a depreciation formula or schedule established by management. Depreciation of long-term assets is discussed in Chapter 8.

Inventory and cost of goods sold expense are important for product companies—manufacturers, wholesalers, and retailers. But before turning to an examination of these accounts at The Home Depot, we should recognize that cost of sales expense is also a critical performance component for many service companies, particularly those who engage in projects for their clients and customers. For fiscal 2020, the consulting firm Accenture PLC reports revenues of $44.3 billion and cost of services of $30.4 billion; the professional staffing company Kelly Services, Inc. reported net service revenues of $4.5 billion and direct costs of services of $3.7 billion; and Alphabet, Inc. reported revenue of $136.8 billion and cost of sales of $59.5 billion. While these companies report no inventory, the relationship of revenues to costs of revenues remains important.

Reporting Inventory Costs in the Financial Statements

To help frame our discussion of inventory, **Exhibits 7.1** and **7.2** present information from the current asset section of the balance sheet and the continuing operations section of the income statement for The Home Depot. We highlight merchandise inventories in the balance sheet as well as cost of goods sold in the income statement.

When inventory is purchased or produced, it is capitalized and carried on the balance sheet as an asset until it is sold, at which time its cost is transferred from the balance sheet to the income statement as an expense (cost of goods sold). Cost of goods sold (COGS) is then subtracted from sales revenue to yield **gross profit**:

Gross profit = Sales revenue − Cost of goods sold

The manner in which inventory costs are transferred from the balance sheet to the income statement affects both the level of inventories reported on the balance sheet and the amount of gross profit (and net income) reported on the income statement.

EXHIBIT 7.1 Balance Sheets (Current Assets Only)

THE HOME DEPOT, INC.
Consolidated Balance Sheets

($ millions)	February 2, 2020	January 3, 2019
Assets		
Current assets:		
Cash and cash equivalents	$2,133	$ 1,778
Receivables, net	2,106	1,936
Merchandise inventories	14,531	13,925
Other current assets	1,040	890
Total current assets	$19,810	$18,529

EXHIBIT 7.2 Income Statement

THE HOME DEPOT, INC.
Consolidated Statement of Earnings

($ millions)	**Fiscal Year Ended February 2, 2020**
Net sales	$110,225
Cost of sales	**72,653**
Gross profit	37,572
Total operating expenses	21,729
Operating income	15,843
Interest and other, net	1,128
Earnings before provision for income taxes	14,715
Provision for income taxes	3,473
Net earnings	$ 11,242

Recording Inventory Costs in the Financial Statements

To illustrate the inventory purchasing and selling cycle, assume that a start-up company purchases 800 units of merchandise inventory at a cost of $4 cash per unit. We account for this transaction as follows:

ANALYZE

Transaction	Cash Asset	+	Noncash Assets	=	Liabil-ities	+	Contrib. Capital	+	Earned Capital	Revenues	−	Expenses	=	Net Income
(1) Purchase 800 units of inventory at $4 cash per unit.	−3,200 Cash		+3,200 Inventory	=							−		=	

JOURNALIZE

		Dr.	Cr.
(1)	Inventory (+A)	3,200	
	Cash (−A)		3,200

POST

+ Inventory (A) −	
(1) 3,200	

+ Cash (A) −	
	3,200 (1)

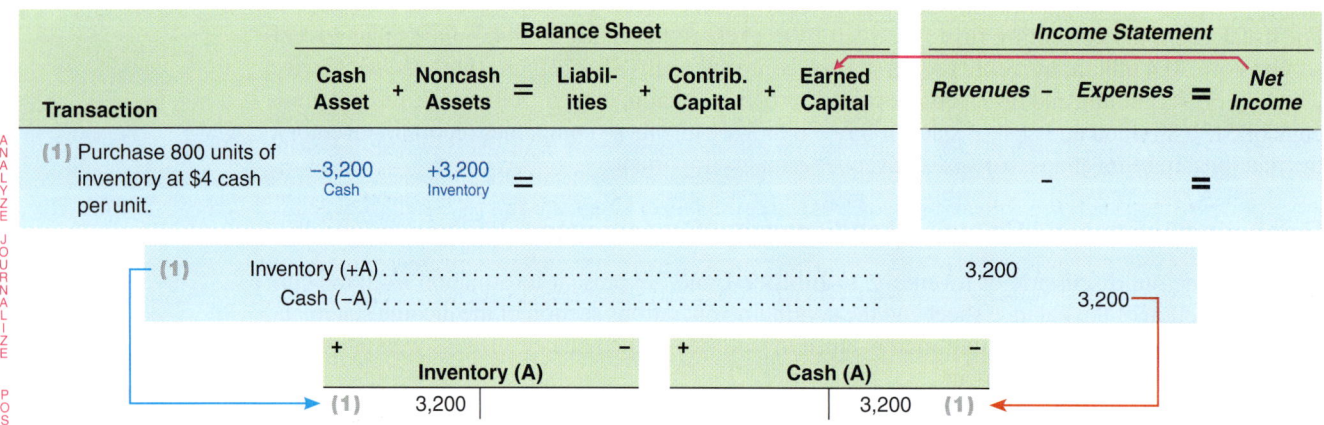

Next, assume this company sells 500 of those units for $7 cash per unit. The two following entries are required to record (a) the sales revenue and (b) the expense for the cost of the inventory sold.

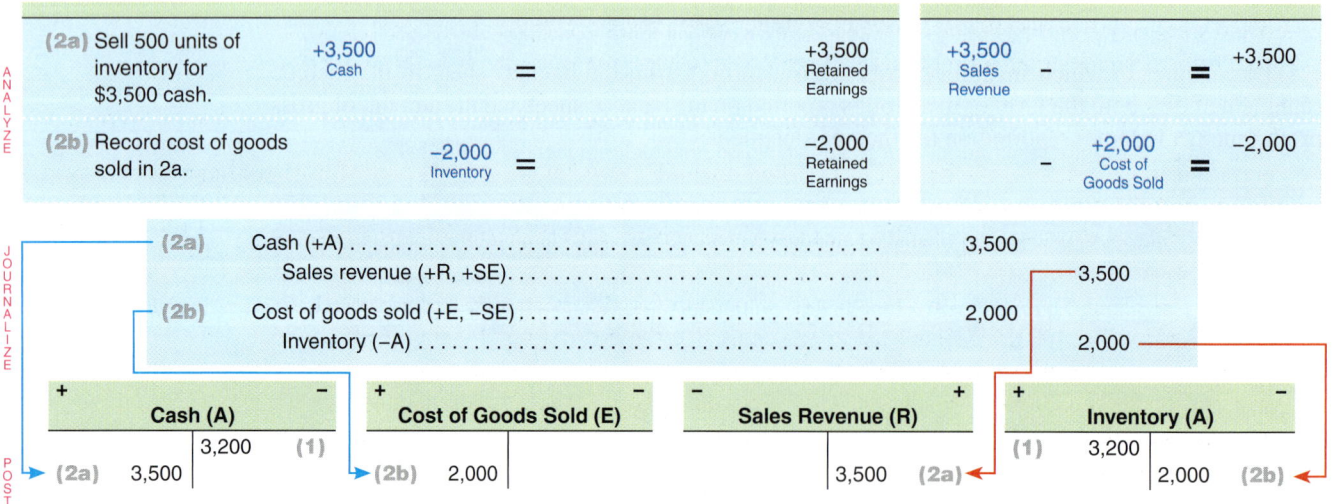

ANALYZE

Transaction	Cash Asset	+	Noncash Assets	=	Liabil-ities	+	Contrib. Capital	+	Earned Capital	Revenues	−	Expenses	=	Net Income
(2a) Sell 500 units of inventory for $3,500 cash.	+3,500 Cash			=					+3,500 Retained Earnings	+3,500 Sales Revenue	−		=	+3,500
(2b) Record cost of goods sold in 2a.			−2,000 Inventory	=					−2,000 Retained Earnings		−	+2,000 Cost of Goods Sold	=	−2,000

JOURNALIZE

		Dr.	Cr.
(2a)	Cash (+A)	3,500	
	Sales revenue (+R, +SE)		3,500
(2b)	Cost of goods sold (+E, −SE)	2,000	
	Inventory (−A)		2,000

POST

+ Cash (A) −	
	3,200 (1)
(2a) 3,500	

+ Cost of Goods Sold (E) −	
(2b) 2,000	

− Sales Revenue (R) +	
	3,500 (2a)

+ Inventory (A) −	
(1) 3,200	
	2,000 (2b)

The gross profit from this sale is $1,500 ($3,500 – $2,000). Also, $1,200 worth of merchandise remains in inventory (300 units × $4 per unit).

Inventory and the Cost of Acquisition

In general, a company should recognize all inventories to which it holds legal title, and that inventory should be recognized at the cost of acquiring the inventory. On occasion, that means that the company will recognize items in inventory that are not on its premises. For instance, if a company purchases inventory from a supplier on an "FOB shipping point" basis, meaning that the purchasing company receives title to the goods as soon as they are shipped by the supplier, the purchasing company should recognize the inventory as soon as it receives notice that the goods have been shipped. A similar situation occurs when a company ships its own products to a customer, but has not yet fulfilled the requirements for recognizing revenue on the shipment. In this case, the cost of the products remains in the selling company's inventory account until revenue (and cost of goods sold) can be recognized.

FYI The term **FOB** ("free on board") **shipping point** means that title passes to the purchaser as soon as it is shipped by the seller. **FOB destination** means that the seller retains title until the item arrives at the purchaser's location.

It is also possible for a company to have physical possession of inventory items, but not to have legal title. **Target Corporation**, for example, reports the following in a recent 10-K.

> We routinely enter into arrangements with vendors whereby we do not purchase or pay for merchandise until the merchandise is ultimately sold to a guest. Under the vast majority of these arrangements, which represent less than 5 percent of consolidated sales, we record revenue and related costs gross. We concluded that we are the principal in these transactions for a number of reasons, most notably because we 1) control the overall economics of the transactions, including setting the sales price and realizing the majority of cash flows from the sale, 2) control the relationship with the customer, and 3) are responsible for fulfilling the promise to provide goods to the customer. Merchandise received under these arrangements is not included in Inventory because the purchase and sale of this inventory are virtually simultaneous.

Inventory is reported in the balance sheet at its cost, including any cost to acquire, transport, and prepare goods for sale. In some cases, determining the cost of inventory requires accounting for various incentives that suppliers offer to purchase more or to pay promptly. If a company qualifies for a supplier's volume discount or rebate, it should immediately recognize the effective reduction in the cost of inventory and cost of goods sold. Or, if the company purchases inventory on credit, suppliers often grant **cash discounts** to buyers if payment is made within a specified time period. Cash discounts are usually established as part of the credit terms and stated as a percentage of the purchase price. For example, credit terms of 1/10, n/30 (one-ten, net-thirty) indicate that a 1% cash discount is allowed if the payment is made within 10 days. If the cash discount is not taken, the full purchase price is due in 30 days. Cash discounts are discussed in greater detail in Chapter 9.

Inventory Reporting by Manufacturing Firms

Retail and wholesale businesses purchase merchandise for resale to customers. In contrast, a manufacturing firm produces the goods it sells. Its inventory reporting is designed to reflect this difference in the nature of its operations.

FYI Only one inventory account appears in the financial statements of a merchandiser. A manufacturer normally has three inventory accounts: Raw Materials, Work-in-Process, and Finished Goods.

Manufacturing firms typically report three categories of inventory account:

- **Raw materials inventory**—the cost of parts and materials purchased from suppliers for use in the production process. When raw materials are used in the production process, the cost of the materials used is transferred from raw materials inventory into the work-in-process inventory account.
- **Work-in-process inventory**—the cost of the inventory of partially completed goods. Work-in-process (abbreviated WIP) includes the materials used in the production of the product as well as labor cost and overhead cost. (Methods by which labor and overhead costs are assigned to products in the WIP account is a *managerial accounting* topic.) When the production process is completed, the **cost of goods produced** is transferred from WIP into the finished goods inventory account.
- **Finished goods inventory**—the cost of the stock of completed product ready for delivery to customers. When finished goods are sold, cost of goods sold is debited and finished goods inventory is credited, much the same as in a retail business.

EXHIBIT 7.3 Components of Inventory for Pfizer, Inc.

	Dec. 31, 2020
Inventories ($ millions):	
Finished goods	$2,878
Work in process	4,430
Raw materials and supplies	738
Total	$8,046

A complete illustration of the accounting process for a manufacturing business is beyond the scope of this text. However, it is useful to understand how these inventory accounts are presented in the financial statements of manufacturing firms. In some cases, each of the three categories of inventory is presented in the balance sheet. Usually, however, the balance sheet only presents the combined total of the three accounts, leaving the detail to be presented in the disclosure notes. Pfizer, Inc. reported inventory of $8,046 million in its balance sheet dated December 31, 2020. **Exhibit 7.3** details the components of Pfizer's inventory balance as presented in its 10-K report. It shows that work in process inventory represented the largest portion of the total inventory balance. **Exhibit 7.3** is representative of the note disclosure provided by many manufacturing companies.

BUSINESS INSIGHT

If a manufacturing company has an unexpected buildup of inventory, the interpretation depends on the type of inventory. A larger-than-normal buildup of finished goods would imply that the company was having difficulty getting customers to purchase its products. However, if the buildup is in work-in-process inventory, it might imply a problem with manufacturing processes, particularly if accompanied by a decrease in finished goods inventory.

Review 7-1 LO7-1

Identifying Inventory Costs

GuidedExample MBC

Determine whether each cost should be included in the initial measurement of merchandise inventory of the seller. Consider each item separately.

a. _____ Transportation costs incurred by the seller to obtain goods purchased by supplier.
b. _____ Advertising costs incurred to sell the merchandise held for sale.
c. _____ Invoice cost of inventory in-transit from a suppler, shipped FOB shipping point.
d. _____ Sales tax incurred by seller on merchandise purchased.
e. _____ Costs incurred by the seller to ship inventory to the customer, sent FOB shipping point.

Solution on p. 7-42.

INVENTORY COSTING METHODS

LO7-2 Account for inventory and cost of goods sold using different costing methods.

eLecture MBC

The computation of cost of goods sold is important and is shown in **Exhibit 7.4**.

EXHIBIT 7.4 Cost of Goods Sold Computation

	Beginning inventory value (prior period ending balance sheet)
+	Cost of inventory purchases and/or production
	Cost of goods available for sale
−	Ending inventory value (current period balance sheet)
	Cost of goods sold (current income statement)

The cost of inventory available at the beginning of a period is a carryover from the ending inventory balance of the prior period. The costs of current period purchases of inventory (or costs of newly manufactured inventories) are added to the costs of beginning inventory on the balance sheet, yielding the total cost of goods (inventory) available for sale. Then, the total cost of goods available either ends up in cost of goods sold for the period (reported on the income statement) or is carried forward as inventory to start the next period (reported on the ending balance sheet). This cost flow is schematically shown in **Exhibit 7.5**.

EXHIBIT 7.5 Inventory Cost Flows to Financial Statements

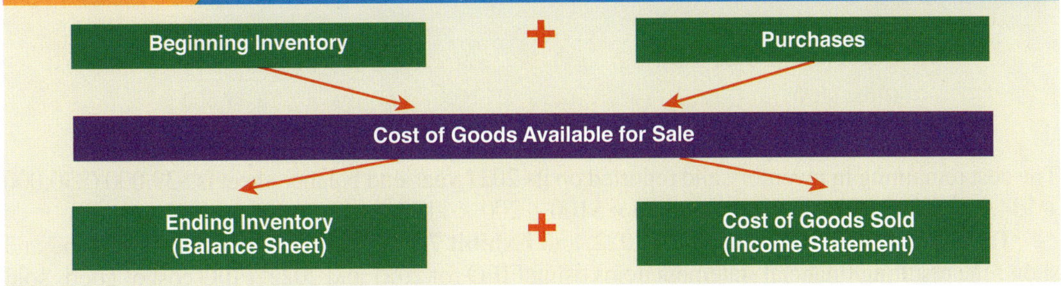

Understanding the flow of inventory costs is important. If the beginning inventory plus all inventory purchased or manufactured during the period is sold, then COGS is equal to the cost of the goods available for sale. However, when inventory remains at the end of a period, companies must identify the cost of those inventories that have been sold and the cost of those inventories that remain.

Most companies will organize the physical flow of their inventories to keep the cost of inventory management low, while minimizing the likelihood of spoilage or obsolescence. However, the accounting for inventory and cost of goods sold does not have to follow the physical flow of the units of inventory, so companies may report using a **cost flow assumption** that does not conform to the actual movement of product through the firm. (For instance, many grocery chains use last-in, first-out to account for inventory costs, but that doesn't mean that they put the newest produce out to sell while keeping the older produce back in the storeroom.)

Illustration To illustrate the possible cost flow assumptions that companies can adopt, assume that **Exhibit 7.6** reflects the inventory records of Butler Company.

EXHIBIT 7.6 Summary Inventory Records for Butler Company

		Number of Units	Cost per Unit	Total Cost	Number of Units	Price per Unit	Total Revenue
January 1, 2021	Beginning inventory . . .	500	$100	$ 50,000			
2021	Inventory purchased . . .	200	170	34,000			
	Inventory sold				450	$250	$112,500
2022	Inventory purchased . . .	600	180	108,000			
	Inventory sold				500	255	127,500

Butler Company began the period with inventory consisting of 500 units it purchased at a total cost of $50,000 ($100 each). During the two-year period, the company purchased an additional 200 units costing $34,000 and 600 units costing $108,000. The total cost of goods available for sale for this two-year period equals $192,000.

Tracking the number of units available for sale each year and in inventory at the end of each year is simple. However, the changing cost per unit makes it more complicated to determine the cost of goods sold and the ending inventory. The relationships depicted in **Exhibit 7.5** can hold in multiple ways, depending on the cost flow assumption chosen. Three inventory costing methods are acceptable under U.S. GAAP.[1]

First-In, First-Out (FIFO)

The **first-in, first-out (FIFO)** inventory costing method transfers costs from inventory in the order that they were initially recorded. That is, FIFO assumes that the first costs recorded in inventory (first-in) are the first costs transferred from inventory (first-out) to cost of goods sold.

FYI First-in, first-out (FIFO) assumes that goods are used in the order in which they are purchased; the inventory remaining represents the most recent purchases.

[1] Of the firms in the Standard and Poor's 500 Index as of March 22, 2021, **13.2%** have a LIFO reserve reported on Compustat in 2019. A few additional firms may be on LIFO but have a zero reserve.

Conversely, the costs of the last units purchased are the costs that remain in inventory at year-end. Applying FIFO to the data in **Exhibit 7.6** means that the costs relating to the 450 units sold are all taken from its *beginning* inventory, which consists of 500 units. The company's 2021 cost of goods sold and gross profit, using FIFO, is computed as follows:

Sales	$112,500
COGS (450 @ $100 each)	45,000
Gross profit	$ 67,500

The cost remaining in inventory and reported on its 2021 year-end balance sheet is $39,000 ($50,000 + $34,000 – $45,000; also computed 50 × $100 + 200 × $170).

The same process can be used for 2022, and **Exhibit 7.7** depicts the FIFO costing method and shows the resulting financial statement items using FIFO for 2021 and 2022. FIFO cost of goods sold for 2022 is 50 units at $100 each plus 200 units at $170 each plus 250 units at $180 each, or $84,000. Ending inventory for 2022 is 350 units at $180 each, or $63,000. Over the two-year period, the total cost of goods available for sale of $192,000 is either recognized as cost of goods sold ($45,000 + $84,000 = $129,000) or remains in ending inventory ($63,000).

EXHIBIT 7.7 Butler Company using FIFO Inventory Costing

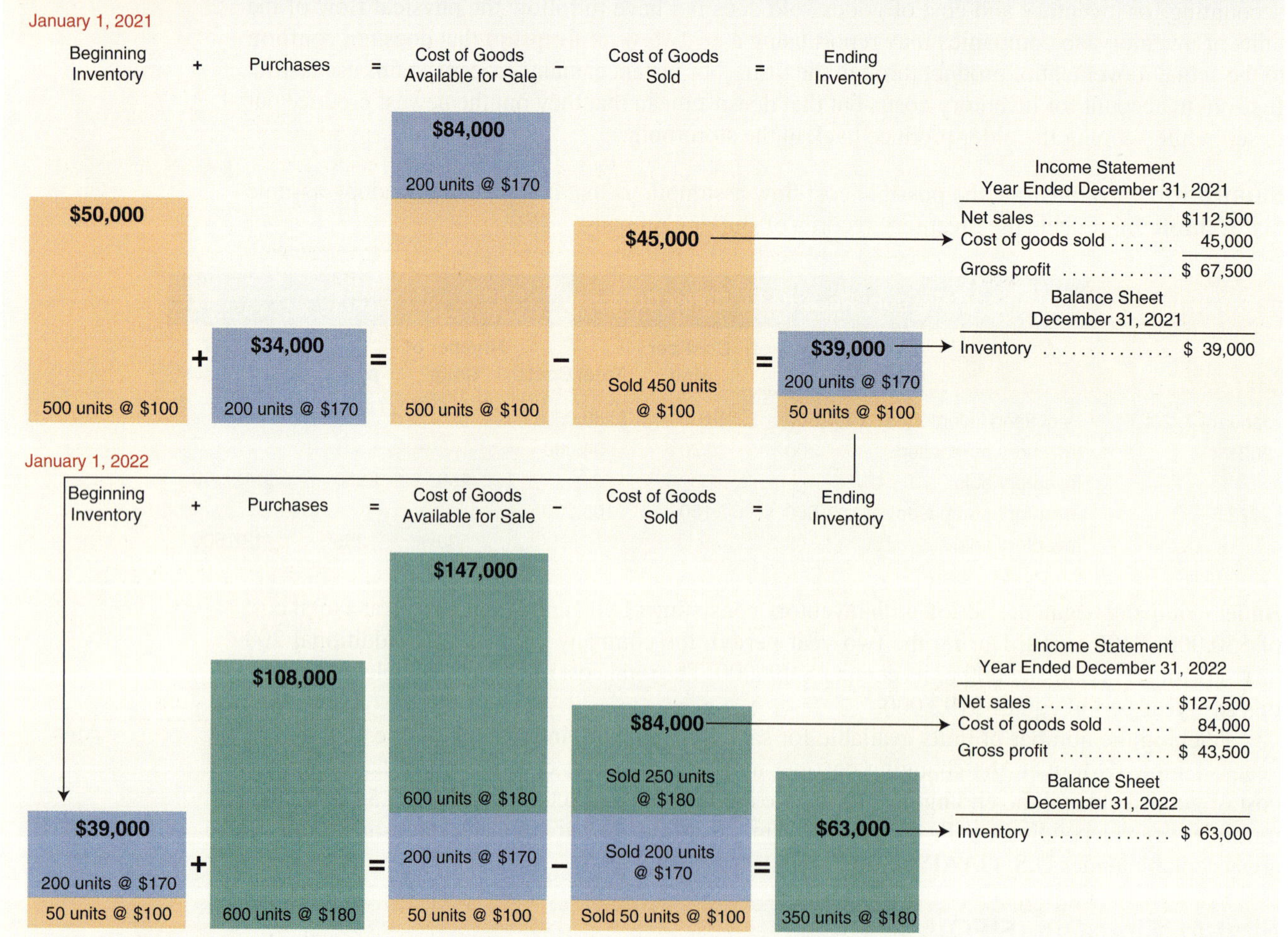

Last-In, First-Out (LIFO)

FYI Last-in, first-out (LIFO) matches the cost of the last goods purchased against revenue.

The **last-in, first-out (LIFO)** inventory costing method transfers to cost of goods sold the most recent costs that were recorded in inventory. That is, we assume that the most recent costs recorded in inventory (last-in) are the first costs transferred from inventory (first-out). Conversely, the costs of the first units purchased are the costs that remain in inventory at year-end. Butler Company's 2021 cost of goods sold and gross profit, using LIFO, are computed as follows:

Sales	$112,500
COGS: (200 @ $170 each = $34,000)	
(250 @ $100 each = $25,000)	59,000
Gross profit	$ 53,500

The cost remaining in inventory and reported on its 2021 balance sheet is $25,000 ($50,000 + $34,000 – $59,000; also computed 250 × $100).

The same process can be used for 2022, and **Exhibit 7.8** depicts the LIFO costing method and shows the resulting financial statement values using LIFO for both years. LIFO cost of goods sold for 2022 is 500 units at $180 each, or $90,000. Ending inventory is 250 units at $100 each plus 100 units at $180 each, or $43,000. Again, the two-year total cost of goods available for sale of $192,000 is either recognized as cost of goods sold ($59,000 + $90,000 = $149,000) or remains in inventory ($43,000).

EXHIBIT 7.8 Butler Company using LIFO Inventory Costing

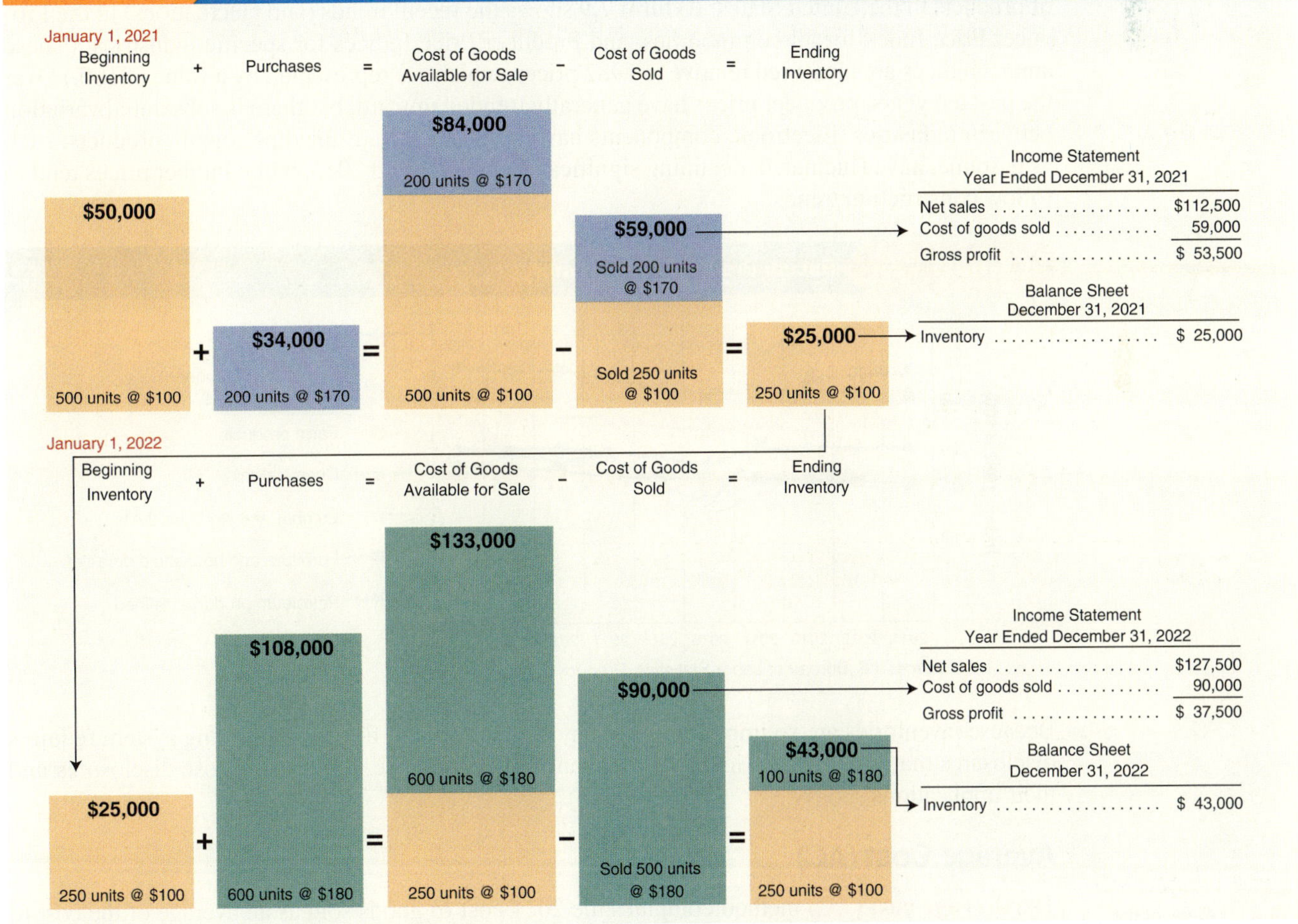

The exhibit shows that **LIFO layers** of inventories added in each year are kept separately. So, the ending inventory in 2022 consists of a pre-2021 layer of 250 units at $100 each plus a 2022 layer of 100 units at $180 each. When unit sales exceed purchases (as we discuss in the appendix), the first costs carried to cost of goods sold are those purchased in the current year, followed by the most recent layer of LIFO inventory and working down to the oldest layers. So, the 2021 beginning inventory value of $100 per unit remains in LIFO inventory as long as there are 250 units remaining at the end of the year. One aspect of this flow assumption is that reported LIFO inventory values can be significantly lower than the current cost of acquiring the same inventory.

LIFO inventory costing is always applied on a periodic, annual basis. This means that Butler's cost of goods sold and ending inventory for 2022 do not depend on the timing of the sales and purchases within the year. Inventory levels might be drawn down below 250 units *during* the year, but the 250 unit LIFO layer at $100 each remains in ending inventory as long as inventory is built up to 250 units by the *end* of the year.

Inventory Costing and Price Changes

There are several important aspects of inventory costing that are illustrated by the Butler Company example. First, both LIFO and FIFO are historical cost methods, though they allocate the costs of inventory differently. All costs are accounted for, but in different ways.

Second, the differences between LIFO and FIFO arise when the costs of inventory change over time. In general, LIFO puts more recent costs into cost of goods sold expense, so LIFO cost of goods sold is higher than FIFO cost of goods sold (and gross profit correspondingly lower) when the costs of inventory are rising over time. This phenomenon can be seen in years 2021 and 2022 for Butler Company. If the costs of inventory are falling, then FIFO cost of goods sold exceeds LIFO cost of goods sold.

One place where we can observe the cost trends of acquiring inventory is in the U.S. Bureau of Labor Statistics' Producer Price Indices. These indices track the costs of producing a wide variety of products in the United States. **Exhibit 7.9** shows the recent trends (and fluctuations) in the Producer Price Index for all commodities, and Producer Price Indices for specific industries. (These annual indices are measured relative to 1982 prices, which are represented by a value of 100.) Over the past ten years, producer prices have generally trended upward, but there is substantial variation between industries. Electronic components have trended down, refined petroleum products, such as gasoline, have fluctuated, declining significantly in 2014 and 2015, while lumber prices tend to follow construction trends.

EXHIBIT 7.9 Recent Producer Price History

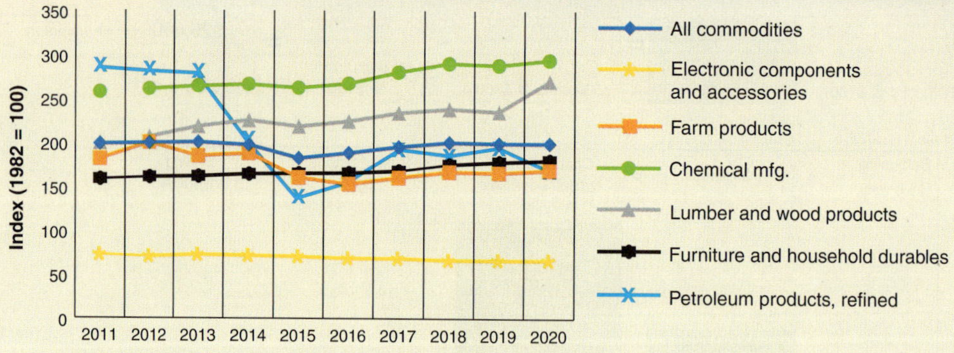

Source: U.S. Bureau of Labor Statistics, Producer Price Indices

Because inventories are so important for many companies, the financial reporting system requires disclosures that are useful in interpreting financial performance. We turn to those disclosures and their implications shortly.

Average Cost (AC)

FYI Average cost values inventory on the basis of the average cost of all similar goods available during the period.

The **average cost (AC)** method computes the 2021 cost of goods sold as an average of the cost to purchase all of the inventories that were available for sale during the period as follows:

Sales	$112,500
COGS (450 @ $120 [{$50,000 + $34,000}/700 units] each)	54,000
Gross profit	$ 58,500

The average cost of $120 per unit is determined from the total cost of goods available for sale divided by the number of units available for sale ($84,000/700 units). The cost remaining in inventory and reported on its 2021 balance sheet is $30,000 ($84,000 – $54,000; also computed 250 × $120).

When average cost is applied to the future years, the beginning inventory balance's average cost is again averaged with the inventory acquisitions made during the year. This new average is used to assign costs to that year's ending inventory and cost of goods sold. For the Butler Company, the average cost is $120 for 2021 and $162.35 (rounded) for 2022. The average cost for 2022 is the opening inventory balance plus the period's purchases ($30,000 + $108,000) divided by the total number of units available for sale (250 + 600). So, 2022 cost of goods sold is 500 units at $162.35 each, and ending inventory is 350 units at that same average cost. **Exhibit 7.10** depicts the average cost method and shows the resulting financial statement values using average cost for both years.

EXHIBIT 7.10 Butler Company using Average Cost Inventory Costing

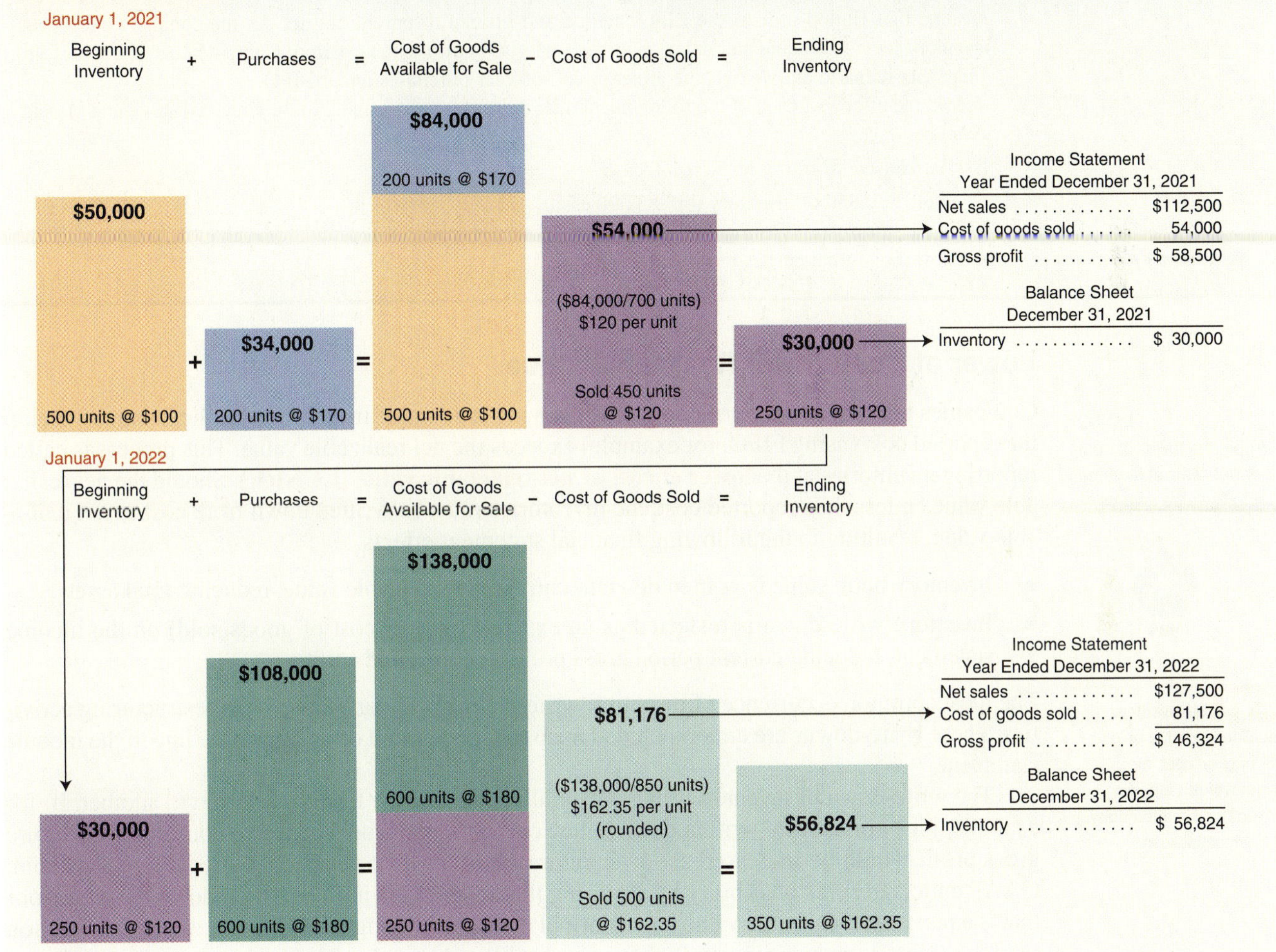

Accounting for Inventory Using Different Cost Methods

LO7-2 **Review 7-2**

GuidedExample MBC

At the beginning of the current period, Hutton Company holds 1,000 units of its only product with a per-unit cost of $18. A summary of purchases during the current period follows:

	Units	Unit Cost	Cost
Beginning Inventory	1,000	$18.00	$18,000
Purchases: #1	1,800	18.25	32,850
#2	800	18.50	14,800
#3	1,200	19.00	22,800
Goods available for sale	4,800		$88,450

During the current period, Hutton sells 2,800 units.

continued

continued from previous page

Required

a. Assume that Hutton uses the first-in, first-out (FIFO) method. Compute the cost of goods sold for the current period and the ending inventory balance.

b. Assume that Hutton uses the last-in, first-out (LIFO) method. Compute the cost of goods sold for the current period and the ending inventory balance.

c. Assume that Hutton uses the average cost (AC) method. Compute the cost of goods sold for the current period and the ending inventory balance.

d. As manager, which one of these three inventory costing methods would you choose:

1. To reflect what is probably the physical flow of goods? Explain.
2. To minimize income taxes for the period? Explain.

e. Assume that Hutton utilizes the LIFO method and instead of purchasing lot #3, the company allows its inventory level to decline and delays purchasing lot #3 until the next period. Compute cost of goods sold under this scenario and discuss the effect of end-of-year purchases under LIFO.

f. Record the effects of each of the following summary transactions 1 and 2 in the financial statement effects template.

1. Purchased inventory for $70,450 cash.
2. Sold $50,850 of inventory for $85,000 cash.

g. Using the information from part *f*, prepare journal entries, set up T-accounts for each of the accounts used, and post the journal entries to those T-accounts.

Solution on p. 7-42.

Lower of Cost or Net Realizable Value

LO7-3 Apply the lower of cost or net realizable value rule to value inventory.

eLecture MBC

Companies are required to write down the carrying amount of inventories on the balance sheet, *if* the reported cost (using FIFO, for example) exceeds the net realizable value. This process is called reporting inventories at the **lower of cost or net realizable value (LCNRV)**. Should the net realizable value be less than reported cost, the inventories must be written down from cost to net realizable value, resulting in the following financial statement effects.

- Inventory book value is written down to current net realizable value, reducing total assets.
- Inventory write-down is reflected as an expense (part of cost of goods sold) on the income statement, reducing current period gross profit, income, and equity.

FYI If inventory declines in value below its original cost, for whatever reason, the inventory is written down to reflect this loss.

The most common occurrence of inventory write-downs is in connection with restructuring activities. These write-downs are either included in cost of goods sold or on a separate line in the income statement.

The write-down of inventories can potentially shift income from one period to another. If, for example, inventories were written down below current replacement cost (too conservative), future gross profit would be increased as lower future costs would be reflected in cost of goods sold. GAAP anticipates this possibility by requiring that inventories not be written down below a floor that is equal to net realizable value less a normal markup. Although this does allow some discretion (and the ability to manage income), the net realizable value and markup values must be confirmed by the company's auditors.

FYI Standards require the consistent application of costing methods from one period to another.

Illustration To illustrate the lower of cost or net realizable value rule, assume Home Depot has the following items in its current period ending inventory:

Item	Quantity	Cost per Unit	Net Realizable Value	LCNRV per Unit	Total LCNRV
Spools of copper wire.	250	$10	$15	$10	250 × $10 = $2,500
Sheets of wood paneling	500	$ 8	$ 6	$ 6	500 × $ 6 = $3,000

A write-down is not necessary for the spools of copper wire because the net realizable value ($15 per unit) is higher than the acquisition cost ($10 per unit). However, the 500 sheets of wood paneling should be recorded in the current period's ending inventory at the net realizable value of $6 per unit because it is lower than the acquisition cost of $8 per unit. When the net realizable value of inventory declines below its acquisition cost, we must record a write-down. Before the write-down, inventory is recorded at cost of $6,500. With the write-down of $1,000, inventory after the write-down is recorded at LCNRV of $5,500. The effects of this write-down and corresponding journal entries follow:

ANALYZE

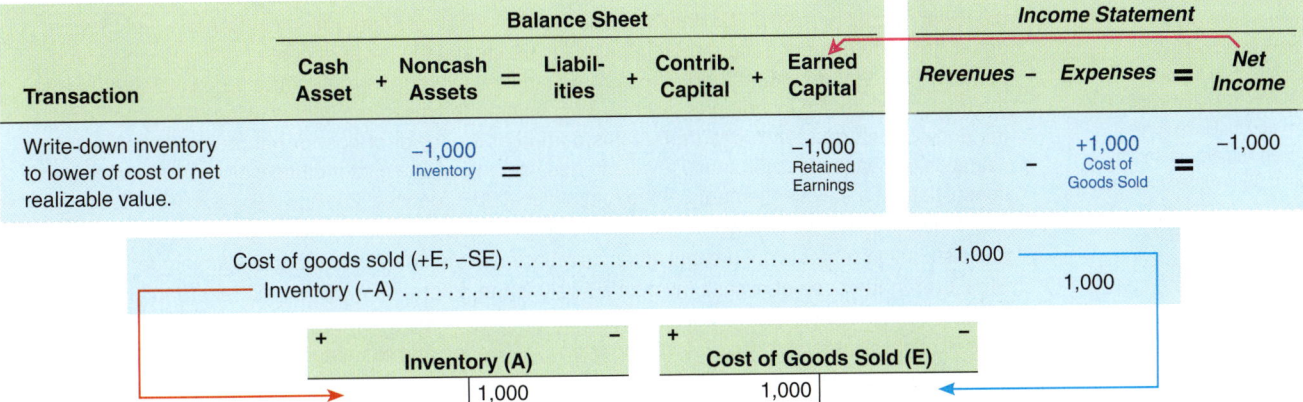

Transaction	Cash Asset	+	Noncash Assets	=	Liabil-ities	+	Contrib. Capital	+	Earned Capital	Revenues	−	Expenses	=	Net Income
	Balance Sheet									**Income Statement**				
Write-down inventory to lower of cost or net realizable value.			−1,000 Inventory	=					−1,000 Retained Earnings		−	+1,000 Cost of Goods Sold	=	−1,000

JOURNALIZE

	Debit	Credit
Cost of goods sold (+E, −SE)	1,000	
Inventory (−A)		1,000

POST

+ Inventory (A) −	
	1,000

+ Cost of Goods Sold (E) −	
1,000	

A GLOBAL PERSPECTIVE

IFRS

Under U.S. GAAP, inventory that has been written down cannot be revalued later at higher levels even if the net realizable value of that inventory increases. IFRS, on the other hand, does allow companies to reverse the write-down of the inventory up to the acquisition cost if market values warrant. The revaluation results in a debit to Inventory and a credit to Cost of Goods Sold. The option to revalue inventory after a write-down differs across countries.

Applying the Lower of Cost or Net Realizable Value Rule

LO7-3 **Review 7-3**

GuidedExample MBC

Venner Company had the following inventory at December 31.

	Quantity	Unit Price Cost	NRV
Fans			
Model X1	300	$18	$19
Model X2	250	22	24
Model X3	400	29	26
Heaters			
Model B7	500	24	28
Model B8	290	35	32
Model B9	100	41	38

Required

1. Determine ending inventory by applying the lower of cost or NRV rule to
   a. Each item of inventory.
   b. Each major category of inventory.
   c. Total inventory.
2. Which of the LCNRV procedures from requirement 1 results in the lowest net income for the year? Explain.

Solution on p. 7-43.

FINANCIAL STATEMENT EFFECTS AND DISCLOSURE

LO7-4 Evaluate how inventory costing affects management decisions and outsiders' interpretations of financial statements.

The notes to the financial statements describe, at least in general terms, the inventory accounting method used by a company. To illustrate, The Home Depot reports $14,531 million in merchandise inventory on its February 2, 2020, balance sheet as a current asset. The following note was taken from that 10-K report:

eLecture MBC

FYI Standards require financial statement disclosure of (1) the composition of the inventory (in the balance sheet or a separate schedule in the notes), (2) significant or unusual inventory financing arrangements, and (3) inventory costing methods employed (which can differ for different types of inventory).

> The substantial majority of our merchandise inventories are stated at the lower of cost (first-in, first-out) or market, as determined by the retail inventory method, which is based on a number of factors such as markups, markdowns, and inventory losses (or shrink). As the inventory retail value is adjusted regularly to reflect market conditions, inventory valued using the retail method approximates the lower of cost or market. Certain subsidiaries, including retail operations in Canada and Mexico, and distribution centers, record merchandise inventories at the lower of cost or net realizable value, as determined by a cost method. These merchandise inventories represent approximately 29% of the total merchandise inventories balance. We evaluate the inventory valued using a cost method at the end of each quarter to ensure that it is carried at the lower of cost or net realizable value. The valuation allowance for merchandise inventories valued under a cost method was not material to our consolidated financial statements at the end of fiscal 2019 or fiscal 2018.
>
> Independent physical inventory counts or cycle counts are taken on a regular basis in each store and distribution center to ensure that amounts reflected in merchandise inventories are properly stated. Shrink (or in the case of excess inventory, swell) is the difference between the recorded amount of inventory and the physical inventory. We calculate shrink based on actual inventory losses occurring as a result of physical inventory counts during each fiscal period and estimated inventory losses occurring between physical inventory counts. The estimate for shrink occurring in the interim period between physical inventory counts is calculated on a store-specific basis based on recent shrink results and current trends in the business.

This note includes several items that would be of interest to financial statement users:

1. The Home Depot uses the FIFO method to determine the cost of most of its inventory suggesting several methods are likely to be in use.
2. Inventory is reported at the lower of cost or net realizable value, and the amount of write-down (the valuation allowance) was not material at the financial statement date.
3. The company periodically takes a physical count of inventory to identify "shrink." Shrink refers to the loss of inventory due to theft, breakage or damage, spoilage (for perishable goods), or other losses, as well as inaccurate records.

When businesses adjust inventory balances for shrink, the loss is debited to cost of goods sold. Hence, cost of goods sold expense on the income statement includes the actual cost of products sold during the period plus the loss due to shrink as well as losses resulting from lower of cost or market adjustments and discounts lost.

Another illustration of inventory disclosure is taken from the notes of **The Timken Company**. Timken reports an inventory of $841.3 million on its December 31, 2020, balance sheet. The following excerpts were taken from note disclosures in its 2020 10-K report ($ millions):

> Notes 1 and 7
>
> Inventories are valued at the lower of cost or net realizable value, with approximately 61% valued by the FIFO method and the remaining 39% valued by the LIFO method. The majority of the Company's domestic inventories are valued by the LIFO method, while all of the Company's international inventories are valued by the FIFO method.
>
> If all inventories had been valued at FIFO, inventories would have been $172.1 million and $168.9 million greater at December 31, 2020 and 2019, respectively. The Company recognized an increase in its LIFO reserve of $3.2 million during 2020, compared to a decrease in its LIFO reserve of $5.0 million during 2019. Inventory and the allowance for surplus and obsolete inventory increased from 2019 primarily as a result of recent acquisitions.

There are several interesting items disclosed in Timken's note:

1. Timken uses LIFO to report the *majority* of its domestic inventories, while *all* of its international inventories are valued using the FIFO method. Neither U.S. GAAP nor tax authorities such as the IRS require the use of a single inventory costing method. That is, companies are allowed to, and frequently do, use different inventory costing methods for different categories of inventory. In addition, multinational companies may use one costing method in the United States and a different method for foreign inventory stocks.

2. Timken reports inventory values at the lower of cost or net realizable value. The FIFO value differs from the LIFO cost. In 2020, the FIFO cost was $172.1 million higher than the LIFO cost, while in 2019, the FIFO cost was $168.9 million higher than LIFO. Companies using LIFO are required to report the difference between the LIFO cost and current value—determined either as market value or replacement cost or as the FIFO cost. The difference between the ending inventory's FIFO cost (or current cost) and its LIFO cost is called the **LIFO reserve**.

Why do companies disclose such details on inventory, and why is so much attention paid to inventory in financial statement analysis? First, the magnitude of a company's investment in inventory is often large—affecting both balance sheets and income statements. Second, risks of inventory losses are often high, as they are tied to technical obsolescence and consumer tastes. Third, it can provide insight into future performance—both good and bad. Fourth, high inventory levels result in substantial costs for the company, such as:

- Financing costs to purchase inventories (when not purchased on credit)
- Storage costs of inventories (such as warehousing and related facilities)
- Handling costs of inventories (including wages)
- Insurance costs of inventories

Consequently, companies seek to keep inventories at levels that balance these costs against the cost of insufficient inventory (stock-out and resulting lost sales and delays in production, as machines and employees sit idle awaiting inventories to process).

Next, we turn our focus on the effects of the different inventory costing assumptions on the financial statements.

Financial Statement Effects of Inventory Costing

The three inventory costing methods described a few pages earlier yield differing levels of gross profit for our illustrative example, as shown in **Exhibit 7.11**.

We emphasize that, even though the various methods produce different financial statements, the underlying events are the same. That is, different accounting methods can make similar situations seem more different than they really are.

LIFO Reserve **Exhibit 7.11** demonstrates one of the income statement/balance sheet links that proves useful in analyzing financial statements. In the beginning inventory for 2021, LIFO and FIFO start from the same point—500 units at $100 each. But during 2021, FIFO would record cost of goods sold that is $14,000 less than LIFO ($45,000 versus $59,000). During 2021, LIFO put $14,000 more into cost of goods sold than FIFO did, but that also means that LIFO put $14,000 less into ending inventory. We can see that the LIFO reserve has grown from zero to $14,000, the same amount. This relationship continues in 2022: the LIFO reserve increased by $6,000 (from $14,000 to $20,000), and the LIFO cost of goods sold was $6,000 greater than the FIFO cost of goods sold ($90,000 versus $84,000). The LIFO reserve equals the ending inventory's FIFO cost less LIFO cost, but it is also the *cumulative* difference between LIFO and FIFO cost of goods sold. The *change* in the LIFO reserve is the difference between LIFO and FIFO cost of goods sold for the current period.

FYI If ending inventory is misstated, then (1) the inventory, retained earnings, working capital, and current ratio in the balance sheet are misstated, and (2) the cost of goods sold and net income in the income statement are misstated.

So, if Butler Company chose to report using LIFO, we could estimate what the company's FIFO cost of goods sold would have been by seeing how the LIFO reserve changed.

FIFO cost of goods sold = LIFO cost of goods sold – Change in the LIFO reserve

That relationship proves useful if we want to compare Butler Company's gross profit to that of another company using FIFO. A change in the LIFO reserve also provides some information about how a company's inventory costs changed over the period.

Income Statement Effects The income differences between inventory accounting methods are a function of two factors. First is the speed and direction of inventory cost changes. For Butler Company, inventory costs have increased from $100 per unit to $180 per unit in a two-year period. If costs increased more slowly, the difference between LIFO and FIFO would decrease. And, if costs decreased, the differences would reverse: FIFO cost of goods sold would be greater than LIFO cost of goods sold.

EXHIBIT 7.11 Financial Statement Effects of Inventory Costing Methods for Butler Company

		FIFO	LIFO	Average Cost
January 1, 2021	**Balance Sheet**			
	Beginning inventory	$ 50,000	$ 50,000	$ 50,000
	LIFO Reserve	—	—	—
Year Ended 2021	**Income Statement**			
	Revenue	$112,500	$112,500	$112,500
	Cost of goods sold:			
	Beginning inventory	50,000	50,000	50,000
	Add: Purchases	34,000	34,000	34,000
	Goods available for sale	84,000	84,000	84,000
	Subtract: Ending inventory	39,000	25,000	30,000
	Cost of goods sold	45,000	59,000	54,000
	Gross profit	67,500	53,500	58,500
	Selling, general and administrative expenses (assumed number)	10,000	10,000	10,000
	Income before income taxes	57,500	43,500	48,500
	Income tax expense (25%)	14,375	10,875	12,125
	Net income	$ 43,125	$ 32,625	$ 36,375
December 31, 2021	**Balance Sheet**			
	Ending inventory	$ 39,000	$ 25,000	$ 30,000
	LIFO Reserve	—	14,000	—
Year Ended 2022	**Income Statement**			
	Revenue	$127,500	$127,500	$127,500
	Cost of goods sold:			
	Beginning inventory	39,000	25,000	30,000
	Add: Purchases	108,000	108,000	108,000
	Goods available for sale	147,000	133,000	138,000
	Subtract: Ending inventory	63,000	43,000	56,824
	Cost of goods sold	84,000	90,000	81,176
	Gross profit	43,500	37,500	46,324
	Selling, general and administrative expenses (assumed number)	10,000	10,000	10,000
	Income before income taxes	33,500	27,500	36,324
	Income tax expense (25%)	8,375	6,875	9,081
	Net income	$ 25,125	$ 20,625	$ 27,243
December 31, 2022	**Balance Sheet**			
	Ending inventory	$ 63,000	$ 43,000	$ 56,824
	LIFO Reserve	—	20,000	—

The second factor determining the differences is the length of time inventory is held by the company. If Butler Company were able to operate with zero inventory (or at least begin and end the reporting period with zero inventory), the three inventory accounting methods would yield exactly the same cost of goods sold. On the other hand, if inventory must be held for a long period, the differences would increase.

Effects of Changing Costs When the cost of a company's products is changing, management usually makes corresponding changes in the prices it charges for those products. If costs are declining, competitive pressures are likely to push down the prices customers are willing to pay. If costs are increasing, the company will try to increase prices to recover at least some of the greater cost. When costs fluctuate (for example, for a commodity), management may act to cause its prices to fluctuate in an effort to maintain its target profit margin.[2]

[2] LIFO has a reporting advantage when inventory costs fluctuate, in that it matches current period costs against current period revenues. For a company that holds one quarter's worth of inventory, FIFO matches the costs from three months ago against current period revenues. Such a "mismatch" might make it difficult for management to convey its success in maintaining its current profit margin.

If costs and prices are rising, then FIFO reports a higher gross margin, because the costs of older, lower-cost inventory are being matched against current selling prices. For tax purposes, the company would prefer to use LIFO because it would decrease gross profit and decrease taxable income. If Butler Company were subject to a 25% income tax rate, the use of LIFO rather than FIFO reduces taxes by $3,500 in 2021 ($14,375 – $10,875 in **Exhibit 7.11**, or 25% of the $14,000 difference in 2021 cost of goods sold) and by $1,500 in 2022 ($8,375 – $6,875 in **Exhibit 7.11**, or 25% of the $6,000 difference in 2022 cost of goods sold). In total over the two years, using LIFO (rather than FIFO) would reduce Butler's tax bill by $5,000 (which equals 25% of the $20,000 LIFO reserve at the end of 2022).

In the United States, LIFO is a popular tax method for accounting for inventories that have an upward trend in costs. But, the Internal Revenue Service has imposed a LIFO conformity requirement. If Butler Company is using LIFO for tax reporting, it must use LIFO for reporting to its shareholders. For inventories with a decreasing trend in costs, FIFO reduces the amount of taxes paid. FIFO is allowed by the Internal Revenue Service, but there is no corresponding conformity requirement for firms that use FIFO.

FYI When a company adopts LIFO in its tax filings, the company is required to use LIFO for reporting to its shareholders (in its 10-K). This requirement is known as the LIFO conformity rule.

Balance Sheet Effects The ending inventory using LIFO for our illustration is less than that reported using FIFO. In prolonged periods of rising costs, using LIFO yields ending inventories that are markedly lower than FIFO. As a result, balance sheets using LIFO do not accurately represent the cost that a company would incur to replace its current investment in inventories.

Timken, for example, reported that the FIFO value of its inventory was $172.1 million higher than the LIFO cost at the end of 2020. That is, the amount presented in its balance sheet was understated (relative to current value) by more than $172 million. For purposes of analysis, the value of the LIFO reserve can be viewed as an **unrealized holding gain**—a gain resulting from holding inventory as prices are rising. That is, there is a holding gain due to rising inventory costs that has not been recorded in the financial statements. This gain is not recognized until the inventory is sold. In its December 31, 2020, balance sheet, Timken reported current assets of $2,000.3 million and current liabilities of $848.0 million, for a current ratio of $2,000.3 ÷ $848.0, or about 2.36. However, Timken's inventory is not reported at an up-to-date amount, while the accounts payable would reflect the current prices owed to suppliers. Therefore, an improved measure of the current ratio would be [$2,000.3 + $172.1] ÷ $848.0, or about 2.56.

In contrast, by assigning the most recently purchased inventory items to ending inventory, FIFO costing tends to approximate current value in the balance sheet. Hence, companies using FIFO tend not to have large unrealized inventory holding gains. However, if prices fall, companies using FIFO are more likely to adjust inventory values to the lower of cost or net realizable value.

FYI Some companies highlight this in their disclosures. For example, another company that uses LIFO, Chevron Corporation, mentions the current ratio effect in the notes to their statements saying "The current ratio was adversely affected by the fact that Chevron's inventories are valued on a last-in, first-out basis."

Cash Flow Effects The increased gross profit using FIFO results in higher pretax income and, consequently, higher taxes payable (assuming FIFO is also used for tax reporting). Conversely, the use of LIFO in an inflationary environment results in a lower tax liability.

Use of LIFO has reduced the dollar amount of Timken inventories by $172.1 million, resulting in a cumulative increase in cost of goods sold and a cumulative decrease in gross profit and pretax profit of that same amount.[3] The decrease in cumulative pretax profits has lowered Timken's tax bill over the life of the company by roughly $43.03 million ($172.1 million × 25% assumed corporate tax rate), which has increased Timken's cumulative operating cash flow by that same amount. The increased cash flow from tax savings is often cited as a compelling reason for management to adopt LIFO.

Adjusting the Balance Sheet to FIFO For analysis purposes, we can use the LIFO reserve to adjust the balance sheet and income statement to achieve comparability between companies that utilize different inventory costing methods. For example, if we wanted to compare Timken with another company using FIFO, we add the LIFO reserve to its LIFO inventory. As explained above, this $172.1 million increase in 2020 inventories increases its cumulative pretax profits by $172.1 million and taxes by $43.03 million. Thus, the balance sheet adjustments involve increasing inventories by $172.1 million, tax liabilities by $43.03 million, and retained earnings by the remaining after-tax amount of $129.07 million (computed as $172.1 million – $43.03 million).

[3] Cost of Goods Sold = Beginning Inventories + Purchases – Ending Inventories. Thus, as ending inventories decrease, cost of goods sold increases.

IFRS

A GLOBAL PERSPECTIVE

One of the important differences in inventory accounting between U.S. GAAP and IFRS is that the latter does not allow the use of last-in, first-out (LIFO) accounting. Only FIFO and Average Cost are allowed for companies reporting under IFRS.

An analyst comparing a U.S. GAAP company to an IFRS company would need to keep an eye on these inventory differences and, when necessary, do the conversions described in the preceding paragraphs. While FIFO firms are not required to disclose what they would have looked like under LIFO, LIFO firms must disclose enough information to do a rough approximation of what they would have looked like under FIFO—making for an improved comparison with an IFRS company.

Adjusting the Income Statement to FIFO To adjust the income statement from LIFO to FIFO, we use the *change* in the LIFO reserve. For Timken, the LIFO reserve changed from $168.9 million in 2019 to $172.1 million in 2020, an increase of $3.2 million. To adjust the income statement to FIFO, we subtract $3.2 million from the cost of goods sold (reported using LIFO) and add the same amount to gross profit and pretax income. To estimate net income, we need to adjust for income taxes. Assuming a corporate tax rate of 25%, the use of LIFO provides Timken with tax savings of additional taxes of $800,000 ($3.2 million × 25%). Thus, 2020 net income using FIFO would be higher by $2.4 million ($3.2 million − $800,000).

RESEARCH INSIGHT

LIFO and Stock Prices The value-relevance of inventory disclosures depends at least partly on whether investors rely more on the income statement or the balance sheet to assess future cash flows. Under LIFO, cost of goods sold reflects current costs, whereas FIFO ending inventory reflects current costs. This implies that LIFO enhances the usefulness of the income statement to the detriment of the balance sheet. This trade-off partly motivates the required LIFO reserve disclosure (the adjustment necessary to restate LIFO ending inventory and cost of goods sold to FIFO).

Research suggests that LIFO-based income statements better reflect stock prices than do pro forma FIFO income statements that are constructed using the LIFO reserve. Research also shows a negative relation between stock prices and LIFO reserve—meaning that higher magnitudes of LIFO reserve are associated with lower stock prices. This is consistent with the LIFO reserve being viewed as an inflation indicator (for either current or future inventory costs) detrimental to company value.

Review 7-4 LO7-4

Interpreting the Effects of Inventory Valuation on Financial Results

GuidedExample MBC

Jasmine Company uses the LIFO costing method to value its inventory. The company reported the following information in its Year 2 annual report.

December 31	Year 2	Year 1
Total inventories at FIFO	$50,000	$60,000
Less LIFO allowance	(15,000)	(12,000)
Total inventories, less allowance	$35,000	$48,000

a. On the company's Year 2 balance sheet, what dollar amount is reported for inventory?

b. Had the company reported inventory under the FIFO method, what dollar amount would be reported on the company's Year 2 balance sheet?

c. If the company reported $100,000 in its Year 2 income statement for cost of goods sold, what is the dollar amount of cost of goods sold under FIFO?

continued

continued from previous page

d. Assuming a 25% tax rate, what is the difference in Year 2 taxes considering the company valued inventory using LIFO (for both financial reporting and tax purposes) instead of FIFO (for both financial reporting and tax purposes)?

e. How do the company's Year 2 results under LIFO compare to results if the company had adopted FIFO instead?

	LIFO compared to FIFO (Higher, lower, same)
1. Ending inventory amount on balance sheet	________
2. Cost of goods sold on income statement	________
3. Sales on income statement	________
4. Gross profit on income statement	________
5. Amount of taxes paid for the year	________

Solution on p. 7-44.

ANALYZING FINANCIAL STATEMENTS

Analysis Objective

We are trying to determine whether Home Depot's sales provide sufficient revenues to cover its operation costs, primarily selling and administrative expenses, after allowing for the costs of acquiring the products and services sold.

LO7-5 Define and interpret gross profit margin and inventory turnover ratios. Use inventory disclosure information to make appropriate adjustments to ratios.

eLecture MBC

Analysis Tool Gross Profit Margin (GPM) Ratio

$$\text{Gross profit margin} = \frac{\text{Sales revenue} - \text{Cost of goods sold}}{\text{Sales revenue}}$$

Applying the Gross Profit Margin Ratio to The Home Depot.

Fiscal Year Ended

Jan. 28, 2018: $\frac{(\$100{,}904 - \$66{,}548)}{\$100{,}904} = 0.340 \text{ or } 34.0\%$

Feb. 3, 2019: $\frac{(\$108{,}203 - \$71{,}043)}{\$108{,}203} = 0.343 \text{ or } 34.3\%$

Feb. 2, 2020: $\frac{(\$110{,}225 - \$72{,}653)}{\$110{,}225} = 0.341 \text{ or } 34.1\%$

Guidance The gross profit margin is commonly used instead of the dollar amount of gross profit as it allows for comparisons across companies and over time. A decline in GPM is usually cause for concern because it indicates that the company has less ability to pass on to customers increased costs in its products. Because companies try to charge the highest price the market will bear, a decline in GPM is often the result of market forces beyond the company's control. Some possible reasons for a GPM decline are:

- Product line is stale. Perhaps it is out of fashion and the company must resort to markdowns to reduce overstocked inventories. Or, perhaps the product lines have lost their technological edge, yielding reduced demand.
- A change in product mix resulting from a change in buyers' behavior (more generic brands, more necessities, fewer big-ticket items).
- New competitors enter the market. Perhaps substitute products or new technologies are now available from competitors, yielding increased pressure to reduce selling prices.
- General decline in economic activity. Perhaps an economic downturn reduces product demand. The weak housing market during the latter half of the decade likely affected the gross profits of home improvement companies.

- Inventory is overstocked. Perhaps the company overproduced goods and finds itself in an overstock position. This can require reduced selling prices to move inventory.

Takeaways The Home Depot's sales revenue has increased from fiscal year ended January 28, 2018 to fiscal year ended February 2, 2020. It would appear that the company is maintaining its gross profit margin. However, to properly evaluate gross profit margin, it is useful to make comparisons with other companies in the same industry. The left-hand chart below compares The Home Depot's gross profit margin with that of its largest (but smaller) competitor, **Lowe's Companies, Inc.**

Home Depot in Context

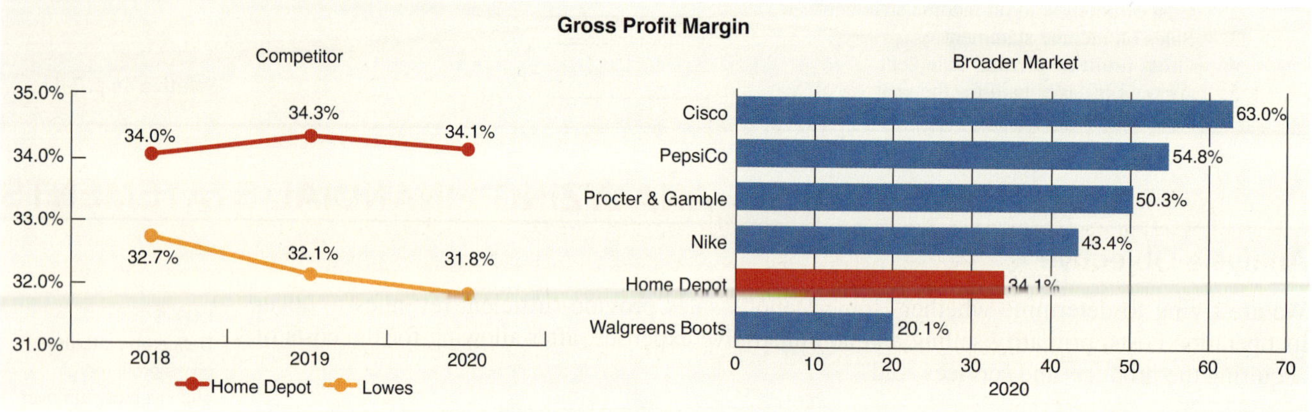

As the line chart illustrates, The Home Depot has reported nearly identical, and very stable, gross profit margins in the last three years while Lowe's has reported a decreasing trend in gross profit margins. In addition, in 2020 The Home Depot's sales revenue increased by 1.9%, while Lowe's revenues increased by 1.2%.

Because of competitive pressures, companies rarely have the opportunity to affect gross margin with price increases. (Of course, an astute choice of product offerings is likely to reduce pricing discounts and improve the gross profit margin.) Most improvements in gross margin that we witness are the result of better management of supply chains, production processes, or distribution networks. Similarly, a decline in gross profit margin suggests problems or inefficiencies in these processes. Companies that succeed typically do so because of better performance on basic business processes. This is one of The Home Depot's primary objectives.

Analysis Objective

We wish to determine how quickly inventory passes through the production process and results in sales.

Analysis Tool Inventory Turnover (INVT) Ratio

$$\text{Inventory turnover} = \frac{\text{Cost of goods sold}}{\text{Average inventory}}$$

Applying Inventory Turnover Ratio to Home Depot

Fiscal Year Ended

Jan. 28, 2018: $\frac{\$66,548}{[(\$12,748 + \$12,549)/2]} = 5.26$ times per year

Feb. 3, 2019: $\frac{\$71,043}{[(\$13,925 + \$12,748)/2]} = 5.33$ times per year

Feb. 2, 2020: $\frac{\$72,653}{[(\$14,531 + \$13,925)/2]} = 5.11$ times per year

Home Depot in Context

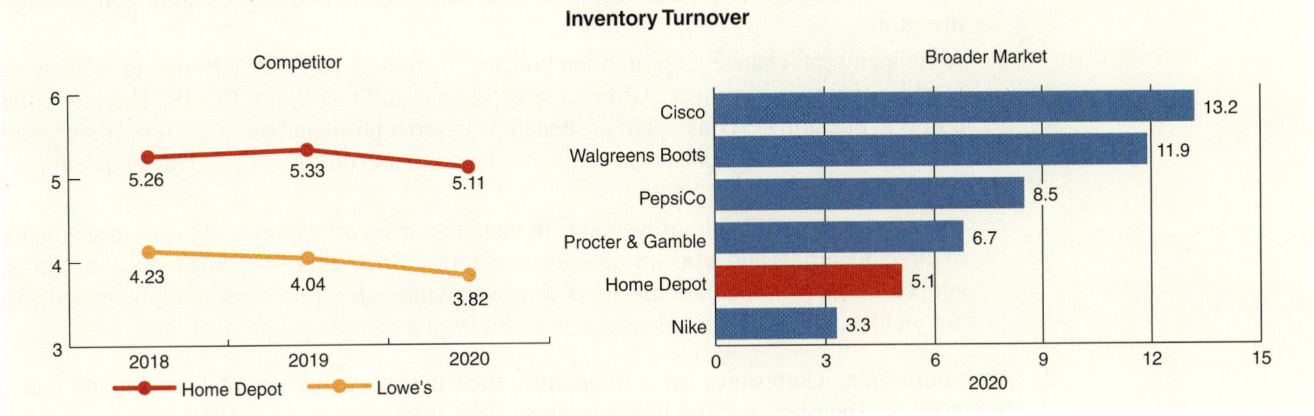

Cost of goods sold is in the numerator because inventory is reported at cost. The denominator is the average of beginning inventory and ending inventory to recognize growth (or decline) in the company's investment in inventory over the period. Inventory turnover indicates how many times inventory turns (is sold) during a period. More turns indicate that inventory is being sold more quickly.

Analysis Tool Average inventory days outstanding (AIDO), also called *days inventory outstanding*:

$$\text{Average inventory days outstanding} = \frac{\text{Average inventory}}{\text{Average daily cost of goods sold}}$$

Applying Average Inventory Days Outstanding Ratio to Home Depot

Fiscal Year Ended

Jan. 28, 2018: $\frac{[(\$12,748 + \$12,549)/2]}{(\$66,548/365)} = 69 \text{ Days}$

Feb. 3, 2019: $\frac{[(\$13,925 + \$12,748)/2]}{(\$71,043/365)} = 69 \text{ Days}$

Feb. 2, 2020: $\frac{[(\$14,531 + \$13,925)/2]}{(\$72,653/365)} = 71 \text{ Days}$

The Average Inventory Days Outstanding (AIDO) contains the same information as the Inventory Turnover (INVT) ratio, but on a different scale. If a company's INVT goes up (down), its AIDO goes down (up). AIDO = 365÷INVT, or INVT = 365÷AIDO.

Home Depot in Context

The average daily cost of goods sold equals cost of goods sold divided by the number of days in the period (for our example, 365 for a year).

Average inventory days outstanding indicates how long, on average, inventories are on the shelves or in production before being sold. For example, if a retailer's annual cost of goods sold is $1,200 and average inventories are $300, inventories are turning four times and are on the shelves 91.25 days [$300/($1,200/365)] on average. This performance might be an acceptable turnover for the retail fashion industry where it needs to sell out its inventories each retail selling season, but it would not be acceptable for the grocery industry.

Guidance Analysis of inventory turnover is important for at least two reasons:

1. *Inventory quality*. Inventory turnover can be compared with those of prior periods and competitors. Higher turnover is viewed favorably, implying that products are salable, preferably without undue discounting of selling prices, or that production processes are functioning smoothly. Conversely, lower turnover implies that inventory is on the shelves for a longer period of time, perhaps from excessive purchases or production, missed fashion trends or technological advances, increased competition, and so forth. Our conclusions about higher or lower turnover must consider alternative explanations including:

a. Company product mix can change to higher-margin, slower-turning inventories or vice-versa. This change can occur from business acquisitions and the resulting consolidated inventories.

b. A company can change its promotion policies. Increased, effective advertising is likely to increase inventory turnover. Advertising expense is in SG&A, not COGS. Therefore, the cost is in operating expenses, but the benefit is in gross profit and turnover. If the promotion campaign is successful, the positive effects in margin and turnover should offset the promotion cost in SG&A.

c. A company can realize improvements in manufacturing efficiency and lower investments in direct materials and work-in-process inventories. Such improvements reduce inventory and, consequently, increase inventory turnover. Although positive, such improvements do not yield any information about the desirability of a company's product line.

2. *Asset utilization.* Companies strive to optimize their inventory investment. Carrying too much inventory is expensive, and too little inventory risks stock-outs and lost sales (current and future). There are operational changes that companies can make to reduce inventory including:

   a. Improved manufacturing processes can eliminate bottlenecks and the consequent build-up of work-in-process inventories.

   b. Just-in-time (JIT) deliveries from suppliers that provide raw materials to the production line when needed can reduce the level of raw materials required.

   c. Demand-pull production, in which raw materials are released into the production process when final goods are demanded by customers instead of producing for estimated demand, can reduce inventory levels. **Dell Technologies** was founded on a business model that produced for actual, rather than estimated, demand; many of its computers are manufactured after the customer order is received.

3. *Risk.* Reducing inventories reduces inventory carrying costs, thus improving profitability and increasing cash flow (asset reduction is reflected as a cash inflow adjustment in the statement of cash flows). However, if inventories get too low, production can be interrupted and sales lost. The COVID-19 pandemic has highlighted some of the supply chain risks of operations that have minimized inventory.

There is normal tension between the sales side of a company that argues for depth and breadth of inventory and the finance side that monitors inventory carrying costs and seeks to maximize cash flow. Companies, therefore, seek to *optimize* inventory investment, not *minimize* it.

RESEARCH INSIGHT

In a *Wall Street Journal* article, it was reported that in 2013, companies reported deficiencies in their procedures to account for inventory and cost of sales, i.e., internal control weaknesses, so numerous that the category ranked number two in areas with such deficiencies.[5] Recent academic research suggests these deficiencies are important. According to a study of companies over 2004–2009, the evidence is consistent with firms that have inventory-related material weaknesses having systematically lower inventory turnover ratios and being more likely to report inventory impairments relative to firms with effective internal control. In addition, the study shows that firms that fix their internal control weaknesses show improvements in inventory turnover rates.[6]

Takeaways The chart above compares inventory turnover for The Home Depot with that of its chief rival, Lowe's. The Home Depot's inventory turnover and AIDO improved in fiscal year 2019 but then weakened in 2020. Lowe's inventory turnover decreased, year to year, but increases in inventories probably helped it to maintain revenues and gross profit in the changing economic climate.

[4] "More Accounting Deficiencies Linked to Inventory," *Wall Street Journal* August 26, 2014.

[5] See Feng, Mei, Chan Li, Sarah E. McVay, and Hollis Skaife, "Does Ineffective Internal Control over Financial Reporting affect a Firm's Operations? Evidence from Firms' Inventory Management." The Accounting Review, March 2015.

When comparing The Home Depot to the broader sample of companies, we can see that The Home Depot is toward the lower end of inventory turnover values. The inventory of technology companies like Cisco is subject to obsolescence and holding inventory reduces its expected value. Walgreen Boots is focused on pharmacy prescriptions, and that inventory has a limited shelf life.

YOU MAKE THE CALL

You are the Plant Manager You are analyzing your inventory turnover report for the month and are concerned that the average inventory days outstanding is lengthening. What actions can you take to reduce average inventory days outstanding? [Answer on page 7-28]

Adjusting Turnover Ratios For a company using the last-in, first-out (LIFO) inventory method, it is advisable to make an adjustment before calculating the inventory turnover ratio. LIFO is most commonly used when management has experienced a trend of rising inventory costs. As a result, LIFO puts higher (newer) costs into cost of goods sold and leaves lower (older) costs in inventory. This creates a potential mismatch between the numerator and denominator of the inventory turnover ratio.

For instance, consider Butler Company's 2022 financial information in **Exhibit 7.11**. Measured in physical terms, Butler started 2022 with 250 units, sold 500 units during 2022, and ended 2022 with 350 units. So, the physical inventory turnover would be

$$\textbf{Physical inventory turnover} = \frac{\textbf{Units sold}}{\textbf{Average units held}} = \frac{500}{(250 + 350)/2} = 1.67 \text{ times}$$

However, the 2022 inventory turnover calculated using the LIFO reported numbers does not agree with the physical inventory turnover.

$$\textbf{LIFO inventory turnover} = \frac{\textbf{Cost of goods solds}}{\textbf{Average inventory}} = \frac{\$90{,}000}{(\$25{,}000 + \$43{,}000)/2} = 2.65 \text{ times}$$

Why is the LIFO inventory turnover higher? The distortion occurs because the LIFO cost of goods sold is 500 units valued at $180 each, while the beginning inventory is 250 units valued at $100 each and the ending inventory is 250 units valued at $100 each plus 100 units valued at $180 each. The difference between 1.67 and 2.65 comes about because LIFO causes the value per unit to be higher in the numerator than in the denominator.

A quick fix would be to use the LIFO reserve information to put the beginning and ending inventory values on a more up-to-date basis. LIFO puts the newer costs in cost of goods sold, while FIFO puts the newer costs in inventory. If Butler were using LIFO, we could use the reported inventory balances and the LIFO reserve information to determine that the beginning FIFO inventory would have been $39,000 ($25,000 + $14,000) and the ending FIFO inventory would have been $63,000 ($43,000 + $20,000).

$$\textbf{Adjusted inventory turnover} = \frac{\textbf{LIFO cost of goods sold}}{\textbf{Average FIFO inventory}} = \frac{\$90{,}000}{(\$39{,}000 + \$63{,}000)/2} = 1.76 \text{ times}$$

This adjusted ratio is much closer to what's actually happening to the inventories at Butler Company.

The magnitude of this adjustment can be significant. For instance, **Chevron Corporation** in its 2020 annual report states that its 2020 expense for "Purchased crude oil and products" was $50,488 million. Chevron's balance sheet totals for inventories were $5,848 million at the end of 2019 and $5,676 million at the end of 2020, for an average of $5,762 million. These numbers would give an inventory turnover ratio of $50,488 million ÷ $5,762 million, or 8.76 times, implying that inventory is held less than 42 days on average.

However, we know that the LIFO inventory balances are out of date. Chevron's LIFO reserve disclosure says that the replacement cost of inventories was higher than the reported amounts by $4,513 million at the end of 2019 and $2,749 million at the end of 2020, making the replacement cost of inventories equal to $10,361 million at the end of 2019 and $8,425 million at the end of 2020. The adjusted inventory turnover ratio would be $50,488/[($10,361 + $8,425)/2] = 5.4, implying that inventory is held about 68 days—more than 60% higher than the LIFO measure.

Following a similar line of analysis, it would be possible to construct a FIFO inventory turnover for Chevron, which could be useful in making comparisons to another company that uses IFRS in its financial reports.

Review 7-5 LO7-5

Calculating Inventory Ratios

GuidedExample MBC

Publix Super Markets Inc. reports inventory and cost of goods sold using the last-in, first-out (LIFO) costing method for a "significant portion" of U.S. inventory. The table below presents financial information from its 2020, 2019, and 2018 10-K reports.

($ millions)	2020	2019	2018
Income statement:			
Sales	$44,864	$38,116	$36,094
Cost of goods sold	32,355	27,740	26,311
Gross profit	12,509	10,376	9,783
Balance sheet:			
Inventory	2,034	1,913	1,849
Notes to financial statements:			
LIFO reserve	549	529	489

Required

a. Compute the gross profit margin for each year, 2018 through 2020, and the inventory turnover ratio for 2019 and 2020.

b. What amount for cost of goods sold and gross profit would Publix report in 2019 and 2020 if FIFO were used to assign costs to inventory and cost of goods sold? (Assume that FIFO cost is equal to the current value of Publix's inventory.)

c. Recalculate Publix's inventory turnover ratio for 2019 and 2020 assuming that FIFO had been used to value inventory.

Solution on p. 7-44.

APPENDIX 7A: LIFO Liquidation

LO7-6 Analyze LIFO liquidations and the impact they have on the financial statements.

eLecture MBC

When companies use LIFO inventory costing, the most recent costs of purchasing inventory are transferred to cost of goods sold, while older costs remain in ending inventory. Each time inventory is purchased at a different price, a new *layer* (also called a **LIFO layer**) is added to the inventory balance. As long as a year's purchases equal or exceed the quantity sold, older cost layers remain in inventory—sometimes for several years. On the other hand, when the quantity sold exceeds the quantity purchased, inventory costs from these older cost layers are transferred to cost of goods sold. This situation is called **LIFO liquidation**. Because these older costs are usually much lower than current replacement costs, LIFO liquidation normally yields a boost to current gross profit as these older costs are matched against current revenues.

To illustrate the effects of LIFO liquidation, we return to the example of Butler Company in **Exhibit 7.6** and add an additional year. At the end of 2022, Butler has 350 units in inventory, 250 at $100 each and 100 at $180 each. Suppose that during 2023, the company purchases 500 units at $190 and sells 650 units at $250. At the end of 2023, Butler will have only 200 units remaining in inventory and, under LIFO, those units will be assigned a cost of $100 each. The determination of cost of goods sold and ending inventory for 2023 can be seen in **Exhibit 7A.1**.

EXHIBIT 7A.1 Calculation of 2023 LIFO Inventory and Cost of Goods Sold

Beginning Inventory	250 units at $100 each plus 100 units at $180 each	$ 43,000
Purchases	500 units at $190 each	95,000
Cost of goods available for sale		138,000
Ending inventory	200 units at $100 each	20,000
Cost of goods sold	500 units at $190 each plus 100 units at $180 each plus 50 units at $100 each	$118,000

Exhibit 7A.2 portrays graphically that the inventory reduction in 2023 eliminated the LIFO layer added in 2022 and reduced the original LIFO layer from the start of 2021.

EXHIBIT 7A.2 Butler Company LIFO Inventory Flows

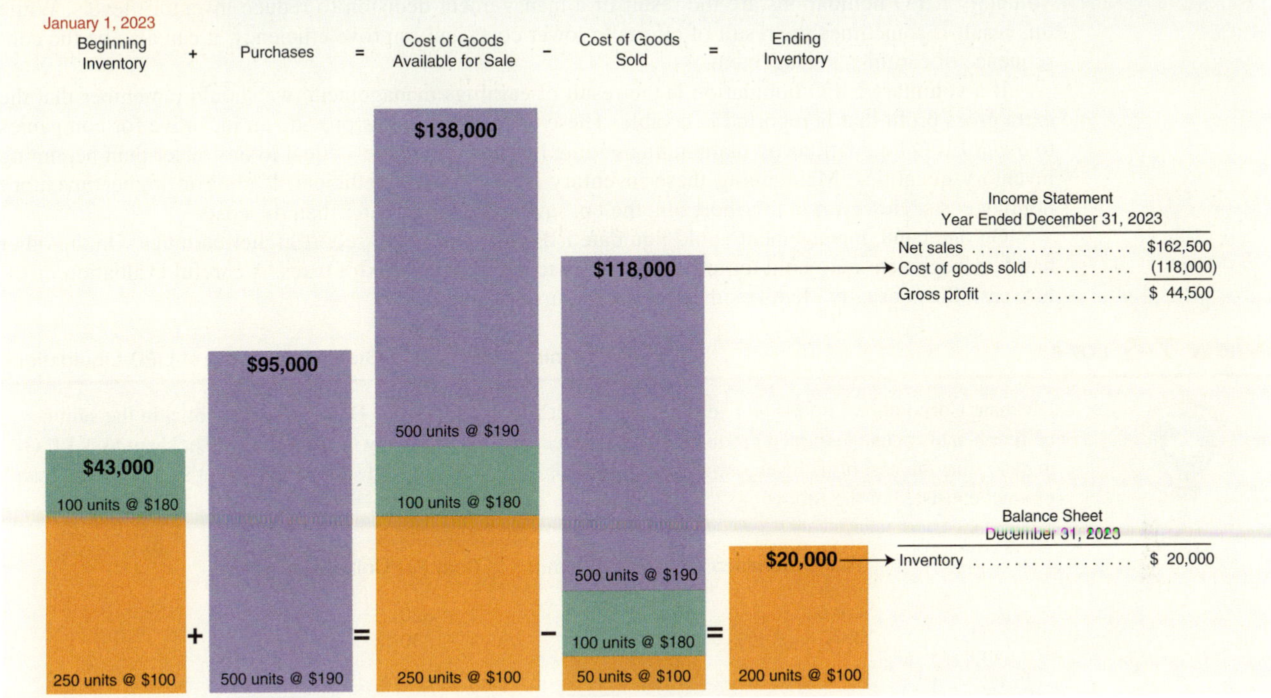

What would have happened if Butler had purchased 650 units at $190 in 2023? The ending inventory would have been identical to the beginning inventory. And, the cost of goods sold would have been $123,500 (650 units at $190 each), $5,500 higher than the $118,000 cost of goods sold in **Exhibit 7A.1**. This difference can be attributed to the differences between the current unit cost of inventory ($190) and the old unit costs ($180 and $100) that had been in inventory but are now in cost of goods sold.

Thus, Butler's cost of goods sold has been *reduced* by $5,500 due to the LIFO liquidation, and its gross profit and income before tax have been *increased* by the same amount. If Butler's tax rate were 25%, the net income would be increased by $4,125. This **LIFO liquidation gain** must be disclosed in the company's disclosure notes.

The effect of LIFO liquidation is evident in the following disclosure information from Note 1 to **Kaiser Aluminum Corporation**'s 2020 annual report.

> Inventories. Inventories are stated at the lower of cost or market value. Finished products, work-in-process and raw material inventories are stated on the last-in, first-out ("LIFO") basis. At December 31, 2020 and December 31, 2019, the cost of our inventory on a first-in, first-out ("FIFO") basis, which approximates the current replacement cost, exceeded its stated LIFO value by $8.4 million and $11.9 million, respectively. During the year ended December 31, 2020, we decremented a prior year, lower cost LIFO layer, which resulted in a benefit of $0.2 million. During the year ended December 31, 2019, we decremented a prior year, higher cost LIFO layer which resulted in a charge of $3.6 million. Other inventories are stated on the FIFO basis and consist of operating supplies, which are materials and supplies to be consumed during the production process.

Kaiser reports that reductions in inventory quantities led to the sale (at current selling prices) of products that carried costs from prior years that were less than current costs in 2020 and greater than current costs in 2019. As a result of these inventory reductions, pretax income increased by $0.2 million in 2020 and decreased by $3.6 million in 2019.

Analysis Implications

LIFO liquidation boosts gross profit when older, lower costs are matched against revenues based on current sales prices. This increase in gross profit is transitory. Once an old LIFO layer is liquidated, it can only be replaced at current prices. The transitory boost in gross profit temporarily distorts the gross profit margin (GPM) ratio.

It is important that we ask why the LIFO liquidation happened. Involuntary LIFO liquidations result from circumstances beyond the company's control, such as disruptions in supply due to a natural disaster. Voluntary LIFO liquidations are the result of a management decision to reduce inventory levels. While this result is sometimes the result of efforts to lower costs and improve efficiency, it can also be the consequence of earnings management.

If a voluntary LIFO liquidation is the result of earnings management, we should remember that the extra gross profit that is reported is taxable. These tax consequences provide an incentive for companies to *avoid* LIFO liquidations by maintaining ending inventories at levels equal to or greater than beginning inventory quantities. Maintaining these inventory levels can be inefficient, leading to higher inventory holding costs. However, in the short run, the tax savings can be greater than the costs.

On one hand, management could liquidate LIFO inventories to report higher earnings. On the other hand, management may hold too much inventory to avoid paying extra taxes. A careful evaluation of future cash flows usually identifies the preferred course of action.

Review 7-6 LO7-6

Determining the Financial Statement Impact of LIFO Liquidations

GuidedExample MBC

Dickhaut Corporation imports and sells a product that is produced in the Dominican Republic. In the summer of Year 8, a hurricane disrupted production and affected Dickhaut's supply of this product. Dickhaut uses LIFO to determine the cost of its inventory and cost of goods sold. On January 1, Year 8, Dickhaut's inventory of this product consisted of the following:

Year Purchased	Quantity (units)	Cost Per Unit	Total Cost
Year 6	2,000	$20	$ 40,000
Year 7	3,000	30	90,000
Total	5,000		$130,000

Through mid-December, purchases were limited to 7,000 units, because the cost had increased to $70 per unit. Dickhaut sold 11,500 units during Year 8 at a price of $65 per unit, which significantly depleted its inventory. However, the cost was expected to drop to $55 per unit by early January Year 9.

Required

a. Assume that Dickhaut makes no further purchases during Year 8. Compute its gross profit for Year 8.

b. Assume that Dickhaut purchases 4,500 units for $70 per unit before the end of December Year 8, so that it maintains its balance of inventory at 5,000 units. Compute its gross profit for Year 8.

c. How should Dickhaut disclose the LIFO liquidation if it chooses not to make a year-end purchase?

d. If Dickhaut's corporate tax rate is 25%, should it make a year-end purchase? If so, how many units should the company purchase before December 31, Year 8? Assume that the management of Dickhaut believes it is efficient (in the long run) to carry 5,000 units in inventory.

Solution on p. 7-45.

SUMMARY

LO7-1 Interpret disclosures of information concerning operating expenses, including manufacturing and retail inventory costs. (p. 7-3)

- Inventory is reported in the balance sheet at its cost, including any cost to acquire, transport and prepare goods for sale.
- Manufacturing inventory consists of raw materials, work in process and finished goods. The cost of manufacturing inventory includes the cost of materials and labor used to produce goods, as well as overhead cost.

LO7-2 Account for inventory and cost of goods sold using different costing methods. (p. 7-7)

- FIFO places the cost of the most recent purchases in ending inventory and older costs in the cost of goods sold.
- LIFO places the cost of the most recent purchases in cost of goods sold and older costs in inventory.
- The average cost method computes an average unit cost, which is used to value inventories *and* cost of goods sold.

Apply the lower of cost or net realizable value rule to value inventory. (p. 7-13) **LO7-3**

- If the net realizable value of inventory falls below its cost, the inventory is written down to net realizable value, thereby reducing total assets.
- The loss is added to cost of goods sold and reported in the income statement (unless it is large enough to warrant separate disclosure).

Evaluate how inventory costing affects management decisions and outsiders' interpretations of financial statements. (p. 7-14) **LO7-4**

- When inventory costs are rising, LIFO costing reports higher cost of goods sold and lower income than either FIFO or average costing.
- If LIFO is used for tax reporting, it must be used for financial reporting.
- LIFO distorts the inventory turnover ratio because inventories are often severely undervalued (relative to current cost of goods sold). Management can boost earnings by liquidating these undervalued inventories.
- International Financial Reporting Standards (IFRS) allows FIFO and average costing methods. LIFO is not permitted.

Define and interpret gross profit margin and inventory turnover ratios. Use inventory disclosure information to make appropriate adjustments to ratios. (p. 7-20) **LO7-5**

- Gross profit margin (GPM)—a measure of profitability that focuses on the amount of revenue in excess of cost of goods sold as a percentage of revenue
- Gross profit margin is defined as Gross profit/Sales revenue.
- Inventory turnover (INVT)—a measure of the frequency at which the average balance in inventory is sold each year
- Inventory turnover is defined as Cost of goods sold/Average inventory.
- These ratios provide insight into how efficiently the company is managing inventory.
- Note disclosures enable a financial statement reader to determine the up-to-date costs of LIFO inventories, to estimate what cost of goods sold would have been under FIFO, and to compute an inventory turnover ratio that is not subject to the distortions noted in LO7-4.

Appendix 7A: Analyze LIFO liquidations and the impact they have on the financial statements. (p. 7-25) **LO7-6**

- LIFO liquidation is the result of selling and not replenishing inventory stocks purchased in previous accounting periods.
- When inventory costs are increasing, LIFO liquidation results in higher net income as the unrealized holding gains from LIFO are realized.
- Companies that use LIFO have an incentive to hold inventories to avoid LIFO *liquidation* and the resulting higher income taxes.

GUIDANCE ANSWERS . . . YOU MAKE THE CALL

You are the Plant Manager Companies need inventories to avoid lost sales opportunities; however, there are several ways to minimize inventory needs. (1) We can reduce product costs by improving product design to eliminate costly features not valued by customers. (2) We can use more cost-efficient suppliers, possibly including production in lower wage-rate parts of the world. (3) We can reduce raw material inventories with just-in-time delivery from suppliers. (4) We can eliminate bottlenecks in the production process that increase work-in-process inventories. (5) We can manufacture for orders rather than for estimates of demand to reduce finished goods inventories. (6) We can improve warehousing and distribution to reduce duplicate inventories. (7) We can monitor product sales and adjust product mix as demand changes to reduce finished goods inventories.

KEY RATIOS

Gross profit (GP)

$$GP = \text{Sales revenue} - \text{Cost of goods sold}$$

Inventory turnover (INVT)

$$INVT = \frac{\text{Cost of goods sold}}{\text{Average inventory}}$$

Gross profit margin (GPM)

$$\text{Gross profit margin} = \frac{\text{Sales revenue} - \text{Cost of goods sold}}{\text{Sales revenue}}$$

Average inventory days outstanding (AIDO)

$$AIDO = \frac{\text{Average inventory}}{\text{Average daily cost of goods sold}}$$

Assignments with the MBC logo in the margin are available in myBusinessCourse. See the Preface of the book for details.

MULTIPLE CHOICE

Multiple Choice Answers
1. c 2. c 3. a 4. d 5. b

MBC **1.** Which of the following is not normally reported as part of total manufacturing inventory cost?

a. work-in-process
b. finished goods
c. property, plant, and equipment
d. raw materials

MBC **2.** When the current year's ending inventory amount is overstated, then the

a. current year's cost of goods sold is overstated.
b. current year's total assets are understated.
c. current year's net income is overstated.
d. next year's income is overstated.

MBC **3.** In a period of rising prices, the inventory cost allocation method that tends to result in the lowest reported net income is

a. LIFO.
b. FIFO.
c. average cost.
d. specific identification.

MBC **4.** Assume that Beyer Corporation has the following initial balance and subsequent purchase of inventory:

Beginning inventory	4,000 units @ $50 each	$200,000
Inventory purchased during the year	10,000 units @ $75 each	750,000
Cost of goods available for sale	14,000 units	$950,000

During the year, Beyer Corporation sold 12,000 units. Which of the following is not true?

a. FIFO cost of goods sold would be $800,000.
b. FIFO ending inventory would be $150,000.
c. LIFO cost of goods sold would be $850,000.
d. LIFO ending inventory would be $150,000.

MBC **5.** Sletten Industries uses the last-in, first-out (LIFO) method of accounting for the inventories of its single product. For the fiscal year, the company reported sales revenue of $160 million and cost of goods sold of $108 million. The following table was reported in the financial statement disclosure notes.

($ millions)	January 1	December 31
Inventory value at LIFO	$20.0	$22.4
LIFO Reserve	11.2	17.6
Inventory value at FIFO	$31.2	$40.0

If Sletten Industries had used FIFO to account for its inventory, its gross profit for the year would be

a. $69.6 million.
b. $58.4 million.
c. $45.6 million.
d. $52.0 million.

Superscript A denotes assignments based on Appendix 7A.

QUESTIONS

Q7-1. Under what circumstances is it justified to include transportation costs in the value of the inventory purchased?

Q7-2. Why do relatively stable inventory costs reduce the importance of management's choice of an inventory costing method?

Q7-3. What is one explanation for increased gross profit during periods of rising inventory costs when FIFO is used?

Q7-4. If inventory costs are rising, which inventory costing method—first-in, first-out; last-in, first-out; or average cost—yields the (a) lowest ending inventory? (b) lowest net income? (c) largest ending inventory? (d) largest net income? (e) greatest cash flow assuming that method is used for tax purposes?

Q7-5. Even though it does not reflect their physical flow of goods, why might companies adopt last-in, first-out inventory costing in periods when costs are consistently rising?

Q7-6. In a recent annual report, Kaiser Aluminum Corporation made the following statement in reference to its inventories: "The Company recorded pretax charges of approximately $19.4 million because of a reduction in the carrying values of its inventories caused principally by prevailing lower prices for alumina, primary aluminum, and fabricated products." What basic accounting principle caused Kaiser Aluminum to record this $19.4 million pretax charge? Briefly describe the rationale for this principle.

Kaiser Aluminum Corporation
NASDAQ :: KALU

Q7-7. Under what conditions would each of the inventory costing methods discussed in the chapter produce the same results?

Q7-8. What is inventory "shrink"? How does a company determine the amount of inventory shrink that may have occurred?

Q7-9. What is a LIFO reserve? How is the LIFO reserve related to unrealized holding gains?

Q7-10. Analysts claim that it is more difficult to forecast net income for a company that uses LIFO. Why might this be true?

Q7-11.[A] LIFO liquidation may be involuntary—that is beyond the control of management. Suggest two situations that might lead to involuntary LIFO liquidation.

Q7-12.[A] LIFO liquidation is often discretionary. What motives might management have to liquidate LIFO inventory?

DATA ANALYTICS

DA7-1. Preparing an Excel Worksheet to Record Inventory at the Lower of Cost or Net Realizable Value

LO7-3

Homework MBC · Data Analytics

The Excel file associated with this exercise includes a sheet (Inventory Data Sheet) with information regarding Lain Company's inventory including unit cost, cost of disposal, unit selling price, and quantity on hand. A second sheet (Inventory Obsolescence Sheet) includes information about inventory markdowns on the selling price due to obsolescence concerns. In this exercise, we calculate the value of inventory at the lower of cost or net realizable value. In doing so, we first update sales data with the latest inventory obsolescence information using a useful Excel function: VLOOKUP.

REQUIRED

1. Download Excel file DA7-1 found in myBusinessCourse.
2. In the Data-Inventory Obsolescence worksheet, use VLOOKUP to pull in the original selling price from the Data-Inventory worksheet. *Hint:* Use the Item number in the first column as the lookup value, the table in the Inventory Data Sheet for the source to pull from, the column titled Selling price per unit for the source data. This must be an exact match.
3. List the formula that is currently in cell D4 of your Inventory Obsolescence sheet.
4. Calculate the updated selling price, considering the mark-down percentage in the Updated Selling Price per Unit column. Round to two decimal places. What is the updated selling price for Item No.1823555?
5. Using the VLOOKUP function, add the updated selling price from the Data-Inventory Obsolescence worksheet to the Updated Selling Price per Unit column in the Data-Inventory worksheet.
6. Eliminate the errors in the cells in the Updated Selling Price per Unit column on the Data-Inventory worksheet by replacing the error with the original selling price per unit using the IFERROR function. *Hint:* Enclose the formula used in part 5 within the IFERRROR function: replace the error sign with the original selling price per unit.
7. List the formula that is currently in cell G5 of your Inventory Data sheet.
8. For each item, enter the net realizable value in the Net Realizable Value per Unit column.
9. Using an IF statement, calculate the lower of cost per unit or net realizable value per unit in the Lower of Cost or NRV per Unit column. *Hint:* If the cost per unit is less than the net realizable value per unit, show the cost per unit value in the cell; otherwise, show the net realizable value per unit in the cell.
10. Calculate the total inventory value at the lower of cost or net realizable value for each item in the Total Inventory Value column. What is the lower of cost or net realizable value for Item no. 1124503 (in total)? Item no. 1122812 (in total)?
11. List the total inventory value at the lower of cost or net realizable value.

LO7-5

Data Analytics

DA7-2. Preparing Excel Visualizations of Gross Profit Data Over Time

Financial information for the following five retailers is included in the Excel file associated with this chapter: **The Home Depot, Inc.** (Home Depot), **Lowe's Companies, Inc.** (Lowe's), **Target Corporation** (Target), **The ODP Corporation** (ODP), and **Costco Wholesale Corporation** (Costco). In this problem we analyze the gross profit percentage of retail companies with different business models. The gross profit percentage measures a company's ability to cover its operating costs from revenues after allowing for costs of goods and services sold. A gross profit percentage will vary by industry (some industries require extensive manufacturing operations for example) and is also affected by a company's business strategy. For example, a company with a lower gross profit percentage (a grocery store) will make up for profits with higher sales volume. A company with a high gross profit percentage (high-end jewelry store) can afford to sell fewer products when each item has a higher gross profit percentage.

REQUIRED

1. Download Excel file DA7-2 found in myBusinessCourse.
2. Calculate the gross profit percentage for each of the three years (with Year 3 being the most recent year).
3. Create a line chart showing the trend of the gross profit percentage for each company over the three-year period.
4. List the companies in order from the highest to the lowest gross profit percentage for each of the three years.
5. Add a trendline to the line chart for each company and forecast one additional period. *Hint:* Right-click on each line in your chart and add trendline. In the format trendline area under Forecast, forward 1 period.
6. List the companies in order from the highest to the lowest gross profit percentage for the forecasted year.
7. Describe the trends in the line chart.
8. Describe the likely source of the difference between the company with the highest gross profit percentage and the lowest gross profit percentage.

Gross Profit Percentage

$$\frac{\text{Sales revenue} - \text{Cost of goods sold}}{\text{Sales revenue}}$$

LO7-5

Data Analytics

DA7-3. Preparing Tableau Visualizations to Analyze Inventory Management

Refer to PB-22 in Appendix B. This problem uses Tableau to create and analyze visualizations of inventory ratios of certain market segments of S&P 500 companies.

LO7-5

Data Analytics

DA7-4. Preparing Tableau Visualizations to Analyze Gross Profit

Refer to PB-21 in Appendix B. This problem uses Tableau to create and analyze visualizations of gross profit percentages of S&P 500 companies.

DATA VISUALIZATION

Data Visualization

Data Visualization Activities are available in myBusinessCourse. These assignments use Tableau Dashboards to expose students to visual depictions of data and introduce students to data analytics through data visualizations. These exercises are easily assignable and auto graded by MBC.

MINI EXERCISES

LO7-1

M7-13. Recording an Inventory Purchase FSET

Shields Company has purchased inventories incurring the following costs: (a) the invoice amount of \$300, financed through a \$250 note with the remainder paid in cash, (b) shipping charges of \$15 on account, (c) interest of \$5 accrued on the \$250 borrowed to finance the purchase, and (d) \$4 on account for the cost of moving the inventory to the company's warehouse.

REQUIRED

a. Determine the cost to be assigned to the inventory.

b. Record the transactions using the financial statement effects template.

M7-14. Recording an Inventory Purchase LO7-1

Using the information included in M7-13, record the purchase using "T" accounts.

M7-15. Recording Inventory Costs LO7-1

Schrand Inc., a merchandiser, is requesting help in determining what costs ought to be considered as costs when incurred or treated as inventory costs, which are expensed as COGS. The costs include: sales persons wages, utilities such as heat and light in the store, the floor supervisor's salary, the cost of merchandise to be sold, costs of packaging and shipping to buyers.

REQUIRED

Determine the items above that should be included in inventory.

M7-16. Determining Cost of Goods Sold for a Manufacturing Company LO7-1

Ybarra Products began operations this year. During its first year, the company purchased raw materials costing $100,800 and used $75,600 of those materials in the production of its products. The company's manufacturing operations also incurred labor costs of $69,600 and overhead costs of $33,600. At year-end, Ybarra had $22,800 of partially completed product in work-in-process inventory and $42,000 in finished goods inventory. What was Ybarra Company's cost of goods sold for the year?

M7-17. Calculating Gross Profit Margin LO7-5

Johnson & Johnson
NYSE :: JNJ

Johnson & Johnson reported the following revenue and cost of goods sold information in its 10-K report for 2020, 2019, and 2018.

($ millions)	2020	2019	2018
Sales to customers	$82,584	$82,059	$81,581
Cost of products sold	28,427	27,556	27,091

Compute Johnson & Johnson's gross profit margin for each year.

M7-18. Calculating Effect of Inventory Errors LO7-1

For each of the following scenarios, determine the effect of the error on income in the current period and in the subsequent period. To answer these questions, rely on the inventory equation:

Beginning inventory + Purchases – Cost of goods sold = Ending inventory

a. Porter Company received a shipment of merchandise costing $64,000 near the end of the fiscal year. The shipment was mistakenly recorded at a cost of $46,000.

b. Chiu, Inc., purchased merchandise costing $32,000. When the shipment was received, it was determined that the merchandise was damaged in shipment. The goods were returned to the supplier, but the accounting department was not notified and the invoice was paid.

c. After taking a physical count of its inventory, Murray Corporation determined that it had "shrink" of $25,000, and the books were adjusted accordingly. However, inventory costing $10,000 was never counted.

M7-19. Calculating LIFO, FIFO, Income and Cash Flows LO7-2, 4

An acquaintance has proposed the following business plan to you. A local company requires a consistent quantity of a commodity and is looking for a reliable supplier. You could become that reliable supplier.

The cost of the commodity is expected to rise steadily over the foreseeable future, but the company is willing to pay more than the price that is current at the time. All you would need to do is make an investment, purchase the inventory and then deliver inventory to the company over the following year. One complication is that the commodity is available for purchase only seasonally, so at the end of every year you would need to purchase the supply for the following year. The customer pays promptly on delivery.

An initial cash investment of $136,400 would be used to purchase $110,000 of inventory in December of Year 1. The remaining cash would be held for liquidity needs. In the following year, you would deliver this inventory to the customer. Inventory costs are expected to increase by $22,000 per year, and the customer agrees to pay $33,000 more than the current cost of inventory. So, during Year 2, you would deliver inventory that originally cost $110,000, receive payment of $165,000 and pay $132,000 to purchase inventory for the current year. This pattern would continue in future years, but with annually increasing costs of inventory and corresponding increases in the price charged the customer.

If you accept this proposal, your objective would be to receive $19,800 in dividends (about a 15% return on the $136,400 investment) at the end of each year. Assume your business would have an income tax rate of 40%.

a. Construct a projected balance sheet as of the end of December, Year 1.

b. Construct financial forecasts of income statements, cash flows (direct method) and balance sheets for the next three years (through Year 4). Assume that your business would operate in a tax jurisdiction that requires the use of FIFO for inventory. Would this opportunity meet your financial objective?

c. Suppose that your business would operate in a tax jurisdiction that allowed the use of LIFO for inventory. Would this opportunity meet your financial objective? Why?

LO7-2 Homework MBC

M7-20. Computing Cost of Goods Sold and Ending Inventory Under FIFO, LIFO, and Average Cost

Assume that Gode Company reports the following initial balance and subsequent purchase of inventory.

Beginning inventory	2,500 units @ $100 each	$ 250,000
Inventory purchased during the year	5,000 units @ $150 each	750,000
Cost of goods available for sale	7,500 units	$1,000,000

Assume that 4,250 units are sold during the year. Compute the cost of goods sold for the year and the balance reported as ending inventory on its year-end balance sheet under the following inventory costing methods:

a. FIFO *b.* LIFO *c.* Average cost

LO7-2 Homework MBC

M7-21. Inferring Purchases Using Cost of Goods Sold and Inventory Balances FSET

Geiger Corporation, a retail company, reported inventories of $66,000 at the beginning of the year, and $73,000 at the end of the year. The annual income statement reported cost of goods sold of $349,000.

a. Compute the amount of inventory purchased during the year.

b. Record (1) purchases of inventory and (2) cost of goods sold in the financial statement effects template to show the effect of these entries on the balance sheet and income statement.

LO7-2 Homework MBC

M7-22. Inferring Purchases Using Cost of Goods Sold and Inventory Balances

Use the information from M7-21 to complete the following.

a. Prepare journal entries to record (1) purchases, and (2) cost of goods sold.

b. Post the journal entries in part *a* to their respective T-accounts.

LO7-2 Homework MBC

M7-23. Computing Cost of Goods Sold and Ending Inventory

Bartov Corporation reports the following beginning inventory and purchases for the year:

Beginning inventory	600 units @ $10 each	$ 6,000
Inventory purchased during the year	1,050 units @ $12 each	12,600
Cost of goods available for sale	1,650 units	$18,600

Bartov sells 900 of these units during the year. Compute its cost of goods sold for the year and the ending inventory reported on its year-end balance sheet under each of the following inventory costing methods:

a. FIFO *b.* LIFO *c.* Average cost

LO7-5 Homework MBC

M7-24. Computing and Evaluating Inventory Turnover

Walmart Inc., and Target Corporation reported the following in their financial reports:

Walmart Inc.
NYSE :: WMT
Target Corporation
NYSE :: TGT

($ billions)	Walmart			Target		
Fiscal Year	Sales	COGS	Inventory	Sales	COGS	Inventory
2020	$519.9	$394.6	$44.4	$77.1	$54.9	$9.0
2019	510.3	385.3	44.3	74.4	53.3	9.5
2018	495.8	373.4	43.8	71.8	51.1	8.6

a. Compute the 2020 and 2019 inventory turnovers for each of these two retailers.

b. Discuss any changes that are evident in inventory turnover across years and companies from part *a*.

c. Describe ways in which a retailer can improve its inventory turnover. Are there ways to increase inventory turnover that are not beneficial to the company's long-term interests?

M7-25. Inferring Purchases Using Cost of Goods Sold and Inventory Balances (FSET) LO7-2 Homework MBC

Penno Company reported ending inventories of $2,945,000 and beginning inventories of $3,223,750. Cost of goods sold totaled $17,848,750 for the year.

a. Calculate inventory purchases for the year.

b. Using the financial statement effects template, show the effects of (a) the purchase of inventory during the year, and (b) cost of goods sold on the balance sheet and income statement.

M7-26. Inferring Purchases Using Cost of Goods Sold and Inventory Balances LO7-2 Homework MBC

Use the information from M7-25 to complete the following.

a. Prepare the journal entry to record cost of goods sold.

b. Set up a T-account for inventory and post the cost of goods sold entry from part *a* to this account.

c. Using the T-account from *b*, determine the amount of inventory that was purchased in 2020. Prepare a journal entry to record those purchases.

M7-27. Determining Lower of Cost or Net Realizable Value (NRV) LO7-3 Homework MBC

The following data refer to Froning Company's ending inventory.

Item Code	Quantity	Unit Cost	Unit NRV
LXC.	84	$45	$48
KWT	295	38	34
MOR	420	22	20
NES	140	27	32

Determine the ending inventory amount by applying the lower of cost or net realizable value rule to (*a*) each item of inventory and (*b*) the total inventory.

EXERCISES

E7-28. Analyzing Inventory and Margin in a Seasonal Business LO7-5 Homework MBC

Power Marine Supply, opened its first boating supply store over 30 years ago. Since that time, the company has grown to be one of the largest boating supply companies in the world, with fiscal year 4 revenues in excess of $1,350 million. The accompanying table provides financial information for two recent years. Power Marine Supply's fiscal year is closely aligned with the calendar year. All amounts are in millions.

Time Period	Net Revenues	Cost of Goods Sold	Ending Inventory
Fiscal Year 4	—	—	$428
First quarter Year 5	$ 254	$ 200	514
Second quarter Year 5	506	324	516
Third quarter Year 5.	388	276	474
Fourth quarter Year 5	260	204	446
Fiscal Year 5	1,408	1,004	446
First quarter Year 6	260	196	538
Second quarter Year 6	504	324	508
Third quarter Year 6.	384	274	464
Fourth quarter Year 6	260	202	424
Fiscal Year 6	1,408	996	424

a. Using the fiscal year (annual) information for Year 5 and Year 6, calculate the gross profit margin and the inventory turnover ratio.

b. Power Marine Supply is in a seasonal business, in which the sales total for the second and third quarters is substantially higher than the sales total for the first and fourth quarters. Calculate the company's gross profit margin by quarter. What do you learn from the seasonal pattern in the gross profit margin?

c. What is the seasonal pattern in inventory balances? What effect does Power Marine Supply's choice of fiscal year-end have on the inventory turnover ratio calculated in *a*?

d. Recalculate Power Marine Supply's inventory turnover ratios for Year 5 and Year 6 using a weighted average of the company's inventory investment over the year.

E7-29.[A] Applying and Analyzing Inventory Costing Methods LO7-2, 4, 6 Homework MBC

At the beginning of the current period, Chen carried 3,000 units of its product with a unit cost of $20. A summary of purchases during the current period follows:

	Units	Unit Cost	Cost
Beginning Inventory	3,000	$20	$ 60,000
Purchases: #1...............	5,400	22	118,800
#2...............	2,400	26	62,400
#3...............	3,600	29	104,400

During the current period, Chen sold 8,400 units.

a. Assume that Chen uses the first-in, first-out method. Compute its cost of goods sold for the current period and the ending inventory balance.

b. Assume that Chen uses the last-in, first-out method. Compute its cost of goods sold for the current period and the ending inventory balance.

c. Assume that Chen uses the average cost method. Compute its cost of goods sold for the current period and the ending inventory balance.

d. Which of these three inventory costing methods would you choose to:

1. Reflect what is probably the physical flow of goods? Explain.
2. Minimize income taxes for the period? Explain.
3. Report the largest amount of income for the period? Explain.

LO7-2 Homework MBC

E7-30. Computing Cost of Sales and Ending Inventory

Stocken Company has the following financial records for the current period:

	Units	Unit Cost
Beginning inventory	150	$46
Purchases: #1....................	975	42
#2....................	825	38
#3....................	300	36

Ending inventory at the end of this period is 525 units. Compute the ending inventory and the cost of goods sold for the current period using (*a*) first-in, first-out, (*b*) average cost, and (*c*) last-in, first-out.

LO7-3 Homework MBC

E7-31. Determining Lower of Cost or Net Realizable Value (NRV)

Crane Company had the following inventory at December 31.

		Unit Price	
	Quantity	Cost	NRV
Desks			
Model 9001...........	105	$190	$210
Model 9002...........	70	280	268
Model 9003...........	30	350	360
Cabinets			
Model 7001...........	180	60	64
Model 7002...........	120	95	88
Model 7003...........	75	130	126

a. Determine the ending inventory amount by applying the lower of cost or net realizable value rule to

1. Each item of inventory.
2. Each major category of inventory.
3. Total inventory.

b. Which of the LCNRV procedures from requirement *a* results in the lowest net income for the year? Explain.

LO7-2, 4, 6 Homework MBC

General Motors
NYSE :: GM

E7-32.[A] Analyzing Inventory Note Disclosure

General Motors Corporation reported the following information in its 10-K report:

Inventories at December 31 ($ millions)	2008	2007
Productive material, work in process, and supplies	$ 4,849	$ 6,267
Finished product, service parts, etc..	9,426	10,095
Total inventories at FIFO.	14,275	16,362
Less LIFO allowance	(1,233)	(1,423)
Total automotive and other inventories, less allowances	$13,042	$14,939

The company reports its inventory using the LIFO costing method during 2007 and 2008.

a. At what dollar amount are inventories reported on its 2008 balance sheet?

b. At what dollar amount would inventories have been reported in 2008 if FIFO inventory costing had been used?

c. What cumulative effect has the use of LIFO had, as of year-end 2008, on GM's pretax income, compared to the pretax income that would have been reported using the FIFO costing method?

d. Assuming a 35% income tax rate, what is the cumulative effect on GM's tax liability as of year-end 2008?

e. In July 2009, GM changed its inventory accounting to FIFO costs. Why do you suppose GM made that choice?

E7-33.[A] Analyzing of Inventory and Note Disclosure

LO7-2, 4, 6

Homework MBC

Deere & Company
NYSE :: DE

The inventory note disclosure from Deere & Company's 2020 10-K follows ($ millions).

A majority of inventory owned by Deere & Company and its U.S. equipment subsidiaries are valued at cost, on the "last-in, first-out" (LIFO) basis. Remaining inventories are generally valued at the lower of cost, on the "first-in, first-out" (FIFO) basis, or net realizable value. The value of gross inventories on the LIFO basis at November 1, 2020 and November 3, 2019 represented 52 percent and 55 percent, respectively, of worldwide gross inventories at FIFO value. The pretax favorable income effect from the liquidation of LIFO inventory during 2020 was $33 million. If all inventories had been valued on a FIFO basis, estimated inventories by major classification at November 1, 2020 and November 3, 2019 in millions of dollars would have been as follows:

($ million)	2020	2019
Raw materials and supplies	$1,995	$2,285
Work-in-process	648	747
Finished goods and parts	4,006	4,613
Total FIFO value	6,649	7,645
Less adjustment to LIFO value	1,650	1,670
Inventories	$4,999	$5,975

We note that not all of Deere's inventories are reported using the same inventory costing method (companies can use different inventory costing methods for different inventory pools).

a. At what dollar amount are Deere's inventories reported on its 2020 balance sheet?

b. At what dollar amount would inventories have been reported on Deere's 2020 balance sheet had it used FIFO inventory costing?

c. What *cumulative* effect has the use of LIFO inventory costing had, as of year-end 2020, on its pretax income compared with the pretax income it would have reported had it used FIFO inventory costing? Explain.

d. Assuming a 25% income tax rate, by what *cumulative* dollar amount has Deere's tax liability been affected by use of LIFO inventory costing as of year-end 2020? Has the use of LIFO inventory costing increased or decreased its cumulative tax liability?

e. What effect has the use of LIFO inventory costing had on Deere's pretax income and tax liability for 2020 (assume a 25% income tax rate)?

f. Deere's 2020 disclosure states: "The pretax favorable income effects from the liquidation of LIFO inventory during 2020 was $33 million." Explain what happened in 2020 with respect to Deere's inventory and why there were favorable income effects.

E7-34. Analyzing Inventories Using LIFO Inventory Disclosure Note

LO7-2, 4, 5

Homework MBC

Casey's General Stores, Inc.
NASDAQ :: CASY

The disclosure note below is from the 2020 10-K report of Casey's General Stores, Inc., an operator of convenience stores ($ thousands).

Inventories

Inventories, which consist of merchandise and fuel, are stated at the lower of cost or market. For fuel, cost is determined through the use of the first-in, first-out (FIFO) method. For merchandise inventories, cost is determined through the use of the last-in, first-out (LIFO) method. The excess of replacement cost over the stated LIFO value was $87,546 and $80,814 at April 30, 2020 and 2019, respectively. There were no material LIFO liquidations during the periods presented. Below is a summary of the inventory values at April 30, 2020 and 2019.

continued

continued from previous page

($ thousands)	Years Ended April 30, 2020	2019
Fuel	$ 33,695	$ 83,204
Merchandise	202,312	189,836
Total inventory	$236,007	$273,040

In 2020, Casey's General Stores reported sales revenue of $9,175.3 million and cost of goods sold of $7,030.6 million.

a. Calculate the amount of inventories purchased by Casey's General Stores in 2020.

b. What amount of gross profit would Casey's General Stores have reported if the FIFO method had been used to value all inventories?

c. Calculate the gross profit margin (GPM) as reported and assuming that the FIFO method had been used to value all inventories.

LO7-5 Homework MBC

Tiffany & Co. NYSE :: TIF
Best Buy NYSE :: BBY
RH, Inc. NYSE :: RH

E7-35. Calculating Gross Profit Margin and Inventory Turnover
The following table presents sales revenue, cost of goods sold, and inventory amounts for three specialty retailers, Tiffany & Co., Best Buy, and RH.

($ millions)	2020	2019
Tiffany & Co.		
Revenues	$ 4,424	$ 4,442
Cost of goods sold	1,662	1,631
Inventory	2,464	2,428
Best Buy		
Revenues	$43,638	$42,879
Cost of goods sold	33,590	32,918
Inventory	5,174	5,409
RH		
Revenues	$ 2,647	$ 2,506
Cost of goods sold	1,552	1,520
Inventory	439	532

a. Compute the gross profit margin (GPM) for each of these companies for 2020 and 2019.

b. Compute the inventory turnover ratio and the average inventory days outstanding for 2020 for each company.

c. What factors might determine the differences among these three companies' ratios?

PROBLEMS

LO7-2, 4, 5 Homework MBC

Caterpillar, Inc. NYSE :: CAT
Komatsu Ltd. (ADR) OTC :: KMTUY

P7-36. Analyzing Inventory and Its Disclosure Note
Caterpillar Inc. and Komatsu Ltd. are international manufacturers of industrial and construction equipment. Caterpillar's headquarters is in the United States, while Komatsu's headquarters is in Japan. The following information comes from their recent financial statements.

Caterpillar—fiscal year ending December 31, 2020 ($ millions)	
Cost of goods sold	$29,082
Beginning inventory	11,266
Ending inventory	11,402
Komatsu—fiscal year ending March 31, 2020 (¥ millions)	
Cost of goods sold	¥1,749,048
Beginning inventory	837,552
Ending inventory	805,309

In its note disclosures, Caterpillar also provides the following information (assume no LIFO liquidation):

Inventories
We state inventories at the lower of cost or net realizable value. We principally determine cost using the last-in, first-out (LIFO) method. The value of inventories on the LIFO basis represented about 60 percent of total inventories at December 31, 2020 and 2019. If the FIFO (first-in, first-out) method had been in use, inventories would have been $2,132 million and $2,086 million higher than reported at December 31, 2020 and 2019, respectively.

REQUIRED

a. Calculate the inventory turnover and average inventory days outstanding ratios for Caterpillar and Komatsu using the information reported in their financial statements. Describe some operational reasons that companies might have differing inventory ratios, even if they are in the same industry.

b. Did the cost of Caterpillar's acquiring (i.e., producing) products go up or down in 2020?

c. Assuming a 25% income tax rate, by what cumulative dollar amount has Caterpillar's tax liability been affected by use of LIFO inventory costing as of fiscal year-end 2020? Has the use of LIFO inventory costing increased or decreased its cumulative tax liability?

d. What effect has the use of LIFO inventory costing had on Caterpillar's pretax income and tax liability for fiscal year 2020? (Assume a 25% tax rate.)

e. In its disclosure notes, Komatsu reports that it "determines cost of work in process and finished products using the specific identification method based on actual costs accumulated under a job-order cost system. The cost of finished parts is determined principally using the first-in, first-out method." What effect does this disclosure note have on your interpretation in question *a* above? Use the information available to make a more appropriate comparison of the two companies' inventory turnover.

P7-37. Analyzing Inventory Disclosure Comparing LIFO and FIFO

LO7-2, 4, 5

Homework MBC

Kroger
NYSE :: KR

The current asset section of the 2020 and 2019 fiscal year-end balance sheets of The Kroger Co. are presented in the accompanying table:

($ millions)	February 1, 2020	February 2, 2019
Current assets		
Cash and temporary cash investments	$ 399	$ 429
Store deposits in-transit	1,179	1,181
Receivables	1,706	1,589
FIFO inventory	8,464	8,123
LIFO reserve	(1,380)	(1,277)
Assets held for sale	—	166
Prepaid and other current assets	522	592
Total current assets	$10,890	$10,803

In addition, Kroger provides the following disclosure note describing its inventory accounting policy (assume the following is their complete disclosure):

Inventories are stated at the lower of cost (principally on a last-in, first-out "LIFO" basis) or market. In total, approximately 91% of inventories in 2019 and 90% of inventories in 2018 were valued using the LIFO method. The remaining inventories, including substantially all fuel inventories, are stated at the lower of cost (on a FIFO basis) or net realizable value. Replacement cost was higher than the carrying amount by $1,380 at February 1, 2020 and $1,277 at February 2, 2019. The Company follows the Link-Chain, Dollar-Value LIFO method for purposes of calculating its LIFO charge or credit.

REQUIRED

a. At what dollar amount does Kroger report its inventory in its February 1, 2020, balance sheet?

b. What is the cumulative effect (through February 1, 2020) of the use of LIFO on Kroger's pretax earnings?

c. Assuming a 25% tax rate, what is the cumulative (through February 1, 2020) tax effect of the use of LIFO to determine inventory costs?

d. Kroger reported net earnings of $1,512 million in its fiscal year 2020 income statement. Assuming a 25% tax rate, what amount of net earnings would Kroger report if the company used the FIFO inventory costing method?

e. Kroger reported merchandise costs (cost of goods sold) of $95,294 million in fiscal year 2020. Compute its inventory turnover for the year.

f. How would the inventory turnover ratio differ if the FIFO costing method had been used?

LO7-5

Homework MBC

Samsung Electronics Co. Ltd.
KRX :: 005930
HP Inc.
NYSE :: HPQ
Apple Inc.
NASDAQ :: AAPL

P7-38. Calculating Gross Profit and Inventory Turnover

The following table presents sales revenue, cost of goods sold, and inventory amounts for three computer/electronics companies, Samsung Electronics Co., HP Inc., and Apple Inc.

($ millions)	Fiscal year ending		
Samsung Electronics Co. Ltd. (S. Korean won)	Dec. 31, 2020	Dec. 31, 2019	Dec. 31, 2018
Revenues	236,806,988	230,400,881	243,771,415
Cost of goods sold	144,488,296	147,239,549	132,394,411
Inventory	32,043,145	26,766,464	28,984,704
HP Inc. (US dollar)	Oct. 31, 2020	Oct. 31, 2019	Oct. 31, 2018
Revenues (products only)	56,639	58,756	58,472
Cost of goods sold	46,202	47,586	47,803
Inventory	5,963	5,734	6,062
Apple Inc. (US dollar)	Sept. 26, 2020	Sept. 28, 2019	Sept. 29, 2018
Revenues	274,515	260,174	265,595
Cost of goods sold	169,559	161,782	163,756
Inventory	4,061	4,106	3,956

REQUIRED

a. Compute the gross profit margin (GPM) for each of these companies for all three fiscal years.

b. Compute the inventory turnover ratio and the average inventory days outstanding for each company for the last two fiscal years. (All three firms use FIFO inventory costing.)

c. What factors might determine the differences among these three companies' ratios?

LO7-2, 4, 6

Homework MBC

Seneca Foods Corporation
NASDAQ :: SENEA

P7-39.[A] Analyzing and Interpreting Inventories and Its Related Ratios and Disclosures

The current asset section from Seneca Foods Corporation, a low-cost producer and distributor of quality fruits and vegetables, March 31, 2020 annual report follows:

($ thousands)	March 31, 2020	March 31, 2019
Current Assets		
Cash and cash equivalents	$ 10,702	$ 11,480
Accounts receivable, less allowance for doubtful accounts of $1,598 and $57, respectively	109,802	84,122
Contracts receivable	7,610	—
Assets held for sale-discontinued operations	182	98
Inventories	411,631	501,684
Assets held for sale	—	1,568
Refundable income taxes	4,350	1,221
Other current assets	7,323	3,075
Total current assets	551,600	603,248

Seneca reports the following related to its gross profit:

	Fiscal Years	
($ thousands)	2020	2019
Net sales	$1,335,769	$1,199,581
Cost of sales	1,193,881	1,160,085
Gross profit	$ 141,888	$ 39,496

Seneca further reports the following disclosure note:

11. Inventories
Effective December 30, 2007 (beginning of 4th quarter of Fiscal Year 2008), the Company changed its inventory valuation method from the lower of cost, determined under the FIFO method, or market to the lower of cost, determined under the LIFO method, or market. In the high inflation environment that the Company was experiencing, the Company believed that the LIFO inventory method was preferable over the FIFO method because it better compares the cost of current production to

continued

continued from previous page

current revenue. The effect of LIFO was to increase continuing net earnings by $12.8 million in 2020 and to reduce net earnings by $30.4 million in 2019, compared to what would have been reported using the FIFO inventory method. The increase in earnings per share was $1.38 ($1.37 diluted) in 2020; and a reduction in earnings per share of $3.14 ($3.14 diluted) in 2019. There were LIFO liquidations of $6.6 million in 2020 and $28.7 million in 2019. Most of this LIFO liquidation in 2019 is reported as Discontinued Operations since it related to the Modesto fruit (see Discontinued Operations Note 3). The inventories by category and the impact of using the LIFO method are shown in the following table:

(In thousands)	2020	2019
Finished products	$351,251	$454,920
In process	31,173	42,045
Raw materials and supplies	173,474	166,060
	555,898	663,025
Less excess of FIFO cost over LIFO cost	144,267	161,341
Total inventories	$411,631	$501,684

In prior financial statements, Seneca has stated that it "manages the Company for cash, not reported earnings" and that the "decision to switch to LIFO has turned out to be a very prudent one of the last five years."

a. Compute the ratio of inventories to total current assets for 2020 and 2019. Is the change observed for the ratio a positive development for a company such as Seneca? Explain.

b. Compute inventory turnover for both 2020 and 2019 (2018 ending inventories were $680,828). Interpret and explain the change in inventory turnover as positive or negative for the company.

c. What inventory costing method does Seneca use? What effect has the use of this method (relative to FIFO or LIFO) had on its reported income for 2020 and 2019? Was the result an increase or decrease? Explain.

d. Seneca claims that it manages its company for cash flow. Does its inventory reporting help the Company to do so? How much in taxes has Seneca saved, assuming a 25% tax rate, by the inventory approach it adopted?

CASES AND PROJECT

C7-40.[A] **Analyzing Effects of LIFO on Inventory Turnover Ratios**

LO7-2, 4, 5, 6

Homework MBC

Exxon Mobil Corp.
NYSE :: XOM
BP, p.l.c.
NYSE :: BP

The current assets of Exxon Mobil Corporation follow:

($ millions)	2020	2019
Current assets		
Cash and cash equivalents	$ 4,364	$ 3,089
Notes and accounts receivable, net	20,581	26,966
Inventories:		
Crude oil, products and merchandise	14,169	14,010
Materials and supplies	4,681	4,518
Other current assets	1,098	1,469
Total current assets	$44,893	$50,052

In addition, the following note was provided in its 2020 10-K report:

Inventories. Crude oil, products and merchandise inventories are carried at the lower of current market value or cost (generally determined under the last-in, first-out method—LIFO). Inventory costs include expenditures and other charges (including depreciation) directly and indirectly incurred in bringing the inventory to its existing condition and location. Selling expenses and general and administrative expenses are reported as period costs and excluded from inventory cost. Inventories of materials and supplies are valued at cost or less.

continued

continued from previous page

Miscellaneous Financial Information. In 2020, 2019, and 2018, net income included gains of $41 million, $523 million and $107 million, respectively, attributable to the combined effects of LIFO inventory accumulations and drawdowns. The aggregate replacement cost of inventories was estimated to exceed their LIFO carrying values by $5.4 billion and $9.7 billion at December 31, 2020, and 2019, respectively.

REQUIRED

a. Exxon Mobil reported a pretax loss of $28,883 million in 2020. What amount of pretax earnings would have been reported by the company if inventory had been reported using the FIFO costing method?

b. Exxon Mobil reported cost of goods sold of $94,007 million in 2020. Compute its inventory turnover ratio for 2020 using total inventories.

c. **BP, p.l.c.** (BP) reports its financial information using IFRS. For fiscal year 2020, BP reported cost of goods sold of $132,104 million, beginning inventory of $20,880 million and ending inventory of $16,873 million. Compute BP's inventory turnover ratio for fiscal year 2020.

d. Compare your answers in parts *b* and *c*. BP can't use LIFO to report under IFRS, so revise your calculations in such a way as to find out which company has faster inventory turnover.

e. What is meant by the statement that "2020 net income included gains of $41 million attributable to the combined effects of LIFO inventory accumulations and draw-downs"?

LO7-2, 4
Virco Manufacturing Corp.
NASDAQ :: VIRC

C7-41. Analyzing Effects of Change from LIFO to FIFO Inventory Costing

Virco Manufacturing Corp. provided the following note in its annual report for the year ended January 31, 2011:

On January 31, 2011, the Company elected to change its costing method for the material component of raw materials, work in process, and finished goods inventory to the lower of cost or market using the first-in first-out ("FIFO") method, from the lower of cost or market using the last-in first out ("LIFO") method. The labor and overhead components of inventory have historically been valued on a FIFO basis. The Company believes that the FIFO method for the material component of inventory is preferable as it conforms the inventory costing methods for all components of inventory into a single costing method and better reflects current acquisition costs of those inventories on our consolidated balance sheets. Additionally, presentation of inventory at FIFO aligns the financial reporting with the Company's borrowing base under its line of credit (see Note 3 for further discussion of the line of credit). Further, this change will promote greater comparability with companies that have adopted International Financial Reporting Standards, which does not recognize LIFO as an acceptable accounting method. In accordance with FASB ASC Topic 250, "Accounting Changes and Error Corrections," all prior periods presented have been adjusted to apply the new accounting method retrospectively. In addition, as an indirect effect of the change in our inventory costing method from LIFO to FIFO, the Company recorded additional inventory lower of cost or market expenses and changes in deferred tax assets and income tax expense. The retroactive effect of the change in our inventory costing method...increased the February 1, 2008, opening retained earnings balance by $4.1 million, and increased our inventory and retained earnings balances by $8.5 million and $5.4 million as of January 31, 2009, by $6.9 million and $4.3 million as of January 31, 2010, and by $7.6 million and $4.7 million as of January 31, 2011, respectively.

REQUIRED

a. What do the stated changes in inventory in each year represent (e.g., the $7.6 million in 2011)? Equity? What is the difference between the two?

b. What were Virco's stated reasons for the change to FIFO?

c. In the Annual Report for the year ended January 2010, Virco states the following: "Inventories are stated at the lower of cost or market. Cost is determined using the last-in, first-out ("LIFO") method of valuation for the material content of inventories and the first-in, first-out ("FIFO") method for labor and overhead. The Company uses LIFO as it results in a better matching of costs and revenues." What are some possible motivations behind why Virco changed to the FIFO method of accounting beyond those listed by management?

SOLUTIONS TO REVIEW PROBLEMS

Review 7-1

a. Yes *b.* No *c.* Yes *d.* Yes *e.* No

Review 7-2

Preliminary computation: Units in ending inventory = 4,800 available − 2,800 sold = 2,000

a. First-in, first-out (FIFO)

Cost of goods sold computation:	Units		Cost		Total
	1,000	@	$18.00	=	$18,000
	1,800	@	$18.25	=	32,850
	2,800				**$50,850**
Cost of goods available for sale		$88,450			
Less: Cost of goods sold		50,850			
Ending inventory ($22,800 + $14,800)		**$37,600**			

b. Last-in, first-out (LIFO)

Cost of goods sold computation:	Units		Cost		Total
	1,200	@	$19.00	=	$22,800
	800	@	$18.50	=	14,800
	800	@	$18.25	=	14,600
	2,800				**$52,200**
Cost of goods available for sale		$88,450			
Less: Cost of goods sold		52,200			
Ending inventory [$18,000 + (1,000 × $18.25)]		**$36,250**			

c. Average cost (AC)

Average unit cost	= $88,450/4,800	= $18.427
Cost of goods sold	= 2,800 × $18.427	= $51,596
Ending inventory	= 2,000 × $18.427	= $36,854

d. 1. FIFO in most circumstances reflects physical flow. For example, FIFO would apply to the physical flow of perishables and to situations where the earlier items acquired are moved out first because of risk of deterioration or obsolescence.

2. LIFO results in the lowest ending inventory amount during periods of rising costs, which in turn yields the lowest net income and the lowest income taxes.

e. Last-in, first-out with LIFO liquidation

Cost of goods sold computation:	Units		Cost		Total
	800	@	$18.50	=	$14,800
	1,800	@	$18.25	=	32,850
	200	@	$18.00	=	3,600
	2,800				**$51,250**
Cost of goods available for sale		$65,650			
Less: Cost of goods sold		51,250			
Ending inventory (800 × $18)		**$14,400**			

The company's LIFO gross profit has increased by $950 ($52,200 − $51,250). This increase is from LIFO liquidation, which is the reduction of inventory quantities that results in matching older (lower) cost layers against current selling prices. The company has, in effect, dipped into lower-cost layers to boost current period profit—all from a simple delay of inventory purchases.

f. Transaction effects shown in the financial statement effects template, journal entries, and T-accounts.

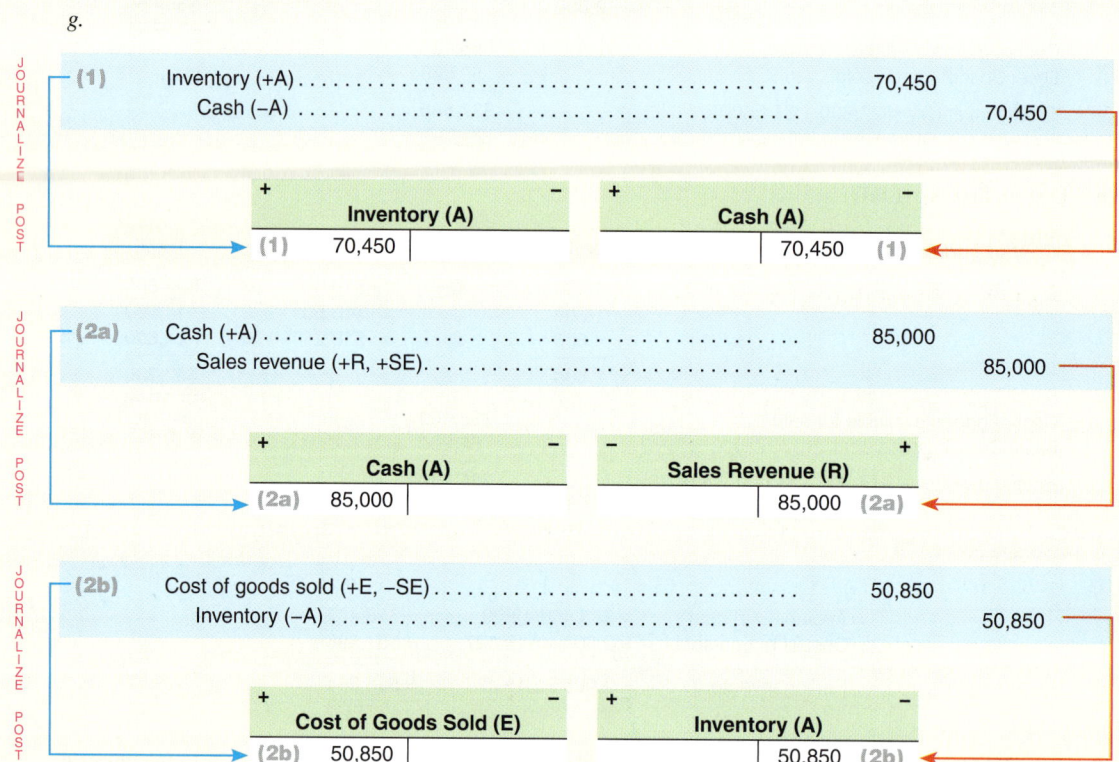

ANALYZE

Transaction	Balance Sheet: Cash Asset	+	Noncash Assets	=	Liabil-ities	+	Contrib. Capital	+	Earned Capital	Income Statement: Revenues	−	Expenses	=	Net Income
(1) Purchase $70,450 of inventory.	−70,450 Cash		+70,450 Inventory	=							−		=	
(2a) Sell Inventory for $85,000 cash.	+85,000 Cash			=					+85,000 Retained Earnings	+85,000 Sales Revenue	−		=	+85,000
(2b) Record cost of goods sold in 2a.			−50,850 Inventory	=					−50,850 Retained Earnings		−	+50,850 Cost of Goods Sold	=	−50,850

g.

JOURNALIZE

		Debit	Credit
(1)	Inventory (+A)	70,450	
	Cash (−A)		70,450

POST

+ Inventory (A) −		+ Cash (A) −	
(1) 70,450			70,450 (1)

JOURNALIZE

		Debit	Credit
(2a)	Cash (+A)	85,000	
	Sales revenue (+R, +SE)		85,000

POST

+ Cash (A) −		− Sales Revenue (R) +	
(2a) 85,000			85,000 (2a)

JOURNALIZE

		Debit	Credit
(2b)	Cost of goods sold (+E, −SE)	50,850	
	Inventory (−A)		50,850

POST

+ Cost of Goods Sold (E) −		+ Inventory (A) −	
(2b) 50,850			50,850 (2b)

Review 7-3

1.

Item	Quantity	Cost	NRV	Inventory Amounts: Cost	NRV	LCNRV (by Item)
Fans						
Model X1	300	$18	$19	$ 5,400	$ 5,700	$ 5,400
Model X2	250	22	24	5,500	6,000	5,500
Model X3	400	29	26	11,600	10,400	10,400
Totals				$22,500	$22,100	$21,300
Heaters						
Model B7	500	24	28	$12,000	$14,000	$12,000
Model B8	290	35	32	10,150	9,280	9,280
Model B9	100	41	38	4,100	3,800	3,800
Totals				26,250	27,080	25,080
Totals				$48,750	$49,180	$46,380

a. As shown in this schedule, applying the lower of cost or NRV rule to each item of the inventory results in an ending inventory amount of $46,380.

b. Applying the lower of cost or NRV rule to each major category of the inventory results in an ending inventory amount of $48,350, calculated as follows:

Fans	$22,100
Heaters.	26,250
	$48,350

c. As shown in this schedule, applying the lower of cost or NRV rule to the total inventory results in an ending inventory amount of $48,750.

2. The LCM procedure that results in the lowest ending inventory amount also results in the lowest net income for the year (the lower the ending inventory amount, the higher the cost of goods sold). Applying the lower of cost or NRV rule to each item of the inventory results in the lowest net income for the year.

Review 7-4

a. $35,000
b. $50,000
c. $97,000 ($100,000 – ($15,000 – $12,000))
d. $750 ($3,000 × 25%)
e. (1) lower (2) higher (3) same (4) lower (5) lower

Review 7-5

a. The gross profit margin and inventory turnover are calculated as follows:

Gross profit margin
2018: $ 9,783 / $36,094 = 0.271 (or 27.1%)
2019: $10,376 / $38,116 = 0.272 (or 27.2%)
2020: $12,509 / $44,864 = 0.279 (or 27.9%)

Inventory turnover
2019: $27,740/[($1,913 + $1,849)/2] = 14.75 times
2020: $32,355/[($2,034 + $1,913)/2] = 16.39 times

b. Cost of goods sold and gross profit must be adjusted by the change in the LIFO reserve to convert to FIFO.

Cost of goods sold
2019: $27,740 – ($529 – $489) = $27,700
2020: $32,355 – ($549 – $529) = $32,335

Gross profit
2019: $10,376 + ($529 – $489) = $10,416
2020: $12,509 + ($549 – $529) = $12,529

The use of LIFO resulted in a lower cost of goods sold and a higher gross profit in 2019 and 2020 because the LIFO reserve grew larger each year.

c. Restated inventory turnover calculations:

Inventory turnover
2019: $27,700/[($2,442 + $2,338)/2] = 11.6 times
2020: $32,335/[($2,583 + $2,442)/2] = 12.9 times

Because inventory values are higher and cost of goods sold is lower in 2019 and 2020 under FIFO, the inventory turnover ratio is lower when FIFO numbers are used.

Review 7-6

a.

Sales revenue	
(11,500 × $65)	$747,500
Cost of goods sold	
(7,000 × $70) + (3,000 × $30) + (1,500 × $20)	610,000
Gross profit	$137,500

b.

Sales revenue	
(11,500 × $65)	$747,500
Cost of goods sold	
(11,500 × $70)	805,000
Gross profit	$ (57,500)

c. Dickhaut should report in its disclosure notes that gross profit was increased by $195,000 [$137,500 – $(57,500)] due to LIFO liquidation. It's worth noting that Dickhaut could report any gross profit between $(57,500) and $137,500 by adjusting its end-of-year purchases.

d. The replenishment decision should depend on the cash flows from each alternative over the planning period (until the point where inventory could be replenished next year at $55). The following table looks at three alternatives—no year-end purchase, a year-end purchase of 4,500 units, and a year-end purchase of 1,500 units. The second alternative would retain all the LIFO layers that were in the beginning inventory, while the third alternative would retain only the Year 6 layer at $20 per unit. For this last alternative, cost of goods sold would be $685,000 (8,500 units at $70 each plus 3,000 units at $30 each).

As the table shows, the third alternative is preferred to the second, but the first alternative is preferred over the other two. (Of course, this analysis is based on the assumption that 5,000 units will be held in inventory for the entire planning horizon. If Dickhaut anticipates future inventory reductions, e.g., due to product changes, end-of-year purchases would only defer the payment of taxes and their relative benefits would decrease.)

	No purchase		Purchase 4,500 units		Purchase 1,500 units	
	Income	**Cash Flows**	**Income**	**Cash Flows**	**Income**	**Cash Flows**
Revenue	$747,500	$747,500	$747,500	$747,500	$747,500	$747,500
COGS	610,000		805,000		685,000	
Gross profit	137,500		(57,500)		62,500	
Tax (25%)	(34,375)	(34,375)	14,375	14,375	(15,625)	(15,625)
Year-end purchases				(315,000)		(105,000)
Year 9 purchases		(247,500)				(165,000)
Total cash flows		$465,625		$446,875		$461,875

Chapter 8 Reporting and Analyzing Long-Term Operating Assets

LEARNING OBJECTIVES

LO8-1 Determine which costs to capitalize and report as tangible assets and which costs to expense.

LO8-2 Apply different depreciation methods to allocate the cost of assets over time.

LO8-3 Determine the effects of asset sales and impairments on financial statements.

LO8-4 Analyze the effect of tangible assets on key performance measure.

LO8-5 Describe the accounting and reporting for intangible assets.

LO8-6 Analyze the effects of intangible assets on key performance measures.

Road Map

LO	Learning Objective | Topics	Page	eLecture	Review	Assignments
LO8-1	Determine which costs to capitalize and report as tangible assets and which costs to expense.	8-3	e8-1	R 8-1	M8-11, E8-25, E8-26, DA8-1
LO8-2	Apply different depreciation methods to allocate the cost of assets over time.	8-5	e8-2	R 8-2	M8-12, M8-13, M8-18, M8-20, M8-21, M8-22, E8-25, E8-26, E8-27, E8-28, E8-29, E8-30, E8-31, E8-32, E8-33, E8-38, E8-39, E8-42, E8-43, DA8-2
LO8-3	Determine the effects of asset sales and impairments on financial statements.	8-10	e8-3	R 8-3	M8-14, M8-15, M8-16, M8-17, E8-25, E8-26, E8-28, E8-29, E8-31, E8-42, , E8-43, P8-44, C8-48, C8-49, C8-52, C8-53
LO8-4	Analyze the effect of tangible assets on key performance measures.	8-13	e8-4	R 8-4	M8-23, E8-34, E8-35, E8-40, C8-48, C8-50, DA8-3
LO8-5	Describe the accounting and reporting for intangible assets.	8-17	e8-5	R 8-5	M8-19, M8-24, E8-36, E8-37, PB-45, P8-46, P8-47, C8-51
LO8-6	Analyze the effects of intangible assets on key performance measures.	8-23	e8-6	R 8-6	M8-24, E8-41, P8-45, C8-50, C8-51, DA8-4

PROCTER & GAMBLE
www.pg.com

The Procter & Gamble Company (P&G) has successfully reinvented itself . . . again. Founded in 1837 by William Procter and James Gamble, P&G is the largest consumer products company in the world today. P&G markets its products in more than 180 countries, and its annual sales now are in excess of $70 billion, far exceeding competitors such as **Colgate-Palmolive Company** and **Kimberly-Clark Corporation**. P&G has focused on its higher-margin products such as those in beauty care. P&G's advertising budget is approximately a little over 10% of sales, which is about the same percentage as Colgate's and more than twice as large as Kimberly-Clark's.

P&G's financial performance has been impressive. Its return on equity (ROE) in fiscal year 2020 was almost 28%. Although more financially leveraged than the average publicly traded company, there is little need for concern because P&G generates more than $17 billion in operating cash flow, which is more than sufficient to cover its $434 million in interest payments. P&G also returned $15.2 billion to shareholders in dividends and repurchases of its own shares in 2020. (Stock repurchases are covered more fully in Chapter 11.)

P&G has made a priority of focusing on top brands to achieve superior products, packaging, brand communications, retail execution and customer value. P&G's product portfolio consists of numerous well-recognized household brands. Surveys in the business press show that the company is widely admired. A partial listing follows by reportable business segments, including some "Billion Dollar Brands" in each segment:

- **Baby, Feminine & Family Care**—Always, Bounty, Charmin, Pampers, Tampax
- **Beauty**— Head & Shoulders, Olay, Old Spice, Pantene
- **Fabric and Home Care**—Febreze, Cascade, Dawn, Downy, Gain, Tide
- **Grooming**—Braun, Gillette, Venus
- **Health Care**—Crest, Oral-B, Metamucil, Pepto-Bismol

While these brands are well-established, substantial risks exist. In the fiscal 2020 annual report, management states that "Our business model relies on continued growth and success of existing brands and products, as well as the creation of new innovative products. The markets and industry segments in which we offer our products are highly competitive. . . Our growth strategy is to provide meaningful and noticeable superiority in all elements of our consumer proposition." External risks also exist. For example, in recent years commodity costs have risen rapidly and significantly, and the coronavirus pandemic has disrupted supply chains. Around 55% of the company's business is generated outside North America, and P&G has "on the ground" operations in about 70 countries. Currency exchange rate fluctuations and trade policies can have a disruptive effect on distribution channels and sales growth.

In this chapter, we explore the reporting and analysis of long-term operating assets. In order to maintain growth in sales, income, and cash flows, capital-intensive companies like P&G must be diligent in managing long-term operating assets. As is the case with P&G, many companies have made large investments in innovation and brand value. These investments are not always reflected adequately in the balance sheet. Management's choices and GAAP rules concerning the reporting of long-term operating assets can have a marked impact on the analysis and interpretation of financial statements.

Sources: *Procter & Gamble* 2018 Annual Report and 10-K.

CHAPTER ORGANIZATION

Reporting and Analyzing Long-Term Operating Assets

Property, Plant, and Equipment

- Determining Costs to Capitalize
- Depreciation Methods
- Changes in Accounting Estimates
- Asset Sales and Impairments
- Note Disclosures
- Analysis Implications

Analyzing Financial Statements

- PPE Turnover
- Percent Depreciated Ratio
- Cash Flow Effects

Intangible Assets

- Research and Development Costs
- Patents, Copyrights, Trademarks, and Franchise Rights
- Amortization and Impairment
- Goodwill
- Note Disclosures
- Analysis Implications

INTRODUCTION

LO8-1 Determine which costs to capitalize and report as tangible assets and which costs to expense.

eLecture MBC

Investments in long-term operating assets often represent the largest component of a company's balance sheet. Effectively managing long-term operating assets is crucial, because these investments affect company performance for several years and are frequently irreversible. To evaluate how well a company is managing operating assets, we need to understand how they are measured and reported.

This chapter describes the accounting, reporting, and analysis of long-term operating assets, including tangible and intangible assets. **Tangible assets** are assets that have physical substance. They are frequently included in the balance sheet as *property, plant, and equipment*, and include land, buildings, machinery, fixtures, and equipment. **Intangible assets**, such as trademarks and patents, do not have physical substance but provide the owner with specific rights and privileges.

Long-term operating assets have two common characteristics. First, unlike inventory, these assets are not acquired for resale. Instead, they are necessary to produce and deliver the products and services that generate revenues for the company. Second, these assets help produce revenues for multiple accounting periods. Consequently, accountants focus considerable attention on how they are reported in the balance sheet and how these costs are transferred over time to the income statement as expenses.

To illustrate the size and importance of long-term operating assets, the asset section (only) of P&G's balance sheet is reproduced in **Exhibit 8.1**. We can see as of June 30, 2020, the end of P&G's fiscal year, P&G's net investment in property, plant, and equipment totaled approximately \$20.7 billion, and its intangible assets represent a \$63.7 billion investment. Together, these two categories of assets make up about 70% of P&G's total assets.

This chapter is divided into two main sections. The first section focuses on accounting for tangible property, plant, and equipment and the related depreciation expense that is reported each period in the income statement. The second section examines the measurement and reporting of intangible assets.

PROPERTY, PLANT, AND EQUIPMENT (PPE)

For many companies, the largest category of operating assets is long-term property, plant, and equipment (PPE) assets. The size and duration of this asset category raises several important questions, including:

- Which costs should be **capitalized** on the balance sheet as assets? Which should be expensed?
- How should capitalized costs be allocated to the accounting periods that benefited from the asset?
- How should asset sales or significant changes in assets' fair values be reported?

This section explains the accounting, reporting, and analysis of PPE assets and related items.

EXHIBIT 8.1 Procter & Gamble Balance Sheet (assets only)

($ millions)	June 30 2020	June 30 2019
Assets		
Current assets		
Cash and cash equivalents	$ 16,181	$ 4,239
Available-for-sale investment securities	—	6,048
Accounts receivable	4,178	4,951
Inventories		
Materials and supplies	1,414	1,289
Work in process	674	612
Finished goods	3,410	3,116
Total inventories	5,498	5,017
Prepaid expenses and other current assets	2,130	2,218
Total current assets	27,987	22,473
Property, plant, and equipment, net	20,692	21,271
Goodwill	39,901	40,273
Trademarks and other intangible assets, net	23,792	24,215
Other noncurrent assets	8,328	6,863
Total assets	$120,700	$115,095

Determining Costs to Capitalize

When a company acquires an asset, it must first decide which portion of the cost should be included among the expenses of the current period and which costs should be capitalized as part of the asset and reported in the balance sheet. Outlays to acquire PPE are called **capital expenditures**. Expenditures that are recorded as an asset must possess each of the following two characteristics:

1. The asset is owned or controlled by the company.
2. The asset is expected to provide future benefits.

All normal costs incurred to acquire an asset and prepare it for its intended use should be capitalized and reported in the balance sheet. These costs would include the purchase price of the asset plus any of the following: installation costs, taxes, shipping costs, legal fees, and setup or calibration costs. If owning an asset carries legal obligations at the end of the asset's life (for example, to remove the asset or to perform environmental remediation), the current cost of those obligations should be included in the asset's cost and recognized as a liability at the time the asset is acquired. This cost will be included in the subsequent depreciation of the asset.

Determining the specific costs that should be capitalized requires judgment. There are two important considerations to address when deciding which costs to capitalize. First, companies can only capitalize costs that are *directly linked* to future benefits. Incidental costs or costs that would be incurred regardless of whether the asset is purchased should not be capitalized. Second, the costs capitalized as an asset can be no greater than the expected future benefits to be derived from use of the asset. This requirement means that if a company reports a $200 asset, we can reasonably expect that it will derive at least $200 in expected future cash inflows from the use and ultimate disposition of the asset.

Sometimes, companies construct assets for their own use rather than purchasing a similar asset from another company. In this case, all of the costs incurred to construct the asset—including materials, labor, and a reasonable amount of overhead—should be included in the cost that is capitalized. In addition, in many cases, a portion of the interest expense incurred during the construction period should also be capitalized as part of the asset's cost. This interest is called **capitalized interest**. Capitalizing some of a company's interest cost as part of the cost of a self-constructed asset reduces interest expense in the current period and increases depreciation expense in future periods when the asset is placed in service.

Once an asset is placed in service, additional costs are often incurred to maintain and improve the asset. Routine repairs and maintenance costs are necessary to realize the full potential benefits of ownership of the asset and should be treated as expenses of the period in which the maintenance is performed. However, if the cost can be considered an *improvement or betterment* of the asset, the cost should be capitalized. An improvement or betterment is an outlay that either enhances the usefulness of the asset or extends the asset's useful life beyond the original expectation.

YOU MAKE THE CALL

You are the Company Accountant Your company has just purchased a plot of land as a building site for an office building. After the purchase, you discover that the building site was once the site of an oil well. Before construction can commence, your company must spend $40,000 to properly cap the oil well and prepare the site to meet current environmental standards. How should you account for the $40,000 cleanup cost? [Answers on page 8-25]

Review 8-1 LO8-1

Determining the Proper Accounting Treatment of Tangible Costs

GuidedExample MBC

For each of the following costs incurred by a manufacturer, indicate whether the cost should be capitalized or immediately expensed.

a. Attorney fees for services provided to prepare a contract to purchase a new manufacturing plant
b. Estimated cost of environmental clean-up at the end of the useful life of the new manufacturing plant
c. Cost of repainting the walls of the plant after five years of use of the facilities
d. Cost of an addition to the plant that allows expansion of current production
e. Invoice cost of purchasing new equipment
f. Sales tax paid on equipment purchased
g. Installation costs of new equipment
h. Costs to pay the salaries of employees during the training sessions on the use of the new equipment
i. Payment of insurance premiums to insure against worker accidents pertaining to the use of manufacturing equipment

Solution on p. 8-41.

Depreciation

LO8-2 Apply different depreciation methods to allocate the cost of assets over time.

eLecture MBC

FYI Depreciation is a systematic allocation of asset cost over the useful life—not a measure of the change in fair value.

Once an asset has been recorded in the balance sheet, the cost must be transferred over time from the balance sheet to the income statement and reported as an expense. The nature of long-term operating assets is that they benefit more than one period. As a consequence, it is impossible to match a specific portion of the cost *directly* to the revenues of a particular period. Accounting principles require that this expense be recognized as equitably as possible over the asset's useful economic life. Therefore, we rely on a *systematic allocation* to assign a portion of the asset's cost to each period benefited. This systematic allocation of cost is called **depreciation**.

The concept of systematic allocation of an asset's cost is important. When depreciation expense is recorded, the reported value of the asset (also called the *book value* or *carrying value*) is reduced. Naturally, it is tempting to infer that the fair value of the asset is lower as a result. However, this reported value does not reflect the fair value of the asset. The fair value of the asset may decline by more or less than the amount of depreciation expense and can even increase in some periods. Depreciation expense should only be interpreted as an assignment of costs to an accounting period and not a measure of the decline in fair value of the asset.

The amount of cost that is allocated to a given period is recorded as depreciation expense in the income statement with a balancing entry in **accumulated depreciation** in the balance sheet. Accumulated depreciation is a contra-asset account (denoted "XA" in the journal entry). Like all contra-asset accounts, it offsets the balance in the corresponding asset account. To illustrate, assume that Dehning Company purchases a heavy-duty delivery truck for $100,000 and decides to record $18,000 of depreciation expense in the first year of operation. The following entries would be recorded with a cash outflow reflected in the investing section of the statement of cash flows.

The asset would be presented in the balance sheet at period-end at its net book value.

Truck, at cost	$100,000	
Less accumulated depreciation	18,000	
Truck, net	$ 82,000	(Book Value)

	Balance Sheet											Income Statement				
Transaction	Cash Asset	+	Noncash Assets	–	Contra Asset	=	Liabil-ities	+	Contrib. Capital	+	Earned Capital	Revenues	–	Expenses	=	Net Income
(1) Purchased delivery truck.	–100,000 Cash		+100,000 Truck	–		=							–		=	
(2) Depreciation of delivery truck.				–	+18,000 Accumulated Depreciation	=					–18,000 Retained Earnings		–	+18,000 Depreciation Expense	=	–18,000

ANALYZE JOURNALIZE POST

(1) Truck (+A) 100,000
  Cash (–A) 100,000

Truck (A): (1) 100,000 (debit)

Cash (A): 100,000 (1) (credit)

ANALYZE JOURNALIZE POST

(2) Depreciation expense (+E, –SE) 18,000
  Accumulated depreciation (+XA, –A) 18,000

Depreciation Expense (E): (2) 18,000 (debit)

Accumulated Depreciation (XA): 18,000 (2) (credit)

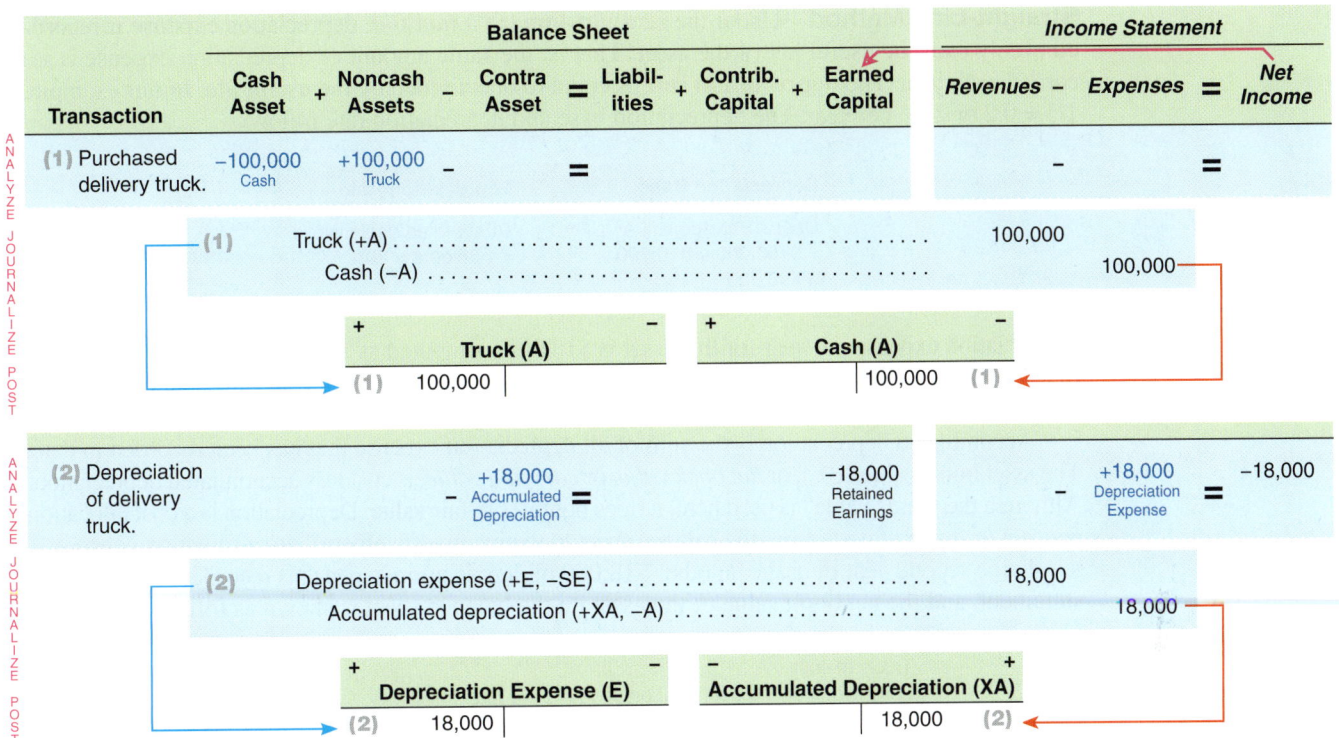

By presenting the information using a contra-asset account, the original acquisition cost of the asset is preserved in the asset account. The net book value of the asset reflects the acquisition cost less the balance in the accumulated depreciation account. The balance in the accumulated depreciation account is the sum of the depreciation expense that has been recorded to date. In a note disclosure accompanying the balance sheet in **Exhibit 8.1**, Procter & Gamble reports that the original cost of its property, plant, and equipment is $43,771 million and the depreciation accumulated as of June 30, 2020, is $23,079 million. The result is a net book value of $20,692 million.

Depreciation Methods

Two estimates are required to compute the amount of depreciation expense to record each period.

1. **Useful life**. The useful life is the period of time over which the asset is expected to provide economic benefits to the company. The useful life is not the same as the physical life of the asset. An asset may or may not provide economic benefits to the company for its entire physical life. This useful life should not exceed the period of time that the company intends to use the asset. For example, if a company has a policy of replacing automobiles every two years, the useful life should be set at no longer than two years, even if the automobiles physically last three years or more.
2. **Residual (or salvage) value**. The residual value is the expected realizable value of the asset at the end of its useful life. This value may be the disposal or scrap value, or it may be an estimated resale value for a used asset.

These factors must be estimated when the asset is acquired. The **depreciation base**, also called the *nonrecoverable cost*, is the portion of the cost that is depreciated. The depreciation base is the capitalized cost of the asset less the estimated residual value. This amount is allocated over the useful life of the asset according to the *depreciation method* that the company has selected.

To illustrate alternative depreciation methods, we return to the example presented earlier. Assume that Dehning Company purchases a delivery truck for $100,000. The company expects the truck to last five years and estimates a residual value of $10,000. The depreciation base is $90,000 ($100,000 – $10,000). We illustrate the three most common depreciation methods:

1. Straight-line method
2. Double-declining-balance method
3. Units-of-production method

Straight-Line Method Under the **straight-line (SL) method**, depreciation expense is recorded evenly over the useful life of the asset. That is, the same amount of depreciation expense is recorded each year. The **depreciation rate** is equal to one divided by the useful life. In our example, 1/5 = 0.2 or 20% per year. The depreciation base and depreciation rate follow.

Depreciation Base	Depreciation Rate
Cost – Salvage value = $100,000 – $10,000 = $90,000	1/Estimated useful life = 1/5 years = 20%

Depreciation expense per year for this asset is $18,000, computed as $90,000 × 20%. For the asset's first full year of usage, $18,000 of depreciation expense is reported in the income statement. At the end of that first year the asset is reported on the balance sheet, as shown earlier in the chapter.

Accumulated depreciation is the sum of all depreciation expense that has been recorded to date. The asset **book value (BV)**, or *net book value* or *carrying value,* is cost less accumulated depreciation. Although the word "value" is used here, it does not refer to fair value. Depreciation is a cost allocation concept (transfer of costs from the balance sheet to the income statement), not a valuation concept.

In the second year of usage, another $18,000 of depreciation expense is recorded in the income statement, and the net book value of the asset on the balance sheet is shown as follows:

Truck, at cost	$100,000
Less accumulated depreciation	36,000
Truck, net	$ 64,000

Accumulated depreciation now includes the sum of the first and second years' depreciation ($36,000), and the net book value of the asset is now reduced to $64,000. After the fifth year, a total of $90,000 of accumulated depreciation will be recorded, yielding a net book value for the truck of $10,000, its estimated salvage value.

Double-Declining-Balance Method GAAP allows companies to use **accelerated depreciation** methods. Accelerated depreciation methods record more depreciation expense in the early years of an asset's useful life and less expense in the later years. The total depreciation expense recorded over the entire useful life of the asset is the same as with straight-line depreciation. The only difference is in the amount of depreciation recorded for any given year.

The **double-declining-balance (DDB) method** is an accelerated depreciation method that computes the depreciation rate as twice the straight-line rate. This double rate is then multiplied by the net book value of the asset, which declines each period as accumulated depreciation increases. For Dehning Company, the depreciation base and the depreciation rate are computed as follows:

Depreciation Base	Depreciation Rate
Net Book Value = Cost – Accumulated Depreciation	2 × SL rate = 2 × 20% = 40%

FYI When calculating DDB depreciation, the depreciation rate is multiplied by the book value; residual value is not subtracted from book value.

The depreciation expense for the first year of usage for this asset is $40,000, computed as $100,000 × 40%. At the end of the first full year, $40,000 of depreciation expense is reported on the income statement (compared with $18,000 under the SL method), and the asset is reported on the balance sheet as follows:

Truck, at cost	$100,000
Less accumulated depreciation	40,000
Truck, net	$ 60,000

In the second year, $24,000 ($60,000 × 40%) of depreciation expense is reported in the income statement, and the net book value of the asset on the balance sheet is shown as follows:

Truck, at cost	$100,000
Less accumulated depreciation	64,000
Truck, net	$ 36,000

The double-declining-balance method continues to record depreciation expense in this manner until the salvage amount is reached, at which point the depreciation process is discontinued. This leaves a net book value equal to the salvage value as with the straight-line method. The DDB depreciation schedule for the life of this asset is illustrated in **Exhibit 8.2**.

EXHIBIT 8.2 Double-Declining-Balance Depreciation Schedule

Year	Book Value at Beginning of Year	Depreciation Expense	Book Value at End of Year
1	$100,000	100,000 × 40% = $40,000	$60,000
2	60,000	60,000 × 40% = 24,000	36,000
3	36,000	36,000 × 40% = 14,400	21,600
4	21,600	21,600 × 40% = 8,640	12,960
5	12,960	12,960 – 10,000 = 2,960*	10,000

*The depreciation expense in the fifth year is not calculated as 40% × $12,960 because the resulting depreciation would reduce the net book value below the $10,000 residual value. Instead, the residual value ($10,000) is subtracted from the remaining book value ($12,960), resulting in depreciation expense of $2,960.

Exhibit 8.3 compares the depreciation expense and net book value for both the SL and the DDB methods. During the first two years, the DDB method yields higher depreciation expense in comparison with the SL method. Beginning in the third year, this pattern reverses and the SL method produces higher depreciation expense. Over the asset's life, the same $90,000 in total depreciation expense is recorded, leaving a residual value of $10,000 on the balance sheet under both methods.

EXHIBIT 8.3 Comparison of Straight-Line and Double-Declining-Balance Depreciation

	Straight-Line		Double-Declining-Balance	
Year	Depreciation Expense	Book Value at End of Year	Depreciation Expense	Book Value at End of Year
1	$18,000	$82,000	$40,000	$60,000
2	18,000	64,000	24,000	36,000
3	18,000	46,000	14,400	21,600
4	18,000	28,000	8,640	12,960
5	18,000	10,000	2,960	10,000
	$90,000		$90,000	

All depreciation methods yield the same salvage value

Total depreciation over asset life is identical for all methods

Units-of-Production Method Under the **units-of-production method**, the useful life of the asset is defined in terms of the number of units of service provided by the asset. For instance, this could be the number of units produced, the number of hours that a machine is operated, or, as with Dehning Company's delivery truck, the number of miles driven. To illustrate, assume that Dehning Company estimates that the delivery truck will provide 150,000 miles of service before it is sold for its residual value of $10,000. The depreciation rate is expressed in terms of a cost per mile driven, computed as follows:

$$\frac{\$100{,}000 - \$10{,}000}{150{,}000 \text{ miles}} = \$0.60 \text{ per mile}$$

If the delivery truck is driven 35,000 miles in year 1, the depreciation expense for that year would be $21,000 (35,000 × $0.60). This method produces an amount of depreciation that varies from year to year as the use of the asset varies.

The units-of-production method is used by companies with natural resources such as oil reserves, mineral deposits, or timberlands. These assets are often referred to as **wasting assets** because the asset is consumed as it is used. The acquisition cost of a natural resource, plus any costs incurred to prepare the asset for its intended use, should be capitalized and reported among PPE assets in the balance sheet.

When the natural resource is used or extracted, inventory is created. The cost of the resource is transferred from the long-term asset account into inventory and, once the inventory is sold, to the income statement as cost of goods sold. The process of transferring costs from the resource account into inventory is called **depletion**.

Depletion is very much like depreciation of tangible operating assets, except that the amount of depletion recorded each period should reflect the amount of the resource that was actually extracted or used up during that period. As a result, depletion is usually calculated using the units-of-production method. The depletion rate is calculated as follows:

$$\textbf{Depletion rate per unit consumed} = \frac{\textbf{Acquisition cost} - \textbf{Residual value}}{\textbf{Estimated quantity of resource available}}$$

The calculation requires an estimate of the quantity of the resource available, which usually requires the assistance of experts, such as geologists or engineers, who are trained to make these determinations.

Depreciation for Tax Purposes Most companies use the straight-line method for financial reporting purposes and an accelerated depreciation method for tax returns.[1] Governments allow accelerated depreciation, in part, to provide incentives for taxpayers to invest. As a result of the differing depreciation methods used for financial accounting and tax purposes, lower depreciation expense (and higher income) is reported for financial accounting purposes early in the life of an asset relative to tax purposes. Even though this difference reverses in later years, companies prefer to defer the tax payments so that the cash savings can be invested to produce earnings. Further, even with the reversal in the later years of an asset's life, if total depreciable assets are growing at a fast enough rate, the additional first-year depreciation on newly acquired assets more than offsets the lower depreciation expense on older assets, yielding a continuing deferral of taxable income and taxes paid. There are other differences between financial reporting and tax reporting that create issues in determining a company's tax expense. In Chapter 10, we explore these differences further and examine deferred tax liabilities and deferred tax assets.

Changes in Accounting Estimates

The estimates required in the depreciation process are made when the asset is acquired. When necessary, companies can, and do, change these estimates during the useful lives of assets. When either the useful life or residual value estimates change, the change is applied prospectively. That is, companies use the new estimates from the date of the change going forward and do not restate the financial statements of prior periods.

To illustrate, assume that, after three years of straight-line depreciation, Dehning Company decided to extend the useful life of its truck from 5 years to 6 years. From **Exhibit 8.3**, the book value of the delivery truck at the end of the third year is $46,000. The change in estimated useful life would not require a formal accounting entry. Instead, depreciation expense would be recalculated for the remaining three years of the truck's useful life:

$$\frac{\$46,000 - \$10,000}{3\text{ years}} = \$12,000\text{ per year}$$

Thus, beginning in year four, depreciation expense of $12,000 (instead of $18,000) would be recorded each year.

[1] The U.S. Congress changes allowable tax depreciation methods from time to time. Some investments may qualify for immediate deduction of as much as 100% of the acquisition cost. Another common method is MACRS (Modified Accelerated Cost Recovery System). This method assumes no salvage value, and generally produces depreciation amounts consistent with the double-declining-balance method with a half year of service in the first and last year. When a declining balance method is used with zero salvage, the depreciation schedule must switch after the midpoint of the asset's life to straight-line depreciation of the remaining balance over the remaining life.

Accounting for Equipment

LO8-2 **Review 8-2**

On January 2, Lev Company purchases equipment for use in fabrication of a part for one of its key products. The equipment costs $95,000, and its estimated useful life is five years, after which it is expected to be sold for $10,000.

Guided Example MBC

Required

a. Compute depreciation expense for each year of the equipment's useful life for each of the following depreciation methods:
   1. Straight-line
   2. Double-declining-balance

b. Assume that Lev Company uses the straight-line depreciation method. Show the effects of these entries on the balance sheet and the income statement using the financial statements effects template.

c. Prepare journal entries to record the initial purchase of the equipment on January 2 and the year-end depreciation adjustment on December 31, and post the journal entries to T-accounts.

d. Show how the equipment is reported on Lev's balance sheet at the end of the third year assuming straight-line depreciation.

Solution on p. 8-41.

Asset Sales and Impairments

This section discusses gains and losses from asset sales and computation and disclosure of asset impairments.

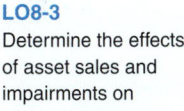

LO8-3 Determine the effects of asset sales and impairments on financial statements.

eLecture MBC

Gains and Losses on Asset Sales The gain or loss on the sale (disposition) of a long-term asset is computed as follows:

Gain or loss on asset sale = Proceeds from sale − Book value of asset sold

The book (carrying) value of an asset is its acquisition cost less accumulated depreciation. When an asset is sold, its acquisition cost and related accumulated depreciation are removed from the balance sheet and any gain or loss is reported in income from continuing operations. To illustrate such a transaction, assume that Dehning Company decided to sell the delivery truck after four years of straight-line depreciation (without the aforementioned change in useful life). From **Exhibit 8.3**, we know that the book value of the truck is $28,000 ($100,000 − $72,000). If the truck is sold for $30,000, the entry to record the sale follows.

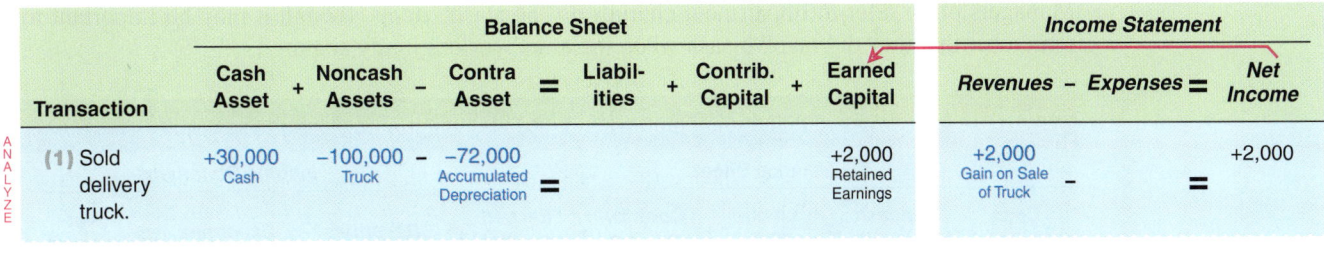

ANALYZE

Transaction	Balance Sheet: Cash Asset	+ Noncash Assets	− Contra Asset	= Liabilities	+ Contrib. Capital	+ Earned Capital	Income Statement: Revenues	− Expenses	= Net Income
(1) Sold delivery truck.	+30,000 Cash	−100,000 Truck	− −72,000 Accumulated Depreciation	=		+2,000 Retained Earnings	+2,000 Gain on Sale of Truck	−	= +2,000

JOURNALIZE

		Dr.	Cr.
(1)	Cash (+A)	30,000	
	Accumulated depreciation (−XA, +A)	72,000	
	Truck (−A)		100,000
	Gain on sale of truck (+R, +SE)		2,000

POST

+ Cash (A) −		− Accumulated Depreciation (XA) +		− Gain on Sale of Truck (R) +		+ Truck (A) −	
(1) 30,000		(1) 72,000			2,000 (1)		100,000 (1)

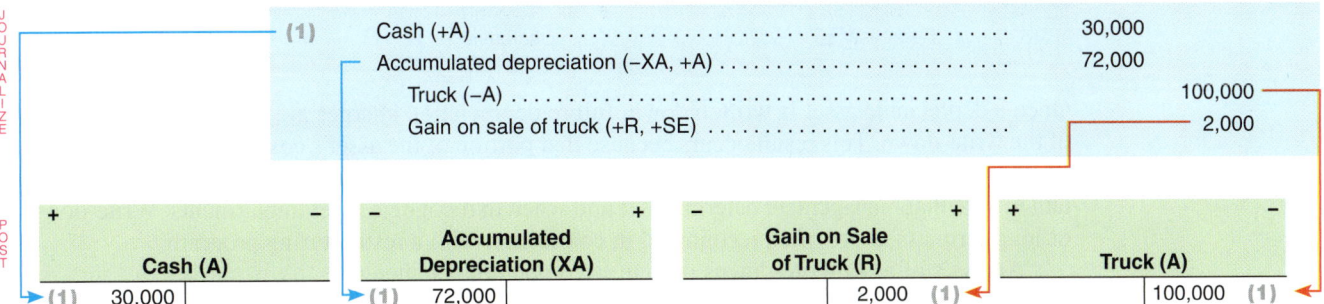

Gains and losses on asset sales can be large, and analysts must be aware of these nonrecurring operating income components. Further, if the gains are deemed immaterial, companies often include such gains and losses in general line items of the income statement—often as a component of selling, general, and administrative expenses. As described in Chapter 4, the $30,000 increase in cash is an investing cash inflow in the statement of cash flows, and the $2,000 gain would be subtracted from net income in an indirect-method statement of cash flows from operating activities.

Asset Impairments Property, plant, and equipment assets are reported at their net book values (original cost less accumulated depreciation). This is the case even if fair values of these assets increase subsequent to acquisition. As a result, there can be unrecognized gains hidden in the balance sheet.

However, if fair values of PPE assets subsequently decrease—and it can be determined that the asset value is permanently impaired—then companies must recognize losses on those assets. For assets that the company intends to keep and use, **impairment** is determined by comparing the sum of *expected* future (undiscounted) cash flows from the asset with its net book value. If these expected cash flows are greater than net book value, no impairment is deemed to exist. However, if the sum of expected cash flows is less than net book value, the asset is deemed impaired and it is written down to its current fair value (generally, the discounted present value of those expected cash flows). **Exhibit 8.4** depicts this impairment analysis.

EXHIBIT 8.4 Impairment Analysis of Long-Term Assets

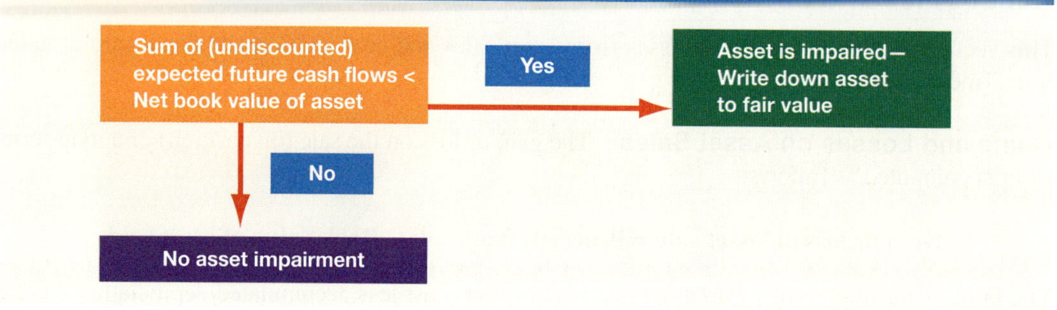

When a company records an impairment charge, assets are reduced by the amount of the write-down and the loss is recognized in the income statement, which reduces current period income. These effects are illustrated in **Exhibit 8.5**. Impairment charges are often included as part of **restructuring costs** along with future costs of workforce reductions. The entry in **Exhibit 8.5** reduces net income but does not affect current cash flows, so the impairment charges would be added back to net income when reporting indirect-method cash flows from operating activities. Managers often refer to impairment charges as "noncash" items, though it may be important to remember that they did involve cash when the asset was originally acquired.

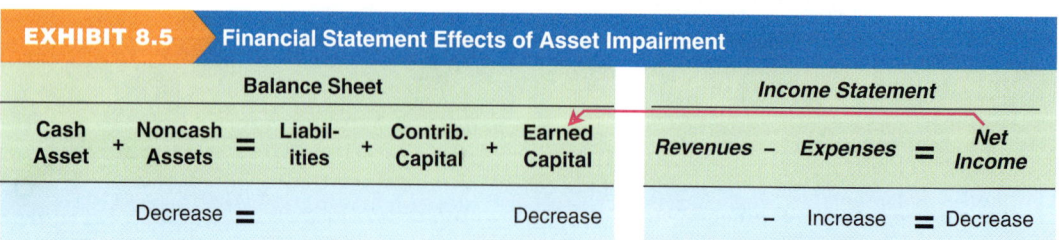

EXHIBIT 8.5 Financial Statement Effects of Asset Impairment

Balance Sheet										Income Statement				
Cash Asset	+	Noncash Assets	=	Liabilities	+	Contrib. Capital	+	Earned Capital		*Revenues*	–	*Expenses*	=	*Net Income*
		Decrease	=					Decrease			–	Increase	=	Decrease

Once a depreciable asset is written down, future depreciation charges are reduced by the amount of the write-down. This result occurs because that portion of the asset's cost that is written down is permanently removed from the balance sheet and cannot be subsequently depreciated. It is important to note that management determines if and when to recognize asset impairments. Write-downs of long-term assets are often recognized in connection with a restructuring program.

Analysis of asset write-downs presents two potential challenges:

1. *Insufficient write-down.* Assets sometimes are impaired to a larger degree than is recognized. This situation can arise if management is overly optimistic about future prospects or is reluctant to recognize the full loss in income. Underestimation of an impairment causes current

income to be overstated and income in future years to be lower relative to income that would have been reported had the impairment been correctly recorded.

2. *Aggressive write-down.* This *big bath* scenario can arise if income is currently and severely depressed by recognizing a larger impairment charge than the actual costs. Management's view is that the market will not penalize the firm for an extra write-off, and that doing so purges the balance sheet of costs that would otherwise reduce future years' income. This leads to income being overstated for several years after the write-down.

Neither of these cases is condoned under GAAP. Yet, because management is estimating future cash flows for the impairment test and such estimates are difficult to verify, it has some degree of latitude over the timing and amount of the write-off and can use that discretion to manage reported income.

Note Disclosure

Procter & Gamble provides the following information in Note 1 of its 2020 Annual Report to describe its accounting for PPE assets.

Property, plant, and equipment
Property, plant, and equipment is recorded at cost reduced by accumulated depreciation. Depreciation expense is recognized over the assets' estimated useful lives using the straight-line method.

Machinery and equipment includes office furniture and fixtures (15-year life), computer equipment and capitalized software (3- to 5-year lives), and manufacturing equipment (3- to 20-year lives). Buildings are depreciated over an estimated useful life of 40 years. Estimated useful lives are periodically reviewed and, where appropriate, changes are made prospectively. Where certain events or changes in operating conditions occur, asset lives may be adjusted and an impairment assessment may be performed on the recoverability of the carrying amounts.

The note details P&G's depreciation method (straight-line) and the estimated useful lives of various classes of PPE assets. Later in the notes, the company reports "asset-related costs" of $372 million included in its restructuring charges for the year ended June 30, 2020. The company describes these costs as follows:

Asset-related costs
Asset-related costs consist of both asset write-downs and accelerated depreciation. Asset write-downs relate to the establishment of a new fair value basis for assets held-for-sale or disposal. These assets were written down to the lower of their current carrying basis or amounts expected to be realized upon disposal, less minor disposal costs. Charges for accelerated depreciation relate to long-lived assets that will be taken out of service prior to the end of their normal service period. These assets related primarily to manufacturing consolidations and technology standardization. The asset-related charges will not have a significant impact on future depreciation charges.

A GLOBAL PERSPECTIVE

IFRS

International Financial Reporting Standards (IFRS) are very similar to U.S. GAAP in the recognition of asset values when acquired and in the depreciation methods allowed. However, IFRS requires that companies recognize depreciation separately on the significant components of an asset. So, a U.S. company that acquires a building might recognize a single asset and depreciate it over the expected useful life of the building. An IFRS company would be required to recognize a bundle of assets like the structure, the roof, the elevators, the HVAC system, etc. Each of these components would be depreciated separately over its expected useful life, generally producing a more accelerated depreciation expense.

One implication of this difference is that subsequent expenditures might be dealt with differently. The U.S. company that replaces the HVAC system after its expected fifteen-year life would classify the expenditure as a maintenance expense. But the IFRS company would have fully depreciated the original HVAC system, and the new system would be treated as a capital expenditure, creating a new asset.

Review 8-3 LO8-3

Analyzing the Financial Statement Impacts of Disposals and Impairments

GuidedExample MBC

The following three equipment items were purchased at different points in time but were all sold during the current year. Assume all equipment items have a zero salvage value.

Equipment item	Original Cost	Estimated Useful Life	Life at Date of Sale	Cash Sale Price
101	$ 55,000	5 years	36 months	$22,000
220	$ 80,000	8 years	84 months	$12,500
380	$125,000	10 years	48 months	$68,000

a. Using the financial statement effects template, show how the sale of each equipment item affects the balance sheet and income statement. Assume that the company applies the straight-line depreciation method.

b. Instead, assume that Item #380 was not sold. However, the company examined the equipment for impairment and estimates $73,000 in future cash inflows related to the use of the equipment. The fair value of the equipment is determined to be $68,000. Use the financial statement effects template to show the impact of an impairment (if an impairment is required to be recorded).

c. Prepare journal entries required for parts *a* and *b*.

Solution on p.8-41.

ANALYZING FINANCIAL STATEMENTS

LO8-4 Analyze the effects of tangible assets on key performance measures.

eLecture MBC

Most companies produce their financial performance with their long-term operating assets like property, plant, and equipment and with their intellectual property. Effective use of these assets represents one of the key components of success for companies. In addition, these assets are acquired with the anticipation that they will provide benefits for an extended period of time. They are often expensive relative to their annual benefit, and most of these assets require replenishment on an ongoing basis.

Analysis Objective

We are trying to gauge the effectiveness of Procter & Gamble's use of its physical productive assets.

Analysis Tool PPE Turnover (PPET)

$$\textbf{PPE Turnover (PPET)} = \frac{\textbf{Sales revenue}}{\textbf{Average PPE, net*}}$$

*PPE, net refers to gross PPE less accumulated depreciation.

Applying the PPE Turnover Ratio to Procter & Gamble

$$\textbf{2018:} \quad \frac{66{,}832}{(19{,}893 + 20{,}600)/2} = 3.30$$

$$\textbf{2019:} \quad \frac{67{,}684}{(20{,}600 + 21{,}271)/2} = 3.23$$

$$\textbf{2020:} \quad \frac{70{,}950}{(21{,}271 + 20{,}692)/2} = 3.38$$

Guidance Property, plant, and equipment turnovers vary greatly by industry and are affected by companies' manufacturing strategies, so it is difficult to give specific guidance. In general, a higher ratio is preferred, as it is one significant component of the company's return on assets.

---

[2] See Christensen, Hans B., and Valeri V. Nikolaev, "Does fair value accounting for non-financial assets pass the market test?" *Review of Accounting Studies*, September 2013.

Procter & Gamble in Context

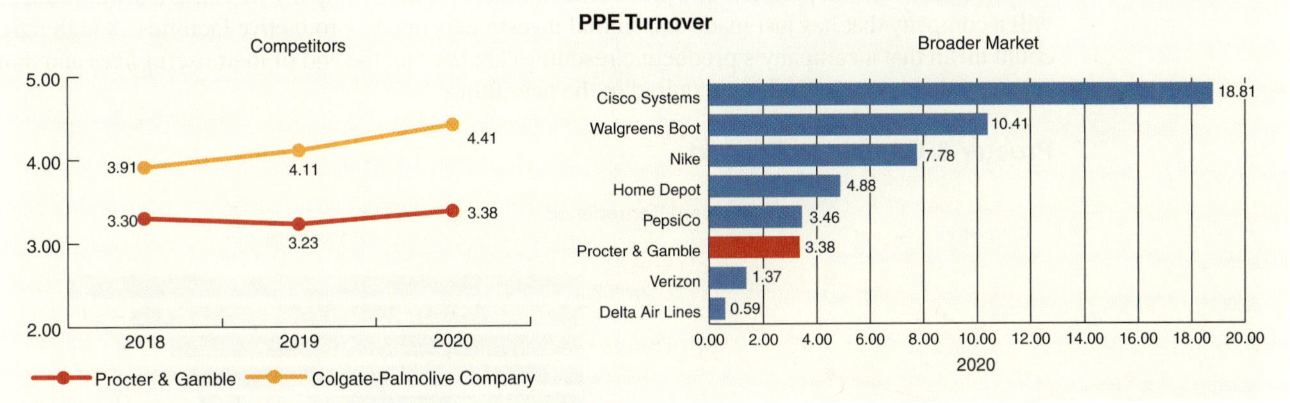

These companies do not have identical fiscal year ends. For each fiscal year listed above and in later charts, fiscal year-end balance sheet dates range from February 2 to December 31.

Takeaways P&G's fiscal 2020 PPET increased slightly from 2019 PPET, but 2019 PPET decreased slightly from 2018 PPET. Companies prefer that PPET be higher rather than lower, because it implies a lower level of capital investment is required to achieve a given level of sales revenue. P&G's PPET is lower than Colgate-Palmolive, though it is higher than a few others in its industry. We can also see that PPET differs considerably by industry—capital-intensive businesses with long-lived assets like Delta Air Lines and Verizon Communications have a low ratio.

Other Considerations Besides effectiveness of asset usage, PPET depends on a number of factors that affect the denominator and that should be taken into account in interpreting the numbers. First, it reflects the company's manufacturing strategy; a company that outsources its production will have a very high PPET, like Nike. Or, a company that has assets that are more fully depreciated will also report a high PPET. In Chapter 12, we discuss how ratios mixing income statement and balance sheet information can be affected by acquisitions of other companies.

Analysis Objective

We are trying to gauge the age of P&G's long-term tangible operating assets relative to their expected useful lives.

Analysis Tool Percent Depreciated

$$\textbf{Percent depreciated} = \frac{\textbf{Accumulated depreciation}}{\textbf{Cost of depreciable assets}}$$

Applying the Percent Depreciated Ratio to Procter & Gamble Accumulated depreciation can be seen in the balance sheet or note disclosures. The original cost of depreciable assets can be found in the same places. (See **Exhibit 8.1** for P&G's presentation.) Two types of property, plant, and equipment are not depreciated. Land is one type, and the other is construction in progress. Land is not depreciated because it has an indefinite life, and construction in progress is not depreciated until the constructed asset is placed in service. For P&G, the $43,771 million original cost of property, plant, and equipment includes $777 million for land and $2,034 million for construction in progress, which must be removed from the denominator.

$$\textbf{2018:}\quad \frac{\$21{,}247}{\$37{,}783} = 56.2\%$$

$$\textbf{2019:}\quad \frac{\$22{,}122}{\$40{,}009} = 55.3\%$$

$$\textbf{2020:}\quad \frac{\$23{,}079}{\$40{,}960} = 56.3\%$$

Guidance Percent depreciated depends on a company's age and on the occurrence of disruptive technological shifts in products and production methods. A new company will have a lower ratio, as will a company that has just made substantial investments in new productive facilities. A high ratio could mean that a company's productive resources are nearing the end of their useful lives and that substantial investments will be required in the near future.[3]

Procter & Gamble in Context

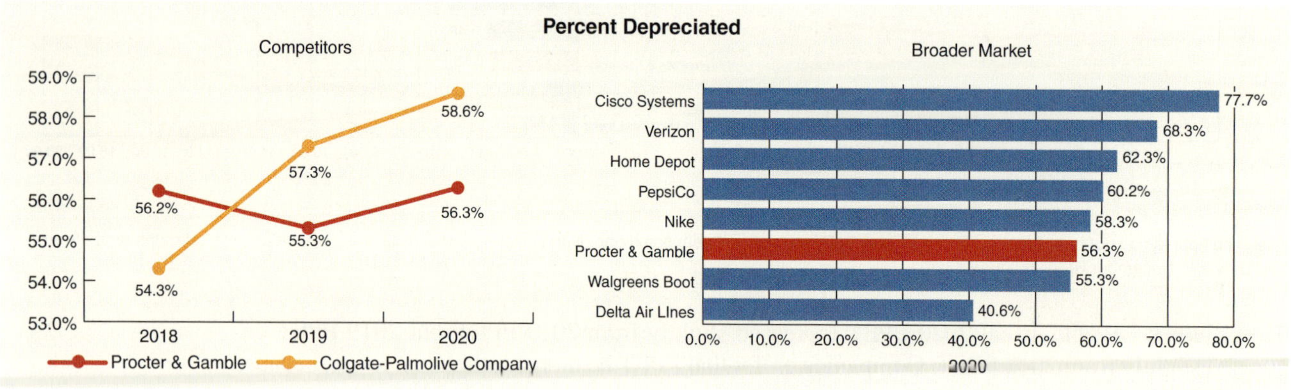

These companies do not have identical fiscal year ends. For each fiscal year listed above and in later charts, fiscal year-end balance sheet dates range from February 2 to December 31.

Takeaways Both Procter & Gamble and Colgate-Palmolive are mature companies experiencing long-term steady growth. They acquire assets on a continuing basis and, as a result, they have some assets that are brand-new and others that are reaching the end of their productive lives. The net result is that the percent depreciated ratio is approximately 54% to 59% for both companies.

Other Considerations Companies' percent depreciated ratio may differ because they are using different depreciation methods (straight-line or accelerated) or because they have chosen different useful lives for their assets. For instance, one airline depreciates its aircraft over twenty-five years to zero salvage value, while another depreciates its aircraft over fifteen years to ten percent salvage. A percent depreciated ratio of 50% for the first company would mean its average aircraft is 12.5 years old, while the same 50% ratio would imply aircraft that was 8.3 years old for the second company. As a result, it is always advisable to check companies' note disclosures to make sure that the ratios are interpreted correctly.

BUSINESS INSIGHT

Federal authorities arrested WorldCom, Inc.'s CEO, Bernie Ebbers, and chief financial officer, Scott Sullivan, in August 2002 for allegedly conspiring to alter the telecommunications giant's financial statements to meet analyst expectations. They were accused of *cooking the books* so the company would not show a loss for 2001 and subsequent quarters.

Specifically, WorldCom incurred large costs in anticipation of an increase in Internet-related business that did not materialize. The executives shifted these costs to the balance sheet and recorded them as PPE, thereby inflating current profitability. By capitalizing these costs (moving them from the income statement to the balance sheet), WorldCom was able to disguise these costs as an asset to be allocated as future costs. Contrary to WorldCom's usual practices and prevailing accounting principles, no support existed for capitalization.

continued

[3] Some companies do not provide complete disclosure for this computation. For example, Cisco Systems combines land and buildings in one line item and thus, an external reader of the statements cannot subtract the book value of land from the denominator to compute the percent depreciated accurately.

continued from previous page

Although the WorldCom case also involved alleged fraud, an astute analyst would have suspected something was amiss from analysis of WorldCom's property, plant, and equipment turnover (Sales/Average property, plant, and equipment) as shown below. The decline in turnover reveals that its assets constituted an ever-increasing percent of total sales during 1995 to 2002, by quarter. This finding does not, in itself, imply fraud. It does, however, raise serious questions that should have been answered by WorldCom executives in meetings with analysts.

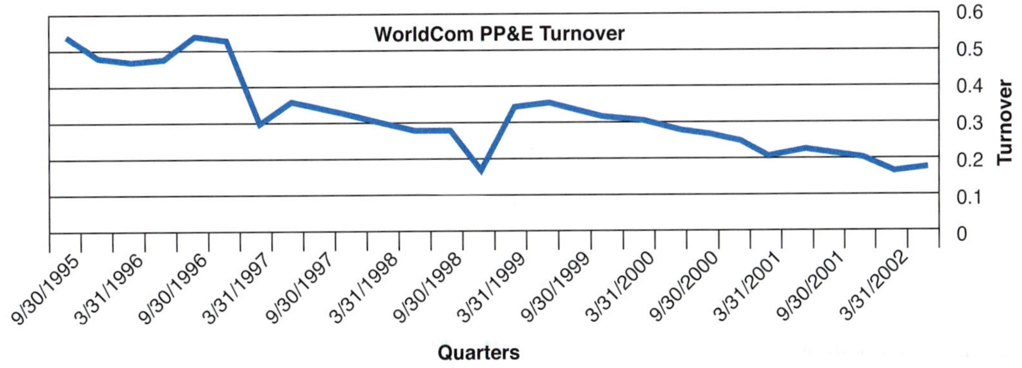

Cash Flow Effects

When cash is involved in the acquisition of plant or equipment, the cash amount is reported as a use of cash in the investment section of the statement of cash flows as discussed in Chapter 4. Any cash received from asset sales is reported as a source of cash. The investing section of Procter & Gamble's 2020 annual report is shown below.

($ millions)	2020
Investing activities.	
Capital expenditures.	$(3,073)
Proceeds from asset sales	30
Acquisitions, net of cash acquired	(58)
Purchases of short-term investments.	—
Proceeds from sales and maturities of investment securities.	6,151
Change in other investments	(5)
Total investing activities	$ 3,045

In 2020, P&G paid cash of $3,073 million to acquire plant assets and received cash of $30 million on the disposal of plant and equipment. The company also received more than $6 billion cash from the maturities and sales of investment securities. Losses (gains) on these disposal transactions would be added (subtracted) as adjustments in the operating section. Acquisitions of other companies cost $58 million in 2020.

For the Dehning Company delivery truck sale described earlier in this chapter, the investing section of the statement of cash flows would show $30,000 of cash proceeds. The gain on the sale would be subtracted from net income in the operating section. No receivable was involved in the sale.

YOU MAKE THE CALL

You Are the Division Manager You are the division manager for a main operating division of your company. You are concerned that a declining PPE turnover is adversely affecting your division's profitability. What specific actions can you take to increase PPE turnover? [Answers on page 8-25]

Review 8-4 LO8-4 Analyzing the Effects of Tangible Assets on Financial Statements

GuidedExample MBC

American Airlines Group, Inc., reported the following information in its annual 10-K reports for the years 2017 to 2020.

	2020	2019	2018	2017
Sales	17,337	45,768	44,541	42,622
Operating property and equipment, net	31,669	34,995	34,098	34,156
Accumulated depreciation	16,757	18,659	17,443	15,646
Operating property and equipment*	47,010	51,980	50,263	48,585

* Amount includes flight equipment and ground property and equipment, but excludes equipment purchase deposits.

a. Compute the PPE turnover for 2020, 2019, and 2018. Comment on the trend over time.

b. Calculate the percentage depreciated of American's depreciable assets at the end of fiscal years 2020, 2019, and 2018. Comment on the trend over time.

Solution on p. 8-42.

INTANGIBLE ASSETS

LO8-5 Describe the accounting and reporting for intangible assets.

eLecture MBC

Intangible assets are assets that lack physical substance but provide future benefits to the owner in the form of specific property rights or legal rights. For many companies, these assets have become an important source of competitive advantage and company value.

For financial accounting purposes, intangible assets are classified as either separately transferable or not separately transferable. Separately transferable intangible assets generally fall into one of two categories. The first category is assets that are the product of contractual or other legal rights. These intangibles include patents, trademarks, copyrights, franchises, license agreements, broadcast rights, mineral rights, and noncompetition agreements. The second category of separately transferable intangible assets includes benefits that are not contractually or legally defined but can be separated from the company and sold, transferred, or exchanged. Examples include customer lists, unpatented technology, formulas, processes, and databases. There are also intangible assets that are not separately transferable, primarily goodwill. Procter & Gamble reports its intangible assets on its 2020 balance sheet in just two categories ($ in millions): Goodwill $39,901; Trademarks and Other Intangible Assets $23,792. A significant portion of these assets resulted from the acquisition of The Gillette Company.

The issues involved in reporting intangible assets are conceptually similar to those of accounting for property, plant, and equipment. We must first decide which costs to capitalize, and then we need to determine how and when those costs will be transferred to the income statement. However, intangible assets often pose a particularly difficult problem for accountants. This problem arises because the benefits provided by these assets are often uncertain and difficult to quantify. In addition, the useful life of an intangible asset is often impossible to estimate with confidence.

As was the case with property, plant, and equipment, intangible assets are either purchased from another individual or company or internally developed. Like PPE assets, the cost of purchased intangible assets is capitalized. Unlike PPE assets, though, we generally do not capitalize the cost of internally developed intangible assets. Research and development (R&D) costs, and the patents and technologies that are created as a result of R&D, serve as useful examples.

Research and Development Costs

R&D activities are a major expenditure for most companies, especially for those in technology and pharmaceutical industries where R&D expenses can exceed 10% of revenues. These expenses include employment costs for R&D personnel, R&D-related contract services, and R&D plant asset costs.

Companies invest millions of dollars in R&D because they expect that the future benefits resulting from these activities will eventually exceed the costs. Successful R&D activities create new products that can be sold and new technologies that can be utilized to create and sustain a competitive advantage. Unfortunately, only a fraction of R&D projects reach commercial production, and it is difficult to predict which projects will be successful. Moreover, it is often difficult to predict when the benefits will be realized, even if the project is successful.

Because of the uncertainty surrounding the benefits of R&D, accounting for R&D activities follows a uniform method—immediate recognition as an expense. This approach applies to all R&D costs incurred prior to the start of commercial production, including the salaries and wages of personnel engaged in R&D activities, the cost of materials and supplies, and the equipment and facilities used in the project. Should any of the R&D activities prove successful, the benefits should result in higher net income in future periods. Costs incurred internally to develop new software products do not satisfy the capitalization requirement of providing expected future profits until the technological feasibility of the product is established. Therefore, until the feasibility requirement can be met, these costs are expensed.

If equipment and facilities are purchased for a specific R&D project and have no other use, their cost is expensed immediately even though their useful life would typically extend beyond the current period. The expensing of R&D equipment and facilities is in stark contrast to the capitalization-and-depreciation of non-R&D plant assets. The expensing of R&D plant assets is mandated unless those assets have alternative future uses (in other R&D projects or otherwise). For example, a general research facility housing multi-use lab equipment should be capitalized and depreciated like any other depreciable asset. However, project-directed research buildings and equipment with no alternate uses must be expensed.

BUSINESS INSIGHT

R&D Costs at Cisco Systems Cisco spends between $6.3 billion and $6.6 billion annually for R&D compared with its revenues of around $49–$52 billion, or about 13%. This level reflects a high percent of revenues devoted to R&D in comparison with nontechnology companies but typifies companies that compete in the high-tech arena. Following is the R&D-expense-to-sales ratio (also called *R&D Intensity*) for Cisco and some related companies.

	2020	2019	2018
Cisco Systems, Inc.	12.87%	12.67%	12.84%
Juniper Networks, Inc.	21.56%	21.50%	21.59%
HP, Inc.	2.61%	2.55%	2.40%

RESEARCH INSIGHT

Research has provided evidence consistent with managers reducing R&D spending when trying to meet certain earnings targets or other earnings goals. Part of this is due to the accounting—research and development costs are expensed immediately, reducing reported earnings in the current period. Thus, although the research and development spending should provide better future performance, it harms current performance leading "myopic" managers to cut back.[4] Recent research also suggests that some firms do not disclose research spending even when it appears that they must have such costs. One theory is that these firms do not want to disclose their research and development spending in order to hide the extent of their costs from their competitors.[5]

Patents

Successful research and development activity often leads a company to obtain a patent for its discoveries. A patent is an exclusive right to produce a product or use a technology. Patents are granted to protect the inventor of the new product or technology by preventing other companies from copying the innovation. The fair value of a patent depends on the commercial success of the product or technology. For example, a patent on the formula for a new drug to treat diabetes could be worth billions of dollars.

[4] See Bushee, Brian, "The Influence of Institutional Investors on Myopic R&D Investment Behavior." *Accounting Review*, 1998; Graham, John R., Cam Harvey and Shiva Rajgopal, "The Economic Implications of Corporate Financial Reporting." *Journal of Accounting and Economics*, 2005; and Sloan, Richard and P. Dechow. "Executive Incentives and the Horizon Problem: An Empirical Investigation," *Journal of Accounting and Economics*, 1991, for examples of research on this topic.

[5] See Koh, P.S., and D. M. Reeb. "Missing R&D," *Journal of Accounting and Economics*, 2015.

If a patent is purchased from the inventor, the purchase price is capitalized and reported in the balance sheet as an intangible asset. On the other hand, if the patent is developed internally, only the legal costs and registration fees are capitalized. The R&D cost to develop the new product or technology is expensed as incurred. This accounting illustrates the marked difference between purchased and internally created intangible assets.

Copyrights

A copyright is an exclusive right granted by the government to an individual author, composer, play writer, or similar individual for the life of the creator plus 70 years. Corporations can also obtain a copyright for varying periods set by law. Copyrights, like patents, can be acquired. The acquisition cost would be capitalized and amortized over the expected remaining economic life.

Trademarks

A trademark is a registered name, logo, package design, image, jingle, or slogan that is associated with a product. Many trademarks are easily recognizable, such as the Nike "swoosh," the shape of a Coca-Cola bottle, McDonald's golden arches, and the musical tones played in computer advertisements featuring Intel computer chips. Companies spend millions of dollars developing and protecting trademarks and their value is enhanced by advertising programs that increase their recognition. If a trademark is purchased from another company, the purchase price is capitalized. However, the cost of internally developed trademarks is expensed as incurred. Likewise, all advertising costs are expensed immediately, even if the value of a trademark is enhanced by the advertisement. For these reasons, many trademarks are not presented in the balance sheet.

BUSINESS INSIGHT

Trademarks and Patents at P&G Procter & Gamble has acquired many of the products it currently markets to consumers. Others were developed internally. The following paragraph from the Management Discussion and Analysis section of P&G's 2020 annual report emphasizes the importance of these intangible assets to the company.

> (Our) trademarks are important to the overall marketing and branding of our products. . . . In part, our success can be attributed to the existence and continued protection of these trademarks, patents, and licenses.

Franchise Rights

A franchise is a contractual agreement that gives a company the right to operate a particular business in an area for a particular period of time. For example, a franchise may give the owner the right to operate a number of fast-food restaurants in a particular geographic region for twenty years. Operating rights and licenses are similar to franchise rights, except that they are typically granted by government agencies. Most franchise rights are purchased and, as a result, the purchase price should be capitalized and presented as an intangible asset in the balance sheet.

Amortization and Impairment of Identifiable Intangible Assets

When intangible assets are acquired and capitalized, a determination must be made as to whether the asset has a definite life. Examples of intangible assets with definite lives include patents and franchise rights. An intangible asset with a definite life must be amortized over the expected useful life of the asset. Amortization is the systematic allocation of the cost of an intangible asset to the periods benefited, similar to depreciation of tangible assets.

Amortization expense is generally recorded using the straight-line method. The expense is included in the income statement as a component of operating income and is often included among selling, general, and administrative expenses. The cost of the intangible asset is presented in the balance sheet net of accumulated amortization.

Amortization To illustrate, assume that Landsman Company spent $100,000 in early 2022 to purchase a patent. The entry to record the capitalization of this cost follows.

ANALYZE

Transaction	Cash Asset	+	Noncash Assets	−	Contra Asset	=	Liabil-ities	+	Contrib. Capital	+	Earned Capital	Revenues	−	Expenses	=	Net Income
(1) Purchased patent.	−100,000 Cash		+100,000 Patent	−		=							−		=	

JOURNALIZE

		Debit	Credit
(1)	Patent (+A)	100,000	
	Cash (−A)		100,000

POST

+ Patent (A) −	
(1) 100,000	

+ Cash (A) −	
	100,000 (1)

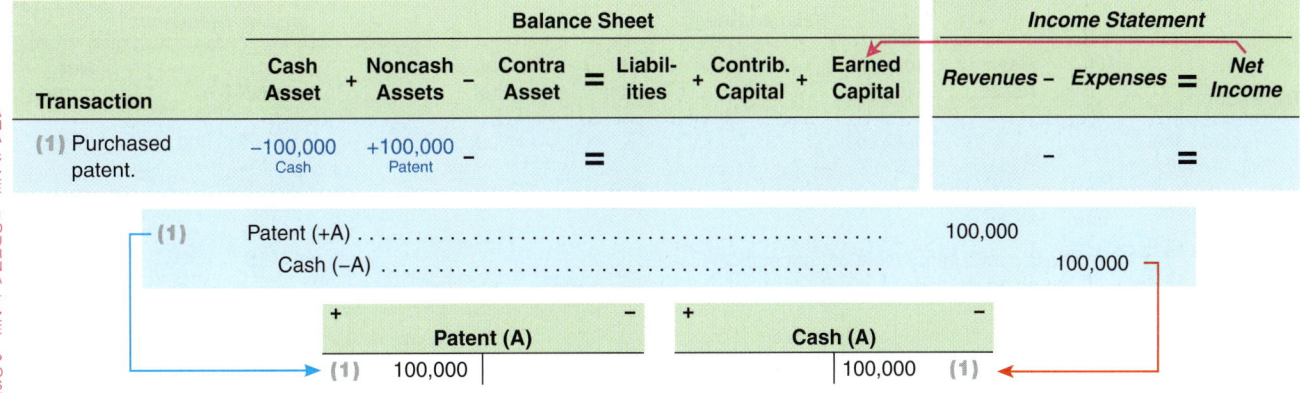

Although the patent had a remaining legal life of 12 years, Landsman estimated that the useful life of the patent was 5 years. Thus, the intangible asset has a definite life. The entry to record the annual amortization expense at the end of 2022 follows.

ANALYZE

Transaction	Cash Asset	+	Noncash Assets	−	Contra Asset	=	Liabil-ities	+	Contrib. Capital	+	Earned Capital	Revenues	−	Expenses	=	Net Income
(2) Record amortization expense.				−	+20,000 Accumulated Amortization	=					−20,000 Retained Earnings		−	+20,000 Amortization Expense	=	−20,000

JOURNALIZE

		Debit	Credit
(2)	Amortization expense (+E, −SE)	20,000	
	Accumulated amortization (+XA, −A)		20,000

POST

+ Amortization Expense (E) −	
(2) 20,000	

− Accumulated Amortization (XA) +	
	20,000 (2)

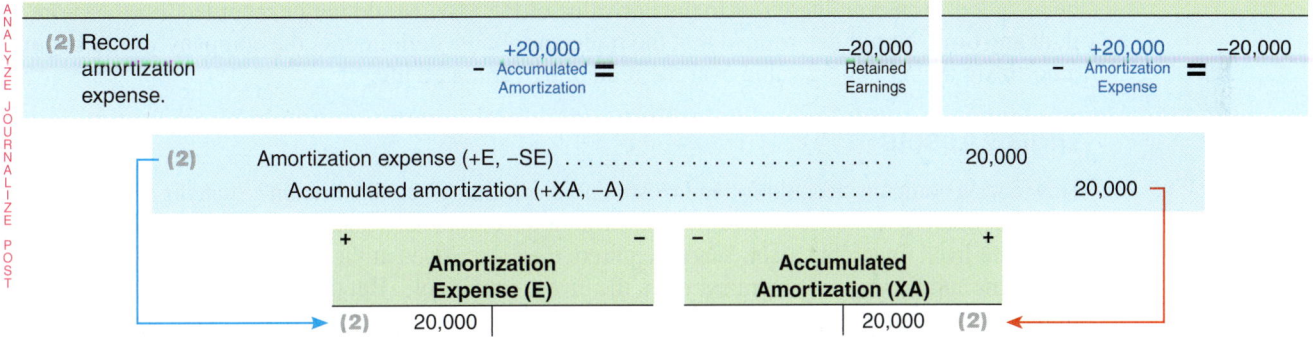

Impairment Some transferable intangible assets, such as some trademarks, have indefinite lives. For these assets, the expected useful life extends far enough into the future that it is impossible for management to estimate a useful life. An intangible asset with an indefinite life should not be amortized until the useful life of the asset can be specified. That is, no expense is recorded until management can reasonably estimate the useful life of the asset.

Although intangible assets with indefinite lives are not subject to amortization, they must be tested annually to determine if their value has been impaired. The impairment test for intangibles is slightly different from the impairment test used to evaluate PPE assets. The intangible asset is impaired if the book value of the asset exceeds its fair value and the write-down is equal to the difference between the book value and the fair value.

To illustrate, assume that Norell Company purchased a trademark in 2020 for $240,000 and determined that the intangible asset had an indefinite life. The entry to record the purchase of the trademark follows.

ANALYZE

Transaction	Cash Asset	+	Noncash Assets	−	Contra Asset	=	Liabil-ities	+	Contrib. Capital	+	Earned Capital	Revenues	−	Expenses	=	Net Income
(1) Purchased trademark for cash.	−240,000 Cash		+240,000 Trademark	−		=							−		=	

JOURNALIZE

		Debit	Credit
(1)	Trademark (+A)	240,000	
	Cash (−A)		240,000

POST

+ Trademark (A) −	
(1) 240,000	

+ Cash (A) −	
	240,000 (1)

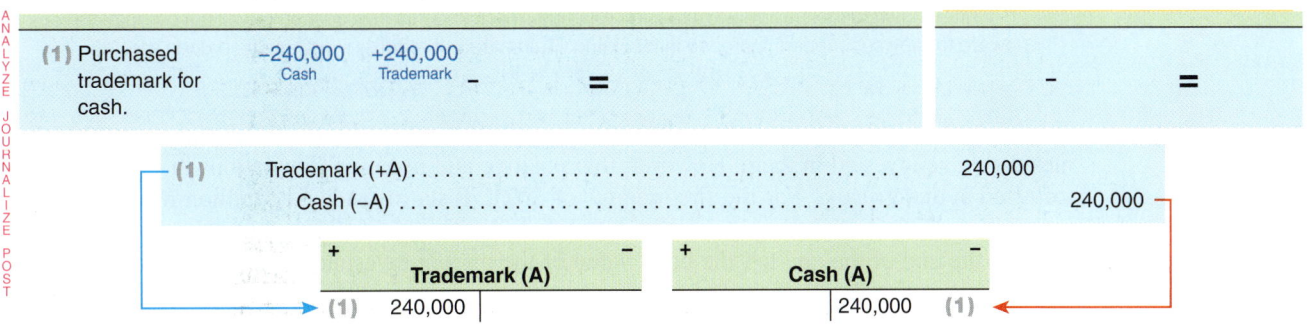

In 2023, changes in regulations caused Norell to conclude that the value of the trademark had been impaired. They estimated the current fair value was $100,000, resulting in a loss of $140,000 ($240,000 – $100,000). The entry to record the impairment of the trademark would be as follows.

ANALYZE

Transaction	Balance Sheet: Cash Asset	+	Noncash Assets	=	Liabilities	+	Contrib. Capital	+	Earned Capital	Income Statement: Revenues	−	Expenses	=	Net Income
(2) Record asset impairment.			−140,000 Trademark	=					−140,000 Retained Earnings		−	+140,000 Loss Due to Impairment	=	−140,000

JOURNALIZE

		Debit	Credit
(2)	Loss due to impairment of trademark (+E, −SE)	140,000	
	Trademark (−A)		140,000

POST

+ Trademark (A) −	
(1) 240,000	
	140,000 (2)

+ Loss Due to Impairment of Trademark (E) −	
(2) 140,000	

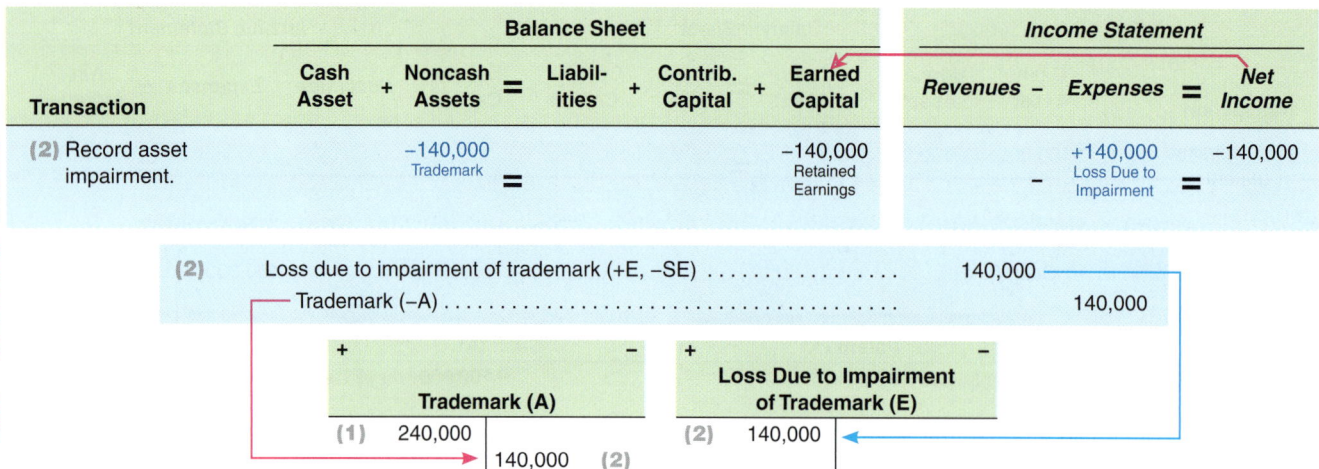

If the value of the trademark subsequently decreases further, additional impairment losses would be recorded. However, increases in the fair value of the asset would not be recorded. Furthermore, if, at any time, Norell determined that the trademark had a definite life, the company would begin amortizing the remaining value over the remaining estimated life.

Digital Assets

How does a company account for an investment in a digital asset, like bitcoin? Such digital assets do not meet the requirements for treatment as cash or as a financial security, so they are considered an indefinite-lived intangible asset. When acquired, they are valued at the cost of acquisition, and realized gains and losses are recognized when the investment is sold. But the asset must be subject to an impairment analysis at the end of a financial reporting period or when there is an indication that the asset has been impaired. It the asset value recovers following an impairment, the asset's book value cannot be written up. The following was reported by **Tesla Inc.** in its March 31, 2021 10-Q.

> During the three months ended March 31, 2021, we purchased an aggregate of $1.50 billion in digital assets, comprised solely of bitcoin. In addition, during the three months ended March 31, 2021, we began accepting bitcoin as a payment for sales of certain of our products in specified regions, subject to applicable laws. . . We currently account for all digital assets held as a result of these transactions as indefinite-lived intangible assets in accordance with ASC 350, Intangibles—Goodwill and Other. We have ownership of and control over our bitcoin and we may use third-party custodial services to secure it. The digital assets are initially recorded at cost and are subsequently remeasured on the consolidated balance sheet at cost, net of any impairment losses incurred since acquisition. . . In determining if an impairment has occurred, we consider the lowest market price of one bitcoin quoted on the active exchange since acquiring the bitcoin. If the then current carrying value of a digital asset exceeds the fair value so determined, an impairment loss has occurred with respect to those digital assets in the amount equal to the difference between their carrying values and the price determined... The impaired digital assets are written down to their fair value at the time of impairment and this new cost basis will not be adjusted upward for any subsequent increase in fair value. Gains are not recorded until realized upon sale(s).

The volatility in digital assets like bitcoin leads to volatility in the financial reports of companies that have invested in them. However, that positive and negative fluctuations in value are not reflected symmetrically. For the first quarter of 2021, Tesla invested $1.5 billion in bitcoin and recognized $27 million of impairment losses and realized gains of $128 million from sales of bitcoin. At the end of the quarter, the book value of the bitcoin investment was $1.33 billion, while the fair value was $2.48 billion, 86% higher.

Goodwill

Goodwill is an intangible asset that is recorded only when one company acquires another company. Goodwill is defined as the excess of the purchase price paid for a company over the fair value of its identifiable net assets (assets minus the liabilities assumed). The identifiable net assets include any identifiable intangible assets acquired in the purchase. Therefore, goodwill can neither be linked to any identifiable source, nor can it be sold or separated from the company. It represents the value of the acquired company above and beyond the specific identifiable assets listed on the balance sheet.

By definition, goodwill has an indefinite life. Once it is recorded in the balance sheet, it is not amortized. Instead, it is subject to an annual impairment test. Goodwill is impaired when the fair value of the acquired business (more specifically, any testable reporting unit) is less than the recorded book value. If this occurs, goodwill is written down to an imputed value. The goodwill write-down (also called a goodwill write-off) results in the immediate transfer of some or all of a company's goodwill book value from the balance sheet to the income statement as an expense. The book value of goodwill is immediately reduced and a corresponding expense is reported in the income statement. Like the impairment write-down of tangible assets, the write-down of goodwill is a discretionary expense whose amount and timing are largely determined by management (with auditor acceptance).

It is commonplace to see goodwill impairment write-downs related to unsuccessful acquisitions, and these usually represent material amounts. For instance, in 2012, Hewlett-Packard wrote down almost $14 billion relating to its 2011 acquisition of Autonomy, a British tech firm, for about $10 billion. Goodwill write downs are usually nonrecurring but are typically reported by companies in income from continuing operations. For analysis purposes, we normally classify them as operating and nonrecurring.

At the time of this writing, the Financial Accounting Standards Board has tentatively decided to require public companies to amortize goodwill over a ten-year period. Such a change would make the accounting for goodwill similar to that of an intangible asset with a definite life, like a patent.

Note Disclosures

The book value of P&G intangible assets is almost 53% of its total asset value in 2020 (refer to **Exhibit 8.1**). In addition to the amount reported in the balance sheet, P&G provides the following in Notes 1 and 2 that more fully describes its intangible asset accounting.

Note 1: Summary of Significant Accounting Policies—
Goodwill and Other Intangible Assets

Goodwill and indefinite-lived intangible assets are not amortized, but are evaluated for impairment annually or more often if indicators of a potential impairment are present. Our annual impairment testing of goodwill is performed separately from our impairment testing of indefinite-lived intangible assets.

We have acquired brands that have been determined to have indefinite lives. We evaluate a number of factors to determine whether an indefinite life is appropriate, including the competitive environment, market share, brand history, underlying product life cycles, operating plans, and the macroeconomic environment of the countries in which the brands are sold.

In addition, when certain events or changes in operating conditions occur, an impairment assessment is performed and indefinite-lived assets may be adjusted to a determinable life.

The cost of intangible assets with determinable useful lives is amortized to reflect the pattern of economic benefits consumed, either on a straight-line or accelerated basis over the estimated periods benefited. Patents, technology, and other intangible assets with contractual terms are generally amortized over their respective legal or contractual lives. Customer relationships, brands, and other non-contractual intangible assets with determinable lives are amortized over periods generally ranging from 5 to 30 years. When certain events or changes in operating conditions occur, an impairment assessment is performed and remaining lives of intangible assets with determinable lives may be adjusted.

Procter & Gamble's largest intangible is goodwill ($39.9 billion). The acquisition of Gillette in 2006 resulted in the recognition of $35.3 billion of goodwill, some of which remains as part of goodwill currently on the balance sheet. P&G paid $53.4 billion for Gillette upon acquisition in 2006, and at the time allocated $29.7 billion to other intangibles.

Note 2: Goodwill and Intangible Assets

Identifiable intangible assets were comprised of:

	2020		2019	
	Gross Carrying Amount	**Accumulated Depreciation**	**Gross Carrying Amount**	**Accumulated Depreciation**
Intangible assets with determinable lives				
Brands	$ 3,820	$ (2,347)	$ 3,836	$ (2,160)
Patents and technology	2,776	(2,513)	2,776	(2,434)
Customer relationships.	1,752	(778)	1,787	(691)
Other.	143	(92)	145	(91)
Total	$ 8,491	$ (5,730)	$ 8,544	$ (5,376)
Brands with indefinite lives	21,031	—	21,047	—
Total	$29,522	$ (5,730)	$29,591	$ (5,376)

There are two observations that we can make from the above disclosures. First, P&G has purchased a significant amount of intangible assets by acquiring other companies. We can infer this from the large amount of goodwill assets reported in the balance sheet. Second, most of P&G's identifiable intangible assets are trademarks, and most have indefinite lives. Hence, we might expect that the amount of amortization expense in any given year would be small, as indicated by the total in the above table. However, goodwill impairment write-offs could be substantial in any given year.

Review 8-5 LO8-5

Accounting for Intangible Assets

GuidedExample MBC

In Year 8, Bowen Company's R&D department developed a new production process that significantly reduced the time and cost required to manufacture its product. R&D costs were $120,000. The process was patented on July 1, Year 8. Legal costs and fees to acquire the patent totaled $12,500. Bowen estimated the useful life of the patent at 10 years.

On July 1, Year 10, Bowen sold the nonexclusive right to use the new process to Kennedy Company for $90,000. Because Bowen retained the patent, the agreement allows Kennedy to use, but not sell, the new technology for a period of 5 years. Both Bowen Company and Kennedy Company have December 31 fiscal years.

On July 1, Year 12, another competitor obtained a patent on a new process that made Bowen's patent obsolete.

Required

a. How should Bowen Company account for the R&D costs? Show the effects of these entries using the financial statement effects template.

b. How should Bowen Company account for legal costs incurred to obtain the patent? Show the effects of these entries using the financial statement effects template.

c. What amount of amortization expense would Bowen record in Year 8? Show the effects of these transactions using the financial statement effects template.

d. How would Kennedy Company record the acquisition of the rights to use the new technology? Show the effects of this transaction using the financial statement effects template.

e. What effect would the new patent registered by the other competitor have on Kennedy Company? Show the effects of this transaction using the financial statement effects template.

f. What effect would the new patent registered by the other competitor have on Bowen Company?

g. Prepare the appropriate journal entries necessary to account for the transactions in parts *a*, *b*, *c*, *d*, and *e* and post the entries to T-accounts.

Solution on p. 8-42.

Analysis Implications

LO8-6 Analyze the effects of intangible assets on key performance measures.

eLecture MBC

Because internally generated intangible assets are not capitalized, an important component of a company's assets is potentially hidden from users of the financial statements. Moreover, differential treatment of purchased and internally created assets makes it difficult to compare companies. If one company generates its patents and trademarks internally, while another company purchases these intangibles, their balance sheets can differ dramatically, even if the two companies are otherwise very similar.

These hidden intangible assets can distort our analysis of the financial statements. For example, when a company expenses R&D costs, especially R&D equipment and facilities that can potentially benefit more than one period, both the income statement and the balance sheet are distorted. Net income, assets, and stockholders' equity are all understated.

The income statement effects may be small if a company regularly purchases R&D assets and the amount of purchases is relatively constant from year to year. Specifically, after the average useful life is reached, say in 5 to 10 years, the expensing of current-year purchases will be approximately the same as the depreciation that would have been reported had the assets been capitalized. Thus, the income statement effect is mitigated. However, the recorded assets and equity are still understated. This accounting produces an upward bias in asset turnover ratios and ROE.

Finally, the statement of cash flows is also affected by the manner in which a company acquires its intellectual assets. A company that generates its patents and trademarks internally recognizes the expenditures as part of cash flow from operating activities. However, a company that purchases its patents and trademarks from an independent party or through acquisitions recognizes the expenditures as part of cash flow from investing activities.

A GLOBAL PERSPECTIVE

IFRS

Under International Financial Reporting Standards, development costs can be capitalized as intangible assets when specific criteria are met. For instance, the company must be able to demonstrate that it has the ability and the intention to complete the development process and to produce an intangible asset that will generate future benefits through use or sale.

Here is an example from GlaxoSmithKline plc's note disclosures:

Research and development

Research and development expenditure is charged to the income statement in the period in which it is incurred. Development expenditure is capitalised when the criteria for recognising an asset are met, usually when a regulatory filing has been made in a major market and approval is considered highly probable. Property, plant, and equipment used for research and development is capitalised and depreciated in accordance with the Group's policy.

Under IFRS, similar to under U.S. GAAP, goodwill must be periodically evaluated for impairment. The overall concepts are very similar between IFRS and GAAP but the details differ. For example, under IFRS companies are required to compare the recoverable amount (defined as the higher of the fair value or value-in-use) of a cash-generating unit to the carrying value of that unit to determine an impairment loss. Just as under U.S. GAAP, once impaired, goodwill cannot be revalued upward. Although, note that this is different from the treatment of PPE under IFRS, as discussed earlier in the chapter.

Analyzing the Effects of Intangible Assets and R&D Expense on the Financial Statements

LO8-6 **Review 8-6**

GuidedExample MBC

Selected income statement data for **Bristol-Myers Squibb Company** and **Pfizer, Inc.**, is presented in the following table:

	2020		2019		2018	
	Bristol-Myers Squibb	Pfizer	Bristol-Myers Squibb	Pfizer	Bristol-Myers Squibb	Pfizer
Sales revenue	$ 42,518	$ 41,908	$ 26,145	$ 41,172	$21,581	$ 40,825
R&D	11,143	9,405	4,871	8,394	4,551	7,760
Other intangible assets	53,243	28,471	63,969	33,936	1,091	35,211
Total assets	118,481	154,229	129,944	167,594	34,986	159,422

a. Compute the percent of net sales that Bristol-Myers Squibb Company and Pfizer, Inc., spent on research and development (R&D) for years 2018, 2019, and 2020.

b. Compute the percent of other intangible assets of total assets for Bristol-Myers Squibb Company and Pfizer, Inc., for years 2018, 2019, and 2020.

c. Comment on any significant trends.

Solution on p. 8-44.

SUMMARY

LO8-1 **Determine which costs to capitalize and report as tangible assets and which costs to expense. (p. 8-3)**

- Tangible assets, including land, buildings, machinery, and equipment, are assets with physical substance and are usually classified as property, plant, and equipment.
- All costs incurred to acquire an asset and prepare it for its intended use should be capitalized and reported in the balance sheet.
- The cost of self-constructed assets should include all costs incurred during construction, including the interest cost of financing the construction.

LO8-2 **Apply different depreciation methods to allocate the cost of assets over time. (p. 8-5)**

- Depreciation methods generally fall into three categories:
  (1) Straight-line depreciation
  (2) Accelerated depreciation, such as the double-declining-balance method
  (3) Units-of-production method

LO8-3 **Determine the effects of asset sales and impairments on financial statements. (p. 8-10)**

- The sale of a long-term asset will result in a gain or loss if the proceeds from the sale are greater than or less than the book value of the asset.
- If the expected benefits (undiscounted cash flows) derived from an asset fall below its book value, the asset is impaired and should be written down to fair value.

LO8-4 **Analyze the effects of tangible assets on key performance measures. (p. 8-13)**

- PPE turnover and long-term asset turnover ratios provide insights into the capital intensity of a company and how efficiently the company is utilizing these investments.
- The ratio of accumulated depreciation divided by the cost of depreciable assets measures the percent depreciated.

LO8-5 **Describe the accounting and reporting for intangible assets. (p. 8-17)**

- Intangible assets are long-term assets lacking in physical substance, such as patents, trademarks, franchise rights, and goodwill.
- For the most part, internally generated intangible assets are not recognized in the balance sheet.
- Intangible assets purchased from other companies are capitalized and presented separately in the balance sheet.
- Intangible assets with definite lives are amortized using the straight-line method.
- Intangible assets with indefinite lives are not amortized, but are checked for impairment.
- Digital assets like cryptocurrencies are treated as intangible assets with indefinite lives.

LO8-6 **Analyze the effects of intangible assets on key performance measures. (p. 8-23)**

- Differential treatment of purchased intangibles and internally generated assets affects financial statement analysis.

GUIDANCE ANSWERS . . . YOU MAKE THE CALL

You are the Company Accountant Any cost that is necessary in order to bring an asset into service should be capitalized as a part of the cost of the asset. In this case, your company cannot build an office building on this property until the oil well is properly capped. Therefore, the $40,000 cost of capping the oil well should be capitalized as part of the cost of the land.

You are the Division Manager To increase PPE turnover one must either increase sales or reduce PPE assets. The first step is to identify unproductive or inefficiently utilized assets. Unnecessary assets can be sold, and some processes can be outsourced. Also, by reducing downtime, effective maintenance practices will increase asset productivity.

KEY RATIOS

$$\text{PPE Turnover (PPET)} = \frac{\text{Sales revenue}}{\text{Average PPE, net}} \qquad \text{Percent depreciated} = \frac{\text{Accumulated depreciation}}{\text{Cost of depreciable assets}}$$

Assignments with the MBC logo in the margin are available in myBusinessCourse. See the Preface of the book for details.

MULTIPLE CHOICE

1. Burgstahler Corporation bought a lot to construct a new corporate office building. An older building on the lot was razed immediately so that the office building could be constructed. The cost of razing the older building should be
   a. recorded as part of the cost of the land.
   b. written off as a loss in the year of purchase.
   c. written off as an extraordinary item in the year of purchase.
   d. recorded as part of the cost of the new building.

2. The purpose of recording periodic depreciation of long-term PPE assets is to
   a. report declining asset values on the balance sheet.
   b. allocate asset costs over the periods benefited by use of the assets.
   c. account for costs to reflect the change in general price levels.
   d. set aside funds to replace assets when their economic usefulness expires.

3. When the estimate of an asset's useful life is changed,
   a. depreciation expense for all past periods must be recalculated.
   b. there is no change in the amount of depreciation expense recorded for future years.
   c. only depreciation expense for current and future years is affected.
   d. only depreciation expense in the current year is affected.

4. If the sale of a depreciable asset results in a loss, the proceeds from the sale were
   a. less than current fair value.
   b. greater than cost.
   c. greater than book value.
   d. less than book value.

5. Which of the following principles best describes the current method of accounting for research and development costs?
   a. Revenue recognition method
   b. Systematic and rational allocation
   c. Immediate recognition as an expense
   d. Income tax minimization

6. Goodwill should be recorded in the balance sheet as an intangible asset only when
   a. it is sold to another company.
   b. it is acquired through the purchase of another business.
   c. a company reports above-normal earnings for five or more consecutive years.
   d. it can be established that a definite benefit or advantage has resulted from some item such as an excellent reputation for service.

Multiple Choice Answers
1. a 2. b 3. c 4. d 5. c 6. b

QUESTIONS

Q8-1. How should companies account for costs, such as maintenance or improvements, which are incurred after an asset is acquired?

Q8-2. What is the effect of capitalized interest on the income statement in the period that an asset is constructed? What is the effect in future periods?

Q8-3. Why is the recognition of depreciation expense necessary for proper expense recognition?

Q8-4. Why do companies use accelerated depreciation for income tax purposes, when the total depreciation taken over the asset's useful life is identical to straight-line depreciation?

Q8-5. How should a company treat a change in an asset's estimated useful life or residual value? Which period(s)—past, present, or future—is affected by this change?

Q8-6. What factors determine the gain or loss from the sale of a long-term operating asset?

Q8-7. When is a PPE asset considered to be impaired? How is the impairment loss determined?

Q8-8. What is the proper accounting treatment for research and development costs? Why are R&D costs not capitalized under GAAP?

Q8-9. Why are some intangible assets amortized while others are not? What is meant by an intangible asset with an "indefinite life"?

Q8-10. Under what circumstances should a company report goodwill in its balance sheet? What is the effect of goodwill on the income statement?

DATA ANALYTICS

LO8-1 Data Analytics MBC

DA8-1. Preparing an Excel Visualization of Property and Equipment Components Over Time

The Excel file associated with this exercise includes information regarding Fastenal Company's disclosures on its property and equipment in its Form 10-Ks over a six-year period. For this exercise, we analyze the changes in the composition of property and equipment over time.

REQUIRED

1. Download Excel file DA8-1 found in myBusinessCourse.
2. Create a Stacked Area chart showing the gross balances (before accumulated depreciation) of its property and equipment accounts. *Hint:* Highlight your data and open the Insert tab. Click Recommended Charts in the Charts group. Open the All Charts tab and click Area. Select the Stacked Area chart.
3. Answer the following questions based on the visualization.
   a. In which two years did total property and equipment rise at a slightly faster pace than the other years shown?
   b. From Year 1 to Year 6, which category of property and equipment showed the most growth?
   c. Which category of property and equipment appeared to drop (in proportion to the other categories) from Year 1 to Year 6?
   d. What is the largest category of property and equipment in Year 6?
4. Create two Pie charts, one for Year 1, and one for Year 6, showing gross balances (before accumulated depreciation) of property and equipment accounts.
5. If necessary, add chart titles to state the year. *Hint:* Click inside the chart and open the Chart Design tab. Click Add Chart Element in the Charts Layout group and select Chart Title.
6. Add data labels to the pie charts and edit data labels to only show percentages and not values. *Hint:* Right-click inside the pie and select Format Data Labels. Select Percentages under Label Options in the sidebar. Deselect Value, if necessary.
7. Answer the following questions based on the visualization.
   a. Which component has the highest proportion in Year 1? What is the percentage?
   b. Which component has the highest proportion in Year 6? What is the percentage?
   c. Which component had the greatest increase in proportion of the total from Year 1 to Year 6? What was the percentage difference?
   d. Which component had the greatest decrease in proportion from Year 1 to Year 6? What was the percentage difference?
   e. Which components showed a 2% or less difference in proportion of the total between Year 1 and Year 6?

LO8-2 Data Analytics MBC

DA8-2. Determining the Method Used to Produce a Depreciation Visualization

The Excel file associated with this exercise includes four charts depicting depreciation under four different methods over the life of a fixed asset with a useful life of five years. In this exercise, we match each depreciation method provided to the appropriate depreciation chart based upon the trend in depreciation over the five-year period.

REQUIRED

1. Download Excel file DA8-2 found in myBusinessCourse.
2. Calculate the fixed asset's original cost if the residual value of the asset is $5,000.
3. Match each of the charts with the depreciation method used: straight-line, sum-of-the-years'-digits, declining-balance, or units-of-production methods.
4. Indicate which chart(s) can be prepared upon purchase of the fixed asset and which chart(s) can only be prepared over time.

LO8-4 Data Analytics MBC

DA8-3. Using Excel Visualizations to Analyze Property and Equipment

The Excel file associated with this exercise includes data for Delta Air Lines, Inc., as reported in its Form 10-K reports over a 10-year period. The percent depreciated of depreciable fixed assets measures the age of the assets compared to useful life. A company that has made substantial investments in new fixed assets will have a lower ratio compared to a company with fixed assets nearing the end of their useful life. In this exercise, we review the trend of percent depreciated of gross property and equipment for Delta Airlines over a 10-year period.

REQUIRED

1. Download Excel file DA8-3 found in myBusinessCourse.
2. Compute the ratio of accumulated depreciation to gross property and equipment for each year. Assume all assets are depreciable.
3. Prepare the following three charts in Excel.
   - Chart 1: A bar chart showing accumulated depreciation and gross property and equipment per year over the 10-year period.
   - Chart 2: A line chart showing property and equipment additions over the 10-year period, with the earliest year on the left hand side. *Hint:* To reverse the order of the years, right-click inside the horizontal axis. A Format Axis sidebar will appear. Open the bar chart icon tab. Click Categories in reverse order under Axis options.
   - Chart 3: A line chart showing the ratio of accumulated depreciation to gross property and equipment over the 10-year period.
4. Answer the following questions based on your visualizations.
   a. In Chart 1, in what year(s) was the trend of increasing values not evident in the chart?
   b. In Chart 2, what year(s) showed a drop in property and equipment additions?
   c. In Chart 2, what year showed the most significant change?
   d. Describe the trend shown in Chart 3.
   e. What is the likely cause of the increase shown in Year 10 in Chart 3.

Percent Depreciated

$$\frac{\text{Accumulated depreciation}}{\text{Cost of depreciable asset}}$$

DA8-4. Using Excel Visualizations to Analyze Research & Development Expense Trends

LO8-6

Homework MBC · Data Analytics

The Excel file associated with this exercise includes six years of financial information including research and development (R&D) expense and sales for seven companies in the Health sector. In this exercise, we analyze trends of the ratio of R&D to total sales. An increase in the ratio means that a higher portion of sales was devoted to R&D activities for the period.

REQUIRED

1. Download Excel file DA8-4 found in myBusinessCourse.
2. Calculate in Excel, R&D expense as a percentage of sales for six years for each of the following companies: **Abbott Laboratories**, **Baxter International, Inc.**, **Bristol-Myers Squibb Co.**, **Boston Scientific Corp.**, **Johnson & Johnson**, **Merck & Co.**, and **Pfizer Inc.**
3. Prepare a line chart in Excel showing the trend of R&D expense as a percentage of sales over the six-year period. *Hint:* The vertical axis should be percentages; the horizontal axis should be Year. The series (lines) should be the seven companies. To edit the chart, open the Chart Design Tab and click Select Data. You may need to switch rows/columns.
4. Describe the trend in the chart for each company. *Hint:* Review the trend but also notice the beginning and ending point of your line chart.
5. Indicate which two companies showed the most growth in research as a percentage of sales over the six-year period.

R&D Expense to Sales

$$\frac{\text{R\&D Expense}}{\text{Total Sales}}$$

DATA VISUALIZATION

Data Visualization Activities are available in myBusinessCourse. These assignments use Tableau Dashboards to expose students to visual depictions of data and introduce students to data analytics through data visualizations. These exercises are easily assignable and auto graded by MBC.

Data Visualization

MINI EXERCISES

M8-11. Determining Whether to Capitalize or Expense

LO8-1

Homework MBC

For each of the following items, indicate whether the cost should be capitalized or expensed immediately:

a. Paid $600 for routine maintenance of machinery
b. Paid $2,700 to rent equipment for two years
c. Paid $1,000 to equip the production line with new instruments that measure quality
d. Paid $10,000 to repair the roof on the building
e. Paid $800 to refurbish a machine, thereby extending its useful life
f. Purchased a patent for $2,500

LO8-2 Homework MBC

M8-12. Computing Depreciation Under Straight-Line and Double-Declining-Balance

A delivery van costing $27,000 is expected to have a $2,000 salvage value at the end of its useful life of 5 years. Assume that the truck was purchased on January 1, Year 1. Compute the depreciation expense for Year 1 and Year 2 under each of the following depreciation methods:

a. Straight-line

b. Double-declining-balance

LO8-2 Homework MBC

M8-13. Computing Depreciation Under Alternative Methods

Equipment costing $195,000 is expected to have a residual value of $15,000 at the end of its six-year useful life. The equipment is metered so that the number of units processed is counted. The equipment is designed to process 1,500,000 units in its lifetime. In Year 1 and Year 2, the equipment processed 280,000 units and 205,000 units respectively. Calculate the depreciation expense for Year 1 and Year 2 using each of the following methods:

a. Straight-line

b. Double-declining-balance

c. Units of production

LO8-3 Homework MBC

M8-14. Recording the Sale of PPE Assets (FSET)

As part of a renovation of its showroom, O'Keefe Auto Dealership sold furniture and fixtures that were eight years old for $6,000 in cash. The assets had been purchased for $65,000 and had been depreciated using the straight-line method with no residual value and a useful life of ten years.

Show how the sale of the furniture and fixtures affects the balance sheet and income statement using the financial statement effects template.

LO8-3 Homework MBC

M8-15. Recording the Sale of PPE Assets

Using the information from M8-14, prepare a journal entry to record the sale of furniture and fixtures.

LO8-3 Homework MBC

M8-16. Recording the Sale of PPE Assets (FSET)

Gaver Company sold machinery that had originally cost $165,000 for $55,000 in cash. The machinery was three years old and had been depreciated using the double-declining-balance method assuming a five-year useful life and a residual value of $11,000.

Using the financial statement effects template, show how the sale of the machinery affects the balance sheet and income statement.

LO8-3 Homework MBC

M8-17. Recording the Sale of PPE Assets

Using the information from M8-16, prepare a journal entry to record the sale of furniture and fixtures.

LO8-2 Homework MBC

M8-18. Computing Depreciation Under Straight-Line and Double-Declining-Balance for Partial Years

A machine costing $218,700 is purchased on May 1, Year 1. The machine is expected to be obsolete after three years (36 months) and, thereafter, no longer useful to the company. The estimated salvage value is $8,100. Compute depreciation expense for both Year 1 and Year 2 under each of the following depreciation methods:

a. Straight-line

b. Double-declining-balance

LO8-5

Siemens AG
NYSE :: SI

M8-19. Accounting for Research and Development Under IFRS

The following information on Siemens AG's treatment of research and development is extracted from its 2020 financial statements. Siemens AG is an integrated technology company with activities in the fields of industry, energy, and healthcare. The company is incorporated under the laws of Germany and reports using International Financial Reporting Standards (IFRS).

> **Research and development costs**—Costs of research activities are expensed as incurred. Costs of development activities are capitalized when the recognition criteria in IAS 38 are met. Capitalized development costs are stated at cost less accumulated amortization and impairment losses with an amortization period of generally three to ten years.

a. How does the reporting under IFRS differ from reporting under U.S. GAAP for research and development?

b. At year-end September 30, 2020, Siemens had a gross carrying amount of Other Intangible Assets of $13.1 billion Euros and accumulated amortization and impairment related to those assets of $8.3 billion Euros. Should the amounts capitalized be tested annually for impairment?

LO8-2 Homework MBC

M8-20. Computing Double-Declining-Balance Depreciation

DeFond Company purchased equipment for $70,000. For each of the following sets of assumptions, prepare a depreciation schedule (all years) for this equipment assuming that DeFond uses the double-declining-balance depreciation method.

Useful Life	Residual Value
a. Four years	$11,200
b. Five years	4,200
c. Ten years	1,400

M8-21. Computing and Recording Depletion (FSET)

LO8-2

Homework MBC

The Nelson Oil Company estimated that the oil reserve that it acquired during the year would produce 4.8 million barrels of oil. The company extracted 360,000 barrels the first year, 600,000 barrels the second year, and 720,000 barrels the third year. Nelson paid $40,800,000 for the oil reserve.

a. Compute depletion for each year—Year 1, Year 2, and Year 3.

b. Using the financial statement effects template, report the (i) acquisition of the oil reserve and (ii) depletion for the year.

M8-22. Computing and Recording Depletion

LO8-2

Homework MBC

Use the information from M8-21 to complete the following.

a. Prepare the journal entries to record (i) the acquisition of the oil reserve and (ii) the depletion for the year.

b. Open T-accounts and post the entries in the accounts.

M8-23. Computing and Comparing PPE Turnover for Two Companies

LO8-4

Homework MBC

Texas Instruments Incorporated
NYSE :: TXN
Intel Corporation
NASDAQ :: INTC

Texas Instruments Incorporated and Intel Corporation report the following information:

	Texas Instruments		Intel Corp	
($ millions)	Sales	PPE, Net	Sales	PPE, Net
2020	$14,461	$3,269	$77,867	$56,584
2019	14,383	3,303	71,965	55,386

a. Compute the 2020 PPE turnover for both companies. Comment on any difference you observe.

b. Discuss ways in which high-tech manufacturing companies like these can increase their PPE turnover.

M8-24. Assessing Research and Development Expenses

LO8-5, 6

Homework MBC

Abbott Laboratories
NYSE :: ABT

Abbott Laboratories reports the following income statement (in partial form):

Year Ended December 31 ($ millions)	2020
Net sales	$34,608
Cost of products sold	15,003
Amortization of intangible assets	2,132
Research and development*	2,420
Selling, general, and administrative	9,696
Total operating cost and expenses	29,251
Operating earnings	$ 5,357

* including acquired in-process and collaborations R&D

a. Compute the percent of net sales that Abbott Laboratories spends on research and development (R&D). How would you assess the appropriateness of its R&D expense level?

b. Using the financial statement effects template, describe how the accounting for R&D expenditures affects Abbott Laboratories' balance sheet and income statement.

EXERCISES

E8-25. Recording Asset Acquisition, Depreciation, and Disposal (FSET)

LO8-1, 2, 3

Homework MBC

On January 2, Year 1, Verdi Company acquired a machine for $240,000. In addition to the purchase price, Verdi spent $5,000 for shipping and installation, and $7,000 to calibrate the machine prior to use. The company estimates that the machine has a useful life of five years and residual value of $19,500.

a. Using the financial statement effects template, report the acquisition of the machine.

b. Calculate the annual depreciation expense using straight-line depreciation. Using the financial statement effects template, show how annual depreciation in the first year affects the balance sheet and income statement.

c. On December 31, Year 4, Verdi sold the machine to another company for $35,000. Using the financial statement effects template, show how the sale of the machinery affects the balance sheet and income statement.

LO8-1, 2, 3 Homework MBC

E8-26. Recording Asset Acquisition, Depreciation, and Disposal
Using the information from E8-25, prepare journal entries for parts *a*, *b*, and *c*.

LO8-2 Homework MBC

E8-27. Computing Straight-Line and Double-Declining-Balance Depreciation
On January 2, Haskins Company purchased a laser cutting machine for use in fabrication of a part for one of its key products. The machine cost $64,000, and its estimated useful life is five years, after which the expected salvage value is $4,000. Compute depreciation expense for each year of the machine's useful life under each of the following depreciation methods:

a. Straight-line
b. Double-declining-balance

LO8-2, 3 Homework MBC

E8-28. Computing Depreciation, Asset Book Value, and Gain or Loss on Asset Sale (FSET)
Sloan Company uses its own executive charter plane that originally cost $1.2 million. It has recorded straight-line depreciation on the plane for six full years, with an $120,000 expected salvage value at the end of its estimated 10-year useful life. Sloan disposes of the plane at the end of the sixth year.

a. At the disposal date, what is the (1) accumulated depreciation and (2) net book value of the plane?
b. Using the financial statement effects template, show how the disposal of the plane affects the balance sheet and income statement, assuming that the sales price is
1. Cash equal to the book value of the plane.
2. $300,000 cash.
3. $900,000 cash.

LO8-2, 3 Homework MBC

E8-29. Computing Depreciation, Asset Book Value, and Gain or Loss on Asset Sale
Using the information from E8-28, prepare journal entries for the three scenarios in part *b*.

LO8-2 Homework MBC

E8-30. Computing Straight-Line and Double-Declining-Balance Depreciation
On January 2, Dechow Company purchased a machine to help manufacture a part for one of its key products. The machine cost $196,830 and is estimated to have a useful life of six years, with an expected salvage value of $21,060.

Compute each year's depreciation expense for the first and second year for each of the following depreciation methods.

a. Straight-line
b. Double-declining-balance

LO8-2, 3 Homework MBC

E8-31. Computing Depreciation, Asset Book Value, and Gain or Loss on Asset Sale
Palepu Company owns and operates a delivery van that originally cost $54,400. Straight-line depreciation on the van has been recorded for three years, with a $4,000 expected salvage value at the end of its estimated six-year useful life. Depreciation was last recorded at the end of the third year, at which time Palepu disposed of this van.

a. Compute the net book value of the van on the sale date.
b. Compute the gain or loss on sale of the van if its sales price is for:
1. Cash equal to book value of van.
2. $30,000 cash.
3. $24,000 cash.

LO8-2 Homework MBC

E8-32. Computing Depreciation and Accounting for a Change of Estimate
Lambert Company acquired machinery costing $88,000 on January 2. At that time, Lambert estimated that the useful life of the equipment was 6 years and that the residual value would be $12,000 at the end of its useful life. Compute depreciation expense for this asset for the first, second, and third year using the

a. straight-line method.
b. double-declining-balance method.
c. Assume that on January 2 of the third year, Lambert revised its estimate of the useful life to 7 years and changed its estimate of the residual value to $8,000. What effect would this have on depreciation expense in the third year for each of the above depreciation methods?

LO8-2 Homework MBC

E8-33. Computing Depreciation and Accounting for a Change of Estimate
In January, Rankine Company paid $10,200,000 for land and a building. An appraisal estimated that the land had a fair value of $3,000,000 and the building was worth $7,200,000. Rankine estimated that the useful life of the building was 30 years, with no residual value.

a. Calculate annual depreciation expense using the straight-line method.

b. Calculate depreciation for the first and second year using the double-declining-balance method.

c. Assume that in the third year, Rankine changed its estimate of the useful life of the building to 25 years. If the company is using the double-declining-balance method of depreciation, what amount of depreciation expense would Rankine record in the third year?

E8-34. Estimating the Percent Depreciated

LO8-4 Homework MBC

Deere & Company NYSE :: DE

The property and equipment note disclosure from the Deere & Company balance sheet follows ($ millions):

PROPERTY AND DEPRECIATION

A summary of property and equipment at November 1, 2020, in millions of dollars follows:

	2020
Land	$ 282
Buildings and building equipment	4,114
Machinery and equipment	5,936
Dies, patterns, tools, etc.	1,662
All other	1,115
Construction in progress	440
Total at cost	13,549
Less accumulated depreciation	7,771
Property and equipment—net	$ 5,778

During 2020, the company reported $800 million of depreciation expense.

Estimate the percent depreciated of Deere's depreciable assets. How do you interpret this figure?

E8-35. Computing and Evaluating Receivables, Inventory, and PPE Turnovers

LO8-6 Homework MBC

3M Company NYSE :: MMM

3M Company reports the following financial statement amounts in its 10-K report:

($ millions)	Sales	Cost of Sales	Receivables	Inventories	PPE, Net
2020	$32,184	$16,605	$4,705	$4,239	$9,421
2019	32,136	17,136	4,791	4,134	9,333
2018	32,765	16,682	5,020	4,366	8,738

a. Compute the receivables, inventory, and PPE turnover ratios for both 2020 and 2019. (Receivables turnover and inventory turnover are discussed in Chapters 6 and 7, respectively.)

b. What changes are evident in the turnover rates of 3M for these years? Discuss ways in which a company such as 3M can improve its turnover within each of these three areas.

E8-36. Identifying and Accounting for Intangible Assets

LO8-5 Homework MBC

On the first day of the year, Holthausen Company acquired the assets of Leftwich Company, including several intangible assets. These include a patent on Leftwich's primary product, a device called a plentiscope. Leftwich carried the patent on its books for $2,100, but Holthausen believes that the fair value is $280,000. The patent expires in seven years, but competitors can be expected to develop competing patents within three years. Holthausen believes that, with expected technological improvements, the product is marketable for at least 20 years.

The registration of the trademark for the Leftwich name is scheduled to expire in 15 years. However, the Leftwich brand name, which Holthausen believes is worth $700,000, could be applied to related products for many years beyond that.

As part of the acquisition, Leftwich's principal researcher left the company. As part of the acquisition, he signed a five-year noncompetition agreement that prevents him from developing competing products. Holthausen paid the scientist $420,000 to sign the agreement.

a. What amount should be capitalized for each of the identifiable intangible assets?

b. What amount of amortization expense should Holthausen record the first year for each asset?

E8-37. Accounting for Digital Assets

LO8-5 Homework MBC

Square, Inc. NYSE :: SQ

As of the end of its fiscal year, December 31, 2020, Square, Inc., reported an investment in bitcoin valued at $50 million. During the first quarter of 2021, Square made a further investment of $170 million. During the first quarter of 2021, the company "recorded an impairment charge of $19.9 million in the three months ended March 31, 2021 due to the observed market price of bitcoin decreasing below the carrying value during the period."

According to its statement of cash flows for the period, Square, Inc., did not sell off any of its investment in bitcoin during the first quarter of 2021.

REQUIRED

a. What will be the balance of Square's bitcoin investment on March 31, 2021?

b. Square reports that the impairment occurred "during the period" when the market price dropped below the carrying value. At the end of the quarter, the fair value of the bitcoin asset was $472.0 million. How would that affect your answer to part *a*? Why?

LO8-2 Homework MBC

E8-38. Computing and Recording Depletion Expense (FSET)

During the year, Eldenburg Mining Company purchased land for $9,000,000 that had a natural resource reserve estimated to be 625,000 tons. Development and road construction costs on the land were $525,000, and a building was constructed at a cost of $62,500. When the natural resources are completely extracted, the land has an estimated residual value of $1,500,000. In addition, the cost to restore the property to comply with environmental regulations is estimated to be $1,000,000. Production in the first and second year was 75,000 tons and 106,250 tons, respectively.

a. Compute the depletion charge for the first and second year.

b. Using the financial statement effects template, report each year's depletion as determined in part *a*.

LO8-2 Homework MBC

E8-39. Computing and Recording Depletion

Using the information from E8-38, prepare journal entries to record each year's depletion.

LO8-4 Homework MBC

Tesla, Inc.: NASDAQ :: ADGF

E8-40. Computing and Interpreting Percent Depreciated and PPE Turnover

The following disclosure is from Note 8 to the 2020 10-K of Tesla, Inc.:

Note 8—Property, Plant and Equipment, Net

Our property, plant, and equipment, net, consisted of the following (in millions):

	Dec. 31, 2020	Dec. 31, 2019
Machinery, equipment, vehicles, and office furniture . . .	$ 8,493	$ 7,167
Tooling . . .	1,811	1,493
Leasehold improvements . . .	1,421	1,087
Land and buildings . . .	3,662	3,024
Computer equipment, hardware and software . . .	856	595
Construction in progress. . .	1,621	764
	17,864	14,130
Less: Accumulated depreciation. . .	(5,117)	(3,734)
Total . . .	$12,747	$10,396

The summary of significant accounting policies included the following description of Tesla's depreciation policies:

Property, plant, and equipment, net, including leasehold improvements, are recognized at cost less accumulated depreciation. Depreciation is generally computed using the straight-line method over the estimated useful lives of the respective assets, as follows:

Machinery, equipment, vehicles, and office furniture . . .	2 to 12 years
Building and building improvements. . .	15 to 30 years
Computer equipment and software . . .	3 to 10 years

Leasehold improvements are depreciated on a straight-line basis over the shorter of their estimated useful lives or the terms of the related leases.

a. Tesla's revenue totaled $31,536 ($ millions) in 2018. Compute its PPE turnover for the year.

b. Compute the percent depreciated ratio for 2020.

c. Comment on these ratios. What effect does Tesla's depreciation policies have on these ratios?

LO8-6

E8-41. Evaluating R&D Expenditures of Companies

R&D intensity is measured by the ratio of research and development expense to sales revenue. The following table compares the R&D intensity for various companies.

Company	R&D Intensity
Callaway Golf Co.	2.91%
Samsung Electronics Co., Ltd (Korea)	8.96%
Apple, Inc.	6.83%
Intel Corporation	17.41%
Microsoft Corporation	13.47%
Baxter International, Inc.	4.46%
Pfizer, Inc.	22.44%
Merck & Co., Inc.	28.25%
Bayer Group Consolidated (Germany)	17.21%
Syngenta AG (Switzerland)	6.76%
Deere & Company	5.26%

Callaway Golf Co.
NYSE :: ELY
Apple, Inc.
NASDAQ :: AAPL
Samsung Electronics Co., Ltd
KS :: 005930
Intel Corporation
NASDAQ :: INTC
Microsoft Corporation
NASDAQ :: MSFT
Baxter International, Inc.
NYSE :: BAX
Pfizer, Inc.
NYSE :: PFE
Merck & Co., Inc
NYSE :: MRK
Bayer
NYSE :: BAYRY
Syngenta AG
NYSE :: SYT
Deere & Co.
NYSE :: DE

a. Comment on the differences among these companies. To what extent are the differences related to industry affiliation?

b. What other factors (besides industry affiliation) might determine a company's R&D intensity?

E8-42. Computing and Assessing Plant Asset Impairment

LO8-2, 3

Homework MBC

Zeibart Company purchased equipment for $180,000 on July 1, 2019, with an estimated useful life of 10 years and expected salvage value of $20,000. Straight-line depreciation is used. On July 1, 2023, economic factors cause the fair value of the equipment to decline to $72,000. On this date, Zeibart examines the equipment for impairment and estimates $100,000 in future cash inflows related to use of this equipment.

a. Is the equipment impaired at July 1, 2023? Explain.

b. If the equipment is impaired on July 1, 2023, compute the impairment loss and prepare a journal entry to record the loss.

c. What amount of depreciation expense would Zeibart record for the 12 months from July 1, 2023 through June 30, 2024? Prepare a journal entry to record this depreciation expense. (*Hint*: Assume no change in salvage value.)

E8-43. Computing and Assessing Plant Asset Impairment (FSET)

LO8-2, 3

Homework MBC

Using the information from E8-42, show how the entries in parts *b* and *c* affect Zeibart Company's balance sheet and income statement by using the financial statement effects template.

PROBLEMS

P8-44. Computing and Recording Proceeds from the Sale of PPE

LO8-3

Homework MBC

Hilton Worldwide Holdings Inc.
NASDAQ :: HLT

The following information was provided in the 2020 10-K of Hilton Worldwide Holdings, Inc.

Note 7: Property and Equipment ($ millions)

	2020	2019
Property and equipment, gross	$832	$889
Accumulated depreciation and amortization	(486)	(509)
Property and equipment, net	$346	$380

During the year ended December 31, 2020, we recognized $28 million of impairment losses related to property and equipment, including $4 million for finance lease ROU assets, which reduced the gross carrying value of property and equipment by $119 million, including finance lease ROU assets by $42 million, and the accumulated depreciation and amortization by $91 million, including finance lease ROU assets by $38 million.

Note 7 also revealed that depreciation and amortization expense on property and equipment totaled $57 million in 2020. The statement of cash flows reported that expenditures for property and equipment totaled $46 million in 2020 and that there were neither proceeds nor gain or loss on the sale of property and equipment during the year.

REQUIRED

1. Using the information provided, prepare a journal entry or FSET to record:
   a. the acquisition of new property and equipment during the year;
   b. the recording of depreciation and amortization expense for the year;

c. the impairment of the company's property and equipment during the year.

2. Do these entries explain the changes in Hilton's balance sheet accounts for property and equipment? Most of the changes? Would a disposal transaction complete the picture?

LO8-5, 6 Homework MBC

Agilent Technologies, Inc. NYSE :: A
HP, Inc. NYSE :: HPQ

P8-45. Analyzing and Assessing Research and Development Expenses

Agilent Technologies, Inc., the high-tech spin-off from HP, Inc., reports the following operating profit for 2020 in its 10-K ($ millions):

Net revenue	
Products	$3,993
Services and other	1,346
Total net revenue	5,339
Costs and expenses	
Cost of products	1,796
Cost of services and other	706
Total costs	2,502
Research and development	495
Selling, general, and administrative	1,496
Total costs and expenses	4,493
Income from operations	$ 846

REQUIRED

a. What percentage of its total net revenue is Agilent spending on research and development?

b. How are its balance sheet and income statement affected by the accounting for R&D costs?

c. In 2003, Agilent's spending on R&D was $1,051 million—17.4% of its total net revenue. What are some possible ways that the company might have reduced its R&D intensity from 2003 to 2020? What are some of the possible implications for the company?

LO8-4 Homework MBC

Target Corporation NYSE :: TGT

P8-46. Analyzing PPE Accounts and Recording PPE Transactions, Including Discontinued Operations

The 2019 and 2018 income statements and balance sheets (asset section only) for Target Corporation follow, along with its note disclosure describing Target's accounting for property and equipment. Target's statement of cash flows for fiscal 2019 (fiscal year ended February 1, 2020) reported capital expenditures of $3,027 million and disposal proceeds for property and equipment of $63 million. No gain or loss was reported on property and equipment disposals. In addition, Target acquired property and equipment through non-cash acquisitions not reported on the statement of cash flows.

Consolidated Statements of Operations

($ millions)	2019	2018
Sales	$77,130	$74,433
Other revenue	982	923
Total revenues	78,112	75,356
Cost of sales	54,864	53,299
Selling, general, and administrative expenses	16,233	15,723
Depreciation and amortization (exclusive of depreciation included in cost of sales)	2,357	2,224
Operating income	4,658	4,110
Net interest expense	477	461
Net other (income)/expense	(9)	(27)
Earnings from continuing operations before income taxes	4,190	3,676
Provision for income taxes	921	746
Net earnings from continuing operations	3,269	2,930
Discontinued operations, net of tax	12	7
Net earnings	$ 3,281	$ 2,937

Consolidated Statements of Financial Position (Asset Section Only) ($ millions)	February 1, 2020	February 2, 2019
Assets		
Cash and cash equivalents	$ 2,577	$ 1,556
Inventory	8,992	9,497
Other current assets	1,333	1,466
Total current assets	12,902	12,519
Property and equipment		
Land	6,036	6,064
Buildings and improvements	30,603	29,240
Fixtures and equipment	6,083	5,912
Computer hardware and software	2,692	2,544
Construction-in-progress	533	460
Accumulated depreciation	(19,664)	(18,687)
Property and equipment, net	26,283	25,533
Operating lease assets	2,236	1,965
Other noncurrent assets	1 ,358	1,273
Total assets	$42,779	$41,290

11. Property and Equipment

Property and equipment, including assets acquired under finance leases, is depreciated using the straight-line method over estimated useful lives or lease terms if shorter. We amortize leasehold improvements purchased after the beginning of the initial lease term over the shorter of the assets' useful lives or a term that includes the original lease term, plus any renewals that are reasonably certain at the date the leasehold improvements are acquired. Depreciation expense for 2019, 2018, and 2017 was $2,591 million, $2,460 million, and $2,462 million, respectively, including depreciation expense included in Cost of Sales. For income tax purposes, accelerated depreciation methods are generally used. Repair and maintenance costs are expensed as incurred. Facility pre-opening costs, including supplies and payroll, are expensed as incurred.

We review long-lived assets for impairment when store performance expectations, events, or changes in circumstances—such as a decision to relocate or close a store or distribution center, discontinue a project, or significant software changes—indicate that the asset's carrying value may not be recoverable. We recognized impairment losses of $23 million, $92 million, and $91 million during 2019, 2018, and 2017, respectively . . . Impairments are recorded in Selling, General, and Administrative Expenses.

REQUIRED

a. Prepare journal entries to record the following for fiscal 2019:
   i. Depreciation expense
   ii. Capital expenditures
   iii. Disposal of property, plant, and equipment
   iv. Impairments and write-downs (Assume that impairments and write-downs reduce the property and equipment account, rather than increasing accumulated depreciation.)

b. Estimate the amount of property and equipment that was acquired, if any, through non-cash transactions.

P8-47. Reporting PPE Transactions and Asset Impairment **LO8-5**

Homework MBC

Williams-Sonoma
NYSE :: WSM

Note B from the fiscal 2018 10-K report of Williams-Sonoma, Inc., (February 3, 2019) follows. Its statement of cash flows reported that the company made capital expenditures of $190,102,000 during fiscal 2018, impaired assets of $9,639,000, and recorded depreciation expense of $182,533,000, excluding amortization of intangibles. In addition, the company reported a loss on the disposal of property and equipment of $570,000.

Note B: Property and Equipment

Property and equipment consists of the following:

($ thousands)	Feb. 3, 2019	Jan. 28, 2018
Leasehold improvements	$ 950,259	$ 950,024
Fixtures and equipment	836,400	800,003
Capitalized software	733,941	621,730
Land and buildings	175,181	173,457
Corporate systems projects in progress	39,416	65,283
Construction in progress	7,205	8,615
Total	2,742,402	2,619,112
Accumulated depreciation and amortization	(1,812,767)	(1,686,829)
Property and equipment—net	$ 929,635	$ 932,283

We review the carrying value of all long-lived assets for impairment, primarily at a store level, whenever events or changes in circumstances indicate that the carrying value of an asset may not be recoverable. We review for impairment all stores for which current or projected cash flows from operations are not sufficient to recover the carrying value of the assets. Impairment results when the carrying value of the assets exceeds the estimated undiscounted future cash flows over the remaining useful life. Our estimate of undiscounted future cash flows over the store lease term is based upon our experience, historical operations of the stores, and estimates of future store profitability and economic conditions. The future estimates of store profitability and economic conditions require estimating such factors as sales growth, gross margin, employment rates, lease escalations, inflation on operating expenses, and the overall economics of the retail industry, and they are therefore subject to variability and difficult to predict. If a long-lived asset is found to be impaired, the amount recognized for impairment is equal to the difference between the net carrying value and the asset's fair value.

REQUIRED

Prepare journal entries to record the following for fiscal 2018:

a. Depreciation expense

b. Capital expenditures

c. Impairment of property and equipment (Assume that impairments and write-downs reduce the property and equipment account, rather than increasing accumulated depreciation.)

d. Disposal of property and equipment

CASES AND PROJECTS

LO8-3, 4 Homework MBC

General Mills, Inc.
NYSE :: GIS

C8-48. Interpreting and Reporting Property, Plant, and Equipment (PPE) Expenditures (FSET) General Mills, Inc., is a global consumer foods company. The firm manufactures and sells a wide range of branded products and is a major supplier to the foodservice and baking industries. The company's core product areas are ready-to-eat cereal, super-premium ice cream, convenient meal solutions, and healthy snacking. The following data are taken from the company's 2020 annual report. From the balance sheet:

($ millions)	May 31, 2020	May 26, 2019
Equipment	$ 6,428.0	$ 6,548.3
Buildings	2,412.6	2,477.2
Capitalized software	668.5	631.6
Construction in progress	373.5	343.8
Land	66.1	73.6
Equipment under finance lease	5.8	5.7
Buildings under finance lease	0.3	0.3
Total land, buildings, and equipment	9,954.8	10,080.5
Less accumulated depreciation	(6,374.2)	(6,293.3)
Total	$ 3,580.6	$ 3,787.2

From the income statement ($ millions):

	2020	2019
Net sales	$17,626.6	$16,865.2

REQUIRED

a. Compute the PPE turnover for 2020. Assuming an average PPE turnover of 4.0 for the company's closest competitors, does General Mills appear to be capital intensive?

b. Calculate the percentage depreciated of General Mills' depreciable assets at the end of fiscal year 2020. What implications might the result suggest for the company's future cash flows?

c. General Mills reported depreciation and amortization (not reported separately) expense of approximately $594.7 million in 2020. Estimate the average useful life of its depreciable assets by dividing average depreciable assets by depreciation expense.

d. During 2020, General Mills purchased $460.8 million of land, buildings, and equipment for cash. Use the financial statement effects template to reflect the asset purchases and the year's depreciation charge.

C8-49. Recording Depreciation and Asset Purchases LO8-3

MBC

Using the information from C8-48, prepare journal entries to record the asset purchases and the year's depreciation expense.

C8-50. Managing Operating Assets to Improve Performance: A Management Application LO8-4, 6

Return on a company's net operating assets is commonly used to evaluate financial performance. One way to increase performance is to focus on operating assets.

REQUIRED

Indicate how this might be done in relation to the following asset categories. Indicate also any potential problems a given action might create.

a. Receivables
b. Inventories
c. Property, plant, and equipment
d. Intangibles

C8-51. Determining the Effects of Capitalizing Versus Expensing Software Development Costs LO8-5, 6

Take-Two Interactive Software, Inc.
NASDAQ :: TTWO
Electronic Arts, Inc.
NASDAQ :: EA

The following information is taken from the March 31, 2020, annual report of Take-Two Interactive Software, Inc., a maker and distributor of video games. All amounts are in thousands of U.S. dollars.

Income Statement Information:	2020
Net sales	$3,088,970
Cost of goods sold	1,542,450
Operating expenses	1,121,253
Income (loss) from operations	$ 425,267

Information from the Management Discussion, Balance Sheet and Note 8:

Software Development Costs and Licenses

Capitalized software development costs include direct costs incurred for internally developed titles and payments made to third-party software developers under development agreements.

We capitalize internal software development costs (including specifically identifiable payroll expense, employee stock-based compensation, and incentive compensation costs related to the completion and release of titles, as well as third-party production and other content costs), subsequent to establishing technological feasibility of a software title. Technological feasibility of a product includes the completion of both technical design documentation and game design documentation. Significant management judgments are made in the assessment of when technological feasibility is established. For products where proven technology exists, this may occur early in the development cycle. Technological feasibility is evaluated on a product-by-product basis. Prior to establishing technological feasibility of a product, we record any costs incurred by third-party developers as research and development expenses . . .

continued

continued from previous page

Amortization of capitalized software development costs and licenses commences when a product is available for general release and is recorded on a title-by-title basis in cost of goods sold. For capitalized software development costs, annual amortization is calculated using (1) the proportion of current year revenue to the total revenue expected to be recorded over the life of the title or (2) the straight-line method over the remaining estimated life of the title, whichever is greater. For capitalized licenses, amortization is calculated as a ratio of (1) current year revenue to the total revenue expected to be recorded over the remaining estimated life of the title or (2) the contractual royalty rate based on actual net product sales as defined in the licensing agreement, whichever is greater. Amortization periods for our software products generally range from 12 to 36 months.

We evaluate the future recoverability of capitalized software development costs and licenses on a quarterly basis. Recoverability is primarily assessed based on the title's actual performance. For products that are scheduled to be released in the future, recoverability is evaluated based on the expected performance of the specific products to which the cost or license relates. We use a number of criteria in evaluating expected product performance, including historical performance of comparable products developed with comparable technology, market performance of comparable titles, orders for the product prior to its release, general market conditions, and past performance of the franchise. When we determine that capitalized cost of the title is unlikely to be recovered by product sales, an impairment of software development and license costs capitalized is charged to cost of goods sold in the period in which such determination is made.

Capitalized Software Development Costs and Licenses	2020
Beginning balance	$632,316
Additions	131,734
Amortization and write-downs	(321,956)
Ending balance	$442,094

Assume an income tax rate of 25% where necessary.

REQUIRED

You wish to compare the performance of Take-Two with one of its competitors, **Electronic Arts, Inc.** However, Electronic Arts does not capitalize any significant amounts of its software development costs. Estimate Take-Two's 2020 Income from operations if it did not capitalize any software development costs. Briefly explain your adjustment(s).

LO8-3 Homework MBC

The Walt Disney Company
NASDAQ :: DWA

C8-52. Analyzing Impairment Charges (FSET)

In its fiscal year ended October 3, 2020, **The Walt Disney Company** recorded a loss. Part of this loss was due to impairment charges. In its annual report the company stated:

Goodwill and Intangible Asset Impairment

Our International Channels reporting unit, which is part of the Direct-to-Consumer & International segment, comprises the Company's international television networks. Our international television networks primarily derive revenues from affiliate fees charged to multi-channel video programming distributors (i.e., cable, satellite, telecommunications, and digital over-the-top service providers) (MVPDs) for the right to deliver our programming under multi-year licensing agreements and the sales of advertising time/space on the networks. A majority of the operations in this reporting unit were acquired in the TFCF acquisition, and therefore the fair value of these businesses approximated the carrying value at the date of the acquisition of TFCF.

The International Channels business has been negatively impacted by the COVID-19 pandemic resulting in decreased viewership and lower advertising revenue related to the availability of content, including the deferral of certain live sporting events. The Company's increased focus on DTC distribution in international markets is expected to negatively impact the International Channels business as we shift the primary means of monetizing our film and television content from licensing of linear channels to use on our DTC services because the International Channels reporting unit valuation does not include the value derived from this shift, which is reflected in other reporting units. In addition, the industry shift to DTC, including by us and many of our distributors, who are pursuing their own DTC strategies, has changed the competitive dynamics for the International Channels business and resulted in unfavorable renewal terms for certain of our distribution agreements.

Due to these circumstances, in the third quarter of fiscal 2020, we tested the International Channels' goodwill and long-lived assets (including intangible assets) for impairment . . .

continued

continued from previous page

> In the third quarter of fiscal 2020, we recorded a non-cash impairment charge primarily on our MVPD agreement intangible assets of $1.9 billion . . . In the third quarter of fiscal 2020, the carrying value of the International Channels exceeded the fair value, and we recorded a non-cash impairment charge of $3.1 billion to fully impair the International Channels reporting unit goodwill. The $1.9 billion impairment of our MVPD relationships and $3.1 billion impairment of goodwill are recorded in "Restructuring and impairment charges" in the Consolidated Statements of Operations.

REQUIRED

a. The Walt Disney Company reported a $1.7 billion pre-tax loss for the fiscal year 2020. What would pre-tax income or loss have been without the above described impairment charges?

b. Show the journal entry for 2020 to record the impairment charges using the financial statement effects template.

c. If circumstances changed in the future and the fair value increased either the MVPD agreement or the goodwill related to the International Channels, could the company reverse a portion of the impairment losses?

C8-53. Analyzing Impairment Charges LO8-3

Using the information from C8-52, prepare journal entries to record the impairment charges.

Homework MBC

SOLUTIONS TO REVIEW PROBLEMS

Review 8-1

a. Capitalize *c.* Expense *e.* Capitalize *g.* Capitalize *i.* Expense
b. Capitalize *d.* Capitalize *f.* Capitalize *h.* Expense

Review 8-2

*a*1. Straight-line depreciation expense = ($95,000 – $10,000)/5 years = $17,000 per year

*a*2. Double-declining-balance (twice straight-line rate = 2 × (1/5) = 40%)

Year	Book Value × Rate	Depreciation Expense
1.	$95,000 × 0.40 =	$38,000
2.	($95,000 – $38,000) × 0.40 =	22,800
3.	($95,000 – $60,800) × 0.40 =	13,680
4.	($95,000 – $74,480) × 0.40 =	8,208
5.	($95,000 – $82,688) × 0.40 =	2,312*

*The formula value of $4,925 is not reported because it would depreciate the asset below residual value. Only the $2,312 needed to reach residual value is depreciated.

b.

	Balance Sheet							Income Statement		
Transaction	Cash Asset	+ Noncash Assets	– Contra Asset	=	Liabil-ities	+ Contrib. Capital	+ Earned Capital	Revenues	– Expenses	= Net Income
(a) Purchased equipment.	–95,000 Cash	+95,000 Equipment	–	=					–	=
(b) Recorded annual depreciation.			– +17,000 Accumulated Depreciation	=			–17,000 Retained Earnings		– +17,000 Depreciation Expense	= –17,000

ANALYZE

c.

JOURNALIZE

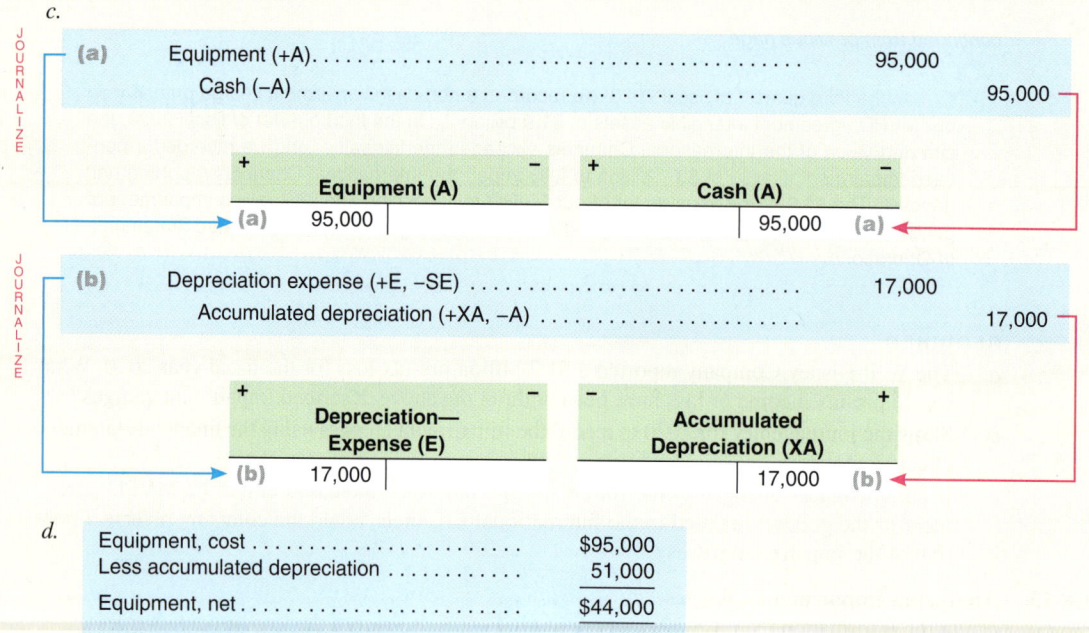

		Debit	Credit
(a)	Equipment (+A)	95,000	
	Cash (−A)		95,000

+ Equipment (A) −		+ Cash (A) −	
(a) 95,000			95,000 (a)

JOURNALIZE

		Debit	Credit
(b)	Depreciation expense (+E, −SE)	17,000	
	Accumulated depreciation (+XA, −A)		17,000

+ Depreciation—Expense (E) −		− Accumulated Depreciation (XA) +	
(b) 17,000			17,000 (b)

d.

Equipment, cost	$95,000
Less accumulated depreciation	51,000
Equipment, net	$44,000

Equipment is reported on Lev's balance sheet at its net book value of $44,000.

Review 8-3

a.

ANALYZE

Transaction	Cash Asset	+ Noncash Assets	− Contra Asset	= Liabilities	+ Contrib. Capital	+ Earned Capital	Revenues	− Expenses	= Net Income
(1) Sold Equipment #101	+22,000 Cash	−55,000 Equipment	−33,000 Accumulated Depreciation						
(2) Sold Equipment #220	+12,500 Cash	−80,000 Equipment	−70,000 Accumulated Depreciation			+2,500 Retained Earnings	+2,500 Gain on Sale of Equipment		+2,500
(3) Sold Equipment #380	+68,000 Cash	−125,000 Equipment	−50,000 Accumulated Depreciation			−7,000 Retained Earnings		+7,000 Loss on Sale of Equipment	−7,000

b.

ANALYZE

Transaction	Cash Asset	+ Noncash Assets	− Contra Asset	= Liabilities	+ Contrib. Capital	+ Earned Capital	Revenues	− Expenses	= Net Income
(1) Impairment of Equipment		−7,000 Equipment				−7,000 Retained Earnings		+7,000 Impairment Loss	−7,000

c.

	Debit	Credit
Cash (+A)	22,000	
Accumulated Depreciation (+XA, −A)	33,000	
Equipment #101 (−A)		55,000
Cash (+A)	12,500	
Accumulated Depreciation (+XA, −A)	70,000	
Equipment #220 (−A)		80,000
Gain on sale of equipment (+R, +SE)		2,500
Cash (+A)	68,000	
Accumulated Depreciation (+XA, −A)	50,000	
Loss on sale of equipment (+E, −SE)	7,000	
Equipment #380 (−A)		125,000
Impairment Loss (+E, −SE)	7,000	
Equipment #380 (−A)		7,000

Review 8-4

a.

	2020	2019	2018
Sales	$17,337	$45,768	$44,541
Avg PPE, net	$33,332	$34,547	$34,127
PPET	0.52	1.32	1.31

The PPE turnover ratio dropped from a stable 1.3 in 2019 and 2018 to 0.5 in 2020. This was due largely to the sharp drop in revenue due to the pandemic.

While the cost of equipment dropped by 9.5%, sales dropped by 62.1% from 2019 to 2020. This illustrates how an unexpected drop in sales has a significant impact on companies with heavy investments in tangible assets.

b.

	2020	2019	2018
Accumulated depreciation	$16,757	$18,659	$17,443
Cost	$47,010	$51,980	$50,263
% deprec	35.6%	35.9%	34.7%

The percentage of assets remained constant from 2019 to 2020, indicating that assets held are at a similar point in their useful lives. This trend was possible even though average assets decreased by 3.5%, which indicates that some older assets in the mix were replaced with newer assets.

Review 8-5

ANALYZE

Transaction	Balance Sheet: Cash Asset	+ Noncash Assets	− Contra Asset	= Liabilities	+ Contrib. Capital	+ Earned Capital	Income Statement: Revenues	− Expenses	= Net Income
(a) Record R&D costs as R&D expense.	−120,000 Cash					−120,000 Retained Earnings		+120,000 R&D Expense	−120,000
(b) Record acquisition of patent.	−12,500 Cash	+12,500 Patent							
(c) Amortization of patent.			+625 Accumulated Amortization			−625 Retained Earnings		+625 Amortization Expense	−625
(d) Purchased rights to use of patent.	−90,000 Cash	+90,000 Technology Rights							
(e) Record impairment of technology rights.		−54,000 Technology Rights				−54,000 Retained Earnings		+54,000 Loss Due to Impairment	−54,000

a. Bowen Company would expense the $120,000 in R&D costs in Year 8.

b. The $12,500 in legal fees to obtain the patent would be capitalized. As a result, the book value of the patent would be $12,500 on July 1, Year 8.

c. Each year, beginning on July 1, Year 8, Bowen would record amortization expense of $1,250 ($12,500/10). For Year 8, six months of amortization expense, or $625, would be recorded ($1,250/2).

d. Because Kennedy purchased the right to use the technology, the purchase price can be capitalized as an intangible asset and amortized over the five-year length of the agreement. Kennedy would record amortization expense of $18,000 ($90,000/5) each year, beginning July 1, 2020. (Bowen would recognize the $90,000 as revenue.)

e. Given that the patent is obsolete, Kennedy Company would record an impairment loss. Kennedy Company would write off the remaining value of the technology agreement, recording an impairment loss of $54,000 [$90,000 − ($18,000 × 2)].

f. Bowen Company would also record an impairment loss. Bowen would write off the unamortized balance in the patent account, resulting in a loss of $7,500 [$12,500 − ($1,250 × 4)].

g.

JOURNALIZE

(a)	R&D expense (+E, −SE)	120,000	
	Cash (−A)		120,000

POST

+	Research & Development Expense (E)	−
(a) 120,000		

+	Cash (A)	−
		120,000 (a)

JOURNALIZE

(b)	Patent (+A)	12,500	
	Cash (−A)		12,500

POST

+	Patent (A)	−
(b) 12,500		

+	Cash (A)	−
		120,000 (a)
		12,500 (b)

JOURNALIZE

(c)	Amortization expense (+E, −SE)	625	
	Accumulated amortization (+XA, −A)		625

POST

+	Amortization Expense (E)	−
(c) 625		

−	Accumulated Amortization (XA)	+
		625 (c)

JOURNALIZE

(d)	Technology rights (+A)	90,000	
	Cash (−A)		90,000

POST

+	Technology Rights (A)	−
(d) 90,000		

+	Cash (A)	−
		90,000 (d)

JOURNALIZE

(e)	Loss due to impairment of technology rights (+E, −SE)	54,000	
	Technology rights (−A)		54,000

POST

+	Loss Due to Impairment of Technology Rights (E)	−
(e) 54,000		

+	Technology Rights (A)	−
(d) 90,000		
		54,000 (e)
Bal. 36,000		

Review 8-6

a.

Bristol-Myers Squibb	Pfizer
2020: 26.21% ($11,143 ÷ $42,518)	2020: 22.44% ($9,405 ÷ $41,908)
2019: 18.63% ($ 4,871 ÷ $26,145)	2019: 20.39% ($8,394 ÷ $41,172)
2018: 21.09% ($ 4,551 ÷ $21,581)	2018: 19.01% ($7,760 ÷ $40,825)

b.

Bristol-Myers Squibb	Pfizer
2020: 44.94% ($53,243 ÷ $118,481)	2020: 18.46% ($28,471 ÷ $154,229)
2019: 49.23% ($63,969 ÷ $129,944)	2019: 20.25% ($33,936 ÷ $167,594)
2018: 3.12% ($ 1,091 ÷ $ 34,986)	2018: 22.09% ($35,211 ÷ $159,422)

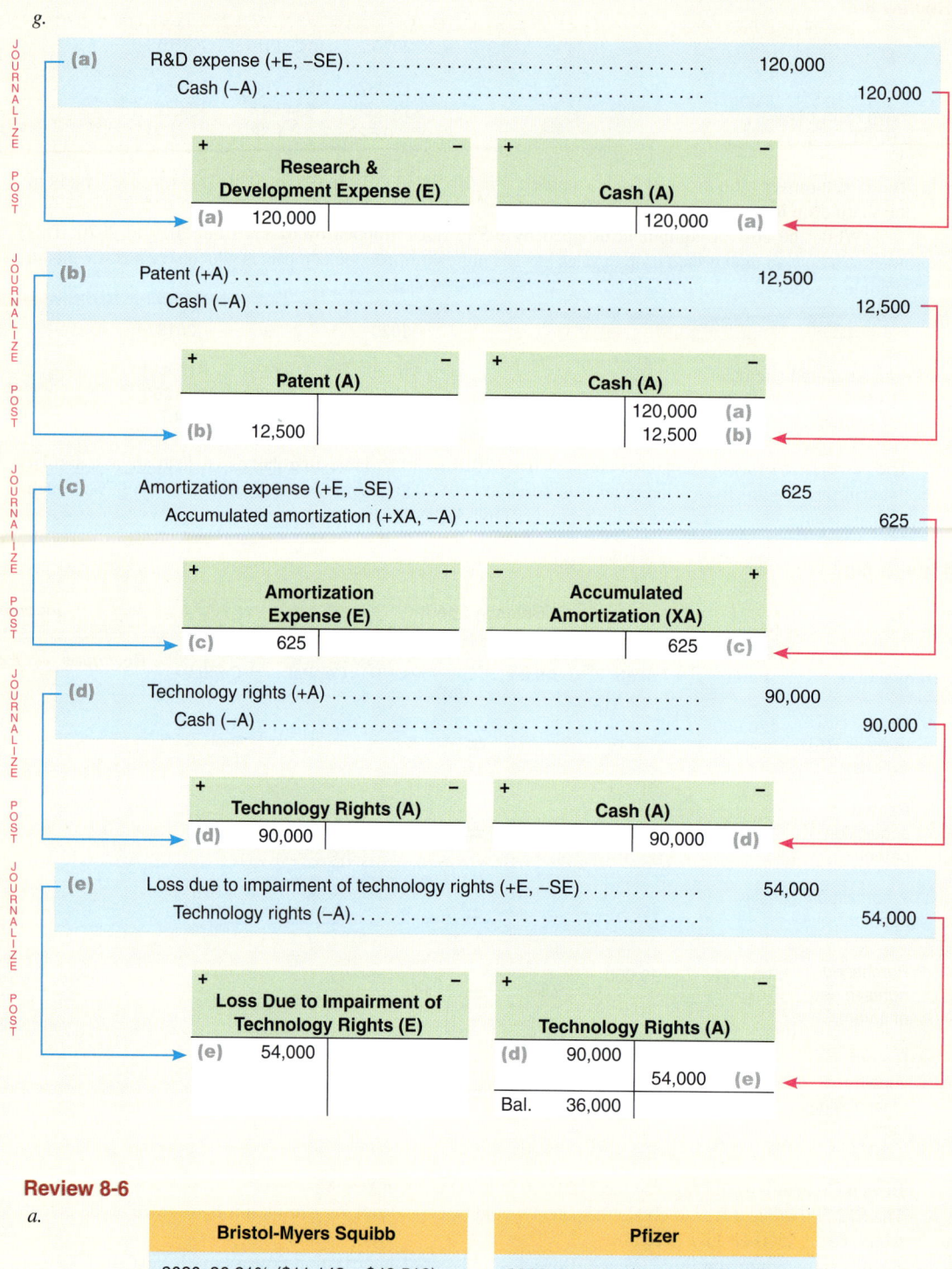

c. R&D as a percentage of sales for Bristol-Myers Squibb fluctuated each year, with the most significant increase from 2019 to 2020 as compared to 2018 to 2019. The company reported in its 10-K that this increase was partially due to an acquisition that increased its operations. R&D as a percentage of sales for Pfizer increased each year, with a slightly larger increase from 2019 to 2020 as compared to 2018 to 2019. The company reported in its 10-K that this increase was partially due to costs to co-develop a COVID-19 vaccine. Other intangible assets as a percentage of total assets for Bristol-Myers Squibb increased significantly from 2018 to 2019. The company reported in its 10-K that this increase was largely due to an acquisition that resulted in purchased intangible assets. Other intangible assets as a percentage of total assets for Pfizer decreased each year from 2018 to 2020. The net intangible asset amounts decrease when the decrease due to amortization or impairment charges of existing intangible assets is not outweighed by additions due to purchased intangibles.

Chapter 9

Reporting and Analyzing Liabilities

LEARNING OBJECTIVES

LO9-1 Identify and account for current operating liabilities.

LO9-2 Describe and account for current nonoperating (financial) liabilities.

LO9-3 Explain and illustrate the pricing of long-term nonoperating liabilities.

LO9-4 Analyze and account for financial statement effects of long-term nonoperating liabilities.

LO9-5 Explain how solvency ratios and debt ratings are determined and how they impact the cost of debt.

Road Map

LO	Learning Objective | Topics	Page	eLecture	Review	Assignments
LO9-1	Identify and account for current operating liabilities.	9-4	e9-1	R9-1	M9-18, M9-19, M9-20, M9-21, M9-24, M9-28, M9-38, E9-44, E9-45, E9-46, E9-50, E9-51, P9-64, P9-78, DA9-1
LO9-2	Describe and account for current nonoperating (financial) liabilities.	9-10	e9-2	R9-2	M9-22, M9-23, M9-24, E9-61
LO9-3	Explain and illustrate the pricing of long-term nonoperating liabilities.	9-13	e9-3	R9-3	M9-25, M9-36, M9-37, M9-39, M9-40, M9-41, M9-42, M9-43, E9-47, E9-49, E9-52, E9-53, E9-54, E9-55, E9-56, E9-57, E9-58, E9-59, E9-60, E9-62, P9-65, P9-66, P9-67, P9-68, P9-69, P9-70, P9-71, P9-72, P9-73, P9-74, P9-75, P9-76, P9-77, C9-79, C9-80
LO9-4	Analyze and account for financial statement effects of long-term nonoperating liabilities.	9-18	e9-4	R9-4	M9-26, M9-27, M9-29, M9-30, M9-31, M9-32, M9-33, M9-34, M9-39, M9-40, M9-41, M9-42, E9-47, E9-48, E9-52, E9-53, E9-54, E9-55, E9-56, E9-57, E9-58, E9-59, E9-60, E9-61, E9-62, P9-65, P9-66, P9-67, P9-68, P9-69, P9-70, P9-71, P9-72, P9-73, P9-74, P9-75, P9-76, P9-77, C9-79, C9-80
LO9-5	Explain how solvency ratios and debt ratings are determined and how they impact the cost of debt.	9-27	e9-5	R9-5	M9-25, M9-35, C9-79, C9-80, DA9-2

VERIZON
www.verizon.com

In 2000, **Bell Atlantic Corporation** merged with **GTE** to form **Verizon Communications**, one of the largest telecommunication providers in the world. Verizon's industry is constantly changing and extremely competitive. Hans Vestberg, who became the CEO in 2018, faces the challenging tasks of fending off a host of competitors including **AT&T**, **Comcast**, and **T-Mobile**, as well as dealing with the disruptions like the coronavirus pandemic that lowered revenues and net income for 2020.

In recent years, Verizon has embarked upon a strategic transformation as advances in technology and the pandemic have changed the ways that people communicate in their personal and professional lives. The company has focused on leveraging their network leadership and retaining and growing their customer base while balancing profitability and safety for employees and customers. This strategy requires significant investments in acquiring wireless spectrum, putting the spectrum into service, expanding the fiber optic network that supports wireless and wireline service, maintaining networks, and developing and maintaining database capacity. The company has been a leading developer in fifth generation (5G) wireless technologies. This investment program requires a significant amount of cash ($20 billion annually) at a time when the company is faced with more than $128 billion in outstanding debt (a total liability balance of $247 billion) and $18 billion in employee benefit obligations. Fortunately, Verizon's operating cash flow remains strong at $41 billion in 2020.

Previous chapters focused on the reporting of operating assets, including receivables, inventories, property, plant, and equipment, and intangible assets, along with the related expenses. We now turn our attention to the other side of the balance sheet. Chapter 9 examines how we value liabilities and how debt financing along with the subsequent payment of interest and principal affect the financial statements. We also discuss the required disclosures that enable us to effectively analyze a company's ability to make its liability payments as they mature. Chapter 10 focuses on the reporting for specific types of liabilities, and Chapter 11 examines the reporting of stockholders' equity.

As Verizon faces increased competition from other telecom companies, cable, and Internet providers, it must continue to innovate to maintain its position as an industry leader. This objective will require large investments in technology and infrastructure, only part of which will come from its operating cash flow. The company faces other substantial risks as well, including (1) the threat of cyberattacks, (2) changes in regulation in their industry, (3) technological and business disruptions, and (4) their significant debt burden and possibility of rising interest rates. To be successful, Vestberg will need to manage Verizon's debt burden and efficiently allocate cash resources between strategic investments and debt payments.

Sources: *Verizon* 2020 10-K.

CHAPTER ORGANIZATION

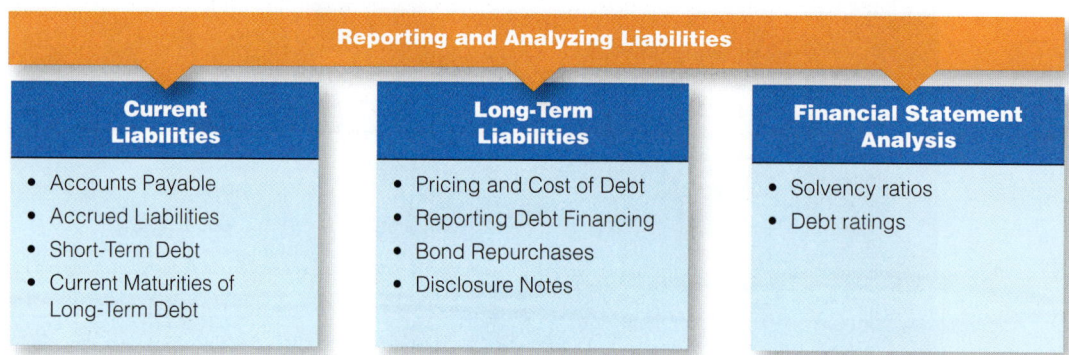

Reporting and Analyzing Liabilities

Current Liabilities
- Accounts Payable
- Accrued Liabilities
- Short-Term Debt
- Current Maturities of Long-Term Debt

Long-Term Liabilities
- Pricing and Cost of Debt
- Reporting Debt Financing
- Bond Repurchases
- Disclosure Notes

Financial Statement Analysis
- Solvency ratios
- Debt ratings

INTRODUCTION

Just as asset disclosures provide us with information on where a company invests its funds, the disclosures concerning liabilities and equity inform us as to how those assets are financed. To be successful, a company must not only invest funds wisely, but be astute in the manner in which it finances those investments.

Companies hope to finance their assets at the lowest possible cost. The cost of financing assets with liabilities is the interest charged by the lender. While many liabilities bear explicit interest rates, many other liabilities (such as accounts payable and accrued liabilities) are non-interest-bearing. This fact does not mean that these liabilities are cost-free. For example, while a supplier may appear to offer interest-free credit terms, the cost of that credit is implicitly included in the price it charges for the goods or services it sells.

Verizon's liabilities and equity, as taken from its 2020 10-K report, are presented in **Exhibit 9.1**. Just as assets are classified as either current or noncurrent, so are liabilities presented in the balance sheet as either current or noncurrent.

Current liabilities, as the name implies, are short-term in nature, generally requiring payment within the coming year. As a result, they are not a suitable source of funding for long-term assets that generate cash flows over several years. Instead, companies often finance long-term assets with long-term liabilities that require payments over several years, so that the cash outflows required by the financing source match the cash inflows produced by the assets to which they relate.

EXHIBIT 9.1 Verizon Communications' Liabilities and Equity

At December 31 ($ millions)	2020	2019
Current liabilities		
Debt maturing within one year	$ 5,889	$ 10,777
Accounts payable and accrued liabilities	20,658	21,806
Current operating lease liabilities	3,485	3,261
Other current liabilities	9,628	9,024
Total current liabilities	39,660	44,868
Long-term debt	123,173	100,712
Employee benefit obligations	18,657	17,952
Deferred income taxes	35,711	34,703
Non-current operating lease liabilities	18,000	18,393
Other liabilities	12,008	12,264
Total liabilities	247,209	228,892
Total equity	69,272	62,835
Total liabilities and equity	$316,481	$291,727

When a company acquires assets and finances them with liabilities, its **financial leverage** increases. Because the magnitude of required liability payments increases with the level of liability financing, those larger payments increase the chance of default should a downturn in business occur. Increasing levels of liabilities make the company riskier to creditors who, consequently, demand a higher return on the financing they provide to the company. The assessment of default risk is part of liquidity and solvency analysis.

This chapter, along with Chapter 10, focuses on liabilities that are reported on the balance sheet and the corresponding interest costs reported in the income statement. All such liabilities represent probable, nondiscretionary, future obligations that are the result of events that have already occurred. Chapter 10 also addresses *off-balance sheet financing*, which encompasses future obligations that are reported in the notes, but not on the face of the balance sheet. An understanding of both on-balance-sheet and off-balance-sheet financing is central to evaluating a company's financial condition and assessing its risk of default.

CURRENT LIABILITIES

LO9-1
Identify and account for current operating liabilities.

Liabilities are separated on the balance sheet into current and noncurrent (long-term). We first focus our attention on current liabilities, which are obligations that must be met (paid) within one year. Most current liabilities, such as those related to utilities, wages, insurance, rent, and taxes, generate a corresponding impact on operating expenses.

Verizon reports three categories of current liabilities: (1) debt maturing within one year, which includes short-term borrowings as well as long-term obligations that are scheduled for payment in the upcoming year, (2) accounts payable and accrued liabilities, and (3) other current liabilities, which consist mainly of customer deposits, dividends declared but not yet paid, and miscellaneous short-term obligations too small to list separately.

It is helpful to separate current liabilities into operating and nonoperating components. These two components primarily consist of:

1. Current operating liabilities
   - **Accounts payable** Obligations to others for amounts owed on purchases of goods and services. These are usually non-interest-bearing.
   - **Accrued liabilities** Obligations for expenses incurred that have not been paid as of the end of the current period. These include, for example, accruals for employee wages earned but yet unpaid, accruals for taxes (usually quarterly) on payroll and current-period profits, and accruals for other liabilities such as rent, utilities, interest, and insurance. Accruals are made to properly reflect the liabilities owed as of the statement date and the expenses incurred in the period. Each one is journalized by a debit to an expense account (an increase in the expense) and a credit to a related liability (an increase in the liability).
   - **Deferred performance liabilities** Obligations that will be satisfied, not by paying cash, but instead, by providing products or services to customers. Examples of deferred performance liabilities include customer deposits, other types of contract liabilities (ASC 606) such as the unconditional right to receive payment from a customer, unearned gift card revenues for retail companies, and liabilities for frequent flier programs offered by airlines.
2. Current nonoperating liabilities
   - **Short-term interest-bearing debt** Short-term bank borrowings and notes expected to mature in whole or in part during the upcoming year.
   - **Current maturities of long-term debt** Long-term borrowings that are scheduled to mature in whole or in part during the upcoming year.

The remainder of this section describes current liabilities.

Accounts Payable

Accounts payable, which are part of current operating liabilities, arise from the purchase of goods and services from others on credit. Verizon reports $20,658 million in accounts payable and accrued liabilities as of December 31, 2020. Its accounts payable represent $6,667 million, or 32%, of this total amount.

Accounts payable are a non-interest-bearing source of financing. Increased payables reduce the amount of net working capital because these payables are deducted from current assets in the computation of net working capital. Also, increased payables improve operating cash flow (because inventories were purchased without using cash). An increase in accounts payable also increases profitability because it causes a reduction in the level of interest-bearing debt that is required to finance operating assets. ROE increases when companies make use of this low-cost financing source. However, management must be careful to avoid excessive "**leaning on the trade**" because short-term income and cash flow gains can result in long-term costs such as damaged supply channels.[1]

When a company purchases goods or services on credit, suppliers often grant **cash discounts** to buyers if payment is made within a specified time period. Cash discounts are usually established as part of the credit terms and stated as a percentage of the purchase price. For example, credit terms of 1/10, n/30 (one-ten, net-thirty) indicate that a 1% cash discount is allowed if the payment is made within 10 days. If the cash discount is not taken, the full purchase price is due in 30 days.

Net-of-Discount Method To illustrate a cash discount, assume that a company purchases 1,000 units of merchandise at $4 per unit on terms of 1/10, n/30. The total purchase price is 1,000 × $4 = $4,000. However, if payment is made within 10 days, the net purchase price would then be $3,960 ($4,000 – $40). While this difference seems like a small amount, consider the cost of not taking the discount. If the discount is missed, the buyer is afforded an extra 20 days to pay for the merchandise, for which it pays a penalty of $40, or $2 per day. Two dollars per day is the equivalent of $730 per year which, in turn, is equivalent to paying interest at an annual rate of 18.4% ($730/$3,960).

When cash discounts are offered, the inventory purchase should be recorded at its cost using the **net-of-discount method**. When the net-of-discount method is used, inventory is capitalized at the net cost, assuming that the discount will be taken by the buyer. Continuing with our example, the following entry would be recorded by the buyer at the time of purchase:

	Balance Sheet									Income Statement			
Transaction	Cash Asset	+	Noncash Assets	=	Liabil-ities	+	Contrib. Capital	+	Earned Capital	Revenues	–	Expenses	= Net Income
ANALYZE: Purchase inventory on account.			+3,960 Inventory	=	+3,960 Accounts Payable						–		=

JOURNALIZE

Inventory (+A)	3,960	
Accounts payable (+L)		3,960

POST

+ Inventory (A) –		– Accounts Payable (L) +	
3,960			3,960

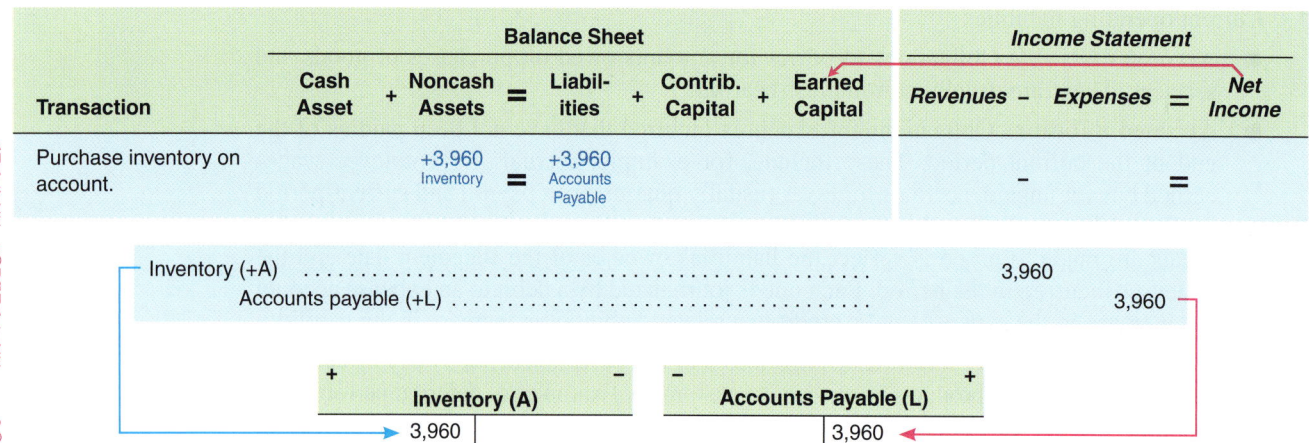

When payment is made within the 10-day discount period, accounts payable is debited and cash is credited:

Transaction	Cash Asset	+	Noncash Assets	=	Liabil-ities	+	Contrib. Capital	+	Earned Capital	Revenues	–	Expenses	= Net Income
ANALYZE: Payment on accounts payable.	–3,960 Cash			=	–3,960 Accounts Payable						–		=

JOURNALIZE

Accounts payable (–L)	3,960	
Cash (–A)		3,960

POST

– Accounts Payable (L) +		+ Cash (A) –	
3,960			3,960

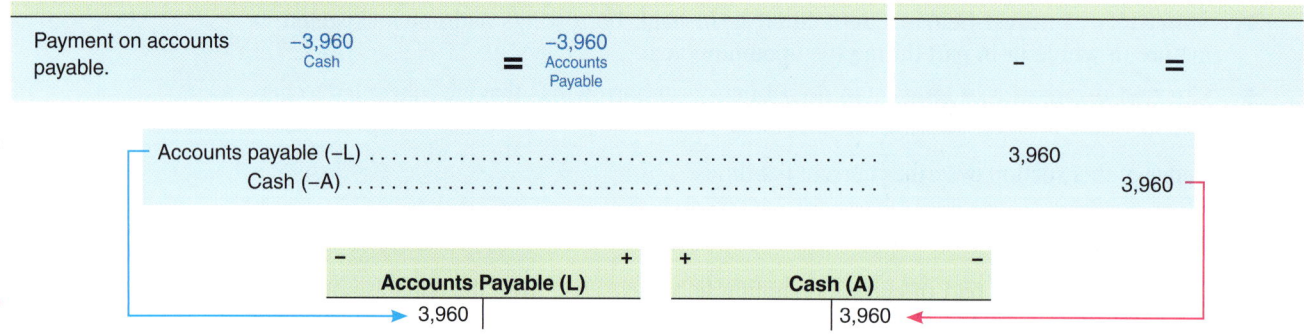

However, when a discount is missed, the lost discount must be recorded. For example, if full payment is made after the 10-day discount period, the payment is recorded as follows:

[1] One must be careful, because excessive delays in the payment of payables can result in suppliers charging a higher price for their goods or, ultimately, refusing to sell to certain buyers. This situation is a hidden "financing" cost that, even though it is not interest, is a real cost.

ANALYZE

	Balance Sheet									Income Statement				
Transaction	Cash Asset	+	Noncash Assets	=	Liabil-ities	+	Contrib. Capital	+	Earned Capital	Revenues	−	Expenses	=	Net Income
Payment on accounts payable.	−4,000 Cash			=	−3,960 Accounts Payable				−40 Retained Earnings		−	+40 Interest Expense (Discounts Lost)	=	−40

JOURNALIZE

Accounts payable (−L)	3,960	
Interest expense, discounts lost (+E, −SE)	40	
Cash (−A)		4,000

POST

− Accounts Payable (L) +	
3,960	

+ Cash (A) −	
	4,000

+ Interest Expense – Discounts Lost (E, SE) −	
40	

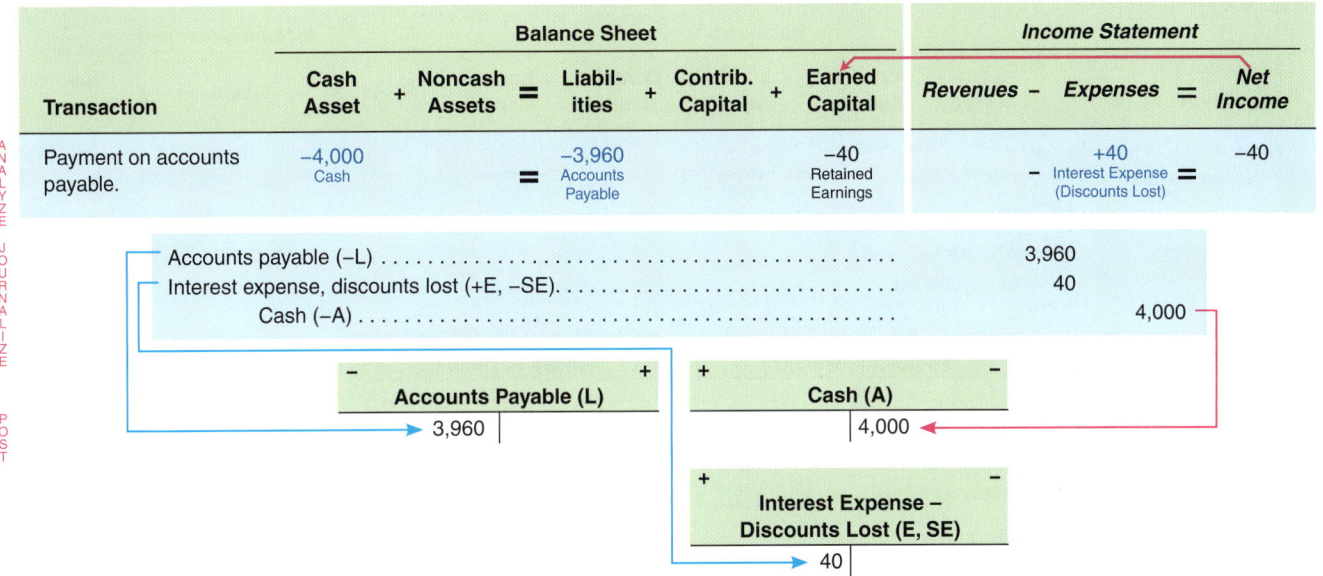

The missed discount is an expense in the period when the discount is lost. This serves two purposes. First, discounts lost are not capitalized as part of inventory and are not added to cost of goods sold. Instead, the lost discounts are treated like a finance charge and recorded as an expense of the period when the discount is missed. Second, the net-of-discount method highlights late payments by explicitly keeping a record of lost discounts. Given the high cost of missed cash discounts, most businesses would likely want to minimize the amount of discounts lost. Thus, keeping a record of discounts lost is useful when it comes to managing cash and accounts payable.

Accrued Liabilities

Accrued liabilities are identified at the end of an accounting period to reflect liabilities and expenses that have been incurred during the period but are not yet paid.[2] **Verizon** reports details of its $20,658 million accounts payable and accrued liabilities, including its $6,667 accounts payable, in Note 15 to its 2020 10-K report:

December 31 ($ millions)	2020	2019
Accounts payable	$ 6,667	$ 7,725
Accrued expenses	6,050	5,984
Accrued vacation, salaries and wages	5,057	4,885
Interest payable	1,452	1,441
Taxes payable	1,432	1,771
Total	$20,658	$21,806

Verizon accrues liabilities for the following expenses: miscellaneous accrued expenses, accrued vacation pay, accrued salaries and wages, interest payable, and accrued taxes. These accruals are typical of most companies. The accruals are recognized with a liability on the balance sheet and a corresponding expense on the income statement. This reporting means that liabilities increase, current income decreases, and reported equity decreases. When an accrued liability is ultimately paid, both cash and the liability are decreased (but no expense is recorded because it was recognized previously).

Accounting for Accrued Liabilities The following entries illustrate the accounting for a typical accrued liability, accrued wages:

[2] Accruals can also be made for recognition of revenue and a corresponding receivable. An example of this situation would be interest earned but not received on an investment in bonds that is still outstanding at period-end.

	Balance Sheet					Income Statement		
Transaction	Cash Asset	+ Noncash Assets	= Liabil-ities	+ Contrib. Capital	+ Earned Capital	*Revenues*	− *Expenses*	= *Net Income*
ANALYZE (1) Accrued $75 for employee wages earned.			= +75 Wages Payable		−75 Retained Earnings		− +75 Wages Expense	= −75
ANALYZE (2) Next period's cash payment of wages.	−75 Cash		= −75 Wages Payable				−	=

JOURNALIZE

		Dr.	Cr.
(1)	Wages expense (+E, −SE)	75	
	Wages payable (+L)		75

POST

+ Wages Expense (E) −	
(1) 75	

− Wages Payable (L) +	
	75 (1)

JOURNALIZE

		Dr.	Cr.
(2)	Wages payable (−L)	75	
	Cash (−A)		75

POST

− Wages Payable (L) +	
(2) 75	

+ Cash (A) −	
	75 (2)

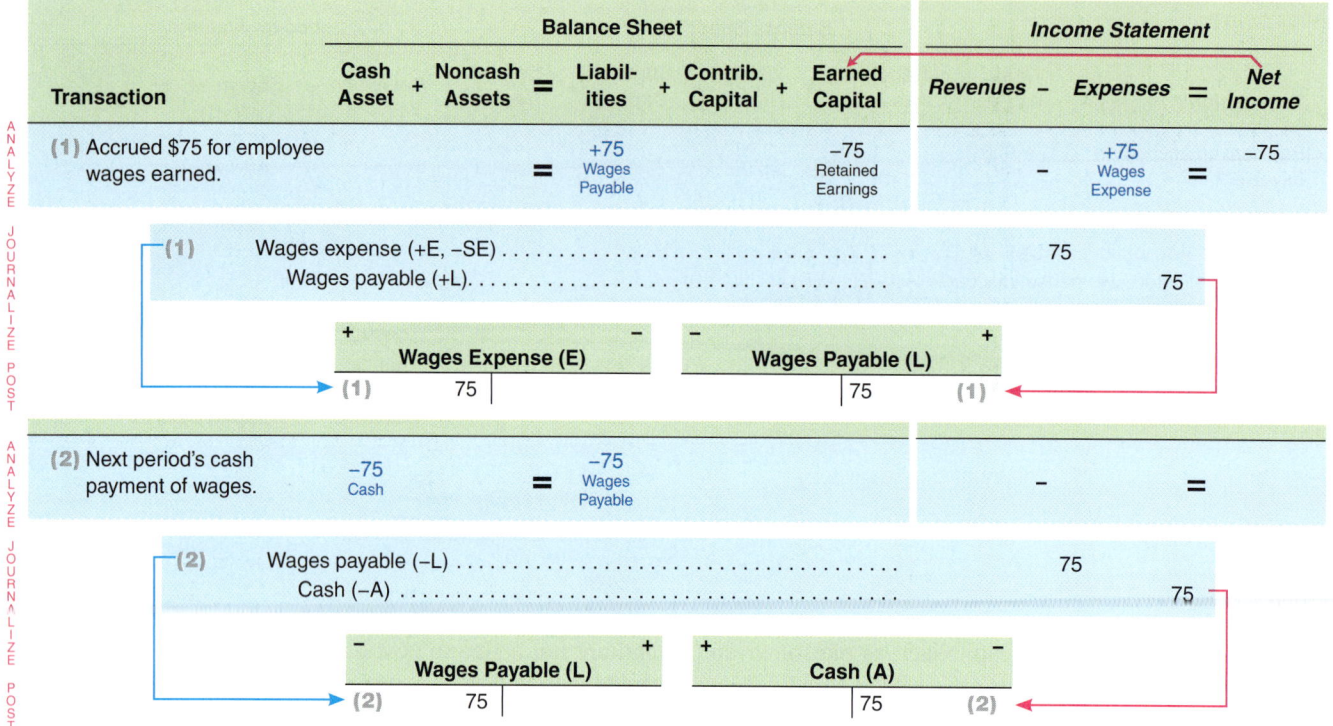

The following financial statement effects result from this accrual of employee wages:

- Employees have worked during a period and have not yet been paid. The effect of this accrual is to increase wages payable on the balance sheet and to recognize wages expense on the income statement. Failure to recognize this liability and associated expense would understate liabilities on the balance sheet and overstate income.
- Employees are paid in the following period, resulting in a cash decrease and a reduction in wages payable. This payment does not result in expense because the expense was recognized in the prior period when incurred.

Contingent Liabilities The accrued wages illustration relates to events that are fairly certain. We know, for example, when wages are incurred but not paid. Other examples of such accruals are rental costs, insurance premiums due but not yet paid, and taxes owed.

Some accrued liabilities, however, are less certain than others. Consider a company facing a lawsuit. Should it record the possible liability and related expense? The answer depends on the likelihood of occurrence and the ability to estimate the obligation. Specifically, if the obligation is *probable* **and** the amount *estimable,* then a company will recognize this obligation, called a **contingent liability**, with a corresponding charge to income. If an obligation is only *reasonably possible,* regardless of the company's ability to estimate the amount, the contingent liability is not reported on the balance sheet and is merely disclosed in the notes to the financial statements (we discuss further below). All other contingent liabilities that are less than reasonably possible are not accrued—disclosure in a note is permitted but not required.

IFRS

A GLOBAL PERSPECTIVE

Reporting Contingent Liabilities U.S. GAAP and IFRS are similar with respect to reporting accrued liabilities. The one exception is contingencies. IFRS uses the term "provisions" to refer to contingent liabilities that are accrued and reported on the balance sheet, while an obligation that is disclosed in the notes is labeled "contingent liability." Both GAAP and IFRS require accrual of the "best estimate" of the liability. However, if the best estimate of the future payments required to settle the obligation is a range of values, IFRS requires that the midpoint of the range be used as the estimated value of the contingent liability or provision. In the same situation, U.S. GAAP requires that the low end of the range be used, with disclosure of the maximum.

Warranties The revenue recognition standard discussed in Chapter 6 has implications for the accounting for warranty obligations. When a company delivers a product with a warranty, is the warranty simply assurance that the product will function as intended, or should it be considered a separate performance obligation? If it is considered a separate performance obligation, then the company would allocate the purchase price between the product and the warranty and recognize a contract liability at the time of purchase. However, if the warranty is not a separate performance obligation (e.g., it cannot be purchased separately from the product and is intended as assurance that the product will perform as expected), none of the purchase price is allocated to the warranty, and a liability accrual for the warranty obligation must be made at the time of purchase, as mentioned in Chapter 6.

The expected cost of the warranty commitment usually is reasonably estimated at the time of sale based on past experience. GAAP requires manufacturers to record the expected cost of warranties as a liability and to record the related expected warranty expense in the income statement to match against the sales revenue reported for that period.

To illustrate, the effects of an accrual of a $1,000 warranty liability are:

	Balance Sheet									*Income Statement*				
Transaction	Cash Asset	+	Noncash Assets	=	Liabilities	+	Contrib. Capital	+	Earned Capital	*Revenues*	–	*Expenses*	=	*Net Income*
ANALYZE (1) Accrued $1,000 of expected warranty costs on goods sold this period.				=	+1,000 Warranty Liability				–1,000 Retained Earnings		–	+1,000 Warranty Expense	=	–1,000
ANALYZE (2) Next period's costs (sent $950 in replacement products) to cover failures under warranty.			–950 Inventory	=	–950 Warranty Liability						–		=	

JOURNALIZE

(1) Warranty expense (+E, –SE) 1,000
Warranty liability (+L) 1,000

POST

+ Warranty Expense (E) –	
(1) 1,000	

– Warranty Liability (L) +	
	1,000 (1)

JOURNALIZE

(2) Warranty liability (–L) 950
Inventory (–A) 950

POST

– Warranty Liability (L) +	
(2) 950	

+ Inventory (A) –	
	950 (2)

Reporting of warranty liabilities has the same effect on financial statements as does the accrual of wages expense in the previous section. That is, a liability is recorded on the balance sheet and an expense is reported in the income statement, reducing income by the warranty accrual. When the defective product is later replaced (or repaired), the liability is reduced together with the cost of the inventory (or other assets) spent to satisfy the claim. (Only a portion of the products estimated to fail does so in the current period; we expect other product failures in future periods. Using methods similar to the aging of accounts in Chapter 6, management monitors this estimate and adjusts it if failure is higher or lower than expected.) As in the accrual of wages, the expense is reported when it is incurred and the liability is estimated at that time, not when payments are made.

Apple Inc. reports $3,354 million of warranty liability in its 2020 balance sheet. The disclosure notes reveal the following additional information:

Several notes are combined below: Accrued Warranty and Indemnification, Warranty, and Warranty Costs The Company offers limited warranties on its new and certified refurbished hardware products and on parts used to repair its hardware products, and customers may purchase extended service coverage, where available, on many of the Company's hardware products. The Company accrues the estimated cost of warranties in the period the related revenue is recognized based on historical and projected warranty claim rates, historical and projected cost per claim, and knowledge of specific product failures outside the Company's typical experience. If actual product failure rates or repair costs differ from estimates, revisions to the estimated warranty liabilities would be required.

Accrued Warranty and Indemnification The following table shows changes in the Company's accrued warranties and related costs for 2020, 2019, and 2018 (in millions):

	2020	2019	2018
Beginning accrued warranty and related costs	$3,570	$3,692	$3,834
Cost of warranty claims	(2,956)	(3,857)	(4,115)
Accruals for product warranty	2,740	3,735	3,973
Ending accrued warranty and related costs	$3,354	$3,570	$3,692

In 2020, Apple incurred $2,956 million in cost to replace or repair defective products during the year, reducing the liability by this amount. This cost can be in the form of cash paid to customers or to employees as wages, and in the form of parts used for repairs. The company accrued an additional $2,740 million in new warranty liabilities in 2020. It is important to realize that only the increase in the liability resulting from additional accruals affects the income statement, reducing income through the additional warranty expense. Warranty payments reduce the warranty liability but have no impact on the income statement.

U.S. GAAP requires that the warranty liability reflect the estimated amount of cost that the company expects to incur as a result of warranty claims. This amount is often difficult to estimate and is prone to error. There is also the possibility that a company might intentionally underestimate its warranty liability to report higher current income, or overestimate it so as to depress current income and create an additional liability on the balance sheet that can be used to absorb future warranty costs without the need to record additional expense. Doing so would shift income from the current period to one or more future periods. Warranty liabilities should be compared with sales levels. Any deviations from the historical relation of the warranty liability to sales may indicate a change in product quality or, alternatively, it may reveal earnings management.

Experience tells us that some accrued liabilities are more prone to misstatement than others. Estimated accruals that are linked with restructuring programs, including severance accruals and accruals for asset write-downs, are often overstated, as are estimated environmental liabilities. Companies sometimes overestimate these "one-time" accruals, resulting in early recognition of expenses (as "nonrecurring items") and a corresponding reduction in current period income. This choice, in turn, boosts income in future years when management decides that the accrual can be reversed because it was initially too large. This may suggest that management is conservative and wants to avoid understating liabilities. It can also reflect a desire by management to show earnings growth in the future by shifting current income to future periods. Accrued liabilities set up to smooth income over future periods are called "**cookie jar reserves**." The terms "clearing the decks" and "taking a big bath" have also been applied to such accounting practices.

YOU MAKE THE CALL

You are the Analyst **DowDuPont Inc.** disclosed the following in their 2020 10-K:

Environmental Matters

Accruals for environmental matters are recorded when it is probable that a liability has been incurred and the amount of the liability can be reasonably estimated based on current law and existing technologies. At December 31, 2020, the Company had accrued obligations of $80 million for probable environmental remediation and restoration costs, inclusive of $36 million retained and assumed following the DWDP Distributions and $44 million of indemnified liabilities.

continued

continued from previous page

What conditions needed to be met before these liabilities could be reported?

The company then stated that "This is management's best estimate of the costs for remediation and restoration with respect to environmental matters for which the Company has accrued liabilities, although it is reasonably possible that the ultimate cost with respect to these particular matters could range up to $170 million above the amount accrued at December 31, 2020."

How does this uncertainty affect the company's balance sheet? [Answers on page 9-33]

Other Current Liabilities

Verizon provides more detailed disclosure for the line item on the balance sheet labeled "other" under current liabilities. Here is the table they provide:

Other Current Liabilities	2020	2019
Dividends payable	$2,618	$2,566
Contract liability	4,843	4,651
Other	2,167	1,807
Total	$9,628	$9,024

Contract liability includes advance billings and customer deposits (under ASC 606). Either customers have prepaid for work (i.e., another term for this is deferred revenue), or the unconditional right to payment has occurred according to the contract terms. If the customer has prepaid, cash is increased (debited) and the liability is increased (credited). If the unconditional right to payment has occurred but no payment has been made, then the company increases a receivable (debits a receivable) and increases the liability (credits the liability).

Dividends payable is a liability for dividends that have been declared but not yet paid. There is a liability for the dividends to be paid in this case, but recall dividends are never expensed. The other side of the entry is a decrease to equity (a debit to equity).

Accounting for Current Operating Liabilities LO9-1 **Review 9-1**

GuidedExample MBC

Part One

On April 12, Waymire Corporation purchased raw materials costing $29,000 on credit. The credit terms were 2/10, n/30.

a. If Waymire paid for the materials on April 19, how much would it pay?

b. Compute the cost of a lost discount as an annual percentage interest rate.

Part Two

The Toro Company reported warranty liabilities of $96,604,000 in its October 31, 2019, balance sheet. On its October 31, 2020, balance sheet, it reported a liability of $107,121,000. It recognized $77,758,000 in net warranty expenses during fiscal year 2020, ending October 31, 2020.

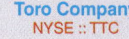

Toro Company
NYSE :: TTC

a. What amount of cost did Toro incur to cover warranty claims in 2020?

b. How would the fulfillment of these claims be recorded using the financial statement effects template?

c. Record the entry described in part *b* in a journal entry.

Solution on p. 9-48.

Current Nonoperating (Financial) Liabilities

Current nonoperating (financial) liabilities include short-term bank loans, the accrual of interest on those loans, and the current maturities of long-term debt. Companies generally try to structure their financing so that debt service requirements (payments) of those financing obligations coincide with the cash inflows from the assets financed. This strategy means that current assets are usually financed with current liabilities and that long-term assets are financed with long-term liability (and equity) sources.

LO9-2
Describe and account for current nonoperating (financial) liabilities.

eLecture MBC

The use of short-term financing is particularly important for companies that have seasonal sales. To illustrate, a seasonal company's investment in current assets tends to fluctuate during the year, as depicted in the graphic below:

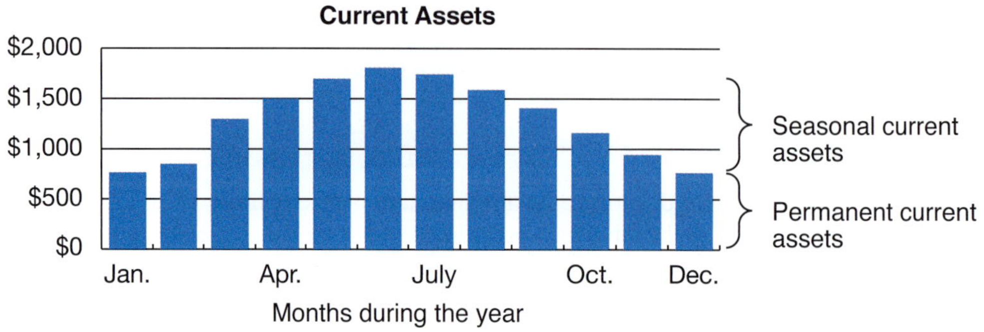

This particular company does most of its selling in the summer months. More inventory is purchased and manufactured in the early spring than at any other time of the year. Sales of the company's manufactured goods are also greater during the summer months, giving rise to accounts receivable that are higher than normal during the summer and fall. The peak working capital level is reached at the height of the selling season and is lowest when the business slows in the off-season. There is a permanent level of working capital required for this business (about $750), and a seasonal component (maximum of about $1,000). Businesses differ in their working capital requirements, but many have permanent and seasonal components.

If a company's working capital needs fluctuate from one season to the next, then the financing needs of the company are also seasonal. Some assets can be financed with short-term operating liabilities. For example, seasonal increases in inventory balances are typically financed with increased levels of accounts payable. However, operating liabilities are unlikely to meet all of the financing needs of a company. Additional financing is provided by short-term interest-bearing debt.

This section focuses on short-term nonoperating liabilities. These include short-term debt and interest as well as current maturities of long-term liabilities.

Short-Term Interest-Bearing Debt Seasonal swings in working capital are often financed with a bank line of credit (short-term debt). In this case the bank provides a commitment to lend up to a given level with the understanding that the amounts borrowed are repaid in full sometime during the year. An interest-bearing note is evidence of such borrowing.

When these short-term funds are borrowed, the cash received is reported on the balance sheet together with an increase in liabilities (notes payable). The note is reported as a current liability because the expectation is that it will be paid within a year. This borrowing transaction has no effect on income or equity, but there will be a financing cash inflow on the statement of cash flows. The borrower incurs (and the lender earns) interest on the note as time passes. U.S. GAAP requires the borrower to accrue the interest liability and the related interest expense each time financial statements are issued.

To illustrate, assume that Verizon borrows $1,000 cash from 1st Bank on January 1. The note bears interest at a 12% annual (3% quarterly) rate, and the interest is payable on the first of each subsequent quarter (April 1, July 1, October 1, January 1). Assuming that Verizon issues calendar-quarter financial statements, this borrowing results in the following financial statement effects for the period January 1 through April 1:

	Balance Sheet									Income Statement				
Transaction	Cash Asset	+	Noncash Assets	=	Liabil-ities	+	Contrib. Capital	+	Earned Capital	*Revenues*	−	*Expenses*	=	*Net Income*
ANALYZE (1) Jan. 1, Borrowed $1,000 cash by issuing note payable.	+1,000 Cash			=	+1,000 Notes Payable						−		=	

JOURNALIZE

		Dr.	Cr.
Jan 1	Cash (+A)	1,000	
	Notes payable (+L)		1,000

POST

+ Cash (A) −	
Jan. 1 1,000	

− Notes Payable (L) +	
	1,000 Jan. 1

Transaction	Cash Asset	+	Noncash Assets	=	Liabil-ities	+	Contrib. Capital	+	Earned Capital	*Revenues*	−	*Expenses*	=	*Net Income*
ANALYZE (2) Mar. 31, Interest accrues on 12% note payable.				=	+30 Interest Payable				−30 Retained Earnings		−	+30 Interest Expense	=	−30

JOURNALIZE

		Dr.	Cr.
March 31	Interest expense (+E, −SE)	30	
	Interest payable (+L)		30

POST

+ Interest Expense (E) −	
March 31 30	

− Interest Payable (L) +	
	30 March 31

Transaction	Cash Asset	+	Noncash Assets	=	Liabil-ities	+	Contrib. Capital	+	Earned Capital	*Revenues*	−	*Expenses*	=	*Net Income*
ANALYZE (3) Apr.1, Cash paid to cover interest due.	−30 Cash			=	−30 Interest Payable						−		=	

JOURNALIZE

		Dr.	Cr.
April 1	Interest payable (−L)	30	
	Cash (−A)		30

POST

− Interest Payable (L) +	
April 1 30	

+ Cash (A) −	
	30 April 1

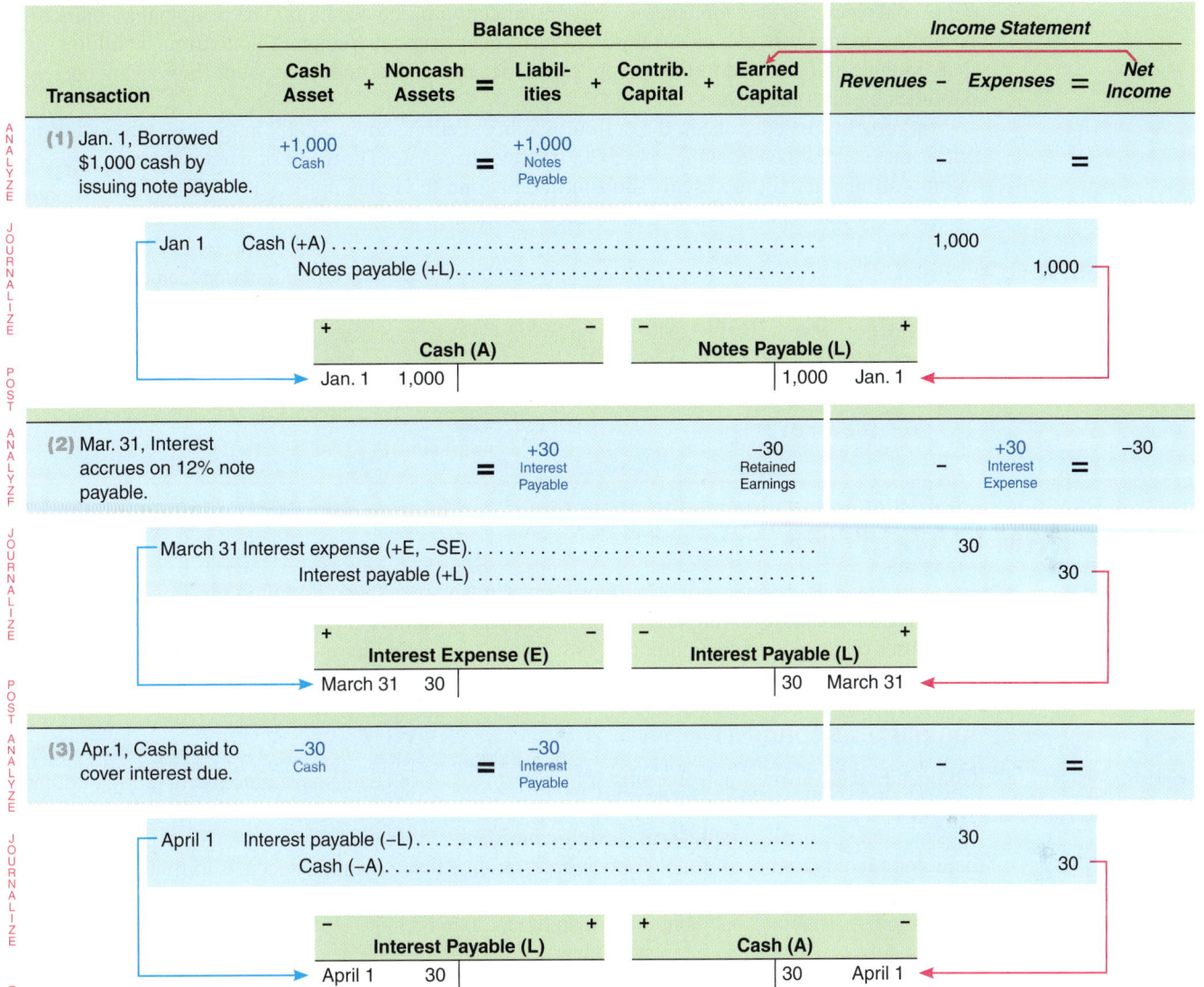

The January 1 borrowing is reflected by an increase in cash and in notes payable. On March 31, this company issues its quarterly financial statements. Although interest is not paid until April 1, the company has incurred three months' interest obligation as of March 31. Failure to recognize this liability and the expense incurred would not fairly present the financial condition of the company. Accordingly, the quarterly accrued interest is computed as follows:

$$\textbf{Interest Expense} = \textbf{Principal} \times \textbf{Annual Rate} \times \textbf{Portion of Year Outstanding}$$
$$\$30 = \$1{,}000 \times 12\% \times 3/12$$

The subsequent interest payment on April 1 is reflected in the financial statements as a reduction of cash and a reduction of the interest payable liability accrued on March 31. There is no expense reported on April 1 because it was recorded the previous day (March 31) when the financial statements were prepared; however, the payment of interest would be an operating cash outflow in the statement of cash flows for the quarter beginning April 1. (For fixed-maturity borrowings specified in days, such as a 90-day note, we use a 365-day year for interest accrual computations; see Review 9-2.)

Current Maturities of Long-Term Debt All companies are required to provide a schedule of the maturities of their long-term debt in the notes to financial statements. Debt payments that must be made during the upcoming 12 months on long-term debt (such as for a mortgage) or the maturity of a bond or note are reported as current liabilities called *current maturities of long-term* *debt.* This change is accomplished by a reclassification in the accounts. The principal amount approaching maturity is debited to the long-term debt account (reducing noncurrent liabilities by that amount) and credited to the current maturities of long-term debt account (increasing current liabilities by that amount).

In Verizon's balance sheet, the current liability section shows $5,889 million in debt maturing within one year of the December 31, 2020, balance sheet date. The disclosure notes reveal that $320 million of this amount represents short-term debt, and the remaining $5,569 million is long-term debt that must be repaid or refinanced sometime during 2021.

Review 9-2 LO9-2

Accounting for Current Nonoperating Liabilities

Gigler Company borrowed $10,000 on a 90-day, 6% note payable dated January 15. The bank accrues interest daily based on a 365-day year.

a. Use the financial statement effects template to show the implications (amounts and accounts) of the January 31 month-end interest accrual.

b. Use journal entries and T-accounts to record the month-end interest accrual.

Solution on p. 9-49.

LONG-TERM LIABILITIES

LO9-3
Explain and illustrate the pricing of long-term nonoperating liabilities.

Companies generally try to fund long-term investments in assets with long-term financing. Long-term financing consists of long-term liabilities and stockholders' equity. The remainder of this chapter focuses on long-term debt liabilities. Other long-term liabilities are discussed in Chapter 10, and stockholders' equity is the focus of Chapter 11.

Installment Loans

Companies can borrow small amounts of long-term debt from banks, insurance companies, or other financial institutions. These liabilities are often designed as installment loans and may be secured by specific assets called **collateral**. Installment loans are loans that require a fixed periodic payment for a fixed duration of time. For example, assume that a company decides to finance an office building with a 15-year mortgage requiring 180 equal monthly payments (180 payments = 15 years × 12 months). The fixed payment on an installment loan includes a portion of the principal (i.e., the amount borrowed) plus any interest that has accrued on the loan.

To illustrate the accounting for installment loans, assume that Shevlin Company borrowed $40,000 from 1st Bank on July 1, 2021. The terms of the loan require that Shevlin repay the loan in 12 equal quarterly payments over a three-year period and require 8% interest per year. The quarterly payment is $3,782 and can be calculated using the Table A.3 (page A-22) present value factor for 12 periods (3 years × 4 quarters) and 2% interest (8% per year ÷ 4 quarters) as follows:

$$\text{Present Value} = \text{Payment} \times \text{Present Value Factor}$$

$$\frac{\text{Present Value}}{\text{Present Value Factor}} = \text{Payment}$$

$$\frac{\$40{,}000}{10.57534} = \$3{,}782$$

Using a financial calculator, we can compute the payment by letting N be the number of quarters and setting I/Yr equal to the interest rate per quarter. The payment can then be calculated as follows: N = 12; I/Yr = 2; PV = 40,000; FV = 0:

Calculator

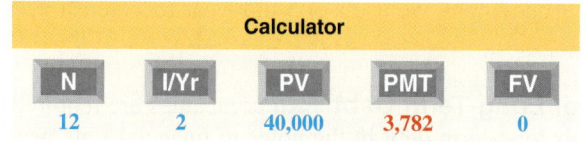

N	I/Yr	PV	PMT	FV
12	2	40,000	3,782	0

When Shevlin Company agrees to the loan terms, it receives the loan amount, $40,000 in cash, and incurs a $40,000 liability (installment loan payable). The loan is recorded on July 1 as follows:

ANALYZE

Transaction	Cash Asset	+	Noncash Assets	=	Liabil-ities	+	Contrib. Capital	+	Earned Capital	Revenues	−	Expenses	=	Net Income
Borrow $40,000 from 1st Bank.	+40,000 Cash			=	+40,000 Installment Loan Payable						−		=	

(Balance Sheet: Cash Asset through Earned Capital; Income Statement: Revenues through Net Income)

JOURNALIZE

	Debit	Credit
Cash (+A)	40,000	
Installment loan payable (+L)		40,000

POST

+ Cash (A) −		− Installment Loan Payable (L) +	
40,000			40,000

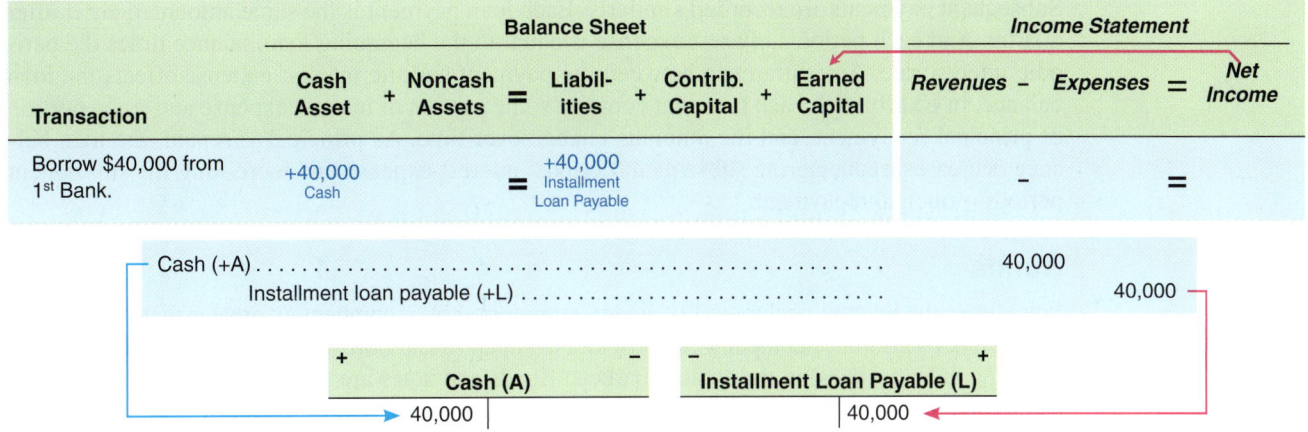

On October 1, 2021, the first payment of $3,782 is due. The payment includes both interest for the three months from July 1 through September 30 and some portion of the original loan amount (the **principal**). The division of the payment between interest and principal is best illustrated using a **loan amortization table**, like the one in **Exhibit 9.2**. (Pages A-14–A-15 in Appendix A demonstrate the use of Excel to calculate the required payment and the amortization table.)

Each payment includes interest and principal. The first loan payment, due on October 1, 2021, is summarized in the second row of the table. Column [B] is the quarterly loan payment. Column [C] is the interest expense, computed by multiplying column [A] by the interest rate (2 percent per quarter). Column [D] is the principal portion of the payment, which is the cash payment (column [B]) less the interest (column [C]). The remaining balance on the loan is in column [E], which is equal to the beginning balance in column [A] less the principal payment from column [D]. The loan balance decreases with each payment until the loan is paid off on July 1, 2024.

EXHIBIT 9.2 Loan Amortization Table

Date	[A] Beginning Balance	[B] Cash Payment	[C] ([A] × interest %) Interest	[D] ([B] − [C]) Principal	[E] ([A] − [D]) Balance
07/01/21					40,000
10/01/21	40,000	3,782	800	2,982	37,018
01/01/22	37,018	3,782	740	3,042	33,976
04/01/22	33,976	3,782	679	3,103	30,873
07/01/22	30,873	3,782	617	3,165	27,708
10/01/22	27,708	3,782	554	3,228	24,480
01/01/23	24,480	3,782	489	3,293	21,187
04/01/23	21,187	3,782	423	3,359	17,828
07/01/23	17,828	3,782	356	3,426	14,402
10/01/23	14,402	3,782	288	3,494	10,908
01/01/24	10,908	3,782	218	3,564	7,344
04/01/24	7,344	3,782	146	3,636	3,708
07/01/24	3,708	3,782	74	3,708	0

The first payment is recorded as follows:

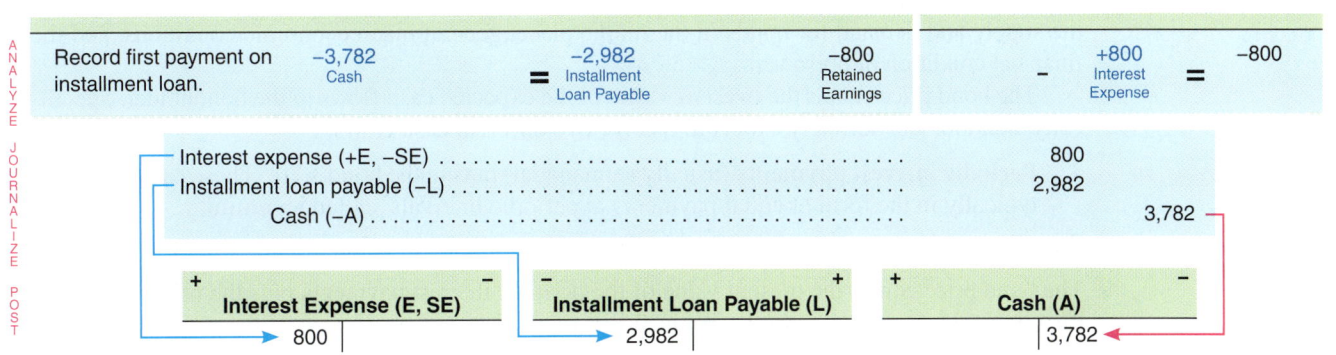

ANALYZE

Transaction	Cash Asset	+	Noncash Assets	=	Liabil-ities	+	Contrib. Capital	+	Earned Capital	Revenues	−	Expenses	=	Net Income
Record first payment on installment loan.	−3,782 Cash			=	−2,982 Installment Loan Payable				−800 Retained Earnings		−	+800 Interest Expense	=	−800

JOURNALIZE

	Debit	Credit
Interest expense (+E, −SE)	800	
Installment loan payable (−L)	2,982	
Cash (−A)		3,782

POST

+ Interest Expense (E, SE) −		− Installment Loan Payable (L) +		+ Cash (A) −	
800		2,982			3,782

Subsequent payments are recorded similarly. Each loan payment is the same amount, quarter after quarter. And each period's interest expense is equal to the beginning loan balance times the periodic interest rate. Any difference between the payment and the interest expense affects the loan balance. In **Exhibit 9.2**, each payment contains some portion of interest expense and some portion of principal repayment, and the amounts change over time. As principal is repaid, the loan balance decreases, reducing the subsequent periods' interest expense and increasing the subsequent periods' principal repayment.

Bonds

Sometimes the amount or duration of financing required by a company is greater than the amount that a bank or insurance company can provide. Companies can borrow larger amounts of money by issuing bonds (or notes) in the capital markets. Bonds and notes are debt securities issued by companies and traded in the bond markets. When a company issues bonds, it is borrowing money. The investors who buy the bonds are lending money to the issuing company. That is, the bondholders are the company's creditors. Because the bond markets provide companies with access to large amounts of capital, bonds represent a very common, cost-effective source of long-term debt financing.

Bonds and notes are structured like any other borrowing. The borrower receives cash and agrees to pay it back with interest. Generally, the entire **face amount** (principal) of the bond or note is repaid at maturity and interest payments are made (usually semiannually) in the interim.

Companies wishing to raise funds in the bond market normally work with an underwriter (e.g., **Goldman Sachs**) to set the terms of the bond issue. The underwriter sells individual bonds (usually in $1,000 denominations) from this general bond issue to its retail clients, corporations, and professional portfolio managers (e.g., **The Vanguard Group**), and it receives a fee for underwriting the bond issue.

Once issued, the bonds can be traded in the secondary market between investors just like stocks. Market prices of bonds fluctuate daily despite the fact that the company's obligation for payment of principal and interest remains fixed throughout the life of the bond. This occurs because of fluctuations in the general level of interest rates and changes in the financial condition of the borrowing company.

The following sections analyze and interpret the reporting for bonds. We first examine the mechanics of bond pricing. In a subsequent section, we address the accounting for and reporting of bonds.

Pricing of Bonds

Two different interest rates are crucial for understanding how a bond is priced.

- **Coupon (contract** or **stated) rate** The coupon rate of interest is stated in the bond contract. It is used to compute the dollar amount of (semiannual) interest payments that are paid to bondholders during the life of the bond issue.
- **Market (yield) rate** The market rate is the interest rate that investors expect to earn on the investment for this debt security. This rate is used to price the bond issue.

The coupon (contract) rate is used to compute interest payments, and the market (yield) rate is used to price the bond. The coupon rate and the market rate are nearly always different. The coupon rate is fixed prior to issuance of the bond and remains so throughout its life (unless the interest rate "floats" with market rates). Market rates of interest, on the other hand, fluctuate continually with the supply and demand for bonds in the marketplace, general macroeconomic conditions, and the financial condition of borrowers.

The bond price equals the **present value** of the expected cash flows to the bondholder. Specifically, bondholders normally expect to receive two different cash flows:

1. **Periodic interest payments** (usually semiannual) during the bond's life. These cash flows are typically in the form of equal payments at periodic intervals, called an **annuity**.
2. **Single payment** of the face (principal) amount of the bond at maturity.

The bond price equals the present value of the periodic interest payments plus the present value of the principal payment at maturity. We next illustrate the issuance of bonds at three different prices: at par, at a discount, and at a premium.

Bonds Issued at Par When a bond is issued at par, its coupon rate is identical to the market rate. Under this condition, a $1,000 bond sells for $1,000 in the market. To illustrate bond pricing, assume that investors wish to value a bond issue with a face amount of $100,000, a 6% annual coupon rate with interest payable semiannually (3% semiannual rate), and a maturity of 4 years.[3] Investors purchasing this issue receive the following cash flows:

	Number of Payments	Dollars per Payment	Total Cash Flows
Semiannual interest payments	4 years × 2 = 8	$100,000 × 3% = $ 3,000	$ 24,000
Principal payment at maturity	1	$100,000	100,000
			$124,000

Specifically, the bond agreement dictates that the borrower makes 8 semiannual payments of $3,000 each, computed as $100,000 × (6%/2), plus the $100,000 face amount at maturity, for a total of $124,000 in cash flows. Each $1,000 bond in this bond issue provides the bondholder with an annuity of 8 payments of $30 and a principal payment of $1,000 at maturity. For an individual bond, the cash flows total $1,240 (= $30 × 8 + $1,000).

When pricing bonds, the number of periods used for computing the present value is the number of interest (coupon) payments required by the bond. In this case, there are 8 semiannual interest payments required, so we use 8 six-month periods to value the bond. The market interest rate (yield) is 6% per year, which is 3% per six-month period.

The bond price is the present value of the interest annuity plus the present value of the principal payment. Assuming that investors desire a 6% annual market rate (yield), the bond sells for exactly $100,000, which is computed as follows:

	Payment	Present Value Factor[a]	Present Value
Interest	$ 3,000	7.01969[b]	$ 21,059
Principal	$100,000	0.78941[c]	78,941
			$100,000

[a] Mechanics of using tables to compute present values are explained in Appendix A at the end of the text. Present value factors are taken from tables provided in Appendix A.

[b] Present value of ordinary annuity for 8 periods discounted at 3% per period.

[c] Present value of single payment in 8 periods, hence discounted at 3% per period.

Because the bond contract pays investors a 6% annual rate when investors demand a 6% market rate, investors purchase these bonds at the **par (face) value** of $1,000 per bond, or $100,000 in total.[4] Using a financial calculator, we can compute the bond value as follows: N = 8; I/Yr = 3; PMT = 3,000; FV = 100,000:

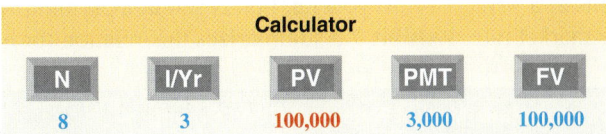

Calculator				
N	I/Yr	PV	PMT	FV
8	3	100,000	3,000	100,000

Bonds Issued at a Discount As a second illustration, assume that market conditions are such that investors demand an 8% annual yield (4% semiannual) for the 6% coupon bond, while all other details remain the same. The bond now sells for $93,267, computed as follows:

	Payment	Present Value Factor	Present Value
Interest	$ 3,000	6.73274[a]	$20,198
Principal	$100,000	0.73069[b]	73,069
			$93,267

[a] Present value of ordinary annuity for 8 periods discounted at 4% per period.

[b] Present value of single payment in 8 periods, hence discounted at 4% per period.

[3] Semiannual interest payments are typical for bonds. With semiannual interest payments, the issuer pays bondholders two interest payments per year. The semiannual interest rate is the annual rate divided by two.

[4] If we purchase a bond after the semiannual interest date, we must pay accrued interest in addition to the purchase price. This interest is returned to us in the regular interest payment. (This procedure makes the bookkeeping easier for the issuer/underwriter.)

Using a financial calculator, the bond is priced as follows: N = 8; I/Yr = 4; PMT = 3,000; FV = 100,000:

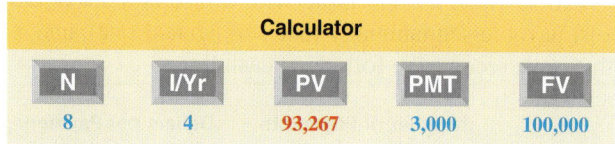

Calculator				
N	I/Yr	PV	PMT	FV
8	4	93,267	3,000	100,000

The market price of the bond issue is, therefore, $93,267. The price of each bond in the bond issue is $932.67 (= $93,267/100).

Because the bond carries a coupon rate *lower* than that which investors demand, the bond is less desirable and sells at a **discount**. In general, bonds sell at a discount whenever the coupon rate is less than the market rate.[5]

Bonds Issued at a Premium As a third illustration, assume that investors in the bond market demand a 4% annual yield (2% semiannual) for the 6% coupon bonds, while all other details remain the same. The bond issue now sells for $107,325, computed as follows:

	Payment	Present Value Factor	Present Value
Interest	$ 3,000	7.32548[a]	$ 21,976
Principal	$100,000	0.85349[b]	85,349
			$107,325

[a] Present value of ordinary annuity for 8 periods discounted at 2% per period.

[b] Present value of single payment in 8 periods, hence discounted at 2% per period.

Using a financial calculator, the bond is priced as follows: N = 8; I/Yr = 2; PMT = 3,000; FV = 100,000:

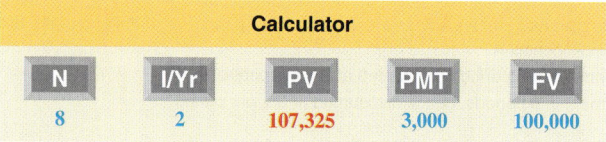

Calculator				
N	I/Yr	PV	PMT	FV
8	2	107,325	3,000	100,000

The market price of the bond issue is, therefore, $107,325. The price of each bond in the bond issue is $1,073.25 (= $107,325/100).

Because the bond carries a coupon rate higher than that which investors demand, the bond is more desirable and sells at a **premium**. In general, bonds sell at a premium whenever the coupon rate is greater than the market rate. **Exhibit 9.3** summarizes this relation for bond pricing.

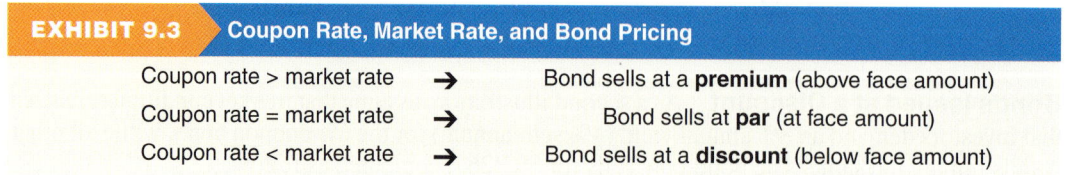

EXHIBIT 9.3 Coupon Rate, Market Rate, and Bond Pricing

Coupon rate > market rate	→	Bond sells at a **premium** (above face amount)
Coupon rate = market rate	→	Bond sells at **par** (at face amount)
Coupon rate < market rate	→	Bond sells at a **discount** (below face amount)

Effective Cost of Debt

When a bond sells for par, the cost to the issuing company is the cash interest paid. In our first illustration where the bond is issued at par, the *effective cost* of the bond is the 6% interest paid by the issuer.

When a bond sells at a discount, the issuer's effective cost consists of two parts: (1) the cash interest paid and (2) the discount incurred. The discount, which is the difference between par and the lower issue price, is a cost that must eventually be reflected in the issuer's income statement

[5] Bond prices are often stated in percent form. For example, a bond sold at par is said to be sold at 100 (that is, 100% of its face value, par). The bond sold at $932.67 is said to be sold at 93.267 (93.267% of par, computed as $932.67/$1,000).

as an expense. This fact means that the effective cost of a discount bond is greater than if the bond had sold at par. A discount is a cost and, like any other cost, must eventually be transferred from the balance sheet to the income statement as an expense. In the previous section's discount example, the economic substance is that the bond issuer has not borrowed $100,000 at 6%, but rather $93,267 at 8%.

When a bond sells at a premium, the issuer's effective cost consists of (1) the cash interest paid and (2) a cost reduction due to the premium received. The premium is a benefit that must eventually find its way from the balance sheet to the income statement as a *reduction* of interest expense. As a result of the premium, the effective cost of a premium bond is less than if the bond had sold at par. Effectively, the bond issuer has borrowed $107,325 at 4% in the premium example above.

Bonds are priced to yield the return (market rate) demanded by investors in the bond market, which results in the effective interest rate of a bond *always* equaling the yield (market) rate, regardless of the coupon (stated) rate of the bond. Bond prices are set by the market so as to always yield the rate required by investors based on the terms and qualities of the bond. Companies cannot influence the effective cost of debt by raising or lowering the coupon rate. We discuss the factors affecting the market yield later in the chapter.

The effective cost of debt is ultimately reflected in the amount reported in the issuer's income statement as interest expense. This amount can be, and usually is, different from the cash interest paid. The two are the same only for a bond issued at par. The next section discusses how management reports bonds on the balance sheet and interest expense on the income statement.

Computing Bond Issue Price LO9-3 **Review 9-3**

GuidedExample MBC

On January 2, Randall, Inc., issues $500,000 of 4% bonds that pay interest semiannually and mature in ten years. Compute the bond issue price assuming the following market interest (yield) rate per year compounded semiannually. Consider each case separately.

a. 4%
b. 6%
c. 2%

Solution on p. 9-49.

Reporting of Bond Financing

This section identifies and describes the financial statement effects of bond transactions.

LO9-4
Analyze and account for financial statement effects of long-term nonoperating liabilities.

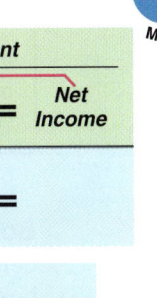

eLecture MBC

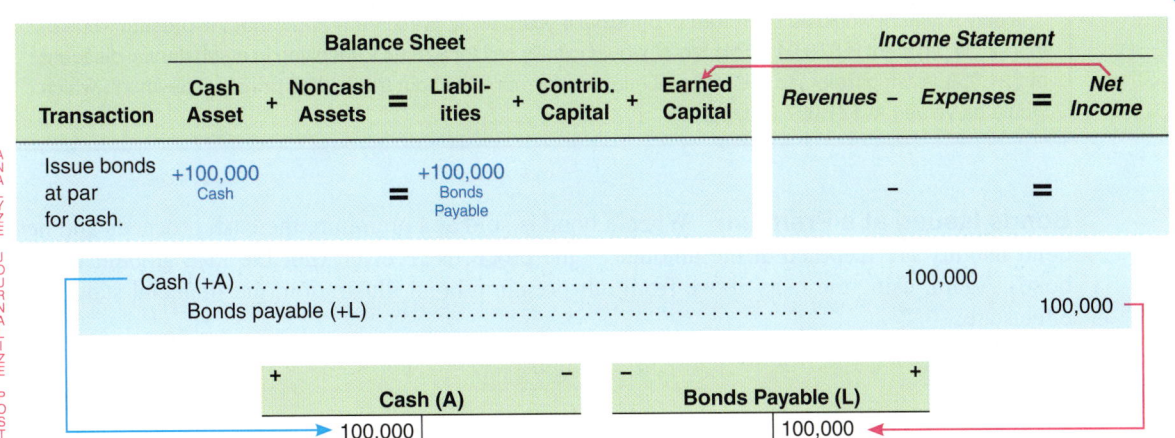

Bonds Issued at Par When a bond sells at par, the issuing company receives the cash proceeds and accepts an obligation to make payments per the bond contract. Specifically, cash is increased and a liability (bonds payable) is increased by the same amount. Using the facts from our earlier illustration, the issuance of bonds at par has the following financial statement effects. (There is no revenue or expense at the date the bond is issued.)

A N A L Y Z E

	Balance Sheet									Income Statement				
Transaction	Cash Asset	+	Noncash Assets	=	Liabilities	+	Contrib. Capital	+	Earned Capital	Revenues	−	Expenses	=	Net Income
Issue bonds at par for cash.	+100,000 Cash			=	+100,000 Bonds Payable						−		=	

J O U R N A L I Z E

Cash (+A)	100,000	
Bonds payable (+L)		100,000

P O S T

+	Cash (A)	−
100,000		

−	Bonds Payable (L)	+
		100,000

Bonds Issued at a Discount For the discount bond case, cash is increased by the proceeds from the sale of the bonds, and the liability increases by the same amount. However, the net liability consisting of the two components shown below (including a bond discount contra liability) is reported on the balance sheet.

> **FYI** "Bonds Payable, Net" is a common title reflecting the face value of the bond less the unamortized discount.

Bonds payable, face	$100,000
Less bond discount	(6,733)
Bonds payable, net	$ 93,267

Using the facts above from our bond discount illustration, the financial statement effects follow:

ANALYZE

Transaction	Cash Asset	+	Noncash Assets	=	Liabilities	−	Contra Liabilities	+	Contrib. Capital	+	Earned Capital	Revenues	−	Expenses	=	Net Income
	Balance Sheet											***Income Statement***				
Issue bonds at a discount for cash.	+93,267 Cash			=	+100,000 Bonds Payable	−	+6,733 Bond Discount						−		=	

JOURNALIZE

Cash (+A)	93,267	
Bond discount (+XL, −L)	6,733	
Bonds payable (+L)		100,000

POST

+ Cash (A) −	+ Bond Discount (XL) −	− Bonds Payable (L) +
93,267	6,733	100,000

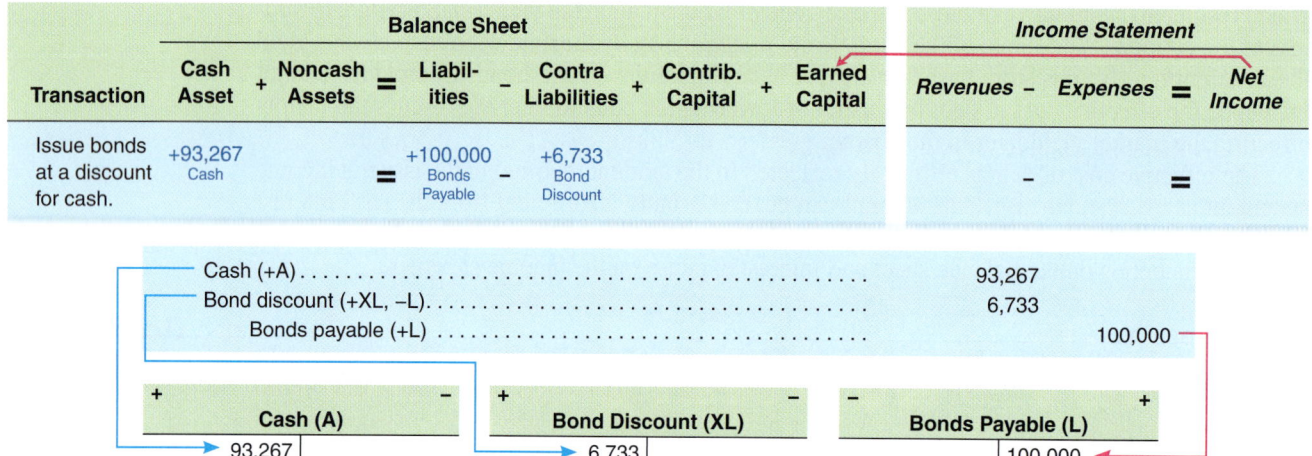

Bonds are reported on the balance sheet net of any discount (or plus any premium). When the bond matures, however, the company is obligated to repay $100,000. Accordingly, at maturity, the bond liability must read $100,000, the amount that is owed. Therefore, between the bond issuance and its maturity, the discount must decline to zero. This reduction of the discount over the life of the bond is called **amortization**. This amortization causes the effective interest expense to be greater than the periodic cash interest payments based on the coupon rate.

> **BUSINESS INSIGHT**
>
> **Zeros and Strips** Zero coupon bonds and notes, called *zeros*, do not carry an explicit coupon rate. However, the pricing of these bonds and notes is done in the same manner as those with coupon rates—the exception is the absence of an interest annuity. This omission means that the price is the present value of just the principal payment at maturity; hence, the bond is sold at a *deep discount*. For example, consider a 4-year, $100,000 zero coupon bond, priced to yield a market rate of 6% that compounds semi-annually. The only payment would be the return of principal 4 years away. We already know that the present value of this single payment is $78,941. This "zero" would initially sell for $78,941, resulting in a substantial discount of $21,059. A "strip" refers to the string of interest payments without the ending principal payment, which would be valued at $21,057 initially.

Bonds Issued at a Premium When a bond is sold at a premium, the cash proceeds and net bond liability are recorded at the amount of the proceeds received (not the face amount of the bond). Again, using the facts above from our premium bond illustration, the financial statement effects are:

	Balance Sheet									Income Statement				
Transaction	Cash Asset	+	Noncash Assets	=	Liabil-ities	+	Contrib. Capital	+	Earned Capital	Revenues	–	Expenses	=	Net Income
Issue bonds at a premium for cash.	+107,325 Cash			=	+100,000 Bonds Payable +7,325 Bonds Premium						–		=	

ANALYZE JOURNALIZE POST

Cash (+A)	107,325	
Bond premium (+L)		7,325
Bonds payable (+L)		100,000

+ Cash (A) –		– Bond Premium (L) +		– Bonds Payable (L) +	
107,325			7,325		100,000

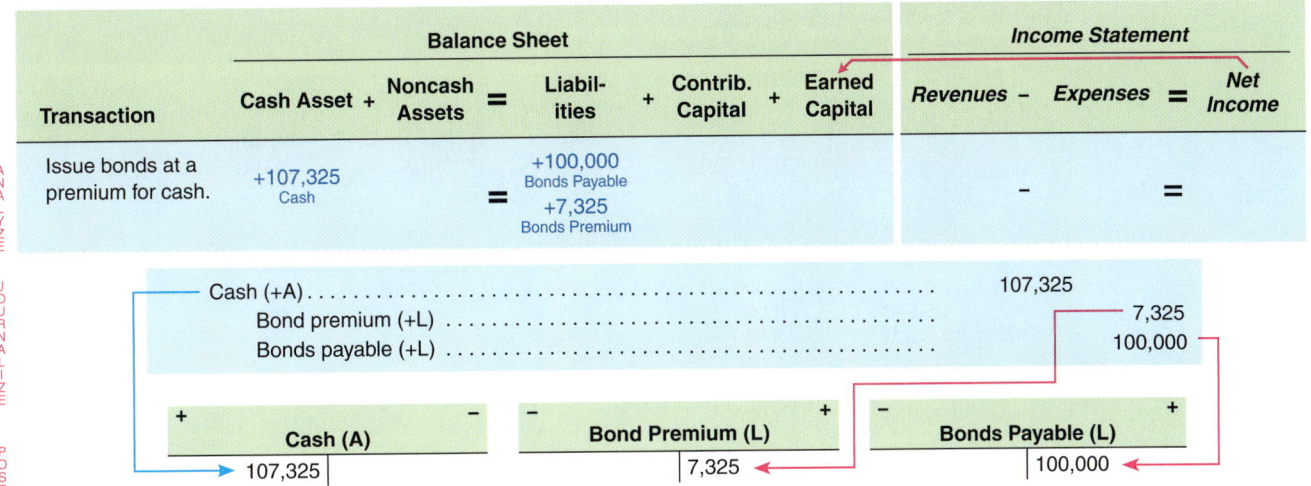

The net bond liability amount reported on the balance sheet, again, consists of two parts:

Bonds payable, face	$100,000
Add bond premium	7,325
Bonds payable, net	$107,325

The $100,000 must be repaid at maturity, and the premium is amortized to zero over the life of the bond. The premium represents a *benefit,* which yields a *reduction* in interest expense on the income statement.

Effects of Discount and Premium Amortization

The amount of interest expense that is reported on the income statement always equals the loan balance at the beginning of the period (bonds payable, net of discount or premium) times the market interest rate at the time of issue. For bonds issued at par, interest expense equals the cash interest payment. However, for bonds issued at a discount or premium, interest expense reported on the income statement equals interest paid adjusted for the amortization of the discount or premium:

Cash interest paid + Amortization of discount	or	Cash interest paid – Amortization of premium
Interest expense		Interest expense

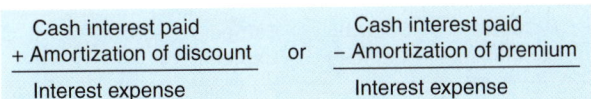

Specifically, periodic amortization of a discount is added to the cash interest paid to get interest expense for a discount bond. Amortization of the discount reflects the additional cost the issuer incurs from issuance of the bonds at a discount and its recognition, via amortization, as an increase to interest expense. For a premium bond, the premium is a benefit the issuer receives at issuance. Amortization of the premium reduces interest expense over the debt term. Consequently, interest expense on the income statement represents the *effective cost* of debt. (The *nominal cost* of debt is the cash interest paid.) This is true whether the bonds are issued at par, at a discount, or at a premium.

Companies amortize discounts and premiums using the effective interest method. To illustrate, recall the assumptions of the discount bond above—face amount of $100,000, a 6% annual coupon rate payable semiannually (3% semiannual rate), a maturity of 4 years, and a market (yield) rate of 8% annual (4% semiannual). These facts resulted in a bond issue price of $932.67 per bond, or $93,267 for the entire bond issue. **Exhibit 9.4** illustrates a bond discount amortization table for this bond.

EXHIBIT 9.4 Bond Discount Amortization Table

Semi-Annual Period	[A] Beginning Balance	[B] *(Face × coupon%)* Cash Interest Paid	[C] *([A] × market%)* Interest Expense	[D] *([C] – [B])* Discount Amortization	[E] *(Prior bal – [D])* Discount Balance	[F] *(Face – [E])* Bond Payable Net
0					$6,733	$ 93,267
1	$93,267	$3,000	$3,731	$731	6,002	93,998
2	93,998	3,000	3,760	760	5,242	94,758
3	94,758	3,000	3,790	790	4,452	95,548
4	95,548	3,000	3,822	822	3,630	96,370
5	96,370	3,000	3,855	855	2,775	97,225
6	97,225	3,000	3,889	889	1,886	98,114
7	98,114	3,000	3,925	925	962*	99,038
8	99,038	3,000	3,962	962	0	100,000

* rounding

The interest period is denoted in the left-most column. Period 0 is the point in time at which the bond is issued. Periods 1–8 are successive six-month interest periods. (Recall, interest is paid semiannually.) Column [B] is cash interest paid, which is a constant $3,000 per period (face amount × coupon rate). Column [C] is interest expense, which is reported in the income statement. This column is computed as the carrying amount of the bond at the beginning of the period (column [A]) multiplied by the 4% semiannual yield rate used to compute the bond issue price. Column [D] is discount amortization, which is the difference between interest expense and cash interest paid. Column [E] is the discount balance, which is the previous balance of the discount less the discount amortization in column [D]. Column [F] is the net bond payable, which is the $100,000 face amount less the unamortized discount from column [E]. Column [A] is the value from the previous period's column [F].

The amortization process continues until period 8, at which time the discount balance is $0 and the net bond payable is $100,000 (the maturity value). An amortization table reveals the financial statement effects of the bond for its duration. Specifically, we see the cash effects in column [B], the income statement effects in column [C], and the balance sheet effects in columns [D], [E], and [F].

To record the interest payment at the end of period 1, we use the values in row 1 of the amortization table. The resulting entry is recorded as follows:

	Balance Sheet											Income Statement				
Transaction	Cash Asset	+	Noncash Assets	=	Liabil-ities	–	Contra Liabilities	+	Contrib. Capital	+	Earned Capital	*Revenues*	–	*Expenses*	=	*Net Income*
Record interest payment and interest expense on bond.	–3,000 Cash			=		–	–731 Bond Discount				–3,731 Retained Earnings		–	+3,731 Interest Expense	=	–3,731

A N A L Y Z E

J O U R N A L I Z E

Interest expense (+E, –SE)	3,731	
Cash (–A)		3,000
Bond discount (–XL, +L)		731

P O S T

+ Interest Expense (E) –	
3,731	

+ Cash (A) –	
	3,000

+ Bond Discount (XL) –	
	731

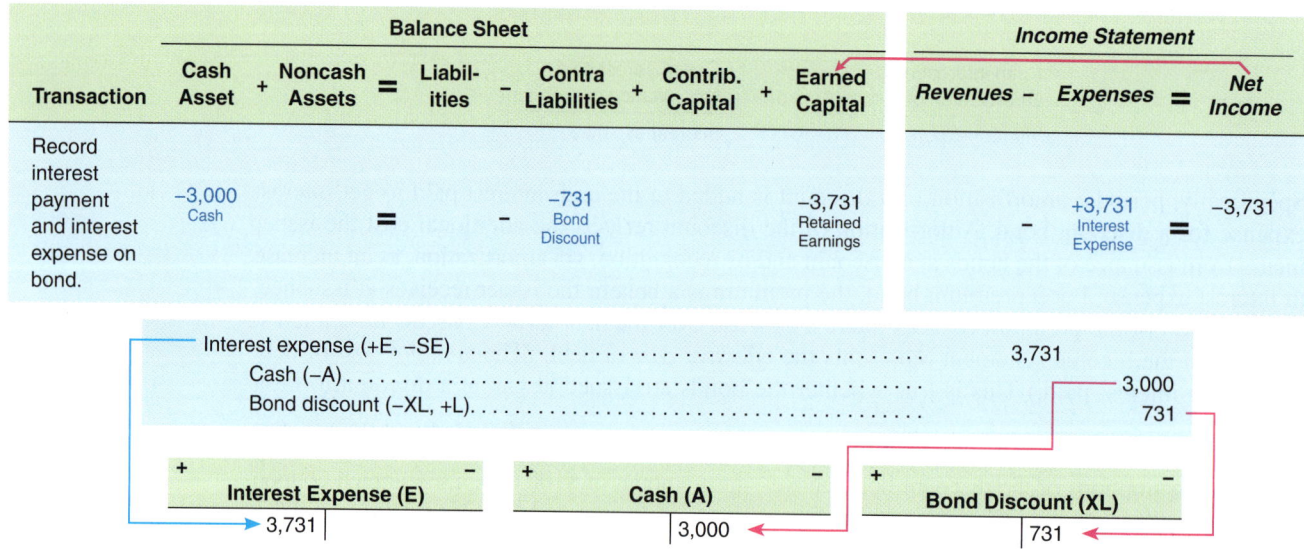

To illustrate amortization of a premium bond, we use the assumptions of the premium bond above—$100,000 face value, a 6% annual coupon rate payable semiannually (3% semiannual rate), a maturity of 4 years, and a 4% annual market (yield) rate (2% semiannual). These parameters resulted in a bond issue price of $1,073.25 per bond or $107,325 for the entire bond issue. **Exhibit 9.5** shows the bond premium amortization table for this bond.

EXHIBIT 9.5 Bond Premium Amortization Table

Semi-Annual Period	[A] Beginning Balance	[B] (Face × coupon%) Cash Interest Paid	[C] ([A] × market%) Interest Expense	[D] ([B] – [C]) Premium Amortization	[E] (Prior bal – [D]) Premium Balance	[F] (Face + [E]) Bond Payable Net
0					$7,325	$107,325
1	$107,325	$3,000	$2,147	$853	6,472	106,472
2	106,472	3,000	2,129	871	5,601	105,601
3	105,601	3,000	2,112	888	4,713	104,713
4	104,713	3,000	2,094	906	3,807	103,807
5	103,807	3,000	2,076	924	2,883	102,883
6	102,883	3,000	2,058	942	1,941	101,941
7	101,941	3,000	2,039	961	980	100,980
8	100,980	3,000	2,020	980	0	100,000

Interest expense is computed using the same process that we used for discount bonds. The difference is that the yield rate is 4% (2% semiannual) in the premium case. Cash interest paid follows from the bond contract (face amount × coupon rate), and the other columns' computations reflect the premium amortization. After period 8, the premium is fully amortized (equals zero) and the net bond payable balance is $100,000, the amount owed at maturity. The book value of bonds issued at a discount starts below the face value and, over time, increases. The book value of bonds issued at a premium starts above the bonds' face value and, over time, decreases. At maturity, the book value of both types of bonds equals the face value that must be paid to the bondholders. Again, an amortization table reveals the financial statement effects of the bond—the cash effects in column [B], the income statement effects in column [C], and the balance sheet effects in columns [D], [E], and [F].

To record the interest payment at the end of period 1, we, again, use the values in row 1 of the amortization table. The resulting entry is recorded as follows:

ANALYZE

Transaction	Cash Asset	+ Noncash Assets	=	Liabilities	+ Contrib. Capital	+ Earned Capital	Revenues	– Expenses	= Net Income
Record interest payment and interest expense on bond.	–3,000 Cash		=	–853 Bond Premium		–2,147 Retained Earnings		– +2,147 Interest Expense	= –2,147

(Balance Sheet: Cash Asset through Earned Capital; Income Statement: Revenues through Net Income)

JOURNALIZE

	Debit	Credit
Interest expense (+E, –SE)	2,147	
Bond premium (–L)	853	
Cash (–A)		3,000

POST

+ Interest Expense (E) –		– Bond Premium (L) +		+ Cash (A) –	
2,147		853			3,000

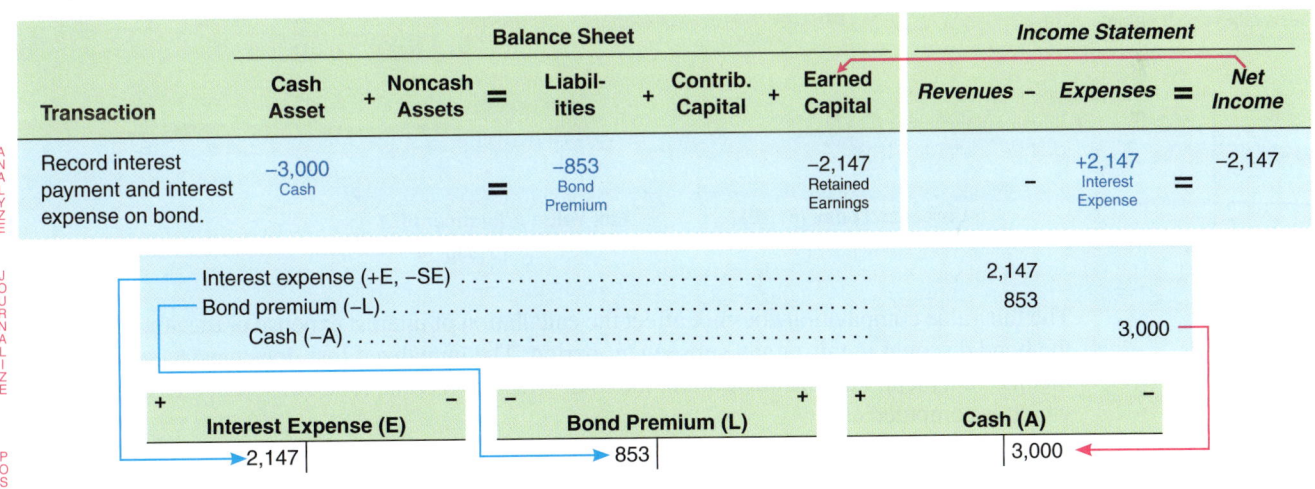

The Fair Value Option

Thus far, we have described the reporting of liabilities at *historical cost*. This means that all financial statement relationships are established on the date that the liability is created and do not subsequently change. For example, the interest rate used to value a bond is the market rate of interest on the date that the bond is issued, and the reported value of the bond is the face value plus the unamortized premium or minus the unamortized discount. Yet, once issued, bonds can be traded in secondary markets. Market interest rates fluctuate and, as a consequence, the market value of a bond is likely to change after the bond is issued.

As an alternative to historical cost, a company may elect to report some or all of its financial liabilities at *fair value*. Moreover, a company may choose to report some of its liabilities at historical cost and others at fair value. It must make this choice at the inception of the liability (e.g., at the time that a bond is issued) and cannot subsequently switch between fair value and historical cost for that liability. If a company elects to report a liability at fair value in its balance sheet, then any changes in fair value are reported as a gain or loss in its income statement. If a liability is to be reported at historical cost, then its fair value is disclosed in the notes.

To illustrate how we report a liability at fair value, we refer to our example of a 4-year, 6% bond issued at a discount to yield 8%. The issue price of this bond is $93,267, and we assume that the bond is issued on June 30, 2021. Six months later, on December 31, the issuing company pays the first of eight coupon payments of $3,000. From **Exhibit 9.4**, we know that after this coupon payment, the bond payable, net of the discount, is equal to $93,998. Now assume that the market value of the bond has increased to $96,943. (This price increase is consistent with a market interest rate that has decreased to 7%.) The bond would now be reported on the balance sheet at a value of $96,943:

Bonds payable	$100,000
Less, unamortized discount	6,002
Bond payable, net (historical cost)	$ 93,998
Plus, fair value adjustment	2,945
Bond payable, net (fair value)	$ 96,943

The increase in the bond's fair value must be added to an account that adjusts the bond payable liability. The balancing entry is included as a loss in the income statement and ends up in retained earnings. The fair value adjustment would be recorded as follows:

	Balance Sheet									*Income Statement*				
Transaction	Cash Asset	+	Noncash Assets	=	Liabilities	+	Contrib. Capital	+	Earned Capital	*Revenues*	–	*Expenses*	=	*Net Income*
Adjust bonds payable to fair value.				=	+2,945 Fair Value Adjustment				–2,945 Retaining Earnings		–	+2,945 Unrealized Loss	=	–2,945

A N A L Y Z E J O U R N A L I Z E P O S T

Unrealized loss (+E, –SE)	2,945	
Fair value adjustment (+L)		2,945

+ Unrealized Loss (E, SE) –	
2,945	

– Fair Value Adjustment (L) +	
	2,945

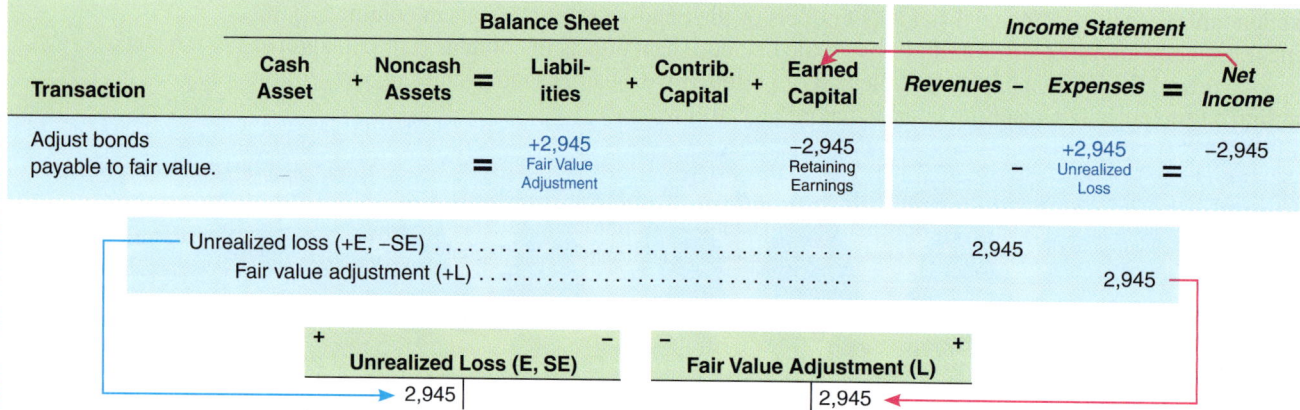

The fair value computation does not affect the calculation of interest expense or the amortization of the bond discount in this or any subsequent period. The unrealized loss does have an effect on the income statement. For this illustration, the total effect on income for 2021 is a decrease of $6,676, which is computed as:

Coupon payment, July 1–December 31	$3,000
Amortization of the bond discount	731
Interest expense	$3,731
Unrealized loss	2,945
Total effect (decrease) on earnings	$6,676

If the fair value of this bond decreases (e.g., because interest rates increase), the fair value adjustment account would be debited and an unrealized gain would be credited and reported in the income statement.[6] We discuss the fair value option further in Chapter 12.

[6] In ASC 825, FASB included a requirement that companies separately report in comprehensive income (rather than in net income) the portion of the total change in the fair value of a liability resulting from a change in the instrument-specific credit risk when the entity has elected to value the instrument using the fair-value option. For example, if the entity's own credit quality deteriorates, the company does not report this reduction of the fair value of the liability as income on their income statement, but rather as an item in other comprehensive income.

Effects of Bond Repurchase

Companies can and sometimes do repurchase (also called *redeem*) their bonds prior to maturity. The bond indenture (contract agreement) often includes a **call provision** giving the company the right to repurchase its bond by paying a small premium above face value. Alternatively, the company can repurchase bonds in the open market. When a company uses historical cost to account for its bonds, a bond repurchase usually results in a gain or loss and is computed as follows:

Gain or loss on bond repurchase = Book value of the bond − Repurchase payment

The *book (carrying) value of the bond* is the net amount reported on the balance sheet. If the issuer pays more to retire the bonds than the amount carried on its balance sheet, a loss is reported on its income statement, usually called *loss on bond retirement.* The issuer reports a *gain on bond retirement* if the repurchase price is less than the book value of the bond.

GAAP dictates that any gains or losses on bond repurchases be reported as part of ordinary income unless they meet the criteria for treatment as part of discontinued operations. Relatively few debt retirements meet these criteria and, hence, most gains and losses on bond repurchases are reported as part of income from continuing operations.

The question arises as to how gains and losses on the redemption of bonds should affect our analysis of a company's profitability. Because bonds and notes payable represent nonoperating items, activities including the refunding of bonds and any gain or loss resulting from such activity should be omitted from our computation of net operating profit.

Financial Statement Disclosure Notes

Companies are required to disclose details about their long-term liabilities, including the amounts borrowed under each debt issuance, the interest rates, maturity dates, and other key provisions. Following is Verizon's disclosure in note 7 to its 2020 10-K for its long-term debt ($ millions):

Long-Term Debt

Outstanding long-term obligations as of December 31, 2020 and 2019 are as follows:

At December 31	Maturities	Interest Rates %	(dollars in millions) 2020	2019
Verizon Communications	< 5 Years	0.85–5.51	$ 17,936	$ 19,885
	5–10 Years	1.38–7.75	35,423	30,038
	> 10 Years	1.75–8.95	65,019	47,777
	< 5 Years	Floating	2,917	2,210
	5–10 Years	Floating	941	1,789
Alltel Corporation	5–10 Years	6.80	38	38
	> 10 Years	7.88	58	58
Operating telephone company subsidiaries—debentures	< 5 Years	7.88–8.00	141	141
	5–10 Years	6.00–8.38	317	286
	> 10 Years	5.13–8.75	308	339
GTE LLC	< 5 Years	8.75	141	141
	5–10 Years	6.94	250	250
Other subsidiaries—asset-backed debt	< 5 Years	0.41–3.56	9,414	8,116
	< 5 Years	Floating	1,216	4,277
Finance lease obligations (average rate of 2.5% and 3.2% in 2020 and 2019, respectively)			1,284	1,116
Unamortized discount, net of premium			(6,057)	(4,480)
Unamortized debt issuance costs			(604)	(492)
Total long-term debt, including current maturities			128,742	111,489
Less long-term debt maturing within one year			5,569	10,777
Total long-term debt			$123,173	$100,712

Verizon reported a book value for long-term debt of $128,742 million at year-end 2020. Of this amount, $5,569 million will mature in the next year—hence, its classification as a current liability (current maturities of long-term debt)—and the remainder will mature after 2021. Verizon also reports $6,057 million in unamortized discount (net of unamortized premium) on this debt.

In addition to amounts, rates, and due dates on its long-term debt, Verizon also reports aggregate maturities for the 5 years subsequent to its balance sheet date:

Maturities of Long-Term Debt

Maturities of long-term debt outstanding at December 31, 2020, are as follows ($ millions):

2021	$ 5,227
2022	8,645
2023	7,511
2024	4,286
2025	8,528
Thereafter	93,865

This reporting reveals that Verizon is required to make principal payments of $34,197 million between 2021 and 2025, and $93,865 million thereafter. Such maturities are important, as a company must meet its required payments, negotiate a rescheduling of the indebtedness, or refinance the debt to avoid default. The latter (default) usually has severe consequences, as debt holders have legal remedies available to them that can result in bankruptcy of the company.

Verizon's disclosure on the fair value of its total debt follows:

The fair value of our debt is determined using various methods, including quoted prices for identical debt instruments . . . as well as quoted prices for similar debt instruments with comparable terms and maturities. . . . The fair value of our short-term and long-term debt, excluding finance leases, was as follows ($ millions):

	2020		2019	
At December 31,	**Carrying Amount**	**Fair Value**	**Carrying Amount**	**Fair Value**
Short-term and long-term debt, excluding finance leases	$127,778	$156,752	$110,373	$129,200

As of December 31, 2020, indebtedness with a book value of $127,778 million had a fair value of $156,752 million, resulting in an unrecognized liability (and loss if the debt is redeemed) of $28,974 million (due mainly to a decline in interest rates subsequent to bond issuance). The justification for not recognizing unrealized gains and losses on the balance sheet and income statement is that such amounts can reverse with future fluctuations in interest rates. Further, because only the face amount of debt is repaid at maturity, unrealized gains and losses that arise during intervening years are not necessarily relevant. (This same logic is used to justify the nonrecognition of gains and losses on held-to-maturity investments in debt securities, a topic covered in Chapter 12.) At this time, Verizon, like most U.S. companies, has elected to report liabilities at historical cost in the financial statements and disclose fair values in the notes.

Sensitivity Analysis

As part of the disclosure, many companies including Verizon also disclose the sensitivity of their estimate of fair value to changes in underlying factors or assumptions. This allows readers to see the effects of changes in assumptions.

The table that follows summarizes the fair values of our long-term debt, including current maturities, and interest rate swap derivatives as of December 31, 2020 and 2019. The table also provides a sensitivity analysis of the estimated fair values of these financial instruments assuming 100-basis-point upward and downward shifts in the yield curve. Our sensitivity analysis does not include the fair

continued

continued from previous page

values of our commercial paper and bank loans, if any, because they are not significantly affected by changes in market interest rates.

(dollars in millions) Long-Term Debt and Related Derivatives	Fair Value	Fair Value Assuming + 100 Basis Point Shift	Fair Value Assuming – 100 Basis Point Shift
At December 31, 2020	$155,695	$142,420	$170,423
At December 31, 2019	128,633	119,288	139,980

Interest and the Statement of Cash Flows

GAAP requires that interest payments (and receipts) be included in cash flows from operating activities. For companies using the indirect method for operating cash flows, net income already includes interest expense. Because interest expense does not equal interest payments, the reconciliation of net income to cash flows from operating activities should include an adjustment for any amortization of bond discounts or premiums.

However, interest income and interest expense are typically related to nonoperating assets (investments in securities) and nonoperating liabilities (interest-bearing bonds and notes), respectively. As such, they should be omitted from all computations of net operating profit (as in Appendix A to Chapter 5) and separated from other cash flows when analyzing a company's operations, even though it sometimes requires some digging in the financial statements to determine their magnitudes.

Disclosure of Commitments and Contingencies

All significant contractual commitments must be disclosed in the notes to the financial statements. We discuss this further in Chapter 10.

As discussed above, for contingent liabilities that have a likelihood of occurrence that is probable and the cost that can be estimated, the amount of the liability is recognized on the balance sheet and expensed on the income statement. However, if the liability is only reasonably possible (i.e., less likely than probable), then the liability is disclosed in the notes to the financial statements. If the liability is even less likely to occur than "reasonably possible," then disclosure is permitted but not required.

Many companies are required to include a line item labeled "Commitments and Contingent Liabilities" or some variant of this on the face of the balance sheet.[7] This line item does not have associated amounts on the balance sheet.

The following is Verizon's liability section of the balance sheet, including this line item:

Liabilities and Equity	2020	2019
Current liabilities		
Debt maturing within one year	$ 5,889	$ 10,777
Accounts payable and accrued liabilities	20,658	21,806
Current operating lease liabilities	3,485	3,261
Other	9,628	9,024
Total current liabilities	$ 39,660	$ 44,868
Long-term debt	$123,173	$100,712
Employee benefit obligations	18,657	17,952
Deferred income taxes	35,711	34,703
Non-current operating lease liabilities	18,000	18,393
Other liabilities	12,008	12,264
Total long-term liabilities	$207,549	$184,024
Commitments and Contingencies (Note 16)		

[7] Recent SEC guidance (S-X 5-02 (25)) and industrial companies that are SEC registrants include this line item. The SEC requires this caption to appear on the balance sheet whenever a disclosure note bears such a title. If no such disclosure note exists or the only disclosed items are immaterial items, then the caption need not appear on the balance sheet.

Note 16 in Verizon's disclosure notes is approximately one page long and discusses various accruals as well as potential litigation and environmental losses, some of which have been accrued (i.e., those that are probable and estimable) and some that have not. The note also discusses various contractual commitments and guarantees. (We discuss in Chapter 10.)[8]

Review 9-4 LO9-4

Accounting for Long-Term Nonoperating Liabilities

GuidedExample MBC

On January 1, Givoly Company issues $300,000 of 15-year, 10% bonds payable for $351,876, yielding an effective interest rate of 8%. Interest is payable semiannually on June 30 and December 31.

a. Show computations to confirm the issue price of $351,876.

b. Complete the financial statement effects template for (1) bond issuance, (2) semiannual interest payment and premium amortization on June 30, and (3) semiannual interest payment and premium amortization on December 31.

c. Provide Givoly's journal entries and T-accounts for the transactions listed in part *b.*

Solution on p. 9-49.

ANALYZING FINANCIAL STATEMENTS

LO9-5 Explain how solvency ratios and debt ratings are determined and how they impact the cost of debt.

A major concern of managers and analysts is the solvency of the corporation. In this chapter we revisit two ratios discussed in previous chapters, both of which are designed to measure a firm's solvency. The first ratio is the debt-to-equity ratio (D/E), first introduced in Chapter 1. It measures the extent to which a company relies on debt financing, also known as financial leverage. The second ratio is times interest earned (TIE), which measures the ability of current operations to cover interest costs.

eLecture MBC

Analysis Objective

We want to gauge the ability of a company to satisfy its long-term debt obligations and remain solvent.

Analysis Tool Debt-to-Equity Ratio

$$\textbf{Debt-to-equity ratio (D/E)} = \frac{\textbf{Total liabilities}}{\textbf{Total stockholders' equity}}$$

Applying the Ratio to Verizon

$$\textbf{2018:}\ \frac{\$210{,}119}{\$54{,}710} = 3.84 \text{ or } 384\%$$

$$\textbf{2019:}\ \frac{\$228{,}892}{\$62{,}835} = 3.64 \text{ or } 364\%$$

$$\textbf{2020:}\ \frac{\$247{,}209}{\$69{,}272} = 3.57 \text{ or } 357\%$$

Guidance A debt-to-equity ratio equal to 1.0 implies that the company is relying on debt and equity financing in equal amounts. As a company's reliance on debt increases and the company's long-term solvency becomes more of a concern, this ratio increases. A debt-to-equity ratio of about 1.3 is about average, though **Exhibit 5.13** (in Chapter 5) shows that the ratio varies by industry, and the median debt-to-equity ratio for telecommunications companies is 1.60.

[8] On the balance sheet after "Commitments and contingencies" is what is known as a mezzanine section of the balance sheet (meaning in between the liabilities section and equity section of the balance sheet). This section contains certain types of redeemable preferred stocks, redeemable noncontrolling interests, and some types of convertible notes. These are debt-equity hybrid securities, meaning they have some characteristics of debt and some characteristics of equity. A detailed discussion of each of these securities is outside the scope of this text. For most ratio analysis in this introductory-level textbook, we include all the securities in the mezzanine section as either debt or equity for the sake of simplicity. Analysts or other financial statement users might go into more detail and view some of these securities as debt and some of the securities as equity in their analyses. We note that IFRS does not have a mezzanine section of the balance sheet.

Verizon in Context

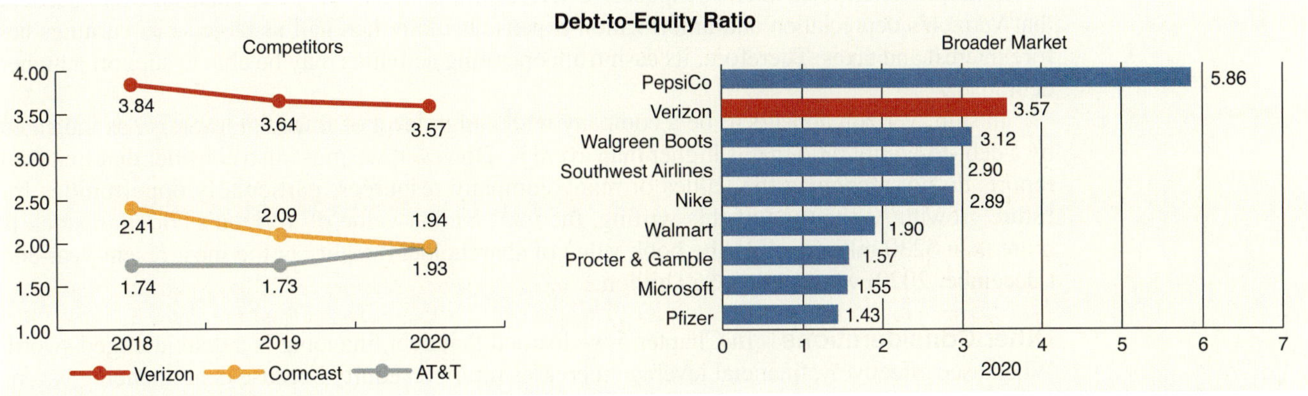

These companies do not have identical fiscal year ends. For each fiscal year listed above and in later charts, fiscal year-end balance sheet dates range from January 31 to December 31. For example, Walmart has a fiscal year-end of January 31, 2020, and Pfizer has a fiscal year-end of December 31, 2020.

Analysis Tool Times Interest Earned

$$\text{Times interest earned (TIE)} = \frac{\text{Earnings before interest and taxes}}{\text{Interest expense}}$$

Applying the Ratio to Verizon

$$\textbf{2018: } \frac{\$24,456}{\$4,833} = 5.1 \text{ times}$$

$$\textbf{2019: } \frac{\$27,463}{\$4,730} = 5.8 \text{ times}$$

$$\textbf{2020: } \frac{\$28,214}{\$4,247} = 6.6 \text{ times}$$

Guidance When a company relies on debt financing, it assumes the burden of paying the interest on the debt. The times interest earned ratio measures the burden of interest costs by comparing earnings before interest and taxes (EBIT) to annual interest expense. A high TIE ratio indicates that a company is able to meet its interest costs without adversely affecting profitability. The median TIE for the telecommunications industry is 3.77.

Verizon in Context

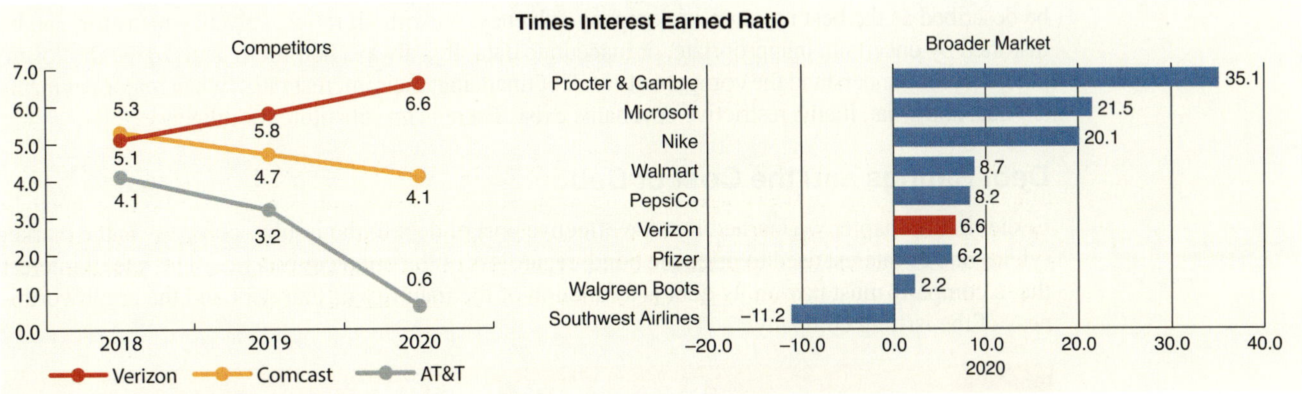

Takeaways Before 2014, Verizon's debt-to-equity ratio was lower than either Comcast or AT&T, two of its competitors. In 2014, Verizon engaged in a transaction to buy out the 45% equity interest of its wireless partner (Vodafone Group Plc) that had the effect of reducing its cash and reducing its shareholders' equity by a substantial amount. Verizon's debt-to-equity ratio increased significantly in 2014; the ratio has been in steady decline ever since. Its times interest earned ratio is lower than the other featured companies in this text, but well in excess of that of its industry and its close competitors. The size of this ratio is driven by two factors—the amount of debt financing, which in turn determines interest expense, as well as profitability. We should also take into account that Verizon's depreciation and amortization expense is more than half as large as its earnings before interest and taxes. Therefore, its cash from operating activities may be able to support a higher debt load.

In sum, Verizon appears to be a company with a high level of financial leverage, as indicated by a debt-to-equity ratio that is higher than average. However, we must also consider that financial reports do not recognize the values of many company resources, particularly opportunities for future growth. At the time of this writing, the total market value of Verizon's common stock is more than $230 billion, while the book value of shareholders' equity at the most recent year-end (December 2020) was roughly $69 billion.

Other Considerations In Chapter 5 we learned that debt financing is a double-edged sword. When used effectively, financial leverage increases return on equity because debt financing is generally less costly than equity financing. However, debt carries with it the risk of **default**, which is the risk that the company will be unable to pay its obligations when they come due (insolvency). To provide some protection against default risk, creditors usually require a company to execute a loan agreement that places restrictions on the company's activities. These restrictions, called covenants, impose indirect costs on a firm beyond the explicit cost of interest, and these indirect costs tend to increase as a company increases its reliance on debt financing. When a company's solvency ratios are close to the limits specified by its covenants, management is more likely to pass up profitable investment opportunities or engage in counterproductive earnings management activities to avoid violating these restrictions.

Walgreens Boots Alliance, Inc., (Walgreens), has several revolving credit facilities with aggregate borrowing capacity of $11.5 billion as of its year-end, August 31, 2020. In a disclosure note and in another section of its 10-K, Walgreens reports:

> Each of the Company's credit facilities described above contain a covenant to maintain, as of the last day of each fiscal quarter, a ratio of consolidated debt to total capitalization not to exceed 0.60:1.00. . . . The credit facilities contain various other customary covenants. As of August 31, 2020, the Company was in compliance with all such applicable covenants. . . .
>
> If we breach any of these restrictions or covenants and do not obtain a waiver from the lenders, then, subject to applicable cure periods, our outstanding indebtedness could be declared immediately due and payable. This could have a material adverse effect on our business operations and financial condition.

In prior years, the company has also mentioned other covenant restrictions more specifically, such as maintaining a minimum net worth and limitations on the sale of assets and purchases of investment. There are several variations on the ratios that we have discussed, and there is no single ratio that can be described as the best measure of company solvency. As with all ratios, solvency measures can be distorted by uncertain, inappropriate, or inaccurate data. It is always helpful to analyze the disclosure notes to better understand the components of debt financing, their interest rates, when major payments are due, and what, if any, restrictive covenants exist. There is no substitute for diligence.

Debt Ratings and the Cost of Debt

Earlier in the chapter we learned that the effective cost of debt to the issuing company is the market (yield) rate of interest used to price the bond, regardless of the bond coupon rate. The rate of interest that a company must pay on its debt is a function of the maturity of that debt and the creditworthiness of the issuing company.

RESEARCH INSIGHT

Accounting Conservatism and Cost of Debt Research indicates that companies applying more conservative accounting methods incur a lower cost of debt. Research also suggests that while accounting conservatism can lead to lower-quality accounting income (because such income does not fully reflect economic reality), creditors are more confident in the numbers and view them as more credible. Evidence also implies that companies can lower the required return demanded by creditors (the risk premium) by issuing high-quality financial reports that include enhanced note disclosures and detailed supplemental reports.

A company's debt rating, also referred to as credit quality and creditworthiness, is related to default risk. Companies seeking to obtain bond financing from the capital markets normally first seek a rating on their proposed debt issuance from one of several rating agencies, such as **Standard & Poor's**, **Moody's Investors Service**, or **Fitch**. The aim of rating agencies is to rate debt so that its default risk is more accurately determined and priced by the market. Such debt issuances carry debt ratings from one or more of the three large rating agencies, as shown in **Exhibit 9.6**. This exhibit includes the general description attached to the debt for each rating class—for example, AAA is assigned to debt of prime maximum safety (maximum creditworthiness). Bonds with credit ratings below investment grade (below Baa or BBB) are referred to as "high yield" bonds or, more pejoratively, "junk bonds," which may not be purchased by many professionally managed portfolios.[9]

EXHIBIT 9.6 Corporate Debt Ratings and Descriptions

Moody's	S&P	Fitch	Description
Aaa	AAA	AAA	Prime Maximum Safety
Aa	AA	AA	High Grade, High Quality
A	A	A	Upper-Medium Grade
Baa	BBB	BBB	Lower-Medium Grade
Ba	BB	BB	Non-Investment Grade
B	B	B	Speculative
Caa	CCC	CCC	Substantial Risk
Ca	CC	CC	Extremely Speculative
C	C	C	Exceptionally High Risk
	D		Default

YOU MAKE THE CALL

You are the Vice President of Finance Your company is currently rated BB by credit rating agencies. You are considering possible financial and other restructurings of the company to increase your credit rating. What types of restructurings might you consider? What benefits will your company receive from those restructurings? What costs will your company incur to implement such restructurings? [Answers on page 9-33]

Walgreens provides detailed disclosures about its ratings in its 2020 10-K.

Credit ratings

As of October 14, 2020, the credit ratings of Walgreens Boots Alliance were:

Rating Agency	Long-Term Debt Rating	Commercial Paper Rating	Outlook
Fitch	BBB–	F3	Stable
Moody's	Baa2	P-2	Negative
Standard & Poor's	BBB	A-2	Negative

In assessing the Company's credit strength, each rating agency considers various factors including the Company's business model, capital structure, financial policies, and financial performance. There can be no assurance that any particular rating will be assigned or maintained. The Company's credit ratings impact its borrowing costs, access to capital markets, and operating lease costs. The rating agency ratings are not recommendations to buy, sell, or hold the Company's debt securities or commercial paper. Each rating may be subject to revision or withdrawal at any time by the assigning rating agency and should be evaluated independently of any other rating.

Two years ago, all three ratings agencies gave an outlook of "stable," but Walgreens credit ratings have slipped a little in recent years. Revenues grew by 2% in 2020, while operating income decreased by 74%. The change in accounting for leases caused Walgreens' debt-to-equity ratio to go

[9] Standard & Poor's and Fitch modify their ratings to more detail with the addition of a plus (+) or minus (–) sign (e.g., BBB+, BBB, BBB–). Similarly, Moody's uses numerical modifiers within ratings (e.g., Aa1, Aa2, Aa3).

from 1.8 to 3.1. The 2020 ratings above are bordering on the "high yield" range, which could affect the company's ability to access the debt market.

It is these ratings that, in conjunction with the maturity of its bonds, establish the market interest rate and consequent selling price. There are a number of considerations that affect the rating of a bond. **Standard & Poor's** lists the following factors among its credit rating criteria:

Business Risk
- Industry characteristics
- Competitive position (e.g., marketing, technology, efficiency, regulation)
- Management

Financial Risk
- Financial characteristics
- Financial policy
- Profitability
- Capital structure
- Cash flow protection
- Financial flexibility

Rating agencies use a number of accounting ratios to help establish creditworthiness, including measures of liquidity, solvency, and profitability. These ratios are variants of the ratios we describe in Chapter 5 and in this chapter, especially those used to assess solvency.

There are other relevant factors in setting debt ratings, including the following:

- **Collateral** Companies can provide security for debt in the form of mortgages on assets. To the extent debt is secured, the debt holder is in a preferred position vis-à-vis other creditors.
- **Covenants** Debt agreements (indentures) can contain restrictions on the issuing company to protect debt holders. Examples are restrictions on excessive dividend payment, on other company acquisitions, on further borrowing, and on maintaining minimum levels for key liquidity and solvency ratios. These covenants provide debt holders some means of control over the issuer's operations because, unlike equity investors, they do not have voting rights.
- **Options** Debt obligations involve contracts between the borrowing company and debt holders. Options are sometimes written into debt contracts. Examples are options to convert debt into stock (so that debt holders have a stake in value creation) and options allowing the issuing company to repurchase its debt before maturity (usually at a premium).

Review 9-5 LO9-5

Computing Solvency Ratios

GuidedExample

MBC

Presented below is information reported in the financial statements of Macy's Inc., Nordstrom Inc., and Bed Bath & Beyond, Inc., for the fiscal years ended in February (or March) of 2020 and 2019 ($ millions).

($ million)	Fiscal Year Ended	Income (Loss) before Income Taxes	Interest Expense
Macy's.	Feb. 01, 2020	$ 728	$ 205
Macy's.	Feb. 02, 2019	1,420	261
Nordstrom.	Feb. 01, 2020	682	112
Nordstrom.	Feb. 02, 2019	733	119
Bed Bath & Beyond	Feb. 29, 2020	(764.9)	64.8
Bed Bath & Beyond	Mar. 02, 2019	(156.6)	69.5

a. Compute the times interest earned ratio for each company for the fiscal years ended in 2020 and 2019.

b. Comment on trends in solvency.

Solution on p. 9-50.

SUMMARY

Identify and account for current operating liabilities. (p. 9-4) LO9-1

- Current liabilities are short-term and generally non-interest-bearing; accordingly, firms try to maximize the financing of their assets using these sources of funds.
- ROE increases when firms make use of accounts payable increases to finance operating assets; a firm must avoid excessive "leaning on the trade" for short-term gains that can damage long-term supplier relationships.
- When cash discounts are offered by creditors, companies use the net of discount method to report accounts payable information.
- Accrued liabilities reflect amounts that have been recognized as expenses in the current (or a prior) period, but not yet paid.
- While all accruals result in a liability on the balance sheet and an expense on the income statement, management has latitude in determining (in some cases, estimating) their amount and timing; this discretion offers the opportunity for managing earnings.

Describe and account for current nonoperating (financial) liabilities. (p. 9-10) LO9-2

- Management will generally try to ensure that the debt service on financial (nonoperating) liabilities coincides with the cash flows from the assets financed.
- When large amounts of financing are required for, say, plant and equipment, firms find that bonds, notes, and other forms of long-term financing provide a cost-efficient means of raising capital.

Explain and illustrate the pricing of long-term nonoperating liabilities. (p. 9-13) LO9-3

- The coupon rate indicated on a bond contract determines the periodic interest payment. The required return on any bond called the market (yield or effective) rate is determined by market conditions and rarely equals the coupon (contract) rate. The market rate is used to price the bond and determines the effective cost of the debt to the issuer.
- If the market rate is below the coupon rate, the bond will sell at a premium to its face value, ensuring that the owner of the bond earns only the market rate of interest. If the market rate exceeds the coupon rate, the bond will sell at a discount so that the bond is issued at less than its face value.

Analyze and account for financial statement effects of long-term nonoperating liabilities. (p. 9-18) LO9-4

- A discount for a bond selling below its face value represents additional interest expense over time to the issuer because the issuer received less than face value upon issuance but must pay the holder the face value at the bond's maturity; this discount represents additional interest beyond the coupon payment to the holder. The premium on a bond selling above its face value lowers the interest cost to the issuer.
- Companies may choose to report liabilities at fair value; if the fair value option is elected, changes in fair value are reported as gains and losses in the income statement.[10]
- Gains and losses on bonds repurchased must be reported in operating income, unless they are part of discontinued operations. Such transactions do not represent operating activities, and gains/losses should be removed when determining cash from operations with the indirect method.

Explain how solvency ratios and debt ratings are determined and how they impact the cost of debt. (p. 9-27) LO9-5

- Two debt-related ratios that are particularly useful in evaluating a company's solvency include the debt-to-equity ratio and the times interest earned ratio.
- The market rate of interest to a firm reflects the creditworthiness of the particular issuer. Credit agencies play an important role in this process by issuing debt ratings.
- Borrowing is typically secured by collateral that places the lender in a superior position to other creditors and covenants that put restrictions on the borrower's activities; bonds can also contain options, including those for conversion or repurchase.

[10] Unless the change in fair value results from a change in instrument-specific credit risk. If it is caused by instrument-specific credit risk (i.e., a change in fair value because of a change in the credit quality of the issuer), that portion of the change in fair value is reported in other comprehensive income.

GUIDANCE ANSWERS . . . YOU MAKE THE CALL

You are the Analyst Accrued liabilities must be probable and estimable before they can be reported in the balance sheet. If DowDuPont's environmental costs turn out to be higher than management estimates, it may be understating its liabilities (and overstating equity). As an analyst, if you suspect that DowDuPont's estimate is too low, you should add an additional estimated liability to the company's balance sheet amounts to conduct analysis.

You are the Vice President of Finance The types of restructurings you might consider are those yielding a strengthening of the financial ratios typically used to assess liquidity and solvency by the rating agencies. Such restructurings include inventory reduction to generate cash, the reallocation of cash outflows from investing activities (PPE or intangible assets) to debt reduction, and reducing the cash outflows for repurchases of the company's stock (treasury stock). These actions increase liquidity or reduce financial leverage and, thus, should yield an improved debt rating. An improved debt rating gives the company access to more debt holders, as the current debt rating is below investment grade and is not a suitable investment for many professionally managed portfolios. An improved debt rating also yields a lower interest rate on debt. Offsetting these benefits are costs such as the following: (1) potential loss of sales from inventory stock-outs; (2) potential future cash flow reductions and loss of market power from reduced investing in PPE and intangibles; and (3) possible reductions in share price if shareholders were expecting more cash to be returned in the form of dividends and stock buybacks. All cost and benefits must be assessed before you pursue any restructurings.

KEY RATIOS

$$\text{Debt-to-equity (D/E)} = \frac{\text{Total liabilities}}{\text{Total stockholders' equity}} \qquad \text{Times interest earned (TIE)} = \frac{\text{Earnings before interest and taxes}}{\text{Interest}}$$

Assignments with the MBC logo in the margin are available in myBusinessCourse. See the Preface of the book for details.

MULTIPLE CHOICE

Multiple Choice Answers
1. a 2. b 3. b
4. c 5. a, b, and d

1. Which of the following statements is correct? A decrease in accrued wages liability:
- *a.* decreases cash flows from operations.
- *b.* decreases working capital.
- *c.* increases net income.
- *d.* increases net nonoperating (financial) assets.

2. On April 1, a firm borrows $18,000 at an annual interest rate of 10% with payments required semiannually on September 30 and March 31. How much interest payable and how much interest expense should appear on the firm's annual report at the end of the firm's fiscal year, December 31?
- *a.* $1,350 payable and $450 expense.
- *b.* $450 payable and $1,350 expense.
- *c.* $900 payable and $900 expense.
- *d.* $1,350 payable and $900 expense.

3. A firm issues $24,000,000 of 10-year bonds and receives $23.5 million in cash. Which of the following statements is correct?
- *a.* The bonds do not have a coupon rate because they are zeros.
- *b.* The market rate exceeds the coupon rate.
- *c.* The contract rate exceeds the market rate.
- *d.* The bonds were issued at par.

4. A firm issues $4 million of 10-year, 6% notes with interest paid semiannually. At issuance the firm received $4,654,057 cash reflecting a 4% yield. What is the amount of premium written off against interest expense in the first year the notes are outstanding?
- *a.* $53,838
- *b.* $19,622
- *c.* $54,376
- *d.* $26,919

5. On May 1 of the current year, Wild, Inc., makes an early repayment of long-term debt due to mature on June 1, two years later. Which of the following ratios for the current year is (are) decreased by this repayment?
- *a.* Current Ratio
- *b.* Quick Ratio
- *c.* Times Interest Earned
- *d.* Debt-to-Equity

QUESTIONS

Q9-1. What does the term "current liabilities" mean? What assets are usually used to settle current liabilities?

Q9-2. What is the justification for using the net-of-discount method to record inventory purchases when cash discounts are offered?

Q9-3. What is an accrual? How do accruals impact the balance sheet and the income statement?

Q9-4. What is the difference between a bond coupon rate and its market interest rate (yield)?

Q9-5. How does issuing a bond at a premium or discount affect the bond's *effective* interest rate vis-à-vis the coupon (stated) rate?

Q9-6. Why do companies report a gain or loss on the repurchase of their bonds (assuming the repurchase price is different from bond book value)?

Q9-7. How do debt ratings affect the cost of borrowing for a company?

Q9-8. How would you interpret a company's reported gain or loss on the repurchase of its bonds?

Q9-9. What do the following terms mean? (a) bonds payable, (b) call provision, (c) face value, (d) coupon, (e) bond discount, (f) bond premium, and (g) amortization of bond premium or discount.

Q9-10. What are the advantages and disadvantages of issuing bonds rather than common stock?

Q9-11. A $2,500,000 issue of 10-year, 9% bonds was sold at 98 plus accrued interest three months after the bonds were dated. What net amount of cash is received?

Q9-12. How does issuing bonds at a premium or discount "adjust the contract rate to the applicable market rate of interest"?

Q9-13. Regardless of whether premium or discount is involved, what generalization can be made about the change in the book value of bonds payable during the period in which they are outstanding?

Q9-14. If the effective interest amortization method is used for bonds payable, how does the periodic interest expense change over the life of the bonds when they are issued (a) at a discount and (b) at a premium?

Q9-15. How should premium and discount on bonds payable be presented in the balance sheet?

Q9-16. On April 30, one year before maturity, Weber Company retired $400,000 of 9% bonds payable at 101. The book value of the bonds on April 30 was $395,200. Bond interest was last paid on April 30, the date of bond retirement. What is the gain or loss on the retirement of the bonds?

Q9-17. Brownlee Company borrowed money by issuing a 20-year mortgage note payable. The note will be repaid in equal monthly installments. The interest expense component of each payment decreases with each payment. Why?

DATA ANALYTICS

DA9-1. Preparing an Excel Map Visualization of Sales Tax Across States

LO9-1 Homework MBC Data Analytics

For this exercise, download the Excel file "Table 3: State Tax Collections by State and Type of Tax 2021" obtained at the United States Census Bureau at https://www.census.gov/data/tables/2021/econ/qtax/historical.html. For this exercise, we extract data for *sales and gross receipts taxes by state* for the first quarter of 2021. We then convert the data to a U.S. map chart and analyze the results.

REQUIRED

1. Download Excel file DA9-1 found in myBusinessCourse.
2. Prepare a table by extracting from the U.S. Census Bureau file: General Sales and Gross Receipts Taxes by state for 2021 Q1. You will only be using the General Sales and Gross Receipts data in your analysis. Do not include Washington, D.C. in your table. *Hint:* Eliminate unnecessary data. Then use the Transpose function. (You may want to unmerge cells before transposing the data. After the transposition, you can line up the amounts with the states.) Convert the data to a table as the final step.
3. List the total of the amounts in your table. (Leave the amounts in thousands.)
4. Using the table as a reference, list the states with no tax.
5. Prepare a map chart of the tax by state. *Hint:* Highlight your data; then click on Insert, Maps, and Filled Map. If you're having trouble with the map, try converting the Xs in the Receipts column for states with no taxes to 0s.
6. What is the top and bottom end of the legend automatically prepared for the chart?
7. Answer the following questions using the map visualization:
   a. What three states have the largest tax?

b. Where is there a visible cluster of mid-range taxes on the map if we consider the map in four quadrants?

c. Where is there the least amount of tax on the map if we consider the map in four quadrants?

8. Is the amount of sales tax dependent only on the volume of sales activity in the state?
9. Does the map visualization provide information on the sales tax rate by state?

LO9-5 Data Analytics Homework MBC

DA9-2. Preparing Excel Schedules to Determine Compliance with Debt Agreements

Monroe Inc. (the Company) obtained financing from Pro Bank in Year 8. Associated with the debt agreement are debt covenants, which place restrictions on the Company's activities. The intention of the covenants is to protect the lender (Pro Bank) from a situation where the Company is unable to pay the debt when it is due. A debt agreement will include any debt covenants along with details on any calculations involved. From the debt agreement between Monroe Inc. and Pro Bank, the financial covenants are included below. Key definitions of certain terms are also included.

FINANCIAL COVENANTS

1. Total Leverage Ratio. The Company will not, as of the last day of any fiscal quarter, permit the Total Leverage Ratio to be greater than 2.00 to 1.00.
2. Minimum EBITDA. The Company will not, as of the last day of any fiscal quarter, permit EBITDA, for the period of the quarter ending on or immediately prior to such date to be less than $300 million.
3. Funded Debt. The Company will not, at any time, permit the aggregate outstanding principal amount of all Funded Debt to exceed an amount equal to 10% of the Company's total assets (as determined as of the last day of the most recently ended fiscal quarter for which financial statements have been provided).

DEFINITIONS

- *Total Leverage Ratio:* As of any date of determination, the ratio of (a) Funded Debt on such date to (b) EBITDA for the quarter ending on or immediately prior to such date.
- *EBITDA:* For any period, the sum of the following, for the Company in accordance with GAAP: Net income for such period plus (b) the sum of the following, to the extent deducted in determining net income for such period: (1) income tax expense during such period, (2) interest expense, net of interest income for such period, and (3) amortization and depreciation expense.
- *Funded Debt:* As of the date of determination with respect to the Company, the sum of all liabilities of the Company due to borrowing money.

The Excel file associated with this exercise includes quarterly financial information for Monroe Inc. from Quarter 1 of Year 10 to Quarter 2 of Year 12.

REQUIRED

1. Download Excel file DA9-2 found in myBusinessCourse.
2. Determine the key financial categories needed to determine whether the company is in compliance with the three financial covenants for each quarter presented.
3. Calculate the key financial amounts within the Excel worksheet.
4. Create an IF statement for each financial covenant per quarter that returns a "YES" if the company is in compliance at quarter end, or a "NO" if the company is not in compliance at quarter end.
5. List the formula for the IF statement for Q1 Year 10 for the first financial statement covenant.
6. Add a rule to your IF statement to shade the cell where YES is contained in green and a rule to shade the cell where NO is contained in red. *Hint:* Under the Home tab, click on Conditional formatting, Highlight cell rules, Text that contains, and then set up two rules.
7. Indicate the quarter ends (if any) where the company is not in compliance with the financial covenants.
8. Create *What-if Scenario 1* by duplicating the original schedule created. Assume that Funded Debt was higher by 10% at each quarter-end. Increase interest expense by 10% as well as Funded Debt. Assume no other changes in the financial data provided.
9. Indicate the quarter ends (if any) where the company is not in compliance with the financial covenants based on the schedule created in part 8.
10. Create *What-if Scenario 2* by duplicating the original schedule created. Assume that total assets were lower by 10% each quarter-end. Assume no other changes in the financial data provided.
11. Indicate the quarter ends (if any) where the company is not in compliance with the financial covenants based on the schedule created in part 10.
12. Determine the minimum required net income for each quarter in order to be in compliance with the second financial covenant, using the original data. Use 30% of earnings before tax as an estimate for tax expense. Round tax expense to one decimal place.

13. Determine the quarter where there is the smallest difference between net income reported and the minimum net income required to meet the second financial covenant.

DATA VISUALIZATION

Data Visualization Activities are available in myBusinessCourse. These assignments use Tableau Dashboards to expose students to visual depictions of data and introduce students to data analytics through data visualizations. These exercises are easily assignable and auto graded by MBC.

Data Visualization

MINI EXERCISES

M9-18. Recording Cash Discounts (FSET) LO9-1

On November 15, Shields Company purchased inventory costing $9,300 on credit. The credit terms were 2/10, n/30.

a. Assume that Shields Company paid the invoice on November 23. Using the financial statement effects template, report entries to record the purchase of this inventory and the cash payment to the supplier applying the net-of-discount method.

	Balance Sheet									Income Statement				
Transaction	Cash Asset	+	Noncash Assets	=	Liabil-ities	+	Contrib. Capital	+	Earned Capital	Revenues	−	Expenses	=	Net Income

b. Compute the cost of a lost discount as an annual percentage rate.

M9-19. Recording Cash Discounts LO9-1

Using the information from M9-18, complete the following.

a. Prepare journal entries to record the purchase of this inventory and the cash payment to the supplier applying the net-of-discount method.

b. Set up the necessary T-accounts and post the journal entries to the T-accounts.

M9-20. Recording Cash Discounts (FSET) LO9-1

Schrand Corporation purchased materials from a supplier that offers credit terms of 2/15, n/60. It purchased $10,000 of merchandise inventory from that supplier on January 20.

a. Assume that Schrand Corporation paid the invoice on February 15. Using the financial statement effects template, report the purchase of this inventory and the cash payment to the supplier using the net-of-discount method.

b. Compute the cost of a lost discount as an annual percentage rate.

M9-21. Recording Cash Discounts LO9-1

Using the information from M9-20, complete the following.

a. Prepare journal entries to record the purchase of this inventory and the cash payment to the supplier applying the net-of-discount method.

b. Set up the necessary T-accounts and post the journal entries to the T-accounts.

M9-22. Analyzing and Computing Financial Statement Effects of Loan Interest (FSET) LO9-2

Huddart Company gave a creditor a 90-day, 8% note payable for $5,400 on December 16. Record the year-end December 31 accounting adjustment Huddart must make in the financial statement effects template. (Round to the nearest dollar.)

M9-23. Analyzing and Computing Financial Statement Effects of Loan Interest LO9-2

Using the information from M9-22, complete the following.

a. Prepare the journal entry to record the year-end December 31 accounting adjustment Huddart must make. (Round to the nearest dollar.)

b. Post the journal entry to its respective T-accounts.

M9-24. Analyzing and Determining the Amount of a Liability LO9-1, 2

For each of the following situations, indicate the liability amount, if any, which is reported on the balance sheet of Hirst, Inc., at December 31.

a. Hirst owes $82,500 at year-end for its inventory purchases.

b. On December 31, Hirst agreed to purchase a $21,000 drill press in January of the following year.

c. During November and December, Hirst sold products to a firm with a 90-day warranty against product failure. Estimated costs in the following year of honoring this warranty are $1,650.

d. Hirst provides a profit-sharing bonus for its executives equal to 5% of its reported pretax annual income. The estimated pretax income for this year is $450,000. Bonuses are not paid until January of the following year.

LO9-3, 5
Microsoft Corporation
NASDAQ :: MSFT

M9-25. Interpreting Relations Between Bond Price, Coupon, Yield, and Rating

In January 2017, Microsoft Corporation issued $17 billion of bonds in seven parts, with maturities ranging from 2020 to 2057. The bond issue was rated Aaa by Moody's. Two of the bond offerings are described below.

Amount: $4 billion; Maturity: February 6, 2027; Coupon: 3.3%; Price: 99.31; Yield: 3.383%.
Amount: $2 billion; Maturity: February 6, 2057; Coupon: 4.5%; Price: 99.49; Yield: 4.528%.

a. Discuss the relation between the coupon rate, issuance price, and yield for the 2027 issue.

b. Compare the yields on the two bond issues. Why are the yields different when the bond ratings are the same?

LO9-4
Homework MBC

M9-26. Determining Gain or Loss on Bond Redemption

On January 1, two years before maturity, Easton Company retired $300,000 of its 8.5% bonds payable at the current market price of 102 (102% of the bond face amount, or $300,000 × 1.02 = $306,000). The bond book value on January 1 was $298,000, reflecting an unamortized discount of $2,000. Bond interest was fully paid and recorded up to the date of retirement. What is the gain or loss on retirement of these bonds?

LO9-4
Pfizer, Inc.
NYSE :: PFE

M9-27. Interpreting Bond Note

In its 2020 10-K, Pfizer, Inc., reported the following maturity schedule for its debt outstanding:

($ millions)	Total	2021	2022–2023	2024–2025	After 2025
Long-term debt, including current portion.	$39,135	$2,002	$4,346	$3,068	$29,719

a. What did Pfizer, Inc., report in its 2020 balance as the current portion of long-term debt?

b. What implications does the payment schedule have for your evaluation of Pfizer's liquidity and solvency?

LO9-1
Homework MBC

M9-28. Classifying Debt Accounts into the Balance Sheet or Income Statement

Indicate the proper financial statement classification (balance sheet or income statement) for each of the following accounts:

a. Gain on Bond Retirement
b. Discount on Bonds Payable
c. Mortgage Notes Payable
d. Bonds Payable
e. Bond Interest Expense
f. Bond Interest Payable (due next period)
g. Premium on Bonds Payable
h. Loss on Bond Retirement

LO9-4

M9-29. Interpreting Bond Note Disclosures

Cencosud SA is a leading Latin American retailer that was listed on the New York Stock Exchange until January 2018. As of December 31, 2017, the company had approximately US$ 4.12 billion in short- and long-term debt. In its last 20-F filing with the Securities and Exchange Commission, Cencosud reports the following:

Our loan agreements and outstanding bonds contain a number of covenants requiring us to comply with certain financial ratios and other tests. The most restrictive financial covenants under these loan agreements and bonds require us to maintain:

- a ratio of consolidated Net Financial Debt to consolidated net worth not exceeding 1.2 to 1;
- a ratio of consolidated Net Financial Debt to EBITDA (as defined in the relevant credit agreements) for the most recent four consecutive fiscal quarters for such period of less than 5.25 to 1;
- unencumbered assets in an amount equal to at least 120% of the outstanding principal amount of total liabilities;
- minimum consolidated assets of at least UF 50.5 million[11]; and
- minimum consolidated net worth of at least UF 28.0 million.

As of the date of this annual report, we are in compliance with all of our loan and debt instruments.

[11] "UF" refers to *Unidades de Fomento*. The UF is an inflation-indexed Chilean monetary unit with a value in Chilean pesos that is adjusted daily to reflect changes in the official Consumer Price Index ("CPI").

a. Why do creditors impose restrictive covenants on borrowers?
b. How might restrictive covenants such as these affect management decisions?
c. What implications do these restrictions have on an analysis of the company and its solvency?

M9-30. Analyzing Financial Statement Effects of Bond Redemption (FSET) LO9-4 Homework MBC

Holthausen Corporation issued $500,000 of 11%, 20-year bonds at 108 on January 1, 2016. Interest is payable semiannually on June 30 and December 31. Through January 1, 2022, Holthausen amortized $5,240 of the bond premium. On January 1, 2022, Holthausen will retire the bonds at 103. Record the issue and retirement of these bonds in the financial statement effects template.

M9-31. Analyzing Financial Statement Effects of Bond Redemption LO9-4 Homework MBC

Using the information from M9-30, complete the following.

a. Prepare journal entries to record the issue and retirement of these bonds.
b. Post the journal entries to their respective T-accounts.

M9-32. Analyzing Financial Statement Effects of Bond Redemption LO9-4 Homework MBC

Dechow, Inc., issued $300,000 of 8%, 15-year bonds at 96 on July 1, 2015. Interest is payable semiannually on December 31 and June 30. Through June 30, 2022, Dechow amortized $3,823 of the bond discount. On July 1, 2022, Dechow will retire the bonds at 101. Record the issue and retirement of these bonds in the financial statement effects template. (Assume the June interest expense has already been recorded.)

M9-33. Analyzing Financial Statement Effects of Bond Redemption LO9-4 Homework MBC

Using the information from M9-32, complete the following.

a. Prepare journal entries to record the issue and retirement of these bonds. (Assume the June interest expense has already been recorded.)
b. Post the journal entries to their respective T-accounts.

M9-34. Analyzing and Computing Accrued Interest on Notes LO9-4 Homework MBC

Compute any interest accrued for each of the following notes payable owed by Penman, Inc., as of December 31. (Use a 365-day year.)

Lender	Issuance Date	Principal	Interest Rate (%)	Term
Nissim.	November 21	$25,000	8%	120 days
Klein	December 13	15,000	6	90 days
Bildersee.	December 19	20,000	5	60 days

M9-35. Debt Ratings and Capital Structure LO9-5 General Mills, Inc. NYSE :: GIS

General Mills, Inc., reports the following information in the statement of cash flows for the year ended May 31, 2020:

Cash Flows from Financing Activities ($ millions)	Year Ended May 31, 2020
Change in notes payable	$(1,158.6)
Issuance of long-term debt.	1,638.1
Payment of long-term debt.	(1,396.7)
Proceeds from common stock issued on exercised options.	263.4
Purchases of common stock for treasury	(3.4)
Dividends paid	(1,195.8)
Dividends to noncontrolling interests and other, net.	(88.5)
Net cash used by financing activities	$(1,941.5)

a. General Mills reported net income of $2,210.8 million in the year ended May 2020. What effect did these financing cash flows have on General Mills solvency measures for the year? Explain.
b. Would the changes in financing tend to lower or increase the firm's debt rating? (Currently General Mills' long-term debt is rated at upper medium grade.)

M9-36. Computing Bond Issue Price LO9-3 Homework MBC

Bushman, Inc., issues $250,000 of 9% bonds that pay interest semiannually and mature in 10 years. Compute the bond issue price assuming that the bonds' market rate is:

a. 8% per year compounded semiannually.
b. 10% per year compounded semiannually.

LO9-3 Homework MBC

M9-37. Computing Issue Price for Zero-Coupon Bonds

Baiman, Inc., issues $250,000 of zero-coupon bonds that mature in 10 years. Compute the bond issue price assuming that the bonds' market rate is:

a. 8% per year compounded semiannually.

b. 10% per year compounded semiannually.

c. If prior to the debt issue at 10%, the firm had total assets of $3.5 million and total equity of $1.5 million, what would be the effect of the new borrowing on the financial leverage of the firm?

LO9-1 Homework MBC

M9-38. Financial Statement Effects of Accounts Payable Transactions

Petroni Company engages in the following sequence of transactions every month:

1. Purchases $450 of inventory on credit.
2. Sells $450 of inventory for $630 on credit.
3. Pays other operating expenses of $165 in cash.
4. Collects $630 in cash from customers.
5. Pays supplier of inventory $450.

a. Create a monthly income statement and statement of operating cash flow (direct method) for four consecutive months.

b. The CFO is disappointed with the cash flows from the business. They do not provide the support for investment and growth that she wants. She proposes delaying supplier payments by a month. That is, each month's inventory purchase will be paid for in the following month. How would this change the monthly income statements and operating cash flows in part *a*? Would it provide the steady flow of cash that the CFO is looking for? Why?

LO9-3, 4 Homework MBC

M9-39. Computing Bond Issue Price and Preparing an Amortization Table in Excel

On December 31, 2021, Kaplan, Inc., issues $400,000 of 9% bonds that pay interest semiannually and mature in 10 years (December 31, 2031).

a. Using the Excel PV worksheet function, compute the issue price assuming that the bonds' market rate is 8% per year compounded semiannually. (Refer to Appendix A for illustration.)

b. Prepare an amortization table in Excel to demonstrate the amortization of the book (carrying) value to the $400,000 maturity value at the end of the 20th semiannual period. (Refer to Appendix A for illustration.)

LO9-3, 4 Homework MBC

M9-40. Classifying Bond-Related Accounts

Indicate the proper financial statement classification for each of the following accounts:

Gain on Bond Retirement (material amount)
Discount on Bonds Payable
Mortgage Notes Payable
Bonds Payable
Bond Interest Expense
Bond Interest Payable
Premium on Bonds Payable

LO9-3, 4 Homework MBC

M9-41. Recording and Assessing the Effects of Installment Loans (FSET)

On December 31, 2021, Thomas, Inc., borrowed $500,000 on a 6%, 15-year mortgage note payable. The note is to be repaid in equal semiannual installments of $25,510 (payable on June 30 and December 31).

Report each of the following transactions using the financial statement effects template: (1) the issuance of the mortgage note payable, (2) the payment of the first installment on June 30, 2022, and (3) the payment of the second installment on December 31, 2022. Round amounts to the nearest dollar.

LO9-3, 4 Homework MBC

M9-42. Recording and Assessing the Effects of Installment Loans

Using the information from M9-41, complete the following.

a. Prepare journal entries to record each of the transactions.

b. Post the journal entries to their respective T-accounts.

LO9-3 Homework MBC

M9-43. Determining Bond Prices

Lunar, Inc., plans to issue $500,000 of 6% bonds that will pay interest semiannually and mature in 5 years. Assume that the effective interest rate is 8% per year compounded semiannually. Compute the selling price of the bonds. Use Tables A.2 and A.3 in Appendix A near the end of the book.

EXERCISES

E9-44. Analyzing and Computing Accrued Warranty Liability and Expense LO9-1

Waymire Company sells a motor that carries a 60-day unconditional warranty against product failure. Waymire estimates that between the sale and lapse of the product warranty, 2% of the 152,000 units sold this period will require repair at an average cost of $50 per unit. The warranty liability for this product had a beginning-of-period balance of $66,000, and $59,000 has already been spent on warranty repairs and replacements during the period.

a. How much warranty expense must Waymire report in its income statement, and what amount of warranty liability must it report on its balance sheet for this year?

b. What analysis issues do we need to consider with respect to the amount of reported warranty liability?

c. What solvency ratios are increased if warranty liabilities rise?

E9-45. Analyzing Contingencies and Assessing Liabilities LO9-1

The following independent situations represent various types of liabilities. Analyze each situation and indicate which of the following is the proper accounting treatment for each company: (1) record in accounts, (2) disclose in a financial statement note, or (3) neither record nor disclose.

a. A stockholder has filed a lawsuit against Clinch Corporation. Clinch's attorneys have reviewed the facts of the case. Their review revealed that similar lawsuits have never resulted in a cash award, and it is highly unlikely that this lawsuit will either.

b. Foster Company signed a 60-day, 10% note when it purchased (and received) items from another company.

c. The Department of Environment Protection notifies Shevlin Company that a state where it has a plant is filing a lawsuit for groundwater pollution against Shevlin and another company that has a plant adjacent to Shevlin's plant. Test results have not identified the exact source of the pollution. Shevlin's manufacturing process often produces by-products that can pollute groundwater.

d. Sloan Company manufactured and sold products to a retailer that sold the products to consumers. The Sloan Company warranty offers replacement of the product if it is found to be defective within 90 days of the sale to the consumer. Historically, 1.2% of the products are returned for replacement.

E9-46. Analyzing and Computing Accrued Wages Liability and Expense LO9-1

Demski Company pays its employees on the 1st and 15th of each month. It is March 31, and Demski is preparing financial statements for this quarter. Its employees have earned $40,000 since the 15th of this month and have not yet been paid. How will Demski's balance sheet and income statement change to reflect the accrual of wages that must be made at March 31? What balance sheet and income statement accounts would be incorrectly reported if Demski failed to make this accrual (for each account indicate whether it would be overstated or understated)?

E9-47. Analyzing and Reporting Financial Statement Effects of Bond Transactions (FSET) LO9-3, 4

On January 1, Hutton Corp. issued $400,000 of 15-year, 11% bonds payable for $503,753, yielding an effective interest rate of 8%. Interest is payable semiannually on June 30 and December 31.

a. Show computations to confirm the issue price of $503,753.

b. Record the bond issuance, semiannual interest payment, and premium amortization on June 30, and semiannual interest payment and premium amortization on December 31 in the financial statement effects template. Use the effective interest rate method.

E9-48. Analyzing and Reporting Financial Statement Effects of Bond Transactions LO9-4

Using the information from E9-47, complete the following.

a. Prepare journal entries to record the bond issuance, semiannual interest payment, and premium amortization on June 30, and semiannual interest payment and premium amortization on December 31. Use the effective interest rate method.

b. Post the journal entries to their respective T-accounts.

E9-49. Computing the Bond Issue Price LO9-3

D'Souza, Inc., issues $600,000 of 11% bonds that pay interest semiannually and mature in seven years. Assume that the market interest (yield) rate is 12% per year compounded semiannually. Compute the bond issue price.

LO9-1 Homework MBC

Siemens AG
OTCMKTS :: SIEGY

E9-50. Interpreting Warranty Liability Disclosures (FSET)
The following disclosures were provided by Siemens AG in its 2020 annual report:

Product-related expenses
Provisions for estimated costs related to product warranties are recorded in line item Cost of sales at the time the related sale is recognized.

Note 18 Provisions

	Provision for Warranties Year Ended September 30*	
(in millions of €)	2020	2019
Beginning balance	€4,300	€4,575
Additions	633	1,621
Usage	(395)	(1,060)
Reversals	(258)	(1,131)
Translation differences and other	(2,706)	294
Ending balance	€1,574	€4,300

* The company rounds amounts, and thus, they may not exactly sum to totals and subtotals.

a. The provision that Siemens reports is an estimated warranty liability. What would constitute "additions" to the provision in 2020? Using the financial statement effects template, record this addition.

b. What constitutes "usage" of the provision? Besides the provision, what other accounts are likely to be affected by usage? Using the financial statement effects template, record usage of €395 million in 2020.

c. "Reversals" are corrections of previous estimates of warranty obligations. Why would it be useful to report reversals separately from additions?

d. Siemens reported sales revenue of €57,139 million in 2020 and €58,483 in 2019. Calculate the ratio of warranty expense to sales for each year.

LO9-1 Homework MBC

E9-51. Interpreting Warranty Liability Disclosures
Using the information from E9-50, complete the following.

Prepare the journal entries for (a) additions to the provision and (b) usage of the provision.

LO9-3, 4 Homework MBC

E9-52. Reporting Financial Statement Effects of Bond Transactions (FSET)
Lundholm, Inc., which reports financial statements each December 31, is authorized to issue $300,000 of 9%, 15-year bonds dated May 1, 2021, with interest payments on October 31 and April 30. Assume the bonds are issued at par on May 1, 2021.

Record the bond issuance, payment of the first semiannual period's interest, and retirement of $100,000 of the bonds at 101 on November 1, 2022, using the financial statement effects template. Assume that interest was paid on October 31, 2022.

LO9-3, 4 Homework MBC

E9-53. Reporting Financial Statement Effects of Bond Transactions
Using the information from E9-52, complete the following.

a. Prepare journal entries for the transactions described.

b. Post the journal entries to their respective T-accounts.

LO9-3, 4 Homework MBC

E9-54. Reporting Financial Statement Effects of Bond Transactions (FSET)
On January 1, McKeown, Inc., issued $450,000 of 8%, 9-year bonds for $397,397, yielding a market (yield) rate of 10%. Semiannual interest is payable on June 30 and December 31 of each year.

a. Show computations to confirm the bond issue price.

b. Record the bond issuance, semiannual interest payment, and discount amortization on June 30, and semiannual interest payment and discount amortization on December 31, using the financial statement effects template. Use the effective interest rate.

LO9-3, 4 Homework MBC

E9-55. Reporting Financial Statement Effects of Bond Transactions
Using the information from E9-54, complete the following.

a. Prepare the journal entries for transactions described in part *b*.

b. Post the journal entries to their respective T-accounts.

E9-56. Reporting Financial Statement Effects of Bond Transactions (FSET) LO9-3, 4 Homework MBC

On January 1, Shields, Inc., issued $500,000 of 9%, 20-year bonds for $549,482, yielding a market (yield) rate of 8%. Semiannual interest is payable on June 30 and December 31 of each year.

a. Show computations to confirm the bond issue price.

b. Record the bond issuance, semiannual interest payment, and premium amortization on June 30, and semiannual interest payment and premium amortization on December 31, using the financial statement effects template. Use the effective interest rate method.

E9-57. Reporting Financial Statement Effects of Bond Transactions LO9-3, 4 Homework MBC

Using the information from E9-56, complete the following.

a. Prepare the journal entries for transactions described in part *b*.

b. Post the journal entries to their respective T-accounts.

E9-58. Analyzing Bond Pricing, Interest Rates, and Financial Statement Effect of a Bond Issue LO9-3, 4 Deere & Company NYSE :: DE

Following is a price quote for $200 million of 6.55% coupon bonds issued by Deere & Company that mature in October 2028:

Ratings/Industry	Issue/Call Information	Coupon/Maturity	Price/YTM
A2/A	Deere & Company	6.550	123.962
Industrial	Non Callable, NYBE, DE	10-01-2028	4.178

This quote indicates that, on this day, Deere's bonds have a market price of 123.962 (123.962% of face value), resulting in a yield of 4.178%.

a. Assuming that these bonds were originally issued at or close to par value, what does the above market price reveal about the direction that interest rates have changed since Deere issued its bonds? (Assume that Deere's debt rating has remained the same.)

b. Does the change in interest rates since the issuance of these bonds affect the amount of interest expense that Deere is reporting in its income statement? Explain.

c. If Deere were to repurchase its bonds at the above market price of 123.962, how would the repurchase affect its current income? Assume that the bonds were issued at face value (100).

d. Assuming that the bonds remain outstanding until their maturity, at what market price will the bonds sell on their due date of October 1, 2028?

E9-59. Analyzing and Reporting Financial Statement Effects of Bond Transactions (FSET) LO9-3, 4 Homework MBC

On January 1, Trueman Corp. issued $400,000 of 20-year, 11% bonds for $369,907, yielding a market (yield) rate of 12%. Interest is payable semiannually on June 30 and December 31.

a. Confirm the bond issue price.

b. Record the bond issuance, semiannual interest payment, and discount amortization on June 30, and semiannual interest payment and discount amortization on December 31, using the financial statement effects template. Use the effective interest rate method.

c. Trueman elected to report these bonds in its financial statements at fair value. On December 31, these bonds were listed in the bond market at a price of 101 (or 101% of par value). Using the financial statement effects template, record the entry to adjust the reported value of these bonds to fair value.

d. Prepare a table summarizing the effect of these bonds on earnings for the year.

E9-60. Analyzing and Reporting Financial Statement Effects of Bond Transactions LO9-3, 4 Homework MBC

Using the information from E9-59, complete the following.

a. Prepare the journal entries for transactions described in part *b*.

b. Post the journal entries to their respective T-accounts.

c. Prepare the journal entry for the transaction described in part *c* to adjust the bonds to fair value.

E9-61. Reporting and Interpreting Bond Disclosures LO9-2, 4 Homework MBC

The adjusted trial balance for the Hass Corporation at the end of 2021 contains the following accounts:

$ 37,500	Bond Interest Payable
900,000	9% Bonds Payable due 2023
750,000	10% Bonds Payable due 2022
28,500	Discount on 9% Bonds Payable
3,000	Premium on 8% Bonds Payable
250,000	Zero-Coupon Bonds Payable due 2024
150,000	8% Bonds Payable due 2026

Prepare the long-term liabilities section of the balance sheet. Indicate the proper balance sheet classification for accounts listed above that do not belong in the long-term liabilities section.

LO9-3, 4 Homework MBC

E9-62. Recording and Assessing the Effects of Installment Loans (FSET)
On December 31, Dehning, Inc., borrowed $600,000 on a 6%, 10-year mortgage note payable. The note is to be repaid in equal quarterly installments of $20,056 (beginning March 31). Using the financial statement effects template, report (1) the issuance of the mortgage note payable, (2) the payment of the first installment on March 31, and (3) the payment of the second installment on June 30. Round amounts to the nearest dollar.

LO9-3, 4 Homework MBC

E9-63. Recording and Assessing the Effects of Installment Loans
Using the information from E9-62, complete the following.

a. Prepare the journal entries for transactions described in E9-62.

b. Post the journal entries to their respective T-accounts.

PROBLEMS

LO9-1
Hewlett-Packard Enterprise Company
NYSE :: HPQ
Cisco Systems, Inc.
NASDAQ :: CSCO

P9-64. Interpreting Warranty Liability Disclosures
The following information was extracted from the 10-K reports for the years ended in 2020 for **Hewlett-Packard Enterprise** and **Cisco Systems, Inc.**

	Hewlett-Packard Enterprise Company		Cisco Systems, Inc.	
($ millions)	2020	2019	2020	2019
Revenue from product sales.	$26,982	$29,135	$49,301	$51,904
Warranty expense.	238	239	561	600
Accrued warranty liability	385	400	331	342

REQUIRED

a. Compute the amount of warranty costs incurred in 2020 for each company. (That is, what amount was spent for warranty repairs and settlements in 2020? Assume no other adjustments to the account are made.)

b. Compare these two companies on the basis of the ratio of warranty expense to sales. What factors might explain any difference that you observe?

LO9-3, 4 Homework MBC

P9-65. Recording and Assessing the Effects of Bond Financing (with Accrued Interest) (FSET)
Eskew, Inc., which closes its books on December 31, is authorized to issue $250,000 of 6%, 15-year bonds dated May 1, 2021, with interest payments on November 1 and May 1.

REQUIRED

1. Assuming that the bonds were sold at 100 plus accrued interest on October 1, 2021, prepare the necessary entries for items *a–f* below using the financial statement effects template.
   a. The bond issuance.
   b. Payment of the first semiannual period's interest on November 1, 2021.
   c. Accrual of bond interest expense at December 31, 2021.
   d. The adjustment to fair value on December 31, 2021, assuming that Eskew, Inc., elected to use the fair value option. On that date, the bond traded at a price of 98.5 (98.5% of par value) in the bond market. (Assume that the change in fair value results from a change in market interest rates rather than a change in instrument-specific credit risk.)
   e. Payment of the semiannual interest on May 1, 2022. (The firm does not make reversing entries.)
   f. Retirement of $100,000 of the bonds at 101 on May 1, 2026 (immediately after the interest payment on that date). Assume that the fair value adjustment account for the entire issue has a debit balance of $11,250 as of that date. *Hint:* Forty percent of the outstanding bonds were retired in this transaction.
2. Suppose fair value adjustments of bond values were not posted to net income, but rather to other comprehensive income. How would Eskew, Inc.'s December 31, 2021, financial statements change?

LO9-3, 4 Homework MBC

P9-66. Recording and Assessing the Effects of Bond Financing (with Accrued Interest)
Using the information from P9-65, prepare journal entries for transactions described in parts *a* to *f* of part (1).

P9-67. Interpreting Debt Disclosures on Interest Rates and Expense

LO9-3, 4
Walgreens Boots Alliance, Inc.
NYSE :: WBA

Walgreens Boots Alliance, Inc. discloses the following in note 7 in its 10-K relating to its debt:

In millions	August 31, 2020	August 31, 2019
Short-term debt		
Commercial paper	$ 1,517	$ 2,400
Credit facilities	1,071	1,624
$8 billion note issuance[1]		
2.700% unsecured notes due 2019	—	1,250
£700 million note issuance[1]		
2.875% unsecured Pound sterling notes due 2020	533	—
Other[2]	418	464
Total short-term debt	**$ 3,538**	**$ 5,738**
Long-term debt		
$1.5 billion note issuance[1]		
3.200% unsecured notes due 2030	$ 497	$ —
4.100% unsecured notes due 2050	990	—
$6 billion note issuance[1]		
3.450% unsecured notes due 2026	1,891	1,890
4.650% unsecured notes due 2046	591	591
$8 billion note issuance[1]		
3.300% unsecured notes due 2021	1,248	1,247
3.800% unsecured notes due 2024	1,993	1,992
4.500% unsecured notes due 2034	496	495
4.800% unsecured notes due 2044	1,493	1,492
£700 million note issuance[1]		
2.875% unsecured Pound sterling notes due 2020	—	488
3.600% unsecured Pound sterling notes due 2025	398	365
€750 million note issuance[1]		
2.125% unsecured Euro notes due 2026	891	824
$4 billion note issuance[1]		
3.100% unsecured notes due 2022	1,198	1,197
4.400% unsecured notes due 2042	493	493
Other[4]	24	25
Total long-term debt, less current portion	**$12,203**	**$11,098**

Walgreens Boots also discloses that its interest expense, net was $639 million and it paid interest of $584 million in fiscal 2020.

REQUIRED

a. What was the average interest rate on Walgreens Boots debt in 2020?

b. Does your computation in part *a* seem reasonable given the disclosure relating to specific bond issues? Explain.

c. Why can the amount of interest paid be different from the amount of interest expense recorded in the income statement?

P9-68. Recording and Assessing the Effects of Bond Financing (with Accrued Interest) (FSET)

LO9-3, 4
Homework MBC

Petroni, Inc., which closes its books on December 31, is authorized to issue $600,000 of 4%, 20-year bonds dated March 1, 2022, with interest payments on September 1 and March 1.

REQUIRED

Assuming that the bonds were sold at 100 plus accrued interest on July 1, 2022, record each transaction in the financial statement effects template.

a. The bond issuance.

b. Payment of the semiannual interest on September 1, 2022.

c. Accrual of bond interest expense at December 31, 2022.

d. Payment of the semiannual interest on March 1, 2023. (The firm does not make reversing entries.)

e. Retirement of $125,000 of the bonds at 101 on March 1, 2023 (immediately after the interest payment on that date).

P9-69. Recording and Assessing the Effects of Bond Financing (with Accrued Interest)

LO9-3, 4
Homework MBC

Using the information from P9-68, complete the following.

a. Prepare journal entries for transactions described in parts *a* to *e*.

b. Post the journal entries to their respective T-accounts.

LO9-3, 4 Homework MBC

P9-70. Preparing an Amortization Schedule and Recording the Effects of Bonds (FSET)
On December 31, 2021, Kasznik, Inc., issued $480,000 of 4%, 10-year bonds for $442,586, yielding an effective interest rate of 5%. Semiannual interest is payable on June 30 and December 31 each year. The firm uses the effective interest method to amortize the discount.

REQUIRED

a. Prepare an amortization schedule showing the necessary information for the first two interest periods. Round amounts to the nearest dollar.

b. In the financial statement effects template, report (1) the bond issuance on December 31, 2021, (2) bond interest expense and discount amortization at June 30, 2022, and (3) bond interest expense and discount amortization at December 31, 2022.

LO9-3, 4 Homework MBC

P9-71. Recording the Effects of Bonds
Using the information from P9-70, complete the following.

a. Prepare journal entries for transactions described in part *b*.

b. Post the journal entries to their respective T-accounts.

LO9-3, 4 Homework MBC

P9-72. Preparing an Amortization Schedule and Recording the Effects of Bonds (FSET)
On April 30 Cheng, Inc., issued $325,000 of 6%, 15-year bonds for $268,801, yielding an effective interest rate of 8%. Semiannual interest is payable on October 31 and April 30 each year. The firm uses the effective interest method to amortize the discount.

REQUIRED

a. Prepare an amortization schedule showing the necessary information for the first two interest periods. Round amounts to the nearest dollar.

b. In the financial statement effects template, report (1) the bond issuance on April 30, (2) the bond interest payment and discount amortization at October 31, (3) the adjusting entry to record bond interest expense and discount amortization at December 31, the close of the firm's accounting year, and (4) the bond interest payment and discount amortization at April 30 of the following year.

LO9-3, 4 Homework MBC

P9-73. Recording the Effects of Bonds
Using the information from P9-72, complete the following.

a. Prepare journal entries for transactions described in part *b*.

b. Post the journal entries to their respective T-accounts.

LO9-3, 4 Homework MBC

P9-74. Recording and Assessing the Effects of Installment Loans: Semiannual Installments (FSET)
On December 31, 2021, Wasley Corporation borrowed $300,000 on a 6%, 10-year mortgage note payable. The note is to be repaid with equal semiannual installments, beginning June 30, 2022.

REQUIRED

a. Compute the amount of the semiannual installment payment. Use the appropriate table (in Appendix A near the end of the book) or a financial calculator, and round the amount to the nearest dollar.

b. In the financial statement effects template, report (1) Wasley's borrowing of funds on December 31, 2021, (2) Wasley's installment payment on June 30, 2022, and (3) Wasley's installment payment on December 31, 2022. (Round amounts to the nearest dollar.)

LO9-3, 4 Homework MBC

P9-75. Recording and Assessing the Effects of Installment Loans: Semiannual Installments
Using the information from P9-74, complete the following.

a. Prepare journal entries for transactions described in part *b*.

b. Post the journal entries to their respective T-accounts.

LO9-3, 4 Homework MBC

P9-76. Recording and Assessing the Effects of Installment Loans: Quarterly Installments (FSET)
On December 31, 2021, Watts Corporation borrowed $750,000 on an 8%, 5-year mortgage note payable. The note is to be repaid with equal quarterly installments, beginning March 31, 2022.

REQUIRED

a. Compute the amount of the quarterly installment payment. Use the appropriate table (in Appendix A near the end of the book) or a financial calculator, and round amount to the nearest dollar.

b. In the financial statement effects template, report (1) the borrowing of funds by Watts Corporation on December 31, 2021, (2) the installment payment by Watts Corporation on March 31, 2022, and (3) the installment payment by Watts Corporation on June 30, 2022.

P9-77. Recording and Assessing the Effects of Installment Loans: Quarterly Installments LO9-3, 4

Homework MBC

Using the information from P9-76, complete the following.

a. Prepare journal entries for transactions described in part *b*.
b. Post the journal entries to their respective T-accounts.

P9-78. Contingent Liabilities LO9-1

BP, PLC
NYSE :: BP

BP operates off-shore oil drilling platforms, including rigs in the Gulf of Mexico. In April 2010, explosions and a fire on the Deepwater Horizon rig led to the death of 11 crew members and a 200-million-gallon oil spill in the Gulf of Mexico. BP's 2010 annual report included the following description of its contingent liabilities (provision) related to this accident:

> In estimating the amount of the provision, BP has determined a range of possible outcomes for Individual and Business Claims, and State and Local Claims.... BP has concluded that a reasonable range of possible outcomes for the amount of the provision at December 31, 2010, is $6 billion to $13 billion. BP believes that the provision recorded at December 31, 2010, of $9.2 billion represents a reliable best estimate from within this range of possible outcomes.

REQUIRED

a. BP prepares its financial statements in accordance with IFRS. How did BP report the $9.2 billion estimate in its 2010 financial statements?
b. How would the accounting for this provision differ if BP prepared its financial statements in accordance with U.S. GAAP?

CASES AND PROJECTS

C9-79. Interpreting Debt Disclosures LO9-3, 4, 5

Comcast
NASDAQ :: CMCSA

Comcast Corporation's 2020 income statement and partial balance sheet (liabilities and equity, only) are presented below. In addition, Note 6 pertaining to Comcast's long-term debt obligations is provided. All $ amounts are presented in millions.

Summarized Consolidated Statement of Income Year Ended December 31 (in millions)	2020	2019
Revenue	$103,564	$108,942
Costs and expenses:		
Programming and production	33,121	34,440
Other operating and administrative	33,109	32,807
Advertising, marketing, and promotion	6,741	7,617
Depreciation	8,320	8,663
Amortization	4,780	4,290
Other operating gains	—	—
Total costs and expenses	86,071	87,817
Operating income	17,493	21,125
Interest expense	(4,588)	(4,567)
Investment and other income (loss), net	1,160	438
Income before income taxes	14,065	16,996
Income tax benefit (expense)	(3,364)	(3,673)
Net income	$ 10,701	$ 13,323

Summarized Consolidated Balance Sheet (Liabilities and Equity only) December 31 (in millions)	2020	2019
Current liabilities:		
Accounts payable and accrued expenses related to trade creditors	$ 11,364	$ 10,826
Accrued participations and residuals	1,706	1,730
Deferred revenue	2,963	2,768
Accrued expenses and other current liabilities	9,617	10,516
Current portion of long-term debt	3,146	4,452
Total current liabilities	28,796	30,292
Long-term debt, less current portion	100,614	97,765
Collateralized obligation	5,168	5,166
Deferred income taxes	28,051	28,180
Other noncurrent liabilities	18,222	16,765
Commitments and contingencies		
Total liabilities	180,851	178,168
Total equity	93,018	85,246
Total liabilities and equity	$273,869	$263,414

Note 6: Long-Term Debt December 31 (in millions)	Weighted-Average Interest Rate as of December 31, 2020	Weighted-Average Interest Rate as of December 31, 2019	2020[b]	2019[b]
Term loans	2.07%	1.87%	$ 7,641	$ 8,078
Senior notes with maturities of 5 years or less, at face value	3.41%	3.29%	19,190	26,378
Senior notes with maturities between 5 and 10 years, at face value	3.47%	3.74%	23,114	21,683
Senior notes with maturities greater than 10 years, at face value	4.03%	4.54%	54,203	46,653
Other, including finance lease obligations			1,261	1,098
Debt issuance costs, premiums, discounts, fair value adjustments for acquisition accounting and hedged positions, net[a]			(1,649)	(1,673)
Total debt	3.60%[a]	3.78%[a]	103,760	102,217
Less: Current portion			3,146	4,452
Long-term debt			$100,614	$ 97,765

[a] Includes the effects of our derivative financial instruments.

[b] As of December 31, 2020, included in our outstanding debt were foreign currency denominated borrowings with principal amounts of £4.7 billion, €7.3 billion, ¥238.5 billion, and ¥16.4 billion RMB. As of December 31, 2019, included in our outstanding debt were foreign currency denominated borrowings with principal amounts of £4.9 billion, €4.9 billion, ¥267 billion, and ¥9 billion RMB.

Our senior notes are unsubordinated and unsecured obligations and are subject to parent and/or subsidiary guarantees. As of December 31, 2020 and 2019, our debt had an estimated fair value of $125.6 billion and $115.8 billion, respectively. The estimated fair value of our publicly traded debt was primarily based on Level 1 inputs that use quoted market value for the debt. The estimated fair value of debt for which there are no quoted market prices was based on Level 2 inputs that use interest rates available to us for debt with similar terms and remaining maturities.

Principal Maturities of Debt December 31 (in millions)	
2021	$ 3,133
2022	4,028
2023	3,925
2024	6,746
2025	6,953
Thereafter	80,624

REQUIRED

a. Comcast provided cash flow information revealing that the company paid interest equal to $3,878 million in 2020. Explain why this amount is different from the amount of interest expense reported in its 2020 income statement.

b. Comcast reports its debt using historical cost. What would be the impact on the financial statements if the company elected to report all of its debt at fair value? (Assume no changes to fair values due to changes in instrument-specific credit risk.) Be specific.

c. The financial ratios specified in Comcast's loan agreements include the solvency measures described in this chapter. Calculate Comcast's debt-to-equity ratio and times interest earned for 2020. Explain why creditors might include these ratios in the restrictive covenants of loan agreements.

d. Violation of debt covenants can be a serious event that can impose substantial costs on a company. What actions might management take to avoid violating debt covenants if the company's ratios are near the covenant limits?

e. Explain what type of disclosures are likely present in Note 16—"Commitment and Contingencies," which is represented as a line item on the balance sheet with no amounts.

C9-80. Assessing Debt Financing, Company Interests, and Managerial Ethics **LO9-3, 4, 5**

Foster Corporation is in the third quarter of the current year, and projections are that net income will be down about $480,000 from the previous year. Foster's return on assets is also projected to decline from its usual 15% to approximately 13%. If earnings do decline, this year will be the second consecutive year of decline. Foster's president is quite concerned about these projections (and his job) and has called a meeting of the firm's officers for next week to consider ways to "turn things around—and fast."

Margot Barth, treasurer of Foster Corporation, has received a memorandum from her assistant, Lorie McNichols. Barth had asked McNichols if she had any suggestions as to how Foster might improve its earnings performance for the current year. McNichols' memo reads as follows:

> As you know, we have $2,400,000 of 4%, 20-year bonds payable outstanding. We issued these bonds 10 years ago at face value, so they have 10 years left to maturity. When they mature, we would probably replace them with other bonds. The economy is expecting a period of greater inflation, and interest rates have increased to about 8%. My proposal is to replace these bonds right now. More specifically, I propose:
>
> 1. Immediately issue $2,400,000 of 20-year, 8% bonds payable. These bonds will be issued at face value.
> 2. Use the proceeds from the new bonds to buy back and retire our outstanding 4% bonds. Because of the current high rates of interest, these bonds are trading in the market at about $1,760,000.
> 3. The benefits to Foster are that (a) the retirement of the old bonds will generate a $640,000 gain for the income statement and (b) there will be an extra $640,000 of cash available for other uses.

Barth is intrigued by the possibility of generating an $640,000 gain for the income statement. However, she is not sure this proposal is in the best long-run interests of the firm and its stockholders.

REQUIRED

a. How is the $640,000 gain calculated from the retirement of the old bonds? Where would this gain be reported in Foster's income statement?

b. Why might this proposal not be in the best long-run interests of the firm and its stockholders?

c. What possible ethical conflict is present in this proposal?

SOLUTIONS TO REVIEW PROBLEMS

Review 9-1

Part One

a. The discount would be $580 ($29,000 × 0.02). Thus, Waymire would pay $28,420 ($29,000 – $580).

b. The cost of the lost discount is $29 per day ($580/20) or $10,585 per year (simple interest). The implicit financing cost of the lost discount is 37.24% ($10,585/$28,420).

Part Two

a. Toro Company incurred $67,241 thousand in warranty claims in 2020 ($000):

$96,604 + $77,758 – warranty claims = $107,121. Warranty claims = $67,241.

b.

Transaction	Cash Asset	+	Noncash Assets	=	Liabil-ities	+	Contrib. Capital	+	Earned Capital	Revenues	–	Expenses	=	Net Income
Payment to satisfy warranty claims.	–67,241 Cash			=	–67,241 Warranty Liability						–		=	

ANALYZE JOURNALIZE POST

c.

Warranty liability (–L)	67,241	
Cash (–A)		67,241

– Warranty Liability (L) +	
67,241	

+ Cash (A) –	
	67,241

The credit entry to cash assumes that cash was paid to satisfy the warranty claims. Toro could also have credited wages payable, or parts inventory as needed.

Review 9-2

a. The related journal entry to recognize the accrual of interest is:

Transaction	Cash Asset	+	Noncash Assets	=	Liabil-ities	+	Contrib. Capital	+	Earned Capital	Revenues	–	Expenses	=	Net Income
Accrued $26 of interest as of January 31*.				=	+26 Interest Payable				–26 Retained Earnings		–	+26 Interest Expense	=	–26

ANALYZE JOURNALIZE POST

b.

Interest expense (+E, –SE)	26	
Interest payable (+L)		26

+ Interest Expense (E) –	
26	

– Interest Payable (L) +	
	26

*Accrued interest for a 16-day period at January 31 = $10,000 × 0.06 × 16/365 = $26.

Review 9-3

The bond issue price: *a.* $500,000 *b.* $425,613 *c.* $590,228

	N	I/Yr	PV	PMT	FV
a.	20	2.0	500,000	10,000	500,000
b.	20	3.0	425,613	10,000	500,000
c.	20	1.0	590,228	10,000	500,000

Review 9-4

a. Issue price for $300,000, 15-year, 10% semiannual bonds discounted at 8%:

Present value of principal payment ($300,000 × 0.30832)	$ 92,496
Present value of semiannual interest payments ($15,000 × 17.29203)	259,380
Issue price of bonds	$351,876

b.

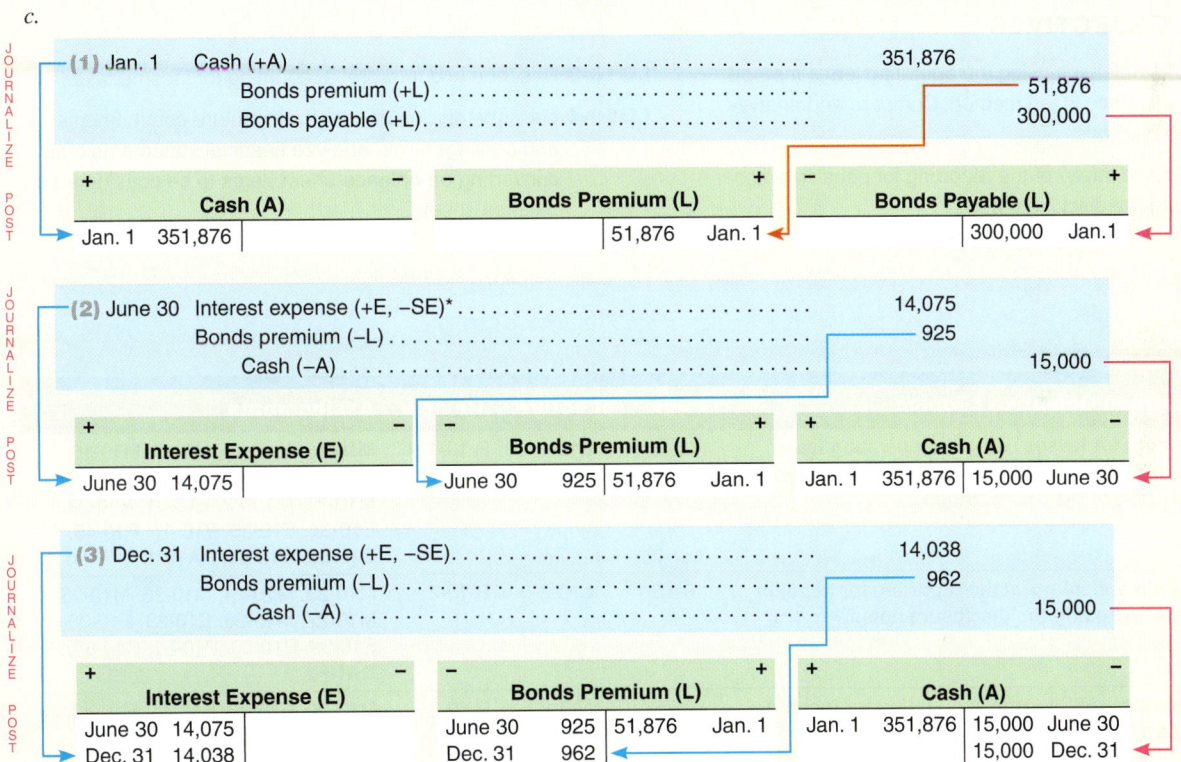

Transaction	Cash Asset	+ Noncash Assets	=	Liabilities	+ Contrib. Capital	+ Earned Capital	Revenues	− Expenses	= Net Income
	Balance Sheet						**Income Statement**		
(1) Jan. 1 Issuance.	+351,876 Cash		=	+300,000 Bonds Payable +51,876 Bonds Premium				−	=
(2) June 30 Interest and amortization[1].	−15,000 Cash		=	−925 Bonds Premium		−14,075 Retained Earnings		− +14,075 Interest Expense	= −14,075
(3) Dec. 31 Interest and amortization[2].	−15,000 Cash		=	−962 Bonds Premium		−14,038 Retained Earnings		− +14,038 Interest Expense	= −14,038

c.

(1) Jan. 1 Cash (+A) 351,876
Bonds premium (+L) 51,876
Bonds payable (+L) 300,000

+ Cash (A) −		− Bonds Premium (L) +		− Bonds Payable (L) +	
Jan. 1 351,876			51,876 Jan. 1		300,000 Jan. 1

(2) June 30 Interest expense (+E, −SE)* 14,075
Bonds premium (−L) 925
Cash (−A) 15,000

+ Interest Expense (E) −		− Bonds Premium (L) +		+ Cash (A) −	
June 30 14,075		June 30 925	51,876 Jan. 1	Jan. 1 351,876	15,000 June 30

(3) Dec. 31 Interest expense (+E, −SE). 14,038
Bonds premium (−L) 962
Cash (−A) 15,000

+ Interest Expense (E) −		− Bonds Premium (L) +		+ Cash (A) −	
June 30 14,075		June 30 925	51,876 Jan. 1	Jan. 1 351,876	15,000 June 30
Dec. 31 14,038		Dec. 31 962			15,000 Dec. 31

[1] $300,000 × 0.10 × 6/12 = $15,000 cash payment; 0.04 × $351,876 = $14,075 interest expense; the difference is the bond premium amortization, a reduction of the net bond carrying amount.

[2] 0.04 × ($351,876 – $925) = $14,038 interest expense. The difference between this amount and the $15,000 cash payment is the premium amortization, a reduction of the net bond carrying amount.

Review 9-5

a.

($ million)	Fiscal Year Ended	Earnings (Loss) before Interest, Tax	Interest Expense	Times Interest Earned
Macy's.	Feb. 02, 2019	$ 1,681	$ 261	6.4 times
Macy's.	Feb. 01, 2020	933	205	4.6 times
Nordstrom.	Feb. 02, 2019	852	119	7.2 times
Nordstrom.	Feb. 01, 2020	794	112	7.1 times
Bed Bath & Beyond . . .	Mar. 02, 2019	(87.1)	69.5	(1.3) times
Bed Bath & Beyond . . .	Feb. 29, 2020	(700.1)	64.8	(10.8) times

b. Based on the times interest earned ratio, Macy's and Bed Bath & Beyond's solvency weakened while Nordstrom's solvency slightly weakened in the fiscal year ended in 2020. Relative to each other, Nordstrom's solvency remained stable and was the strongest. Macy's solvency is weaker than Nordstrom's, but with two years of losses, Bed Bath & Beyond clearly has the weakest solvency of the three companies.

Chapter

10 Reporting and Analyzing Leases, Pensions, Income Taxes, and Commitments and Contingencies

LEARNING OBJECTIVES

LO10-1 Account for leases using the operating lease method and the finance lease method. Compare and analyze the two methods.

LO10-2 Explain and interpret the reporting for pension plans, including the disclosure notes.

LO10-3 Describe and interpret accounting for income taxes.

LO10-4 Describe disclosures regarding future commitments and contingencies. Analyze financial statements after converting off-balance-sheet items to be considered on balance sheet.

Road Map

LO	Learning Objective | Topics	Page	eLecture	Review	Assignments
LO10-1	**Account for leases using the operating lease method and the finance lease method. Compare and analyze the two methods.**	10-3	e10-1	R 10-1	M10-13, M10-14, M1-15, M10-16, M10-17, M10-18, M10-19, M10-20, M10-21, M10-22, E10-31, E10-32, E10-34, E10-35, P10-47, P10-48, C10-59, C10-60, **DA10-1**
LO10-2	**Explain and interpret the reporting for pension plans, including the disclosure notes.**	10-15	e10-2	R 10-2	M10-23, M10-24, M10-25, M10-26, M10-27, M10-28, E10-33, E10-38, E10-39, P10-50, P10-51, C10-58, **DA10-2**
LO10-3	**Describe and interpret accounting for income taxes.**	10-25	e10-3	R 10-3	M10-30, E10-40, E10-41, E10-42, E10-43, E10-44, E10-45, E10-46, P10-52, P10-53, P10-54, P10-55, P10-56, P10-57, C10-61, C10-62, C10-63, **DA10-3**
LO10-4	**Describe disclosures regarding future commitments and contingencies. Analyze financial statements after converting off-balance-sheet items to be considered on balance sheet.**	10-36	e10-4	R 10-4	M10-29, E10-35, E10-36, E10-37, P10-49, C10-59

DEERE & COMPANY

www.Deere.com

Deere & Company has a storied American history. John Deere invented the self-scouring plow in the mid-1800s in Grand Detour, Illinois. His business grew quickly, and he moved to Moline, Illinois, on the Mississippi River for water power and ease of transportation. Today, Deere & Company is a large, multinational corporation and has one of the best-known brands, logos, and slogans: *Nothing runs like a Deere*.

The company makes a wide array of products including lawn mowers, gators, all sizes of tractors used in the agricultural sector, construction equipment, and more. The technological advances have been swift in the industry; for example, Deere produces self-driving tractors and large spraying drones. As of the year-ended November 1, 2020, the company had revenues of $35.5 billion and net income of $2.8 billion. Total assets are $75 billion, and liabilities are $62 billion. Deere employs a large workforce in its manufacturing facilities, and many of the company's employees are covered by a defined benefit pension plan. The company both owns some assets and leases some assets in its operations. In addition, Deere has some commitments that are not required to be on the balance sheet, and the company discloses information about those items so its financial statement users are informed about these future cash commitments. Finally, the company has income tax obligations to many states, the U.S. government, and foreign jurisdictions. We explain the accounting for these items in this chapter.

Source: Deere 2020 10K Report

CHAPTER ORGANIZATION

Reporting and Analyzing Leases, Pensions, and Income Taxes

Leases
- Lessee Reporting of Operating and Finance Leases
- Disclosures
- Analyzing Financial Statements Including the Comparability of Financial Statements

Pensions
- Reporting of Defined Benefit Pension Plans
- Disclosures
- Other Postretirement Benefits

Income Taxes
- Reporting Tax Expense
- Book-Tax Differences
- Disclosures
- Computation and Analysis

INTRODUCTION

Investors, creditors, and other users of financial statements assess the composition of a company's balance sheet and its relation to the income statement. Chapter 6 introduced the concept of earnings quality to refer to the extent to which reported income reflects the underlying economic performance of a company. Similarly, the quality of the balance sheet refers to the extent to which the assets and liabilities of a company are reported in a manner that accurately reflects its economic resources and obligations. For example, in previous chapters, we highlighted the reporting of LIFO inventories and noncapitalized intangible assets to illustrate how some assets can be undervalued or even excluded from the balance sheet.

Financial managers are keenly aware of the importance that financial markets place on the quality of balance sheets. This importance sometimes creates pressure on companies to *window dress* their financial statements in order to report their financial condition and performance in the best possible light. One means of improving the perceived financial condition of the company is by keeping debt off the balance sheet. **Off-balance-sheet financing** refers to financial obligations of a company that are not reported as liabilities in the balance sheet. We note, however, that there are many fewer items that can remain 'off balance sheet' under today's accounting standards relative to the past. It is also important to be cognizant that some items that represent scheduled future cash outflows are required to remain unrecorded, that is 'off balance sheet,' because they do not rise to the level of a liability or cannot be accurately estimated in amount. We discuss off-balance sheet financing in this chapter as well as an analytical procedure for external financial statement users to employ to estimate "as if" balance sheets that include estimates of the off-balance-sheet items.

The first part of this chapter focuses on three common financial obligations (along with any related assets) that companies report in their financial statements—leases, pensions, and income taxes. We discuss other commitments and contingencies and off-balance-sheet financing arrangements at the end of the chapter.

Deere & Company's balance sheet is presented in **Exhibit 10.1**. The amounts reported on Deere's balance sheet related to leases, pensions, taxes, and commitments and contingencies are highlighted.

LEASES

LO10-1 Account for leases using the operating lease method and the finance lease method. Compare and analyze the two methods.

eLecture MBC

A lease is a contract between the owner of an asset (the **lessor**) and the party desiring to use that asset (the **lessee**). Because this is a private contract between two willing parties, it is governed only by applicable commercial law and can include whatever provisions are negotiated between the parties. The lessor and lessee can be any legal form of organization, including private individuals, corporations, partnerships, and joint ventures.

Leases generally contain the following terms:

- The lessor allows the lessee the unrestricted right to use the asset during the lease term.
- The lessee agrees to make periodic payments to the lessor and to maintain the asset.

EXHIBIT 10.1 Deere & Company Balance Sheets (excerpts)

DEERE & COMPANY Consolidated Balance Sheet (excerpts) As of November 1, 2020, and November 3, 2019 (in millions of dollars)	2020	2019
ASSETS		
Cash and cash equivalents	$ 7,066	$ 3,857
Marketable securities	641	581
Receivables from unconsolidated affiliates	31	46
Trade accounts and notes receivable—net	4,171	5,230
Financing receivables—net	29,750	29,195
Financing receivables securitized—net	4,703	4,383
Other receivables	1,220	1,487
Equipment on operating leases—net	7,298	7,567
Inventories	4,999	5,975
Property and equipment—net	5,817	5,973
Investments in unconsolidated affiliates	193	215
Goodwill	3,081	2,917
Other intangible assets—net	1,327	1,380
Retirement benefits	863	840
Deferred income taxes	1,499	1,466
Other assets	2,432	1,899
Total Assets	$75,091	$73,011
LIABILITIES AND STOCKHOLDERS' EQUITY		
LIABILITIES		
Short-term borrowings	$ 8,582	$10,784
Short-term securitization borrowings	4,682	4,321
Payables to unconsolidated affiliates	105	142
Accounts payable and accrued expenses	10,112	9,656
Deferred income taxes	519	495
Long-term borrowings	32,734	30,229
Retirement benefits and other liabilities	5,413	5,953
Total liabilities	62,147	61,580
Commitments and contingencies (Note 21)		
Redeemable noncontrolling interest (Note 5)		14
STOCKHOLDERS' EQUITY		
Total stockholders' equity	12,944	11,417
Total Liabilities and Stockholders' Equity	$75,091	$73,011

- The legal title to the asset remains with the lessor. At the end of the lease, either the lessor takes physical possession of the asset, or the lessee purchases the asset from the lessor at a price specified in the lease contract.

From the lessor's standpoint, lease payments are set at an amount that yields an acceptable return on investment, commensurate with the credit standing of the lessee. The lessor, thus, obtains a quality investment, and the lessee gains use of the asset.

From the lessee's perspective, the lease serves as a financing vehicle, similar to an intermediate-term secured bank loan. However, there are several advantages to leasing over bank financing:

- Leases often require less equity investment than bank financing. That is, banks often only lend a portion of the asset's cost and require the borrower to make up the difference from its available cash.
- Leases often require payments to be made at the beginning of the period (e.g., the first of the month). However, because leases are contracts between two parties, their terms can be structured in any way to meet their respective needs. For example, a lease can allow variable payments to match seasonal cash inflows of the lessee or have graduated payments for companies in their start-up phase.

- If the lessee requires the use of the asset for only a part of its useful life, leasing avoids the need to sell a used asset.
- Because the lessor retains ownership of the asset, leases provide the lessor with tax benefits such as accelerated depreciation deductions. This fact can lead to lower payments for lessees.

Lessee Reporting of Leases

FASB's Topic 842, *Leases* (hereafter, the lease standard) became effective for public firms with fiscal years and interim periods beginning after December 15, 2018 (the effective date was delayed for private firms to three years later). The standard requires lessees to recognize a **right-of-use asset** and a lease liability for all leases (with the exception, if so elected, of short-term leases) at the commencement date and recognize expenses on their income statements related to the leases. This is a substantial change from the prior standard, in which leases classified as operating leases under the prior accounting standards were "off-balance" sheet—meaning there was no lease asset or lease liability on the balance sheet. Many leases were structured to achieve operating lease classification and, thus, off-balance-sheet financing.

Estimates by the International Accounting Standards Board were that, worldwide, public firms had more than $3 trillion in off-balance-sheet leases before the lease standard took effect.[1] The new accounting standard has significantly changed the balance sheets of lessees.

There are two classifications of leases for lessees: operating leases and finance leases. The main distinction between the categories is that some leases are considered equivalent to a sale/purchase (finance lease), whereas others are not (operating lease). The lease standard requires lessees to record a right-of-use asset and lease liability for *all* leases (with an exception for leases of less than 12 months—also called a short-term lease). However, the income statement treatment is not the same across the two classifications of leases under U.S. GAAP; we discuss the differences below. There are also different lease classifications for the lessor. In fact, you can see that Deere includes within its assets on its balance sheet (see **Exhibit 10-1**) net equipment of $ 7,298 million that the company, as the lessor, has leased out through operating leases. However, in this text, we focus primarily on the accounting from the lessee's perspective.[2]

An overall summary of lease classification and accounting treatment for lessees is as follows:

Lessee			
Finance Lease			
Classification Rule	**Accounting**		
	Balance Sheet	**Income Statement**	**Cash Flows**
Meets at least one of the five lease classification criteria.	Recognize a right-of-use asset and test for impairment. Recognize a lease liability.	Recognize amortization expense on the right-of-use asset (typically straight line over lease term or useful life). Recognize interest expense on the lease liability using the effective interest method.	Interest is operating cash flow; principal is financing.
Operating Lease			
Classification Rule	**Accounting**		
	Balance Sheet	**Income Statement**	**Cash Flows**
Meets none of the five lease classification criteria.	Recognize a right-of-use asset and test for impairment. Recognize a lease liability.	Recognize lease expense on a straight-line basis as a single line item.	Lease payment is operating cash flow.

Note that finance leases require a recording of interest expense and amortization. The operating leases are expensed on a straight-line basis (rather than high interest costs early in the term of the lease).

[1] IFRS Fact Sheet—IFRS 16 Leases

[2] There are classifications of leases for lessors as well: sales-type leases, direct financing leases, and operating leases. The accounting for leases for lessors is essentially unchanged.

The current lease accounting standard is aligned in concept with the current revenue recognition standard that we discussed in Chapter 6. Specifically, the parties need to identify the contract and the consideration. Whether a lease exists is to be determined on the date the contract is signed or authorized (the inception of the lease). The company must determine if the contract is a lease or includes a lease. Next, the consideration for the lease must be determined. Lease payments can consist of five amounts: fixed payments, variable payments, a purchase option, a lease termination penalty, and residual value guarantee. Lease payments are critical because these are the basis for determining the classification of the lease and the amount of the lease liability.

Classification Rules The classification rules are intended to classify leases based on the extent of control of the asset that is passed to the lessee in the contract. If control has passed (the lease meets one of the criteria), the lease is a finance lease. The lease is to be classified (and measurement of the right-of-use asset and lease liability measured) on the lease commencement date (when the asset is available for use). FASB uses five criteria to classify leases; if a lease meets *at least one* of the criteria, it is classified as a finance lease (lessee) and a sales-type lease (lessor).[3] The five criteria, briefly, are as follows:

1. *Ownership transfer*: the lease transfers ownership of the underlying asset to the lessee by the end of the lease term.
2. *Purchase option*: the lease grants the lessee an option to purchase the underlying asset that the lessee is reasonably expected to exercise.
3. *Lease term length*: the lease term is for the major part of the remaining economic life of the underlying asset.
4. *Present value of lease payments*: the present value of the lease payments (and any residual value guaranteed by the lessee that is not already reflected in the lease payments) equals or exceeds substantially all of the fair value of the underlying asset.
5. *Alternative use*: the underlying asset is expected to have no alternative use to the lessor at the end of the lease term.

To illustrate the accounting for the two classifications of leases, we use the following example. Gillette Electronics agrees to lease retail store space in a shopping center. The lease is a 5-year lease with annual payments of $10,000 due at each year-end. (Many leases require payments up front; we generally use end-of-year annual payments in this textbook for simplicity.) Using a 7% interest rate, the present value of the five annual future lease payments equals $41,002, computed as $10,000 × 4.10020 (Appendix A, Table A.3). Using a calculator, the present value of the annual lease payments is computed as follows:[4]

Calculator

N	I/Yr	PV	PMT	FV
5	7	41,002	10,000	0

Finance Lease When the lease is a finance lease, the lessee records a lease liability equal to the present value of the remaining lease payments discounted using the rate implicit in the lease (or if that rate is not available, the lessee's incremental borrowing rate). The lease is recorded on the lease commencement date. In our example, the liability is recorded for $41,002 as follows:

[3] Though, the lessor and lease make the determination independently.

[4] The result produced by the financial calculator is actually −41,002. The present value will always have the opposite sign from the payment. So, if the payment is positive, the present value will be negative. **Appendix A** illustrates the use of a financial calculator to compute present values. In this calculation, it is important to set the payments per year (period) to 1 and make sure that the payments are set to occur at the end of each period.

ANALYZE

Transaction	Cash Asset	+	Noncash Assets	−	Contra Assets	=	Liabilities	+	Contrib. Capital	+	Earned Capital	*Revenues*	−	*Expenses*	=	*Net Income*
(1) Leased store space under finance lease.			+41,002 Right-of-use Asset—Finance Lease	−		=	+41,002 Finance Lease Liability						−		=	

JOURNALIZE

		Dr.	Cr.
(1)	Right-of-use asset—Finance lease (+A).	41,002	
	Finance lease liability (+L).		41,002

POST

+ Right-of-Use Asset—Finance Lease (A) −	
(1) 41,002	

− Finance Lease Liability (L) +	
	41,002 (1)

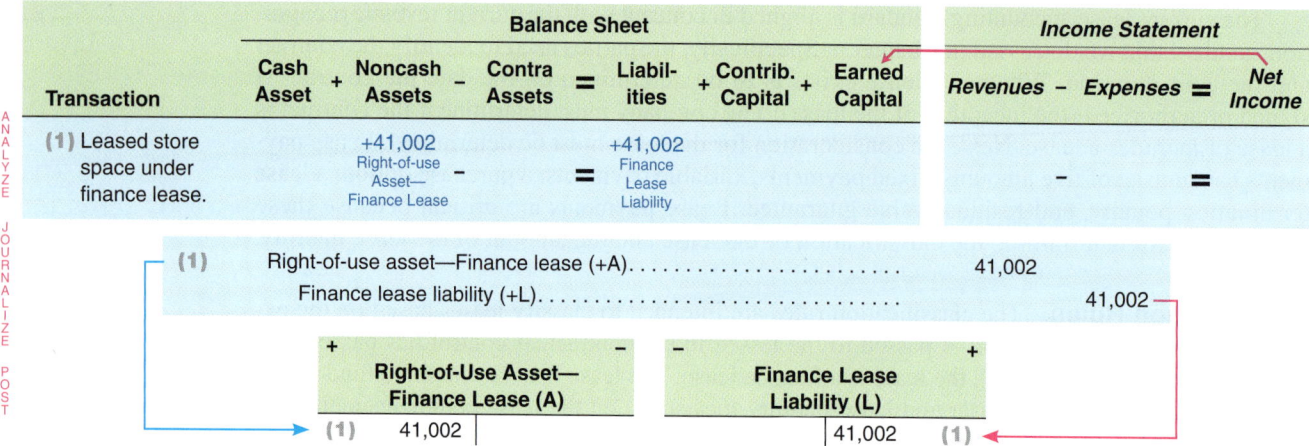

The asset is reported among long-term (PPE) assets in the balance sheet, and the liability is reported both in current and long-term debt.

At the end of the first year, two entries are required: one to account for the asset and the other to account for the lease payment. The right-of-use asset must be amortized, similar to how purchased long-term assets must be depreciated. The entry to amortize Gillette's leased asset (assuming straight-line amortization, a useful life of 5 years, and zero residual value [$41,002/5 = $8,200]) is:[5]

ANALYZE

Transaction	Cash Asset	+	Noncash Assets	−	Contra Assets	=	Liabilities	+	Contrib. Capital	+	Earned Capital	*Revenues*	−	*Expenses*	=	*Net Income*
(2) Annual amortization expense.				−	+8,200 Accumulated Amortization	=					−8,200 Retained Earnings		−	+8,200 Amortization Expense	=	−8,200

JOURNALIZE

		Dr.	Cr.
(2)	Amortization expense (+E, −SE)	8,200	
	Accumulated amortization—Right-of-use asset (+XA, −A)		8,200

POST

+ Amortization Expense (E) −	
(2) 8,200	

− Accumulated Amortization—Right-of-Use Asset (XA) +	
	8,200 (2)

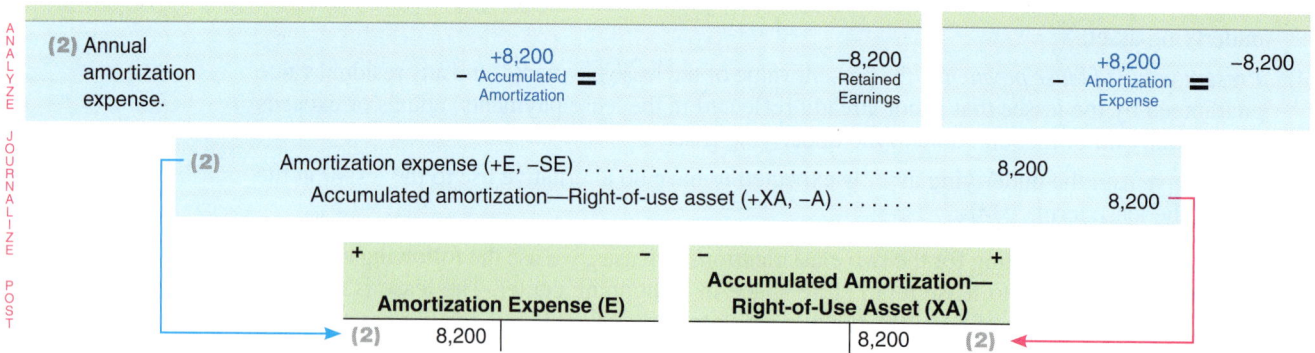

The second entry is to account for the lease payment. This involves recording the cash payment, recording interest expense, and recording the amount of principal repayment. In our example, we first determine how much of the cash payment is interest and how much is principal repayment.

ANALYZE

Transaction	Cash Asset	+	Noncash Assets	−	Contra Assets	=	Liabilities	+	Contrib. Capital	+	Earned Capital	*Revenues*	−	*Expenses*	=	*Net Income*
(3) Lease payment.	−10,000 Cash			−		=	−7,130 Finance Lease Liability				−2,870 Retained Earnings		−	+2,870 Interest Expense	=	−2,870

JOURNALIZE

		Dr.	Cr.
(3)	Finance lease liability (−L)	7,130	
	Interest expense (+E, −SE).	2,870	
	Cash (−A)		10,000

POST

− Finance Lease Liability (L) +	
(3) 7,130	

+ Cash (A) −	
	10,000 (3)

+ Interest Expense (E) −	
(3) 2,870	

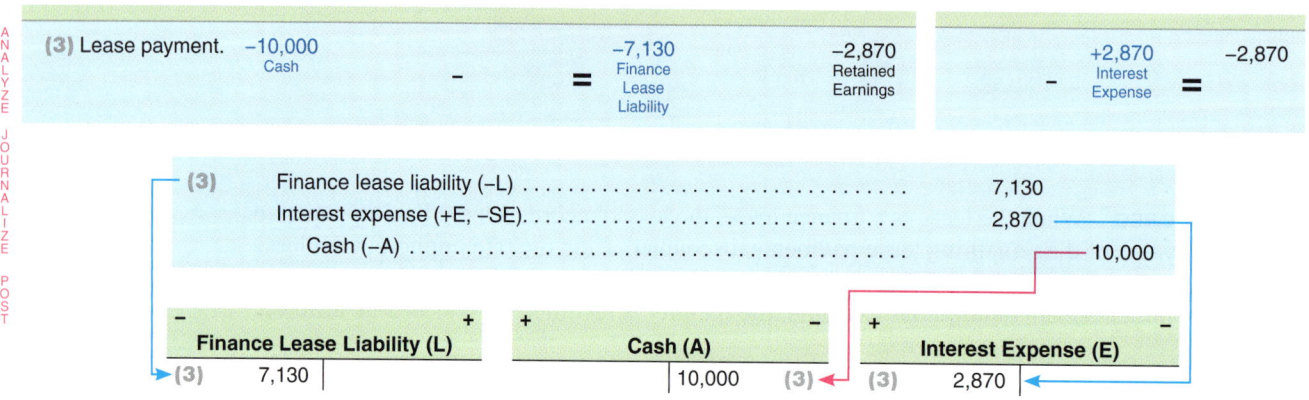

[5] Companies can choose whether to create an accumulated amortization account (contra-asset) or to simply reduce (credit) the right-of-use asset directly.

Interest expense of $2,870 is computed by multiplying the unpaid balance in the lease liability by the interest rate ($41,002 × 7%). The difference between the lease payment and interest expense ($10,000 – $2,870) is the principal repayment, which is recorded as a reduction, or debit, to the lease liability. The year-end balance in the lease liability account is $33,872, calculated as ($41,002 – $7,130).

Exhibit 10.2 presents the amortization table for Gillette's lease liability under the finance lease method. The amortization of finance leases is identical to the amortization of installment loans introduced in Chapter 9.

EXHIBIT 10.2 Amortization Table for a Finance Lease Liability

A Year	B Beginning-Year Lease Liability	C Interest Expense (B × 7%)	D Payment	E Principal Repayment (D – C)	F Ending-Year Lease Liability (B – E)
1	$41,002	$2,870	$10,000	$7,130	$33,872
2	33,872	2,371	10,000	7,629	26,243
3	26,243	1,837	10,000	8,163	18,080
4	18,080	1,266	10,000	8,734	9,346
5	9,346	654	10,000	9,346	0

Operating Lease When the lease is an operating lease, the initial measurement of the right-of-use asset and liability is measured at the same time and in the same manner as we just discussed for finance leases. Gillette will need to prepare an amortization schedule as shown in **Exhibit 10.2** for the operating lease liability. Even though control has not passed to the lessee, the lessee still has a right-of-use asset and an obligation to make lease payments. The difference in accounting occurs subsequent to the initial measurement. Unlike a finance lease, for operating leases an equal amount of expense is recorded each period on the income statement, using the straight-line method for expense recognition.

To illustrate, let's assume the Gillette Electronics lease from our example above is classified as an operating lease. Again, initial measurement is the same as above, and the initial entry is as follows:

ANALYZE

Transaction	Cash Asset	+	Noncash Assets	=	Liabil-ities	+	Contrib. Capital	+	Earned Capital	Revenues	–	Expenses	=	Net Income
	Balance Sheet									**Income Statement**				
Lease store space under operating lease.			+41,002 Right-of-Use Asset—Operating Lease	=	+41,002 Operating Lease Liability						–		=	

JOURNALIZE

Right-of-use asset—Operating lease (+A)	41,002	
Operating lease liability (+L)		41,002

POST

+ Right-of-Use Asset—Operating Lease (A) –		– Operating Lease Liability (L) +	
41,002			41,002

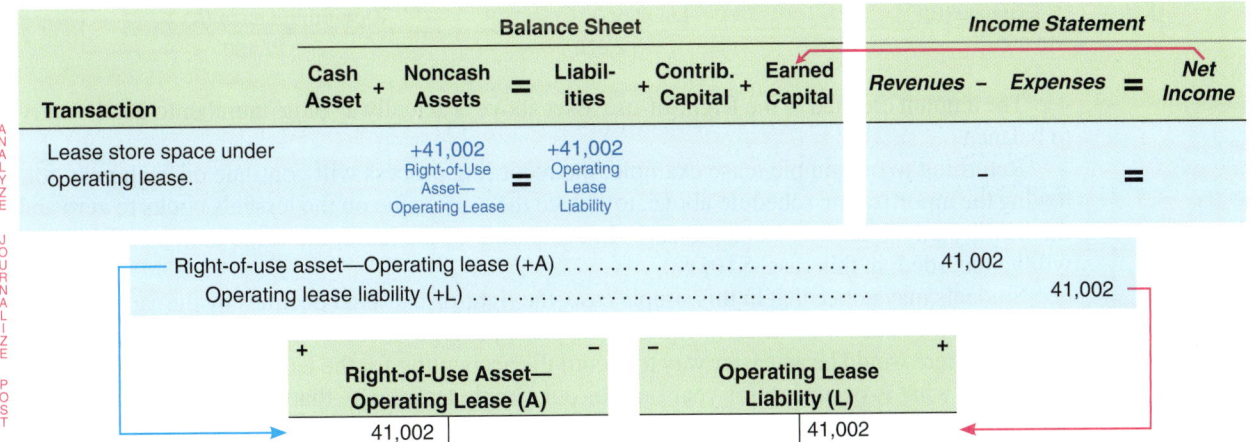

At the end of the first year, Gillette will record the straight-line expense amount related to the lease and will record the lease payment in cash. The straight-line expense is computed by taking the total cost of the lease divided by the total number of lease payments. The total cost of the lease in our example is straightforward because this is a simple lease (we briefly discuss more complicated cases below). The total cost of the lease is $50,000, and if we divide by the 5-year term, we obtain $10,000 as the annual straight-line expense amount. As stated above, Gillette still needs to prepare the amortization schedule for the liability. Though no interest expense line item is recorded for the operating lease liability, Gillette needs to compute the "interest" on the lease liability. Gillette also needs to compute the amortization of the right-of-use asset. The amortization is computed as the straight-line expense amount less the computed "interest" amount (though again no actual amortization expense line item or interest expense line item is recorded). The entries to record the payment of the lease payment as well as the recording of the straight-line expense are as follows:

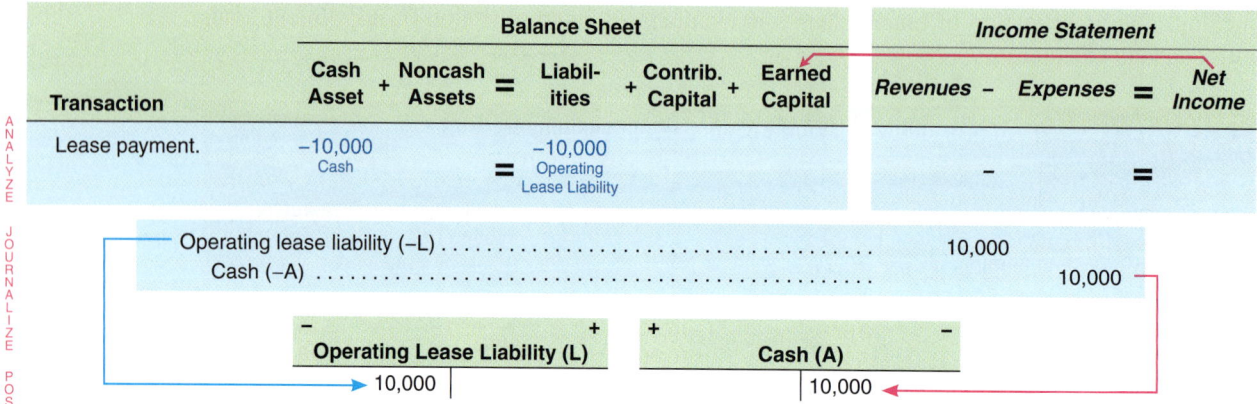

Recording of the lease payment:

ANALYZE

Transaction	Cash Asset	+ Noncash Assets	=	Liabil-ities	+ Contrib. Capital	+ Earned Capital	Revenues	− Expenses	=	Net Income
	Balance Sheet						***Income Statement***			
Lease payment.	−10,000 Cash		=	−10,000 Operating Lease Liability				−	=	

JOURNALIZE

Operating lease liability (−L)	10,000	
Cash (−A)		10,000

POST

Operating Lease Liability (L) (− | +)
10,000 |

Cash (A) (+ | −)
| 10,000

Recording of the straight-line expense:

ANALYZE

Transaction	Cash Asset	+ Noncash Assets	=	Liabil-ities	+ Contrib. Capital	+ Earned Capital	Revenues	− Expenses	=	Net Income
Record lease expense.		−7,130 Right-of-Use Asset—Operating Lease	=	+2,870 Operating Lease Liability		−10,000 Retained Earnings		− +10,000 Operating Lease Expense	=	−10,000

JOURNALIZE

Operating lease expense (+E, −SE)	10,000	
Operating lease liability (+L)		2,870
Right-of-use asset—Operating lease (−A).		7,130

POST

Operating Lease Expense (E) (+ | −)
10,000 |

Operating Lease Liability (L) (− | +)
| 2,870

Right-of-Use Asset—Operating Lease (A) (+ | −)
| 7,130

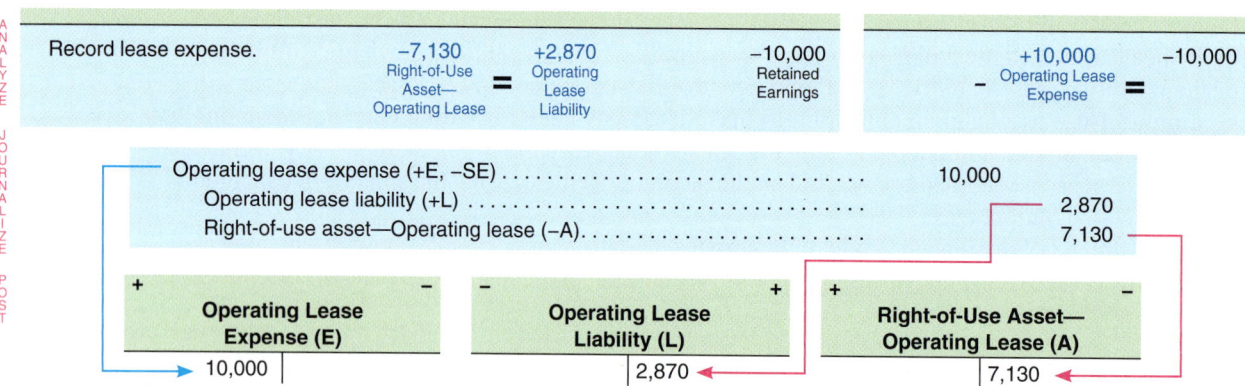

The amount credited to the Right-of-use asset above is actually a "plug" number to get the entry to balance.

Returning to our simple lease example, the recording process will continue on each year, following the amortization schedule above, to reduce the asset value on the lessee's books to zero and the liability on the lessee's books to zero. In every year of the lease, the same amount of expense will be recorded, in this case, $10,000.

Students may notice that in this simple case, the right-of-use asset declines by the same amount that the liability declines (which is equal to the principal repayment from the schedule above) and think that there would be an easier way to record the accounting for the lease. Indeed, an alternative way to see what is occurring for year one for our simple lease case, that may be more obvious to students, is to look at a net entry of the two entries above:

Year 1 net entry:

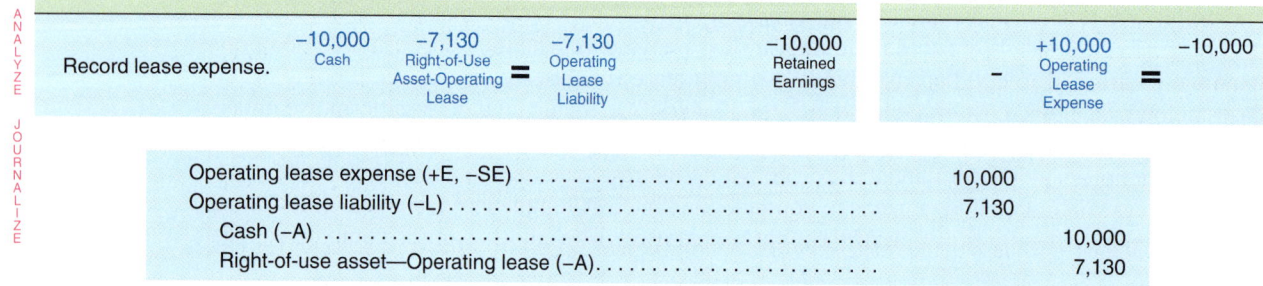

ANALYZE

Transaction	Cash Asset	+ Noncash Assets	=	Liabil-ities	+ Contrib. Capital	+ Earned Capital	Revenues	− Expenses	=	Net Income
Record lease expense.	−10,000 Cash	−7,130 Right-of-Use Asset-Operating Lease	=	−7,130 Operating Lease Liability		−10,000 Retained Earnings		− +10,000 Operating Lease Expense	=	−10,000

JOURNALIZE

Operating lease expense (+E, −SE)	10,000	
Operating lease liability (−L)	7,130	
Cash (−A)		10,000
Right-of-use asset—Operating lease (−A).		7,130

This is correct in this case, however, this relation—that the decline in the lease liability is the same as the decline in the right-of-use asset—will not always hold. The lease in our case is a simple lease with payments due at the end of the year. If the lease were one with payments due at the beginning of the year, or if the lease were more complex, for example, if it included prepayments, escalation provisions, other required or optional payments, lessee initial direct costs, lease incentives, or other items, then the accounting would be different. In such cases, the decline ("amortization") of the right-of-use asset will not equal reduction of the liability (i.e., the principal repayment). Indeed, in the more complex leases, the right-of-use asset value will not even equal the liability value when the lease commences. As a result, the only way to compute the decline the right-of-use asset value (the "amortization") in more complex cases is as a "plug" number equal to the straight-line expense amount less the computed "interest" amount for the reporting period. In these more complex cases (which are common), the two-entry method originally presented is necessary to correctly record the accounting for the lease.

In year 5 of this lease for Gillette, the entries would be as follows:

Operating lease liability (–L)	10,000	
Cash (–A)		10,000

The entry for the straight-line-expense amount is:

ANALYZE JOURNALIZE POST

Transaction	Cash Asset	+	Noncash Assets	=	Liabilities	+	Contrib. Capital	+	Earned Capital	Revenues	–	Expenses	=	Net Income
Record lease expense.			−9,346 Right-of-Use Asset—Operating Lease	=	+654 Operating Lease Liability				−10,000 Retained Earnings		–	+10,000 Operating Lease Expense	=	−10,000

(Balance Sheet: Cash Asset through Earned Capital; Income Statement: Revenues through Net Income)

Operating lease expense (+E, –SE)	10,000	
Operating lease liability (+L)		654
Right-of-use asset—Operating lease (–A)		9,346

+ Operating Lease Expense (E) –	– Operating Lease Liability (L) +	+ Right-of-Use Asset—Operating Lease (A) –
10,000 |	| 654	| 9,346

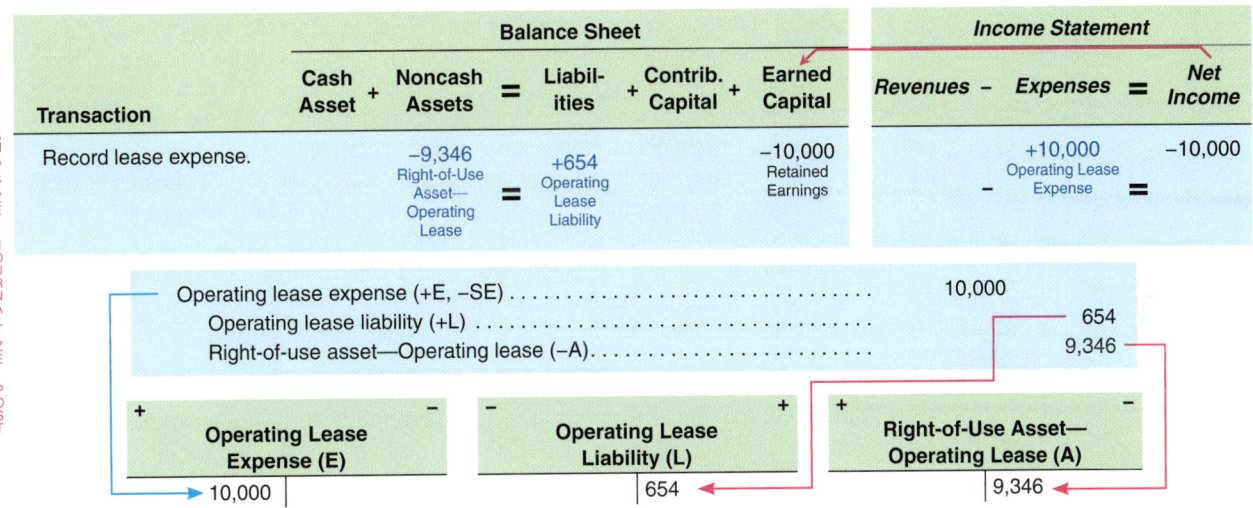

Thus, at the end of the lease term, the liability will be zero ($41,002 – $10,000 + $2,870 – $10,000 + $2,371 – $10,000 + $1,837 – $10,000 + 1,266 – $10,000 + $654). The asset also will have a zero balance ($41,002 – $7,130 – $7,629 – $8,163 – $8,734 – $9,346).

Comparison of Operating and Finance Lease Treatment The accounting for operating leases might seem odd in some ways to readers. Gillette is required to compute an "interest" cost using the amortization of the liability table to adjust the lease liability account and to compute the "amortization" of the right-of-use asset to adjust the right-of-use asset account. But there is no interest expense or amortization expense ever recorded in the income statement—only one straight-line Lease Expense. The goal (in the end, anyway) of the standard was to achieve (retain) straight-line expensing for these leases: the related expenses are not greater in the earlier part of the lease relative to the latter part of the lease, as they are with finance lease treatment. For example, even in our simple lease illustration above, the total expense in the first year for Gillette if the lease was a finance lease is $11,070. (Amortization of the right-of-use asset is $8,200, and interest expense is $2,870.) However, with the operating lease classification, the first year expense amount is $10,000. Note that the balance of the asset on the balance sheet differs—the balance of the asset declines faster for the finance lease than the operating lease (i.e., amortization is faster for the finance lease). The balance of the lease liability each year is the same for the finance lease as it is for the operating lease. A full comparison is below:

EXHIBIT 10.3 Comparison of Expenses and Right-of-Use Asset Balance

	Finance Lease Method					Operating Lease Method		
Year	Interest Expense	Amortization Expense	Total Expense	Right-of-Use Asset Balance End of Year	Operating Lease Liability Balance End of Year	Lease Expense	Right-of-Use Asset Balance End of Year	Operating Lease Liability Balance End of Year
1......	$2,870	$ 8,200	$11,070	$32,802	$33,872	$10,000	$33,872	$33,872
2......	2,371	8,200	10,571	24,602	26,243	10,000	26,243	26,243
3......	1,837	8,200	10,037	16,401	18,080	10,000	18,080	18,080
4......	1,266	8,201	9,467	8,200	9,346	10,000	9,346	9,346
5......	654	8,201	8,855	0	0	10,000	0	0
Total ...	$8,998	$41,002	$50,000			$50,000		

Exhibit 10.3 shows how the finance lease method reports a higher total expense (amortization plus interest) in the early years of the lease and a lower total expense in the later years. But the operating lease method reports the same expense every year. Total expense over the 5-year life of the lease is the same under both methods.

IFRS

A GLOBAL PERSPECTIVE

In 2008, the FASB and IASB (collectively, the "boards") initiated a joint project to develop a new standard to account for leases. Although many of the perceived problems with the previous leasing guidance related to a lessee's accounting for operating leases, the boards thought it beneficial to reflect on lease accounting holistically and to consider lease accounting while concurrently developing a proposal on revenue recognition (ASC 606, Revenue from Contracts with Customers). Although the project began as a joint project, the boards ended up diverging in some key areas. Most significantly, the boards did not agree on whether all leases should be accounted for using the same model. After significant deliberation, the IASB decided that lessees should apply a single model to all leases, which is reflected in *IFRS 16, Leases*, released in January 2016. The FASB decided that lessees should apply a dual model. Under the FASB model, lessees will classify a lease as either a finance lease or an operating lease, while a lessor will classify a lease as either a sales-type, direct financing, or operating lease.

Other Issues A detailed, expanded discussion of more complicated issues surrounding leases is beyond the scope of this text. However, we briefly mention two aspects that are likely to be of interest.

Multiple components: In determining whether a lease exists, management will need to determine if a contract contains a lease. It is possible that a contract could contain both lease and non-lease components and/or multiple lease components. In such a case, consideration in the contract is allocated to the separate components based on relative standalone selling prices.

As a disclosure example of such issues, the following excerpt is from Delta Airlines' 2020 10-K:

> In addition, we have regional aircraft leases that are embedded within our capacity purchase agreements and included in the operating right-of-use ("ROU") asset and lease liability. We allocated the consideration in each capacity purchase agreement to the lease and nonlease components based on their relative standalone value. Lease components of these agreements consist of 125 aircraft as of December 31, 2020, and nonlease components primarily consist of flight operations, in-flight, and maintenance services. We determined our best estimate of the standalone value of the individual components by considering observable information including rates paid by our wholly owned subsidiary, Endeavor Air, Inc., and rates published by independent valuation firms. See Note 12, "Commitments and Contingencies," for additional information about our capacity purchase agreements.

We note that companies can elect a simpler method of not separating the lease and non-lease components in certain cases. For example, Deere & Co., disclose the following:

> The company has elected to combine lease and nonlease components, such as maintenance and utilities costs included in a lease contract, for all asset classes.

Impairment: Lessees need to determine if the leased asset (finance or operating) is impaired. If a lessee records an impairment charge on a right-of-use asset associated with a finance lease, it should revise the amortization expense by calculating a new straight-line amortization based on the revised asset value.

If the lease is an operating lease and the right-of-use asset requires an impairment, once impaired, lease expense will no longer be recognized on a straight-line basis. A lessee should continue to amortize the lease liability using the same effective interest method as before the impairment charge. The right-of-use asset, however, should be subsequently amortized on a straight-line basis.

As can be seen in **Exhibit 10.3** the unamortized value of a right-of-use asset resulting from an operating lease is typically greater than it would have been had the lease been classified as a finance lease. Because of this higher value, a right-of-use asset arising from an operating lease may have a higher risk of impairment.

BUSINESS INSIGHT

A *Wall Street Journal* article discusses an interesting consequence of the new accounting lease standard. The new standard requires companies to collect and disclose lease data to a much greater extent than had been the case previously. While this was a large task for many companies, it provided a more detailed look into their lease spending than they had performed before enabling management to implement cost cutting and achieve greater efficiency. The article provides several examples:

> Tyson Foods Inc. spent about three years analyzing and digitizing its leases to get the comprehensive view of the portfolio required under the new rules. As a result, the Springdale, Ark., meat producer expects to reduce roughly $450 million in lease obligations it has for transportation and material handling equipment and real estate. "The improved visibility gives us a lot better management of our overall lease portfolio," said Brian Martfeld, the company's senior director for controls and automation. CVS Health Corp. spent about $2.5 billion on operating leases in 2017, according to a company spokesman. As it wrangled more than 10,000 lease agreements, the Woonsocket, R.I.-based health-care company found some areas it could trim. "We are considering curtailing the leasing of certain low-dollar equipment in the future," a company spokesman said. "Laptop and desktop computers would be two common examples."

Because many of these leases are long term it may take time to realize the savings.

Source: *Wall Street Journal*, January 22, 2019, "CFOs Uncover Surprise Savings as They Implement New Lease-Accounting Rules"

Lease Disclosures

Deere & Company adopted the new lease standard during the first quarter of 2020. Based on Deere's fiscal year-end, the company was not required to adopt the standard earlier. However, many companies were required or opted to adopt the lease standard earlier than fiscal year 2020, such as Caterpillar Inc. (as of January 1, 2019), American Airlines (as of January 1, 2018), and PepsiCo, Inc. (as of first quarter of 2019).

Deere recognizes operating leases and finance leases as a lessee. Deere discloses that its right-of-use assets and lease liabilities for operating leases and finance leases are embedded in balance sheet accounts shown in Exhibit 10-1. For example, right-of-use assets for operating leases of $324 million are included in the amount of $2,432 million, labeled as "other assets" on the balance sheet. These lease accounts are not stated separately because they are not material to the balance sheet; thus, they do not require separate line items. In the notes to their 2020 financial statements, Deere discloses the following (excerpted and reordered to some extent):

> Lessee
> The company recognizes on the balance sheet a lease liability and a right of use asset for leases with a term greater than one year for both operating and finance leases.
>
> The amounts of the lease liability and right of use asset are determined at lease commencement and are based on the present value of the lease payments over the lease term. The lease payments are discounted using the company's incremental borrowing rate since the rate implicit in the lease is generally not readily determinable. The company determines the incremental borrowing rate for each lease based primarily on the lease term and the economic environment of the country where the asset will be used,

continued

continued from previous page

adjusted as if the borrowings were collateralized. Leases with contractual periods greater than one year and that do not meet the finance lease criteria are classified as operating leases.

Operating and finance lease right of use assets and lease liabilities follow in millions of dollars:

	2020
Operating leases:	
Other assets	$324
Accounts payable and accrued expenses	305
Finance leases:	
Property and equipment—net	$ 63
Short-term borrowings	21
Long-term borrowings	39
Total finance lease liabilities	$ 60
Weighted-average remaining lease terms:	
Operating leases	5
Finance leases	3
Weighted-average discount rates:	
Operating leases	2.1%
Finance leases	2.2%

The lease expense by type consisted of the following in millions of dollars:

(in millions)	2020
Operating lease expense	$126
Short-term lease expense	23
Variable lease expense	41
Finance lease:	
Depreciation expense	20
Interest on lease liabilities	2
Total lease expense	$212

Cash paid for amounts included in the measurement of lease liabilities follows in millions of dollars:

	2020
Operating cash flows from operating leases	$124
Operating cash flows from finance leases	2
Financing cash flows from finance leases	17

Companies are required to disclose their future lease payments for the next five years and thereafter. Deere & Co. discloses the following:

Operating Leases

Lease payment amounts in each of the next five years at November 1, 2020, follow in millions of dollars:

Due in:	Operating Leases	Finance Leases
2021	$ 90	$22
2022	74	18
2023	52	12
2024	42	5
2025	24	3
Later years	41	2
Total lease payments	323	62
Less imputed interest	18	2
Total minimum lease payments	$305	$60

Notice that the "Total minimum lease payments" is the present value of the lease payments because imputed interest is subtracted. This present value is the liability recorded in the balance sheet as shown in Deere's disclosures above where they show that $305 million is included in "Accounts payable and accrued expenses" in the balance sheet.

Going forward, all firms will report operating leases under this standard. Financial statement users need to be cautious, however, if comparing a year where leases are reported under the new standard to a year where leases are reported under the old standard. For example, 2020 was Deere's first year of adoption so comparing 2020 to 2019 could be misleading because in 2020 the operating lease assets and the associated liabilities are included in the balance sheet and in 2019 the operating lease assets and their associated liabilities are not included in the balance sheet. Many ratios, such as debt-to-equity, debt-to-assets, return-on-assets, and others would be impacted.

Financial statement users could perform better year-over-year analysis in the year of adoption by adjusting the prior year financial statement numbers to 'as if' amounts—'as if' the new standard applied in 2019. We cover this notion of analyzing financial statements after adjusting them such that off-balance sheet debt is treated as if it were on-balance sheet debt below in our discussion of commitments and contingencies.[6]

Leases and the Statement of Cash Flows A lease results in an increase to long-term operating assets and an increase in liabilities. However, in many cases, there is no effect on cash flows at the inception of the lease—see entry (1) on page 10-7. As a consequence, the initial inception of the lease should be reported as a material noncash transaction and not presented in the statement of cash flows under either investing or financing cash flows. Subsequently, the amortization of the leased asset for a finance lease is added (in an indirect method statement of cash flows) to cash flow from operations (an expense that does not require a cash outlay), and the principal portion of the lease payment is treated as debt repayment under cash flows from financing activities. Note that because amortization is added back to earnings to compute operating cash flows in the indirect method Statement of Cash flows, and the principal repayment is a financing cash flow, operating cash flows will likely be higher for a finance lease relative to an operating lease. This is because, again, in the case of the operating lease, the lease expense is in the operating section of the Statement of Cash Flows either as part of net income in an indirect method statement or as a cash outflow in a direct method statement. In a direct method Statement of Cash Flows, the interest on a finance lease is an operating cash flow and the principal repayment is a financing cash flow. For an operating lease when the direct method Statement of Cash Flows is used, the full lease payment is shown as an operating cash flow.

YOU MAKE THE CALL

You are the CEO While implementing the new lease accounting standard, your CFO gathers more information on your lease contracts than your company has ever had before. What are some decisions and potential outcomes that this information might lead to? [Answer on page 10-40]

Accounting for Leases LO10-1 **Review 10-1**

Assume that **The Gap Inc.** leased a vacant retail space with the intention of opening another store. The lease calls for annual lease payments of $32,000, due at the end of each of the next ten years. Assume the appropriate discount rate is 7%.

GuidedExample MBC

continued

[6] Estimating the liability and asset amounts for operating leases under the old standard when only the future payments were disclosed and no asset or liability was included in the balance sheet would require the following steps (briefly stated): 1) estimate a discount rate, such as the rate on comparable debt, 2) compute the present value of the disclosed required future lease payments as of the end of the current reporting period, 3) estimate the associated asset value (could do this several ways but most easily one could look at the relative asset to liability ratio of the leases under the new standard), and 4) assume the difference between the 'as if' asset and 'as if' liability under the old standard reduces shareholder equity.

continued from previous page

Part One
First, assume that the lease is treated as a finance lease.
1. Using a financial statement effects template, report the entry that Gap would make to record the commencement of the lease agreement.
2. Using a financial statement effects template, report the entries to record amortization expense and the first lease payment at the end of the first year of the lease.
3. For parts 1 and 2, prepare the journal entries and post to the corresponding T-accounts.

Part Two
Now assume that the lease is treated as an operating lease.
1. Using a financial statement effects template, report the entries necessary for Gap for the first year.
2. For part 1, prepare journal entries and post to the corresponding T-accounts.

Solution on p. 10-64.

PENSIONS

LO10-2 Explain and interpret the reporting for pension plans, including the note disclosures.

eLecture MBC

Companies frequently offer retirement or pension plans as a benefit for their employees. There are two general types of pension plans:

1. **Defined contribution plan**. This type of plan is one in which the employer, employee, or both make contributions on a regular basis. Individual accounts are set up for participants. Future benefits are not guaranteed but instead fluctuate on the basis of investment earnings. Following retirement, the employee makes periodic withdrawals from that account. The amount that can be withdrawn is determined by how much is contributed to the plan and the rate of return earned on the investment. A tax-advantaged 401(k) account is a typical example. Under a 401(k) plan, the employee makes contributions that are exempt from federal taxes (as are the returns on the contributions) until they are withdrawn after retirement.
2. **Defined benefit plan**. This type of plan is one in which benefits are defined (promised). Defined benefit plans require the company to make periodic payments to a third party, which then makes payments to an employee after retirement. Retirement benefits are usually based on years of service and the employee's salary, not on the amount invested or the rate of return. It is possible for companies to set aside insufficient funds to cover these obligations. As a result, defined benefit plans can be overfunded or underfunded. (Federal law does set minimum funding requirements.) All pension investments are retained by the third party until paid to the employee. In the event of bankruptcy, employees have the standing of a general creditor, but usually have additional protection from the Pension Benefit Guaranty Corporation (PBGC), an independent agency of the U.S. government funded by premiums paid from the participating companies.

For a defined contribution plan, any company contribution is recorded as an expense in the income statement when the cash is paid or the liability is accrued. A defined benefit plan is more complex. Although the company contributes cash or securities to the pension investment account, the pension obligation is not satisfied until the employee receives pension benefits, which may be many years into the future. This section focuses on how a defined benefit plan is reported in the financial statements and how we assess company performance and financial condition when such a plan exists.

We note that the use of defined benefit plans has declined significantly. Many companies are instead establishing defined contribution plans for employees. For example, as of 2018, IRS data (Form 5500 summary data from the Department of Labor website, so including private companies) reveal that there are 675,007 defined contribution plans covering 105.8 million total, and 83.4 million active, employees compared with 46,869 defined benefit plans covering 34 million total, and 13.1 million active, employees. Many companies disclose that their defined benefit pension plans are closed to new entrants. Despite this decline in the use or contribution to defined benefit plans, such plans still constitute a significant liability for many companies.

Balance Sheet Effects of Defined Benefit Pension Plans

Pension plan assets are primarily investments in stocks and bonds (mostly of other companies, but it is not uncommon for companies to invest pension funds in their own stock). Pension liabilities (called the **projected benefit obligation** or **PBO**) are the company's obligations to pay current and former employees. The difference between the fair value of the pension plan assets and the projected benefit obligation is called the **funded status** of the pension plan. If the PBO exceeds the pension plan assets, the pension is **underfunded**. Conversely, if pension plan assets exceed the PBO, the pension plan is **overfunded**. Under current U.S. GAAP, companies are required to record only the funded status on their balance sheets (that is, the *net* amount, not the pension plan assets and PBO separately), either as an asset if the plan is overfunded, or as a liability if it is underfunded.

Pension plan assets consist of stocks and bonds whose value changes each period in three ways. First, the value of the investments increases or decreases as a result of interest, dividends, and gains or losses on the stocks and bonds held. Second, the pension plan assets increase when the company contributes additional cash or stock to the investment account. Third, the pension plan assets decrease by the amount of benefits paid to retirees during the period. These three changes in the pension plan assets are articulated below.

	Pension Plan Assets
	Pension plan assets, beginning balance
+	Actual returns on investments (interest, dividends, gains and losses)
+	Company contributions to pension plan
−	Benefits paid to retirees
=	Pension plan assets, ending balance

The pension liability, or PBO (projected benefit obligation), is computed as the present value of the expected future benefit payments to employees. The future payments depend on the number of years the employee is expected to work (years of service) and the employee's salary level at retirement. Consequently, companies must estimate future wage increases, as well as the number of employees expected to reach retirement age (or the vesting requirement) with the company. In addition, in order to compute the present value of benefit payments, the company has to estimate how long the plan participants are likely to receive pension benefits following retirement (that is, how long the employee—and often surviving spouse—will live). Once the future retiree pool is determined and the expected future payments under the plan are estimated, the expected payments are then discounted to arrive at the present value of the pension obligation. This is the PBO. A reconciliation of the PBO from beginning balance to year-end balance follows.

	Projected Benefit Obligation
	Projected benefit obligation, beginning balance
+	Service cost
+	Interest cost
+/−	Actuarial losses (gains)
−	Benefits paid to retirees
=	Projected benefit obligation, ending balance

As this reconciliation shows, the balance in the PBO changes during the period for four reasons.

- First, as employees continue to work for the company, their pension benefits increase. The annual **service cost** represents the additional (future) pension benefits earned by employees during the current year.
- Second, **interest cost** accrues on the outstanding pension liability, just as it would with any other long-term liability (see the accounting for bond liabilities in Chapter 9). Because there are no scheduled interest payments on the PBO, the interest cost accrues each year; that is, interest is added to the existing liability.
- Third, the PBO can increase (or decrease) due to **actuarial losses (and gains)**, which arise when companies make changes in their pension plans or make *changes in actuarial assumptions* (including assumptions that are used to estimate the PBO, such as the rate of wage inflation, termination and mortality rates, and the discount rate used to compute the present value of future

obligations). For example, if a company increases the discount rate used to compute the present value of future pension plan payments from, say, 8% to 9%, the present value of future benefit payments declines (just like bond prices), and the company records a gain. Conversely, if the discount rate is reduced to 7%, the present value of the PBO increases and a loss is recorded. Other assumptions used to estimate the pension liability (such as the expected wage inflation rate or the expected life span of current and former employees) can create similar actuarial losses or gains.

- Fourth, pension benefit payments to retirees reduce the PBO. (That portion of the liability is now paid.)

Finally, the net pension liability (or asset) that is reported in a company's balance sheet, then, is computed as follows.

Net Pension Asset (or Liability)
Pension plan assets (at fair value)
− Projected benefit obligation (PBO)
Funded status

If the funded status is positive (assets exceed liabilities), the overfunded pension plan is reported on the balance sheet as an asset, typically called prepaid pension cost. If the funded status is negative (liabilities exceed assets), it is reported as a liability.[7] During the early 2000s, long-term interest rates declined drastically, and many companies lowered their discount rate for computing the present value of future pension payments. Lower discount rates meant higher PBO values. This period also witnessed two bear markets—the "dot com crash" in 2000–2001 and the financial crisis of 2008–2010—and pension plan assets declined in value. The combined effect of the increase in PBO and the decrease in asset values caused many pension funds to become severely underfunded. Willis Towers Watson, a compensation consulting firm, analyzed the Fortune 1000 corporations that sponsor a defined benefit plan (between 350–400 companies) and found that in 2009, aggregate funding was 81% of the projected liability. The companies' funded status was 87% in 2019 and is projected to be 87% for 2020 as well.[8] Deere & Company reported an underfunded pension obligation of $447 million in 2020. This amount was equal to less than 1% of its total assets. Many companies with a defined benefit plan report that their plans are underfunded. The underfunded (overfunded) liability as a percent of total assets for Deere and several other companies is reported in the chart below. One company, Cummins Inc., actually has an overfunded status because plan assets exceed obligations.

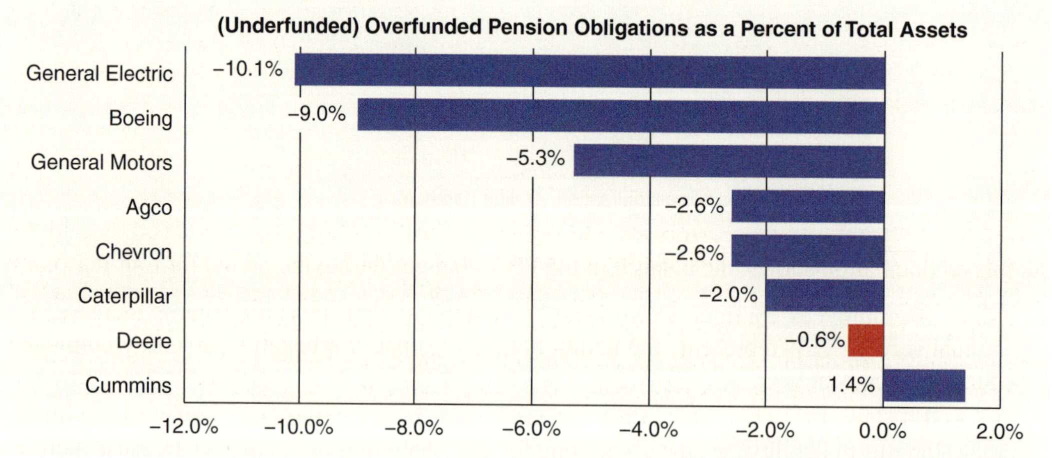

[7] Companies that have a defined benefit plan typically maintain many pension plans. Some are overfunded and others are underfunded. Current U.S. GAAP requires companies to group all of the overfunded and underfunded plans together and to present a net asset for the overfunded plans and a net liability for the underfunded plans.

[8] Source: https://www.willistowerswatson.com/en-US/News/2021/01/health-of-largest-us-corporate-pension-plans-showed-no-improvement-in-2020

Income Statement Effects of Defined Benefit Pension Plans

In a defined benefit plan, pension expense is not determined by the company's contribution to the pension fund. Instead, net pension expense is computed as follows.

	Net Pension Expense
	Service cost
+	Interest cost
−	*Expected* return on pension plan assets
±	Amortization of deferred amounts
	Net pension expense

The net pension expense is rarely reported separately on the income statement.

As shown above, the net pension expense has four components. The previous section about the PBO described the first two components: service costs and interest costs. The third component of pension expense relates to the return on pension plan assets, which *reduces* total pension expense. To compute this component, companies use the long-term *expected* rate of return on the pension plan assets, rather than the *actual* return, and multiply that expected rate by the balance in the pension plan assets account. Use of the expected return rather than actual return is an important distinction. Company CEOs and CFOs dislike income variability because they believe that stockholders react negatively to it, so company executives intensely (and successfully) lobbied the FASB to use the more stable expected long-term investment return, rather than the actual return, in computing pension expense. Thus, the pension plan assets' expected return is subtracted to compute net pension expense.

Any difference between the expected and the actual return is accumulated, together with other deferred amounts, off-balance-sheet and reported in the note disclosures. Other deferred amounts include changes in PBO resulting from changes in estimates used to compute the PBO and from amendments to the pension plans made by the company. However, if the deferred amounts exceed certain limits, the excess is recognized on-balance-sheet with a corresponding amount recognized as amortization in the income statement.[9] This amortization is the fourth component of pension expense and can be either a positive or a negative amount depending on the sign of the difference between expected and actual return on plan assets.

YOU MAKE THE CALL

You are a Consultant to the FASB The Board has asked your input on whether the assets in the pension fund should be netted against Pension Benefit Obligation (PBO) or whether the pension asset and the pension obligation should be reported separately. How would you advise the Board? [Answer on page 10-40]

Note Disclosures—Components of Plan Assets and PBO

GAAP requires extensive disclosures for pensions (and other postretirement benefits that we discuss later). These notes provide details relating to the net pension liability reported in the balance sheet and the components of pension expense reported as part of SG&A expense in the income statement.

Deere & Company indicates in Note 8 to its 2020 10-K that the funded status of its pension plan is $(447) million on December 31, 2020. This means Deere's plan is underfunded. Following are excerpts from the disclosures Deere makes in its pension note (excerpted and reordered to some extent):

[9] To avoid amortization, the deferred amounts must be less than 10% of the PBO or pension investments, whichever is less. The excess, if any, is amortized until no further excess remains. When the excess is eliminated (by investment returns or company contributions, for example), the amortization ceases. Alternatively, U.S. GAAP allows for any systematic and rational recognition of gains and losses as a component of net periodic pension cost if the method results in recognition of at least the minimum amortization amount required, is applied consistently, and is applied to all gains and losses on both plan assets and PBOs. Any method that accelerates recognition of gains and losses is generally preferable.

8. PENSION AND OTHER POSTRETIREMENT BENEFITS

The company has several funded and unfunded defined benefit pension plans and other postretirement benefit (OPEB) plans, primarily health care and life insurance plans, covering its U.S. employees and employees in certain foreign countries. The company uses an October 31 measurement date for these plans.

	Pensions	
	2020	**2019**
Change in benefit obligations		
Beginning of year balance	$(14,250)	$(12,108)
Service cost	(321)	(261)
Interest cost	(347)	(447)
Actuarial gain (loss)	(771)	(2,174)
Benefits paid	749	705
Settlements/curtailments	15	
Foreign exchange and other	(96)	35
End of year balance	(15,021)	(14,250)
Change in plan assets (fair value)		
Beginning of year balance	14,024	12,602
Actual return on plan assets	1,144	2,081
Employer contribution	108	70
Benefits paid	(749)	(705)
Settlements	(12)	
Foreign exchange and other	59	(24)
End of year balance	14,574	14,024
Funded status	$ (447)	$ (226)

The amounts recognized at November 1, 2020, and November 3, 2019, respectively, in millions of dollars consist of the following:

	Pensions	
	2020	**2019**
Amounts recognized in balance sheet		
Noncurrent asset	$ 863	$ 840
Current liability	(72)	(56)
Noncurrent liability	(1,238)	(1,010)
Total	$ (447)	$ (226)
Amounts recognized in accumulated other comprehensive income—pretax		
Net actuarial loss	$ 4,475	$ 4,312
Prior service cost (credit)	21	32
Total	$ 4,496	$ 4,344

Deere's PBO began in 2020 with a balance of $14,250 million. It increased by the accrual of $321 million in service cost and $347 million in interest cost. During the year, Deere also realized an actuarial loss of $771 million and a loss on foreign exchange and other of $96 million, which increased the pension liability. The PBO decreased as a result of $749 million in benefits paid to retirees and $15 million in settlements, leaving a balance of $15,021 million at year-end.

Pension plan assets began the year with a fair value of $14,024 million, which increased by $1,144 million from investment returns and increased by $108 million from company contributions. The company drew down its investments to make pension payments of $749 million to retirees, and made $12 million in settlements. Finally, plan assets increased for foreign exchange and other of $59 million, leaving the pension plan assets with a year-end balance of $14,574 million. The funded status of Deere's pension plan at year-end is $(447) million ($15,021 million – $14,574 million). The negative balance indicates that its pension plan is underfunded. The PBO and pension plan assets account cannot be separated into operating and nonoperating components; thus, most analysts treat the entire funded status as an operating item (either asset or liability). Deere disclosed that the net $(447) underfunded amount is included in three categories on the balance sheet (**Exhibit 10-1**): as a noncurrent liability ($1,238) and a current liability ($72), offset by a noncurrent asset ($863).

Note Disclosures—Components of Pension Expense

Deere & Company incurred $143 million of pension expense in 2020. Details of this expense are found in its pension note disclosure. Deere reported $160 million in pension cost related to defined contribution plans. In addition, Deere reported its expense (benefit) related to its defined benefit plans as follows ($ millions):

	2020	2019
Pensions		
Service cost	$ 321	$ 261
Interest cost	347	447
Expected return on plan assets	(819)	(802)
Amortization of actuarial loss	256	148
Amortization of prior service cost	13	11
Settlements/curtailments	25	5
Net cost	$ 143	$ 70

Most analysts have long considered the service cost portion of pension expense to be an operating expense, similar to salaries and other benefits. In contrast, the other components were considered nonoperating. The accounting standards require companies to report the service cost component in the same line item as compensation. Meanwhile, the other components of net (benefit) cost are required to be presented outside of income from operations. We note that Deere states that service cost is recorded in the line item "Other operating expenses" in the statement of consolidated income.

RESEARCH INSIGHT

Valuation of Pension Disclosures The FASB requires disclosure of the major components of pension cost presumably because it is useful for investors. Pension-related research has examined whether investors assign different valuation multiples to the components of pension cost when assessing company market value. Research finds that the market does, indeed, attach different interpretation to pension components, reflecting differences in information about recurring vs. nonrecurring expenses.

Interest cost is the product of the PBO and the discount rate. This discount rate is set by the company. The expected dollar return on pension assets is the product of the pension plan asset balance and the expected long-run rate of return on the investment portfolio. This rate is also set by the company. Further, the PBO is affected by the expected rate of wage inflation, termination, and mortality rates, all of which are estimated by the company.

U.S. GAAP requires disclosure of several rates used by the company in its estimation of PBO and the related pension expense. Deere discloses the following table in its pension note disclosure:

Weighted-Average Assumptions	2020	2019
Discount rates—service cost	2.9%	4.0%
Discount rates—interest cost	2.7%	4.0%
Rate of compensation increase	3.8%	3.8%
Expected long-term rates of return	6.4%	6.5%
Interest crediting rate—U.S. cash balance plan	2.1%	3.3%

During 2020, Deere decreased its assumed discount rate used to compute the present value of the PBO and service cost. The expected rate of compensation remained constant. Deere decreased its expected long-term rates of returns on plan assets and its interest crediting rate.

Changes in these assumptions have the following general effects on pension expense and, thus, profitability. This table summarizes the effects of increases in the various rates used to compute the pension cost. Decreases have the exact opposite effects of increases. In the computation of the PBO, the higher the discount, the lower the obligation.

Estimate Change	Probable Effect on Pension Expense	Reason for Effect
Discount rate increase	Increases	If the PBO is discounted at a higher rate, the PBO liability will be smaller. This will increase the actuarial gain, which may have to be amortized into pension cost (benefit) over time (along with other items). If the rate used to compute the interest cost increases, then the PBO is multiplied by a higher interest rate, resulting in an increased interest cost component of the pension expense. Often, the interest cost effect dominates.
Investment return increase	Decreases	The dollar amount of expected return on plan assets is the product of the plan assets balance and the expected long-term rate of return. Increasing the return increases the expected return on plan assets, thus reducing pension expense.
Wage inflation increase	Increases	The expected rate of wage inflation affects future wage levels that determine expected pension payments. An increase, thus, increases PBO, which increases both the service and the interest cost components of pension expense.

In the case of Deere, net actuarial losses increased their end-of-year benefit obligation by $771 million in 2020. The company discloses that the loss is due primarily to a decrease in the discount rate used to compute the PBO partially offset by a decrease in mortality assumptions.

BUSINESS INSIGHT

Pension Buyout at GM General Motors' pension obligation was at one time the largest of any company in the world. In 2011, its defined benefit plans were underfunded by $25.4 billion. Because pension fund assets are invested in securities, the underfunded balance can increase if the stock market falls. Analysts argued that the size, risk, and long duration of these obligations depressed GM's credit rating and its stock price.

In an effort to remove some of the projected obligations from its balance sheet, GM offered to buy out the pensions of 42,000 retirees in 2012. The pensions of an additional 76,000 retirees were transferred to Prudential Financial, who will make the annuity payments to the retirees. Although the buyout required an immediate cash payment, the move removed approximately $26 billion of pension obligations from GM's 2012 balance sheet, thus improving solvency ratios. In addition, the reduced obligation means that future income statements will reflect lower pension expense due to reduced interest costs. GM's 2020 financial statement shows that the defined benefit pension plans are still underfunded by $12.4 billion. Note that this is a considerable improvement from 2014, when the plans were underfunded by $24.1 billion. The related pension expense included in the income statement for 2020 was a benefit of $1,023 million.

Note Disclosures and Future Cash Flows

The net periodic defined benefit pension cost for Deere in 2020 is $143 million; this is different from the $108 million in cash that Deere contributed to its defined benefit plans. In addition, Deere paid $160 million into its defined contribution plans. Thus, its total pension cost for 2020 was $303 million ($143 + $160), and its cash contributions totaled $268 million ($108 + $160).

Companies use their pension plan assets to pay pension benefits to retirees. When markets are booming, as was true during the 1990s, pension plan assets can grow rapidly. However, when markets reverse, as in the bear market of the early 2000s and in 2008–2009, the value of pension plan assets can decline. The company's annual pension plan contribution is an investment decision influenced, in part, by market conditions and minimum required contributions specified by law.[10] Companies' cash contributions come from borrowed funds or operating cash flows.

[10] The Pension Protection Act of 2006 tightens funding requirements so employers make greater cash contributions to pension funds, closes loopholes that allow companies with underfunded plans to skip cash pension payments, prohibits employers and union leaders from promising extra benefits if pension plans are markedly underfunded, and strengthens disclosure rules to give workers and retirees more information about the status of their pension plan.

RESEARCH INSIGHT

Why Do Companies Offer Pensions? Research examines why companies choose to offer pension benefits. It finds that deferred compensation plans and pensions help align the long-term interests of owners and employees. Research also examines the composition of pension investments. It finds that a large portion of pension fund assets are invested in fixed-income securities, which are of lower risk than other investment securities. This implies that pension assets are less risky than nonpension assets. However, in severe economic downturns, some corporations curtail their pension plan contributions in order to protect cash flow.

Deere paid $749 million in pension benefits to retirees in 2020, yet it contributed only $108 million to pension assets that year. The remaining amount was paid out of available funds in the investment account. Cash contributions to the pension plan assets are the relevant amounts for an analysis of projected cash flows. Benefits paid in relation to the pension liability balance can provide a clue about the need for *future* cash contributions. Companies are required to disclose the expected benefit payments for five years after the statement date and the remaining obligations thereafter. Following is Deere's benefit disclosure statement:

The following table summarizes the benefit payments that are scheduled to be paid in the years ending December 31 ($ millions):

	Pensions
2021	$ 765
2022	724
2023	711
2024	707
2025	699
2026–2030	3,450

Deere's unfunded pension amount increased by roughly $221 million from 2019 to 2020. The company contributed $108 million, and the plan assets had an actual return of $1,144 million. The reason for the increase in the net unfunded balance in its pension plan is from increase in the pension liability essentially because of the actuarial losses. The low interest rate environment we have been in for several years, is keeping the estimated pension liabilities relatively high (because the discounting is at a low rate).

BUSINESS INSIGHT

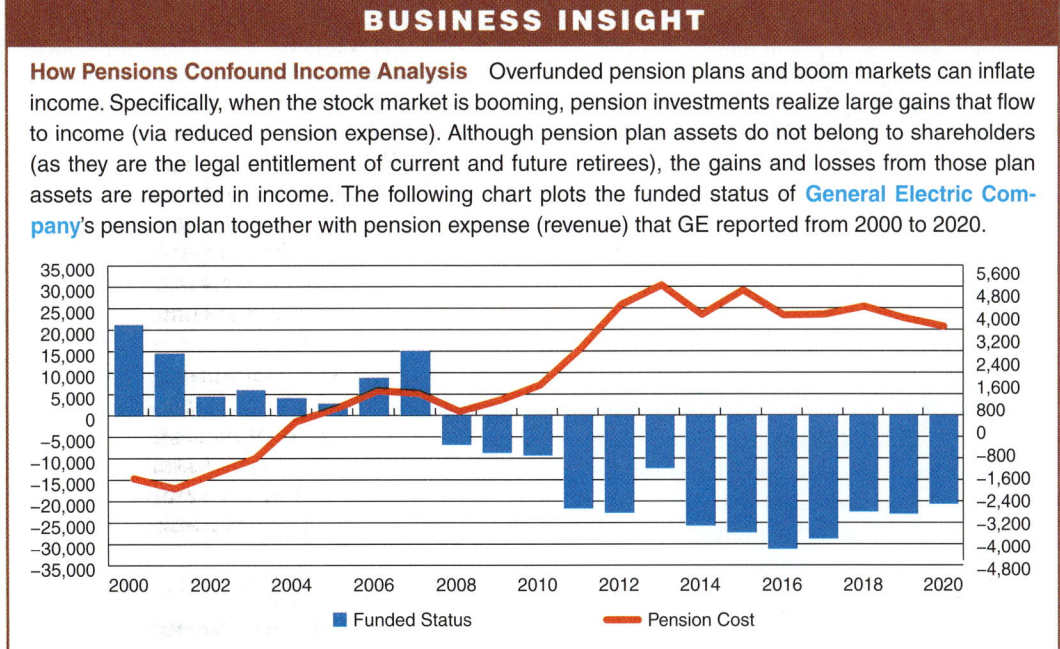

How Pensions Confound Income Analysis Overfunded pension plans and boom markets can inflate income. Specifically, when the stock market is booming, pension investments realize large gains that flow to income (via reduced pension expense). Although pension plan assets do not belong to shareholders (as they are the legal entitlement of current and future retirees), the gains and losses from those plan assets are reported in income. The following chart plots the funded status of General Electric Company's pension plan together with pension expense (revenue) that GE reported from 2000 to 2020.

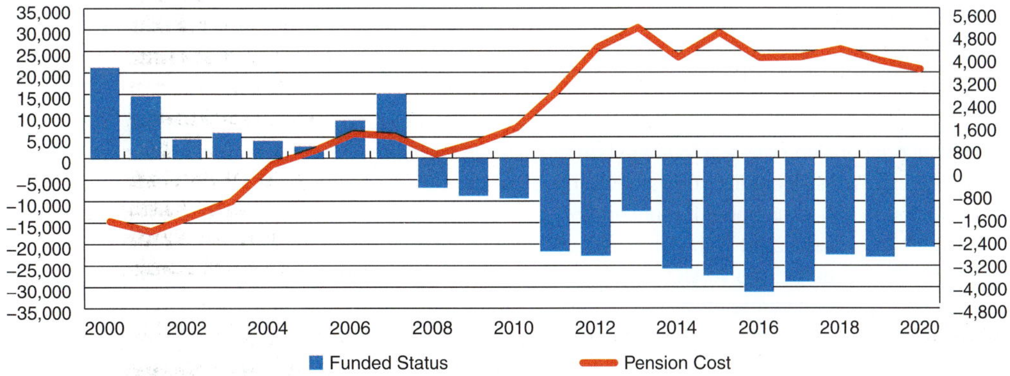

continued

continued from previous page

GE's funded status was consistently positive (indicating an overfunded plan) until 2008. The degree of overfunding peaked in 1999 at the height of the stock market and began to decline during the bear market of the early 2000s. GE reported pension *revenue* (not expense) during this period. In 2001, GE's reported pension *revenue* was $2,095 million (10.6% of its pretax income). Because of the plan's overfunded status, the expected return and amortization of deferred gains components of pension expense amounted to $5,288 million, far in excess of the service and interest costs of $3,193 million. Since 2004, GE has recorded pension expense (rather than revenue) as the pension plan's overfunding and expected long-term rates of return declined, and in 2008 the funded status turned negative. In 2020, GE reported an unfunded liability of $20.6 billion and a pension expense of roughly $3.6 billion.

One application of the pension note disclosure is to assess the likelihood that the company will be required to increase its cash contributions to the pension plan. This estimate is made by examining the funded status of the pension plan and the projected payments to retirees. For severely underfunded plans, the projected payments to retirees will not be covered by existing pension assets. When this occurs, the company will need to divert operating cash flow from other prospective projects to cover its pension plan. Alternatively, if operating cash flows will not be sufficient, it will likely need to borrow to fund those payments. This decision can be especially troublesome as the debt service payments include interest, thus, effectively increasing the cost of the pension contribution.

Other Post-Employment Benefits

In addition to pension benefits, many companies provide health care and insurance benefits to retired employees. These benefits are referred to as **other post-employment benefits (OPEB)**. These benefits present reporting challenges similar to pension accounting. However, companies most often provide these benefits on a "pay-as-you-go" basis, and it is rare for companies to make contributions in advance for OPEB. As a result, this liability, known as the **accumulated post-employment benefit obligation (APBO)**, is largely, if not totally, unfunded. GAAP requires that the unfunded APBO liability be reported in the balance sheet and the annual service costs and interest costs be accrued as expenses each year. This requirement is controversial for two reasons. First, future health care costs are especially difficult to estimate, so the value of the resulting APBO (the present value of the future benefits) is fraught with error. Second, these benefits are provided at the discretion of the employer and can be altered or terminated at any time. Consequently, employers argue that without a legal obligation to pay these benefits, the liability should not be reported in the balance sheet.

Other post-employment benefits can produce large liabilities. For example, Deere & Company reports underfunded health care and insurance obligations of $3,892 million and a related expense of $198 million in 2020. Our analysis of cash flows related to pension obligations can be extended to other post-employment benefit obligations. For example, in addition to its pension payments, Deere discloses that it is obligated to make health care and insurance payments to retirees totaling $2,947 million over the next 10 years. Our analysis of projected cash flows must consider this potential cash outflow.

RESEARCH INSIGHT

Valuation of Nonpension Post-Employment Benefits The FASB requires employers to accrue the costs of all nonpension post-employment benefits; known as *accumulated post-employment benefit obligation* (APBO). These benefits consist primarily of health care and insurance. This requirement is controversial due to concerns about the uncertainty inherent in the liability estimate. Research finds that the APBO (alone) is associated with company value. However, when other pension-related variables are included in the research, the APBO liability is no longer useful in explaining company value. Research concludes that the pension-related variables do a better job at conveying value-relevant information than the APBO number alone, which implies that the APBO number is less reliable.

A GLOBAL PERSPECTIVE

IFRS

Pension Fund Status IFRS and U.S. GAAP require companies to report the funded status of their defined benefit pension plans on the balance sheet. IFRS, however, calculates pension expense differently. First, unlike U.S. GAAP, IFRS requires that the expected return on pension assets must be the same rate as the discount rate used to value the PBO. In addition, IFRS recognizes the cost of plan amendments in the income statement immediately, rather than amortizing those costs over the service life of employees. There are also other differences that make direct comparison across IFRS and U.S. GAAP firms difficult.

Analyzing Pension Disclosures

LO10-2 **Review 10-2**

GuidedExample MBC

The following pension data is taken from Note 16 of The Boeing Company 10-K report.

($ millions)	2020
Change in Benefit Obligation	
Beginning balance	$77,645
Service cost	3
Interest cost	2,455
Actuarial loss (gain)	7,759
Settlement/curtailment/other	(68)
Gross benefits paid	(5,386)
Exchange rate adjustment	7
Ending balance	$82,415
Change in Plan Assets	
Beginning balance at fair value	$61,711
Actual return on plan assets	9,275
Company contribution	3,013
Settlement payments	(68)
Benefits paid	(5,241)
Exchange rate adjustment	6
Ending balance at fair value	$68,696

Components of Net Periodic Benefit (Income)/Cost	Pension 2020
Service cost	$ 3
Interest cost	2,455
Expected return on plan assets	(3,756)
Amortization of private service credits	(80)
Recognized net actuarial loss/(gain)	1,032
Settlement/curtailment loss/(gain)	9
Net periodic benefit (income)/cost	$ (337)

Required

1. In general, what factors affect a company's pension benefit obligation during a period?
2. In general, what factors affect a company's pension plan investments during a period?
3. What amount is reported on the balance sheet relating to the Boeing Company pension plan?
4. How does the expected return on plan assets affect pension cost?
5. How does Boeing's expected return on plan assets compare with its actual return (in $s) for 2020?
6. How much net pension cost is reflected in Boeing's 2020 income statement?
7. Assess Boeing's ability to meet payment obligations to retirees.

Solution on p. 10-67.

ACCOUNTING FOR INCOME TAXES

LO10-3 Describe and interpret accounting for income taxes.

eLecture MBC

Companies maintain two sets of books: one for reporting to their shareholders and creditors and one to report to tax authorities. This is not unethical or illegal. In fact, it is often required. Companies with publicly traded securities compute and report financial accounting income under the rules (e.g., GAAP or IFRS) provided by the financial accounting standards setters (e.g., FASB in the United States). As we have discussed, this income computation is done on the accrual basis, and it is meant to provide information about firm performance to outside stakeholders, such as investors and creditors.[11] Companies must also compute taxable income and report the amount on their tax return(s) filed with the tax authorities in the jurisdictions in which they are required to file (e.g., the Internal Revenue Service and state tax authorities in the United States). Taxable income is determined under the rules promulgated by the government of the taxing jurisdiction (e.g., the Internal Revenue Code in the United States). Tax authorities have different objectives from financial accounting standard setters. The tax rules are set in order to raise money to fund government activities, to encourage or discourage certain behaviors, and (hopefully) based on some sense of fairness and equity. In contrast, financial accounting income is meant to provide information about firm performance to investors, creditors, and other stakeholders so that these parties can make informed decisions about such things as investments and loans. The rules and objectives are very different for the two income measures, and as a result, the two resulting income numbers for a company can be very different.

Our objective here is to learn how to determine a corporation's income tax expense that is reported on the income statement for financial accounting purposes. Financial accounting uses accrual accounting; thus, income tax expense is determined using accrual accounting just like all other expenses. As a result, income tax expense on the income statement is not the cash taxes paid for the reporting period. Instead, it is the accrual-based expense measure, meaning it is the total income tax expense related to the financial accounting income reported in the period regardless of whether those income taxes are actually paid in the current period or not. Furthermore, because it is accrual-based, there will be resulting assets and liabilities that need to be accounted for on the balance sheet. These include what are called deferred tax assets and deferred tax liabilities.

The U.S. enacted tax reform through legislation known as the Tax Cuts and Jobs Act (TCJA) in 2017. We provide an overview of the provisions of this legislation where it is relevant for our discussion because the legislation is still affecting and being discussed in many financial statements. One of the key features of the legislation was a reduction in the top statutory corporate income tax rate from 35% to 21%. As mentioned previously early on in the textbook, we employ a 25% rate for our calculations (mainly for ease of mental math but also because raising the rate is being considered).

Book-Tax Differences

There are two general types of differences between taxable income and financial accounting (book) income, also known as book-tax differences: permanent differences and temporary differences.

A difference that would be considered permanent is an item of income or expense that is accounted for differently for book and tax purposes in the current year and never reverses in a future year. A simple example of a permanent difference is interest income on municipal bonds. Municipal bond interest income is included in financial accounting income. However, municipal bond interest is tax exempt at the federal level, meaning it is not included in taxable income. Thus, if a company has municipal bond interest income, its financial accounting income will be higher than its taxable income by the amount of municipal bond interest. This difference will not reverse in the future because the municipal bond interest is never included in taxable income. The accounting for income tax with respect to a permanent difference is straightforward; no deferred tax assets or liabilities are created. Income tax expense is lower (in this case) in the current year as a result of the (explicit) income taxes saved by investing in municipal bonds.

A temporary difference is an item of income or expense that is different between book and taxable income in the current year but will reverse in a future year such that the same amount is included in taxable income and book income over time. Temporary differences are:

1. created by using accrual accounting for book, and cash accounting for tax, and/or
2. created by using different rules for determining the accrual amount for book than for tax.

FYI We use the term "book income" to refer to income before income taxes, as reported in financial statements. "Taxable income" refers to income reported in the income tax return.

[11] All companies have to report to tax authorities, but many privately held companies do not have to comply with GAAP.

A common example of a temporary difference is depreciation. For financial accounting purposes, companies often use straight-line depreciation, as discussed in Chapter 8. For U.S. tax purposes, however, companies use an accelerated method of depreciation (the Modified Accelerated Cost Recovery System (MACRS)). Thus, early in an asset's life, tax depreciation will be greater than book depreciation. However, over the life of the asset, the same amount of depreciation will be recorded for book and tax (assuming zero salvage value). This is a temporary difference because tax depreciation is higher earlier on but will be equal to or less than book depreciation in later years in the asset's life. In other words, the book-tax difference will reverse. The computation of the income tax expense is more difficult in this case. We need to account for the taxes due on taxable income (the cash taxes) *and* an accrual of taxes that are known to be due in a future period when the depreciation difference reverses. In other words, total income tax expense is the tax expense related to financial accounting income for the period regardless of whether the taxes are actually paid this year. The accrual for the portion not yet paid creates a **deferred tax liability**—the book-tax difference in this period will lead to higher taxable income relative to book income in the future. This higher relative taxable income means higher cash taxes to be paid in the future—that is, a liability. Furthermore, as part of the TCJA, businesses are now allowed to "fully expense" certain asset purchases (generally with useful lives of 20 years or less) in the first year the asset is put into service. This means that for tax purposes the taxpayer can deduct the entire cost of the qualifying asset as depreciation in the first year. In such cases, the difference between financial accounting treatment and tax treatment is extreme. This full expensing provision is optional to the taxpayer and is currently in the law for assets purchased between December 2017 and December 31, 2022. (The extra [bonus] depreciation phases down for assets purchased after that and will be zero at the start of 2027.) For our purposes, we first provide an example using accelerated depreciation for tax purposes and then modify the example to illustrate what happens when the asset is fully deducted for tax purposes in the first year. The concepts are the same, but the illustration is useful nonetheless.

Example Assume Clark Corporation is in its first year of business. It purchases a piece of equipment that costs $200,000 with a useful life of 4 years and no net salvage value. The firm uses straight-line depreciation for financial reporting purposes and accelerated depreciation under MACRS for tax purposes. (We will use double declining balance depreciation as an approximation for our example.) Comparing the depreciation schedules reveals the following information:

FYI Income tax expense is also titled **provision for income tax**.

	Tax Reporting	Financial Reporting		
Year	DDB Depreciation	Straight-Line Depreciation	Tax vs. Book Difference	Cumulative Tax-Book Difference
1	$100,000	$50,000	$50,000	$50,000
2	50,000	50,000	0	50,000
3	25,000	50,000	(25,000)	25,000
4	25,000	50,000	(25,000)	0

Assume the corporate statutory tax rate is 25%. We expect the tax rate to stay at 25% for the entire 4 years, and that depreciation is the only book-tax difference for the Clark Corporation. The deferred tax liability at the end of each year is the cumulative book-tax difference times the tax rate. The tax rate to be used is the enacted tax rate expected to be in effect when the book-tax difference reverses. The deferred tax expense each period is the current year book-tax difference (which is the change in the cumulative book-tax difference) times the tax rate. The deferred tax liability at the end of each year and the deferred tax expense for each year for Clark Corporation would be:

Year	Cumulative Tax-Book Difference	Tax Rate	Deferred Tax Liability, End of Year	Deferred Tax Expense
1	$50,000	25%	$12,500	$12,500
2	50,000	25%	12,500	0
3	25,000	25%	6,250	(6,250)
4	0	25%	0	(6,250)

Now assume for illustration that financial accounting earnings each year before depreciation and taxes are $325,000 and there are no other book-tax differences. The yearly calculation of financial reporting and taxable income along with the income tax expense is as follows:

Year	Tax Reporting 1	2	3	4
Earnings before depreciation	$325,000	$325,000	$325,000	$325,000
Depreciation deduction	(100,000)	(50,000)	(25,000)	(25,000)
Taxable income	225,000	275,000	300,000	300,000
Tax due on the tax return (@ 25%)	56,250	68,750	75,000	75,000

Year	Financial Accounting Reporting 1	2	3	4
Earnings before depreciation	$325,000	$325,000	$325,000	$325,000
Depreciation expense	(50,000)	(50,000)	(50,000)	(50,000)
Earnings before tax	275,000	275,000	275,000	275,000
Tax expense	68,750	68,750	68,750	68,750

The entry to record income tax expense in Year 1 follows using the financial statement effects template and journal entry form. (We show the entries as if the company is paying in cash at the time the entry is recorded. If the company pays in cash at a later time, a short-term liability account, income tax payable, would be credited in the entries below.)

ANALYZE

Transaction	Balance Sheet: Cash Asset	+ Noncash Assets	= Liabilities	+ Contrib. Capital	+ Earned Capital	Income Statement: Revenues	− Expenses	= Net Income
Recording income tax expense in Year 1.	−56,250 Cash		= +12,500 Deferred Tax Liability		−68,750 Retained Earnings		− +68,750 Provision for Income Taxes	= −68,750

JOURNALIZE

	Debit	Credit
Provision for income taxes (+E, −SE)	68,750	
Deferred tax liability (+L)		12,500
Cash (−A)		56,250

POST

+ Provision for Income Taxes (E) −	− Deferred Tax Liability (L) +	+ Cash (A) −
68,750 |	| 12,500	| 56,250

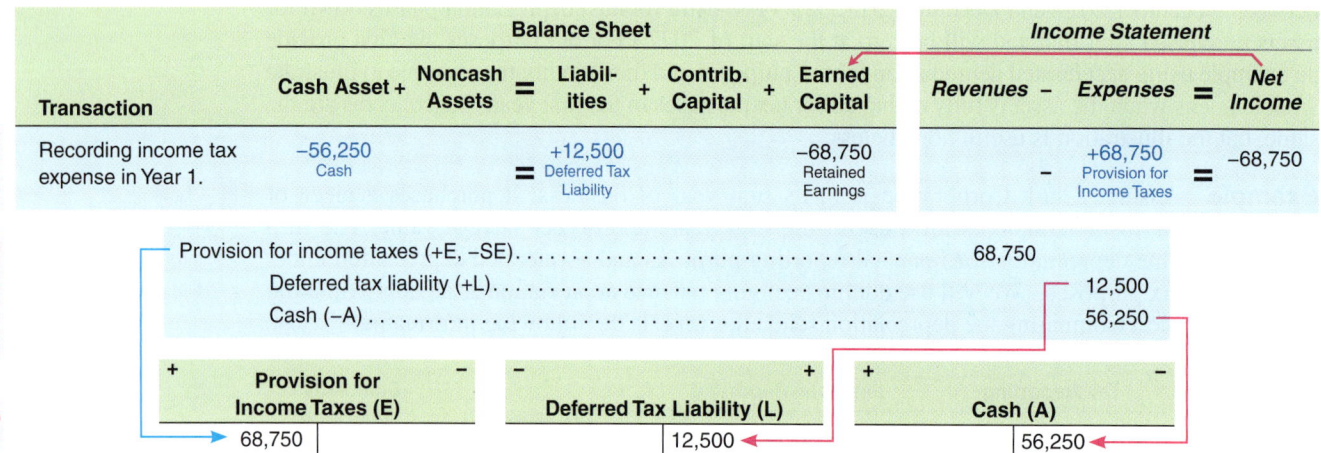

Clark Corporation would record income tax expense in each of the years of operation. For example, in Year 4, Clark Corporation records its income tax expense as follows:

ANALYZE

Transaction	Cash Asset	+ Noncash Assets	= Liabilities	+ Contrib. Capital	+ Earned Capital	Revenues	− Expenses	= Net Income
Recording income tax expense in Year 4.	−75,000 Cash		= −6,250 Deferred Tax Liability		−68,750 Retained Earnings		− +68,750 Provision for Income Taxes	= −68,750

JOURNALIZE

	Debit	Credit
Provision for income taxes (+E, −SE)	68,750	
Deferred tax liability (−L)	6,250	
Cash (−A)		75,000

POST

+ Provision for Income Taxes (E) −	− Deferred Tax Liability (L) +	+ Cash (A) −
68,750 |	6,250 |	| 75,000

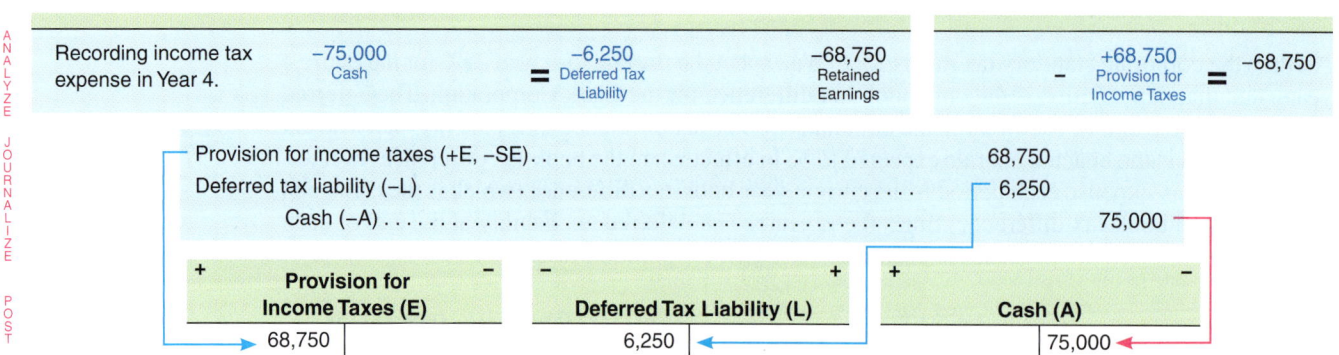

The analysis highlights several facts:

1. Over the 4 years, tax payments to the IRS total $275,000 = $56,250 + $68,750 + $75,000 + $75,000. Total tax expense on the books for the 4 years also equals $275,000 = 4 × $68,750.
2. The timing of the tax payments differs from the tax expense recognized on the books.
3. The deferred tax liability created in the first year is reduced to zero in the 4th year when the useful life of the asset is over.

4. The cash flow takes place consistent with the tax code. The accounting expense amount is an accrual-basis measure.
5. In year 1, the corporation's provision for income tax consists of current income tax expense of $56,250 and deferred income tax expense of $12,500 for the total income tax expense of $68,750. In year 4, the corporation has current income tax expense of $75,000 and deferred income tax expense of $(6,250) for a total income tax expense of $68,750. The total income tax expense is shown on the income statement, and the more detailed breakout into current and deferred expense is disclosed in the notes to the financial statements.

What would occur if Clark Corporation deducted the full cost of the asset for tax purposes under the new rules in the TCJA?

Now we would have the following comparative depreciation schedules:

	Tax Reporting	Financial Accounting Reporting		
Year	Full Deduction	Straight-Line Depreciation	Tax vs. Book Difference	Cumulative Tax-Book Difference
1	$200,000	$50,000	$150,000	$150,000
2	0	50,000	(50,000)	100,000
3	0	50,000	(50,000)	50,000
4	0	50,000	(50,000)	0

The deferred tax liability schedule would be as follows:

Year	Cumulative Tax-Book Difference	Tax Rate	Deferred Tax Liability, End of Year	Deferred Tax Expense
1	$150,000	25%	$37,500	$37,500
2	100,000	25%	25,000	(12,500)
3	50,000	25%	12,500	(12,500)
4	0	25%	0	(12,500)

If we assume the same income and facts otherwise, the calculation of taxable income and tax on the tax return is as follows:

	Tax Reporting			
	1	2	3	4
Earnings before depreciation	$325,000	$325,000	$325,000	$325,000
Depreciation deduction	(200,000)	0	0	0
Taxable income	125,000	325,000	325,000	325,000
Tax due on the tax return (@ 25%)	31,250	81,250	81,250	81,250

Note that the computation of financial accounting income and total tax expense for financial accounting is exactly the same as it was before! Financial accounting depreciation did not change, and neither did total tax expense. What changed is the amount of tax Clark Corporation pays in cash each year versus the amount that is recognized as a deferred tax liability (or reversal of deferred tax liability).

For example, in year 1, the journal entry would be as follows:

Provision for income taxes (+E, −SE)	68,750	
Deferred tax liability (+L)		37,500
Cash (−A)		31,250

Notice that Clark Corporation saves a significant amount of cash taxes in year one between the two different tax treatments of the assets – the tax savings are $25,000 ($56,250 – $31,250; can also compute as additional depreciation deduction of $100,000 multiplied by the tax rate of 25%). However, for financial accounting purposes the deferred tax liability and deferred tax expense must increase because the company needs to account for all the taxes on the reported financial accounting income of $275,000, and that has not changed. Thus, the new tax law saves Clark Corporation cash taxes early in the asset's life and saves Clark Corporation money overall in terms of the time value of money. (Note that Clark Corporation's total cash taxes over the life of the asset did not change.) However, these savings are not reflected on GAAP financial statements because GAAP financial statements are accrual based and do not take the time value of money into account when accounting for income taxes.

RESEARCH INSIGHT

As tax reform was debated over the last decade in the U.S., this issue about the tax versus financial accounting treatment entered into the conversation. The question is whether publicly traded companies, whose financial statements (not tax returns) are the focus of the capital markets, would respond to the tax incentives provided by the immediate expensing of assets. Research suggests that publicly traded companies will respond less than private companies, and maybe less than policymakers would otherwise estimate, because the benefits of the accelerated depreciation, even full expensing, are not reflected on financial statements. One of the authors of this text testified about these issues to both the U.S. House Ways and Means Committee and the Senate Finance Committee. Actual evidence on how companies respond to the TCJA will be forthcoming over time once data are available. However, testing the effects of immediate deducting of asset purchases for tax purposes will be more difficult than it may seem because of confounding factors.

There are also transactions that generate the necessity to record a **deferred tax asset**. For example, bad debts, warranty expense, and many other accrued expenses usually require an associated deferred tax asset to be recorded. For financial accounting purposes, bad debt expense and warranty expense are expensed using management estimates before the receivable actually goes bad and before the warranty costs are actually paid. Again, this is because financial accounting is done on the accrual method and expenses that are associated with the revenue recorded generally are estimated and accrued before they are paid in cash. This is the conservative nature of financial reporting. For tax purposes, these expenses cannot be estimated but instead are deductible generally only when paid. This difference in timing between tax reporting and financial accounting leads to temporary differences where the tax deduction is later in time than the financial accounting expense (opposite of what we just illustrated for depreciation). Because in this case a tax deduction will occur in the future due to a transaction or event in the current period, the company has a deferred tax asset (future benefit) that needs to be recorded.

Temporary book-tax differences also occur with items of revenue. Take, for example, unearned revenue (also called deferred revenue or contract liability) we described in Chapter 6. If a company receives cash in advance of being able to recognize revenue, the company will record unearned revenue (a liability) until the revenue can be recognized. For tax purposes, however, the cash received is generally recorded as income in the period it is received.[12] Thus, there is often a book-tax difference. In this case, the revenue is recorded for tax in an earlier period than for financial accounting, meaning that in some future year(s), taxable income will be less than financial accounting income when the revenue is recognized according to the GAAP rules. That means the company has a deferred tax asset to record in the year the cash is received in the amount of the book-tax difference for revenue times the applicable tax rate.

As a brief example, let's say that the corporation Josie's Jewelry, Inc., makes sales of $100,000 in the current period and estimates and records a bad debt expense of $5,000. This is an expense for financial reporting purposes, but there is no deduction allowed for tax purposes in the current period. The tax deduction is not allowed until the receivable actually goes bad (i.e., is deemed to be uncollectible). Using a tax rate of 25%, Josie's Jewelry would report an increase in a deferred tax asset in the current period of $1,250 ($5,000 × 25%) and a corresponding deferred tax benefit (i.e., a negative deferred tax expense) on the income statement. When the receivable is deemed uncollectible and written off in a future period and the deduction is taken for tax purposes, the corporation will reverse

[12] The TCJA codified the principles in a 2004 tax ruling—Revenue Procedure 2004-34. Taxpayers are able to defer income recognition for tax purposes as well as long as the taxpayer is an accrual-basis taxpayer and the income is deferred for financial accounting purposes. The rule is that the taxpayer must recognize the income for tax purposes in gross income in the year of receipt unless they make an election to defer the income. The deferred income must be recognized in the year following the year of receipt (and is accelerated if the taxpayer ceases to exist).

the deferred tax asset to zero (assuming the full $5,000 is the amount that eventually is deducted for tax purposes) and record a $1,250 deferred tax expense. Notice that in this future period, the deduction is taken for tax purposes so the actual tax paid is lower, and thus, current tax expense is lower by $1,250. Thus, the net effect on income in the future period is zero. (Deferred tax expense is higher by $1,250, and current tax expense is lower by $1,250, netting to a zero total effect.) This is correct because the tax benefit was accrued (recognized) in the first period when the revenue was earned, bad debt expense was recorded, and deferred tax asset was established.

BUSINESS INSIGHT

As part of the TCJA, the United States changed the manner in which the foreign earnings of U.S. businesses are taxed. Previously, the U.S. had a regime that was a worldwide tax system, with deferral. This meant that the U.S. taxed the worldwide earnings of U.S. companies, but the U.S. taxation of certain foreign earnings (i.e., foreign operating earnings of a subsidiary of a U.S. company) was deferred until repatriation to the U.S. When the earnings were repatriated back to the U.S. (e.g., as a dividend to the parent company), then U.S. taxes were due (net of a foreign tax credit). This led to many negative economic consequences, such as U.S. multinational enterprises having an estimated $2 trillion in foreign earnings "locked out" of the U.S. In addition, it led to varied financial accounting outcomes because companies could accrue the U.S. taxes for financial accounting or not accrue the U.S. taxes because of an exception to deferred tax accounting (based on management's plans for the use of the foreign earnings).

The TCJA fundamentally changed the U.S. international tax system. The U.S. now has what some are calling a modified territorial tax system (and some are calling it a sort of worldwide minimum tax system). At a very high level, the new system exempts foreign earnings of U.S. multinationals from U.S. taxation unless the earnings are "high return" earnings in "low tax" jurisdictions, in which case the U.S. will tax those earnings currently (albeit at a lower rate). The system includes other base erosion protections that require companies to compute a type of alternative tax after disallowing certain payments to foreign parties that are considered "base eroding." Much of this is far beyond an introductory accounting textbook; however, one feature that affected financial statements for many multinational companies in 2017 was a mandatory deemed repatriation tax on the accumulated foreign earnings of the company as of the time the TCJA was passed (roughly). As part of the transition to the modified territorial system from the worldwide system, the U.S. required a tax payment on the accumulated earnings at a rate of 15.5% if the earnings were held in cash or cash equivalents, or a rate of 8% if the earnings were in noncash assets. (This tax is sometimes referred to as the transition tax.) This was a mandatory tax but could be paid over installments that stretch eight years. For financial accounting, the standard setters required companies to accrue the tax expense for this tax in the fiscal year containing December 2017, with no discounting for the time value of money, consistent with the rest of the accounting for income taxes.

Because of the variation in the accounting prior to the TCJA, there was some marked variation in terms of the effects of this mandatory tax for financial accounting. If a company had already accrued significant U.S. taxes on its unremitted foreign earnings, the accounting charge for the repatriation tax might not have been very large. Apple, Inc., for example, had substantial unremitted foreign earnings, but had accrued U.S. tax on a portion of these earnings. The accrued U.S. tax, recorded as a deferred tax liability before the TCJA, was $36.4 billion. Apple reports that it owed a deemed repatriation tax of $37.3 billion. Thus, there was very little of the mandatory repatriation tax that needed to have additional U.S. tax expense recorded for financial accounting. On the other hand, Cisco reported that it had $76 billion of unremitted earnings on which it owed a mandatory repatriation tax of $8.1 billion. Cisco did not have any deferred tax liability recorded (meaning no U.S. tax was previously accrued on those earnings). Thus, Cisco had to record all of the $8.1 billion as additional tax expense in their year ended July 28, 2018. The company's effective tax rate for the year was 99.2%!

Net Operating Losses Another book-tax difference is a net operating loss carryover. For tax purposes, corporations can carry over operating losses to future years.[13] Financial accounting does not have such a rule; if a corporation has a loss for financial reporting, the loss is recorded and the corporation starts the next year with a clean slate and measures income for that next year only. Thus,

[13] Prior to the TCJA, corporations could carry net operating losses back two years for tax purposes and forward for 20 years. The TCJA changed the rules. Now corporations cannot carry losses (starting with losses generated in 2018) back in time, but can only carry them forward. The TCJA also changes the carryforward period to be indefinite. However, another change in the TCJA is that tax loss carryforwards can only be used to offset 80% of taxable income in the future period. In essence, the concept of allowing loss carryovers for tax purposes approximates an averaging of income over time so companies with volatile income are not required to pay high taxes in years with high income and then get no relief in years with losses. We note that during the COVID-19 pandemic, the U.S. government temporarily made the net operating loss carryover rules more generous.

the net operating loss carryover is a temporary book-tax difference. Because the loss carry over represents future deductions for tax purposes, the company has and must record an increase to deferred tax assets and a deferred tax benefit (i.e., negative deferred tax expense) in the amount of the loss carryover times the tax rate (the enacted tax rate expected to be in effect when the loss carryover will be used to offset taxes). Thus, even though the corporation is not getting the cash benefits of the deduction yet, the accounting rules require the company to accrue the benefit to the current period.

Valuation Allowance After a corporation computes its income tax expense and records its deferred tax assets and liabilities, the corporation has yet another step to complete. The corporation must evaluate the realizability of the deferred tax assets. This means that management must estimate whether the company will have sufficient future taxable income to offset the future deductions represented by the deferred tax assets. If management does not think the company will have enough future taxable income to be able to use all the deferred tax assets, then a contra-asset must be established against the deferred tax assets. Thus, the deferred tax assets on the balance sheet will not be overstated. As an analogy, recall that when a company has accounts receivables, it must evaluate the collectability of those receivables and establish an allowance for doubtful accounts to ensure the accounts receivable asset is not overstated. Similarly, if a corporation has deferred tax assets that management does not expect to be able to use to offset future taxable income, then the company must record a **valuation allowance**. When the contra-asset is recorded, deferred tax expense is increased, which decreases accounting income (and if a valuation allowance is reduced, deferred tax expense is reduced, increasing income). A more detailed discussion is beyond the scope of this text, but net operating losses and associated valuation allowances have been an important part of many companies' accounting for income taxes.

Unrecognized Tax Benefit (Uncertain Tax Positions) Another step in accounting for income taxes is the computation of what is known as an unrecognized tax benefit. Essentially, corporations must estimate what amount tax authorities might assess in additional tax during future audits by the tax authorities (e.g., the IRS). In other words, this is a contingent liability—the corporation might owe more tax if the tax authority disagrees with the tax positions the company has taken on past tax returns. U.S. GAAP requires companies to record additional tax expense for this amount as well as an additional liability. The liability is included in total liabilities on the balance sheet (it is not an off-balance-sheet amount) but is not a separate line item. Details about the account are in the notes to the financial statements.

An example of disclosure about this amount is from Apple, Inc.'s most recent 10-K.

Apple, Inc.
Uncertain Tax Positions

The aggregate changes in the balance of gross unrecognized tax benefits, which excludes interest and penalties, for 2020, 2019, and 2018, is as follows (in millions):

	2020	2019	2018
Beginning balances	$15,619	$9,694	$8,407
Increases related to tax positions taken during a prior year	454	5,845	2,431
Decreases related to tax positions taken during a prior year	(791)	(686)	(2,212)
Increases related to tax positions taken during the current year	1,347	1,697	1,824
Decreases related to settlements with taxing authorities	(85)	(852)	(756)
Decreases related to expiration of statute of limitations	(69)	(79)	—
Ending balances	$16,475	$15,619	$9,694

Revaluation of Deferred Tax Assets and Liabilities Due to a Tax Rate Change

As we have mentioned, deferred tax assets and liabilities are measured using the enacted corporate statutory tax rate expected to be in effect when the deferred tax asset or liability reverses. In addition, as we have also mentioned, the TCJA lowered the U.S. corporate statutory tax rate to 21% from a top rate of 35%. This specific example provides an excellent illustration of the required accounting. When this occurred, companies had to revalue their deferred tax assets and liabilities on their financial statements. For financial accounting, the rules require that the revaluation occur in the period the tax law is enacted, not when it is effective (again, because the rate used to value the deferred tax assets and liabilities is the enacted rate expected to be in effect when the items reverse, not the rate applicable to the current period). Thus, if the company had net deferred tax liabilities, the company would reduce the value of the liability on the balance sheet and record a reduction to deferred tax expense. As a result, accounting income increases (because tax expense is lower). To illustrate a simple case, the Koehler Company had net deferred tax liabilities (meaning deferred tax liabilities in excess of deferred tax assets) of $1 million at the end of 2017 valued at the pre-TCJA tax rate of 35%. The simplest way to think about the tax rate change is that there was a 40% reduction in the tax rate. Thus, Koehler Company is required to devalue its deferred tax liabilities by 40%.[14] In 2017, the company would record the following entry to revalue the deferred tax liabilities at 21% and show the reduction to deferred tax expense:

Deferred tax liability (−L).	400,000	
Deferred tax benefit (−E, +SE)		400,000

The balance sheet equation would be as follows:

Transaction	Cash Asset +	Noncash Assets	=	Liabilities +	Contrib. Capital	+ Earned Capital	Revenues −	Expenses =	Net Income
Revalue deferred tax liabilities for a tax rate change			=	−400,000 Deferred Tax Liability		+400,000 Retained Earnings	−	−400,000 Deferred Tax Benefit =	+400,000

Conversely, if the company had net deferred tax assets, the company would revalue those assets at the lower rate and increase deferred tax expense. This would result in a higher expense and a "hit" to (a decrease in) accounting earnings.

CVS, one of our focus companies in the text, is a relatively simple company (with little to no foreign operations). Thus, their discussion of this issue is illustrative for our purposes.

The following is a portion of the tax note disclosure in CVS's 2017 10-K:

> On December 22, 2017, the President signed into law the Tax Cuts and Jobs Act (the "TCJA"). Among numerous changes to existing tax laws, the TCJA permanently reduces the federal corporate income tax rate from 35% to 21% effective on January 1, 2018. The effects on deferred tax balances of changes in tax rates are required to be taken into consideration in the period in which the changes are enacted, regardless of when they are effective. As the result of the reduction of the corporate income tax rate under the TCJA, the Company estimated the revaluation of its net deferred tax liabilities and recorded a provisional income tax benefit of approximately $1.5 billion for [the] year ended December 31, 2017. The Company has not completed all of its processes to determine the TCJA's final impact. The final impact may differ from this provisional amount due to, among other things, changes in interpretations and assumptions the Company has made thus far and the issuance of additional regulatory or other guidance. The accounting is expected to be completed by the time the 2017 federal corporate income tax return is filed in 2018.

Income Tax Disclosures

Deere & Company reported income of the consolidated group before income taxes of $3,883 million in 2020. Deere reported an income tax expense of $1,082 million in 2020. In 2019, Deere reported income of consolidated group before income taxes of $4,088 million and income tax expense of $852 million.

To fully understand how income tax expense is determined, we refer to the disclosure notes. Note 9 to Deere's 2020 10-K report contains the table shown in **Exhibit 10.4**.

[14] More specifically, the deferred tax liability is $1,000,000 and was computed using a 35% tax rate. Thus, the cumulative book-tax difference was $2,857,143 ($1,000,000/.35). To find the new deferred tax liability, multiply the cumulative book-tax difference by 21%. This yields $600,000 for the new deferred tax liability balance. To get to this balance, the deferred tax liability needs to be reduced by $400,000.

EXHIBIT 10.4 Deere & Company Income Tax Expense

($ millions)	2020	2019
Current:		
U.S.:		
Federal	$ 400	$ 545
State	53	72
Foreign	640	700
Total current	$1,093	$1,317
Deferred:		
U.S.:		
Federal	$ (68)	$ (345)
State	9	(26)
Foreign	48	(94)
Total deferred	(11)	(465)
Provisions for income taxes	$1,082	$ 852

The income tax expense or benefit reported in the income statement consists of two primary components:

Current tax expense—this can be thought of for our purposes as the amount that has been paid or is payable to tax authorities in the current period. (It also usually contains the income effects of some tax accruals that are beyond the scope of this text.)

Deferred tax expense—this is the effect on tax expense due to changes in deferred tax liabilities and assets. It is the result of temporary differences between the reported income statement and the tax return.

Based on the table shown in **Exhibit 10.4**, Deere reported a tax provision of $1,093 million for current taxes in 2020 and a provision of $1,317 for current taxes in 2019. It also reported a net deferred tax benefit of $11 million in 2020, down from $465 million in 2019.

Companies must also disclose the components of deferred tax assets and liabilities. The components of Deere's deferred tax assets and liabilities are presented in **Exhibit 10.5**.

EXHIBIT 10.5 Components of Deere & Company's Deferred Income Tax Assets and Liabilities

Deferred income taxes arise because there are certain items that are treated differently for financial accounting than for income tax reporting purposes. An analysis of the deferred income tax assets and liabilities at November 1, 2020, and November 3, 2019, in millions of dollars follows:

	2020		2019	
($ millions)	Deferred Tax Assets	Deferred Tax Liabilities	Deferred Tax Assets	Deferred Tax Liabilities
OPEB liabilities	$ 804		$1,015	
Lessor lease transactions		$ 489		$ 599
Tax loss and tax credit carryforwards	937		781	
Accrual for sales allowances	362		518	
Tax over book depreciation		196		339
Goodwill and other intangible assets		368		378
Pension liability – net	316		186	
Allowance for credit losses	81		70	
Accrual for employee benefits	249		207	
Share-based compensation	41		68	
Deferred compensation	40		39	
Lessee lease transactions	56	56		
Other items	366	305	375	311
Less valuation allowances	(858)		(661)	
Deferred income tax assets and liabilities	$2,394	$1,414	$2,598	$1,627

We can reconcile the amounts from this disclosure back to the amounts shown on the balance sheet in **Exhibit 10-1**. The net deferred tax asset on the balance sheet equals $980 million or

$1,499 million – $519 million. The net deferred tax asset in the disclosure above is $980 million or $2,394 – $1,414.[15]

The largest component in the deferred tax asset balance is due to tax loss credits and carryforwards. A portion of these losses and credits is reported to expire during the years 2021 to 2040, while a portion can be carried forward indefinitely. Notice also that Deere has a large deferred tax asset for pensions and OPEB (other postretirement benefit) plans. As we discussed earlier in the chapter, Deere has a large unfunded pension liability. The company has to record the liability and a pension expense for financial accounting on the accrual basis but does not get a tax deduction until funds are contributed to the plan. Thus, larger expenses have been recorded for book relative to the deductions taken for tax. In the future, this will reverse (assuming Deere eventually funds its pension), and the deductions for tax will be greater than the expenses for book. Thus, Deere has a deferred tax asset. (Again, the total income tax expense is the accrual-basis expense related to financial accounting income, not cash taxes paid.) Deere also recognizes a deferred tax asset for sales allowances. Although an estimate for sales returns, for example, is an expense for financial accounting purposes, it is not deductible for tax purposes unless the allowance is actually granted resulting in a deferred tax asset. Finally, notice the subtraction for the valuation allowance. The company discloses in its 2020 10-K that its deferred tax assets "are regularly assessed for the likelihood of recoverability from estimated future taxable income, reversal of deferred tax liabilities, and tax planning strategies. To the extent the company determines that it is more likely than not a deferred income tax asset will not be realized, a valuation allowance is established." The valuation allowance is 26% and 20% of deferred tax assets (before the allowance) in the years 2020 and 2019, respectively.

In terms of where deferred tax assets and liabilities are reflected on the balance sheet, under the current accounting standards all are recorded in the noncurrent section of the balance sheet. A net amount (asset or liability) is shown.

Companies also report in the disclosure notes a reconciliation of differences between the statutory U.S. tax rate (currently 21%) and the tax expense reported in the income statement. The **effective tax rate** is determined by dividing the provision for income taxes (tax expense) by the income before income taxes. Deere's effective tax rate for 2020 was 27.9% ($1,082 million/$3,883 million: income tax expense/pre-tax accounting income from the income statement). Deere's rate reconciliation lists the principal reasons for the difference between the provision for income taxes calculated using effective tax rate and the U.S. federal statutory income tax rate:

A comparison of the statutory and effective income tax provision and reasons for related differences in millions of dollars follow:

	2020	2019	2018
U.S. federal income tax provision at the U.S. statutory rate (2020 and 2019—21 percent, 2018—23.3 percent)	$ 815	$859	$ 950
Increase (decrease) resulting from:			
Net deferred tax asset remeasurement		6	414
Deemed earnings repatriation tax		(74)	290
Effects of GILTI and FDII	39	(33)	
Other effects of tax reform			42
Differences in taxability of foreign earnings	38	(94)	(92)
Valuation allowance on deferred taxes	139	28	50
Research and business tax credits	(50)	(85)	(43)
State and local income taxes, net of federal income tax benefit	59	47	59
Excess tax benefits on equity compensation	(87)	(40)	(49)
Tax rates on foreign earnings	68	183	44
Unrecognized tax benefits	(32)	(28)	30
Other—net	93	83	32
Provision for income taxes	$1,082	$852	$1,727

[15] Readers will note that the asset and liability amounts do not separately, directly tie to the balance sheet, however. It is not clear what classification method Deere is using (but the net amount does tie out). It is possible the company has separated the amounts by jurisdiction, as the GAAP guidance says that an entity shall not offset deferred tax assets and liabilities from different tax jurisdictions. Prior to 2017, companies classified deferred tax assets and liabilities as short term and long term. However, US GAAP changed such that all are now netted and recorded in long term assets or liabilities. We also note that for some companies the disclosures will be impossible to tie to the financial statements at all if, for example, the net amount is small and the company combines with other items into the 'other' category.

Effective tax rates can vary considerably from one company to another due to permanent differences, tax credits, and other factors. A comparison of the effective tax rate for several companies is presented in **Exhibit 10.6**. The leftmost chart shows companies' 2020 ETR split by current and deferred portions of the tax expense. The rightmost chart compares ETRs for companies in 2020 and 2019.

EXHIBIT 10.6 Comparison of Effective Tax Rates

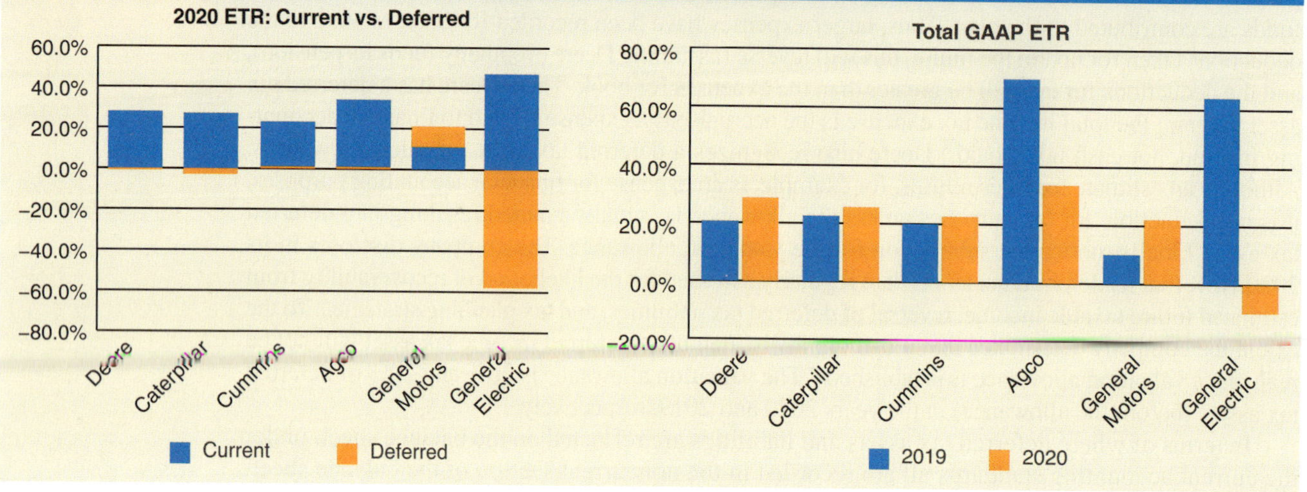

Even though 2020 was the year of the pandemic, the ETRs look quite reasonable, in the range of −10% to +33%. One may wonder why Agco's rate in 2019 was so high. An examination of their 10-K reveals a large impairment charge in 2019. Such a charge would reduce financial accounting income but would not be deductible for tax purposes. Thus, tax expense would not be affected (the numerator) but pre-tax accounting income (the denominator) is lower resulting in a higher effective tax rate (a higher ratio). For GE in 2019 and 2020, it appears from their disclosures that their effective tax rate was significantly impacted by the sale of their BioPharma business. Events such as these in any given year can cause the ETR to be very high or very low but not really indicate a change in tax planning activities. It is important to note again that these rates do not represent cash taxes paid. Thus, even though GE has a negative tax expense in 2020, it does not necessarily mean they received a cash refund of any kind.

Deferred Taxes in the Statement of Cash Flows

Income taxes, including deferred income taxes, are reported in the operating section of the statement of cash flows. When the statement of cash flows is prepared using the direct method, deferred income taxes are excluded from taxes paid in cash. When the indirect (or reconciliation) method is used, the deferred portion of the income tax expense must be added back to net income as an expense not requiring the use of cash. The amount of income taxes paid in cash is then reported at the bottom of the statement of cash flows or in the disclosures.

Computation and Analysis of Taxes

An analysis of deferred taxes can yield useful insights. An increase in deferred tax liabilities indicates that a company is reporting higher profits in its income statement than in its tax return. The difference between reported corporate profits and taxable income increased substantially in the late 1990s, just prior to the stock market decline.

Although an increase in deferred tax liabilities can be the result of legitimate differences between financial reporting standards and tax rules, we must be aware of the possibility that such differences can also be caused by tax avoidance or by earnings management, improper revenue recognition, or other questionable accounting practices. More advanced courses cover the accounting for income taxes in more depth.

RESEARCH INSIGHT

Recent research has studied the accounting for income tax. Several papers have examined whether the overall difference between a company's taxable income and its financial accounting income contains any information about earnings quality. The idea is that if managers use accruals to manage financial accounting earnings upward, taxable income would not likely be similarly managed because there are fewer accruals for tax purposes (e.g., allowance for doubtful accounts, warranty reserves, etc.). The evidence is generally consistent with this hypothesis.[16]

Accounting for Income Taxes LO10-3 **Review 10-3**

GuidedExample MBC

The following note is from the annual report of Adler Corporation.

Note 9: Income Taxes
The provision for income taxes includes the following

($ thousands)	
Current provision	
Domestic	$1,342
Foreign	146
Deferred provision (credit)	
Domestic	960
Foreign	(58)
Total	$2,390

Required

a. (1) What is the amount of income tax expense reported on its income statement? (2) How much of the income tax expense is payable in cash (estimated)? (3) Assuming that the deferred tax liability increased, identify an example that could account for such a change.

b. Prepare the entry, using the financial statement effects template, to record its income tax expense for the year.

c. Prepare the journal entry to record its income tax expense. Post journal entries to the appropriate T-accounts.

Solution on p. 10-67.

COMMITMENTS AND CONTENGENCIES AND OTHER DISCLOSURES

LO10-4
Describe disclosures regarding future commitments and contingencies. Analyze financial statements after converting off-balance-sheet items to be considered on balance sheet.

eLecture MBC

FASB and SEC guidance also require entities to provide additional detail and disclosure about various commitments and contingencies. Often companies will list a line item on the balance sheet "Commitments and Contingencies" with no corresponding amount. **Exhibit 10.1** shows that Deere includes such a line item on their balance sheet.

In the notes to the financial statements, Deere provides disclosure about such items as 1) warranty liability, 2) guarantees to banks related to third-party receivables for the financing of John Deere equipment, 3) commitments for the construction and acquisition of property and equipment, 4) miscellaneous contingent liabilities and 5) unresolved legal actions.

Generally, many of the items in such disclosures are not on the balance sheet as liabilities (though some are); thus, financial statement users need to evaluate how to treat such items. As discussed in the introduction, off-balance-sheet financing refers to financial obligations of a company that are not reported as liabilities in the balance sheet. Off-balance-sheet financing reduces the amount of debt reported on the balance sheet, thereby lowering the company's financial leverage ratios. Additionally, many off-balance-sheet financing techniques (e.g., contract manufacturing) remove assets from the balance sheet, along with the liabilities, without reducing revenues or markedly affecting net income. Such techniques cause operation ratios, such as return on assets (ROA),

[16] See the following studies: 1) Phillips, John, Mort Pincus, and Sonja Rego, "Earnings Management: New Evidence Based on Deferred Tax Expense." *The Accounting Review*, 1999, 2) Lev, Baruch and Doron Nissim, "Taxable Income, Future Earnings, and Equity Values," *The Accounting Review*, October 2004, and 3) Hanlon, Michelle, "The Persistence and Pricing of Earnings, Accruals, and Cash Flows When Firms Have Large Book-Tax Differences," *The Accounting Review*, January 2005.

to appear stronger than they are. Interestingly, the accounting standards have moved many of the "off-balance-sheet" items onto the balance sheet (e.g., parts of pensions, special-purpose entities, and now operating leases). However, there are still some off-balance-sheet items such as contractual obligations that do not meet the FASB definition of a liability. One example is the set of endorsement contract obligations a company such as Nike has when it endorses high-profile athletes.

Nike, Inc., includes the line item "commitments and contingencies" on their balance sheet and discloses the details in a note to their financial statements. Nike also includes a broader disclosure about contractual obligations and off-balance-sheet commitments in the Management Discussion and Analysis section of their annual 10-K. The disclosure in their May 31, 2020, annual report is as follows:

Off-Balance-Sheet Arrangements

In connection with various contracts and agreements, we routinely provide indemnification relating to the enforceability of intellectual property rights, coverage for legal issues that arise and other items where we are acting as the guarantor. Currently, we have several such agreements in place. Based on our historical experience and the estimated probability of future loss, we have determined that the fair value of such indemnification is not material to our financial position or results of operations.

Contractual Obligations

Our significant long-term contractual obligations as of May 31, 2020, and significant endorsement contracts, including related marketing commitments, entered into through the date of this report are as follows:

Description of Commitment (Dollars in millions)	Cash Payments Due During the Year Ended May 31						
	2021	2022	2023	2024	2025	Thereafter	Total
Operating Leases	$ 550	$ 514	$ 456	$ 416	$ 374	$1,474	$ 3,784
Long-Term Debt	289	286	786	275	1,275	11,541	14,452
Endorsement Contracts	1,330	1,471	1,178	1,064	1,135	3,164	9,342
Product Purchase Obligations	4,234	—	—	—	—	—	4,234
Other Purchase Obligations	1,085	345	189	136	127	345	2,227
Transition tax related to the Tax Act	86	86	86	161	215	268	902
Total	$7,574	$2,702	$2,695	$2,052	$3,126	$16,792	$34,941

Note: Footnotes to the tables excluded for brevity.

The endorsement contracts have included contracts with well-known athletes such as Serena Williams, LeBron James, Maria Sharapova, Roger Federer, Tiger Woods, and of course, Michael Jordan. The athletes sign long-term, multimillion dollar contracts to use and promote Nike shoes, apparel, and accessories. These long-term endorsement contracts are just one of Nike's off-balance-sheet obligations.

In the table above, long-term debt, operating leases, and the transition tax related to the Tax Act (discussed previously) are included in the balance sheet. The endorsement contracts, one of the largest items, are not included on the balance sheet as liabilities. If an analyst desires to estimate the associated "as if" liability with such contracts, the following approach could be used. (This process can be used for other off-balance sheet 'liabilities' as long as one has estimates of the future cash outflows.)

1. Estimate a discount rate. One reasonable proxy is the interest rate on Nike's debt, which is roughly 3% per their debt note disclosure.
2. Estimate the future payments and the number of years those payments will be made. One limitation of the above disclosure is that the first five years show the annual payment, but the remaining payments are lumped in a column "thereafter." An estimate of the number of years for the amount in the "thereafter" column can be computed by dividing the amount ($3,164) by the previous year's payment ($1,135). In this case, this estimate yields almost 3 years. To estimate using full years, divide the amount in the "thereafter" column by three and arrive at an estimate of the payment amount for each of the next three years. In this case, it is $1,055 million ($3,164/3).
3. Find the present value of the future payments. The present value of the payments listed above for years 2021 through 2028 (including the estimated payments), at 3% over the 8 years, is roughly $8.3 billion. This can be computed using one of several methods; for example, 1) the

present value tables in Appendix A to find the present value of each payment or 2) Excel's NPV function.

This yields a rough approximation of the "as if" liability related to these payments. However, the associated asset value, if any, for this off-balance-sheet item—the value of advertising through endorsements—is very hard to estimate.

ANALYZING FINANCIAL STATEMENTS

Analysis Objective

We want to assess the effect of financial obligations, including off-balance-sheet commitments, on financial solvency and liquidity.

Analysis Tool Fixed Commitments Ratio

$$\textbf{Fixed commitments ratio} = \frac{\textbf{Operating cash flow before fixed commitments}}{\textbf{Fixed commitments}}$$

Applying the Fixed Commitments Ratio to Deere & Company Some fixed commitments, such as operating lease payments and purchase commitments, are cash outflows that are classified as operating activities in the statement of cash flows. Others (for example, payments due on long-term debt) are classified as financing cash flows, and some can be classified as investing (for example, commitments to purchase plant assets). Deere reports total fixed commitments of $17,562 million in its 10-K report. Of these, $10,926 million is for noninterest payments on long-term debt and finance leases (financing), and $159 is for equipment purchase commitments (investing). Subtracting these amounts leaves the amount of fixed commitments that are part of operating cash flows ($17,562 – $10,926 – $159 = $6,477). To compute the **fixed commitments ratio**, we start with operating cash flows, add back the fixed commitments that are classified as operating, and then divide by the total amount of fixed commitments.

($ millions)

$$\textbf{2018:}\quad \frac{(\$1,822 + \$7,023)}{\$20,538} = 0.43$$

$$\textbf{2019:}\quad \frac{(\$3,412 + \$6,289)}{\$19,544} = 0.50$$

$$\textbf{2020:}\quad \frac{(\$7,483 + \$6,477)}{\$17,562} = 0.79$$

Guidance A fixed commitments ratio less than 1.0 generally indicates that a company is generating insufficient cash flows from operations to meet its contractual obligations. Some commitments may be met by selling assets or by raising additional financing. For example, when long-term debt comes due, it can be refinanced with new debt if the company is otherwise in sound financial health.

Deere & Company in Context

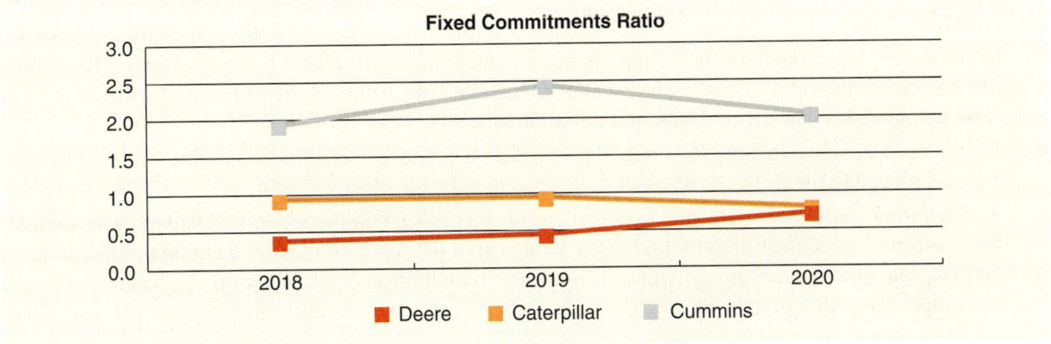

Takeaways Deere and Caterpillar are consistently below 1.0 for these three years, which might be a cause for some concern. However, Deere's ratios have increased over the three years suggesting improvement.

The key takeaway from this section is that off-balance sheet obligations can have a significant impact on our analysis and understanding of a company's future obligations, solvency, and liquidity.

Other Considerations The fixed commitments ratio is but one measure of financial solvency and liquidity. It should be used in conjunction with other ratios, such as the debt-to-equity ratio and the current ratio in an effort to gauge the ability of the firm to meet its financial obligations.

Review 10-4 LO10-4

Analyzing Commitments and Contingencies

Guided Example MBC

Cummins Inc. provides the following disclosure in the notes to its 2020 financial statements:

Guarantees and Commitments

Periodically, we enter into guarantee arrangements, including guarantees of non-U.S. distributor financings, residual value guarantees on equipment under operating leases, and other miscellaneous guarantees of joint ventures or third-party obligations. At December 31, 2020, the maximum potential loss related to these guarantees was $44 million.

We have arrangements with certain suppliers that require us to purchase minimum volumes or be subject to monetary penalties. At December 31, 2020, if we were to stop purchasing from each of these suppliers, the aggregate amount of the penalty would be approximately $32 million. Most of these arrangements enable us to secure supplies of critical components. We do not currently anticipate paying any penalties under these contracts.

We enter into physical forward contracts with suppliers of platinum and palladium to purchase certain volumes of the commodities at contractually stated prices for various periods, which generally fall within two years. At December 31, 2020, the total commitments under these contracts were $79 million. These arrangements enable us to guarantee the prices of these commodities, which otherwise are subject to market volatility.

We have guarantees with certain customers that require us to satisfactorily honor contractual or regulatory obligations, or compensate for monetary losses related to nonperformance. These performance bonds and other performance-related guarantees were $100 million at December 31, 2020.

a. How would the following items from the disclosure above be shown on the financial statements?
1. $44 million of guarantees
2. $32 million in penalties
3. $79 million in commitments on contracts
4. $100 million in performance-related guarantees

b. Compute the present value of the future payments related to purchase commitments of $79 million. (Note: Assume that the amount will be paid evenly over the next two years, with payments made at the end of each year. Assume a discount rate of 4%.)

Solution on p. 10-67.

SUMMARY

LO10-1 **Account for leases using the operating lease method and the finance lease method. Compare and analyze the two methods. (p. 10-3)**

- For both a finance lease and an operating lease, a right-of-use asset and a lease liability are recorded by the lessee. The amount of the liability is the present value of the future lease payments. The amount recognized for the right-of-use asset is equal to the amount of the liability adjusted for items such as lease prepayments, lease incentives, and initial direct costs.
- For finance leases, the income statement reports interest expense related to the liability and amortization expense related to the right-of-use asset.
- For operating leases, a straight-line lease expense is recognized on the income statement. The straight-line lease expense is measured by taking the total cost of the lease divided by the total number of lease periods. The amortization of the right-of-use asset (reduction in book value on the balance sheet) is determined by subtracting the interest on the lease liability from the straight-line-expense amount. Thus,

while the expense is straight-line, a loan amortization table like that used for finance leases is used to determine the reduction in book value of the asset and reduction in liability as payments are made.

- Right-of-use book value declines more quickly with the finance lease method.
- An asset leased using a finance lease will have higher related expenses early in the asset's life relative to an asset leased using an operating lease.
- For companies that utilize operating leases, in order to compare financial statements before and after the new lease standard, an analyst or other financial statement user needs to compute the present value of the future lease payments and treat this present value as an "as-if" liability. In addition, an estimate of the asset would need to be determined.

Explain and interpret the reporting for pension plans, including the disclosure notes. (p. 10-15) LO10-2

- Pension and other postretirement obligations represent a large obligation for many companies.
- The projected benefit obligation is the present value of the estimated future benefits that a company expects to pay retired employees.
- The net liability that a company reports on the balance sheet is the projected benefit obligation offset by the plan assets.
- Pension note disclosures provide detailed information about changes in pension obligations, changes in plan assets, and the determinants of pension expense.
- Pension note disclosures provide information allowing us to interpret pension expenses and cash flows.

Describe and interpret accounting for income taxes. (p. 10-25) LO10-3

- While income tax expense is reported below income from operations, it is an operating expense. The initial item in an indirect statement of cash flows is net income, which reflects the subtraction of the tax expense.
- Income tax expense is determined as the sum of the tax computed due to the government and the net change in deferred assets and liabilities (and potentially other accruals).
- Deferred taxes occur because of differences between U.S. GAAP reporting and the tax due based on the rules of the tax authority. The former are based on accrual accounting, while the latter are often based on a hybrid accrual and cash-based accounting system.
- Deferred tax assets and liabilities are valued at the enacted tax rate expected to be in effect when the temporary differences between financial accounting and tax bases reverse.

Describe disclosures regarding future commitments and contingencies. Analyze financial statements after converting off-balance-sheet items to be considered on balance sheet. (p. 10-36) LO10-4

- Disclosure of future commitments and contingent payments is required.
- Off-balance-sheet financing refers to financial obligations of the company that are not recognized as liabilities in the balance sheet. Recognizing these obligations often requires recognizing off-balance-sheet assets.
- Off-balance-sheet financing improves financial leverage ratios, and the corresponding unrecognized assets improve performance measures.
- Some of these disclosed commitments and contingencies will be recognized on the balance sheet, and some are off-balance-sheet. If the item is off-balance-sheet but an analyst or creditor desires to analyze the company's financials as if the item were treated as a liability, the present value of the future payments should be computed and included in liabilities for analysis purposes.

GUIDANCE ANSWERS . . . YOU MAKE THE CALL

You are the CEO Normally we think that managers inside the firm have full information about firm activities and performance. However, they likely do not have perfect information. Gathering a new level of data regarding lease contracts and terms may lead corporations to consolidate leases, negotiate better lease terms, or potentially reduce the quantity of assets leased. You, as the CEO, may even decide to invest in machine learning software or textual analysis software to gather more data and help your company be more efficient and cost-effective in setting lease contracts.

You are a Consultant to the FASB Normally accountants do not favor offsetting liabilities against the related assets as is currently the reporting practice required under GAAP for pensions. However, because the pension fund is a separate legal entity, there is a problem with reporting the pension plan assets among the firm's assets. A company does not have unilateral control over a pension trust. It can put assets into the trust but can not easily get them out of the trust. For this reason, the pension assets do not meet the criteria we normally require for recognition. Thus, reporting a net amount (PBO – pension assets) seems the best course of action.

KEY RATIOS

$$\text{Fixed commitments ratio} = \frac{\text{Operating cash flow before fixed commitments}}{\text{Fixed commitments}}$$

$$\text{Effective tax rate} = \frac{\text{Provision for income taxes}}{\text{Income before income taxes}}$$

Assignments with the MBC logo in the margin are available in myBusinessCourse. See the Preface of the book for details.

MULTIPLE CHOICE

Multiple Choice Answers
1. a 2. d 3. d 4. b 5. d 6. c 7. c

1. U.S. GAAP requires that certain leases be accounted for as *finance leases*. The reason for this treatment is that this type of lease
- *a.* is essentially viewed as a sale/purchase.
- *b.* is an example of form over substance.
- *c.* provides the use of the leased asset to the lessee for a limited period of time.
- *d.* is an example of off-balance-sheet financing.

2. For a lease that is accounted for as an operating lease by the lessee, the rent expense should be
- *a.* allocated and recorded as interest expense and depreciation expense.
- *b.* allocated and recorded as a reduction in the liability for leased assets and interest expense.
- *c.* recorded as rent expense with no other entries recorded.
- *d.* recorded as a straight-line lease expense with associated entries to record the cash payment, reduce the liability, and amortize the right-of-use asset on the balance sheet.

3. The balance sheet liability for a finance lease would be reduced each period by the
- *a.* lease payment.
- *b.* lease payment plus the amortization of the related asset.
- *c.* lease payment less the amortization of the related asset.
- *d.* lease payment less the periodic interest expense.

4. Which of the following statements characterizes defined benefit pension plans?
- *a.* The employer's obligation is satisfied by making the necessary periodic contribution.
- *b.* Retirement benefits are based on the plan's benefit formula.
- *c.* Retirement benefits depend on how well pension fund assets have been managed.
- *d.* Contributions are made in equal amounts by employer and employees.

5. When the value of pension plan assets is greater than the projected benefit obligation,
- *a.* the difference is added to pension expense.
- *b.* the difference is reported as deferred pension cost.
- *c.* the difference is reported as a contra equity adjustment.
- *d.* the pension plan is overfunded.

6. Which of the following is *not* a component of net pension expense?
- *a.* Interest cost
- *b.* Expected return on plan assets
- *c.* Benefits paid to retirees
- *d.* Amortization of actuarial gains or losses

7. Deferred tax assets and liabilities should be reported using
- *a.* the tax rate in effect in the current period.
- *b.* the tax rates management thinks will be passed in the next year.
- *c.* the enacted tax rate that will be in effect when the temporary differences reverse.
- *d.* the enacted tax rate that was in effect when the temporary difference was created.

QUESTIONS

Q10-1. Under the lease accounting standard (Topic 842), what are the financial reporting differences between an operating lease and a finance lease? Explain.

Q10-2. Explain the cash flows and Statement of Cash Flow effects of a finance lease and an operating lease.

Q10-3. Is the expense of a lease over its entire life the same whether it is a finance or an operating lease? Explain.

Q10-4. What are the economic and accounting differences between a defined contribution plan and a defined benefit plan?

Q10-5. Under what circumstances will a company report a net pension asset? A net pension liability?

Q10-6. What are the components of pension expense that is reported in the income statement?

Q10-7. What effect does the use of expected returns on pension investments and the deferral of unexpected gains and losses on those investments have on income?

Q10-8. How is the initial valuation determined for lease liability and the right-of-use asset for both an operating lease and a finance lease?

Q10-9. Over what time period should the cost of providing retirement benefits to employees be expensed?

Q10-10. What is the conceptual reason why income tax expense on the income statement is not equal to cash taxes paid?

Q10-11. Under what circumstances would a tax payment be made that also requires the recording of a deferred tax asset or liability?

Q10-12. Explain what an unrecognized tax benefit is and where it is recorded on the balance sheet.

DATA ANALYTICS

DA10-1 Using Excel Visualizations to Analyze the Impact of an Accounting Change

LO10-1

The new lease standard (ASC 842) resulted in significant changes for companies that had large operating lease obligations. Prior to the new lease standard, operating lease obligations were disclosed but a liability was not recorded on the balance sheet. Upon transitioning to the new leasing standard, **Walgreens Boots Alliance, Inc.** (Walgreens Boots) and **Verizon Communications Inc.** (Verizon) disclosed the impact on the beginning balances of the accounting period in which the transition to the new lease standard took place. (The standard was adopted through a modified retrospective approach.)

Information included in the Excel file associated with this exercise was extracted or inferred from disclosures made by Walgreens Boots and Verizon in the year of adoption of the lease standard. Using this data, we calculate ratios before and immediately after the adoption of the lease standard to better understand the impact of the accounting standard on financial statement results.

Total liabilities-to-total assets

$$\frac{\text{Total liabilities}}{\text{Total assets}}$$

Current Ratio

$$\frac{\text{Current assets}}{\text{Current liabilities}}$$

Total liabilities-to-total equity

$$\frac{\text{Total liabilities}}{\text{Total stockholders' equity}}$$

REQUIRED

1. Download Excel file DA10-1 found in myBusinessCourse.
2. Calculate the following ratios in Excel for both companies on the balances shown before and directly after the new lease standard adoption:
   a. Total liabilities-to-total assets
   b. Current ratio
   c. Total liabilities-to-total equity
3. Create a bar chart for each company comparing the three ratios before and after adoption of the new lease standard. For the y-axis, use increments of 0.5 in both charts. Add data labels to the bars. *Hint:* Highlight the data, Insert, Bar. Right-click on the bars and click Add data labels.
4. Indicate which ratio results looked more favorable and which ratio results looked less favorable after adoption of the new lease standard for each company.
5. Answer the following questions:
   a. Did the economics of leasing change the day after the new lease standard became effective?
   b. Would investors or creditors have understood the impact of operating leases on the balance sheet before the adoption of the new lease standard by companies?
   c. Which compar y showed a more significant relative impact from the adoption of the new lease standard, based on the change in ratios before and after adoption of the new lease standard?
   d. Does the company from your answer to part *c* have the larger liabilities-to-total equity ratio of the two companies before adoption of the new lease standard?
6. Prepare two pie charts in Excel for each company, showing the components of liabilities before and after the adoption of the new lease standard. *Hint:* Add data labels (percentages).
7. Answer the following questions based upon the pie chart visualizations.

a. For Verizon, how many proportions of the pie are there before and after the new lease standard? For Walgreens Boots?

b. What is the difference in the proportion of total current liabilities, long-term debt, long-term operating lease liabilities, and other long-term debt for Verizon after the adoption of the new lease standard? For Walgreens Boots?

c. Why did one company show a larger impact (identified in part *b*) from the adoption of the new lease standard that can be seen in the pie charts?

LO10-2 Data Analytics

DA10-2. Analyzing the Trends of Plan Asset and PBO Balances and Service Cost Over Time in Excel

The **Boeing Company** (Boeing) has sponsored a defined pension benefit plan for many years for its employees. Information obtained from Form 10-K statements over a 10-year period is included in the file associated with this exercise. We analyze the trend of (and the relations between) balances of the PBO and Plan assets over time. We also analyze the trends in service cost over time and determine possible causes of the trends.

REQUIRED

1. Download Excel file DA10-2 found in myBusinessCourse.
2. Prepare a line chart showing the trend of PBO balances and Plan Asset balances over the 10-year period. *Hint:* Highlight data; click Insert, Line.
3. Indicate in which years the plans were overfunded and underfunded.
4. Indicate the year (by visually looking at the chart) where the relation of Plan Assets to PBO differed from the other years most clearly.
5. Describe the trend in the PBO balance over time.
6. Prepare a line chart showing the trend of service cost over the 10-year period.
7. Describe the trend in service cost over time.
8. Answer the following questions based upon the service cost chart.
   a. In what two years did service cost change the most significantly? *Hint:* Use the gridlines in the chart to help you estimate the largest change.
   b. What would be a likely cause of the changes identified in part *a*?
9. Compare and contrast the trend from year 9 to year 10 between the PBO balance and service cost.

LO10-3 Data Analytics

DA10-3. Analyzing Excel Visualizations of Deferred Tax Accounts

The Excel file associated with this exercise includes balance sheet tax account data for two years for 14 large companies in the Consumer Discretionary segment. In this exercise, we analyze trends in the deferred tax allowance as a percentage of the gross deferred tax asset balance. An increase in the percentage means that management expects a larger portion of deferred tax asset to not be realized.

REQUIRED

1. Download Excel file DA10-3 found in myBusinessCourse.
2. Create a schedule in Excel showing each company's deferred tax allowance balance divided by the gross deferred tax asset balance.
3. Sort the data in the table based on the 2020 column data, ordering from largest to smallest, using the Sort function.
4. Create a bar chart visualization showing a bar for 2019 and 2020 for each company. *Hint:* Highlight the data; click Insert, Bar.
5. List the companies in which the ratio did not increase from year 2019 to 2020.
6. List the company that visually showed the largest change in the ratio from 2019 to 2020.
7. What is the most likely reason for the common trend in the ratios from 2019 to 2020?
8. Create a separate schedule in Excel with a column for each company's net deferred tax asset balance and a column for each company's deferred tax liability balance as of 2020.
9. Create a stacked bar chart for each company's net deferred tax asset balance and deferred tax liability balance as of 2020. *Hint:* Select the Insert tab, Recommended charts, and choose the 100% stacked bar chart.
10. Indicate which company has the highest percentage of net deferred tax assets to deferred tax liabilities.
11. Indicate which company has the lowest percentage of net deferred tax assets to deferred tax liabilities.
12. Indicate a factor that could have had a significant impact on the relation of net deferred tax assets to deferred tax liabilities described in part 11.

DATA VISUALIZATION

Data Visualization Activities are available in myBusinessCourse. These assignments use Tableau Dashboards to expose students to visual depictions of data and introduce students to data analytics through data visualizations. These exercises are easily assignable and auto graded by MBC.

Data Visualization

MINI EXERCISES

M10-13. Accounting for Leases (FSET) LO10-1 Homework MBC

On January 3, Hanna Corporation signed a lease on a machine for its manufacturing operation and the lease commences on the same date. The lease requires Hanna to make six annual lease payments of $15,000 with the first payment due December 31. Hanna could have financed the machine by borrowing the purchase price at an interest rate of 7%.

a. Using the financial statement effects template, report the entries that Hanna Corporation would make on January 3 and December 31 to record this lease assuming

i. the lease is reported as an operating lease.

ii. the lease is reported as a finance lease.

b. Explain how the financial statement effects differ between the two treatments.

M10-14. Accounting for Leases LO10-2 Homework MBC

Using the information from M10-13, prepare the journal entries for part *a* and post to the appropriate T-accounts.

M10-15. Accounting for Leases (FSET) LO10-1 Homework MBC

On July 1, Shroff Company leased a warehouse building under a 10-year lease agreement. The lease requires quarterly lease payments of $5,000. The first lease payment is due on September 30, 2020. The lease was reported as a finance lease using an 8% annual interest rate.

a. Using the financial statement effects template, report the entry to record the commencement of the lease on July 1.

b. Using the financial statement effects template, report the entries that would be necessary on September 30 and December 31.

M10-16. Accounting for Leases LO10-1 Homework MBC

Using the information from M10-15, (1) prepare the journal entries for parts *a* and *b*, and (2) post to the appropriate T-accounts.

M10-17. Accounting for Operating and Finance Leases (FSET) LO10-1 Homework MBC

On January 1, Weber, Inc., entered into two lease contracts. The first lease contract was a six-year lease for computer equipment with $20,000 annual lease payments due at the end of each year. Weber took possession of the equipment on January 1. The second lease contract was a six-month lease, beginning January 1, for warehouse storage space with $1,500 monthly lease payments due the first of each month. Weber made the first month's payment on January 1. The present value of the lease payments under the first contract is $99,359. The present value of the lease payments under the second contract is $8,895.

REQUIRED

a. Assume that the first lease contract is a finance lease. Prepare a financial statement effects template to show the effects of the entry on January 1.

b. Assume the second lease contract is an operating lease. Prepare a financial statement effects template to show the effects of the entry on January 1.

M10-18. Accounting for Operating and Finance Leases LO10-1 Homework MBC

Using the information from M10-17, prepare the journal entries for parts *a* and *b*.

M10-19. Accounting for Operating Leases (FSET) LO10-1 Homework MBC

On January 1 of the current year, Samuels, Inc., purchased a building for $2.5 million to be leased. The building is expected to have a 45-year life with no salvage value. The building was leased immediately by Verdi Corp. (a calendar year-end company) for $162,500 a year payable December 31 of each year. The lease term is five years. The rate of interest implicit in the lease is 7%. The lease is classified as an operating lease.

a. Prepare an amortization schedule of the lease liability.

b. Prepare an amortization schedule for the right-of-use asset.

c. Prepare a financial statement effects template to show the effects of the entries for Verdi Corp. for the current and following year.

LO10-1 Homework MBC

M10-20. Accounting for Operating Leases

Using the information from M10-19, prepare the journal entries for the current year and the following year.

LO10-1 Homework MBC

M10-21. Accounting for Operating Leases (FSET)

Redo Mini-Exercise M10-19 but now assume the payments are made on January 1 of each year (including the first year on January 1).

LO10-1 Homework MBC

M10-22. Accounting for Operating Leases

Redo Mini-Exercise M10-20, but now assume the payments are made on January 1 of each year (including the first year on January 1).

LO10-2 Homework MBC

M10-23. Accounting for Pension Benefits (FSET)

Bartov Corporation has a defined contribution pension plan for its employees. Each year, Bartov contributes to the plan an amount equal to 4% of the employee payroll for the year. Bartov's current year payroll was $320,000. Bartov also provides a life insurance benefit that pays a $40,000 death benefit to the beneficiaries of retired employees. At the end of the current year, Bartov estimates that its liability under the life insurance program is $500,000. Bartov has assets with a fair value of $140,000 in a trust fund that are available to meet the death benefit payments.

REQUIRED

a. Prepare a financial statement effects template to show the effects of the entry at December 31 to record Bartov's annual defined contribution to a pension trustee who will manage the pension funds for the firm's employees.

b. What amount of liability for death benefit payments must Bartov report in its December 31 balance sheet? Explain.

LO10-2 Homework MBC

M10-24. Accounting for Pension Benefits

Using the information from M10-23, prepare the journal entry for part *a*.

LO10-2

Exxon Mobil Corporation
NYSE :: XOM

M10-25. Analyzing and Interpreting Pension Disclosures—Expenses and Returns

Exxon Mobil Corporation discloses the following information in its pension note disclosure in its 10-K report:

(In millions)	2020
Service cost	$1,672
Interest cost	1,365
Expected return on plan assets	(1,600)
Amortization of actuarial loss (gain)	726
Amortization of prior service cost	73
Net pension enhancement and curtailment/settlement cost	329
Net periodic pension benefit cost	$2,565

a. How much pension expense does Exxon Mobil Corporation report in its 2020 income statement?

b. What effect does its "expected return on plan assets" have on its reported pension expense? Explain.

c. Explain use of the word "expected" as it relates to results of pension plan investments.

LO10-2

YUM! Brands
NYSE :: YUM

M10-26. Analyzing and Interpreting Pension Disclosures—Expenses and Returns

YUM! Brands, Inc., discloses the following pension note disclosure in its 10-K report:

	Pension Benefits	
(In millions)	2020	2019
Service cost	$ 8	$ 6
Interest cost	35	39
Amortization of prior service cost	5	6
Expected return on plan assets	(43)	(44)
Amortization of net loss	14	1
Net periodic benefit cost	$19	$ 8

a. How much pension expense does Yum report in its 2020 income statement?

b. What effect does its "expected return on plan assets" have on its reported pension expense? Explain.

c. Explain use of the word "expected" as it relates to results of pension plan investments.

M10-27. Analyzing and Interpreting Retirement Benefit Disclosure (FSET)

LO10-2
Abercrombie & Fitch
NYSE :: ANF
Homework MBC

Abercrombie & Fitch Co. discloses the following disclosure note relating to its retirement plans in its fiscal 2020 10-K report:

> **16. SAVINGS AND RETIREMENT PLANS:** The Company maintains the Abercrombie & Fitch Co. Savings and Retirement Plan, a qualified plan. All U.S. associates are eligible to participate in this plan if they are at least 21 years of age. In addition, the Company maintains the Abercrombie & Fitch Co. Nonqualified Savings and Supplemental Retirement, composed of two sub-plans (Plan I and Plan II). Plan I contains contributions made through December 31, 2004, while Plan II contains contributions made on and after January 1, 2005. Participation in these plans is based on service and compensation. The Company's contributions to these plans are based on a percentage of associates' eligible annual compensation. The cost of the Company's contributions to these plans was $14.1 million, $14.8 million, and $15.1 million for Fiscal 2020, Fiscal 2019, and Fiscal 2018, respectively.

a. Does Abercrombie have a defined contribution or defined benefit pension plan? Explain

b. Prepare a financial statement effects template to show the effects of the contributions to its retirement plan for fiscal 2020.

c. How is Abercrombie's obligation to its retirement plan reported on its balance sheet?

M10-28. Analyzing and Interpreting Retirement Benefit Disclosure

LO10-2
Homework MBC

Using the information from M10-27, prepare the journal entry for the company's contributions to its retirement plans in fiscal 2020.

M10-29. Analyzing and Interpreting Disclosures on Contract Manufacturers

LO10-4
Nike
NYSE :: NKE

Nike, Inc., reports the following information relating to its manufacturing activities in Part 1 of its 2020 10-K report:

> We are supplied by 122 footwear factories located in 12 countries. Virtually all of our footwear is manufactured outside of the United States by over 15 independent contract manufacturers, which often operate multiple factories. The largest single footwear factory accounted for approximately 9% of total fiscal 2020 NIKE Brand footwear production.
>
> For fiscal 2020, contract factories in Vietnam, Indonesia, and China manufactured approximately 50%, 24%, and 22% of total NIKE Brand footwear, respectively. We also have manufacturing agreements with independent contract manufacturers in Argentina and India to manufacture footwear for sale primarily within those countries. For fiscal 2020, four footwear contract manufacturers each accounted for greater than 10% of footwear production and in the aggregate accounted for approximately 61% of NIKE Brand footwear production.

a. What effect does the use of contract manufacturers have on Nike's balance sheet?

b. Nike executes purchase contracts with its contract manufacturers to purchase their output. How are executory contracts reported under GAAP? Does your answer suggest a possible motivation for the use of contract manufacturing?

M10-30. Computing and Reporting Deferred Income Taxes

LO10-3
Homework MBC

Fisk, Inc., purchased $480,000 of construction equipment on January 1, 2022. The equipment is being depreciated on a straight-line basis over six years with no expected salvage value. MACRS depreciation is being used on the firm's tax returns. At December 31, 2024, the equipment's book value is $240,000, and its tax basis is $138,400. (This is Fisk's only temporary difference.) Over the next three years, straight-line depreciation will exceed MACRS depreciation by $24,800 in 2025, $24,800 in 2026, and $52,000 in 2027. Assume that the income tax rate in effect for all years is 25%.

a. What amount of deferred tax liability should appear in Fisk's December 31, 2024, balance sheet?

b. What amount of deferred tax liability should appear in Fisk's December 31, 2025, balance sheet?

c. What amount of deferred tax liability should appear in Fisk's December 31, 2026, balance sheet?

d. Where should the deferred tax liability accounts be classified in Fisk's balance sheets?

EXERCISES

LO10-1 Homework MBC

E10-31. Account for and Compare Leases Using Finance and Operating Lease Methods (FSET)
Core Co. leased a piece of manufacturing equipment from E-So Co. with the following terms:

Annual lease payment:	$550,000
Term of lease:	5 years
Interest rate:	4.0%
Lease commences on January 1, 2023	
Payments are made on December 31 of each year in the lease term	

a. Compute the value of the right-of-use asset and the lease liability on the date the lease commences.

b. Prepare a lease liability amortization schedule and right-of-use asset amortization schedule for the lessee.

c. Prepare a financial statement effects template to show the effects for Core Co. for January 1, 2023–December 31, 2024, if the lease is classified as a finance lease.

d. Prepare a financial statement effects template to show the effects for Core Co. for January 1, 2023–December 31, 2024, if the lease is classified as an operating lease.

e. Explain the differences in the operating lease and finance lease treatments for the financial accounting statements including showing the right-of-use asset value over the term of the lease.

LO10-1 Homework MBC

E10-32. Accounting for Leases Using Finance and Operating Lease Methods
Using the information from E10-31, prepare the journal entries for parts *c* and *d*.

LO10-2
Target
NYSE :: TGT

E10-33. Analyzing and Interpreting Pension Plan Benefit Note Disclosures
Target Corporation provides the following note relating to its retirement plans in its 2020 10-K report: (Note the disclosure is excerpted, simplified, and altered for simplicity.)

> **Defined Contribution Plans** Team members who meet eligibility requirements can participate in a defined contribution 401(k) plan by investing up to 80 percent of their eligible earnings, as limited by statute or regulation. We match 100 percent of each team member's contribution up to 5 percent of eligible earnings. Company match contributions are made to funds designated by the participant, none of which are based on Target common stock. Benefits expense related to these matching contributions was $321 million, $278 million, and $215 million as of January 2021, 2020, and 2019 respectively.

a. Does Target have a defined contribution or defined benefit pension plan? Explain.

b. How would Target account for its contributions to its retirement plan?

c. How is Target's obligation to its retirement plan reported on its balance sheet?

d. Do you see any problems for employees in Target's plan?

LO10-1
JetBlue Airways Corporation
NASDAQ :: JBLUE
Deere & Company, Inc.
NYSE :: DEL

E10-34. Analyzing Lease Disclosures Regarding the Adoption of the New Lease Standard and Analyzing Across Companies
JetBlue's balance sheet and discussion of the new lease standard is as follows in their 2018 10-K:

(in millions)	2018	2017
Total assets	$10,426	$9,781
Total liabilities	5,815	5,049
Total equity	4,611	4,732

In February 2016, the FASB issued ASU 2016-02, *Leases (Topic 842)* of the Codification, which requires lessees to recognize leases on the balance sheet and disclose key information about leasing arrangements. . . . Under the new standard, a lessee will recognize liabilities on the balance sheet, initially measured at the present value of the lease payments, and right-of-use (ROU) assets representing its right to use the underlying asset for the lease term. . . .
For JetBlue, we believe the most significant impact of the new standard relates to the recognition of new assets and liabilities on our balance sheet for operating leases related to our aircraft, engines, airport terminal space, airport hangars, office space, and other facilities and equipment. Upon adoption, we expect to recognize additional lease assets and lease liabilities ranging from $1.0 billion to $1.4 billion.

1. If JetBlue records $1.2 billion of the operating leases as both an asset and a liability on January 1, 2019, how much will their debt-to-equity ratio from December 31, 2018, change? (Assume no other changes for JetBlue.)
2. If an analyst wants to compare Delta, who adopted in the fourth quarter of 2018, to JetBlue, who is adopting in 2019, what would the analyst need to consider and do?

E10-35. Analyzing and Interpreting Lease Disclosures Prior to and Upon Conversion to the New Lease Standard **LO10-1, 4**

Verizon
NYSE :: VZ

Verizon Communications Inc. provides the following balance sheet (excerpted and abbreviated) and discussion and disclosure of leases:

Verizon Communications Inc. and Subsidiaries
2018 Annual Report
Consolidated Balance Sheet information (in millions)

	2018	2017
Total assets	$248,829	$257,143
Total liabilities	210,119	212,456
Total equity	54,710	44,687

The aggregate minimum rental commitments under noncancelable leases for the periods shown at December 31, 2018, are as follows:

Years	Operating Leases
2019	$ 4,043
2020	3,678
2021	3,272
2022	2,871
2023	2,522
Thereafter	10,207
Total minimum rental commitments	$26,593

The company also discloses the following in the summary of significant accounting policies:

In February 2016, the FASB issued this standard update to increase transparency and improve comparability by requiring entities to recognize assets and liabilities on the balance sheet for all leases, with certain exceptions. In addition, through improved disclosure requirements, the standard update will enable users of financial statements to further understand the amount, timing, and uncertainty of cash flows arising from leases. . . . Upon adoption of this standard, there will be a significant impact in our consolidated balance sheet as we expect to recognize a right-of-use asset and liability related to substantially all operating lease arrangements, which we currently estimate will range between $21.0 billion and $23.0 billion. Verizon's current operating lease portfolio included in this range is primarily comprised of network equipment including towers, distributed antenna systems, and small cells, real estate, connectivity mediums including dark fiber, and equipment leases.

a. As of the end of 2018, what asset amount is included on the balance sheet with respect to operating leases? What amount of liabilities?

b. What amount does Verizon state they need to add to the balance sheet as a right-of-use asset for operating leases and a lease liability for operating leases?

c. If Verizon would have adopted the new lease standard on December 31, 2018, and had determined that the right-of-use lease asset for operating leases and the liability amount were both $22 billion, how would the company's debt-to-equity ratio change? Assume no other changes on the balance sheet. (Note that they would not necessarily be the same amount; we are just assuming the same amount for simplicity.)

d. What do you predict will happen to ratios such as return-on-assets using reported numbers for both before and after the new standard is adopted?

E10-36. Analyzing Commitments and Contingencies **LO10-4**

Under Armour, Inc.
NYSE :: UA

Under Armour, Inc., provides the following disclosure in the notes to its 2020 financial statements:

7. Commitments and Contingencies
(excerpts only)

Sports Marketing and Other Commitments
Within the normal course of business, the Company enters into contractual commitments in order to promote the Company's brand and products. These commitments include sponsorship agreements with teams and athletes on the collegiate and professional levels, official supplier agreements, athletic event sponsorships, and other marketing commitments. The following is a schedule of the Company's future minimum payments under its sponsorship and other marketing agreements as of December 31, 2020, as well as significant sponsorship and other marketing agreements entered into during the period after December 31, 2020, through the date of this report:

(In thousands)	
2021	$106,727
2022	85,090
2023	69,454
2024	55,525
2025	32,370
2024 and thereafter	12,453
Total future minimum sponsorship and other payments	$361,619

The amounts listed above are the minimum compensation obligations and guaranteed royalty fees required to be paid under the Company's sponsorship and other marketing agreements. The amounts listed above do not include additional performance incentives and product supply obligations provided under certain agreements. It is not possible to determine how much the Company will spend on product supply obligations on an annual basis as contracts generally do not stipulate specific cash amounts to be spent on products. The amount of product provided to the sponsorships depends on many factors including general playing conditions, the number of sporting events in which they participate, and the Company's decisions regarding product and marketing initiatives. In addition, the costs to design, develop, source, and purchase the products furnished to the endorsers are incurred over a period of time and are not necessarily tracked separately from similar costs incurred for products sold to customers.

a. The above amounts of promised contractual payments to sponsored athletes are not reported on the financial statements. How might financial analysts think about these payments?

b. Compute an estimate of the present value of these payments, using Under Armour's interest rate on its debt, roughly 3%.

LO10-4 Apple Inc. NYSE :: AAPL Homework MBC

E10-37. Analyzing Commitments and Contingencies

Apple Inc. provides the following disclosure in the notes to its 2020 financial statements:

Other Off-Balance-Sheet Commitments

Unconditional Purchase Obligations
The Company has entered into certain off–balance sheet commitments that require the future purchase of goods or services ("unconditional purchase obligations"). The Company's unconditional purchase obligations primarily consist of payments for supplier arrangements, Internet and telecommunication services, intellectual property licenses, and content creation. Future payments under noncancelable unconditional purchase obligations having a remaining term in excess of one year as of September 26, 2020, are as follows (in millions):

2021	$3,476
2022	2,885
2023	1,700
2024	357
2025	104
Thereafter	130
Total	$8,652

Contingencies
The Company is subject to various legal proceedings and claims that have arisen in the ordinary course of business and that have not been fully resolved. The outcome of litigation is inherently uncertain. If one or more legal matters were resolved against the Company in a reporting period for amounts above management's expectations, the Company's financial condition and operating

continued

continued from previous page

results for that reporting period could be materially adversely affected. In the opinion of management, there was not at least a reasonable possibility the Company may have incurred a material loss, or a material loss greater than a recorded accrual, concerning loss contingencies for asserted legal and other claims, except for the following matters:

iOS Performance Management Cases

Various civil litigation matters have been filed in state and federal courts in the U.S. and in various international jurisdictions alleging violation of consumer protection laws, fraud, computer intrusion, and other causes of action related to the Company's performance management feature used in its iPhone operating systems, introduced to certain iPhones in iOS updates 10.2.1 and 11.2. The claims seek monetary damages and other non-monetary relief. On April 5, 2018, several U.S. federal actions were consolidated through a Multidistrict Litigation process into a single action in the U.S. District Court for the Northern District of California (the "Northern California District Court"). On February 28, 2020, the parties in the Multidistrict Litigation reached a settlement to resolve the U.S. federal and California state class actions. Under the terms of the settlement, which the Northern California District Court preliminarily approved in May 2020, the Company has agreed to pay up to $500 million in the aggregate to certain U.S. owners of iPhones if certain conditions are met. The final amount of the settlement will be determined based on the number of consumers who file valid claims and the attorneys' fee award. However, the Company has agreed to pay at least $310 million to settle the claims. In addition to civil litigation, the Company is also responding to governmental investigations and requests for information relating to the performance management feature. The Company continues to believe that its iPhones were not defective, that the performance management feature introduced with iOS updates 10.2.1 and 11.2 was intended to, and did, improve customers' user experience, and that the Company did not make any misleading statements or fail to disclose any material information. The Company has accrued its best estimate for the ultimate resolution of these matters.

1. Apple discloses that its rate of interest on 5-year debt securities is roughly 2.5%. Compute the present value of the future payments related to their off-balance-sheet purchase obligations. (Note: Assume that the "Thereafter" amount on the table is all paid in 2026.)
2. What would an analyst consider this to be—an asset, a liability, or equity?
3. Has Apple recorded a liability with respect to the litigation and contract for its iOS performance management cases? What amount is recorded, if any?

E10-38. Analyzing and Interpreting Pension Disclosure—Funded and Reported Amounts LO10-2

YUM! Brands, Inc., reports the following pension note disclosure in its 10-K report.

YUM! Brands
NYSE :: YUM

December 27 (in millions)	Pension Benefits 2020
Change in benefit obligation:	
Benefit obligation at beginning of year	$1,015
Service cost	8
Interest cost	35
Plan amendments	1
Special termination benefits	2
Benefits paid	(46)
Settlement payments	—
Actuarial (gain) loss	118
Benefit obligation at end of year	$1,133
Change in plan assets:	
Fair value of plan assets at beginning of year	$ 886
Actual return on plan assets	168
Employer contributions	6
Benefits paid	(46)
Fair value of plan assets at end of year	$1,014
Funded status at end of year	$ (119)

a. Describe what is meant by *service cost* and *interest cost.*
b. What is the source of funds to make payments to retirees?
c. Show the computation of the 2020 funded status for Yum.
d. What net pension amount is reported on its 2020 balance sheet?

LO10-2 **E10-39. Analyzing and Interpreting Pension Disclosures—Funded and Reported Amounts**

Verizon
NYSE :: VZ

Verizon Communications Inc. reports the following pension data in its 2020 10-K report.

At December 31 ($ millions)	**Pension 2020**
Change in Benefit Obligations:	
Beginning of year	$21,248
Service cost	305
Interest cost	505
Plan amendments	—
Actuarial (gain) loss, net	2,308
Benefits paid	(842)
Settlements paid	(1,288)
End of year	$22,236
Change in Plan Assets:	
Beginning of year	$19,451
Actual return on plan assets	2,750
Company contributions	57
Benefits paid	(842)
Settlements paid	(1,288)
End of year	$20,128
Funded Status—End of year	$ (2,108)

a. Describe what is meant by *service cost* and *interest cost*.
b. What is the source of funds to make payments to retirees?
c. Show the computation of Verizon's 2020 funded status.
d. What net pension amount is reported on its 2020 balance sheet?

LO10-3 **E10-40. Computing and Reporting Deferred Income Taxes (FSET)**

Early in January 2022, Oler, Inc., purchased equipment costing $12,800. The equipment had a 2-year useful life and was depreciated in the amount of $6,400 in 2022 and 2023. Oler deducted the entire $12,800 on its tax return in 2022. This difference was the only one between its tax return and its financial statements. Oler's income before depreciation expense and income taxes was $188,800 in 2022 and $196,000 in 2023. The tax rate in each year was 25%.

REQUIRED

a. What amount of deferred tax liability should Oler report in 2022 and 2023?
b. Prepare the entries to record income taxes for 2022 and 2023 using the financial statement effects template.
c. Repeat requirement *b* if in 2022 the U.S. enacts a permanent tax rate change to be effective in 2023; the rate will increase to 35%.

LO10-3 **E10-41. Computing and Reporting Deferred Income Taxes**

Using the information from E10-40, prepare the journal entries for (i.) part *b* and (ii.) part *c*.

LO10-3 **E10-42. Calculating and Reporting Deferred Income Taxes**

Bens' Corporation paid $18,000 on December 31, 2022, for equipment with a three-year useful life. The equipment will be depreciated in the amount of $6,000 each year. Bens' took the entire $18,000 as an expense in its tax return in 2022. Assume this is the only timing difference between the firm's books and its tax return. Bens' tax rate is 25%.

REQUIRED

a. What amount of deferred tax liability should appear in Bens' 12/31/2022 balance sheet?
b. Where in the balance sheet should the deferred tax liability appear?
c. What amount of deferred tax liability should appear in Bens' 12/31/2023 balance sheet?

LO10-3 **E10-43. Recording Income Tax Expense (FSET)**

Nike
NYSE :: NKE

Nike, Inc., reports the following tax information in the notes to its 2020 financial report.

Income before income taxes is as follows:

Year Ended May 31 (In millions)	2020	2019	2018
Income before income taxes:			
United States	$2,954	$ 593	$ 744
Foreign	(67)	4,208	3,581
Total income before income taxes	$2,887	$4,801	$4,325

The provision for income taxes is as follows:

Year Ended May 31 (In millions)	2020	2019	2018
Current:			
United States			
Federal	$(109)	$ 74	$1,167
State	81	56	45
Foreign	756	608	533
Total current	728	738	1,745
Deferred:			
United States			
Federal	(231)	(33)	595
State	(47)	(9)	25
Foreign	(102)	76	27
Total deferred	(380)	34	647
Total income tax	$348	$772	$2,392

Nike also states the following:

> The effective tax rate for the fiscal year ended May 31, 2020, was lower than the effective tax rate for the fiscal year ended May 31, 2019, due to increased benefits from discrete items such as stock-based compensation. The foreign earnings rate impact shown above for the fiscal year ended May 31, 2020, includes withholding taxes of 6.5% and held for sale accounting items of 2.9%, offset by a benefit for statutory rate differences and other items of 3.5%. The foreign derived intangible income benefit reflects U.S. tax benefits introduced by the Tax Act for companies serving foreign markets. This benefit became available to the Company as a result of a restructuring of its intellectual property interests. Income tax audit and contingency reserves reflect benefits associated with the modification of the treatment of certain research and development expenditures of 2.9% offset by an increase related to the resolution of an audit by the U.S. Internal Revenue Service ("IRS") and other matters of 1.5%. Included in other is the deferral of income tax effects related to intra-entity transfers of inventory of 2.3% and other items of 0.6%.

a. Record Nike's provision for income taxes for 2020 using the financial statement effects template.

b. Explain how the provision for income taxes affects Nike's financial statements.

c. Calculate and compare Nike's effective tax rate for 2020, 2019, and 2018.

E10-44. Recording Income Tax Expense — LO10-3 (Homework MBC)

Using the information from E10-43, record Nike's provision for income taxes for 2020 using journal entries.

E10-45. Recording Income Tax Expense (FSET) — LO10-3 (Homework MBC)

Procter & Gamble, Inc. reports the following tax information in its 2020 financial report.

Procter & Gamble, Inc.
NYSE :: PG

Year Ended June 30	2018	2019	2020
Current:			
Federal and state	$4,178	$1,255	$1,558
Foreign	1,131	1,259	1,769
Total	5,309	2,514	3,327
Deferred:			
Federal and state	(1,989)	(296)	39
Foreign	145	(115)	(635)
Total	(1,844)	(411)	(596)
Provisions for income taxes	$3,465	$2,103	$2,731

a. Record P&G's provision for income taxes for 2020 using the financial statement effects template.

b. Explain how the provision for income affects P&G's financial statements.

LO10-3 Homework MBC **E10-46. Recording Income Tax Expense**
Using the information from E10-45, record P&G's provision for income taxes for 2020 using journal entries.

PROBLEMS

LO10-1 United Continental Holdings, Inc. NASDAQ :: UAL **P10-47. Analyzing and Interpreting Leases**
United Continental Holdings, Inc., did not adopt the new lease standard in 2018 but provides the following disclosure its 2018 10-K report ($ millions).

Consolidated Balance Sheets as of December 31

	As Reported		New Lease Standard Adjustments		As Adjusted	
	2018	2017	2018	2017	2018	2017
Operating property and equipment:						
Other property and equipment (owned)	$ 7,919	$ 6,946	$(1,041)	$(922)	$ 6,878	$ 6,024
Less-accumulated depreciation and amortization (owned)	(12,760)	(11,159)	140	92	(12,620)	(11,067)
Flight equipment (finance leases)[a]	1,029	1,151	(37)	(211)	992	940
Less-accumulated amortization	(654)	(777)	8	169	(646)	(608)
Operating lease assets						
Flight equipment	—	—	2,380	3,102	2,380	3,102
Other property and equipment	—	—	2,882	2,975	2,882	2,975
Current liabilities:						
Current maturities of finance leases[a]	149	128	(26)	(50)	123	78
Current maturities of operating leases	—	—	719	949	719	949
Other	619	576	(66)	(58)	553	518
Long-term obligations under finance leases[a]	1,134	996	(910)	(766)	224	230
Long-term obligations under operating leases	—	—	5,276	5,789	5,276	5,789

[a] Finance leases, under the New Lease Standard, are the equivalent of capital leases under Topic 840.

> The adoption of the New Lease Standard primarily resulted in the recording of assets and obligations of our operating leases on our consolidated balance sheets. Certain amounts recorded for prepaid and accrued rent associated with historical operating leases were reclassified to the newly captioned Operating lease assets in the consolidated balance sheets. Also, certain leases designated under Topic 840 as owned assets and capitalized finance leases will not be considered assets under the New Lease Standard and will be removed from the consolidated balance sheets, along with the related lease liability.

a. What is the amount United discloses that it would have capitalized for operating leases as right-of-use lease assets for the year ended December 31, 2018?

b. What is the amount of additional liability United discloses that it would have recorded for operating leases had United adopted the new lease standard in 2018?

c. What is the amount of asset under the new lease standard for finance leases? For the lease liability related to finance leases?

d. Why do you think the amount of operating leases is so much greater than finance leases?

e. United reported total assets of $44,792 million, total liabilities of $34,797 million, and total shareholders' equity of $9,995 million. Net income for the year was reported as $2,129 for the year and is essentially unchanged as a result of the new lease standard. Compute the reported return-on-assets and debt-to-equity ratios. Compute the ratios adjusted for the new lease standard, only taking into account the changes for operating leases (ignore all other changes).

LO10-1 American Airlines Group, Inc. NASDAQ :: AAL Homework MBC **P10-48. Analyzing Lease Disclosures**
American Airlines Group, Inc., provides the following disclosures in the notes to their 2020 financial statements (excerpted for brevity):

4. Leases

American leases certain aircraft and engines, including aircraft under capacity purchase agreements. As of December 31, 2020, American had 641 leased aircraft, with remaining terms ranging from less than one year to 12 years.

Supplemental balance sheet information related to leases was as follows (in millions, except lease term and discount rate):

	December 31	
	2020	2019
Operating leases:		
Operating lease ROU assets	$7,994	$8,694
Current operating lease liabilities	$1,641	$1,695
Noncurrent operating lease liabilities	6,739	7,388
Total operating lease liabilities	$8,380	$9,083
Finance leases:		
Property and equipment, at cost	$1,021	$ 954
Accumulated amortization	(539)	(447)
Property and equipment, net	$ 482	$ 507
Current finance lease liabilities	$ 100	$ 112
Noncurrent finance lease liabilities	472	558
Total finance lease liabilities	$ 572	$ 670

The components of lease expense were as follows (in millions):

	Year Ended December 31		
	2020	2019	2018
Operating lease cost	$1,943	$2,012	$1,889
Finance lease cost:			
Amortization of assets	92	79	78
Interest on lease liabilities	38	43	48
Variable lease cost	1,786	2,542	2,353
Total net lease cost	$3,859	$4,676	$4,368

a. What is the right-of-use asset for operating leases as of the end of 2020?

b. What is the net asset recorded for finance leases?

c. What is the lease liability balance for operating leases as of the end of 2020? What does this amount represent?

d. What is the amount of amortization expense recorded in 2020 for finance leases? For operating leases?

e. What is the amount of interest expense recorded in 2020 for finance leases? For operating leases?

P10-49. Analyze Commitment and Contingency Disclosures

LO10-4

Cisco Systems, Inc.
NASDAQ :: CSCO
Homework MBC

Cisco Systems, Inc., reports the following in the Commitments and Contingencies note to their 10-K for the year ended July 2020.

Purchase Commitments with Contract Manufacturers and Suppliers

We purchase components from a variety of suppliers and use several contract manufacturers to provide manufacturing services for our products. During the normal course of business, in order to manage manufacturing lead times and help ensure adequate component supply, we enter into agreements with contract manufacturers and suppliers that either allow them to procure inventory based upon criteria as defined by us or establish the parameters defining our requirements. A significant portion of our reported purchase commitments arising from these agreements consists of firm, noncancelable, and unconditional commitments. Certain of these purchase commitments

continued

continued from previous page

with contract manufacturers and suppliers relate to arrangements to secure long-term pricing for certain product components for multi-year periods. In certain instances, these agreements allow us the option to cancel, reschedule, and adjust our requirements based on our business needs prior to firm orders being placed. As of July 25, 2020, and July 27, 2019, we had total purchase commitments for inventory of $4.4 billion and $5.0 billion, respectively.

We record a liability for firm, noncancelable, and unconditional purchase commitments for quantities in excess of our future demand forecasts consistent with the valuation of our excess and obsolete inventory. As of July 25, 2020, and July 27, 2019, the liability for these purchase commitments was $141 million and $129 million, respectively, and was included in other current liabilities.

a. What effect does the use of contract manufacturers have on Cisco's balance sheet?

b. Assuming an interest rate of 4% and payments due in 1 year of $3.4 billion and in years 2-5, $250 million, what is the present value of these commitments as of July 2020?

c. What amount does Cisco state that it has accrued as a liability as of July 2020?

LO10-2 **P10-50. Analyzing and Interpreting Pension Disclosures**

Homework MBC

Hoopes Corporation's December 31, 2022, 10-K report has the following disclosures related to its retirement plans.

The following table provides a reconciliation of the changes in the pension plans' benefit obligations and fair value of assets over the two-year period ended December 31, 2022, and a statement of the funded status as of December 31, 2022 and 2021 (in millions):

	Pension Plans	
(in millions)	**2022**	**2021**
Changes in Projected Benefit Obligation ("PBO")		
PBO at beginning of year	$17,381	$13,260
Service cost	625	500
Interest cost	1,080	988
Actuarial (gain) loss	2,250	3,128
Benefits paid	(562)	(469)
Other	72	(26)
PBO at end of year	$20,846	$17,381
Change in Plan Assets		
Fair value of plan assets at beginning of year	$15,954	$12,974
Actual return on plan assets	2,910	2,393
Company contributions	668	1,080
Benefits paid	(562)	(469)
Other	38	(24)
Fair value of plan assets at end of year	$19,008	$15,954

Net periodic benefit cost for the three years ended December 31 were as follows (in millions):

	Pension Plans		
(in millions)	**2022**	**2021**	**2020**
Service cost	$ 625	$500	$ 599
Interest cost	1,080	988	958
Expected return on plan assets	(1,274)	(1,146)	(1,271)
Recognized actuarial (gains) losses and other	221	28	(73)
Net periodic benefit cost	$ 652	$370	$ 213

Weighted-average actuarial assumptions for our primary U.S. pension plans, which represent substantially all of our PBO, are as follows:

continued

continued from previous page

(in millions)	Pension Plans 2022	2021	2020
Discount rate used to determine benefit obligation	5.76%	6.37%	7.68%
Rate of increase in future compensation levels used to determine benefit obligation	4.58	4.63	4.42
Expected long-term rate of return on assets	8.00	8.00	8.50

REQUIRED

a. How much pension expense (revenue) does Hoopes report in its 2022 income statement?

b. Hoopes reports a $1,274 million expected return on plan assets as an offset to 2022 pension expense. Approximately, how is this amount computed? What is the actual gain or loss realized on its 2022 plan assets? What is the purpose of using this estimated amount instead of the actual gain or loss?

c. What factors affected its 2022 pension liability? What factors affected its 2022 plan assets?

d. What does the term *funded status* mean? What is the funded status of the 2022 Hoopes retirement plans? What amount of asset or liability does Hoopes report on its 2022 balance sheet relating to its retirement plans?

e. Hoopes decreased its discount rate from 6.37% to 5.76% in 2022. What effect(s) does this have on its balance sheet and its income statement?

f. Hoopes changed its estimate of expected annual wage increases used to determine its defined benefit obligation in 2022. What effect(s) does this change have on its financial statements? In general, how does such a change affect income?

P10-51. Analyzing and Interpreting Pension Disclosures—Funded and Reported Amounts

LO10-2

Johnson and Johnson NYSE :: JNJ

Homework MBC

Johnson and Johnson reports the following pension note disclosure as part of its 2020 10-K report.

(in millions)	Pension Benefits 2020
Change in Benefit Obligation:	
Projected benefit obligation—beginning of year	$37,188
Service cost	1,380
Interest cost	955
Plan participant contributions	61
Amendments	(1,780)
Actuarial (gains) losses	5,716
Divestitures and acquisitions	(88)
Curtailments, settlements, and restructuring	(24)
Benefits paid from plan	(1,111)
Effect of exchange rates	1,003
Projected benefit obligation—end of year	$43,300
Change in Plan Assets:	
Plan assets at fair value—beginning of year	$32,201
Actual return on plan assets	5,524
Company contributions	870
Plan participant contributions	61
Settlements	(13)
Divestitures and acquisitions	(84)
Benefits paid from plan assets	(1,111)
Effect of exchange rates	747
Plan assets at fair value—end of year	$38,195
Funded status—end of year	$ (5,105)

a. Describe what is meant by *service cost* and *interest cost.*

b. What is the actual return on pension investments in 2020?

c. Provide an example under which an "actuarial loss," such as the $5,716 million loss that Johnson and Johnson reports in 2020, might arise.

d. What is the source of funds to make payments to retirees?

e. How much cash did Johnson and Johnson contribute to its pension plans in 2020?

f. How much cash did the company pay to retirees in 2020?

g. Show the computation of its 2020 funded status.

h. What net pension amount is reported on its 2020 balance sheet?

LO10-3 **P10-52. Interpreting the Income Tax Expense Disclosure**

Cummins, Inc. NYSE :: CMI Homework MBC

Cummins, Inc., reports the following tax information in its fiscal 2020 financial report.

The provision for income taxes by taxing jurisdiction and by significant component consisted of the following in millions of dollars:

	2020	2019	2018
Current:			
U.S. federal and state	$ 162	$ 288	$ 303
Foreign	358	282	348
Impact of tax law changes	—	—	153
Total current income tax expense	$ 520	$ 570	$ 804
Deferred:			
U.S. federal and state	$ 2	$ (32)	$ (71)
Foreign	22	28	(26)
Impact of tax law changes	(17)	—	(141)
Total deferred income tax expense (benefit)	7	(4)	(238)
Income tax expense	$ 527	$ 566	$ 566
Earnings before taxes on the income statement	$2,338	$2,834	$2,753

REQUIRED

a. What amount of tax expense is reported in Cummins' 2020 income statement? In 2019? In 2018? How much of each year's income tax expense is current tax expense, and how much is deferred tax expense?

b. Compute Cummins' effective tax rate for each year.

c. Assume that Cummins' deferred tax in 2020 is due to deferred tax liabilities. Provide one possible example that would be consistent with this situation.

LO10-3 **P10-53. Calculating and Reporting Income Tax Expense (FSET)**

Homework MBC

Lynch Company began operations in 2022. The company reported $36,000 of depreciation expense on its income statement in 2022 and $39,000 in 2023. On its tax returns, Lynch deducted $48,000 for depreciation in 2022 and $55,500 in 2023. The 2023 tax return shows a tax obligation (liability) of $18,000 based on a 25% tax rate.

REQUIRED

a. Determine the temporary difference between the book value of depreciable assets and the tax basis of these assets at the end of 2022 and 2023.

b. Calculate the deferred tax liability for each year.

c. Calculate the income tax expense for 2023.

d. Record the company's provision for income taxes for 2023 using the financial statement effects template.

LO10-3 **P10-54. Calculating and Reporting Income Tax Expense**

Homework MBC

Using the information from P10-53, prepare the journal entry to record income tax expense for 2023 and post the entry to the appropriate T-accounts.

LO10-3 **P10-55. Calculating and Reporting Income Tax Expense (FSET)**

Homework MBC

Carter Inc. began operations in 2022. The company reported $104,000 of depreciation expense on its 2022 income statement and $102,400 in 2023. Carter Inc. deducted $112,000 for depreciation on its tax return in 2022 and $97,600 in 2023. The company reports a tax obligation of $36,120 for 2023 based on a tax rate of 25%.

REQUIRED

a. Determine the temporary difference between the book value of depreciable assets and the tax basis of these assets at the end of 2022 and 2023.

b. Calculate the deferred tax liability at the end of each year.

c. Calculate the income tax expense for 2023.

d. Record the company's provision for income taxes for 2023 using the financial statement effects template.

P10-56. Calculating and Reporting Income Tax Expense LO10-3 Homework MBC

Using the information from P10-55, prepare the journal entry to record income tax expense for 2023 and post the entry to the appropriate T-accounts.

P10-57. Computing and Reporting Deferred Income Taxes LO10-3 Macy's, Inc. NASDAQ :: M

Macy's, Inc., reported the following in its fiscal 2017 annual report:

On December 22, 2017, H.R. 1 was enacted into law. This new tax legislation, among other things, reduced the U.S. federal corporate tax rate from 35% to 21% effective January 1, 2018.

In applying the impacts of the new tax legislation to its 2017 income tax provision, the Company remeasured its deferred tax assets and liabilities based on the rates at which they are expected to reverse in the future, which is generally a 21% federal tax rate and its related impact on the state tax rates. The resulting impact was the recognition of an income tax benefit of $571 million in the fourth quarter of 2017. In addition, applying the new U.S. federal corporate tax rate of 21% on January 1, 2018, resulted in a federal income tax statutory rate of 33.7% in 2017. Combining the impacts on the Company's current income tax provision and the remeasurement of its deferred tax balances, the Company's effective income tax rate was a benefit of 1.9% in 2017.

The tax effects of temporary differences that give rise to significant portions of the deferred tax assets and deferred tax liabilities are as follows:

(millions)	Feb. 3, 2018	Jan. 28, 2017
Deferred tax assets		
Postemployment and postretirement benefits	$ 188	$ 405
Accrued liabilities accounted for on a cash basis for tax purposes	218	379
Long-term debt	25	63
Unrecognized state tax benefits and accrued interest	39	76
State operating loss and credit carryforwards	101	79
Other	165	347
Valuation allowance	(65)	(36)
Total deferred tax assets	671	1,313
Deferred tax liabilities		
Excess of book basis over tax basis of property and equipment	(923)	(1,381)
Merchandise inventories	(389)	(604)
Intangible assets	(276)	(380)
Other	(205)	(391)
Total deferred tax liabilities	(1,793)	(2,756)
Net deferred tax liability	$(1,122)	$(1,443)

a. What was the amount of income tax expense or benefit that Macy's reported related to revaluing deferred tax assets and liabilities to the new, lower tax rate?

b. Explain why Macy's reported an income tax *benefit* when it revalued its deferred income tax liabilities and deferred income tax assets to the new, lower tax rate.

CASES AND PROJECTS

C10-58. Analyzing and Interpreting Pension Disclosures LO10-2 DuPont De Nemours, Inc. (abbreviated "DuPont") NYSE :: DD

DuPont De Nemours, Inc. (abbreviated "DuPont") provides the following disclosures in its 10-K report relating to its pension plans. (Footnotes to the tables excluded for brevity.)

Net Periodic Benefit Costs for All Significant Plans for the Year Ended December 31	**Defined Benefit Pension Plans**		
In millions	**2020**	**2019**	**2018**
Net Periodic Benefit Costs:			
Service cost	$ 70	$ 184	$ 651
Interest cost	57	630	1,638
Expected return on plan assets	(110)	(988)	(2,846)
Amortization of prior service credit	(5)	(9)	(24)
Amortization of unrecognized loss (gain)	16	128	649
Curtailment/settlement/other	9	—	(10)
Net periodic benefit costs (credits)—Total	$37	$(55)	$58
Less: Net periodic benefit (credits) costs—discontinued operations	—	(45)	90
Net periodic benefit costs (credits)—Continuing operations	$ 37	$ (10)	$ (32)
Changes in plan assets and benefit obligations recognized in other comprehensive loss (income):			
Net loss (gain)	$ 99	$ 350	$ 1,490
Prior service (credit) cost	—	(65)	34
Amortization of prior service credit	5	3	24
Amortization of unrecognized (loss) gain	(16)	(7)	(649)
Curtailment loss	(4)	(2)	—
Settlement loss	(9)	(2)	2
Effect of foreign exchange rates	21	(2)	1
Total recognized in other comprehensive loss (income)	$ 96	$ 275	$902
Noncontrolling interest	$ 2	$ —	$ —
Total recognized in net periodic benefit costs (credits) and other comprehensive loss (income)	$ 131	$ 265	$ 870

Change in Projected Benefit Obligations of All Plans	**Defined Benefit Pension Plans**	
In millions	**2020**	**2019**
Change in projected benefit obligations:		
Benefit obligations at beginning of year	$4,784	$ 53,014
Service cost	70	184
Interest cost	57	630
Plan participants' contributions	11	11
Actuarial changes in assumptions and experience	298	515
Benefits paid	(268)	(1,247)
Plan amendments	—	(76)
Acquisitions/divestitures/other	—	20
Effect of foreign exchange rates	347	31
Termination benefits/curtailment cost/settlements	(4)	(4)
Spin-off of Dow	—	(29,285)
Spin-off of Corteva	—	(19,009)
Benefit obligations at end of year	$5,295	$ 4,784

Change in Plan Assets and Funded Status of All Plans	**Defined Benefit Pension Plans**	
In millions	**2020**	**2019**
Change in plan assets:		
Fair value of plan assets at beginning of year	$3,757	$ 41,462
Actual return on plan assets	309	1,191
Employer contributions	98	697
Plan participants' contributions	11	11
Benefits paid	(268)	(1,247)
Acquisitions/divestitures/other	—	10
Effect of foreign exchange rates	251	60
Spin-off of Dow	—	(22,626)
Spin-off of Corteva	—	(15,801)
Fair value of plan assets at end of year	$4,158	$ 3,757

Weighted Average Assumptions for All Pension Plans	Benefit Obligations at December 31	
	2020	2019
Discount rate	0.84%	1.21%
Interest crediting rate for applicable benefits	1.25%	1.25%
Rate of compensation increase	3.09%	3.14%
Expected return on plan assets	N/A	N/A

REQUIRED

a. How much pension expense (revenue) does DuPont report in its 2020 income statement?

b. DuPont reports a $110 million expected return on plan assets as an offset to 2020 pension expense. Estimate the rate of return DuPont expected to earn on its plan assets in 2020.

c. What factors affected its 2020 pension liability? What factors affected its 2020 plan assets?

d. What does the term "funded status" mean? What is the funded status of the 2020 DuPont retirement plans at the end of 2020? What amount of asset or liability should DuPont report on its 2020 balance sheet relating to its retirement plans?

e. DuPont changed its discount rate from 1.21% to 0.84% in 2020. What effect(s) does this change have on its balance sheet and its income statement?

f. Suppose DuPont increased its estimate of expected returns on plan assets in 2021. What effect(s) would this increase have on its income statement? Explain.

g. DuPont provides us with its weighted-average discount rate. The company has manufacturing operations in about 40 countries and has roughly 34,000 employees all over the world. Would you expect that the discount rate differed in the United States from the average rate outside the United States? Explain. What would you expect for future compensation levels?

C10-59. Interpreting Finance and Operating Leases (FSET)

LO10-1, 4
Target Corporation
NYSE: TGT
Homework MBC

Target Corporation disclosed the following in the notes to their fiscal year 2020 10-K.

Leases (millions)	Classification	Jan. 30, 2021	Feb. 1, 2020
Assets			
Operating	Operating lease assets	$2,227	$2,236
Finance	Buildings and improvements, net of accumulated depreciation[(a)]	1,504	1,180
Total leased assets		$3,731	$3,416
Liabilities			
Current			
Operating	Accrued and other current liabilities	$ 211	$ 200
Finance	Current portion of long-term debt and other borrowings	88	67
Noncurrent			
Operating	Noncurrent operating lease liabilities	2,218	2,275
Finance	Long-term debt and other borrowings	1,766	1,303
Total lease liabilities		$4,283	$3,845

Note: We use our incremental borrowing rate based on the information available at commencement date in determining the present value of lease payments.

[(a)] Finance lease assets are recorded net of accumulated amortization of $550 million and $441 million as of January 30, 2021, and February 1, 2020, respectively.

Lease Cost (millions)	Classification	2020	2019	2018
Operating lease cost[(a)]	SG&A expenses	$332	$287	$251
Finance lease cost				
Amortization of leased assets	Depreciation and amortization[(b)]	105	82	65
Interest on lease liabilities	Net interest expense	62	51	42
Sublease income[(c)]	Other revenue	(11)	(13)	(11)
Net lease cost		$484	$407	$347

[(a)] 2020 includes $44 million of short-term leases and variable lease costs. Short-term and variable lease costs were insignificant for 2019 and 2018.

[(b)] Supply chain-related amounts are included in Cost of Sales.

[(c)] Sublease income excludes rental income from owned properties of $48 million, $48 million, and $47 million for 2020, 2019, and 2018, which is included in Other Revenue.

Maturity of Lease Liabilities (millions)	Operating Leases[(a)]	Finance Leases[(b)]	Total
2021	$ 289	$ 152	$ 441
2022	290	159	449
2023	283	158	441
2024	269	155	424
2025	256	154	410
After 2025	1,694	1,687	3,381
Total lease payments	$3,081	$2,465	$5,546
Less: Interest	652	611	
Present value of lease liabilities	$2,429	$1,854	

[(a)] Operating lease payments include $847 million related to options to extend lease terms that are reasonably certain of being exercised and exclude $231 million of legally binding minimum lease payments for leases signed but not yet commenced.

[(b)] Finance lease payments include $160 million related to options to extend lease terms that are reasonably certain of being exercised and exclude $1.1 billion of legally binding minimum lease payments for leases signed but not yet commenced.

a. What is the right-of-use asset for operating leases as of the end of fiscal 2020?
b. What is the net asset recorded for finance leases at the end of fiscal 2020?
c. What is the lease liability balance for operating leases as of the end of fiscal 2020? What does this amount represent?
d. What is the amount of amortization expense recorded in 2020 for finance leases?
e. What is the amount of interest expense recorded in 2020 for finance leases?
f. What is recorded on the income statement for operating leases?
g. Assume the lease payment for 2020 for finance leases is $125 million. Report the entries for 2020 (year ended February 2, 2021) for finance leases, using the financial statement effects template.
h. Discuss the implications of the different line items on the income statement for expensing lease costs for both types of leases that Target discloses.
i. Target has reported total assets for 2020 (year ended January 30, 2021) of $51,248, total liabilities of $36,808, and equity of $14,440. Explain the effect on debt-to-equity from having the operating leases "on-balance sheet."

LO10-1 Homework MBC

C10-60. Interpreting Finance and Operating Leases
Using the information from C10-59, prepare the journal entries for part *g*.

LO10-3 Williams-Sonoma NYSE :: WSM Homework MBC

C10-61. Interpreting Income Tax Disclosures (FSET)
The following information is taken from Williams-Sonoma, Inc.'s 10-K.

Note D: Income Taxes

The components of earnings before income taxes, by tax jurisdiction, are as follows:

	Fiscal Year Ended		
(in thousands)	Fiscal 2020 (52 weeks)	Fiscal 2019 (52 weeks)	Fiscal 2018 (53 weeks)
United States	$773,317	$353,215	$333,594
Foreign	121,149	103,806	95,653
Total	$894,466	$457,021	$429,247

continued

continued from previous page

The provision for income taxes consists of the following:

(in thousands)	Fiscal Year Ended		
	Fiscal 2020 (52 weeks)	**Fiscal 2019 (52 weeks)**	**Fiscal 2018 (53 weeks)**
Current			
Federal	$171,821	$76,873	$43,745
State	39,498	14,205	15,357
Foreign	15,494	12,438	12,822
Total current	226,813	103,516	71,924
Deferred			
Federal	(7,575)	(606)	23,507
State	(5,997)	(870)	1,562
Foreign	511	(1,081)	(1,430)
Total deferred	(13,061)	(2,557)	23,639
Total provision	$213,752	$100,959	$95,563

In thousands	**Jan. 31, 2021**	**Feb. 2, 2020**
Deferred tax (liabilities)		
Operating lease liabilities	$ 319,599	$ 347,693
Compensation	20,852	14,350
Merchandise inventories	20,631	22,311
Gift cards	19,345	19,520
Accrued liabilities	13,451	8,440
Stock-based compensation	9,926	9,860
Loyalty rewards	9,609	5,252
Executive deferred compensation	8,647	7,543
State taxes	7,460	7,546
Federal and state net operating loss	2,609	3,443
Operating lease right-of-use assets	(283,856)	(309,801)
Deferred lease incentives	(31,672)	(46,701)
Property and equipment	(54,724)	(37,309)
Other	(317)	(3,277)
Valuation allowance	(2,819)	(3,648)
Total deferred tax assets, net	$ 58,741	$ 45,222

As of January 31, 2021, we had $38,696,000 of gross unrecognized tax benefits, of which $34,026,000 would, if recognized, affect the effective tax rate.

We accrue interest and penalties related to unrecognized tax benefits in the provision for income taxes. As of January 31, 2021, and February 2, 2020, our accruals for the payment of interest and penalties totaled $8,225,000 and $7,251,000, respectively.

Due to the potential resolution of tax issues, it is reasonably possible that the balance of our gross unrecognized tax benefits could decrease within the next twelve months by a range of $0 to $15,800,000.

We file income tax returns in the U.S. and foreign jurisdictions. We are subject to examination by the tax authorities in these jurisdictions. Our U.S. federal taxable years for which the statute of limitations has not expired are fiscal years 2017 to 2020. Substantially all material states, local and foreign jurisdictions' statutes of limitations are closed for taxable years prior to 2017.

REQUIRED

a. What amount of income tax expense did Williams-Sonoma report for the year ended January 31, 2021?

b. Calculate Williams-Sonoma's effective tax rate for each year reported. In addition, calculate the rate of U.S. federal taxes on U.S. income in the fiscal year ended January 31, 2021.

c. Williams-Sonoma reported income taxes payable of $69,476,000 in its January 31, 2021, balance sheet, and $22,501,000 at February 2, 2020. What amount of income taxes did it pay in cash during the fiscal year ended January 31, 2021?[17]

d. Report the entry to record income tax expense for the fiscal year ended January 31, 2021, using the financial statement effects template.

e. The company reported a net book value of property, plant, and equipment of $873,894,000 on January 31, 2021. Given a tax rate of 21% (assume they are all in the U.S.), what is an estimate of the tax basis of these assets on that date?

f. The company reported $34,988,000 in other long-term liabilities related to deferred compensation obligations on its January 31, 2021, balance sheet. The company provided the following explanation of this asset in Note H to its 10-K:

> We also have a nonqualified executive deferred compensation plan that provides supplemental retirement income benefits for a select group of management. This plan permits eligible employees to make salary and bonus deferrals that are 100% vested. We have an unsecured obligation to pay in the future the value of the deferred compensation adjusted to reflect the performance, whether positive or negative, of selected investment measurement options chosen by each participant during the deferral period.

Explain how this expense results in a temporary difference between tax and financial reporting.

g. Williams-Sonoma has a valuation allowance listed in its schedule of deferred tax assets and liabilities. Briefly and in general explain what a valuation allowance is and how it affects deferred taxes and reported income.

h. In fiscal year 2017, Williams-Sonoma stated that the company recorded a $28.3 million additional tax expense for the remeasurement of deferred tax assets. This remeasurement is related to the drop in the U.S. statutory tax rate of 33.9% to a lower rate of 21%. Explain what this is and why the company had to record this expense.

LO10-3 Homework MBC

C10-62. Interpreting Income Tax Disclosures

Using the information from C10-61, prepare the journal entries for part *d*.

LO10-5

Alphabet Inc.
NASDAQ :: GOOG

C10-63. Interpreting Income Tax Disclosures

Alphabet Inc. reported the following in Note 14 to its 2020 10-K report:

Note 14. Income Taxes

Income from continuing operations before income taxes consists of the following (in millions):

	Year Ended December 31		
	2018	2019	2020
Domestic operations	$15,779	$16,426	$37,576
Foreign operations	19,134	23,199	10,506
Total	$34,913	$39,625	$48,082

	Year Ended December 31		
	2018	2019	2020
Current:			
Federal and state	$2,153	$2,424	$4,789
Foreign	1,251	2,713	1,687
Total	3,404	5,137	6,476
Deferred:			
Federal and state	907	286	1,552
Foreign	(134)	(141)	(215)
Total	773	145	1,337
Provision for income taxes	$4,177	$5,282	$7,813

continued

[17] For this problem, assume a simple case. The complicating factors that would change the answer are beyond the scope of this text. For those readers aware of these complicating factors, assume there are no acquisitions of other companies during the year and that Williams-Sonoma has no unrecognized tax benefits.

continued from previous page

Tax Contingencies

We are subject to income taxes in the United States (federal and state) and numerous foreign jurisdictions. Significant judgment is required in evaluating our tax positions and determining our provision for income taxes. During the ordinary course of business, there are many transactions and calculations for which the ultimate tax determination is uncertain. We establish reserves for tax-related uncertainties based on estimates of whether, and the extent to which, additional taxes will be due. These reserves are established when we believe that certain positions might be challenged despite our belief that our tax return positions are fully supportable. We adjust these reserves in light of changing facts and circumstances, such as the outcome of tax audits. The provision for income taxes includes the impact of reserve provisions and changes to reserves that are considered appropriate.

The reconciliation of our tax contingencies is as follows (in millions):

	2018	2019	2020
Gross tax contingencies—January 1	$2,309	$3,414	$3,923
Gross increases to tax positions in prior periods	164	216	88
Gross decreases to tax positions in prior periods	(90)	(181)	(465)
Gross increases to current period tax positions	1,088	707	507
Settlements with tax authorities	(36)	(207)	(1,207)
Lapse of statute of limitations	(21)	(26)	(26)
Gross tax contingencies—December 31	$3,414	$3,923	$2,820

We are under examination, or may be subject to examination, by the Internal Revenue Service ("IRS") for the calendar year 2013 and thereafter. These examinations may lead to ordinary course adjustments or proposed adjustments to our taxes or our net operating losses with respect to years under examination as well as subsequent periods. During Q3 2020, we resolved the audits of tax years 2007 through 2012 with the IRS for amounts that were materially consistent with our accrual. In October 2014, the European Commission opened a formal investigation to examine whether decisions by the tax authorities in Luxembourg with regard to the corporate income tax paid by certain of our subsidiaries comply with European Union rules on state aid. On October 4, 2017, the European Commission announced its decision that determinations by the tax authorities in Luxembourg did not comply with European Union rules on state aid. Based on that decision the European Commission announced an estimated recovery amount of approximately €250 million, plus interest, for the period May 2006 through June 2014, and ordered Luxembourg tax authorities to calculate the actual amount of additional taxes subject to recovery. Luxembourg computed an initial recovery amount, consistent with the European Commission's decision, that we deposited into escrow in March 2018, subject to adjustment pending conclusion of all appeals. In December 2017, Luxembourg appealed the European Commission's decision. In May 2018, we appealed. We believe the European Commission's decision to be without merit and will continue to defend ourselves vigorously in this matter. We are also subject to taxation in various states and other foreign jurisdictions including China, Germany, India, Japan, Luxembourg, and the United Kingdom. We are under, or may be subject to, audit or examination and additional assessments by the relevant authorities in respect of these particular jurisdictions primarily for 2009 and thereafter.

REQUIRED

a. Compute Alphabet's effective tax rate for each year presented. Also, compute Alphabet's domestic tax rate (federal plus state) and its foreign tax rate on income from foreign operations.

b. What is Alphabet's amount of unrecognized tax benefit at the end of 2020? Briefly describe what this is and how it is shown in the company's income statement and balance sheet.

SOLUTIONS TO REVIEW PROBLEMS

Review 10-1

The present value of the lease payments is $224,755, computed as $32,000 × 7.02358 (from Appendix A, Table A-3) or computed using a financial calculator or Excel. At the commencement of the finance lease, The Gap would record a Right-of-Use Asset for the finance lease and a Finance Lease Liability.

The amortization table for the loan is as follows:

Amortization Table for a Lease Liability*

A	B	C	D	E	F
Year	Beginning of Year Lease Liability	Interest Expense (B × 7%)	Payment	Principal Payment (D – C)	Ending-Year Lease Liability (B – E)
1	$224,755	$15,733	$32,000	$16,267	$208,488
2	208,488	14,594	32,000	17,406	191,082
3	191,082	13,376	32,000	18,624	172,458
4	172,458	12,072	32,000	19,928	152,530
5	152,530	10,677	32,000	21,323	131,207
6	131,207	9,184	32,000	22,816	108,391
7	108,391	7,587	32,000	24,413	83,978
8	83,978	5,878	32,000	26,122	57,856
9	57,856	4,050	32,000	27,950	29,906
10	29,906	2,093	32,000	29,907	0

* Small differences due to rounding

Part One

Entry for finance lease treatment—commencement of lease.

Initially, the company records the lease asset and lease liability at the lease commencement. At the end of the first year, Gap would record amortization expense of $22,476 ($224,755/10), interest expense of $15,733 ($224,755 × 0.07; and see table above), and the lease payment.

ANALYZE

Transaction	Cash Asset	+ Noncash Assets	– Contra Assets	= Liabilities	+ Contrib. Capital	+ Earned Capital	Revenues	– Expenses	= Net Income
	Balance Sheet						***Income Statement***		
(1) Lease store space using finance-type lease.		+224,755 Right-of-Use Asset—Finance Lease		+224,755 Finance Lease Liability					
(2a) Annual amortization expense.			+22,476 Accumulated Amortization			–22,476 Retained Earnings		+22,476 Amortization Expense	–22,476
(2b) Lease payment and interest expense.	–32,000 Cash			–16,267 Finance Lease Liability		–15,733 Retained Earnings		+15,733 Interest Expense	–15,733

JOURNALIZE

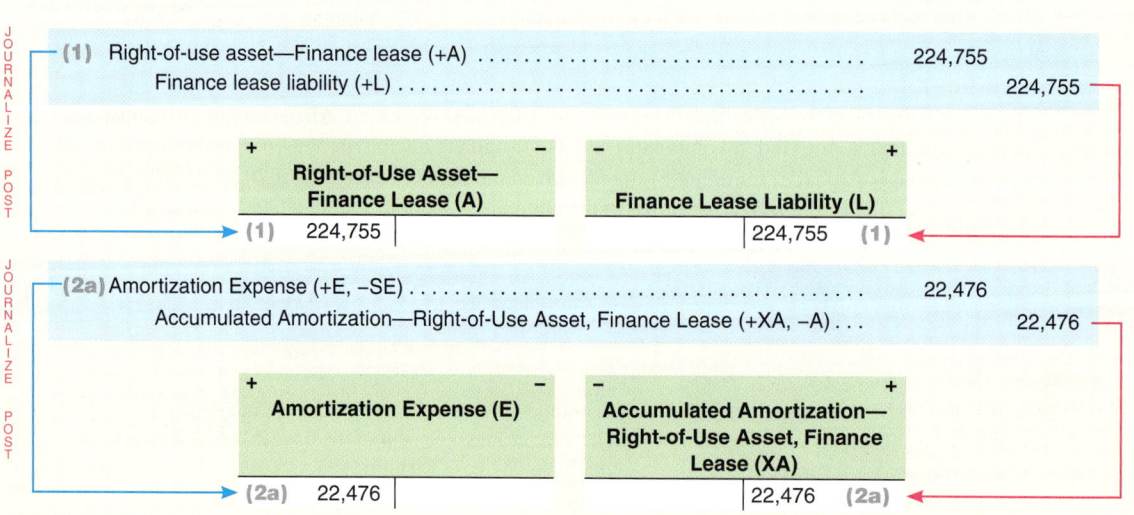

(1)	Right-of-use asset—Finance lease (+A)	224,755	
	Finance lease liability (+L)		224,755

POST

+ Right-of-Use Asset—Finance Lease (A) –	
(1) 224,755	

– Finance Lease Liability (L) +	
	224,755 (1)

JOURNALIZE

(2a)	Amortization Expense (+E, –SE)	22,476	
	Accumulated Amortization—Right-of-Use Asset, Finance Lease (+XA, –A)		22,476

POST

+ Amortization Expense (E) –	
(2a) 22,476	

– Accumulated Amortization—Right-of-Use Asset, Finance Lease (XA) +	
	22,476 (2a)

JOURNALIZE

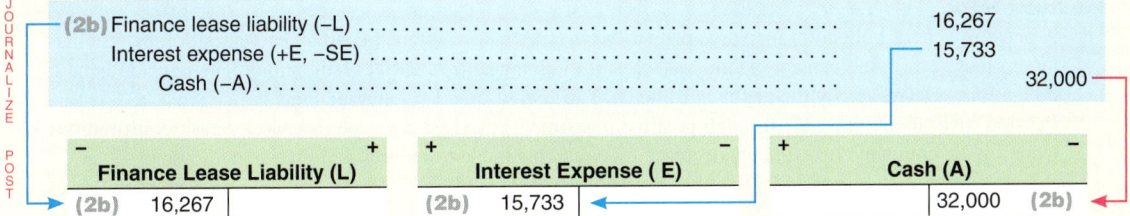

(2b) Finance lease liability (−L)	16,267	
Interest expense (+E, −SE)	15,733	
Cash (−A)		32,000

POST

− Finance Lease Liability (L) +		+ Interest Expense (E) −		+ Cash (A) −	
(2b) 16,267		(2b) 15,733			32,000 (2b)

Part Two

If the lease were an operating lease, the entries would be as follows:

(1a) To record lease asset and liability at commencement of lease.

(1b) At the end of the year the lease payment is recorded.

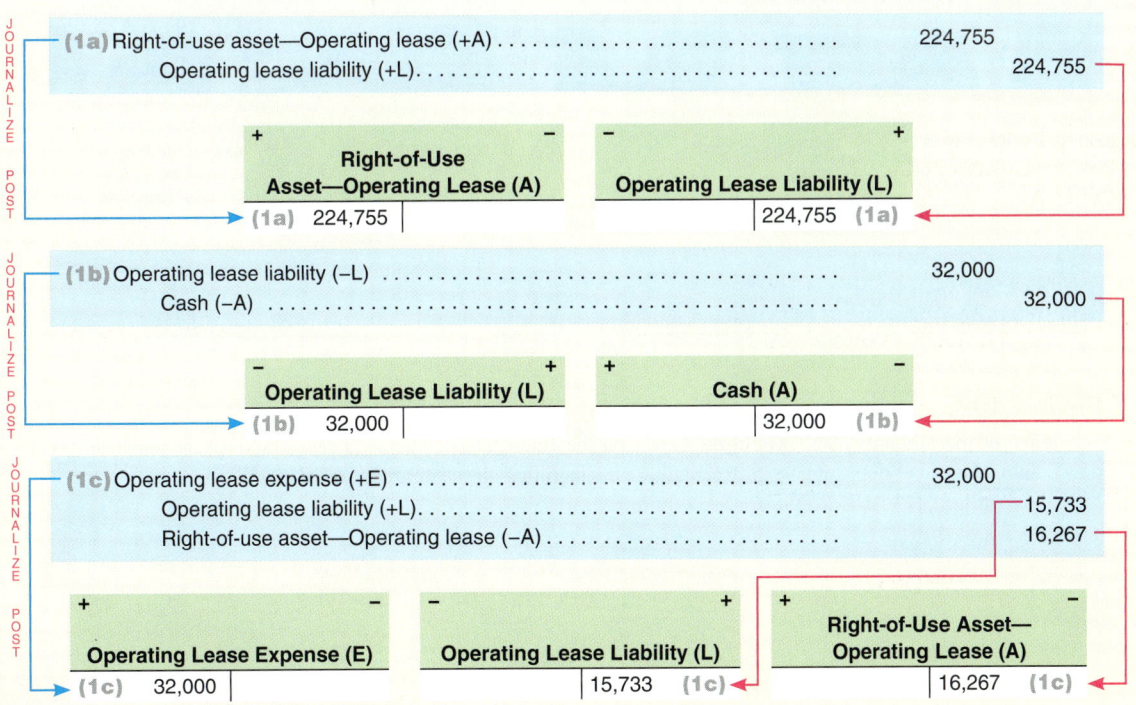

(1c) At the end of the year, the straight-line lease expense is recorded and the balance sheet items are adjusted.

ANALYZE

Transaction	Cash Asset	+	Noncash Assets	−	Contra Assets	=	Liabil-ities	+	Contrib. Capital	+	Earned Capital	Revenues	−	Expenses	=	Net Income
(1a) Lease store space using operating-type lease.			+224,755 Right-of-Use Asset—Operating Lease	−		=	+224,755 Operating Lease Liability						−		=	
(1b) Lease payment.	−32,000 Cash			−		=	−32,000 Operating Lease Liability						−		=	
(1c) Record lease expense.			−16,267 Right-of-Use Asset—Operating Lease	−		=	+15,733 Operating Lease Liability				−32,000 Retained Earnings		−	+32,000 Operating Lease Expense	=	−32,000

JOURNALIZE

(1a) Right-of-use asset—Operating lease (+A)	224,755	
Operating lease liability (+L)		224,755

POST

+ Right-of-Use Asset—Operating Lease (A) −		− Operating Lease Liability (L) +	
(1a) 224,755			224,755 (1a)

JOURNALIZE

(1b) Operating lease liability (−L)	32,000	
Cash (−A)		32,000

POST

− Operating Lease Liability (L) +		+ Cash (A) −	
(1b) 32,000			32,000 (1b)

JOURNALIZE

(1c) Operating lease expense (+E)	32,000	
Operating lease liability (+L)		15,733
Right-of-use asset—Operating lease (−A)		16,267

POST

+ Operating Lease Expense (E) −		− Operating Lease Liability (L) +		+ Right-of-Use Asset—Operating Lease (A) −	
(1c) 32,000			15,733 (1c)		16,267 (1c)

Review 10-2

1. A pension benefit obligation increases primarily by service cost, interest cost, and actuarial losses. The latter are increases in the pension liability as a result of changes in actuarial assumptions. The pension benefit obligation is decreased by the payment of benefits to retirees and by actuarial gains.
2. Pension investments increase through positive investment returns for the period and by cash contributions made by the company. Investments decrease by payments made to retirees and investment losses.
3. Boeing's funded status is $(13,719) million ($82,415 million PBO – $68,696 million pension assets) as of 2020. The negative amount indicates that the plan is underfunded. Therefore, this amount is reported as a liability on the company's balance sheet.
4. Expected return on plan assets acts as an offset to service cost and interest cost in computing the net pension cost. As the expected return increases (decreases), net pension cost decreases (increases).
5. Boeing's expected return of $3,756 million was less than its actual return of $9,275 million in 2020.
6. Boeing reports net pension income of $337 million due to the expected return on plan assets that more than offset the costs of the plan for the year.
7. Boeing's funded status is negative, indicating an underfunded plan. The company contributed $3,013 million to the pension plan in 2020. The funding status has improved somewhat; for example, in 2019 the plan was underfunded by $(15,934). It is likely that the company will need to increase its future funding levels to cover the plan's requirements. This action is likely to have negative consequences for its ability to fund other operating needs and could damage its competitive position in the future. The company disclosed that most employees have transitioned to defined contribution plans. This is evidenced by the relatively small ($3 million) increase in service cost for the 2020 period. Thus, the company is not materially increasing liabilities based on new commitments but is mainly managing existing obligations from past contracts.

Review 10-3

a. 1. $2,390.

2. $1,488 = $1,342 + $146 is an estimate of the amount currently payable or that has already been paid during the year.

3. The most obvious example would be depreciation allowed by the tax code that exceeded the amount calculated by the straight-line method used for financial accounting.

b.

ANALYZE

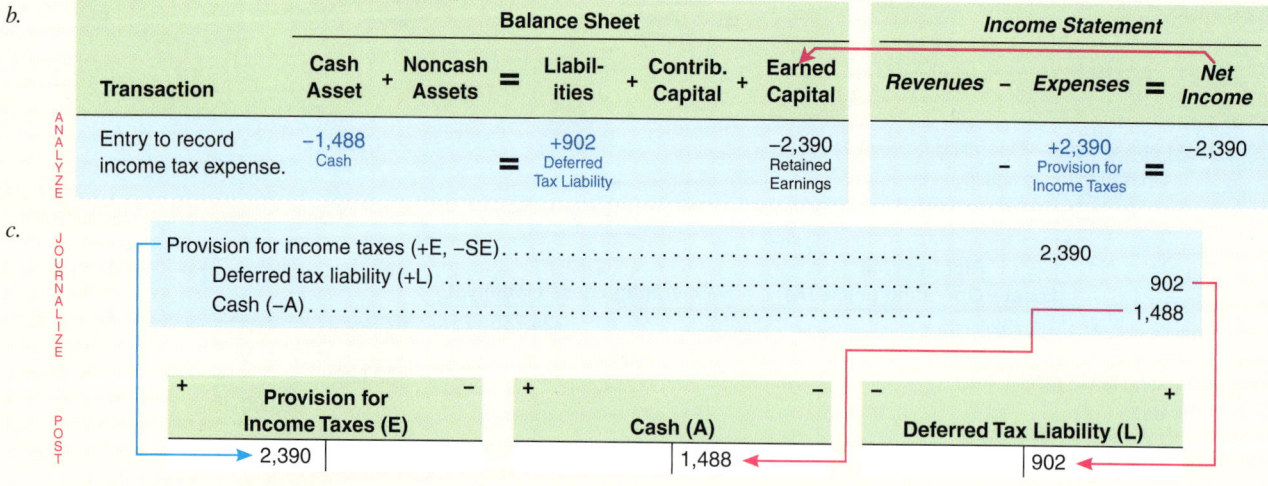

	Balance Sheet									Income Statement				
Transaction	Cash Asset	+	Noncash Assets	=	Liabil-ities	+	Contrib. Capital	+	Earned Capital	*Revenues*	–	*Expenses*	=	*Net Income*
Entry to record income tax expense.	–1,488 Cash			=	+902 Deferred Tax Liability				–2,390 Retained Earnings		–	+2,390 Provision for Income Taxes	=	–2,390

c.

JOURNALIZE

Provision for income taxes (+E, –SE)	2,390	
Deferred tax liability (+L)		902
Cash (–A)		1,488

POST

+ Provision for Income Taxes (E) –		+ Cash (A) –		– Deferred Tax Liability (L) +	
2,390			1,488		902

Review 10-4

a. None of the amounts listed would be shown on the financial statements. These amounts are disclosed as contingencies but don't qualify for recognition as liabilities on the company's balance sheet.

b. $74.5 million [PV(0.04,2,-39.5) = $74.5 million]

Chapter 11 Reporting and Analyzing Stockholders' Equity

LEARNING OBJECTIVES

LO11-1 Describe and account for business financing through stock issuances and repurchases.

LO11-2 Describe the effect on equity of earnings, dividends, and stock splits.

LO11-3 Define and illustrate comprehensive income.

LO11-4 Describe and illustrate the basic and diluted earnings per share computations.

LO11-5 Appendix 11A: Analyze the accounting for convertible securities, stock rights, stock options, and restricted stock.

Road Map

LO	Learning Objective | Topics	Page	eLecture	Review	Assignments
LO11-1	Describe and account for business financing through stock issuances and repurchases.	11-3	e11-1	R11-1	M11-19, M11-20, M11-21, M11-22, M11-24, M11-27, M11-42, M11-43, E11-45, E11-46, E11-47, E11-48, E11-49, E11-53, E11-63, E11-65, P11-66, P11-67, P11-68, P11-69, P11-70, P11-71, P11-72, P11-73, P11-74, P11-75, C11-79, C11-80, C11-81, C11-82
LO11-2	Describe the effect on equity of earnings, dividends, and stock splits.	11-11	e11-2	R11-2	M11-23, M11-28, M11-29, M11-30, M11-31, M11-32, M11-33, M11-34, M11-35, M11-36, M11-42, M11-43, E11-50, E11-52, E11-54, E11-55, E11-56, E11-57, E11-58, E11-59, E11-60, E11-61, E11-62, E11-65, P11-66, P11-67, P11-68, P11-69, P11-70, P11-71, P11-72, P11-73, C11-80, C11-81, DA11-3
LO11-3	Define and illustrate comprehensive income.	11-16	e11-3	R11-3	M11-22, M11-27, M11-43, E11-49, E11-53, E11-62, E11-63, E11-65, P11-68, P11-74, P11-76
LO11-4	Describe and illustrate the basic and diluted earnings per share computations.	11-19	e11-4	R11-4	M11-25, M11-26, M11-27, M11-37, M11-38, M11-39, M11-42, M11-43, M11-44, E11-49, E11-51, E11-52, E11-61, P11-66, P11-68, P11-70, P11-74, P11-76, C11-81, DA11-1
LO11-5	Appendix 11A: Analyze the accounting for convertible securities, stock rights, stock options, and restricted stock.	11-22	e11-5	R11-5	M11-40, M11-41, E11-64, P11-74, P11-76, P11-77, C11-78, C11-82, DA11-2

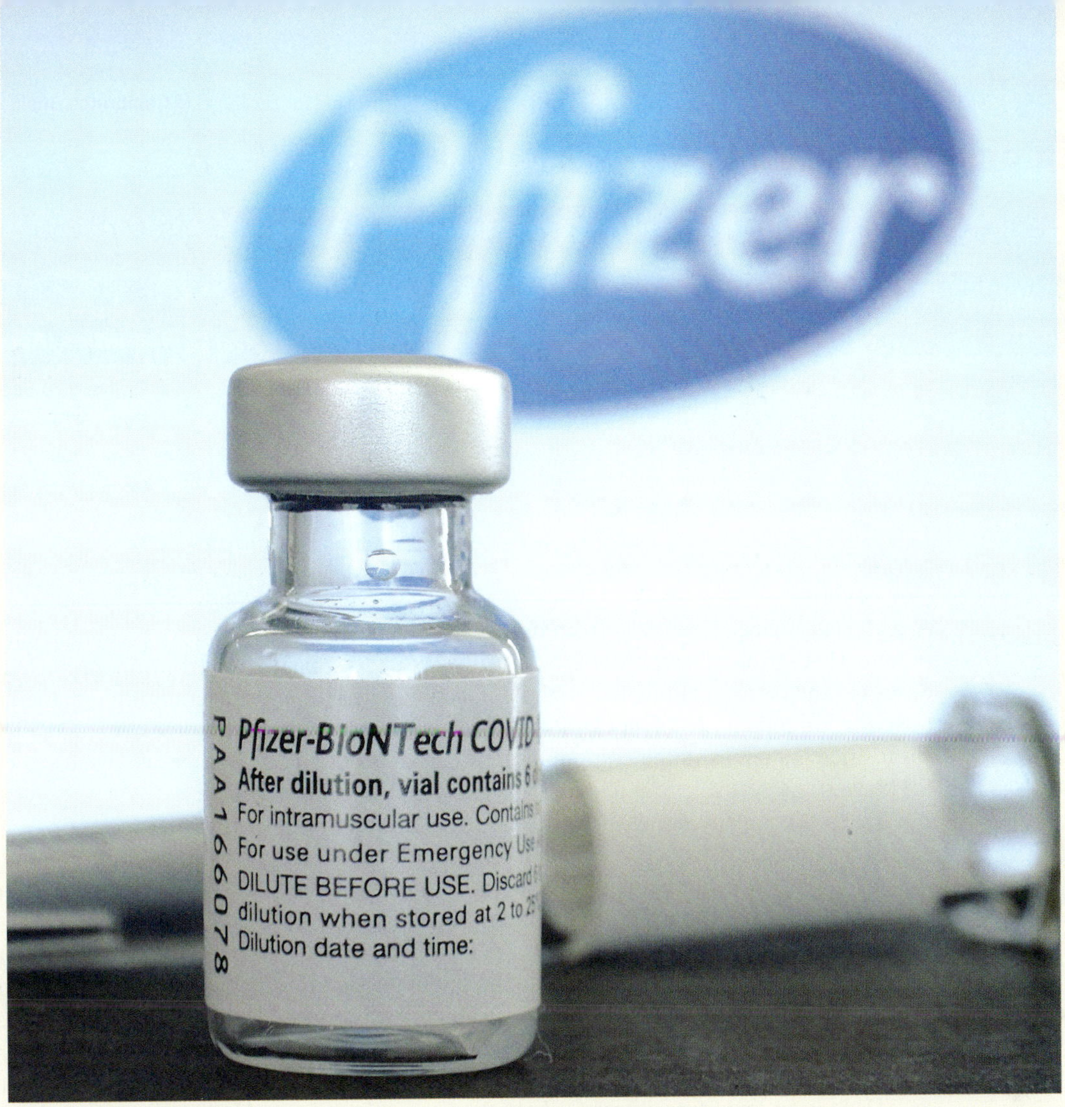

PFIZER
www.pfizer.com

Pfizer Inc. is a research-based, global pharmaceutical company that discovers, develops, manufactures, and markets prescription medicines. Pfizer's 2020 revenues were almost $42 billion. Pfizer was a very well-known company before 2020. With the global pandemic and Pfizer's joint work with BioNTech on one of the widely used COVID-19 vaccines, the company is prominently in the news every day. During 2020, Pfizer spun-off (divested) part of its business. Prior to this, the company had three operating segments. Now the company operates as a single operating segment.

Revenues at pharmaceutical firms are substantially dependent on patent protection following the research and development to discover and produce the drug. As patent protections expire, revenues fall. To counter expiring patents, Pfizer must either acquire companies with innovative drug pipelines (in-process research and development), enter into collaborations to develop drugs with other companies or develop new drugs in-house. To discover new drugs, Pfizer spends sizeable amounts each year on research and development: $8.4 billion in 2019 and $9.4 billion in 2020.

Pfizer must balance the capital needs of its acquisition strategy and its heavy commitment to research and development with the expectations of shareholders. From 2018 to 2020, the company reported $42.9 billion of net cash flow from operating activities, but it also paid $45.5 billion in cash to shareholders in the form of dividends and share repurchases. Other transactions involving shareholders' equity included share-based compensation for employees and conversions of one form of shareholders' equity to another.

This chapter describes the reporting and analysis of equity transactions, including sales and repurchases of stock, dividends, comprehensive income, and convertible securities.

Sources: Pfizer 2020 10-K Report.

CHAPTER ORGANIZATION

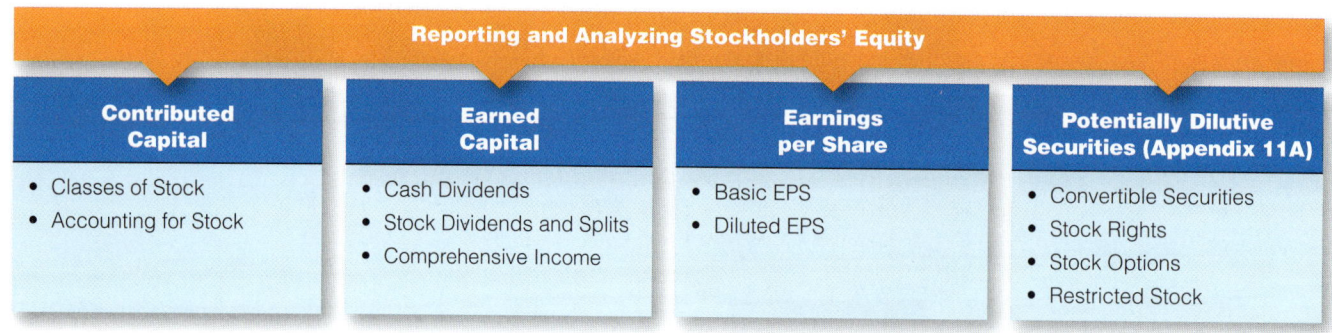

Reporting and Analyzing Stockholders' Equity

Contributed Capital	Earned Capital	Earnings per Share	Potentially Dilutive Securities (Appendix 11A)
• Classes of Stock • Accounting for Stock	• Cash Dividends • Stock Dividends and Splits • Comprehensive Income	• Basic EPS • Diluted EPS	• Convertible Securities • Stock Rights • Stock Options • Restricted Stock

INTRODUCTION

LO11-1 Describe and account for business financing through stock issuances and repurchases.

eLecture MBC

A company finances its assets from one of three sources: either it borrows funds from creditors, it obtains funds from shareholders, or it reinvests excess cash flow from operations. This chapter describes the issues relating to stockholders' equity, including the accounting for stock transactions (issues and repurchases of stock, and dividends), the accounting for stock options, the accounting for restricted stock, and the computation of earnings per share. Finally, we discuss the accounting for convertible securities, an increasingly prevalent financing vehicle.

When a company issues stock to the investing public, it records the receipt of cash (or other assets) and an increase in contributed capital, a part of stockholders' equity, representing investment in the company by shareholders. The increases in cash and equity equal the issue price of the stock on the issue date multiplied by the number of shares sold.

Contributed capital is accounted for at *historical cost.* Consequently, fluctuations in the market price of the issuer's stock subsequent to the initial public offering do not directly affect the financial statements of the issuing company. These fluctuations are the result of transactions between outside parties not involving the issuer. When and if stock is repurchased and subsequently resold, the issuer's contributed capital decreases (increases) by the current purchase (sales) price of the shares.

FYI Corporations never record gains or losses on the purchase or sale of the company's own stock or the payment of dividends.

There is an important difference between accounting for stockholders' equity and accounting for transactions involving assets and liabilities: *there is never any gain or loss reported on the purchase and sale of the company's own stock or the payment of dividends.* Instead, these "gains and losses" are reflected as increases and decreases in the contributed capital component of the issuing company's stockholders' equity.

This chapter focuses on the two broad categories of shareholder investment: contributed capital and earned capital. **Exhibit 11.1** provides an illustration of this breakdown using Pfizer's stockholders' equity as of December 31, 2020.

EXHIBIT 11.1 Stockholders' Equity from Pfizer's Balance Sheet

	Shareholders' Equity (millions except preferred stock issued and per common share data)	Dec. 31, 2020
Contributed capital	Preferred stock, no par value, at stated value; 27 shares authorized; issued: 2020—0; 2019—431	$ —
	Common stock, $0.05 par value; 12,000 shares authorized; issued: 2020—9,407; 2019—9,369	470
	Additional paid-in capital	88,674
	Treasury stock, shares at cost: 2020—3,840; 2019—3,835	(110,988)
Earned capital	Retained earnings	96,770
	Accumulated other comprehensive loss	(11,688)
	Total Pfizer Inc. shareholders' equity	63,238
	Equity attributable to noncontrolling interests	235
	Total equity	$63,473

Pfizer, like other companies, has two broad categories of stockholders' equity:

1. **Contributed capital** This section reports the proceeds received by the issuing company from original stock issuances. Contributed capital often includes common stock, preferred

stock, and additional paid-in capital. Netted against these capital accounts is treasury stock, the amounts paid to repurchase shares of the issuer's stock from its investors less the proceeds from the resale of such shares. Collectively, these accounts are generically referred to as contributed capital (or *paid-in capital*).

2. **Earned capital** This section consists of (a) retained earnings (or accumulated deficit, if negative), which represent the cumulative income and losses of the company less any dividends to shareholders, and (b) accumulated other comprehensive income (AOCI), which includes changes to equity that are not included in income and are, therefore, not reflected in retained earnings. For Pfizer, AOCI includes foreign currency translation adjustments, changes in market values of derivatives, unrecognized gains and losses on available-for-sale securities, and pension adjustments.

Before turning to a discussion of contributed capital and earned capital, we note one other item in **Exhibit 11.1**—Equity attributable to **noncontrolling interests**. This amount results from the practice of consolidating subsidiaries that are controlled, but not wholly owned, and it represents neither capital contributed to Pfizer nor capital earned by Pfizer's shareholders. Chapter 12 provides a brief introduction to this topic.

CONTRIBUTED CAPITAL

We begin our discussion with contributed capital. Contributed capital represents the cumulative cash inflow that the company has received from the sale of various classes of stock, less the net cash that it has paid out to repurchase its stock from the market.

Pfizer's contributed capital consists of preferred and common stock, additional paid-in capital, less costs of treasury stock (repurchased shares).

Classes of Stock

There are two general classes of stock: preferred and common. The difference between the two lies in the respective legal rights conferred upon each class.

Common Stock Shares of **common stock** represent the primary ownership unit in a corporation. Common stockholders have voting rights that allow them to participate in the governance of the corporation. The total number of common shares is usually presented on the face of the balance sheet. There are three numbers of shares to be aware of:

- The number of **shares authorized** represents the upper limit on the number of shares that the corporation can issue. This number is established in the *articles of incorporation* and can only be increased by an affirmative shareholder vote.
- The number of **shares issued** is the actual number of shares that have been sold to stockholders by the corporation.
- The number of **shares outstanding** is the number of issued shares less the number of shares repurchased as treasury stock.

Pfizer's common stock is described as follows in its 2020 balance sheet (shares in millions):

Common stock, $0.05 par value; 12,000 shares authorized; issued: 2020—9,407

The Pfizer common stock has the following important characteristics:

- Pfizer common stock has a par value of $0.05 per share. The **par value** is an arbitrary amount set by company organizers at the time of formation. Generally, par value has no substance from a financial reporting or statement analysis perspective. (There are some legal implications, which are usually minor.) Its main impact is in specifying the allocation of proceeds from stock issuances between the two contributed capital accounts on the balance sheet: common stock and additional paid-in capital.
- Pfizer has authorized the issuance of 12,000 million shares. As of December 31, 2020, 9,407 million shares are issued yielding a total par value of $470 million = $0.05 × 9,407 million shares.

When shares are first issued, the number of shares outstanding equals those issued. Any shares subsequently repurchased are subtracted from issued shares to derive outstanding shares.

Some corporations issue multiple classes of stock, with differential voting rights. For instance, **Alphabet Inc.** has Class A common stock with one vote per share, Class B common stock with ten votes per share, and Class C capital stock with no voting rights at all. All shares participate equally in dividends, but this structure has allowed the original management team to raise capital while retaining significant voting rights.

Preferred Stock **Preferred stock** generally has some preference, or priority, with respect to common stock but does not have voting rights. Two typical preferences are:

1. **Dividend preference** Preferred shareholders receive dividends on their shares before common shareholders do. If dividends are not paid in a given year, those dividends are normally forgone. However, some preferred stock contracts include a *cumulative provision* stipulating that any forgone dividends must first be paid to preferred shareholders, together with the current year's dividends, before any dividends are paid to common shareholders.
2. **Liquidation preference** If a company fails, its assets are sold (liquidated), and the proceeds are paid to the creditors and shareholders, in that order. Shareholders, therefore, have a greater risk of loss than do creditors. Among shareholders, the preferred shareholders receive payment in full before any proceeds are paid to common shareholders. This liquidation preference makes preferred shares less risky than common shares. Any liquidation payment to preferred shares is normally at its par value, although it is sometimes specified in excess of par, called a **liquidating value**.

The preferred stock of Pfizer is described in Note 12 to its 2019 10-K:

> The Series A convertible perpetual preferred stock . . . is held by an employee stock ownership plan (Preferred ESOP) Trust and provides dividends at the rate of 6.25%, which are accumulated and paid quarterly. The per-share stated value is $40,300, and the preferred stock ranks senior to our common stock as to dividends and liquidation rights. Each share is convertible, at the holder's option, into 2,574.87 shares of our common stock with equal voting rights. The conversion option is indexed to our common stock and requires share settlement, and, therefore, is reported at the fair value at the date of issuance. We may redeem the preferred stock at any time or upon termination of the Preferred ESOP, at our option, in cash, in shares of common stock, or a combination of both at a price of $40,300 per share.

The preferred stock of Pfizer is described in Note 12 to its 2020 10-K:

> Prior to May 4, 2020, our Series A convertible perpetual preferred stock (the Series A Preferred Stock) was held by an ESOP trust (the Trust). All outstanding shares of Series A Preferred Stock were converted, at the direction of the independent fiduciary under the Trust and in accordance with the certificate of designations for the Series A Preferred Stock, into shares of our common stock on May 4, 2020. The Trust received an aggregate of 1,070,369 shares of our common stock upon conversion, with zero shares of Series A Preferred Stock remaining outstanding as a result of the conversion. In December 2020, we filed a certificate of elimination and a restated certificate of incorporation with the Delaware Secretary of State, which eliminated the Series A Preferred Stock.

Following are several important features of the Pfizer preferred stock:

- As of the end of 2019, the company, had 27 million preferred shares authorized and 431 shares issued. Zero shares are issued as of December 31, 2020, because all preferred shares were converted into common shares. The articles of incorporation set the number of shares authorized for issuance, when that limit is reached, shareholders must approve any increase in authorized shares.
- Pfizer preferred stock has a preference with respect to dividends and liquidation, meaning that preferred shareholders are paid before common shareholders.
- Pfizer preferred stock is convertible into common stock at the option of the holder and at a predetermined exchange rate. A preferred share is convertible, at the holder's option, into common shares. Indeed, on May 4, 2020, all preferred shares outstanding were converted into 1,070,369 common shares.

- In December 2020, the Series A Preferred Stock was eliminated, leaving a zero balance in preferred stock on December 31, 2020.

Pfizer's cumulative preferred shares carried a dividend yield of 6.25%. This dividend yield compared favorably with the $1.52 per share (3.9% yield) paid to its common shareholders (as of December 31, 2019). Generally, preferred stock can be an attractive investment for shareholders seeking higher dividend yields, especially when tax laws wholly or partially exempt such dividends from taxation.

There are additional features sometimes seen in preferred stock agreements:[1]

1. **Call feature** The call feature provides the issuer with the right, but not the obligation, to repurchase the preferred shares at a specified price (also called redeemable preferred stock). This price can vary according to a specified time. A decline in the market rate of interest is one event that can lead to the firm exercising the call provision. While of value to the issuer of the preferred stock, the call provision makes the issue less attractive to potential investors. The result is a lower offering price per share.
2. **Conversion feature** The yield on preferred stock, especially when coupled with a cumulative feature, is similar to the interest rate on a bond or note. Further limited protection is offered because preferred shareholders receive the par value at liquidation like debtholders receive face value. The fixed yield and liquidation value for the preferred stock limit the upside potential return of preferred shareholders. This constraint can be overcome by inclusion of a *conversion feature* that allows preferred stockholders to convert their shares into common shares at their option at a predetermined conversion ratio. Some preferred contracts give the company an option to force conversion.

   The conversion feature causes the shares to be more attractive to potential investors because the preferred stockholders now have the opportunity to share in the fruits of a successful company with the common stockholders. Indeed, the market price of preferred stock tends to reflect the added value of the conversion feature.
3. **Participation feature** Preferred shares sometimes carry a *participation feature* that allows preferred shareholders to share ratably with common stockholders in dividends. The dividend preference over common shares can be a benefit when dividend payments are meager, but a fixed dividend yield limits upside potential if the company performs exceptionally well. This limitation can be overcome with a participation feature.

A GLOBAL PERSPECTIVE

IFRS

Under IFRS, convertible debt securities are termed compound financial instruments because the conversion feature has a value even if it is not legally detachable for sale. IFRS splits the convertible bonds' value into the separate debt and conversion option values for reporting purposes. GAAP splits the value when the conversion option is determined to be a derivative liability. If the conversion option is determined to be equity, U.S. GAAP does not require bifurcation of the security into separate components. New GAAP rules effective in 2021 make differences between GAAP and IFRS more common (bifurcation less often under GAAP). Another difference is that GAAP has a mezzanine section of the balance sheet between equity and liabilities where securities with both equity and debt features are recorded. IFRS does not allow a mezzanine section of the balance sheet.

[1] Preferred shares, in general, are somewhat debt-like. For example, preferred shares have a higher and more certain rate of dividends, approaching something more like interest. In addition, they have preference over common stockholders in the event of bankruptcy. More features can be added to the preferred shares that make them even more debt-like. In some cases, the classification for accounting changes accordingly. For example, if entities have mandatorily redeemable preferred stock that do not contain a conversion option, these securities are to be included as liabilities on the balance sheet, not in equity and not in the mezzanine section of the balance sheet (i.e., the section between the liabilities section and the equity section in the balance sheet). Entities are required to present contingently redeemable preferred stock—meaning redeemable upon the occurrence of an event outside the control of the issuer—and preferred stock that is redeemable at the option of the holder in the mezzanine section of the balance sheet (i.e., the section between the liabilities section and the equity section). The purpose of this classification is to convey to the reader that such a security may not permanently be part of equity and could result in a demand for cash or other assets of the entity in the future. These are the accounting rules, but as discussed elsewhere in the text, analysts and other financial statement users may treat these securities differently than FASB (and may treat some of the securities as debt and some as equity) when conducting ratio-analysis or other evaluations of company performance. For example, in much of the analyses sections of this text, we include these items as either debt or equity: noncontrolling equity interests are included in shareholders' equity, and mezzanine items—redeemable noncontrolling interests in subsidiaries and redeemable preferred stock—are included in equity. But other financial statement users may include them in debt under certain circumstances for analysis purposes.

Accounting for Stock Transactions

We cover the accounting for stock transactions in this section, including the accounting for stock issuances and for stock repurchases.

Stock Issuance Stock issuances, whether common or preferred, yield an increase in both assets and stockholders' equity. Companies use stock issuances to obtain cash and other assets for use in their business.

Stock issuances increase assets (cash) by the number of shares sold multiplied by the issuance price of the stock on the issue date. Equity increases by the same amount, which is reflected in contributed capital accounts. Specifically, assuming the issuance of common stock, the common stock account increases by the number of shares sold multiplied by its par value, and the additional paid-in capital account is increased for the remainder of the purchase price.[2]

BUSINESS INSIGHT

Airbnb's IPO In December of 2020, Airbnb offered its shares to the general public for the first time. The first public sale of common stock by a corporation is called an initial public offering, or IPO for short. After the IPO, any offering of stock to the public is called a seasoned equity offering.

The Airbnb IPO was long awaited by employees who had received equity-based pay and potential new investors alike. The company's stock has a par value of $0.0001. The IPO raised about $3.5 billion with an IPO price of $68 per share. The company stock opened on the Nasdaq at $146 per share. It rose to a high of nearly $220 and as of August, 2021 trades at around $155 per share.

To illustrate, assume that Davis Company issues 10,000 shares of $1 par value common stock at a market price of $43 cash per share. The financial statement effects and entries for this stock issuance follow.

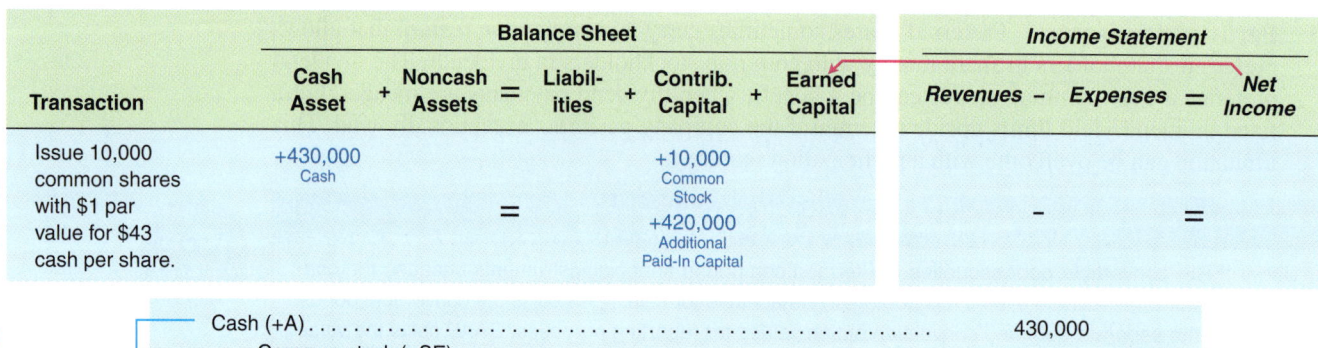

ANALYZE

	Balance Sheet									Income Statement				
Transaction	Cash Asset	+	Noncash Assets	=	Liabil-ities	+	Contrib. Capital	+	Earned Capital	*Revenues*	–	*Expenses*	=	*Net Income*
Issue 10,000 common shares with $1 par value for $43 cash per share.	+430,000 Cash			=			+10,000 Common Stock +420,000 Additional Paid-In Capital				–		=	

JOURNALIZE

Cash (+A)	430,000	
Common stock (+SE)		10,000
Additional paid-in capital (+SE)		420,000

POST

+ Cash (A) –		– Additional Paid-in-Capital (SE) +		– Common Stock (SE) +	
430,000			420,000		10,000

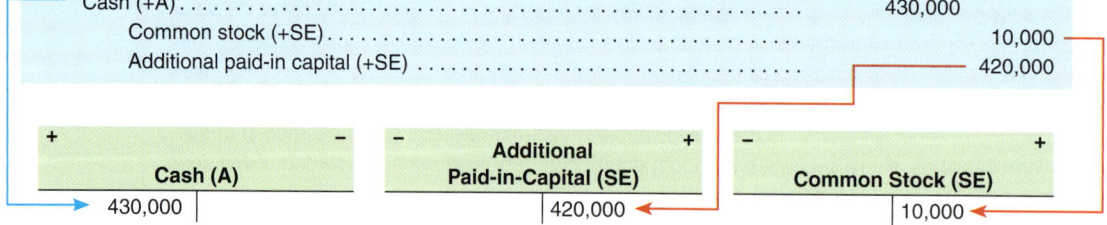

FYI Stock issuance affects the balance sheet, the statement of cash flows, and the statement of stockholders' equity. There is no revenue or gain from stock issuance reported in the income statement.

Specifically, the following financial statement effects of the stock issuance are:

1. Cash increases by $430,000 (10,000 shares × $43 per share) and is reported as a cash inflow from financing activities on the statement of cash flows.
2. Common stock increases by the $10,000 par value of shares sold (10,000 shares × $1 par value).[3]

[2] Companies that offer their shares for sale to the general public are called *public corporations*. In a *private company*, ownership is limited to a smaller number of investors, and the stock is not available to the general public. The distinction between public and private corporations should not be confused with media references to the public sector and the private sector. The *public sector* refers to government entities. Virtually all business entities, including public corporations, are considered part of the *private sector*.

[3] Common stock can also be issued as "no par" or as "no par with a stated value." For no par stock, the common stock account is increased by the entire proceeds of the sale, and no amount is assigned to additional paid-in capital. For no par stock with a stated value, the stated value is treated just like par value; that is, common stock is increased by the number of shares multiplied by the stated value, and the remainder is assigned to the additional paid-in capital account.

3. Additional paid-in capital increases by the $420,000 difference between the issue price and par value ($430,000 – $10,000).

Once shares are issued, they are freely traded in the market among investors. The proceeds of those sales and any gains and losses on those sales do not affect the issuing company and are not recorded in its accounting records. Further, fluctuations in the issuing company's stock price subsequent to issuance do not directly affect its financial statements. Hence, the equity section of the balance sheet cannot be used to determine the current market value of the company. The market value (or market capitalization) is given by the product of the number of common shares outstanding times the current per-share market price of the stock.

Pfizer's outstanding common shares, repeated from **Exhibit 11.1**, are (in millions):

Common stock, $0.05 par value; 12,000 shares authorized; issued: 2020—9,407	$ 470
Additional paid-in capital.	88,674

Pfizer's common stock, in the amount of $470 million, equals the number of shares issued multiplied by the common stock's par value: 9,407 million × $0.05 = $470 million.[4] The balance of the proceeds from stock issuances is included in the additional paid-in capital account. Total proceeds from stock issuances are $89,144 ($470 + $88,674) million, or $9.48 per share ($89,144/9,407 million shares).

RESEARCH INSIGHT

Stock Issuance and Stock Returns Seasoned equity offerings are issuances of common stock by firms that already have outstanding shares. On average, stock price declines when a company announces that it will issue additional shares of common stock. Investors infer that issuing common stock rather than debt is an indication that management believes the stock is overvalued in the market, making it a more attractive form of financing. In addition, research has found that companies engage in earnings management around seasoned equity offerings, using both accrual estimates (e.g., underestimating bad debt expense or warranty expense) and real transactions (e.g., cutting R&D or accelerating sales). As a result, both earnings and stock returns decline in subsequent periods.

Stock Repurchase Pfizer provides the following description of its stock repurchase program in notes to its 10-K report.

We purchase our common stock through privately negotiated transactions or in the open market as circumstances and prices warrant. Purchased shares under each of the share-purchase plans, which are authorized by our BOD, are available for general corporate purposes. In December 2015, the BOD authorized an $11 billion share repurchase program, which was exhausted in the third quarter of 2018. In December 2017, the BOD authorized an additional $10 billion share repurchase program, which was exhausted in the first quarter of 2019. In December 2018, the BOD authorized another $10 billion share repurchase program to be utilized over time and share repurchases commenced thereunder in the first quarter of 2019.

In March 2018, we entered into an accelerated share repurchase agreement (ASR) with Citibank, N.A. to repurchase $4 billion of our common stock pursuant to our previously announced share repurchase authorization. We paid $4 billion and received an initial delivery of 87 million shares of stock at a price of $36.61 per share, which represented approximately 80% of the notional amount of the ASR. In September 2018, the ASR was completed, resulting in Citibank owing us an additional 21 million shares of our common stock. The average price paid for all of the shares delivered under the ASR was $36.86 per share. The common stock received is included in Treasury stock.

In February 2019, we entered into an ASR with Goldman Sachs & Co. LLC to repurchase $6.8 billion of our common stock pursuant to our previously announced share repurchase authorization. We paid $6.8 billion and received an initial delivery of 130 million shares of common stock, which

continued

[4] The number of shares issued and the par value of those shares are both rounded to the nearest million.

continued from previous page

represented approximately 80% of the notional amount of the ASR. In August 2019, the ASR with Goldman Sachs & Co. LLC was completed, resulting in Goldman Sachs & Co. LLC owing us an additional 33.5 million shares of our common stock. The average price paid for all of the shares delivered under the ASR was $41.42 per share. The common stock received is included in Treasury stock.

The following table provides the number of shares of our common stock purchased and the cost of purchases under our publicly announced share repurchase plans, including our ASRs [accelerated share repurchase agreements]:

(SHARES IN MILLIONS, DOLLARS IN BILLIONS)	2020	2019(b)	2018(c)
Shares of common stock purchased	—	213	307
Cost of purchase	—	$8.9	$12.2

(a) Represents shares purchased pursuant to the ASR with Goldman Sachs & Co. LLC entered into in February 2019, as well as open market share repurchases of $2.1 billion.

(b) Represents shares purchased pursuant to the ASR with Citibank entered into in March 2018, as well as open market share repurchases of $8.2 billion.

Our remaining share-purchase authorization was approximately $5.3 billion at December 31, 2020.

Pfizer has initiated multiple stock buyback programs over time. One reason a company will repurchase shares is if it feels that the market undervalues them. Management reasons that the repurchase sends a positive signal to the market about the company's financial condition that favorably affects its share price. Recent research provides evidence that share prices generally increase following the announcement of a share repurchase program. Any gain on resale is *never* reflected in the income statement. Instead, the excess of the resale price over the repurchase price is added to additional paid-in capital. GAAP prohibits companies from reporting gains via stock transactions with their own shareholders.

Another reason shares are repurchased is to offset the dilutive effects of an employee stock option program. When employees are compensated with equity-based pay, the number of shares outstanding will increase over time as the shares are given to employees. These additional shares reduce earnings per share and are, therefore, viewed as *dilutive.* In response, many companies repurchase a roughly equivalent number of shares in a desire to keep outstanding shares somewhat constant. Corporations also buy back their own shares in order to concentrate ownership to avoid an unwelcome takeover action. Repurchased shares do not participate in dividends or in shareholder votes.

A stock repurchase has the opposite financial statement effects from a stock issuance. That is, cash is reduced by the price of the shares repurchased (number of shares repurchased multiplied by the purchase price per share), and stockholders' equity is reduced by the same amount. The reduction in equity is achieved by increasing a contra equity account called **treasury stock**. *A contra equity account is a negative equity account with a debit balance,* which reduces stockholders' equity. Thus, when a contra equity account increases, total equity decreases.

Any subsequent reissuance of treasury stock does not yield a gain or loss. Instead, the difference between the proceeds received and the repurchase price of the treasury stock is reflected as an increase or decrease to additional paid-in capital.[5]

To illustrate, assume that 3,000 common shares of Davis Company stock previously issued for $43 are later repurchased for $40. The financial statement effects and entries for this stock repurchase follow.

[5] Repurchased shares do not have to be held in treasury but could be retired by the company.

ANALYZE

Transaction	Cash Asset	+ Noncash Assets	= Liabilities	+ Contrib. Capital	+ Earned Capital	− Contra Equity	*Revenues*	− *Expenses*	= *Net Income*
Repurchase 3,000 common shares for $40 cash per share.	−120,000 Cash		=			− +120,000 Treasury Stock		−	=

JOURNALIZE

Treasury stock (+XSE, −SE)	120,000	
Cash (−A)		120,000

POST

+ Treasury Stock (XSE) −	
120,000	

+ Cash (A) −	
	120,000

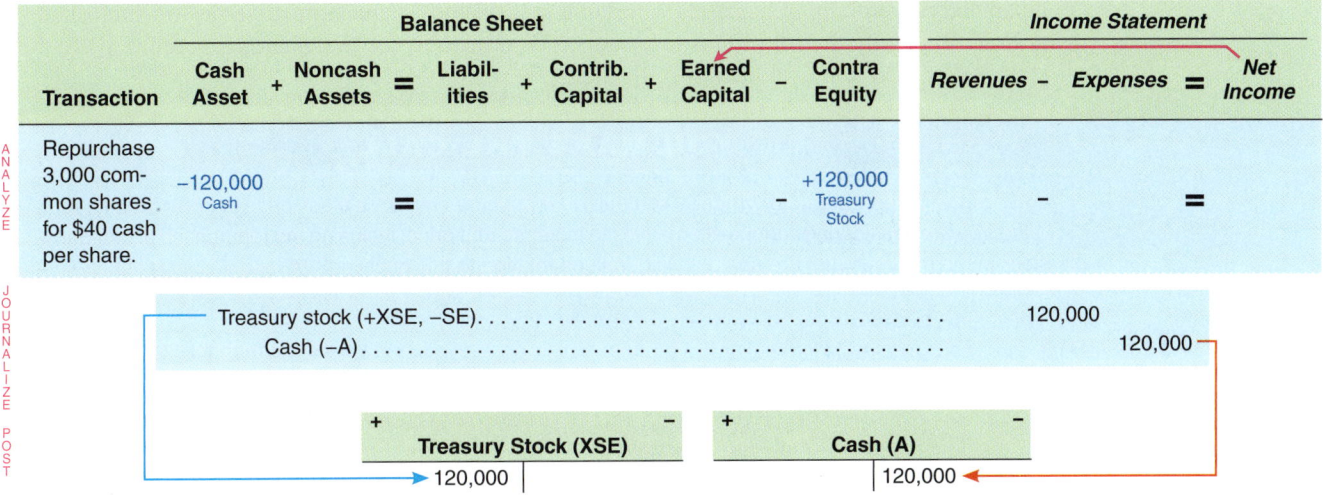

Assets (cash) and equity both decrease. Treasury stock (a contra equity account) increases by $120,000, which reduces stockholders' equity by that same amount.

Assume that these 3,000 shares are then subsequently resold for $42 cash per share. The financial statement effects and entries for this treasury stock sale follow.

ANALYZE

Transaction	Cash Asset	+ Noncash Assets	= Liabilities	+ Contrib. Capital	+ Earned Capital	− Contra Equity	*Revenues*	− *Expenses*	= *Net Income*
Reissue 3,000 treasury (common) shares for $42 cash per share.	+126,000 Cash		=	+6,000 Additional Paid-In Capital		− −120,000 Treasury Stock		−	=

JOURNALIZE

Cash (+A)	126,000	
Treasury stock (−XSE, +SE)		120,000
Additional paid-in capital (+SE)		6,000

POST

+ Cash (A) −	
126,000	

− Additional Paid-In Capital (SE) +	
	6,000

+ Treasury Stock (XSE) −	
	120,000

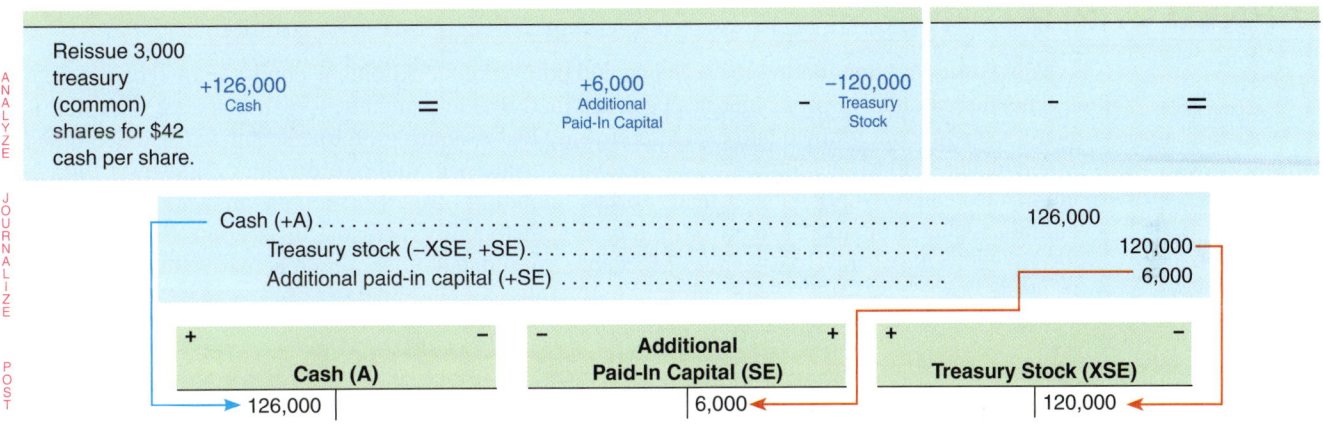

Cash assets increase by $126,000 (3,000 shares × $42 per share), the treasury stock account is reduced by the $120,000 cost of the treasury shares issued, and the $6,000 excess (3,000 shares × $2 per share) is reported as an increase in additional paid-in capital.[6] Again, there is no effect on the income statement—companies are prohibited from reporting gains and losses from repurchases and reissuances of their own stock.

The treasury stock section of Pfizer's 2020 balance sheet is reproduced below.

At December 31 (millions)	2020
Treasury stock, shares at cost: 2020—3,840	$(110,988)

Pfizer has repurchased a cumulative total of 3,840 million shares of its common stock for $110,988 million, an average repurchase price of $28.90 per share. This compares with total contributed capital of $89,144 million ($0 million + $470 million + $88,674 million). When a

[6] If the reissue price is below the repurchase price, then additional paid-in capital is reduced until it reaches a zero balance, after which retained earnings is reduced.

company has several repurchases and sales of treasury stock, a question arises as to which shares were sold. Typically the solution is to assume a flow such as the first shares repurchased are the first ones assumed to be sold (first-in, first-out).

YOU MAKE THE CALL

You are the Chief Financial Officer You believe that your company's stock price is lower than its real value. You are considering various alternatives to increase that price, including the repurchase of company stock in the market. What are some considerations relating to this decision? [Answer on page 11-29]

Review 11-1 LO11-1

Accounting for Stock Issuances

GuidedExample MBC

Plesko Corporation reported the following transactions relating to its stock accounts during the year.

Jan.	15	Issued 10,000 shares of $5 par value common stock at $17 cash per share.
Mar.	31	Purchased 2,000 shares of its own common stock at $15 cash per share.
June	25	Reissued 1,000 shares of its treasury stock at $20 cash per share.

a. Show the financial impact of each transaction using the financial statement effects template.

b. Provide the appropriate journal entry for each transaction, and post the journal entries to the related T-accounts.

Solution on p. 11-51.

EARNED CAPITAL

LO11-2 Describe the effect on equity of earnings, dividends, and stock splits.

eLecture MBC

We now turn our attention to the earned capital portion of stockholders' equity. Earned capital represents the cumulative profit that has been retained by the company. Recall that earned capital is increased by income earned and decreased by any losses incurred. Earned capital is also decreased by dividends paid to shareholders. Not all dividends are paid in the form of cash, however. In fact, companies can pay dividends in many forms, including property (such as land, for example) or additional shares of stock. We cover both cash and stock dividends in this section. Earned capital also includes the positive or negative effects of accumulated other comprehensive income (AOCI). The earned capital of Pfizer is highlighted in the following graphic:

Shareholders' Equity (millions except preferred stock issued and per common share data)	Dec. 31, 2020
Preferred stock, no par value, at stated value; 27 shares authorized; issued: 2020—0; 2019—431	$ —
Common stock, $0.05 par value; 12,000 shares authorized; issued: 2020—9,407; 2019—9,369	470
Additional paid-in capital	88,674
Treasury stock, shares at cost: 2020—3,840; 2019—3,835	(110,988)
Retained earnings	97,770
Accumulated other comprehensive loss	(11,688)
Total Pfizer Inc. shareholders' equity	63,238
Equity attributable to noncontrolling interests	235
Total equity	$63,473

Cash Dividends

Many companies, but certainly not all, pay dividends. Their reasons for dividend payments are varied. Most dividends are paid in cash on a quarterly basis. The following is a description of Pfizer's dividend policy from its 2020 10-K.

> **Dividends on Common Stock**
> In December 2020, our BOD declared a first-quarter dividend of $0.39 per share, payable on March 5, 2021, to shareholders of record at the close of business on January 29, 2021. The first-quarter 2021 cash dividend will be our 329th consecutive quarterly dividend.

continued

continued from previous page

Our current and projected dividends provide a return to shareholders while maintaining sufficient capital to invest in growing our business. Our dividends are not restricted by debt covenants. While the dividend level remains a decision of Pfizer's BOD and will continue to be evaluated in the context of future business performance, we currently believe that we can support future annual dividend increases, barring significant unforeseen events. Viatris is expected to begin paying a quarterly dividend in the second quarter of 2021, at which time Pfizer's quarterly dividend is expected to be reduced such that the combined dividend dollar amount received by Pfizer shareholders, based upon the combination of continued Pfizer ownership and approximately 0.124079 shares of Viatris common stock which were granted for each Pfizer share in the spin-off, will equate to Pfizer's dividend amount in effect immediately prior to the initiation of the Viatris dividend.

Outsiders closely monitor dividend payments. It is generally perceived that the level of dividend payments is related to the expected long-term core income. Accordingly, dividend increases are usually accompanied by stock price increases, and companies rarely reduce their dividends unless absolutely necessary. Dividend reductions are, therefore, met with substantial stock-price declines.

BUSINESS INSIGHT

General Electric (GE) was one of the biggest dividend payers in the U.S. However, in 2017, the company cut its dividend in half, from 24 cents/share to 12 cents per share, in an effort to save cash—about $4 billion per year. GE's dividend cut was one of the largest in the history of the S&P 500 and the biggest since the great recession era (2009). Even after this dividend cut, it was projected that about 85% of the company's free cash flow would go toward dividends, which illuminates the change in the company and its business over time. The stock price fell around 7% on the day the dividend cut was announced and almost 6% the next day (though other negative news was simultaneously announced, so not all of the price drop was likely due to the dividend news). In December of 2018, the company slashed the dividend further to only 1 cent per share.

Financial Effects of Cash Dividends Cash dividends reduce both cash and retained earnings by the amount of the cash dividends paid. To illustrate, Pfizer paid over $8.4 billion in 2020 cash dividends on its common and preferred shares (prior to converting the preferred shares). The financial statement effects of this cash dividend payment are reflected as a reduction in assets (cash) and a reduction in retained earnings as follows.

ANALYZE

($ billions)	Balance Sheet									Income Statement				
Transaction	Cash Asset	+	Noncash Assets	=	Liabil-ities	+	Contrib. Capital	+	Earned Capital	Revenues	−	Expenses	=	Net Income
Paid $8.4 billion cash dividends on common and preferred shares.	−8.4 Cash			=					−8.4 Retained Earnings		−		=	

JOURNALIZE

Retained earnings (−SE)	8.4	
Cash (−A)		8.4

POST

− Retained Earnings (SE) +		+ Cash (A) −	
8.4			8.4

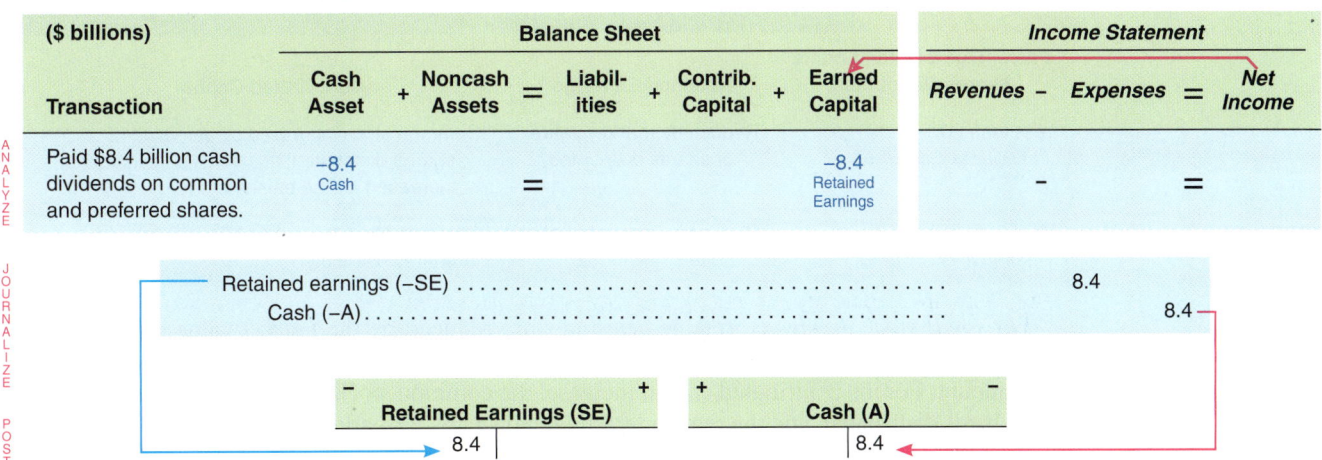

Dividend payments have no effect on profitability. They are a direct reduction to retained earnings (and cash) and bypass the income statement.

Preferred stock dividends have priority over those for common shares, including unpaid prior years' preferred dividends (dividends in arrears) when preferred stock is cumulative. To illustrate, assume that Hanna Company has 15,000 shares of $50 par value, 8% preferred stock outstanding, and 50,000 shares of $5 par value common stock outstanding. During its first three years in business, assume that Hanna declares $20,000 dividends in the first year, $260,000 of dividends in the second year, and $60,000 of dividends in the third year. If the preferred stock is cumulative, the total amount of dividends paid to each class of stock in each of the three years would be:

	Preferred Stock	Common Stock
Year 1		
Current-year dividend ($15,000 × $50 × 8%; but only $20,000 is paid, leaving $40,000 in arrears)	$20,000	
Balance to common		$ 0
Year 2		
Arrearage from Year 1 [($15,000 × $50 × 8%) − $20,000]	40,000	
Current-year dividend ($15,000 × $50 × 8%).	60,000	
Balance to common [$260,000 − ($40,000 + $60,000)].		160,000
Year 3		
Current-year dividend ($15,000 × $50 × 8%).	60,000	
Balance to common		0

Stock Dividends and Splits

Dividends need not be paid in cash. Many companies pay **stock dividends**—that is dividends in the form of additional shares of stock. Companies can also distribute additional shares to their stockholders with a stock split. We cover both of these distributions in this section.

Stock Dividends When dividends are paid in the form of the company's stock, retained earnings are reduced and contributed capital is increased. However, the amount by which retained earnings are reduced depends on the proportion of the outstanding shares distributed to the total outstanding shares on the issue date. **Exhibit 11.2** illustrates two possibilities depending on whether a stock dividend is classified as either a small stock dividend or a large stock dividend. When the additional number of shares issued as a stock dividend is so great that it is likely to have a negative impact on the market price per share of the stock, the dividend must be treated as a large stock dividend. Dividends of less than 20%–25% of the outstanding shares are considered to be small stock dividends, while dividends of more than 20%–25% are classified as large stock dividends.[7]

EXHIBIT 11.2 Analysis of Stock Dividend Effects

Percentage of Outstanding Shares Distributed	Retained Earnings	Contributed Capital
Less than 20%–25% *(small stock dividend)*	Reduce by **market value** of shares distributed	Common stock increased by par value of shares distributed; additional paid-in capital increased for the balance
More than 20%–25% *(large stock dividend)*	Reduce by **par value** of shares distributed	Common stock increased by par value of shares distributed

For *small stock dividends,* retained earnings are reduced by the *market* value of the shares distributed (dividend shares × market price per share), and contributed capital is increased by the same amount. For the contributed capital increase, the common stock is increased by the par value of the shares distributed, and the remainder [dividend shares × (market value per share − par value

[7] Standard setters did not want a "bright-line" test and allow facts and circumstances to dictate the treatment between 20% and 25%. The determining factor is the effect on price. For example, if a 25% stock dividend does not affect the stock price, it would be treated as a small stock dividend. Likewise, if a 20% stock dividend does affect price, it would be treated as a large stock dividend for accounting purposes.

per share)] increases additional paid-in capital. For *large stock dividends,* retained earnings are reduced by the *par* value of the shares distributed (dividend shares × par value per share), and common stock is increased by the same amount (no change to additional paid-in capital). A large stock dividend is referred to as a stock split effected in the form of a dividend in the financial statements.

To illustrate the financial statement effects of stock dividends, assume that a company has 1 million shares of $5 par common stock outstanding. It then declares a small stock dividend of 15% of the outstanding shares (1,000,000 shares × 15% = 150,000 shares) when the market price of the stock is $30 per share. This small stock dividend has the following financial statement effects:

ANALYZE

	Balance Sheet									Income Statement				
Transaction	Cash Asset	+	Noncash Assets	=	Liabilities	+	Contrib. Capital	+	Earned Capital	Revenues	−	Expenses	=	Net Income
Distribute 150,000 shares as a *small* stock dividend.				=			+750,000 Common Stock +3,750,000 Additional Paid-In Capital		−4,500,000 Retained Earnings		−		=	

JOURNALIZE

Retained earnings (−SE)	4,500,000	
Common stock (+SE)		750,000
Additional paid-in capital (+SE)		3,750,000

POST

Retained Earnings (SE): − 4,500,000 | +

Additional Paid-in-Capital (SE): − | + 3,750,000

Common Stock (SE): − | + 750,000

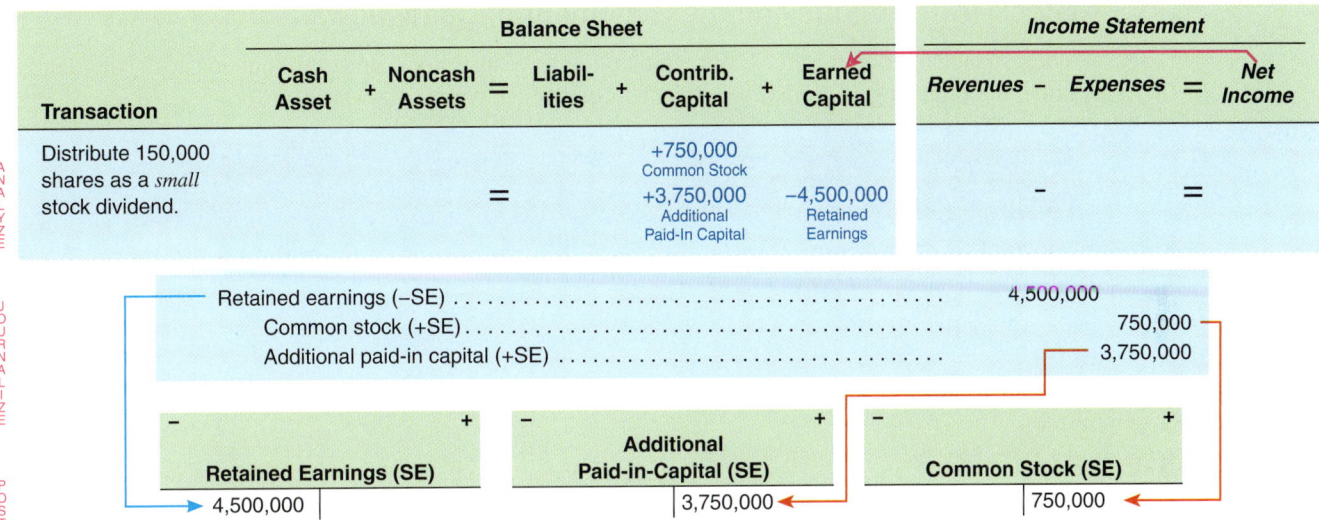

Retained earnings are reduced by $4,500,000, which equals the market value of the small stock dividend (150,000 shares × $30 market price per share). The increase in contributed capital is treated as follows: common stock is increased by the par value of $750,000 (150,000 shares × $5 par value), and the remainder of $3,750,000 increases additional paid-in capital. Similar to cash dividend payments, the stock dividends, whether large or small, never impact income. But unlike cash dividends, stock dividends do not affect the cash flows from financing activities.

Next, assume instead that a company declares a large stock dividend of 70% of the 1 million outstanding common ($5 par) shares when the market price of the stock is $30 per share. This large stock dividend has the following financial statement effects and related entries:

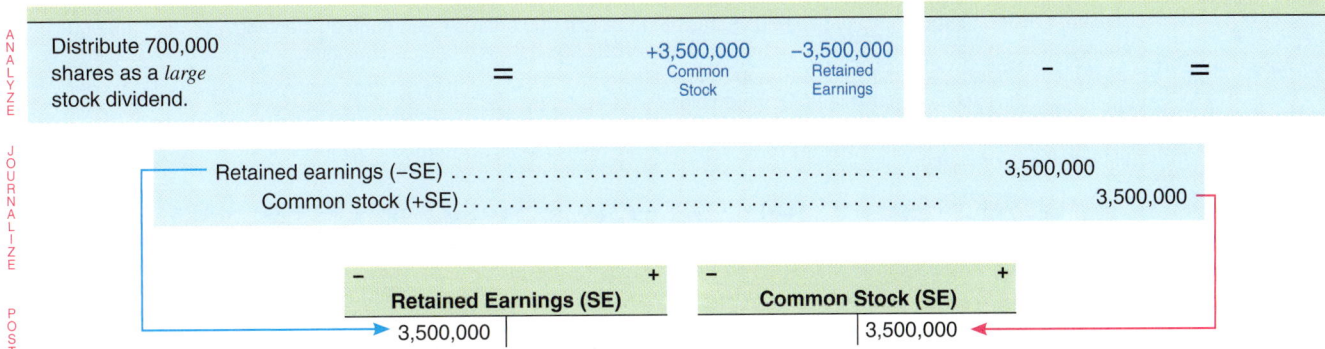

ANALYZE

Transaction	Cash Asset	+	Noncash Assets	=	Liabilities	+	Contrib. Capital	+	Earned Capital	Revenues	−	Expenses	=	Net Income
Distribute 700,000 shares as a *large* stock dividend.				=			+3,500,000 Common Stock		−3,500,000 Retained Earnings		−		=	

JOURNALIZE

Retained earnings (−SE)	3,500,000	
Common stock (+SE)		3,500,000

POST

Retained Earnings (SE): − 3,500,000 | +

Common Stock (SE): − | + 3,500,000

Retained earnings are reduced by $3,500,000, which equals the par value of the large stock dividend (700,000 shares × $5 par value per share). Common stock is increased by the par value of $3,500,000. There is no effect on additional paid-in capital because the dividend is reported at par value.

For both large and small stock dividends, companies are required to show comparable shares outstanding for all prior periods for which earnings per share (EPS) is reported in the statements. The reasoning is that a stock dividend has no effect on the ownership percentage of each common stockholder. As such, to show a dilution in reported EPS would erroneously suggest a decline in profitability when it is simply due to an increase in shares outstanding.

Stock Splits A **stock split** is a proportionate distribution of shares and, as such, is similar in substance to a stock dividend. A typical stock split is 2-for-1, which means that the company distributes one additional share for each share owned by a shareholder. Following the distribution, each investor owns twice as many shares, yet their percentage ownership in the company is unchanged.

A stock split is not a monetary transaction and, as such, there are no financial statement effects. However, companies must disclose the new number of shares outstanding for all periods presented in the financial statements. Further, many states require that the par value of shares be proportionately adjusted as well (for example, halved for a 2-for-1 split).

Stock Transactions and the Statement of Cash Flows

The issuance of common stock, the acquisition of treasury stock, and cash (but not stock) dividends affect the financing section of the statement of cash flows as follows:

Transaction	Effect on Cash Flow from Financing Activities
Issuance of Common Stock	Increase
Acquisition of Treasury Stock	Decrease
Sale of Treasury Stock	Increase
Cash Dividends Paid	Decrease

Stock splits and stock dividends do not influence the statement of cash flows.

Review 11-2 LO11-2

Accounting for Cash Dividends, Stock Dividends, and Stock Splits

GuidedExample MBC

Part One

Finn Corporation has outstanding 10,000 shares of $100 par value, 5% preferred stock, and 50,000 shares of $5 par value common stock. During its first three years in business, Finn declared no dividends in the first year, $300,000 of cash dividends in the second year, and $80,000 of cash dividends in the third year.

a. If the preferred stock is cumulative, determine the total amount of dividends paid to each class of stock for each of the three years.

b. If the preferred stock is not cumulative, determine the total amount of dividends paid to each class of stock for each of the three years.

Part Two

The stockholders' equity of Zhang Corporation at December 31 follows.

5% preferred stock, $100 par value, 10,000 shares authorized; 4,000 shares issued and outstanding	$ 400,000
Common stock, $5 par value, 200,000 shares authorized; 50,000 shares issued and outstanding	250,000
Paid-in capital in excess of par value—Preferred stock	40,000
Paid-in capital in excess of par value—Common stock	300,000
Retained earnings	656,000
Total stockholders' equity	$1,646,000

a. The following transactions occurred during the following year. Show the financial impact of each transaction using the financial statement effects template.

Apr. 1 Declared and issued a 100% stock dividend on all outstanding shares of common stock when the market value of the stock was $11 per share.

Dec. 7 Declared and issued a 3% stock dividend on all outstanding shares of common stock when the market value of the stock was $7 per share.

Dec. 31 Declared and paid a cash dividend of $1.20 per share on all outstanding common shares.

b. Provide the appropriate journal entry for each transaction listed in part *a* and post the journal entries to the related T-accounts.

c. Determine the end of year balance in retained earnings if the company reported $288,000 in earnings for the year.

d. If instead of the 100% stock dividend on April 1, the company initiated a 2-for-1 stock split, record the resulting journal entry

Solution on p. 11-52.

Comprehensive Income

LO11-3
Define and illustrate comprehensive income.

eLecture MBC

Comprehensive income is a more inclusive notion of company performance than net income. It includes all recognized changes in equity that occur during a period except those resulting from contributions by and distributions to owners.

Specifically, comprehensive income includes net income *plus* additional gains and losses not included in the income statement. These additional gains and losses are called *other comprehensive income* and include, for example, foreign currency adjustments, unrealized gains or losses on available-for-sale debt securities, unrealized gains and losses on some derivatives, and adjustments to pension and other benefit plans. Comprehensive income includes the effects on a company of some economic events that are often outside of management's control. Accordingly, some observers assert that net income is a measure of management's performance, while comprehensive income is a measure of company performance.

Comprehensive income can be reported by firms in one of two ways. The first reporting method is to present a statement of comprehensive income that combines net income and other comprehensive income in one statement. Such a statement begins much like any income statement, with revenues, cost of goods sold, operating expenses, and so forth. However, in the statement of comprehensive income, net income is a subtotal, followed by the gains and losses that are classified as other comprehensive income, along with their tax effect. The second reporting approach presents other comprehensive income (after tax) in a separate statement immediately following the income statement. Pfizer follows the second reporting approach. Its statement of comprehensive income is presented in **Exhibit 11.3**.

EXHIBIT 11.3 Pfizer's 2020 Abridged Consolidated Statement of Comprehensive Income ($ millions)

Net income before allocation to noncontrolling interests		$9,652
Other comprehensive income:		
Foreign currency translation adjustments, net	$ 957	
Reclassification adjustments	(17)	
Unrealized holding gains/(losses) on derivative financial instruments, net	(582)	
Reclassification adjustments for (gains)/losses included in net income	21	
Unrealized holding gains/(losses) on available-for-sale securities, net	361	
Reclassification adjustments for (gains)/losses included in net income	(188)	
Benefit plans: actuarial gains/(losses), net	(1,128)	
Reclassification adjustments related to amortization	276	
Reclassification adjustments related to settlements, net	278	
Other	(189)	
Benefit plans: prior service (costs)/credits and other, net	52	
Reclassification adjustments related to amortization of prior service costs and other, net	(176)	
Tax provision/(benefit)on other comprehensive income/(loss)	(349)	
Total other comprehensive income/(loss)		14
Comprehensive income before allocation to noncontrolling interests		9,666
Less: Comprehensive income attributable to noncontrolling interests		27
Comprehensive income attributable to Pfizer Inc.		$9,639

Unlike net income, other comprehensive income is not closed to retained earnings at the end of each accounting period. Instead, other comprehensive income is closed to a separate earned capital account called **accumulated other comprehensive income** (abbreviated AOCI).

In its 2020 balance sheet, Pfizer reports accumulated other comprehensive loss of $(11,688), compared to $(11,640) in 2019. The $48 decrease from 2019 to 2020 is (almost) equal to the $14 other comprehensive income for 2020 that Pfizer reported in its statement of comprehensive income (**Exhibit 11.3**) less a $71 million loss for the spin-off of the Upjohn Business.[8] (The $9 million difference is due to noncontrolling interests' share of other comprehensive income items. Note also that the noncontrolling interest is $36 million in net income and [$9] million in other comprehensive income for a total of $27, which ties to the amount shown in Exhibit 11.3.)

[8] Pfizer reported in its 2020 10-K that "the spin-off also resulted in a net increase to Accumulated other comprehensive loss of $71 million for the derecognition of net gains on foreign currency translation adjustments of $397 million and actuarial losses net of prior service credits associated with benefit plans of $326 million, which were reclassified to Retained earnings."

Summary of Stockholders' Equity

A summary of transactions that affect stockholders' equity is included in the statement of stockholders' equity. This statement reports a reconciliation of the beginning and ending balances of important stockholders' equity accounts. Pfizer's statement of stockholders' equity is shown in **Exhibit 11.4**. Pfizer's statement of shareholders' equity reveals the following key transactions for 2020:

- Total comprehensive income increased shareholders' equity by $9,639 million (net income of $9,616 million plus other comprehensive income of $23 million).
- Dividends to preferred and common shareholders decreased stockholders' equity by $8,571 million.
- Employee share-based compensation increased equity by $1,044 million.
- Conversion of preferred stock into common stock and redemptions decreased the preferred stock account, for a net decrease in stockholders' equity of $1 million.
- The spin-off of the Upjohn business resulted in a decrease in stockholders' equity of $2,015 million.

EXHIBIT 11.4 **Pfizer's Stockholders' Equity (December 31, 2020)**

(Millions, Except Preferred Shares)	Preferred Stock Shares	Preferred Stock Stated Value	Common Stock Shares	Common Stock Par Value	Additional Paid-In Capital	Treasury Stock Shares	Treasury Stock Cost	Retained Earnings	Accum. Other Comp. Loss	Share-holders' Equity	Non-controlling Interests	Total Equity
Balance December 31, 2019	431	$17	9,369	$468	$87,428	(3,835)	$(110,801)	$97,670	$(11,640)	$63,143	$303	$63,447
Net income								9,616		9,616	36	9,652
Other comprehensive income/(loss), net of tax									23	23	(9)	14
Cash dividends declared:												
Common stock								(8,571)		(8,571)		(8,571)
Noncontrolling interests											(91)	(91)
Share-based payment transactions			37	2	1,261	(6)	(218)			1,044		1,044
Preferred stock conversions and redemptions	(432)	(17)			(15)	1	31			(1)		(1)
Distribution of Upjohn Business								(1,944)	(71)	(2,015)	(3)	
Other											(1)	(1)
Balance December 31, 2020	—	$—	9,407	$470	$88,674	(3,840)	$(110,988)	$96,770	$(11,688)	$63,238	$235	$63,473

*Amounts may be off by $1 due to rounding.

ANALYZING FINANCIAL STATEMENTS

Analysis Objective

We want to measure the return on investment by common shareholders.

Before getting to the specifics of the performance ratio, we must address a complexity introduced when a company (like Pfizer) has a subsidiary that is not 100% owned. Suppose Company A owns 85% of the common stock of Company B. The remaining 15% of B's shareholders are called a "noncontrolling interest." Company A would be required to incorporate the assets, liabilities, revenues, and expenses of Company B in its reports. As a result, Company A's reported net income would include all the income from both A and B. But then there is an adjustment in which 15% of B's income is subtracted (as "net income attributable to noncontrolling interests"), and the resulting number is "net income attributable to common shareholders." We use this information to develop the following measure of profit that can be attributed to common shareholders of the reporting company.

Net income
– Net income attributable to noncontrolling interests
– Preferred dividends
Net income available for common shareholders

A similar adjustment is required on the balance sheet, where total equity consists of "equity attributable to noncontrolling interests" plus "common shareholders' equity" (as can be seen in **Exhibit 11.4**).

Total equity
– Equity attributable to noncontrolling interests
– Preferred stock equity
Common shareholders' equity

Analysis Tool Return on Common Equity (ROCE)

$$\text{Return on Common Equity (ROCE)} = \frac{\text{Net income available for common shareholders}}{\text{Average common shareholders' equity}}$$

Applying the Ratio to Pfizer

$$\textbf{2018: } \text{ROCE} = \frac{\$11{,}188 - \$36 - \$19}{[(\$63{,}758 - \$351 - \$19) + (\$71{,}656 - \$348 - \$21)]/2} = 0.165, \text{ or } 16.5\%$$

$$\textbf{2019: } \text{ROCE} = \frac{\$16{,}302 - \$351 - \$19}{[(63{,}447 - \$303 - \$17) + (\$63{,}758 - \$351 - \$19)]/2} = 0.252, \text{ or } 25.2\%$$

$$\textbf{2020: } \text{ROCE} = \frac{\$9{,}652 - \$36 - \$0}{[(\$63{,}473 - \$235 - \$0) + (\$63{,}447 - \$303 - \$17)]/2} = 0.152, \text{ or } 15.2\%$$

Guidance ROCE is similar to ROE except that when we compute ROCE, we remove the effect of noncontrolling interests and preferred stock from both the numerator and the denominator.

Pfizer in Context

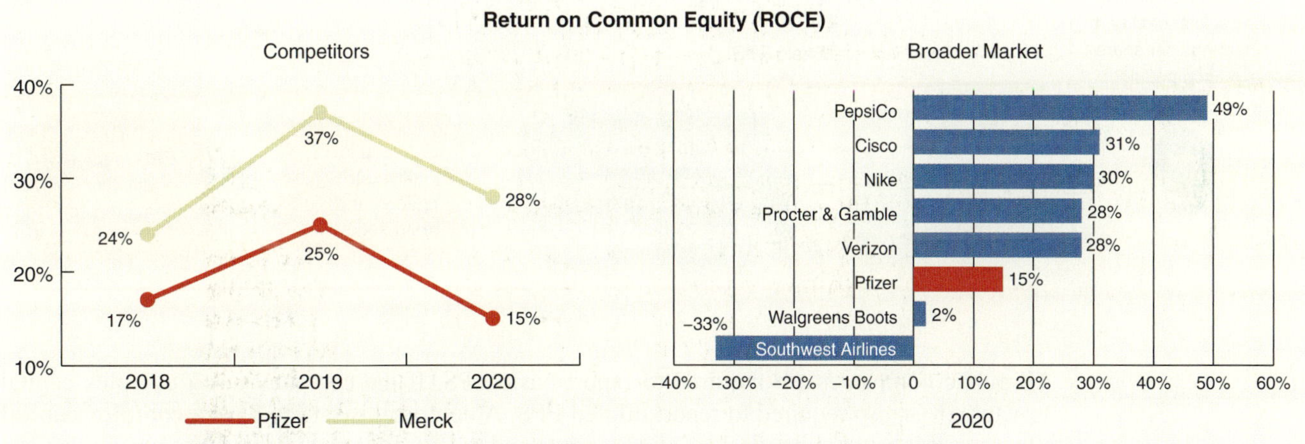

Takeaways Neither Pfizer's nor Merck's ROCE has been stable for the past few years. Such volatility can occur from changes in equity, perhaps due to large share repurchases in a year, which decreases equity, or large changes in income, either from operations or one-time items such as gains (losses) on sales of discontinued operations. Pfizer's 2020 ROCE is on the lower end, relative to many of the other focus companies in this textbook.

Many companies have little or no preferred stock or noncontrolling interests. So the difference between return on common equity (ROCE) and return on equity (ROE) will be immaterial for these firms. When preferred stock is present, ROCE is a more accurate measure of return to common shareholders.

Other Considerations In Chapter 5, we learned that ROE can be decomposed into two components: return on assets and return on financial leverage. Differences between firms may reflect a difference in performance, or a difference in the reliance on debt financing. A similar division can be done with ROCE with the caveat that ROCE essentially treats preferred stock as debt rather than equity.

One final point: the financial press sometimes refers to a measure called **book value per share**. This amount is the net book value of the company that is available to common shareholders, defined as: stockholders' equity less preferred stock less equity attributable to noncontrolling interest divided by the number of common shares outstanding (issued common shares less treasury shares). Pfizer's 2020 book value per share is computed as: ($63,473 million – $235 million – $0 million)/(9,407 million shares – 3,840 million shares) = $11.36 book value per common share.

Review 11-3 LO11-3 — Presenting Other Comprehensive Income

GuidedExample MBC

Fastenal Company and Subsidiaries
NYSE: FAST

In its 2020 10-K, **Fastenal Company and Subsidiaries** reported the following items ($ millions):

Sales	$5,647.3
Net earnings	859.1
Earnings before income taxes	1,132.7
Foreign currency translation adjustment (net of tax)	17.2
Accumulated other comprehensive (loss), Dec. 31, 2020	(21.2)
Accumulated other comprehensive (loss), Dec. 31, 2019	(38.4)
Total stockholders' equity, Dec. 31, 2020	2,733.2

a. Prepare a statement of comprehensive income that would immediately follow the company's income statement.

b. Prepare a reconciliation of accumulated other comprehensive income that would be included as part of the company's statement of stockholders' equity.

Solution on p. 11-53.

EARNINGS PER SHARE

LO11-4
Describe and illustrate the basic and diluted earnings per share computations.

eLecture MBC

The income statement reports at least one, and potentially two, earnings per share (EPS) numbers: basic and diluted. The difference between the two measures is illustrated as follows:

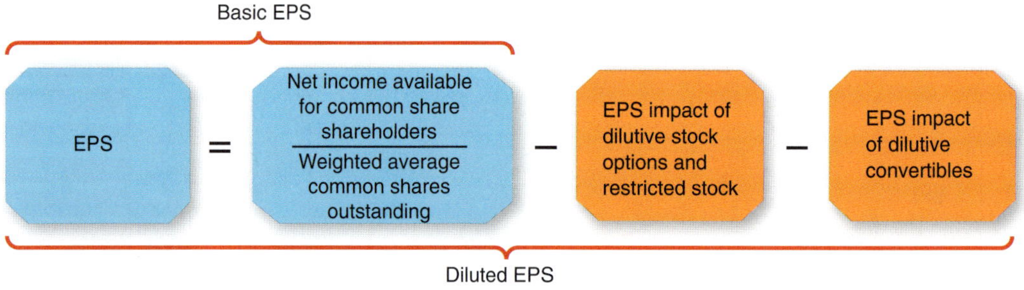

All public companies are required to report basic EPS. If the company has a complex capital structure, it is also required to report diluted EPS. A company is said to have a **complex capital structure** if it has certain *dilutive securities* outstanding. **Dilutive securities** are securities that can be converted into shares of common stock and would therefore reduce (or dilute) the earnings per share upon conversion. A few of the more prominent types of potentially dilutive securities are:

- Equity-based pay, including stock options and restricted stock
- Convertible debt
- Convertible preferred stock

The Appendix at the end of this chapter details the accounting for these securities. A company with none of these dilutive securities outstanding is said to have a **simple capital structure**.

Basic EPS (BEPS) is computed as earnings available for common shareholders (net income less net income attributable to noncontrolling interests and preferred dividends) divided by the weighted average number of common shares outstanding for the year. (The number of shares is "weighted" by the amount of time each share was outstanding during the year.) The subtraction of net income attributable to noncontrolling interests and preferred stock dividends yields the income per common share available for dividend payments to common shareholders. The preferred dividends are subtracted because this portion of net income does not accrue to the common stockholders.

Computation of **Diluted EPS (DEPS)** reflects the added shares that would have been issued if all "in the money" stock options, unvested restricted stock, and other convertible securities had been exercised at the beginning of the year. When DEPS is calculated, the corporation needs to consider the maximum potential reduction (dilution) of its BEPS that could occur if the conversion of these securities took place. To do so means that only securities that reduce BEPS upon conversion are to be considered converted. The result (DEPS) must be a figure that is lower than BEPS. The actual calculation can be quite complex. This does not detract from the importance of the DEPS value. The diluted earnings per share figure is favored by analysts as a better indicator of performance compared to basic earnings per share. Because reported DEPS never exceeds reported BEPS, the calculation is considered conservative.

Computation and Analysis of EPS

The computation of basic EPS is relatively straightforward, particularly when the firm neither issues nor buys any of its shares during the year. The formula is:

$$\textbf{Basic EPS (BEPS)} = \frac{\textbf{Net income available for common shareholders}}{\textbf{Weighted average number of common shares outstanding}}$$

To illustrate this calculation, assume that United Bridge Corporation reported net income of \$200,000 in 2021 and paid \$24,000 in preferred dividends. At the beginning of the year, the company had 44,000 shares of common stock outstanding. On June 30 (exactly the midpoint of the year) United Bridge purchased 8,000 shares of stock as treasury stock. Thus, the number of shares outstanding for the first six months of 2021 was 44,000 and, for the second half of the year, the company had 36,000 shares outstanding. The weighted average number of shares outstanding was, therefore, 40,000 [(44,000 + 36,000)/2]. Basic EPS would be calculated as follows:

$$\textbf{Basic EPS} = \frac{\textbf{\$200,000} - \textbf{\$24,000}}{\textbf{40,000 shares}} = \textbf{\$4.40 per share}$$

The computation of diluted EPS is more complex in that it requires adjusting the basic EPS calculation for the effect of dilutive securities. This will typically require adjusting both the numerator and the denominator of the calculation, using the if-converted method.

$$\textbf{Diluted earnings per share (DEPS)} = \frac{\textbf{Net income available for common shareholders + Add-backs}}{\textbf{Weighted average number of common shares + Shares of convertible securities and stock options assumed to be converted}}$$

To illustrate, assume that United Bridge Corporation's preferred stock is convertible into 8,000 shares of common stock. To calculate diluted EPS, we must assume that the convertible preferred shares were converted at the beginning of the year. If this had occurred, two things would have been different for United Bridge. First, the weighted average number of shares outstanding would be higher by 8,000 shares. Second, the company would not have paid preferred dividends of \$24,000. The resulting calculation would be:

$$\textbf{Diluted EPS} = \frac{\textbf{\$200,000}}{\textbf{48,000 shares}} = \textbf{\$4.17 per share}$$

A full description of the procedures for calculating diluted EPS is beyond the scope of this text.[9] However, as the calculation above illustrates, diluted EPS adjusts basic EPS for the effect of dilutive securities. Reported DEPS must be no larger than BEPS to reflect its conservative message.

Pfizer reports both basic and diluted EPS. The table below, drawn from Pfizer's 2020 consolidated income statement, presents its basic and diluted EPS figures.

[9] Also, some more complicated securities, including securities in the mezzanine section of the balance sheet, may lead to required adjustments to the numerator of basic EPS at times, and to both the numerator and the denominator of diluted EPS. We note also that while there were previously two methods to compute diluted EPS with respect to convertible instruments; entities may only use one method now under U.S. GAAP. The "if-converted" method is required to be used and the "treasury stock method" should no longer be used (ASU 2020-06). These are beyond the scope of this text, but we note them here for those interested in studying the topic more.

Year Ended December 31	2020	2019
Earnings per common share—basic		
Income from continuing operations attributable to Pfizer Inc. common shareholders	$1.26	$1.95
Income from discontinued operations—net of tax	0.47	0.98
Net income attributable to Pfizer Inc. common shareholders	$1.73	$2.92
Earnings per common share—diluted		
Income from continuing operations attributable to Pfizer Inc. common shareholders	$1.24	$1.91
Income from discontinued operations—net of tax	0.47	0.96
Net income attributable to Pfizer Inc. common shareholders	$1.71	$2.87
Weighted average shares—basic (millions)	5,555	5,569
Weighted average shares—diluted (millions)	5,632	5,675

Several observations should be made regarding Pfizer's EPS disclosures:

1. Pfizer reports basic EPS of $1.73 in 2020 and $2.92 in 2019. Diluted EPS is $0.02 lower and $0.05 lower in 2020 and 2019, respectively, relative to basic EPS. The difference between basic and diluted EPS is caused by the effect of dilutive securities. Specifically, Pfizer has outstanding stock options and convertible preferred stock (in 2019 and part of 2020), and accelerated share repurchase agreements. Most publicly traded companies have at least one type of dilutive security outstanding. The dilutive effect of these securities on Pfizer's EPS is small.
2. The income statement further separates these EPS figures into EPS from continuing operations and EPS from discontinued operations. Discontinued operations resulted in an increase to EPS in both 2020 and 2019. GAAP requires separate reporting of the effects of nonrecurring items on EPS, including discontinued operations (see Chapter 6).
3. Pfizer used weighted average shares outstanding of 5,555 million shares to calculate basic EPS in 2020. This number is not the same as the number of shares outstanding in its December 31, 2020, balance sheet. Nor is it the simple average of the beginning and ending numbers of shares outstanding. The precise number of shares used in the EPS calculations requires knowing exactly when common stock and treasury stock transactions occurred during the year so that the weighted average number of shares outstanding can be calculated. Such detailed information is seldom available in a company's 10-K report.

EPS figures are sometimes used as a method of comparing operating results for companies of different sizes under the assumption that the number of shares outstanding is proportional to the income level (that is, a company twice the size of another will report double the income and will have double the common shares outstanding, leaving EPS approximately equal for the two companies). This assumption is erroneous. Management controls the number of common shares outstanding. Different companies also have different philosophies regarding share issuance and repurchase. For example, consider that most companies report annual EPS of less than $5, while **Berkshire Hathaway Inc.** reported EPS of $26,668 for 2020! The large amount occurs because Berkshire Hathaway has so few common shares outstanding, not necessarily because it has stellar profits.

Most analysts prefer to concentrate their attention on diluted EPS versus basic EPS as the more important measure, but the value of the EPS number is influenced by a number of factors including the number of common shares outstanding. For this reason, comparisons are more useful over time than across firms, but a careful reader should differentiate between EPS growth that comes from increases in the numerator and EPS growth that comes from decreases in the denominator. For these reasons, EPS may be of limited use in evaluating a firm's operational performance.

BUSINESS INSIGHT

It is possible that reported earnings declines but Basic EPS increases. For example, for its year ended July 2020, Cisco Systems, Inc., had a decline in earnings of 3.5% but its basic EPS increased by 2 cents a share. Another example in recent years is Signet Jewelers who one year had a decline in earnings of almost 5% and an increase in Basic EPS of 8%. A similar relation held for IBM in the years 2012–2014. Often this is due to reductions in the number of shares due to share repurchases.

Computing Basic and Diluted Earnings per Share LO11-4 **Review 11-4**

Petroni Corporation reported net income of $1,750 million for the year. The weighted average number of common shares outstanding during the year was 760 million shares. Petroni paid $40 million in dividends on preferred stock, which was convertible into 10 million shares of common stock.

a. Calculate Petroni's basic earnings per share.
b. Calculate Petroni's diluted earnings per share.
c. What EPS numbers should Petroni report on its annual income statement?

GuidedExample MBC

Solution on p. 11-54.

APPENDIX 11A: Dilutive Securities: Accounting for Convertible Securities, Stock Options, and Restricted Stock

Convertible Securities

LO11-5 Analyze the accounting for convertible securities, stock rights, stock options, and restricted stock.

eLecture MBC

Convertible securities are debt and equity securities that provide the holder with an option to convert those securities into other securities. Convertible debentures, for example, are debt securities that give the holder the option to convert the debt into common stock at a predetermined conversion price. Preferred stock can also contain a conversion privilege.

To illustrate, assume 5,000 shares of preferred stock were issued at a stated value of $100 per share, with each share convertible into 12 shares of $5 par value common stock. The appropriate journal entry would be:

Cash (+A)	500,000	
Preferred stock (stated value) (+SE)		500,000

Now assume that 2,000 shares are converted to (2,000 × 12) = 24,000 shares of common stock. The appropriate journal entry is:

Preferred stock (stated value) (−SE)	200,000	
Common stock (par $5) (+SE)		120,000
Additional paid-in capital (+SE)		80,000

Conversion privileges offer an additional benefit to the holder of a security. That is, debtholders and preferred stockholders carry senior positions as claimants in bankruptcy and carry a fixed-interest or dividend yield. With a conversion privilege, they can enjoy the residual benefits of common shareholders should the company perform well.

A conversion option is valuable and yields a higher price for the securities than they would otherwise command. However, conversion privileges impose a cost on common shareholders. That is, the higher market price received for convertible securities is offset by the cost imposed on the subordinate (common) securities. Conversion of these securities into common shares dilutes the ownership percentage of existing holders of the firm's common stock.

The accounting for the conversion features at issuance was previously complex at times as GAAP had five models for convertible debt instruments. One model recorded the instrument as a single debt instrument and the other four required separation of the debt instrument and conversion option. Convertible preferred stock was assessed under similar models. Described at a high level here, in 2021, FASB simplified the accounting such that convertible debt will be accounted for at issuance as one security unless the conversion option is required to be accounted for as a derivative security or the convertible debt is issued with a substantial premium for which the premiums are recorded as paid-in capital. If the conversion option is equity, no separation or bifurcation is required. The accounting treatment for convertible preferred stock is similar in the sense that generally only when the conversion feature is required to be accounted for as a derivative will the security be bifurcated for accounting purposes. The new guidance (ASU 2020-06) also requires more disclosures.

When securities are converted, the book value of the converted security is removed from the balance sheet and a corresponding increase is made to contributed capital. To illustrate the most commonly used method, assume that a company has convertible bonds with a face value of $1,000 and an unamortized premium of $100. Its holders convert them into 20 shares of $10 par value common stock. The financial statement effects and related entries of this conversion would be:

ANALYZE

	Balance Sheet									Income Statement				
Transaction	**Cash Asset**	+	**Noncash Assets**	=	**Liabil-ities**	+	**Contrib. Capital**	+	**Earned Capital**	***Revenues***	–	***Expenses***	=	***Net Income***
$1,100 book value bonds are converted into 20 common shares of $10 par value.				=	−1,000 Bonds Payable −100 Bonds Premium		+200 Common Stock +900 Additional Paid-In Capital				–		=	

JOURNALIZE

Bonds payable (−L)	1,000	
Bonds premium (−L)	100	
Common stock (+SE)		200
Additional paid-in capital (+SE)		900

POST

− Bonds Payable (L) +	
1,000	

− Additional Paid-in Capital (SE) +	
	900

− Bonds Premium (L) +	
100	

− Common Stock (SE) +	
	200

The key financial statement effects of this transaction are:

- The bond's face value ($1,000) and unamortized premium ($100) of the bonds are removed from the balance sheet.
- Common stock increases by the par value of the shares issued (20 shares × $10 par = $200), and additional paid-in capital increases for the balance ($900).
- There is no effect on income from this conversion unless an interest accrual is required.

One final note: the potentially dilutive effect of convertible securities is taken into account in the computation of diluted earnings per share (DEPS). Specifically, the diluted EPS computation assumes conversion at the beginning of the year (or when the security is issued if during the year). The earnings available to common shares in the numerator are increased by any forgone after-tax interest expense or preferred dividends, and the additional shares to be issued in the conversion increase the shares outstanding in the denominator.

Stock Rights

Corporations often issue **stock rights** that give the holder an option to acquire a specified number of shares of capital stock under prescribed conditions and within a stated period. The evidence of stock rights is a certificate called a **stock warrant**. Stock rights are issued for several reasons that include the following:

- To compensate outside parties (such as underwriters, promoters, board members, and other professionals) for services provided to the company;
- As a preemptive right that gives existing stockholders the first chance to buy additional shares when the corporation decides to raise additional equity capital through share issuances;
- To enhance the marketability of other securities issued by the company (an example is issuing rights to purchase common stock with convertible bonds).

Stock rights or warrants specify the:

- Number of rights represented by the warrant
- Option price per share (which can be zero)
- Number of rights needed to obtain a share of the stock
- Expiration date of the rights
- Instructions for the exercise of rights

Accounting for stock rights is complex. The goals of this discussion are to understand the essence of stock rights issued to current stockholders.

Stock rights issued to current stockholders have three important dates: (1) Announcement date of the rights offering; (2) Issuance date of the rights; and (3) Expiration date of the rights. Between the announcement date and the issuance date, the price of the stock will reflect the value of the rights. After the issuance date, the shares and the rights trade separately. Shareholders can exercise their rights, sell their stock, or allow the rights to lapse.

To illustrate, assume on December 10, 2021, a company announces the issue of rights to purchase one additional share of its $5 par value common stock for every 10 shares currently held on January 1, 2022. The exercise price per share is $20, and the rights expire September 1, 2022. Assume further that 7,000 of the rights are exercised.

- No recognition is required at the announcement date and at the issuance date.
- The first entry is made when the first stock right is exercised. We give only the summary entry that would be appropriate after September 1, 2022.

Sept 1: To record the issuance of 7,000 shares of common stock on exercise of stock rights:
The financial statement effects and related entries would be (amounts in millions): .

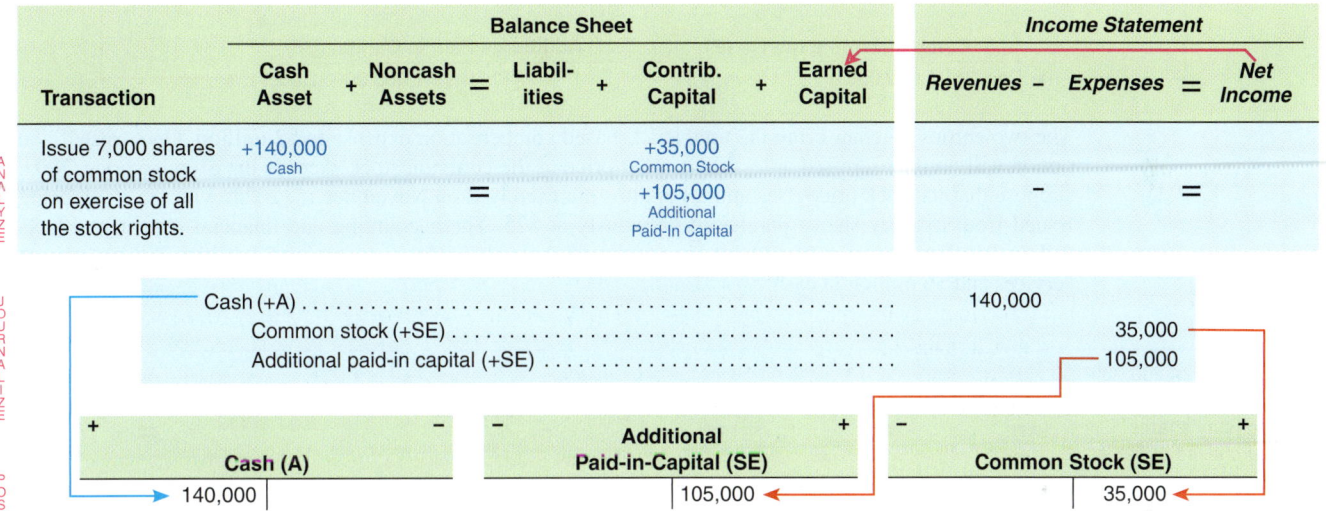

ANALYZE

	Balance Sheet									Income Statement				
Transaction	**Cash Asset**	+	**Noncash Assets**	=	**Liabilities**	+	**Contrib. Capital**	+	**Earned Capital**	***Revenues***	−	***Expenses***	=	***Net Income***
Issue 7,000 shares of common stock on exercise of all the stock rights.	+140,000 Cash			=			+35,000 Common Stock +105,000 Additional Paid-In Capital				−		=	

JOURNALIZE

Cash (+A)	140,000	
Common stock (+SE)		35,000
Additional paid-in capital (+SE)		105,000

POST

+ Cash (A) −		− Additional Paid-in-Capital (SE) +		− Common Stock (SE) +	
140,000			105,000		35,000

Employee Stock Options

Employee stock options are granted to employees in exchange for service. The option gives the employee the right, but not the obligation, to purchase a share of stock in the future at a price specified today. Generally, options are granted with a strike price (or exercise price) equal to the market price on the date of grant. Stock options are expensed for financial accounting purposes in an amount equal to the fair value of the options on the date of grant. For example, in Note 13 to its 10-K report, Pfizer reported the fair value of stock option grants to be $6.4 million on December 31, 2020 (1.8 million options granted × 3.56 per option).

Stock option grants normally require a vesting period. The **vesting period** is a period of time during which the employee is not allowed to exercise the stock option. For example, a stock option may expire in 5 years and vest over a period of 3 years. Such an option would be exercisable in the fourth or fifth year of its life. Rather than recognizing the entire option value as compensation expense at the time that the option grant is awarded, GAAP requires that the fair value of the option be recorded ratably over the vesting period.

To illustrate stock option accounting, suppose that on January 1, 2021, a company grants options to purchase 200,000 shares to senior management as part of its performance bonus plan. The options are granted with an exercise price of $30 (the current price) and can be exercised after vesting in 2 years. The firm uses an accepted valuation method (not discussed here) to obtain a fair value of $10 per option. The accounting and financial statement effects and related entries for 2021 would be:

January 1—grant date

The total compensation cost is determined at the grant date, but no journal entry is recorded on the grant date.

December 31, 2021 and 2022—record compensation expense:

ANALYZE JOURNALIZE POST

Transaction	Cash Asset +	Noncash Assets =	Liabilities +	Contrib. Capital +	Earned Capital −	Contra Equity	Revenues −	Expenses =	Net Income
Record compensation expense for 200,000 options granted at $30, valued at $10 per share, vested at 50% per year.				+1,000,000 Additional Paid-In Capital	−1,000,000 Retained Earnings			+1,000,000 Compensation Expense	−1,000,000

Dec. 31	Compensation expense (+E, −SE)	1,000,000	
	Additional paid-in capital (+SE)		1,000,000

+ Compensation Expense (E) −		− Additional Paid-in Capital (SE) +	
Dec. 31 1,000,000			1,000,000 Dec. 31

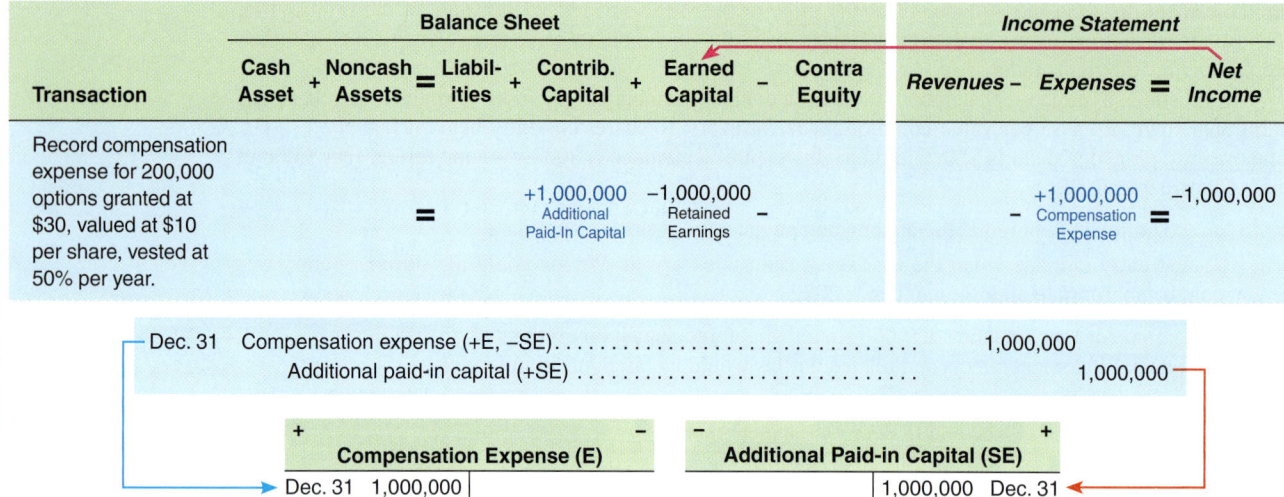

The two entries together bring the total stock-based compensation expense to $2 million. Once vested, the option will not be exercised unless the market price of the common stock exceeds the exercise price. Next, suppose that its stock price rises and all options are exercised on November 15, 2023, with the stock being issued from treasury shares purchased previously at $25. The accounting and financial statement effects follow. In effect, senior management has purchased these shares by contributing $2 million in employment services and $6 million in cash.

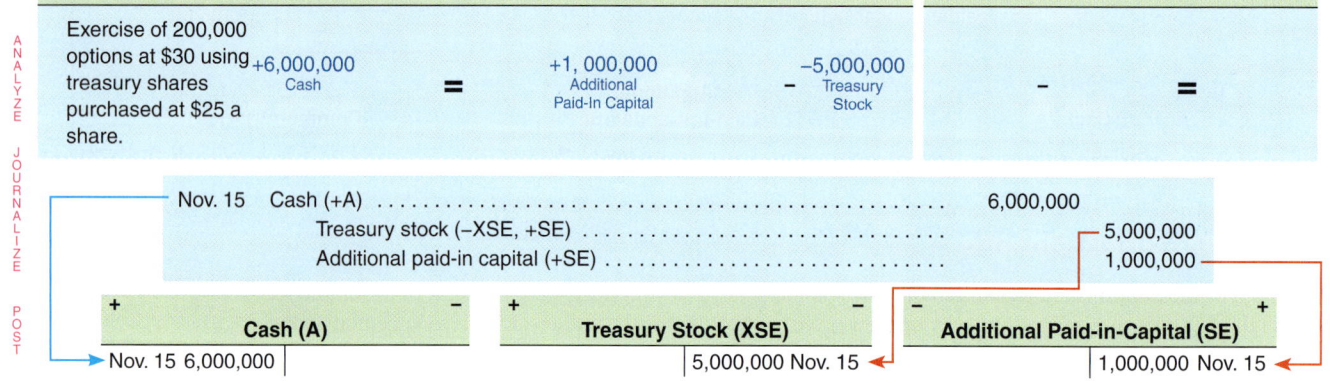

ANALYZE JOURNALIZE POST

Transaction	Cash Asset +	Noncash Assets =	Liabilities +	Contrib. Capital +	Earned Capital −	Contra Equity	Revenues −	Expenses =	Net Income
Exercise of 200,000 options at $30 using treasury shares purchased at $25 a share.	+6,000,000 Cash			+1, 000,000 Additional Paid-In Capital		−5,000,000 Treasury Stock			

Nov. 15	Cash (+A)	6,000,000	
	Treasury stock (−XSE, +SE)		5,000,000
	Additional paid-in capital (+SE)		1,000,000

+ Cash (A) −		+ Treasury Stock (XSE) −		− Additional Paid-in-Capital (SE) +	
Nov. 15 6,000,000			5,000,000 Nov. 15		1,000,000 Nov. 15

Restricted Stock

Companies are increasingly moving away from stock options to other types of performance-based pay. One type that is commonly used is restricted stock, either in the form of restricted stock share awards or restricted stock unit awards (which we refer to hereafter as **restricted stock awards (RSAs)** and **restricted stock units (RSUs)** for convenience). Indeed, Pfizer awarded no options under its stock option plan in 2018, 2019, or 2020. In 2020, Pfizer granted $272 million in value of RSUs.

Restricted stock plans give employees shares or rights to shares, but these are restricted (meaning the employee does not have full ownership) until the employee has satisfied vesting requirements. If the employee leaves before the awards vest, the shares or rights would be lost. Pfizer states that it has a three-year vesting period.

While unvested, both RSAs and RSUs are potentially dilutive securities in the calculation of diluted EPS. We note that, generally, unvested RSAs are not included in the calculation of basic EPS, even though as we will see below, the shares are outstanding. (However, sometimes they are considered participating securities and included in the calculation of basic EPS. For example, CISCO excludes them from basic EPS and Facebook includes them.) RSUs are not outstanding shares and are not included in the calculation of basic EPS. RSUs are considered potentially dilutive in the calculation of diluted EPS.

Restricted Stock Award (RSA)

An RSA is a form of equity compensation that transfers stock to the recipient on the date of the grant. It is not an option to buy shares but rather an award of shares. The recipient's rights in shares are restricted until the shares vest.

On the grant date of an RSA, the company increases (debits) a contra-equity account, Unearned Compensation—Equity (also called Deferred Compensation), for the fair value of the shares at the grant date. Common Stock at par and Paid-in Capital in Excess of Par are increased (credited). Over the vesting period, this Unearned Compensation-Equity amount is reversed to Compensation Expense using the straight-line method. Note that compensation is valued at the fair value of the shares at the grant date and is unaffected by any change in stock value during the vesting period.

To illustrate, suppose that on January 1, 2022 a company grants 1,000 shares (RSAs) with a total fair value of $30,000 and a 3-year vesting period. Common stock has a $1 per share par value. The accounting and financial statement effects and related entries on the grant date would be:

ANALYZE

	Balance Sheet											Income Statement			
Transaction	Cash Asset	+	Noncash Assets	=	Liabilities	+	Contrib. Capital	+	Earned Capital	−	Contra Equity	*Revenues*	− *Expenses*	=	*Net Income*
1,000 restricted stock awards				=			+1,000 Common Stock +29,000 Paid-in Capital—Common Stock			−	+30,000 Unearned Comp.—Equity		−	=	

JOURNALIZE

Jan. 1	Unearned compensation—Equity (+XSE, −SE)	30,000	
	Common stock (+SE)		1,000
	Paid-in capital in excess of par—Common stock (+SE)		29,000

POST

+ Unearned Compensation—Equity (XSE) −		− Common Stock (SE) +		− Paid-in Capital in Excess of Par—CS (SE) +	
30,000			1,000		29,000

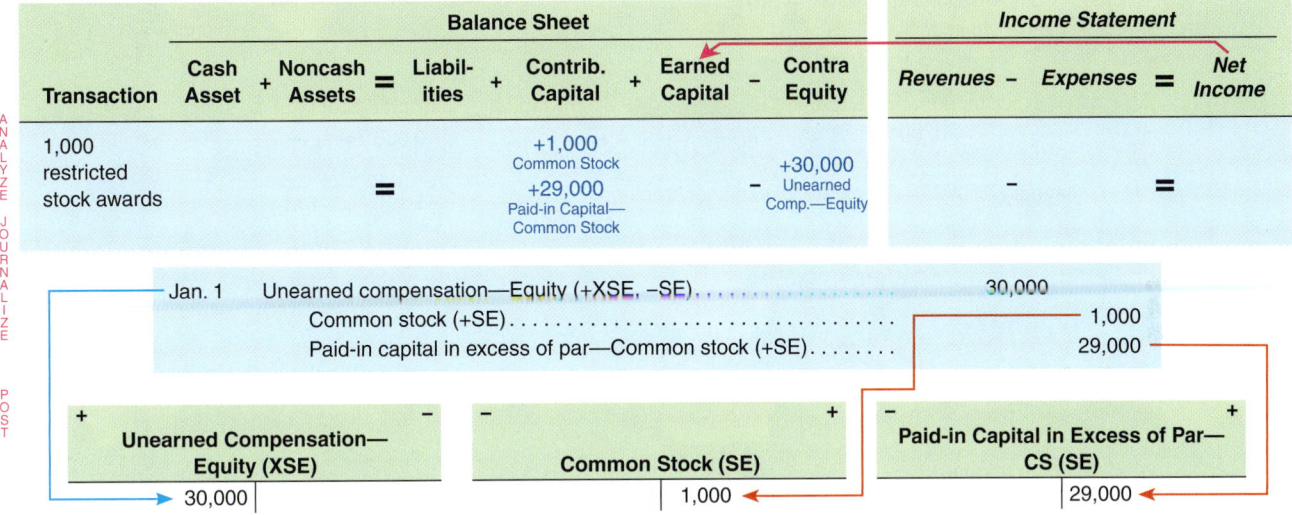

December 31, 2022, 2023, and 2024—To record compensation expense

ANALYZE

Transaction	Cash Asset	+	Noncash Assets	=	Liabilities	+	Contrib. Capital	+	Earned Capital	−	Contra Equity	Revenues	− Expenses	=	Net Income
Record compensation expense				=					−10,000 Retained Earnings	−	−10,000 Unearned Comp—Equity		− +10,000 Compensation Expense	=	−10,000

JOURNALIZE

Dec. 31	Compensation expense (+E, −SE)	10,000	
	Unearned compensation—Equity (−XSE, +SE)		10,000

POST

+ Compensation Expense (E) −		+ Unearned Compensations—Equity (XSE) −	
10,000			10,000

Restricted Stock Unit (RSU)

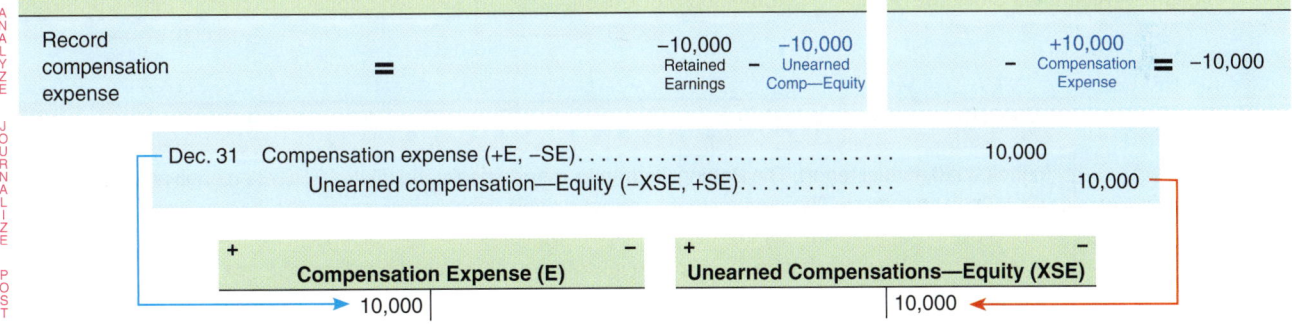

An RSU is not an actual transfer of stock on the grant date, but rather a commitment to transfer stock once vesting conditions are met. Thus, upon the grant of an RSU, the employee is granted the right to receive a certain number of shares of stock at a future date under certain conditions. There is no issuance of shares on the grant date, in contrast to the RSA discussed above; thus, no accounting entry is required on the grant date. The compensation value is determined at the grant date, however. Over the vesting period as the compensation is earned, the company records Compensation Expense (debit) and increases (credits) an account called Paid-in Capital—Restricted Stock for the proportionate share of the value each reporting period (using the straight-line method). After the employee meets the vesting requirements (the restrictions lapse), the amount from Paid-in Capital—Restricted Stock is transferred to Common Stock at par and Paid-in Capital—Common Stock.

To illustrate, suppose that on January 1, 2022, a company grants 1,000 RSUs. Each RSU may be exchanged for 1 share of $1 par common stock. The fair value of the shares on the grant date is $30, and the requisite service period is 3 years. (Assume no forfeitures and no expectation of forfeitures.) The accounting and financial statement effects and related entries would be:

January 1, 2022—Grant of RSUs

No entry.

December 31, 2022, 2023, and 2024—To record compensation expense

ANALYZE

	Balance Sheet						Income Statement		
Transaction	Cash Asset	+ Noncash Assets	= Liabilities	+ Contrib. Capital	+ Earned Capital	− Contra Equity	Revenues	− Expenses	= Net Income
Record compensation expense			=	+10,000 Paid-in Capital—Restricted Stock	−10,000 Retained Earnings	−		− +10,000 Compensation Expense	= −10,000

JOURNALIZE

Dec. 31	Compensation expense (+E, −SE)	10,000	
	Paid-in capital—Restricted stock (+SE)		10,000

POST

+ Compensation Expense (E) −	
10,000	

− Paid-in Capital—Restricted Stock (SE) +	
	10,000

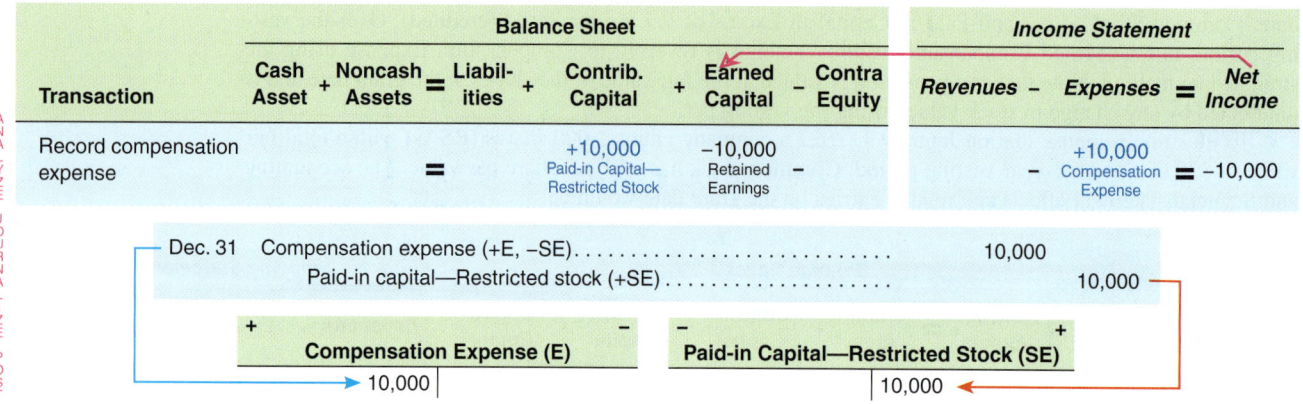

January 1, 2022—To record issuance of stock

ANALYZE

Transaction	Cash Asset	+ Noncash Assets	= Liabilities	+ Contrib. Capital	+ Earned Capital	− Contra Equity	Revenues	− Expenses	= Net Income
Issuance of stock			=	-30,000 Paid-in Capital—Restricted Stock +1,000 Common Stock +29,000 Paid-in Capital—Common Stock		−		−	=

JOURNALIZE

Jan. 1	Paid-in capital—Restricted stock (−SE)	30,000	
	Common Stock (+SE)		1,000
	Paid-in Capital excess of par—Common stock (+SE)		29,000

POST

− Paid-in Capital—Restricted Stock (SE) +	
30,000	

− Common Stock (SE) +	
	1,000

− Paid-in Capital in Excess of Par—CS (SE) +	
	10,000

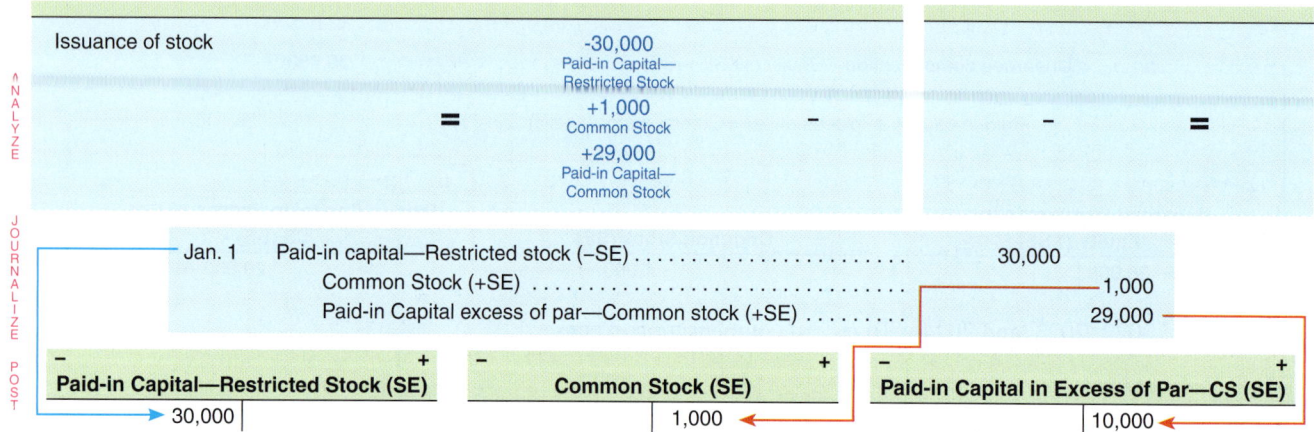

BUSINESS INSIGHT

In their 2020 annual report, The Boeing Company, reports basic and diluted EPS at an equivalent amount of ($20.88) per share. The company states that diluted (loss)/earnings per share includes any dilutive impact of stock options, restricted stock units, performance-based restricted stock units, and performance awards. They also state that for 2020, potential common shares of 1.6 million were excluded from diluted loss per share because the effect would have been antidilutive. Why is this? Because of the loss—if the loss is spread out over more shares, the effect is anti-dilutive.

Review 11-5 LO11-5

Accounting for Convertible Debt

GuidedExample MBC

Kallapur, Inc., has issued convertible debentures: each $1,000 bond is convertible into 200 shares of $1 par common stock. Assume that the bonds were sold at a discount and that each bond has a current unamortized discount equal to $150.

Required

a. Using the financial statement effects template, illustrate the effects of the conversion of one of its bonds.

b. Prepare journal entries for the transaction assuming conversion of one bond.

c. Post the journal entries to the related T-accounts.

Solution on p. 11-54.

SUMMARY

Describe and account for business financing through stock issuances and repurchases. (p. 11-3) LO11-1

- Contributed capital represents the cumulative cash (or other asset) inflow that the company has received from the sale of various classes of stock, preferred and common.
- Preferred stock receives preference in terms of dividends before common and, if cumulative, receives all dividends not paid in the past before common dividends can be paid. Preferred stock can also be designated as convertible into common stock at the holder's option and at a predetermined conversion ratio. Voting privileges reside only with the common stock.
- Common stock is often repurchased by the firm for use in stock award programs, to signal management confidence in the company, or simply to return cash to shareholders. Repurchased stock is either cancelled or held for reissue. If held for reissue, the repurchase is debited to a contra equity account titled treasury stock.

Describe the effect on equity of earnings, dividends, and stock splits. (p. 11-11) LO11-2

- Earned capital includes retained earnings, which represents the cumulative profit that has been retained by the company. Earned capital is increased by income earned and decreased by losses and dividends declared by the firm. Earned capital also includes the effects of items included in other comprehensive income.
- Dividends in the form of stock decrease retained earnings and increase contributed capital by an equivalent amount.
- A stock split is a proportionate distribution similar in substance to a stock dividend. The new number of shares outstanding must be disclosed. Otherwise, no further accounting is required unless the state of incorporation requires that the par value be proportionally adjusted.

Define and illustrate comprehensive income. (p. 11-16) LO11-3

- Comprehensive income includes several additional items not recognized in net income, including: adjustments for changes in foreign exchange rates, unrealized changes in available-for-sale debt securities, and pension liability adjustments. The concept is designed to highlight impacts on net assets that are beyond management's control.

Describe and illustrate the basic and diluted earnings per share computations. (p. 11-19) LO11-4

- Earnings per share is a closely watched number reported for all publicly traded firms. Basic EPS is computed as the ratio of net income (less preferred dividends and noncontrolling interests) to the weighted average number of outstanding shares for the period. The value of this performance metric is subject to all the difficulties in measuring net income, including the fact that net income can increase due to an acquisition or divestiture that can have no impact on the number of outstanding shares.
- Most analysts are more interested in what is termed diluted earnings per share. This conservative calculation, which, if reported, never exceeds basic EPS, reflects the maximum reduction in basic EPS possible assuming conversion of the convertible securities.
- Stock options that are "in the money" are always dilutive.
- Convertible securities that would be antidilutive are treated as if they were not converted.

Appendix 11A: Analyze the accounting for convertible securities, stock rights, stock options, and restricted stock. (p. 11-22) LO11-5

- Convertible securities are debt and equity instruments, including stock rights, that allow these securities to be exchanged for other securities, typically common stock. The convertible feature adds value to the security to which it is attached.
- Stock options, one form of stock right, allow the holders to exchange them at a specified (strike) price for common stock. This right is valuable and creates an expense when granted to an employee or other individual. Expense recognition is appropriate, using the value obtained by applying an options-pricing model, even though the calculation is not precise. The option will not be exercised unless the market price of the common stock exceeds the strike price.
- Convertible preferred stock and convertible debt securities need to be considered in the calculation of DEPS to the extent conversion reduces reported BEPS.
- Restricted stock awards and restricted stock units are recorded as compensation expense as the vesting period expires (as the employee works over the vesting period).
- Generally, unvested restricted stock awards and restricted stock units are excluded from the denominator of basic EPS. If dilutive, they are taken into account in the calculation of diluted EPS. Once vested, the shares are included in the computation of basic EPS.

GUIDANCE ANSWERS . . . YOU MAKE THE CALL

You are the Chief Financial Officer Several points must be considered. (1) Treasury shares are likely to prop up earnings per share (EPS). While the numerator (earnings) is likely dampened by the use of cash for the stock repurchase (because the cash cannot be reinvested in operations), EPS is likely to increase because of the reduced shares in the denominator. (2) If the shares are sufficiently undervalued (in management's opinion), the stock repurchase and subsequent resale can provide a better return than some alternative investments. (3) Stock repurchases send a strong signal to the market that management feels its stock is undervalued. This is more credible than merely making that argument with analysts. On the other hand, company cash is diverted from other investments. This is bothersome if such investments are mutually exclusive either now or in the future.

KEY RATIOS

Net income available for common shareholders =
Net income − Net income attributable to noncontrolling interests − Preferred dividends

Common shareholders' equity =
Total equity − Equity attributable to noncontrolling interests − Preferred stock equity

$$\text{Return on Common Equity (ROCE)} = \frac{\text{Net income available for common shareholders}}{\text{Average common shareholders' equity}}$$

$$\text{Basic earnings per share (BEPS)} = \frac{\text{Net income available for common shareholders}}{\text{Weighted average number of common shares outstanding}}$$

Diluted earnings per share (DEPS) =

$$\frac{\text{Net income available for common shareholders + Add-backs}}{\text{Weighted average number of common shares + Shares of convertible securities and stock options assumed to be converted}}$$

Assignments with the MBC logo in the margin are available in myBusinessCourse.
See the Preface of the book for details.

MULTIPLE CHOICE

Multiple Choice Answers
1. d 2. a 3. a 4. d 5. d

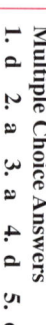

1. Suppose Pfizer issues 100,000 shares of its common stock, $0.05 par value, to obtain a warehouse and the accompanying land when the price of the stock is $28.00. Which one of the following statements is not true?
   a. The newly acquired assets will increase total assets by $2.8 million.
   b. Retained earnings are unaffected.
   c. The common stock account increases by $5,000.
   d. Total shareholders' equity increases by $2,795,000.

2. Assume Pfizer resells 15,000 shares of its stock that were purchased when the market price of the stock was $25. If the shares are resold for $22, which one of the following statements holds?
   a. Additional paid-in capital decreases by $45,000.
   b. The treasury stock account increases by $45,000.
   c. Additional paid-in capital increases by $45,000.
   d. The treasury stock account decreases by $45,000.

3. Suppose Pfizer declares a 200,000 common stock dividend (par $0.05) when the market value of a share is $30.00. Which one of the following statements is true?
   a. The common stock account increases by $10,000.
   b. Additional paid-in capital decreases by $5.99 million.
   c. Retained earnings increases by $6 million.
   d. Additional paid-in capital increases by $6 million.

4. Which of the following statements is true?
   a. When a *large stock dividend* is paid, retained earnings are reduced by the market value of the shares distributed.
   b. Neither stock dividends nor stock splits affect basic earnings per share calculations.
   c. A three-for-one stock split increases the total outstanding shares by 300%.
   d. A stock split has no financial statement effects because it is not a monetary transaction.

Homework MBC

5. Which of the following statements is not true in relation to diluted EPS (DEPS)?
   a. Stock options that are in the money will always cause DEPS to be less than basic EPS.
   b. Convertible bonds, if dilutive, will cause changes in both the numerator and the denominator of DEPS.
   c. Stock analysts tend to concentrate their attention on DEPS instead of basic EPS.
   d. A company's only equity contract that can lead to dilution is stock options.

Homework MBC

QUESTIONS

Q11-1. Define *par value stock.* What is the significance of a stock's par value from an accounting and analysis perspective?

Q11-2. What are the basic differences between preferred stock and common stock? What are the typical features of preferred stock?

Q11-3. What features make preferred stock similar to debt? Similar to common stock?

Q11-4. What is meant by dividend arrearage on preferred stock? If dividends are two years in arrears on $400,000 of 6% preferred stock, and dividends are declared at the end of this year, what amount of total dividends must preferred shareholders receive before any distributions are made to common shareholders?

Q11-5. Distinguish between authorized stock and issued stock. Why might the number of shares issued be more than the number of shares outstanding?

Q11-6. Describe the difference between contributed capital and earned capital. Specifically, how can earned capital be considered as an investment by the company's shareholders?

Q11-7. How does the account "additional paid-in capital" (APIC) arise? What inferences, if any, can you draw from the amount of APIC as reported on the balance sheet relative to the common stock amount in relation to the financial condition of the company?

Q11-8. Define *stock split.* What are the major reasons for a stock split?

Q11-9. Define *treasury stock.* Why might a corporation acquire treasury stock? How is treasury stock reported in the balance sheet?

Q11-10. If a corporation purchases 600 shares of its own common stock at $10 per share and resells them at $14 per share, where would the $2,400 increase in capital be reported in the financial statements? Why is no gain reported?

Q11-11. A corporation has total stockholders' equity of $3,471,000 and one class of $2 par value common stock. The corporation has 375,000 shares authorized; 225,000 shares issued; 195,000 shares outstanding; and 30,000 shares as treasury stock. What is its book value per share?

Q11-12. What is a stock dividend? How does a common stock dividend distributed to common shareholders affect their respective ownership interests?

Q11-13. What is the difference between the accounting for a small stock dividend and the accounting for a large stock dividend?

Q11-14. Employee stock options have a potentially dilutive effect on earnings per share (EPS) that is recognized in the diluted EPS computation. What can companies do to offset these dilutive effects, and how might this action affect the balance sheet?

Q11-15. What information is reported in a statement of stockholders' equity?

Q11-16. What items are typically reported under the stockholders' equity category of other comprehensive income (OCI)?

Q11-17. What is a stock option vesting period? How does the vesting period affect the recognition of compensation expense for stock options?

Q11-18. Describe the accounting for the conversion of a convertible bond to equity. Would this accounting ever result in the recognition of a gain in the income statement?

DATA ANALYTICS

LO11-4 **DA11-1. Analyzing Trends in the Price-to-Earnings Ratio using Excel**

Data Analytics

The Excel file associated with this exercise includes market price and ratio information for companies in the S&P 500. (Data obtained from https://datahub.io/core/s-and-p-500-companies#data on August 26, 2021, made available under the Public Domain Dedication and License v1.0 whose full text can be found at: http://opendatacommons.org/licenses/pddl/1.0/.)

For this exercise, we examine trends in the price-to-earnings ratio of S&P 500 companies by industry segment. The price-to-earnings ratio measures the amount an investor is willing to pay per share of stock for each dollar of earnings per share. An increase in this ratio generally means that an investor would have a higher expectation for company profits in the future. In the first analysis, we calculate the average value or mean of the price-to-earnings ratio for each segment. In the second analysis, we calculate the median value of the price-to-earnings ratio for each segment. Lastly, we compare the average and median ratio results and analyze the cause of the differences.

Price-to Earnings Ratio

$$\frac{\text{Market price per share}}{\text{Earnings per share}}$$

REQUIRED

1. Download Excel file DA11-1 found in myBusinessCourse.
2. Create a PivotTable (PivotTable 1) showing the average Price/Earnings ratio by sector. *Hint:* With your cursor in your data, select Insert, PivotChart. Add Sector to Rows and Price/Earnings to Values; select Average for the display of Price/Earnings by right-clicking on an amount in the PivotTable, clicking Value Field Settings, and selecting Average.
3. Remove the grand total row (which is irrelevant for this table). *Hint:* Click on the Design tab, Grand totals, Off for rows & columns.
4. Change display of your data to show two decimal places. *Hint:* Right-click on an amount in the PivotTable, click on number format, and make change.
5. Sort your PivotTable in the order of highest to lowest values. *Hint:* Right-click on an amount in the PivotTable; click Sort, Sort Largest to smallest.
6. Indicate which sector has the highest and which sector has the lowest average price/earnings ratio.
7. Copy original PivotTable, paste below the original to create PivotTable 2, change the calculation of price/earnings to now display maximum value, and sort Price/Earnings values from largest to smallest values. *Hint:* Right-click on an amount in the PivotTable, and click Value Field Settings.
8. Indicate which sector has the highest and which sector has the lowest maximum price/earnings ratio.
9. Copy original PivotTable, paste below PivotTable 2 to create PivotTable 3, change the calculation of price/earnings to now display minimum value, and sort Price/Earnings values from largest to smallest values. *Hint:* Click the i button next to Average of Price/Earnings and select Min.
10. Indicate which sector has the highest and which sector has the lowest minimum price/earnings ratio.
11. Read the following article, "Stuck in the Middle—Mean vs. Median," by Dr. Dieter Schremmer found at the following link: https://www.clinfo.eu/mean-median/.
12. Compute the median value of the Price/Earnings ratio for the Energy sector and for the Industrials sector. *Hint:* Median is not a calculation option within the PivotTables. Instead, double-click on the dollar amount in the PivotTable for Energy to open up a new sheet with the underlying data. In a new cell (at least two rows below the table) calculate the median of the Price/Earnings data: =MEDIAN(xx). Repeat steps for the Industrials sector.
13. Compute the difference between the Maximum Price/Earnings (see PivotTable 2) and the Minimum Price/Earnings (see PivotTable 3) for both sectors: Energy and Industrials.
14. Compare the median values obtained in part 12 to the average values listed in PivotTable 1 and answer the following question: What caused the differences between the mean and median values in your calculations?

LO11-5 **DA11-2. Constructing and Analyzing a Dataset on Share-Based Compensation in Excel**

Data Analytics

For this exercise, we create and analyze a dataset in Excel of the changes in the composition of share-based compensation plans (restricted stock unit, performance share, and stock option plans) for **Target Corporation** over a 10-year period.

REQUIRED

1. Download Excel file DA11-2 found in myBusinessCourse.

2. Create a dataset that will provide information on the composition of Target's share-based compensation plans over a 10-year period from fiscal year 2011 to fiscal year 2020.
    - In your dataset, for each of the share-based awards (restricted stock unit, performance share, and stock options) include the following: number of units granted during the year and the unrecognized compensation expense at year-end.
    - Also include in your dataset the total share-based compensation expense included on the income statement for each year and the fair value per unit at grant date of the restricted stock units for each year.
    - *Hints*:
        - This information can be found in the note disclosures in the annual 10-K reports.
        - When collecting your data, note that some amounts are in thousands, and some in millions.
        - Fiscal years end in January or February of the following year; for example, Fiscal Year 2020 ends January 30, 2021.
3. Prepare a line chart in Excel over the 10-year period showing the trends in units granted of the three different types of share-based awards. *Hint:* Highlight data; click Insert, Line. Chart should show the earliest year on the left and the latest year on the right. To change the order, right-click inside the horizontal axis. In the Format Axis sidebar, check Categories in reverse order.
4. Describe the 10-year trend in the data visualization for each of the three awards.
5. Prepare a line chart in Excel showing the trend of share-based compensation expense over the 10-year period.
6. Indicate which year(s) in the data visualization prepared in part 5 showed a highly visible decline in share-based compensation expense.
7. Indicate which year seems to be the start of an increasing trend in the visualization created in part 5.
8. Prepare a line chart in Excel showing the trend of unrecognized share-based compensation expense over the 10-year period for all three share-based plan types.
9. Indicate which share-based plan type in the data visualization prepared in part 8 showed the highest value and lowest value in Fiscal Year 2011, 2015, and 2020.
10. Prepare a schedule for the total fair value of the restricted stock share awards at the date of grant for each of the 10 years. *Hint:* Multiply the number of restricted stock units by the unit price at the date of grant.
11. Indicate which year(s) showed a decrease in total value based on the data visualization prepared in part 10.
12. Describe the trend shown in fair value of restricted stock share awards from fiscal year 2016 to fiscal year 2020.
13. Summarize the result of your analysis.

DA11-3. Preparing Tableau Visualizations to Analyze Dividend Payout Policies Through Ratios LO11-2

Refer to PB-28 in Appendix B. This problem uses Tableau to analyze dividend payout policies of S&P 500 companies through the dividend yield and dividend payout ratio.

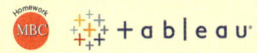

Homework MBC +tableau Data Analytics

DATA VISUALIZATION

Data Visualization Activities are available in myBusinessCourse. These assignments use Tableau Dashboards to expose students to visual depictions of data and introduce students to data analytics through data visualizations. These exercises are easily assignable and auto graded by MBC.

Data Visualization

MINI EXERCISES

M11-19. Analyzing and Identifying Financial Statement Effects of Stock Issuances LO11-1

On June 1, Beatty Corp. issues (*a*) 16,000 shares of $50 par value preferred stock at $68 cash per share, and it issues (*b*) 24,000 shares of $1 par value common stock at $10 cash per share.

a. Do these transactions increase contributed capital or earned capital?

b. What is the effect of these transactions on Beatty Corp.'s income statement?

c. What are the differences between the preferred stock and the common stock issued by Beatty Corp.?

LO11-1 Homework MBC

M11-20. Analyzing and Identifying Financial Statement Effects of Stock Issuances (FSET)
On September 1, Magliolo, Inc., (*a*) issues 13,500 shares of $10 par value preferred stock at $48 cash per share and (*b*) issues 90,000 shares of $2 par value common stock at $37 cash per share. Using the financial statement effects template, illustrate the effects of these two issuances.

LO11-1 Homework MBC

M11-21. Analyzing and Identifying Financial Statement Effects of Stock Issuances
Using the information from M11-20, answer the following.

a. Prepare the journal entries for the two issuances.

b. Post the journal entries to the related T-accounts.

LO11-1, 3 Homework MBC

Cisco Systems
NASDAQ :: CSCO

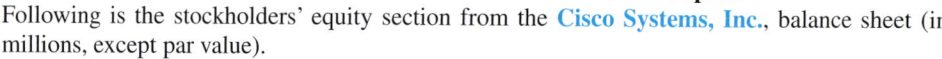

M11-22. Distinguishing between Common Stock and Additional Paid-in Capital
Following is the stockholders' equity section from the Cisco Systems, Inc., balance sheet (in millions, except par value).

Shareholders' equity	July 25, 2020
Preferred stock, no par value: 5 shares authorized; none issued and outstanding	$ —
Common stock and additional paid-in capital, $0.001 par value: 20,000 shares authorized; 4,237 shares issued and outstanding at July 25, 2020	41,202
Accumulated deficit	(2,763)
Accumulated other comprehensive loss	(519)
Total equity	$37,920

a. For the $41,202 million reported as "common stock and additional paid-in capital," what portion is common stock, and what portion is additional paid-in capital? Explain.

b. The company reported $11.2 billion in net income and $273 million in other comprehensive income for the fiscal year ended July 25, 2020. In what shareholders' equity accounts are these amounts accumulated?

LO11-2 Homework MBC

M11-23. Identifying and Analyzing Financial Statement Effects of Stock Issuance and Repurchase (FSET)
On January 1, Bartov Company issues 3,000 shares of $100 par value preferred stock at $250 cash per share. On March 1, the company repurchases 3,000 shares of previously issued $1 par value common stock at $78 cash per share.

Using the financial statement effects template, illustrate the effects of these two transactions.

LO11-1 Homework MBC

M11-24. Analyzing and Identifying Financial Statement Effects of Stock Issuance and Repurchase
Using the information from M11-23, answer the following.

a. Prepare the journal entries for the two transactions.

b. Post the journal entries to the related T-accounts.

LO11-4

Tesla, Inc.
NYSE :: TSLA

M11-25. Assessing the Financial Statement Effects of a Stock Split
In its 2020 10-K, Tesla, Inc., included the following information:

> On August 10, 2020, our Board of Directors declared a five-for-one split of the Company's common stock effected in the form of a stock dividend (the "Stock Split"). Each stockholder of record on August 21, 2020 received a dividend of four additional shares of common stock for each then-held share, distributed after close of trading on August 28, 2020. All share and per share amounts presented herein have been retroactively adjusted to reflect the impact of the Stock Split.

Tesla effected this stock split as a large stock dividend. What changes has Tesla made to its balance sheet as a result of this action?

LO11-4 Homework MBC

M11-26. Computing Basic and Diluted Earnings per Share
Zeller Corporation began the year with 168,000 shares of common stock and 22,000 shares of convertible preferred stock outstanding. On March 1 an additional 14,000 shares of common stock

were issued. On August 1, another 22,000 shares of common stock were issued. On November 1, 8,400 shares of common stock were acquired for the treasury. The preferred stock has a $2 per-share dividend rate, and each share may be converted into one share of common stock. Zeller Corporation's net income for the year is $701,000.

a. Compute basic earnings per share for the year.

b. Compute diluted earnings per share for the year.

c. If the preferred stock were not convertible, Zeller Corporation would have a simple capital structure. How would this change Zeller's earnings per share presentation?

M11-27. Assessing Common Stock and Treasury Stock Balances

LO11-1, 3, 4

Homework MBC

Toyota Motor Corporation (ADR)
NYSE :: TM

Following is the stockholders' equity section from the Toyota Motor Corporation's balance sheet for the 2020 fiscal year, which ended on March 31, 2020.

Toyota Motor Corporation Shareholders' Equity (Millions of Yen)	March 31, 2020
Common stock, no par value: authorized 10,000,000,000 shares in 2019 and 2020; issued: 3,262,997,492 shares at March 31, 2020	¥ 397,050
Additional paid-in capital	489,334
Retained earnings	23,427,613
Accumulated other comprehensive income (loss)	(1,166,273)
Treasury stock, at cost: 496,844,960 shares at March 31, 2020	(3,087,106)
Total Toyota Motor Corporation shareholders' equity	¥20,060,618

a. Toyota has repurchased 496,844,960 shares that comprise its March 31, 2020, treasury stock account. Compute the number of outstanding shares as of March 31, 2020.

b. Assume that all of this treasury stock had been acquired in one purchase on July 1, 2019. What would have been the effect on the denominator of the basic EPS calculation?

c. The company reported ¥(916,650) in accumulated other comprehensive income (loss) and ¥21,987,515 in retained earnings on March 31, 2019. Given this information, what would the company report as other comprehensive income (loss) for the fiscal year ended March 31, 2020?

M11-28. Identifying and Analyzing Financial Statement Effects of Cash Dividends (FSET)

LO11-2

Homework MBC

Freid Corp. has outstanding 9,000 shares of $50 par value, 6% preferred stock, and 60,000 shares of $1 par value common stock. The company has $492,000 of retained earnings. At year-end, the company declares and pays the regular $3 per share cash dividend on preferred stock and a $2.20 per share cash dividend on common stock.

Using the financial statement effects template, illustrate the effects of these two dividend payments.

M11-29. Identifying and Analyzing Financial Statement Effects of Cash Dividends

LO11-2

Homework MBC

Using the information from M11-28, answer the following.

a. Prepare the journal entries for the two dividend payments.

b. Post the journal entries to the related T-accounts.

M11-30. Analyzing and Identifying Financial Statement Effects of Stock Dividends (FSET)

LO11-2

Homework MBC

Dutta Corp. has outstanding 85,000 shares of $5 par value common stock. At year-end, the company declares and issues a 4% common stock dividend when the market price of the stock is $21 per share.

Using the financial statement effects template, illustrate the effects of this dividend declaration and payment.

M11-31. Analyzing and Identifying Financial Statement Effects of Stock Dividends

LO11-2

Homework MBC

Using the information from M11-30, answer the following.

a. Prepare the journal entries for the stock dividend declaration and payment.

b. Post the journal entries to the related T-accounts.

M11-32. Analyzing, Identifying, and Explaining the Effects of a Stock Split

LO11-2

Homework MBC

On September 1, Weiss Company has 225,000 shares of $15 par value ($165 market value) common stock that are issued and outstanding. Its balance sheet on that date shows the following account balances relating to the common stock.

Common stock	$3,375,000
Paid-in capital in excess of par value	2,025,000

On September 2, Weiss splits its stock 3-for-2 and reduces the par value to $10 per share.

a. How many shares of common stock are issued and outstanding immediately after the stock split?

b. What is the dollar balance of the common stock account immediately after the stock split?

c. What is the likely reason that Weiss Company split its stock?

LO11-2 Homework MBC

M11-33. Distributing Cash Dividends to Preferred and Common Shareholders

Dechow Company has outstanding 24,000 shares of $50 par value, 6% cumulative preferred stock, and 96,000 shares of $10 par value common stock. The company declares and pays cash dividends amounting to $192,000.

a. If no arrearage on the preferred stock exists, how much in total dividends, and in dividends per share, is paid to each class of stock?

b. If one year's dividend arrearage on the preferred stock exists, how much in total dividends, and in dividends per share, is paid to each class of stock?

LO11-2 Homework MBC

M11-34. Analyzing and Preparing a Retained Earnings Reconciliation

Use the following data to prepare the 2022 retained earnings reconciliation for Maffett Company.

Total retained earnings, December 31, 2021	$555,000
Stock dividends declared and paid in 2022	45,000
Cash dividends declared and paid in 2022	56,000
Net income for 2022	150,000

LO11-2 Homework MBC

M11-35. Accounting for Large Stock Dividend and Stock Split (FSET)

Watts Corporation has 32,000 shares of $10 par value common stock outstanding and retained earnings of $656,000. The company declares a 100% stock dividend. The market price at the declaration is $17 per share.

a. Using the financial statement effects template, illustrate the effects of the stock dividend.

b. Assume that the company splits its stock two shares for one share and reduces the par value from $10 to $5 rather than declaring a 100% stock dividend. How does the accounting for the stock split differ from the accounting for the 100% stock dividend?

LO11-2 Homework MBC

M11-36. Accounting for Large Stock Dividend and Stock Split

Using the information from M11-35, prepare the general journal entry for the stock dividend in part *a* and stock split in part *b*.

LO11-4 Homework MBC

M11-37. Computing Basic and Diluted Earnings per Share

During the year, Park Corporation had 75,000 shares of $10 par value common stock and 15,000 shares of 8%, $50 par value convertible preferred stock outstanding. Each share of preferred stock may be converted into three shares of common stock. Park Corporation's net income was $702,000 for the year.

a. Compute the basic earnings per share for the year.

b. Compute the diluted earnings per share for the year.

LO11-4 Homework MBC

M11-38. Computing Earnings per Share

Kingery Corporation began the calendar (and fiscal) year with a simple structure consisting of 47,500 shares of common stock outstanding. On May 1, 12,500 additional shares were issued, and another 2,000 shares were issued on September 1. The company had a net income for the year of $300,000.

a. Compute the earnings per share of common stock.

b. Assume that the company also had 7,500 shares of 6%, $50 par value cumulative preferred stock outstanding throughout the year. Compute the basic earnings per share of common stock.

LO11-4
Siemens AG (ADR)
OTCMKTS :: SIEGY

M11-39. Defining and Computing Earnings per Share

Siemens AG reports the following basic and diluted earnings per share in its 2020 annual report.

(shares in thousands; earnings per share in €)	Year Ended September 30 2020
Income from continuing operations attributable to shareholders of Siemens AG...	€ 3,979
Less: Dilutive effect from share-based payment resulting from Siemens Healthineers	3
Income from continuing operations attributable to shareholders of Siemens AG to determine dilutive earnings per share	3,976
Weighted average shares outstanding—basic	806,335
Effect of dilutive share-based payment	11,029
Effective of dilutive warrants	—
Weighted average shares outstanding—diluted	817,364
Basic earnings per share (from continuing operations)	€ 4.93
Diluted earnings per share (from continuing operations)	€ 4.86

a. Describe the accounting definitions for basic and diluted earnings per share.
b. Identify the Siemens numbers that make up both EPS computations.
c. What calculation limits the reported value of diluted EPS?

M11-40.[A] Analyzing Stock Option Expense for Income (FSET) LO11-5 Homework MBC

Merck & Co.
NYSE :: MRK

Merck & Co., Inc., reported net income attributable to Merck & Co., Inc., of $7,067 million for the 2020 fiscal year. Its 2020 10-K report contained the following information regarding its stock options.

> Employee stock options are granted to purchase shares of Company stock at the fair market value at the time of grant. These awards generally vest one-third each year over a three-year period, with a contractual term of 7–10 years . . . The weighted average exercise price of options granted in 2020 was $77.67 per option . . . The weighted average fair value of options granted in 2020 was $9.93 per option.

a. Merck granted 3,564 options to employees in 2020. Using the financial statement effects template, show how the stock option grants would be reported in 2020. (Assume all grants took place on January 1, 2020.)
b. How does the granting of stock options affect EPS?
c. Merck employees exercised 1,685,000 options in 2020, paying a total of $89 million in cash to the company. Using the financial statement effects template, show how these option exercises would be reported in 2020.
d. How does the exercise of stock options affect EPS?

M11-41.[A] Analyzing Stock Option Expense for Income LO11-5 Homework MBC

Using the information from M11-40, answer the following.

a. Prepare the journal entry to show how stock option grants would be recorded in 2020.
b. Using a summary journal entry, show how the option exercises described in part *c* would be recorded in 2020.

M11-42. Examining the Effect of Stock Transactions LO11-1, 2, 4 Homework MBC

Year 1: Noreen Company issues 20,000 shares of its no-par common stock for $30/share in cash.
Year 2: Noreen Company buys 2,000 shares of its no-par common stock for $28/share in cash.
Year 3: Noreen Company declares but has not yet paid a dividend on its no-par common stock of $2 per share. The company's basic earnings per share were $10 in the third year.

Indicate the effect (increase, decrease, no effect) of each of these stock decisions for each year on the items listed.

Year	Total Assets	Total Liabilities	Total Stockholders' Equity	EPS	Operating Income
1					
2					
3					

LO11-1, 2, 3, 4 **M11-43. Reporting Stockholders' Equity**

Homework MBC

Bonner Company began business this year and immediately sold 500,000 common shares for $13,500,000 cash and paid $750,000 in common dividends. At midyear, the firm bought back some of its own shares. The company reports the following additional information at year-end:

Net income	$3,750,000
Unrealized gain on available-for-sale debt securities	$ 66,000
Common stock, at par	$5,000,000
Retained earnings beginning of year	$ 0
Common shares authorized	750,000
Common shares outstanding at year's end	425,000

a. What was the average sales price of a common share when issued?
b. What is the par value of the common shares?
c. How much is in the Additional paid-in capital account at the end of the year?
d. How much is accumulated other comprehensive income (loss) at the end of the year?
e. Determine the retained earnings amount at the end of the year.
f. How many shares of stock are in the treasury at the end of the year?
g. Compute BEPS.

LO11-4 **M11-44. Analyzing Earnings Per Share Effects of Convertible Securities**

Homework MBC

JetBlue
NASDAQ :: JBLU

JetBlue Airways Corporation reports the following data in its 2019 10-K. The data relate to the corporation's computation of its earnings per share calculations. (Dollar and share data are in millions.)

	2019
Net income[(1)]	$ 569
Weighted average basic shares	296.6
Effect of dilutive securities	1.8
Weighted average diluted shares	298.4

[(1)] See JetBlue Airways 2019 10-K

REQUIRED

a. What is the objective behind the calculation of diluted EPS?
b. Calculate JetBlue's basic EPS.
c. Calculate JetBlue's diluted EPS.
d. In a previous year, JetBlue stated that it excluded 6.9 million stock options from the computation of diluted EPS. Under what circumstances would this be appropriate?

EXERCISES

LO11-1 **E11-45. Identifying and Analyzing Financial Statement Effects of Stock Transactions (FSET)**

Homework MBC

Lipe Company reports the following transactions relating to its stock accounts.

Feb. 20	Issued 12,000 shares of $1 par value common stock at $25 cash per share.
Feb. 21	Issued 18,000 shares of $100 par value, 8% preferred stock at $250 cash per share.
Jun. 30	Purchased 2,400 shares of its own common stock at $15 cash per share.
Sep. 25	Sold 1,200 shares of the treasury stock at $21 cash per share.

Using the financial statement effects template, illustrate the effects of these transactions.

LO11-1 **E11-46. Identifying and Analyzing Financial Statement Effects of Stock Transactions**

Homework MBC

Using the information from E11-45, answer the following.

a. Prepare the journal entries for these transactions.
b. Post the journal entries to the related T-accounts.

E11-47. Analyzing and Identifying Financial Statement Effects of Stock Transactions (FSET) LO11-1 Homework MBC

McNichols Corp. reports the following transactions relating to its stock accounts.

Jan. 15 Issued 40,000 shares of $5 par value common stock at $17 cash per share.
Jan. 20 Issued 9,000 shares of $50 par value, 8% preferred stock at $78 cash per share.
Mar. 31 Purchased 4,500 shares of its own common stock at $20 cash per share.
June 25 Sold 3,000 shares of the treasury stock at $26 cash per share.
July 15 Sold the remaining 1,500 shares of treasury stock at $19 cash per share.

Using the financial statement effects template, illustrate the effects of these transactions.

E11-48. Analyzing and Identifying Financial Statement Effects of Stock Transactions LO11-1 Homework MBC

Using the information from E11-47, answer the following.

a. Prepare the journal entries for these transactions.
b. Post the journal entries to the related T-accounts.

E11-49. Analyzing and Computing Average Issue Price and Treasury Stock Cost LO11-1, 3, 4 Homework MBC

The Coca-Cola Company
NYSE :: KO

Following is the stockholders' equity section from The Coca-Cola Company 2020 balance sheet. (All amounts in millions except par value.)

The Coca-Cola Company Shareowners' Equity	December 31, 2020
Common stock—$0.25 par value; authorized—11,200 shares; issued—7,040 shares	$ 1,760
Capital surplus . . .	17,601
Reinvested earnings. . .	66,555
Accumulated other comprehensive income (loss) . . .	(14,601)
Treasury stock, at cost—2,738 shares . . .	(52,016)
Equity attributable to shareowners of The Coca-Cola Company . . .	$19,299

a. Compute the number of shares outstanding.
b. At what average price were the Coca-Cola shares issued?
c. At what average cost were the Coca-Cola treasury stock shares purchased?
d. Coca-Cola reported a balance of $(13,544) million in Accumulated other comprehensive income (loss) on December 31, 2019, and Net income attributable to shareowners of the Coca-Cola Company of $7,747 million for 2020. What is (1) comprehensive income and (2) other comprehensive income in 2020?
e. How should treasury stock be treated in calculating EPS?

E11-50. Analyzing and Distributing Cash Dividends to Preferred and Common Stocks LO11-2 Homework MBC

Moser Company began business on March 1, 2021. At that time, it issued 40,000 shares of $60 par value, 5% cumulative preferred stock, and 200,000 shares of $5 par value common stock. Through the end of 2023, there has been no change in the number of preferred and common shares outstanding.

a. Assume that Moser declared and paid cash dividends of $0 in 2021, $270,000 in 2022, and $400,000 in 2023. Compute the total cash dividends and the dividends per share paid to each class of stock in 2021, 2022, and 2023.
b. Assume that Moser declared and paid cash dividends of $0 in 2021, $120,000 in 2022, and $200,000 in 2023. Compute the total cash dividends and the dividends per share paid to each class of stock in 2021, 2022, and 2023.

E11-51. Computing Basic and Diluted Earnings per Share LO11-4 Homework MBC

Soliman Corporation began the year with 50,000 shares of common stock and 15,000 shares of convertible preferred stock outstanding. On May 1, an additional 18,000 shares of common stock were issued. On July 1, 12,000 shares of common stock were acquired for the treasury. On September 1, the 12,000 treasury shares of common stock were reissued. The preferred stock has a $4 per-share dividend rate, and each share may be converted into two shares of common stock. Soliman Corporation's net income is $540,000 for the year.

a. Compute earnings per share for the year.
b. Compute diluted earnings per share for the year.
c. If the preferred stock were not convertible, Soliman Corporation would have a simple capital structure. How would this change Soliman's earnings per share presentation?

LO11-2, 4 Homework MBC

E11-52. Analyzing and Distributing Cash Dividends to Preferred and Common Stocks

Potter Company has outstanding 12,000 shares of $50 par value, 6% preferred stock, and 40,000 shares of $5 par value common stock. During its first three years in business, it declared and paid no cash dividends in the first year, $225,000 in the second year, and $36,000 in the third year.

a. If the preferred stock is cumulative, determine the total amount of cash dividends paid to each class of stock in each of the three years.

b. If the preferred stock is noncumulative, determine the total amount of cash dividends paid to each class of stock in each of the three years.

c. How should each type of preferred dividends be treated in calculating EPS?

LO11-1, 3 Homework MBC

Chipotle Mexican Grill
NYSE :: CMG

E11-53. Analyzing and Computing Issue Price, Treasury Stock Cost, Shares Outstanding, and Net Income

The following is the stockholders' equity section from **Chipotle Mexican Grill, Inc.**'s balance sheet (in thousands, except per share data).

Shareholders' Equity	**December 31, 2020**
Preferred stock, $0.01 par value, 600,000 shares authorized, no shares issued as of December 31, 2020	$ —
Common stock, $0.01 par value, 230,000 shares authorized, and 36,704 shares issued as of December 31, 2020	367
Additional paid-in capital	1,549,909
Treasury stock, at cost, 8,703 common shares at December 31, 2020	(2,802,075)
Accumulated other comprehensive income (loss)	(4,229)
Retained earnings	3,276,163
Total shareholders' equity	$2,020,135

a. Show the computation to derive the $367 thousand for common stock.

b. At what average price has Chipotle issued its common stock?

c. How many shares of Chipotle common stock are outstanding as of December 31, 2020?

d. At what average cost has Chipotle repurchased its treasury stock as of December 31, 2020?

e. Give three reasons why a company such as Chipotle would want to repurchase $2,802 million of its common stock.

f. Chipotle reported a foreign currency translation adjustment, net of tax, of $1,134 thousand and comprehensive income of $356,900 thousand for 2020. What did Chipotle report as net income for the year?

LO11-2 Homework MBC

E11-54. Analyzing and Distributing Cash Dividends to Preferred and Common Stocks

Skinner Company began business on June 30. At that time, it issued 28,000 shares of $50 par value, 6% cumulative preferred stock, and 100,000 shares of $10 par value common stock. Through the end of Year 3, there has been no change in the number of preferred and common shares outstanding.

a. Assume that Skinner declared and paid cash dividends of $96,000 in Year 1, $0 in Year 2, and $560,000 in Year 3. Compute the total cash dividends and the dividends per share paid to each class of stock in Year 1, Year 2, and Year 3.

b. Assume that Skinner declared and paid cash dividends of $0 in Year 1, $168,000 in Year 2, and $239,000 in Year 3. Compute the total cash dividends and the dividends per share paid to each class of stock in Year 1, Year 2, and Year 3.

LO11-2 Homework MBC

E11-55. Analyzing and Identifying Financial Statement Effects of Dividends (FSET)

Chaney Company has outstanding 20,000 shares of $10 par value common stock. It also has $325,000 of retained earnings. Near the current year-end, the company declares and pays a cash dividend of $1.90 per share and declares and issues a 4% stock dividend. The market price of the stock at the declaration date is $25 per share.

Using the financial statement effects template, illustrate the effects of these two separate dividends.

LO11-2 Homework MBC

E11-56. Analyzing and Identifying Financial Statement Effects of Dividends

Using the information from E11-55, answer the following.

a. Prepare the journal entries for these two separate dividend transactions.

b. Post the journal entries to the related T-accounts.

E11-57. Identifying and Analyzing Financial Statement Effects of Dividends (FSET) LO11-2 Homework MBC

The stockholders' equity of Palepu Company at December 31, 2021, appears below.

Common stock, $10 par value, 300,000 shares authorized; 120,000 shares issued and outstanding	$1,200,000
Paid-in capital in excess of par value	720,000
Retained earnings	450,000

During 2022, the following transactions occurred:

May 12 Declared and issued a 7% stock dividend; the common stock market value was $18 per share.

Dec. 31 Declared and paid a cash dividend of 75 cents per share.

Using the financial statement effects template, illustrate the effects of these transactions.

E11-58. Identifying and Analyzing Financial Statement Effects of Dividends LO11-2 Homework MBC

Using the information from E11-57, answer the following.

a. Prepare the journal entries for these transactions.

b. Post the journal entries to the related T-accounts.

c. Prepare a retained earnings reconciliation for 2022 assuming that the company reports 2022 net income of $425,000.

E11-59. Analyzing and Identifying Financial Statement Effects of Dividends (FSET) LO11-2 Homework MBC

The stockholders' equity of Kinney Company at December 31, 2021, is shown below:

5% preferred stock, $100 par value, 10,000 shares authorized; 3,500 shares issued and outstanding	$ 350,000
Common stock, $5 par value, 200,000 shares authorized; 45,000 shares issued and outstanding	225,000
Paid-in capital in excess of par value—preferred stock	36,000
Paid-in capital in excess of par value—common stock	270,000
Retained earnings	590,400
Total stockholders' equity	$1,471,400

The following transactions, among others, occurred during 2022.

Apr. 1 Declared and issued a 100% stock dividend on all outstanding shares of common stock. The market value of the stock was $11 per share.

Dec. 7 Declared and issued a 3% stock dividend on all outstanding shares of common stock. The market value of the stock was $14 per share.

Dec. 20 Declared and paid (1) the annual cash dividend on the preferred stock and (2) a cash dividend of 80 cents per common share.

Using the financial statement effects template, illustrate the effects of these transactions.

E11-60. Analyzing and Identifying Financial Statement Effects of Dividends LO11-2 Homework MBC

Using the information from E11-59, answer the following.

a. Prepare the journal entries for these transactions.

b. Post the journal entries to the related T-accounts.

c. Prepare a 2022 retained earnings reconciliation assuming that the company reports 2022 net income of $227,700.

E11-61. Analyzing, Identifying, and Explaining the Effects of a Stock Split LO11-2, 4 Homework MBC

On March 1 of the current year, Xie Company has 360,000 shares of $20 par value common stock that are issued and outstanding. Its balance sheet shows the following account balances relating to common stock.

Common stock	$7,200,000
Paid-in capital in excess of par value	3,060,000

On March 2, Xie Company splits its common stock 2-for-1 and reduces the par value to $10 per share.

a. How many shares of common stock are issued and outstanding immediately after the stock split?
b. What is the dollar balance in its common stock account immediately after the stock split?
c. What is the dollar balance in its paid-in capital in excess of par value account immediately after the stock split?
d. What is the effect of a stock split on the calculation of EPS?

LO11-2, 3 **E11-62. Analyzing and Computing Dividends, Effect of Options Exercises, and Comprehensive Income**

Homework MBC

Intuit Inc.
NASDAQ :: INTU

Following is the stockholders' equity section of the **Intuit Inc.** balance sheet (dollars in millions, except par value; shares in thousands). Changes in the company's outstanding shares are due to (1) treasury share purchases by the company and (2) issues of treasury shares for employee stock options.

Stockholders' Equity ($ millions)	July 31, 2020	July 31, 2019
Preferred stock, $0.01 par value		
Authorized—1,345 shares total; 145 shares designated Series A; 250 shares designated Series B Junior Participating		
Issued and outstanding—none	$ —	$ —
Common stock, $0.01 par value		
Authorized—750,000 shares		
Outstanding—261,740 shares at July 31, 2020, and 260,180 shares at July 31, 2019	3	3
Additional paid-in capital	6,179	5,772
Treasury stock, at cost	(11,929)	(11,611)
Accumulated other comprehensive loss	(32)	(36)
Retained earnings	10,885	9,621
Total stockholders' equity	$ 5,106	$ 3,749

a. In the fiscal year ended July 31, 2020, Intuit reported net income of $1,826 million. How much did Intuit pay in dividends to its common shareholders?
b. In the fiscal year ended January 31, 2020, Intuit repurchased 1,176 thousand of its common shares. How many shares were issued to employees under stock option plans?
c. Intuit's issuance of shares for stock option plans decreased the Additional paid-in capital balance by $31 million. Was the (average) option exercise price greater or less than the (average) amount Intuit paid to acquire the treasury shares that were reissued?
d. What did Intuit report as comprehensive income in 2020?

LO11-1, 3 **E11-63. Analyzing and Computing Issue Price, Treasury Stock Cost, and Shares Outstanding**

Homework MBC

Merck & Co.
NYSE :: MRK

Following is the stockholders' equity section of the **Merck & Co., Inc.**, balance sheet.

Merck & Co., Inc., Stockholders' Equity ($ millions)	Dec. 31, 2020	Dec. 31, 2019
Common stock, $0.50 par value		
Authorized—6,500,000,000 shares		
Issued—3,577,103,522 shares in 2020 and 2019	$ 1,788	$ 1,788
Other paid-in capital	39,588	39,660
Retained earnings	47,362	46,602
Accumulated other comprehensive loss	(6,634)	(6,193)
	82,104	81,857
Less treasury stock, at cost:		
1,046,877,695 shares in 2020 and 1,038,087,496 shares in 2019	56,787	55,950
Total Merck & Co., Inc., stockholders' equity	$25,317	$25,907

a. Explain the derivation of the $1,788 million in the common stock account.
b. Using December 31, 2020, balances, at what average issue price were the Merck common shares issued?
c. At what average cost was the Merck treasury stock as of December 31, 2020?
d. How many common shares are outstanding as of December 31, 2020?
e. Did Merck report a net other comprehensive income or a net other comprehensive loss in 2020? Compute the amount.

E11-64.[A] **Analyzing the Accounting and Effects of Convertible Securities, Stock Options, and Restricted Stock**

LO11-5

Homework MBC

Facebook, Inc.
NASDAQ :: FB

A portion of Note 2: Earnings per Share from Facebook, Inc.'s 10-K is as follows:

	2020 Class A Stock	2019 Class A Stock
Basic EPS:		
Numerator		
Net income attributable to common shareholders.	$24,607	$15,569
Denominator		
Weighted ave. shares outstanding.	2,407	2,404
Basic EPS.	$ 10.22	$ 6.48
Diluted EPS:		
Numerator		
Net income attributable to common shareholders.	$24,607	$15,569
Reallocation of net income as a result of conversion of Class B to Class A common stock.	4,539	2,916
Net income for diluted EPS.	$29,146	$18,485
Denominator		
Number of shares used for basic EPS computation	2,407	2,404
Conversion of Class B to Class A common stock	444	450
Weighted average effect of dilutive RSUs and employee stock options	37	22
Number of shares used for diluted EPS computation	2,888	2,876
Diluted EPS	$ 10.09	$ 6.43

a. Explain why employee stock options and restricted stock units are adjustments to the denominator for diluted EPS.

b. Facebook computes EPS separately for its Class B shares (not shown here) and states that the computation of the diluted EPS for its Class A stock assumes the conversion of its Class B common stock to Class A common stock. Based on the table above, what were the effects of the assumed conversion?

E11-65. Interpreting Information in the Statement of Shareholders' Equity

LO11-1, 2, 3

Homework MBC

Walt Disney Co.
NYSE :: DIS

The 2020 statement of stockholders' equity for Walt Disney Co. is presented below. (Disney includes both par value and additional paid-in capital under the heading "Common Stock." Noncontrolling interests have been excluded for simplicity, so the rows may not add up to the total shown. All amounts in millions.)

	Equity Attributable to Disney					
	Shares	Common Stock	Retained Earnings	Accumulated Other Comprehensive Income (Loss)	Treasury Stock	Total Disney Equity
Balance at September 28, 2019. . . .	1,802	$53,907	$42,494	$ (6,617)	$ (907)	$88,877
Comprehensive income (loss) . . .	—	—	(2,864)	(1,705)	—	(4,569)
Equity compensation activity.	8	590	—	—	—	590
Dividends		9	(1,596)			(1,587)
Contributions.	—	—	—	—	—	—
Adoption of new lease accounting guidance.	—	—	197	—	—	197
Distributions and other	—	(9)	84	—	—	75
Balance at October 3, 2020	1,810	$54,497	$38,315	$ (8,322)	$ (907)	$83,583

REQUIRED

a. Did Disney issue any additional common shares in fiscal year 2020 (ending on September 29, 2020)?

b. What was Disney's total comprehensive income in fiscal year 2020?

c. According to its statement of cash flows, Disney paid common dividends of $1,587 million in fiscal year 2020. What might be a possible explanation for the fact that dividends reduced retained earnings by $1,596 million?

d. Compute Disney's return on common equity in 2020.

PROBLEMS

LO11-1, 2, 4 Homework MBC

P11-66. Analyzing and Identifying Financial Statement Effects of Stock Transactions (FSET)
The stockholders' equity section of Gupta Company at December 31, 2021, follows.

8% preferred stock, $25 par value, 50,000 shares authorized; 10,200 shares issued and outstanding	$255,000
Common stock, $10 par value, 200,000 shares authorized; 75,000 shares issued and outstanding	750,000
Paid-in capital in excess of par value—preferred stock	102,000
Paid-in capital in excess of par value—common stock	300,000
Retained earnings	405,000

During 2022, the following transactions occurred.

Jan. 10	Issued 42,000 shares of common stock for $17 cash per share.
Jan. 23	Purchased 12,000 shares of common stock for the treasury at $19 cash per share.
Mar. 14	Sold one-half of the treasury shares acquired January 23 for $21 cash per share.
July 15	Issued 4,800 shares of preferred stock for 192,000 cash.
Nov. 15	Sold 1,500 of the treasury shares acquired January 23 for $24 cash per share.

REQUIRED

a. Using the financial statement effects template, illustrate the effects of each transaction.

b. Indicate the impact of each transaction on the calculation of basic EPS.

c. Prepare the December 31, 2022, stockholders' equity section of the balance sheet assuming the company reports 2022 net income of $88,500.

LO11-1, 2 Homework MBC

P11-67. Analyzing and Identifying Financial Statement Effects of Stock Transactions
Using the information from P11-66, answer the following.

a. Prepare the journal entries for these transactions.

b. Post the journal entries to the related T-accounts.

LO11-1, 2, 3, 4 Homework MBC

P11-68. Analyzing and Identifying Financial Statement Effects of Stock Transactions (FSET)
The stockholders' equity of Sougiannis Company at December 31 of the prior year follows.

7% preferred stock, $100 par value, 30,000 shares authorized; 7,500 shares issued and outstanding	$ 750,000
Common stock, $15 par value, 150,000 shares authorized; 60,000 shares issued and outstanding	900,000
Paid-in capital in excess of par value—preferred stock	36,000
Paid-in capital in excess of par value—common stock	540,000
Retained earnings	487,500
Total stockholders' equity	$2,713,500

The following transactions, among others, occurred during the current year.

Jan. 12	Announced a 3-for-1 common stock split, reducing the par value of the common stock to $5 per share. The authorized shares were increased to 450,000 shares.
Sept. 1	Acquired 15,000 shares of common stock for the treasury at $10 cash per share.
Oct. 12	Sold 2,250 treasury shares acquired September 1 at $12 cash per share.
Nov. 21	Issued 7,500 shares of common stock at $11 cash per share.
Dec. 28	Sold 1,800 treasury shares acquired September 1 at $9 cash per share.

REQUIRED

a. Using the financial statement effects template, illustrate the effects of each transaction.

b. Indicate the impact of each transaction on the calculation of basic EPS.

c. Prepare the December 31 stockholders' equity section of the balance sheet assuming that the company reports net income of $124,500.

d. Compute return on common equity for the year.

P11-69. Analyzing and Identifying Financial Statement Effects of Stock Transactions LO11-1, 2

Using the information from P11-68, answer the following.

a. Prepare the journal entries for these transactions.

b. Post the journal entries to the related T-accounts.

P11-70. Identifying and Analyzing Financial Statement Effects of Stock Transactions (FSET) LO11-1, 2, 4

The stockholders' equity of Verrecchia Company at December 31 of the prior year follows.

Common stock, $5 par value, 280,000 shares authorized; 120,000 shares issued and outstanding	$600,000
Paid-in capital in excess of par value	480,000
Retained earnings	276,800

During the current year, the following transactions occurred.

Jan. 5 Issued 8,000 shares of common stock for $12 cash per share.

Jan. 18 Purchased 3,200 shares of common stock for the treasury at $14 cash per share.

Mar. 12 Sold one-fourth of the treasury shares acquired January 18 for $17 cash per share.

July 17 Sold 400 shares of the remaining treasury stock for $13 cash per share.

Oct. 1 Issued 4,000 shares of 8%, $25 par value preferred stock for $35 cash per share. This is the first issuance of preferred shares from 40,000 authorized shares.

REQUIRED

a. Using the financial statement effects template, illustrate the effects of each transaction.

b. Prepare the December 31 of the current year stockholders' equity section of the balance sheet assuming that the company reports net income of $58,000 for the year.

c. How will each transaction affect the calculation of basic EPS?

P11-71. Identifying and Analyzing Financial Statement Effects of Stock Transactions LO11-1, 2

Using the information from P11-70, answer the following.

a. Prepare the journal entries for these transactions.

b. Post the journal entries to the related T-accounts.

P11-72. Identifying and Analyzing Financial Statement Effects of Stock Transactions (FSET) LO11-1, 2

Following is the stockholders' equity of Dennis Corporation at December 31 of the previous year.

8% preferred stock, $50 par value, 8,000 shares authorized; 5,600 shares issued and outstanding	$ 280,000
Common stock, $20 par value, 40,000 shares authorized; 20,000 shares issued and outstanding	400,000
Paid-in capital in excess of par value—preferred stock	56,000
Paid-in capital in excess of par value—common stock	308,000
Retained earnings	190,400
Total stockholders' equity	$1,234,400

The following transactions, among others, occurred during the current year.

Jan. 15 Issued 800 shares of preferred stock for $62 cash per share.

Jan. 20 Issued 3,200 shares of common stock at $36 cash per share.

May 18 Announced a 2-for-1 common stock split, reducing the par value of the common stock to $10 per share. The authorization was increased to 80,000 shares.

June 1 Issued 1,600 shares of common stock for 48,000 cash.

Sept. 1 Purchased 2,000 shares of common stock for the treasury at $18 cash per share.
Oct. 12 Sold 720 treasury shares at $21 cash per share.
Dec. 22 Issued 400 shares of preferred stock for $59 cash per share.

REQUIRED

Using the financial statement effects template, illustrate the effects of each transaction.

LO11-1, 2 **P11-73. Identifying and Analyzing Financial Statement Effects of Stock Transactions**

Homework MBC

Using the information from P11-72, answer the following.

a. Prepare the journal entries for these transactions.
b. Post the journal entries to the related T-accounts.

LO11-1, 3, 4, 5 **P11-74.[A] Analyzing and Interpreting Stockholders' Equity and EPS (FSET)**

Homework MBC

Procter & Gamble
NYSE :: PG

Following is the stockholders' equity section of the balance sheet for The Procter & Gamble Company along with selected earnings and dividend data. For simplicity, balances for noncontrolling interests have been left out of income and shareholders' equity information.

($ millions except per share amounts)	2020	2019
Net earnings attributable to Procter & Gamble shareholders	$13,027	$ 3,897
Common dividends	7,551	7,256
Preferred dividends	263	263
Basic net earnings per common share	$ 5.13	$ 1.45
Diluted net earnings per common share	$ 4.96	$ 1.43
Shareholders' equity:		
Convertible class A preferred stock, stated value $1 per share (600 shares authorized)	$ 897	$ 928
Nonvoting class B preferred stock, stated value $1 per share (200 shares authorized)	—	—
Common stock, stated value $1 per share (10,000 shares authorized) shares issued: 2020—4,009.2; 2019—4,009.2	4,009	4,009
Additional paid-in capital	64,194	63,827
Reserve for ESOP debt retirement	(1,080)	(1,146)
Accumulated other comprehensive income (loss)	(16,165)	(14,936)
Treasury stock, at cost (shares held: 2020—1,529.5, 2019—1,504.5)	(105,573)	(100,406)
Retained earnings	100,239	94,918
Shareholders' equity attributable to Procter & Gamble shareholders	$46,521	$47,194

a. Compute the number of shares outstanding at the end of each fiscal year. Estimate the average number of shares outstanding during 2020. How do these two computations compare?
b. Calculate the average cost per share of the shares held as treasury stock at the end of each fiscal year.
c. In 2020, preferred shareholders elected to convert 3.74 million shares of preferred stock ($31 million book value) into common stock. Rather than issue new shares, the company granted to the preferred shareholders 3.74 million common shares held in treasury stock with a total cost of $26 million. Prepare the entry to illustrate how this transaction would have been recorded using the financial statement effects template.
d. P&G has no convertible debt outstanding. What could explain the reported diluted EPS?
e. Calculate P&G's return on common equity (ROCE) for fiscal 2020.

LO11-1 **P11-75. Analyzing and Interpreting Stockholders' Equity**

Homework MBC

Using the information from P11-74, prepare a journal entry to illustrate how the transaction in part *c* would be recorded.

LO11-3, 4, 5 **P11-76.[A] Analyzing and Interpreting Equity Accounts and Earnings per Share (FSET)**

Homework MBC

Alphabet Inc.
NASDAQ :: GOOGL

The 2019 and 2020 statements of stockholders' equity for Alphabet Inc. are presented below along with portions on Notes 11 and 13 relating to stockholders' equity and equity-based compensation.

ALPHABET INC.
Consolidated Statements of Stockholders' Equity
(In millions, except per share amounts, which are reflected in thousands)

	Class A and Class B Common Stock, Class C Capital Stock and Paid-in Capital		Accumulated Other Comprehensive Income (Loss)	Retained Earnings	Total Stock-holders' Equity
	Shares	Amount			
Balance as of December 3,1, 2018	695,556	$45,049	$(2,306)	$134,885	$177,628
Cumulative effect of accounting change	0	0	(30)	(4)	(34)
Common and capital stock issued	8,120	202	0	0	202
Stock-based compensation expense	0	10,890	0	0	10,890
Tax withholding related to vesting of restricted stock units and other	0	(4,455)	0	0	(4,455)
Repurchases of capital stock	(15,341)	(1,294)	0	(17,102)	(18,396)
Sale of interest in consolidated entities	0	160	0	0	160
Net income	0	0	0	34,343	34,343
Other comprehensive income (loss)	0	0	1,104	0	1,104
Balance as of December 31, 2019	688,335	50,552	(1,232)	152,122	201,442
Common and capital stock issued	8,398	168	0	0	168
Stock-based compensation expense	0	13,123	0	0	13,123
Tax withholding related to vesting of restricted stock units and other	0	(5,969)	0	0	(5,969)
Repurchases of capital stock	(21,511)	(2,159)	0	(28,990)	(31,149)
Sale of interest in consolidated entities	0	2,795	0	0	2,795
Net income	0	0	0	40,269	40,269
Other comprehensive income (loss)	0	0	1,865	0	1,865
Balance as of December 31, 2020	675,222	$58,510	$ 633	$163,401	$222,544

Note 11: Stockholders' Equity

Convertible Preferred Stock

Our board of directors has authorized 100 million shares of convertible preferred stock, $0.001 par value, issuable in series. As of December 31, 2019 and 2020, no shares were issued or outstanding.

Class A and Class B Common Stock and Class C Capital Stock

Our board of directors has authorized three classes of stock, Class A and Class B common stock, and Class C capital stock. The rights of the holders of each class of our common and capital stock are identical, except with respect to voting. Each share of Class A common stock is entitled to one vote per share. Each share of Class B common stock is entitled to 10 votes per share. Class C capital stock has no voting rights, except as required by applicable law. Shares of Class B common stock may be converted at any time at the option of the stockholder and automatically convert upon sale or transfer to Class A common stock.

Share Repurchases

In July 2020, the Board of Directors of Alphabet authorized the company to repurchase up to an additional $28.0 billion of its Class C capital stock. The repurchases are being executed from time to time, subject to general business and market conditions and other investment opportunities, through open market purchases or privately negotiated transactions, including through Rule 10b5-1 plans. The repurchase program does not have an expiration date.

During the years ended December 31, 2019 and 2020, we repurchased and subsequently retired 15.3 million and 21.5 million shares of Alphabet Class C capital stock for an aggregate amount of $18.4 billion and $31.1 billion, respectively.

Note 13: Compensation Plans

Stock Plans

Our stock plans include the Alphabet 2012 Stock Plan and Other Bet stock-based plans. Under our stock plans, RSUs and other types of awards may be granted. An RSU award is an agreement to issue shares of our publicly traded stock at the time the award vests. RSUs granted to participants under the Alphabet 2012 Stock Plan generally vest over four years contingent upon employment or service with us on the vesting date.

continued

continued from previous page

As of December 31, 2020, there were 38,777,813 shares of stock reserved for future issuance under our Alphabet 2012 Stock Plan.

Stock-Based Compensation

For the years ended December 31, 2018, 2019, and 2020, total stock-based compensation expense was $10.0 billion, $11.7 billion, and $13.4 billion, including amounts associated with awards we expect to settle in Alphabet stock of $9.4 billion, $10.8 billion, and $12.8 billion, respectively.

For the years ended December 31, 2018, 2019, and 2020, we recognized tax benefits on total stock-based compensation expense, which are reflected in the provision for income taxes in the Consolidated Statements of Income, of $1.5 billion, $1.8 billion, and $2.7 billion, respectively.

For the years ended December 31, 2018, 2019, and 2020, tax benefit realized related to awards vested or exercised during the period was $2.1 billion, $2.2 billion, and $3.6 billion, respectively. These amounts do not include the indirect effects of stock-based awards, which primarily relate to the research and development tax credit.

Stock-Based Award Activities

The following table summarizes the activities for our unvested Alphabet RSUs for the year ended December 31, 2020:

	Unvested Restricted Stock Units	
	Number of Shares	**Weighted-Average Grant-Date Fair Value**
Unvested as of December 31, 2019	19,394,236	$1,055.22
Granted	12,647,562	1,407.97
Vested	(11,643,670)	1,089.31
Forfeited/canceled	(1,109,335)	1,160.01
Unvested as of December 31, 2020	19,288,793	$1,262.13

The weighted-average grant-date fair value of RSUs granted during the years ended December 31, 2018 and 2019 was $1,095.89 and $1,092.36, respectively. Total fair value of RSUs, as of their respective vesting dates, during the years ended December 31, 2018, 2019, and 2020 were $14.1 billion, $15.2 billion, and $17.8 billion, respectively.

As of December 31, 2020, there was $22.8 billion of unrecognized compensation cost related to unvested employee RSUs. The amount is expected to be recognized over a weighted-average period of 2.6 years.

Note 11. Net Income Per Share (in part)

We compute net income per share of Class A and Class B common stock and Class C capital stock using the two-class method. Basic net income per share is computed using the weighted-average number of shares outstanding during the period. Diluted net income per share is computed using the weighted-average number of shares and the effect of potentially dilutive securities outstanding during the period. Potentially dilutive securities consist of restricted stock units and other contingently issuable shares. The dilutive effect of outstanding restricted stock units and other contingently issuable shares is reflected in diluted earnings per share by application of the treasury stock method. The computation of the diluted net income per share of Class A common stock assumes the conversion of Class B common stock, while the diluted net income per share of Class B common stock does not assume the conversion of those shares.

REQUIRED

a. What is the difference between Alphabet's Class A common stock and its Class B common stock? Why do they have two different classes of common stock? In fiscal year 2014, Alphabet created shares of Class C capital stock, which participate in any common dividends but have no voting rights. What might be the purpose of the Class C stock?

b. Alphabet repurchased some of their Class C shares in 2020. Prepare the journal entry to show the repurchase transaction using the financial statement effects template.

c. Using the information in the notes, estimate the stock-based compensation expense for 2021 related to the 2020 grants of restricted stock units. Show the entry using the financial statement effects template.

d. Alphabet states that there is $22.8 billion of unrecognized compensation cost related to unvested employee RSUs. What are these, and why isn't this a liability on the balance sheet for Alphabet?

e. Alphabet reported net income of $40,269 million in 2020 and basic EPS of $59.15 per share. Estimate the weighted average number of shares used to calculate basic EPS.

f. Assume Alphabet has 15.0 million stock options outstanding at the end of 2020. If all outstanding stock options were exercised in 2020, what would be the impact on Alphabet's basic EPS?

g. Alphabet reported diluted EPS of $58.61 in 2020. What are the primary dilutive securities that Alphabet mentions?

P11-77.[A] **Analyzing and Interpreting Equity Accounts** LO11-5

Homework MBC

Using the information from P11-76, complete the following.

a. Prepare the journal entry for part *b*.

b. Prepare the journal entry for part *c*.

CASES AND PROJECTS

C11-78.[A] **Interpreting Disclosure on Convertible Preferred Securities** LO11-6

Broadcom, Inc.
NASDAQ: AVGO

On September 30, 2019, Broadcom, Inc. issued 4 million shares of 8.00% Mandatory Convertible Stock, Series A, $0.001 par value. The issuance generated revenue of approximately $3,679 million. The company disclosed the following in their 10-K:

> The holders of Mandatory Convertible Preferred Stock are entitled to receive, when, as and if declared by our Board of Directors, or an authorized committee thereof, out of funds legally available for payment, cumulative dividends at the annual rate of 8.00% of the liquidation preference of $1,000 per share (equivalent to $80 annually per share), payable in cash or, subject to certain limitations, by delivery of shares of our common stock or any combination of cash and shares of our common stock, at our election; provided, however, that any undeclared and unpaid dividends will continue to accumulate.
>
> Subject to limited exceptions, no dividends may be declared or paid on shares of our common stock, unless all accumulated dividends have been paid or set aside for payment on all outstanding shares of our Mandatory Convertible Preferred Stock for all past completed dividend periods. In the event of our voluntary or involuntary liquidation, dissolution or winding-up, no distribution of our assets may be made to holders of our common stock until we have paid to holders of our Mandatory Convertible Preferred Stock a liquidation preference equal to $1,000 per share plus accumulated and unpaid dividends.
>
> On September 30, 2022, unless earlier converted, each outstanding share of Mandatory Convertible Preferred Stock will automatically convert into shares of our common stock at a rate between the then minimum and maximum conversion rates. At any time prior to September 30, 2022, holders may elect to convert each share of Mandatory Convertible Preferred Stock into shares of our common stock at the then minimum conversion rate. . . . As of November 1, 2020, the minimum conversion rate was 3.0567, and the maximum conversion rate was 3.5729.
>
> We recognized $27 million and $29 million of accrued preferred stock dividends, which were presented as temporary equity in our consolidated balance sheets as of November 1, 2020, and November 3, 2019, respectively.

REQUIRED

a. What is meant by the term "mandatory convertible" prior to the words "preferred stock"?

b. What is reflected on Broadcom's balance sheet at December 31, 2019?

c. The fair market value of a preferred share is $1,422 on December 28, 2020, and the fair value on the date of issue was $1,083. What could account for the substantial increase in the value per share?

d. How should preferred stock be treated in an analysis of a company?

e. Discuss the general effects of the conversion feature on current computations of EPS and also of the future conversion on Broadcom's balance sheet.

C11-79. **Identifying Corporate Takeover, Stock Ownership, and Managerial Ethics** LO11-1

Ron King, chairperson of the board of directors and chief executive officer of Image, Inc., is pondering a recommendation to make to the firm's board of directors in response to actions taken by Jack Hatcher. Hatcher recently informed King and other board members that he (Hatcher) had purchased

15% of the voting stock of Image at $12 per share and is considering an attempt to take control of the company. His effort to take control would include offering $16 per share to stockholders to induce them to sell shares to him. Hatcher also indicated that he would abandon his takeover plans if the company would buy back his stock at a price 50% over its current market price of $13 per share.

King views the proposed takeover by Hatcher as a hostile maneuver. Hatcher has a reputation of identifying companies that are undervalued (that is, their underlying net assets are worth more than the price of the outstanding stock), buying enough stock to take control of such a company, replacing top management, and, on occasion, breaking up the company (that is, selling off the various divisions to the highest bidder). The process has proven profitable to Hatcher and his financial backers. Stockholders of the companies taken over also benefited because Hatcher paid them attractive prices to buy their stock.

King recognizes that Image is currently undervalued by the stock market but believes that eventually the company will significantly improve its financial performance to the long-run benefit of its stockholders.

REQUIRED

What are the ethical issues that King should consider in arriving at a recommendation to make to the board of directors regarding Hatcher's offer to be "bought out" of his takeover plans?

LO11-1, 2 **C11-80. Understanding Shareholders' Meeting, Managerial Communications, and Financial Interpretations**

The stockholders' equity section of Pillar Corporation's comparative balance sheet at the end of 2021 and 2022 is presented below. It is part of the financial data just reviewed at a stockholders' meeting.

	December 31, 2022	December 31, 2021
Common stock, $10 par value, 600,000 shares authorized; issued at December 31, 2022, 220,000 shares; 2021, 200,000 shares	$2,200,000	$2,000,000
Paid-in capital in excess of par	3,660,000	3,300,000
Retained earnings (see Note)	2,368,000	2,260,000
Total stockholders' equity	$8,228,000	$7,560,000

Note: Availability of retained earnings for cash dividends is restricted by $1,600,000 due to a planned plant expansion.

The following items were also disclosed at the stockholders' meeting: net income for 2022 was $976,000; a 10% stock dividend was issued December 14, 2022; when the stock dividend was declared, the market value was $28 per share; the market value per share at December 31, 2022, was $26; management plans to borrow $400,000 to help finance a new plant addition, which is expected to cost a total of $1,840,000; and the customary $1.54 per share cash dividend had been revised to $1.40 when declared and issued the last week of December 2022. As part of its investor relations program, during the stockholders' meeting management asked stockholders to write any questions they might have concerning the firm's operations or finances. As assistant controller, you are given the stockholders' questions.

REQUIRED

Prepare brief but reasonably complete answers to the following questions:

a. What did Pillar do with the cash proceeds from the stock dividend issued in December?

b. What was my book value per share at the end of 2021 and 2022?

c. I owned 6,000 shares of Pillar in 2021 and have not sold any shares. How much more or less of the corporation do I own at December 31, 2022, and what happened to the market value of my interest in the company?

d. I heard someone say that stock dividends don't give me anything I didn't already have. Why did you issue one? Are you trying to fool us?

e. Instead of a stock dividend, why didn't you declare a cash dividend and let us buy the new shares that were issued?

f. Why are you cutting back on the dividends I receive?

g. If you have $1,600,000 put aside in retained earnings for the new plant addition, which will cost $1,840,000, why are you borrowing $400,000 instead of just the $240,000 needed?

C11-81. Assessing Stock Buybacks, Corporate Accountability, and Managerial Ethics **LO11-1, 2, 4**

Liz Plummer, vice president and general counsel, chairs the Executive Compensation Committee for Sunlight Corporation. Four and one-half years ago, the compensation committee designed a performance bonus plan for top management that was approved by the board of directors. The plan provides an attractive bonus for top management if the firm's earnings per share grows each year over a five-year period. The plan is now in its fifth year; for the past four years, earnings per share has grown each year. Last year, earnings per share was $1.95 (net income was $5,850,000 and the weighted average common shares outstanding was 3,000,000). Sunlight Corporation has no preferred stock and has had 3,000,000 common shares outstanding for several years. Plummer has recently seen an estimate that Sunlight's net income this year will decrease about 5% from last year because of a slight recession in the economy.

Plummer is disturbed by an item on the agenda for the board of directors meeting on June 20 and an accompanying note from Rob Lundy. Lundy is vice president and chief financial officer for Sunlight. Lundy is proposing to the board that Sunlight buy back 450,000 shares of its own common stock on July 1. Lundy's explanation is that the firm's stock is undervalued now and that Sunlight has excess cash available. When the stock subsequently recovers in value, Lundy notes, Sunlight will reissue the shares and generate a nice increase in contributed capital.

Lundy's note to Plummer merely states, "Look forward to your support of my proposal at the board meeting."

REQUIRED

Why is Plummer disturbed by Lundy's proposal and note? What possible ethical problem does Plummer face when Lundy's proposal is up for a vote at the board meeting?

C11-82.[A] Redeemable Preferred Shares **LO11-1, 5**

Restaurant Brands International Inc.
NYSE :: QSR

Restaurant Brands International, Inc., reports the following in disclosure Note 13 to their financial statements in their 2017 10-K related to redeemable preferred stock.

Note 13

Redeemable Preferred Shares

On December 12, 2014, we issued 68,530,939 Class A 9.0% cumulative compounding perpetual voting preferred shares (the "Preferred Shares") to a subsidiary of Berkshire Hathaway, which were outstanding until the Redemption Date (as defined below). A 9.0% annual dividend accrued on the purchase price of $43.775848 per Preferred Share, and was payable quarterly in arrears, when declared and approved by our board of directors. The Preferred Shares were redeemable at our option on and after December 12, 2017. During 2014, we adjusted the carrying value of the Preferred Shares to their redemption price of $48.109657 per Preferred Share (the "redemption price"). The Preferred Shares were classified as temporary equity while outstanding because redemption was not solely within our control, as the Preferred Shares also contained provisions that allowed the holder to redeem the Preferred Shares for cash beginning in December 2024 or upon a change in control.

On December 12, 2017 (the "Redemption Date"), we redeemed all of the issued and outstanding Preferred Shares for aggregate consideration of $3,115.6 million (the "Redemption Consideration"), consisting of (i) $3,297.0 million, which is the redemption price of $48.109657 per Preferred Share multiplied by the number of Preferred Shares outstanding, plus (ii) $54.0 million of accrued and unpaid preferred dividends up to the Redemption Date, minus (iii) an adjustment of $235.4 million, . . . The $235.4 million adjustment, net of $1.6 million of related transaction costs, is reflected as a $233.8 million increase to net income attributable to common shareholders and common shareholder's equity. . . . Upon redemption, the Preferred Shares were deemed canceled, dividends ceased to accrue, and all rights of the holder terminated.

The company's balance sheet, in part, reflected the following:

Restaurant Brands International Inc. and Subsidiaries
Excerpt from Consolidated Balance Sheet
December 31, 2017 and 2016 (millions of USD)
LIABILITIES, REDEEMABLE PREFERRED SHARES AND SHAREHOLDERS' EQUITY

	2017	2016
Current liabilities:		
Accounts and drafts payable	$ 412.9	$ 369.8
Other accrued liabilities	838.2	469.3
Gift card liability	214.9	194.4
Advertising fund liabilities	110.8	83.3
Current portion of long-term debt and capital leases	78.2	93.9
Total current liabilities	1,655.0	1,210.7
Term debt, net of current portion	11,800.9	8,410.2
Capital leases, net of current portion	243.8	218.4
Other liabilities, net	1,455.1	784.9
Deferred income taxes, net	1,508.1	1,715.1
Total liabilities	16,662.9	12,339.3
Redeemable preferred shares; no par value; 68,530,939 shares authorized, issued and outstanding at December 31, 2016	—	3,297.0
Shareholders' equity:		
Common shares, no par value; unlimited shares authorized at December 31, 2017, and December 31, 2016; 243,899,476 shares issued and outstanding at December 31, 2017; 234,236,678 shares issued and outstanding at December 31, 2016	2,051.5	1,955.1
Retained earnings	650.6	445.7
Accumulated other comprehensive income (loss)	(475.7)	(698.3)
Total Restaurant Brands International Inc. shareholders' equity	2,226.4	1,702.5
Noncontrolling interests	2,334.2	1,786.1
Total shareholders' equity	4,560.6	3,488.6
Total liabilities, redeemable preferred shares and shareholders' equity	$21,223.5	$19,124.9

a. Where were the redeemable preferred shares listed on the balance sheet before they were redeemed?

b. What was the aggregate sales price of the redeemable preferred shares in 2014?

c. When issued, $250 million of the issue price was allocated to warrants that were issued as part of the transaction in 2014. Later in 2014, the company adjusted the carrying value of the redeemable preferred shares to their redemption price of $3,297 million. What was the increase in the carrying value of the shares? Where would this have been reported, if at all?

d. If you were an analyst of the company, how would you have viewed these shares?

SOLUTIONS TO REVIEW PROBLEMS

Review 11-1

a.

ANALYZE

Transaction	Cash Asset +	Noncash Assets =	Liabilities +	Contrib. Capital +	Earned Capital −	Contra Equity	Revenues −	Expenses =	Net Income
(1) Jan. 15 Issued 10,000 shares of common stock.	+170,000 Cash	=		+50,000 Common Stock +120,000 Additional Paid-in Capital		−	−	=	
(2) Mar. 31 Purchased 2,000 shares of treasury stock.	−30,000 Cash	=				− +30,000 Treasury Stock	−	=	

continued

continued from previous page

Transaction	Cash Asset	+	Noncash Assets	=	Liabil-ities	+	Contrib. Capital	+	Earned Capital	−	Contra Equity	*Revenues*	−	*Expenses*	=	*Net Income*
(3) June 25 Reissued 1,000 shares of treasury stock purchased Mar. 31.	+20,000 Cash			=			+5,000 Additional Paid-in Capital			−	−15,000 Treasury Stock		−		=	

b.

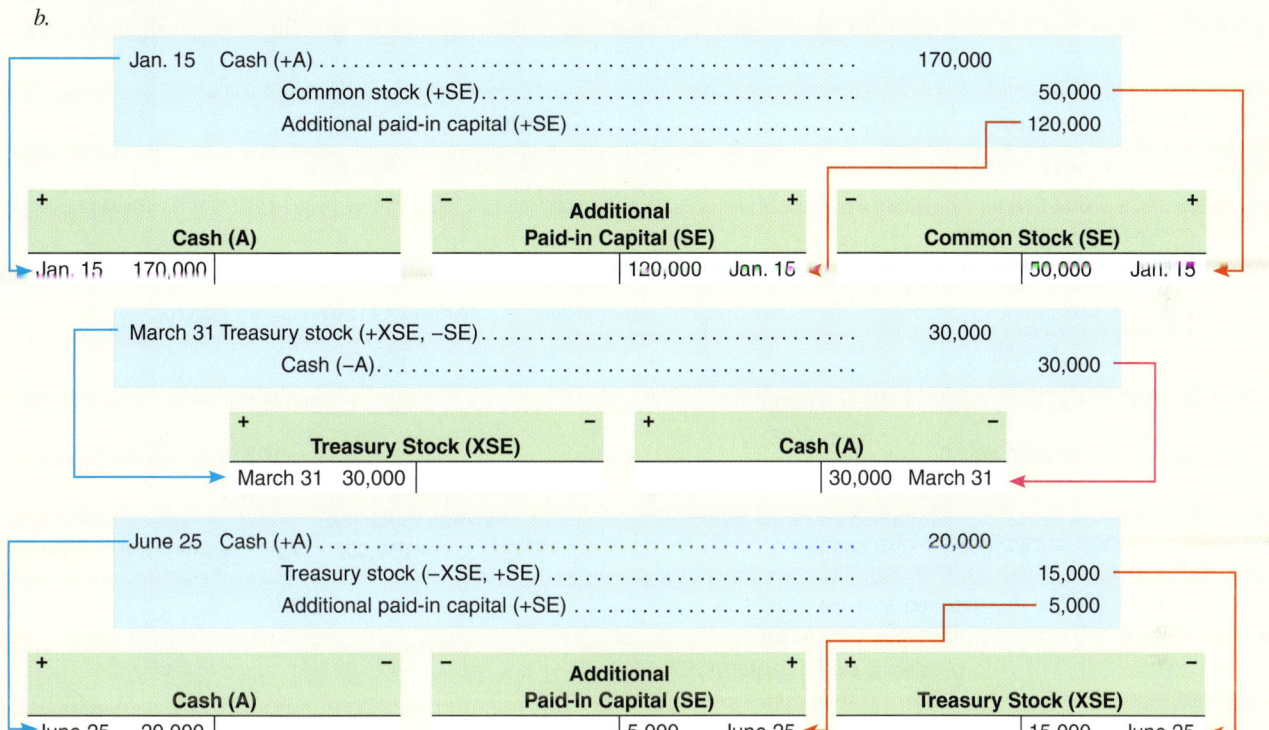

Jan. 15 Cash (+A)	170,000	
Common stock (+SE)		50,000
Additional paid-in capital (+SE)		120,000

+ Cash (A) −				− Additional Paid-in Capital (SE) +				− Common Stock (SE) +	
Jan. 15	170,000				120,000	Jan. 15		50,000	Jan. 15

March 31 Treasury stock (+XSE, −SE)	30,000	
Cash (−A)		30,000

+ Treasury Stock (XSE) −			+ Cash (A) −	
March 31	30,000		30,000	March 31

June 25 Cash (+A)	20,000	
Treasury stock (−XSE, +SE)		15,000
Additional paid-in capital (+SE)		5,000

+ Cash (A) −				− Additional Paid-In Capital (SE) +				+ Treasury Stock (XSE) −	
June 25	20,000				5,000	June 25		15,000	June 25

Review 11-2

PART ONE

a.

	Preferred Stock	Common Stock
Year 1	$ 0	$ 0
Year 2		
Arrearage from Year 1 ($1,000,000 × 5%)	50,000	
Current-year dividend ($1,000,000 × 5%)	50,000	
Balance to common		200,000
Year 3		
Current-year dividend ($1,000,000 × 5%)	50,000	
Balance to common		30,000

b.

	Preferred Stock	Common Stock
Year 1	$ 0	$ 0
Year 2		
Current-year dividend ($1,000,000 × 5%)	50,000	
Balance to common		250,000
Year 3		
Current-year dividend ($1,000,000 × 5%)	50,000	
Balance to common		30,000

PART TWO

a.

ANALYZE

	Balance Sheet									Income Statement				
Transaction	Cash Asset	+	Noncash Assets	=	Liabil-ities	+	Contrib. Capital	+	Earned Capital	Revenues	–	Expenses	=	Net Income
(1) Apr. 1 Declared a 100% stock dividend.				=			+250,000 Common Stock		–250,000[1] Retained Earnings		–		=	
(2) Dec. 7 Declared a 3% stock dividend.				=			+15,000 Common Stock +6,000 Additional Paid-in Capital		–21,000[2] Retained Earnings		–		=	
(3) Dec. 31 Declared and paid a cash dividend.	–123,600 Cash			=					–123,600[3] Retained Earnings		–		=	

1 This large stock dividend reduces retained earnings at the par value of shares distributed (50,000 shares × 100% × $5 par value = $250,000). Contributed capital (common stock) increases by the same amount.

2 This small stock dividend reduces retained earnings at the market value of shares distributed (3% × 100,000 shares × $7 per share = $21,000). Contributed capital increases by the same amount ($15,000 to common stock and $6,000 to paid-in capital).

3 At the time of the cash dividend, there are 103,000 shares outstanding. The cash paid is, therefore, 103,000 shares × $1.20 per share = $123,600.

b.

JOURNALIZE

			Debit	Credit
(1)	April 1	Retained earnings (–SE)	250,000	
		Common stock (+SE)		250,000

POST

– Retained Earnings (SE) +		– Common Stock (SE) +	
April 1 250,000			250,000 April 1

JOURNALIZE

			Debit	Credit
(2)	Dec. 7	Retained earnings (–SE)	21,000	
		Common stock (+SE)		15,000
		Additional paid-in capital (+SE)		6,000

POST

– Retained Earnings (SE) +		– Additional Paid-in Capital (SE) +		– Common Stock (SE) +	
Dec. 7 21,000			6,000 Dec. 7		15,000 Dec. 7

JOURNALIZE

			Debit	Credit
(3)	Dec. 31	Retained earnings (–SE)	123,600	
		Cash (–A)		123,600

POST

– Retained Earnings (SE) +		+ Cash (A) –	
Dec. 31 123,600			123,600 Dec. 31

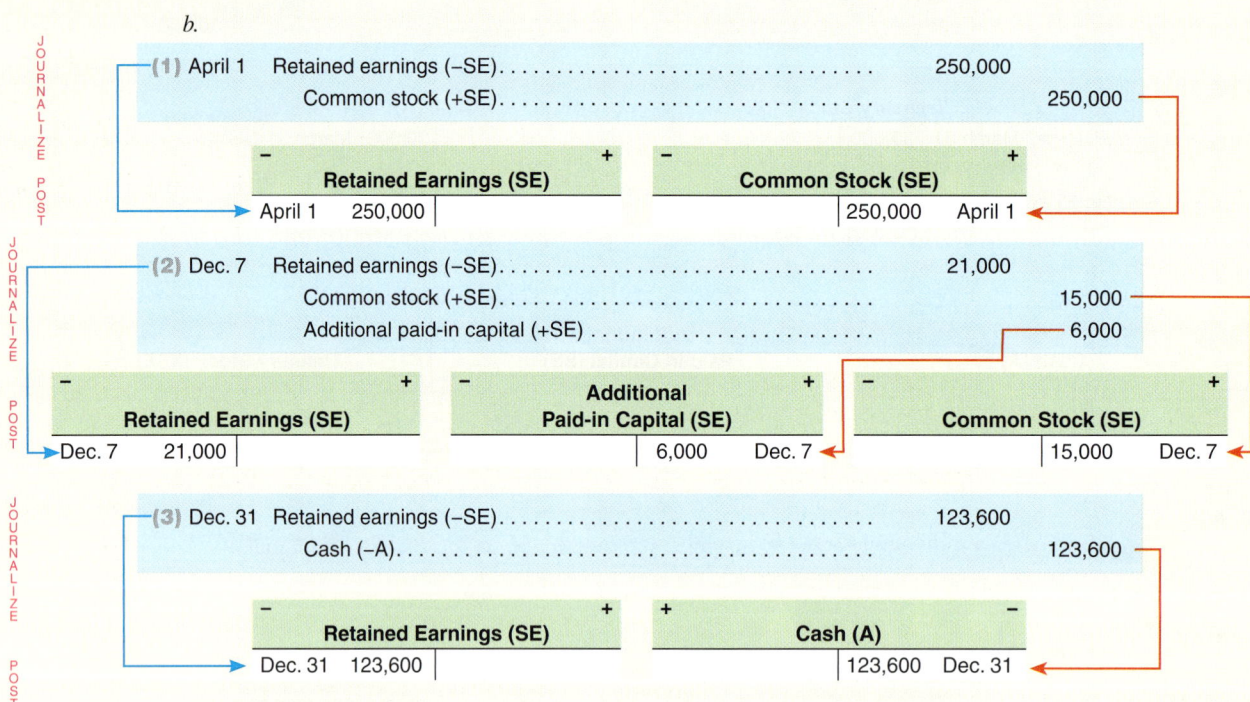

c. The ending retained earnings balance is $549,400 ($656,000 – $250,000 – $21,000 – $123,600 + $288,000 = $549,400)

d. If a company initiates a stock split, no journal entry is required.

Review 11-3

a.

Fastenal Company and Subsidiaries
Consolidated Statement of Comprehensive Income
For the Year Ended December 31, 2020 ($ millions)

Net earnings	$859.1
Other comprehensive income (loss), net of tax:	
Foreign currency translation adjustment, net of tax	17.2
Comprehensive income	$876.3

b.

Accumulated Other Comprehensive Income (Loss) Reconciliation For the Year Ended December 31, 2020 ($ millions)	
Accumulated other comprehensive income (loss), December 31, 2019	$ (38.4)
Other comprehensive income (loss)..................................	17.2
Accumulated other comprehensive income (loss), December 31, 2020	$ (21.2)

Review 11-4

a. Basic EPS would be calculated as follows (millions, except per share amount):

$$\text{Basic EPS} = \frac{\$1{,}750 - \$40}{760 \text{ shares}} = \$2.25 \text{ per share}$$

b. Diluted EPS is calculated as follows (millions, except per share amounts):

$$\text{Diluted EPS} = \frac{\$1{,}750}{770 \text{ shares}} = \$2.27 \text{ per share}$$

c. Petroni would only report basic EPS on its income statement. Diluted EPS, as calculated in requirement *b*, is actually higher than basic EPS because the convertible preferred stock is anti-dilutive. GAAP requires that reported diluted EPS be lower than basic EPS. Consequently, Petroni would not report the diluted EPS number.

Review 11-5

a.

ANALYZE

Transaction	Cash Asset	+	Noncash Assets	=	Liabilities	−	Contra Liabilities	+	Contrib. Capital	+	Earned Capital	Revenues	−	Expenses	=	Net Income
	Balance Sheet											***Income Statement***				
Conversion of an $850 book-value bond into 200 common shares of $1 par value.				=	−1,000 Bonds Payable	−	−150 Bond Discount		+200 Common Stock +650 Additional Paid-In Capital				−		=	

b.

JOURNALIZE

Bonds payable (−L)...	1,000	
Bond discount (−XL, +L)		150
Common stock (+SE)		200
Additional paid-in capital (+SE)............................		650

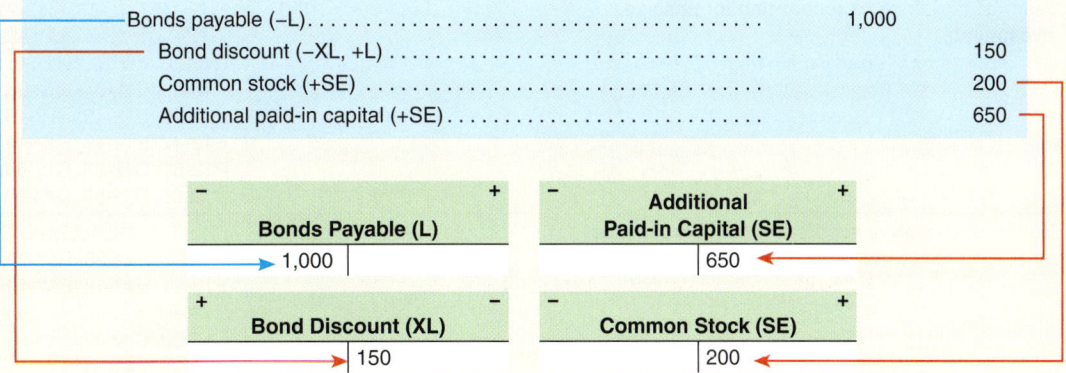

c.

POST

− Bonds Payable (L) +	
1,000	

− Additional Paid-in Capital (SE) +	
	650

+ Bond Discount (XL) −	
	150

− Common Stock (SE) +	
	200

Chapter 12 Reporting and Analyzing Financial Investments

LEARNING OBJECTIVES

LO12-1 Explain and interpret the three levels of investor influence over an investee—passive, significant, and controlling.

LO12-2 Describe the term "fair value" and the fair value hierarchy.

LO12-3 Describe and analyze accounting for passive investments.

LO12-4 Explain and analyze accounting for investments with significant influence.

LO12-5 Describe and analyze accounting for investments with control.

LO12-6 Appendix 12A: Illustrate and analyze accounting mechanics for equity method investments.

LO12-7 Appendix 12B: Apply consolidation accounting mechanics.

LO12-8 Appendix 12C: Discuss the reporting of derivative securities.

Road Map

LO	Learning Objective | Topics	Page	eLecture	Review	Assignments
LO12-1	Explain and interpret the three levels of investor influence over an investee-passive, significant, and controlling.	12-3	e12-1	R 12-1	M12-11, E12-28, E12-29, E12-30, E12-31, E12-33, E12-34, E12-41, E12-42, E12-43, E12-45, E12-46, E12-47, E12-48, E12-49, E12-50, P12-59, P12-61, P12-62, C12-63, C12-64, C12-65, C12-66, C12-67
LO12-2	Describe the term "fair value" and the fair value hierarchy.	12-5	e12-2	R 12-2	M12-14, E12-49, P12-59, P12-61, C12-66, C12-67
LO12-3	Describe and analyze accounting for passive investments.	12-6	e12-3	R 12-3	M12-12, M12-13, M12-21, M12-22, M12-23, M12-24, M12-25, M12-26, E12-28, EU-29, E12-30, E12-31, E12-33, E12-34, E12-36, E12-41, E12-42, E12-43, E12-45, E12-46, E12-47, E12-48, E12-49, P12-59, P12-61, C12-63, C12-64, C12-65, C12-66, C12-67, DA12-1
LO12-4	Explain and analyze accounting for investments with significant influence.	12-17	e12-4	R 12-4	M12-15, M12-16, M12-17, M12-20, E12-37, E12-38, E12-39, E12-40, E12-41, E12-42, E12-49, E12-50, P12 -61, P12-62, C12-64, C12-65, C12-66, C12-67
LO12-5	Describe and analyze accounting for investments with control.	12-22	e12-5	R 12-5	M12-18, M12-19, M12-20, M12-27, E12-32, E12-35, E12-44, E12-55, E12-56, P12-60, P12-62, C12-66
LO12-6	Appendix 12A: Illustrate and analyze accounting mechanics for equity method investments.	12-31	e12-6	R 12-6	E12-57, P12-62
LO12-7	Appendix 12B: Apply consolidation accounting mechanics.	12-33	e12-7	R 12-7	E12-51, E12-52, E12-53, E12-54, E12-56, PU-60, P12-62
LO12-8	Appendix 12C: Discuss the reporting of derivative securities.	12-35	e12-8	R 12-8	E12-58

ALPHABET
www.Alphabet.com

When Sergey Brin and Larry Page, Stanford computer science students, started **Google Inc.**, in September, 1998, they were probably unaware that their fortune would be made in the advertising field that now generates nearly all its revenue.

Google went public in August 2004, with an offering price below $100 a share. As of the time of this writing, the stock price is greater than $2,600 and there have been two splits! **Alphabet, Inc.** (the new parent company name for what was previously Google, Inc.), faces competition in general-purpose search engines from **Yahoo, Inc.**, and **Microsoft Corporation**, and in social networks from **Facebook, Inc.**, and **Twitter, Inc.** The company also competes fiercely with **Apple Inc.**, in the mobile applications market. In addition, the company faces legal challenges from competitors and anti-trust investigations in the United States and other countries. Alphabet, Inc., faces substantial scrutiny in international markets. The company faces pressure from its employees' objections to some of its contracts with customers, from privacy concerns of users and regulators, and from customers who object to the placement of their advertisements in proximity to certain types of content.

Alphabet, Inc., addresses these growth challenges in several ways. Roughly 15% of Alphabet's 2020 revenue was spent on research and development to advance the company's provision of cutting-edge products and services to its users and its diversification away from advertising. In addition, Alphabet, Inc., acquires companies with technology that the company can leverage. Most of these acquisitions are small, but Alphabet, Inc., acquired **YouTube, Inc.**, in 2006 for $1.19 billion, **DoubleClick, Inc.**, in 2008 for $3.19 billion, **Motorola Mobility Holdings, Inc.**, in 2012 for $12.4 billion, **Waze**, in 2013 for over $1 billion, **Nest Labs, Inc.**, in 2014 for roughly $3 billion, an operation of **HTC Corporation** in 2020 for $1.1 billion to work on hardware development, and **Fitbit**, in 2021, for approximately $2 billion. In addition to these investments for operating growth, Alphabet, Inc.'s 2020 balance sheet shows that roughly 48% of its reported assets are cash and securities.

As we discuss in this chapter, the accounting method used to report investments depends on the investor company's purpose in making the investment and on the degree of influence or control that the investor company can exert over the investee company (the company whose securities are being purchased). One consequence of these accounting methods is that small changes in the amount invested can produce significant changes in the investor's financial statements.

Sources: Alphabet 2020 10-K report, *Wall Street Journal*, February 5, 2019.

CHAPTER ORGANIZATION

Reporting and Analyzing Financial Investments

Passive Investments

- Trading Securities
- Available-for-Sale Securities
- Held-to-Maturity Securities

Investments with Significant Influence

- Accounting and Reporting
- Equity Method and Effects on Ratios

Investments with Control

- Accounting and Reporting
- Acquired Assets and Liabilities
- Accounting for Goodwill
- Noncontrolling Interest

Further Considerations

- Equity Method Mechanics (Appendix 12A)
- Consolidation Accounting Mechanics (Appendix 12B)
- Reporting Derivative Securities (Appendix 12C)

INTRODUCTION

LO12-1 Explain and interpret the three levels of investor influence over an investee—passive, significant, and controlling.

Most companies invest in government securities or the securities of other companies. These investments often have the following strategic goals:

- **Short-term investment of excess cash.** Companies often generate excess cash for investment either during slow times of the year (after receivables are collected and before seasonal production begins) or for liquidity needs (such as to counter strategic moves by competitors or to quickly respond to acquisition opportunities).
- **Alliances for strategic purposes.** Companies often acquire an equity interest in other companies for strategic purposes, such as gaining access to their research and development activities, to supply or distribution markets, or to their production and marketing expertise.
- **Market penetration or expansion.** Acquisitions of controlling interests in other companies can achieve vertical or horizontal integration in existing markets or can be avenues to penetrate new and growing markets.

Investments in government securities and in the securities of other companies are usually referred to as **financial investments**. Firms make these investments for different purposes, so accounting for the investments can follow one of five different methods, each of which affects the balance sheet and the income statement differently. To help assimilate the materials in this chapter, **Exhibit 12.1** provides a graphical depiction of accounting for financial investments as we will explore it.

EXHIBIT 12.1 Financial Investment Diagram

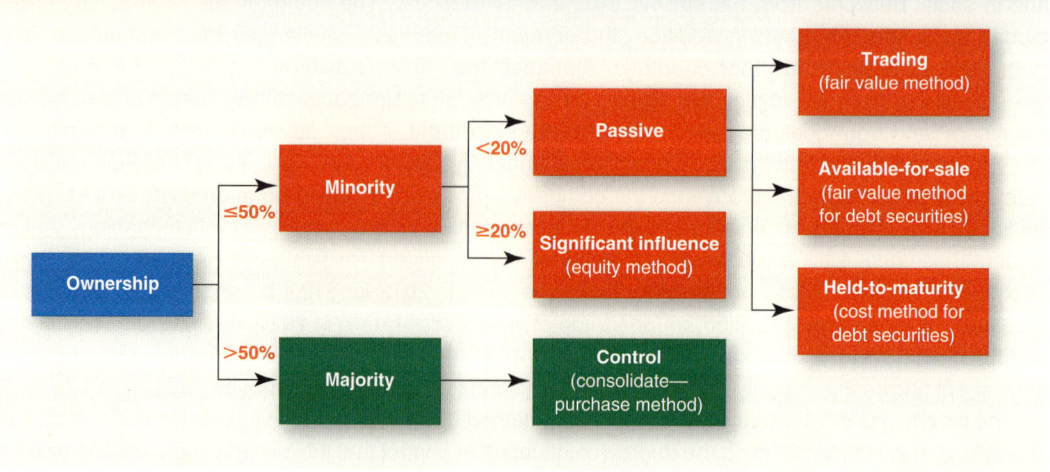

The degree of influence or control that the investor company (purchaser) can exert over the investee organization (the company or government whose securities are being purchased) determines the accounting method. U.S. GAAP identifies three levels of influence/control:

1. **Passive influence**. In this case, the purchasing company is merely an investor and cannot exert influence over the investee organization. The purchaser's goal for this investment is to realize interest, dividends, and capital gains. Generally, passive investor status is presumed if the investor company owns less than 20% of the outstanding voting stock of the investee. Investments in debt securities, such as bonds or notes of other organizations, are also classified as passive investments.
2. **Significant influence**. An investor company can sometimes exert significant influence over, but not control, the activities of an investee company. This level of influence can result from the percentage of voting stock owned. It also can result from legal agreements, such as a license to use technology, a formula, or a trade secret like production know-how. It also can occur when the investor company is the sole supplier or customer of the investee. Generally, significant influence is presumed if the investor company owns 20% to 50% of the voting stock of the investee.
3. **Controlling influence**. When a company has control over another, it has the ability to elect a majority of the board of directors and, as a result, the ability to determine its strategic direction and hiring of executive management. Control is generally presumed if the investor company owns more than 50% of the outstanding voting stock of the investee company. Control can sometimes occur at less than 50% stock ownership by virtue of legal agreements, technology licensing, or other contractual means.

Once the type of investment and the level of influence/control is determined, the appropriate accounting method is applied, as outlined in **Exhibit 12.2**.

EXHIBIT 12.2 Investment Type, Accounting Treatment, and Financial Statement Effects

	Accounting	Balance Sheet Effects	Income Statement Effects	Cash Flow Effects
Passive	Trading (Debt or equity investments)	Investment balance reported as end-of-period fair value	Interest and dividend payments from investee are included in income Capital gain/loss recognized in the period in which it occurs	Purchase/sale of investee yields investing cash flows Interest and dividend payments received from investee are operating cash inflows
	Available-for-Sale (Debt investments only)	Investment balance reported as end-of-period fair value	Interest payments from investee are included in income Capital gain/loss recognized when investment sold; interim gain/loss reported as AOCI*	Purchase/sale of investee yields investing cash flows Interest payments received from investee are operating cash inflows
	Held-to-Maturity (Debt investments only)	Investment balance reported at adjusted acquisition cost	Interest payments from investee are included in income Capital gain/loss recognized when investment sold	Purchase/sale of investee yields investing cash flows Interest payments received from investee are operating cash inflows
Significant Influence	Equity Method	Investment balance reflects purchase price and subsequent changes in proportion owned of investee's earned equity	Investor reports income equal to percent owned of investee income Sale of investee yields gains/losses	Purchase/sale of investee yields investing cash flows Dividend payments received from investee are operating cash inflows
Control	Consolidation	Balance sheets of investor and investee are presented as if one entity	Income statements of investor and investee are presented as if one entity Sale of investee yields gains/losses	Purchase/sale of investee yields investing cash flows Cash flows of investor and investee are presented as if one entity

*AOCI (Accumulated Other Comprehensive Income) is defined in Chapter 11 and discussed further in the following pages.

There are two basic reporting issues with investments: (1) how investment income should be recognized and (2) at what amount (cost or fair value) the investment should be reported on the balance sheet. We next discuss both of these issues under each of the three investment types.

Review 12-1 LO12-1

Classifying Investments as Passive, Significant, or Controlling

GuidedExample MBC

Autos Unlimited Inc., a large auto manufacturer, is considering an investment in one of its suppliers. For each of the separate situations below, determine if the investment by the auto manufacturer should be reported as a passive investment (P), an investment reflecting significant influence (SI), or a controlling interest (C).

1. _____ Autos Unlimited purchases $500,000 of bonds issued by its supplier.
2. _____ Autos Unlimited purchases $5 million of bonds issued by its supplier.
3. _____ Autos Unlimited purchases common stock of its supplier representing 69% of the outstanding common stock of the supplier.
4. _____ Autos Unlimited purchases common stock of its supplier representing 45% of the outstanding common stock of the supplier.
5. _____ Autos Unlimited purchases common stock of its supplier representing 10% of the outstanding common stock of the supplier.

Solution on p. 12-57.

FAIR VALUE: AN INTRODUCTION

LO12-2 Describe the term "fair value" and the fair value hierarchy.

eLecture MBC

The term **fair value** is finding increasing use in the language of accounting, but it is particularly prevalent in the accounting for financial investments. When an investor purchases a security for $100, the relevance of that acquisition cost fades rather quickly. If the investor considers selling the security a year later, the original $100 cost is much less meaningful than the current price for the security in the markets. Or, if we were to look at the balance sheet of a company, it would be useful to know how much its investments are worth today, rather than what was paid for them at various points in the past.

When accounting requires the use of fair value, U.S. GAAP defines fair value as the amount that an independent buyer would be willing to pay for an asset (or the amount that would need to be paid to discharge a liability) in an orderly transaction. For an asset that is actively traded on financial markets, fair value is the amount that we would receive by selling that asset at the balance sheet date. But fair value is also used when there is no active market for the asset. When Microsoft accounts for its acquisition of LinkedIn, it must report the fair value of the intellectual property that it obtained in that transaction. In such cases, fair value is not "mark-to-market," but rather "mark-to-model." For instance, fair value might be determined by a discounted cash flow analysis as in Chapter 9. U.S. GAAP allows various methods to be used in determining the "most representative" fair value at the appropriate date.

While fair values are often deemed to be more relevant than historical cost, they are also viewed as more subjective—particularly when fair value is determined by reference to a model rather than a liquid market. For this reason, U.S. GAAP requires that firms disclose the methods used to determine fair value for their assets using a **fair value hierarchy**.

Level 1: Values based on quoted prices in active markets for identical assets/liabilities. An example would be a common share of a company traded on an active exchange. For instance, Alphabet, Inc.'s class A common stock closed at a price of $1,739.52 per share on December 31, 2020. That price would be used to determine the fair value of another company's investment in Alphabet, Inc., stock.

Level 2: Values based on observable inputs other than Level 1 (e.g., quoted prices for similar assets/liabilities or interest rates or yield curves). An example would be a bond that is infrequently traded but that is similar to bonds that are actively traded. Moody's rates Alphabet, Inc., bonds at Aa2. Other bonds with that rating would likely have a similar yield, which could be used to compute the present value of the bond payments to estimate the fair value of a bond investment.

Level 3: Values based on inputs observable only to the reporting entity (e.g., management estimates or assumptions). An example would be an operating asset that is judged to be impaired.

Alphabet, Inc.'s use of fair value to report its investments is presented in the coming pages. The purpose of the classification is to provide an assessment of the subjectivity that underlies the numbers in the balance sheet (and sometimes, the income statement), with Level 1 being the least subjective and Level 3 being the most subjective.

In addition, companies have a **fair value option** that provides them with the *option* of using fair value to measure the value of many financial assets and liabilities. This option extends the use of fair value to a wide range of financial assets and liabilities, including accounts and notes receivable, accounts and notes payable, and bonds payable. Other assets that *must* be reported at fair value include (1) investments in other companies' equity securities, (2) derivative securities, such as options, futures, and forward contracts, that are purchased to hedge price, interest rate, or foreign exchange rate fluctuations, (3) long-term assets that are impaired, and (4) inventories that have been written down to fair value based on the lower-of-cost-or-market rule.

Classifying Investments Using the Fair Value Hierarchy LO12-2 **Review 12-2**

GuidedExample MBC

Indicate the level of the fair value hierarchy (Level 1, Level 2, or Level 3) that is described in the following excerpts from recent 10-K statements of Pfizer Inc. and Coca Cola Company.

a. Level _____ Investments may include securities that are valued using alternative pricing sources, such as investment managers or brokers, which use proprietary pricing models that incorporate unobservable inputs. (Pfizer 2020 10-K)

b. Level _____ Investments may include individual securities that are valued at the closing price or last trade reported on the major market on which they are traded. (Pfizer 2020 10-K)

c. Level _____ Investments may include corporate bonds, government and government agency obligations, and other fixed income securities valued using bid evaluation pricing models or quoted prices of securities with similar characteristics. (Pfizer 2020 10-K)

d. Level _____ We value assets and liabilities included in this level using dealer and broker quotations, certain pricing models, bid prices, quoted prices for similar assets and liabilities in active markets, or other inputs that are observable or can be corroborated by observable market data. (Coca-Cola Company 2020 10-K)

e. Level _____ Unobservable inputs that are supported by little or no market activity and that are significant to the fair value of the assets or liabilities. This includes certain pricing models, discounted cash flow methodologies, and similar techniques that use significant unobservable inputs. (Coca-Cola Company 2020 10-K)

f. Level _____ The fair values of our investments in debt and equity securities using quoted market prices from daily exchange traded markets are based on the closing price as of the balance sheet date. (Coca-Cola Company 2020 10-K)

Solution on p. 12-57.

PASSIVE INVESTMENTS IN DEBT SECURITIES

LO12-3
Describe and analyze accounting for passive investments.

eLecture MBC

The term "passive" refers to the investor's role in trying to influence the operations of the investee organization. So, short-term investments of excess cash are typically passive investments, usually in liquid, low-risk securities. In addition, investors seeking trading profits from short-term capital gains would be considered passive investors, even though their trading style may be active. Debt securities have no ownership interest, so they are always passive, and we leave the accounting for passive equity investments for the next section. Passive debt investments can be broadly grouped into two categories: those reported at cost and those reported at fair value. Furthermore, there are two methods for reporting investments at fair value. These alternative treatments are discussed below.

Acquisition of the Investment

When a debt investment is acquired, regardless of the amount purchased, the investment is initially recorded on the balance sheet at its fair value—that is, its price on the date of purchase. This accounting is the same as that for the acquisition of other assets such as inventories or plant assets. Subsequent to acquisition, investments are carried on the balance sheet as current or long-term assets, depending on management's expectations about their ultimate holding period. (The assets are reported as current assets if management expects to dispose of them within one year.)

When investments are sold, any recognized gain or loss on sale usually is equal to the difference between the proceeds received and the book (carrying) value of the investment on the balance sheet. However, there is one passive investment method where that is not true.

To illustrate entries for a passive debt investment, assume that—on January 1 of Year 1—Pownall Company wants to earn a return on a cash balance for which it has no immediate need. King Company has just issued high-quality bonds that mature in five years. Each bond has a face value of $1,000 and an annual coupon rate of interest equal to 10% (paid semi-annually on June 30 and December 31). The bonds have a current market price of $1,000, implying a 10% annual discount rate. At the start of the year, Pownall Company purchases 500 of King Company's bonds for $500,000. The financial statement effects of this transaction for Pownall are the following:

ANALYZE

	Balance Sheet									Income Statement				
Transaction	Cash Asset	+	Noncash Assets	=	Liabil-ities	+	Contrib. Capital	+	Earned Capital	*Revenues*	–	*Expenses*	=	*Net Income*
(1) Purchase 500 bonds at $1,000 each.	–500,000 Cash		+500,000 Investments	=							–		=	

JOURNALIZE

(1) Investment in King Company bonds (+A)	500,000	
Cash (–A)		500,000

POST

+ Investment in King Company (A) –		+ Cash (A) –	
(1) 500,000			500,000 (1)

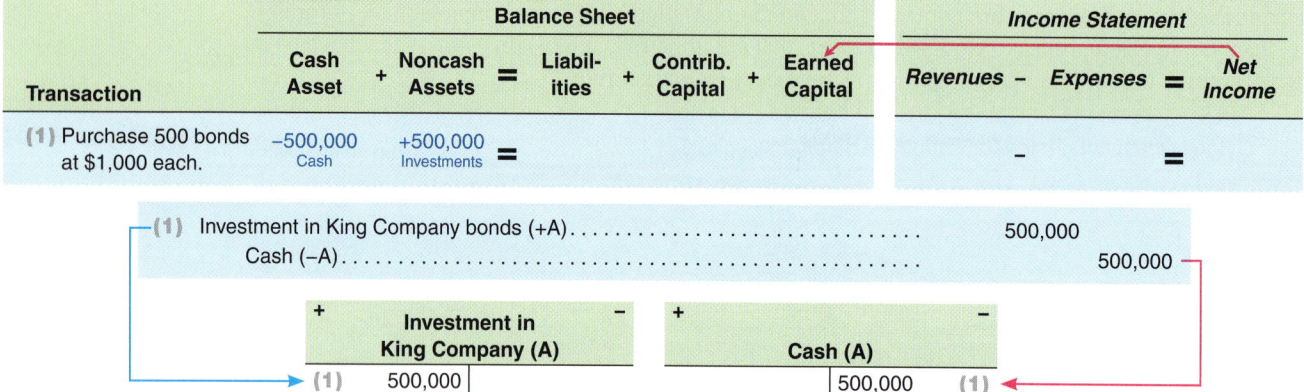

While accounting for the initial investment is straightforward, the subsequent reporting can follow one of three paths.

Investments Reported at Cost

When a company purchases a debt security, and it has the positive intent and the ability to hold that security until it matures, the value fluctuations between purchase and maturity are not relevant for financial statement readers. In such cases, these debt securities are classified as **held-to-maturity (HTM)**. **Exhibit 12.3** summarizes the reporting of these securities.

EXHIBIT 12.3

Investment Classification	Reporting of Fair Value Changes	Reporting Interest Received and Gains and Losses on Sale
Held-to-Maturity (HTM)	Fair value changes are not reported in either the balance sheet or the income statement	Reported as other income in income statement

In our illustrative example, we assume (for the moment) that Pownall Company has the ability and the intent to hold the bonds until they mature. For the King Company bonds, Pownall Company's use of the held-to-maturity method would have the following interest income and book value pattern over the five years (mirroring the accounting for a bond from Chapter 9). At the end of each six-month period, Pownall would receive an interest payment of $25,000 and recognize investment income of the same amount. Fluctuations in the market value of King Company bonds are not reflected in the accounting for the investment. At the end of year 5, Pownall would also receive a principal repayment of $500,000.

Year	Beginning Book Value (A)	Interest Income	Interest Received	Principal Payment	Ending Book Value
	(a)	(b) = (a) × 10%/2	(c)		(d) = (a) + (b) – (c)
½	$500,000	$25,000	$25,000	$-0-	$500,000
1	500,000	25,000	25,000	-0-	500,000
1½	500,000	25,000	25,000	-0-	500,000
2	500,000	25,000	25,000	-0-	500,000
2½	500,000	25,000	25,000	-0-	500,000
3	500,000	25,000	25,000	-0-	500,000
3½	500,000	25,000	25,000	-0-	500,000
4	500,000	25,000	25,000	-0-	500,000
4½	500,000	25,000	25,000	-0-	500,000
5	500,000	25,000	25,000	500,000	-0-

Investments Marked to Fair Value

If Pownall Company does not have the ability or the intent to hold the King Company bonds to maturity, then it cannot use the held-to-maturity accounting method. Instead, it must reflect changes in the fair value of those bonds at the end of a reporting period. In this illustration, we assume that Pownall closes its accounts and issues financial statements at the end of every calendar year. At the end of the first six months after the investment, Pownall Company makes the following entry:

ANALYZE

	Balance Sheet					Income Statement		
Transaction	Cash Asset +	Noncash Assets =	Liabilities +	Contrib. Capital +	Earned Capital	Revenues −	Expenses =	Net Income
(2) Receive interest payment.	+25,000 Cash	=			+25,000 Retained Earnings	+25,000 Investment Income	−	= +25,000

JOURNALIZE

		Dr.	Cr.
(2)	Cash (+A)	25,000	
	Investment income (+R, +SE)		25,000
	Received interest payment from King Company Bonds		

POST

+ Cash (A) −	
(2) 25,000	

− Investment Income (R) +	
	25,000 (2)

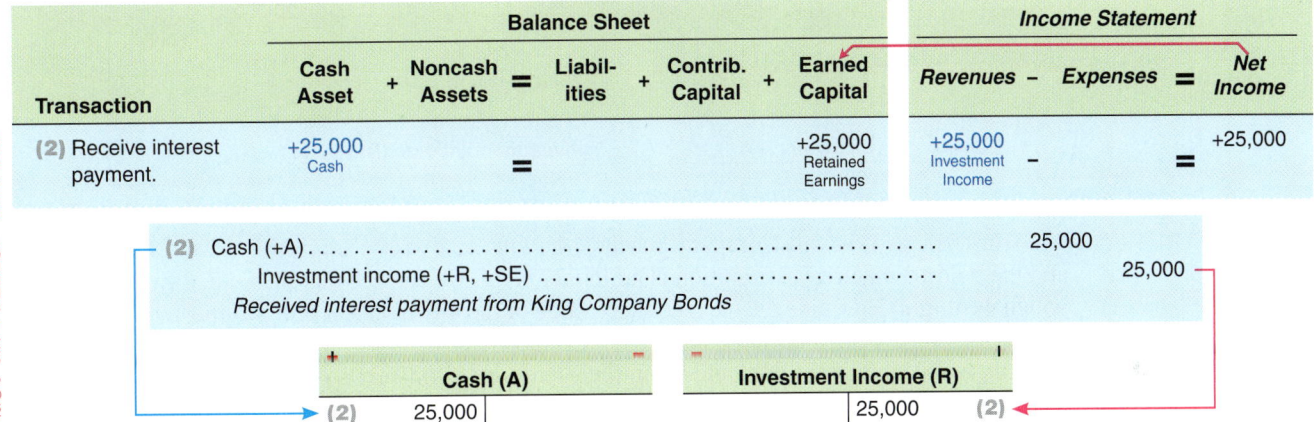

Sale of the Investment

On July 1, Year 1, an unexpected liquidity need causes Pownall to sell 100 of the 500 bonds for $950 cash per bond. The financial statement effects of this transaction and its related entries for Pownall follow.

ANALYZE

	Balance Sheet					Income Statement		
Transaction	Cash Asset +	Noncash Assets =	Liabilities +	Contrib. Capital +	Earned Capital	Revenues −	Expenses =	Net Income
(3) Sell 100 bonds at a price of $950 each.	+95,000 Cash	−100,000 Investments =			−5,000 Retained Earnings	−	+5,000 Realized Loss	= −5,000

JOURNALIZE

		Dr.	Cr.
(3)	Cash (+A)	95,000	
	Realized loss on sale of investment (+E, −SE)	5,000	
	Investment in King Company bonds (−A)		100,000

POST

+ Cash (A) −	
(3) 95,000	

+ Realized Loss (E) −	
(3) 5,000	

+ Investment in King Company (A) −	
	100,000 (3)

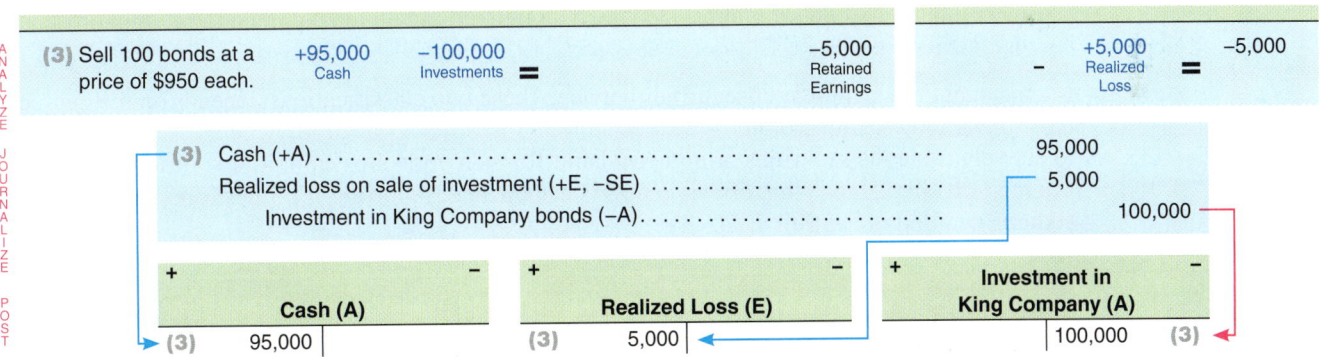

The gain or loss on sale is reported as a component of *other income,* which is commonly commingled with interest and dividend revenue in the income statement.

On the statement of cash flows, the $500,000 purchase (transaction 1) would be an investing cash outflow, and the $95,000 proceeds (transaction 2) would be an investing cash inflow. If Pownall Company presents its cash flows from operating activities using the indirect method, we would see an addition of the $5,000 loss on sale among the adjustments from net income to cash from operations.

Accounting for the purchase and sale of investments is similar to any other asset. Further, there is no difference in accounting for purchases and sales across the different types of passive investments when those purchases and sales occur in the same reporting period.

Pownall Company continues to receive interest payments from its remaining King Company bonds. On December 31, it would make the following entry:

Transaction	Cash Asset	+ Noncash Assets	= Liabil-ities	+ Contrib. Capital	+ Earned Capital	Revenues	− Expenses	= Net Income
(4) Receive interest payment.	+20,000 Cash		=		+20,000 Retained Earnings	+20,000 Investment Income	−	= +20,000

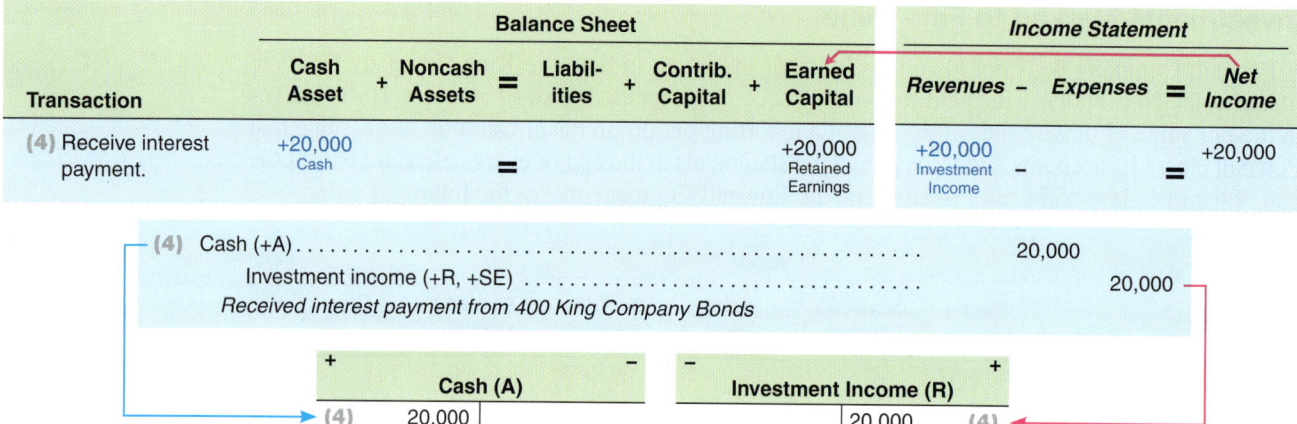

ANALYZE JOURNALIZE POST

(4) Cash (+A)	20,000	
Investment income (+R, +SE)		20,000
Received interest payment from 400 King Company Bonds		

+ Cash (A) −	
(4) 20,000	

− Investment Income (R) +	
	20,000 (4)

However, as Pownall Company reaches the end of its fiscal reporting period (a year-end), and the hold-to-maturity assumption is no longer valid, we can see that there are different ways in which we might determine the balance sheet value of the 400 bonds of King Company that Pownall Company still owns. And, that balance sheet value will be the asset's book value going forward, affecting gains and losses now and when the shares are ultimately sold.

Debt Investments Marked to Fair Value

The following two classifications of marketable debt securities require the investment to be reported on the balance sheet at current fair value:

1. **Trading (T) securities**. These are investments in debt securities that management intends to actively buy and sell for trading profits as market prices fluctuate.
2. **Available-for-sale (AFS) securities**. These are investments in debt securities that management intends to hold for interest income, although it may sell them if the price is right or if the organization needs cash.

Management's assignment of securities between these two classifications depends on the degree of turnover (transaction volume) it expects in the investment portfolio, which reflects its intent to actively trade the securities or not. Available-for-sale portfolios exhibit less turnover than do trading portfolios. Once that classification is established, reporting for a portfolio follows procedures detailed in **Exhibit 12.4**.

FYI GAAP permits companies to have multiple portfolios, each with a different classification. Management can change portfolio classification provided it adheres to strict disclosure and reporting requirements if its expectations of turnover change.

EXHIBIT 12.4 Accounting Treatment for Trading and Available-for-Sale Debt Investments

Investment Classification	Reporting of Fair Value Changes	Reporting Gains and Losses on Sale	Reporting Interest Income
Trading (T)	Balance sheet values are updated to reflect fair value changes; unrealized gains and losses are reported as investment income; affects equity via retained earnings	Gain or loss on sale equals proceeds minus the most recent book (fair) value	Reported as investment income in income statement
Available-for-Sale (AFS)	Balance sheet values are updated to reflect fair value changes; unrealized gains and losses bypass the income statement and are reported directly in the statement of comprehensive income and then in accumulated other comprehensive income (AOCI), a component of equity	Gain or loss on sale equals proceeds minus the original acquisition cost of the investment; any unrealized gains or losses in accumulated other comprehensive income must be eliminated	Reported as investment income in income statement

Both trading (T) and available-for-sale (AFS) investments are reported at fair values on the balance sheet on the statement date. Whether the change in fair value affects current income depends on the investment classification: available-for-sale debt securities have no immediate income effect; trading securities have an income effect. The impact on shareholders' equity is similar for both classifications, with the only difference being whether the change is reflected in retained earnings or in accumulated other comprehensive income (AOCI) in equity. Interest income and any gains or losses on security sales are reported in the investment income section of the income statement for both classifications.

> **FYI** When trading securities are marked-to-fair value, the unrealized gain/loss is recorded as income and reported in the income statement. For available-for-sale investments, unrealized gains/losses are reported as other comprehensive income.

Fair Value Adjustments To illustrate the accounting for changes in fair value subsequent to purchase (and before sale), assume that Pownall's investment in King Co. (400 remaining bonds purchased for $1,000 per bond) could be sold for $1,010 per bond at year-end. The investment must be marked to fair value in an adjusting entry to reflect the $4,000 unrealized gain ($10 per bond increase for 400 bonds).

If the investment is classified as trading securities (T), the entry would be:

Transaction	Cash Asset	+ Noncash Assets	= Liabilities	+ Contrib. Capital	+ Earned Capital	Revenues	− Expenses	= Net Income
	Balance Sheet					***Income Statement***		
If trading portfolio:								
(5T) $10 increase in market value of King Co. investment.		+4,000 Investments	=		+4,000 Retained Earnings	+4,000 Unrealized Gain	−	= +4,000

ANALYZE

	Dr.	Cr.
(5T) Investment in King Company bonds (+A)	4,000	
Unrealized gain (+R, +SE)		4,000

JOURNALIZE

+ Investment in King Company (A) −		− Unrealized Gain (R) +	
(5T) 4,000			4,000 (5T)

POST

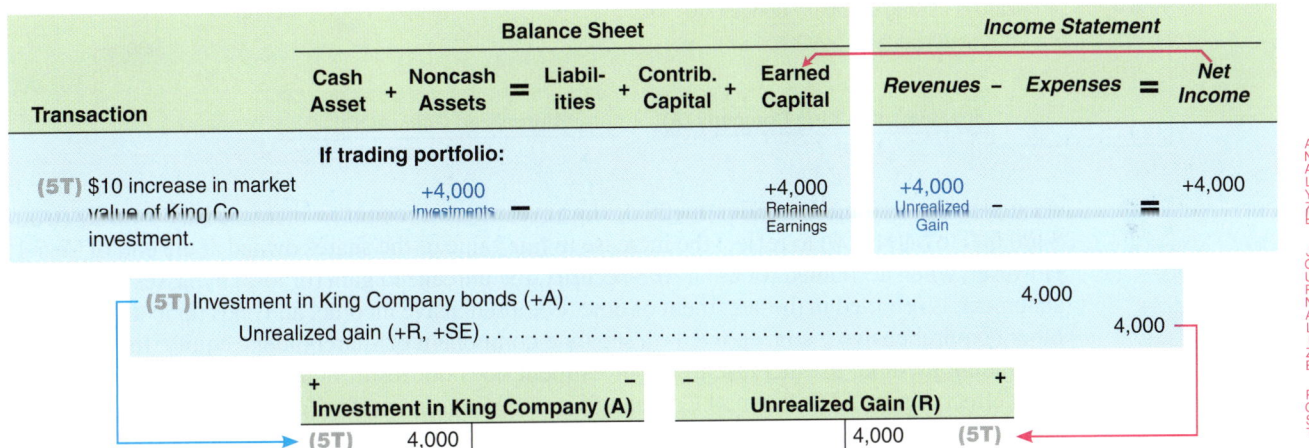

The investment account is increased by $4,000, making the end-of-year book value of Pownall's investment equal to $404,000, its fair value. Total investment income reported on Pownall's income statement would be $44,000, consisting of a realized holding loss of $5,000, interest income of $45,000 (= 500 × 10% × $1,000/2 + 400 × 10% × $1,000/2), and $4,000 in unrealized holding gains. If Pownall is actively trading to achieve capital gains, then this approach seems like the correct way to "keep score."

This entry to adjust the balance sheet to reflect the fair value of the securities is an adjusting entry. It would need to be made at the end of every fiscal period as financial reports are being prepared.

What happens when the securities are subsequently sold? Assume that Pownall Company sells its 400 bonds of King Company for $990 per bond on July 1 of Year 2. Pownall Company would receive the interest payment of $20,000 on June 30 of Year 2, as in transaction (4) above. On July 1, Year 2, Pownall receives $396,000 (= 400 × $990) in cash, and it no longer owns bonds of King Company. When the trading securities method is used, the accounting for the sale of shares is relatively simple:

Transaction	Cash Asset	+ Noncash Assets	= Liabilities	+ Contrib. Capital	+ Earned Capital	Revenues	− Expenses	= Net Income
(6T) Sell 400 bonds for $990 per bond.	+396,000 Cash	−404,000 Investments	=		−8,000 Retained Earnings		− +8,000 Realized Loss	= −8,000

ANALYZE

	Dr.	Cr.
(6T) Cash (+A)	396,000	
Realized loss (+E, −SE)	8,000	
Investment in King Company bonds (−A)		404,000

JOURNALIZE

+ Cash (A) −		+ Investment in King Company (A) −		+ Realized Loss (E) −	
(6T) 396,000			404,000 (6T)	(6T) 8,000	

POST

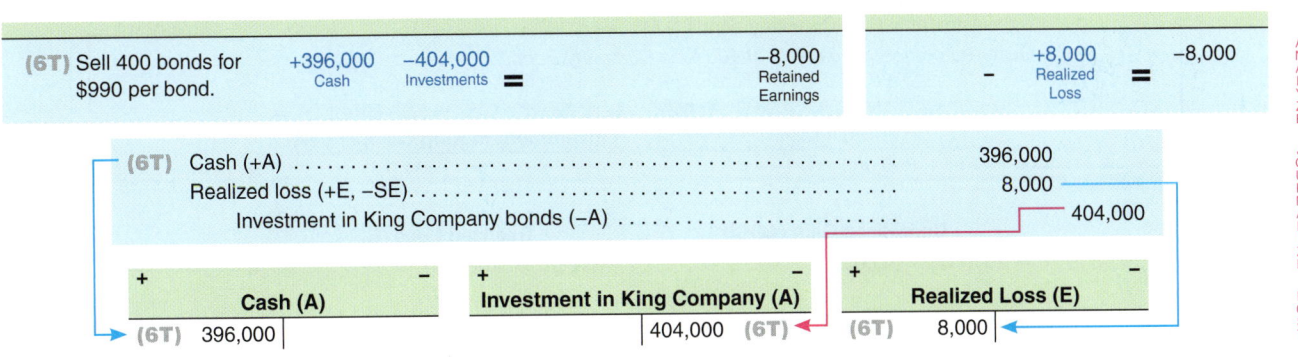

Under the trading securities method, holding gains and losses (both realized and unrealized) are recognized in income in the period in which they occur. Holding these 400 bonds caused a holding gain of $4,000 in Year 1 and a holding loss of $8,000 in Year 2. Again, if Pownall Company were actively seeking capital gains, we would say that they were less successful in Year 2 than they had been in Year 1.

Now let's assume that Pownall Company had classified its investment in King Company as available-for-sale (AFS) securities; the end-of-year adjusting entry would be the following:

ANALYZE

Transaction	Cash Asset	+ Noncash Assets	=	Liabilities	+ Contrib. Capital	+ Earned Capital	Revenues	− Expenses	= Net Income
If available-for-sale portfolio:									
(5AFS) $10 increase in market value of King Co. investment.		+4,000 Investments	=			+4,000 Unrealized Gain (AOCI)		−	=

JOURNALIZE

		Debit	Credit
(5AFS)	Investment in King Company bonds (+A)	4,000	
	Unrealized gain (+AOCI, +SE)		4,000

POST

+ Investment in King Company (A) −	
(5AFS) 4,000	

− Unrealized Gain (AOCI) +	
	4,000 **(5AFS)**

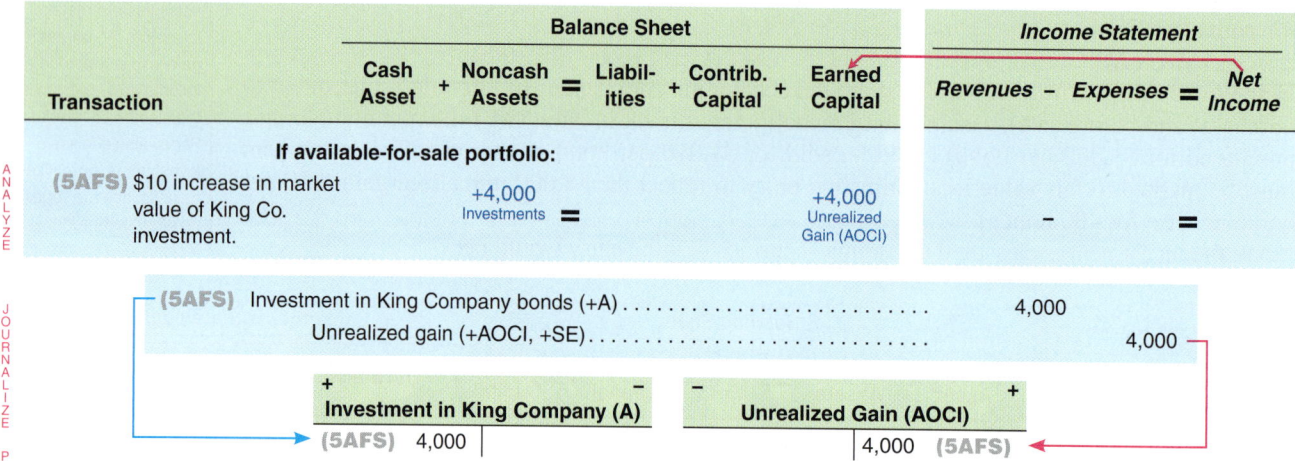

As under the trading securities method, the investment account is increased by $4,000 (from $400,000 to $404,000) to reflect the increase in fair value of the shares owned at the end of Year 1. However, when accounted for as an AFS security, the unrealized gain (or loss) bypasses the income statement, is reported in the statement of other comprehensive income, and ends up in accumulated other comprehensive income (AOCI), a separate component of shareholders' equity. In contrast to the trading method, the increase in the investment does not result in an immediate income statement effect. Under AFS, Pownall Company's investment income for Year 1 would reflect only the $5,000 realized loss from the sale of 100 bonds, plus the interest income of $45,000. The $4,000 unrealized gain is reflected in stockholders' equity but not reported on the income statement. In a sense, the balance sheet has been updated to reflect the current values, but the income statement has been left out of the picture for the time being.

When Pownall Company sells the 400 bonds for $396,000 in the subsequent period, the entry under AFS would be the following:

ANALYZE

Transaction	Cash Asset	+ Noncash Assets	=	Liabilities	+ Contrib. Capital	+ Earned Capital	Revenues	− Expenses	= Net Income
(6AFS) Sell 400 King bonds for $990 per bond.	+396,000 Cash	−404,000 Investment	=			−4,000 Unrealized Gain (AOCI) −4,000 Retained Earnings		− +4,000 Realized Loss	= −4,000

JOURNALIZE

		Debit	Credit
(6AFS)	Cash (+A)	396,000	
	Unrealized gain (−AOCI, −SE)	4,000	
	Realized loss on King bonds (+E, −SE)	4,000	
	Investment in King Company bonds (−A)		404,000
	Received proceeds from sale of 400 King Company Bonds		

POST

+ Cash (A) −	
(6AFS) 396,000	

+ Investment in King Company (A) −	
	404,000 **(6AFS)**

− Unrealized Gain (AOCI) +	
(6AFS) 4,000	

+ Realized Loss (E) −	
(6AFS) 4,000	

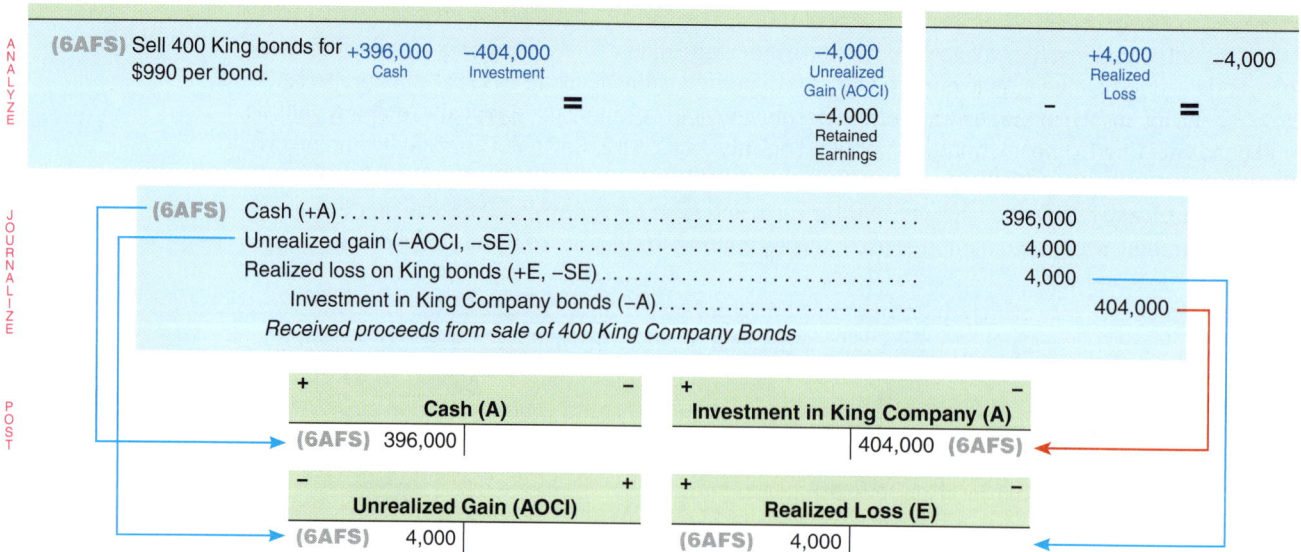

Under AFS, the realized gain (loss) goes into income when the security is sold, and the amount is determined by comparing the amount received when the shares are sold ($990 per bond) to the amount paid for the shares when originally purchased ($1,000 per bond). When the investment is sold, the entry must remove the investment (which was valued at $1,010 per bond at the end of last period) *and* the unrealized holding gain ($10 per bond) that was put into accumulated other comprehensive income when the shares were revalued. Both the Investment in King Company account and the AOCI for King Company have zero balances after this transaction.

The principal difference between trading and available-for-sale accounting for debt securities is in the income statement, as summarized in the following table. Under the trading security method, Pownall Company records income of $44,000 in Year 1 and $12,000 in Year 2. Under available-for-sale, Pownall Company records income that is $4,000 lower in Year 1 and $4,000 higher in Year 2. The total income from the investment in King Company is the same, but the timing is different.

	Income Reported in Income Statement From Investment in King Company Bonds	
	Trading	Available-for-Sale
Year 1		
Interest income	$45,000	$45,000
Realized holding loss	(5,000)	(5,000)
Unrealized holding gain	4,000	—
Total Year 1 investment income	$44,000	$40,000
Year 2		
Interest income	$20,000	$20,000
Realized holding loss	(8,000)	(4,000)
Total year 2 investment income	12,000	16,000
Total investment income—Year 1 plus Year 2	$56,000	$56,000

Because of the difference in the way unrealized gains and losses are reported, the classification of investments as either trading or available-for-sale will have an effect on key ratios that might be used to evaluate the performance of a company. Ratios that use net income in the calculation are affected. Return on equity (ROE), return on assets (ROA), and profit margin (PM) are among those ratios affected. Return on net operating assets (RNOA), which is discussed in Appendix A at the end of Chapter 5, would not be affected by this classification because passive investments would be considered nonoperating assets and excluded from the calculation of net operating assets, and the gains and losses would be excluded from net operating profit after taxes (NOPAT).

Another difference between trading security classification and available-for sale security classification is that under some circumstances, current GAAP requires the recording of an allowance for credit losses on available-for-sale debt securities and the use of the current expected credit loss methodology. This is a recent change to GAAP. A detailed explanation is beyond the scope of an introductory book, thus, we just briefly mention it here. Estimates of expected credit losses are based on historical loss experience as well as on current conditions and reasonable and supportable forecasts. Subsequent to the purchase of the security, changes in expected credit losses are recorded in an allowance for credit losses, a contra-asset account (the investment is not directly written down) and a credit loss expense is recorded in the income statement (or in some cases, Other Comprehensive Income). This treatment maintains the asset at a net realizable value.

PASSIVE INVESTMENTS IN EQUITY SECURITIES

While passive investments in debt securities may be accounted for in three different ways, passive investments in equity securities should be reported based on the trading securities method. That is, passive equity investments should be marked to fair value, and changes in fair value should be reported in the income statement in the period they occur. The available-for-sale method—which lets unrealized holding gains and losses go into AOCI until the security is sold—is not allowed for passive investments in equity securities.

When an equity security is purchased, the cost of the purchase increases (debits) the investment asset. Dividends received are reported as income by the investing company. At the end of every reporting period, the investing company must adjust the investment asset's value to its current fair value. If the value has increased, the change produces an unrealized holding gain in the investing company's income statement. If the investment asset's value has decreased, then marking the asset's value down to fair value produces an unrealized holding loss in the investing company's income statement. Fluctuations in the fair value of an equity security are presented as they occur in the investing company's balance sheet and income statement. When the equity security is sold, the realized holding gain or loss is determined by subtracting the fair value from the investing company's most recent balance sheet from the proceeds of the sale.

In the investing company's statement of cash flows, the original investment would be an investing cash outflow, and the sale proceeds would appear as an investing cash inflow (assuming that the purchase and sale were cash transactions). Cash dividends received would be operating cash inflows (under US GAAP). If the investing company uses the indirect method to report its operating cash flows, it would have to subtract any unrealized holding gain (or add back any unrealized holding loss) that was reporting in its income statement.

As an example, assume that Pownall Company used $50,000 cash to purchase 1,000 common shares of King Company on January 1, Year 1. One thousand shares represent 5% of King's outstanding common stock, so Pownall's investment is considered passive. During Year 1, King pays dividends to its common shareholders equal to $1.50 per share. Assume that King Company shares are traded actively on a national stock exchange. At the end of Year 1, the price for a common share of King Company is $55. Shortly after the end of Year 1, Pownall sells its investment and receives $52,000 in cash. These events would be accounted for in the following way:

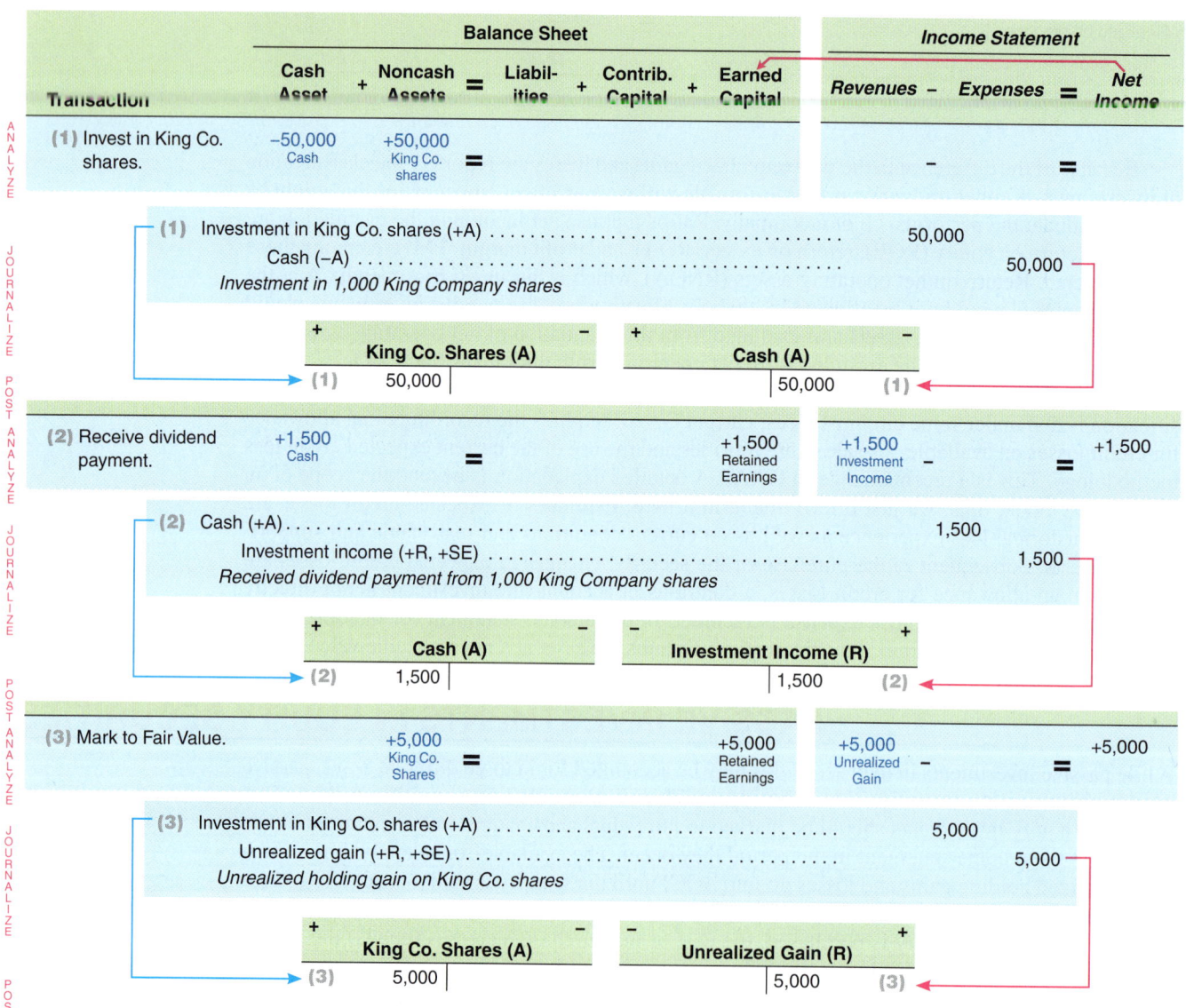

	Balance Sheet									Income Statement				
Transaction	Cash Asset	+	Noncash Assets	=	Liabil-ities	+	Contrib. Capital	+	Earned Capital	*Revenues*	–	*Expenses*	=	*Net Income*
ANALYZE (1) Invest in King Co. shares.	−50,000 Cash		+50,000 King Co. shares	=							–		=	
ANALYZE (2) Receive dividend payment.	+1,500 Cash			=					+1,500 Retained Earnings	+1,500 Investment Income	–		=	+1,500
ANALYZE (3) Mark to Fair Value.			+5,000 King Co. Shares	=					+5,000 Retained Earnings	+5,000 Unrealized Gain	–		=	+5,000

JOURNALIZE

(1) Investment in King Co. shares (+A)	50,000	
Cash (−A)		50,000
Investment in 1,000 King Company shares		

POST

+	King Co. Shares (A)	−
(1)	50,000	

+	Cash (A)	−
		50,000 (1)

JOURNALIZE

(2) Cash (+A)	1,500	
Investment income (+R, +SE)		1,500
Received dividend payment from 1,000 King Company shares		

POST

+	Cash (A)	−
(2)	1,500	

−	Investment Income (R)	+
		1,500 (2)

JOURNALIZE

(3) Investment in King Co. shares (+A)	5,000	
Unrealized gain (+R, +SE)		5,000
Unrealized holding gain on King Co. shares		

POST

+	King Co. Shares (A)	−
(3)	5,000	

−	Unrealized Gain (R)	+
		5,000 (3)

ANALYZE

Transaction	Cash Asset	+	Noncash Assets	=	Liabil-ities	+	Contrib. Capital	+	Earned Capital	Revenues	−	Expenses	=	Net Income
	Balance Sheet									**Income Statement**				
(4) Sell King Co. shares.	+52,000 Cash		−55,000 King Co. shares	=					−3,000 Retained Earnings		−	+3,000 Realized Loss	=	−3,000

JOURNALIZE

		Debit	Credit
(4)	Cash (+A)	52,000	
	Realized loss (+E, −SE)	3,000	
	Investment in King Co. shares (−A)		55,000
	Sell King Co. shares and recognize $3,000 realized holding loss		

POST

+ Cash (A) −		+ Realized Loss (E) −		+ King Co. Shares (A) −	
(4) 52,000		(4) 3,000			55,000 (4)

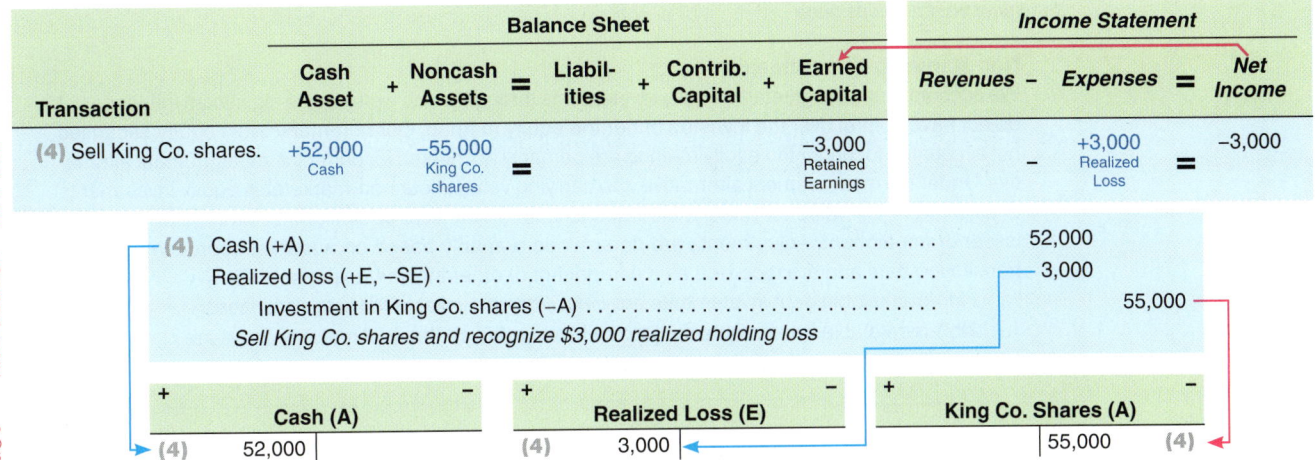

The available-for-sale method is not allowed for equity investments, so the holding gain/loss component of Pownall Company's investment income always reflects the events of that period. There is no opportunity for the investing company to "store up" holding gains or losses and to recognize them at a desired time.

As described earlier, the fair value of financial investments can be determined using a variety of mark-to-market or mark-to-model techniques, including hiring experts in valuation. When those approaches are prohibitively expensive, accounting standard setters also allow a version of a **cost method** for equity investments with no readily determinable fair value. The investing company uses the investment's cost but then adjusts that cost for any impairments and for any observed price changes in orderly transactions for the identical (or similar) investment from the same issuer. This approach—known as the "measurement alternative"—requires the investing company to establish systems to identify such transactions on a continuing basis.

Financial Statement Disclosures

Companies are required to disclose cost and fair value information on their investment portfolios in disclosures to financial statements. **Alphabet, Inc.**, reports its accounting policies for its investments in Note 1 to its 2020 10-K report:

Cash, Cash Equivalents, and Marketable Securities

We invest all excess cash primarily in government bonds, corporate debt securities, mortgage-backed and asset-backed securities, time deposits, and money market funds.

We classify all marketable debt securities that have stated maturities of three months or less from the date of purchase as cash equivalents and those with stated maturities of greater than three months as marketable securities on our Consolidated Balance Sheets.

We determine the appropriate classification of our investments in marketable debt securities at the time of purchase and reevaluate such designation at each balance sheet date. We have classified and accounted for our marketable debt securities as available-for-sale. After consideration of our risk versus reward objectives, as well as our liquidity requirements, we may sell these debt securities prior to their stated maturities. As we view these securities as available to support current operations, we classify highly liquid securities with maturities beyond 12 months as current assets under the caption marketable securities on the Consolidated Balance Sheets. We carry these securities at fair value, and report the unrealized gains and losses, net of taxes, as a component of stockholders' equity, except for the changes in allowance for expected credit losses, which are recorded in other income (expense), net. For certain marketable debt securities we have elected the fair value option, for which changes in fair value are recorded in other income (expense), net. We determine any realized gains or losses on the sale of marketable debt securities on a specific identification method, and we record such gains and losses as a component of other income (expense), net.

Our investments in marketable equity securities are measured at fair value with the related gains and losses, realized and unrealized, recognized in other income (expense), net.

continued

continued from previous page

Non-Marketable Investments

We account for non-marketable equity investments through which we exercise significant influence but do not have control over the investee under the equity method. Our non-marketable equity securities not accounted for under the equity method are primarily accounted for under the measurement alternative. Under the measurement alternative, the carrying value of our non-marketable equity investments is adjusted to fair value for observable transactions for identical or similar investments of the same issuer or impairment. Adjustments are determined primarily based on a market approach as of the transaction date and are recorded as a component of other income (expense), net.

Non-marketable debt investments are classified as available-for-sale securities.

Non-marketable investments that do not have stated contractual maturity dates are classified as non-current assets on the Consolidated Balance Sheets.

This note reveals that Alphabet, Inc., reports investments in debt securities with maturities of three months or less as cash equivalents. These investments are most likely treated as trading securities, and any changes in their fair value would result in a gain or loss that would be reported in the income statement. Because of the short maturity of these investments, the gains and losses due to changes in fair value are generally very small. Liquid investments in debt securities with longer maturities are reported as marketable securities and classified as available-for-sale. Consistent with this accounting treatment, Alphabet, Inc., notes that its marketable debt securities are carried in the balance sheet at fair value, and it reports the "unrealized gains and losses, net of taxes, as a component of stockholders' equity." Alphabet then states that investments in marketable equity securities are measured at fair value with the related gains and losses recognized in the income statement. The cash, cash equivalents, and marketable securities are presented under current assets in the balance sheet:

December 31 ($ millions)	2020
Cash and cash equivalents	$ 26,465
Marketable securities	110,229
Total cash, cash equivalents, and marketable securities	$136,694

In Note 3 to its 10-K, Alphabet, Inc., provides further information about the composition of its investment portfolio starting with its investments in debt securities.

The following table summarizes Alphabet, Inc.'s debt securities by significant investment categories (in millions):

	As of December 31, 2020					
	Adjusted Cost	Gross Unrealized Gains	Gross Unrealized Losses	Fair Value	Cash and Cash Equivalents	Marketable Securities
Level 2:						
Time deposits[1]	$ 3,564	$ 0	$ 0	$ 3,564	$3,564	$ 0
Government bonds	55,156	793	(9)	55,940	2,527	53,413
Corporate debt securities	31,521	704	(2)	32,223	8	32,215
Mortgage-backed and asset-backed securities	16,767	364	(7)	17,124	0	17,124
Total	$107,008	$1,861	$(18)	$108,851	$6,099	$102,752

[1] The majority of our time deposits are domestic deposits.

A large portion of Alphabet, Inc.'s investment in debt securities is in government bonds. The various types of securities are labeled "Level 2." This label refers to the method used to determine the fair value of each investment. The fair values of the investments listed as Level 2 are determined based on a combination of quoted prices for identical or similar instruments in active markets and models with significant observable market inputs. No portion of Alphabet, Inc.'s debt investments is listed as Level 3. In past years, Alphabet, Inc., had listed Level 3 debt investments representing preferred stock and convertible debt investments that are issued by private companies and have no quoted market prices.

For each type of investment, Alphabet, Inc., reports its cost, its fair value, and the gross unrealized gains and losses; the latter equals the difference between the cost and fair value. Alphabet reports the cost of its debt investments at $107,008 million and its fair value at $108,851 million. The fair value total is then divided into cash and cash equivalents of $6,099 million and marketable securities of $102,752 million. Alphabet accounts for the investments in this table as available-for-sale investments. Alphabet also has about $2 billion of investments in debt securities for which they have elected the fair value option.

In addition to information about its investments in debt securities, Alphabet must report on its equity investments. As seen in the table below, the investments in marketable equity securities are of a much smaller magnitude than the debt securities and are almost all reported using Level 1 fair values. There is no reporting of unrealized holding gains and losses, because equity investments are recorded at fair value, with gains and losses (both realized and unrealized) going through income as they occur.

	As of December 31, 2020	
	Cash and Cash Equivalents	Marketable Equity Securities
Level 1:		
Money market funds	$12,210	$ 0
Marketable equity securities	0	5,470
	12,210	5,470
Level 2:		
Mutual funds	0	388
Total	$12,210	$5,858

Alphabet, Inc., has also invested in nonmarketable equity securities and, at the end of 2020, these securities had a Level 2 or Level 3 fair value totaling $18,893 million.

Potential for Earnings Management

When a company owns an asset with a disparity between its fair value and its book value, there is a potential for "real earnings management" or "transaction smoothing." Real earnings management refers to the use of transactions (rather than estimates) to arrive at an attractive earnings number. Examples from previous chapters would include the liquidation of LIFO inventory or the sale of a fully depreciated physical asset with remaining life. Such transactions would increase reported income and—perhaps—disguise disappointing results in a company's fundamental operations.

These concerns are also relevant in the accounting for financial investments. Suppose financial investments were kept on the books at their original cost. Over time, some would appreciate in value while others would decline. Keeping the investments at cost reduces financial statement usefulness in two ways. First, it fails to keep financial statement readers informed about changes in the company's asset values. Second, it provides management with an earnings management tool. Selling off assets with accumulated gains (losses) would increase (decrease) reported earnings, thereby providing an income smoothing tool that might disguise the company's performance.

The reporting rules for passive investments are designed to limit this sort of problem. For instance, the requirement to mark equity securities to their fair value every reporting period means that holding gains and losses cannot build up over an extended time period. And, on the last day of a reporting period, the holding gain/loss reported in income would be the same—whether the security was sold or not. However, it is still useful for a financial statement reader to identify gains and losses to clarify a company's sources of income. For instance, Alphabet's nonmarketable equity securities' holding gains and losses accounted for a $1.5 billion increase in the company's investment income for 2020.

Fair value fluctuations are ignored for debt securities under the held-to-maturity method. But if a bond is held until its maturity, there will be no gain or loss at that point. The book value and the fair value will coincide. The requirements for using held-to-maturity are that the investing company has both the intent and the ability to hold the debt instrument until it matures, and transfers to another accounting method are generally not permitted.

The available-for-sale method "disconnects" the balance sheet and the income statement, so the balance sheet reports up-to-date values for financial assets, but the unrealized holding gains and losses do not go through the income statement until realized in a transaction. This practice does provide an opportunity for management to affect the current period's income by selling selected securities. Alphabet, Inc., could sell the debt securities with accumulated unrealized holding gains of $1,861 million to increase pre-tax income or sell those with accumulated unrealized holding losses to decrease pre-tax income by $18 million. But limiting this method to debt securities reduces the potential magnitude of these effects, and the financial statement reader can look in the disclosures to find the realized holding gains and losses included in income.

Review 12-3 LO12-3 — Accounting for Passive Investments

Part One: Available-for-sale securities

The following investing transactions by Lateral Inc. took place during the current year.

1. On January 1, purchased 500 Pincus Corporation bonds for $470,000 cash. The bonds have a face value of $1,000 each and an annual coupon rate of interest of 6% that is paid semi-annually on June 30 and December 31.
2. On June 30, receive interest of $15,000.
3. On June 30, the fair value of a Pincus Corporation bond is $920.
4. On July 31, all of the Pincus Corporation bonds are sold for $450,000 cash.

Required

Assume Lateral Inc.'s books are closed and financial reports are issued semiannually on June 30 and December 31.

a. Show the effects (amount and account) of the four transactions involving investments in marketable securities classified as available-for-sale in the financial statement effects template.

b. Prepare the journal entries, and post the journal entries to the appropriate T-accounts.

Part Two: Trading securities

Use the same transaction information 1 through 4 from part 1 to answer the following, assuming that the investments are now classified as trading securities.

Required

a. Enter the effects (amount and account) relating to these transactions in the financial statement effects template.

b. Prepare the journal entries, and post the journal entries to the related T-accounts.

Solution on p. 12-57.

INVESTMENTS WITH SIGNIFICANT INFLUENCE

LO12-4 Explain and analyze accounting for investments with significant influence.

Many companies make investments in other companies that yield them significant influence over those other companies. These intercorporate investments are usually made for strategic reasons including:

- **Prelude to acquisition.** Significant ownership can allow the investor company to gain a seat on the board of directors from which it can learn much about the investee company, its products, and its industry.
- **Strategic alliance.** One example of a strategic alliance is an investment in a company that provides critical inputs for the investor's production process or distribution of finished products. This relationship is closer than the usual supplier-buyer relationship, often because the investor company provides trade secrets or technical know-how of its production process.
- **Pursuit of research and development.** Many research activities in the pharmaceutical, software, and oil and gas industries are conducted jointly. The common motivation is to reduce risk or the amount of capital invested by the investor. The investor company's equity investment often carries an option to purchase additional shares or the entire company, which it can exercise if the research activities are fruitful.

A crucial feature in each of these investments is that the investor company has ownership sufficient to exert *significant influence* over the investee company. GAAP requires that such investments be accounted for using the *equity method.*

Significant influence is the ability of the investor to affect the financing or operating policies of the investee. Ownership levels of 20% to 50% of the outstanding common stock of the investee presume significant influence. Significant influence can also exist when ownership is less than 20%. Evidence of such influence can be that the investor company is able to gain a seat on the board of directors of the investee by virtue of its equity investment, or the investor controls technical know-how or patents that are used by the investee, or the investor is able to exert significant influence by virtue of legal contracts between it and the investee. There is growing pressure for determining significant influence by the facts and circumstances of the investment instead of the strict ownership percentage rule reflected in current corporate reporting.

Accounting for Investments with Significant Influence

Investments with significant influence must be accounted for using the **equity method**. The equity method of accounting for investments reports the investment on the balance sheet at an amount equal to the proportion of the investee's equity owned by the investor; hence, the name equity method. (This accounting assumes acquisition at book value. Acquisition at an amount greater than book value is covered in Appendix 12A.) Contrary to passive investments that are reported at fair value, equity method investments increase (decrease) with increases (decreases) in the earned equity of the investee.

Equity method accounting is summarized as follows:

- Investments are initially recorded at their purchase cost.
- Dividends received are treated as a recovery of the investment and, thus, reduce the investment balance. (Unlike passive investments, dividends are *not* reported as income.)
- The investor reports income equal to its proportionate share of the reported income of the investee; the investment account is increased by that income or decreased by its share of any loss.
- The investment is *not* reported at fair value, as is the case with most passive investments.

To illustrate the accounting for investments using the equity method, consider the following scenario: Assume that Alphabet, Inc., acquires a 30% interest in Mitel Networks, a company seeking to develop a new technology in a strategic alliance with Alphabet. At acquisition, Mitel reports \$1,000 of stockholders' equity, the book values of its assets and liabilities equal their fair values, and Alphabet purchases its 30% stake for \$300. At the first year-end, Mitel reports profits of \$100 and pays \$20 in cash dividends to its shareholders (\$6 to Alphabet). Following are the financial statement effects for Alphabet (the investor company) for this investment using the equity method:

	Balance Sheet									Income Statement				
Transaction	Cash Asset	+	Noncash Assets	=	Liabilities	+	Contrib. Capital	+	Earned Capital	Revenues	−	Expenses	=	Net Income
(1) Purchased 30% investment in Mitel for \$300 cash.	−300 Cash		+300 Investment in Mitel	=							−		=	
(2) Mitel reports \$100 income.			+30 Investment in Mitel	=					+30 Retained Earnings	+30 Investment Income	−		=	+30
(3) Mitel pays \$20 cash dividends, \$6 to Alphabet.	+6 Cash		−6 Investment in Mitel	=							−		=	
End. bal. of Alphabet's investment account.			324											

The related journal entries and T-accounts are:

(1) Investment in Mitel (+A)	300	
Cash (−A)		300

+ Investment in Mitel (A) −		+ Cash (A) −	
(1) 300			300 (1)

(2) Investment in Mitel (+A)	30	
Investment income (+R, +SE)		30

+ Investment in Mitel (A) −		− Investment Income (R) +	
(1) 300			30 (2)
(2) 30			

(3) Cash (+A)	6	
Investment in Mitel (−A)		6

+ Cash (A) −		+ Investment in Mitel (A) −	
	300 (1)	(1) 300	
(3) 6		(2) 30	6 (3)

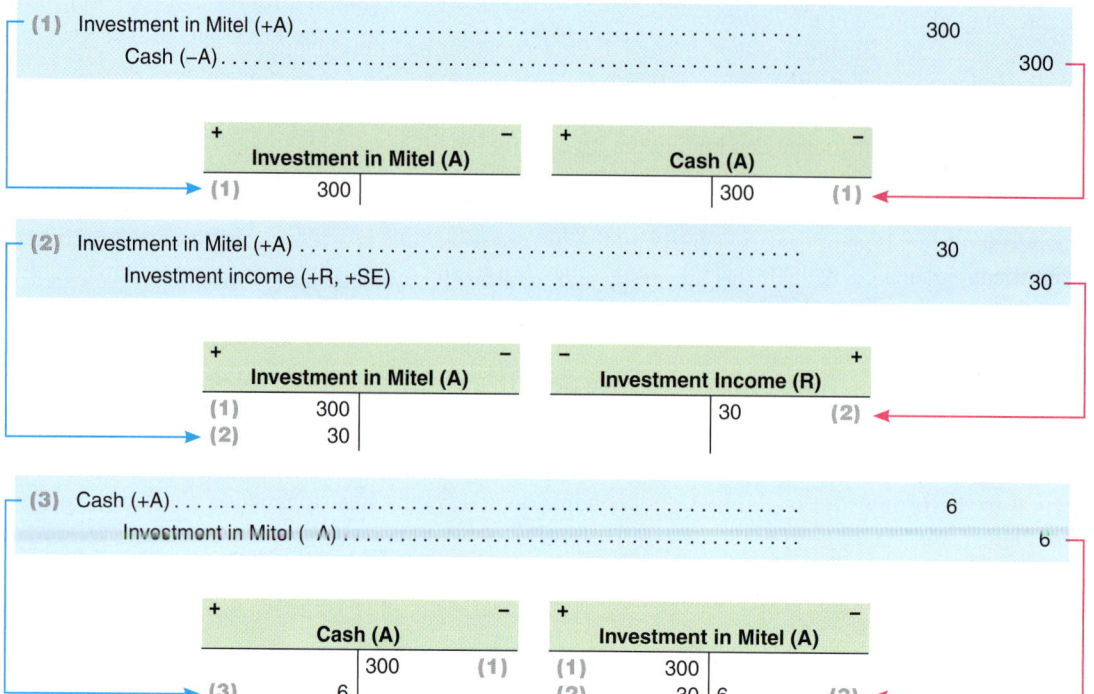

The investment is initially reported on Alphabet's balance sheet at its purchase price of $300, representing a 30% interest in Mitel's equity of $1,000. During the year, Mitel's equity increases to $1,080 ($1,000 plus $100 income and less $20 dividends). Likewise, Alphabet's investment increases by $30 to reflect its 30% share of Mitel's $100 income and decreases by $6 from Mitel's $20 of dividends (30% × $20). After these transactions, Alphabet's investment in Mitel is reported on Alphabet's balance sheet at 30% of $1,080, or $324. Appendix 12A covers the case in which Alphabet might have paid a premium over 30% of the fair value of Mitel's net assets.

On the statement of cash flows, the original investment in Mitel would be seen as a $300 investing cash outflow. The $6 dividend received would be an operating cash inflow. However, the indirect method presentation would start with net income, which includes $30 in income from Mitel. Therefore, a negative $24 adjustment would be necessary (entitled something like "excess of equity income over dividends received") to arrive at the correct operating cash inflow.

Two final points about equity method accounting: First, just as the equity of a company is different from its fair value, so is the balance of the equity investment account different from its fair value. Indeed, there can be a substantial difference between the book value of an investment and its fair value. Second, if the investee company reports income, the investor company also reports income. Recognition of equity income by the investor, however, does not mean that it has received that income in cash. Cash is only received if the investee's directors declare a dividend payment.

FYI Investee dividend-paying ability can be (a) restricted by regulatory agencies or foreign governments, (b) prohibited under debt agreements for highly leveraged borrowers, and/or (c) influenced by directors that the investor does not control.

RESEARCH INSIGHT

Equity Income and Stock Prices The equity method of accounting for investments does not recognize any dividends received from the investee or any fair value changes for the investee in the investor's income until the investment is sold. However, research has found a positive relationship between investors' and investees' stock prices at the time of investees' earnings and dividend announcements. This relationship suggests that the fair value includes information regarding investees' earnings and dividends when assessing the stock prices of investor companies. This finding implies the market looks beyond the book value of the investment account in determining stock prices of investor companies. The finding also reflects the fact that the earnings from the operations of subsidiaries are considered earnings of the parent corporation.

Equity Method Accounting and Effects on Ratios

Under equity method accounting, only the net equity owned is reported on the balance sheet (not the assets and liabilities to which the investment relates), and only the net equity in earnings is reported in the income statement (not the investee's sales and expenses). Both the balance sheet and income statements are, therefore, markedly affected. Further, because the gross assets and liabilities are left off the balance sheet, and because the sales and expenses are omitted from the income statement, several financial ratios are also affected. Some important examples are highlighted:

- **Net operating profit margin** (NOPM = NOPAT/Sales revenue). Many analysts include equity income (sales less expenses) in NOPAT when it relates to operating investments. (For example, when the entities are performing operating activities, such as bottling companies owned by Coca-Cola.) However, the investee's sales are omitted from the investor's sales. The reported NOPM is, thus, *overstated.*
- **Asset turnover ratios** (Sales revenue/Average assets). Because the investee's sales and its assets are omitted from the investor's financial statements, asset turnover ratios such as inventory turnover, receivables turnover, and PPE turnover are affected. The direction of the effect is, however, *indeterminable*.
- **Financial leverage** (Debt-to-equity = Total liabilities/Total stockholders' equity). Financial leverage is *understated* because the liabilities of the investee are omitted from the numerator of the debt-to-equity ratio.

Profitability ratios like ROE and ROA are also affected by the use of equity method investments, though the exact direction would require a careful analysis of the noncontrolling interests described on page 12-28. Analysts frequently adjust reported financial statements for equity investments before conducting their analysis. One approach to adjusting the reported financial statements would be to consolidate the equity method investee with the investor company.

Financial Statement Disclosures

Coca-Cola Company reports its interest in its equity method investees as follows in its 2020 and 2019 financial statements:

Coca-Cola—Financial Statement Effects of Equity Investments

($ millions)	2020	2019
Balance sheet		
Equity method investments	$19,273	$19,025
Income statement		
Equity income—net	$ 978	$ 1,049
Statement of Cash Flows		
Equity (income) loss, net of dividends	$ (511)	$ (421)

Coca-Cola's equity method investment of $19,273 million represents 22.1% of its total assets of $87,296 million. Its equity income of $978 million is 12.6% of its consolidated net income of $7,768 million. And, while Coca-Cola recognized $978 million in income from its equity investees, $511 million was not received in dividends, meaning that Coca-Cola received $467 million ($978 million – $511 million) in dividends.

Pertinent portions of Note 6 from Coca-Cola's 2020 10-K report are presented below:

> The Company's equity method investments include, but are not limited to, our ownership interests in Coca-Cola European Partners plc ("CCEP"), Monster, AC Bebidas, Coca-Cola FEMSA, Coca-Cola HBC AG ("Coca-Cola Hellenic"), and Coca-Cola Bottlers Japan Holdings Inc. ("CCBJHI"). As of December 31, 2020, we owned approximately 19 percent, 19 percent, 20 percent, 28 percent, 23 percent, and 19 percent, respectively, of these companies' outstanding shares. As of December 31, 2020, our investments in our equity method investees in the aggregate exceeded our proportionate share of the net assets of these equity method investees by $8,762 million. This difference is not amortized.

continued

continued from previous page

A summary of financial information for our equity method investees in the aggregate is as follows (in millions):

Year ended December 31[1]	2020
Net operating revenues	$69,384
Cost of goods sold	41,139
Gross profit	28,245
Operating income	7,056
Consolidated net income	$ 4,176
Less: Net income attributable to noncontrolling interests	54
Net income attributable to common shareowners	$ 4,122
Company equity income (loss)—net	$ 978

[1] The financial information represents the results of the equity method investees during the Company's period of ownership.

December 31	2020
Current assets	$29,431
Noncurrent assets	67,900
Total assets	$97,331
Current liabilities	20,033
Noncurrent liabilities	33,613
Total liabilities	$53,646
Equity attributable to shareowners of investees	42,622
Equity attributable to noncontrolling interests	1,063
Total equity	$43,685
Company equity method investment	$19,273

One can see that there is a substantial amount of economic activity in these equity method investees relative to that of Coca-Cola. Coca-Cola reports 2020 revenues of $33.0 billion, which is less than half of the $69.4 billion in revenues reported by the equity method investees.

YOU MAKE THE CALL

You are the Chief Financial Officer A substantial percentage of your company's sales are made through a key downstream producer, who combines your product with other materials to make the product that is ultimately purchased by consumers. In the last two years, this downstream producer has been branching out into other products that limit the capacity that can be devoted to your product. As a result, the growth prospects for your company have been diminished. What potential courses of action can you consider? Explain. (Answer on page 12-39.)

Review 12-4 LO12-4

Accounting for Investments Using the Equity Method

GuidedExample

MBC

Maplewood Inc., completed the following four transactions in the current year for its investments accounted for using the equity method.

1. Purchased 5,000 shares of Hribar common stock at $10 cash per share. These shares reflect 30% ownership of Hribar.
2. Received a $2 per share cash dividend on Hribar common stock.
3. Made an adjustment to reflect $100,000 income reported by Hribar.
4. Sold all 5,000 shares of Hribar common stock for $90,000.

continued

continued from previous page

Required

a. Show the effects (amount and account) relating to the four transactions in the financial statement effects template.

b. Prepare the journal entries and post the journal entries to the related T-accounts.

Solution on p. 12-59.

INVESTMENTS WITH CONTROL

LO12-5
Describe and analyze accounting for investments with control.

eLecture MBC

If the investor company owns enough of the voting stock of the investee company such that it can exercise control over the investee, it must report **consolidated financial statements**. For example, in Note 1 to its 2020 10-K describing its accounting policies, Alphabet, Inc., reports:

> **Basis of Consolidation**
> The consolidated financial statements of Alphabet include the accounts of Alphabet and entities consolidated under the variable interest and voting models. All intercompany balances and transactions have been eliminated.

This statement means that Alphabet, Inc.'s financial statements are an aggregation of those of the parent company and all its subsidiary companies to create the financial statements of the total economic entity. This process involves adding up the separate financial statements, while being careful to remove the effect of transactions between the separate entities.

Accounting for Investments with Control

Accounting for business combinations (acquisitions) can be thought of as requiring one additional step to equity method accounting. Under the equity method, the investment balance represents the proportion of the investee's equity owned by the investor, and the investor company income statement includes its proportionate share of the investee's income. Consolidation accounting (1) replaces the investment balance with the investee's assets and liabilities to which it relates, and (2) replaces the equity income reported by the investor with the investee's sales and expenses to which it relates. Specifically, the consolidated balance sheet includes the gross assets and liabilities of the investee company, and the income statement includes the gross sales and expenses of the investee.

To illustrate, consider the following scenario. Penman Company acquires all of the common stock of Nissim Company by exchanging $3,000 cash for all of Nissim's common stock. Nissim will continue to exist as a separate legal company—a subsidiary of Penman Company, the parent.

In this case, the $3,000 purchase price is equal to the book value of Nissim's stockholders' equity (contributed capital of $2,000 and retained earnings of $1,000), and we assume that the fair values of Nissim's assets and liabilities are the same as their book values. On Penman's balance sheet, the investment in Nissim Co. appears as a financial investment (GAAP only requires consolidation for financial statements issued to the public, not for the internal financial records of the separate companies). Penman records an initial balance in the investment account of $3,000, which equals the purchase price. The balance sheets for Penman and Nissim immediately after the acquisition, together with the required consolidating adjustments (or eliminations), and the consolidated balance sheet that the two companies report are shown in **Exhibit 12.5**.

Penman controls the activities of Nissim, so GAAP requires consolidation of the two balance sheets. That is, Penman must report a balance sheet as if the two companies were one economic entity. For the most part, this process involves adding together the companies' resources and obligations. However, if one company has a claim on the other (e.g., a receivable) and the other company has an obligation to the first (e.g., a payable), the consolidation process must eliminate both the claim and the obligation. In the case of Penman Company and Nissim Company, the consolidated balances for current assets, PPE, and liabilities are the sum of those accounts on each balance sheet. Penman's asset investment in Nissim represents a claim on Nissim Company, and Nissim's stockholders' equity accounts represent an obligation that is held by Penman, and this intercompany claim/obligation must be eliminated to complete the consolidation. This elimination is accomplished by removing the financial investment of $3,000 and removing Nissim's equity to which that investment relates.

EXHIBIT 12.5 **Mechanics of Acquisition Accounting (Purchased at Book Value, where Book Values = Fair Values)**

	Penman Company	Nissim Company	Consolidating Adjustments*	Consolidated
Current assets	$ 5,000	$1,000		$ 6,000
Investment in Nissim	3,000	0	$(3,000)	0
PPE, net	10,000	4,000		14,000
Total assets	$18,000	$5,000		$20,000
Liabilities	$ 5,000	$2,000		$ 7,000
Contributed capital	10,000	2,000	(2,000)	10,000
Retained earnings	3,000	1,000	(1,000)	3,000
Total liabilities and equity	$18,000	$5,000		$20,000

*The accounting equation remains in balance with these adjustments.

The consolidated balance sheet is shown in the far right column of **Exhibit 12.5**. It shows total assets of $20,000, total liabilities of $7,000, and stockholders' equity of $13,000. Consolidated equity equals that of the parent company—this is always the case when the parent owns 100% of the subsidiary's shares.

Comparing the first and last columns of **Exhibit 12.5** demonstrates the difference between the equity method and consolidation. In the left column, it appears that Penman spent $3,000 to acquire a financial asset. However, in the last column, it appears that Penman spent $3,000 to acquire a "bundle" of assets and liabilities consisting of $1,000 in cash plus $4,000 in PPE minus $2,000 in liabilities. The purchase of the financial asset was the means by which this bundle was acquired. The net value of this bundle is $3,000, so the net assets don't change. But the financial statement reader gets more information about what was acquired.

Penman Company's statement of cash flows would show an investing cash outflow for the acquisition of Nissim Company. However, the outflow is shown net of the cash received in the acquisition, which was $1,000. Therefore, the investing section would have a line item showing something like "Cash paid for acquisitions, net of cash acquired" with an outflow of $2,000.

In addition, the changes in Penman's operating assets and liabilities on this year's balance sheet from last year's balance sheet will no longer match the adjustments for operating assets and liabilities on the indirect method statement of cash flows from operations. For instance, the change in Penman's receivables will be changes due to its own operations (including Nissim after the acquisition) plus any receivables acquired in the Nissim acquisition.

The illustration above assumes that the purchase price of the acquisition equals book value and the fair values of the acquired company's assets and liabilities are equal to their book values. What changes, if any, occur when the purchase price and book value are different? To explore this case, consider an acquisition where purchase price exceeds book value (the typical scenario). This situation might arise, for example, if an investor company believes it is acquiring something of value that is not reported on the investee's balance sheet—such as tangible assets whose fair values have risen above book value, or unrecorded intangible assets like patents or corporate synergies. When an acquisition occurs, all assets and liabilities acquired (both tangible and intangible) must be recognized at their fair value on the consolidated balance sheet.

To illustrate an acquisition where purchase price exceeds book value, assume that Penman Company acquires 100% of Nissim Company for $4,000 instead of the $3,000 purchase price we used in the previous illustration. Also assume that in determining its purchase price, Penman feels that the additional $1,000 ($4,000 vs. $3,000) is justified because (1) Nissim's PPE is worth $300 more than its book value, and (2) Penman expects to realize $700 in additional value from corporate synergies.

The $4,000 investment account reflects two components: the book value acquired of $3,000 (as before) and an additional $1,000 of newly acquired assets. The post-acquisition balance sheets of the two companies, together with the consolidating adjustments and the consolidated balance sheet, are shown in **Exhibit 12.6**.

EXHIBIT 12.6 Mechanics of Acquisition Accounting (Purchased above Book Value)

	Penman Company	Nissim Company	Consolidating Adjustments	Consolidated
Current assets	$ 4,000	$1,000		$ 5,000
Investment in Nissim	4,000	0	$(4,000)	0
PPE, net	10,000	4,000	300	14,300
Goodwill			700	700
Total assets	$18,000	$5,000		$20,000
Liabilities	$ 5,000	$2,000		$ 7,000
Contributed capital	10,000	2,000	(2,000)	10,000
Retained earnings	3,000	1,000	(1,000)	3,000
Total liabilities and equity	$18,000	$5,000		$20,000

The consolidated balances for current assets, PPE, and liabilities are the sum of those accounts on each company's balance sheet. The investment account, however, includes newly acquired assets that must be reported on the consolidated balance sheet. The consolidation process in this case has two steps. First, the $3,000 equity of Nissim Company is eliminated against the investment account as before. Then, the remaining $1,000 of the investment account is eliminated through the adjustments for revised asset and liability balances on the consolidated balance sheet ($300 of PPE and $700 of goodwill not reported on Nissim's balance sheet). Thus, the consolidated balance sheet reflects the book value of Penman and the *fair value* (book value plus the excess of Nissim's fair value over book value) for Nissim Company at the acquisition date.

Reporting of Acquired Assets and Liabilities

Acquisitions are often made at a purchase price in excess of the book value of the acquired company's equity. The excess purchase price must be allocated to all of the assets and liabilities acquired, including those that do not currently appear on the balance sheet of the acquired company. This allocation can be done in three steps:

Step 1: Adjust the book value of all tangible assets acquired and all liabilities assumed to fair value. This adjustment addresses the issue of misvalued assets and liabilities on the acquired firm's balance sheet.

Step 2: Assign a fair value to any identifiable intangible assets. Recall from Chapter 8 that intangible assets are only reported on the balance sheet if they are purchased; internally created intangible assets (other than software) are not capitalized. This step requires the acquiring firm to assign a value to the acquired company's intangible assets, even if those assets are not reported on the acquired firm's balance sheet.

Step 3: Assign the residual amount to goodwill. Goodwill is the excess of the acquisition price over the fair value of identifiable net assets acquired. That is, whatever value cannot be assigned to identifiable tangible and intangible assets is considered goodwill.[1]

The acquiring company is required to disclose relevant information about the allocation of the purchase price in its disclosure notes.

For example, consider Alphabet's reported allocation of its total $2.4 billion purchase price in December 2019 for Looker, a unified platform for business intelligence as reported in Note 8 to its 2019 10-K report:

[1] What happens if goodwill is negative? Such a "bargain purchase" is uncommon, because it implies that the "whole" of the acquired company is worth less than the sum of its parts. Therefore, when an acquirer believes that it has made a bargain purchase, it must carefully check its valuation of all the components of the goodwill calculation. If that review confirms that the acquirer has made a bargain purchase, then it recognizes a gain in its income from continuing operations.

Note 8. Acquisitions
2019 Acquisitions
Looker
In December 2019, we obtained all regulatory clearances necessary to close the acquisition of Looker, a unified platform for business intelligence, data applications, and embedded analytics for $2.4 billion, with integration pending approval from a UK regulatory review. The addition of Looker to Google Cloud is expected to help customers accelerate how they analyze data, deliver business intelligence, and build data-driven applications.

The fair value of assets acquired and liabilities assumed was recorded based on a preliminary valuation and our estimates and assumptions are subject to change within the measurement period. The $2.4 billion purchase price includes our previously held equity interest and excludes post acquisition compensation arrangements. In aggregate, $91 million was cash acquired, $290 million was attributed to intangible assets, $1.9 billion to goodwill, and $48 million to net assets acquired. Goodwill was recorded in the Google segment and primarily attributable to synergies expected to arise after the acquisition. Goodwill is not expected to be deductible for tax purposes.

Other Acquisitions
During the year ended December 31, 2019, we completed other acquisitions and purchases of intangible assets for total consideration of approximately $1.0 billion. In aggregate, $28 million was cash acquired, $282 million was attributed to intangible assets, $901 million to goodwill, and $185 million to net liabilities assumed. These acquisitions generally enhance the breadth and depth of our offerings and expand our expertise in engineering and other functional areas.

Pro forma results of operations for these acquisitions, including Looker, have not been presented because they are not material to the consolidated results of operations, either individually or in the aggregate.

For all intangible assets acquired and purchased during the year ended December 31, 2019, patents and developed technology have a weighted-average useful life of 3.5 years, customer relationships have a weighted average useful life of 6.3 years, and trade names and other have a weighted-average useful life of 4.5 years.

Pending Acquisition of Fitbit
In November 2019, we entered into an agreement to acquire Fitbit, a leading wearables brand, for $7.35 per share, representing a total purchase price of approximately $2.1 billion as of the date of the agreement. The acquisition of Fitbit is expected to be completed in 2020, subject to customary closing conditions, including the receipt of regulatory approvals. Upon the close of the acquisition, Fitbit will be part of Google segment.

Of the approximate $3.4 billion paid for acquisitions during 2019, Alphabet assigned $2.8 billion to goodwill. The remaining $600 million includes $119 million in cash plus $572 million in intangible assets, less $137 million in net liabilities. The $572 million in intangible assets and the $137 million in net liabilities were recorded at fair value at the time of the acquisition.

Alphabet reports its aggregated goodwill separately on its balance sheet but combines its other intangible assets in its balance sheet under the title "Intangible assets, net." Goodwill can only be recognized as an asset in an acquisition and only then in the amount by which the purchase price exceeds the fair value of the identifiable net assets acquired, including all identifiable intangible assets.

For the acquisitions it made in 2019, Alphabet, Inc., estimates customer relationships have a weighted average useful life of 6.3 years. Patents and developed technology have a weighted average useful life of 3.5 years. Tradenames and other intangibles have a weighted average useful life of 4.5 years. These estimated lives determine the annual amortization expense associated with these assets on the firm's financial books. For publicly traded companies, goodwill is not currently amortized under GAAP, but is instead subject to impairment testing and impairment write-downs when appropriate. FASB has been re-evaluating the proper accounting for goodwill. In 2014, the board decided to allow amortization of goodwill for private companies in an effort towards simplicity. In December, 2020 FASB tentatively decided to move to a 10-year amortization period for goodwill for public companies, with impairment testing also required. This 2020 decision is not a rule, but still being worked on and considered by FASB. Below we discuss the current impairment rules. Impairment testing will still be required even if FASB moves to an amortization rule for public company goodwill.[2]

Reporting of Goodwill GAAP requires companies to test goodwill annually for impairment just like any other asset. To begin, the investor company can judge qualitatively—based on economic events and conditions—whether it is more likely than not that the fair value of the subsidiary is less than its book value. If that is not the case (i.e., if fair value exceeds book value), then no further testing is needed.

If it is more likely than not that the subsidiary's fair value is less than its book value (or the investor bypassed the optional qualitative test), then the fair value of that subsidiary is determined and compared with the book value of the parent company's investment account.[3] If the fair value is greater than the investment balance, the investment's goodwill is deemed not to be impaired. If the subsidiary's book value exceeds its fair value, then its goodwill must be written down by the amount of the difference, resulting in an impairment loss that is reported in the consolidated income statement. The impairment loss recognized may not exceed the carrying value of goodwill.

To illustrate the impairment computation, assume that a subsidiary's current book value is reported at $1 million on the parent company's balance sheet, but the subsidiary is found to have a current fair value of $900,000. Under these conditions, goodwill is impaired by $100,000, which is computed as follows.

Fair value of subsidiary	$ 900,000
Minus book value of net assets	(1,000,000)
Impairment loss	$ (100,000)

The financial statement effects and related journal entry and T-accounts are:

ANALYZE

	Balance Sheet					Income Statement		
Transaction	Cash Asset +	Noncash Assets =	Liabil-ities +	Contrib. Capital +	Earned Capital	Revenues −	Expenses =	Net Income
(1) Impairment adjustment to Goodwill.		−100,000 Goodwill			−100,000 Retained Earnings		+100,000 Goodwill Impairment Expense	−100,000

JOURNALIZE

(1) Goodwill impairment expense (+E, −SE)	100,000	
Goodwill (−A)		100,000

POST

+ Goodwill Impairment Expense (E) −	
(1) 100,000	

+ Goodwill (A) −	
	100,000 (1)

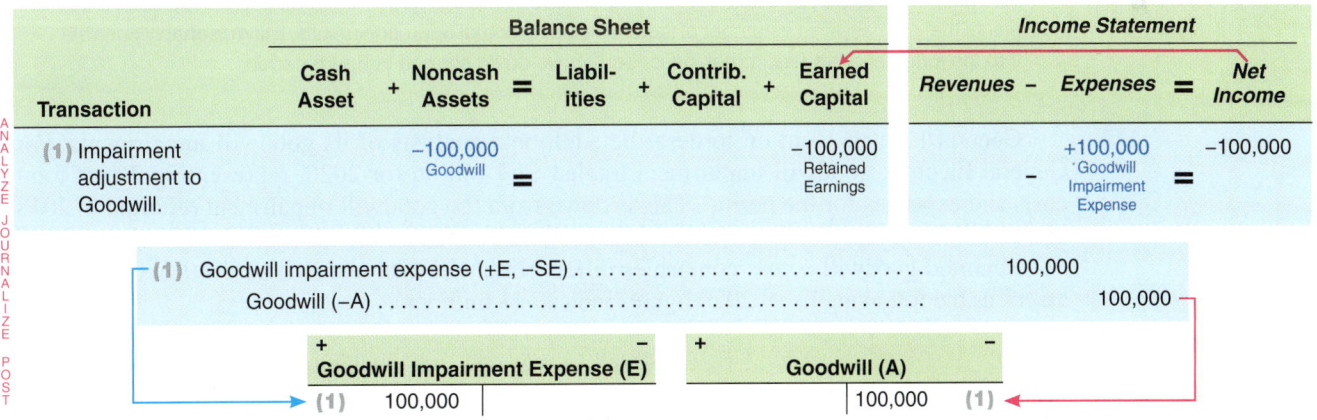

This analysis of investee company implies that goodwill must be written down by $100,000. The impairment loss is reported as a separate line item in the consolidated income statement. The related note disclosure describes the reasons for the write-down.

General Electric reports the following goodwill impairment in excerpts from its 10-K report for 2020:

[2] Whether to amortize goodwill or not is an old debate. Prior to the issuance of Financial Accounting Statement number 141, goodwill was amortized over 40 years.

[3] The fair value of the subsidiary company can be determined using market comparables or another valuation method (such as the discounted cash flow model, residual operating income model, or P/E multiples).

NOTE 8. GOODWILL AND OTHER INTANGIBLE ASSETS
GOODWILL
CHANGES IN GOODWILL BALANCES

(In millions)	Balance at December 31, 2019	Acquisitions	Impairments	Currency Exchange and Other	Balance at December 31, 2020
Power	$ 145	$—	$ —	$ —	$ 146
Renewable Energy	3,290	—	—	111	3,401
Aviation	9,859	—	(877)	266	9,247
Healthcare	11,728	89	—	37	11,855
Capital	839	—	(839)	—	—
Corporate[(a)]	873	—	—	2	876
Total*	$26,734	$90	$(1,717)	$417	$25,524

* Difference due to rounding.
[(a)] Corporate balance at December 31, 2020 and 2019 is our Digital business.

In the fourth quarter of 2020, we performed our annual impairment test. Based on the results of this test, the fair values of each of our reporting units exceeded their carrying values.

We continue to monitor the operating results and cash flow forecasts of our Additive reporting unit in our Aviation segment as the fair value of this reporting unit was not significantly in excess of its carrying value. At December 31, 2020, our Additive reporting unit had goodwill of $243 million.

In the second quarter of 2020 we performed an interim impairment test at our Additive reporting unit within our Aviation segment and GECAS reporting unit within our Capital segment, both of which incorporated a combination of income and market valuation approaches. The results of the analysis indicated that carrying values of both reporting units were in excess of their respective fair values. Therefore, we recorded non-cash impairment losses of $877 million and $839 million for the Additive and GECAS reporting units, respectively, in the caption Goodwill impairments in our consolidated Statement of Earnings (Loss). All of the goodwill in Additive was the result of the Arcam AB and Concept Laser GmBH acquisitions in 2016. Of the $839 million of goodwill for GECAS, $729 million arose from the acquisition of Milestone Aviation, our helicopter leasing business, in 2015. After the impairment charges, there was no goodwill remaining in our GECAS reporting unit. . . .

Determining the fair value of reporting units requires the use of estimates and significant judgments that are based on a number of factors including actual operating results. It is reasonably possible that the judgments and estimates described above could change in future periods.

General Electric went on to describe additional analysis of its goodwill impairments. For General Electric, goodwill impairment totaled $1.7 billion for 2020, representing 2% of total costs and expenses for the period. This is down from the goodwill impairment reported in 2018 of $22.1 billion, representing 18% of total costs and expenses for the period.

Reported goodwill across companies differs widely in total and as a percentage of company assets, as the following fiscal 2020 figures indicate ($ millions).

	Total Reported Assets	Reported Goodwill	Goodwill Percentage
Alphabet, Inc.	$275,909	$20,624	7.5%
Facebook, Inc.	159,316	19,050	12.0%
United Airlines, Inc.	52,605	4,523	8.6%
Adobe Inc.	24,284	10,742	44.2%
PepsiCo, Inc.	92,918	18,757	20.2%
The Coca-Cola Company	87,296	17,506	20.1%
The Procter & Gamble Company	120,700	39,901	33.1%
Colgate-Palmolive Company	15,920	3,824	24.0%
Bausch Health Companies Inc.	31,199	13,044	41.8%
Bristol-Myers Squibb Co.	118,481	20,547	17.3%

Reported goodwill is an indicator of whether a company has developed its business opportunities or purchased them and, in the same fashion, reported intangible assets are an indicator of whether a company has acquired its intellectual property in-house or by purchasing it. The purchase of intellectual properties and business opportunities allows a company to react quickly to conditions, but it is often a more expensive way to achieve growth.

BUSINESS INSIGHT

In competitive bidding situations, the winning bidder is likely to be the one who most overvalued the item, a phenomenon known as the "winner's curse." Therefore, acquisition goodwill is viewed with some skepticism by financial analysts. Does the goodwill represent synergies like future cost savings or business opportunities that are available only to the combined companies? Or, does it represent an overpayment?

A *Financial Times* article described multi-billion dollar goodwill impairment charges by General Electric and ascribes a significant portion of these charges to a 2015 acquisition of Alstom in which the $10.1 billion purchase price resulted in $17.3 billion in goodwill. The article said that "the company was so keen to get the deal done that it paid too much."

When companies record a goodwill impairment charge, they often emphasize that the impairment was a "non-cash charge," implying that it is therefore less important. That statement is true as far as the current period is concerned, but acquisitions involve cash or some other item of value. Goodwill impairment requires no current cash outflows, but it does reflect on the wisdom of past cash outflows.

Source: Ed Crooks, "GE's $23 Billion Writedown Is a Case of Goodwill Gone Bad," *Financial Times*, October 3, 2018.

Noncontrolling Interest

Noncontrolling interest represents the equity of shareholders who own a minority of the shares of one or more of the subsidiaries in a consolidated entity. When a company acquires a controlling interest in another company, it must consolidate that subsidiary when preparing its financial statements by reporting all of the subsidiary's assets and liabilities in the consolidated balance sheet and all of the subsidiary's revenues and expenses in the consolidated income statement. This is true even when the controlling parent company acquires less than 100% of the subsidiary. When less than 100% of the subsidiary's shares are acquired, there are two groups of shareholders: the parent company's shareholders and the noncontrolling shareholders who own a minority of the subsidiary's shares. These noncontrolling shareholders have a claim on the net assets and the earnings of the subsidiary company, and this claim is considered part of the consolidated company's shareholders' equity.

To illustrate the reporting of noncontrolling interest, assume that Penman Company acquires 80% of Nissim Company for $2,400 (80% of $3,000). Because Penman must consolidate 100% of the assets and liabilities of Nissim, Penman's equity must increase to maintain the accounting equation. A new equity account titled noncontrolling interests is added to Penman's stockholders' equity. The consolidation worksheet is presented in **Exhibit 12.7**.

EXHIBIT 12.7 Mechanics of Consolidation Accounting (Less than 100% of Subsidiary Shares Purchased with Fair Values = Book Values)

	Penman Company	Nissim Company	Consolidating Adjustments	Consolidated
Current assets	$ 5,600	$1,000		$ 6,600
Investment in Nissim	2,400	0	$(2,400)	0
PPE, net	10,000	4,000		14,000
Total assets	$18,000	$5,000		$20,600
Liabilities	$ 5,000	$2,000		$ 7,000
Contributed capital	10,000	2,000	$(2,000)	10,000
Retained earnings	3,000	1,000	(1,000)	3,000
Penman shareholders' equity	13,000			13,000
Noncontrolling interests			600	600
Total equity	13,000			13,600
Total liabilities and equity	$18,000	$5,000		$20,600

The contributed capital of the consolidated entity (common stock, additional paid-in capital, treasury stock, etc.) refers to the parent company's shareholders' equity (in this example, Penman Company). The net assets owned by the noncontrolling shareholders are represented in one account, labeled noncontrolling interests, which is considered to be part of shareholders' equity of the consolidated company. Each period, the noncontrolling interests equity account is increased by the noncontrolling shareholders' share of the subsidiary's net income and decreased by any dividends paid to those shareholders.

The consolidated income statement lists total consolidated revenues and expenses and consolidated net income. After net income is computed, the portion of net income that is attributed to noncontrolling interests is subtracted. If the noncontrolling shareholders own 20% of the subsidiary's shares, then 20% of the earnings of the subsidiary are subtracted from the consolidated entity's income statement. (This is not 20% of the consolidated company's earnings, only 20% of the subsidiary's earnings.)

The stockholders' equity section of The Walt Disney Company's 2020 balance sheet is shown as an illustration of the presentation of noncontrolling interests in the balance sheet:

The Walt Disney Company Consolidated Balance Sheet (Stockholders' equity section only) ($ millions)	**October 3, 2020**
Equity	
Preferred stock	$ —
Common stock, $0.01 par value, authorized—4.6 billion shares, issued—1.8 billion shares	54,497
Retained earnings	38,315
Accumulated other comprehensive loss	(8,322)
Treasury stock, at cost, 19 million shares	(907)
Total Disney shareholders' equity	83,583
Noncontrolling interests	4,680
Total equity	$88,263

Total Disney Company's shareholders' equity is listed at $83,583 million. This is the equity claim of those investors who own shares in Disney. Next, the $4,680 million of noncontrolling interests is listed. This amount represents the share of The Walt Disney Company subsidiaries' net assets that is owned by noncontrolling shareholders (e.g., Hong Kong Disneyland Resort and Shanghai Disney Resort). The final line lists the total equity, which is the sum of Disney's stockholders' equity and the noncontrolling interests.

The Walt Disney Company's income statement presents noncontrolling interests as follows:

The Walt Disney Company Consolidated Income Statement (excerpts) ($ millions)	**Year Ended October 3, 2020**
Net income (loss)	$(2,474)
Net income from continuing operations attributable to noncontrolling and redeemable noncontrolling interests	(390)
Net income from discontinued operations attributable to noncontrolling interests	—
Net income (loss) attributable to The Walt Disney Company (Disney)	$(2,864)

The Walt Disney Company presents a net loss of $(2,864) million. This is the loss for the consolidated entity, including the share of income for Disney's shareholders as well as that portion that is for the noncontrolling interests. Next, the income attributable to noncontrolling and redeemable noncontrolling interests ($390 million) is subtracted, leaving net loss attributable to Disney's shareholders ($2,864 million).

IFRS

A GLOBAL PERSPECTIVE

U.S. GAAP and IFRS are very similar in their treatment of the accounting for investments as covered in this chapter. Unlike GAAP, however, IFRS still allows equity investments to be accounted for under available-for-sale. Under this option for equity investments in IFRS, another difference is that the unrealized holding gains and losses remain in AOCI and are never recognized in income.

GAAP uses the term "equity" or "affiliate" to describe an investment involving significant influence (usually between 20% and 50%). IFRS uses the term "associate" to describe such an investment, with the same 20% threshold.

The process of accounting for an acquisition and issuing subsequent consolidated financial statements is very similar to that described in the previous section.

Limitations of Consolidation Reporting Consolidation of financial statements is meant to present a financial picture of the entire set of companies under control of the parent. Because investors typically purchase stock in the parent company and not in the subsidiaries, the view is more relevant than would be one of the parent company's own balance sheet with subsidiaries reported as equity investments. Still, we must be aware of certain limitations that the consolidation process entails:

1. Consolidated income does not imply that cash is received by the parent company and is available for subsidiaries. The parent can only receive cash via dividend payments, and dividend payments may trigger tax obligations. It is readily possible, therefore, for an individual subsidiary to experience cash flow problems even though the consolidated group has strong cash flows. Likewise, debts of a subsidiary are not obligations of the consolidated group. Thus, even if the consolidated balance sheet is strong, creditors of a failing subsidiary are often unable to sue the parent or other subsidiaries to recoup losses.
2. Consolidated balance sheets and income statements are a mix of the subsidiaries, often from different industries. Comparisons across companies, even if in similar industries, are often complicated by the different mix of subsidiary companies. Companies are required to report some financial results for their business segments. For instance, General Electric reports revenues, operating profits, and assets for each of its five operating segments—Power, Renewable Energy, Aviation, Healthcare, and Capital.
3. Segment disclosures on individual subsidiaries are affected by intercorporate transfer-pricing policies that can artificially inflate the profitability of one segment at the expense of another. Companies also have considerable discretion in the allocation of corporate overhead to subsidiaries, which can markedly affect segment and subsidiary profitability.

FINANCIAL STATEMENT ANALYSIS

This section introduces no new ratios, but the topics covered in Chapter 12 do have implications for ratios covered in other chapters. For instance, gains and losses on available-for-sale securities are not recognized in income until those securities are sold. Therefore, management can increase net income by selling securities on which it has gains or decrease net income by selling securities on which it has losses. As a result, management may have a means to smooth the variations in income over time, using gains and losses from previous periods that have nothing to do with current performance. As careful financial statement users, we can read the disclosure notes to find the realized gains and losses included in income for the period.

Financial ratio comparisons are also affected by the percentage ownership of affiliated companies. For instance, suppose Naughton Group has 50% ownership in the company that distributes its products. Chapman Enterprises, a competitor of Naughton, owns 55% of the shares of the company that distributes its products. While the difference between 50% and 55% ownership probably has little economic significance, the accounting reports for Naughton and Chapman will look very different. Naughton's income statement will report only its own revenues and expenses, while Chapman's income statement will report its own revenues and expenses *and* the revenues and expenses of the distribution company (less any intercompany adjustments). Naughton's balance sheet will report its own assets, including its 50% equity in the distributor, while Chapman's balance sheet will report its own assets and liabilities *plus* those of the distribution company. Financial statement readers should interpret comparisons of ratios like PPE Turnover in light of these effects.

A similar "quantum" change in accounting occurs at 20% ownership. There may appear to be little economic difference between owning 19% of a company's shares and owning 20% of those shares. But there is a significant difference in the accounting for those two alternatives, and this difference sometimes affects the choice between a 19% investment and a 20% investment. If the investee is a start-up earning losses, a 20% investment would require the investor to recognize 20% of those losses in its own income. A 19% investment would not recognize any share of the losses, though the fair value fluctuations of the investment will be recognized in income as they occur.

Finally, acquisitions disrupt the usual relationships between income statements and between the income statement and balance sheet items. When one company acquires another, the acquirer consolidates the acquired company as of the date that the deal closes. At that point, it includes the acquired company's assets and liabilities on the consolidated balance sheet, and it begins to report the acquired company's revenues and expenses from that time forward. So, if Hoskin Corp. acquires 100% of Lynch, Inc., on December 31, 2022, how will the inventory turnover ratio be affected? The 2022 cost of goods sold for Hoskin will reflect a year of Hoskin's COGS plus one day of Lynch's COGS. The beginning-of-year inventory will be 100% of Hoskin's inventory at that time, but the end-of-year inventory will be 100% of Hoskin's inventory plus 100% of Lynch's inventory. The inventory turnover ratio is likely to decrease significantly, but that decrease is due to the acquisition, not necessarily a decline in Hoskin's operating performance.

The acquisition's effect on reported sales growth should be carefully examined as well. Suppose that Hoskin Corp and Lynch, Inc., both have a December 31 fiscal year and that Hoskin acquired Lynch on June 30, 2021—halfway through the fiscal year for both companies. When looking at Hoskin's reported revenue and its growth, one should recognize that the 2020 revenues will be Hoskin's alone, and the 2021 revenues will reflect Hoskin's sales plus half a year of Lynch's sales. Finally, the 2022 revenues will reflect a full year of sales for the combined firms. A careful reader of the financial statements should use the disclosure notes to try to separate out the effects of the acquisition from the ongoing, organic performance of the combined company.

Review 12-5 LO12-5

Accounting for a Consolidation

GuidedExample

On January 1 of the current year, Bradshaw Company purchased all of the common shares of Dukes Company for $600,000 cash—this is $200,000 in excess of Dukes' book value of its equity. The balance sheets of the two firms immediately after the acquisition follow:

	Bradshaw (Parent)	Dukes (Subsidiary)	Consolidating Adjustments	Consolidated
Current assets	$1,000,000	$100,000		
Investment in Dukes	600,000	—		
PPE, net	3,000,000	400,000		
Goodwill	—	—		
Total assets	$4,600,000	$500,000		
Liabilities	$1,000,000	$100,000		
Contributed capital	2,000,000	200,000		
Retained earnings	1,600,000	200,000		
Total liabilities and equity	$4,600,000	$500,000		

During purchase negotiations, Dukes' PPE was appraised at $500,000, and all of Dukes' remaining assets and liabilities were appraised at values approximating their book values. Also, Bradshaw concluded that payment of an additional $100,000 was warranted because of anticipated corporate synergies.

Required

a. Show the impact of the consolidating adjusting entry in the financial statement effects template.
b. Prepare the appropriate consolidating adjusting journal entry and post the journal entry to the related T-accounts.
c. Prepare the consolidated balance sheet at acquisition.

Solution on p. 12-60.

APPENDIX 12A: Equity Method Mechanics

LO12-6 Illustrate and analyze accounting mechanics for equity method investments.

eLecture MBC

The appendix provides a comprehensive example of accounting for an equity method investment. Assume that Petroni Company acquires a 30% interest in the outstanding voting shares of Wahlen Company on January 1, 2019, for $234,000 in cash. On that date, Wahlen's book value of equity is $560,000. Petroni agrees to pay $234,000 for a company with a book value of equity equivalent to $168,000 ($560,000 × 30%) because it feels that (1) Wahlen's balance sheet is undervalued by $140,000 (Petroni estimates PPE is undervalued by $50,000 and that Wahlen has unrecorded patents valued at $90,000) and (2) the investment is expected to yield intangible benefits valued at $24,000. (The $140,000 by which the balance sheet is undervalued translates into an investment equivalent of $42,000 [$140,000 × 30%]. This, plus the intangible benefits valued at $24,000, comprises the $66,000 difference between the purchase price [$234,000] and the book value equivalent [$168,000].)

The effect of the investment on Petroni's books is to reduce cash by $234,000 and to report the investment in Wahlen for $234,000. The investment is reported at its fair value at acquisition, just like all other asset acquisitions, and it is reported as a noncurrent asset because the expected holding period of equity method investments is in excess of one year. Subsequent to this purchase there are three main aspects of equity method accounting:

1. Dividends received from the investee are treated as a return *of* the investment rather than a return *on* the investment (investor company records an increase in cash received and a decrease in the investment account).
2. When the investee company reports net income for a period, the investor company reports its proportionate ownership of that income. This amount is usually reported in the investment income section of its income statement. Thus, both income and the investment account increase from equity method income. If the investee company reports a net *loss* for the period, income of the investor company is reduced as well as its investment account by its proportionate share.
3. The investment balance is not marked-to-fair value (market) as with passive investments. Instead, it is recorded at its historical cost and is increased (decreased) by the investor company's proportionate share of investee income (loss) and decreased by any cash dividends received. Unrecognized gains (losses) can, therefore, occur if the fair value of the investment differs from this adjusted cost. (If a decline in value is deemed "other than temporary," then the investment would be written down.)

To illustrate these mechanics, let's return to our illustration and assume that subsequent to acquisition, Wahlen reports net income of $50,000 and pays $10,000 cash dividends. Petroni would reflect these events in the FSET as follows:

Transaction	Balance Sheet: Cash Asset	+ Noncash Assets	= Liabilities	+ Contrib. Capital	+ Earned Capital	Income Statement: Revenues	− Expenses	= Net Income
(1) Purchase 30% of Wahlen Co. stock.	−234,000 Cash	+234,000 Investment in Wahlen	=				−	=
(2) Recognize 30% of Wahlen net income.		+15,000 Investment in Wahlen	=		+15,000 Retained Earnings	+15,000 Investment Income	−	= +15,000
(3) Receive 30% of Wahlen dividends.	+3,000 Cash	−3,000 Investment in Wahlen	=				−	=

After these entries, the investment balance is $246,000. Petroni has an investing cash outflow of $234,000 and an operating cash inflow of $3,000. Retained earnings increase by $15,000 from recognizing the 30% share of Wahlen's net income.

However, Petroni must also account for the differential values that accounted for the purchase premium. If Wahlen's PPE is undervalued by $50,000 and has an expected remaining life of twenty years, Petroni must depreciate $750 (= 30%*$50,000/20 years) in value for each of the next twenty years. And, if the unrecorded patents have an expected useful life of nine years, Petroni must amortize $3,000 (= 30%*$90,000/9 years) of the investment's value for each of the coming nine years. These amortizations are deducted from the investment income recognized by Petroni. The entries are the following:

Transaction	Balance Sheet: Cash Asset	+ Noncash Assets	= Liabilities	+ Contrib. Capital	+ Earned Capital	Income Statement: Revenues	− Expenses	= Net Income
(4) Depreciate additional PPE value.		−750 Investment in Wahlen	=		−750 Retained Earnings	−750 Investment Income	−	= −750
(5) Amortize additional patent assets.		−3,000 Investment in Wahlen	=		−3,000 Retained Earnings	−3,000 Investment Income	−	= −3,000

A part of the premium paid by Petroni is attributed to items that have definite lives (PPE and patents), and we must account for those amounts in judging the investment's performance. In this case, Petroni records income of $11,250 on its $234,000 investment – $15,000 for its share of Wahlen's income, minus the $3,750 amortization of the premium paid for PPE and patents. The Investment in Wahlen asset has a value of $242,250 ($234,000 + 15,000 – 3,000 – 750 – 3,000) after all entries.

The amount attributed to goodwill is tested for impairment annually, but it is not subject to periodic amortization (under current GAAP, though this may change in the future).

Review 12-6 LO12-6

Accounting for Equity Investments

GuidedExample

Harper purchased 35% of the outstanding shares of Maxwell Company on January 1 of the current year for $80,000 in cash. Maxwell's plant assets with a book value of $164,000 were appraised at $170,000, and Maxwell has an unrecorded patent with a fair value of $5,000. All of the remaining assets and liabilities were appraised at values approximating their book values. Assume that the undervalued plant assets have an estimated remaining useful life of 20 years, and the unrecorded patent has a useful life of 5 years. During the year, Maxwell reported net income of $65,000 and paid cash dividends to shareholders totaling $35,000.

Required

a. Prepare the entry to record Harper Company's equity in the earnings of Maxwell Company, including any amortization of the excess of fair value over book value of assets acquired in the financial statement effects template.

b. Prepare the journal entry to record Harper Company's equity in the earnings of Maxwell Company, including any amortization of the excess of fair value over book value of assets acquired.

Solution on p. 12-61.

APPENDIX 12B: Consolidation Accounting Mechanics

LO12-7
Apply consolidation accounting mechanics.

eLecture
MBC

This appendix is a continuation of the example we introduced in Appendix 12A, extended to the consolidation of a parent company and one wholly owned subsidiary. Assume that Petroni Company acquires 100% (rather than 30% as in Appendix 12A) of the outstanding voting shares of Wahlen Company on January 1, 2022. To obtain these shares, Petroni pays $420,000 cash and issues 20,000 shares of its $10 par value common stock. On this date, Petroni's stock has a fair value of $18 per share, and Wahlen's book value of equity is $560,000. Petroni is willing to pay $780,000 ($420,000 plus 20,000 shares at $18 per share) for this company with a book value of equity of $560,000 because it believes Wahlen's balance sheet is understated by $140,000. (Its PPE is undervalued by $50,000, and it has unrecorded patents valued at $90,000.) The remaining $80,000 of the purchase price excess over book value is ascribed to corporate synergies and other unidentifiable intangible assets (goodwill). Thus, the purchase price consists of the following three components:

Investment ($780,000)	Book value of Wahlen ($560,000) Excess fair value over book ($140,000) Goodwill ($80,000)

The investment in Wahlen appears as a financial asset on Petroni's books. This means that at acquisition, Petroni's assets increase by $360,000 (cash decreases by $420,000, and the investments account increases by $780,000), and its equity (contributed capital) increases by the same amount.

The balance sheets of Petroni and Wahlen at acquisition follow, including the adjustments that occur in the consolidation process and the ultimate consolidated balance sheet.

Accounts	Petroni Company	Wahlen Company	Consolidation Adjustments* Entry S	Consolidation Adjustments* Entry A	Consolidated Balance Sheet
Cash	$ 168,000	$ 80,000			$ 248,000
Receivables, net	320,000	180,000			500,000
Inventory	440,000	260,000			700,000
Investment in Wahlen	780,000	0	$(560,000)	$(220,000)	0
Land	200,000	120,000			320,000
PPE, net	1,040,000	320,000		50,000	1,410,000
Patents	0	0		90,000	90,000
Goodwill	0	0		80,000	80,000
Totals	$2,948,000	$960,000			$3,348,000
Accounts payable	$ 320,000	$ 60,000			$ 380,000
Long-term liabilities	760,000	340,000			1,100,000
Contributed capital	1,148,000	80,000	$ (80,000)		1,148,000
Retained earnings	720,000	480,000	(480,000)		720,000
Totals	$2,948,000	$960,000			$3,348,000

*Entry S refers to elimination of subsidiary stockholders' equity, and Entry A refers to adjustment of assets and liabilities acquired.

The initial balance of the investment account at acquisition ($780,000) reflects the $700,000 fair value of Wahlen's net tangible assets and patents ($560,000 book value + $140,000 undervaluation of assets) plus the goodwill ($80,000) acquired. Goodwill is the excess of the purchase price over the fair value of the net assets acquired. It does not appear on Petroni's balance sheet as an explicit asset at this point. It is, however, included in the investment balance and will emerge as a separate asset during consolidation.

The process of completing the initial consolidated balance sheet involves eliminating Petroni's investment account and replacing it with the assets and liabilities of Wahlen Company to which it relates. Recall the investment account consists of three items: the book value of Wahlen ($560,000), the excess of net asset fair value over book value ($140,000), and goodwill ($80,000). The consolidation process eliminates each item as follows:

Entry S: Elimination of Wahlen's book value of equity: Investment account is reduced by the $560,000 book value of Wahlen, and each of the components of Wahlen's equity ($80,000 common stock and $480,000 retained earnings) is eliminated.

Entry A: Elimination of the excess of purchase price over book value: Investment account is reduced by $220,000 to zero. The remaining adjustments increase assets (A) by the additional purchase price paid. PPE is written up by $50,000, and a $90,000 patent asset and an $80,000 goodwill asset are reported.

Stepping back from the consolidation process, we can see its effects by comparing the Petroni Company (parent) balance sheet to the consolidated balance sheet. The Petroni Company balance sheet shows a financial asset valued at $780,000. Consolidation gives us a different perspective. Rather than viewing this as a financial investment, consolidation views the financial investment as the *means* by which Petroni Company acquired a bundle of assets and liabilities. That is, the financial asset of $780,000 has been replaced by Cash ($80,000), Receivables ($180,000), Inventory ($260,000), Land ($120,000), PPE – net ($370,000), Patent ($90,000), Goodwill ($80,000), Payables ($60,000) and Long-term liabilities ($340,000). This bundle has a net value equal to the $780,000, but it provides much more detail about the transaction in which Petroni engaged.

The one part of the balance sheet that is not changed by the consolidation is the shareholders' equity section. The consolidated shareholders' equity accounts are the same as the parent company shareholders' equity accounts when the parent owns 100% of the subsidiary.

Consolidation is similar in successive periods. To the extent that the excess purchase price has been assigned to depreciable assets, or identifiable intangible assets that are amortized over their useful lives, the new assets recognized initially are depreciated. If the PPE value adjustment has an estimated life of 20 years, then the consolidated income statement would include depreciation of 1/20 of this $50,000 each year. Amortization of the $90,000 patent would also appear in the consolidated income statement. Finally, because goodwill is not amortized under GAAP, it remains at its carrying amount of $80,000 on the consolidated balance sheet unless and until it is impaired and written down.

Recording a Consolidating Adjustment — LO12-7 Review 12-7

On January 1 of the current year, Harper Company purchased all of the common shares of Maxwell Company for $200,000 cash. Balance sheets of the two firms at the acquisition date follow.

	Harper Company	Maxwell Company	Consolidating Adjustments	Consolidated
Current assets	$ 680,000	$ 48,000		
Investment in Maxwell	200,000	—		
Plant assets, net	1,200,000	164,000		
Goodwill	—	—		
Total assets	$2,080,000	$212,000		
Liabilities	$ 280,000	$ 36,000		
Contributed capital	1,400,000	160,000		
Retained earnings	400,000	16,000		
Total liabilities and equity	$2,080,000	$212,000		

During purchase negotiations, Maxwell's plant assets were appraised at $170,000, and Maxwell had an unrecorded patent with a fair value of $5,000. All of the remaining assets and liabilities were appraised at values approximating their book values. The remaining $13,000 of the purchase price was ascribed to goodwill.

continued

continued from previous page

Required

a. Prepare the consolidating adjustments and the consolidated balance sheet at acquisition.

b. Prepare the journal entry to record the consolidating adjustments at acquisition.

c. Record the consolidating adjusting entry in the financial statement effects template.

Solution on p. 12-61.

APPENDIX 12C: Accounting for Investments in Derivatives

LO12-8
Discuss the reporting of derivative securities.

eLecture

Derivatives refer to financial instruments that are utilized by companies to reduce various kinds of risks. Some examples follow:

- A company expects to purchase raw materials for its production process and wants to reduce the risk that the purchase price increases prior to the purchase.
- A company has an accounts receivable on its books that is payable in a foreign currency and wants to reduce the risk that exchange rates move unfavorably prior to collection.
- A company borrows funds on a floating rate of interest (such as linked to the prime rate) and wants to convert the loan to a fixed rate of interest.

Companies are commonly exposed to these and many similar types of risk. Although companies are generally willing to assume the normal market risks that are inherent in their business, many of these financial-type risks can add variability to income and are uncontrollable. Fortunately, commodities, currencies, and interest rates are all traded on various markets and, further, securities have been developed to manage all of these risks. These securities fall under the label of derivatives. They include forward contracts, futures contracts, option contracts, and swap agreements.

Companies use derivatives to manage many of these financial risks. The reduction of risk comes at a price: the fee that another party (called the counterparty) is charging to assume that risk. Most counterparties are financial institutions, and managing financial risk is their business and a source of their profits. Although derivatives can be used effectively to manage financial risk, they can also be used for speculation with potentially disastrous results. It is for this reason that regulators passed standards regarding their disclosure in financial statements.

Reporting of Derivatives Derivatives work by offsetting the gain or loss for the asset or liability to which they relate. Derivatives thus shelter the company from such fluctuations. For example, if a hedged receivable denominated in a foreign currency declines in value (due to a strengthening of the $US), the derivative security will increase in value by an offsetting amount, at least in theory. As a result, net equity remains unaffected and no gain or loss arises, nor is a loss reported in income.[4]

Although accounting for derivatives is complex, it essentially boils down to this: The derivative contract and the asset or liability to which it relates are both reported on the balance sheet at fair value. The asset and liability are offsetting *if* the hedge is effective and, thus, net equity is unaffected. Likewise, the related gains and losses are largely offsetting, leaving income unaffected. Income is impacted only to the extent that the hedging activities are ineffective or result from speculative activities. It is this latter activity, in particular, that regulators were concerned about in formulating accounting standards for derivatives.

Disclosure of Derivatives Companies are required to disclose both qualitative and quantitative information about derivatives in notes to their financial statements and elsewhere (usually in Management's Discussion and Analysis section). The aim of these disclosures is to inform outsiders about potential risks underlying derivative securities.

Following is **Southwest Airlines Co.**'s disclosures from Note 1 to its 2020 10-K report relating to its use of derivatives.

Financial Derivative Instruments
The Company accounts for financial derivative instruments at fair value and applies hedge accounting rules where appropriate. The Company utilizes various derivative instruments, including jet fuel, crude oil, unleaded gasoline, and heating oil-based derivatives, to attempt to reduce the risk of its exposure to jet fuel price increases. These instruments are accounted for as cash flow hedges upon proper qualification.

continued

[4] Unrealized gains and losses on cash flow and net investment hedges are accumulated in other comprehensive income (OCI) and are not recognized in current income until the time when the hedged item affects earnings (for example, when the commodity is used). Unrealized gains and losses on derivatives classified as *fair value hedges* (such as those relating to interest rate hedges and swaps, and the hedging of asset values such as relating to securities) are recorded in current income on the same line that includes the hedged item's impact on earnings.

continued from previous page

> The Company also has had interest rate swap agreements to convert certain floating-rate debt to a fixed-rate and had interest rate swap agreements to convert portions of its fixed-rate debt to floating rates. The Company has forward-stating interest rate swap agreements, the primary objective of which is to hedge forecasted debt issuances. These interest rate hedges are appropriately designated as cash flow hedges.
>
> Since the majority of the Company's financial derivative instruments are not traded on a market exchange, the Company estimates their fair values. Depending on the type of instrument, the values are determined by the use of present value methods or option value models with assumptions about commodity prices based on those observed in underlying markets.
>
> All cash flows associated with purchasing and selling derivatives are classified as operating cash flows in the Consolidated Statement of Cash Flows, within Changes in certain assets and liabilities. The Company classifies its cash collateral provided to or held from counterparties in a "net" presentation on the Consolidated Balance Sheet against the fair value of the derivative positions with those counterparties. See Note 11 for further information.

Southwest Airlines' derivative use is mainly to hedge against fuel cost. Those hedges act to place a ceiling on fuel cost. The company reports that 77% of its 2020 fuel consumption was covered by hedging activity.

From a reporting standpoint, unrealized gains and losses on these derivative contracts are accumulated in the accumulated other comprehensive income (AOCI) portion of its stockholders' equity until the fuel is consumed. Once that fuel is consumed, those unrealized gains and losses are removed from AOCI, and the gain (loss) on the option is used to offset the loss (gain) on fuel.

Although the fair value of derivatives and their related assets or liabilities can be substantial, the net effect on earnings and stockholders' equity is usually minor because companies are mainly using them as hedges and not as speculative securities. The accounting standards for derivative instruments were enacted in response to a concern that speculative activities were not adequately disclosed. Subsequent to its passage, the financial effects have often appeared modest (with occasional exceptions such as **JP Morgan Chase**'s "London Whale" in 2012). Either these companies were not speculating to the extent expected, or they have since reduced their level of speculation in response to increased scrutiny from better disclosures.

Significant economic disruptions can also impact hedge accounting results. Most recently, for example, during the Coronavirus pandemic, air travel essentially stopped and oil prices plunged. This left many airlines with 'over-hedged' positions. Basically, they hedged more fuel than they ended up using (and fuel was much cheaper than expected as well). For example, British Airways' parent company, International Airlines Group, recorded a €1.325 billion charge, and Air France-KLM recorded a charge of €455 million related to over-hedging.[5] Southwest Airlines disclosed the following in their 2020 10-K: "During 2020, as a result of the drastic drop in demand for air travel due to the COVID-19 pandemic, the Company's forecast for 2020 and 2021 fuel purchases and consumption was significantly reduced, causing the Company to be in an estimated "over-hedged" position for second, third, and fourth quarter 2020, and full year 2021. Therefore, the Company de-designated a portion of its fuel hedges related to these periods, and has reclassified approximately $39 million in losses from AOCI into Other (gains) losses, net, during 2020."

Analyzing Derivative Instruments

LO12-8 Review 12-8

GuidedExample

Colgate-Palmolive Company reported the following information regarding its derivative instruments in its 2020 10-K report.

Excerpts from Note 7: Fair Value Measurements and Financial Instruments

> The Company is exposed to market risk from foreign currency exchange rates, interest rates, and commodity price fluctuations. Volatility relating to these exposures is managed on a global basis by utilizing a number of techniques, including working capital management, sourcing strategies, selling price increases, selective borrowings in local currencies and entering into selective derivative instrument transactions, issued with standard features, in accordance with the Company's treasury and risk management policies, which prohibit the use of derivatives for speculative purposes and leveraged derivatives for any purpose. It is the Company's policy to enter into derivative instrument contracts with terms that match the underlying exposure being hedged. Provided below are details of the Company's exposures by type of risk and derivative instruments by type of hedge designation. . . .
>
> The following table presents the location and amount of gains (losses) on hedges recognized on the Company's Consolidated Statements of Income:

continued

[5] The Wall Street Journal, May 15, 2020 https://www.wsj.com/articles/overhedging-oil-prices-lands-some-coronavirus-battered-global-airlines-in-further-trouble-11589555843.

continued from previous page

	Twelve Months Ended December 31, 2020		
	Cost of Sales	Selling, General, and Administrative Expenses	Interest (Income) Expense, Net
Gain (loss) on hedges recognized in income:			
Interest rate swaps designated as fair value hedges:			
Derivative instrument	$—	$ —	$(10)
Hedged items	—	—	10
Foreign currency contracts designated as fair value hedges:			
Derivative instrument	—	29	—
Hedged items	—	(29)	—
Foreign currency contracts designated as cash flow hedges:			
Amount reclassified from OCI	1	—	—
Commodity contracts designated as cash flow hedges:			
Amount reclassified from OCI	(1)	—	—
Total gain (loss) on hedges recognized in income	$—	$ —	$ —

Required

a. What types of risks would the contracts listed above be designed to hedge against?

b. What is the net gain or loss recognized on the company's 2020 income statement related to the risks described in part a?

Solution on p. 12-62.

SUMMARY

LO12-1 Explain and interpret the three levels of investor influence over an investee—passive, significant, and controlling. (p. 12-3)

- Ownership of 20% or less in another corporation is presumed to be a passive investment by the investor.
- Significant influence is assumed to be available to the investor corporation if it owns more than 20% but not over 50% of the outstanding voting stock of the investee corporation.
- Control is generally presumed if the investing firm owns more than 50% of the outstanding voting stock of the investee corporation.

LO12-2 Describe the term "fair value" and the fair value hierarchy. (p. 12-5)

- Fair value is the amount that an independent buyer would be willing to pay for an asset (or the amount that would need to be paid to discharge a liability) in an orderly transaction.
- Fair value can be determined by reference to a market price when available, but it may also be determined by other methods (discounted cash flow analysis, pricing of comparable assets, etc.). GAAP defines three levels of fair value determination:
  - Level 1: Values based on quoted prices in active markets for identical assets/liabilities
  - Level 2: Values based on observable inputs other than Level 1 (e.g., quoted prices for similar assets/liabilities or interest rates or yield curves)
  - Level 3: Values based on inputs observable only to the reporting entity (e.g., management estimates or assumptions)
- GAAP requires that companies disclose their fair value determinations in the disclosure notes of their financial statements.

LO12-3 Describe and analyze accounting for passive investments. (p. 12-6)

- Ownership of a debt security or 20% or less of the equity of another corporation is treated as a passive investment by the investor. Investing for returns is the objective rather than influencing another corporation's decisions. The investment is reported as a long-term asset only if the intention is to retain the asset for longer than a year. Investments in debt securities are segregated into three types—trading securities, held-to-maturity securities, and securities available-for-sale.
- Debt securities that management intends to hold to maturity are carried at (amortized) cost unless their value is considered impaired, in which case the security is written down. Otherwise changes in fair value are not recognized on the balance sheet or the income statement.

- Debt securities treated as trading securities have an objective of short-term gain and will be converted into cash in a very short period of time. Any trading securities held at the end of an accounting period are marked to their fair value. The value change is recognized as an unrealized gain (or loss) in the income statement.
- Debt securities treated as available-for-sale securities are those that classify as neither held-to-maturity nor trading. Any securities held at the end of an accounting period are also marked to their fair value. However, the value change bypasses the income statement to become part of retained earnings called other comprehensive income. Holding gains and losses are recognized in income when the security is sold.
- Investments in equity securities are always marked to fair value, with holding gains and losses (both realized and unrealized) going through income in the period they occur.
- Gains and losses realized on sale, and dividends on passive investments, are reported as other income in the income statement.

Explain and analyze accounting for investments with significant influence. (p. 12-17) **LO12-4**

- Significant influence is assumed to be available to the investor corporation if it owns more than 20% but not over 50% of the outstanding voting stock of the investee corporation. Typically, the investment is initially recorded as a long-term asset at the purchase price.
- In the case of significant influence, the equity method of reporting is followed.
- Under the equity method, the investor recognizes its proportionate share of the investee's net income as income and an increase in the investment account. Any dividends received by the investor are treated as a recovery of the investment and reduce the investment balance.

Describe and analyze accounting for investments with control. (p. 12-22) **LO12-5**

- If a corporation is considered to have control of another corporation, the financial statements of both firms are consolidated and reported as though they were a single entity.
- Control means that the investor has the ability to affect the strategic direction of the investee. Control is generally presumed if the investing firm owns more than 50% of the outstanding voting stock of the investee corporation.
- At the time of the acquisition, acquired assets and liabilities are restated at fair value in the consolidated balance sheet.
- If the purchase price exceeds the fair value of acquired net assets, the remainder is labeled "goodwill." Goodwill is not amortized, but tested for impairment annually. Though, these rules are currently under consideration by FASB, and amortization of goodwill may be required in the future.

Appendix 12A: Illustrate and analyze accounting mechanics for equity method investments. (p. 12-31) **LO12-6**

- Under the equity method of accounting, neither the investee's assets nor its liabilities are reported on the investor's balance sheet. Only the proportionate investment is reported. Further, only the investor's net equity is reported in income; and the investee's sales and expenses are omitted.
- The result is that revenues and expenses, but not NOPAT, are understated; NOPM (NOPAT/Sales) is overstated; and net operating assets (NOA) are understated. Also, financial leverage is understated. ROE remains unaffected.

Appendix 12B: Apply consolidation accounting mechanics. (p. 12-33) **LO12-7**

- Identifiable intangible assets (such as patents, trademarks, customer lists) often result from the acquisition of one corporation by another. This is a situation in which the acquirer will have control and consolidation accounting is required.
- Intangibles are valued at the purchase date and then (unless indefinite-lived) amortized over their economic life. Any remaining purchase price not allocated to tangible or identifiable intangible assets is treated as goodwill.
- Goodwill and other indefinite-lived intangibles are not amortized but written down when and if considered impaired. The write-down is an expense of the period. We note again, however, that goodwill accounting is being reviewed by FASB. Private companies are currently allowed to amortize goodwill and amortization is currently under FASB consideration for public companies as well.
- Reports of consolidated corporations are often difficult to understand because they commingle the assets, liabilities, revenues, expenses, and cash flows of several businesses that can be very different.

Appendix 12C: Discuss the reporting of derivative securities. (p. 12-35) **LO12-8**

- Derivatives refer to financial instruments that are utilized by companies to reduce various kinds of risks.
- Derivatives work by offsetting the gain or loss for the asset or liability to which they relate.
- The accounting for derivatives boils down to this: The derivative contract and the asset or liability to which it relates are both reported on the balance sheet at fair value. The asset and liability are offsetting if the hedge

works. Likewise, the related gains and losses are largely offsetting, leaving income unaffected. For cash flow and net investment hedges, the gains and losses are accumulated in AOCI until the hedged item affects earnings. For fair value hedges, the gains and losses are recorded in the income statement in the same line item as the income effects from the hedged item.

GUIDANCE ANSWERS . . . YOU MAKE THE CALL

You are the Chief Financial Officer When a key component of a company's distribution process begins to turn its attention to other products, it can have a detrimental effect of the prospects for future growth. For instance, the soft-drink companies depend heavily on their bottling companies to get the product to the consumer. In these circumstances, companies may purchase enough shares in the distribution company to exert significant influence (or even control) over the key distributor.

Assignments with the MBC logo in the margin are available in myBusinessCourse. See the Preface of the book for details.

MULTIPLE CHOICE

Multiple Choice Answers
1. c 2. e 3. a 4. b

1. Corporation A owns 35% of corporation B. This is a case where:
- *a.* Corporation A controls corporation B.
- *b.* Corporation A does not control corporation B.
- *c.* Corporation A has significant influence on corporation B.
- *d.* Corporation A does not have a significant influence on corporation B.
- *e.* Both *a* and *c* are correct.

2. In accounting for available-for-sale debt securities, the
- *a.* securities are reported on the balance sheet at their fair value.
- *b.* securities are reported at cost.
- *c.* increases in fair value are reported in income.
- *d.* increases in fair value are not reported in income.
- *e.* both *a* and *d* are correct.

3. Which of the following statements is true of investments accounted for under the equity method?
- *a.* Investor reports its percentage share of the investee's income in its income.
- *b.* Investor reports dividends received from the investee in its operating income.
- *c.* Investment is reported at its fair value.
- *d.* Investment is reported at cost plus any dividends received from the investee.
- *e.* Investment is reported at fair value less any dividends received from the investee.

4. Which of the following statements is true about goodwill?
- *a.* Current reporting standards require that goodwill be amortized over its economic life.
- *b.* Goodwill is written down when the fair value of the investee is less than the book value.
- *c.* Goodwill can be recognized only when the acquisition price does not exceed the value of the tangible and identifiable intangible assets acquired.
- *d.* The recording of goodwill can be based on the acquisition of assets such as patents and trademarks.
- *e.* Goodwill equals retained earnings.

Superscript $^{A\ (B,\ C)}$ denotes assignments based on Appendix 12A (12B, 12C).

QUESTIONS

Q12-1. For investments in debt securities, what measure (fair value or amortized cost) is used for the balance sheet to report (a) trading securities, (b) available-for-sale securities, and (c) held-to-maturity securities?

Q12-2. What is an unrealized holding gain (loss)? Explain. For passive investments in equity securities, how are unrealized holding gains (losses) treated?

Q12-3. Where are unrealized holding gains and losses related to trading securities reported in the financial statements? Where are unrealized holding gains and losses related to available-for-sale debt securities reported in the financial statements?

Q12-4. What does *significant influence* imply regarding financial investments? Describe the accounting procedures used for such investments.

Q12-5. On January 1 of the current year, Yetman Company purchases 40% of the common stock of Livnat Company for $200,000 cash. During the year, Livnat reports $64,000 of net income and pays $48,000 in cash dividends. At year-end, what amount should appear in Yetman's balance sheet for its investment in Livnat?

Q12-6. What accounting method is used when a stock investment represents more than 50% of the investee company's voting stock? Explain.

Q12-7. What is the underlying objective of consolidated financial statements?

Q12-8. Finn Company purchases all of the common stock of Murray Company for $600,000 when Murray Company has $240,000 of common stock and $360,000 of retained earnings. Book values of the assets and liabilities of Murray Company equal their fair values. If a consolidated balance sheet is prepared immediately after the acquisition, what amounts are eliminated in preparing it? Explain.

Q12-9.[B] Bradshaw Company owns 100% of Dee Company. At year-end, Dee owes Bradshaw $150,000. If a consolidated balance sheet is prepared at year-end, how is the $150,000 handled? Explain.

Q12-10. What are some limitations of consolidated financial statements?

DATA ANALYTICS

DA12-1. Using Excel Visualizations to Analyze Changes in Other Comprehensive Income

LO12-3

Homework MBC | Data Analytics

The Excel file associated with this exercise includes data for Amazon.com, Inc., and Apple Inc., as reported in Form 10-Q and 10-K reports over a two-year period ($ millions). In this exercise, we analyze the change in unrealized gains and losses reported in other comprehensive income by quarter over a two-year period for Amazon and Apple.

REQUIRED

1. Download Excel file DA12-1 found in myBusinessCourse.
2. Prepare Waterfall charts in Excel for each year for Amazon and Apple, showing the quarterly change in unrealized gains/losses on securities. *Hint:* Add totals for each year, highlight data, select Insert, Chart, Waterfall.
3. Label the last bar as "total" per the legend. *Hint:* Double-click on bar (last) to open the Format Data Point sidebar. Single-click on the same bar. Check Set as total under Series Options on the bar column icon tab.
4. Indicate how many columns are shown in each chart.
5. Indicate how many orange bars are displayed in each chart. What do the orange bars represent?
6. Indicate how many blue bars are displayed in each chart. What do the blue bars represent?
7. Indicate what type of securities are the source for the gains and losses displayed in the charts.
8. Indicate which chart showed the most volatility over the course of the year. What total amount of gain or loss would be shown on the Form 10-K for that particular year?
9. Indicate whether the trends shown in the charts are similar across companies for each year.
10. Compute the percentage change in the net gain/(loss) from Year 1 to Year 2 for Amazon and for Apple.
11. Indicate why GAAP requires the gains and losses analyzed above to be reported in other comprehensive income rather than net income.

DATA VISUALIZATION

Data Visualization Activities are available in myBusinessCourse. These assignments use Tableau Dashboards to expose students to visual depictions of data and introduce students to data analytics through data visualizations. These exercises are easily assignable and auto graded by MBC.

Data Visualization

MINI EXERCISES

LO12-1

Homework MBC

M12-11. Classifying Investments as Passive, Significant, or Controlling

For each of the situations below, determine if the investment should be reported as a passive investment (P), an investment reflecting significant influence (SI), or a controlling interest (C).

a. ____ Griffin Company purchased 25% of the common stock of Wright, Inc., Griffin is one of several suppliers that Wright, Inc., relies on to supply subcomponents.

b. ____ Dye Corporation purchased 20% of the $40 million bond issue offered by Glover Company.

c. ____ Zhao, Inc., purchased 2,000 shares of Alphabet, Inc., common stock, paying $1.1 million.

d. ____ Watts Corporation purchased 65% of the common stock of Zimmerman, Inc., common stock for cash. Watts and Zimmerman had been engaged in several strategic alliances prior to the purchase.

e. ____ Shevlin, Inc., purchased 15% of Bowen Company's common stock. Shevlin is Bowen Company's largest customer, buying more than 60% of its output.

LO12-3

Homework MBC

Cisco Systems, Inc.
NASDAQ :: CSCO

M12-12. Interpreting Disclosures of Available-for-Sale Securities

Use the following year-end note disclosure information from Cisco Systems, Inc.'s 2020 10-K report to answer parts *a* and *b*.

($ millions)	2020
Amortized cost of available-for-sale debt investments	$17,163
Gross unrealized gains	454
Gross unrealized losses	(7)
Fair value of available-for-sale debt investments	$17,610

a. At what amount is its available-for-sale investments reported on Cisco's 2020 balance sheet? Explain.

b. How is its net unrealized gain of $447 million ($454 million – $7 million) reported by Cisco in its financial statements?

LO12-3

Homework MBC

M12-13. Accounting for Passive Investments in Equity Securities

Assume that Wu Company purchases 8,500 common shares of Pincus Company for $12 cash per share. Shares of Pincus Company are actively traded. During the year, Wu receives a cash dividend of $1.30 per common share from Pincus, and the year-end market price of Pincus common stock is $13 per share. How much income does Wu report relating to this investment for the year?

LO12-2

Microsoft Corporation
NASDAQ :: MSFT

M12-14. Analyzing Disclosures of Investment Securities

In its June 30, 2020, balance sheet, Microsoft Corporation reports short-term investments with a value of $122,951 million. The amount of debt investments excluding the value of derivatives of $35 million is $122,916 million. These debt investments are recognized at fair value, and Microsoft provides information in its disclosure notes related to fair value measurements summarized in the table that follows.

June 30, 2020 (In $ millions)	Level 1	Level 2	Level 3	Gross Fair Value
Commercial paper	$ 0	$3,070	$ 0	$ 3,070
Certificates of deposit	0	1,252	0	1,252
U.S. government and agency securities	95,393	1,992	0	97,385
Foreign government bonds	0	6,984	0	6,984
Mortgage- and asset-backed securities	0	4,900	0	4,900
Corporate notes and bonds	0	8,810	58	8,868
Municipal securities	0	366	91	457

a. Explain the differences between the three columns labeled Level 1, Level 2, and Level 3.

b. Are all of these investments "marked-to-fair value"? If not, which ones are not marked-to-fair value? Which investment values do you regard as most subjective? Least subjective?

c. If Microsoft needed to raise cash to take advantage of an investment opportunity, which of these investments do you regard as most liquid (i.e., most easily turned into cash)? Least liquid?

M12-15. Analyzing and Interpreting Equity Method Investments (FSET) LO12-4

Stober Company purchases an investment in Lang Company at a purchase price of $1.5 million cash, representing 30% of the outstanding stock and book value of Lang. During the year, Lang reports net income of $150,000 and pays cash dividends of $60,000. At the end of the year, the fair value of Stober's investment is $1.8 million.

a. At what amount is the investment reported on Stober's balance sheet at year-end?

b. What amount of income from investments does Stober report? Explain.

c. Stober's $300,000 unrealized gain in investment fair value (choose one and explain):

(1) is not reflected on either its income statement or its balance sheet.

(2) is reported in its current income.

(3) is reported on its balance sheet only.

(4) is reported in its other comprehensive income.

d. Record each of the transactions and events from above in the financial statement effects template.

M12-16. Analyzing and Interpreting Equity Method Investments LO12-4

Using the information from M12-15, answer the following.

a. Prepare journal entries to record the transactions and events.

b. Post the journal entries to their respective T-accounts.

M12-17. Calculating Income for Equity Method Investments LO12-4

Kross Company purchases an equity investment in Penno Company at a purchase price of $6 million, representing 40% of the outstanding stock and book value of Penno. During the current year, Penno reports net income of $720,000 and pays cash dividends of $240,000. At the end of the year, the market value of Kross' investment is $6.5 million. What amount of income does Kross report relating to this investment in Penno for the year? Explain.

M12-18. Computing Consolidating Adjustments and Noncontrolling Interest LO12-5

Philipich Company purchases 80% of Hirst Company's common stock for $480,000 cash when Hirst Company has $240,000 of common stock and $360,000 of retained earnings, and the fair values of Hirst's assets and liabilities equal their book values. If a consolidated balance sheet is prepared immediately after the acquisition, what amounts are eliminated when preparing that statement? What amount of noncontrolling interest appears in the consolidated balance sheet? Where does it appear?

M12-19. Computing Consolidated Net Income LO12-5

Benartzi Company purchased a 90% interest in Liang Company on January 1 of the current year. Benartzi Company had $840,000 net income for the current year *before* recognizing its share of Liang Company's net income. If Liang Company had net income of $210,000 for the year, what is the consolidated net income for the year? How would it be presented?

M12-20. Effect of Investing on Ratios LO12-4, 5

DeFond Company wishes to secure a reliable supply of a key component for its production processes, and its management is considering two alternative investments. Verduzco Company produces exactly the supply that DeFond needs, so DeFond could use cash to purchase 100% of the common stock of Verduzco. Lin Company produces twice as much of the component that DeFond needs, but DeFond could form a joint venture with another company where each would purchase 50% of Lin Company's common stock and each take 50% of Lin Company's output.

The table that follows gives the balance sheet information for all three companies prior to any investment by DeFond. For the questions below, assume that DeFond would be able to purchase shares at the investee companies' book values and that the investee companies' assets and liabilities have fair values equal to their book values.

	DeFond Company	Verduzco Company	Lin Company
Cash	$1,000	$ 125	$ 250
Investment	—	—	—
Noncash assets	2,500	1,125	2,250
Liabilities	2,750	875	1,750
Shareholders' Equity	750	375	750

a. Suppose that DeFond purchases 100% of Verduzco's common stock for $375. Produce the consolidated balance sheet for DeFond immediately after the acquisition.

b. Suppose that DeFond purchases 50% of Lin's common stock for $375. Produce the balance sheet for DeFond immediately after the investment (using the equity method).

c. From a business perspective, either of these investments will accomplish the objective of obtaining a reliable supply of components. How will the financial ratios differ between the two alternatives?

LO12-3 Homework MBC

M12-21. Reporting of and Analyzing Financial Effects of Trading (Debt) Securities (FSET)
Hartgraves Company had the following transactions and adjustments related to a bond investment that is a trading security.

Year 1

Oct. 1 Purchased $900,000 face value of Skyline, Inc.'s 7% bonds at 97 plus a brokerage commission of $1,800. The bonds pay interest on September 30 and March 31 and mature in 20 years. Hartgraves Company expects to sell the bonds in the near future.

Dec. 31 Made the adjusting entry to record interest earned on investment in the Skyline bonds.

31 Made the adjusting entry to record the current fair value of the Skyline bonds. At December 31, the fair value of the Skyline bonds was $882,000.

Year 2

Mar. 31 Received the semiannual interest payment on investment in the Skyline bonds.

Apr. 1 Sold the Skyline bond investment for $886,140 cash.

Record each of the transactions in the financial statement effects template.

LO12-3 Homework MBC

M12-22. Reporting of and Analyzing Financial Effects of Trading (Debt) Securities
Using the information from M12-21, answer the following.

a. Prepare journal entries to record these transactions.

b. Post the journal entries to their respective T-accounts.

LO12-3 Homework MBC

M12-23. Reporting of and Analyzing Financial Effects of Investments in Equity Securities (FSET)
Blouin Company had the following transactions and adjustment related to a stock investment that is a trading security.

Year 1

Nov. 15 Purchased 15,000 shares of Lane, Inc.'s common stock at $17 per share plus a brokerage commission of $1,800. Blouin expects to sell the stock in the near future.

Dec. 22 Received a cash dividend of $1.00 per share of common stock from Lane.

31 Made the adjusting entry to reflect year-end fair value of the stock investment in Lane. The year-end fair value of the Lane common stock is $15.50 per share.

Year 2

Jan. 20 Sold all 15,000 shares of the Lane common stock for $225,000.

Record each of the transactions in the financial statement effects template.

LO12-3 Homework MBC

M12-24. Reporting of and Analyzing Financial Effects of Investments in Equity Securities
Using the information from M12-23, answer the following.

a. Prepare journal entries to record these transactions.

b. Post the journal entries from *a* to their respective T-accounts.

LO12-3 Homework MBC

M12-25. Reporting of and Analyzing Financial Effects of Available-for-Sale (Debt) Securities (FSET)
Refer to the data for Hartgraves Company in Mini Exercise 12-21. Assume that when the shares were purchased, management did not intend to sell the stock in the near future. Record the transactions and adjustments for Hartgraves Company as an available-for-sale security in the financial statement effects template.

LO12-3 Homework MBC

M12-26. Reporting of and Analyzing Financial Effects of Available-for-Sale (Debt) Securities
Using the information from M12-25, answer the following.

a. Prepare journal entries to record these transactions.

b. Post each of the transactions to their respective T-account.

LO12-5 Homework MBC

M12-27. Computing Stockholders' Equity in Consolidation
On January 1 of the current year, Halen Company purchased all of the common shares of Jolson Company for $460,000 cash. On this date, the stockholders' equity of Halen Company consisted of $480,000 in common stock and $248,000 in retained earnings. Jolson Company had $280,000 in common stock and $180,000 in retained earnings. What amount of total stockholders' equity appears on the consolidated balance sheet?

EXERCISES

E12-28. Assessing Financial Statement Effects of Trading and Available-for-Sale (Debt) Securities (FSET)

LO12-1, 3

Homework MBC

Four transactions involving investments in marketable debt securities classified as trading follow.

(1) On July 1, purchased US Treasury Bonds for $610,000 in cash. The bonds have a face value of $600,000 and pay interest semi-annually (June 30 and December 31) at an annual rate of 4.00%.

(2) Received cash interest payment of $12,000 on December 31.

(3) Year-end market price of bonds is $616,000.

(4) Received cash interest payment of $12,000 and sold all bonds on June 30 for $612,000.

a. Record each of the transactions above in the financial statement effects template.

b. Using the same transaction information as above and assuming the investments in marketable securities are classified as available-for-sale, record each of the transactions in the financial statement effects template.

E12-29. Assessing Financial Statement Effects of Trading and Available-for-Sale (Debt) Securities

LO12-1, 3

Homework MBC

Using the information from E12-28, answer the following.

a. Assuming that the debt securities are classified as trading, (i.) prepare the journal entries to record the four transactions, and (ii.) post the journal entries to their respective T-accounts.

b. Assuming that the debt securities are classified as available-for-sale, (i.) prepare the journal entries to record the four transactions, and (ii.) post the journal entries to their respective T-accounts.

E12-30. Assessing Financial Statement Effects of Passive Investments in Equity Securities (FSET)

LO12-1, 3

Homework MBC

For the following transactions involving investments in marketable securities, assume that:

1. Ohlson Co. purchases 6,000 common shares of Freeman Co. at $16 cash per share.
2. Ohlson Co. receives a cash dividend of $1.25 per common share from Freeman.
3. Year-end market price of Freeman common stock is $17.50 per share.
4. Ohlson Co. sells all 6,000 common shares of Freeman for $103,680 cash.

Record each of the transactions in the financial statement effects template.

E12-31. Assessing Financial Statement Effects of Passive Investments in Equity Securities

LO12-1, 3

Homework MBC

Using the information from E12-30, answer the following.

a. Prepare journal entries to record the four transactions.

b. Post the journal entries to their respective T-accounts.

E12-32. Acquisitions and Trend Analysis

LO12-5

Homework MBC

Microsoft Corporation
NASDAQ :: MSFT

In its 2018 10-K annual report, Microsoft Corporation reported the following revenues:

($ millions)	Fiscal Year Ended June 30 2018	2017	2016
Total revenues	$110,360	$96,571	$91,154

a. Calculate the yearly revenue growth for this period. Based on this trend, what revenue would you forecast for fiscal year 2019?

In December of 2016 (i.e., almost in the middle of fiscal year 2017, Microsoft completed its $27.0 billion acquisition of LinkedIn Corporation. In the 10-K disclosures for 2018, Microsoft reports

Following are the supplemental consolidated financial results of Microsoft Corporation on an unaudited pro forma basis, as if the acquisition had been consummated on July 1, 2015:

(In millions, except earnings per share) Year Ended June 30	2017	2016
Revenue	$98,291	$94,490

b. How does the acquisition of LinkedIn affect your interpretation of the growth trend in part *a*?

c. Using the disclosure information, revise the growth calculations to separate the measures of "organic growth" from "purchased growth."

LO12-1, 3 Homework MBC

E12-33. Reporting of and Analyzing Financial Effects of Trading (Debt) Securities (FSET) Barclay, Inc., had the following transactions and adjustments related to a bond investment that is classified as a trading security.

Year 1

Nov. 1 Purchased $500,000 face value of Joos, Inc.'s 9% bonds at 102 plus a brokerage commission of $1,500. The bonds pay interest on October 31 and April 30 and mature in 15 years. Barclay expects to sell the bonds in the near future.

Dec. 31 Made the adjusting entry to record interest earned on investment in the Joos bonds.

31 Made the adjusting entry to record the current fair value of the Joos bonds. At December 31, the fair value of the Joos bonds was $502,500.

Year 2

Apr. 30 Received the semiannual interest payment on investment in the Joos bonds.

May 1 Sold the Joos bond investment for $501,500 cash.

Record each of the transactions in the financial statement effects template.

LO12-1, 3 Homework MBC

E12-34. Reporting of and Analyzing Financial Effects of Trading (Debt) Securities Using the information from E12-33, answer the following.

a. Prepare journal entries to record these transactions.

b. Post the journal entries to their respective T-accounts.

LO12-5 Homework MBC

E12-35. Reporting of Stockholders' Equity in Consolidation Baylor Company purchased 75% of the common stock of Reed Company for $480,000 in cash when the stockholders' equity of Reed Company consisted of $400,000 in common stock and $240,000 in retained earnings. On the acquisition date, the stockholders' equity of Baylor Company consisted of $720,000 in common stock and $352,000 in retained earnings. Prepare the stockholders' equity section in the consolidated balance sheet as of the acquisition date.

LO12-3
CNA Financial Corporation
NYSE :: CNA

E12-36. Interpreting Note Disclosures for Investments CNA Financial Corporation provides the following information from its 2020 10-K report (excerpts from Notes A and B):

Investments

The Company classifies its fixed maturity securities as either available-for-sale or trading, and as such, they are carried at fair value. Changes in fair value of trading securities are reported within Net investment income on the Consolidated Statements of Operations. Changes in fair value related to available-for-sale securities are reported as a component of Other comprehensive income.

Credit Losses

The allowances for credit losses on fixed maturity securities, mortgage loans, reinsurance receivables, and insurance receivables are valuation accounts that are reported as a reduction of a financial asset's cost basis and are measured on a pool basis when similar risk characteristics exist. Management estimates the allowance using relevant available information from both internal and external sources. Historical credit loss experience provides the basis for the estimation of expected credit losses and adjustments may be made to reflect current conditions and reasonable and supportable forecasts. Adjustments to historical loss information are made for any additional factors that come to the Company's attention. This could include significant shifts in counterparty financial strength ratings, aging of past due receivables, amounts sent to collection agencies, or other underlying portfolio changes. Amounts are considered past due when payments have not been received according to contractual terms. The Company also considers current and forecast economic conditions, using a variety of economic metrics and forecast indices. . . .

December 31, 2020 (In millions)	Cost or Amortized Cost	Gross Unrealized Gains	Gross Unrealized Losses	Allowance for Credit Losses[1]	Estimated Fair Value
Fixed maturity securities available-for-sale:					
Corporate and other bonds	$20,792	$3,578	$22	$23	$24,325
States, municipalities, and political subdivisions	9,729	1,863	—	—	11,592
Asset-backed:					
Residential mortgage-backed	3,442	146	1	—	3,587
Commercial mortgage-backed	1,933	93	42	17	1,967
Other asset-backed	2,179	81	9	—	2,251
Total asset-backed	7,554	320	52	17	7,805
U.S. Treasury and obligations of government-sponsored enterprises	339	2	3	—	338
Foreign government	512	32	—	—	544
Redeemable preferred stock	—	—	—	—	—
Total fixed maturity securities available-for-sale	38,926	5,795	77	40	44,604
Total fixed maturity securities trading	27	—	—	—	27
Total fixed maturity securities	$38,953	$5,795	$77	$40	$44,631

[1] As of January 1, 2020, the Company adopted ASU 2016-13, Financial Instruments-Credit Losses (Topic 326): Measurement of Credit Losses on Financial Instruments. The Unrealized OTTI Losses (Gains) column that tracked subsequent valuation changes on securities for which a credit loss had previously been recorded has been replaced with the Allowance for Credit Losses column.

a. At what amount is its investment portfolio reflected on its balance sheet? In your answer identify its fair value, cost, any unrealized gains and losses, and any allowance for credit losses.

b. How are its unrealized gains and/or losses reflected in CNA's balance sheet and income statement?

c. How are any credit losses and the gains and losses realized from the sale of securities reflected in CNA's balance sheet and income statement?

E12-37. Assessing Financial Statement Effects of Equity Method Securities (FSET) LO12-4 Homework MBC

The following transactions involve investments in marketable securities and are accounted for using the equity method.

1. Purchased 18,000 common shares of Barth Co. at $9 cash per share; the shares represent 30% ownership in Barth.
2. Received a cash dividend of $1.25 per common share from Barth.
3. Recorded income from Barth stock investment when Barth's net income is $120,000.
4. Sold all 18,000 common shares of Barth for $180,500.

Record each of the transactions in the financial statement effects template.

E12-38. Assessing Financial Statement Effects of Equity Method Securities LO12-4 Homework MBC

Using the information from E12-37, answer the following.

a. Prepare journal entries to record these four transactions.

b. Post the journal entries to their respective T-accounts.

E12-39. Assessing Financial Statement Effects of Equity Method Securities (FSET) LO12-4 Homework MBC

The following transactions involve investments in marketable securities and are accounted for using the equity method.

1. Healy Co. purchases 30,000 common shares of Palepu Co. at $8 cash per share; the shares represent 25% ownership of Palepu.
2. Healy receives a cash dividend of $0.80 per common share from Palepu.
3. Palepu reports annual net income of $240,000.
4. Healy sells all 30,000 common shares of Palepu for $280,000 cash.

Record each of the transactions in the financial statement effects template.

E12-40. Assessing Financial Statement Effects of Equity Method Securities LO12-4 Homework MBC

Using the information from E12-39, answer the following.

a. Prepare journal entries to record these four transactions.

b. Post the journal entries to their respective T-accounts.

LO12-1, 3, 4

Homework MBC

E12-41. Assessing Financial Statement Effects of Passive and Equity Method Investments (FSET) On January 1, Ball Corporation purchased, as a stock investment, 5,000 shares of Leftwich Company common stock for $15 cash per share. On December 31, Leftwich announced net income of $40,000 for the year and paid a cash dividend of $1.10 per share. At December 31, the market value of Leftwich's stock was $19 per share.

a. Assume that the stock acquired by Ball represents 15% of Leftwich's voting stock—a passive equity investment. Record each of the following transactions in the financial statement effects template.

(1) Ball purchased 5,000 common shares of Leftwich at $15 cash per share; the shares represent a 15% ownership in Leftwich.

(2) Leftwich reported annual net income of $40,000.

(3) Received a cash dividend of $1.10 per common share from Leftwich.

(4) Year-end market price of Leftwich common stock is $19 per share.

b. Assume that Ball's $75,000 investment purchased 30% of Leftwich's voting stock and that Ball accounts for this investment using the equity method since it is able to exert significant influence. For the same four transactions as above, record each of the transactions in the financial statement effects template.

LO12-1, 3, 4

Homework MBC

E12-42. Assessing Financial Statement Effects of Passive and Equity Method Investments Using the information from E12-41, answer the following.

For the transactions described in parts *a* and *b*, (i.) prepare journal entries and (ii.) post the journal entries to their respective T-accounts.

LO12-1, 3

Homework MBC

Amazon.com, Inc.
NASDAQ :: AMZN

E12-43. Allocation of Acquisition Purchase Price In 2017, Amazon.com, Inc., made two significant acquisitions intending to expand the company's retail presence. On May 12, 2017, Amazon acquired Souq Group Ltd. ("Souq"), an e-commerce company, for approximately $583 million, net of cash acquired and on August 28, 2017, acquired Whole Foods Market, a grocery store chain, for approximately $13.2 billion, net of cash acquired. Other acquisitions were also made for consideration of $204 million, making a total of $13,963 million (net of cash acquired) for the year.

From the disclosure in its 2018 10-K, Amazon provides the following information:

The aggregate purchase price of these acquisitions was allocated as follows (in millions):

December 31	2017
Purchase Price	
Cash paid, net of cash acquired	$13,963
Allocation	
Goodwill	?
Intangible assets:	
Marketing-related	1,987
Contract-based	440
Technology-based	166
Customer-related	54
	2,647
Property and equipment	3,810
Deferred tax assets	117
Other assets acquired	1,858
Long-term debt	(1,165)
Deferred tax liabilities	(961)
Other liabilities assumed	(1,844)
	$13,963

a. How are the values in the above table determined?

b. How much goodwill would Amazon.com recognize from these acquisitions? How will that goodwill be treated in subsequent periods?

c. Do you think Amazon.com shareholders would prefer to see an allocation that gives a lot of value to separately identifiable assets or an allocation where most of the acquisition price goes to goodwill? Why?

E12-44. Allocation of Acquisition Purchase Price

LO12-5
Gilead Sciences, Inc.
NASDAQ :: GILD

On October 23, 2020, Gilead Sciences completed its acquisition of Immunomedics, a company focused on the development of antibody-drug conjugate ("ADC") technology. Immunomedics researches and develops biopharmaceutical products, particularly antibody-based products for patients with solid tumors and blood cancers. The company also manufactures and markets Trodelvy, a Trop-2-directed ADC developed by Immunomedics that is the first ADC the FDA approved for the treatment of adult patients with metastatic triple-negative breast cancer. Immunomedics is a wholly owned subsidiary of Gilead Sciences following the acquisition. Gilead paid $20.6 billion in cash for the stock of Immunomedics.

Gilead Sciences's 2020 10-K reports the following for purchase price allocation:

(in millions)	Amount
Cash and cash equivalents	$ 726
Inventories	946
Intangible assets	
Finite-lived intangible asset	4,600
Acquired R&D	15,760
Outlicense contract	175
Deferred income taxes	(4,565)
Liability related to future royalties	(1,100)
Other assets (and liabilities), net	04
Total identifiable net assets	16,606
Goodwill	?

a. How are the values in the above table determined?

b. How much goodwill would Gilead recognize from this acquisition? How will that goodwill be treated in subsequent periods?

c. Do you think Gilead's shareholders would prefer to see an allocation that gives a lot of value to separately identifiable assets or an allocation where most of the acquisition price goes to goodwill? Why?

E12-45. Reporting of and Analyzing Financial Effects of Passive Equity Securities (FSET)

LO12-1, 3
Homework MBC

Guay Company had the following transactions and adjustment related to a passive equity investment.

Year 1

Nov. 15 Purchased 7,500 shares of Core, Inc.'s common stock at $16 per share plus a brokerage commission of $1,350. Guay Company expects to sell the stock in the near future.

Dec. 22 Received a cash dividend of $1.25 per share of common stock from Core.

31 Made the adjusting entry to reflect year-end fair value of the stock investment in Core. The year-end market price of the Core common stock is $17.50 per share.

Year 2

Jan. 20 Sold all 7,500 shares of the Core common stock for $129,600.

Record each of the transactions in the financial statement effects template.

E12-46. Reporting of and Analyzing Financial Effects of Passive Equity Securities

LO12-1, 3
Homework MBC

Using the information from E12-45, answer the following.

a. Prepare journal entries to record these transactions.

b. Post the journal entries to their respective T-accounts.

E12-47. Reporting of and Analyzing Financial Effects of Equity Securities Under International Standards (FSET)

LO12-1, 3
Homework MBC

Refer to the data for Guay Company in Exercise 12-45. Assume that Guay Company reports under International Financial Reporting Standards (IFRS). Under IFRS, Guay can designate an equity investment for accounting based on FVOCI (fair value—other comprehensive income). While holding the equity investment, dividends are recorded in income and unrealized holding gains and losses go to AOCI, much like AFS securities. However, the difference is that these gains and losses are never recognized in income. Rather, they remain in AOCI. Assume that when the shares were purchased, management designated its investment in Core, Inc., for FVOCI treatment.

a. Record the transactions and adjustments for Guay Company under this assumption in the financial statement effects template.

b. Why might the standard setters have allowed this option to companies reporting under IFRS?

LO12-1, 3 Homework MBC

E12-48. Reporting of and Analyzing Financial Effects of Equity Securities Under International Standards

Using the information from E12-47, (a) prepare the journal entries and (b) post the journal entries to their respective T-accounts.

LO12-1, 2, 3, 4 Homework MBC

E12-49. Reporting and Interpreting Financial Investment Performance

Kasznik Company began operations on January 2, and by year-end (December 31) had made the following investments in financial securities. Year-end information on these investments follows.

Investment	Cost or End-of-Year Equity Basis (as appropriate)	Year-End Fair Value	Investment Classification
Common stock of Barth, Inc.	$102,000	$ 97,950	Fair value (Trading)
Common stock of Foster, Inc.	243,750	240,000	Fair value (Trading)
30-Year US Treasury Bond	295,500	288,000	Available-for-sale
10-Year US Treasury Note	235,500	232,050	Available-for-sale
Ertimur, Inc.	150,000	153,600	Equity method
Soliman, Inc..	204,000	199,800	Equity method

a. At what total amount are the trading stock investments reported in the December 31 balance sheet?

b. At what total amount are the available-for-sale debt investments reported in the December 31 balance sheet?

c. At what total amount are the equity method stock investments reported in the December 31 balance sheet?

d. What total amount of unrealized holding gains or unrealized holding losses related to the investments appears in the annual income statement?

e. What total amount of unrealized holding gains or unrealized holding losses related to the investments appears in the stockholders' equity section of the December 31 balance sheet?

LO12-1, 4 Homework MBC

AT&T, Inc.
NYSE :: T

E12-50. Analyzing Equity Method Investment Disclosures

AT&T, Inc., reports a December 31, 2019, balance of $3,695 million in "Investments in and advances to equity affiliates." Provide the entries for the following events for fiscal year 2020:

a. AT&T's share of income from its affiliates was $95 million.

b. AT&T received dividends and distributions from its affiliates of $133 million during fiscal year 2020.

c. After these events, what should be the balance in AT&T's investments in affiliates account at December 31, 2020? The actual balance was $1,780 million. What might explain any differences between these two values?

LO12-7 Homework MBC

E12-51.[B] Constructing the Consolidated Balance Sheet at Acquisition (FSET)

On January 1 of the current year, Healy Company purchased all of the common shares of Miller Company for $400,000 cash. Balance sheets of the two firms at acquisition follow.

	Healy Company	Miller Company	Consolidating Adjustments	Consolidated
Current assets	$1,360,000	$ 96,000		
Investment in Miller.	400,000	—		
Plant assets, net.	2,400,000	328,000		
Goodwill	—	—		
Total assets.	$4,160,000	$424,000		
Liabilities.	$ 560,000	$ 72,000		
Contributed capital	2,800,000	320,000		
Retained earnings	800,000	32,000		
Total liabilities and equity	$4,160,000	$424,000		

During purchase negotiations, Miller's plant assets were appraised at $340,000; and all of its remaining assets and liabilities were appraised at values approximating their book values. Healy also concluded that an additional $36,000 (in goodwill) demanded by Miller's shareholders was warranted because Miller's earning power was better than the industry average. (1) Prepare the consolidating adjustments, (2) prepare the consolidated balance sheet at acquisition, and (3) record the consolidated transaction in the financial statement effects template.

E12-52.[B] Recording a Consolidation Adjustment LO12-7

Using the information from E12-51, (a) prepare the journal entry and (b) post the journal entry to its respective T-accounts.

E12-53.[B] Constructing the Consolidated Balance Sheet at Acquisition (FSET) LO12-7

Rayburn Company purchased all of Kanodia Company's common stock for cash on January 1, at which time the separate balance sheets of the two corporations appeared as follows:

	Rayburn Company	Kanodia Company	Consolidating Adjustments	Consolidated
Investment in Kanodia	$ 480,000	—		
Other assets	1,840,000	$560,000		
Goodwill	—	—		
Total assets	$2,320,000	$560,000		
Liabilities	$ 720,000	$128,000		
Contributed capital	1,120,000	240,000		
Retained earnings	480,000	192,000		
Total liabilities and equity	$2,320,000	$560,000		

During purchase negotiations, Rayburn determined that the appraised value of Kanodia's other assets was $576,000; and all of its remaining assets and liabilities were appraised at values approximating their book values. The remaining $32,000 of the purchase price was ascribed to goodwill. (1) Prepare the consolidating adjustments, (2) prepare the consolidated balance sheet at acquisition, and (3) record the consolidated transaction in the financial statement effects template.

E12-54.[B] Constructing the Consolidated Balance Sheet at Acquisition LO12-7

Using the information from E12-53, (a) prepare the journal entry and (b) post the journal entry to its respective T-accounts.

E12-55. Assessing Goodwill Impairment LO12-5

On January 1, Engel Company purchases 100% of Ball Company for $23.5 million. At the time of acquisition, Ball's stockholders' equity (and the fair value of its identifiable net assets) is reported at $14.3 million. Engel ascribes the excess of $9.2 million to goodwill. Assume that the fair value of Ball declines to $17.5 million.

a. Provide computations to determine if the goodwill has become impaired and, if so, the amount of the impairment.

b. What impact does the impairment of goodwill have on Engel's financial statements?

E12-56.[B] Constructing the Consolidated Balance Sheet at Acquisition LO12-5, 7

Easton Company acquires 100% of the outstanding voting shares of Harris Company on January 1. To obtain these shares, Easton pays $252,000 in cash and issues 6,000 of its $10 par value common stock. On this date, Easton's stock has a fair value of $36 per share, and Harris' book value of stockholders' equity is $336,000. Easton is willing to pay $468,000 for a company with a book value for equity of $336,000 because it believes that (1) Harris buildings are undervalued by $48,000, and (2) Harris has an unrecorded patent that Easton values at $36,000. Easton considers the remaining balance sheet items to be fairly valued (no book-to-fair value difference). The remaining $48,000 of the purchase price excess over book value is ascribed to corporate synergies and other general unidentifiable intangible assets (goodwill). The January 1, 2019, balance sheets at the acquisition date follow:

	Easton Company	Harris Company	Consolidating Adjustments	Consolidated
Cash	$ 100,800	$ 48,000		
Receivables	192,000	108,000		
Inventory	264,000	156,000		
Investment in Harris	468,000	—		
Land	120,000	72,000		
Buildings, net	480,000	132,000		
Equipment, net	144,000	60,000		
Total assets	$1,768,800	$576,000		

continued

continued from previous page

	Easton Company	Harris Company	Consolidating Adjustments	Consolidated
Accounts payable	$ 192,000	$ 36,000		
Long-term liabilities	456,000	204,000		
Common stock	600,000	48,000		
Additional paid-in capital	88,800	—		
Retained earnings	432,000	288,000		
Total liabilities & equity	$1,768,800	$576,000		

a. Show the breakdown of the investment into the book value acquired, the excess of fair value over book value, and the portion of the investment representing goodwill.

b. Prepare the consolidating adjustments and the consolidated balance sheet. Identify the adjustments by whether they relate to the elimination of stockholders' equity [S] or the excess of purchase price over book value [A].

c. How will the excess of the purchase price over book value acquired be treated in years subsequent to the acquisition?

LO12-6 Homework MBC

E12-57.[A] Accounting for Equity Method Investments

Refer to the Easton Company acquisition described in E12-56. Instead of a 100% acquisition, assume that Easton purchased 40% of the outstanding shares of Harris Company on January 1 for $187,200 in cash. Also assume that the undervalued buildings have an estimated remaining useful life of 20 years and the unrecorded patent has a useful life of 5 years.

During the year, Harris reported net income of $96,000 and paid cash dividends to shareholders totaling $48,000.

a. Prepare journal entries to record Easton Company's equity in the earnings of Harris Company, including any amortization of the excess of fair value over book value of assets acquired.

b. What is the value of the investment in Harris Company reported on Easton Company's balance sheet as of December 31?

LO12-8

Hewlett Packard Enterprise Company
NYSE :: HPE

E12-58.[C] Reporting and Analyzing Derivatives

Hewlett Packard Enterprise Company reports the following information on its cash-flow hedges (derivatives) in comprehensive income (net income plus other comprehensive income) in its 2020 10-K report:

($ millions)	Total
Net earnings	$(322)
Change in net unrealized gains/(losses) on available-for-sale securities	(5)
Change in net unrealized gains/(losses) on cash flow hedges	(61)
Change in unrealized components of defined benefit pension plans	(99)
Change in cumulative translation adjustment	(12)
Benefit for income taxes	8
Comprehensive income	$(491)

a. Identify and describe the usual applications for derivatives.

b. How are derivatives and their related assets (and/or liabilities) reported on the balance sheet?

c. By what amount has the unrealized gain or loss on the HPE derivatives affected its current income? What are the analysis implications?

PROBLEMS

LO12-1, 2, 3

Metlife Inc.
NYSE :: MET

Homework MBC

P12-59. Analyzing and Interpreting Available-for-Sale Securities Disclosures

Following is a portion of the investments Note 8 from MetLife Inc.'s 2020 10-K report. Investment earnings are a crucial component of the financial performance of insurance companies such as MetLife, and investments comprise a large part of its assets. MetLife accounts for its bond investments as available-for-sale securities.

Fixed Maturity Securities Available-for-Sale

The following tables present the fixed maturity securities AFS by sector.

(in millions)	December 31, 2020 Amortized Cost	ACL	Gross Unrealized Gains	Gross Unrealized Losses	Estimated Fair Value
U.S. corporate	$ 79,788	$(44)	$13,924	$ 252	$ 93,416
Foreign government	63,243	(21)	8,883	406	71,699
Foreign corporate	60,995	(16)	8,897	468	69,408
U.S. government and agency	39,094	—	8,095	89	47,100
RMBS	28,415	—	2,062	42	30,435
ABS	16,963	—	231	75	17,119
Municipals	10,982	—	2,746	6	13,722
CMBS	11,331	—	681	102	11,910
Total fixed maturity securities AFS	$310,811	$(81)	$45,519	$1,440	$354,809

(in millions)	December 31, 2019 Amortized Cost	Gross Unrealized Gains	Gross Unrealized Temporary Losses	Gross Unrealized OTTI Losses	Estimated Fair Value
U.S. corporate	$ 79,115	$ 8,943	$ 305	$—	$ 87,753
Foreign government	58,840	8,710	321	—	67,229
Foreign corporate	59,342	5,540	717	—	64,165
U.S. government and agency	37,586	4,604	106	—	42,084
RMBS	27,051	1,535	72	(33)	28,547
ABS	14,547	83	88	—	14,542
Municipals	11,081	2,001	29	—	13,053
CMBS	10,093	396	42	—	10,447
Total fixed maturity securities AFS	$297,655	$31,812	$1,680	$(33)	$327,820

MetLife abbreviates allowance for credit loss as "ACL" and other than temporary impairment as "OTTI."

REQUIRED

a. At what amount does MetLife report its bond investments on its balance sheets for 2020 and 2019?

b. What are its net unrealized gains (losses) for 2020 and 2019? By what amount did these unrealized gains (losses) affect its reported income?

c. What is the difference between *realized* and *unrealized* gains and losses? Are realized gains and losses treated differently in the income statement than unrealized gains and losses? MetLife's 2020 pre-tax income was $6,927 million. What is the maximum amount MetLife could have increased pre-tax income by selling available-for-sale securities on the last day of 2020?

d. Many analysts compute a *mark-to-market investment return* as follows: Net investment income + Realized gains and losses + Change in unrealized gains and losses. Do you think that this metric provides insights into the performance of MetLife's investment portfolio beyond that which is included in GAAP income statements? Explain.

P12-60.[B] Preparing the Consolidated Balance Sheet LO12-5, 7

Homework MBC

On January 1, Gem Company purchased for $490,000 cash a 70% stock interest in Alpine, Inc., which then had common stock of $525,000 and retained earnings of $175,000. Balance sheets of the two companies immediately after the acquisition were as follows:

	Gem	Alpine
Current assets	$ 322,500	$200,000
Stock investment—Controlling (Alpine)	490,000	—
Plant and equipment (net)	331,250	575,000
Total assets	$1,143,750	$775,000
Liabilities	$ 62,500	$ 75,000
Common stock	875,000	525,000
Retained earnings	206,250	175,000
Total liabilities and stockholders' equity	$1,143,750	$775,000

At the time of Gem's investment, the fair values of Alpine's assets and liabilities were equal to their book values.

REQUIRED

Prepare the consolidated balance sheet on the acquisition date; include a column for consolidating adjustments (see **Exhibit 12.7** for guidance).

LO12-1, 2, 3, 4

Homework MBC

P12-61. Analyzing and Reporting Debt Investment Performance

Columbia Company began operations in the current year and by year-end (December 31) had made six bond investments. Year-end information on these bond investments follows.

Company	Face Value	Cost or Amortized Cost	Year-End Fair Value	Classification
Ling, Inc.	$150,000	$153,600	$157,950	Trading
Wren, Inc.	375,000	393,750	405,000	Trading
Olanamic, Inc.	300,000	295,500	298,500	Available for sale
Fossil, Inc.	225,000	231,000	240,000	Available for sale
Meander, Inc.	150,000	151,800	153,600	Held to maturity
Resin, Inc.	210,000	204,000	205,500	Held to maturity

REQUIRED

a. At what total amount will the trading bond investments be reported in the December 31 balance sheet?

b. At what total amount will the available-for-sale bond investments be reported in the December 31 balance sheet?

c. At what total amount will the held-to-maturity bond investments be reported in the December 31 balance sheet?

d. What total amount of unrealized holding gains or unrealized holding losses related to bond investments will appear in the annual income statement?

e. What total amount of unrealized holding gains or unrealized holding losses related to bond investments will appear in the stockholders' equity section of the December 31 balance sheet?

LO12-1, 4, 5, 6, 7

Deere & Company
NYSE :: DE

P12-62.[A, B] Analyzing and Interpreting Disclosures on Consolidations

Deere & Company consists of two business units: the equipment operations (parent corporation) and a wholly owned finance subsidiary. These two units are consolidated in Deere's fiscal 2020 10-K report (for the year ended January 31, 2021). Following is a supplemental disclosure that Deere includes in its 10-K report that shows the separate balance sheets of the parent and its subsidiary, as well as consolidating adjustments and the consolidated balance sheet presented to shareholders. This supplemental disclosure is not mandated under GAAP but is voluntarily reported by Deere as useful information for investors and creditors.

Deere & Company
January31, 2021
Supplemental Consolidating Data•

(in millions)	Equipment Operations	Financial Services	Eliminations	Consolidated
Assets				
Cash and cash equivalents	$ 6,074	$ 888		$ 6,962
Marketable securities	8	659		667
Receivables from unconsolidated affiliates	5,151		$ (5,123)	28
Trade accounts and notes receivable—net	900	5,341	(1,204)	5,037
Financing receivables—net	103	29,335		29,438
Financing receivables securitized—net	18	3,913		3,931
Other receivables	1,010	151	(20)	1,141
Equipment on operating leases—net		7,030		7,030
Inventories	5,956			5,956
Property and equipment—net	5,703	38		5,741
Investments in unconsolidated affiliates	157	21		178
Investment in financial services	5,345		(5,345)	—
Goodwill	3,194			3,194
Other intangible assets—net	1,342			1,342
Retirement benefits	903	60	(57)	906
Deferred income taxes	1,797	51	(292)	1,556
Other assets	1,485	891	(3)	2,373
Total assets	$39,146	$48,378	$(12,044)	$75,480

continued

continued from previous page

Deere & Company
January31, 2021
Supplemental Consolidating Data•

(in millions)	Equipment Operations	Financial Services	Eliminations	Consolidated
Liabilities and stockholders' equity				
Liabilities				
Short-term borrowings	$ 394	$ 8,830		$ 9,224
Short-term securitization borrowings	17	3,952		3,969
Payables to unconsolidated affiliates	119	5,123	$ (5,123)	119
Accounts payable and accrued expenses . . .	8,672	1,959	(1,227)	9,404
Deferred income taxes	394	430	(292)	532
Long-term borrowings.	10,139	22,633		32,772
Retirement benefits and other liabilities	5,325	106	(57)	5,374
Total liabilities	25,060	43,033	(6,699)	61,394
Commitments and contingencies				
Redeemable noncontrolling interest				
Stockholders' equity				
Deere stockholders' equity	14,083	5,345	(5,345)	14,083
Non-controlling interests.	3			3
Adjusted total stockholders' equity	14,086	5,345	(5,345)	14,086
Total liabilities and stockholders' equity	$39,146	$48,378	$(12,044)	$75,480

* presentation adjusted slightly by authors for simplicity

REQUIRED

a. Does each individual company (unit) maintain its own financial statements? Explain. Why does GAAP require consolidation instead of providing the financial statements of individual companies (units)?s

b. What is the balance of Investments in Financial Services as of January 31, 2021, on the parent's balance sheet (Equipment Operations)? What is the equity balance of the financial services subsidiary to which this relates as of January 31, 2021? Do you see a relationship? Will this relationship always exist?

c. Refer to your answer for *a*. How does the equity method of accounting for the investment in the subsidiary company obscure the actual financial condition of the parent company that is revealed in the consolidated financial statements?

d. Refer to the Consolidating Adjustments column reported—it is used to prepare the consolidated balance sheet. Generally, what do these adjustments accomplish?

e. Compare the consolidated balance of stockholders' equity with the stockholders' equity of the parent company (Equipment Operations). Will the relation that is evident always hold? Explain.

f. Recall that the parent company uses the equity method of accounting for its investment in the subsidiary, and that this account is eliminated in the consolidation process. What is the relation between consolidated net income and the net income of the parent company? Explain.

g. What do you believe is the implication for the consolidated balance sheet if the fair value of the Financial Services subsidiary is greater than the book value of its stockholders' equity?

CASES AND PROJECTS

C12-63. Effect of Investment Accounting on Performance Ratios

LO12-1, 3

Homework MBC — Apple Inc. NASDAQ :: AAPL

Apple Inc., is one of the most successful enterprises of all time. Its computers, tablets, phones, and watches are all highly desired by consumers, and the company's product innovations keep arriving at a steady pace. Apple's financial success can also be attributed to its supply chain management and to its management of its income taxes. Apple has for many years maintained high balances of cash and marketable securities. This was historically partially due to prior tax laws which made it costly to pay dividends from foreign subsidiaries back to the U.S. parent. It is also partially due to other reasons, perhaps that the company desires to maintain sufficient liquidity. In any case, Apple's balance sheet reports substantial investments in marketable securities, as shown in the following:

($ millions)	September 26, 2020	September 28, 2019
Total assets.	$323,888	$338,516
Marketable securities	153,814	157,054
Net operating assets (operating assets – operating liabilities)	23,961	41,481

The following information is taken from the company's fiscal 2020 income statement and disclosure notes:

($ millions)	Year Ended September 26, 2020
Operating income	$66,288
Other income/(expenses), net*.	803
Income before provision for income tax	67,091
Provision for income tax	(9,680)
Net income	$57,411

*Apple reported that this amount included interest expense of $2,873 million, interest and dividend income of $3,763, and other income/(expense), net of $(87).

Finally, the following table is taken from Note 2 of Apple's 2020 10-K annual report. The reported numbers are slightly higher than those reported from Apple's balance sheet above because some AFS securities are classified as cash equivalents on the balance sheet, rather than marketable securities.

Fixed-income (debt) investments—AFS:

($ millions)	Adjusted Cost	Unrealized Gains	Unrealized Losses	Fair Value
2020	$189,431	$2,784	$(385)	$191,830
2019	204,977	1,202	(281)	205,898

REQUIRED

a. Calculate Apple's return on assets for fiscal year 2020. Assume an income tax rate of 25%.

b. Calculate Apple's RNOA for 2020. (Refer to Appendix A of Chapter 5 for further discussion.) What factors contribute to this RNOA?

c. What method does Apple use to account for its fixed-income investments? What value is included in its 2020 balance sheet?

d. From its balance sheet, it would appear that a significant portion of Apple's resources are devoted to investing in financial instruments. Calculate the after-tax return to Apple's financial assets. Apple's Statement of Other Comprehensive Income reports an after-tax unrealized holding gain on AFS investments equal to $1,202 million? What would have been Apple's return to financial investments if it had used the trading security method for these investments?

LO12-1, 3, 4 **C12-64. Analyzing Financial Statement Effects of Passive and Equity Investments (FSET)**

Homework MBC

On January 2, 2022, Magee, Inc., purchased, as a stock investment, 28,000 shares of Dye, Inc.'s common stock for $21 per share, including commissions and taxes. On December 31, 2022, Dye announced a net income of $392,000 for the year and declared a dividend of 80 cents per share, payable January 15, 2023, to stockholders of record on January 5, 2023. At December 31, 2022, the market value of Dye's stock was $18 per share. Magee received its dividend on January 18, 2023.

REQUIRED

a. Assume that the stock acquired by Magee represents 10% of Dye's voting stock and is classified in the trading category. Prepare all entries appropriate for this investment, beginning with the purchase on January 2, 2022, and ending with the receipt of the dividend on January 18, 2023, using the financial statement effects template.

b. Assume that the stock acquired by Magee represents 40% of Dye's voting stock. Prepare all entries appropriate for this investment, beginning with the purchase on January 2, 2019, and ending with the receipt of the dividend on January 18, 2023, using the financial statement effects template.

LO12-1, 3, 4 **C12-65. Analyzing Financial Statement Effects of Passive and Equity Investments**

Homework MBC

Using the information from C12-64, answer the following.

For the transactions described in parts *a* and *b*, (i.) prepare journal entries and (ii.) post the journal entries to their respective T-accounts.

C12-66. Assessing Management Interpretation of Consolidated Financial Statements LO12-1, 2, 3, 4, 5

Demski, Inc., manufactures heating and cooling systems. It has a 75% interest in Asare Company, which manufactures thermostats, switches, and other controls for heating and cooling products. It also has a 100% interest in Demski Finance Company, created by the parent company to finance sales of its products to contractors and other consumers. The parent company's only other investment is a 25% interest in the common stock of Knechel, Inc., which produces certain circuits used by Demski, Inc. A condensed consolidated balance sheet of the entity for the current year follows.

DEMSKI, INC., AND SUBSIDIARIES
Consolidated Balance Sheet
December 31, 2019

Assets		
Current assets		$13,510,000
Stock investment—Influential (Knechel)		1,820,000
Other assets		49,980,000
Excess of cost over equity acquired in net assets of Asare Company		1,190,000
Total assets		$66,500,000
Liabilities and shareholders' equity		
Current liabilities		$ 7,210,000
Long-term liabilities		9,940,000
Shareholders' equity		
Common stock	$35,000,000	
Retained earnings	11,690,000	
Demski, Inc., shareholders' equity	46,690,000	
Noncontrolling interests	2,660,000	
Total shareholders' equity		49,350,000
Total liabilities and shareholders' equity		$66,500,000

This balance sheet, along with other financial statements, was furnished to shareholders before their annual meeting, and all shareholders were invited to submit questions to be answered at the meeting. As chief financial officer of Demski, you have been appointed to respond to the questions at the meeting.

REQUIRED

Answer the following shareholder questions.

a. What is meant by *consolidated* financial statements?

b. Why is the investment in Knechel shown on the consolidated balance sheet, but the investments in Asare and Demski Finance are omitted?

c. Explain the meaning of the asset Excess of Cost over Equity Acquired in Net Assets of Asare Company.

d. What is meant by *noncontrolling interest*, and to what company is this account related?

C12-67. Understanding Intercorporate Investments, Accounting Practices, and Managerial Ethics LO12-1, 2, 3, 4

Gayle Sayres, controller of Nexgen, Inc., has asked her Deputy Controller, Doug Stevens, for suggestions as to how the company can improve its reported financial performance for the year. The company is in the last quarter of the year, and projections to the end of the year show the company will have a net loss of about $320,000 before tax.

"My suggestion," said Stevens, "is that we sell 800 of the 160,000 common shares of Heflin Company that we own. The 160,000 shares give us a 20% ownership of Heflin, and we have been using the equity method to account for this investment. We have owned this stock a long time and the current market value of the 160,000 shares is about $600,000 above our book value for the stock."

"That sale will only generate a gain of about $3,000," replied Sayres.

"The rest of the story," continued Stevens, "is that once we sell the 800 shares, we will own less than 20% of Heflin. We can then reclassify the remaining 159,200 shares from the influential category to the passive equity/fair value category. Then we value the stocks at their current fair value, include the rest of the $600,000 gain in this year's income statement, and finish the year with a healthy net income."

"But," responded Sayres, "we aren't going to sell all the Heflin stock; 800 shares maybe, but certainly not any more. We own that stock because they are a long-term supplier of ours. Indeed, we even have representation on their board of directors. The 159,200 shares do not belong in the passive category."

Stevens rolled his eyes and continued, "The classification of an investment as passive or not depends on management's intent. This year-end we claim it was our intent not to exert influence over Heflin. Next year we change our minds and take the stock out of the trading category. Generally accepted accounting principles can't legislate management intent, nor can our outside auditors read our minds. Besides, why shouldn't we take advantage of the flexibility in GAAP to avoid reporting a net loss for this year?"

REQUIRED

a. Should generally accepted accounting principles permit management's intent to influence accounting classifications and measurements?

b. Is it ethical for Gayle Sayres to implement the recommendation of Doug Stevens?

SOLUTIONS TO REVIEW PROBLEMS

Review 12-1

1. P 2. P 3. C 4. SI 5. P

Review 12-2

a. Level 3 *b.* Level 1 *c.* Level 2 *d.* Level 2 *e.* Level 3 *f.* Level 1

Review 12-3

SOLUTION TO PART 1

a.

Transaction	Balance Sheet: Cash Asset	+ Noncash Assets	= Liabilities	+ Contrib. Capital	+ Earned Capital	Income Statement: Revenues	− Expenses	= Net Income
ANALYZE (1) Purchased 500 Pincus bonds.	−470,000 Cash	+470,000 Investments (AFS)						
ANALYZE (2) Receive $15,000 interest payment from Pincus bonds.	+15,000 Cash				+15,000 Retained Earnings	+15,000 Interest Income		+15,000
ANALYZE (3) June 30 fair value of Pincus bonds is $460,000.		−10,000 Investments (AFS)			−10,000 Unrealized Loss (AOCI)			
ANALYZE (4) On July 31, sell all 500 Pincus bonds for $450,000.	+450,000 Cash	−460,000 Investments (AFS)			+10,000 Unrealized Loss (AOCI) −20,000 Retained Earnings		+20,000 Realized Loss	−20,000

b.

JOURNALIZE

		Dr.	Cr.
(1)	Investment in Pincus bonds (+A)	470,000	
	Cash (−A)		470,000

POST

+ Investment in Pincus (A) −		+ Cash (A) −	
(1) 470,000			470,000 (1)

JOURNALIZE

		Dr.	Cr.
(2)	Cash (+A)	15,000	
	Interest income (+R, +SE)		15,000

POST

+ Cash (A) −		− Interest Income (R) +	
(2) 15,000	470,000 (1)		15,000 (2)

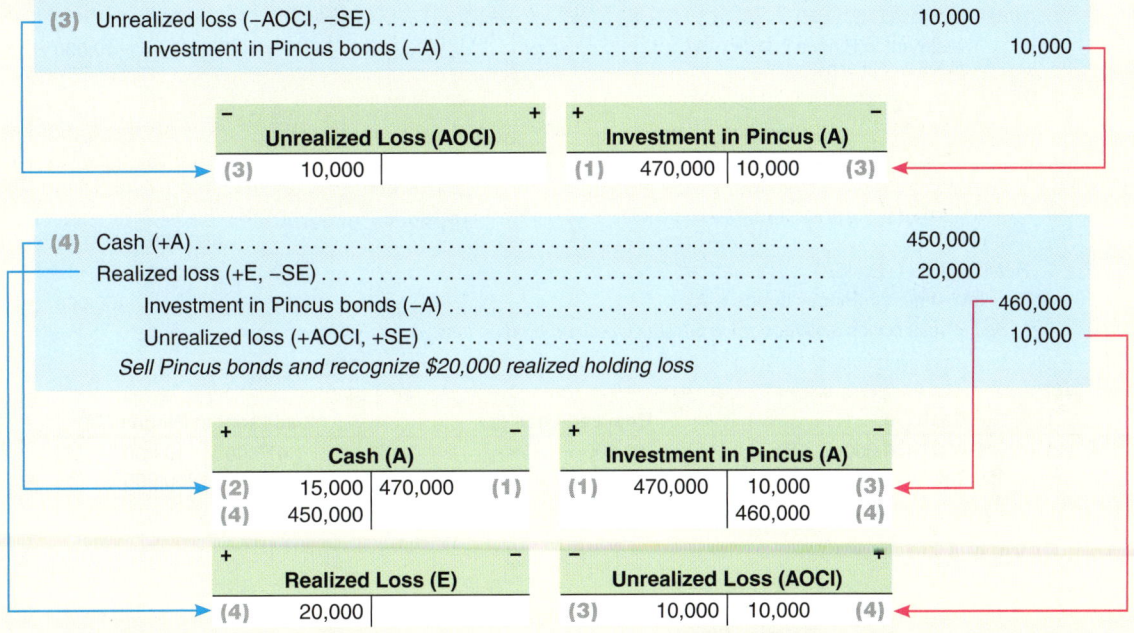

		Debit	Credit
(3)	Unrealized loss (−AOCI, −SE)	10,000	
	Investment in Pincus bonds (−A)		10,000

− Unrealized Loss (AOCI) +				+ Investment in Pincus (A) −			
(3)	10,000			(1)	470,000	10,000	(3)

		Debit	Credit
(4)	Cash (+A)	450,000	
	Realized loss (+E, −SE)	20,000	
	Investment in Pincus bonds (−A)		460,000
	Unrealized loss (+AOCI, +SE)		10,000
	Sell Pincus bonds and recognize $20,000 realized holding loss		

+ Cash (A) −				+ Investment in Pincus (A) −			
(2)	15,000	470,000	(1)	(1)	470,000	10,000	(3)
(4)	450,000					460,000	(4)

+ Realized Loss (E) −				− Unrealized Loss (AOCI) +			
(4)	20,000			(3)	10,000	10,000	(4)

SOLUTION TO PART 2

a.

ANALYZE

Transaction	Balance Sheet: Cash Asset	+ Noncash Assets	=	Liabilities	+ Contrib. Capital	+ Earned Capital	*Income Statement: Revenues*	− *Expenses*	=	*Net Income*
(1) Purchased 500 Pincus bonds.	−470,000 Cash	+470,000 Investments (Trading)	=					−	=	
(2) Receive $15,000 interest payment from Pincus bonds.	+15,000 Cash		=			+15,000 Retained Earnings	+15,000 Interest Income	−	=	+15,000
(3) June 30 fair value of Pincus bonds is $460,000.		−10,000 Investments (Trading)	=			−10,000 Retained Earnings		− +10,000 Unrealized Loss	=	−10,000
(4) On July 31, sell all 500 King Co. bonds for $450,000.	+450,000 Cash	−460,000 Investments (Trading)	=			−10,000 Retained Earnings		− +10,000 Realized Loss	=	−10,000

b.

JOURNALIZE POST

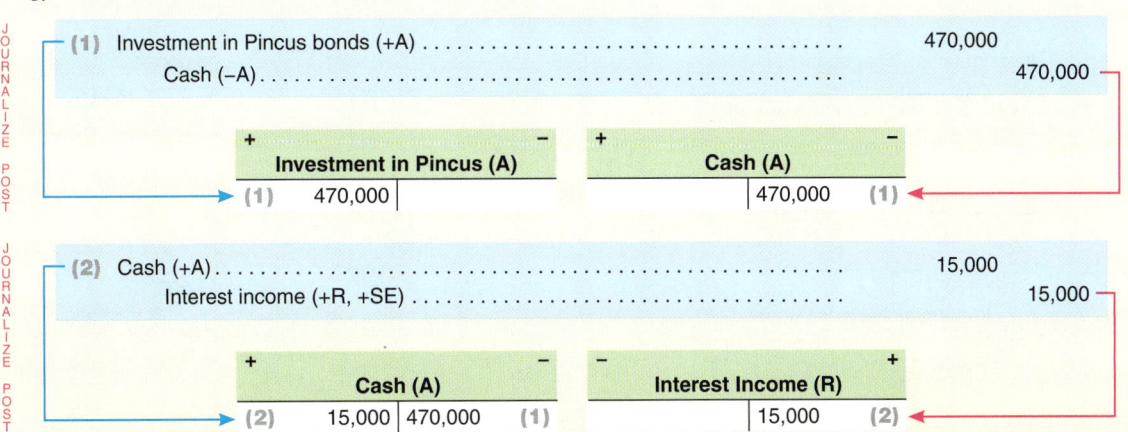

		Debit	Credit
(1)	Investment in Pincus bonds (+A)	470,000	
	Cash (−A)		470,000

+ Investment in Pincus (A) −				+ Cash (A) −			
(1)	470,000					470,000	(1)

JOURNALIZE POST

		Debit	Credit
(2)	Cash (+A)	15,000	
	Interest income (+R, +SE)		15,000

+ Cash (A) −				− Interest Income (R) +			
(2)	15,000	470,000	(1)			15,000	(2)

JOURNALIZE / POST

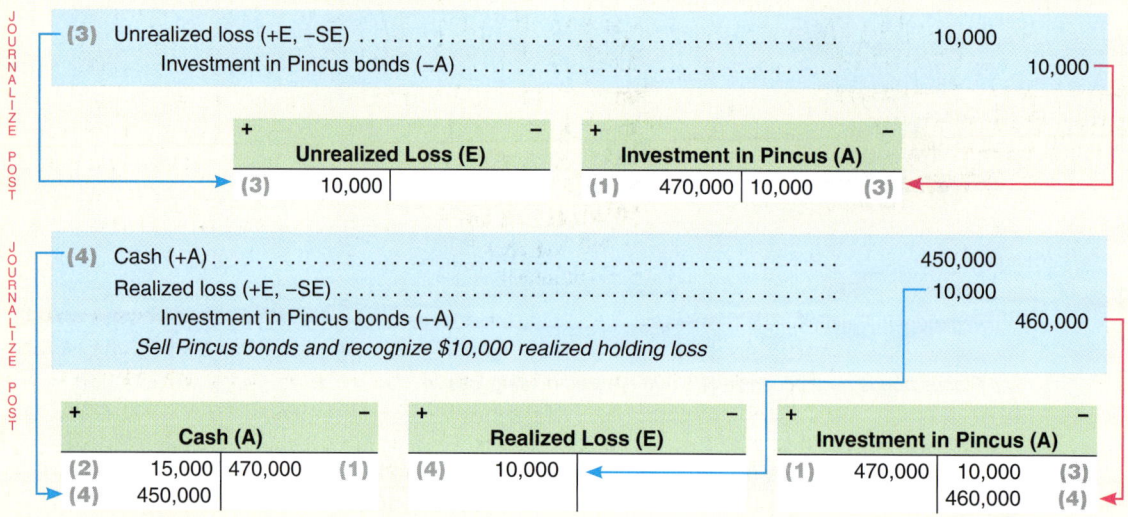

		Dr.	Cr.
(3)	Unrealized loss (+E, −SE)	10,000	
	Investment in Pincus bonds (−A)		10,000

Unrealized Loss (E)

+	−
(3) 10,000	

Investment in Pincus (A)

+	−
(1) 470,000	10,000 (3)

JOURNALIZE / POST

		Dr.	Cr.
(4)	Cash (+A)	450,000	
	Realized loss (+E, −SE)	10,000	
	Investment in Pincus bonds (−A)		460,000
	Sell Pincus bonds and recognize $10,000 realized holding loss		

Cash (A)

+	−
(2) 15,000	470,000 (1)
(4) 450,000	

Realized Loss (E)

+	−
(4) 10,000	

Investment in Pincus (A)

+	−
(1) 470,000	10,000 (3)
	460,000 (4)

Review 12-4

a.

	Balance Sheet									Income Statement				
Transaction	Cash Asset	+	Noncash Assets	=	Liabilities	+	Contrib. Capital	+	Earned Capital	*Revenues*	−	*Expenses*	=	*Net Income*
(1) Purchased 5,000 Hribar shares at $10 cash per share. These shares reflect 30% ownership of Hribar.	−50,000 Cash		+50,000 Investment in Hribar	=							−		=	
(2) Received a $2 per share on cash dividend on Hribar stock.	+10,000 Cash		−10,000 Investment in Hribar	=							−		=	
(3) Made an adjustment to reflect $100,000 income reported by Hribar.			+30,000 Investment in Hribar	=					+30,000 Retained Earnings	+30,000 Investment Income	−		=	+30,000
(4) Sold all 5,000 Hribar shares for $90,000.	+90,000 Cash		−70,000 Investment in Hribar	=					+20,000 Retained Earnings	+20,000 Gain on Sale	−		=	+20,000

b.

JOURNALIZE / POST

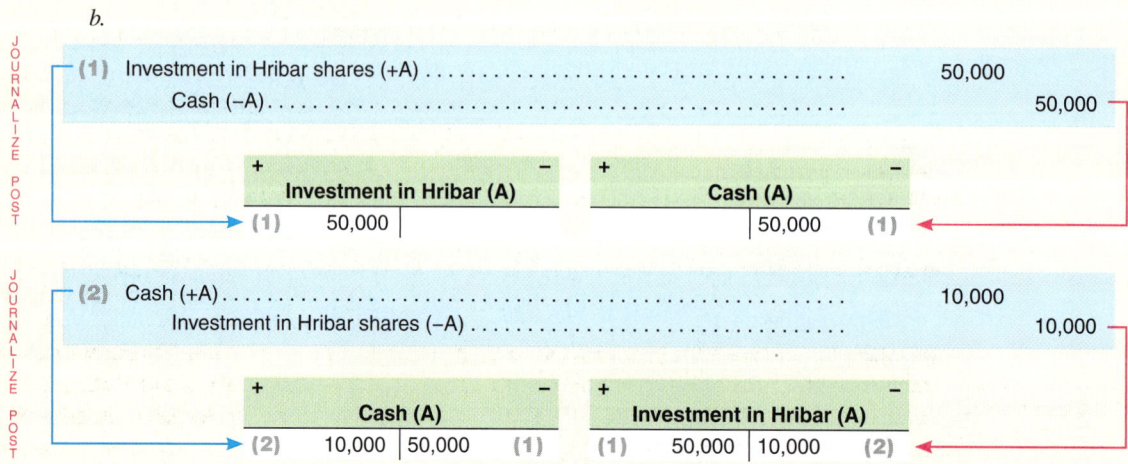

		Dr.	Cr.
(1)	Investment in Hribar shares (+A)	50,000	
	Cash (−A)		50,000

Investment in Hribar (A)

+	−
(1) 50,000	

Cash (A)

+	−
	50,000 (1)

JOURNALIZE / POST

		Dr.	Cr.
(2)	Cash (+A)	10,000	
	Investment in Hribar shares (−A)		10,000

Cash (A)

+	−
(2) 10,000	50,000 (1)

Investment in Hribar (A)

+	−
(1) 50,000	10,000 (2)

JOURNALIZE / POST

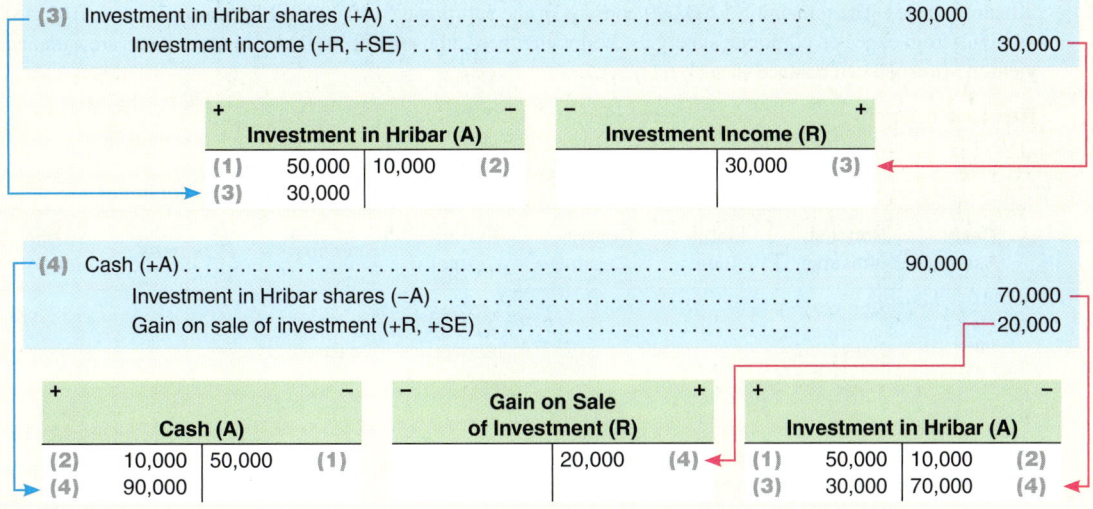

(3) Investment in Hribar shares (+A)	30,000	
Investment income (+R, +SE)		30,000

+ Investment in Hribar (A) −			
(1)	50,000	10,000	(2)
(3)	30,000		

− Investment Income (R) +			
		30,000	(3)

JOURNALIZE / POST

(4) Cash (+A)	90,000	
Investment in Hribar shares (−A)		70,000
Gain on sale of investment (+R, +SE)		20,000

+ Cash (A) −			
(2)	10,000	50,000	(1)
(4)	90,000		

− Gain on Sale of Investment (R) +			
		20,000	(4)

+ Investment in Hribar (A) −			
(1)	50,000	10,000	(2)
(3)	30,000	70,000	(4)

Review 12-5

a.

ANALYZE

Transaction	Balance Sheet: Cash Asset	+ Noncash Assets	= Liabilities	+ Contrib. Capital	+ Earned Capital	Income Statement: Revenues	− Expenses	= Net Income
(1) Consolidation adjustment for Bradshaw.		+100,000 PPE, net +100,000 Goodwill −600,000 Investment in Dukes		−200,000 Dukes Common Stock	−200,000 Dukes Retained Earnings		−	=

b.

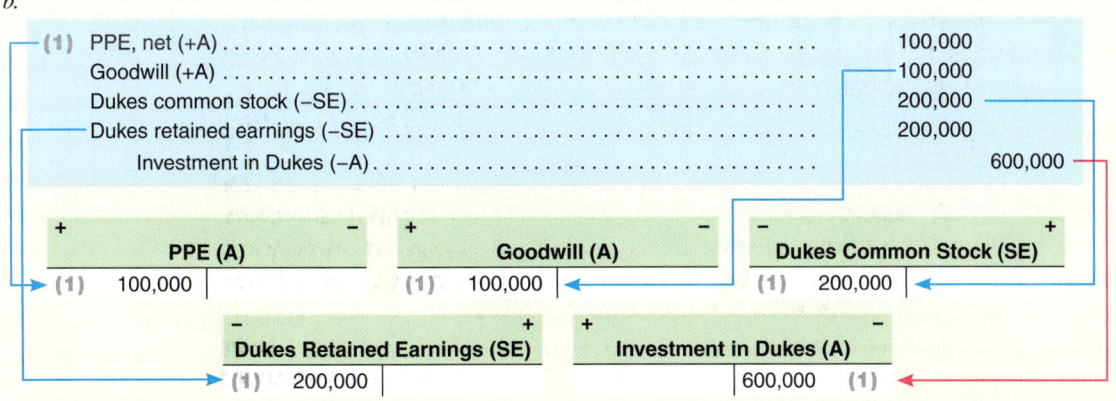

(1) PPE, net (+A)	100,000	
Goodwill (+A)	100,000	
Dukes common stock (−SE)	200,000	
Dukes retained earnings (−SE)	200,000	
Investment in Dukes (−A)		600,000

+ PPE (A) −			
(1)	100,000		

+ Goodwill (A) −			
(1)	100,000		

− Dukes Common Stock (SE) +			
(1)	200,000		

− Dukes Retained Earnings (SE) +			
(1)	200,000		

+ Investment in Dukes (A) −			
		600,000	(1)

c.

	Bradshaw (Parent)	Dukes (Subsidiary)	Consolidating Adjustments	Consolidated
Current assets	$1,000,000	$100,000		$1,100,000
Investment in Dukes	600,000	—	$(600,000)	
PPE, net	3,000,000	400,000	100,000	3,500,000
Goodwill	—	—	100,000	100,000
Total assets	$4,600,000	$500,000		$4,700,000
Liabilities	$1,000,000	$100,000		$1,100,000
Contributed capital	2,000,000	200,000	(200,000)	2,000,000
Retained earnings	1,600,000	200,000	(200,000)	1,600,000
Total liabilities and equity	$4,600,000	$500,000		$4,700,000

Notes: The $600,000 investment account is eliminated with the $400,000 book value of Dukes' equity to which it mainly relates. The remaining $200,000 consists of the additional $100,000 in PPE assets and the $100,000 in goodwill from expected corporate synergies. Following these adjustments, the balance sheet items are summed to yield the consolidated balance sheet.

Review 12-6

a.

ANALYZE

	Balance Sheet					Income Statement		
Transaction	Cash Asset +	Noncash Assets =	Liabilities +	Contrib. Capital +	Earned Capital	Revenues –	Expenses =	Net Income
		+22,295 Investment in Maxwell Co. =			+22,295 Retained Earnings	+22,295 Investment Income –	=	+22,295

b.

Investment in Maxwell Company (+A)	22,295	
Investment Income (+R, +SE)		22,295
$22,295 = 35% × ($65,000 – ($6,000/20) – ($5,000/5))		

Review 12-7

a.

	Harper Company	Maxwell Company	Consolidating Adjustments	Consolidated
Current assets	$ 680,000	$ 48,000		$ 728,000
Investment in Maxwell	200,000	—	$(200,000)	—
Plant assets	1,200,000	164,000	6,000	1,370,000
Patent	—0	—	5,000	5,000
Goodwill	—	—	13,000	13,000
Total assets.	$2,080,000	$212,000		$2,116,000
Liabilities.	$280,000	$ 36,000	$ —	$316,000
Contributed capital	1,400,000	160,000	(160,000)	1,400,000
Retained earnings	400,000	16,000	(16,000)	400,000
Total liabilities and equity	$2,080,000	$212,000		$2,116,000

b.

Maxwell contributed capital (–SE)	160,000	
Maxwell retained earnings (–SE)	16,000	
Plant assets (+A)	6,000	
Patent (+A).	5,000	
Goodwill (+A)	13,000	
Investment in Maxwell (–A)		200,000

c.

	Balance Sheet					Income Statement		
Transaction	Cash Asset +	Noncash Assets =	Liabilities +	Contrib. Capital +	Earned Capital	Revenues –	Expenses =	Net Income
		+6,000 Plant Assets +5,000 Patent +13,000 Goodwill –200,000 Investment in Maxwell =		–160,000 Maxwell Contrib. Capital	–16,000 Maxwell Retained Earnings	–	=	

Review 12-8

a. The company executes hedging contracts in order to counter market risks. Interest rate swaps are designed to mitigate fluctuations in earnings and cash flows that may result from interest rate volatility. For example, the company states that it "utilizes forward-starting interest rate swaps to mitigate the risk of variability in interest rate for future debt issuances." Foreign currency contracts are designed to mitigate the impact on net income of changes in foreign currency exchange rates. For example, the company states that it hedges "portions of its foreign currency purchases, assets and liabilities arising in the normal course of business…". Commodity contracts are designed to mitigate risks of price changes of materials purchases. The company states that it "is exposed to price volatility related to raw materials used in production, such as essential oils, resins, pulp, tropical oils, tallow, corn, poultry and soybeans."

b. The aim of the company in executing a derivate contract is to offset the gain or loss for the asset or liability to which they relate. This means that the company would be sheltered from losses, but it also would not realize any gains on the held asset or liability. In the table disclosure, it is evident that the gain or loss on a hedged items was completely offset by a corresponding loss or gain of the derivative instrument. The net result is that the income statement reflected no net gain or loss related to the risks outlined in part a.

Appendix A

Compound Interest and the Time-Value of Money

Suppose you were lucky enough to hold a winning lottery ticket that allowed you to choose when you would receive your prize. Most of us would answer: Now! But let's say this ticket gave you the option of receiving \$20,000 now, or \$24,000 two years from now. Which would you choose?

Of course, \$24,000 is better than \$20,000. But the choice is not that simple. If you take the \$20,000 today, you can buy a new car, pay next semester's tuition, or invest the money in the stock market. If you wait, you'll receive the larger prize, but you may have to take the bus for the next two years, postpone your college studies, or pass up on a great investment opportunity.

This is the essence of what is called the **time-value of money**. A dollar received today is worth more than a dollar received two years in the future. Having cash in our possession gives us the opportunity to spend or invest that cash today. Cash received in the future cannot be spent or invested today.[1]

The easiest way to illustrate the time-value of money is to assume that we collect the \$20,000 cash prize today and invest it in a money-market account that guarantees a 10% return on our investment. In one year, the investment would be worth \$22,000—which is the original \$20,000 investment plus \$2,000 interest (\$20,000 × 10%). At the end of two years, the investment would be worth \$24,200 [= \$22,000 + (\$22,000 × 10%) = \$22,000 × 1.10].

In the second year, the investment earns a return of \$2,200, which is \$22,000 × 10%. The interest earned in the second year is greater than the interest earned in year one because the interest earned in the first year earns interest in year two. This interest earned on interest is called **compound interest**. As interest accumulates on an investment, both the original investment and the accumulated interest will earn a return in subsequent periods. Interest calculated on the original investment, but not on interest accrued in prior periods, is called **simple interest**.

This Appendix explains and illustrates the concepts of time-value of money and compound interest. It is divided into three sections. The first two address future value concepts and present value concepts, respectively. In the last section, we illustrate the use of spreadsheet software to compute present and future values.

[1] The time-value of money is primarily due to lost opportunities. However, the risk associated with some future cash flows will influence our assessment of their time-value. That is, there may be some uncertainty associated with a future payment. For instance, in our lottery ticket example, there may be a possibility that the payer could default on the \$24,000 payment. Risk is reflected in time-value calculations by using higher interest rates for risky cash flows.

FUTURE VALUE CONCEPTS

As illustrated above, $20,000 invested today to earn a return of 10% per year will accumulate interest and be worth $24,200 in two years. The $24,200 is referred to as the *future value* of $20,000 because it represents what $20,000 invested today at 10% would be worth two years in the future. The **future value** of any amount is the amount that an investment is worth at a given future date if invested at a given rate of compound interest.

Assume that we allow our $20,000 investment to continue to earn interest for three years. The interest will continue to compound and the future value will continue to grow. This is illustrated in **Exhibit A.1**.

EXHIBIT A.1 Future Value of $20,000

Initial investment	$20,000
Interest earned in year 1 (initial investment × 10%)	2,000
Investment plus accumulated interest (future value) in 1 year	22,000
Interest earned in year 2 (year 1 amount × 10%)	2,200
Investment plus accumulated interest (future value) in 2 years	24,200
Interest earned in year 3 (year 2 amount × 10%)	2,420
Investment plus accumulated interest (future value) in 3 years	$26,620

As **Exhibit A.1** illustrates, the future value of $20,000 invested for three years at 10% per year is $26,620. This can be calculated as $26,620 = $20,000 × 1.10 × 1.10 × 1.10 = $20,000 × $(1.10)^3$. Similarly, if the interest rate is 8%, the future value is $25,194 = $20,000 × $(1.08)^3$. That is, to determine the future value of an amount n periods in the future, we multiply the present value by one plus the interest rate, raised to the nth power:

$$\textbf{Future Value} = \textbf{Present Value} \times (1 + \textbf{interest rate})^n$$

The future value of any amount depends on two factors: time and rate. That is, how many periods (e.g., years or months) into the future do we want to project the future value, and what rate of return (or interest rate) do we use? There are two simple methods that we can use to obtain future values. The first method uses tables presented at the end of this Appendix. **Table A.1** presents the future value of a single amount. To use the table, move across the top of the table to choose the appropriate interest rate, and then move down the column to choose the number of periods in the future. **Table A.1** shows that future value increases as the number of periods and as the interest rate increase.

For example, if we move across the top to the 10% column and then down to period 3, **Table A.1** provides a value of 1.33100. This is the future value of $1 in three periods at 10% interest per period and is called the **future value factor**. If we want to calculate the future value of $20,000, we multiply the *future value factor* from **Table A.1** by $20,000:

Initial Amount	×	Future Value Factor	=	Future Value
$20,000	×	**1.33100**	=	**$26,620**

The future value can also be calculated using a financial calculator. Financial calculators require four inputs to calculate a fifth value, which is the solution. We illustrate the use of a calculator with the following graphic:

Calculator

N	I/Yr	PV	PMT	FV
3	10	20,000	0	26,620

On the financial calculator, N is the number of periods (3), I/Yr is the interest rate per period (10), PV is the current, or present, value ($20,000), PMT refers to a periodic payment (0 in our example), and FV is the future value. Because we are calculating the future value in this illustration, that value is highlighted in red as the solution.[2]

Whether we use the tables at the end of the Appendix or a financial calculator, it is important to recognize that these computations are based on an interest rate *per period*. Most interest rates are stated on an annual, or *per year*, basis. However, for compound interest calculations, a period need not be equal to a year.

[2] Actually, most calculators return a solution of −26,620. The calculator interprets the PV as an investment (cash out) and FV as the return (cash in). So, if PV is entered as a positive amount, then FV will come back negative, and vice versa.

Therefore, we must always be careful to adjust our interest rate *per year* to the appropriate interest rate *per period* and use the corresponding number of time periods in our calculations.

To illustrate, assume that our \$20,000 investment paid 8% annual interest, *compounded quarterly*. Although the interest rate is quoted as 8% *per year*, the rate is actually 2% every three-month *period* (=8%/4). Hence, in three years, we would have twelve periods. To determine the future value, we would go down the 2% column in **Table A.1** to the 12-period row to get a future value factor of 1.26824.

Initial Amount	×	**Future Value Factor**	=	**Future Value**
\$20,000	×	**1.26824**	=	**\$25,365**

Alternatively, using the financial calculator:

Calculator

N	I/Yr	PV	PMT	FV
12	2	20,000	0	25,365

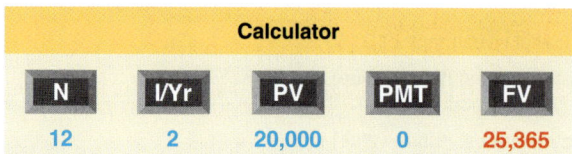

That is, the future value of \$20,000 invested for three years at 8%, compounded quarterly, is \$25,365.

PRESENT VALUE CONCEPTS

The concept of *present value* is the inverse of future value. Rather than determining how much an amount today is worth in the future, present value determines how much a future amount is worth today. The **present value** of an amount is the value *today* of a cash flow occurring at a future date given a rate of compound interest. As was the case with future value, present values depend on two factors: time and rate.

Present value is a particularly useful concept because it allows us to compare cash flows occurring at different times in the future. We can do this because we can calculate the value of each cash flow at a common point in time—today. For example, let's say we want to compare two investments. Investment A pays \$15,000 in two years. Investment B pays \$16,000 in three years. We cannot compare these two investments directly, because the payoffs occur in different amounts at different times in the future.[3] However, we can determine how much each payoff is worth today. If the appropriate interest rate is 8%, the present value of Investment A is \$12,860 and the present value of Investment B is \$12,701. (We demonstrate how to compute these amounts below.) Hence, Investment A is worth more today than Investment B. By determining the value of each cash payoff at the same point in time (today), we can easily compare the alternatives.

Present Value of a Single Amount

To determine the present value of a single cash payment occurring one period in the future, we simply divide the future cash flow by one plus the interest rate (the interest rate is also called the **discount rate**):[4]

$$\textbf{Present Value} = \frac{\textbf{Future Value}}{\textbf{(1 + discount rate)}}$$

If the cash flow occurs n periods in the future, we rearrange the equation from the previous page and divide by one plus the discount rate raised to the nth power:

$$\textbf{Present Value} = \frac{\textbf{Future Value}}{\textbf{(1 + discount rate)}^{n}}$$

[3] The reason that this comparison is difficult is that Investment A pays a return in two years, while Investment B doesn't pay a return until year 3. One way to understand this complexity is to ask: What will happen to the cash earned on Investment A during the third year? Or, alternatively, if we invest the return on Investment A for an additional year, how much would we earn after three years? By comparing present values, we are implicitly assuming that any cash payoffs from either investment could be reinvested at the rate of return used to calculate the present value.

[4] The term "discount rate" is often used when referring to present values. This is because when future cash flows are valued using present value calculations, the present value is always less than the future cash amount. Hence, we say that the future value is "discounted" to the present value using the "discount rate."

There are two simple methods for obtaining the present value of a single cash flow occurring at any date in the future. The first method relies on **Table A.2** at the end of this Appendix. We use **Table A.2** in the same way we used **Table A.1** to calculate future values. First, we choose the column representing the appropriate discount rate, and then we move down the column to select the number of periods in the future. The value in the table is the **present value factor**, which decreases as the number of periods and the interest rate increase. We then multiply the future amount by the *present value factor* to get the present value.

For example, consider Investment A. From **Table A.2**, the present value factor for 8% and two periods is 0.85734. The present value of $15,000 received in two years, discounted at 8% per year, is calculated as follows:

Future Amount	×	**Present Value Factor**	=	**Present Value**
$15,000	×	**0.85734**	=	**$12,860**

The present value can also be computed using a financial calculator. In this case, N=2; I/Yr = 8; PMT = 0; FV = 15,000 and PV is our answer (highlighted in red).

Calculator

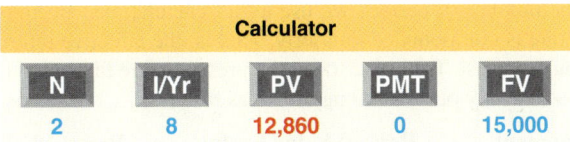

N	I/Yr	PV	PMT	FV
2	8	12,860	0	15,000

By similar means we can compute the present value of Investment B. The present value factor for 8% and three periods is 0.79383. The present value of $16,000 received in three years, discounted at 8% per year is:

Future Amount	×	**Present Value Factor**	=	**Present Value**
$16,000	×	**0.79383**	=	**$12,701**

Or, using the financial calculator, we get the same answer as follows:

Calculator

N	I/Yr	PV	PMT	FV
3	8	12,701	0	16,000

Present Value of an Annuity

Sometimes, we are faced with determining the present value of a series of regular, equal payments, called an **annuity**. For example, let's say we have an investment that pays $7,000 each year for the next three years. We can calculate the present value of each payment and then sum the results to get the present value of the entire annuity. Assume the appropriate discount rate is 6% per year. From **Table A.2**, the present value factors for a 6% discount rate are 0.94340 for one period, 0.89000 for two periods, and 0.83962 for three periods. The calculation of the present value is presented in **Exhibit A.2** (rounded to the nearest whole dollar):

EXHIBIT A.2 Present Value of an Annuity of 3 Payments of $7,000 Discounted at 6%

	Future Payment	×	Present Value Factor	=	Present Value
1	$7,000		0.94340		6,604
2	7,000		0.89000		6,230
3	7,000		0.83962		5,877
					$18,711

While this method of computing the present value of an annuity is accurate, it can be tedious for annuities with many cash payments. **Table A.3** at the end of this Appendix presents present value factors for annuities of various lengths. This table is used in the same way as **Table A.2**: first we choose the column reflecting our discount rate, and then we choose the row representing the number of payments. From **Table A.3**, the present value factor for an annuity of three payments discounted at 6% is 2.67301. To calculate the present value of an annuity, we multiply the periodic payment by the present value factor:

Payment	×	**Present Value Factor**	=	**Present Value**
$7,000	×	**2.67301**	=	**$18,711**

Or alternatively, using a financial calculator, we enter N=3, I/Yr=6, PMT=7,000, FV=0, and the solution is the PV, highlighted in red:

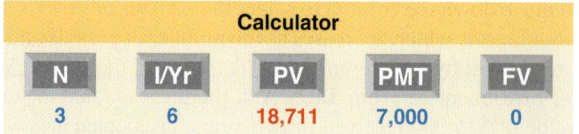

Calculator				
N	I/Yr	PV	PMT	FV
3	6	18,711	7,000	0

Installment Loans

One useful application of the present value of an annuity is to value an *installment loan*. An **installment loan** is a loan that requires a series of equal payments, or installments, each of which includes interest and some of the original principal. Assume that we take out a bank loan requiring 12 quarterly payments of $2,000 and an annual interest rate of 8%. When working with annuities, a period is the time between payments, and the number of payments is the number of periods we use in our calculations. Because the payments are made quarterly, the 8% annual rate is compounded quarterly. That is, the effective interest rate is 2% per quarter. To calculate the loan amount, we use **Table A.3** to get the present value factor for 12 payments discounted at 2%, and then multiply the factor by our $2,000 payment, as follows:

Payment	×	Present Value Factor	=	Present Value
$2,000	×	10.57534	=	$21,151

Calculator				
N	I/Yr	PV	PMT	FV
12	2	21,151	2,000	0

That is, if we agreed to make 12 quarterly payments of $2,000, including an interest charge of 2% per quarter, we could borrow $21,151.

A more common calculation would be to determine the loan payment given the amount borrowed. For example, if we borrow $30,000 and agree to repay the loan in 24 equal monthly payments at a 12% annual interest rate (1% per month), what monthly payment would we need to make to repay the loan plus interest? To compute the payment, we divide the present value (the loan amount) by the present value factor from **Table A.3** (1%, 24 periods) as follows:

Present Value	÷	Present Value Factor	=	Payment
$30,000	÷	21.24339	=	$1,412.20

Using a financial calculator, we can calculate the payment (PMT) directly, given the other inputs:

Calculator				
N	I/Yr	PV	PMT	FV
24	1	30,000	1,412.20	0

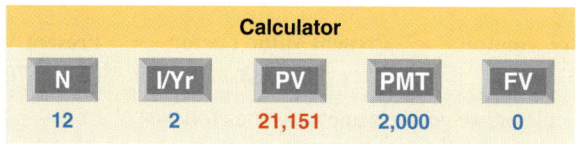

Bond Valuation

From Chapter 9, we know that a typical corporate bond has a face value of $1,000 and pays periodic interest payments every six months based on the stated (or coupon) interest rate. That is, the face value and the stated rate of a bond allow us to lay out the cash flows that will be paid to the bondholder. We also know that bonds are valued using the market interest rate, which may be different from the stated rate.

Bonds represent a combination of an annuity of the periodic interest payments and a single future payment of the face value, or principal payment, sometimes called a **balloon payment**. In order to value a bond, we must calculate the present value of each of these two components. Let's assume that we wish to value a $1,000, 5-year, 7% bond that pays a semi-annual coupon payment. The face value is $1,000, and the semi-annual payment is $35 (= $1,000 × 7%/2). Let's assume a market interest rate (yield) of 8% (which is 4% every six months). The bond is valued as the sum of two parts:

1. Use **Table A.2** to compute the value of the principal (balloon) payment.
2. Use **Table A.3** to compute the value of the annuity of interest (coupon) payments.

This calculation is illustrated in **Exhibit A.3**:

EXHIBIT A.3 Calculating a Bond Value Using Present Value Tables (4%, 10 periods)

	Cash Flow	×	Present Value Factor	=	Present Value
Face value: 1 payment of $1,000 at the end of 5 years (**Table A.2**—4%, 10 periods)	$1,000	×	0.67556	=	$675.56
Semi-annual coupon payments: 10-payment annuity of $35 every six months (**Table A.3**—4%, 10 periods)	$35	×	8.11090	=	283.88
					$959.44

The bond value can also be calculated using a financial calculator, with the following inputs: N=10; I/Yr=4; PMT=35; FV=1,000. The solution is the PV:

Calculator

N	I/Yr	PV	PMT	FV
10	4	959.45	35	1,000

The calculator automatically adds the present value of the annuity (10 payments of $35) to the present value of the single amount ($1,000 principal value) to get the bond value. That is, the market is willing to invest $959.45 in a $1,000, 5-year, 7% bond that pays interest semi-annually, and this amount is what would be received in proceeds from issuing the bond. The difference between $1,000 and $959.45 can be attributed to the difference between the 7% coupon rate of interest and the 8% required by investors.

Calculating Bond Yields

Sometimes we know the future cash payments and the present value of those payments, but not the discount rate used to compute the present value. This would be useful, for example, if we knew the price of a bond but wanted to determine the yield.

To illustrate the calculation of a bond yield, assume that we have a $1,000, 8-year, 5% bond that is currently priced at 104 (104% of par value or $1,040). The semiannual interest payment is $25 (= $1,000 × 5%/2), and the principal amount of $1,000 is due in 8 years (16 semiannual periods). We input the following values: N=16; PV=1,040; PMT=25; FV=1,000. The solution is returned by pressing the I/Yr button:

Calculator

N	I/Yr	PV	PMT	FV
16	2.20	1,040	25	1,000

In this case, the calculator returns a solution of 2.20%. This is the interest rate *per period* that discounts the future payments on the bond to the present value of $1,040. Because each period is six months, we must double this rate to get the bond yield (or market rate of interest), which is always quoted on an annual basis. Thus, the yield on this bond is 4.4% (= 2.2% × 2).[5]

Future Value of Annuities

On occasion, we may have a future funding target that will be met by making period payments. For instance, we may wish to accumulate a down payment for a residence or accumulate a retirement balance to draw upon in future years. For this analysis, we must examine the future value created by an annuity, i.e., a series of payments.

Suppose we wish to accumulate a down payment by making quarterly payments into an account that earns 4% per year (1% per quarter). Payments of $2,000 would be made at the beginning of each quarter and

[5] Technically, in order to obtain the result illustrated here, the amounts for PMT and FV must be entered with the same sign, but the PV amount must be entered with the opposite sign. For example, if we enter PV = −1,040, PMT = 25 and FV = 1,000, we would get the result above.

would continue for five years. How much would accumulate over the five years? The future value of each payment can be determined using **Table A.1**, but **Table A.4** accumulates the amounts in a convenient format. An annuity of $2,000 per quarter for 20 quarters at 1% per period would produce a future value of:

Payment	×	Future Value Factor	=	Future Value
$2,000	×	22.2392	=	$44,478.40

This analysis would also allow for testing the sensitivity of the amount to various factors. For instance, making payments for 6 years would increase the balance to $54,486.40. Investing in an account that provided 2% interest per quarter would accumulate $49,566.60 after five years.

USING EXCEL TO COMPUTE TIME-VALUE

Spreadsheet software, such as Microsoft Excel, is extremely useful for performing a variety of time-value calculations. In this section, we illustrate a few of the features of Excel.

Future Value Calculations

Calculating future value in Excel is straightforward by using the formula for future value or using the function wizard feature. Assume we wish to compute the future value of $12,000 invested today at 6% interest for four years. The formula for this calculation is:

=12000*1.06^4

Excel returns the value 15149.72. An alternative method of making this calculation is by using the function wizard. The function wizard is accessed by clicking on the *fx* icon in the formula bar at the top of the spreadsheet.

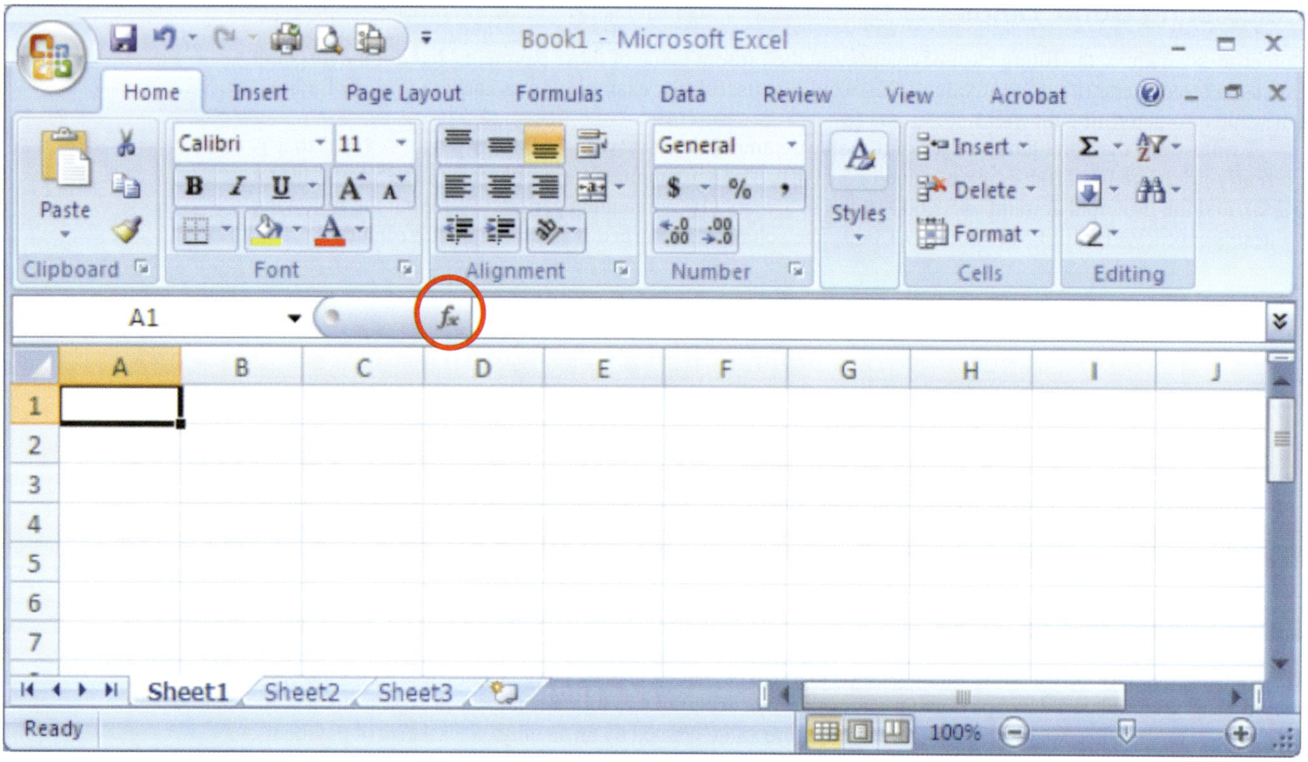

Clicking on the *fx* icon opens a dialog box that offers a variety of built-in functions. The dialog box appears as follows:

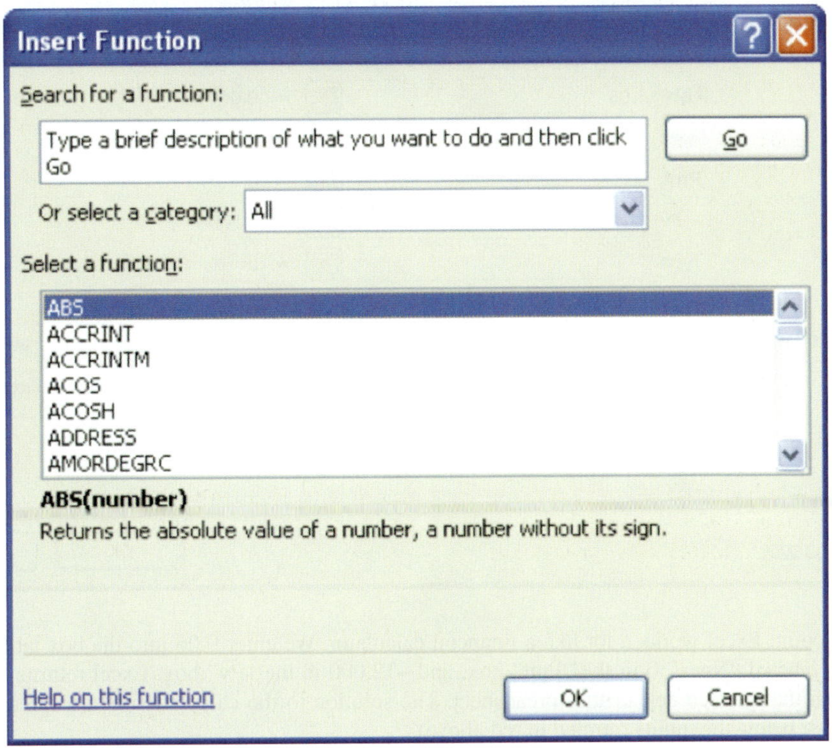

The user can scroll through the long list of built-in Excel functions or customize the search by selecting a category of functions. In the screen shot below, the category of functions described as "Financial" is selected. Scrolling through the list, we select the FV function (for future value).

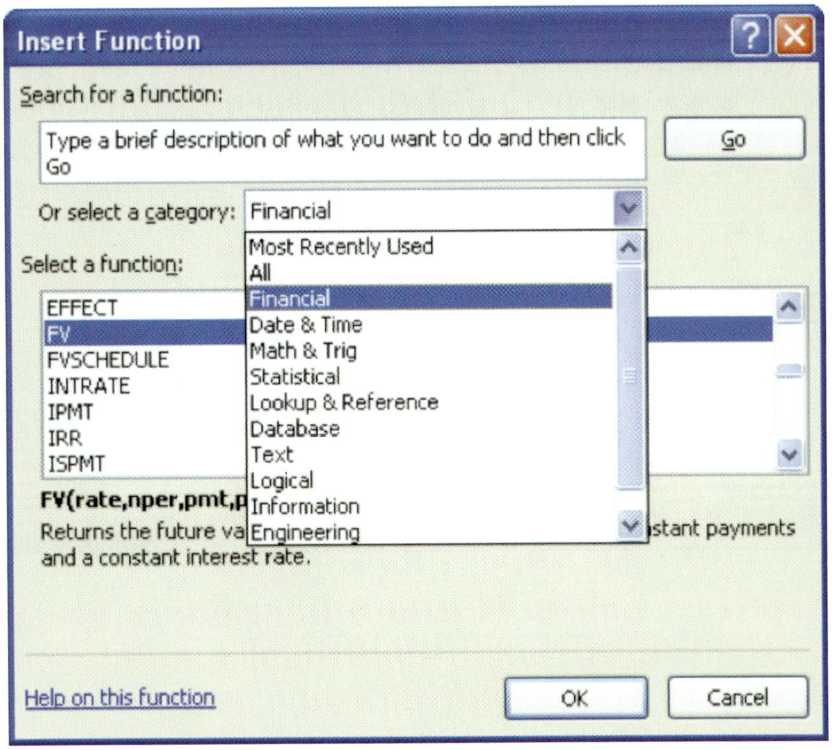

Once the FV function is selected, a new dialog box appears:

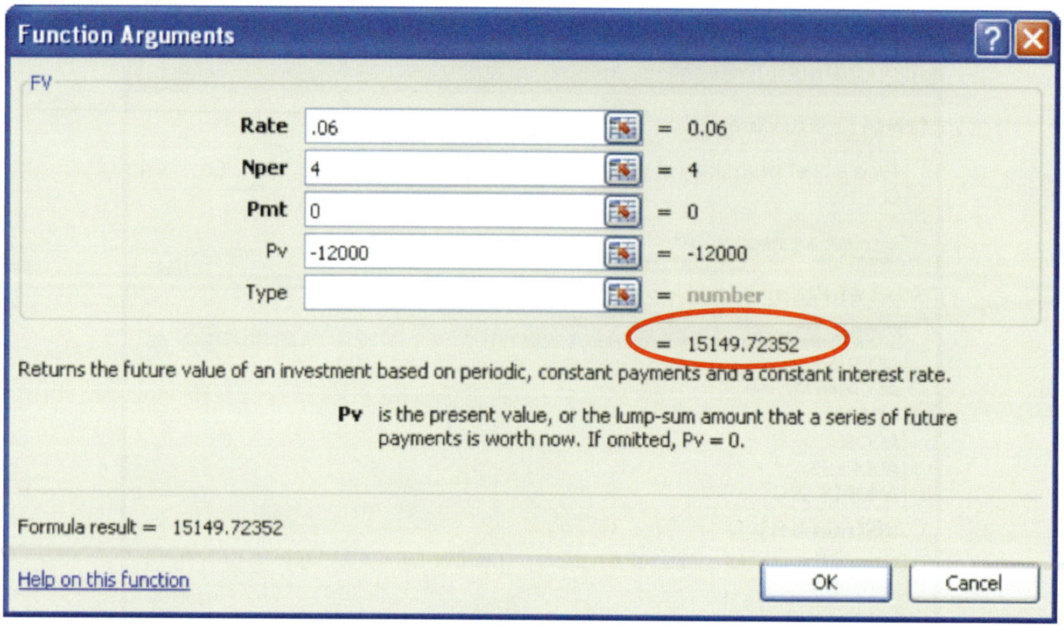

At this point, Excel works a lot like a financial calculator. We enter 0.06 into the box labeled "Rate," 4 in the box labeled "Nper," 0 in the "Pmt" box, and −12,000 in the "Pv" box. Excel returns the value of $15,149.72 in the selected cell in the spreadsheet. The solution to the calculation is also presented in the dialog box just below the inputs (circled in red above).

One advantage of Excel is that it allows the user to enter cell locations as function arguments in the dialog box. This can be useful if we wish to gauge the impact of changing an argument. For instance, we could enter the following in a spreadsheet:

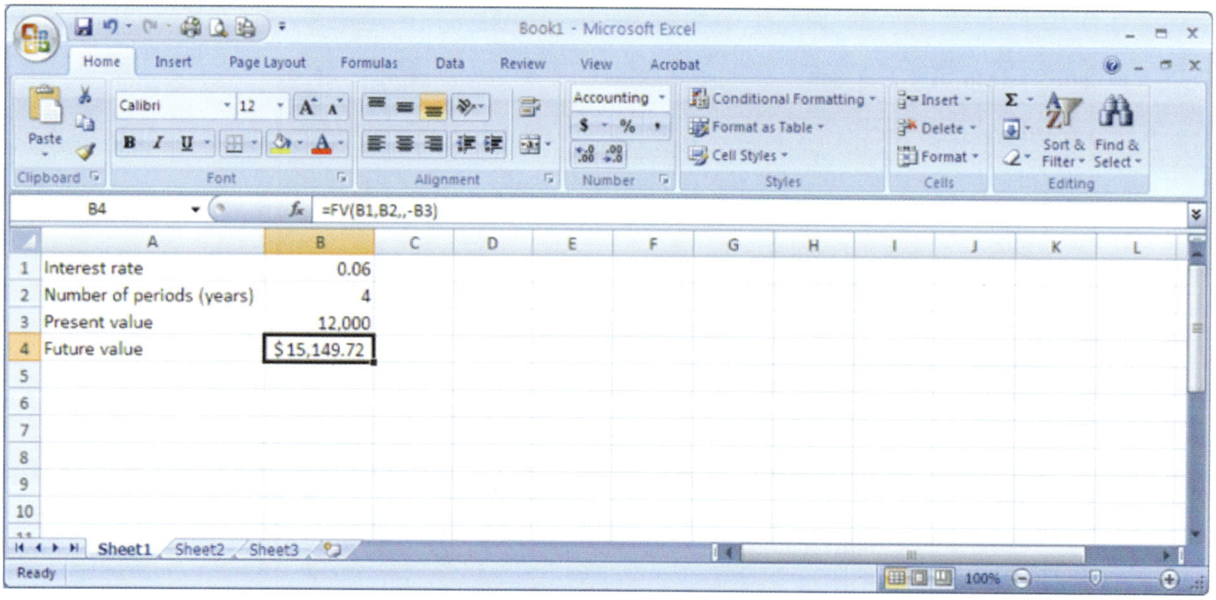

The amount presented as the "Future value" is actually returned by the dialog box below:

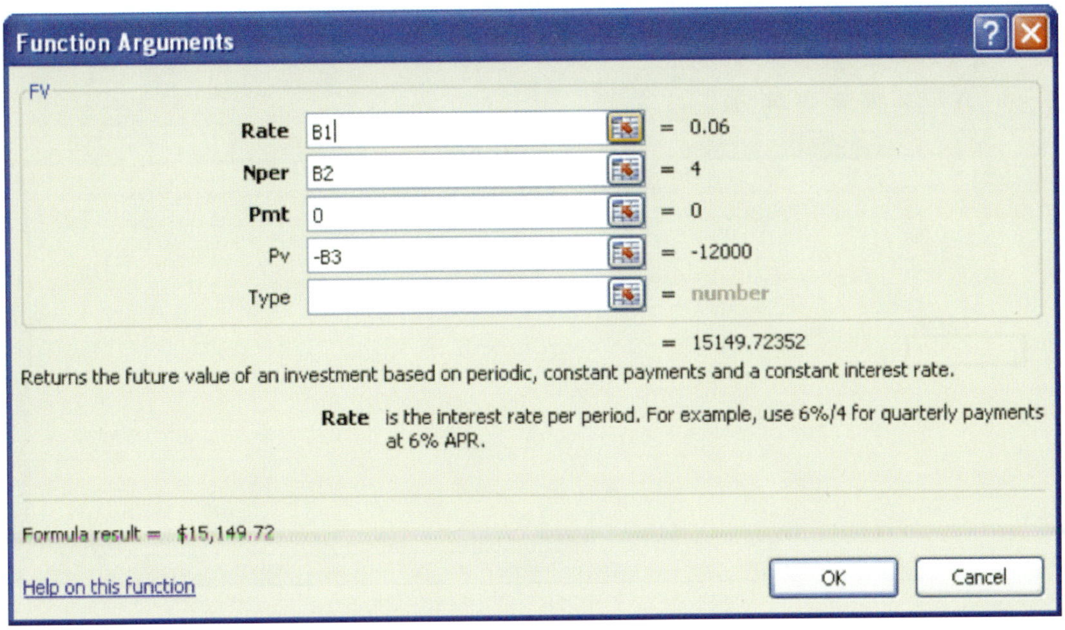

When we enter cell locations (e.g., "B1") in the boxes for function arguments, the function wizard uses the value in that cell as the argument. The benefit of this is that we can now change an argument and recalculate the future value without revisiting the function wizard dialog box. For example, let's say we wish to determine what the future value of our investment would be if we held our investment for five years instead of four years. We simply replace the "4" in cell B2 with a "5" as follows:

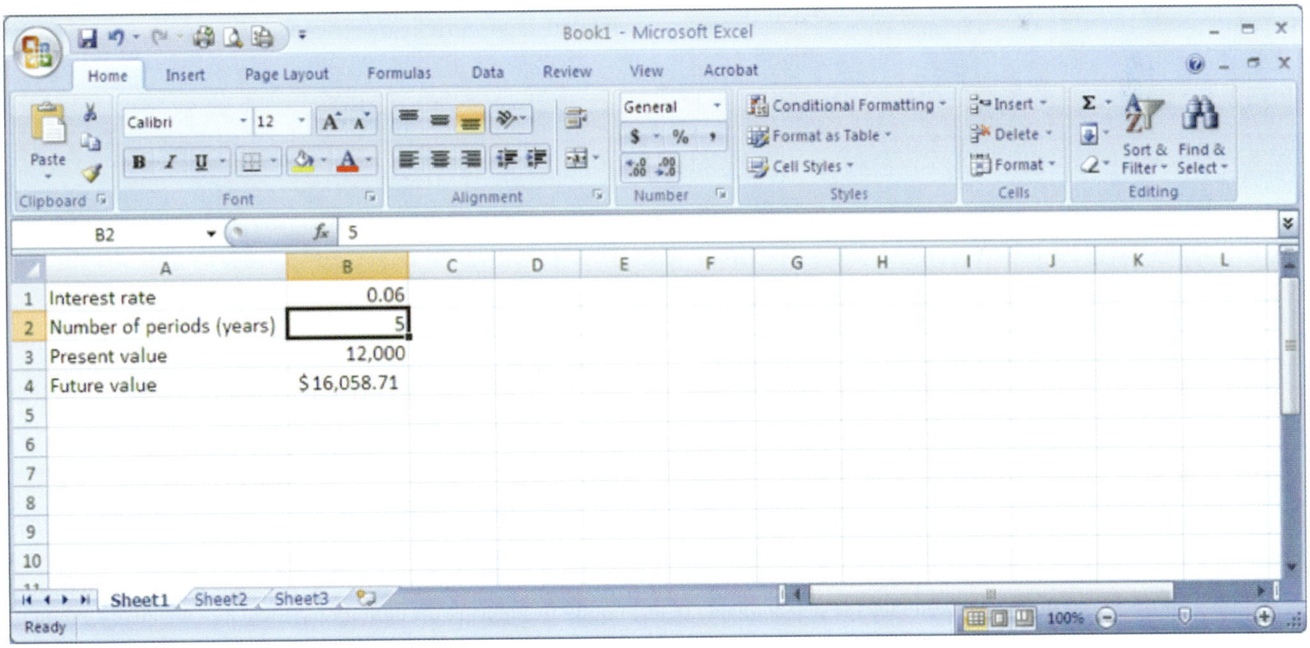

Excel automatically returns the value of $16,058.71 as the future value (cell B4).

Present Value Calculations

Computing present value is as straightforward as future value. The function to use is "PV" for present value. Let's assume we wish to calculate the present value of $15,000 that we expect to receive in two years discounted at 8% per year. Earlier, we determined that the present value is $12,860. To make this calculation using Excel, we enter each of the arguments in the spreadsheet as follows:

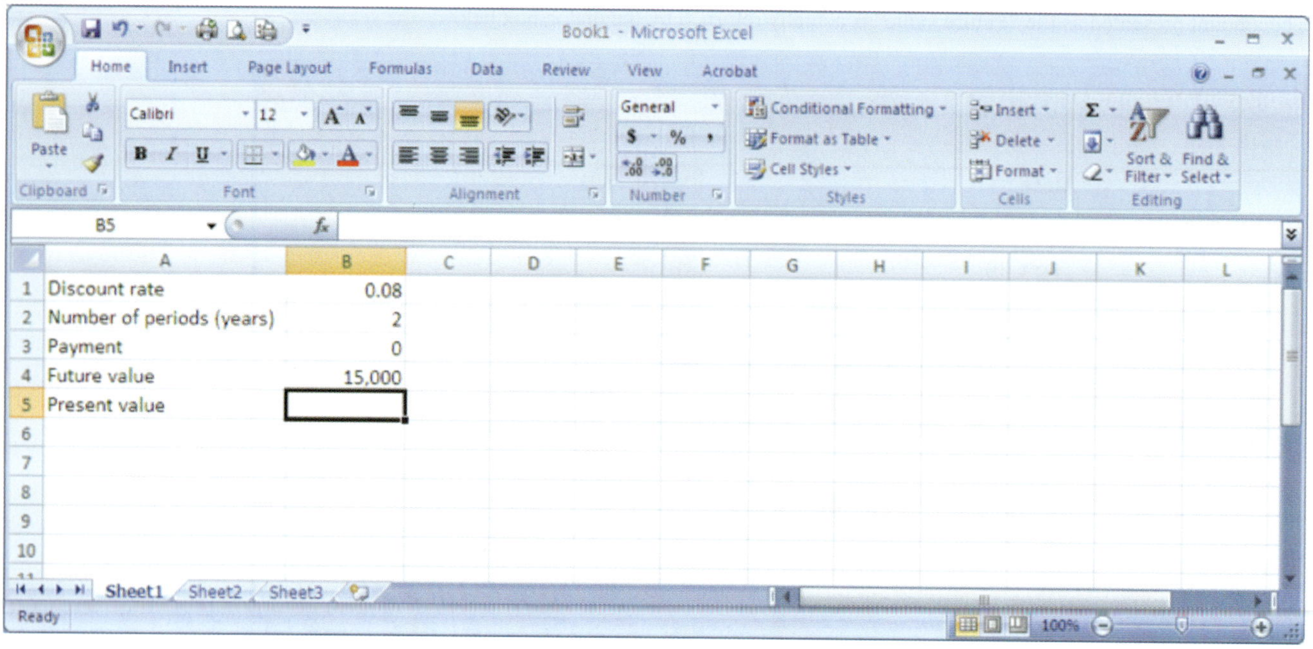

We then use the function wizard to access the "PV" function:

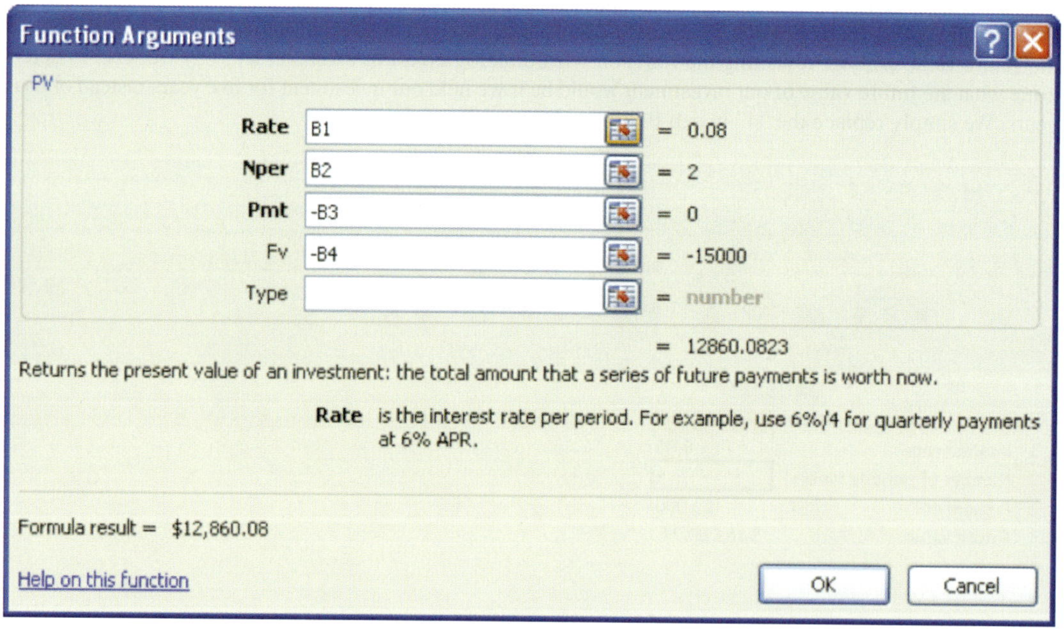

The PV function is similar to the FV function. The amount returned is the present value of $12,860.08. The "Pmt" argument in the PV function is used for annuity payments. In this example, we wanted the present value of a lump-sum amount paid in two years, so the payment was set to 0. However, we can use the same function to compute the present value of an annuity by entering the annuity payment as a negative amount in the "Pmt" argument or in the payment cell of our spreadsheet. Earlier, we determined that the present value of a series of $7,000 payments received annually for three years and discounted at 6% is $18,711. To compute this amount using Excel, we list the payment (Pmt) as 7,000 and the future value (FV) as 0:

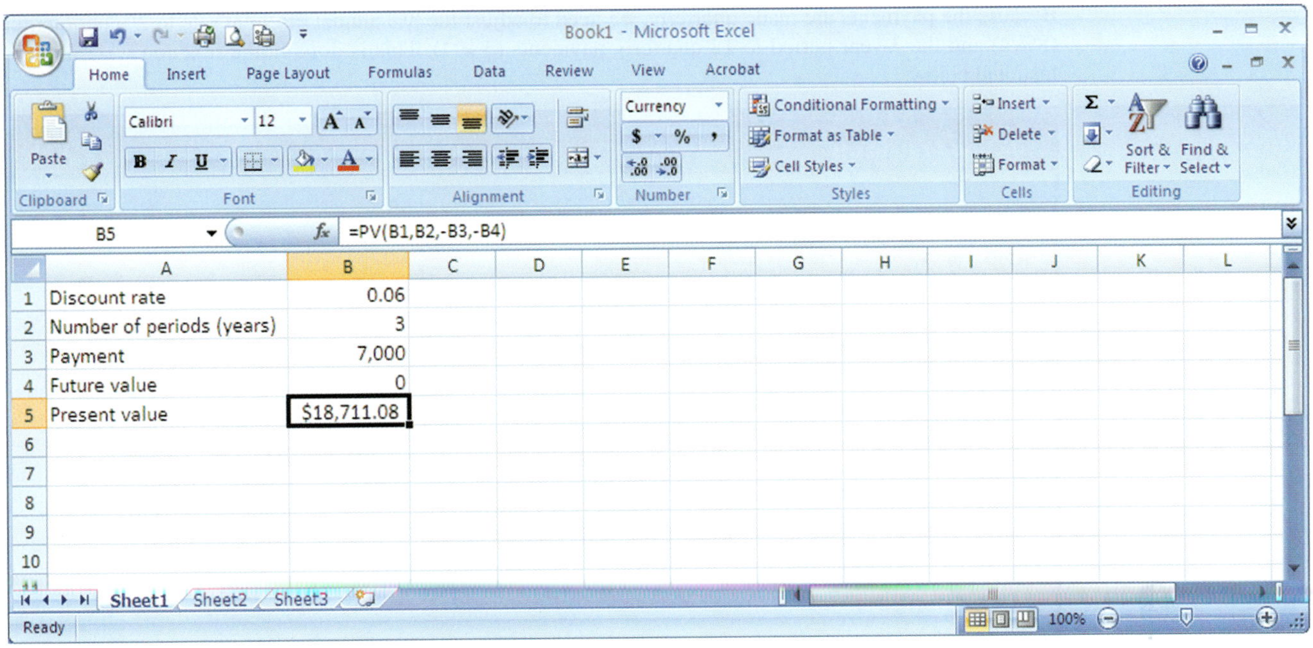

Similarly, our installment loan that requires 12 quarterly payments of $2,000 at 8% interest per year (2% per quarter) would have a present value of $21,150.68, which is computed as follows:

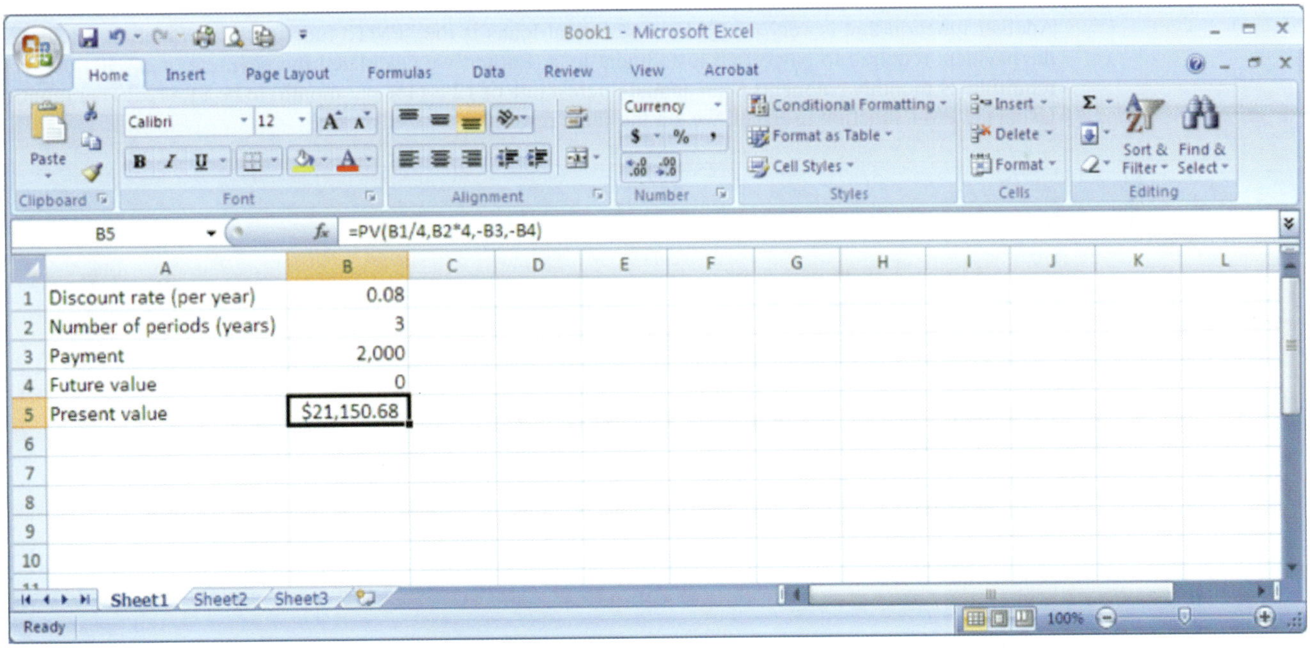

Because the payments are made quarterly, we need to adjust the 8% annual discount rate to 2% per quarter (8%/4) and the 3-year period to 12 quarterly payments (3 × 4). This is done in the function wizard, as illustrated below:

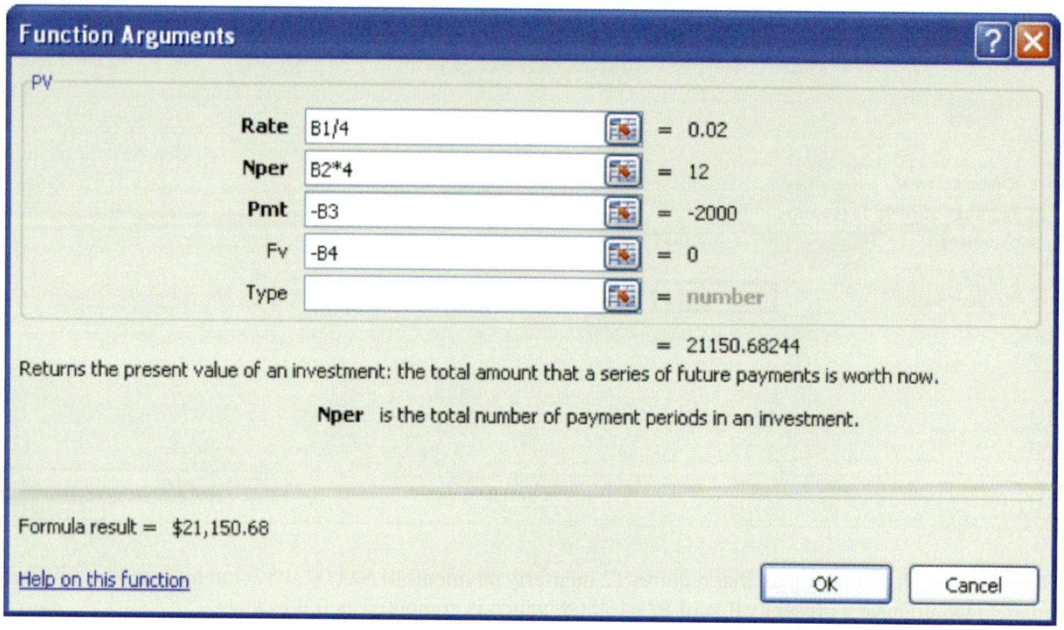

Another function that is very useful for installment loans is the "PMT" function. This function calculates the payment required to pay off an installment loan. Earlier, we calculated the payment on a $30,000 loan requiring 24 monthly payments at an annual interest rate of 12% (1% per month) to be $1,412.20 per month. Using the PMT function in Excel, we get the same result:

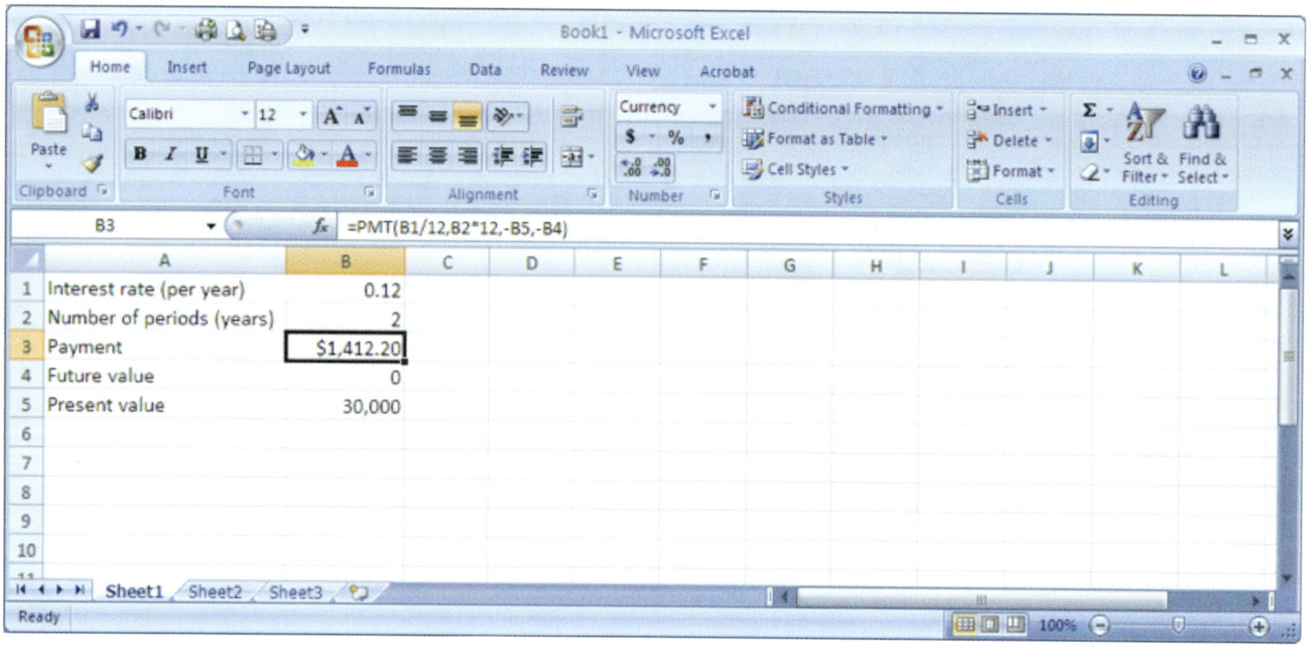

Here we need to divide the annual interest rate by 12 and multiply the number of years by 12 in order to allow for monthly compounding.

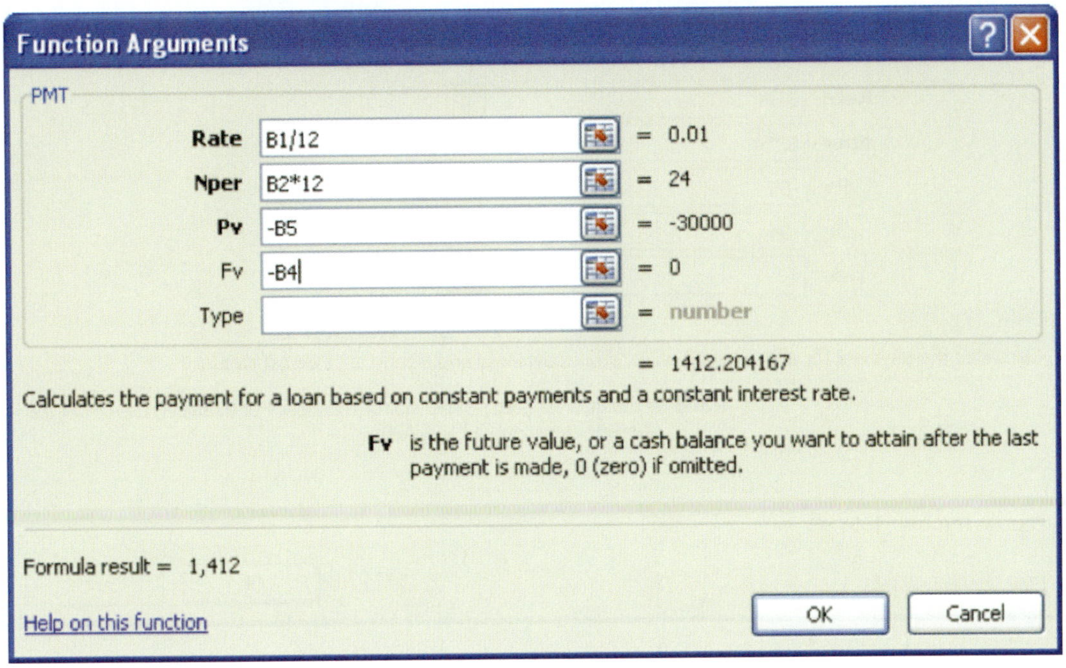

Excel is very useful for setting up loan amortization tables. These tables lay out the loan payments and calculate the interest and principal included in each payment. To illustrate, assume we borrow $5,000 at 4% annual interest and agree to repay the loan in 8 quarterly payments (four payments per year for two years). The quarterly payment is $653.45, calculated as follows:

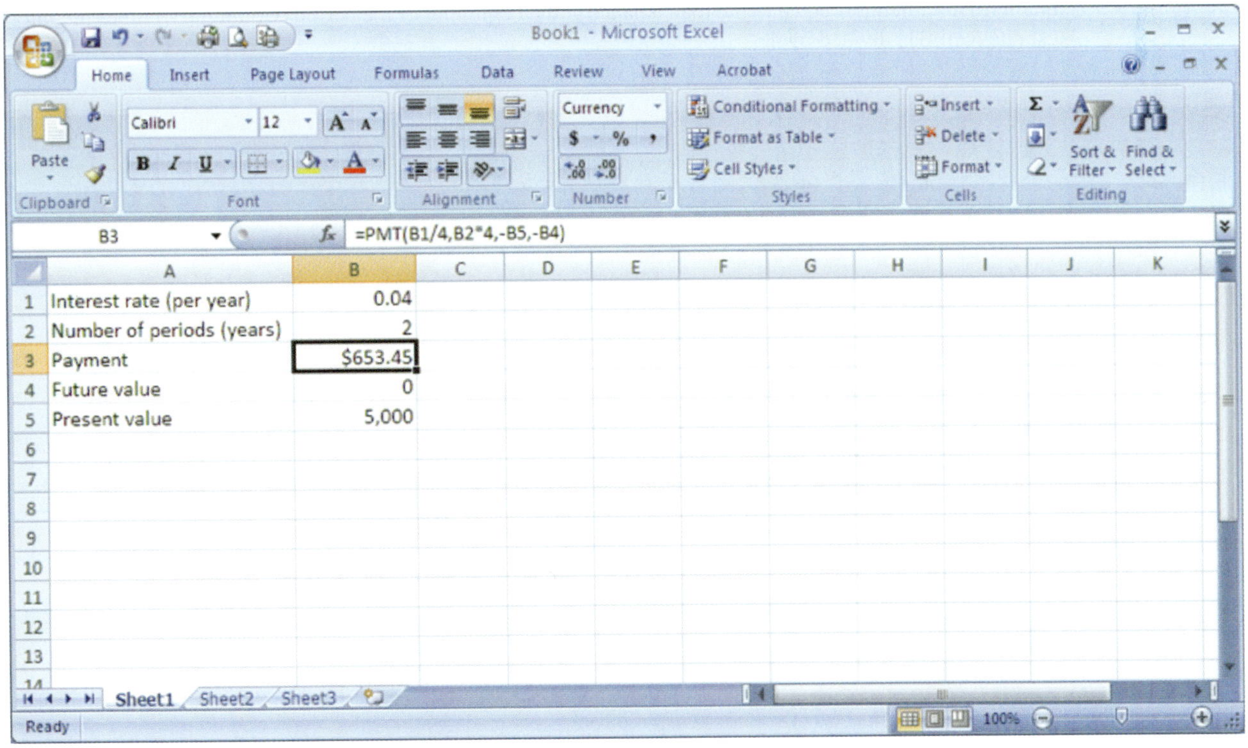

The function box appears as follows:

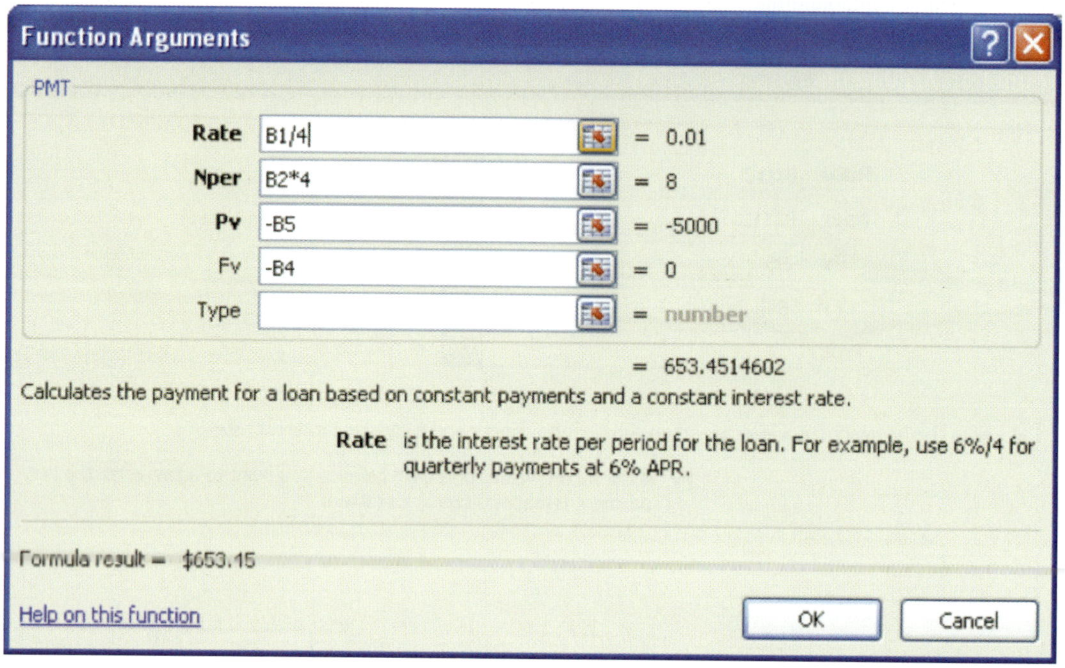

The loan amortization table can be set up on the same worksheet or in a separate sheet linked to the payment calculation. Here we use the same worksheet.

The first column [D] lists the period (1 through 8). In the second column [E], we list the loan balance at the beginning of each period. For the first period, the beginning balance is the loan amount of $5,000. Thereafter, the beginning balance is set equal to the ending balance from the previous period, which is in column [I]. Column [F] lists the quarterly payment of $653.45. In column [G], we compute the interest each quarter. This amount is equal to the loan balance at the beginning of the period (Column [E]) times the interest rate (cell B1) divided by 4.

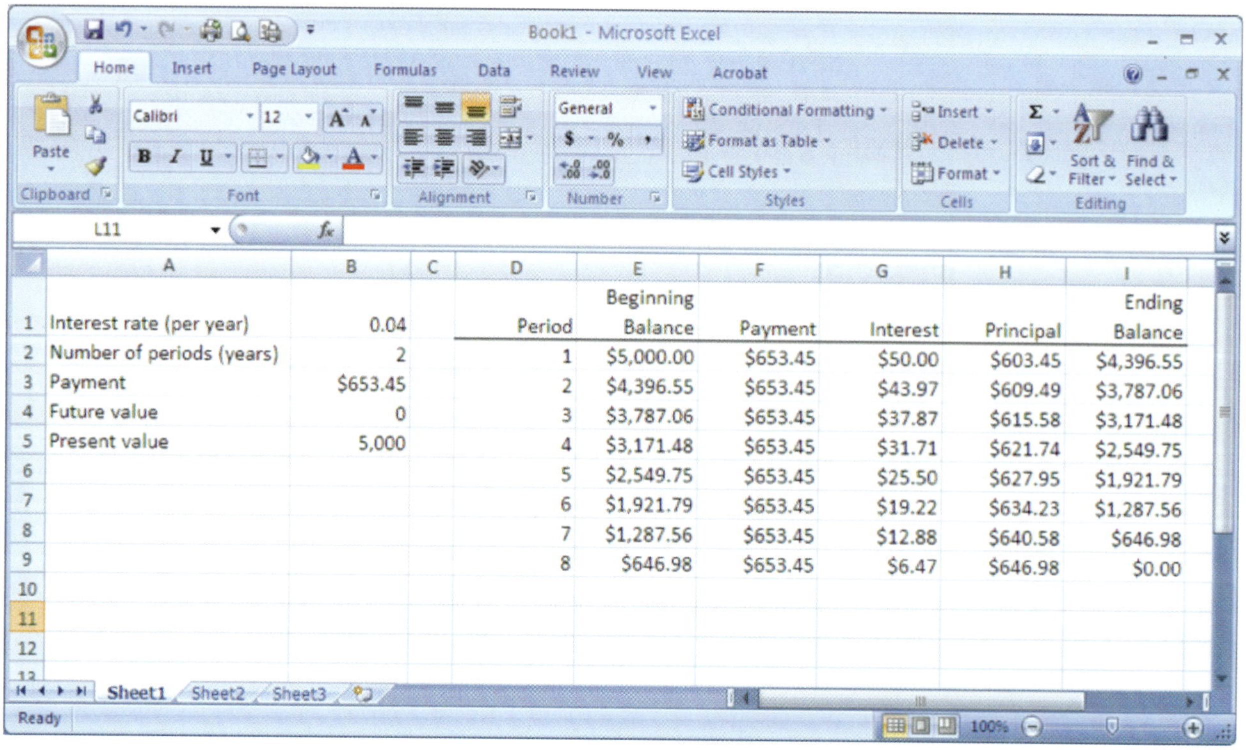

	A	B	C	D	E	F	G	H	I
1	Interest rate (per year)	0.04		Period	Beginning Balance	Payment	Interest	Principal	Ending Balance
2	Number of periods (years)	2		1	$5,000.00	$653.45	$50.00	$603.45	$4,396.55
3	Payment	$653.45		2	$4,396.55	$653.45	$43.97	$609.49	$3,787.06
4	Future value	0		3	$3,787.06	$653.45	$37.87	$615.58	$3,171.48
5	Present value	5,000		4	$3,171.48	$653.45	$31.71	$621.74	$2,549.75
6				5	$2,549.75	$653.45	$25.50	$627.95	$1,921.79
7				6	$1,921.79	$653.45	$19.22	$634.23	$1,287.56
8				7	$1,287.56	$653.45	$12.88	$640.58	$646.98
9				8	$646.98	$653.45	$6.47	$646.98	$0.00

In column [H] we compute the principal component of each payment. This amount is the payment (column [F]) minus the interest (column [G]). Finally, the ending balance (column [I]) is the beginning balance (column [E]) minus the principal (column [H]). Note that the ending balance in period 8 is $0. (The loan has been completely paid off.)

Loan amortization tables are especially useful for accountants because the table computes the amounts we enter for each payment. To illustrate, to record the original $5,000 loan, we make the following journal entry:

Cash (+A)	5,000.00	
Loan payable (+L)		5,000.00

Now, each period, we make a loan payment of $653.45, and that payment is part interest expense and part loan principal. To determine the split between interest and principal, we consult the loan amortization table. For instance, in period 1, the payment is split as $50.00 of interest and $603.45 of principal. To record this payment, we would make the following journal entry:

Interest expense (+E, −SE)	50.00	
Loan payable (−L)	603.45	
Cash (−A)		653.45

Finally, Excel allows us to easily compute the present value of a series of irregular cash flows. To do this we use the NPV function. (NPV stands for *Net Present Value.*) To compute NPV we need a series of cash flows at regular time intervals, such as one payment per year. If we skip a period, we must enter a 0 for that period. The cash flows can be a mixture of positive and negative cash flows (for instance, receipts and payments). In the following spreadsheet, we present a series of seven cash flows and calculate the present value of these payments discounted at 5% using the NPV function.

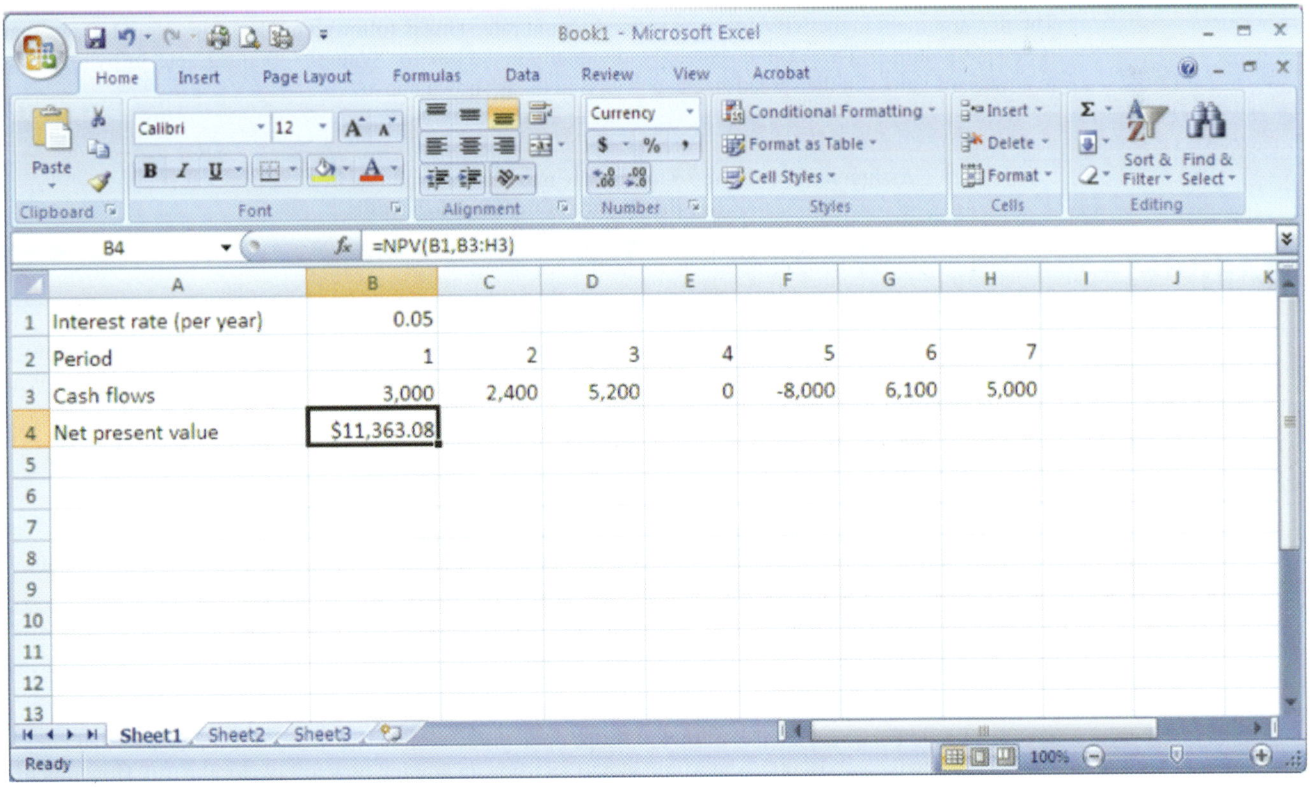

The spreadsheet shows a net present value of $11,363.08. The function wizard dialog box for the NPV function is presented below:

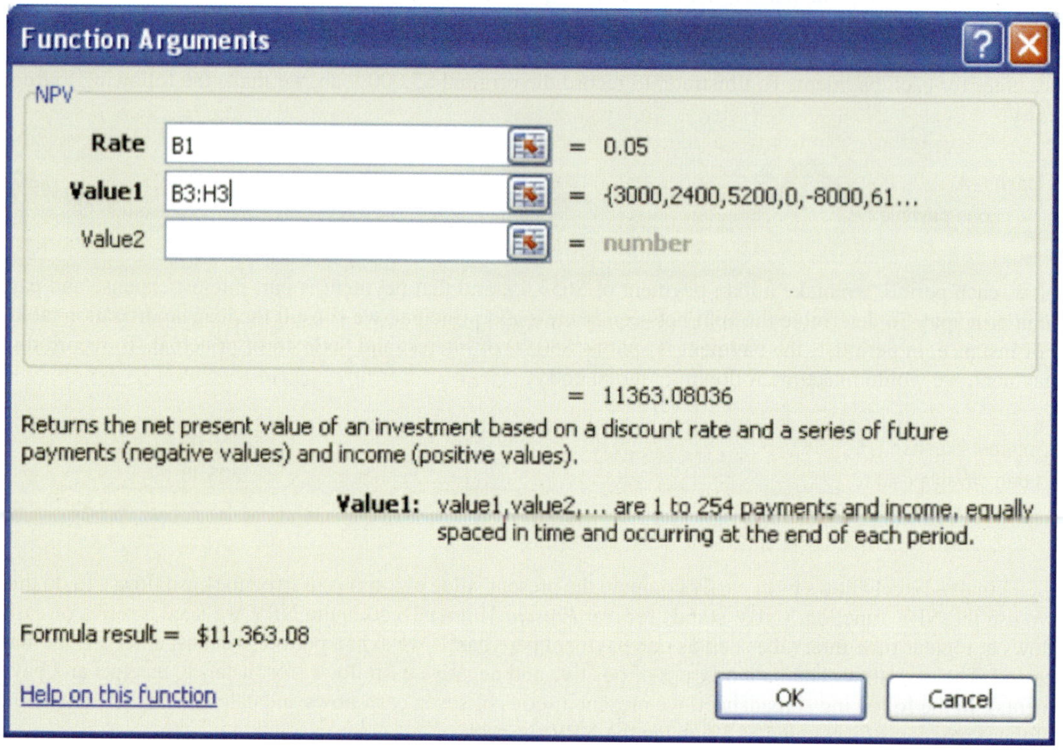

The first argument in the NPV function is the discount rate. This is followed by the series of cash flows that is being discounted. These can be entered individually in the box for "Value1," "Value2," etc. or by referring to a range of values in the spreadsheet, such as B3:H3, as shown above.

Assignments with the MBC logo in the margin are available in myBusinessCourse.
See the Preface of the book for details.

EXERCISES

EA-1. Dawn Riley deposited $6,000 in a money market account on January 2 of the current year. How much will her savings be worth on January 2, six years later, if the money market account earns a return of

a. 4%?
b. 6%?
c. 8%?

EA-2. Jason Shields invested $4,800 in an account that pays a 12% return. How much will the account be worth in four years if the interest is compounded

a. annually?
b. quarterly?
c. monthly?

EA-3. Leslie Porter is planning a trip to Europe upon graduation in two years. She anticipates that her trip will cost $18,000. She would like to set aside an amount now to save for the trip. How much should she set aside if her savings earns 4% interest compounded quarterly?

EA-4. Matt Wilson has an investment opportunity that promises to pay him $30,000 in four years. He could earn 6% if he invested his money elsewhere. What is the maximum amount that he should be willing to invest in this opportunity?

EA-5. Robert Smith purchased a used car for $16,000. To pay for his purchase, he borrowed $14,000 from a local bank at 12%. The loan requires that Robert repay the loan by making 36 monthly payments. How much will Robert have to pay each month to repay the loan?

EA-6. Refer to Exercise EA-5. How much interest will Robert Smith pay as part of his first monthly payment?

EA-7. Sandy Nguyen just graduated from college and has $50,000 in student loans. The loans bear interest at a rate of 8% and require quarterly payments.

a. What amount should Sandy pay each quarter if she wishes to pay off her student loans in six years?

b. Sandy can only afford to pay $1,800 per quarter. How long will it take Sandy to repay these loans?

EA-8. In 2022, Cart Inc. adopted a plan to accumulate funds for environmental remediation beginning July 2, 2027 at an estimated cost of $30 million. Cart plans to make five equal annual payments into a fund earning 6% interest compounded annually. The first deposit is scheduled for July 1, 2022. Determine the amount of the required annual deposit.

EA-9. On May 1, 2022, Ott, Inc., sold merchandise to Fox Inc. Fox signed a noninterest bearing note requiring payment of $50,000 annually for 7 years. The first payment is due May 1, 2023. The prevailing rate for similar notes on that date is 9%. What amount should Ott, Inc., report as revenue in 2022 and 2023?

EA-10. Rex Corporation accepted an $8,500, 5% interest bearing note from Brooks Inc. on December 1 of the current year in exchange for machinery with a list sales price of $8,000. The note is payable on December 1, three years later. If the prevailing interest rate is 8%, what revenues should Rex report in its income statement for the year ended December 31 of the current year?

EA-11. Rye Company is considering purchasing a new machine with a useful life of ten years, at which time its salvage value is estimated to be $60,000. Management estimates a net increase in operating cash inflow due to the new machine at $240,000 per year. What is the maximum amount the company should be willing to pay for the machine if the relevant cost of capital associated with this type of investment is 12%?

EA-12. Debra Wilcox won $10 million in the California lottery. She must choose how she wants the prize to be paid to her. First, Debra can elect to receive 26 annual payments, with the first payment due immediately. Second, she can elect to receive a single payment immediately for the entire amount. However, if she elects the single payment option, the winning prize is reduced to one-half the winnings ($5 million). Which option should Debra choose if her cost of capital (discount rate) is

a. 8%?

b. 4%?

c. What rate would make Debra indifferent between these two options?

EA-13. Linda Reed, an executive at VIP Inc., has earned a performance bonus. She has the option of accepting $30,000 now or $50,000 5 years from now. What would you advise her to do? Explain and support with calculations.

EA-14. On September 1 of the current year, Luft, Inc., deposited $320,000 in a debt retirement fund. The company needs $764,000 cash to settle a maturing debt September 1, eight years later. What is the minimal rate of compound interest required to ensure the debt will be paid when due?

EA-15. Wolf Inc. establishes a construction fund on July 1, 2022, by making a single deposit of $280,000. At the end of each year, Wolf will deposit an additional $45,000. The fund guarantees a 12% return each year. How much will be in the fund on June 30, 2026?

EA-16. Sylvia Owen, owner of I-Haul Trucking, is considering expanding operations from Seattle to the Portland area. Expansion is estimated to cost $15 million, including the required new facilities and additional trucks. Sylvia has elected to finance the expansion by borrowing from her local bank at a yearly interest rate of 10%. She has agreed to repay the loan in twenty equal payments over a 10-year period to begin in six months. (Payments will be made at the end of every half-year period.)

a. What will Sylvia's periodic payments be?

b. How much of her first payment will be interest expense?

c. Assume that after five years, Sylvia decided to pay off the loan early. How much would she owe at that time?

EA-17. On November 1 of the current year, Ybarra Construction Company issued $180,000 of 5-year bonds that pay interest at an annual rate of 5%. The interest payments are due every six months. (That is, the interest is compounded semi-annually.) At the end of the five-year period, Ybarra must pay the bond holders a balloon payment of $180,000.

a. What would the issue price of the bonds be if the prevailing interest rate is (i) 4%? (ii) 6%?

b. Compute the market price of these bonds on November 1, two years later assuming that the prevailing market interest rate at that time is 8%.

EA-18. On August 1 of the current year, Paradise Airlines agreed to lease a passenger jet from Boeing Corporation. The 20-year lease requires an annual payment of $550,000. If Paradise were to purchase the jet, it could borrow the necessary funds at a 9% interest rate.

a. What is the present value of the lease payments if the first payment is due on August 1 of the current year?

b. What is the present value of the lease payments if the first payment is due on August 1, one year later?

EA-19. Burnham Corporation is comparing two alternatives for leasing a machine.

Alternative A is a lease that requires six annual payments of $12,000, with the first payment due immediately.

Alternative B is a lease that requires two payments of $16,500 and three payments of $13,500, with the first payment due one year from now.

a. Which alternative should Burnham choose if the relevant discount rate is 5%?

b. Which alternative should Burnham choose if the relevant interest rate is 7%?

EA-20. On January 2, DeSantis Company is comparing two alternatives for leasing a machine.

Alternative A is a lease that requires 24 quarterly payments of $2,000, with the first payment due on March 31.

Alternative B is a lease that requires five annual payments of $10,000, with the first payment due on December 31.

Which alternative should DeSantis choose if the appropriate discount rate is 8% compounded quarterly?

EA-21. Despite his relative youth, Samuel Hunter has started planning for his retirement. At present, he has $3,000 he can invest, and he believes that he will be able to invest that amount each year for the next 39 years—40 contributions in total.

a. If his investment earns 4% per year for the 40 years, how much will Samuel have accumulated at the end of 40 years?

b. If Samuel delays investing for 10 years, how will that affect the balance accumulated at the end of 40 years?

c. If Samuel begins investing now and finds an investment earning 5% per year for 40 years, how much more will he have accumulated than if he earns 4%?

EA-22. Janice Utley is saving for a real estate investment. If she invests $1,500 now and then at the beginning of each of the next 35 months (36 months in total) at an interest rate of 1% per month, what will be the investment balance at the end of month 36?

TABLE A.1 Future Value of Single Amount

$f = (1 + i)^t$

	Interest Rate											
Period	**0.01**	**0.02**	**0.03**	**0.04**	**0.05**	**0.06**	**0.07**	**0.08**	**0.09**	**0.10**	**0.11**	**0.12**
1	1.01000	1.02000	1.03000	1.04000	1.05000	1.06000	1.07000	1.08000	1.09000	1.10000	1.11000	1.12000
2	1.02010	1.04040	1.06090	1.08160	1.10250	1.12360	1.14490	1.16640	1.18810	1.21000	1.23210	1.25440
3	1.03030	1.06121	1.09273	1.12486	1.15763	1.19102	1.22504	1.25971	1.29503	1.33100	1.36763	1.40493
4	1.04060	1.08243	1.12551	1.16986	1.21551	1.26248	1.31080	1.36049	1.41158	1.46410	1.51807	1.57352
5	1.05101	1.10408	1.15927	1.21665	1.27628	1.33823	1.40255	1.46933	1.53862	1.61051	1.68506	1.76234
6	1.06152	1.12616	1.19405	1.26532	1.34010	1.41852	1.50073	1.58687	1.67710	1.77156	1.87041	1.97382
7	1.07214	1.14869	1.22987	1.31593	1.40710	1.50363	1.60578	1.71382	1.82804	1.94872	2.07616	2.21068
8	1.08286	1.17166	1.26677	1.36857	1.47746	1.59385	1.71819	1.85093	1.99256	2.14359	2.30454	2.47596
9	1.09369	1.19509	1.30477	1.42331	1.55133	1.68948	1.83846	1.99900	2.17189	2.35795	2.55804	2.77308
10	1.10462	1.21899	1.34392	1.48024	1.62889	1.79085	1.96715	2.15892	2.36736	2.59374	2.83942	3.10585
11	1.11567	1.24337	1.38423	1.53945	1.71034	1.89830	2.10485	2.33164	2.58043	2.85312	3.15176	3.47855
12	1.12683	1.26824	1.42576	1.60103	1.79586	2.01220	2.25219	2.51817	2.81266	3.13843	3.49845	3.89598
13	1.13809	1.29361	1.46853	1.66507	1.88565	2.13293	2.40985	2.71962	3.06580	3.45227	3.88328	4.36349
14	1.14947	1.31948	1.51259	1.73168	1.97993	2.26090	2.57853	2.93719	3.34173	3.79750	4.31044	4.88711
15	1.16097	1.34587	1.55797	1.80094	2.07893	2.39656	2.75903	3.17217	3.64248	4.17725	4.78459	5.47357
16	1.17258	1.37279	1.60471	1.87298	2.18287	2.54035	2.95216	3.42594	3.97031	4.59497	5.31089	6.13039
17	1.18430	1.40024	1.65285	1.94790	2.29202	2.69277	3.15882	3.70002	4.32763	5.05447	5.89509	6.86604
18	1.19615	1.42825	1.70243	2.02582	2.40662	2.85434	3.37993	3.99602	4.71712	5.55992	6.54355	7.68997
19	1.20811	1.45681	1.75351	2.10685	2.52695	3.02560	3.61653	4.31570	5.14166	6.11591	7.26334	8.61276
20	1.22019	1.48595	1.80611	2.19112	2.65330	3.20714	3.86968	4.66096	5.60441	6.72750	8.06231	9.64629
21	1.23239	1.51567	1.86029	2.27877	2.78596	3.39956	4.14056	5.03383	6.10881	7.40025	8.94917	10.80385
22	1.24472	1.54598	1.91610	2.36992	2.92526	3.60354	4.43040	5.43654	6.65860	8.14027	9.93357	12.10031
23	1.25716	1.57690	1.97359	2.46472	3.07152	3.81975	4.74053	5.87146	7.25787	8.95430	11.02627	13.55235
24	1.26973	1.60844	2.03279	2.56330	3.22510	4.04893	5.07237	6.34118	7.91108	9.84973	12.23916	15.17863
25	1.28243	1.64061	2.09378	2.66584	3.38635	4.29187	5.42743	6.84848	8.62308	10.83471	13.58546	17.00006
26	1.29526	1.67342	2.15659	2.77247	3.55567	4.54938	5.80735	7.39635	9.39916	11.91818	15.07986	19.04007
27	1.30821	1.70689	2.22129	2.88337	3.73346	4.82235	6.21387	7.98806	10.24508	13.10999	16.73865	21.32488
28	1.32129	1.74102	2.28793	2.99870	3.92013	5.11169	6.64884	8.62711	11.16714	14.42099	18.57990	23.88387
29	1.33450	1.77584	2.35657	3.11865	4.11614	5.41839	7.11426	9.31727	12.17218	15.86309	20.62369	26.74993
30	1.34785	1.81136	2.42726	3.24340	4.32194	5.74349	7.61226	10.06266	13.26768	17.44940	22.89230	29.95992
31	1.36133	1.84759	2.50008	3.37313	4.53804	6.08810	8.14511	10.86767	14.46177	19.19434	25.41045	33.55511
32	1.37494	1.88454	2.57508	3.50806	4.76494	6.45339	8.71527	11.73708	15.76333	21.11378	28.20560	37.58173
33	1.38869	1.92223	2.65234	3.64838	5.00319	6.84059	9.32534	12.67605	17.18203	23.22515	31.30821	42.09153
34	1.40258	1.96068	2.73191	3.79432	5.25335	7.25103	9.97811	13.69013	18.72841	25.54767	34.75212	47.14252
35	1.41660	1.99989	2.81386	3.94609	5.51602	7.68609	10.67658	14.78534	20.41397	28.10244	38.57485	52.79962
36	1.43077	2.03989	2.89828	4.10393	5.79182	8.14725	11.42394	15.96817	22.25123	30.91268	42.81808	59.13557
37	1.44508	2.08069	2.98523	4.26809	6.08141	8.63609	12.22362	17.24563	24.25384	34.00395	47.52807	66.23184
38	1.45953	2.12230	3.07478	4.43881	6.38548	9.15425	13.07927	18.62528	26.43668	37.40434	52.75616	74.17966
39	1.47412	2.16474	3.16703	4.61637	6.70475	9.70351	13.99482	20.11530	28.81598	41.14478	58.55934	83.08122
40	1.48886	2.20804	3.26204	4.80102	7.03999	10.28572	14.97446	21.72452	31.40942	45.25926	65.00087	93.05097

TABLE A.2 Present Value of Single Amount $p = 1/(1 + i)^t$

	Interest Rate											
Period	**0.01**	**0.02**	**0.03**	**0.04**	**0.05**	**0.06**	**0.07**	**0.08**	**0.09**	**0.10**	**0.11**	**0.12**
1	0.99010	0.98039	0.97087	0.96154	0.95238	0.94340	0.93458	0.92593	0.91743	0.90909	0.90090	0.89286
2	0.98030	0.96117	0.94260	0.92456	0.90703	0.89000	0.87344	0.85734	0.84168	0.82645	0.81162	0.79719
3	0.97059	0.94232	0.91514	0.88900	0.86384	0.83962	0.81630	0.79383	0.77218	0.75131	0.73119	0.71178
4	0.96098	0.92385	0.88849	0.85480	0.82270	0.79209	0.76290	0.73503	0.70843	0.68301	0.65873	0.63552
5	0.95147	0.90573	0.86261	0.82193	0.78353	0.74726	0.71299	0.68058	0.64993	0.62092	0.59345	0.56743
6	0.94205	0.88797	0.83748	0.79031	0.74622	0.70496	0.66634	0.63017	0.59627	0.56447	0.53464	0.50663
7	0.93272	0.87056	0.81309	0.75992	0.71068	0.66506	0.62275	0.58349	0.54703	0.51316	0.48166	0.45235
8	0.92348	0.85349	0.78941	0.73069	0.67684	0.62741	0.58201	0.54027	0.50187	0.46651	0.43393	0.40388
9	0.91434	0.83676	0.76642	0.70259	0.64461	0.59190	0.54393	0.50025	0.46043	0.42410	0.39092	0.36061
10	0.90529	0.82035	0.74409	0.67556	0.61391	0.55839	0.50835	0.46319	0.42241	0.38554	0.35218	0.32197
11	0.89632	0.80426	0.72242	0.64958	0.58468	0.52679	0.47509	0.42888	0.38753	0.35049	0.31728	0.28748
12	0.88745	0.78849	0.70138	0.62460	0.55684	0.49697	0.44401	0.39711	0.35553	0.31863	0.28584	0.25668
13	0.87866	0.77303	0.68095	0.60057	0.53032	0.46884	0.41496	0.36770	0.32618	0.28966	0.25751	0.22917
14	0.86996	0.75788	0.66112	0.57748	0.50507	0.44230	0.38782	0.34046	0.29925	0.26333	0.23199	0.20462
15	0.86135	0.74301	0.64186	0.55526	0.48102	0.41727	0.36245	0.31524	0.27454	0.23939	0.20900	0.18270
16	0.85282	0.72845	0.62317	0.53391	0.45811	0.39365	0.33873	0.29189	0.25187	0.21763	0.18829	0.16312
17	0.84438	0.71416	0.60502	0.51337	0.43630	0.37136	0.31657	0.27027	0.23107	0.19784	0.16963	0.14564
18	0.83602	0.70016	0.58739	0.49363	0.41552	0.35034	0.29586	0.25025	0.21199	0.17986	0.15282	0.13004
19	0.82774	0.68643	0.57029	0.47464	0.39573	0.33051	0.27651	0.23171	0.19449	0.16351	0.13768	0.11611
20	0.81954	0.67297	0.55368	0.45639	0.37689	0.31180	0.25842	0.21455	0.17843	0.14864	0.12403	0.10367
21	0.81143	0.65978	0.53755	0.43883	0.35894	0.29416	0.24151	0.19866	0.16370	0.13513	0.11174	0.09256
22	0.80340	0.64684	0.52189	0.42196	0.34185	0.27751	0.22571	0.18394	0.15018	0.12285	0.10067	0.08264
23	0.79544	0.63416	0.50669	0.40573	0.32557	0.26180	0.21095	0.17032	0.13778	0.11168	0.09069	0.07379
24	0.78757	0.62172	0.49193	0.39012	0.31007	0.24698	0.19715	0.15770	0.12640	0.10153	0.08170	0.06588
25	0.77977	0.60953	0.47761	0.37512	0.29530	0.23300	0.18425	0.14602	0.11597	0.09230	0.07361	0.05882
26	0.77205	0.59758	0.46369	0.36069	0.28124	0.21981	0.17220	0.13520	0.10639	0.08391	0.06631	0.05252
27	0.76440	0.58586	0.45019	0.34682	0.26785	0.20737	0.16093	0.12519	0.09761	0.07628	0.05974	0.04689
28	0.75684	0.57437	0.43708	0.33348	0.25509	0.19563	0.15040	0.11591	0.08955	0.06934	0.05382	0.04187
29	0.74934	0.56311	0.42435	0.32065	0.24295	0.18456	0.14056	0.10733	0.08215	0.06304	0.04849	0.03738
30	0.74192	0.55207	0.41199	0.30832	0.23138	0.17411	0.13137	0.09938	0.07537	0.05731	0.04368	0.03338
31	0.73458	0.54125	0.39999	0.29646	0.22036	0.16425	0.12277	0.09202	0.06915	0.05210	0.03935	0.02980
32	0.72730	0.53063	0.38834	0.28506	0.20987	0.15496	0.11474	0.08520	0.06344	0.04736	0.03545	0.02661
33	0.72010	0.52023	0.37703	0.27409	0.19987	0.14619	0.10723	0.07889	0.05820	0.04306	0.03194	0.02376
34	0.71297	0.51003	0.36604	0.26355	0.19035	0.13791	0.10022	0.07305	0.05339	0.03914	0.02878	0.02121
35	0.70591	0.50003	0.35538	0.25342	0.18129	0.13011	0.09366	0.06763	0.04899	0.03558	0.02592	0.01894
36	0.69892	0.49022	0.34503	0.24367	0.17266	0.12274	0.08754	0.06262	0.04494	0.03235	0.02335	0.01691
37	0.69200	0.48061	0.33498	0.23430	0.16444	0.11579	0.08181	0.05799	0.04123	0.02941	0.02104	0.01510
38	0.68515	0.47119	0.32523	0.22529	0.15661	0.10924	0.07646	0.05369	0.03783	0.02673	0.01896	0.01348
39	0.67837	0.46195	0.31575	0.21662	0.14915	0.10306	0.07146	0.04971	0.03470	0.02430	0.01708	0.01204
40	0.67165	0.45289	0.30656	0.20829	0.14205	0.09722	0.06678	0.04603	0.03184	0.02209	0.01538	0.01075

TABLE A.3 Present Value of Ordinary Annuity $p = \{1 - [1/(1+i)^t]\}/i$

	Interest Rate											
Period	**0.01**	**0.02**	**0.03**	**0.04**	**0.05**	**0.06**	**0.07**	**0.08**	**0.09**	**0.10**	**0.11**	**0.12**
1	0.99010	0.98039	0.97087	0.96154	0.95238	0.94340	0.93458	0.92593	0.91743	0.90909	0.90090	0.89286
2	1.97040	1.94156	1.91347	1.88609	1.85941	1.83339	1.80802	1.78326	1.75911	1.73554	1.71252	1.69005
3	2.94099	2.88388	2.82861	2.77509	2.72325	2.67301	2.62432	2.57710	2.53129	2.48685	2.44371	2.40183
4	3.90197	3.80773	3.71710	3.62990	3.54595	3.46511	3.38721	3.31213	3.23972	3.16987	3.10245	3.03735
5	4.85343	4.71346	4.57971	4.45182	4.32948	4.21236	4.10020	3.99271	3.88965	3.79079	3.69590	3.60478
6	5.79548	5.60143	5.41719	5.24214	5.07569	4.91732	4.76654	4.62288	4.48592	4.35526	4.23054	4.11141
7	6.72819	6.47199	6.23028	6.00205	5.78637	5.58238	5.38929	5.20637	5.03295	4.86842	4.71220	4.56376
8	7.65168	7.32548	7.01969	6.73274	6.46321	6.20979	5.97130	5.74664	5.53482	5.33493	5.14612	4.96764
9	8.56602	8.16224	7.78611	7.43533	7.10782	6.80169	6.51523	6.24689	5.99525	5.75902	5.53705	5.32825
10	9.47130	8.98259	8.53020	8.11090	7.72173	7.36009	7.02358	6.71008	6.41766	6.14457	5.88923	5.65022
11	10.36763	9.78685	9.25262	8.76048	8.30641	7.88687	7.49867	7.13896	6.80519	6.49506	6.20652	5.93770
12	11.25508	10.57534	9.95400	9.38507	8.86325	8.38384	7.94269	7.53608	7.16073	6.81369	6.49236	6.19437
13	12.13374	11.34837	10.63496	9.98565	9.39357	8.85268	8.35765	7.90378	7.48690	7.10336	6.74987	6.42355
14	13.00370	12.10625	11.29607	10.56312	9.89864	9.29498	8.74547	8.24424	7.78615	7.36669	6.98187	6.62817
15	13.86505	12.84926	11.93794	11.11839	10.37966	9.71225	9.10791	8.55948	8.06069	7.60608	7.19087	6.81086
16	14.71787	13.57771	12.56110	11.65230	10.83777	10.10590	9.44665	8.85137	8.31256	7.82371	7.37916	6.97399
17	15.56225	14.29187	13.16612	12.16567	11.27407	10.47726	9.76322	9.12164	8.54363	8.02155	7.54879	7.11963
18	16.39827	14.99203	13.75351	12.65930	11.68959	10.82760	10.05909	9.37189	8.75563	8.20141	7.70162	7.24967
19	17.22601	15.67846	14.32380	13.13394	12.08532	11.15812	10.33560	9.60360	8.95011	8.36492	7.83929	7.36578
20	18.04555	16.35143	14.87747	13.59033	12.46221	11.46992	10.59401	9.81815	9.12855	8.51356	7.96333	7.46944
21	18.85698	17.01121	15.41502	14.02916	12.82115	11.76408	10.83553	10.01680	9.29224	8.64869	8.07507	7.56200
22	19.66038	17.65805	15.93692	14.45112	13.16300	12.04158	11.06124	10.20074	9.44243	8.77154	8.17574	7.64465
23	20.45582	18.29220	16.44361	14.85684	13.48857	12.30338	11.27219	10.37106	9.58021	8.88322	8.26643	7.71843
24	21.24339	18.91393	16.93554	15.24696	13.79864	12.55036	11.46933	10.52876	9.70661	8.98474	8.34814	7.78432
25	22.02316	19.52346	17.41315	15.62208	14.09394	12.78336	11.65358	10.67478	9.82258	9.07704	8.42174	7.84314
26	22.79520	20.12104	17.87684	15.98277	14.37519	13.00317	11.82578	10.80998	9.92897	9.16095	8.48806	7.89566
27	23.55961	20.70690	18.32703	16.32959	14.64303	13.21053	11.98671	10.93516	10.02658	9.23722	8.54780	7.94255
28	24.31644	21.28127	18.76411	16.66306	14.89813	13.40616	12.13711	11.05108	10.11613	9.30657	8.60162	7.98442
29	25.06579	21.84438	19.18845	16.98371	15.14107	13.59072	12.27767	11.15841	10.19828	9.36961	8.65011	8.02181
30	25.80771	22.39646	19.60044	17.29203	15.37245	13.76483	12.40904	11.25778	10.27365	9.42691	8.69379	8.05518
31	26.54229	22.93770	20.00043	17.58849	15.59281	13.92909	12.53181	11.34980	10.34280	9.47901	8.73315	8.08499
32	27.26959	23.46833	20.38877	17.87355	15.80268	14.08404	12.64656	11.43500	10.40624	9.52638	8.76860	8.11159
33	27.98969	23.98856	20.76579	18.14765	16.00255	14.23023	12.75379	11.51389	10.46444	9.56943	8.80054	8.13535
34	28.70267	24.49859	21.13184	18.41120	16.19290	14.36814	12.85401	11.58693	10.51784	9.60857	8.82932	8.15656
35	29.40858	24.99862	21.48722	18.66461	16.37419	14.49825	12.94767	11.65457	10.56682	9.64416	8.85524	8.17550
36	30.10751	25.48884	21.83225	18.90828	16.54685	14.62099	13.03521	11.71719	10.61176	9.67651	8.87859	8.19241
37	30.79951	25.96945	22.16724	19.14258	16.71129	14.73678	13.11702	11.77518	10.65299	9.70592	8.89963	8.20751
38	31.48466	26.44064	22.49246	19.36786	16.86789	14.84602	13.19347	11.82887	10.69082	9.73265	8.91859	8.22099
39	32.16303	26.90259	22.80822	19.58448	17.01704	14.94907	13.26493	11.87858	10.72552	9.75696	8.93567	8.23303
40	32.83469	27.35548	23.11477	19.79277	17.15909	15.04630	13.33171	11.92461	10.75736	9.77905	8.95105	8.24378

TABLE A.4 Future Value of Annuity Paid at Beginning of Period

$$FVAD = \left[\frac{(1+i)^n - 1}{i}\right] \times (1+i)$$

	Interest Rate											
Period	**0.01**	**0.02**	**0.03**	**0.04**	**0.05**	**0.06**	**0.07**	**0.08**	**0.09**	**0.10**	**0.11**	**0.12**
1	1.0100	1.0200	1.0300	1.0400	1.0500	1.0600	1.0700	1.0800	1.0900	1.1000	1.1100	1.1200
2	2.0301	2.0604	2.0909	2.1216	2.1525	2.1836	2.2149	2.2464	2.2781	2.3100	2.3421	2.3744
3	3.0604	3.1216	3.1836	3.2465	3.3101	3.3746	3.4399	3.5061	3.5731	3.6410	3.7097	3.7793
4	4.1010	4.2040	4.3091	4.4163	4.5256	4.6371	4.7507	4.8666	4.9847	5.1051	5.2278	5.3528
5	5.1520	5.3081	5.4684	5.6330	5.8019	5.9753	6.1533	6.3359	6.5233	6.7156	6.9129	7.1152
6	6.2135	6.4343	6.6625	6.8983	7.1420	7.3938	7.6540	7.9228	8.2004	8.4872	8.7833	9.0890
7	7.2857	7.5830	7.8923	8.2142	8.5491	8.8975	9.2598	9.6366	10.0285	10.4359	10.8594	11.2997
8	8.3685	8.7546	9.1591	9.5828	10.0266	10.4913	10.9780	11.4876	12.0210	12.5795	13.1640	13.7757
9	9.4622	9.9497	10.4639	11.0061	11.5779	12.1808	12.8164	13.4866	14.1929	14.9374	15.7220	16.5487
10	10.5668	11.1687	11.8078	12.4864	13.2068	13.9716	14.7836	15.6455	16.5603	17.5312	18.5614	19.6546
11	11.6825	12.4121	13.1920	14.0258	14.9171	15.8699	16.8885	17.9771	19.1407	20.3843	21.7132	23.1331
12	12.8093	13.6803	14.6178	15.6268	16.7130	17.8821	19.1406	20.4953	21.9534	23.5227	25.2116	27.0291
13	13.9474	14.9739	16.0863	17.2919	18.5986	20.0151	21.5505	23.2149	25.0192	26.9750	29.0949	31.3926
14	15.0969	16.2934	17.5989	19.0236	20.5786	22.2760	24.1290	26.1521	28.3609	30.7725	33.4054	36.2797
15	16.2579	17.6393	19.1569	20.8245	22.6575	24.6725	26.8881	29.3243	32.0034	34.9497	38.1899	41.7533
16	17.4304	19.0121	20.7616	22.6975	24.8404	27.2129	29.8402	32.7502	35.9737	39.5447	43.5008	47.8837
17	18.6147	20.4123	22.4144	24.6454	27.1324	29.9057	32.9990	36.4502	40.3013	44.5992	49.3959	54.7497
18	19.8109	21.8406	24.1169	26.6712	29.5390	32.7600	36.3790	40.4463	45.0185	50.1591	55.9395	62.4397
19	21.0190	23.2974	25.8704	28.7781	32.0660	35.7856	39.9955	44.7620	50.1601	56.2750	63.2028	71.0524
20	22.2392	24.7833	27.6765	30.9692	34.7193	38.9927	43.8652	49.4229	55.7645	63.0025	71.2651	80.6987
21	23.4716	26.2990	29.5368	33.2480	37.5052	42.3923	48.0057	54.4568	61.8733	70.4027	80.2143	91.5026
22	24.7163	27.8450	31.4529	35.6179	40.4305	45.9958	52.4361	59.8933	68.5319	78.5430	90.1479	103.6029
23	25.9735	29.4219	33.4265	38.0826	43.5020	49.8156	57.1767	65.7648	75.7898	87.4973	101.1742	117.1552
24	27.2432	31.0303	35.4593	40.6459	46.7271	53.8645	62.2490	72.1059	83.7009	97.3471	113.4133	132.3339
25	28.5256	32.6709	37.5530	43.3117	50.1135	58.1564	67.6765	78.9544	92.3240	108.1818	126.9988	149.3339
26	29.8209	34.3443	39.7096	46.0842	53.6691	62.7058	73.4838	86.3508	101.7231	120.0999	142.0786	168.3740
27	31.1291	36.0512	41.9309	48.9676	57.4026	67.5281	79.6977	94.3388	111.9682	133.2099	158.8173	189.6989
28	32.4504	37.7922	44.2189	51.9663	61.3227	72.6398	86.3465	102.9659	123.1354	147.6309	177.3972	213.5828
29	33.7849	39.5681	46.5754	55.0849	65.4388	78.0582	93.4608	112.2832	135.3075	163.4940	198.0209	240.3327
30	35.1327	41.3794	49.0027	58.3283	69.7608	83.8017	101.0730	122.3459	148.5752	180.9434	220.9132	270.2926
31	36.4941	43.2270	51.5028	61.7015	74.2988	89.8898	109.2182	133.2135	163.0370	200.1378	246.3236	303.8477
32	37.8690	45.1116	54.0778	65.2095	79.0638	96.3432	117.9334	144.9506	178.8003	221.2515	274.5292	341.4294
33	39.2577	47.0338	56.7302	68.8579	84.0670	103.1838	127.2588	157.6267	195.9823	244.4767	305.8374	383.5210
34	40.6603	48.9945	59.4621	72.6522	89.3203	110.4348	137.2369	171.3168	214.7108	270.0244	340.5896	430.6635
35	42.0769	50.9944	62.2759	76.5983	94.8363	118.1209	147.9135	186.1021	235.1247	298.1268	379.1644	483.4631
36	43.5076	53.0343	65.1742	80.7022	100.6281	126.2681	159.3374	202.0703	257.3759	329.0395	421.9825	542.5987
37	44.9527	55.1149	68.1594	84.9703	106.7095	134.9042	171.5610	219.3159	281.6298	363.0434	469.5106	608.8305
38	46.4123	57.2372	71.2342	89.4091	113.0950	144.0585	184.6403	237.9412	308.0665	400.4478	522.2667	683.0102
39	47.8864	59.4020	74.4013	94.0255	119.7998	153.7620	198.6351	258.0565	336.8824	441.5926	580.8261	766.0914
40	49.3752	61.6100	77.6633	98.8265	126.8398	164.0477	213.6096	279.7810	368.2919	486.8518	645.8269	859.1424

TABLE A.5 **Present Value of an Annuity Paid at Beginning of Period:** $PVAD = \left[\frac{1 - 1(1+i)^n}{i}\right] \times (1 + i)$

	Interest Rate											
Period	**0.02**	**0.03**	**0.04**	**0.05**	**0.06**	**0.07**	**0.08**	**0.09**	**0.10**	**0.11**	**0.12**	**0.15**
1	1.00000	1.00000	1.00000	1.00000	1.00000	1.00000	1.00000	1.00000	1.00000	1.00000	1.00000	1.00000
2	1.98039	1.97087	1.96154	1.95238	1.94340	1.93458	1.92593	1.91743	1.90909	1.90090	1.89286	1.86957
3	2.94156	2.91347	2.88609	2.85941	2.83339	2.80802	2.78326	2.75911	2.73554	2.71252	2.69005	2.62571
4	3.88388	3.82861	3.77509	3.72325	3.67301	3.62432	3.57710	3.53130	3.48685	3.44371	3.40183	3.28323
5	4.80773	4.71710	4.62990	4.54595	4.46511	4.38721	4.31213	4.23972	4.16987	4.10245	4.03735	3.85498
6	5.71346	5.57971	5.45182	5.32948	5.21236	5.10020	4.99271	4.88965	4.79079	4.69590	4.60478	4.35216
7	6.60143	6.41719	6.24214	6.07569	5.91732	5.76654	5.62288	5.48592	5.35526	5.23054	5.11141	4.78448
8	7.47199	7.23028	7.00205	6.78637	6.58238	6.38929	6.20637	6.03295	5.86842	5.71220	5.56376	5.16042
9	8.32548	8.01969	7.73274	7.46321	7.20979	6.97130	6.74664	6.53482	6.33493	6.14612	5.96764	5.48732
10	9.16224	8.78611	8.43533	8.10782	7.80169	7.51523	7.24689	6.99525	6.75902	6.53705	6.32825	5.77158
11	9.98259	9.53020	9.11090	8.72173	8.36009	8.02358	7.71008	7.41766	7.14457	6.88923	6.65022	6.01877
12	10.78685	10.25262	9.76048	9.30641	8.88687	8.49867	8.13896	7.80519	7.49506	7.20652	6.93770	6.23371
13	11.57534	10.95400	10.38507	9.86325	9.38384	8.94269	8.53608	8.16073	7.81369	7.49236	7.19437	6.42062
14	12.34837	11.63496	10.98565	10.39357	9.85268	9.35765	8.90378	8.48690	8.10336	7.74987	7.42355	6.58315
15	13.10625	12.29607	11.56312	10.89864	10.29498	9.74547	9.24424	8.78615	8.36669	7.98187	7.62817	6.72448
16	13.84926	12.93794	12.11839	11.37966	10.71225	10.10791	9.55948	9.06069	8.60608	8.19087	7.81086	6.84737
17	14.57771	13.56110	12.65230	11.83777	11.10590	10.44665	9.85137	9.31256	8.82371	8.37916	7.97399	6.95423
18	15.29187	14.16612	13.16567	12.27407	11.47726	10.76322	10.12164	9.54363	9.02155	8.54879	8.11963	7.04716
19	15.99203	14.75351	13.65930	12.68959	11.82760	11.05909	10.37189	9.75563	9.20141	8.70162	8.24967	7.12797
20	16.67846	15.32380	14.13394	13.08532	12.15812	11.33560	10.60360	9.95012	9.36492	8.83929	8.36578	7.19823
21	17.35143	15.87747	14.59033	13.46221	12.46992	11.59401	10.81815	10.12855	9.51356	8.96333	8.46944	7.25933
22	18.01121	16.41502	15.02916	13.82115	12.76408	11.83553	11.01680	10.29224	9.64869	9.07507	8.56200	7.31246
23	18.65805	16.93692	15.45112	14.16300	13.04158	12.06124	11.20074	10.44243	9.77154	9.17574	8.64465	7.35866
24	19.29220	17.44361	15.85684	14.48857	13.30338	12.27219	11.37106	10.58021	9.88322	9.26643	8.71843	7.39884
25	19.91393	17.93554	16.24696	14.79864	13.55036	12.46933	11.52876	10.70661	9.98474	9.34814	8.78432	7.43377

Appendix

B Data Analytics and Blockchain Technology

Road Map

Learning Objectives		Page	eLecture	Assignments
1	Define Big Data and describe its four attributes.	B-2	e.1	1, 7, 8, 9, 10, 15, 32, 33, 34
2	Identify and define the four types of data analytics.	B-2	e.1	2, 7, 8, 9, 10, 15, 23, 24, 25, 32, 33, 34, 39, 40, 41
3	Describe the use of data analytics within the accounting profession.	B-3	e.2	15, 16, 17, 18, 19, 20, 21, 22, 23, 24, 25, 26, 27, 28, 29, 30, 31, 35, 36, 37, 38, 39, 40, 41
4	Describe the analytics mindset.	B-4	e.3	3, 16, 17, 18, 19, 20, 21, 22, 23, 24, 25, 26, 27, 28, 29, 30, 31, 35, 36, 37, 38, 39, 41
5	Describe data visualization best practices.	B-6	e.4	4, 5
6	Describe how blockchain technology works and its use within the accounting profession.	B-10	e.5	6, 11, 12, 13, 14

DATA ANALYTICS

Data analytics can broadly be defined as the process of examining sets of data with the goal of discovering useful information from patterns found in the data. Increasingly, this process is aided by computers running programs ranging from basic spreadsheet software, such as Microsoft Excel and Google Sheets, to specialized software, such as Tableau or Power BI. This technology can reveal trends and insights that would otherwise be lost in the overwhelming amount of data.

LO1 Define Big Data and describe its four attributes.

eLecture MBC

Big Data

The concept of data analytics is intertwined with the concept of **big data**. Although no precise definition exists for big data, a commonly accepted definition is that big data is a collection of data that is both extremely large and also extremely complex, thus making its analysis beyond the scope of traditional tools. Important attributes of big data, commonly referred to as the four V's, are Volume, Variety, Velocity, and Veracity. **Volume** refers to the amount of data. According to IDC (a market intelligence company), there were 33 available zettabytes of data globally in 2018. IDC predicted that the amount of data would increase to 175 zettabytes by 2025. (Just so you know, there are 21 zeros in one zettabyte.) Total amounts of data are growing because we are creating more data (through new technologies) and because we are able to store more data (using cloud storage services like Amazon Web Services [AWS] and Microsoft Azure). Massive datasets can't be managed on a single machine. They must be stored in clusters over multiple physical or virtual machines.

Variety refers to the source of data. Data can be structured, semi-structured, or unstructured. Structured data can be contained in rows and columns and stored in spreadsheets or relational databases. Although most accounting data is structured, it is estimated that less than 20 percent of all data is structured.

Unstructured data cannot be easily contained in rows and columns and is, therefore, difficult to search and analyze. Photos, video and audio files, and social media content are examples of unstructured data.

Semi-structured data has characteristics of both structured and unstructured data. It may include some defining details but doesn't completely conform to a rigid structure. For example, the words in an email are unstructured data. The email date and the addresses of the sender and the recipient are structured data. Artificial intelligence algorithms are used to process unstructured and semi-structured data in a way that makes the information useable.

Velocity refers to the speed at which the data is being produced. The amount of data is not only growing; it's growing exponentially as more people gain internet access, and more technology is created that connects humans to machines and machines to machines. Collecting and translating data (especially unstructured data) into usable information is complicated by how quickly new data is generated.

Veracity refers to the quality of the data. Data quality can be negatively affected by untrustworthy data sources, inconsistent or missing data, statistical biases, and human error. The veracity of unstructured data is especially difficult to determine. Machine learning, a type of artificial intelligence based on the idea that systems can learn from data and can identify patterns, is often used to assess data quality.

In summary, a set of data would be considered "big data" if:

- The dataset is too large to be managed by traditional methods.
- The dataset includes a variety of types of data (structured, semi-structured, and unstructured).
- The amount of data in the dataset is expanding rapidly.
- The accuracy and reliability of the data may be uncertain.

eLecture MBC

Types of Data Analytics

LO2 Identify and define the four types of data analytics.

Data analytics can be categorized into four main types, ranging in sophistication from relatively straightforward to very complex. The first category is **descriptive analytics**, which describes what has happened over a given period of time. Simple examples include determining sales trends over a period of time and the relative effectiveness of various social media promotions based on click-through rates. Microsoft Excel and other spreadsheet programs include built-in functions that greatly simplify performing descriptive analytics.

Diagnostic analytics focuses more on why something occurred. This data analytics technique is used to monitor changes in data and often includes a certain amount of hypothesizing: Did the marketing campaign lead to the increase in sales? Did changing the beverage items affect food choices? Did the opening of competing restaurants negatively impact sales growth? Diagnostic analytics is useful because past performance is often a reliable predictor of future outcomes and can greatly aid in planning and forecasting.

Whereas descriptive and diagnostic analytics use data to try to understand what happened and why, **predictive analytics** uses data to try to determine what *will* happen. The movie ***Moneyball*** made the general manager of the **Oakland Athletics**, Billy Beane, famous for using predictive analytics to make personnel decisions in professional baseball. In his evaluation of baseball players, Beane used data to predict player performance so he could assemble the team with the greatest likelihood of winning the World Series. Banks also use predictive analytics to identify and prevent fraudulent transactions by monitoring customer credit card transactions and red flagging those that deviate from a customer behavior profile that was developed from previous transaction and geographic data.

Prescriptive analytics moves beyond what is going to happen to suggesting a course of action for what *should* happen to optimize outcomes. The forecasts created using predictive analytics can be used to make recommendations for future courses of action. For example, if we own a sports bar and determine there is a high likelihood of our local sports team winning the championship this year, we should expand the bar area and add more big-screen televisions to maximize revenues. **Exhibit B.1** summarizes the four types of data analytics.

EXHIBIT B.1 The Four Types of Data Analytics

Type of Data Analytics	Purpose	Example
Descriptive	To explain what happened	What were sales by month last year?
Diagnostic	To understand why it happened	Did the new advertising campaign cause sales to increase last quarter?
Predictive	To predict what will happen	Does this credit card charge deviate (amount, location, etc.) from past purchases by this credit card holder?
Prescriptive	To determine what should happen	How many servers should be on the schedule for game nights?

Data Analytics in the Accounting Profession

LO3 Describe the use of data analytics within the accounting profession.

eLecture MBC

Accountants are already preparing descriptive analytic reports regularly. Comparative income statements, sales reports by location, inventory valuation reports, and ratio calculations (average collection periods, days' sales in inventory, etc.) are all examples of descriptive analytics.

Budget variance reports and segment reports by region or product line prepared by accountants can be used for diagnostic analytics. Accountants may also work with sales and production managers to analyze the reasons behind changes in operating results. A distributor might want to know how much of the increase in overall sales last year was caused by the transfer of two of its representatives to other sales regions. A grocery store manager might want to know if the winter storm last month impacted sales in all or just some of the various departments. A production manager might work with the accounting department to determine any correlation between equipment repair costs and the number of units produced over the last two years.

Data analytics should not be limited to only descriptive and diagnostic analysis. Accountants can provide even more value by employing predictive and prescriptive analytics. Accountants can obtain data from a variety of company sources, including enterprise resource planning systems, customer relationship management systems, and point-of-sale systems, to aid them in obtaining insight into future outcomes and providing guidance for future actions. The area of credit granting provides an example. Predictive analytics can help compute credit scores to predict the likelihood of future payments. As a result, prescriptive analytics can aid in suggesting terms for granting credit. Predictive analytics can also be used to help analyze outstanding accounts receivables and determine estimated credit losses based on how much time has elapsed since the credit sale took place.

Many other opportunities exist for accountants to utilize data analytics. Tax accountants can apply data analysis to unique tax issues to suggest optimal tax strategies. Accountants serving as investment advisors can use big data to find patterns in consumer behavior that others can use to build analytic models for identifying investment opportunities.

Perhaps no area of accounting can benefit more from an understanding of data analytics than auditing. Auditors employ data analytics to shift from the sample-based audit model to one based on continuous modeling of much larger datasets. This allows auditors to identify the riskiest areas of an audit by focusing on outliers and exceptions.

The major accounting firms have fully embraced the power of data analytics. **PricewaterhouseCoopers** (PWC), **Deloitte**, **Ernst & Young** (EY), and **KPMG** all devote significant staffing resources to provide data analytics services to their clients. These firms claim they can help their clients optimize their data assets to aid in faster and better decisions. For example, PWC provides a flowchart starting with the building of a data foundation and applies advanced analytics to improving business performance, ultimately leading to opportunities for innovation.

While computers and software are instrumental in the entire process, the human element is the most critical factor in the success of any data analytics program. One commonality among surveys of top company managers is the value placed on data analytics for the company's future. Another commonality is the need for professionals trained in data analytics to help the company attain its goals.

DATA ANALYTICS IN ACCOUNTING

Benford's Law provides an example of how data analytics has been used to uncover fraud in a national call center. Forensic accountants utilized their knowledge of Benford's Law to form evidence of a problem by observing patterns in the data. According to Benford's Law, in any list of financial transactions, the number one should occur as the first digit 30.1 percent of the time, with each successive number occurring as the first digit in lesser percentages, with the number nine occurring less than 5 percent of the time. Forensic accountants examined issued refunds and noticed an excessively high occurrence of the number four. The forensic accountants learned that the company had a policy that required supervisor approval of refunds that exceeded $50. The accountants were able to identify a small group of operators who had been issuing fraudulent refunds to family, friends, and themselves. These fraudulent $40 refunds totaled several hundred thousand dollars.

In order to be useful, data needs to be analyzed. Technology has provided the analyst with powerful tools that allow big data to provide insights that would not have been possible in the past. Still, the most important tool in the analytics toolkit comes from the analyst. Without critical thinking and good judgement, the value would remain locked within the data.

The Analytics Mindset[1]

LO4 Describe the analytics mindset.

eLecture MBC

The analytics mindset consists of a four-step process of (1) asking the right questions; (2) extracting, transforming, and loading the necessary data; (3) applying appropriate data analytics techniques; and (4) interpreting and presenting the results. **Exhibit B.2** summarizes the steps and requirements of an analytics mindset.

Note that while technology is imbedded in this process, the process still begins and ends with the human element of asking the right questions and interpreting the results. Nothing is more critical than the first step of knowing what to ask. The right questions guide the process to find the right data to analyze and interpret.

[1] The analytics mindset discussed here is an approach developed by the Ernst & Young Foundation.

EXHIBIT B.2 Steps of an Analytics Mindset

Steps in the Analytics Mindset	Requirements
Ask the right questions	Understand the objectives of the end user Understand the underlying business processes
Extract, transform, and load the data	Know what to ask for Manage the data security Transform the data into the required format Cleanse the data for completeness and accuracy
Apply the appropriate analytics techniques	Determine whether the need is for a confirmatory or an exploratory approach
Interpret and present the results	Use appropriate critical judgement regarding what you see Visually display the results in a format that is easy to understand without unnecessary clutter

Asking the right questions requires a few prerequisites. First, you need to know the audience that the analysis is for and what their objectives are. Next, you need to understand the context underlying the problem. For example, to analyze a marketing question you should understand the industry characteristics and the consumer demographics. Without this knowledge, you may not select the correct indicators to analyze.

Along with knowing the right questions to ask, an analytical mindset requires you to form an idea of what to expect from the data. For example, when analyzing inventory salability, you would expect to see certain associated movements in sales and receivables.

After your questions are formed, you need to determine the data needed to aid in finding answers to those questions. This requires a knowledge of the data characteristics of the four V's previously mentioned. With this knowledge you can begin the data extraction process. Here you will need to know what data to ask for, how to manage data security, and what form the data will take.

Once you have the data, you will need to transform it into a format suitable for analysis. This is often referred to as data cleaning. Data is rarely found in the form of a nicely organized Excel spreadsheet. Rather, the data will often need to be converted into a proper format and tested for completeness and accuracy. Further, unnecessary data should be removed from the dataset.

The data should then be loaded into the proper analysis tool, such as Tableau or Microsoft's Power BI. Once loaded, the data should again be cleansed to be sure it is ready for analysis in the chosen software.

It is necessary to determine the appropriate technique to analyze the data within the analysis tool. There are a multitude of ways that the data can be analyzed. Possible choices include computing ratios between associated measures, identifying trends among various measures, creating comparisons between dates, and sorting measures. The proper technique to use will be guided by the questions being asked.

In your interpretation of the data, you should ask yourself what do you see and is this what you expected? In other words, do these results make sense or did the results create new questions that require further analysis?

Eventually, the results must be packaged into a presentation that can be shared with the intended audience. Software such as Tableau, Power BI, or Excel can greatly enhance these presentations through their ability to create **visualizations** and **dashboards**. These visualizations can take many forms, from simple tables to bar or pie charts, to more sophisticated scatter plots, map charts, heat maps, and more. Dashboards are created by combining multiple visualizations. Interactive dashboards allow users to filter out or drill down on content included in the charts and tables, on demand.

Data Analytic Tools

Technologies used by organizations to analyze data and communicate information to users are known as Business Intelligence (BI) tools. Data warehousing (data storage), data mining (extracting usable insights from data), and reporting and querying software are all BI tools.

Excel and Tableau are two popular BI tools that you will be using in the exercises and problems at the end of this Appendix.

Although Excel and Tableau can be used in similar ways, there are some important differences. Excel is a software application that is used for creating, organizing, and analyzing data. Tableau is a data visualization tool. Although calculations can be performed in Tableau, those calculations are made to create new fields for use in visualizations, not as support for accounting transactions. For example, Excel might be used to calculate sales commission amounts, which are then inputted into the accounting system. Tableau would not be used for that purpose.

Users in both Excel[2] and Tableau can

- Connect with different data sources
- Create visualizations and dashboards
- Work with big datasets

Tableau has much stronger interactivity tools and a more comprehensive selection of chart options. Excel generally has more flexibility and more extensive analytics tools.[3]

Python and **R** are popular programming languages that are used for data analysis, particularly when working with big datasets. Although these are programming languages and not application software (Business Intelligence tools), they are relatively easy to code compared to other languages and can be used to write software programs that perform powerful data analyses and visualizations.

ACCESSING EXCEL AND TABLEAU

Excel, if not available to you through your school, can be accessed for free by creating a Microsoft account at https://office.live.com/start/Excel.aspx. A free version of Tableau (Tableau Public) is available to you at https://public.tableau.com/en-us/s/. Tableau Public has most of the functions of Tableau Desktop (the full version). However, you can't save your workbooks locally if you're using Tableau Public. Instead, all workbooks are saved online and are accessible to any Tableau user unless you elect to hide your visualizations. Hiding visualizations is done in Settings after you've registered for Tableau on the Tableau website. Walk-through videos are available for every exercise and problem at cambridgepub.com. Tableau tutorial videos are available at https://www.tableau.com/learn/training/.

Data Visualization

LO5 Describe data visualization best practices.

eLecture MBC

As noted previously, the final step in the analytics mindset is to present your results. This is often done in the form of a visualization. While it is possible to present results as a bunch of tables full of numbers, visualizations with imagery are often a far better means to convey the raw numbers. Visualizations can be thought of as a blending of the art of design with the science of data.

There is an unlimited number of ways that data can be presented; however, certain best practices exist that can serve as a guide when building a visualization. For example, the exact same data on GDP levels are shown in the three charts in **Exhibit B.3**, but each displays the data differently. The table presents the raw data; however, the reader cannot easily rank the different economies. The two bar charts both show the same data; however, the one all in blue makes it far easier to compare economies by showing the data in sorted order. Also, note that adding multiple colors to the other bar chart does nothing to aid the reader, rather it just adds confusion.

Visualizations can be divided into two primary categories, exploratory and explanatory. **Exploratory visualizations** are meant to allow the reader to explore the data presented in order to do additional analysis. Exploratory visualizations would normally include interactive tools like filters that allow the user to change the level of data displayed. This can be useful when the problem is not clearly defined, and the reader wishes to gain a further understanding of the data.

In contrast to exploratory visualizations, **explanatory visualizations** are used to convey information to the audience. A classic example of such a visualization was prepared in 1854 by the British physician Dr. John Snow. Dr. Snow plotted cholera deaths in central London on a map that also showed the location of water pumps. The visualization identified the relationship between these

[2] Full functionality in Excel is only available if you have Excel 2010 or newer and you are running a 64-bit version of Windows. To determine the version of Windows on your computer, go to Settings>System>About. The version will be listed in the Device specifications section.

[3] Pan and Blankley, Excel vs. Tableau: See your data differently, *Journal of Accountancy*, February 29, 2020.

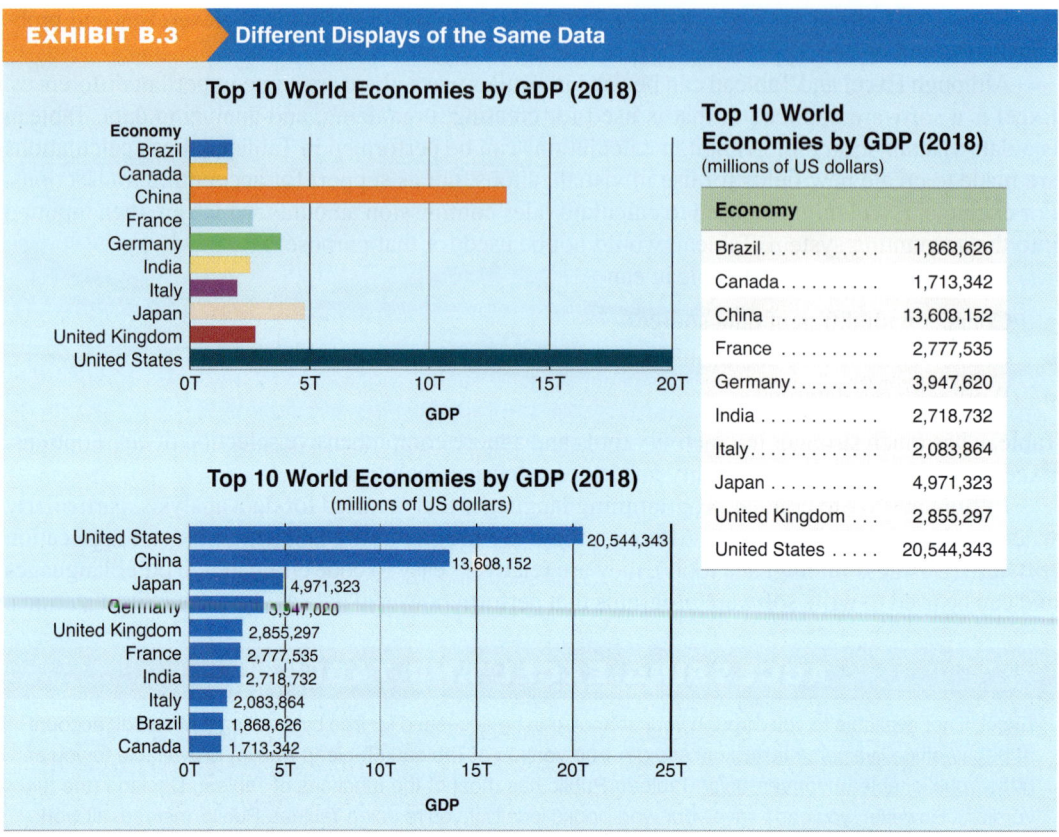

EXHIBIT B.3 Different Displays of the Same Data

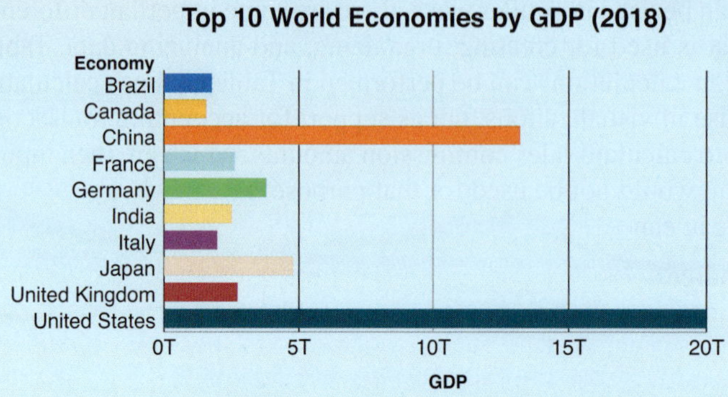

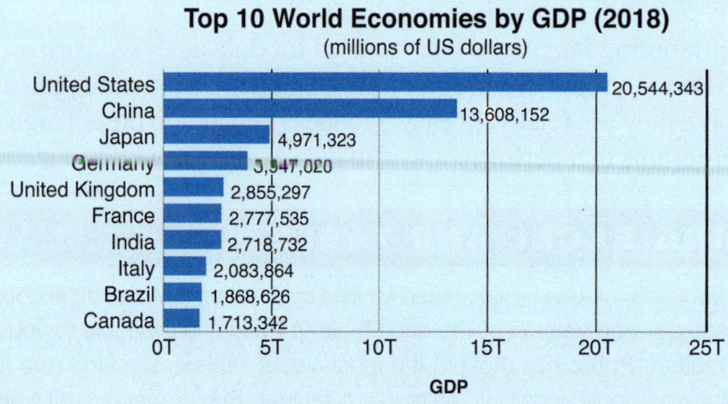

Top 10 World Economies by GDP (2018)
(millions of US dollars)

Economy	
Brazil	1,868,626
Canada	1,713,342
China	13,608,152
France	2,777,535
Germany	3,947,620
India	2,718,732
Italy	2,083,864
Japan	4,971,323
United Kingdom	2,855,297
United States	20,544,343

deaths and the Broad Street water pump and lead to a change in the water and waste systems. Dr. Snow's visualization is shown in **Exhibit B.4**.

EXHIBIT B.4 Cholera Deaths in London in 1854

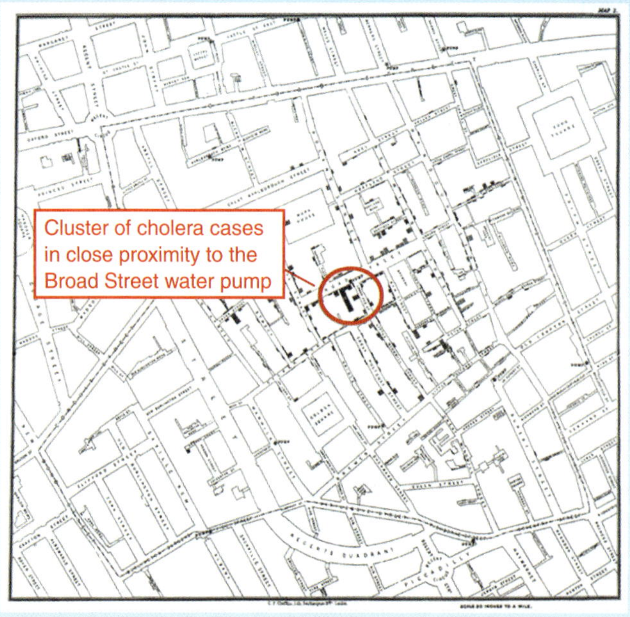

Good visualization design can be enhanced by considering how our brains process visual details such as form, position, and color.

For example, items that are different from the rest become the focus of attention as shown in **Exhibit B.5**. An item that is longer, wider, or in a different orientation will stand out, as will an item that is of a different size, shape, in a different position, or has a different hue or intensity of color.

EXHIBIT B.5 **Displays that Emphasize How Differences Focus Our Attention**

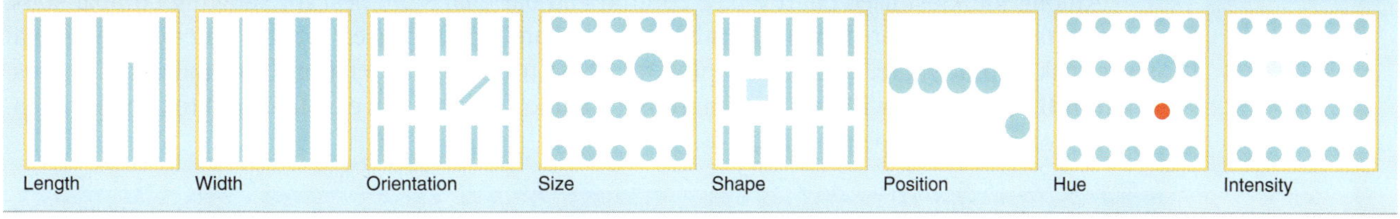

While the use of color can help an item to stand out, it is important to use color correctly. The use of too much color can add to visual clutter. And it's important that color is used consistently, such as always representing a certain year or category. The choice of color is also important since color can convey meanings that differ from one culture to another. For example, red may mean good luck, and green may mean jealousy.

Good visualization design requires the removal of items that detract from the message that we are trying to communicate. **Visual clutter** confuses the audience and lessens the chance that they will be able to easily understand the information that is being conveyed. The concept that less is more is the essence of the visualization design principles developed by Edward Tufte, a statistician and professor emeritus at Yale University. Tufte uses the term chart-junk to refer to any unnecessary or confusing elements included in information displays. His principles show that "excellence in statistical graphics consists of ideas communicated with clarity, precision and efficiency."[4]

Exhibit B.6 illustrates **Tufte's principles**. Note in the first visualization all of the visual clutter only serves to distract the audience from seeing the main point that the United States is the largest economy based on its GDP. Now notice how much cleaner the second visualization is after removing the distracting yellow background, the color coding of each economy, the redundant labeling, and the unnecessary grid lines.

EXHIBIT B.6 **Illustration of Tufte's Principles**

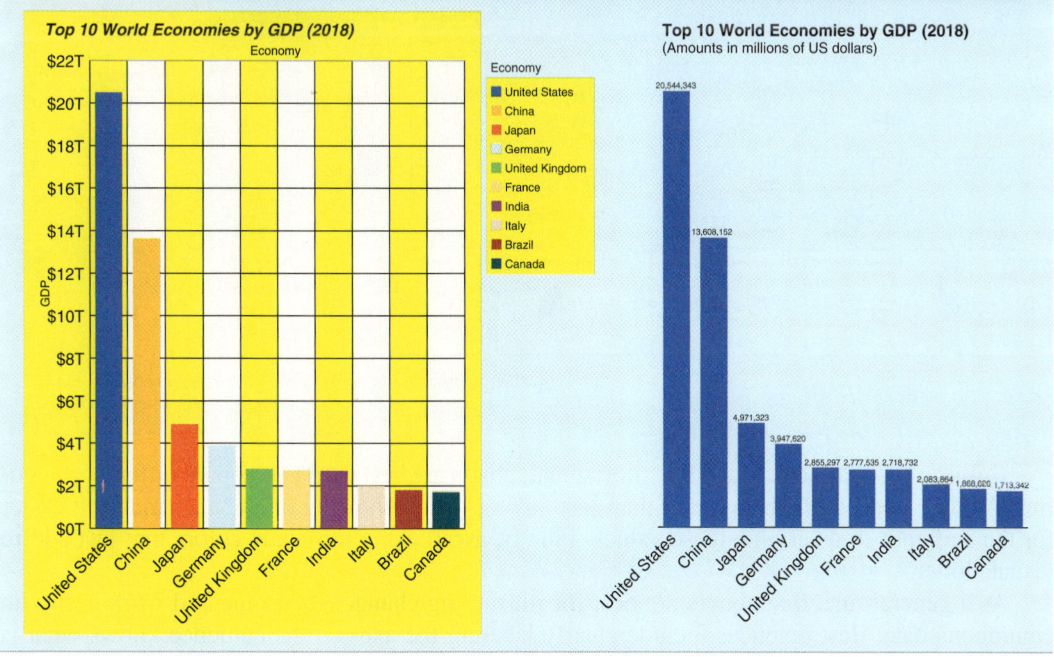

Good visualization construction also involves choosing the most effective chart type depending on what information is being presented.

---

[4] E.R. Tufte, *The Visual Display of Quantitative Information* (Graphics Press, Cheshire, CT 2001).

The starting point for all of the visualizations we will be discussing is a simple table of data. While the table is excellent for looking up values and can precisely communicate numerical values, visualizations in the form of charts provide the audience an easier method to see what the analyst is attempting to convey.

Among the most used chart types, column and bar charts are best for showing comparisons, line charts are useful for showing trends, pie charts are typically used for showing how individual parts make up a whole, and scatter plots are best for showing relationships and distributions. **Exhibit B.7**, reprinted with permission from the author, provides an excellent tool to help in choosing the correct chart type.[5]

EXHIBIT B.7 **Chart Types**

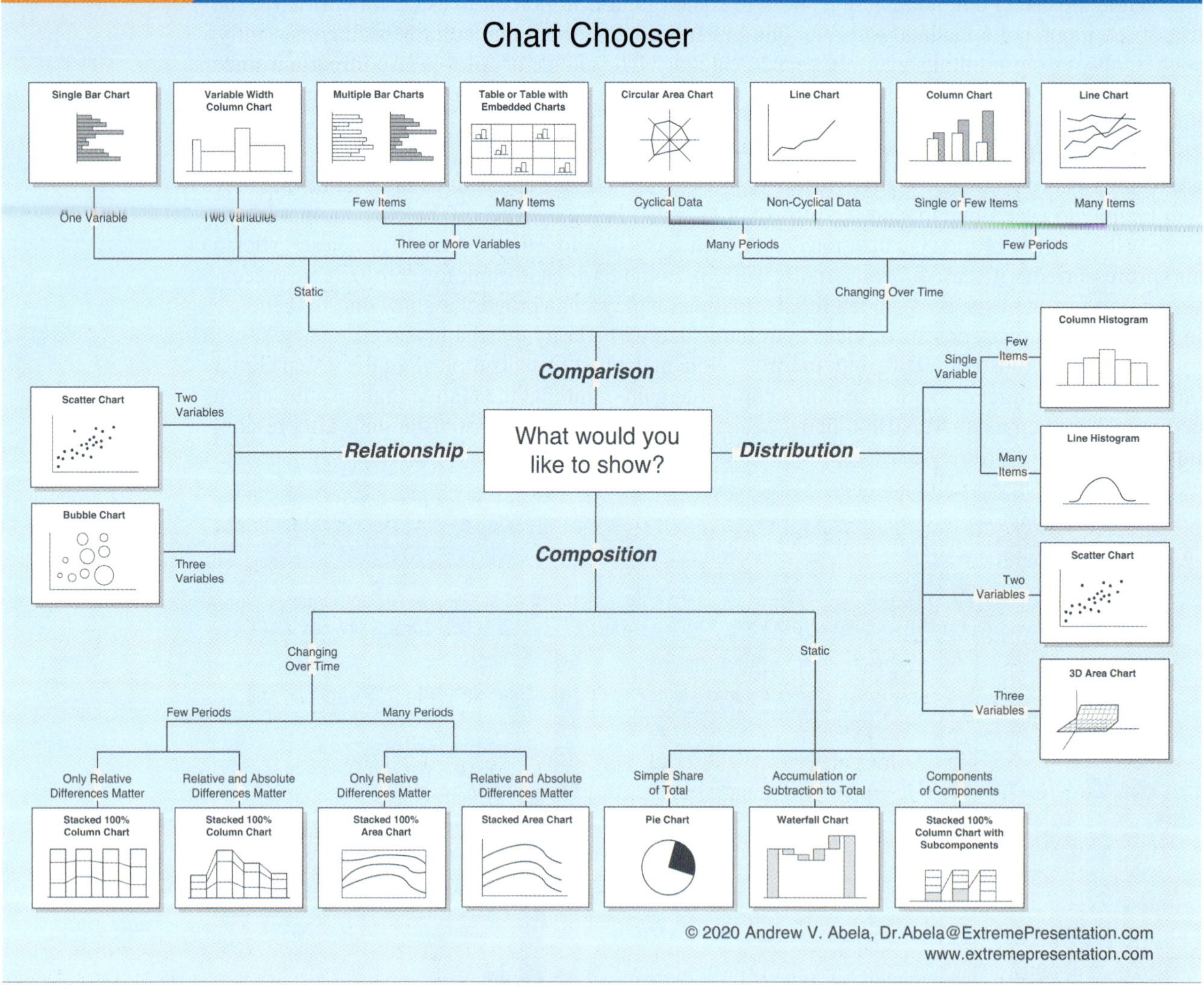

Column (vertical) charts and **bar** (horizontal) charts are best used to compare different categories. Adding labels to the bars rather than just having values showing on the axes makes it easier for the audience to determine these values. Finally, avoid using too many colors that just add to visual clutter.

As a general rule, **line charts** are best for illustrating changes over time and work best with continuous data. Best practices include clearly labeling the axes so the audience knows what is being shown, removing excess clutter such as grid lines and redundant labeling, and avoiding comparing more than five to seven lines.

Pie charts are best used to show parts of a whole. Be sure the parts add up to 100 percent. Pie charts work best when there are just a few categories. If there are many categories of similar size,

[5] Abela, Andrew V. (2013). *Advanced Presentations by Design: Creating Communication that Drives Action*. John Wiley & Sons.

consider using a bar or column chart instead. Finally, avoid the temptation to get "fancy" with 3-D imagery and tilting the pie chart.

Scatter plots are useful if the goal is to show correlations between two variables. They are also useful for showing data distributions and clustering, which can identify anomalies and outliers. A **bubble chart** can extend the capability of a scatter plot by adding an additional dimension through changing the size of each bubble in the scatter plot. The more data that is included in a scatter plot or bubble chart, the better are the comparisons that can be made. If the elements being graphed are distributed over a very wide range, the horizontal axis can be converted from a linear to a logarithmic scale (where the numbers on the horizontal axis increase by multiples of a number). Bubble charts should use only circles rather than other shapes. Bubble charts should be scaled based on the area of the circle and not the diameter.

A **map chart** is a good choice if the data being conveyed in the visualization includes geographic locations. Map charts are best at showing relative differences in numerical values among geographic locations rather than precise differences since the values are usually portrayed as differences in a color gradient.

There are several general rules to follow regardless of the chart type. The following list was found from a search of best practices for data visualization charts.[6]

- Time axis. When using time in charts, set it on the horizontal axis. Time should run from left to right. Do not skip values (time periods), even if there are no values.
- Proportional values. The numbers in a chart (displayed as bar, area, bubble, or other physically measured element in the chart) should be directly proportional to the numerical quantities presented.
- Visual clutter. Remove any excess information, lines, colors, and text from a chart that do not add value.
- Sorting. For column and bar charts, to enable easier comparison, sort your data in ascending or descending order by the value, not alphabetically. This applies also to pie charts.
- Legend. You don't need a legend if you have only one data category.
- Labels. Use labels directly on the line, column, bar, pie, etc., whenever possible, to avoid indirect look-up.
- Colors. In any chart, don't use more than six colors.
- Colors. For comparing the same value at different time periods, use the same color in a different intensity (from light to dark).
- Colors. For different categories, use different colors. The most widely used colors are black, white, red, green, blue, and yellow.
- Colors. Keep the same color palette or style for all charts in the series and the same axes and labels for similar charts to make your charts consistent and easy to compare.

BLOCKCHAIN TECHNOLOGY

LO6 Describe how blockchain technology works and its use within the accounting profession.

eLecture MBC

Blockchain technology differs from the traditional accounting ledger in a fundamental way that has immense implications for the accounting profession. A traditional ledger system is a closed system controlled at a centralized location with individuals at the centralized location responsible for the maintenance and integrity of the ledger. In contrast, a blockchain is an open, decentralized ledger, where the ledger is distributed across multiple computers called **nodes**. The blockchain ledger is managed autonomously by the distributed nodes such that data is authenticated by mass collaboration rather than by a central authority. Each node on the blockchain maintains a complete copy of all past transactions that have been added to the ledger. Thus, by comparing to the other nodes' copies, the ledger is continuously synchronized. Unlike traditional accounting ledgers, none of the nodes has any special rights that differ from those of the other nodes.

Blockchains get their name because new ledger data are periodically bundled into blocks, which are then added to previous blocks to form a chain. Each block can contain a cryptocurrency exchange, as is the case with **Bitcoin**, but other possibilities include sales transactions, equity

[6] https://eazybi.com/blog/data_visualization_and_chart_types/

trades, loan payments, election votes—pretty much any contract transaction. In addition, the block contains a **time stamp** and a **hash #**, which together form a cryptographic signature associated with the previous blocks. This time stamp and hash make the blockchain essentially tamper-proof because the blocks cannot be changed without the change being apparent to all other nodes. While the chain propagates in only a single chronological order, it can be audited in both directions. **Exhibit B.8** is a visual depiction of the blockchain process.

EXHIBIT B.8 Blockchain Process

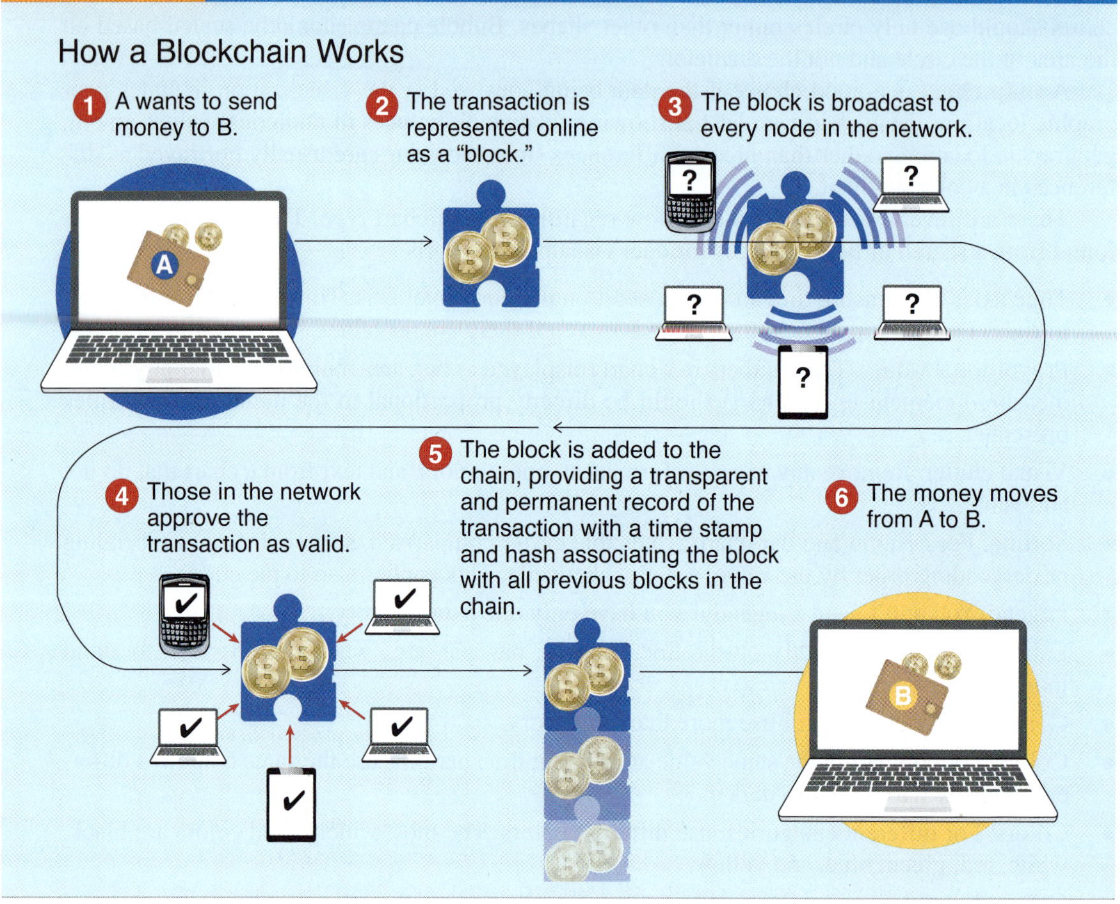
How a Blockchain Works
1 A wants to send money to B.
2 The transaction is represented online as a "block."
3 The block is broadcast to every node in the network.
4 Those in the network approve the transaction as valid.
5 The block is added to the chain, providing a transparent and permanent record of the transaction with a time stamp and hash associating the block with all previous blocks in the chain.
6 The money moves from A to B.
A
B

The accounting profession has seen changes arising from a vast array of technological innovations, from computer spreadsheets to general ledger software to enterprise resource systems. Blockchain technology represents another innovation in the way accounting is and will be performed. The invention of double-entry accounting, the bedrock of financial accounting, allowed managers to trust their own financial recordkeeping. Unfortunately, the same level of trust does not exist with outsiders, which is why companies rely on independent auditors for an opinion on the integrity of an entity's financial statements. These audits are often very time consuming and costly.

Accountants working in the traditional centralized-ledger environment are likely to spend a large amount of time reconciling accounts and amounts. This involves comparing balances at their company with external documents from outside entities, including banks, brokerages, and business partners, among others. In addition to the time-consuming process of acquiring all the needed sources of information and performing the comparisons, additional time and effort are often needed to reconcile any differences. In a blockchain's distributed ledger system, all node participants can continually confirm all transactions, greatly reducing the effort involved in periodic reconciliations.

Accountants working in the traditional environment are expected to produce internal, ad hoc reports. This often requires considerable effort reconciling internal documents, perhaps from multiple departments or divisions. In a blockchain environment, accountants spend far less time verifying transactional data, freeing up time for more valuable advisory activities.

As a final example of the many ways blockchain technology will change the way accountants work, consider the traditional closing of the books at the end of each period. Instead of needing to acquire the necessary data, verify its accuracy, and make all the necessary adjustments, one could envision a far more automated process with the use of blockchain technology. Financial statements could be updated continuously from data provided by the blockchain, making the period-ending closing process much less time consuming.

Blockchain technology is widely viewed as the next major step in financial accounting. Instead of keeping separate records documenting each transaction, transactions can be written directly into the decentralized ledger. Thus, each transaction is distributed and cryptographically signed to ensure against later falsification or destruction. This has the potential to allow auditors to automatically verify much of the data in a traditional audit, freeing them to provide value in more important areas, such as the analysis of complex transactions or operational efficiencies.

Some accountants may worry that these evolving technologies will diminish the need for accountants. If history is any indication, the opposite is likely. The accountant's role in the financial process will certainly change, but this change will be evolution, not extinction. Information will still need to be interpreted and categorized before entering the blockchain, and this is where future accountants will provide their value. The Big Four accounting firms realize this and are at the forefront in research on how blockchain technology will be used.

SUMMARY

Define Big Data and describe its four attributes. (p. B-2) **LO1**

- Big data is a collection of data that is both extremely large and also extremely complex, thus making its analysis beyond the scope of traditional tools.
- The four attributes of Big Data are volume, variety, velocity, and veracity.

Identify and define the four types of data analytics. (p. B-2) **LO2**

- Data analytics can broadly be defined as the process of examining sets of data with the goal of discovering useful information from patterns found in the data.
- Data analytics can be categorized into four types: descriptive, diagnostic, predictive, and prescriptive.

Describe the use of data analytics within the accounting profession. (p. B-3) **LO3**

- Many accountants are already performing descriptive and diagnositc data analytics.
- Accountants can add value by performing predictive and prescriptive data analytics.
- The large accounting firms have devoted large resources to data analytics.
- Being well trained in data analytics is important for future accountants.

Describe the analytics mindset. (p. B-4)

- Analytics is the process of deriving value from the data.
- An analytics mindset requires critical thinking and judgement.
- The four steps of the analytics mindset include (1) asking the right questions; (2) extracting, transforming, and loading the data; (3) applying the proper analytics techniques; and (4) interpreting and presenting the results.

Describe data visualization best practices. (p. B-6) **LO5**

- Form, position, and color can be used to have elements stand out without any conscious effort by the audience.
- Tufte's principles of design emphasize the elimination of visual clutter that serves to distract from the ability of a visualization to convey its message.
- Use of the proper chart type can help the intended audience to visualize comparisons, compositions, distributions, and relationships in the data.

Describe how blockchain technology works and its use within the accounting profession. (p. B-10) **LO 6**

- A blockchain represents a decentralized ledger system and each decentralized computer on the blockchain is called a node.

- Unlike a traditional ledger system where authority for maintenance and integrity rests at a centralized location, each node on the blockchain has the same rights as each other node.
- Each block in the blockchain contains information, such as transaction details, along with a time stamp and a hash linking the block to previous blocks in a chronological order.
- Blockchains are essentially tamperproof because alteration to a block by a node would be apparent to every other node on the blockchain.
- Blockchain technology represents another innovation that will change the way accountants perform their work. Blockchain technology will fundamentally change the way audits are performed, and greatly reduce the time and effort spent on tasks, such as reconciling source documents, producing ad hoc reports, and performing period-ending book closings.

VIDEO RESOURCES FOR TABLEAU

Many assignments require the use of Tableau. For anyone new to Tableau, the following videos are recommended. In addition to these videos, Tableau offers many more free training videos on its website under the learning tab.

A general introduction to the software. (25 minutes). https://www.tableau.com/learn/tutorials/on-demand/getting-started?playlist=484034

An introduction to the Tableau interface. (4 minutes). https://www.tableau.com/learn/tutorials/on-demand/tableau-interface?playlist=484034

Gaining an understanding of relationships in order to connect to outside data. Stop at 14 minutes and 33 seconds. https://www.tableau.com/learn/tutorials/on-demand/relationships?playlist=484036

A general introduction to visual analytics. (6 minutes). https://www.tableau.com/learn/tutorials/on-demand/getting-started-visual-analytics?playlist=484037

How to use sorting. (5 minutes). https://www.tableau.com/learn/tutorials/on-demand/sorting?playlist=484037

An introduction to filtering. (2 minutes). https://www.tableau.com/learn/tutorials/on-demand/ways-filter?playlist=484037

A deeper look at filtering. (7 minutes). https://www.tableau.com/learn/tutorials/on-demand/using-filter-shelf?playlist=484037

Using interactive filters. (4 minutes). https://www.tableau.com/learn/tutorials/on-demand/interactive-filters?playlist=484037

An introduction to formatting. (7 minutes). https://www.tableau.com/learn/tutorials/on-demand/formatting?playlist=484037

The formatting pane. (7 minutes). https://www.tableau.com/learn/tutorials/on-demand/formatting-pane?playlist=484037

An introduction to calculation in Tableau. (3 minutes). https://www.tableau.com/learn/tutorials/on-demand/getting-started-calculations?playlist=484040

Calculation syntax in Tableau. (4 minutes). https://www.tableau.com/learn/tutorials/on-demand/calculation-syntax?playlist=484040

MULTIPLE CHOICE

LO 1 Homework MBC

1. Which of the following are four characteristics of big data?
   a. Volume, variety, vagueness, veracity
   b. Volume, variety, velocity, veracity
   c. Volume, validate, velocity, veracity
   d. Volume, variety, velocity, vulnerability

LO 2 Homework MBC

2. Which of the following are the four categories of data analytics?
   a. Descriptive, diagnostic, predictive, prescriptive
   b. Expressive, diagnostic, predictive, prescriptive
   c. Descriptive, analytical, predictive, prescriptive
   d. Descriptive, diagnostic, prognostic, prescriptive

3. What is the correct order of the steps in the analytics mindset? **LO 4**

a. Extract, transform, and load the data; ask the right questions; apply the proper analytics techniques; interpret and present the results.

b. Ask the right questions; extract, transform, and load the data; apply the proper analytics techniques; interpret and present the results.

c. Ask the right questions; extract, transform, and load the data; interpret and present the results; apply the proper analytics techniques.

d. Ask the right questions; apply the proper analytics techniques; extract, transform, and load the data; interpret and present the results.

4. Charts are used in visualizations to convey the following primary types of information: **LO 5**

a. comparisons, compositions, distributions, and relationships.

b. comparisons, historical, distributions, and relationships.

c. comparisons, compositions, forecasts, and relationships.

d. geographical, compositions, distributions, and relationships.

5. Which of the following statements is not true regarding the use of color in a chart? **LO 5**

a. Use at most six different colors in a chart.

b. To show changes in an item over time use a color gradient rather than different colors.

c. Always use color in a chart to differentiate items.

d. Use the same color palette in a chart series.

6. The glue that binds blocks in a blockchain consists of what? **LO 6**

a. Time stamps

b. Sequential numbering

c. Regulatory approval

d. Hashes

e. Both *a.* and *d.*

Assignments with the MBC logo in the margin are available in myBusinessCourse. See the Preface of the book for details.

EXERCISES

EB-7. Public accounting firms and data analytics. **LO 1, 2**
Go to PWC.com and select "Services" and then "Data and Analytics." Choose a topic and write about how PWC is using data analytics to help its clients.

EB-8. Public accounting firms and data analytics. **LO 1, 2**
Go to KPMG.com and select "Insights." Under "Areas of interest," select "Special Attention" and then "Data and Analytics." Choose a topic and write about how KPMG is using data analytics to help its clients.

EB-9. Public accounting firms and data analytics. **LO 1, 2**
Go to Deloitte.com and select "Services" and then "Analytics." Choose a topic and write about how Deloitte is using data analytics to help its clients.

EB-10. Public accounting firms and data analytics. **LO 1, 2**
Go to EY.com and enter Big data and analytics in the search bar. Choose a topic and write about how Ernst & Young is using data analytics to help its clients.

EB-11. Public accounting firms and blockchain technology. **LO 6**
Go to PWC.com and search for "blockchain." Choose a topic and write about how PWC is using blockchain to help its clients.

EB-12. Public accounting firms and blockchain technology. **LO 6**
Go to KPMG.com and search for "blockchain." Choose a topic and write about how KPMG is using blockchain to help its clients.

EB-13. Public accounting firms and blockchain technology. **LO 6**
Go to Deloitte.com and search for "blockchain." Select "Blockchain—Perspectives, insights, and analysis." Choose a topic and write about how Deloitte is using blockchain to help its clients.

EB-14. Public accounting firms and blockchain technology. **LO 6**
Go to EY.com and search for "blockchain." Choose a topic and write about how Ernst & Young is using blockchain to help its clients.

PROBLEMS

Problems PB-15 through PB-16 use data on employee statistics. The data is contained in the Excel file Employee Data Tableau.xlsx and is accessible in myBusinessCourse.

LO 1, 2, 3 **PB-15. Using Tableau to create summary statistics.**

Homework MBC

+tableau

Go to myBusinessCourse and download the Excel file **Employee Data Tableau.xlsx**. Connect Tableau Public to this Excel file. Go to the worksheet and drag the measures "Education," "Jobcat," and "Jobtime" up to Dimensions. Compare the average salaries by gender and minority status by dragging "Gender" to Rows and "Minority" to Columns and then "Salary" to the canvas. Change salary from a sum to an average.

a. How do average salaries compare by gender and minority status?

Next, explore how education level affects this relation by dragging "Education" to Columns. It may be easier to make this comparison by switching the order of "Minority" and "Education" on the Columns bar.

b. Does education level affect how average salaries compare by gender and minority status?

Next, change salary from average to maximum.

c. Does education level affect how maximum salaries compare by gender and minority status?

LO 3,4 **PB-16. Using Tableau to calculate a visualization.**

Homework MBC

+tableau

Starting with the results from PB-15, change salary back to average. Select the side-by-side bar chart (ninth selection) from the "show me" selections.

Based on this visualization of the data, what can you say about relative salaries for males and females and for caucasians and minorities?

Problems PB-17 through PB-19 use data on executive compensation from S&P 500 companies for the years 2015 through 2019. The data is contained in the Excel file Compensation Data 2015_2019 SP500.xlsx that is available in myBusinessCourse.

LO 3, 4 **PB-17. Executive Compensation Visualizations with Tableau—Part I.**

Homework MBC

+tableau

As a researcher in executive compensation you desire to learn more about the compensation differences between men and women in the roles of Chief Executive Officer (CEO) and Chief Financial Officer (CFO). Data including salary and total compensation, including salary, bonus, stock option awards, and miscellaneous income, for both men and woman serving as CEOs and CFOs for S&P 500 companies for the five years 2015 through 2019 is contained in the Excel file **Compensation Data 2015_2019 SP500.xlsx**. First connect to this file with Tableau and change the Year field from a number to a date type. Next create the following visualizations:

a. A crosstab showing median salary by gender for the entire database. One method to accomplish this is to drag the dimension Gender to the rows shelf and then drag the measure Salary directly to the canvas. Next change the measure of Salary from Sum to Median. Do men or women have a higher median salary and by how much?

b. Create a crosstab that separates CEO median total compensation (Measure Comp1) by gender and Sector. Also show how many individual CEOs are shown by gender and sector. One method to accomplish this is to drag the dimension Sector Name to the columns shelf and the dimensions Position and Gender to the rows shelf. Next drag the measures Comp1 and WRDS(Count) directly to the canvas. Finally change the measure of Comp1 to median. In the consumer Staples sector, how many men and how many women are CEOs, and what is their median total compensation? Note that the totals shown are combined for all five years.

c. Create a separate visualization in the form of a vertical bar chart that displays CEO total compensation by sector, position, and gender. Provide interactive filters for Year, Position, Gender, and Sector Name. Finally, use colors to highlight gender. Within the information technology sector, how much higher is the median compensation for male CEOs than for female CEOs in 2019? What is the name of the highest paid female CEO in this segment and where does she work? One method to accomplish this is to drag the dimensions Sector Name, Position, and Gender to the columns shelf. Next drag the measure Comp1 to the rows shelf and change the measure to Median. Drag Year, Position, Gender, and Sector Name to the Filters shelf and then select Show Filter from each dimension pull down arrow. Select CEO from the Position filter and 2018 from the Year filter. Finally drag Gender to the Color card and WRDS (Count) and Comp1 to the Label card. To see the data behind each of the bars simply hover over the bar and right click and then select Full Data.

d. Save the file for future use.

PB-18. Executive Compensation Visualizations with Tableau—Part II. **LO 3, 4**

To further your research in executive compensation you would like to see the location by state, the level of executive compensation, and also where females hold the position of CFO.

a. Create a map visualization that shows the location of companies that employ female CFOs. In 2016, which state had the highest level of median compensation for a female CFO? Who was the CFO, how much was she paid, and what company did she work for? One way to accomplish this is to first create a map by holding the control key on a Windows machine or the command key on a Mac and select the measures Latitude and Longitude, and then select the map from the Show Me menu. Next drag Total Comp 1 over the Color card and change the measure to Median. Drag the dimension State over the Detail card and the measure WRDS(Count) over the Label card. Drag Gender, Position, Sector Name, and Year to the Filter shelf and select to show these filters. Select 2016 from the Year filter, CFO from the Position filter, and Female from the Gender filter. The state of Washington should appear the darkest indicating the highest median compensation. Click on this state and then click on the View data icon in the top right corner. Select the Full Data tab.

b. Save the file for future use.

PB-19. Executive Compensation Visualizations with Tableau—Part III. **LO 3, 4**

In order to present your findings, you decide to construct a dashboard in Tableau that integrates the visualizations you created in problems PB-17 and PB-18. You wish to allow the user of the dashboard to interact by having the bar chart serve as a filter for the map visualization.

a. Create a dashboard with the bar chart visualization created in problem PB-17 on the top and the map visualization created in problem PB-18 on the bottom. Make the bar chart serve as a filter for the map. What state had the most female CFOs in 2018 from the financials sector and what companies did they work for? How many male CFOs worked in the financials sector in 2018 in that state? Who was the only female CEO in the real estate sector in 2018 and in what state did she work and for what company? What was her total compensation in 2018? How many male CEOs were there in the real estate sector in 2018, and what state employed the largest number? One way to create this dashboard is to open a new dashboard and drag in the bar chart visualization to the top and the map visualization under it. Next click on the bar chart visualization and click on the funnel icon to turn it on as a filter. In order to see the number of individuals in each bar, you can go back to the bar chart and modify the visualization by dragging WRDS(Count) over the Tooltip card.

b. Save the file for future use.

Problems PB-20 through PB-22 use financial statement data for S&P 500 companies for the years 2015 through 2019. The data is contained in the Excel file Compustat SP500 2015_2019.xlsx that is available in myBusinessCourse.

PB-20. Building Basic Tableau Financial Accounting Visualizations. **LO 3, 4**

a. Connect the Tableau software to the Excel file **Compustat SP500 2015_2019.xlsx**. This file consists of four worksheets. First bring in the Balance sheet worksheets and then join both the cash flow statement and the income statement worksheets to the balance sheet worksheets using both of the fields company name and year.

b. What is the sum of net income for all firms in the database for all years combined? One way to determine this is to drag the measure Net income to the canvas.

c. How many unique companies are included in the database? One way to determine this is to drag the dimension Company name to the rows shelf and then select Measure Count (Distinct) from the pull-down menu on the Company name pill.

d. How many distinct firms are there in each segment? One way to determine this is to drag the dimension Segment to the Columns shelf in the visualization created in part *c*. The totals for each segment will appear if the Show marks label is checked in the Label card.

e. What is the sum of total assets for all companies in each segment for the year 2018? One way to determine this is to drag the dimension Segment to the Columns shelf and then drag the Total Assets measure to the Rows shelf. Next drag the Year dimension to the filters shelf, select year as the filter, click next, and then check 2018. Totals for total assets can be seen in the tool tip by hovering over any bar or by checking Show marks label in the Label card.

f. What firm had the most sales in 2018? What segment was this firm in? One way to determine this is to drag the dimension Company name to the rows shelf and drag the measure Sales to the columns shelf. Next drag the Year dimension to the filters shelf, select year as the filter, click next, and then check 2018. Segments can be highlighted by dragging the dimension Segment over the color card. Finally sort the Company names by Sales by clicking the sort icon in the tool bar.

g. Save the file for future use.

LO 3, 4 **PB-21. Tableau Visualizations to Analyze Accounting Performance Measures.**

Homework MBC

+ableau

You recently joined a firm as a junior financial analyst, and you would like to make a good impression by showing your manager the power of visualizations for analyzing data. In order to get a feel for the Tableau software and the dataset you created of financial statement data for S&P 500 firms, you decided to create a few very basic visualizations.

Two widely used ratios to analyze company performance are gross profit percentage and return on sales. You would like to create a visualization that compares these two ratios by segment and further compares segment performance to the median values of these ratios for the entire database of companies.

a. Because of the way cost of goods sold is reported for companies in the real estate segment you decide to exclude this segment from the visualization. After excluding real estate, for the year 2017, which segment reported the highest median value for gross profit percentage and for return on sales?

b. Did any segment report a higher median return on sales than the upper band of the 95 percent confidence interval of overall median return on sales in 2015?

c. Which company had the highest gross profit percentage in 2018 for the segment with the highest median gross profit percentage?

LO 3, 4 **PB-22. Using Tableau to Analyze Inventory.**

Homework MBC

+ableau

You have learned of the importance of a company being able to sell its products in a timely fashion, and that the ratio of days sales in inventory provides this useful information. You decide a dashboard would be helpful in seeing whether this ratio is improving or declining in the consumer discretionary and the consumer staples segments between 2017 and 2018. You build two sheets that are included in the dashboard. The first sheet shows the level of the ratio for each segment for the two years in question. The second sheet shows the change in the ratio between the two years.

Has the ratio days sales in inventory improved or declined in the consumer discretionary and the consumer staples segments between 2017 and 2018. By how much?

LO 2, 3, 4 **PB-23. Using Tableau for Accounts Receivable Aging—Hugo Enterprises.**

Homework MBC

+ableau

Hugo Enterprises has been performing its aging of accounts receivable manually; however, the task is becoming too time consuming. The company has recently acquired Tableau for some data visualizations; however, it was mentioned that the software could be used for receivables aging. You have been asked to perform Hugo's accounts receivable aging using Tableau.

- The Excel file **Hugo Aging Tableau.xlsx** can be found in myBusinessCourse with Hugo's accounts receivable amounts and due dates.
- The first step is to link the Excel file to Tableau. Within Tableau, within the Connect column on the left, select Microsoft Excel. Locate **Hugo Aging Tableau.xlsx** and then click Open.
- If the file needs to be cleaned up for further use, select the checkbox for using the built-in Data Interpreter. This particular file has already been completely cleaned up, so no further work is required here. Now there should appear three columns with customer, amount, and due date data.
- Click on Sheet 1 (this can be renamed) in order to begin creating the aging table.
- A calculated field will need to be created that computes the number of days each invoice is past due. Select Analysis and then select Create Calculated Field. Name this measure Past Due. Next use the formula DateDiff('day',[Due Date],#2023-12-31#). Note the formula is case sensitive and then click OK.
- We now want to put these past due amounts into groupings. We will do this by creating bins and each of the bins will be 30 days. Right-click on the newly created Past Due pill from the Measures shelf on the left of the screen and then select Create and then select Bins. Change the size of the bins to 30 and click OK. A Past Due bin now shows up under Dimensions on the

top left of the screen. Double-click the Past Due (bin) in the Dimensions shelf to see a list of the aging groups. To fill in the table with invoice amounts, simply double-click on the Amount measure in the Measures shelf.

- In order to see the data that makes up each total in the aging table, simply click on the amount and then select the view data icon on the top right corner and select Full Data at the bottom of the pop-up window.
- In order to see a visualization of the data, simply select an appropriate chart from the show me selections.

a. What is Hugo's total dollar value of the invoices that are between 31 and 60 days past due?

b. What is its largest invoice within the 91- to 120-day grouping?

PB-24. Using Tableau for Accounts Receivable Aging—Javier Enterprises. **LO 2, 3, 4**

Homework MBC

+ableau

Javier Enterprises has been performing its aging of accounts receivable manually; however, the task is becoming too time consuming. The company has recently acquired Tableau for some data visualizations; however, it was mentioned that the software could be used for receivables aging. You have been asked to perform Javier's accounts receivable aging using Tableau.

- The Excel file **Javier Aging Tableau.xlsx** can be found in myBusinessCourse with Javier's accounts receivable amounts and due dates.
- The first step is to link the Excel file to Tableau. Within Tableau, within the Connect column on the left, select Microsoft Excel. Locate **Javier Aging Tableau.xlsx** and then click Open.
- If the file needs to be cleaned up for further use, select the checkbox for using the built-in Data Interpreter. This particular file has already been completely cleaned up, so no further work is required here. Now there should appear three columns with customer, amount, and due date data.
- Click on Sheet 1 (this can be renamed) in order to begin creating the aging table.
- A calculated field will need to be created that computes the number of days each invoice is past due. Select Analysis and then select Create Calculated Field. Name this measure Past Due. Next use the formula DateDiff('day',[Due Date],#2023-12-31#). Note the formula is case sensitive and then click OK.
- We now want to put these past due amounts into groupings. We will do this by creating bins, and each of the bins will be 30 days. Right-click on the newly created Past Due bill from the Measures shelf on the left of the screen and then select Create and then select Bins. Change the size of the bins to 30 and click OK. A Past Due bin now shows up under Dimensions on the top left of the screen. Double-click the Past Due (bin) in the Dimensions shelf to see a list of the aging groups. To fill in the table with invoice amounts, simply double-click on the Amount measure in the Measures shelf.
- In order to see the data that makes up each total in the aging table, simply click on the amount and then select the view data icon on the top right corner and select Full Data at the bottom of the pop-up window.
- In order to see a visualization of the data, simply select an appropriate chart from the show me selections.

a. What is Javier Enterprises' total dollar value of the invoices that are between 31 and 60 days past due?

b. What is its largest invoice within the 91- to 120-day grouping?

PB-25. Using Tableau for Fraud Detection. **LO 2, 3, 4**

Homework MBC

+ableau

Benford's Law represents a powerful tool in the forensic accountant's toolkit to aid in the detection of fraud. Benford's Law is a mathematical law that recognizes the leading (first) digit in many real-life number sets is distributed in a certain manner, and often not in the manner that a fraudster would expect. Specifically the number 1 occurs as the first digit approximately 30 percent of the time, with each succeeding digit appearing less often as follows: 1–30%, 2–18%, 3–12%, 4–10%, 5–8%, 6–7%, 7–6%, 8–5%, and 9–5%. Fraudsters who are unaware of this natural ordering will often arrange digits in a random order that deviates from Benford's Law.

In Part A of this problem you will use Tableau to show how a natural dataset of GDP by country conforms to Benford's Law and how a random set of numbers does not. In Part B you will use the same data used in an actual court case to convict a fraudster of embezzlement. Finally, in Part C you will use Benford's Law to test a new reimbursement procedure for possible fraud. A video demonstrating the Tableau tools used in this problem is available on this textbook's website.

Part A Use Tableau to show how a natural dataset of GDP by country conforms to Benford's Law and how a random set of numbers does not.

- Download the file **GDP Tableau.xlsx** from myBusinessCourse. The file contains World Bank GDP data by country for 2018, along with a separate column of random numbers that was generated in Excel using the command =RAND()*1000.
- After you have uploaded the workbook to Tableau, create two calculated fields.
- The first calculated field will pull the first digit from each country's GDP amount. Choose Analysis > Create Calculated Field and name the calculation First Integer. Then either type or paste the following formula in the formula area: LEFT(STR([GDP]),1)
- Next create a second calculated field named Benfords Law by typing or pasting the following in the formula area: LOG(INT([First Integer])+1)- LOG(INT([First Integer]))
- To create the visualization, drag First Integer from the Dimensions area to Columns and drag Number of Records from the Measures area to Rows. Click Sum(Number of Records) on Rows to show the pull-down menu and choose Quick Table Calculation > Percent of Total. The visualization should now show a bar chart with the bars conforming to Benford's Law.
- While it is relatively easy to see that the data conforms to Benford's Law, with a little more work the visualization can be significantly enhanced. To do this, drag Benfords Law from the Measures area of the Data pane to Detail on the Marks card, and then click Benfords Law on the Marks card and choose Measure > Minimum.
- Next switch from the current Data pane to the Analytics pane and then drag Distribution Band over the chart and drop it on the cell icon in the pop-up. A dialog box will appear. Under computation change the value to percentages of 90,100,110 and select Percent of to be Min(Benfords Law). Choose a fill line as the thick black line and then click OK.
- Finally click on the Label icon in the Marks section and select the Show marks labels box.

a. Does the GDP data appear to conform to Benford's Law?

Now return to the Data pane and create a new calculated field for the random numbers by naming the calculation Random Values and typing or pasting the following formula in the formula area: LEFT(STR([Random]),1)

- Drag the Min(Benfords Law) pill out of the Marks area to remove the bands and drag Random Values from the Dimensions area on top of First Integer to replace it in the visualization. If both pills remain in the columns section, simply drag First Integer away.

b. Do the random values appear to conform with Benford's Law?

Part B Use the same data used in an actual court case to convict a fraudster of embezzlement.

In the 1993 court case *State of Arizona v. Wayne James Nelson* Benford's Law was used to convict the defendant of defrauding the state of nearly $2 million by diverting money to a nonexistent vendor. Nelson tried to make the checks appear random; however, he was unaware that these check amounts should actually follow Benford's Law much closer than the random distribution he created. Download the file **Arizona Fraud.xlsx** from myBusinessCourse and follow the same procedure as you did in Part A above and use Tableau to show how the data conforms to Benford's Law.

a. From a casual observation of the checks, can you detect anything suspect?
b. After using Benford's Law, does the list of checks appear suspect?

Part C Use Benford's Law to test a new reimbursement procedure for possible fraud.

Wally's Enterprises has been reimbursing its employees for business expenses after the employee submits detailed evidence of the expense, such as paid receipts. Management has recently changed the reimbursement policy because of the time spent checking all the submitted evidence, with an especially high volume of smaller reimbursement requests. The new policy only requires evidence be submitted if the reimbursement request exceeds $50. As the company's internal auditor, you are concerned that this policy change may result in fraudulent reimbursement requests. In order to test the new policy, you have gathered a random sample of 100 reimbursement requests from both before and after the policy change. This data is located in the file **Expense Reimbursement.xlsx** in myBusinessCourse. Download this file and using Tableau, apply Benford's Law to test whether the new policy appears to have resulted in any fraud.

a. Do the reimbursement requests prior to the policy change appear to follow Benford's Law?
b. Do the reimbursement requests occurring after the policy change appear to follow Benford's Law?
c. What, if anything, leads you to believe that fraud may be occurring?

Problems PB-26 through PB-31 use financial statement data for S&P 500 companies for the years 2015 through 2019. The data is contained in the Excel file Compustat SP500 2015_2019.xlsx. The file can be downloaded myBusinessCourse.

PB-26. Using Tableau to Analyze Fixed Assets. LO 3, 4

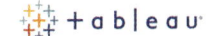

One of the ratios that provides information on how well a company utilizes its assets is the ratio asset turnover. As part of your analysis of different segments of the S&P 500 you would like to have a visualization that ranks companies within various segments by their asset turnover.

a. For the year 2019 what firm in the consumer discretionary segment had the second highest asset turnover? How did the same firm rank in 2018? Did the segment Consumer Discretionary or Consumer Staples have a higher median level of asset turnover in 2017? One way to determine this is to create a visualization by first creating a calculated field of the ratio asset turnover and then dragging the dimensions Segment and Company Name to the rows shelf and the ratio asset turnover to the columns shelf. Using the pull-down arrow of the ratio's pill, change the measure to median. Next sort the horizontal bar chart by Company Name. Drag the dimension Year to the filter shelf and select Show filter. Finally switch from the Data pane to the Analytics pane and drag Median with 95% Cl on the canvas and place the distribution band on Pane.

b. Save the file for future use.

PB-27. Using Tableau to Analyze Liquidity. LO 3, 4

A popular ratio for analyzing a company's short-term liquidity is the current ratio. In your continuing analysis of S&P 500 companies, you have decided to build a simple visualization that uses color highlighting and tooltip labeling to show current ratios by segment over the five-year period 2015 through 2019. You also desire to do some further analysis in Excel, so you will want to export this data as a crosstab to Excel. Finally, you want to include your visualization in a PowerPoint presentation.

a. What segment has the highest current ratio in each year? One way to create this visualization is to first create the calculated field current ratio. Next drag the dimension Year to the Columns shelf and the ratio Current ratio to the Rows shelf. Next change the ratio's measure to median. Finally drag the dimension Segment over the Color card. In order to export the data as a crosstab to Excel click on the worksheet tab in the menu bar and choose Export > Crosstab to excel. If you would prefer to see the data as a crosstab in Tableau, right-click on the Tableau workbook icon and choose Duplicate as crosstab. Finally, to export the visualization to PowerPoint, select File from the menu bar and choose Export as PowerPoint.

b. Save the file for future use.

PB-28. Using Tableau to Analyze Dividend Policy. LO 3, 4

Many equity investors are particularly interested in the dividend paying policy of a company. Two ratios that provide information in this regard are the dividend payout ratio and the dividend yield. As an analyst you would like to build a visualization that looks at these two ratios together and in particular which segments outperform the S&P500 in general.

a. For the year 2015, did any segment outperform or underperform the median S&P500 company for both the dividend payout and dividend yield by more than a 95 percent confidence level? One way to determine this is to first create calculated fields for both dividend yield and dividend payout and then build a scatter graph visualization with median dividend payout on the columns shelf and median dividend yield on the rows shelf. Next drag Segment to the Color card to color highlight the segments. Drag Year to the filter shelf in order to filter on Year. Finally, switch to the Analytics pane and drag Median with 95% Cl to the canvas.

b. Save the file for future use.

PB-29. Using Tableau to Study ROE with the Dupont Method—Part I. LO 3, 4

One of the basic tools in any analyst's toolkit is the DuPont method of Return on Equity (ROE) decomposition. You would like to build a series of visualizations to exploit the DuPont method to find value in equities. To do this you will need visualizations that show, by segment, both ROE and the components of ROE, namely Return on Sales (ROS), Asset Turnover (AT), and Leverage (LEV).

a. Which segment had the highest ROE in both 2017 and 2018? Which component of ROE was mostly responsible? The first step in determining this is to create calculated fields for ROE, ROS, AT, and LEV. The next step is to create a vertical bar chart visualization by dragging the dimensions Segment and Year to the Columns shelf and the median measure of the four new calculated fields to the Rows shelf. The dimension Year needs to be dragged to the filter shelf with the years 2017 and 2018 selected. Finally, Segment can be dragged over the Color card to highlight by color.

b. Which segment showed the largest gain and the largest decline in ROE between 2017 and 2018? This is best shown on a dashboard by combining two separate visualizations. The first visualization in the form of a vertical bar chart can be constructed by dragging the dimensions Segment and Year to the Column shelf and the measure of Median ROE to the rows shelf. The dimension Year should be dragged to the filters shelf and the years 2017 and 2018 selected. To make segments easier to see in the visualization, Segment can be dragged over the Color card to highlight by color. The second visualization, which will show the change in the ratio between 2017 and 2018, can be accomplished by first dragging the dimensions Segment and Year to the Columns shelf and also dragging the dimension Year to the filters shelf and selecting the years 2017 and 2018. Next drag the ratio ROE to the rows shelf and change its measure to median. In order to show the change between years use the pull-down arrow on the ratio's pill and select Quick table calculation and then Difference. Finally, right-click on the year 2017 on the horizontal axis and select hide. To make segments easier to see in the visualization, Segment can be dragged over the Color card to highlight by color. As the last step, create a new dashboard and drag the two visualizations in.

c. Save the file for future use.

LO 3, 4 **PB-30. Using Tableau to Study ROE with the Dupont Method—Part II.**

Homework MBC

tableau

You wish to continue your analysis of segment ROE by looking at trends within segments and then identifying which companies rank the highest for ROE within those segments.

a. For the period 2015 through 2019, which segments showed the best positive trends in ROE growth? One way to create a line chart visualization showing this trend is to drag the dimensions Segment and Year to the Columns shelf and drag the Median measure of ROE to the Rows shelf. To make segments easier to see in the visualization, Segment can be dragged over the Color card to highlight by color. Finally, switch to the Analytics pane and drag Trend line to the canvas, selecting "linear."

b. For the segments identified in part *a*, which firms reported the highest ROE in 2019? A horizontal bar chart visualization can be created by dragging the dimensions Segment and Company name to the Rows shelf and the Median measure of ROE to the columns shelf. Segment and Year can be dragged to the filters shelf to allow filtering on these two dimensions. Finally, to aid in the analysis, the company names can be sorted by clicking on the sort icon located on the tool bar.

c. Save the file for future use.

LO 3, 4 **PB-31. Using Tableau to Study ROE with the Dupont Method—Part III.**

Homework MBC

tableau

To complete your analysis of the DuPont method, you would like to have an interactive dashboard that allows the user to select any of the S&P 500 companies and see its segment, its change in ROE between 2017 and 2018, along with the changes in each of the items making up components of ROE.

a. How much did Alphabet's (the parent company of Google) ROE improve between 2017 and 2018 and which component showed the largest increase? Pick any other company and answer the same question. One approach to build this dashboard is to first create five visualizations. The first horizontal bar chart visualization can be created by dragging the dimensions Company name and Year to the Rows shelf and the measure ROE to the Columns shelf. The dimension Year needs to be dragged to the filters shelf and the years 2017 and 2018 selected. Next drag the dimension Company name to the filters shelf and click on Show filter from the pills pull-down menu. To allow segments to be highlighted by color in the visualization, Segment can be dragged over the Color card. This process can be repeated to create separate visualizations for the components of ROE, namely ROS, AT, and LEV. The fifth visualization, a line chart, can be created by dragging the dimension Year to the Columns shelf and the measures Net Income, Stockholders Equity, Sales, and Total Assets to the rows shelf. The dimension Year should be dragged to the filters shelf and the years 2017 and 2018 selected. The dimension Company name should also be dragged to the filters shelf and then have Show filter selected. Finally, to allow segments to be highlighted by color in the visualization, Segment can be dragged over the Color card. Now that each of the visualizations are complete, create a dashboard by dragging the first four visualizations, one under the other, on the left side of the dashboard and drag the fifth visualization to the right side of the dashboard. Convert the filter of Company name to a Single Value drop-down floating filter by selecting those two options and position the filter at the top of the dashboard.

b. Save the file for future use.

PB-32. Using Microsoft Excel for descriptive analytics. LO 1, 2

Go to myBusinessCourse and download the Excel file **Employee Data Excel.xlsx**. You will need to have the Analysis Toolpak add-in installed in Excel. It can be found under the Tools tab. If it does not appear, select Excel Add-ins under the Tools tab, and then check Analysis Toolpak. From the Excel ribbon, select Data and then Data Analysis. From the pop-up window, choose Descriptive Statistics and then click OK. Select the salary column as the input range and check the box for labels in the first row. Choose "New Worksheet" as the output option, click summary statistics, and click OK. Report the following:

a. Mean (average) salary

b. Median salary

c. Minimum salary

d. Maximum salary

e. Number of salary observations in the database

PB-33. Using the Microsoft Excel PivotTable function for descriptive analytics. LO 1, 2

Go to myBusinessCourse and download the Excel file **Employee Data Excel.xlsx**. Place your cursor anywhere in the table of data. From the Excel ribbon, select Insert and then Pivot Table. The entire table should be selected automatically along with the choice to output the PivotTable to a new worksheet. Select OK. From the PivotTable Fields section, select and drag "Gender" and "Minority" to the "Rows" box below. Select and drag the variable "Education" to the "Columns" box. Select and drag the variable "Salary" to the "Values" box. Change the sum of salary to the average of salary by clicking the "i" icon to the right of the "Sum of Salary," choosing "Average," and then clicking OK. Report the following:

a. Does additional education appear to be associated with a higher average salary?

b. Do males (1) or females (0) appear to earn higher average salaries?

c. Do minorities (1) or nonminorities (0) appear to earn higher average salaries? Does this hold for both genders?

d. What is the average salary of the entire population? What is the average salary of the entire population of males? What is the average salary of the entire population of females? What is the average salary of the entire population of male minorities? What is the average salary of the entire population of female minorities?

PB-34. Using Microsoft Excel for diagnostic analytics. LO 1, 2

Go to myBusinessCourse and download the Excel file **Employee Data Excel.xlsx**. You will need to have the Analysis Toolpak add-in installed in Excel. It can be found under the Tools tab. If it does not appear, you will need to select Excel Add-ins under the Tools tab and then check Analysis Toolpak. From the Excel ribbon, select Data and then Data Analysis. From the pop-up window, choose "Regression," and then click OK. Select values in the "Salary" column as the Input Y Range and values in the columns for "Gender" through "Education" for the Input X Range. Choose "New Worksheet" as the output option, and then click OK. Report the following:

a. A measure on how well the independent variables gender, minority, and education are able to explain the variation in average salary is the adjusted R Squared. What percentage of the variation in average salaries is described by these variables?

b. The *t* Stat is a measure of how an individual independent variable explains variation in the dependent variable average salary. An absolute value greater than 2 is generally considered a significant value in explaining variation. What do the *t* Stats tell us about the ability of the variables gender, minority, and education to explain average salary?

Problems PB-35 through PB-38. will be using the Excel file Compensation Data 2015_2019 SP500.xlsx that can be downloaded from myBusinessCourse.

PB-35. Building a basic Excel PivotTable. LO 3, 4

You have been tasked by a compensation consulting firm to research compensation amounts being paid to executives in large public companies. In particular you wish to learn more about amounts being paid to CEOs and CFOs within certain industries and how these amounts differ by gender.

You have gathered a large database of amounts paid by the S&P500 companies during the period 2015 through 2019.

a. Your first task is to build a PivotTable that separately shows the average salaries paid to CEOs and CFOs by gender on the rows and these amounts by industry segment on the columns. You do not need to separate the data by year at this time. What was the average salary paid to female CEOs in the healthcare segment? How does this compare to male CEOs in the same segment? Were there more male or female CFOs in the Consumer Staples segment?

b. What was the total average salary of all CEOs and CFOs in the information technology segment? Did CEOs or CFOs get paid more? Did males or females get paid more?

LO 3, 4 **PB-36. Sorting, grouping, and filtering a basic PivotTable.**

Homework MBC

You have been asked to construct a basic PivotTable that shows by position and gender the average salary, average total compensation, and number of executives in each of the industry segments.

a. Construct a PivotTable with Position, Gender, and Sector name on the rows and the average salary, average total compensation, and the count of executives in the columns. To make things easier to read, sort the Sector names by the average of salaries. What sector paid its female CEOs the highest average salary and how many female CEOs made up this calculation? Answer the same question for female CFOs.

b. Rather than combining all five years together you would like to answer similar questions for a single year. Add the year measure to the filter and select 2017. Repeat the questions from part *a*, but this time report the lowest paying segment.

c. Copy the entire PivotTable to the right on the same worksheet, but this time sort by the count of the executives rather than by the average salary. Again, filter by year, but this time select 2018. Which industry segment employs the second most male CFOs?

d. You would like for the reader of these PivotTables to interact with them so that they can answer specific questions regarding the data within the PivotTables. In order to add interactivity, insert four slicers, one for position and one for gender, one for years and one for segment. Connect each slicer to both of the PivotTables through the report connections. Also, make each slicer multi-select. What was the average salary and number of male CFOs in the consumer staples segment in 2018?

e. Finally, you are interested in how much of an executive's total compensation is from salary. Rather than doing the calculation for each industry segment, you decide to create a calculated field of salary as a percentage of total compensation. What percentage of the female CFOs in the industrials segment during 2016 was from salary?

LO 3, 4 **PB-37. Adding a PivotChart to a PivotTable.**

Homework MBC

Your audience is having difficulty reading through all the numbers in the PivotTables and would like an easier method to visualize the data. In particular they are interested in seeing the relative salaries among the executives within the various industry segments.

a. Create a PivotTable with position, gender, and sector name in the rows and the average of salary for values. Format the average of salary using number format as currency with zero decimal places. Sort the rows using the field sector name by the value average of salary. Add slicers for gender, year, position, and sector name. Finally, add a PivotChart in the form of a bar chart and give it the title "Salary by position, gender, and industry" and add data labels to the bars. Observe how making selections in the slicers updates both the PivotTable and the PivotChart. Select female CFOs in 2017. What industry segment paid the fifth highest average salary? Answer the same question for male CFOs in 2016.

LO 3, 4 **PB-38. Creating a PivotTable Dashboard.**

Homework MBC

Your audience was happy with the PivotTable produced in Problem PB-37, however they would like to see several visualizations at one time. Specifically, they would like to see total compensation by industry, number of executives by industry, and the state locations where these executives are employed. You decide to make a dashboard with a bar PivotChart of total compensation by industry, a pie PivotChart for the number of executives by industry, and a column PivotChart with the top five states by number of executives.

a. Create the dashboard described previously. Add slicers for gender, position, and year and link the slicers to all of the PivotTables and PivotCharts. Format the dashboard so as to create a visually pleasing layout that is easy to read. In 2018, for male CEOs, how many executives were there and what was the average salary paid in the information technology segment? Also, in 2018, what state employed the most male CEOs?

PB-39. Using Excel for Accounts Receivable Aging—Bella Co.

LO 2, 3, 4

MBC

Bella Co. has been performing its aging of accounts receivable manually; however, the task is becoming too time consuming. The CFO has heard that the PivotTable function within Microsoft Excel could make the task much easier; however, she has never used this technique before. You have been asked to perform Bella's accounts receivable aging using an Excel PivotTable.

- The Excel file Bella Aging Pivot.xlsx can be found in myBusinessCourse with Bella's accounts receivable amounts and due dates.
- Assume that you are performing the aging as of December 31, 2023, the date already entered in cell G1.
- Create new data within column D for the number of days that each invoice is past the due date by entering in cell D2 the formula of cell G1 as an absolute reference minus the cell C2 as a relative reference =$G$1-C2. Next copy this formula down column D to include the entire list of receivables. We now have a list that identifies for each invoice the number of days past due.
- In order to create the PivotTable, simply place the cursor anywhere within columns A through D and select Insert; then select PivotTable. A pop-up should appear with the table range including all the data from columns A through D already selected and the location of the PivotTable being a new worksheet. If this is correct, click OK.
- In the new PivotTable worksheet, locate the PivotTable Fields to the right of the worksheet. Drag the Days Past field down to the rows section and the Amount field down to the values section.
- Finally, in order to do some groupings, place the cursor within the data in column A and right-click and select Group. In the Grouping pop-up, change the starting value to 1, the ending value to 180, and the by value to 30, and click OK. The aging table should appear.
- To add visual impact, a column chart can be added to the worksheet. In order to see all the invoices that make up any grouping, simply place the cursor on the dollar value of the grouping and double-click.

a. What is Bella's total dollar value of the invoices that are between 61 and 90 days past due?

b. What is its largest invoice within the 151- to 180-day grouping?

PB-40. Using Excel for Accounts Receivable Aging—Remus Co.

LO 2, 3

MBC

Remus Co. has been performing its aging of accounts receivable manually; however, the task is becoming too time consuming. The CFO has heard that the PivotTable function within Microsoft Excel could make the task much easier; however, she has never used this technique before. You have been asked to perform Remus' accounts receivable aging using an Excel PivotTable.

- The Excel file Remus Again Pivot.xlsx can be found in myBusinessCourse with Remus' accounts receivable amounts and due dates.
- Assume that you are performing the aging as of December 31, 2023, the date already entered in cell G1.
- Create new data within column D for the number of days that each invoice is past the due date by entering in cell D2 the formula of cell G1 as an absolute reference minus the cell C2 as a relative reference =$G$1-C2. Next copy this formula down column D to include the entire list of receivables. We now have a list that identifies for each invoice the number of days past due.
- In order to create the PivotTable, simply place the cursor anywhere within columns A through D and select Insert; then select PivotTable. A pop-up should appear with the table range including all the data from columns A through D already selected and the location of the PivotTable being a new worksheet. If this is correct, click OK.
- In the new PivotTable worksheet, locate the PivotTable Fields to the right of the worksheet. Drag the Days Past field down to the rows section and the Amount field down to the values section.
- Finally, in order to do some groupings, place the cursor within the data in column A and right-click and select Group. In the Grouping pop-up, change the starting value to 1, the ending value to 180, and the by value to 30, and click OK. The aging table should appear.
- To add visual impact, a column chart can be added to the worksheet. In order to see all the invoices that make up any grouping, simply place the cursor on the dollar value of the grouping and double-click.

a. What is Remus' total dollar value of the invoices that are between 61 and 90 days past due?

b. What is its largest invoice within the 151- to 180-day grouping?

LO 2, 3, 4 **PB-41. Using Excel for Fraud Detection.**

Homework MBC

Benford's Law represents a powerful tool in the forensic accountant's toolkit to aid in the detection of fraud. Benford's Law is a mathematical law that recognizes the leading (first) digit in many real-life number sets is distributed in a certain manner, and often not in the manner that a fraudster would expect. Specifically, the number 1 occurs as the first digit approximately 30 percent of the time, with each succeeding digit appearing less often as follows: 1–30%, 2–18%, 3–12%, 4–10%, 5–8%, 6–7%, 7–6%, 8–5%, and 9–5%. Fraudsters who are unaware of this natural ordering will often arrange digits in a random order that deviates from Benford's Law.

In Part A of this problem, you will use Microsoft Excel to show how a natural dataset of GDP by country conforms to Benford's Law and how a random set of numbers does not. In Part B you will use the same data used in an actual court case to convict a fraudster of embezzlement. Finally, in Part C you will use Benford's Law to test a new reimbursement procedure for possible fraud.

Part A Use Microsoft Excel to show how a natural dataset of GDP by country conforms to Benford's Law and how a random set of numbers does not.

- Download the Excel file **GDP Excel.xlxs** from myBusinessCourse. The file contains World Bank GDP data by country for 2018.
- In order to use Benford's Law, you need to first extract the leading digit from each country's GDP amount. To do this, place the cursor in cell C2 and input the formula =Left(B2,1). Copy this formula down column C for each country.
- Next in cells F2 through F10 input the numbers 1 through 9. In cell G2 input the formula =COUNTIF(c2:$C$205,F2) and copy the formula down for each number 1 through 9. This formula goes through the entire range of extracted first digits in column C and records the count of these digits in the cell if it matches the number in column F.
- Sum the column total in cell G11.
- Next determine the percentage that each leading digit appears by dividing the amount in column G by the total of these amounts in cell G11 and place this figure in column H.
- In column I compute the predicted occurrences of each digit (given above) by placing the formula =Log10(1/F2+1) in cell I2 and copying the formula down the column.
- Finally create a Combo chart to visualize these results by highlighting cells H1:I10 and selecting Combo chart.

a. Do the naturally occurring GDP amounts appear to follow Benford's law?

- Next replace the GDP amounts with random numbers to see if random numbers also obey Benford's Law.
- Input the formula =Rand()*1000 in cell B2 and copy this formula down the column.
- Observe the results in the table and the chart. Try to recalculate the spreadsheet several times to obtain different sets of random numbers.

b. Do random numbers appear to follow Benford's Law?

Part B Use the same data used in an actual court case to convict a fraudster of embezzlement.

In the 1993 court case *State of Arizona v. Wayne James Nelson* Benford's Law was used to convict the defendant of defrauding the state of nearly $2 million by diverting money to a nonexistent vendor. Nelson tried to make the checks appear random; however, he was unaware that these check amounts should actually follow Benford's Law much closer than the distribution he created. Download the file **Arizona Fraud.xlsx** from myBusinessCourse and follow the same procedure as you did in Part A above to use Excel to show how the data conforms to Benford's Law.

a. From a casual observation of the checks, can you detect anything suspect?

b. After using Benford's Law, does the list of checks appear suspect?

Part C Use Benford's Law to test a new reimbursement procedure for possible fraud.

Jimmy's Enterprises has been reimbursing its employees for business expenses after the employee submits detailed evidence of the expense, such as paid receipts. Management has recently changed the reimbursement policy because of the time spent checking all the submitted evidence, with an especially high volume of smaller reimbursement requests. The new policy requires evidence be submitted only if the reimbursement request exceeds $50. As the company's internal auditor, you are concerned that this policy change may result in fraudulent reimbursement requests. In order to test the new policy, you have gathered a random sample of 100 reimbursement requests from both before and after the policy change. This data is located in the file **Expense Reimbursement.xlxs** in myBusinessCourse. Download this file and within Excel use Benford's Law to test whether the new policy appears to have resulted in any fraud.

a. Do the reimbursement requests prior to the policy change appear to follow Benford's Law?
b. Do the reimbursement requests occurring after the policy change appear to follow Benford's Law?
c. What, if anything, leads you to believe that fraud may be occurring?

Index

A

B

Note: Exhibits included in the index with *e* following the page numbers.

C

Note: Exhibits included in the index with *e* following the page numbers.

Note: Exhibits included in the index with *e* following the page numbers.

F

Note: Exhibits included in the index with *e* following the page numbers.

Note: Exhibits included in the index with *e* following the page numbers.

Note: Exhibits included in the index with *e* following the page numbers.

Note: Exhibits included in the index with *e* following the page numbers.

P

Q

R

Note: Exhibits included in the index with *e* following the page numbers.

Note: Exhibits included in the index with *e* following the page numbers.

U

V

W

Y

Z

Note: Exhibits included in the index with *e* following the page numbers.